THE INTERNATIONAL ENCYCLOPEDIA OF EDUCATION

SECOND EDITION

THE INTERNATIONAL ENCYCLOPEDIA OF EDUCATION

SECOND EDITION

Volume 2

Editors-in-Chief

TORSTEN HUSÉN
University of Stockholm, Sweden

T. NEVILLE POSTLETHWAITE
University of Hamburg, Germany

PERGAMON

UK	Elsevier Science Ltd, The Boulevard, Langford Lane, Kidlington, Oxford OX5 1GB, England
USA	Elsevier Science Inc, 660 White Plains Road, Tarrytown, New York 10591-5153,USA
JAPAN	Elsevier Science Japan, Tsunashima Building Annex, 3-20-12 Yushima, Bunkyoku, Tokyo 113, Japan

Second edition 1994

Library of Congress Cataloging in Publication Data
International encyclopedia of education (2nd ed.)
The international encyclopedia of education / editors-in-chief Torsten Husén, T. Neville Postlethwaite. — 2nd ed.
p. cm.
1. Education—Dictionaries. 2. Education—Research—Dictionaries. I. Husén, Torsten, 1916– II. Postlethwaite, T. Neville.
LB15.I569 1994
370'.3—dc20 94–3059

British Library Cataloguing in Publication Data
A catalogue record for this book is available from the British Library.

ISBN 0–08–041046–4 (cloth : set : alk. paper)

∞™ The paper used in this publication meets the minimum requirements of the American National Standard for Information Sciences—Permanence of Paper for Printed Library Materials, ANSI Z39.48–1984.

Printed in Great Britain by BPC Wheatons Ltd, Exeter

CONTENTS

HONORARY EDITORIAL ADVISORY BOARD

EDITORIAL BOARD

C

Cameroon: System of Education

1. General Background

The Republic of Cameroon lies in a triangular wedge between West and Central Africa. Its rugged terrain rises steeply from the Atlantic Ocean and flattens out towards Lake Chad, covering about 475,000 square kilometers. There are tropical rain forests in the South and Saharan desert in the North.

Cameroon is surrounded by English-speaking Nigeria to the west and French-speaking African countries to the north, east, and south. Cameroon's bilingual education policy, although imposed by history, enhances this geopolitical position.

Cameroon was formally created by European colonization which ended in 1960 and 1961 when the country achieved Independence. Since 1571, when Cameroon appeared in recorded world history, Portuguese, Spanish, Dutch, English, and French explorers and traders came to trade along the River Wouri where the waters abound in prawns (or *cameroes*—the Portuguese word from which Cameroon derives its name). By the late eighteenth century when the Slave Trade reached its peak, the English held supremacy. Pidgin English became the language of business and of communication among the multiethnic groups of the region. Pidgin English is not officially used for instruction in the schools, but remains as the third language of mass communication after French and English.

From 1884 to 1914, Germany controlled the region and determined the general boundaries that define the present republic. After the First World War, the German State of Kamerun was divided between France and Britain through a League of Nations mandate. France was assigned three-fourths of the eastern and northern portion of the country and Britain the remaining western fourth. The British administered their portion as part of their neighboring Nigerian colony and set up schools in which pupils were taught in English. English became the language of literacy, creating a local elite which eventually took over political leadership from the largely illiterate traditional rulers. The French established schools which became the instrument for assimilating "natives" into the French culture. By 1946, when the United Nations designated these mandated territories as "trusteeships," the former German State of Kamerun had indeed become French Cameroon and British Cameroon, thanks to the schools!

Following Independence, the southern part of British Cameroon opted to reunite with the new Republic of Cameroon, while the northern part remained within the Federation of Nigeria. In 1961, the new constitution of the Federal Republic of Cameroon declared English and French to be the official languages. Since then, the development of French–English bilingualism has become the greatest hope for national unity, yet also one of the greatest problems in education.

In 1972, the governance structure was changed to that of a united republic, and, in 1984, to the Republic of Cameroon. However, the coexistence of two educational systems ensures that Cameroonians still see themselves as either Anglophones or Francophones.

The population of nearly 12 million in 1991 was 60 percent rural, 55 percent under 20 years of age, and 50 percent female. The annual birthrate is nearly 3 percent. The population increase is about 5.5 percent in urban areas and about 1.8 in rural areas. It reaches 20 percent in the larger towns where the concentration of schools makes them the greatest pools for rural exodus.

Cameroon has over 230 ethnolinguistic communities. Language is therefore a crucial problem in both sociopolitical life and schooling. Although pioneer religious missionaries established schools in local languages, none of them is used today as the medium of instruction in the schools. Most youngsters in Cameroon begin schooling in either English or French, although the school is not their first contact with these languages. Although there are some experiments in mother-tongue teaching in schools, fear of ethnic conflict makes official policy shy away from encouraging the development of one local language into a national language.

Since the establishment of the German protectorate, the structure of the economy has undergone enormous transformation. Originally it was a subsistence agricultural economy but at the beginning of the 1990s there were also modern agropastoral enterprises, industries, and petroleum exploration. Plantation agriculture had a very great early influence on the sociocultural life of the people, especially in terms in introducing salaried jobs, integrating multiethnic groups and, in spreading the importance of literacy and schooling into the hinterlands. However, few private individuals engage in plantation farming; nor have plantations had an impact on modernizing farming methods. Agriculture remains dominated by small household farms on which over 70 percent of the population depends for subsistence. Small one-family farms are the major producers of coffee, cocoa, and cotton, which until the advent of the oil industry in 1975 were the mainstay of the country's export earnings. Cattle rearing by nomadic herdsmen is the mainstay of the economy of the northern grasslands. Here, too, traditional methods prevail although increasing conflict between farmers and graziers is forcing government agencies to intensify the education of farmers in modern methods.

Family farm incomes, especially in rural areas, have had an enormous influence on financing schooling, enabling children in rural areas to stay longer in school, obtain higher diplomas, earn salaries, and climb the social ladder. This background applies to every elite or political leader. Agriculture accounts for about 30 percent of the Gross Domestic Product (GDP). The secondary and tertiary sectors cover 27 and 42 percent respectively. Since 1975, when Cameroon's first refinery went into production, oil revenues have accounted for about 30 percent of the national budget, although their contribution to educational expenditure is hard to determine.

The active population aged 15 to 55 constitutes about 50 percent of the total population. Of these, over 70 percent are engaged in subsistence agriculture where most of the work is still done by women. In 1987, the number of salaried workers in the public and para-public sectors was estimated at about 500,000. The literacy rate is about 60 percent which is one reason for the high number of unskilled workers. However, many school leavers still shy away from manual jobs, despite increasing unemployment.

Government social and economic development planning started in 1960, making 1986–91 the sixth quinquennial. Three major goals of these plans are: to modernize, diversify, and expand the economy by creating new industries and services; to increase the productive capacity of the people; and to double the per capita income at the end of each plan (it was US$ 40 in 1960).

Education is intended as the main instrument to achieve these goals. It aims to instill a modern outlook in place of retrogressive traditional beliefs, attitudes, and practices. More importantly, technical education seeks to impart the new skills needed by industries and services. Thus, investment in human resources gave great impetus to the expansion of secondary and university education in the 1960s and 1970s.

Since the late 1970s, however, school graduates at all levels have outnumbered the capacity of the socioeconomic system to provide jobs. In the early 1990s massive unemployment is placing in doubt the goals of development plans of the past 30 years.

The federal government structure adopted in 1961 brought together the French and English parts of Cameroon under a presidential system which was dissolved in 1972. This was a logical corollary to the creation of a one-party political system in 1966. The system of administration is, therefore, highly centralized with little initiative for local school authorities, especially in matters regarding the school curriculum. However, 1990 began a new era in which, as elsewhere in Africa, there appeared to be a total rejection of the centralized totalitarian one-party system of government. It is difficult to predict the course of the turbulence affecting the country at the beginning of the 1990s and disrupting the school system. Nevertheless, the demand is for decentralization and popular democracy. Hopefully, the present political leadership will yield to the winds of change so that future developments will see greater harmony between the socioeconomic, political, and educational systems.

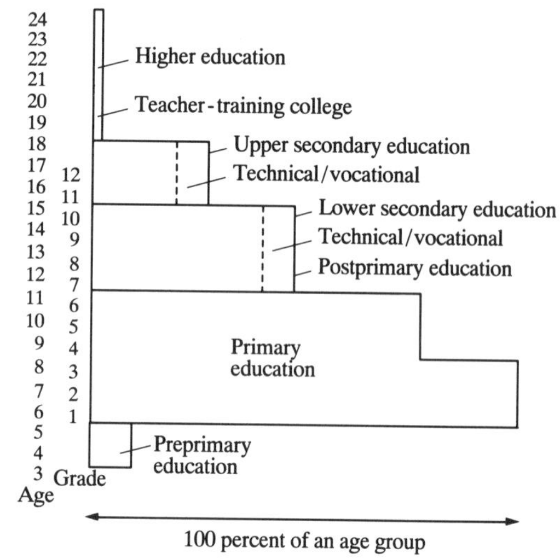

Figure 1
Cameroon: Structure of the formal education system

2. Politics and the Goals of the Education System

From its inception about 150 years ago, the school in Cameroon has been conceived as an instrument for achieving political and social goals. Religious missionaries who were pioneers of the present school system directed schooling toward evangelization. Colonial powers were anxious to train auxiliaries for the administration and to educate the "native" in the ways of the Europeans. Nationalists who fought for independence saw educaion as the means to produce the labor force needed to replace foreigners and to develop the citizens of the new nation. Thus, schooling was geared to salaried jobs and the diploma was highly prized. In addition to these goals, the reunification of the former French and British Cameroons brought national unity and integration as major goals to be pursued, especially through English–French bilingualism.

The advent of a multiparty system is producing

Table 1
Expansion of enrollment from 1965–66 to 1990–91

	1965–66	1970–71	1975–76	1980–81	1985–86	1990–91
Nursery education	—	—	—	41,000	—	91,000
Primary education	742,000	923,000	112,300	1,380,000	1,705,000	2,100,000
Secondary grammar	29,000	310,000	105,000	169,000	259,000	397,000
Secondary technical	—	17,400	31,000	56,000	83,000	128,000
Teacher training	—	—	—	2,100	4,000	—
University education	—	2,600	7,200	10,400	24,650	30,000

much rhetoric about educational reforms. There is, however, no major divergence from earlier conceptions of the role of the school in society. Popular expectation is still for school graduates to get jobs commensurate with their level of schooling. The school remains the instrument for upward social mobility. However, the general direction of future policy seems to be toward greater individual opportunities in a less centralized school system which will fit into a diversified economic system in which the private sector will employ more than the public sector.

3. *The Formal System of Education*

Figure 1 show the structure of the formal English and French education systems. Key statistical information on enrollments and resources in the major educational sectors are provided in Table 1. Education is not yet compulsory in Cameroon, although a government white paper of 1980 advocated free and compulsory primary-school education by the year 2000. This may not be possible but, with careful planning Cameroon should be able to afford free education for over 80 percent of children of primary-school age.

In 1990 there were over 90,000 children receiving nursery-school education. Tuition is free in all public nursery schools which, in 1990, constituted over 60 percent of this level of education for children aged 4 and 5. Nursery education is available either in a separate institution, or, more generally, in a section of a primary school. Only a very small proportion of the age group attends nursery schools although enrollments have been increasing. The demand is greatest especially in the urban areas and is stimulated by the ever-growing number of working-class mothers.

All nursery schools follow the same programs directed by a special section of the inspectorate division of the Ministry of National Education. This division is also responsible for the training and certification of kindergarten teachers, many of whom have been instructed in the Montessori Method. Nursery schools function for only part of the school day, usually in the morning hours, between 8 a.m. and midday. The cost of education is much higher than in primary schools. Parents pay a subsidy in public nursery schools and must pay full fees in private schools.

3.1 Primary, Secondary, and Tertiary Education

Primary schooling begins officially at age 6, although many children begin at age 5. It lasts six years in Francophone schools and seven in Anglophone schools. In 1990 there were over 2.22 million primary-school pupils of whom over 60 percent were enrolled in public schools. All primary schools are coeducational.

The primary-school program in Cameroon is still organized by subjects distributed over 5 hours for each school day, 5 days a week, and about 35 weeks a year. The economic crisis which has hit Cameroon since 1985 has greatly affected the quality of primary-school education, as can be judged from the diminishing number of trained teachers. Many classrooms are poorly equipped. Failure, grade-repeating, and dropout rates are high, often reaching over 40 percent for each cohort between the first and final years of primary school.

Language poses a major problem as the majority of school children begin learning to read and write in a foreign language. Schooling in the mother tongue is still in its experimental phase and even then concerns only about 5 of the 230 languages.

Primary schooling ends with the primary-school leaving certificate examination and a competitive examination to enter secondary school. The national percentage passing the examination was over 40 percent in 1990, an improvement from the previous five years.

Two-year training courses after primary school are available in rural artisan training centers and home economics centers for primary-school children who are too old for admission to secondary schools.

The development of secondary-school education since 1960 has been phenomenal (see Table 1). However, less than 30 percent of primary-school leavers can continue into this level of schooling, which begins at age 11 or 12 and lasts for 7 years. The number of girls is rapidly increasing and was over 40 percent in 1990.

The duration of the secondary-school day is about 5.5 hours and schooling is divided into 3 terms totaling about 35 weeks per year.

Secondary-school education still bears the imprint of the British and French systems. Attempts at harmonizing the two systems in order to create a national system have not succeeded largely for political reasons. However, both systems are dominated by the grammar type of general education school where the goals of instruction are the General Certificate of Education and the baccalauréat.

Stimulated by the lack of employment opportunities for secondary grammar school leavers the demand for secondary technical and vocational education was increasing at the end of the 1980s.

Expansion of public schools continues at a very rapid pace, while religious organizations have been reluctant to open new schools because of the difficulty of paying teachers' salaries. The number of private secondary schools established by private individuals increases every year as only about 30 percent of each primary-school graduating cohorting can be absorbed into existing secondary schools.

The introduction of bilingual schooling in which students receive instruction in both French and English is the most noteworthy curricular innovation since Independence. Modifications in subject matter content have kept abreast of changes introduced in the United Kingdom and France, especially through school textbooks supplied by publishers in those countries.

There was no university in the country in 1960. In 1979, four university centers were added to Cameroon's first university which were created in 1962. A free public higher education policy allows all successful candidates from secondary grammar schools to enter one of the three faculties of the University. Admission into the university centers and higher educational institutions is through competitive examinations. About 40,000 students were enrolled at this level in 1990. Over 35,000 were in the three faculties of Yaounde University. Higher education lasts from three to about seven years and prepares students for university degrees in the faculties and professional diplomas in professional higher educational institutions (French-type grandes écoles).

Language is one of the major problems in higher education, especially due to differences in the secondary-school background of students who must follow lecturers in either French or English depending on the lecturer. Along with inadequate facilities, these problems produce failure rates reaching over 80 percent in some faculties.

In 1990, a Catholic University Institute was established inaugurating private higher education and ending the state monopoly of higher education.

3.2 Preschool Eduation

Preschool education constitutes a very small part of the education effort. Preschool is available in the form of daycare centers run by private individuals and organizations who charge high fees. As with nursery schools, the number of these centers is on the increase in urban areas. Organized games and the basics of picture reading and drawing constitute the main program of these centers.

3.3 Special Education

Like preschool education, special education forms a very small part of education in Cameroon. There was no information on handicapped persons reported in the population census of 1987. Their welfare and education are handled by special services in a government ministry responsible for Social and Women's Affairs. Four main types of special education programs date back to the colonial period. Rehabilitation centers for lepers are run at hospitals by religious missionaries. Centers for the blind are surprisingly few, especially as blindness is a very common phenomenon in the northern part of the country. Students are introduced to the basic elements of braille and are taught handicrafts and gardening. (It is worth noting that the first blind Cameroonian graduated with a PhD from Howard University in the United States in 1984.)

Psychiatric patients were once interned in penitentiary centers, but Cameroon now runs a major psychiatric hospital in the capital city, where one of the biggest centers specializes in treating the disabled. This center also runs a primary-school program for both physically and mentally handicapped children of school age. Finally, a number of institutes admit young delinquents sent from the law courts. In addition to rehabilitation programs, inmates prepare for the primary-school leaving certificate.

The majority of handicapped persons are generally taken care of by their families. However, physically handicapped persons who are able to attend school are generally admitted into regular school programs where no special provisions are made for them.

A small number of physically handicapped teachers are found in schools at all levels. They obtain employment on the basis of similar qualifications like and other person. Blind workers are less evident. However, in the Muslim north of the country, blind persons are teachers or *modibos* in the Koranic schools.

3.4 Vocational, Technical, and Business Education

Formal vocational, technical, and business education begins after primary-school education from about age 13. Government policy, announced in the five-year development plans, has been directed to encouraging this sector which enrolled about 237,000 students in 1990. Business education, in which students receive training in secretarial skills and bookkeeping, dominates this sector where the teaching of computer skills is being introduced even in some remote rural institutions. Vocational training in areas such as motor mechanics, carpentry, masonry, electronics, and similar trade skills enrolls mainly boys. Domestic arts centers remain reserved for girls, although such traditional biases are breaking down with the demand for trained personnel by the expanding hotel, tourist, and catering business.

The building industry in urban centers is the greatest stimulus for the growth of apprenticeship workshops which enroll more primary-school leavers than secondary technical and vocational schools.

The structure of technical and vocational education at this level has been greatly influenced by curricular models of the French education and certificate system. This tradition also persists in professional training at the higher educational level.

The economic boom of 1975–85 gave this sector a great boost. It has since been declining because of the economic crisis, although many parents still advise their children to opt for this sector rather than secondary general education because of the possibilities it offers for self-employment. This sector is still a major priority in government planning.

3.5 Adult and Nonformal Education

Since 1960, great effort has been put into developing adult and nonformal education in three major directions. Extension agriculture through village agricultural officers has greatly contributed to modernizing agricultural techniques, resulting in significant increases in the production of some cash crops (coffee, cocoa, cotton, etc.). Community development has been directed to improving life in rural areas, especially for women. Adult literacy campaigns have not been very successful despite the enormous effort put in by the government and UNESCO in the 1970s.

The Ministry of Women's Affairs, which was created in 1985, has directed much of its energy to programs in which the major goal is to enhance the place of women in society.

The rapid expansion of evening classes in which adults prepare for primary- and secondary-school certificate examinations is one of the major developments in education since the 1970s. Female students are in the majority in these institutions which are generally run by private individuals outside school hours. They are regulated by the Law on Private Education and are fee-paying.

4. Administrative and Supervisory Structure and Operation

Constitutional responsibility for the education of the citizen devolves on the state which exercises this duty through free tuition in all public schools at all levels and also by granting subsidies to private schools. Major national education policies are published through laws and presidential decrees. For example, university institutions are established by these decrees. Thus, a highly centralized control of education is established in which two ministers execute presidential directives on elementary and secondary education on the one hand, and higher education on the other.

Public primary and secondary schools are the responsibility of the Ministry of National Education which establishes and equips schools, recruits teachers, and determines school programs and textbooks. Teachers in public schools are civil servants and enjoy the same salary conditions as other government workers.

In 1990, public primary and secondary schools, absorbed over 13 percent of the national budget.

The administration of the public school system is structured like a giant pyramid with the Ministry at the apex and a provincial delegate or school superintendent in each of the ten provinces at the base.

The inspectorate system is also bureaucratic in structure with an Inspector General of Pedagogy (IGP) for each sector: primary, secondary grammar, and secondary technical and vocational. Each IGP is assisted by national subject inspectors who in turn have assistants in each province. National inspectors are responsible for school syllabuses, textbooks, school examinations, and the supervision of teachers.

The minister in charge of higher education takes final policy decisions regarding universities, although each university has a governing council. Councils have direct responsibility for personnel recruitment, promotion, and dismissal. However, the creation of new departments, degrees, courses, and changes in general regulations, such as admissions, must receive ministerial consent. Universities are public institutions and do not charge tuition fees. Each university receives a budget from the state. Most students receive a grant from the government in addition to free tuition. Student grants consume over 50 percent of the budget of each university and are the greatest source of unrest at Cameroon's first and biggest university.

Over 14 percent of the education budget in 1990 was spent on higher education. In addition, Cameroon spends about 2 percent of its education budget annually on scholarships for training students in foreign universities.

Several higher educational institutions do not fall directly under the Minister of Higher Education, but the Minister must ascertain that they meet academic standards. Some of these are directly run by other ministers and offer specialized training in areas such as agriculture, health, post and telecommunications, forestry, youth and sports, planning, public works, and so on. They award diplomas generally recognized as equivalent to a first degree, although these institutions do not have university status.

Private primary and secondary schools enrolled about 35 percent of the 2.5 million students receiving education at this level in 1990. Private schools are established by private individuals and organizations with the approval of the Minister of National Education. Proprietors must provide the initial funds for buildings and equipment. Personnel are recruited and paid by them although the government gives subsidies which cover about 60 percent of private-school teacher salaries.

The Catholic Church is the largest private education organization. In 1990 it owned over 60 percent of private primary schools and, together with Protestant churches, owned 90 percent of private primary schools. Lay proprietors own 55 percent of the private secondary schools, although most of the old and more prestigious schools are owned by religious organizations.

Private schools are administered under conditions laid down in the Private Education Laws of 1976 and 1987. These provide for national representatives for each of the Catholic, Protestant, Islamic and lay private school authorities. Each national representative is assisted in each province by denominational supervisors, known as education secretaries.

All private schools must follow the same syllabuses and textbooks as public schools. They must be open to inspection by Ministry inspectors, and must prepare their students for official examinations.

Since the abolition of the federal structure in 1972, the administration and supervision of schools have become more centralized. However, the double dualism of Anglophone and Francophone schools on the one hand, and of public and private schools, on the other creates great imbalances in the implementation of national policies, especially curricular innovations.

5. *Educational Finance*

The state, in the final analysis, bears the major financial burden for running both public and private schools. Parents are the next major source of educational financing as they bear the social cost of education. In addition, through Parent–Teacher Associations, they fund buildings and equipment, and, in some cases, pay teachers' salaries.

Before Independence and until the early 1970s, expenditure for school buildings, equipment, and teachers was a very significant part of foreign aid. In the early 1990s, this source has considerably diminished due to the establishment of indigenous churches.

In the 1990–91 fiscal year, US$ 300 million were allocated to education at all levels from the national budget of about US$ 1,500 million. Despite cuts in government expenditures because of the economic crisis, popular demand for education has put pressure on the government to expand schools and increase the education budget. Investment in education will remain a major priority for the next decade.

Table 2 presents the government budgetary allocations for each level of education in the fiscal year 1990–91.

Financial support for private education derives mainly from state subsidies and school fees paid by parents. The bulk of state subsidies (6 billion francs CFA in 1990) is paid to schools run by religious bodies and especially to the older and more prestigious secondary grammar schools. In 1990, over 80 percent of the expenditure on private primary and secondary schools was derived from school fees which were fixed by the Minister of National Education on the advice of a National Commission for Private Education, where all private school proprietors are represented.

At the levels of schooling, in both the public and private sectors, teacher salaries absorb over 70 percent of the school budget. In 1990, over 90 percent of the budgetary allocation for public primary and secondary schools was spent on salaries. Private school proprietors try to tackle this problem by employing part-time or temporary teachers, who made up over 70 percent of the staff of the majority of the schools in 1990.

The costs per pupil in 1990 were US$ 160 for primary, US$ 600 for secondary academic, and US$ 10,000 for secondary technical and vocational schools.

6. *Supplying Personnel for the Education System*

In 1990 there were over 67,000 teachers in primary and secondary schools. Men are in the majority, although the proportion of female teachers has begun to increase, reaching 35 percent of the 41,000 primary-school teachers in 1988. Men are in the majority as heads of schools, although one of the four university centers is headed by a woman.

Shortage of teachers is a chronic problem. Since 1987, there have been drastic cuts in the annual recruitment of teachers for public schools. Admissions to government primary-school teacher-training colleges have also been stopped. The number of qualified experienced teachers is rapidly diminishing. About 50 percent of primary-school teachers in 1990 has only a primary-school leaving certificate.

At the secondary-school level the situation is improving, especially for private secondary schools where unemployed university graduates are willing to accept low salaries. In general, schools in remote rural areas attract fewer female teachers, although they were in the majority in public primary-school teacher-training colleges in the late 1980s.

Pre-service training for primary-school teachers prepares for three grades of certificates—Grade III, II, and I—awarded respectively after three years of training after primary school, two years after GCE

Table 2
Provisions for education in the national budget 1987–90 (in billions of francs CFA)

	1987–88	1988–89	1989–90
Total			
Education	123 (19%)	91 (16%)	112 (18%)
National	650 (100%)	600 (100%)	600 (100%)
Running			
Schools	66.9 (16.7%)	59.8 (10.8%)	67.3 (16%)
Universities	34 (9.6%)	27 (7.1%)	34 (8%)
Subsidies			
Private	6 (1.5%)	6 (1.6%)	6.5 (1.5%)
National	400 (100%)	375 (100%)	425 (100%)
Investment			
Schools	12 (4.8%)	5.3 (2.4%)	6 (3.4%)
Universities	12 (4.8%)	5.3 (2.4%)	6 (3.4%)
National	250 (100%)	225 (100%)	175 (100%)

Ordinary level, and one year after GCE Advanced level. Secondary-school teachers are trained at the Higher Teachers School of Education at Yaounde University (*Ecole Normale Supérieure*) which offers three years of training after secondary high school and two years after the first degree. The majority of the teacher-training colleges are owned by the government and train teachers mainly for public schools. Only two private primary-teacher-training centers exist for Presbyterian and Catholic training schools.

All teacher-training colleges follow official syllabuses from the Minister of National Education. Special training programs are offered for teachers destined for nursery schools, home economics, and technical vocational schools. Inservice training for all categories of teachers takes the form of correspondence courses, seminars, workshops, refresher courses, and travel abroad. Distance education as such does not yet exist.

Probationary periods are provided for in the salary conditions of untrained primary and secondary teachers. All teachers must be inspected every year by either national or provincial inspectors and headmasters, as a condition for earning a bi-annual salary increase.

One of the greatest problems in the schools is the rapid decline in the number of qualified experienced teachers because of aging. By 1970, Anglophone primary schools had over 70 percent trained teachers. Today, these schools have been depleted of the bulk of the experienced teachers produced in the 1960s and 1970s when this part of the country had over 12 primary-school teacher-training colleges. The requirement of the International Monetary Fund in its Structural Adjustment Plan that Cameroon reduce teacher training and recruitment will certainly worsen the standard of education which, in countries like Cameroon, depends greatly on the quality of teachers.

7. Curriculum Development and Teaching Methodology

Although the curricula of primary and secondary schools is given for all schools by the Ministry of National Education, a formal statement of a core curriculum is nowhere stated as such. Statements of national goals can only be deduced from official educational statements and reports such as the Five-Year Socioeconomic Development Plans. Hence there is a disparity between some national goals and curricular practices.

The primary-school curriculum comprises language (English or French), mathematics, natural sciences, history, geography, physical education, and manual work. The curricula of secondary schools is subject-oriented and similar to that of high schools in many Anglophone and Francophone countries. Technical and vocational schools provide training in a wide range of trade areas: motor mechanics, electronics, carpentry, masonry, painting, and so on. Religious instruction is permitted in public schools, but it is compulsory in institutions run by churches. Anglo-Arab and Franco-Arab primary schools exist for Muslim children.

Most instructional materials especially textbooks, are imported from either France or the United Kingdom. Some foreign publishers use local authors to write or adapt materials to suit local syllabuses. However, new textbooks are generally approved by national inspectors who may seek the opinion of classroom teachers. Dissemination of textbooks is undertaken by local bookshops. In 1991 Cameroon negotiated financial subsidies with France in order to reduce prices for some primary-school textbooks. This move could lead to a new textbook policy involving funding agencies which have so far been concerned only with building and equipping schools. Foreign organizations occasionally donate books to school libraries to help alleviate the pathetic dearth of reading materials in Cameroon schools. However, many of these books are not appropriate for Cameroonian children.

The *baccalauréat* usually provides for literary or science subject options. Some options contain electives such as Spanish and German. The GCE allows a choice from among 15 subjects. The best students take 10 subjects English, French, and mathematics are compulsory for all candidates.

Beyond chalk and blackboard, improvements in learning facilities depend on the financial possibilities of each school. A few schools use videotapes for specific programs.

Since 1960, efforts made to harmonize the Anglophone and Francophone school curricula have not been very successful. Attempts to produce nationwide uniformity in school syllabuses have often provoked mutual antagonism between Francophones and Anglophones, erupting in strikes in 1983 and 1987.

Literary subject options attract more candidates, although this trend is changing in favor of science subjects in response to the general impression that students following science options easily find training opportunities in technical and professional training.

As official languages, French and English are compulsory subjects at all levels of the school system. However, from the third year of secondary school, students can choose to study an additional language: Spanish, German, Latin, or Greek.

All schools must follow the official curriculum under the supervision of the inspectorate division of the Ministry of National Education. Private school proprietors must pledge to follow official regulations and syllabuses. Otherwise, they face prosecution under the Private Education Law.

The overall inadaptability of the school curriculum to the socioeconomic realities of Cameroon is a general problem. This has further been aggravated by the use of imported textbooks and of foreign languages for instruction. Poor command of English or French is the major cause of failure at all levels of the school system.

8. *The System of Examinations, Promotions, and Certifications*

Promotion from one year to the next throughout the school system is based on the results gained on tests devised by teachers, while promotion to a higher level of schooling is based on success at the national certificate competitive or selection examinations.

Francophone secondary schools still follow the *baccalauréat* while Anglophone secondary schools prepare students for the General Certificate of Education of the University of London. Both examinations were "Cameroonized" in 1969 and 1976 respectively. However, they still maintain the broad organizational features inherited from the 1960s. There is a dire need to introduce modern techniques of evaluation, as well as culturally appropriate subjects and tests into the examination system.

The job value of the diploma makes preparation for national examinations the major goal of instruction. The centralized examination system could facilitate the introduction of a Standardized Achievement Test which could provide a useful basis for curriculum evaluation throughout the school system and especially for nonexamination classes. However, such a development could take a decade to introduce! Examination questions are generally directed to testing knowledge rather than skills and competencies.

9. *Educational Assessment, Evaluation, and Research*

The planning divisions of the ministries of national and higher education are responsible for assessment, evaluation, and research. A nationwide assessment (Labrousse 1970) of the school system was carried out in the 1970s focusing on factors including dropout, repetition, and per capita costs, in order to compare inputs and outputs. Some startling findings were made which continue to be valid in the early 1990s. For example, it was found that repeating classes was the greatest source of financial loss as many children took double the amount of time to complete their schooling. Fewer than 44 of every cohort of 10,000 first-year primary-school pupils obtained the high-school diploma. These findings led to a policy of automatic promotion in Anglophone primary schools in 1970, and the plan to staff the schools with only trained teachers in the following decade. These innovations were abandoned in the early 1980s.

However, annual statistical surveys by the Ministry of National Education on indicators such as age, sex, enrollments, teacher qualifications, and so forth provide an overall picture of trends in the school system. Studies of achievement levels in writing, numeracy, and literacy skills at various stages of schooling would be very useful in providing an overall picture of the quality of education in schools.

Some form of annual evaluation is carried out in private schools by the National Commission for Private Education. This is based on indicators such as qualifications of teachers, organization, facilities, investment, and performance in official examinations. Such evaluation reports enable the Ministry to categorize schools for the purpose of distributing government subsidies. There have been suggestions that similar appraisals be extended to public schools which are not subjected to any systematic assessment or accountability.

Two research institutes were established in 1969 and 1974 to direct an ambitious effort to introduce massive changes in the primary-school curriculum. Their impact has not been impressive. In 1973, the National Institute for Education was established and given a broad mandate for educational research on all aspects of education. An initial effort to review secondary-school syllabuses and textbooks was abandoned in 1976. Since then this institute has not found a clear direction and focus for its activities. Therefore, in the absence of substantial research studies on crucial national policies such as bilingualism, it is difficult to assess the attitudes of policymakers toward research findings.

Expenditure on educational research and evaluation is difficult to estimate but it must be quite small if not negligible. However, occasional assessments of the functioning of the system are carried out through studies commissioned by international organizations such as the World Bank and UNESCO. In 1988, a World Bank study advised a drastic restructuring of the university system to reduce student numbers and cutting expenditure on scholarships. The pressure for more places at the university level has forced the government to create two full-fledged universities and to increase scholarships.

10. Major Reforms in the 1980s and 1990s

Several reform projects were attempted in the 1970s and 1980s. The ruralization of primary education with its key goal of getting school leavers back to the land and thereby checking rural exodus was introduced in 1969, but in 1990 this received little attention in policy statements. This reform has virtually been forgotten in its original ambitious form. However, one result is that manual work has been established as an important activity in the primary schools.

Bilingual education programs in which Anglophone and Francophone children attend the same schools have expanded since 1963. The teaching of a second foreign language has extended to most primary schools, although it is difficult to evaluate its effectiveness.

At the secondary-school level, bilingual experiments which started in the late 1960s have crystallized into two models. Several cohabitational schools offer both the Francophone and Anglophone secondary schooling programs. Some schools use both English and French as the media of instruction in teaching content subjects.

Great interest has been generated among Francophone parents to send their children to Anglophone schools. An increasing number of Francophone students also undertake university studies in Anglophone countries. Although the 1983 reform of the GCE did not take place in the form that was planned, it has established French, along with mathematics and English, as compulsory subjects for this examination.

Latin and Greek were reintroduced into the secondary-school curriculum in 1987 as electives, but it is not easy to ascertain the number of students taking these subjects at the *baccalauréat* level.

In 1979, four university centers were established. All but one are operating with maximum enrollment. The one exception is the university center in the Anglophone part of the country. The original plan to make this university English-speaking and in the Anglo-Saxon tradition was repeated again in 1991. Many technical and professional institutions of higher education have been established in an effort to provide advanced training in various aspects of the socioeconomic system such as agriculture, post and telecommunications, hotel management, forestry, food technology, and so on.

11. Major Problems for the Year 2000

Overcrowding in classrooms at all levels in consequence of the phenomenal demographic explosion the country has experienced since 1960 is one problem the school system will continue to face in the 1990s. Ongoing efforts to cope with this include involving local associations in funding school projects.

Greater decentralization in which more responsibility for school and curriculum improvement is given to local authorities is a much needed direction for future change.

The quality of education has fallen because of teacher shortage, and poorer and overcrowded facilities. Poor handwriting at the upper levels of schooling is a strong pointer to falling standards. A sustained system of teacher training must be put in place, along with greater attention to factors that ensure greater retention of trained and experienced teachers who should be given security in a professional association.

A strategy for school curriculum renovation has still to be worked out so that reforms can be based on rationales that are clearly stated. Such reforms must be linked to the socioeconomic goals of the 1990s in ways that are realistic. The education system should impart marketable skills without making this the only goal of schooling. Greater diversity in the curriculum should replace the present rigid system. National goals of education should be more clearly stated. Finally, Cameroon must devote greater financial resources to education.

Bibliography

Blakemore K, Cooksey B 1981 *A Sociology of Education for Africa*. Allen and Unwin, London

Fanso G 1989 *History of Cameroon*. Longman, London

Gwei S N 1975 Education in Cameroon: Western precolonial and colonial antecedents and the development of higher education. Doctoral dissertation, University of Michigan, Ann Arbor, Michigan

Kale, J, Yembe O W 1980 Reforms in the educational system: A case study of IPAR Buea. In: Kofele-Kale N (ed.) 1980 *An African Case Study in Nation Building: The Bilingual Republic of Cameroon since Reunification*. Westview Press, Boulder, Colorado

Labrousse A 1970 *Le Financement de l'Education au Cameroun*. UNESCO, Paris
Lallez R 1975 *La Réforme de l'education au Cameroun*. International Bureau of Education, Geneva
Le Vine V T 1964 *The Cameroons: From Mandate to Independence*. University of California Press, Berkeley, California
Mveng E 1963 *Histoire du Cameroun*. Presence Africaine, Paris
Rudin H 1938 *The Germans in Cameroon*. Yale University Press, Princeton, New Jersey
Société Internationale de Linguistique (SIL) 1981 *Rapport Annuel 1980–81*. SIL, Yaounde
UNESCO 1962 *Report of the Advisory Commission for the Development of Higher Education in the Federal Republic of Cameroon*. UNESCO, Paris
UNESCO 1965 *Report of the Second Planning Mission to Cameroon, September–December 1963*. UNESCO, Paris
Vernon-Jackson H O 1967 *Language, Schools, and Government in Cameroon*. Teachers College Press, New York
Yembe O W 1979 Bilingualism and academic achievement in Cameroon secondary schools. Doctoral dissertation, Teachers College, Columbia University, New York

O. W. Yembe

Canada: System of Education

1. General Background

Canada is the second largest country in the world in area, but ranks only thirty-first in population. Its nearly 27 million people represent cultural backgrounds as diverse as the land they inhabit. Geographically, the country encompasses large metropolitan areas, fertile plains, and farmlands, and great stretches of mountains, lakes, northern wilderness, and Arctic tundra.

Almost two-thirds of the population occupy urban areas concentrated in a more or less unbroken band along the border between Canada and the United States, and over 60 percent of Canadians live in two provinces—Ontario, with its largely English-speaking population, and Quebec where the primary language is French. In keeping with its history, Canada is a bilingual country. Its two official languages are French and English.

Politically, Canada is a federal state, divided into ten provinces and two territories. The Confederation Act of 1867 which brought together the four original provinces, was designed to build a strong central government, while ensuring autonomy and self-government for the participants in matters relating to their specific socioeconomic interests, language, religion, law (in the case of Quebec) and, significantly, education. These rights were extended to other communities as they joined the federation. Thus, Canada does not have a national system of education, nor a central office of education. Subject to the observance of certain guaranteed minority religious and language rights, education is exclusively under the control of each province and territory. A few exceptions exist for which the federal government has assumed direct responsibility. These include the education of Canada's aboriginal people (North American Indian, Inuits, and Métis), who represent about 3 percent of the population, armed forces personnel, and inmates of federal prisons. In order to ensure the provision of education in the official language of minorities (e.g., French in Ontario), the federal government also provides financial assistance to support the additional costs of developing and maintaining these programs.

Natural increase accounts for about 65 percent of Canada's population growth. The 1990 annual rate of approximately 7.0 percent was one of the highest in the industrial world, but the lowest in Canada's history. In the decade of the 1980s, the birthrate declined, resulting in a much smaller preschool and primary age group in 1986 than in the "baby boom" years of the 1960s. However, indications are that the rate (almost 15 per thousand in 1991) will stabilize, or increase slightly, through the 1990s. Although the number of people under age 14 did not change much in the 1980s, the secondary-school age group (14–18) decreased by 15 percent between 1981 and 1986. As a consequence of the declining birthrate and a gain in life expectancy, Canada has an aging population. The median age in 1986 was 31.6, the highest in the country's history.

Immigration is also a major factor in Canada's growth. Traditionally, most immigrants came from Britain, but in the 1986 census, 25 percent of all Canadians reported ethnic origins other than British or French. This included, in addition to European immigrants, an influx of West Indians and Africans in the 1970s, together with refugees from Latin America, the Middle East, and Asia in the 1980s. In 1989, Canada received approximately 190,000 immigrants, half of whom came from Asia. Although children under 18 normally represent only about 1 percent of the annual immigration, 70 percent of this number settle in the six major cities. The fact that as many as two-thirds of such children understand neither of the two official languages has created special problems for some urban school systems.

Canada has grown from a largely agricultural and resource-based economy to a prosperous industrialized country, although, like other such economies, it experienced recessionary periods in the 1980s and 1990s. According to the 1986 census, only 6 percent of the population was employed in agriculture, fishing, and mining, in contrast to almost half the population in 1891. Manufacturing industries employed 17 percent, service industries 40 percent, and trade and transportation accounted for 22 percent.

Canada has a major financial commitment to education, which is second only to social welfare as a consumer of government funding. In 1990, educational expenditure represented about 7.0 percent of Gross Domestic Product (GDP). This commitment is reflected in the labor force; in 1989, 15 percent of workers had university degrees, and 42 percent had some post-secondary education compared with 29 percent a decade earlier. However, at the other end of the spectrum, 9 percent of the labor force had less than a Grade 9 education, and it has been estimated that as many as one-fourth of Canadians suffer from basic or functional illiteracy.

2. Politics and the Goals of the Education System

In addition to the Prime Minister of Canada and the cabinet, each province has its own elected legislature, headed by a premier, to administer and delegate the responsibilities, including education, which fall under provincial control.

While the political parties in power in the various jurisdictions may differ and espouse philosophies either slightly to the left or right of center, Canada is not a country of political extremes. Moderation and pragmatism are Canadian characteristics. In a nation founded on democractic principles, the majority of its citizens share an ethic of equal opportunity, and the provision of universal, free schooling to the college or university level. Education is viewed as a process of imparting the necessary knowledge and skills to achieve a productive, rewarding, and fulfilling life. Differences, therefore, tend to focus on the interpretation of concepts such as "knowledge" and "skills" and the methods for acquiring them, rather than on the underlying principles.

It is also notable that with the growth in size and importance of education in the second half of the twentieth century, the federal government has inevitably played a more important role, even though direct participation is prohibited by the Constitution. Since 1963, when the Department of the Secretary of State was designated as the advisor to the Cabinet on post-secondary education, its responsibilities have grown to encompass the development, formulation, and implementation of all federal policies and programs on education. Most significant is its important role in the provision of financial support, especially at the postsecondary level. As a result, the economic and social priorities of the federal government inevitably have consequences for education which may conflict with provincial or regional objectives.

In the closing years of the twentieth century, Canada is faced with serious economic and political decisions. The federal government's commitment to cut budget deficits implies less government spending on services. Federal policies on bilingualism and multiculturalism have been questioned. Most importantly, the resolution of Quebec's status as a "distinct society," either within the federation or as a sovereign state, as well as the question of self-government for native peoples, cannot help but affect all levels of education.

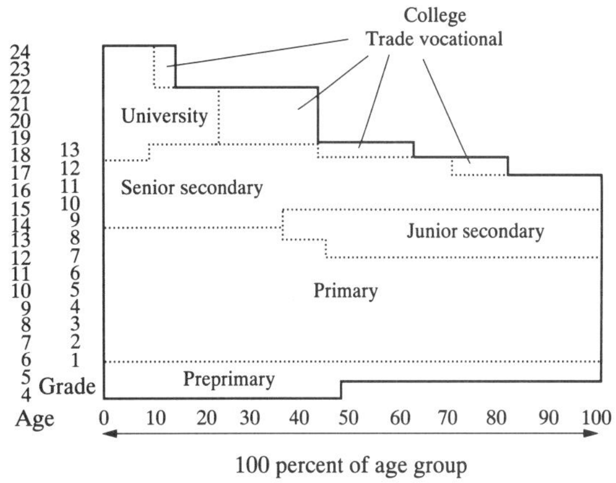

Figure 1
Canada: Structure of the formal education system
Source: *Statistics Canada*

3. The Formal System of Education

3.1 Primary, Secondary, and Tertiary Education

Figure 1 illustrates the range of educational structures and years of study within provincial systems. There are three levels of education offered in Canada: elementary, secondary, and postsecondary. Attendance is compulsory for about ten years in every province. The starting age is 6 or 7, and the minimum leaving age, 15 or 16. The combined elementary–secondary program, however, usually extends over 12 years, although there are provincial differences. The definition of "elementary" and "secondary" also varies from province to province. In most jurisdictions, "elementary" refers to the first six grades; in others, Grade 7 and/or Grade 8 are included. The secondary level, therefore, may consist of five or six grades and may be further subdivided into junior and senior high schools. Quebec has a unique program of five years at the secondary level (Grades 7 to 11), followed by two or three years at a *collège d'enseignment général et professionel* (CEGEP).

At one time, secondary schools were primarily academic and prepared students for university. Vocational and technical schools were often separate institutions. Although some of these still exist, most secondary schools are composite and offer both academic and vocational courses.

The majority of Canada's over 15,500 elementary–secondary schools are public, meaning that they offer free, tax-supported education. In several provinces, provision is made for tax-supported "separate schools" on a denominational basis (usually Roman

Catholic). Private schools, which represent only 4.6 percent of the total, are independent of the public system and charge fees, although provision is made for financial assistance in some provinces. Most public schools, with the exception of a few separate schools, are coeducational. In contrast, many private schools were established exclusively for either boys or girls, although some subsequently became coeducational.

Secondary-school education to at least the Grade 12 level is often specified by business and industry as a minimum for employment. Despite Canada's commitment to education, retention rates at the secondary level are a concern. This situation has serious implications both for the country and for the young people themselves because of the increasing need for highly skilled workers and fewer opportunities for the unskilled or functionally illiterate.

Postsecondary education in Canada is essentially government-financed and has undergone a remarkable expansion since the Second World War. In 1991, Canada had 273 postsecondary institutions which included 69 degree-granting universities (compared to 28 in 1939) and 204 non-degree-granting "community colleges." The latter designation is used in the general sense because of provincial variations in terminology. These institutions offer a broad range of vocational, technical, and semi-professional programs and, in some cases, university transfer programs. Others specialize in specific areas such as art, fisheries, marine technology, or agriculture.

The structure of universities is relatively standard and degrees are offered almost universally at three levels: bachelor's (BA or BSc) and first professional, master's (MA or MSc), and doctoral (PhD) or professional degrees, such as Doctor of Medicine (MD). Each university sets its own admission standards, but the basic requirement is normally secondary school (or in the case of Quebec, CEGEP) graduation. Most institutions make allowance for the admission of "mature students," typically defined as people over 21 years of age who have been out of school for several years.

The school year at the elementary–secondary level averages 180 to 200 teaching days over the period from September to late June. At the postsecondary level, the academic year normally begins in September and continues until late April or early May. Most universities offer both full (two semesters) and half (one semester) courses, and some institutions operate year-round on a three-semester basis. Several universities have work-study programs in which students alternate between classroom study and supervised regular employment. The majority of universities accept either full-time or part-time students, especially at the undergraduate level, and many offer off-campus courses, correspondence courses, or make use of communications technology. In a country as vast as Canada with many sparsely populated

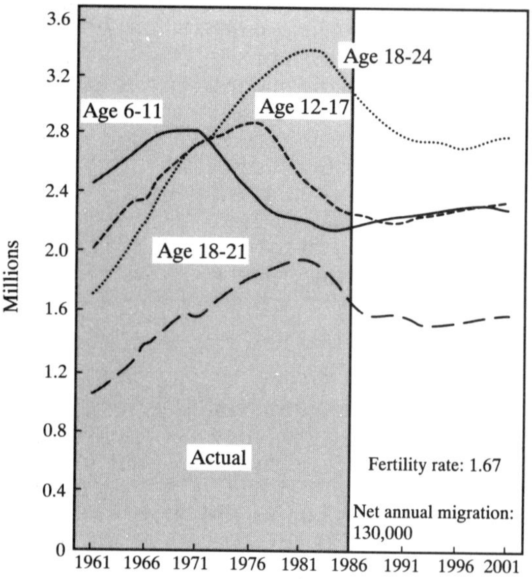

Figure 2
Selected age-group populations of relevance to school enrollment 1961–2001
Source: *Statistics Canada*

areas and severe climate, there are well-developed and innovative programs of distance education at all levels.

In 1989–90, close to six million Canadians, slightly less than one-fourth of the population, were enrolled full-time in educational institutions. Since education is compulsory until age 15 or 16, virtually all of this age group attend school. Of the total enrollment, elementary and secondary schools accounted for just over five million; nonuniversity postsecondary institutions for approximately 315,000, and universities for about 514,000. When part-time students attending universities are taken into account, the total enrollment was approximately 716,000 undergraduates and 100,000 graduate students. Figure 2 shows the actual and projected age-group population relevant to the three levels of education from 1961 through the year 2001.

In 1990, almost 110,000 bachelor's and first professional degrees were granted, an increase of 23,500 over 1980. In fact, between 1981 and 1986, the number of university graduates rose 432 percent, nearly seven times the growth rate of 65 percent for the population as a whole. Since 1981, the number of bachelor's degrees granted to women has exceeded those granted men, reaching about 56 percent in 1990. The number of master's and doctoral degrees awarded also increased over the decade, as did the percentage granted to women. Nevertheless, women are still underrepresented in senior administrative positions and full-time, tenured academic appointments.

Student enrollment includes an increasingly significant number of international students. In the fall of 1991, there were about 87,000 foreign students enrolled at all levels, the majority at the post-secondary level. Over half of these students were from Asian countries with Hong Kong sending about 16 percent of all international students.

Canadian university fees are heavily subsidized and average CDN$1500 a year for undergraduate tuition. Comparable fees for out-of-country students are about five times higher, but still considered competitive with the United States and many European countries.

3.2 Preschool Education

Although the starting age for Grade 1 is usually 6 or 7, preschool programs, commonly called "kindergarten classes," are provided in most provinces in public elementary schools for 5-year olds. Some school boards in Manitoba, Ontario, and Quebec include 4- and 5-year old children in two years of noncompulsory schooling. Alberta operates a unique publicly supported program called "Early Childhood Services," which integrates educational, health, social, and recreational services, and enrolls children as young as $3\frac{1}{2}$ years old. In other provinces, or as an alternative to public school programs, pre-Grade 1 classes are offered in privately operated schools under varying degrees of provincial supervision. For 1991–92, it was estimated that 484,500 children would be in preschool programs. Pre-elementary enrollment has shown an upward trend since 1978–79, partly because of increases in the 4- and 5-year old population and partly because of a greater participation rate. The latter may be due to the considerable increase in the number of families in which both parents work and the growing number of single-parent families. In 1988, for example, both parents were employed, either full- or part-time, in 64 percent of homes with children; in the case of single parents, the figure was 69 percent. In general, day-care facilities are considered to be inadequate to cope with this trend. In some provinces, child care spaces are being incorporated in both elementary and secondary schools to provide facilities for older as well as younger children before and after the formal school day.

3.3 Special Education

Canada emphasizes the concept of equal educational opportunity for all children and attempts to provide for individual differences. Since the 1970s, there has been a trend to integrate "special needs students" (roughly 5 to 10 percent of all students) into regular classrooms. This often requires considerable adjustments in both curriculum and teacher training because of the diverse groups that fall into this category. Included are physically handicapped children and the learning disabled, as well as academically gifted children who are usually directed into enriched or accelerated programs. Special language and cultural needs of children who have recently emigrated to Canada, or of aboriginal children who enter the public school system, are also recognized. In addition, programs have been incorporated in some schools to encourage girls to participate in science and mathematics, subjects which have traditionally been male-dominated. Some critics have argued that the policy of equality of opportunity affects the quality of education and that gifted students, for example, receive less attention than those who lack ability.

There are also separate schools, both public and private, for various categories of disability, such as the severely mentally handicapped, or the visually or hearing impaired.

The education of registered Indian and Inuit children falls within the responsibility of the federal government through its Department of Indian and Northern Affairs. The department is authorized to maintain schools for these children directly or to provide access to education in public or private schools. About half of Canada's aboriginal children attend provincial public schools. In 1986–87, the federal government owned and operated 141 schools on Indian reserves and, in addition, native band councils managed 244 schools under ministerial regulations. Since the 1980s, native peoples have become increasingly vocal in their demands for self-government. The dropout rate among native youth and problems relating to drug and alcohol use, together with a high suicide rate, have caught the attention of all Canadians and efforts are being made to remedy the mistakes of the past. One potential model for the future is a provincially funded secondary school opened in 1991 in Winnipeg, Manitoba. This school replaced a reserve school and has a program which, in addition to university and general courses, emphasizes instruction in native languages, history, and culture.

3.4 Vocational, Technical, and Business Education

Vocational preparation played an increasingly important role in secondary schools in the 1980s, although the earlier system of "streaming" students into vocational programs at age 14 was not reinstated. As a result of studies of the relationship between school and work, emphasis is given to a positive work attitude and ability to learn, rather than to specific job-related skills. The objective is to provide broader, transferable skills to enable young people to function in a society and a job market requiring flexibility to adapt to rapid technological change.

The prevalent Canadian view of education as preparation for work and the emphasis given to the relationship between income and formal qualifications was undoubtedly a factor in the widespread "community college" movement in the 1960s. These institutions originated a number of semiprofessional and technical diploma programs as adjuncts to, or replacements for, inservice training. Focus on the labor market is also reflected at the university level. Professional degrees have proliferated and are considered as prerequisites to employment not only in traditional areas such as law and medicine, but also in social work, teaching, librarianship, business administration, etc.

In addition to formal programs in composite secondary schools and postsecondary institutions, vocational and trade training is offered variously in community colleges, public trade schools, and vocational centers. In 1988–89, over 234,000 trainees were enrolled in such programs. On a small scale, training may also take place within industry in on-the-job apprenticeship programs. Most courses offered can be completed in less than a year and some for less complex occupations may last only a few weeks. Only people who have left the regular school system and who are older than the compulsory age are eligible to attend, and admission standards may range from Grade 8 to Grade 12. Historically, this kind of training was one of the first educational fields in which the federal government was involved since public schools and universities only rarely offered such programs. Initial participation was mainly financial and began with support of provincial programs after the First World War. After 1967, the federal government became more concerned with the types of training and the geographic distribution of programs. One of its current priorities is to encourage business and industry to play a more active role in training.

3.5 Adult and Nonformal Education

Continuing education is an important element in Canada and more than three million Canadians register in adult education programs each year. Courses are offered by a variety of institutions, including school boards, provincial departments of education, universities, and community colleges. Programs are also sponsored or conducted by nonprofit organizations, professional associations, government departments, and business and industry. Instruction is offered by a variety of methods in addition to the conventional classroom. Communications technology has popularized "open learning" and enables learners in remote areas to gain access to educational opportunities.

University extension programs developed rapidly after the Second World War. At the postsecondary level, some courses are offered for academic credit, others are noncredit cultural or recreational programs for personal development. Professional development and refresher courses are also popular.

Programs to counteract illiteracy have been strengthened in all educational jurisdictions. Some embody an institutional approach and are offered through community colleges and evening courses in community-based schools. There are also a number of voluntary organizations that have developed informal and individualized assistance. These methods have received broad recognition and appear to be a more amenable approach to illiteracy at the adult level than formal programs.

4. Administrative and Supervisory Structure and Operation

Each province has a department of education headed by a minister who is an elected member of the provincial cabinet, or in the case of the Yukon and Northwest territories, a councillor. In some provinces, postsecondary education is a separate ministry.

While a provincial minister has responsibility for the overall policy and management of the system, the day-to-day operation and supervision of the department is carried out by the deputy minister and his staff who are permanent civil servants. Functions of ministries include the supervision and inspection of elementary and secondary schools; provision of curriculum and school organization guidelines; production of curriculum materials; finance; teacher certification; prescription of regulations for school trustees and teachers; and support services such as libraries, health, and transportation.

In all provinces, schools are operated by local authorities (boards of education), which are made up of elected or appointed trustees or commissioners. School board areas are delineated by the province. In recent years, many small boards have been consolidated into central, regional, or county units. The powers of the board are delegated by the province and pertain principally to the business and management aspects of education, including the establishment, maintenance, and purchase of facilities and equipment; the appointment of teachers; and budget preparation. The extent to which provincial school systems are decentralized varies. However, in most cases, there is an ideological commitment to local control in response to community needs.

The institutional structure of universities is established by provincial legislative acts. Traditionally, universities are governed by a two-tier system: a board of governors who are responsible for final policy decisions, and a senate which is the university's senior academic body. Although subject to the authority of the board, the senate is responsible for academic policy relating to matters such as admission requirements, approval of courses and programs, qualifications for degrees, and academic planning.

The majority of community colleges also have a board of governors whose members may be appointed by the provincial government, chosen by the municipality, or elected, although a few institutions, mainly institutes of technology, are under direct government control. Boards usually include lay people, as well as faculty and students. Other management models include a partnership between government, colleges, and school district boards

(British Columbia), and, in Quebec, a partnership between the department of education and college boards, supplemented by a nongovernmental college association.

Provincial and territorial governments make every effort to accommodate individual transfers and movements between schools and from province to province. To assist this process, the Council of Ministers of Education, Canada (CMEC) regularly publishes *A Student Transfer Guide* describing secondary-school structures and programs. The Council was established in 1967 to provide a forum and a voice for provincial ministers on matters of common interest, and to facilitate cooperation among its members. As concern with education as a pan-Canadian priority has increased, the CMEC has undertaken a number of significant national activities. One example is the establishment, along with Statistics Canada, of the Canadian Education Statistics Council, whose primary objective is to collect and disseminate comparable, agreed upon interprovincial data.

5. *Educational Finance*

In the period of expansion in the 1960s, expenditures on education grew by 15 to 20 percent annually, absorbing more than 22 percent of government spending and reaching a high of around 8.6 percent of GDP. From 1981–82 to 1991–92 spending almost doubled from CDN$25.5 billion to an estimated CDN$50.6 billion, an annual average increase of 7.1 percent. Elementary and secondary education accounted for nearly 65 percent of this total. Like other industrialized nations, Canada experienced downturns in the economy in the 1980s and 1990s. Increasing concern about high government deficits and the range of services to be supported, contributed to the lowering of the GDP ratio in 1990–91 to about 7.0 percent. The per-student cost for primary and secondary education was CDN$5,817 in the school year 1989–90.

More than 90 percent of educational revenue comes from government with the balance generated from private sources such as tuition fees, donations, and investment income. Traditionally, financing of elementary–secondary education was a municipal responsibility with local property taxes paying most of the cost of basic education. While local taxes are still important, the municipal share in 1991–92 dropped to an estimated 20.5 percent from 49 percent in 1960. In half of the provinces, the bulk, or all, of school board revenues come directly from the province. In the remainder of the jurisdictions, revenues from local taxation range from approximately 35 to 50 percent. The relative contributions of local and provincial levels are adjusted to ensure minimum standards and to moderate local differences in income and wealth. The federal government's direct financing of programs under its jurisdiction amounted to an estimated 8.7 percent in 1991–92. In addition, part of provincial support actually consists of federal funds channelled through the provinces.

Postsecondary education is also essentially government financed, with the federal and provincial governments contributing over 80 percent of the total funding. Direct operating grants to eligible universities and colleges, in effect from 1951 to 1966, were replaced in 1967, except for sponsored research, by a system of transfer payments to provinces. A new method of financing was instituted in 1977, whereby federal contributions to post-secondary education, hospital insurance, and medicare were consolidated. Although about one-third of the allocation is expected to go to support education, provinces may allocate funds to the three programs as they see fit.

The federal government also operates the Canada Student Loans Program for students who do not have sufficient resources to cover the cost of full- or part-time studies at the postsecondary level. Interest on loans is paid by the government during a student's enrollment and repayment arrangements are made 6 to 18 months after the student graduates.

There is growing pressure from the universities for additional funding, with both faculty and students complaining of out-of-date facilities and equipment, crowded classrooms, and insufficient funds for research. Various proposals have been made from increasing fees to instituting a system whereby graduates would pay additional income taxes based on their salary levels once they are employed.

6. *Supplying Personnel for the Education System*

With the doubling of enrollment between 1951 and 1971, the number of elementary–secondary school teachers reached a new high of 284,900 in 1976–77, declined slightly until the mid-1980s, but has shown a steady increase since that time. Based on a student–teacher ratio of 17.5:1 (number of students per full-time teacher), the estimated number of teachers for the school year 1991–92 was 298,700. It is probable that the increase is the result of educational reforms and new programs such as ESL (English as a Second Language) to accommodate a growing immigrant population, as well as the increased focus on computer technology.

About 94 percent of elementary–secondary teachers are employed in public schools, 5 percent in private schools, and the remaining 1 percent in federal schools. In 1988–89, 58 percent of teachers were female, although three out of four public school administrators were men. As is the case with the labor force in general, the average age of teachers has increased owing to low recruitment and a high retention rate; in 1989, only 10 percent were under 30 years of age, compared to 40 percent 15 years earlier.

Teachers' working conditions depend on rules and regulations established by ministries or departments of education, as well as stipulations and policies of school boards who do the actual hiring. All provinces and territories require teachers to hold valid teaching certificates, or to be eligible for certification status. The eligibility requirement is normally a four-year Bachelor of Education (BEd) degree, or equivalent, from a recognized university. Alternatively, a one-year BEd degree may follow a first bachelor's degree in any field of study. Candidates for certification are assessed by the provincial department which also classifies the certificate level (general or specialist), subject area of specialization, and grade level. New teachers are usually required to complete a two-year probationary period. Salary levels are determined by certificate classification level and the number of years of successful teaching experience.

Canadian schools have faced many demands for new programs, ranging from second language instruction and computer technology to AIDS awareness, multicultural orientation, and integration of exceptional children in the regular classroom. The majority of provinces and territories offer inservice programs to help teachers adapt to innovations and learn new skills. Summer programs are also regularly offered by universities and departments of education.

At the postsecondary level, universities, with the exception of certain professional sectors of training, require a doctoral degree as part of the qualifications for entry to faculty tenure-stream positions. Some community college teachers also hold doctoral degrees, although work experience is the principal criterion for certain vocational and technical instructors. Universities and colleges employ a number of part-time or contractually-limited lecturers and instructors as well. Virtually no provision is made for formal pedagogical training of postsecondary educators. This lack, and the importance many universities accord to academic research rather than teaching, was the subject of a 1991 report on Canadian university education (Smith 1991). While the relative importance of research and publications versus teaching is not a new issue, it is likely to receive more attention in the 1990s.

7. *Curriculum Development and Teaching Methodology*

Educational systems in Canada underwent sweeping reforms in the 1960s and early 1970s. Concepts such as child-centered learning, continuous progress, team teaching, discovery method, open-plan schools, and audiovisual aids were adopted, sometimes with little attention to the consequences for educational outcomes or teacher training. School programs that had been made up largely of compulsory subjects and texts specified by provincial departments of education also underwent considerable modification and many new programs were introduced.

Structurally, educational systems became more decentralized. Provinces continued to issue general guidelines, but local boards and individual schools had more control over implementation, materials, and methods. Teaching became less formal and more participatory as a counter-trend to the traditional lecture method and learning by rote. Less emphasis was placed on the learning of "facts," and more on the acquisition of skills to facilitate learning.

While these educational reforms had positive outcomes, especially in terms of providing for individual differences and community needs, and for implementing equal access policies, since the mid-1980s schools have become the target of considerable criticism from employers, from universities, and from parents. Complaints focus on a perceived decline in academic standards, and in literacy and mathematical ability. Public pressure has been exerted in two somewhat conflicting directions: the expectation that schools will incorporate programs pertaining to social and ethical issues, and, at the same time, provide a solid foundation in "the basics." The result has been a trend to redefining an essential "core" curriculum incorporating more compulsory academic courses, mainly in mathematics, sciences, language arts, and social studies (usually history and geography). Elective courses which proliferated in the 1970s have undergone scrutiny. There is, however, a recognition of essential new knowledge and skills beyond the traditional "3 R's." Curricula therefore incorporate computer technology and components such as critical and creative thinking, independent learning, and environmental studies.

In response to national social and cultural policies, considerable effort is made to eliminate racial and sexual stereotypes from learning materials. Second-language learning is emphasized, and in some provinces students have the opportunity to study the less commonly taught languages. Alberta, for example, offers Cree (a native Indian language) and Ukranian, two groups that have contributed to the provincial culture. Sex equity is also fostered by depicting role models for girls and encouraging them to consider nontraditional careers, especially in disciplines and professions involving science or mathematics.

Curriculum materials produced by departments or ministries of education are normally pilot-tested in the schools and revised before receiving official ministry sanction. Curriculum materials produced by the private sector are usually subject to an approval process involving ministry and school board officials before being sanctioned officially. Other materials are considered to be curriculum-support materials.

8. *The System of Examinations, Promotions, and Certifications*

Continuous progress is the norm in elementary

schools. At the secondary level, credit systems are the rule and promotion by subject rather than grade is prevalent. Some jurisdictions have partially or entirely eliminated age-grouped classes. In general, the policy in Canada of open access to secondary education may be summarized as follows: although there is no automatic promotion, the school curriculum provides courses of studies at various levels so that differing abilities can be accommodated.

Graduation from secondary school is based on completion of the number of course credits specified by provincial guidelines. In most systems, examinations are prepared and students are assessed at the local level. However, in several provinces, notably British Columbia, Alberta, and Quebec (as well as the Northwest and Yukon territories which generally follow the programs of Alberta and British Columbia, respectively), graduation diploma examinations in certain subjects are centrally set by the department of education. The type and level of diplomas awarded differ within jurisdictions, but most provinces provide for general and advanced high-school diplomas in recognition of modified programs followed by students who do not intend to enter university. An average of over 60 percent of high-school graduates go on to some form of postsecondary education.

9. Educational Assessment, Evaluation, and Research

The trend to redefining a "core curriculum" and including more compulsory subjects has been accompanied by an emphasis on the measurement of educational outcomes. These focus not only on the assessment of student achievement, but also on the evaluation of programs, teachers, schools, and school systems.

At the elementary level, more attention is being given to the development of evaluation techniques to monitor student progress on a day-to-day basis, rather than summatively at the end of a term. Some provinces have instituted large-scale student testing in specific subjects at selected grade levels, a process which allows individual school systems and schools to be evaluated as well as students.

In 1989, the members of the CMEC combined their expertise in educational evaluation in order to develop the School Achievement Indicators Program. The program provides data to assist each province and territory in making policy decisions and planning program improvement. Indicators of student participation in the systems, as well as graduation rates, will form part of a profile that also includes indicators of the achievement of 13- and 16-year old students in reading, writing, and mathematics. Current plans call for the CMEC to report to the Canadian public on all indicators in the fall of 1993.

Research in education is carried out in all provinces and territories, although the level of activity varies because of differences in population density. A significant number of studies are undertaken by members of university faculties of education, as well as by educational organizations and teachers' federations. The federal government, through the Social Sciences and Humanities Research Council, is a major source of funding, especially for university researchers. Provincial departments and some larger school boards also direct research efforts to matters of regional or local concern, such as program evaluation. Although there is a recognition of the need for national studies, such as the proposed CMEC assessment, because of the political structure of Canadian education, such undertakings are often difficult to implement and fund.

There are a number of channels for the distribution of research results, including scholarly journals, and manual and computer access to references to published papers by services such as the *Canadian Education Index*, published by the Canadian Education Association, ONTERIS (Ontario Educational Research Information System), and EDUQ (Education Quebec). At the national level, Statistics Canada, the official governmental body responsible for the census and the collection of data on all aspects of Canadian life, produces regular statistical reports, analyses, and projections relating to all levels of education.

10. Major Problems for the Year 2000

It is probable that agreement on appropriate curricula, the measurement of educational outcomes, and remedies for functional illiteracy will still be major issues in the year 2000.

It is also likely that there will be an increasing recognition of the need to define the role of the school in a complex society and to identify priorities. In the last several decades, Canadian educational systems have given an almost "kneejerk" response to the multiple demands placed on them. It seems questionable whether schools can continue to pursue academic excellence and, at the same time, be expected to ameliorate social problems by providing the young with life skills, counseling, and moral and social values that were traditionally acquired within the family setting.

It has also been suggested that Canadians, despite their apparent commitment to education, do not value learning to the extent of some other cultures. Although Canada has one of the highest participation rates in the world in postsecondary education, it still lacks the highly skilled workers, particularly in scientific and technological areas, that are necessary if the country is to compete and prosper in a global economy. It has been estimated that nearly two-thirds of the jobs created between 1989 and 2000 will require a minimum of 12 years of schooling and 40 percent will require more than 16 years of training.

The present dropout rate in secondary schools will potentially create a large pool of unemployable, unskilled workers at the turn of the century. Opportunities for returning to school and for retraining are therefore likely to become priorities, as well as the development of new learning environments to promote continuing education.

Financial constraints will be the major concern for universities and other institutions offering post-secondary education. Alternative methods of financing and more efficient delivery systems may be debated. For example, there may be a trend to more specialization within institutions which presently offer programs across a range of academic disciplines and professions.

Finally, one cannot overlook the constitutional crisis of the 1990s which is likely to extend well into the twenty-first century. Educational systems cannot be considered in isolation from the politics, priorities, and culture of the society they serve, and any realignment among provinces, or between provinces and the federal government, will inevitably have a profound effect on education, as it will on all social institutions in Canada.

References

Council of Ministers of Education, Canada 1991a *Secondary Education in Canada: A Student Transfer Guide*, 6th edn. CMEC, Toronto

Smith S L 1991 *Report of the Commission of Inquiry on Canadian University Education.* The Commission, Ottawa

Further Reading

Canadian Education Statistics Council 1990 *A Statistical Portrait of Elementary and Secondary Education in Canada.* Statistics Canada and Council of Ministers of Education, Canada, Ottawa and Toronto

Corpus Almanac and Canadian Sourcebook 1991, 26th edn. Southam, Don Mills

Council of Ministers of Education, Canada 1988 *Recent Trends in Curriculum Reform at the Elementary and Secondary Levels in Canada.* Report presented to the OECD's Centre for Educational Research and Innovation (CERI). CMEC, Toronto

Council of Ministers of Education, Canada 1989 *Education in Canada, 1986–88.* Report to the 41st Session, International Conference on Education, Geneva, Jan. 9–17, 1989. CMEC, Toronto

Council of Ministers of Education, Canada 1990a *Adult Literacy, Canada.* Report to the 42nd Session, International Conference on Education, Geneva, Sept. 3–8, 1990. CMEC, Toronto

Council of Ministers of Education, Canada 1990b *Improving the Quality of Basic Education in Canada.* Prepared for the Eleventh Conference of Commonwealth Education Ministers. CMEC, Toronto

Council of Ministers of Education, Canada 1991b *Teachers' Working Conditions in Canada.* Report prepared in response to the International Labour Office questionnaire on The Conditions of Work of Teachers. CMEC, Toronto

Learning Well . . . Living Well. Draft discussion paper for pre-consultation meetings 1990. Government of Canada, Ottawa

Statistics Canada 1986 *Canadian Social Trends.* (Quarterly) Statistics Canada, Ottawa

Statistics Canada 1989 *Canada Year Book, 1990.* Statistics Canada, Ottawa

Statistics Canada 1990 *Education in Canada. A Statistical Review for 1989–90.* Statistics Canada, Ottawa (Cat. No. 81–229)

Statistics Canada 1991a *Advance Statistics of Education, 1991–92.* Statistics Canada, Ottawa (Cat. No. 81–220)

Statistics Canada 1991b *Canada, a Portrait.* Official handbook of present conditions and recent progress. Statistics Canada, Ottawa (Cat. No. 81–220)

D. L. Berg

Canonical Analysis

During the 1970s and 1980s there was increasing acceptance and use of multivariate analytic procedures that examined the interrelations between the latent variables formed from defined sets of observed variates. Canonical variate analysis was first developed as early as 1935 by Hotelling (1935) and was largely unused because of the complexity of the computations that had to be carried out by hand. With the introduction of the electronic computer, programs which permit its use have become more readily available. However, the power of this analytical procedure is not generally acknowledged. Canonical variate analysis is in fact the general analytic method of which most other parametric statistical procedures, varying from t-tests and analysis of variance through to principal components analysis, factor analysis, and regression analysis and discriminant analysis are but special cases. Both historically and conceptually the basic analytical procedure employed in multivariate analysis is that of canonical variate analysis. Thus a sound understanding of the ideas and principles involved in canonical variate analysis provides an excellent foundation for the development of an understanding of other analytical procedures, such as partial least squares path analysis (PLS), linear structural relations (LISREL) analysis, and multivariate analysis of covariance (MANCOVA). This entry is concerned with the analytical procedure of canonical variate analysis. In this treatment, following Bartlett (1941), the term "variate" is used to refer to those observed measures that are introduced into the analysis, while the term "variable" is reserved for the latent constructs that are formed as a combination of the observed measures or variates.

1. Introduction

Canonical analysis or canonical variate analysis

(CVA) is one of the statistical methods used for studying relations between two sets (X and Y) of variates. Each set may contain one or more than one variate. In this situation, Darlington et al. (1973) envisage three different types of questions that can be asked concerning the correlation matrix of the $(n_x + n_y)$ variates.

(a) Questions about the number and nature of mutually independent relations between the two sets of variates.

(b) Questions about the degree of overlap or redundancy between the two sets. This implies questions about the extent to which one set may be predicted from the other, and vice versa.

(c) Questions about the similarity between the two within-set correlation or covariance matrices.

The use of CVA is often appropriate in answering questions of type (a), sometimes appropriate for those of type (b), and never appropriate for those of type (c).

In order for the purpose of CVA to be more clearly understood, Darlington et al. (1973 p. 439) set out in a table the relationship of CVA to the techniques of analysis of variance, multiple regression analysis, and multivariate analysis of variance. They also point out that by the appropriate use of dummy variables, CVA can perform multiple discriminant analyses and simple contingency table analyses. Canonical variate analysis is thus a technique to be used when either set X or set Y contains one or more variates, and the variates in either set may be continuous, categorical, or mixed.

In canonical variate analysis, the first canonical correlation is the highest correlation that can be found between a weighted composite of the X variates and a weighted composite of the Y variates (the composites being the first pair of canonical variables). The second canonical correlation is the highest correlation that can be found between the X and Y weighted composites which are uncorrelated (orthogonal) with the first pair of canonical variables. The significance of the first, the second, and each subsequent canonical correlation (there being in all n_{min} correlations where n_{min} is the minimum of n_x and n_y) is tested by Bartlett's chi-square approximation to the distribution of Wilks's lambda or by an F-ratio.

The canonical correlation coefficient (Rc_i) between each pair of variables describes the strength of the relationship between the two variables. The square of this relationship Rc_i^2 describes the proportion of the variance of one variable predictable from the other variable both within the same pair of canonical variables.

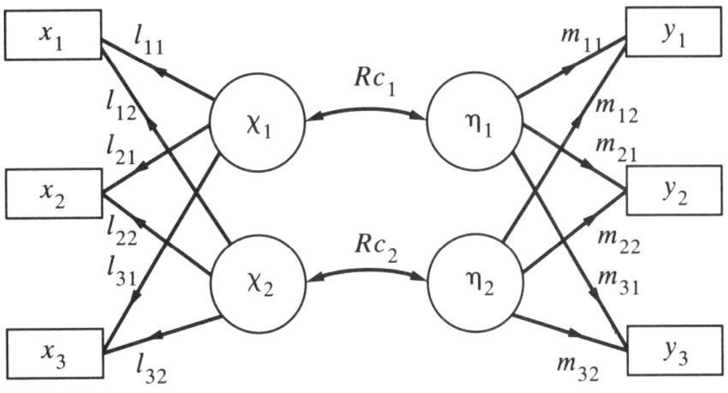

Figure 1
Canonical variate analysis seen as double factor analysis with two orthogonal latent variables.

2. *Relationship of CVA with Regression Analysis and Principal Components Analysis*

The description of the first and subsequent canonical correlations given above can be compared with two other types of analysis.

First, multiple regression analysis where the Y set contains only one variate and a weighted composite of X variates is obtained to maximize the correlation (R_y) between the Y variable (often called the criterion) and the X composite (called the predictor variable). In this situation R_y^2 can be thought of as the proportion of the variance of the criterion that can be "predicted" (or "accounted for," or "explained") from a knowledge of the set of X variates, in particular, the predictor variable.

Second, within each set, the formation of the first, second, and subsequent variables has a univariate analogue in factor analysis, where each factor is a weighted composite of, say, the X variates. In principal components analysis the first composite is formed to maximize the variance extracted. The effect of this first factor is then removed from the original correlation matrix and a second composite formed which is orthogonal to the first composite. The factor loadings of each composite (or variable, or factor), when squared and summed enable the proportion of variance extracted by the factor to be determined. The relationships between regression analysis and CVA, and between factor analysis and CVA, are discussed by Van de Geer who gives two overviews of multivariate models. The first, a pictorial overview, and the second, an overview in terms of operations of matrices, emphasize "that multivariate techniques do not fall into separate categories as special techniques for special situation, but instead form a close family" (Van de Geer 1971 p. 91).

3. *A Pictorial Representation of Canonical Variate Analysis*

In examining and presenting the results of canonical variate analysis (see Van de Geer 1971) it is generally

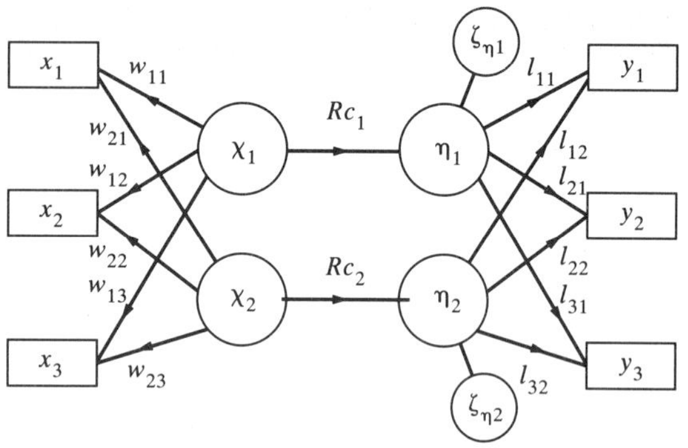

Figure 2
Canonical variate analysis seen as a regression model with two pairs of orthogonal latent variables

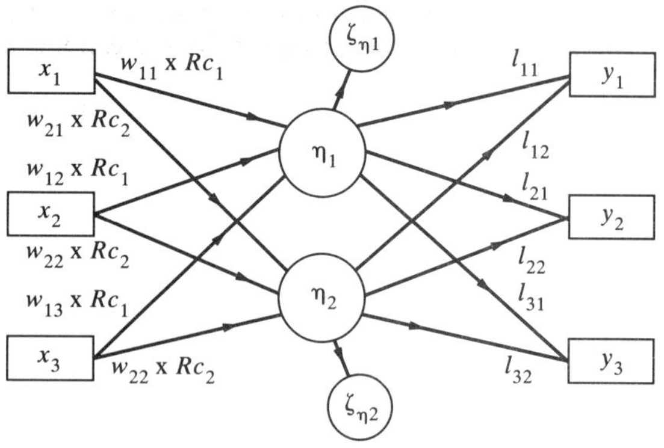

Figure 3
Canonical variable analysis seen as a reduced regression model with two orthogonal latent variables

appropriate to provide a pictorial representation of the results. It is common to indicate observed variates by boxes and latent variables by circles, and to identify the former by normal alphabetical symbols and the latter by Greek alphabetical symbols. If a variable χ is merely considered to be correlated with variable η, the bidirectional nature of the association is indicated by a curved line with arrow heads at both ends. The analytical procedure of canonical variate analysis does not itself distinguish between the different conceptualizations that may be applied to interpret the results of the analysis. These conceptualizations are models derived from theory that have been postulated. The nature of a model is predicated upon theory. If no causal relationship is assumed between the X and Y sets of variates then canonical correlation may be viewed as a double factor analysis. This model is shown pictorially in Fig. 1.

If, however, the variates in set X are viewed as determining the variates in set Y the model is conceptually different and the relationships between the variates and the variables are shown in a different way. This model is shown pictorially in Fig. 2.

For simplicity in pictorial representation the latent variables χ and η in Fig. 2 corresponding to the X set of variates and the Y set of variates respectively, can be combined and the model reduces to the simplified or equivalent form shown in Fig. 3.

4. *Structure Coefficients and Transformation Weights*

Two types of coefficients are available to assist in the interpretation of canonical variate analysis, namely "transformation weights" and "structure coefficients." Sometimes the terms "function coefficient" or "canonical weights" are used instead of "transformation weights," and sometimes the term "standardized canonical loadings" is used instead of "structure coefficients." The interpretation of the factors formed in a canonical variate analysis has traditionally been based on the standardized transformation weights which are analogous to the beta weights in multiple regression analysis and which are assigned to the original variates in forming each latent variable as a linear combination of the variates. Alternatively, the structure coefficients which are the correlations between each of the derived canonical variables and the original variates may be used. From the view of multiple factor analysis these structure coefficients or loadings enable the pairs of canonical variables to be identified and related to the relevant variates in their respective batteries. Moreover, the sum of the squared structure coefficients enables the proportion of variance (V_i) of each set that is extracted by each factor to be determined.

Tatsuoka has commented on the use of structure coefficients:

> That this is a more reasonable approach in attempting to *interpret* the canonical factors (as against assessing the relative contribution of each original variable to the factors) becomes obvious when we recall that the standardized weights (canonical or discriminant) are partial coefficients with the effects of other variables removed or controlled. This is fine when the purpose is to gauge the contribution of each variable in the company of others, but is inappropriate when we wish to give substantive interpretations. (Tatsuoka 1973 p. 280)

Nevertheless, different meanings can be extracted from each set of coefficients with respect to the nature of the model in terms of which the canonical variate analysis is interpreted.

In the path model shown in Fig. 2 it is assumed that the X variates completely determine the latent variables χ_1 and χ_2 and that these latent variables determine, in part, the latent variables η_1 and η_2 with residual error term $e_{\eta 1}$ and $e_{\eta 2}$. The paths from the X variates to the χ variables are given by the transformation weights (w), while the paths from the η variables to the Y variates are given by the structure coefficients l. The influences of the χ latent variables on the η latent variables are given by the canonical correlations Rc_1 and Rc_2 as shown in Fig. 2.

In Fig. 3 where the χ latent variables are omitted, arrows are drawn directly from the X variates to the two η, latent variables, and the values of the path coefficients are given by the products of the corresponding transformation weights and canonical correlations. The residual error terms also act on the η latent variables as shown in Fig. 3.

In Fig. 1 where the model employed uses canonical variate analysis to examine two sets of variables as a double factor analysis, then the paths from the latent variables to the observed variates are given by the appropriate structure coefficients (l). Thus both the structure coefficients and the transformation weights have different uses in the interpretation of the data depending upon the nature of the model that is postulated from theory.

It should be noted that not all readily available computer programs provide both the structure coefficients and the transformation weights and since the models employed may require for full understanding both sets of coefficients, care must be taken in selecting which computer program is employed for the canonical variate analysis with a particular set of data to test a specific model derived from a relevant theoretical perspective.

5. *Variance Considerations*

Some computer programs commonly used for canonical analysis, for example, (Cooley and Lohnes 1971) also include in their printout, measures of redundancy. These measures combine the proportion of variance of one canonical variable predictable from the other canonical variable Rc_i^2 and the proportion of variance (V_i) of each test battery is predictable from a knowledge of scores on the variates in the other battery. This is determined for each canonical variable and is called the factor redundancy: $Rc_i^2 \times V_i$. The factor redundancies are totaled to give the total factor redundancy for each battery given the other battery. Thus it is the redundancy (and not Rc_i^2) that describes how much variance is predictable from one battery to another, whereas for the univariable criterion model of regression analysis, the value of R_y^2 describes this proportion of predictable variance. These measures of redundancy tell much more than do the canonical correlation coefficients about the outcome of the canonical analysis. However, Pugh and Hu (1991) endorse avoiding the interpretation of redundancy coefficients because of their lack of multivariate properties.

6. *Partitioning of Redundancy*

Mayeske et al. (1969) in their re-examination of the data available from the Equality of Educational Opportunity Survey in A *Study of Our Nation's Schools* partitioned the estimates of variance accounted for into unique and joint effects following a procedure which has been discussed more fully by Wisler (1969) and Mood (1971). This technique had been advanced earlier by Newton and Spurrell (1967) and was employed by Peaker (1971) in the report of the Plowden Follow-up Study. Mood (1971) noted a shortcoming of the measure—under certain circumstances the joint contributions to variance explained could be negative. These effects are similar in kind to suppressor relationships. In spite of this shortcoming in the interpretation of the results of partitioning variance, the technique is a useful one for drawing attention to the confounding that occurs between both individual predictor variates and between domains of predictor variates which account for the variation in the criterion variates.

Subsequently, Cooley and Lohnes (1976) developed procedures for the partitioning of variance in

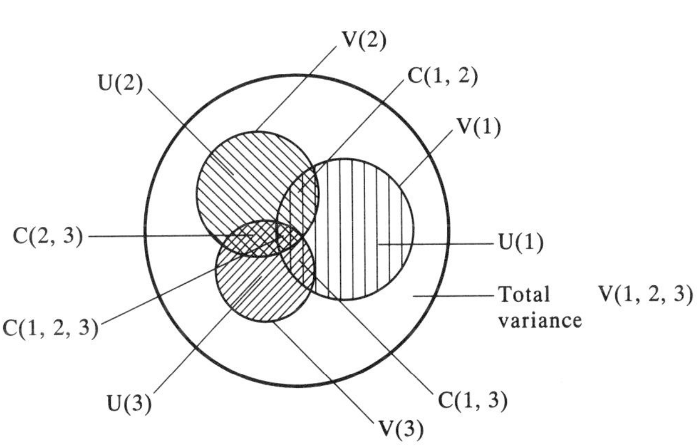

Figure 4
Venn Diagram for three predictor sets

canonical analysis. The unique contribution of a domain of predictors to the multivariate prediction of a set of criterion measures is that part of the variance of the criteria explained by the full model which cannot be obtained without using the particular domain of predictor variables. It is that part of the total redundancy which the particular domain of predictors will account for when these predictors are added to the other predictors included in the canonical analysis. The joint contribution for each predictor domain is the redundancy explained by the full model less the sum of the unique contributions. Thus the total redundancy is partitioned into unique and joint contributions, and the commonality or confounded contribution is separated from the contributions which are not so confounded.

The procedures for partitioning variance and redundancy are simply those of separating quantities associated with overlapping sets. Where there are more than two domains of predictors the possibility exists of partitioning the redundancy into pieces associated with various subsets of the predictors, but where more than four domains exist, the number of possible partitions becomes large and not very meaningful.

Cooley and Lohnes (1976) have prouded the rules for the partitioning of redundancy where $V(j, k, l)$ is the redundancy for a canonical regression model with the predictor sets of J, K, and L. These rules are derived with the use of the Venn diagram shown in Fig. 4.

Two Predictor Sets

Uniqueness for Set 1 $= U(1) = -V(2) + V(1,2)$
Uniqueness for Set 2 $= U(2) = -V(1) + V(1,2)$
Commonality for Set 1 and Set 2 $= C(1,2) = V(1) + V(2) - V(1,2)$

Three Predictor Sets

Uniqueness for Set 1 $= U(1) = -V(2,3) + V(1,2,3)$
Uniqueness for Set 2 $= U(2) = -V(1,3) + V(1,2,3)$
Uniqueness for Set 3 $= U(3) = -V(1,2) + V(1,2,3)$
Commonality C(1,2) $= -V(3) + V(1,3) + V(2,3) - V(1,2,3)$
Commonality C(1,3) $= -V(2) + V(1,2) + V(2,3) - V(1,2,3)$
Commonality C(2,3) $= -V(1) + V(1,2) + V(1,3) - V(1,2,3)$
Commonality C(1,2,3) $= V(1) + V(2) + V(3) - V(1,2) - V(1,3) - V(2,3) + V(1,2,3)$

Examples of canonical analysis showing both pictorial representation and the partitioning of redundancy are given by Keeves (1975, 1986). In the latter case the results of the analysis of data using this analytical procedure may be compared with those obtained through the use of alternative procedures.

7. *Significance Testing*

While significance tests are available for the extraction of latent roots from the complete body of data in canonical variate analysis, which also provide a test for the level of significance of the canonical correlations obtained, such tests assume a simple random sample of cases. However, simple random samples are the exception rather than the rule in the examination of educational data sets. As a consequence the significance tests employed are totally inappropriate. Furthermore, there are no commonly used procedures for testing the significance of transformation weights and structure coefficients or redundancy coefficients. The investigator is thus left to examine critically the magnitudes of these different coefficients and to make a decision regarding which coefficients it is appropriate to include in the interpretation of the data.

8. *Some Developments*

Pugh and Hu (1991) have reviewed the use and interpretation of canonical analysis. Of particular interest is their discussion of the number of subjects needed in relation to the number of variates included in an analysis. No simple rules seem adequate, and the use of the largest possible sample size to be recommended with a ratio of at least 20:1, for subjects to variates, is necessary for accurate interpretation. Furthermore, they strongly endorse the use of cross-validation to examine the invariance of the analysis.

In both the predictive and descriptive uses of canonical analysis, it is possible to employ stepwise procedures for the inclusion of variables in the analysis. However, where such procedures are used some form of cross-validation is desirable if not essential. In addition, by calculating the appropriate matrices of residual correlations it is possible to undertake a part (or partial) canonical analysis, but such procedures have not been widely used in substantive studies (Thorndike 1978).

In addition, Van de Geer (1971 pp. 169–70) considers the application of canonical analysis procedures in situations when the first and second pairs of canonical variables are considered correlated and not orthogonal. Furthermore, Horst (1965) and Van de Geer (1968) provide treatments of problem situations where there are three or more data matrices which are simultaneously matched by canonical variate analysis. However, the development of LISREL has tended to supplant the use of canonical variate analysis in the testing of these and more complex models.

See also: Regression Analyses of Quantified Data; Latent Trait Measurement Models; Factorial Modeling

References

Bartlett M S 1941 The significance of canonical correlations. *Biometrika* 32: 29–38
Cooley W W, Lohnes P R 1971 *Multivariate Data Analysis*. Wiley, New York
Cooley W W, Lohnes P R 1976 *Evaluation Research in Education*. Irvington, New York
Darlington R B, Weinberg S L, Walberg H J 1973 Canonical variate analysis and related techniques. *Rev. Educ. Res.* 43: 433–54
Horst P 1965 *Factorial Analysis of Data Matrices*. Holt, Rinehart and Winston, New York
Hotelling H 1935 The most predictable criterion. *J. Exp. Psychol.* 26: 139–42
Keeves J P 1975 The home, the school and achievement in mathematics and science. *Sci. Educ.* 59(4): 207–18
Keeves J P 1986 Canonical variate analysis. *Int. J. Educ. Res.* 10(2): 164–73
Mayeske G W et al. 1969 *A Study of Our Nation's Schools*. United States Government Printing Office, Washington, DC
Mood A M 1971 Partitioning variance in multiple regression analyses as a tool for developing learning models. *Am. Educ. Res. J.* 8: 191–202
Newton R G, Spurrell D J 1967 A development of multiple regression for the analysis of routine data. *Appl. Stat.* 16: 51–64
Peaker G F 1971 *The Plowden Children Four Years Later*. National Foundation for Educational Research, Slough
Pugh R C and Hu Y 1991 Use and interpretation of canonical correlation analysis. *J. Educ. Res.* Articles: 1978–1989; *J. Educ. Res.* 84(3): 147–52
Tatsuoka M M 1973 Multivariate analysis in educational research. In: Kerlinger F N (ed.) 1973 *Review of Research in Education 1*. Peacock, Itasca, Illinois
Thorndike R M 1978 *Correlation Procedures for Research*. Gardner, New York
Van de Geer J P 1968 *Matching k Sets of Configurations*. University of London, Department of Data Theory, London (Report RN-005-68)
Van de Geer J P 1971 *Introduction to Multivariate Analysis for the Social Sciences*. Freeman, San Francisco, California
Wisler C F 1969 Partitioning the explained variation in a regression analysis. In: Mayeske G W et al. 1969

Further Reading

Pedhazur E J 1982 *Multiple Regression in Behavioral Research*. Holt, Rinehart and Winston, New York
Thompson B 1984 *Canonical Correlation Analysis: Uses and Interpretation*. Sage University Paper Series on Quantitative Applications in the Social Sciences, 07-001. Sage, Beverly Hills, California

J. P. Keeves; J. D. Thomson

Career Education for Special Needs Students

The concept of career education, first formulated in 1971, was developed in the United States. It has been of special importance for educators working with special needs children. The reforms proposed under the heading career education were hailed as having the potential to reduce the huge dropout rate occurring at that time in United States schools. The career education concept that evolved was broader than vocational education. Career education was viewed as preparation for both paid and unpaid work. It included work roles, but also the roles of family member, citizen (including volunteer work), and of a person involved in productive leisure time or recreational activities. This entry will discuss the importance of career education as part of education in general in the context of the educational reform and restructuring movement of the 1990s.

1. Historical Development

Career education became a significant force in United States education in the 1970s and early 1980s. The United States Department of Education established an Office of Career Education in 1974, with Kenneth B Hoyt as director. In 1977 the Career Education Implementation Incentive Act was passed to support activities over a five-year period. Federal monies became available to institute pilot research and demonstration projects, hire personnel, secure materials, and move toward an infusion of career education into the curriculum of the schools. Many state and local educational agencies hired career education coordinators to facilitate this effort.

The concept of career education was also viewed as an important educational reform by many special educators. In 1973 the Council for Exceptional Children (CEC) collaborated with the American Vocational Association (AVA) to conduct a National Topical Conference on Career Education for Exceptional Children and Youth. In 1976 CEC approved a Division on Career Development (DCD). In 1978 CEC issued a position paper supporting career education, and the following year sponsored special institutes and a national topical conference.

In 1982 the federal Career Education Incentive Act expired and the Office of Career Education began phasing itself out. But career education has continued to be a significant component of United States education. Annual and biannual conferences by national career education organizations (including

DCD) continue to be conducted and attended by many staunch supporters and dedicated advocates.

Although "career education" is no longer a commonly used term in the United States, its basic tenets have remained and have been implemented for students with disabilities, under terms such as career development, vocational special education, transition, life skills, and functional skills. One particular exception is the *Life Centered Career Education Curriculum* (Brolin 1993), which will be described later in this entry.

2. Need for Career Education

Most students with disabilities face serious troubles after leaving the educational system. This fact was well-documented in the 1980s, when a multitude of statewide and national studies clearly revealed the limited employment, social, and independent-living achievements of most of these individuals, particularly as young adults. A National Longitudinal Transition Study (SRI International 1988) of 1,326 randomly selected former special education students found that only 29.2 percent were employed one year after leaving school.

The "quality of life" outcome of the former students in the SRI study was even more disappointing. Only 17.3 percent of the entire group were living independently, and only 40 percent were considered by their parents to have adequate "mental skills" (e.g., able to look up telephone numbers, use a telephone, count change, tell time, read common signs). Many experts in the field strongly believe that the curricula for students with disabilities must transcend the traditional academic approach to incorporate specific training in independent living skills, interpersonal and social skills, employability skills, and leisure-time activities.

The education of students with disabilities must equip them with the functional skills needed for employment, social relationships, leisure and recreation, community participation, and independent living. Educational programs cannot assume that students with special learning needs will acquire such skills without direct, competency-based instruction over the entire span of the educational career (K-12). The need of these students is clear: more relevant and appropriate education that will help them build the self-esteem and functional competence required to become a fully participating member of the community. The educational system must become significantly more responsive to the needs of these children and youth if they are to be independent, contributing members of society.

The evidence shows that a substantial career education approach (now more commonly referred to as "functional curriculum") is of critical importance if students with disabilities and other special-needs students are to become successful and productive adults.

3. Barriers to Career Education Implementation

A National Study of High School Programs for Handicapped Youth (Knowlton and Clark 1989) concluded that a major impediment to successful implementation of a functional curriculum was the lack of administrative commitment to the program. The study revealed that teacher commitment to implementing a functional curriculum is not likely to be strong if the administration does not highly value this type of approach. The Knowlton and Clark study supported studies of the Life Centered Career Education (LCCE) Curriculum (Roessler et al. 1990), in which five elements were found to be critical for implementing such a curriculum; administrative support; teacher involvement; school–agency coordination; parental participation; and community placements.

4. Theoretical Foundations and Models

The career education approach is based on the premise that work (paid and unpaid) is, for almost everyone, an important psychological and economic need. Thus, the development of an adequate work personality is critical for each student if he or she is to build a positive self-concept and feelings of dignity and worth. Although the career education concept includes the unpaid aspects of work (e.g., the work of a family member, citizen or volunteer, and avocational activities), the approach has been built on several theories of vocational or career development. In this section, three theoretical models are presented as illustration.

4.1 Hershenson's Theory of Work Adjustment

Hershenson's theory is a developmental model, based on the interaction of the individual and the environment over the individual's life span. The model comprises three domains: (a) work personality, which consists of the person's self-concept as a worker and the person's system of motivation for work; (b) work competencies, consisting of the person's work habits, physical and mental skills applicable to jobs, and work-related interpersonal skills; and (c) work goals, which reflect the individual's specific career objectives at a specific point in time. Hershenson believes that these three domains develop sequentially, in the order listed, and interact over the person's lifetime to affect the person's work adjustment.

According to the theory, one's work personality first develops during infancy under the influence of family; the work competencies during the school years; and the work goals vary over time and are influenced by peers and others while preparing for the transition from school to work. Work adjustment is a dynamic process, occurring over the lifetime, influenced by changes in each of the domains. Work adjustment has three components: task performance, work role behavior, and work satisfaction. Each component is linked primarily to one of the domains: task performance to work competencies, work role behavior to work personality, and work satisfaction to work goals.

Hershenson's theory acknowledges the impact disability can have on work adjustment, recognizing that those with congenital disabilities may be influenced adversely during the formative years, affecting the home-to-school transition and making the development of work competencies difficult. Persons with acquired disabilities would be affected in the work competencies domain, but such disabilities could also impact the work personality and work goals domains (Hershenson 1981).

4.2 Clark's School-based Career Development and Transition Model

Clark's model focuses on work but gives equal consideration to other related competencies that are critical for successful career development and the transition from school to community functioning. He conceived curricula from elementary to junior high school as based on four important elements: (a) values, attitudes, and habits; (b) human relationships; (c) occupational information; and (d) the acquisition of job and daily-living skills. These four elements are considered a solid foundation for the more specific career preparation that students will undertake in high school, postsecondary, and adult and continuing education programs.

The career development and transition education model advocated by Clark is conceived as appropriate for special education students from preschool through the working and retirement years. It is a content model, one that is proposed as an appropriate framework for all exceptionalities at the high school level, irrespective of the administrative placement of students. However, as Clark and Kolstoe (1990) indicated, the school reforms started in the 1980s make implementation of this type of program very difficult.

4.3 Brolin's Life-centered Career Education (LCCE) Model

The LCCE Curriculum (Brolin 1993) is a competency-based educational program that focuses on 22 major skills, categorized under daily living, personal–social, and occupational curriculum areas. The competencies are considered critical for students' employment and avocational activities. The curriculum is based on career development theory and the active involvement of three major instructional settings: home, community, and school. The concept of "infusion" is important; that is, teaching the 22 competencies and their 97 subcompetencies in mainstream regular school subjects whenever possible.

The LCCE approach offers curriculum-based assessment materials to determine the strengths and weaknesses of each student, relative to the 22 competencies. There are knowledge and performance batteries that have been extensively field tested, a basic curriculum guide, and a set of over 1,000 lesson plans. The system includes staff development training materials and programs available for schools interested in implementation. It is probably the most comprehensive functional skills or transition approach available in special education. It has been the object of several research studies and national projects to verify its importance and usefulness for special education students.

5. Career Education in Other Countries

Different countries hold varying points of view and definitions about the nature of career education. Many still conceive the concept more from a vocational or career guidance activity rather than the more expanded view that is presented in this entry. With regard to the former, the Commission of the European Communities (CEC) proposed a program for practical cooperation among member states in secondary education, and set the following priorities: (a) prepare teachers better for their new roles in the transition process; (b) promote closer links between education and economic development; (c) combat school failures; (d) strengthen the specific role of the school in the guidance process; (e) promote gender equality in education; and (f) strengthen the partnership between parents and secondary schools (Commission of the European Communities 1988). The Commission has since been active in developing an action program for the training and preparation of young people for adult and working life. However, no information is available on services to students with disabilities.

The literature includes little information on specific career education programs for students with disabilities in countries other than the United States, but the work being done in three countries will be presented below.

5.1 Australia

In Australia, Parmenter of MacQuarie University has provided leadership in promoting career education programs for students with disabilities. His research team has worked with the Commonwealth Rehabilitation Service in developing seven innovative Work Preparation Centres to train students with intellectual disabilities in the skills needed for employment and independent living. After many years of experience and research, Parmenter has concluded that career education must begin early for students with disabilities if they are to benefit from the later stages of the transition process from school to work and adult living.

Research by Parmenter and his associates has

shown that more emphasis must be given to training these students not only in getting and keeping a job, but also in communication, social, and interpersonal skills. For students with intellectual impairments, a functional skills curriculum is recommended, rather that forcing these students to follow curricula for students who are preparing for an academic career (Parmenter 1986)

5.2 Israel

In Israel, Shoshani of the Centre for Educational Technology in Ramat Aviv, has conducted a special project entitled Education Toward Career Independence for Special Education Students for seventh to ninth graders, to reduce the dropout rate and improve employment opportunities.

A career education program was designed to provide training in the following areas: self-awareness; beginning competency; career awareness; decision-making; employability skills; attitudes and appreciations; economic awareness; and educational awareness. The curriculum is being taught over a period of three years to 13 to 16 years olds, for two to four hours a week. The project has attempted to integrate the LCCE Curriculum with a program developed by the New York City Board of Education, Division of Special Education. In the mid-1990s the Shoshani project was still in progress, though the research relating to comprehensive methodological guidelines for effective implementation was still in the formative stages (Shoshani 1988).

5.3 Taiwan

In Taiwan, researchers in the National Changhua University of Education have launched studies using the LCCE approach for special education students. With the assistance of Kolstoe from the United States, a research team found that the LCCE model could serve as a guide for the content of a career education program for junior high school-aged students in Taiwan who are significantly handicapped (Sheu et al. 1986). Their work identified 180 subcompetencies considered appropriate by the teachers in their study.

Based on the above study, Sheu and Chou collaborated with Brolin in the United States to field test newly developed instructional materials covering the personal–social skills domain of the curriculum. This study (Sheu et al. 1989) of four personal–social skills competency units, found that junior high students with mild mental disabilities significantly improved in two of the four competency areas after studying for only one semester. In the mid-1990s the Taiwan research team was continuing to study the effects of the LCCE materials and to make adaptations so that a career education curriculum approach could be more widely implemented throughout the country.

6. Conclusion

Referring to students with disabilities, Clark et. al. (1991) noted: "special attention to the unique career development needs of these children is as, if not more, important than the general educational deficits that exist. Instructional or guidance time should not be guided by the unwarranted assumption that attention to basic academic skills is all that is needed to provide positive long-term functional outcomes" (p. 15). In essence, it is clear that educators cannot wait until the high school years to provide career education if these individuals are to gain the competence they need for adult success.

Many societies are becoming more complex and technological every year. It is critical that students learn the skills they need to survive in the labor market, and for independent living. Employers want persons who are adaptable, possess self-esteem, have the ability to set goals and motivate themselves, are able to move among jobs, and have the ability to work as a team member. Unless they learn these skills, students with disabilities will at best be destined for the "secondary labor market," that is, jobs that pay little more than minimum wage, offer no fringe benefits, demand few skills, are insecure, and lack advancement opportunities. Career education is not advocated as a replacement for conventional education, but rather as a major curriculum element to be incorporated into the educational mainstream. Few reject its basic premise but, unfortunately, most fail to fully implement it. However, unlike other educational innovations, which have lasted only 3 to 5 years, career education has already endured for over 20 years and has again gained momentum as a worthy educational reform. No other curricular approach has incorporated all the components that are needed to prepare students for all the work roles, paid and unpaid, that they will need to survive.

In the 1990s, there has been a greater emphasis on integrating special education students into regular classes (see *Integrated Services for Children and Youth with Special Needs; Mainstreaming*). While most will argue with this philosophical approach, it is critical that students also learn the daily living, personal–social, and occupational skills needed for adult functioning. A major issue is whether or not special education students can be successfully integrated with regular class students to learn both academic skills and the functional/career education skills they will need for adult success.

See also: Technical and Vocational Education and Training; Transition to Adult and Working Life for Persons with Handicaps

References

Brolin D E (ed.) 1993 *Life-centered Career Education: A Competency-based Approach.* Council for Exceptional Children, Reston, Virginia

Clark G M, Kolstoe O P 1990 *Career Development and Transition Education for Adolescents with Disabilities*. Allyn and Bacon, Boston, Massachusetts
Clark G M, Carlson B C, Fisher S, Cook I D, D'Alonzo B J 1991 *Career Development for Students with Disabilities in Elementary Schools: A Position Statement of the Division on Career Development*. Council for Exceptional Children, Reston, Virginia
Commission of the European Communities 1988 *The European Community Action Programme for the Vocational Training of Young People and Their Preparation for Adult and Working Life*. Commission of the European Communities, Brussels
Hershenson D B 1981 Work adjustment, disability, and the three r's of vocational rehabilitation: A conceptual model. *Rehabilitation Counseling Bulletin* 25(2): 91–97
Knowlton H E, Clark G M 1989 *National Study of High School Special Education Programs for Handicapped Youth in Transition. Vol. 1: Qualitative Component*. Department of Special Education, University of Kansas, Lawrence, Kansas
Parmenter T R 1986 *Bridges from School to Working Life for Handicapped Youth: The View from Australia*. World Rehabilitation Fund, Durham, New Hampshire
Roessler R T, Loyd R J, Brolin D E 1990 Implementing life-centered career education: Contextual barriers and implementation recommendations. *Acad. Ther.* 25(4): 523–33
Sheu T, Chou T, Kolstoe O P, Shyu S 1986 A study of the suitability of the life-centered career education program for the junior high school mentally retarded students in Taiwan, Republic of China. *J. Spec. Educ.* 1: 153–253
Sheu T, Chou T, Lin J 1989 *A Study of the Effects of Life-centered Career Education (LCCE) Personal–Social Skills Training with Mild Mentally Retarded Students in Junior High Schools: The Republic of China*. National Changhua University of Education, Changhua City
Shoshani Y 1988 *Education toward Career Independence for Special Education Students*. Max Rowe Educational Centre, Ramat Aviv
SRI International 1988 *OSEP National Longitudinal Study*. United States Department of Education, Office of Special Education Programs, Washington, DC

D. E. Brolin

Caribbean and Central America: Adult Education

This entry introduces adult education and training in the Caribbean and Central America. It highlights the experience of Cuba, Nicaragua, and Mexico, and gives attention to popular education as a means of promoting conscientization and mobilization among the disadvantaged.

1. Context

"Only one enterprise flourished in war-ridden El Salvador: funeral parlours, a trade not considered in the curriculum of the National Council for Professional Training." This is not just a cynic's view of one moment in time of one Central American country but a hard fact depicting the explosive and convulsive past and present of Central America and the Caribbean. Such situations determine the ups and downs of adult education and training in the region.

Although the Caribbean and Central American countries (the Caribbean with islands stretching from the Bahamas in the north to Trinidad and Tobago, Curaçao, and Aruba in the south, and the mainland countries of Belize, Guyana, Suriname, and French Guiana; Central America with Mexico, Guatemala, Honduras, El Salvador, Nicaragua, Costa Rica, and Panama) are extremely diverse in terms of ethnic groups, language, culture, and history. Most of them share a common fate: they are beset by revolutions and civil wars, and stanced by their colonial past and their neocolonial present. In Costa Rica, Cuba, Mexico, or Nicaragua, for example, a Spanish past is reflected; the Commonwealth Caribbean with, for example, Belize, the Bahamas, Jamaica, and Grenada reflects a British past; the Netherlands Antilles and Suriname share a Dutch past; and Guadeloupe, French Guiana, or Haiti, for example, show a French influence. Nowadays, most of these countries, with the exception of Cuba, are economically dependent on the United States.

Within most countries, as well as from country to country in the region, wealth is distributed unequally, ranging from the relatively high per capita Gross National Product (GNP) of US$3,350 in Trinidad and Tobago through US$1,820 in Mexico to the relatively low per capita income of US$360 in Haiti. With political systems varying ideologically from the Marxist socialist Left as in Cuba to the liberal democratic Right of Barbados, the region is characterized by ideological variety. Large disparities can also be observed in education, in primary school enrollment and dropout rates, and in particular in adult illiteracy rates, ranging from 0.7 percent in Barbados in 1970 to 65.2 percent in Haiti in 1982 (see Table 1). Unlike the situation in most African or Asian countries, women in many Caribbean countries have an illiteracy rate equal to that or even lower than that of men (see, e.g., Barbados or Jamaica in Table 1).

Adult education in the Caribbean and Central America reflects and has, in return, started to shape the region's variety of historical, linguistic, cultural, economic, ideological, and educational traits. Adult education in many countries of the region has developed from a position of being rejected as an unnecessary or even dangerous luxury for a cheap workforce to one of being integrated—without the expected success, however—into governmental economic development plans during the 1960s and 1970s. Adult education has finally turned into a social movement, into popular education, spreading not only over the region but also being exported by writers like Paolo Freire and Illich to Western academics and practitioners. From its inception by Euro-

Table 1
Illiteracy rates in Central America and the Caribbean (adults over 15)

	Year of census	Male	Female	Overall	Estimated rates 1990 Male	Female	Overall
Anguilla[f]	—	—	—	—	—	—	—
Antigua (with Barbuda)	—	—	—	—	—	—	—
Aruba[d]	—	—	—	—	—	—	—
Bahamas	—	—	—	—	—	—	—
Barbados	1970	0.7	0.7	0.7	—	—	—
Belize	1970	8.8	8.8	8.8	—	—	—
British Virgin Islands[f]	1970	1.9	1.5	1.7	—	—	—
Cayman Islands[f]	1970	2.5	2.4	2.5	—	—	—
Costa Rica	1984	7.3	7.4	7.4	7.4	6.9	7.2
Cuba	1981	3.8	3.8	3.8	5.0	7.0	6.0
Dominica	1970	6.0	5.8	5.9	—	—	—
Dominican Republic	1981	31.8	30.9	31.4	15.2	18.2	16.7
El Salvador	1985*	27.4	34.7	31.2	23.8	30.0	27.0
French Guiana[c]	1982	16.4	17.7	17.0	—	—	—
Grenada	1970	2.0	2.4	2.2	—	—	—
Guadeloupe[c]	1982	10.4	9.6	10.0	—	—	—
Guatemala	1973	46.4	61.5	54.0	36.9	52.9	44.9
Guyana	1970	5.7	11.0	8.4	2.5	4.6	3.6
Haiti	1982	62.7	67.5	65.2	40.9	52.6	47.0
Honduras	1974	41.1	44.9	43.1	24.5	29.4	26.9
Jamaica	1970	4.4	3.5	3.9	1.8	1.4	1.6
Martinique[c]	1982	8.0	6.6	7.2	—	—	—
Mexico	1980	13.8	20.1	17.0	10.5	14.9	12.7
Monserrat[f]	1970	3.2	3.4	3.4	—	—	—
The Netherlands Antilles (incl. Curaçao)[e]	1981	5.8	6.6	6.2	—	—	—
Nicaragua	1971	42.0	42.9	42.5	—	—	—
Panama	1980	13.7	15.1	14.4	11.9	11.8	11.9
Puerto Rico[a]	1980	10.3	11.5	10.9	—	—	—
St Kitts-Nevis	1970	2.4	2.3	2.4	—	—	—
St Lucia	1970	19.2	17.6	18.3	—	—	—
St Vincent and the Grenadines	1970	4.2	4.5	4.4	—	—	—
Suriname	1978	31.6	37.1	35.0	4.9	5.3	5.1
Trinidad and Tobago	1980	3.5	6.6	5.1	—	—	—
Turks and Caicos Islands[f]	1970	1.4	2.3	1.9	—	—	—
Virgin Islands[b]	—	—	—	—	—	—	—

Sources: UNESCO 1990, 1991
*Estimates a Autonomous part of the United States b Unincorporated territory of the United States c Overseas departments of France d Autonomous part of the Kingdom of the Netherlands e Integral part of the Kingdom of the Netherlands f British dependencies

pean missionaries and other private initiatives via ministry provision (initially educational but nowadays also intersectoral)—in short, from top down—adult education in the Caribbean and Central America has become a form of popular—bottom-up—education, providing compensatory, second-chance education for the out-of-school population and even espousing a revolutionary potential. Education is no longer "education for the people" but "education by the people."

Since it is impossible to cover here the whole variety of adult education and training in the Caribbean and Central America, one Caribbean and two Central American countries will be given special attention: Cuba, Nicaragua, and Mexico. Cuba is atypical of the Caribbean, but was chosen because its literacy campaign, linked with a revolutionary process, has been seen worldwide as a textbook model. Nicaragua, which provides another example of a literacy campaign, was selected because its revolution of 1979 gave popular educators an opportunity to implement their ideas on a national scale. Mexico—the largest, most populated, and, since the revolution in 1910, one of the most stable of the countries in the region—stands as an example of the incremental introduction and expansion of adult education and training (see *Adult Education for Development*).

2. Cuba

In Cuba, adult education is fully integrated into the

national educational system as a subsystem, offering all Cubans various opportunities for continuing education. Adult education has been unique in training a large proportion of the population in functional literacy, as well as in primary and secondary education. For example, in 1989 only 1.9 percent of 10–49-year olds were illiterate, and the average school level reached the eighth grade (Cuba, Ministry of Education 1990).

Before the socialist revolution in 1959, education was designed to serve the country's elite and to maintain the export-oriented economic system. Since 1959 education has been considered crucial for the transformation of society and has been regarded as an intrinsic part of the revolution. Education in general was not only expected to upgrade the overall educational level but also to mobilize the population. The main goal of adult education was the creation of a general culture of conscientization leading to a strong sense of national pride and identity (see *Conscientization and Mobilization*).

The illiteracy rate in 1953 of 22.1 percent of a population of about 6 million declined to 3.8 percent of the total population of about 10 million in 1981. Statistics on educational attainment show that the discrepancy between rural and urban areas also decreased but was not eradicated; for example, 37.5 percent of the rural population did not complete primary education compared to 16.8 percent of the urban population (UNESCO 1991).

After the 1959 revolution the educational system in Cuba underwent a change of focus from quantitative to qualitative growth. At first the priority was equal accessibility. When this had been largely attained, the emphasis shifted to achieving higher levels of education. Technical and vocational education proved to be an especially urgent need, in order to replace those lost with the brain drain of highly qualified professionals that followed the revolution. The loss was estimated at between 15,000 and 25,000 (Torres 1990 p. 80).

In the 1960s Cuba pursued a massive expansion of education at all levels, especially in rural areas. The "battle for literacy," from 1959 to 1962, largely influenced the following "battle for the sixth grade," set up for new literates and undereducated adults and which had its greatest impact during the mid- and late 1970s. By 1989, 1.5 million participants of the program had achieved the sixth grade. Literacy classes continued only for the remaining minority groups, training about 1,000 participants every year. The strategy of emphasizing socialization was replaced by a return to material incentives in the 1970s, which in turn led to the promotion of academic excellence. In 1989 there existed 96 varieties of technical and vocational education, of which 18 led to a certificate qualifying skilled workers and 78 designating mid-level technicians. With increasing specialization, adult education became more formalized. Enrollments continued to rise, especially at secondary levels. Two new types of adult education developed: lower secondary education for adults and preuniversity education for workers and farmers. The "battle for the ninth grade" had its greatest impact from 1980 to 1985. It upgraded general education, so that by 1989 approximately 900,000 participants of the program had achieved the ninth grade. By the same time, about 90,000 adults had participated in preuniversity education and some 25,000 in language schools for workers (Cuba, Ministry of Education 1990 pp. 62–64).

Adult education in Cuba is characterized by flexibility and continuity and the principle of combining academic study and manual work. The latter is applied in all types and levels of education. For example, students from urban schools on the scheme "school to the countryside" spend 30–45 days per year doing agricultural work; those on the scheme "school in the countryside," from rural schools, do agricultural work for three hours per day. The structural design of adult education courses, provided by and channeled through political and mass organizations, takes into consideration the needs of the working population: many classes take place in the evenings or afternoons, often at working places or at special boarding schools. Changes in curricula and syllabi of all subsystems of education, including adult education, have been introduced since the 1987–88 academic year according to the Continuous Improvement of Education plan. In the early 1990s the situation was also influenced by economic difficulties resulting from the end of support from the Socialist Bloc in Europe and the continuation of the economic blockade by the United States. Nevertheless, "education for all" continued to be a high priority of the government.

Perhaps the most widely acknowledged achievement in education in Cuba was that it became a right for everybody—not only according to official propaganda but in reality, as education became a matter of course for the young generation. Evaluations of Cuban achievements differ according to political and ideological standpoints (Richmond 1990): while opponents of socialist Cuba tended to emphasize problems such as communist indoctrination, progressive educational specialists engaged in both praise and criticism, whereas communist representatives regarded the outcomes of the educational reforms with great satisfaction.

3. Nicaragua

Two events that attracted worldwide interest have drastically shaped adult education and training in Nicaragua: the National Literacy Crusade (CNA) and the Popular Basic Education for Adults program (PBEA). Both were products of the nation's political, social, and cultural transformation process initiated by the Popular Sandinista Revolution (PSR), which overthrew Anastasio Somoza's dictatorship in July 1979.

The Sandinistas, who took power in 1979, inherited from the Somoza dynasty one of the least developed and most erratic adult education histories in the whole Central American region. It can be characterized as a succession of isolated and unrelated projects. A literacy campaign in 1951, following a Pan American proposition advocated in 1949, ended in the bureaucracy of the National Directorate of the National Literacy Campaign. Schemes organized at ministerial level, such as the Workers' Culture School (a training unit for basic stills, aimed at urban workers) or the accelerated primary education program (a night school offering adults six years of children's primary school curriculum) catered mainly for the urban population, while the majority of people in need of adult education opportunities lived in rural areas. Only 6 percent of rural children completed primary school and up to 90 percent of the adult population were illiterate.

Some short-lived radio school experiments in the early 1960s, organized around 120 literacy centers, were a failure. Fewer than 25,000 students participated in adult education programs offered by nongovernmental organizations, religious groups, and the private sector. The government's central attention was given to "antisubversive" adult education activities, such as the 1955 Rio Coco Pilot Project or the "Plan Waslala" (1977–79), which trained 108 "literacy teachers" to act as security agents to identify peasants sympathizing with the Sandinista National Liberation Front. Nicaragua's adult education and its school system were characterized and determined by one family's economic profit-making interest. Although about 45 percent of the population were employed in agriculture and related work, fewer than 1 percent were enrolled in agricultural classes. Training emphasized commerce and services. In 1979, out of a total population of 2.4 million, some 720,000 persons aged 10 years or more were counted as illiterate.

3.1 Nicaragua's National Literacy Crusade

Confronted with the institutions and structures of the Somoza society, which had neither met basic human needs nor served the interests of the majority of the population, the Sandinista revolutionary leadership aimed at achieving a rapid transformation of society. The vision of a new society creatively involving each citizen, "the new man" and "the new woman," in new participatory forms of social organization implied an educational model that would help bring about the transformation. The National Literacy Crusade was advocated as a first step toward this aim. It was stressed by Fernando Cardenal, coordinator of the Literacy Crusade, that the Crusade "is not an educational event with political implications but a political event with educational implications" (Archer and Costello 1990 p. 24).

On the wave of revolutionary triumph, enthusiasm, and struggle for self-determination, the Crusade mobilized the whole country from March 23 to August 23, 1980. The organization of the Crusade was warlike, modeled on the organization of the liberation struggle, and dependent on the cooperation of all ages and interest groups. "Every home a classroom, every table a school desk, every Nicaraguan a teacher" was not just one of the Crusade slogans but reflected reality. About 65,000 volunteers, trained in short-term multiplier-courses, went to the countryside to learn from and teach the illiterate peasants, applying an adapted Freire method. In addition, 26,000 volunteers worked in the cities. Within 5 months 400,000 Nicaraguans were taught basic literacy skills. The illiteracy rate consequently dropped from 50 percent to 13 percent. A follow-up campaign along the Atlantic Coast, targeted at people speaking the indigenous languages of Miskito, Sumo, and Creole English, extended literacy skills to another 13,000 people.

3.2 Popular Basic Education for Adults

After the Crusade, the newly established vice-ministry of adult education (VIMEDA) launched a system of popular basic education for adults, comprising an adult-centered, community-based, productive, and labor-related alternative to the formal school system. Volunteers, some of whom had been learners themselves during the crusade, worked as popular teachers with groups of 10 to 12 persons in Popular Education Collectives (CEPs). In 1984, when about 17,000 CEPs reached 195,000 persons (including out-of-school children), VIMEDA decided to extend the program from six to nine levels to counteract difficulties arising in channeling PBEA graduates into formal secondary schools or into the national inservice training system (SINAFORP) which had insufficient capacity to absorb the students. The additional three PBEA levels were to teach mainly vocational skills.

Intersectoral cooperation, for example with the ministry of agricultural development and land reform (MIDINRA), which had the lead in desinging nonformal labor force training, caused conflict. Lack of resources and teaching personnel, inadequate relationships with the formal education system, and permanent aggression from the "contras" (the anti-Sandinista fighters), threatened the original idealism and flexibility of the PBEA program. Between 1984 and 1987 PBEA started losing its nonformal character and became more rigid and institutionalized. Although PBEA had some impact on formal education, the dream of finally permeating the whole formal educational system began to fade. Resources and time to revive nonformal adult education were missing. It is estimated that by 1990 the illiteracy rate was once again on the rise, reaching a level of 30–35 percent of adults (Arnove and Dewees 1991).

Both the National Literacy Crusade and the Popular Basic Education for Adults contributed to a number of changes in Nicaraguan society. Among these: the integration of rural populations into a national society; adaptation of education to the needs of the agricultural and occupational sectors; conscientization of the people; and strengthening of mass organizations. Self-critical voices of the Sandinista leadership admitted, however, that their approach was too centralized and did not take sectorial or geographical differences sufficiently into account.

Opposition groups viewed both the National Literacy Crusade and the Popular Basic Education for Adults as massive efforts of political indoctrination. This is exactly the stand expressed in the *Guidelines of the Ministry of Education for the New Government of National Salvation*: "Learning was subordinated to the ideological political project of a party which distorted conscience. Everybody was exposed to indoctrination." According to these guidelines, adult education under the government elected in 1991 intended to emphasize family education and civic education with a focus on the individual—without neglecting the need for national reconciliation.

4. Mexico

Adult education in Mexico has focused on basic literacy for marginalized groups of the population, such as women and indigenous people. Mexico's illiteracy rate has decreased from 25.8 percent in 1970 to 12.4 percent in 1990. There is and will continue to be a strong demand for adult education: 13.4 percent of 6–14-year old children have received no schooling and 22.8 percent have not completed primary education. There are deep regional disparities: the low illiteracy rate of 4.0 percent in the Federal District (Mexico City), followed by the state of Neuvo León with 4.6 percent, contrasts with more disadvantaged states, which have a high percentage of indigenous population and high illiteracy rates—for example, 26.8 percent in Guerrero and 30.0 percent in Chiapas (Instituto Nacional de Estadística Geográfica e Informática 1990).

Bilingual training in Spanish and 13 indigenous Indian languages (out of a total of 52) was advocated in a context of the nation seeking to give increased attention to Indian culture to increase feelings of national identity. Assimilation of Indian culture has a long history in Mexico and its only alternative, diversification allowing for cultural pluralism, is not guaranteed by the bilingual method, since the "implicit message of hispanic superiority seems unavoidable in the curriculum" (Epstein 1985 p. 69).

The National Institute for Adult Education (INEA), an agency of the ministry for public education founded in 1981, carries out most literacy activities through its 354 area offices. Participants in literacy courses are taught directly (in groups or as individuals) or via the media. Television and radio programs, supported by local tutors, are offered and enjoy much popularity. Teaching via TV consists of a series of programs with intermittent teaching sessions while the radio courses are based on interviews between an illiterate and an instructor. Besides the national literacy program (PRONALF), created in 1981, INEA also offers primary and secondary education for adults, cultural education, and vocational training.

Apart from INEA and the ministry of education, many other governmental agencies and nongovernmental institutions take part in adult education, concentrating especially on vocational training and technical education. Vocational training is mainly a male activity. This contrasts with general adult education. An age structure analysis shows that two-thirds of the participants in adult education are female and that, on average, users are 26 years of age at the primary and 23 at the secondary level (Torres 1990).

After the change of national president every six years new development plans are formulated. The national development plan 1989–94, valid for the presidency of Carlos Salinas de Gortari, has three main aspects regarding education: (a) a focus on deprived areas of Mexico and on deprived social groups, with high illiteracy rates; (b) a focus on 10–14-year old out-of-school children; and (c) adaptation of course contents to the needs of the learners (Instituto Nacional para la Educación de los Adultos 1991).

In 1987 adult education experienced severe cuts because of austerity measures required by an International Monetary Fund structural adjustment program. Most job-training and on-the-job-training programs were discontinued. It was supposed that the private sector would assume responsibility for the provision of such training, but it did not.

5. Conclusion

In the 1990s the whole of Central America and the Caribbean was suffering from cutbacks in adult education and training, because of the region's severe structural economic crisis (regarded as the worst crisis to affect the region since the depression of the 1930s). The achievements gained were placed at risk and in many countries educational provision was stagnating if not declining (see also Table 1). The crisis also jeopardized The Major Educational Project for Latin America and the Caribbean, as planned by the ministers of education and economic planning of Latin America and the Caribbean during a conference held in Mexico in 1979 (Mexico Declaration), and operationalized in 1981 during a follow-up meeting in Quito, Ecuador. The Major Project's objective was to eradicate illiteracy before the end of the twentieth century and to develop services for adults. The former aim became impossible but collective cooperation was strengthened.

See also: Latin America: Adult Education; China, People's Republic of: Adult Education; Conscientization and Mobilization; Adult Education for Development; Community Education and Community Development; Critical Approaches to Adult Education; Cuba: System of Education; Mexico: System of Education; Nicaragua: System of Education; Planning Education: Latin America; Empowerment Skills, Acquisition of

References

Archer D, Costello P 1990 *Literacy and Power: The Latin American Battleground*. Earthscan, London
Arnove R F, Dewees A 1991 Education and revolutionary transformation in Nicaragua, 1979–90. *Comp. Educ. Rev.* 35(1): 92–109
Cuba, Ministry of Education 1990 *Cuba—Organization of Education: Report of the Republic of Cuba to the 42nd International Conference on Public Education*. Ministry of Education, Havana
Epstein E E 1985 National consciousness and education in Mexico. In: Brock C, Lawlor H (eds.) 1985 *Education in Latin America*. Croom Helm, London
Instituto Nacional de Estadística Geográfica e Informática 1990 *Perfíl Sociodemográfico—XI Censo General de Población y Vivienda, 1990*. Mexico City
Instituto Nacional para la Educación de los Adultos 1991 *La Educación de Adultos en el Marco de la Modernización Educativa, 1989–1991*. INEA, Mexico City
Richmond M 1990 The Cuban educational model and its influence on the Caribbean region. In: Brock C, Clarkson D (eds.) 1990 *Education in Central America and the Caribbean*. Routledge, London
Torres C A 1990 *The Politics of Nonformal Education in Latin America*. Praeger, New York
UNESCO 1990 *Statistical Yearbook*. UNESCO, Paris
UNESCO 1991 *Statistical Yearbook*. UNESCO, Paris

Further Reading

Arnove R F 1986 *Education and Revolution in Nicaragua*. Praeger, New York
Arrien J B, Matus Lazo R 1989 *Nicaragua: Diez Años de Educación en la Revolución: Contexto, Avances, Problemas y Perspectivas de un Proceso de Transformación*. Ministerio de Educación, Mexico City
Carnoy M et al. 1990 *Education and Social Transition in the Third World*. Princeton University Press, Princeton, New Jersey
Leirman W, Salgado J 1985 Basic adult education in Latin America: The case of Mexico in comparison to Brasil, Chile and Nicaragua. In: Knoll J H (ed.) 1985 *Internationales Jahrbuch der Erwachsenenbildung*. Böhlau, Köln
Mexico, Ministry of Public Education 1990 *Report on Education in Mexico: Forty-second Meeting of the International Conference on Education*. International Bureau of Education, Geneva
Miller V 1984 *Between Struggle and Hope: The Nicaraguan Literacy Crusade*. Westview Press, Boulder, Colorado.
Miller V 1985 The Nicaraguan literacy crusade: Education for transformation. In: Duke C (ed.) 1985 *Combating Poverty Through Adult Education: National Development Strategies*. Croom Helm, London
Nicaragua, Ministerio de Educación 1990 *Lineamientos del Ministerio de Educación en el Nuevo Gobierno de Salvación Nacional*. Ministerio de Educación, Managua
Ramesar E D 1985 Adult education: Regional organization in the Caribbean. In: Husén T, Postlethwaite T N (eds.) 1985 *The International Encyclopedia of Education*, 1st edn. Pergamon Press, Oxford
Richmond M 1985 Education and revolution in socialist Cuba: The promise of democratisation. In: Brock C, Lawlor H (eds.) 1985 *Education in Latin America*. Croom Helm, London
Rivero J 1990 *Latin America and the Caribbean: A Major Project for Literacy*. International Bureau of Education, UNESCO, Paris
Schmelkes S 1990 *Post-Alfabetización y Trabajo en América Latina*. UNESCO/OREALC, Santiago, Chile
Torres C A 1989 Political culture and state bureaucracy in Mexico: The case of adult education. *Int. J. Educ. Dev.* 9(1): 53–68
UNESCO 1963 *Statistical Yearbook*. UNESCO, Paris

U. Giere; S. Hielscher

Case Study Methods

"Case study" is a generic term for the investigation of an individual, group, or phenomenon. While the techniques used in the investigation may be varied, and may include both qualitative and quantitative approaches, the distinguishing feature of case study is the belief that human systems develop a characteristic wholeness or integrity and are not simply a loose collection of traits. As a consequence of this belief, case study researchers hold that to understand a case, to explain why things happen as they do, and to generalize or predict from a single example requires an in-depth investigation of the interdependencies of parts and of the patterns that emerge.

Kaplan refers to methodology as a "generalization of technics and a concretization of philosophy" (see *Research Methodology: Scientific Methods*). While the techniques relate to the specific strategies that are used in different types of case study, the philosophy is concerned with the place that case study has in educational inquiry, such as the extent to which it can be used to generalize, predict, or explain as opposed to being used to understand or simply to describe.

The following section deals with the philosophical dimension of case study and this is followed by a discussion of the technical dimension.

1. Case Study and the "Concretization of Philosophy"

Diesing (1972) places case study within the holist tradition of scientific inquiry. According to this tradition, the characteristics of a part are seen to be largely determined by the whole to which it belongs. The holist argues that to understand these parts requires an understanding of their interrelationships, and accounts of wholes need to capture and express this holistic quality.

This view is expressed in a different way by Salomon (1991) who has distinguished the analytical and systemic approaches to educational research. The analytic approach mainly assumes that discrete elements of complex educational phenomena can be isolated for study leaving all else unchanged. The systemic approach, on the other hand, mainly assumes that elements are interdependent and inseparable and a change in one element changes everything else. It follows, therefore, that what is required is a study of patterns not single variables.

A holistic or systemic approach quite often entails qualitative techniques in order to tease out the interrelationships of complex variables. Quantitative research also addresses the interrelationships between variables, and statistical modeling procedures enable the testing of complex theories on the way systems operate. While it may be true that much quantitative research has failed to take account of the complexities of human systems and has reduced them to simplistic hypotheses and law-like relations, this is a failure of the research design and not of quantitative research per se. In addition, although holists frequently use qualitative techniques, they are not a distinguishing feature of case study.

While there are those who still argue that qualitative and quantitative approaches are incompatible because of the different philosophical traditions from which they draw their credibility and in particular because of the underlying assumptions that each make about the validity or dependability of findings, in general there is an acceptance that the two traditions can work together. It is accepted that qualitative research is useful both in developing concepts and theories that can be further tested through quantitative approaches—the approach used in the 150 Schools Project, a current Australian study of effective schooling—and also in explaining more fully findings from quantitative research—the approach adopted in the Australian Staffing and Resources Study (see Sturman 1982).

1.1 Case Study and the Development of Theory

Glaser and Strauss (1968) distinguished "grounded theory," that is, theory grounded in the data collected, from theory generated from logical deduction from *a priori* assumptions. They argued that grounded theory is likely to generate more useful hypotheses in that it has been inductively developed from observational research in the real world. Similarly, Wilson (1977) argued that there is room in research for more inductive approaches where the role of preformed hypotheses is reduced to a minimum.

While case study is an ideal methodology for grounding theory, it does not follow that case study researchers approach or should approach settings without guiding theories and hypotheses. In fact, it is unlikely that they would be able to do this even if they wished. Popper (1963) argues that it is impossible to start with pure observation, that is, without anything in the nature of a theory. Selection within observation takes place and this selection is based on conjectures and anticipations and on other theories which act as a frame of reference for investigators.

Glaser and Strauss (1968) also acknowledged that researchers entered settings with a "general sociological perspective." However, what they were warning against was allowing preconceived theories or ideas to dictate relevances in concepts and hypotheses in the conduct of research. Wilson (1977) talked of "suspending" or "bracketing" preconceptions. Researchers should not be expected to be free of conjectures, but these should not preclude other avenues of inquiry.

Where case studies are providing a detailed description and understanding of a case and where researchers are open to new ideas that may challenge existing propositions, they provide not only the means by which existing conjectures and theories can be tested, but also the capacity to develop new theoretical positions. The process involved is what Kemmis (1980) called "iterative retroduction":

> With each cycle of retroduction, new "surprises". . .are encountered and new hypotheses (interpretations) are advanced. These, in turn, suggest new implications and avenues for disconfirmation which, when pursued may generate new surprises. (p. 115)

1.2 Case Study and Explanation, Understanding, and Description

Kaplan (1964) has distinguished explanation from understanding: the difference between having an explanation and "seeing" it. He argued that the reason for something is known either when it can be fitted into a known pattern (the pattern model) or when it can be deducted from other known truths (the deductive model). According to the pattern model, something is explained when it is so related to a set of other elements that together they constitute a unified system. In other words, an explanation exists for something when it can be understood.

Case study researchers or holists are more likely to be concerned with pattern explanation than deductive explanation because the pattern model is more appropriate when there are many diverse factors and where the pattern of relations between them is important. To arrive at an explanation, therefore, requires a rich description of the case and an understanding of it, in particular the relationship of its parts.

1.3 Case Study and Prediction and Generalization

Diesing (1972) held the view that because it is not

possible to deduce an unknown part of a pattern from a known part, the symmetry of prediction and explanation that occurs in the deductive model, (i.e., in a model where one or more basic factors or laws determine what is to be explained) is not present.

However, this distinction does not always hold. Parsons (1976) commented, for example:

> Interpretation, explanation and understanding in social science contribute to prediction—they are not at odds with it. If one understands, one can attempt prediction and hopefully thereby plan better for the future. Theory organizes description, explanation and prediction in a multi-symbiotic process. (p. 133)

One of the earliest and lingering criticisms of case study methodology relates to the extent that it can be used to generalize to other cases or other settings. In 1975, Campbell referred to this problem in an article entitled *Degrees of Freedom and the Case Study*. The title of his article reflected what was at that time one of the major concerns about case study held by some quantitative researchers. Campbell (1975 p. 175) argued that the difference between qualitative and quantitative research had nothing to do with legitimacy of knowing—he argued that comparative social science engaged in "commonsense knowing"—but was related to confidence in the findings:

> If we achieve a meaningful quantitative 100-nation correlation, it is by dependence on this kind of knowing at every point, not by replacing it with a "scientific" quantitative methodology which substitutes for such knowing. The quantitative multination generalization will contradict such anecdotal, single-case, naturalistic observation at some points, but it will do so only by trusting a much larger body of such anecdotal, single-case, naturalistic observations.

The development of multisite case study, where case study methodology is applied to a number of settings or cases, makes such criticism too simplistic but, in any case, the holist argues that even single case study can be used for generalizations.

For example, Diesing (1972) argued that science deals with uniqueness and regularities: if the primary focus is on regularities, the unique shows up, and if it is on particulars, regularities show up. Case study methods include both the particular and the universal instead of segregating the two, and moves from the particular to the universal and back in graded steps.

Stake (1980 p. 69) has also advocated a process of naturalistic generalization arrived at "from the tacit knowledge of how things are, why they are, how people feel about them, and how these things are likely to be, later on or in other places with which this person is familiar." Naturalistic generalization is arrived at, therefore, by recognizing the similarities of the objects and issues in different contexts and "sensing the covariations of happenings." Stake argued that policymakers attain and amend their understandings, for the most part, through personal experience, and knowledge is often transferred through a process of empathetic understanding. Therefore, demands for typicality and representativeness often yield to needs for assurance that the target case is properly described.

For naturalistic generalizations to be possible, it is essential to ensure that the salient features of a case are documented so that a new situation can be illuminated by a very thorough understanding of a known case. This is so whether it is the researcher who is attempting the generalization or practitioners using the description of the known case and applying it to their settings.

2. Case Study and the "Generalization of Technics"

The specific techniques that are employed in case study depend on the type of study that is being conducted. These types can vary considerably, in part because case study embraces both the quantitative and qualitative paradigms.

2.1 Types of Case Study

Leaving aside narrative historical studies, documentary films, and personal case studies such as those used in medical diagnosis and psychology, Stenhouse (1985) has referred to four styles of case study methodology:

(a) Ethnographic case study which involves single in-depth study usually by means of participant observation and interview. An example from the United Kingdom is the study by Hargreaves (1967).

(b) Action research case study where the focus is on bringing about change in the case under study. An example from a developing country is the group of projects initiated under the Collaborative Action Research in Education (CARE) program in Sierra Leone and reported by Wright (1988).

(c) Evaluative case study which involves the evaluation of programs and where quite often condensed fieldwork replaces the more lengthy ethnographic approach. An example from the United States is the study by Stake and Gjerde (1974).

(d) Educational case study which is designed to enhance the understanding of educational action. An example from Australia is the study by Sturman (1989).

While the first and second styles—ethnographic case study and action research case study—are likely, because of the in-depth nature of such research, to

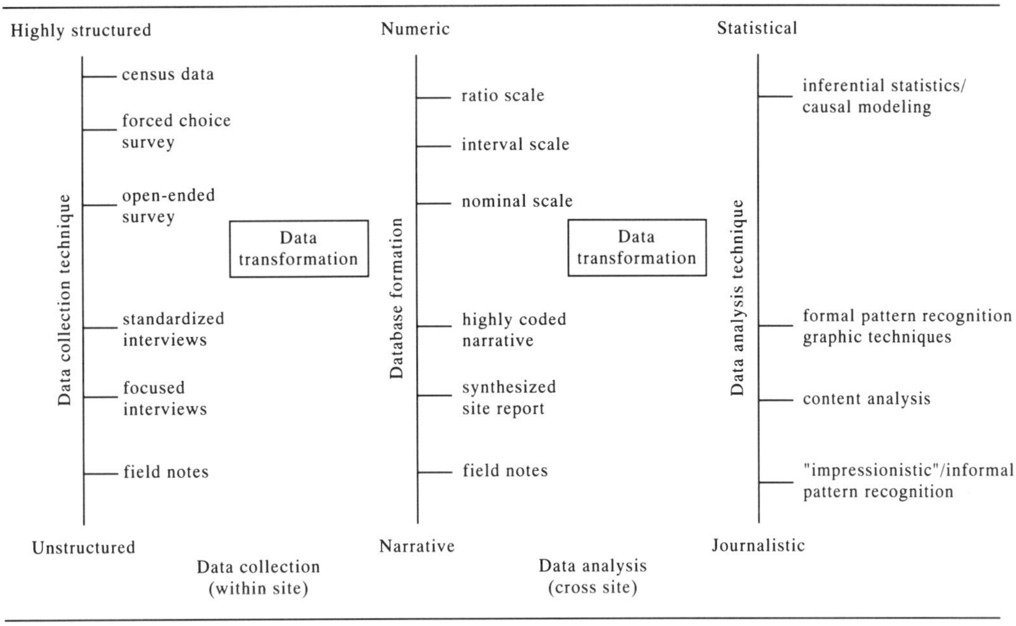

Figure 1
Dimensions of variation in multisite/multimethod studies

Source: Louis K S 1982 Multisite/multimethod studies: An introduction. *American Behavioral Scientist* 26(1): 10, © Sage Publications, Inc. (Reprinted by permission of Sage Publication, Inc.)

be single case study, evaluative and educational case study can involve a single case or can be incorporated into multisite methods. The introduction of multisite methods is particularly noticeable in policy research, which has led Herriott and Firestone (1983) to refer to this as "multisite qualitative policy research."

2.2 Dimensions of Variation in Techniques in Case Study Methods

The degree to which case study research can be structured or unstructured is often ignored in methodological discussions. Louis (1982) has noted:

> In an increasing number of cases, data collected through very unstructured techniques may be transformed through coding into quantitative data bases, which are then analyzed using descriptive or inferential statistical techniques. Conversely, data may be collected through open-ended survey methods and analyzed "holistically" by site. In fact, to understand the variety of methods currently being employed, we must examine the nature of the design and practice at three points in the study: during data collection, during data-base formulation, and during the actual data analysis. (p. 9)

Figure 1, taken from Louis (1982), depicts this. The data collection phase ranges from the unstructured to the structured and can include ethnography, structured or unstructured interviews or surveys, and census data. The data formation stage ranges from the narrative to the numeric and includes the use of field notes; site reports; and nominal, interval, and ratio scales. Similarly, the data analysis phase ranges from the journalistic to the statistical and may include impressionistic analysis, content analysis, or inferential statistics and causal modeling.

2.3 Techniques in Multisite Case Studies

Multisite methodology emerged in response to the perceived limitations of much policy and evaluation research for policymakers. Firestone and Herriott (1983 p. 438) have discussed the demands on policy researchers and the implications that these have for case study. They refer to the formalization of qualitative research and they list five major elements of this:

(a) Whereas traditional qualitative research tends to emphasize in-depth description, formalized qualitative research emphasizes explanation.

(b) Whereas traditional qualitative research tends to emphasize the conduct of inquiry by a single individual, formalized qualitative research emphasizes the use of a multiperson team.

(c) Whereas traditional qualitative research tends to emphasize the discovery of relevant questions and variables within the field, formalized qualitative research emphasizes the codification of questions and variables before beginning fieldwork.

(d) Whereas traditional qualitative research tends to

emphasize unstructured questioning and observation, formalized qualitative research emphasizes the standardization of data collection procedures through the use of semistructured interview and observation protocols.

(e) Whereas traditional qualitative research tends to emphasize extended presentation of verbal narrative, formalized qualitative research emphasizes the systematic reduction of verbal narrative to codes and categories.

In response to demands of policymakers, one of the major outcomes of such techniques, compared with ethnographic case study, is that researchers engaged in multisite case study usually spend much less time in each site. They trade in-depth inquiry for comparisons across a number of sites.

2.4 Case Study and Credibility

One concern that has been expressed about case study techniques, in particular ethnographic case study, is the credibility of what is seen as subjective research techniques. Although Wilson (1977) has argued that ethnographic case study challenges the traditional stance of the objective outsider, personal judgment forms an essential part of all science and is neither objective or subjective.

An assertion is an act of believing—to this extent it is subjective—but that assertion, whether it emerges from ethnographic research or multivariate statistical modeling, rests on personal judgment which includes an appraisal of evidence within the tenets of acceptable practice as perceived by the research community—to this extent it is objective. To say that science is more than its practitioners and their skills and judgments is a failure to perceive how science and its methods have historically progressed.

At the root of case study research as in all science lays the problem of "justified true belief":

> In every case in which someone would want to claim—however tentatively—to have established a scientific truth, he does so by making one set of assumptions about what counts as justification, along with another set of assumptions about the nature of belief. (Kemmis 1980 p. 102)

The problem of justified true belief is then a double problem which involves reconciling the beliefs (private knowledge) of researchers and readers with the forms of knowledge of public discourse.

Instead of the blanket condemnation of subjectivity or the universal approbation of objectivity, what is needed is an opportunity to appraise those personal judgments being made by scientific colleagues. Case study methodology can achieve its own form of precision. Wilson (1977) has referred to this as "disciplined subjectivity." This requires that evidence must be open to scrutiny, and that the study must be reported in a way capable of "conveying credibility" (Glaser and Strauss 1968) and subjected to standards of "trustworthiness," that is, credibility, transferability, dependability, and confirmability (Guba and Lincoln 1985).

Among the strategies that practitioners have suggested for achieving credibility in case study are the following:

(a) Procedures for data collection should be explained.

(b) Data collected should be displayed and ready for re-analysis.

(c) Negative instances should be reported.

(d) Biases should be acknowledged.

(e) Fieldwork analyses need to be documented.

(f) The relationship between assertion and evidence should be clarified.

(g) Primary evidence should be distinguished from secondary and description from interpretation.

(h) Diaries or logs should track what was actually done during different stages of the study.

(i) Methods should be devised to check the quality of data.

The concept of "triangulation" (Tawney 1975) is central to achieving credibility. Triangulation may involve the use of different data sources, different perspectives or theories, different investigators, or different methods. This process is, according to Diesing (1972), the holist's response to the issue of validity and reliability in survey research. The holist is concerned with contextual validity. This can take two forms: the validity of a piece of evidence which can be assessed by comparing it with other kinds of evidence on the same point, and the validity of the source of the evidence which can be evaluated by collecting other kinds of evidence about that source (see *Triangulation in Educational Research*).

To distinguish contextual validity from the validity important to the survey researcher, Diesing referred to the dependability of a source of evidence.

2.5 Case Study and Data Handling and Retrieval

Where case study involves in-depth observations and interviews, one of the problems faced by the researcher is how to store and retrieve such information.

Examples of how to address these issues come mainly from the fields of information and library science (see, e.g., Levine 1985), although the sourcebook prepared by Miles and Huberman (1984) provides one model for preparing qualitative data for analysis (see *Descriptive Data, Analysis of*).

3. Ethics and the Conduct of Case Study

The problem of ethics is not unique to case study methodology, but where case study involves the portrayal of persons or institutions in forms that may enable recognition, the ethical issues are paramount.

These problems are usually resolved through negotiations between researchers and those researched. This may take the form of an official contract or may be more informal, involving discussions over the content of written reports. While it may not be possible to have one set of rules that governs all situations, there is a responsibility on case study researchers to address in a responsible way ethical issues that emerge in their work.

4. Linking Research Methodologies

While conflicts about different methologies have not disappeared, in recent years there has developed in the research community a suspicion of "scientism," that is, an exaggerated regard for techniques which have succeeded elsewhere in contrast to a scientific temper which is open to whatever techniques hold promise for the inquiry in hand (Kaplan 1964).

There has also developed a recognition of the value of blending different methodologies. In one major study into the characteristics of effective schools in Australia, key concepts and variables were defined through reference both to prior quantitative studies as well as case studies of selected schools. From this a quantitative study of 150 schools is being conducted, but case studies will again complement and help to illuminate the findings from this study. The process is cyclical and case study methodology enters the process at various stages.

See also: Research Paradigms in Education

References

Campbell D 1975 Degrees of freedom and the case study. *Comparative Political Studies* 8(2): 178–93

Diesing P 1972 *Patterns of Discovery in the Social Sciences*. Routledge and Kegan Paul, London

Firestone W A, Herriott R E 1983 The formalization of qualitative research: An adaptation of "soft" science to the policy world. *Eval. Rev.* 7(4): 437–66

Glaser B G, Strauss A L 1968 *The Discovery of Grounded Theory: Strategies for Qualitative Research*. Weidenfeld and Nicolson, London

Guba E G, Lincoln Y S 1985 Naturalistic and rationalistic enquiry. In: Husén T, Postlethwaite T N (eds.) 1985 *International Encyclopedia of Education*, 1st edn. Pergamon Press, Oxford

Hargreaves D H 1967 *Social Relations in a Secondary School*. Routledge and Kegan Paul, London

Herriott R E, Firestone W A 1983 Multisite qualitative policy research: Optimizing descriptions and generalizability. *Educ. Researcher* 12(2): 14–19

Kaplan A 1964 *The Conduct of Inquiry: Methodology for Behavioral Science*. Chandler, San Francisco, California

Kemmis S 1980 The imagination of the case and the invention of the study. In: Simons H (ed.) 1980

Levine H G 1985 Principles of data storage and retrieval for use in qualitative evaluations. *Educ. Eval. Policy Anal.* 7(2):169–86

Louis K S 1982 Multisite/multimethod studies: An introduction. *American Behavioral Scientist* 26(1): 6–22

Miles M B, Huberman A M 1984 *Qualitative Data Analysis: A Sourcebook of New Methods*. Sage, Beverly Hills, California

Parsons C 1976 The new evaluation: A cautionary note. *J. Curric. St.* 8(2): 125–38

Popper K R 1963 *Conjectures and Refutations: The Growth of Scientific Knowledge*. Routledge and Kegan Paul, London

Salomon G 1991 Transcending the qualitative-quantitative debate: The analytic and systemic approaches to educational research. *Educ. Researcher* 20(6): 10–18

Stake R E 1980 The case study in social inquiry. In: Simons H (ed.)1980

Stake R E, Gjerde C 1974 *An Evaluation of T. City*. American Educational Research Association (AERA) Monograph Series in Curriculum Evaluation No. 7. Rand McNally, Chicago, Illinois

Stenhouse L 1985 Case study methods. In: Husén T, Postlethwaite T N (eds.) 1985 *International Encyclopedia of Education*, 1st edn. Pergamon Press, Oxford

Sturman A 1982 *Patterns of School Organization: Resources and Responses in Sixteen Schools*. ACER Research Monograph No.18. ACER, Hawthorn

Sturman A 1989 *Decentralisation and the Curriculum: Effects of the Devolution of Curriculum Decision Making in Australia*. ACER Research Monograph No.35. ACER, Hawthorn

Tawney D A 1975 Evaluation and science curriculum projects in the UK. *Stud. Sci. Educ.* 3: 31–54

Wilson S 1977 The use of ethnographic techniques in educational research. *Rev. of Educ. Res.* 47(2): 245–65

Wright C A H 1988 Collaborative action research in education (CARE)—reflections on an innovative paradigm. *Int. J. Educ. Dev.* 8(4): 279–92

Further Reading

Adelman C, Jenkins D, Kemmis S 1976 Re-thinking case study: Notes from the second Cambridge Conference. *Camb. J. Educ.* 6(3): 139–50

Hamilton D, Jenkins D, King C, MacDonald B, Parlett M (eds.) 1977 *Beyond the Numbers Game: A Reader in Educational Evaluation*. MacMillan Education, Basingstoke

Husén T 1988 Research paradigms in education. *Interchange* 19(1): 2–13

Keeves J 1988 The unity of educational research. *Interchange* 19(1): 14–30

Marshall C 1985 Appropriate criteria of trustworthiness and goodness for qualitative research on education organizations. *Quality and Quantity* 19: 353–73

Simons H (ed.) 1980 *Towards a Science of the Singular: Essays about Case Study in Educational Research and Evaluation*. Occasional Publications No. 10. Centre for Applied Research in Education, University of East Anglia, Norwich

Smith J K, Heshusius L 1986 Closing down the conversation: The end of the quantitative–qualitative debate

among educational inquirers. *Educ. Researcher* 15(1): 4–12
Tripp D H 1985 Case study generalisation: An agenda for action. *Br. Educ. Res. J.* 11(1): 33–43

A. Sturman

CD Technology

Compact Disc (CD) is a system for the reproduction of high density digital data from an optical disc. The common characteristics of the CD are: the diameter of the disc (12 cm), the high capacity (about 650 Megabytes), the type of data handled (exclusively digital), and the fact that they are played by means of a LASER (Philips New Media Systems 1986, Miller et al. 1991).

Compact Discs were introduced between 1980 and 1990 and represent an exceptional advance in the technology for the digital storage of data. The CD has become a new publishing medium, an essential component for completely new types of computer applications, and an instrument of enormous potential in the field of education.

This entry aims to give an overview of the technical characteristics and of the possible applications offered by CDs, as well as highlighting the limits that this technology presents. With technological solutions such as CD-ROM (Compact Disc Read Only Memory), CD-ROM XA (Compact Disc Read Only Memory eXtended Architecture), CD-I (Compact Disc Interactive), all based on CD, it is also possible to process data of a multimedia type. Some of the educational applications available for these systems will be described.

1. CD-DA and CD-ROM

The first CD to be launched in October 1982 was the CD-DA (Compact Disc Digital Audio, normally called simply CD). Produced jointly by Philips and Sony, the Compact Disc Digital Audio has revolutionized high fidelity music, with its near perfect reproduction of sound, reduced size, and the impossibility of accidentally ruining the surface by scratching.

A Compact Disc Audio can record music (up to 72 minutes in stereo), in the form of digital data, eliminating all problems of dynamic range, background noise, wow and flutter. One of the factors that has represented a fundamental contribution to the success of the CD-DA (over 100 million players and three billion discs sold by the end of 1991) was the existence of a standard defined by Philips and Sony in a document called the "Red Book." This standard guaranteed the possibility of playing any Compact Disc on any player.

The great potential offered by the CD-DA led Philips and Sony to think of the possibilities of use for data application with the creation of the CD-ROM. Announced in October 1983, it was launched in March 1986. The standard defined for the CD-ROM is described in a document known as the "Yellow Book," and uses the same technology for recording the data by laser, and the same method of mastering and replication, as already used for the CD-DA. The CD-ROM, however, has a more reliable error correction code and a more accurate addressing system to the data blocks. In addition to the standardization of the physical form (the specification of the sector, the smallest unit of addressable data, etc.), the specifications on the logical format were also defined. Indeed, as soon as the industry began to take its first steps in 1985, it was immediately realized that if each software house and data preparation service used its own logical format, each one would be illegible by the file management systems of others. Moreover, for the CD-ROM to become a publishing medium, it had to have a logical format that was accessible to the whole public domain. The format for placing files and directories on the disc was therefore defined. This standard, referred to as the High Sierra Group proposal, which emerged from a proposal of an ad hoc committee of computer vendors, software developers, and system integrators, was subsequently approved by the international standards bodies as ISO 9660. The standard guarantees the interchangeability between any type of CD-ROM disc created in ISO 9660 and the most popular operating systems (MS-DOS, UNIX, VMS, and Apple DOS) (Einberger 1987). As a result of this adaptability the CD-ROM has penetrated all world markets. At the end of 1991 over 2 million drives and 12 million discs had been sold worldwide (Schwerin 1992).

The CD-ROM has several advantages, but also a few disadvantages with respect to other types of media. The advantages include: a high density storage capacity; low cost duplication for high volume applications; local distribution of archival information; inexpensive hardware; virtual indestructibility of data; the fact that it is a removable medium; access and local control through a personal computer; data integrity due to freedom from head crashes; and a fixed user cost that encourages use. Finally, a highly attractive feature of the system is its increasing simplicity and ease of use. The disadvantages of the CD-ROM include: the relatively high costs of data preparation; limited system performance characteristics, particularly in the area of data access time; and a transfer rate that is slow compared to magnetic media (Struckhoff 1989).

The CD-ROM is well-adapted to handling large quantities of text, for example, the equivalent of 150,000 pages in A4 format. However, it can also contain other data: up to 72 minutes of audio in CD-DA format. Nevertheless, the extremely high quality of sound reproduction that music demands (i.e., 20KHz bandwidth) is completely wasted when reproducing speech (3.4 KHz bandwidth), which is often the case in educational programs. For that reason audio in other nonstandard formats are also sometimes used. For still images a very good resolution can be obtained by inserting extended VGA cards into the computer.

At the end of 1991, more than 3,500 titles had been printed on CD-ROM worldwide. The majority of these are of a textual type. However, applications of a multimedia type also exist. One of the most famous in the educational market is "Ecodisc", produced by the BBC Interactive Television Unit. "Ecodisc" is directed at students aged between 14 and 18 studying ecology and presents a simulation of a real nature reserve, where the students are free to explore and carry out experiments. The menu offers the possibility of walking through the reserve, obtaining all the statistical data on it and the projections for the next 50 years, observing and collecting specimens of the various species, listening to expert opinions and analyzing the problems of management. "Ecodisc" operates on a Macintosh platform with a CD-ROM drive.

2. *CD and Multimedia*

The enormous capacity available on CD offers the possibility of recording not only text, audio, software, and data on this memory, but also media that require much more space. It is therefore possible to think of multimedia applications where the user can take advantage of all types of information, still and moving images, graphics and animation, text, speech, and music in a completely transparent way through a computer and a Graphical User Interface (GUI).

In order to bring multimedia to a wide public, the existence of a standard—a key concept of the modern information industry—is emerging as essential. There are *de jure* standards, approved by international bodies, *de facto* standards, accepted for their diffusion on the market and "standards by consensus," created by agreements between several manufacturers. The multimedia solutions proposed on the market as an evolution of the CD-ROM, which are analyzed below, are based on one of the three types of standards.

2.1 *CD-ROM XA (Compact Disc Read Only Memory eXtendend Architecture)*

Launched by Sony, Philips, and Microsoft in August 1988, CD-ROM XA is an extension of the CD-ROM data format consistent with ISO 9660, with the addition of a selection of CD-I characteristics. It is necessary to insert a card into the personal computer for a CD-ROM XA to be played. This system offers the following innovative possibilities:

(a) Recording up to 19 hours of compressed audio, with different standards of quality. The diversification of the levels allows the quality of the audio, and consequently the amount of memory taken up, to be adapted to the design needs.

(b) Switching instantaneously to 16 different audio channels.

(c) Reproducing audio during data transfer operation.

(d) Reproducing synchronized audio while visualizing very good quality color still frames or partial screen, partial motion sequences.

In the education arena, the CD-ROM XA can be profitably used in combination with the videodisc to produce a multimedia title which combines the requirements of motion sequences and a large quantity of audio. Language teaching is just one of the applications that would be guaranteed to derive great benefit from the combined use of these two technologies.

2.2 *DVI (Digital Video Interactive)*

The problems associated with digital motion sequences began to be solved effectively when the ISO (International Standards Organization) recently defined the MPEG (Motion Picture Expert Group) standard for the compression of video. While standardization is still pending, a number of proprietary solutions have been proposed to the market in the late 1980s, the best known of which is DVI. The DVI is not a disc but a set of compression and decompression algorithms and a series of chips on a card that is inserted into a computer, with which the following alternatives can be obtained from a CD-ROM:

(a) 650,000 pages of text;

(b) 22 hours of mid-range monoaural audio;

(c) 5,000 very high resolution stills; or

(d) 72 minutes of full-screen, full-motion video.

The advantages offered by DVI from the point of view of educational applications are many. A wide variety of media can be used to achieve the most complete educational effectiveness. In addition a completely digital recording of data offers a high degree of flexibility, which includes the possibility of transmission of the information via a network. The disadvantages are associated with the quality of the moving images, which, though it is perfectly adequate for many purposes, is still poor (comparable to that of a VCR) for educational applications which include images of a scientific type. Furthermore, the production of applications is relatively costly, even if this is true for all multimedia platforms.

As far as the educational applications of DVI are concerned, in the early 1990s prototype applications are being investigated, for example, at institutions such as Carnegie-Mellon University, Lehigh University, and Bank Street College of Education, all in the United States. The "Palenque Project" has been created at Bank Street College. This is a surrogate travel experience that is spatially organized, a multimedia database with a thematic and hierarchical structure, and a highly visual, intuitive interface. All of these have been intricately interwoven to offer the students an experience of visiting a photographically realistic ancient Mayan site at Palenque, Mexico. While exploring, the students can decide where they want to go on the site and what aspects they want to investigate.

2.3 Integrated Solutions Based on CD

The solutions outlined above are all for the professional market, to be integrated in a platform that includes a computer. However there are also solutions, integrated at the manufacturing stage, which offer a computer already equipped with all the hardware and software necessary for the production or use of multimedia products.

Some educational programs have been created for the Multimedia-PC (MPC). One of the best known titles is *Compton's Multimedia Encyclopedia*, published by Compton's New Media. The encyclopedia offers 31,200 articles, 15,000 illustrations, maps, charts and graphs, 60 minutes of sound, animation, an on-line dictionary, and seven multiple entry paths.

Another application for MPC is *Multimedia Beethoven: The Ninth Symphony*. Users can listen to the symphony played by the Vienna Philharmonic Orchestra, read simultaneously the original German text and the English translation, gain an insight into the musical structure of the symphony and the instruments that play in it, be given an in-depth analysis of each movement, and be supplied with a definition of musical terms. In addition, users can test their knowledge in the "Ninth Game," an interactive quiz for up to four players.

Two further integrated solutions are Ultimedia, a system proposed by IBM, and that based on the software QuickTime, presented by Apple in June 1991.

2.4 CD *for the Consumer Market*

In addition to the solutions for the professional market, there are some solutions designed for the consumer market which have a more contained cost. The most well-known of these is the CD-I (Compact Disc Interactive).

The approach in the design of the CD-I has radically differed from that followed in the design of other systems. It was in fact conceived not as a peripheral of a personal computer, but as an additional part of the home hi-fi system, to be connected to the television. The type and format of the multimedia data that can be used are defined in a standard laid down in the "Green Book." The hardware required to process the data was defined by an agreement between Philips and Sony (the former in particular has given major support since March 1987, when the CD-I was fully specified).

On a one-sided 4.75-inch CD there are several alternatives:

(a) 8,700 images of good television quality;

(b) 65 minutes of cartoon animation plus AM quality mono sound;

(c) more than 19 hours of AM quality mono sound'

(d) 150,000 pages of text; or

(e) 72 minutes of motion video, partial screen, partial motion.

The possibility of a full-screen, full-motion facility now also exists.

From the educational point of view, CD-I has all the features required for a digital multimedia program. In the early 1990s, most of the applications are for entertainment. Some applications are for the "edutainment" area, for example, the photography course program. The CD leads the student photographer step by step, from the choice of the camera to that of the lenses. The student is able to photograph subjects in motion from a film on the video. The result is immediate: the image is blocked and the photo discussed.

3. Educational Impact of CD *and Multimedia Technology*

As well as examining the technology available, it is appropriate to query what the real impact of multimedia technologies in the education world is likely to be. It is not yet possible, given the limited number of applications, to reach a definite conclusion on their effectiveness. Initial studies have been on the effectiveness of interactive videodisc training, as the videodisc is the system with the longest history of use in schools. One of these studies states:

> Interactive videodisc instruction which is thoughtfully and systematically developed, and shows creative new instructional strategies is beginning to demonstrate consistent positive results. Typically, learners who use interactive systems are achieving scores which are significantly higher than learners using other approaches. They often do this although they spend less time in instruction. Uniformly these learners report they enjoy and prefer working with interactive videodisc systems over conventional mediated approaches. (De Bloois 1984 p. 53)

Nevertheless, the impression is that multimedia will not have a far-reaching impact on education until the consumer market has fully taken off, allowing the prices of equipment and program production costs to be reduced. Moreover, up to the early 1990s, the absence of any definitive standards has dissuaded substantial investment by publishers in the educational market.

However, the world of education must investigate and assess from now on what the real contribution of multimedia to teaching may be, in order to acquire in-depth knowledge so that pondered decisions may be taken. A great deal of research is being carried out in universities and schools, revealing the great interest of innovators in the use of technologies that allow flexible teaching and provide an interactive and highly stimulating learning environment which is more adapted to the needs of contemporary teachers and learners and, at the same time, is focused on higher-order thinking skills and enhanced communication skills, collaborative problem-solving and lifelong learning.

See also: Multimedia Packages, Production of; Multimedia Systems in Education; Media Selection

References

De Bloois M 1984 *Effectiveness of Interactive Videodisc Training: A Comprehensive Review*. Monitor Information Services, Future Systems Inc., Falls Church, Virginia

Einberger J 1987 CD-ROM characteristics In: Ropiequet S, Eiberger J, Zoellick B (eds.) 1987 *CD ROM Optical Publishing*. Microsoft Press, Washington, DC

Miller R L, Sayers J H, Reeve V L, Kasten A S 1991 *Multimedia and Related Technologies: A Glossary of Terms*. Monitor Information Services, Future Systems Inc., Falls Church, Virginia

Philips New Media Systems 1986 *Dictionary of Terms*, 2nd edn. Philips International, New Media Information Center, Eindhoven

Schwerin J B 1992 *OPIA 92 Optical Publishing Industry Assessment*. Infotech, Woodstock, Vermont

Strukhoff R 1989 What is CD-ROM? In: Oberlin S, Cox J 1989 *CD-ROM 1989–1990 Yearbook* Microsoft Press, Washington, DC

Further Reading

Greenberger M 1990 *On Multimedia*. Voyager Company, Santa Monica, California

Luther A C 1989 *Digital Video in the PC Environment. Featuring DVI Technology*. McGraw-Hill, New York

Roth J P (ed.) 1991 *Rewritable Optical Storage Technology*. Meckler, Westport,

Philips International Staff 1988 *Compact Disc Interactive. A Designer's Overview*. McGraw-Hill, New York

Sherman C 1988 *The CD-ROM Handbook*. McGraw-Hill, New York

P. Ghislandi

Census and National Survey Data

Most national governments conduct a population census every 5 or 10 years. High income countries also carry out sample surveys of the working-age population, on a monthly basis. Annual censuses of particular institutions such as primary and secondary schools and tertiary institutions are also usually conducted. This entry provides an overview of: (a) what is collected; (b) how and when it is published; (c) some of the major uses in research related to planning and policy; and (d) limitations of the data.

The census of a population is an expensive, time-consuming undertaking, carried out by questionnaire delivered to all residences by a national bureau of census and statistics. The aim is to provide basic demographic, social, and economic data for government and private decision-making and research. Between censuses sample surveys are used to obtain up-to-date information and to provide detail on matters not covered in the census. The best known example of the national sample survey is the monthly or current population survey carried out by trained interviewers on a stratified random sample of households: in the United States, 60,000 households; in Canada, 48,000; in Japan, 40,000; and in Australia, 33,000. In a few countries longitudinal studies of a sample population are carried out by national statistical bodies.

Special education collections such as censuses and samples of schools are often handled by a body separate from that concerned with producing social and economic statistics about the national population. For example, in the United States the National Center for Education Statistics was set up to "collect, and analyse and disseminate statistics and other data related to education in the United States and in other nations."

The method of undertaking a census or a survey is usually clearly detailed in the publications of the national body that undertakes them. This entry will give only minor attention to these methods and to problems of validity and reliability of the data (see UNESCO 1991; *Questionnaires; Interviewing for Selection and Clinical Research*).

1. What is Collected?

Any country's five yearly census will vary over time in size and content. The census collects demographic, economic, and social information by means of a questionnaire from all residents of the country on a particular night. Its range is limited by issues of privacy, the past success in collecting the data and its usefulness, the cost of collection and processing, and the difficulty in obtaining particular information by questionnaire. Examples of problem areas for the census are income and religion and, in some countries, age. The census yields estimates of population by age and sex and region. It usually provides details on employment, educational participation and attainment, main language spoken, ethnicity, housing, mode of transport, and income.

The monthly household population survey is fairly standard in its basic collection of demographic, employment, and unemployment data for persons of working age across the many countries that have adopted most if not all the labor force concepts agreed by the International Labour Organisation (1982), which were based on developmental work carried out in the United States. On an annual or occasional basis, supplementary surveys seek a wide range of information including educational participation and attainment.

National estimates (e.g., of educational participation in postcompulsory education) based on the monthly survey may be provided with an apparently small margin of error. However, the estimates for regions and particular age or social groups are subject to a much larger sampling error. The reliability of estimates may also vary with the way the household questionnaire is administered. If one person answers all questions on behalf of the household there is a tendency on some matters, such as part-time work and part-time study, to underestimate participation compared with the findings of questionnaires administered directly to all members of the household (see, e.g., Freeman and Medoff 1982).

Government censuses of educational institutions always include data on the number and type of institutions, students, and staff. The degree of detail in such collections can vary but student data are usually provided by full-time and part-time status, by age and sex, and by level and type of course. Financial data are sometimes provided in these collections. Comparability across institutions and regions of the data collected in such censuses of educational institutions may be less than desired if (a) common definitions of key concepts such as student, full-time, and teacher are not rigorously defined; and (b) compliance is not assured by institutions surveyed.

Though there may be gaps and deficiencies in the data collected in such censuses of formal educational institutions, they are minor compared with the deficiencies in the data on training in the workplace and on other nonformal types of education. In the 1980s surveys were carried out on modes of training and employee expenditure on training (Australian Bureau of Statistics 1992).

2. *Publication of Data*

Only part of the data collected by national bodies is published in hard copy. Data from government surveys are increasingly released on CD-ROM and floppy disk as well as on microfiche and tape. The restrictions of confidentiality, and concern about the misuse of estimates for which sampling error may be high, place limits on the data that national statistical bodies are willing to release. Special tables with variables as specified by the user, or unit records, or in the case of the population census the 1 percent sample tapes, may be requested.

These new forms of publication represent a potentially vast increase in access to very detailed information for a wide range of users. This is enhanced by the decline in the costs of computers with their amazingly increased capacity, and improved software. A major concern is the level of charges that governments now make for the data, which may limit access to governments, large companies, and well-funded research institutes. The individual researcher and the interested citizen may find their access limited to the holdings of major libraries.

Sample survey data are often available some months after collection. The release of census data, however, may in some countries be delayed for several years.

3. *Major Uses and Limitations*

Any government body or private researcher is likely to make use of census and sample survey data from time to time. Use is made of current data and of time series built up from previous collections, though changes in definitions and in methods of collection may affect comparability over time. To classify all the uses is an impossible task. As an illustration, attention will be focused on the major use of the national data collections by governments and researchers concerned with policy and planning about education, about education and society, and about education and the economy.

The methods of finance, ownership, and regulation of the education system may be important in determining the type of data that will be needed in policymaking. If education were largely financed and provided in an unregulated private sector then there might seem to be little need for government planning and therefore little need for national and regional data collections. But only the most devout advocates of the free market could believe that a government should accept whatever outcomes the market yields, without concern either for market failure or for social costs and benefits that the market might ignore. The data needs may vary with the type of education system, but the necessity for national monitoring exists even with a market system.

While market elements in the provision of education have expanded since the 1980s, across the world it is still governments that dominate the provision and finance of education. The case is overwhelming that some planning should take place. For example, if schooling is provided free by governments in government schools to all who wish to enroll, then the government needs some means of estimating the numbers wishing to enroll. It needs this information to ensure that schools and teachers are in place when the students seek to enroll.

To illustrate the use of national data sets in planning it is necessary to discuss briefly some of the key elements of planning (see *Projections of Educational Statistics*).

3.1 Demography

One of the base elements is demographic analysis. This involves projections of the population by age and gender and by region based on data collected in the census and supplemented through sample data, migration data, and registrations of births and deaths.

3.2 Demand for Education

A second factor in planning involves the consideration of the demand to participate in any particular sector of education. This is a matter of family income and tastes, of rewards to the particular type of education, and of the costs of that type of education. To some extent these factors are influenced by direct government action on the curriculum and the assessment system; by financial factors such as student financial aid and unemployment benefits; or indirectly by government through the effects of its economic policy on the economy—successful or unsuccessful. The direct action of government, such as provision of financial assistance for students, may stem from concerns for social justice (e.g., reducing youth unemployment) or concern for the needs of industry.

Part, but only part, of the data required for analysis of demand is provided by the national census and sample surveys of the population, and collections from educational institutions. For example, data on trends in enrollments are available from institutions; family income and the recent pattern of earnings by age and qualification level are collected in the national surveys in many countries.

There is often the need to supplement the national collections with administrative data collected within government departments or by sample surveys undertaken by research organizations. This is illustrated by the experience of national or state or provincial committees of inquiry which are regularly established to investigate aspects of education. Almost invariably the nationally compiled census and survey data are inadequate for the particular questions under scrutiny by the inquiry.

Even if the data were apparently adequate, the relationships between the important variables cannot be easily specified. Moreover, relationships estimated on the basis of past data may not hold into the future. A major factor affecting analysis of demand for postcompulsory education in many countries is that enrollments may be determined by the supply of places funded by the government. Current or past enrollments may reflect supply but underestimate demand, leaving the estimation of demand as an extremely difficult exercise.

3.3 Supply of Education by Government

A third factor in planning is the extent to which a government wishes to finance or provide the places to meet demand. Government policy on educational provision is affected by the needs of the economy, its policy on social justice and the environment, and its willingness or capacity to finance the activity. The relevance of national census and survey data to consideration of the needs of the economy and the issue of social justice are briefly considered here.

Governments make judgments on the role of education in meeting the labor force needs of the economy. These judgments are supported through "manpower forecasting," "international comparisons," or through "rate-of-return analysis."

Manpower or labor market forecasting requires detailed data on educational attainment by occupation by age. Most censuses and some surveys provide data on these. The problem arises from the meaning that attaches to the myriad of qualification levels and the extent to which job skills are represented by educational qualifications. Furthermore, any occupation, even at the finest detail in the census, will nearly always encompass a fairly wide range of qualification levels. Medical practitioners or secondary teachers may be fairly homogeneous groups in many countries and entry to such jobs may be restricted by law to those possessing particular qualifications. However, this is not true of most jobs, and in most jobs there will be persons with little formal education and persons with high levels of qualifications.

Refinement of the data is important. Defining occupations in terms of the type and level of skill they require rather than in historical groupings is important. Similarly, educational qualifications could be defined in terms of sets of competencies in communication, mathematics, and so on. But it must be recognized that the nature of occupations is changing due to technological change and changes in work practices. With almost any form of equipment, alternative forms of job organization may be possible. The mix of persons with high or low qualification levels within an occupation may therefore vary among firms in an industry as well as between industries. An attempt to reach exact correspondence of educational qualifications and occupation may not be desirable either for work or education. So while the inadequacies of data should be diminished, they must always be quite substantial.

Even with good data the task of labor market forecasting is not easy. Changes in key parameters, such as the rate of resignation or retirement from particular occupations, can have drastic implications for the need for new recruits. The effect of apparently small changes is magnified since in most occupations recruits are but a small flow into the large existing stock within the occupation.

International comparisons are frequently used in support of policy changes in education but they remain hazardous. The Organisation for Economic Co-operation and Development (OECD) and UNESCO, the major international organizations with concern for education, are the main compilers of international data (OECD 1990, UNESCO 1991). Where nations differ in demographic structure, level of development, and in structure of the education system comparisons would be difficult to interpret even with similarly defined key concepts such as enrollments, teachers, and expenditure. However, efforts to achieve agreement in definitions and uniformity in data collection are yielding significant results in meeting the need for a set of indicators that will permit effective international comparisons (Boltani et al. 1992).

Rate-of-return studies and other variants of cost–benefit analysis are advocated as a means of considering the worth of alternative forms of education. The method requires data on education by employment by earnings as well as cost data. These are rarely collected in the national collections in the detail required for the analysis. In any case there are considerable reservations about the technique (Woodhall 1987).

A government's concern for social justice and related concerns for democracy and for the environment are factors in its willingness to provide or subsidize education. For intervention for these reasons a government needs information on inequalities in education, in work and living standards, and on the connections between them. For example, participation rates by ethnicity and language, region, and socioeconomic background may be obtained from census and in part from survey data. However, these data would need to be supplemented with data from cohorts over time for analysis of the connections between educational inequalities and other inequalities in society and the likely effects of government intervention.

3.4 Resources per Student

Even if a government decides to provide places in schools or postsecondary education for all who wish to attend (at the going structure of fees and student assistance), a fourth step is to determine the level of provision of resources: that is, the rate of staffing of schools, nonstaff resources, and buildings; and the rate of payment to staff relative to the general level of wages in society.

Data relevant to such considerations involve staffing data, some of which will be collected in the census of institutions. Some of the information will be available from other forms of data collection undertaken by national statistical bodies. Data on teachers' salaries relative to other pay rates are usually compiled in national collections on pay rates and form part of the data in cost deflators used in the national accounts on national income and expenditure.

4. Conclusion

Data compiled by national statistical bureaus and national educational bodies provide an indispensable input to research for policy and planning in education. However such collections cannot provide all the data required in policy and planning. The national data collections often provide only context data for more basic educational research. Consider, for example, a study on education and ethnicity. Data from the national census and surveys may provide details on the language and ethnicity of persons in the geographical area under consideration, the level of income and unemployment, the type of jobs of the employed, and the particular characteristics of the unemployed compared with the employed. The researcher concerned with the influence of school organization and curriculum or the values and aspirations of young people in various ethnic groups will, however, still have to collect and analyze data relevant to that study. Connections and relationships between the data from national collections and data collected by the researcher still depend on the researcher and the theories by which the research is guided.

See also: Comparative Statistics in Education; Educational Achievement: Comparative Studies; Education Indicators: Use in Policy and Management; Survey Research Methods

References

Australian Bureau of Statistics 1992 *Education and Training in Australia*. Australian Bureau of Statistics, Canberra

Boltani N, Duchesne C, Tuijnman A 1992 *Education at a Glance: OECD Indicators*. Organisation for Economic Co-operation and Development (OECD), Paris

Freeman R B, Medoff J L 1982 Why does youth labor force activity differ across surveys? In: Freeman R B, Wise D B (eds.) 1982 *The Youth Labor Market Problem: Its Nature, Causes and Consequences*. University of Chicago Press, Chicago, Illinois

International Labour Organisation 1982 *Statistics of Labor Force, Employment, Unemployment and Underemployment*. Report Prepared for the Thirteenth International Conference of Labor Statisticians. International Labor Office, Geneva

OECD 1990 *Education in* OECD Countries 1987–88: A Compendium of Statistical Information. OECD, Paris

UNESCO 1991 *Statistical Yearbook, 1991*. UNESCO, Paris

Woodhall M 1987 Earnings and education. In: Psacharopoulos G (ed.) 1987 *Economics of Education, Research and Studies*. Pergamon Press, Oxford

United Nations 1991 *Demographic Yearbook*. United Nations, New York

Further Reading

United States Department of Education 1991 *Digest of Education Statistics, 1991*. National Center for Education Statistics (NCES), Washington, DC

G. Burke

Central African Republic: System of Education

1. General Background

The Central African Republic is a nation of approximately 623,000 square kilometers located in the central region of Africa. Landlocked, it is surrounded by Chad, the Sudan, Congo, Zaire, and Cameroon. Topographically, the country lies on a high plateau, which serves as the watershed between Lake Chad and the Congo River basins. This area includes a system of inland waterways, which is important for transportation, commerce, and communications. Important river ports include the one at the nation's capital, Bangui, and those at Salo and Nola. The central plains rise to mountainous areas, including the Massif du Tondou and the Chaine des Mongos in the east and northeast and the Monts Karre in the west.

In 1988 the population was estimated to be about 2.7 million persons. Nearly 43 percent was under the age of 14 years. Some 63 percent of the population lives in rural areas and the density is 4 inhabitants per square kilometer. The population growth rate is 2.5 percent per year. The population includes a variety of ethnic groups. The largest are the Banda and the Baya, followed in number by the Mandjia, the Ubangi, the Sara, the Mboum, the Fertit, the nomadic Bororo-Fulani, and the Pygmies. A number of Europeans, mainly of French nationality, are concentrated around Bangui. French and Sango serve as the official languages. Some 60 percent of the population have traditional (mainly animist) beliefs, 20 percent are Roman Catholic, 15 percent are Protestant, and 5 percent are Moslem.

In 1989, the per capita Gross National Product (GNP) was estimated at US $390 (or US $290 per capita GDP). The majority of persons work in the agricultural sector and much of the agricultural production is at subsistence level. About 6 percent were employed in manufacturing, industry, and construction; 4 percent in commerce; and 1 percent in administration. Nearly 45 percent were unemployed. The main exports are cotton, coffee, and groundnuts. Minerals include diamonds, and there is the possibility of substantial uranium production. There is a deficit in the balance of payments.

Transportation is one of the main problems confronting economic development. There is a fairly extensive road network, but it has not been well maintained. Due to seasonal factors, the roads are only dependable at certain times during the year. The major source of transportation is the river system, especially the stretch of the Ubangi River which flows between Bangui and Brazzaville, Congo. There is a proposal for a Bangui–Yaoundé railway, and air transportation is facilitated by the major airport at Bangui and several smaller ones. The most widespread means of internal communication is radio.

The Central African Republic gained official independence from France in 1960. In 1976, the Constitution was amended and a new Constitution was adopted. In 1987, a democratic election was held and members of parliament were elected. In 1991, there was an amendment to the Constitution to create the post of a prime minister and to install a multiparty system.

In 1988, the illiteracy rate was 63 percent among all those aged 10 years or more. The primary school gross enrollment ratio was 67 percent (6- to 11-year olds) giving a net enrollment ratio of 49 percent. Average class sizes are 83 at primary level and 72 at secondary school in 1990. Of those in primary school, 17 percent succeeded in the end-of-primary-school exams and 19 percent of those in secondary school in the end-of-secondary-school exams.

2. Politics and the Goals of the Education System

The system of education was inherited from the colonial period at Independence and remained unchanged for 20 years. This academic system was geared towards the production of a small elite of administrators. The system was not appropriate for the socioeconomic needs of the country and it became increasingly apparent that there was a major crisis. For those in school, the majority were in academic tracks and few were educated in vocational and technical education because of only skeletal provision. At the end of secondary school, there was high enrollment in the arts subjects and little enrollment in the science subjects. This resulted in many graduates of secondary schools being unemployed. With the population increase and the democratization of education, the insufficiency of human and material resources for the school system exacerbated the crisis. Not only was there a decrease in the quality of education, but also in the internal and external efficiency of the system.

In 1982, a national effort was focused on the problems of education and training. This has resulted in the establishment of a new school system responding to the realistic needs of the Republic. The goals of the new school system are to ensure the child's full intellectual, physical, moral, civic, and vocational development. The child must learn to read, write, calculate, and, at the same time, develop a sense of productive work and a sense of the responsibilities involved in being a citizen. The overall aim is for

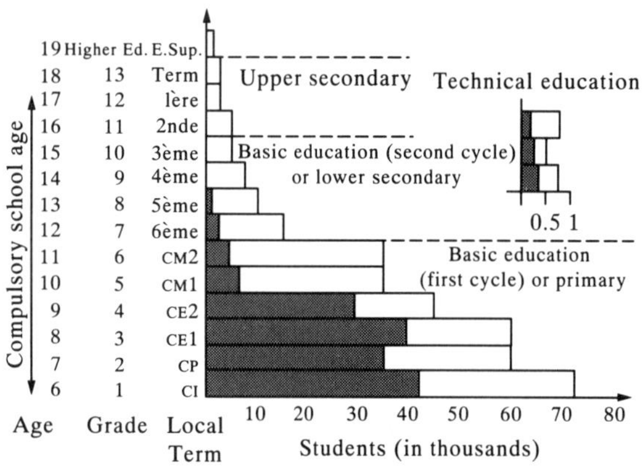

Figure 1
Central African Republic: Structure of the formal education system[a]

a The nonshaded part of each grade level indicates the number of children over age. The shaded part indicates the number of pupils of the equivalent age.

the system to provide a basic education for all, an education that is both general and practical, and relevant to the environment. Instruction will be conducted in French and Sango, the two official languages. The teacher has three roles: to teach, to be a leader in the community, and to involve parents and other members of the community in school affairs. The reform envisaged more emphasis on mathematics, science, and technology in the higher levels of secondary school.

3. The Formal Structure Of Education

3.1 Primary, Secondary, and Tertiary Education

Education is compulsory from the age of 6 to 17 (primary and secondary education). Figure 1 presents a diagram of the new educational system. Primary education (*Enseignement Fondamental, Niveau* 1) lasts for five years. Students enter at age 6 after having completed two years of pre-primary school. After five years, the students enter either lower-secondary school or vocational centers. Lower-secondary education (*Enseignement Fondamental, Niveau* 2) lasts for four years and has three tracks: general, vocational and technical, and agricultural and artisan. Upper-secondary school lasts three years and has general and vocational tracks. Higher education trains persons to a high level of proficiency either for the higher echelons of administration, the teaching service, or research. The University of Bangui has faculties of law, law and economics, the humanities, science, and medicine. There are also four *grandes écoles* for administration, business, and rural development, and a polytechnic. The University had an enrollment of 2,472 students and the *grandes écoles* an enrollment of 346 in the academic year 1989–90.

Grade-repeating rates in primary and lower-secondary school are high and in the order of 30 percent per year. There are 279 days (including Sundays) in the school year. This was computed by deducting all official holidays from 365 days. Officially, there are 4.5 hours of instruction per day in primary school.

3.2 Preschool Education

Preprimary education lasts two years. Children enter at the age of 4 years. The aim is to facilitate the transition from the family to school and to instill work habits in the children.

3.3 Vocational, Technical, and Business Education

Following primary school, students can either enter lower-secondary school or go to local vocational centers where they learn practical skills for the type of employment that exists in the local communities. For those entering lower-secondary school, students opt to enter either the academic track or vocational and technical tracks. The same is true at the upper-secondary school. The curriculum training centers cover such areas as masonry, carpentry, and metal work. The technical college attached to the *Lycée Technical* in Bangui runs courses for automechanics, electricians, and administrators. The Technical College for Women in Bangui has courses in domestic science. Finally, the National Center for the Training of Artisans runs courses in jewelry, basket-weaving and furniture-making, leatherwork, and metalwork.

Efforts are being made to increase the percentage of an age-group entering school and to encourage more students to take vocational courses.

3.4 Adult and Nonformal Education

Nonformal education is regarded as an integrated and indispensable part of the formal educational system. Literacy programs are run by the Division for Nonformal Education of the Ministry of Basic Secondary and Technical Education. This division is responsible for the production of literacy and post-literacy materials, the collection of data to do with literacy and recurrent education, follow-up and evaluation of the various literacy programs, and sensitizing the population to participate in mass literacy programs.

It should be noted, however, that there are difficulties in supplementing literacy activities because of a lack of funding. In 1992 there were only eight zones where these programs were in operation: three of these zones were in Bangui and five in the countryside.

Other bodies are involved in functional literacy programs, sometimes working on their own and sometimes in cooperation with the Division for Nonformal Education. Examples of such bodies are the Regional Centers of Education and Training (CREF), the Central African Agency for the Development of Ouham-Pende (ACADOP), the Evangelical Associations' Project for Agricultural Development (PREDAS), organizations for community and social development, and the National Civic Service for the Promotion of Youth (SCNPJ). The government has also created an ad hoc committee in the campaign against illiteracy in order to strengthen all literacy activities.

Another form of education that exists is that of Koranic education. This consists of teaching the Koran to children in Moslem communities. However, it is beginning to take on a more modern form in that new subjects are being introduced. These include grammar, Arabic, mathematics, and literature. It is said that the Arab–Islamic school comprises a pure Koran study part and an Arabic study part which is identical to the lay school.

4. *Administrative and Supervisory Structure and Operation*

Before 1986 all administration was centralized and in the hands of the Ministry of Education. After 1986 there was a reorganization of the administration in order to make it more effective. Decentralization took place and six *"inspections académiques"* were created. Modern methods of management and a permanent system of "control" (*Inspection Générale de l'Education*) were introduced. In addition, two institutions were established to help in the improvement of the administrative system. These were the National Center for Recurrent Training (*Centre National de Formation Continue*) and the National Institute for Educational Research and Development (*Institut National de Recherche et d'Animation Pédagogiques*).

The Ministry of Education has several tasks, among which are: the general administration of the educational system; the conceptualization, development, implementation, and monitoring of education as formulated in governmental decrees; the planning of all educational activities; the monitoring of the private school system; the conduct of all examinations and national competitions; research on the sources of financing; and the coordination of aid organizations in the field of education. One of its main tasks is funding of school buildings, school furniture and supplies, and teacher training, as well as the general administration of the system. A large amount of funding comes from France, and other funds in the form of loans or gifts come from the World Bank, the African Development Bank, and the United Nations Development Program.

5. *Educational Finance*

The percentage of the state budget allocated to education was 29 in 1980, 21 in 1989, and 19 in 1990. Two programs of structural adjustment took place in this period of time. These included the curtailment of the funds allocated to the social services and, in particular, to education. It should also be noted that the gross enrollment ratios in education decreased from 72 to 67 percent from 1980 to 1990.

In 1990, the education budget (19% of the state budget) was allocated as follows: Primary education (53.8%), lower-secondary education (14.4%), higher-secondary education (21.0%), administration (4.6%), and miscellaneous (6.2%).

The per student expenditures were US$47 for primary, US$86 for secondary, and US$1,710 for higher education in 1990 (US$1 = 282.5 CFA).

6. *Supplying Personnel for the Education System*

Primary school teachers are trained at the *Ecole National d'instituteurs* (ENI). The course lasts two years. To enter the ENI, a candidate must have passed the *baccalauréat*.

Up to 1986, those having a *baccalauréat* could compete for places at the *Ecole Normale Supérieure* (ENS) where there was a two-year training course to become a teacher in the second cycle of basic education (lower-secondary). In 1992, the training of second-cycle basic education teachers had been suspended.

Teachers for the upper-secondary school were recruited from university graduates possessing a degree (*licence*) for a one-year teacher training course at the ENS. By 1992, these teachers received a two-year teacher-training course at the ENS and qualified for a Certificate of Educational Aptitude in Secondary Education (*CAPES*). They are recruited from among those having a licence, as well as from practicing teachers in the second cycle of basic education.

Because of a deficit of primary school teachers, a crash program has been mounted. Candidates are recruited from university students who have not only the *baccalauréat* qualification, but also one or two university certificates obtained in the first or second year at the University. Thus far, this nine-month crash program has produced 234 teachers.

In some provincial schools, there are community teachers who have been recruited from pupils having graduated from the second cycle of basic education. They are employed by the local communities. In 1990, about 60 percent of all primary school teachers were of this category.

In 1990, there were 3,582 primary school teachers, 953 lower- and higher-secondary school teachers, and 410 faculty members in all institutions of higher education. In higher education there were 79 national, 57 foreign, and 274 part-time faculty members.

7. The System of Examinations, Promotions, and Certifications

In primary school, there are monthly assessments by teachers and an end-of-the-year examination. A certain standard must be reached in the end-of-year examination in order to be promoted to the next grade. However, for those pupils who have been working at the time of the monthly assessments or end-of-year examinations the teacher can decide on promotion. At the end of primary school there are two types of examinations: the first results in a Certificate of Primary Education (CEPE) and the second is a competitive examination in order to enter the second cycle of basic education.

In the second cycle of basic education (lower-secondary) there are term assessments. The average of the three term results determines promotion to the next grade. At the end of lower-secondary school there is a national examination for the *Brevet d'Etudes du Premier Cycle* (BEPC). Depending on a pupil's results in the different subjects, he or she is oriented to the general or technical streams in upper-secondary school.

The same form of assessment is undertaken in the upper-secondary school as in the lower-secondary school. At the end of upper-secondary, the pupils sit for the *baccalauréat* (*Second Degré*). The passing of the *baccalauréat* gives the right for admission to higher education.

8. Major Reforms in the 1980s and 1990s

In 1986, the reform of education was legislated and was to begin in the period of the five-year plan from 1986–90. Priority was awarded to the reform of primary education and the aims were to increase enrollment and improve the quality of education. At the secondary-school level, priority was awarded to the training of science and vocational teachers, and at the university level to the initiation of more science courses.

In 1990–91 there was a teachers' strike with the result that nothing happened in the schools, and this obviously affected any improvement in the system. There is a severe deficit in the number of teachers. Above all, there is a lack of funding to deal with the many problems of buildings, supplies, and teachers. Until this situation is improved little can be accomplished.

9. Major Problems for the Year 2000

As already mentioned, the lack of funding is likely to be a major problem for several years to come. Many noble words have been written about the rights of children to education, and the Central African Republic has endorsed the aims for education emanating from the World Conference on Education for All held in Jomtiem in 1990. However, there is much to be achieved in practice. The main aims in this country will be to decrease illiteracy (especially for girls), promote productive work at school, help students to enter the labor market, introduce health and environment education, improve teachers' conditions, and develop a private school system.

Given that education is the responsibility of each and every citizen, efforts will need to be made to involve local communities and parents in the educational school system in the communities. This is a necessary, but long and arduous task. The challenge is great.

D. Limbassa

Central and Eastern Europe: Adult Education

The position of adult education and industrial training in the Central and Eastern European countries is discussed, the focus being on Albania, Bulgaria, the Czech and Slovak Republics, Hungary, Poland, and Romania. The goals and main characteristics of adult education under communism are presented while the new, democratic approach to adult education is also discussed.

1. Development of Adult Education until 1945

The origin of formal adult education in Central and Eastern Europe is strongly connected with the ethnic and national awakening and popular enlightment movement of the nineteenth century. However, in countries such as Hungary and Poland some sort of independent education for both children and adults was organized even earlier. A large number of educational societies, voluntary associations, libraries, reading centers and self-education circles were established in the cities and rural areas of the region during the nineteenth and early twentieth centuries.

Educational societies were set up in Poland in 1822 (the Polish Foundation), in Czechoslovakia in 1831 (the Bohemian Foundation), in Romania in 1861 (the Association of Romanian Literature), and in Bulgaria in 1869 (the Bulgarian Scholars' Society).

The first handbook for self-education entitled *Friendly Advice*, and written by J K Szaniawski, was published in 1805 in Warsaw. So was the first textbook in writing, reading, and elementary arithmetic for adults, which was published by K Wolski in 1811 (Nowak and Cieślak 1982 pp. 14–15). In addition, the first Sunday school for adults in the region was established in Poland in 1815. In 1819 Sunday schools were attended by 800 adults in Kielce, Lublin, Łomża, Radom, and Siedlce in Poland. Sunday schools not only provided useful literacy skills, but also fostered a national cultural identity, which was needed in the process of nation-state building. The primary task, however, was to eradicate illiteracy. Some countries were less successful than others in accomplishing this task. The level of illiteracy was quite high in the 1930s, although it varied from region to region. Some 83 percent of the population in Albania was considered illiterate at that time. The comparative figure for Bulgaria was 28 percent, Czechoslovakia 4 percent, Hungary 7 percent, Poland 23 percent, and Romania 39 percent (Kulich 1989 p. 408). Toward the end of the nineteenth century, Sunday schools were transformed into adult evening schools. From the outset these schools provided an elementary education for adults; secondary education was added subsequently. Adult education was strengthened by the establishment of correspondence schools as well as the appearance of university public lectures in such countries as Czechoslovakia (Charles University in Prague), Poland (the universities of Cracow, Lvov, and Warsaw), and Romania (Cluj University). These university extension programs were eventually reinforced by the establishment of people's universities—popular educational institutions without formal institutional links with regular universities—throughout the region.

This brief description of the history of adult education in Central and Eastern Europe would not be complete without mentioning the role of various amateur circles and ensembles practicing folk art, music, and dancing, which cultivated traditional elements of national heritage and contributed to the creation of a national identity.

2. *Development of Adult Education 1945–89*

According to the Yalta and Potsdam agreements, Central and Eastern European countries found themselves under the dominance of communism after the end of the Second World War. The consolidation of the new system, which was accompanied by far-reaching social, economic, and political change, was completed by the end of the 1940s. The Communist Party had assumed full control of social and political life in all the countries of the region by that time.

The new context of course had major repercussions on adult education too. The main function of adult education had become a compensatory one. Systemic changes in the organization of adult education followed as well. Instead of encouraging social initiatives, the state educational administration took full responsibility for the coordination of all adult education activities. Centralized planning and curricular-organizational unification were two characteristic features of the development of adult education in all Central and Eastern European countries at that time. Individual initiatives in adult education and traditional voluntary associations were nearly completely eliminated. There were, however, some notable achievements as well. The new system was particularly successful in reducing illiteracy through mass campaigns (Pachociński 1989 p. 144).

The political crises of the 1950s and 1960s led to social renewal and limited liberalization of social life, especially in the former German Democratic Republic, Hungary, Czechoslovakia, and Poland. The changes also affected adult education, which became an element of an integrated national system of education in the 1960s and 1970s. The legal provisions enforced by the countries of the region emphasized the necessity of developing workers' education. The role of industrial enterprises, trade unions, local educational authorities, and social organizations and associations in the field of adult education was precisely defined. As a result, a unified system of adult education was established, consisting of schools for working adults, out-of-school professional adult education, and out-of-school general education. By the 1980s Central and Eastern Europe encountered a prolonged socioeconomic and political crisis of stupendous proportions. It appeared that communism as a socioeconomic system had been eroded beyond repair. Adult education as part of the social structure was, of course, influenced by the course of events. As the state economy that had shaped the systems of adult education in the region collapsed, so did state-controlled adult education encounter a dramatic decline in all major spheres of activity.

3. *Goals of Adult Education under Communism*

Educational theory was allegedly based on the Marxist ideal of man to be "developed from all sides." This was not the case in practice, however, since theory was mainly derived from the political doctrines of communism. Didacticism answered the genuine purposes of this theory. The technique refers to an extreme application of technicalities in the teaching process. The process is split into minute parts and attention is paid more to technical concerns than to the discovery of subject-matter using methods such as free discussion on the basis of different and possibly conflicting sources, for example, in history lessons. The main goal of didacticism may be viewed as indoctrination, through a constant repetition of carefully selected subject-matter, serving to reinforce the communist *Weltanschauung*.

Adult education played an important role in the totalitarian state. Its main functions were to supply the labor market with the workforce required for extensive industrialization and to produce, by means of political and ideological indoctrination, politically reliable and loyal citizens. With respect to the second function, one can note that teachers were not only supposed to act within their professional capacity, but also as officials of the bureaucratic system. Thus instructors were also political "agents," charged with the task of transforming the personal convictions of the students in accordance with Marxist ideology.

The sociopolitical system governing adult education was relatively stable in the Central and Eastern European countries from 1945 to about 1980. During this period, state adult education fulfilled mainly two funtions: (a) a compensatory function, and (b) an indoctrination function. The compensatory function was manifested in the form of organizing mass literacy campaigns and providing general and vocational education for adults at the primary and secondary level. Vocational education and industrial training developed rapidly during the 1970s. The main recipients of this training were the workers employed in the state economy. The educational policy of the 1970s was characterized by extreme centralization; quantity was much more important than quality. Courses were held by every ministry and by a large number of educational and cultural associations. However, in spite of the enormous educational efforts made to carry on the compensatory function of adult education, the outcomes were far from satisfactory.

The indoctrination function was carried out by both enterprises and educational institutions. Examples are the enterprise schools, the vocational schools for workers, and the induction or probation courses offered by firms. The enterprises were expected to create an atmosphere favorable to ideological indoctrination. In the interdependent process of education and work, attitudes, behaviors, and ways of thinking favorable to communism were promoted.

There were many other organizations that were expected to contribute to this reinforcement of communist ideas. The trade unions were among the most prominent in this respect. They were responsible for coordination in education, which aimed at strengthening the correspondence between the principles taught in school and those practiced in work and everyday life. Apart from the unions, there were literally hundreds of other sociopolitical organizations that played a major role in official adult education. They were usually handsomely paid from the state budget. A distinction can be made between several groups: political organizations providing citizenship education; professional associations, such as the unions of writers, journalists, lawyers, and teachers; and organizations for popular education such as the so-called "Houses of Culture." This list would not be complete without mentioning the role in the official adult education system of the mass media, museums, theaters, and public libraries.

4. State Systems of Adult Education and Training

Adult education in the Central and Eastern European countries has traditionally comprised two branches: the official or state sector and the "gray," mostly unofficial sector of adult education. The state system was in turn also divided:

(a) School-based adult education. This sector consisted of a variety of schools for adults, which provided a formal education at the primary, secondary, and tertiary level.

(b) Vocational adult education was provided by both enterprises and educational organizations.

(c) The out-of-school subsystem provided mainly politically-oriented adult education dispensed by means of various educational and cultural organizations.

4.1 School-based Adult Education

From about 1945 to 1989 the Central and Eastern European countries ran an extensive system of education for adults. These systems commonly comprised the following types of institutions: (a) elementary schools; (b) general secondary schools providing mainly evening classes or distance and correspondence courses; (c) vocational schools offering a basic and upper secondary education for adults; (d) postsecondary schools; and (e) higher education establishments catering mainly for working adults by means of evening, distance, and correspondence courses.

Several types of schools were established during the interwar period but, on the whole, the system developed mainly after the Second World War. It provided adults with opportunities to study while being in employment and to acquire additional qualifications through an alternative educational route. In general, the system may be described as comprehensive and well-developed; it provided a precisely defined education in all kinds of schools for adults (Savićević 1985 p. 137).

There were more similarities than differences in the school-based system of adult education among the various countries of the region. Albania, Bulgaria, and Romania were particularly concerned with eradicating illiteracy and increasing the supply of skilled workers during the 1970s. By comparison, Czechoslovakia, Hungary, and Poland assigned a higher priority to the provision of secondary and tertiary education for adults in the labor force.

Education was mainly dispensed in evening, distance, and correspondence courses. However, in some countries, notably Czechoslovakia and Poland, full-time day schools for "exemplary" workers were also established. These aimed to provide them with a chance to enter regular universities, and large numbers of adults seized upon this opportunity. In Poland about 40 percent of all students in tertiary education were enrolled on a part-time basis. The corresponding figure for Bulgaria, Czechoslovakia, and Romania was about 30 percent.

Vocational and technical schools for adults at both

basic and upper secondary level developed in large numbers throughout the region. A skilled labor force was needed for planned industrialization. In Poland school classes for adults were often established by, or jointly with, industrial enterprises.

There were also more similarities than differences among the countries of the region with respect to the provision of adult education. The differences concerned mainly the forms of provision. Evening courses were less popular in Bulgaria than Hungary. Evening programs enrolled about 5 percent of the students in Bulgaria, compared with over 30 percent in Hungary. Nearly all of the adult students in Czechoslovakia attended distance courses. In turn, in Poland, evening and distance classes were equally popular at the basic and upper secondary levels.

It should be stressed that school-based adult education in all the Central and Eastern European countries was well-developed under communism. It had become an integral part of the entire delivery system.

4.2 Vocational Adult Education

Vocational education in the Central and East European countries was provided by vocational schools at basic, upper secondary, and tertiary levels, and by various educational agencies in the form of vocational and technical training on-the-job. Generally, there was an imbalance between general and vocational education. Compared with general education, the latter was more highly valued as representing the status and ideology of the working class, and vocational training was thoroughly implicated as an element of political and ideological indoctrination. General adult education of a liberal type was not encouraged since it was identified with middle-class ideals.

Vocational education played an important role in supplying a skilled labor force to the state economy. There were many similarities and some differences in the forms of provision of training for new workers, re-training for those transferring to other jobs, and training to upgrade workers' qualifications.

In Poland this type of training was mainly provided by enterprises. It reached nearly 70 percent of the labor force, and the costs of vocational education corresponded on average to 2 percent of their income (Pachociński and Półturzycki 1979 p. 33). It is acknowledged, however, that it is hardly possible to measure the real cost or the extent of participation in the system. In Poland, the annual enrollment estimates varied from 10 to 20 percent of the overall population in the 1970s (Pachociński and Półturzycki 1979 p. 33). According to official data nearly 5.4 million employees in the Polish state economy took part in various general and vocational courses, seminars, lectures, etc. in 1987—even though about 50 percent referred to safety and hygiene courses (Pachociński 1989 p. 147). However, from the early 1970s onward, the situation was reversed in Hungary. Vocational training, re-training and upgrading were each acquired together with political and general education in vocational schools. Industrial enterprises were mainly responsible for bearing the training costs and for sustaining the wages of trainees (Fukász 1978 p. 41). The same model was followed by Bulgaria, where 628 vocational study centers with 192 branches catering for over 400,000 workers were established in the 1970s (Micheva et al. 1982 p. 43). Czechoslovakia, in turn, elaborated an intricate model of on-the-job training based on task analysis. On-the-job training was reinforced by school forms of adult education (Skalka and Livečka 1977 pp. 47–64). In other countries of the region (e.g., Albania and Romania), some mixed models of vocational training for workers developed. In these, vocational and technical education in schools and on-the-job training in industrial enterprises were alternated in the course of providing vocational education.

There are some differences, however, in defining on-the-job training in Western and Eastern European countries. In the former on-the-job training is mainly viewed as a separate phenomenon, disconnected from the system of education as such, which is not the case in the latter, where on-the-job training is considered an integral part of the comprehensive system of education. At the same time, occupational training in Central and Eastern Europe served not only vocational and technical objectives, but also political and ideological ends.

4.3 Out-of-School Adult Education

Traditionally out-of-school adult education was carried out by voluntary associations in the Western tradition. The same applied to the Central and Eastern European countries in the period before the communist states were established in the late 1940s.

Adult education was viewed by the communists as a strategic means to reinforce the social system. A stable communist state could not be achieved without full control over all types of education. Voluntary associations were eliminated, and a large number of new organizations—for example, trade unions, youth clubs, peace movements, and defense leagues, etc.—were set up with the aim of enhancing conformity with respect to communist principles and ideals.

In all countries of the region, associations for the dissemination of scientific knowledge modeled after the Soviet *Znanie* Society were established. The principal concern of these societies was to dispense a carefully constructed education to the adult population by means of public lectures given by university staff, writers and journalists, and school teachers.

The oldest of these societies, The Polish Society (TWP) was established in 1950. By 1980 the number of lecturers exceeded 40,000. They gave on average three to four public lectures a year, reaching an audience of millions of people and they owned a publishing house for popular books, leaflets, and periodicals. Similar societies for the dissemination of scientific knowledge were established in Czechoslovakia (1952), Hungary (1953), and Bulgaria (1971). The Hungarian Society opened a Free University in 1954 and regularly organized summer universities for adult students from Hungary and abroad.

Many other institutions were set up within the out-of-school sector in nearly all the countries of Central and Eastern Europe. Important were the "Houses of Culture," which served to satisfy the general cultural needs of the people and the socialization needs of the state. Such institutions usually included a cinema, theater and/or exhibition halls, library, and amateur and hobby circles, and they might have run a variety of educational courses.

Among the other providers of adult education the people's universities of Czechoslovakia, Poland, and Romania should be mentioned. The main purpose of these universities was to update the general and vocational education that adults had previously acquired. In 1973–74 there were nearly 5,000 such people's universities in Poland, and 164,000 adults participated in the various courses and about 5 million people attended public lectures (Pachociński and Półturzycki 1979 p. 49). Note should also be taken of the residential folk high schools in Poland—the only country in the region that followed the Danish tradition. The 10 residential schools for adults in Poland served the rural population, and functioned as training centers for village cultural workers.

5. *Independent Adult Education under Communism*

In all Central and Eastern European countries, independent adult education during the communist era was organized by groups in political opposition: dissidents, freedom fighters, and solidarity activists. In one form or another, these groups or social movements strived for the attainment of goals such as human rights, independence, and democratic pluralism. It was understood that these goals would not be easily achieved.

The anti-communist opposition organized people committed to the goal of working for a future in which the communist system would be replaced by parliamentary democracy. The educational activities of the social movements, which were not numerous and mostly illegal, depended on self-education and participation in group discussions. Topics for discussion were the types of political systems that might emerge in a post-communist state, the balance of power in such a future political system—biparty or multiparty—and the place and role of parliament in the new political system. Study circles were also formed around other major themes. Examples are groups discussing privatization and market economism, education, philosophy, publishing, and cultural life. This form of "underground" community education had become well-established toward the mid-1980s. Even some state-controlled institutions such as public libraries, theaters, and museums participated in the illegal circuit, helping in carrying on "alternative" cultural life.

The educational effort of religious leaders and the Roman Catholic Church in Czechoslovakia, Poland, and Hungary was also important. The Church was the only institution besides the communist state apparatus with an independent social structure and a real power basis in society. The Church could not only make its own decisions and rules but also, to a certain extent, implement them. Even though the Church was primarily concerned with religion, it had an important role to play even in philosophy and cultural life; such issues as human rights are deeply embedded in Christian philosophy. It preached passive disobedience to communist rule through "internal freedom" and "internal migration." The Church was important for keeping up morale, for example, by taking care of political prisoners and their families.

In conclusion, a large part of adult education took place not in the official, but in the independent system. It may be noted in the case of Poland that from 1982 to 1989 the leaders of the Solidarity Movement initiated a so-called "Long March" to freedom of thought. The distribution of illegal publications—books, dailies, and magazines—formed the core of this strategy of conscience-raising. About 800 books were printed by underground publishing houses during this period. This shows the importance of independent adult education in Poland in the years preceding independence, and the extent of the educational activity that was carried on.

6. *Adult Education in Transition*

The Central and Eastern European countries have experienced great changes since the revolutions of 1989 and 1990 which, with the exception of Romania, have been peaceful ones. Although the precise nature of the changes is not yet understood, they embrace the following: (a) a gradual disappearing of the remnants of the totalitarian communist state; (b) the adoption of democracy and market economic principles; (c) the endorsement of pluralism as the principal instrument for building free market democracy; and (d) an acceptance of the need to model a post-communist society on humanism and religious and moral values.

The transition from communism to democracy is mainly an educational process. Adult education in particular has an important role to play in off-setting the consequences of decades of ideological indoctrination. The introduction of free market economics may not be possible without a re-orientation of the scale of values and attitudes which communism has instilled in people. Building democracy is done mostly at the grassroots level. Hence the importance of community-based adult education. People have to be made to understand that hard work, personal initiative, and, especially, risk-taking in investment are indispensible for success in a market economic system.

With little open unemployment in the former command economy there were few incentives for further education and training, because workers could expect to remain in the same job or career path for the duration of their working lives. The lack of competition did not motivate firms to invest in training either. As a result, vocational adult education and industrial training were generally neglected, although the situation varied between the different countries of the region. Poland and the former German Democratic Republic, for example, had extensive training systems, although much of this capacity was obsolete and slow in responding to changes in demand. The training systems of Bulgaria and Romania were underdeveloped by comparison.

There is little doubt that the structure and direction of adult education and training are in need of urgent reform, particularly in comparison with the competitor countries of the European Community. The former system of adult education was directed to the acquisition of skills needed to service uncompetitive economic sectors favoring heavy over light industry and workers over professionals. The system was not preparing for change and innovation; hence the acquisition of new skills was hardly encouraged or rewarded.

Unemployment has risen as a result of the transition from a command to a market economy. Skills shortages are also becoming visible. Enterprises hoarded labor under the former system, and labor offices were mainly responsible for allocating the labor force to firms. Unemployment was low in all Central and Eastern European countries in 1989. By the end of 1993, unemployment rates had risen dramatically.

The economic transformation of the Central and Eastern European countries depends crucially on the quality of the labor force. Hence it is essential that adult education be reformed in accordance with the demands of a competitive labor market. The development of the informal sector, which encompasses a wide variety of economic activities, must also be taken into account. The reason for emphasizing training for self-reliance within the informal sector is motivated by the fact that opportunities for wage-employment in the modern sector are limited. Training in the informal sector may contribute to creating employment stability and raising productivity.

7. Research in Adult Education and Training

Due to lack of financial resources, the volume of research into adult education and training has been drastically reduced in the Central and Eastern European countries since 1989. The focus of the research has also changed. For example, the European Center for Leisure and Education in Prague has shifted its research emphasis from comparative adult education to human rights education. Research in adult education in the Central and Eastern European countries is undertaken both within and outside universities. However, because of a scarcity of funds, research studies tend to be based on small populations as a rule; hence results are hardly generalizable. A survey carried out in Poznań in Poland showed that 76 percent of adults had an indifferent attitude to education, 16 percent were negative, and only 8 percent positive; 67 percent of workers neither showed any interest in adult education nor any aspiration to upgrade their education (Solarczyk-Ambrozik 1988 p.27).

8. Conclusion

The former system of adult education and training in Central and Eastern European countries fell apart together with the demise of communism. A new system of education reflecting liberal democracy and free market economy has not yet been created. Although investment in adult education and training is a high priority, the economy at present is not capable of freeing the required financial resources. Because the public system cannot satisfy the social demand, many tasks of adult education are now being carried out by private schools and institutions. The education they offer is accessible only by those who are able to pay for the services rendered. The educational needs of a large section of the adult population is therefore not being catered for.

See also: Adult Education, Reform Strategies in; Russia: System of Education; Hungary: System of Education; Poland: System of Education; Soviet Union: Vocational Education and Training

References

Fukász G 1978 *Adult Education in the Hungarian People's Republic*. Studies and Documents 3. ECLE, Prague

Kulich J 1989 Provision in Eastern Europe and the Soviet Union. In: Titmus C J (ed.) 1989 *Lifelong Education for Adults: An International Handbook*. Pergamon Press, Oxford

Micheva P, Bizhkov G, Petkov I 1982 *Adult Education in the People's Republic of Bulgaria*. Studies and Documents 12. ECLE, Prague

Nowak J, Cieślak A 1982 *Adult Education in Poland and Abroad* (in Polish). Common Knowledge, Warsaw

Pachociński R 1989 History and present situation of adult education policy and adult education research in Poland. In Knoll J (ed.) 1989 *Internationales Jahrbuch der Erwachsenenbildung*, Vol. 17. Böhlau, Cologne

Pachociński R, Półturzycki J 1979 *Adult Education in the*

People's Poland. Studies and Documents 6. ECLE, Prague
Savićević D M 1985. Adult education in Eastern Europe. In: Husén T, Postlethwaite T N (eds.) 1985 *The International Encyclopedia of Education*, 1st edn. Pergamon Press, Oxford
Skalka J, Livečka E 1977 *Adult Education in the Czechoslovak Socialist Republic*. Studies and Documents 1. ECLE, Prague
Solarczyk-Ambrozik E 1988 Research in adult education in Poland. In: Czerniawska O (ed.) 1988 *The Functioning of Adult Education in the 1980s in Poland*. Lublin University, Lublin

Further Reading

Organisation for Economic Co-operation and Development (OECD) 1992 *Education and Training for a New Society: The Case of Romania*. General Distribution Document. OECD, Paris
Organisation for Economic Co-operation and Development 1992 *Education in the Czech and Slovak Federal Republic: Country Report*. General Distribution Document. OECD, Paris
Organisation for Economic Co-operation and Development 1992 *Policy Motives in Education and Training in Bulgaria*. General Distribution Document. OECD, Paris
Organisation for Economic Co-operation and Development 1992 *Report on Education and Training in Poland During the Transformation of the Socio-economic System*. General Distribution Document. OECD, Paris
Organisation for Economic Co-operation and Development 1992 *Transition of Education and the Economy in Hungary in the early 1990s*. General Distribution Document. OECD, Paris
Schweitzer J 1991 The Transition to a Market Economy in Central and Eastern Europe—Employment, Training and Education. World Bank, Washington, DC.

R. Pachociński

Certification of Adult Education

Certification refers to the process by which knowledge, skills, and competencies are measured and recognized. There is a demonstrated need in adult education for clarifying differences between concepts such as certification and validation as well as between individual-based approaches and program-based approaches to these issues. Drawing on experiences in different countries, this article presents a discussion of major trends and issues concerning the certification and validation of skills and competencies acquired by means of adult education, experiential learning, and firm-based training. Although the focus is mainly on the industrialized countries, the problems dealt with are of general concern and applicability.

1. Challenges to Conventional Approaches to Certification

Since the 1970s several changes have occurred that justify a rethinking of certification procedures in education. One important aspect is the emergence of a global economy, which in many countries has led to a debate concerning the competitiveness of labor markets. The concomitant restructuring of labor markets and the transformation of social policies have, in the industrialized countries, given rise to a new appreciation of the social and economic imperative of developing lifelong education, including not only skills training but also "second chance" education and recurrent education for leisure and personal development (OECD 1975, 1977, 1991a). Certification has assumed vastly greater significance as a result.

The expansion of formal education is a second factor that has influenced the debate concerning certification. In a context of spreading education to the masses, diversification in funding, and rapid growth of upper secondary and higher education, the meaning and function of certification is changing. For example, in many countries, school diplomas and university degrees no longer have a common and unique meaning. This often leads to a discussion concerning the social and professional value of different qualifications. Conventional certification practices in formal education are increasingly challenged by these developments.

A third factor concerns the development of "parallel" educational structures (Figeat 1984, Tanguy 1986). During the 1980s and early 1990s, many countries pursued a policy of simultaneously encouraging the development of public training schemes for the unemployed and strengthening private initiatives in adult education and continuing vocational training. Opportunities for adult learning have both increased and become more diverse as a result. Many adults are now in a position to acquire knowledge and skills by means of adult recurrent education, industrial training, and self-directed learning activities. The emergence and growth of the training market has considerably modified the certification issue (Cervero and Azzaretto 1988, Gehin 1989, Carnevale et al. 1990, Eurich 1990) (see *Adult Education and Training Markets; Education and Labor Markets in Developing Nations; Market Failure in Firm-based Education and Training*).

The need to recognize skills and competencies not acquired in a traditional school setting has given rise to alternative assessment and certification practices. A distinction can be made between, firstly, certification as a formal qualification and, secondly, other means for recognizing and validating skills and competencies (OECD 1990).

2. Validation and Certification

Certification usually relates to "officially" endorsed diplomas and degrees. Recognition is typically provided by public authorities, boards in charge of educational institutions, professional bodies, or through collective bargaining. Certification is thus a concern mainly identified with formal education. It does not normally take into account the full range of an individual's personal and professional competencies, even where recognition results from a collective bargaining agreement. However, as adult education and continuing vocational training have expanded and assumed increased economic importance, the call for another approach to certification has become stronger and more urgent. The emphasis on the development of a more broadly based approach to validation has to be examined in this context.

As opposed to formal certification, validation refers to the process of assessing and recognizing a wide range of skills and competencies which people develop throughout their lives and in different contexts, for example, through education, work, and leisure activities. These skills and competencies are "acquired" in the sense that they are tested under everyday conditions. Such acquired abilities have of course always existed; for example, they are implicit in systems of promotion by seniority. Whereas the expansion of formal education called established certification procedures into doubt, the demand for new approaches to validation resulted from technological change, the transformation of work, and the emergence of training markets (see *Adult Education and Training Markets*). Validation has become very complex since the set of acquired abilities that may have to be taken into account has grown very large.

In meritocratic societies, in order to be valuable for individuals and firms, the acquired skills and competencies need to be identified, assessed, and given both professional and social professional recognition. The validation process thus confers a currency value to assessed abilities (Liétard 1991.) Validation is often focused on those abilities that are transferable from one work situation to another, from a life situation to a work situation, or from a life situation to a training situation. Indeed, facilitating transfer is one of the aims of validation. Portability may not prove valuable to the individual unless the skills and competencies previously acquired are "officially" recognized. Validation thus involves an assessment of the equivalency of recognized skills and competencies in relation to a defined standard of achievement, for example, those accepted by institutions of formal education.

3. *Individual-based Approaches to Validation*

Skills assessment has a long history. In the United States, for example, such assessment began on a large scale with the GI Bill passed after the Second World War, which made it possible for veterans to enroll in educational institutions in order to undertake studies interrupted or delayed by the war (see *Experiential and Open Learning for Adults*). Similar procedures were also used in Canada, especially in Quebec. Following on the Continuing Education Act that came into effect in 1971, France introduced a system of credits in short-cycle secondary education. The main purpose was to make this education accessible to adults facing redundancy (Elie 1969, Schwartz 1969). Nevertheless, in France, a need for fuller recognition of work-related skills emerged. This led, in 1986, to the creation of the assessment centers.

These centers are based on the idea that, pending full certification, some validation of acquired skills and competencies should occur (Colardyn and Parlier 1986). The assessment centers can recognize both formally taught and experiential learning, as well as skills and competencies acquired outside the educational system. The aim is to provide individuals with a permanent record of recognized skills and competencies acquired through courses or by other means. A second aim is to encourage individuals to make use of these records in negotiations concerning employment and/or further training. A third aim is to instill in individuals an awareness of the importance of their human "capital" for professional, educational, social, and cultural life (Liétard 1991).

In future, the recognition given by the assessment centers or similar institutions could be taken into account in decisions concerning formal certification, for example, in the form of credit units leading to a diploma. Such an integrated validation system would articulate knowledge-based teaching in educational institutions with competence-based learning at the workplace.

4. *Program-based Approaches to Validation*

There is at present a search for linkages between formal certification and the experiential learning of workers at different occupational levels. Examples of linkages between knowledge-based certification and competence-based recognition can be found in the United Kingdom (Vaughan and Squires 1991). These projects are limited, however, in that they mostly concern the validation of skills and competencies acquired by well-educated employees, for example, engineers and managers. Examples are programs such as CATS, which is promoted by the Council for National Academic Awards and, on a smaller scale, CONTACT (Drake 1991). Similar projects have also developed in Australia.

Adult education is characterized by a wide variety of provision, ranging from formal courses provided in schools, universities, and other institutions, to nonformal education offered by nonprofit associations, to training and retraining managed by public institutions and private, profit-making firms. The sources for funding and the quality and quantity of provision vary accordingly (see *Providers of Adult Education*). This condition of diversity, which to an extent has been intentionally created through policies aimed at establishing "flexible pathways" for adult learning (OECD 1991b), raises many questions concerning the assessment and validation of skills and competencies acquired outside the system of formal education. The apparent contradiction between diversified provision and a lack of flexibility in certification can be studied by examining practices in the three sectors of the training market (see *Adult Education and Training Markets*):

(a) The *formal sector* confers recognized qualifications such as diplomas, degrees, and certificates at the secondary and tertiary levels of the educational system. These formal qualifications are essentially knowledge-based, even in the case of vocational education. Demands for employable skills are usually not determinate, in part because many employers underline the value of a broad education, which they see as providing a useful basis for further education and training.

(b) The *nonformal sector* comprises the most active partners in continuing vocational education: firms, professional associations, and trade unions. The content of the training is usually competence based. Certification can vary from a simple attendance testimony—the most frequent case—to a certificate that can be integrated with a formal qualification. These attempts at integration reflect the search for broadly based approaches to validation.

(c) The *commercial sector* takes advantage of a generally "overloaded" educational system. It is made up of profit-making training firms and schools, often privately financed, that are flexible in adjusting to changes in market demands. Here too the attendance certificate is the rule. Partly for this reason, the value of commercial adult education has been called into doubt in some countries.

The previously mentioned Council of National Academic Awards (CNAA) in the United Kingdom presents an example of a program that has, with some success, developed linkages between formal qualifications and the certificates awarded by providers of further education or training in the three sectors. The CNAA began its work in the mid-1970s by approving certificates awarded by polytechnics and colleges for continuing education which, unlike the universities, could not set up their own degrees and had to refer to the CNAA Accreditation Commission (see *Polytechnical Education*). The various parties having a stake in the proposed educational program (e.g., public authorities, professors, employers, and trade unions) each had a representative on this commission. Based on experience gained with this initiative, the Credit Accumulation and Transfer Scheme (CNAA 1989) was a natural next step. In contrast to the approach taken in France with the assessment centers, recognition is not awarded to an individual but to a specific education or training program. The criteria for approval are duration of study in relation to orientation and program quality, and recognition may be given regardless of the sector—formal, nonformal and, commercial—in which the provider operates.

5. *Integrated Approaches to Certification*

The Accreditation Commission in the United Kingdom presents an interesting example of an attempt to improve coherence by linking provision to certification and validation issues. In future this could be enlarged. For example, one could define the equivalency of certificates awarded in the formal sector of provision with those given in other sectors, and combine these into a new qualification. This would make it possible to integrate formal education with experiential learning and firm-based training, for example, by establishing a system of credit units that collectively form a full and certified course. Such an integrated credit unit or module approach may facilitate the design of systems for continuous vertical upgrading. These systems would take the qualifications (diplomas, apprenticeship certificates, etc.) that are conferred by second-level educational institutions as their point of departure. The purpose of integrating knowledge-based certification with competence-based recognition would be to facilitate upward mobility while allowing for lateral movement across educational tracks that otherwise might lead to occupational "dead ends."

Integrated approaches to certification have several advantages. First, the relationship between initial and postinitial education and training would become more flexible and permeable. Second, from a labor market viewpoint, such practices would help in making the various learning options open to individuals clearer and, hence, in influencing the way individuals and firms devise their learning strategies. An additional advantage is that an integrated approach to certification may offer incentives for investment in further education and training. Such incentives could act without destroying the structure of labor markets and industrial relations systems specific to countries. Third, an integrated approach to accreditation has implications for financing. Public funding could be more easily earmarked for investment in initial education and training, whereas private resources would be particularly needed for continuing vocational education and training. The dilemma of balancing efficiency and social equity would no longer rest mainly or only with public authority but lie in the hands of all constituencies of society.

See also: Adult Education and Training Markets; Market Failure in Firm-based Education and Training; Professional

Associations for Adult Education; University Adult Education

References

Carnevale A P, Gainer L J, Villet J 1990 *Training in America. The Organization and Strategic Role of Training*. Jossey-Bass, San Francisco, California
Council of National Academic Awards (CNAA) 1989 *Background Papers on the Credit Accumulation and Transfer Scheme*. CNNA, London
Cervero R M, Azzaretto J F 1988 *Visions for the Future of Continuing Professional Education*. Research report. University of Georgia, Atlanta, Georgia
Colardyn D, Parlier M 1986 *Bilan des compétences personnelles et professionnelles. Approche historique des pratiques indispensables et diversifiées*. Centre INFFO, Paris
Drake K 1991 Recent developments of continuing professional education. United Kingdom's National Report to OECD. In: OECD 1991 *Higher Education and Employment*, OECD, Paris
Elie A 1969 Action de formation dans le bassin ferrifère. *Educ. Permanente* 1(3): 87–102
Eurich N P 1990 *The Learning Industry: Education for Adult Workers*. The Carnegie Foundation for the Advancement of Teaching, New Jersey
Figeat M 1984 *Politiques de formation de la main-d'oeuvre en France*. Collection Rapports de Recherches, INRP, Paris
Gehin J-P 1989 L'évolution de la formation continue dans les secteur d'activité. *Formation emploi* 25: 19–35
Liétard F 1991 *Institutionalisation d'une pratique: les bilans. Point de vue d'un acteur*. Education Permanente à paraître, Paris
Organisation for Economic Co-operation and Development 1975 *Recurrent Education*. OECD, Paris
Organisation for Economic Co-operation and Development 1977 *Learning Opportunities for Adults*, Vol. 1. OECD, Paris
Organisation for Economic Co-operation and Development 1990 *Assessment and Recognition of Skills and Competencies: Developments in France*. OECD, Paris
Organisation for Economic Co-operation and Development 1991a *Alternatives to Universities*. OECD, Paris
Organisation for Economic Co-operation and Development 1991b Enterprise-related training. In: OECD *Employment Outlook* (July): 135–75
Schwartz B 1969 Pour une education permanente. *Educ. Permanente* 1: 63–86
Tanguy L 1986 *L'introuvable relation formation-emploi. Un état des recherches en France*. La Documentation Française, Paris
Vaughan P, Squires G 1991 *Maintaining Professional Competence*. A survey of the Role of Professional Bodies in the Development of Credit-Bearing CDP courses. The University of Hull, Hull

Further Reading

Aamodt P O 1990 A new deal for Norwegian higher education? *Eur. J. Educ.* 25(2): 171–85
Blanchard S, Francequin-Chartier G, Stassinet G, Vrignaud P 1989 *Outils et procédures de bilan pour la définition d'un projet de formation personnalisée*. Institut National d'Etude du Travail et d'Orientation Professionelle, Paris
de Larminat P 1991 Historique des travaux français de prospective emploi-formation. In: *Pour une prospective des métiers et des qualifications*. La Documentation Française Paris
Madigan K 1990 *Further Education and Training and Collective Bargaining: The Experience of Five Countries*. OECD, Paris
Organisation for Economic Co-operation and Development 1977 *Selection and Certification in Education and Employment*. OECD, Paris
Organisation for Economic Co-operation and Development 1987 *Adults in Higher Education*. OECD, Paris
Organisation for Economic Co-operation and Development 1992 *Adult Illiteracy and Economic Performance*. OECD, Paris
Parry G, Wake C 1990 *Access and Alternative Futures for Higher Education*. Hodder and Stoughton, London
TAFE (Training and Further Education) 1990 *Assessment and Standards in Vocational Education and Training*. Conference Report. TAFE, Leabrook

D. Colardyn

Chad: System of Education

1. General Background

The Republic of Chad is situated in the heart of Africa. In 1979, it was dubbed the "soft lower chest of Africa" by journalists. It covers 1,284,000 square kilometers, stretches 1,440 kilometers from north to south and 720 kilometers from east to west and is land-locked. To the north is Libya; to the east, Sudan; to the south, the Central African Republic; and to the west; Niger, Nigeria, and Cameroon. The capital city is N'Djamena. The population was estimated at just over 5 million in 1984. In the period 1980 to 1985, the population growth rate was estimated to be 2.36 percent and could have been near 3 percent at the beginning of the 1990s. Over 30 percent of the population is under 20 years of age and there are over 1 million children in the age range 6 to 15 years. Of these 1 million, less than 50 percent (i.e., 300,000) of the children are in school.

There are two climatic zones separated by a wide transitional Sudano–Sahelian area. The northern zone tends to be barren and cattle-raising is the main activity. The southern zone is wooded savanna with humid river valleys and agriculture is the main activity. The inhabitants in the north tend to be nomadic or seminomadic Moslem herders, and in the south they are farming people who live in fixed abodes and tend to be animists or Christians.

The mainstays of the economy are cotton and livestock. The agricultural sector accounts for 90 percent of export earnings and 57 percent of Gross National Product (GNP). The most productive area is in the south (the *préfectures* of middle Chari, Mayo-Kekki, Tandjile, and the eastern and western

Logones). Cotton alone accounts for 70 percent of export earnings. Animal husbandry, the traditional activity of the northern nomads, is the second largest earner (mostly to neighboring countries).

Through a process of partnership with France, a certain number of companies have been created in the south, including the Chadian textile company (STT) and a brewery (*Brasseries du Logone*). Pending the exploitation of oil discovered in the Lake Chad area and in the Valley of Logone, three oil companies (Mobil, Total, and Shell) operating a joint facility for the storage, sale, and distribution of refined oil, were established in the capital city, N'Djamena. Esso and its subcontractors operate in the south of Chad for a consortium of Esso, Shell, and Chevron.

French and Arabic are the two official languages. Chadian Arabic, the language of the north is also the *lingua franca* of the capital city. The most common languages spoken in the south are those of Sara-Bongo-Baguirmian or Sara Group—the Sara Madjingay, the Ngambay, and the Mbay Moissala to name but a few. Many other more or less structurally related languages are the Toubou, Kanembou, Kotoko, Massa, and so forth.

Chad became an independent republic in 1960. A succession of kingdoms characterize the early history of Chad. The cultural and political strife and tension between the Arabized northeast and animist south date back to those times. During the last half of the nineteenth century, the United Kingdom and France disputed the territory, and only in 1899 was agreement reached that France would assume control of the area. The colony of Chad was formally established by the French in 1920 and the territory of Chad was founded in 1946. After Independence, there was fighting between the north and the south. This was severe at the end of the 1970s. Despite numerous peace agreements and ceasefires, the civil war continued. The war had international ramifications, with France and the United States supporting one group and Libya the other. The relentless civil war, compounded by the protracted Sahelian droughts, resulted in all efforts and much of the resources going into the war and fighting the drought. Resource priority for education was limited until 1982.

Economic and social well-being deteriorated during the period of droughts and war. School enrollment is one of the lowest in Africa. The literacy rate is only 25 percent. The pattern of schooling is still the same as that of the colonial power. Chad has few paved roads, no rail network, and only a few airfields capable of handling commercial aircraft at prohibitive costs. The Chari River, the largest in Chad, and one that runs through the capital, had no bridge until the end of the 1980s when the *Pont de la Chanson* was built. The name comes from the fact that the money to build the bridge was raised at a concert. Before the bridge was built, only means of transport across the Chari was by ferry.

2. *Politics and the Goals of the Education System*

At Independence, the aim was to provide basic education opportunities to all children and, when possible, to adults. Several efforts were made, over a 10-year period, to improve the formal system of education. However, because of the enormous financial constraints and the perceived nonrelevance of such education on the part of the parents, they have basically failed.

In 1962, within the framework of a large project named "Operation Mandoul" attempts were made to introduce farming into a number of pilot schools in the Koumra region of the country. This also included reforming the curriculum and revising teaching approaches. This costly venture had no substantial effects because the needs of the local population had not been taken into account. In 1968, attempts were made to extend some of the ideas of the 1962 experiment to more rural schools. This was primarily concerned with the integration of agricultural and handicraft subjects into the normal school curriculum in order to make it practically oriented.

In 1973, another project was begun. This was to change the colonial school structure. It was an ambitious scheme to create a school structure of four cycles, each cycle having its own specific goal:

(a) The first cycle was to last 5 years—children were to acquire basic knowledge and the ability to change according to the changing social environment and to think on their own.

(b) The second cycle was to last 3 years—this was aimed toward reinforcing and consolidating the previously acquired skills and knowledge.

(c) The third cycle was to last 4 years and included the main components of vocational training.

(d) The last cycle could be likened to an advanced training for the elite, with the focus being on the training of highly qualified persons needed for the socioeconomic development of the country.

This highly selective project planned ways and means for the school leavers to enter socioeconomic life from each stage of schooling. The most important outcome of the project was the creation of the Institute for Educational Sciences (*Institut National des Sciences de l'Education*—INSE) and, above all, legislation instituting the reform of the Chadian school system. The main idea behind this reform was to adapt the school system to socioeconomic development needs, promote Chadian cultural identity, reinforce national unity, and rationalize the utilization of human resources in order to foster economic development. In the wake of this reform process, the creation of "pilot schools" constituted the only concrete outcome.

By 1978, this philosophy resulted in the primary

school providing basic conventional teaching coupled with about two hours of practical work each week for boys in intermediate classes and workshops where they were initiated into crop husbandry, ironwork, and carpentry by practical work instructors. The objective was to integrate the pupils into the productive system of the area where they lived. This objective was consistent with the new teaching philosophy and was to be extended later to secondary school in order to establish the structural link "elementary–secondary–vocational teaching complexes" combining regional production activities and formal education. The new school would be open to parent associations and village communities in collaboration with the regional development authorities.

In 1979 the civil war brought the whole process to a halt. None of the good intentions and schemes were translated into programs of action and no operational strategy was defined to implement the educational policy. Nevertheless, a few rewarding elements of these projects were kept, notably the "parent association" and "village community" which ushered in a sort of "local school system" era in Chad, providing a new educational partner for the future Chadian school system. It was this "partner" that operated the school system during the period of the war (1979–82), even without discontinuity in certain areas where the structures had been completely destroyed. In 1992, legislation was underway to institute and legalize the "Parent Association."

In 1982, schools all over the country opened again. The main objective of the Ministry of National Education was focused on restoring the school system to its prewar structure. Emergency schemes were implemented from 1985 to late 1988 to refurbish school buildings and train and retrain teaching staff. It was a challenging period, by the end of which most of the school system had been put on track again. The main education issues had been reassessed and rationally addressed, paving the way for the new Chadian School in the year 2000.

3. The Formal System of Education

The Chadian formal educational system is structured approximately according to the French educational structure. It includes preschool institutions, the basic or elementary institutions, and secondary and higher education institutions. Figure 1 depicts the overall structure of the educational system.

3.1 Primary, Secondary, and Tertiary Education

Basic or primary school lasts for six years. Pupils can enter at the ages of 6 or 7. At the end of primary school an examination is taken. On the basis of the results, students enter either secondary school or centers of vocational training.

Secondary school is composed of two cycles. The first cycle lasts for four years at the end of which students obtain the *Brevet d'Etudes du Premier Cycle* (BEPC) which is nothing more than the first secondary cycle leaving certificate. The second cycle leading to the *baccalauréat* is a prerequisite for admission to the higher education institutions such as the University of Chad.

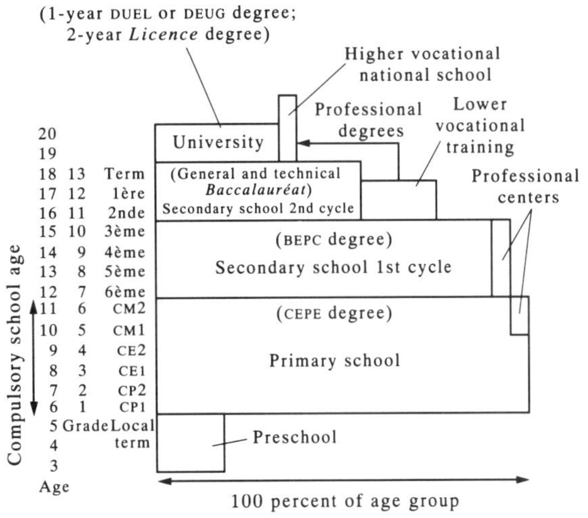

Figure 1
Chad: Structure of the formal education system

The University of Chad, one of the most outstanding higher training institutions, constitutes the third level of the educational system. The University has four faculties: arts and social sciences, law and economics, exact and applied sciences, and medical studies. Each of these faculties is divided into two cycles: the first cycle terminating with the DEUG (*Diplome d'Etudes Universitaires Général*) which is the first cycle diploma. The second cycle ends with the *licence* usually equated with a BA degree. The University of Chad has discontinued conducting the master degree program which was started in the late 1970s.

3.2 Preschool Education

Preschool education (*enseignement préscolaire*) institutions are more or less a combination of *écoles maternelles* and kindergartens. Children can enter these institutions at any time between the ages of three and five years. A very small proportion of an age group attends the *écoles maternelles*. They tend to exist in urban areas only. Attendance is free. The content of work is play-centered and basically socializes children for entering the primary school.

3.3 Special Education

Although there are mentally and physically handicapped children, there are no special provisions for them. They do not go to school but remain with their families.

3.4 Vocational, Technical, and Business Education

Following primary school, students can enter either vocational training centers or industrial–technical schools. The vocational centers are multipurpose school complexes that integrate technical and professional training along with manual and practical work in the forms of production in the areas where the centers are created.

There are two kinds of technical school. The first is a technical training school (*collège*) where the course lasts three years. To enter, a student must have completed one year of lower-secondary education. At the end of the course, the student receives a professional aptitude certificate (CAP). The second type of technical school is parallel to the upper-secondary school and is known as a *Lycée Technique Industriel*. To enter, a student must have successfully completed the BEPC at the end of the lower-secondary school and passed a special entrance examination. Courses last three years, at the end of which, upon successful completion of examinations, the student will receive a *Brevet de Technique* or a *baccalauréat* for technicans. There is also a parallel *Lycée Technique Commercial* which is similar to the *Lycée Technique Industriel* but focuses on commercial subjects.

At the higher education level, there are a number of professional training institutions. Students must have the academic, technical, or commercial *baccalauréat* to enter. Many of the professional institutions also have their own selective entrance examinations. The major institutions are:

(a) *Ecole Normale Supérieure* (ENS) where secondary school teachers and elementary school inspectors are trained. Those eligible for admission must be holders of the *baccalauréat* and pass a very selective test. There is just one ENS in the country and it is in N'Djamena.

(b) *Ecoles Normales* (of which, there are five) are in N'Djamena, Sarh, Moundou, Bongor, and there is also the Bilingual Normal school of Abeché (French and Arabic). They train elementary school teachers.

(c) *The Ecole Nationale d'Administration et de Magistrature* (ENAM) is located in N'Djamena and trains administrators and magistrates and other administrative agents. The holders of the *baccalauréat* are eligible for entrance and must also pass a competitive examination.

(d) Students can enter the public work school from the first and second cycles and are trained as public works engineers. It is located in N'Djamena.

(e) The National Public Health and Social School is located in N'Djamena and trains social workers, nurses, and midwives.

(f) The National School of Telecommunications is located in Sarh and trains post and telecommunication technicians.

(g) There are two agricultural schools located in Bahili and Sarh which train agricultural and forestry technicians.

4. Administrative and Supervisory Structure and Operations

The Ministry of Education is responsible for the administration of education and for carrying out the government's educational policies. The Ministry has five major departments: (a) cabinet; (b) *diréction générale*; (c) *diréction de services* (for the separate divisions for primary education, secondary education, and technical and professional education)–literacy and the protection of national languages; planning, examinations, and competitions; educational projects; sport, youth, and civic education; higher education and scholarships; scientific and technical research; and administrative, financial, and equipment; (d) *des services exterieurs* (meaning *préfectures* outside of the capital); and (e) *des établissements sous tutelle* (the higher education institutions). The Ministry of Education is headed by the Minister of Education who is backed up by the Secretary of State for Higher Education and a Secretary of State for Youth and Sport.

There are, however, other ministries which are responsible for certain aspects of education. These are the ministries of Agriculture and Rural Development, Public Health, Public Works, and Post and Telecommunications.

There are 14 *préfectures* and in each *préfecture* there is a *délégué à l'éducation*. There is a certain amount of decentralization, and since the end of the civil war there has been an increasing effort to involve village communities and parent associations in education through the *préfectures*. Inspectors are based at each large sub-*préfecture* and *préfecture*.

5. Educational Finance

In the past, the state financed all education. In 1992, the position was that there were three partners involved in the financing of education: the state (33%), external aid (61%), and parent associations (6%). The education budget in 1992 was 13.8 percent of the state budget. The state has pledged to raise this to 20 percent by the year 2000.

6. Supplying Personnel for the Education System

In the period up to Independence and up to 1987 there were two types of teacher-training institution: normal schools (*Ecoles Normale des Instituteurs*), for the training of elementary school teachers, the main intake of which came directly from the primary and

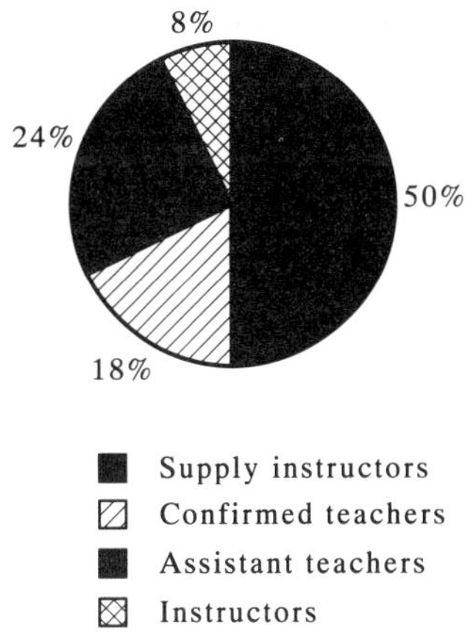

Figure 2
Distribution of teachers in elementary schools

the first cycle of secondary schools; and the normal higher training school (*Ecole Normale Superieure*) and the University of Chad.

In order to upgrade and improve the quality of teachers, it was decreed in 1987 that elementary or primary teachers should be holders of the *baccalauréat* (an *Ecole Normale des Instituteurs bacheliers* was therefore created) and those destined to teach in secondary schools should have at least the first university degree (DUEL or DEUG) or license.

Two of the main characteristics of the Chadian elementary schools are the lack of required educational standards and understaffing. Yet the number of elementary school teachers has been estimated to be 6,215–90 percent of whom are actually teaching in classes and the remaining 10 percent being administrative personnel and supervisory staff. The distribution in terms of the level of education is the following: 1,098 are qualified primary school teachers (*instituteurs et institrices pleins*), 1,513 assistant primary teachers, 469 institutors (*moniteurs*), and 3,135 supply teachers with no pedagogical qualification at all (*maitres suppléants*). In other words, at least 50 percent of elementary school teachers in Chad have no professional teaching qualification. The distribution of school personnel by category can be seen in Fig. 2. According to the 1989 census, there were 25,653 civil scrvants in thc public scctor so that the figure of 6,215 elementary teachers or about 24 percent is low. The total number of the elementary school pupils in 1988–89 was 425,000 pupils, and hence the pupil–teacher ratio was 68:1. This is very high compared to the median ratio for countries in the region where the ratio is 39:1. Even the ratio of 68:1 blurs disparities in the country because in urban areas such as N'Djamena, Sarh, Moundou, and Bongor, the size of classes reaches about 150 pupils.

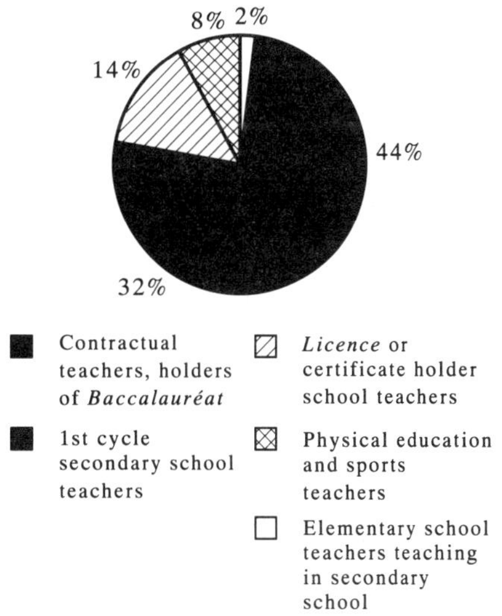

Figure 3
Distribution of secondary school teachers by level of qualification

There were about 1,210 secondary teachers in 1989, 45 percent of whom were not qualified to teach in secondary school. Moreover, there is a total lack of teachers in scientific subjects. The distribution of teachers according to their level of qualification is presented in Fig. 3.

In order to tackle the serious problem of understaffing in secondary schools, the structure of the unique Higher Normal Training School (*Ecole Normale Superieure*—ENS) has been streamlined in such a way that first and second cycle secondary schools teachers are trained and recycled to acquire the required qualification.

In higher education in the academic year 1988–89, the total number of lecturers at the University of Chad was 57. There were 30 *maitre assistant* holders of doctorates and 27 assistant lecture holders of MA or MSc, and 10 laboratory assistants. Owing to the lack of full-time lecturers, the University has resorted to using the service of 67 part-time lecturers. Nevertheless, the lecturers and their assistants are still burdened by an enormous amount of teaching, leaving them with extremely little time for their research work.

7. Curriculum Development and Teaching Methodology

The whole process of curriculum development and design is the responsibility of the ISSED (*Institut Superieur de Science de l'Education*). In this process, the educational goals and objectives set by the government are taken into account. In terms of content, the curriculum is designed in such a way as to provide fundamental "know-how." Yet the curriculum had to be updated in 1983 in order to take account of social reality and adapt schools to the needs of the Chadian pupil. One of the main features of this adaptation was the attempt to introduce a national language into the school system. Through the international Francophone organization called CONFEMEN (*Conference des Ministres de l'Education Nationale*), the Chadian government realized that a child could easily learn the "3Rs" in its mother tongue. So the introduction of national language into the school system was considered to be a must. But there are two main obstacles to this:

(a) With a mosaic of Chadian languages, it has not been possible to choose one or two languages as a national language from among about 270 languages.

(b) Parents refused to accept that their children should be taught in a Chadian language—they prefer French.

8. Assessment, Evaluation, and Research

Docimology or the science of evaluation and assessment is one of the educational areas in which there is no systematic work in Chad. Evaluation is administered at random according to the vagary of the educational background of the person involved. The prevailing evaluation system is that inherited from the French system, and there is no systematic evaluation at all. The only examples of evaluation are those related to examination enabling students to move from one class to another. In this respect the traditional examination taken by candidates is not related to any set of specific objectives, but rather to subject matter and topics. This is, in part, because the Chadian curriculum is designed in terms of topics rather than specific objectives. The traditional examinations ranging from the "CEPE" of the elementary school to the *Maitrise* of the university are meant to evaluate the content of what is taught. In the early 1990s, such matters were improved. A *service d'evaluation et programme* was created within the Department of National Education. New goals and new objectives are being determined and tried out. The education system is expected to come to terms with the problems of assessment and evaluation in the near future.

9. Major Reforms in the 1980s

Since the civil war virtually wiped out the education system there was ample opportunity to create a new and modern system of education. However, little has been achieved except for the introduction of the new partnerships of "parent associations" and "village communities." Since the government was unable to rebuild and re-equip school buildings, the new partnership was essential if an educational system was to be re-established.

At the same time, it was important to identify the key aspects which had been responsible for the previous system's failing. The diagnosis of the weak points and proposals for the introduction of reforms has begun.

10. Major Problems for the Year 2000

The period of the two decades following Independence was marked by an education system evolving through false starts, and trial and error. Following the civil war, there was a great opportunity to capitalize on previous experience and to inaugurate a new era of a more reliable and stable system of education. This new system would:

(a) avoid wasting money on "white elephant" educational projects (as in the 1960s and 1970s);

(b) provide more incentives to parents associations to be involved in school affairs;

(c) set well-defined priorities along the lines of the Jomtien "Education for All" Conference in 1990

(d) place more emphasis on preparation for the working life in the Chad population.

It is also important to increase school enrollment. At the primary school level, plans are in hand to increase the enrollment rates from 48 percent (1989) to 60 percent (2000) and ensure, at the same time, that dropout decreases and that the number of children receiving a primary school-leaving certificate triples. At the secondary school level, the increase in the number of students enrolled should move from 45,000 in 1989 to 76,000 in the year 2000. The increase would be more at the lower than at the higher secondary levels. In the industrial and commercial schools there would be a 20 percent increase. At the higher education level, the plans are to decrease by 10 percent the number of students at the University of Chad but, at the same time, increase enrollment in the Science Faculty and decrease enrollment in the faculties of arts and social sciences and law and economics.

Bibliography

Doromon M 1991 Problematique du système Educatif au Tchad. Unpublished paper

N'Djaména 1990 *Réunion se Suivi de la Table Ronde Genève III*. Conference held in Geneva

Pamdegue A 1991 Système éducatif Tchadien. Unpublished paper

Bourdon J, Orivel F 1991 *Cadrage macro-Economique de la Stratégie Education et Formation du Tchad*. Dijon

T. D. Moadjidibaye

Change, Measurement of

Why is the measurement of change over time so important in educational research? The answer is straightforward. When people acquire new skills, when they learn something new, when they grow intellectually and physically, when their attitudes and interests develop, they are changing in fundamental and interesting ways. By being able to measure change over time, it is possible to map phenomena at the heart of the educational enterprise. Education is intended to foster learning, to bring about changes in attitude, achievement, and values. Only by measuring individual change is it possible to document each person's progress and, consequently, to evaluate the effectiveness of educational systems.

Unfortunately, despite its obvious substantive importance, there has been much controversy over the years about the measurement of change. Influential methodologists concerned about the technical properties of change measurement have argued that it is impossible to measure change well. Empirical researchers were advised to avoid its measurement. Policymakers were told to mistrust research findings based on that measurement.

However, in reality these traditional conclusions and recommendations are incorrect. Change can not only be measured; with a little foresight and planning it can be measured well. Well-publicized false conclusions about the difficulty of change measurement are rooted in a simple misconception: the misconception that individual change should be viewed as an *increment*, as the difference between "before" and "after." Early methodologists and empirical researchers saw each person under study as acquiring a quantum of achievement (or attitude, or value, or whatever) between the "pre" and the "post" measurement. They thought that investigators should only be concerned with the size of the acquired chunk. This was a mistaken perception. Individual change takes place continuously over time; it is not purely a "before" and "after" phenomenon. The failure to perceive change as a continuous process of development hamstrung the creation of decent statistical methods for its measurement.

However, methodologists have recently modified their position. They have concluded that individual change can be measured well, providing that research moves beyond the limitations of the "before and after," or "two wave," design. They now understand that the continuous process of human development can be easily and efficiently documented if each person is measured repetitively over extended periods of time. In this entry the new "multiwave" perspective is presented, and it is argued that, with a little planning, all questions about change can be answered. Because there has been such controversy, this entry begins by reconsidering traditional methods for the measurement of change.

1. Traditional Methods for Measuring Change

Implicit in any discussion of change are two important kinds of question. The first treats each person as an individual and asks about within-person change. For example, in an evaluation of different reading curricula, it can be asked: Does this person's reading achievement improve over time? Is there rapid improvement, or is improvement more gradual? Does reading achievement grow at a steady rate, or does it level out after one or two years?—and so on for every person in the sample. The second type of question asks about between-person differences in change. Do certain types of people change in different ways? Does the reading achievement of girls change faster than that of boys? Does progress in reading achievement differ by type of first-grade reading program? These are questions about the way in which individual change is related, over people, to background, training, environment, and so forth.

Answering questions about within-person change logically precedes the asking of questions about between-person differences in change. It is necessary to know how each person changes before asking whether the individual changes differ in some systematic way from one person to the next. However, the latter questions about between-person differences in change often have the greatest practical importance in educational research.

Traditionally, in research on change, investigators collected only two waves of data on each person in the sample. They observed each person's "status"—their achievement, attitude, or other attribute, say—at the beginning and the end of the investigation. Then, to answer questions about within-person change, they used the "pre" and "post" data to construct a summary measure of individual change for each person in the study. Subsequently, when questions about between-person differences in change were addressed, the two-wave change summaries were simply regressed on, or correlated with, other variables (the "predictors of change") describing background, training, or treatment.

This seems straightforward, but the apparent simplicity masks serious pitfalls. For one thing, for the strategy to be effective the researcher must be able to use the two waves of data that have been collected to construct a decent measure of change for each person in the sample. Methodologists differ as to how this should be done and psychometric history is littered with strategies proposed for the purpose. Some of these strategies are better than others, but they are all inferior to the multiwave methods introduced in Sect. 2.

The simplest two-wave measure of change is the *observed difference score*, obtained by subtracting the initial measurement from the final one for each person. Originally the difference score was highly favored but then fell into disrepute, being much maligned in the 1960s and 1970s. This led to the birth of a coterie of alternative two-wave measures of change, including *regression-based estimators of true change* and *residual change* scores. Although the use of two-wave change measurement is not advocated in practice, it is desirable to comment briefly below on these measures in order to clarify the continuing controversy.

1.1 Two-wave Measures of Within-person Change

Because of the uncompromising vicissitudes of nature, when a test or rating instrument is administered the obtained measurement combines a measure of the person's true capability and whatever random error happens to accompany measurement. Of course, research interest focuses squarely on *true status*—a commodity that, if *measurement error* is large, may differ considerably from *observed status*. Similarly, when members of a group of people are changing over time on some important attribute, it is not the fallible *observed changes* that are of critical interest but the underlying *true changes*. Measures of observed change simply provide a fallible lens through which the hidden nature of true change may be discerned.

Typically, on the ith occasion of measurement (i.e., at time t_i), methodologists have been content to assume that observed status, Y_{ip}, is simply the sum of true status, η_{ip}, and measurement error, ε_{ip} (the second subscript indicating that the pth person is being referenced). These errors of measurement, ε_{ip} are usually assumed to be drawn independently from a normal distribution with zero mean and variance σ_ε^2. When two waves of data have been collected, observed "pretest" and "post-test" status (measured at times t_1 and t_2) can be represented by their requisite sums: $Y_{1p} = \eta_{1p} + \varepsilon_{1p}$ and $Y_{2p} = \eta_{2p} + \varepsilon_{2p}$. Then, the observed difference score for the pth person, D_p—obtained by subtracting Y_{1p} from Y_{2p}—is the sum of the underlying true change, $\Delta_p = (\eta_{2p} - \eta_{1p})$, and the difference between the two measurement errors, $(\varepsilon_{2p} - \varepsilon_{1p})$.

Statistically speaking, the observed difference score is a reasonable commodity. It is intuitively appealing and easy to compute. It is an unbiased estimator of the underlying true change. Despite these advantages, the difference score has been resoundingly criticized for both its purported unreliability and its correlation with initial status. Although these deficiencies have been shown recently to be largely imaginary, they are discussed here briefly in order to set the record straight.

Some have said that the difference score is always unreliable; others have argued that it cannot be both reliable and valid simultaneously (Bereiter 1963, Linn and Slinde 1977). In general, neither of these claims is correct. They are misconceptions arising from misinterpretation of the concepts of reliability and validity in the context of change over time (Rogosa et al. 1982, Rogosa and Willett 1983, 1985, Willett 1988). Thus, it has been argued that an instrument can only be regarded as measuring the same construct on both occasions of measurement if the correlation of time-1 and time-2 scores is high. This is fallacious. Even when the instrument is perfectly construct-valid, growth may be heterogeneous across people (i.e., different people may be growing at different rates). Then the individual growth trajectories will naturally intersect as time passes, the rank order of people in the group will fluctuate from occasion to occasion, and the between-wave correlation will be less than unity. It is perfectly possible, in the context of highly heterogeneous growth, for the time-1/time-2 correlation to be large and negative even when the instrument is perfectly construct-valid.

As a consequence of misinterpreting the observed pretest–post-test correlation as an index of construct validity in expressions for the reliability of the difference score, authors have misguidedly focused on hypothetical situations in which there is little variation in true change across people. By choosing to examine situations in which the variance of true change is close to zero, they have ensured that the numerator of the expression for the reliability of the difference score (which is defined as the ratio of the variances of true and observed change) is very small and so the reliability is almost zero. In reality, in perfectly ordinary situations, the reliability of the difference score can be quite respectable (Rogosa and Willett 1983). And when variation in true change from one person to the next is large, the reliability of the difference score can even be greater than the reliabilities of the constituent pretest and post-test scores (Willett 1988).

Anyway, even if the difference score were always unreliable, this would not necessarily be a problem for the measurement of within-person change. Low difference-score reliability does not imply unilaterally that within-person change has been measured imprecisely. Low reliability often occurs in practice because most of the people in the sample are changing at about the same rate (especially over the short term). So even though the 20 points (say) that everyone has changed can be measured very precisely, the changes of different people cannot be distinguished from one another and the difference score appears unreliable. This problem of interpretation does not call the difference-score itself into question, since it is possible to know quite precisely that everyone has changed by 20 points. On the contrary, it simply undermines the credibility of reliability as a worthwhile indicator of measurement quality.

The difference score has also been falsely condemned for at least three other reasons, all of which originate in critics' misunderstanding of the association between it and pretest status (Linn and Slinde

1977, Plewis 1985). If there is a positive correlation between change and pretest status, for instance, then people with high initial status will tend to have high gains subsequently. If the correlation is negative, then people with low initial scores will tend to change more rapidly than those with high initial scores. This has led some critics to claim that any measure of change that is not independent of initial status must be unfair because it gives "an advantage to persons with certain values of the pretest scores" (Linn and Slinde 1977 p. 125). But such prejudice is unreasonable: why should change and status be unrelated? The intimate connection between change and status is a consequence of growth history. Current status is a product of prior change; current change determines future status. A correlation between change and status is an almost inevitable fact of life.

Second, numerous investigators have empirically estimated the correlation between change and initial status and have worried because their findings often disagreed. Even when investigating similar populations in similar settings with the same measures, some have found the correlation to be positive, some zero, and some strongly negative. But why should they expect a single value for this correlation? When different people are changing in different ways, individual trajectories are likely to crisscross with time and the correlation between change and initial status can fluctuate markedly as different times are selected as the occasion for "initial" measurement (see Rogosa and Willett 1985). Unless some important occasion can be agreed upon substantively to be *the* initial time, researchers should expect to disagree when they ask: What is the correlation between change and initial status? Because the answer, of course, is, "It depends on the time that you define as 'initial'."

Third, the difference score has been inappropriately criticized because some people have convinced themselves that its correlation with pretest score is always negative. In reality this claim is false (for an example of a positive correlation between the difference score and change see Thorndike 1966). Those who condemn the difference score in this way have usually committed one of two mistakes. Either they have spuriously created the negative correlation themselves by "standardizing" the pretest and posttest scores to the same standard deviation before computing the difference score (an ill advised process that destroys legitimate growth information). Or they are simply being confused by the vaguenesses of their statistical estimation. In this latter case, they have usually thoughtlessly used the sample correlation of observed initial status and the difference score to estimate the population correlation of true initial status and true change (the real correlation of interest). Unfortunately, because the pretest measurement error appears with a negative sign in the difference score, this estimator is negatively biased. It is often negative even when the underlying true correlation is positive. However, the bias is easily corrected (see Willett 1988) and, anyway, as Rogosa et al. (1982) noted, an unbiased estimate of within-person change—the difference score—should not be rejected because a poorly conceived estimator of the association between true change and true initial status is biased. It is the latter that needs fixing, not the former.

So even though the difference score is not the outcast that many critics have claimed, several modifications of it have been proposed in order to estimate true change, Δ_p, better: for example, Webster and Bereiter's (1963) reliability-weighted measure of change, and Lord's (1956) regression-based estimated true change. These modified estimators improve the measurement of within-person change by trading off unbiasedness for a reduction in mean-squared error. Under very broad assumptions, these modified measures are simply weighted linear combinations of the observed difference score for the particular person and the average observed difference score over the entire group, with weights that depend on the reliability of the difference score. Essentially, the weighting scheme places emphasis on those aspects of the change measurement that are the most "trustworthy"—favoring the difference score when it is reliable but, otherwise, setting each person's change equal to the average change for everyone when there is little real between-person variation in change to be detected. Even though the modified scores are better estimates of true within-person change, they are usually perfectly correlated with the corresponding difference scores and have (almost) identical reliabilities. Therefore, parallel investigations of between-person differences in change using either of these modified scores usually lead to identical conclusions.

The creation of the residual-change score was motivated by an unnecessary desire to create measures of change that were uncorrelated with pretest score. Residual-change scores are obtained by estimating the residuals that would be obtained in the population regression of true final status on true initial status. They are intended to describe the true change that each person would have experienced, if everyone had "started out equal." Various methods have been proposed for their computation (see Rogosa et al. 1982). Much energy has been dissipated in the psychometric literature detailing the properties of the many estimators of residual change and considerable argument has been aroused. When discussing residual-change scores, methodologists disagree as to exactly what is being estimated, how well it is being estimated, and how it can be interpreted. In addition to the many technical and practical problems that arise in the empirical application of residual change scores, there also remain unresolved issues of logic and substance that are too extensive to detail here (but see Rogosa et al. 1982, Rogosa and Willett 1985, Willett 1988). The researcher is strongly advised to avoid these scores as measures of within-person change.

1.2 Detecting Between-person Differences in Change

Once a two-wave measure of change has been computed for each person, the relationship between change and other "background" variables is often investigated by the common methods of correlation and regression analysis. For instance, to find out if changes in achievement are related to gender, the data-analyst might simply correlate pre/post differences in test score with a dummy variable representing gender. Unfortunately, while straightforward, this rudimentary strategy is flawed. As has been seen, the difference score is a *fallible* measure of change that contains both true change and measurement error. This latter random noise attenuates the between-person findings, causing the obtained sample correlations to underestimate the true relationship between change and the covariates. This problem can be avoided by correcting between-person analyses for the fallibility of the difference score (for methods of correction, see Willett 1988). However, the disattenuation process requires that additional information be available to the data-analyst, usually in the form of an external estimate of the reliability of the difference score. Furthermore, because the disattenuation is sensitive to minor fluctuations in the magnitude of the reliability estimate and because the quality of these estimates themselves is often dubious, there exists the very real possibility of glorious imperfection.

If the difference score is abandoned and an estimate of true change is used instead, information in addition to the pre/post measurement is still required for the estimate of true change to be constructed in the first place. In fact, regardless of the measure of change adopted, acceptable between-person analyses can only be conducted if the researcher possesses information in addition to the pair of pretest and post-test scores. This emphasizes the real and fundamental weakness of the two-wave design: there is insufficient information in two waves of data to measure individual change well. To do a satisfactory job, multiwave data are required.

2. Modern Methods of Change Measurement

Taking a "snapshot" of a person's observed status "before" and "after" is not the best way to reveal the intricacies of their progress. Changes might be occurring smoothly over time with some complex and substantively interesting trajectory. Crude pre/post measurement can never reveal the details of that trajectory. To do a good job of describing individual change over time, a truly longitudinal perspective must be adopted.

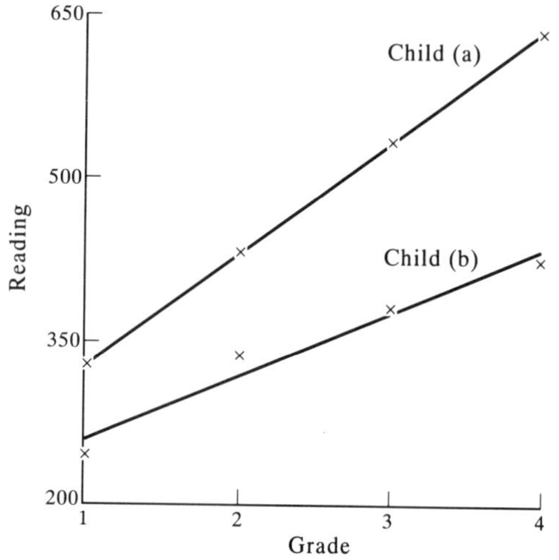

Figure 1
Observed growth records of two children whose reading achievement was measured in Grades 1 through 4. The included trend-lines were fitted by OLS linear regression analysis, conducted separately for each child

2.1 Assembling and Inspecting the Observed Growth Record

People must be followed carefully over time, with multiple "waves" of data collected on their status at sensibly spaced intervals. The investigator must assemble an *observed growth record* for each person in the dataset. If the attribute of interest is changing steadily and smoothly over a long period of time, perhaps three or four widely spaced measurements on each person will be sufficient to capture the shape and direction of the change. But, if the trajectory of individual change is complex, then many more closely spaced measurements may be required (see Willett 1989).

Once collected, preliminary analyses of the observed growth records are aided by plotting an *empirical growth-trajectory* for each person—a graph of observed status displayed against time, perhaps with some type of fitted or sketched trend-line included on the graph to summarize broadly the person's observed growth. Separate inspection of the empirical growth trajectory of each person in the dataset then provides evidence as to whether, and how, each person is changing over time. Fig. 1, for instance, presents the empirical growth trajectories of a pair of children whose reading achievement (scale scores on the Comprehensive Test of Basic Skills) was followed yearly from Grade 1 through Grade 4. In both cases, each child's observed growth in reading achievement is summarized by a linear trend-line, fitted by ordinary least-squares regression analysis. Comparing trend-line and data suggests that a straight line is a reasonable summary of the

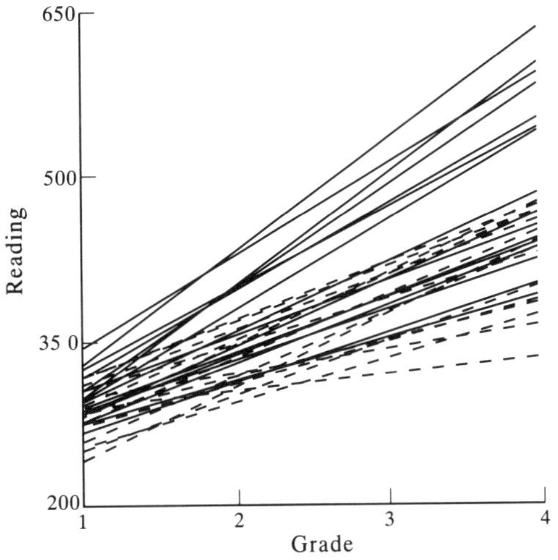

Figure 2
A collection of fitted trajectories summarizing the observed growth in reading achievement between Grades 1 and 4 for 32 children. The fitted trajectories are coded to display reading readiness in kindergarten (solid line for children above the sample median, dashed line for children below the sample median)

observed growth, although Child (b)'s datapoints are a little more widely scattered around the fitted line than are the datapoints for Child (a). Child (a)'s reading achievement is growing at more than double the rate of Child (b), with the latter child having the additional disadvantage of scoring lower initially.

The empirical growth trajectories of everyone under investigation can also be collected together in a single picture. This provides a simple and straightforward way of exploring questions about between-person differences in change. Eyeball comparisons across people may suggest systematic differences in trajectory—children in a phonics-based reading curriculum may tend to change more rapidly than those using a sight-reading curriculum; girls may be growing faster than boys, and so forth. Fig. 2, for instance, adds the fitted growth trajectories of 30 more children to the two already displayed in Fig. 1. The observed data themselves have been omitted to avoid clutter but the trend-lines have been coded to indicate whether the child was judged "ready for reading" in the kindergarten year (solid line = high reading readiness; dashed line = low reading readiness). Inspection of Fig. 2 suggests that children who were rated highly on reading readiness in kindergarten tended to have both higher reading achievement in Grade 1 and more rapid rates of growth between Grades 1 and 4. Similar plots could be created to display the effects of other interesting predictors.

2.2 Choosing a Statistical Model to Represent Within-person Change

Corresponding to the exploratory inspection of observed growth records and empirical growth-trajectories, a more formal multiwave analysis of change requires that a statistical model be chosen to represent individual change over time. Of course, as has been noted earlier, it is each person's underlying true change that is of critical interest. Consequently, when a statistical model is selected to represent change, it consists of two parts: (a) a "structural" part that represents the dependence of true status on time; (b) a "stochastic" part that represents the random effects of measurement error.

But what does an individual growth model look like? In drawing the empirical growth trajectories in Figs. 1 and 2, a linear or "straight-line" function of time was chosen as a valid representation of individual change in reading achievement between Grades 1 and 4. In this case the observed reading achievement Y_{ip} of child p at time t_i is represented as follows:

$$Y_{ip} = [\pi_{0p} + \pi_{1p}t_i] + \varepsilon_{ip} \tag{1}$$

where the structural part of the model, describing the dependence of true reading achievement η_{ip} on time, has been bracketed to separate it from the measurement error ε_{ip}.

The structural part of an individual growth model contains unknown constants called the individual growth parameters. The values of these parameters completely determine the trajectory of true change over time. In Eqn. (1), for instance, there are two individual growth parameters: π_{0p} and π_{1p}. The first parameter, π_{0p}, is the "intercept" of the straight-line growth model, representing person p's true status when t_i is equal to zero (usually defined as the time at which the study began, and therefore π_{0p} represents the true initial status of person p). The second parameter, π_{1p}, is the "slope" of the straight-line growth model, representing the rate at which person p's true status is growing over time. If π_{1p} is positive, then person p's true status is increasing with time; if it is negative then person p's true status is decreasing with time.

Of course, when analyses of multiwave data are conducted, the straight-line model is not the only available representation of individual change. Many different models—perhaps an infinite number—can be hypothesized. Some are simple, like the straight-line model, while others, like the negative-exponential and quadratic curves, are more complex. It is even possible to join several different models together, creating a piecewise individual growth function.

Perhaps the investigator's most important task is to select the individual growth model that will be used. Usually this decision is made via extensive preliminary data-analyses in which the observed growth records are systematically and carefully explored. However, the choice of a particular model for a specific purpose can often be informed by a theory of psychological, social, or educational development. Theory may suggest, for instance, that individual change in a specific domain is constrained to rise to a ceiling. So, by entertaining a growth model that includes an asymptote, the researcher can test this hypothesis and ultimately investigate whether substantively interesting features of the change are associated with differences in people's background, training, and environment. It may be, for instance, that certain background characteristics predict the ultimate limits on growth (the asymptotes), while others predict the rate at which the ceiling is approached. When substantive theory informs model choice, a richer research arena is revealed.

2.3 A Model for Between-person Differences in Change

Once a particular model has been selected to represent true change in a particular domain, everyone in the sample is assumed to have the same generic functional form for their growth. Different people, however, can have different values of the individual growth parameters. For instance, as in the case of Figs. 1 and 2, when within-person change is linear individuals may differ in intercept and slope. Even more interestingly, the individual growth parameters may differ from person to person in a way that is systematically related to variables describing critical attributes of the people involved (the "predictors of change"). Under the straight-line growth model for reading achievement, for instance, the investigator can ask: Is there a systematic relationship between true rate of change in reading achievement and reading readiness in kindergarten?; between true initial status and reading readiness?; between the individual growth parameters and gender?; home environment?; type of reading program?; and so forth.

Hypothesized relationships between individual growth parameters and predictors of change can be formalized in statistical models for between-person differences in change that are similar to the more familiar regression models (see Rogosa and Willett 1985). Eqn. (2), for instance, presents a pair of between-person models, the true intercepts and true slopes of the straight-line reading achievement growth model in Eqn. (1) as a function of a pair of predictors, FEMALE (0=boy, 1=girl) and READYREAD (teacher rating of reading readiness in kindergarten):

$$\pi_{0p} = \beta_{00} + \beta_{01}\text{FEMALE}_p + \beta_{02}\text{READYREAD}_p + u_{0p}$$
$$\pi_{1p} = \beta_{10} + \beta_{11}\text{FEMALE}_p + \beta_{12}\text{READYREAD}_p + u_{1p} \quad (2)$$

where u_{0p} and u_{1p} represent residuals (the parts of π_{0p} and π_{1p} that are "unexplained" by FEMALE and READYREAD). In these models, the β coefficients summarize the population relationship between the individual growth parameters and the predictors of change. They can be interpreted in the same way as regular regression coefficients. A nonzero value of β_{01}, β_{02}, β_{11}, or β_{12} indicates that the corresponding covariate is a predictor of true initial status or true rate of change respectively. For instance, if girls tend to grow more rapidly than boys (i.e., if they have larger values of π_{1p}) then β_{11} will be positive. If children who had higher reading readiness scores in kindergarten have higher initial reading achievement in Grade 1, then β_{02} will be positive, and so on. All of the β coefficients in Eqn. (2) are estimated in the between-person phase of a growth study.

One of the main advantages of the longitudinal perspective is that the investigator is not limited to the simple within- and between-person models presented here. Substantively valid curvilinear functions can be used to model within-person growth, and complex between-person models can be used to relate interindividual differences in several growth parameters to many predictors simultaneously. Systematic interindividual variation in the rate parameter of the negative-exponential growth model, or in the acceleration parameter of the quadratic growth model, can be examined. A new universe for measuring change, far from the worlds of the pre/post design, is revealed.

3. Doing the Statistical Analyses

In an investigation of change, within-person and between-person statistical models—like Eqns. (1) and (2)—are fitted to data and their parameters estimated and interpreted. Many methods of model-fitting and parameter estimation are available. Some are very simple and can easily be implemented on the popular commercially available statistical computer packages; others are more sophisticated and require dedicated computer software. In this section, in order of increasing complexity, a taxonomy of such data-analytic strategies is briefly reviewed.

3.1 Estimating the Within-person Growth Parameters by Ordinary Least-squares Regression Analysis

Once a sensible within-person growth model has been adopted, it can be fitted separately to each of the individual observed growth records by ordinary least-squares (OLS) regression analysis (in the same way that the fitted trend-lines were created for Figs. 1 and 2). This person-by-person growth modeling leads to individual estimates of the several growth parameters that can then become the dependent variables in subsequent second-round between-person data analyses. In the case of the straight-line growth model in Eqn. (1), OLS-obtained intercepts and slopes estimate the true initial status and rate of change for each of the people in the sample and can be related directly to background predictors in follow-up correlation or regression analyses corresponding to Eqn. (2). This strategy is straightforward and easy to implement, and the OLS-estimated intercept and growth rates provide more precise measurement of individual change than was possible with the difference score.

3.2 *Improving the Between-person Analyses with Weighted Least-squares Regression Analysis*

Due to the idiosyncracies of measurement, some people usually have empirical growth records whose entries are smoothly ordered and for whom the growth data fall very close to the underlying true growth trajectory. Other less fortunate people have more erratic growth records and their datapoints are scattered, deviating widely from the underlying growth trajectories. These differences in scatter affect the precision (the standard errors) with which the first-round growth parameter estimation is carried out. People with "smooth and systematic" growth records will have highly precise growth parameter estimates with smaller standard errors; people with "erratic and scattered" observed growth records will have less precise growth parameter estimates with larger standard errors.

Between-person analyses of the relationship between the estimated growth parameters and predictors of change can be improved (made asymptotically efficient) if the precision of the first-round growth parameter estimates is taken into account. To achieve this, weighted least-squares (WLS) regression analysis can be used to fit the between-person models using weights that are inversely related to the square of the standard errors of the first-round parameter estimates. Then, more precisely estimated individual growth parameters (those with the smallest standard errors) will play a more important role in determining the outcomes of the second-phase analyses. Willett (1988) presented an expression for weights that can be used in conjunction with Eqns. (1) and (2).

Any growth analysis will automatically be improved if the first-round estimation of individual growth parameters is more precise. In practice, this is easily achieved by collecting more waves of data on each person in the sample. In the case of straight-line growth, for instance, the standard errors of fitted growth-rates decrease dramatically as extra waves of data are added. It is for this reason alone that multiwave designs provide superior methods for measuring change. Ultimately, researchers can control the quality of their findings; they can simply "add waves" to their design until some desired level of precision is reached (see Willett 1989).

3.3 *Estimating the Within-person and Between-person Growth Models Simultaneously Using Dedicated Computer Software*

In this entry it has been argued that high-quality measurement of change is possible via the collection of longitudinal data and the fitting of within-person and between-person models such as those in Eqns. (1) and (2). Such models constitute an algebraic "hierarchy" describing the statistical structure of growth data to be analyzed. Methodology for fitting such hierarchical models has advanced rapidly. In the early 1990s there were several dedicated computer programs available for simultaneously estimating all of the parameters of such models, and for providing appropriate standard errors and goodness-of-fit statistics. Kreft et al. (1990) provide a comprehensive description of four of them and compare their workings. They conclude that, in general, "all four programs tend to converge to the same solution" (p. 100). One of them—called "HLM"—has been widely used in the empirical literature and is well-supported (Bryk and Raudenbush 1992).

3.4 *Estimating the Within-person and Between-person Models using Covariance Structure Analysis*

There have also been advances in applying the methods of covariance structure analysis to the measurement of change. Covariance structure methods are powerful and general and can be applied easily to many problems in a wide variety of settings. Pioneering work on the application of these methods to the estimation and comparison of mean growth curves was conducted by McArdle and his colleagues (McArdle and Epstein 1987) and other authors have demonstrated how these methods can be used to answer questions about predictors of change (Muthén 1991, Willett and Sayer, in press).

See also: Measurement in Educational Research; Intellectual Development across the Lifespan; Human Development: Research Methodology; Cognitive Development: Individual Differences

References

Bereiter C 1963 Some persisting dilemmas in the measurement of change. In: Harris C W (ed.) 1963 *Problems in Measuring Change*. University of Wisconsin Press, Madison, Wisconsin

Bryk A S, Raudenbush S W 1992 *Hierarchical Linear Models: Applications and Data-analysis Methods*. Sage, Beverly Hills, California

Kreft I G G, de Leeuw J, Kim K S 1990 Comparing four different statistical packages for hierarchical linear regression: GENMOD, HLM, ML2, and VARCL. Center for the Study of Evaluation, University of California, Los Angeles, California

Linn R L, Slinde J A 1977 The determination of the significance of change between pre-and post-testing periods. *Rev. Educ. Res.* 47(1): 121–150

Lord F M 1956 The measurement of growth. *Educ. Psychol. Meas.* 16: 421–37

McArdle J J, Epstein D 1987 Latent growth curves within developmental structural equation models. *Child Dev.* 58: 110–33

Muthén B O 1991 Analysis of longitudinal data using latent variable models with varying parameters. In: Collins L M, Horn J L (eds.) 1991 *Best Methods for the Analysis of Change: Recent Advances, Unanswered Questions,*

Future Directions. American Psychological Association, Washington, DC
Plewis I 1985 *Analyzing Change: Measurement and Explanation using Longitudinal Data*. Wiley, New York
Rogosa D R, Brandt D, Zimowski M 1982 A growth curve approach to the measurement of change. *Psych. Bul.* 93: 726–48
Rogosa D R, Willett J B 1983 Demonstrating the reliability of the difference score in the measurement of change. *J. Educ. Meas.* 20(4): 335–43
Rogosa D R, Willett J B 1985 Understanding correlates of change by modeling individual differences in growth. *Psychometrika* 50(2): 203–28
Thorndike R L 1966 Intellectual status and intellectual growth. *J. Educ. Psychol.* 57(3): 121–27
Webster H, Bereiter C 1963 The reliability of changes measured by mental test scores. In: Harris C W (ed.) 1963 *Problems in Measuring Change*. University of Wisconsin Press, Madison, Wisconsin
Willett J B 1988 Questions and answers in the measurement of change. *Review of Research in Education* 15: 345–422
Willett J B 1989 Some results on reliability for the longitudinal measurement of change: Implications for the design of studies of individual growth. *Educ. Psychol. Meas.* 49: 587–602
Willett J B, Sayer A G in press Using covariance structure analysis to detect correlates and predictors of change. *Psych. Bull.*

J. B. Willett

Childcare and Preschool Effects

Many labels are used to designate institutions devoted to the education and care of children under 6. A nonexhaustive list of the terms used in the field includes: preschool (sessional, Australia), preschool program (as in, Head Start, USA), daycare and child center (USA), infant care center (USA), family daycare (USA), nursery school (UK, USA, etc.), nursery class (UK), day nursery (UK, etc.), reception/transition class (UK), playgroup and play center (UK, NZ, Australia, and others), under-fives and rising fives (UK and others), infant class or school (UK and others), early childhood program, crèche (several English and French-speaking countries), child-minders, école maternelle (France, Belgium), école gardienne (Belgium), garderie (Canada), gardiennes encadrées, jardin d'enfants, Kindergarten (many countries), and so forth. There is also some disarray in the occupational titles of adults who work in these settings (e.g., teacher, childcare worker, nurse, sister, *institutrice, enseignante, puéricultrice, Lehrerin*, social pedagog, *Erzieherin*, etc.). To some extent these occupational titles are related to the type of employing institution, and to some extent to the type and amount of occupational training they provide and/or require.

This terminological diversity is one major characteristic of preprimary education which marks it as a "sub-culture" within the general "culture" of education. Without belaboring the historical, social, and linguistic causes of this terminological diversity, it is sufficient for our purposes to indicate that these lists reflect the controversies and the ideological dissension in the field. To some extent, these controversies are fueled by deep differences in values and attitudes toward the place of women, the functions of the family, the relevance of schooling in the early years, pressures for industrialization, and so forth.

In the field of elementary education there is general agreement that reading, writing, and mathematics are relevant skills, while acquisition of other competencies (e.g., fluency in a second language) may be controversial issues.

The examination of the literature indicates that the value of preprimary education is recognized in some countries (e.g., Belgium, France, and the Netherlands) and social or political demands for scientific demonstration of its benefits are not required. Thus it is interesting to note in some French and Belgian literature, that teachers explain some school failures by the fact that some children did not attend the *école maternelle*. According to these teachers, as with parents, the "passage" through the *école maternelle* is an unquestionable prerequisite for success at the elementary level. On the other hand, in other countries, the value of preprimary education is not taken for granted and empirical demonstration of its positive effects is required. This is especially the case in the United States, where most studies demonstrating the positive effects of preprimary education have been conducted. Therefore, the following review of literature is mainly grounded in the United States research tradition. However, studies conducted in developing countries will also be reviewed.

Since the start of the War Against Poverty and the Head Start operation in the 1960s, American research concerning preschool education has been conducted in three waves of studies: (a) evaluative studies, especially the longitudinal ones; (b) comparative studies; and (c) studies of the quality of life in childcare settings.

1. First Wave: Evaluative Studies

The first wave of preprimary studies addresses the question: Does preschool education make a difference? In the first step, the studies were focused on the immediate effects of the preschool programs provided for underprivileged children. Rapidly, the question of the long-term effects of preschool education was addressed by the researchers. The first generation of studies related to this issue was rather disappointing. When Bronfenbrenner (1974) asked the question "Is early intervention effective?" he introduced a search for the conditions which would make preschool education influential. The second generation of studies in the field are clearly conclusive: preschool education makes a lasting difference.

The report published by the Consortium for Longitudinal Studies (Lazar 1977) and the Perry Preschool Longitudinal Study conducted by Weikart and his team (Schweinhart and Weikart 1980, Berrueta-Clement et al. 1984) demonstrate that success in school and in life is significantly greater for children who participate in a preschool program, than for children from similar low socioeconomic status families who do not participate in a preschool program.

1.1 The Consortium for Longitudinal Studies

The Consortium for Longitudinal Studies (Lazar 1977) regroups and analyzes 14 studies. In the secondary analysis of the data, assignment to special education classes and whether a child was retained in a particular grade were used as indexes of long-term effectiveness. In Lazar's (1977) view

> the advantage of using these two outcomes as measures of effectiveness of early education programs is that they are concrete and stringent indicators of whether a child has performed acceptably within his or her educational institution. (p. 20)

The analysis revealed a reliable program effect. Early intervention reduces the number of students assigned to special education classes and held back in their grade. On the basis of these findings, Lazar and his colleagues conclude that "early education programs can in some way improve the ability of low-income children to meet the requirements of their school" (Lazar 1977 p. 28).

However, some programs are less efficient than others. In order to identify the influential component of early intervention, three groups of programs were distinguished: center-based, home-based, and interventions combining both components. Lazar (1977 p. 28) concludes that "all the projects which found significant effects on special education either were home visiting programs or had some visiting components."

Moreover, in a more recent secondary analysis, Lazar and Darlington (1979) assert that

> the family environment was also apparently affected. Specifically, mothers of children who attend preschool had higher vocational aspirations for their children than the children had for themselves. This discrepancy was not found in mothers of control children. (p. 20)

Thus, one may hypothesize that the long-term effects of preschool intervention are "due in part to increased parental concern and competence to deal with the school system—an indirect effect of parental sensitization by the preschool experiences of their children" (Lazar 1977 p. 28).

This finding confirms Bronfenbrenner's report of 1974 in which he observed that children involved in parent intervention programs and who simultaneously participated in a group program, achieved greater and more enduring gains. He interpreted this observation from an ecological theoretical perspective.

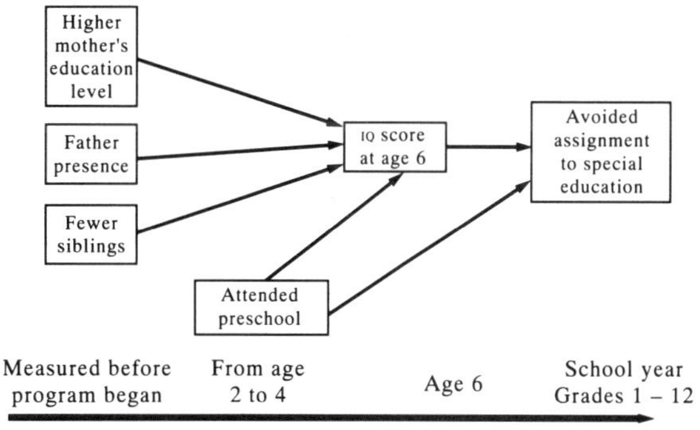

Figure 1
Assignment to special education classes: diagram showing network of variables suggested by data, significant paths only (Lazar and Darlington 1979 p. 18)

> Thus, from the third year onward, parent intervention seemed to serve as a catalyst for sustaining and enhancing the effects of group intervention (. . .). It is as if the child himself has no way of internalizing the process which fosters his growth, whereas the parent–child system does possess this capability. (Bronfenbrenner 1974)

These findings suggest that if early education is to play a role in the development of children, the familial microsystem has to be influenced.

The effect of preschool intervention on cognitive abilities and especially on IQ measures was also a problematic issue. Indeed, during the early studies early intervention seemed to have only a short-lived effect on IQ scores (two or three years). However, the path analysis conducted by Lazar and Darlington (1979) indicates that "IQ scores at age 6 and preschool attendance importantly affected later school performance" (p. 19) as measured by avoidance of placement in special education. Moreover, a path between attendance at a preschool program and the IQ scores is observed (see Fig. 1).

According to the authors, preschool intervention influences the intellectual functioning of children during the critical period of school entrance. However, Lazar and Darlington (1979) remarked:

> by partialling out the effect of preschool on IQ scores at age 6, we essentially found that the preschool affected children in ways that were relevant to school performance but not related to cognitive skills and abilities. Perhaps children's achievement motivation, values, aspirations or coping style were influenced . . . Perhaps children's classroom behaviors were affected . . . Children's families may have been influenced by, for example, changing parents' perceptions of their children, affecting the family dynamics, increasing their hopes for the children's future.

1.2 The Transactional Approach of Schweinhart and Weikart

The Perry Preschool Longitudinal Study (Schweinhart and Weikart 1980) addressed the questions raised by the first wave of studies by proposing a causal model in which the effects of preschool intervention become causes of other subsequent effects.

> Our basic approach has been transactional, emphasizing the changing relationship between the individual and the environment over time. The analysis began with children in poverty. Despite a variety of adaptive strengths, the poor child experiences conditions which inhibit development and may lead to school failure. Preschool education provides extra cognitive stimulation for such children, leading them to demonstrate greater cognitive ability at school entry. Then the rigid stratification process of the school takes over, and they must assume defined positions with respect to school success or failure. Throughout their years of schooling, they perform in terms of this student role—believing it themselves, forming a level of commitment to schooling consistent with their expectations for success or failure, and even attaining a level of school achievement consistent with their expected position. Teachers, parents, and peers accept this position and reinforce it, so that everyone, including the child, has similar expectations and supporting attitudes for the child's scholastic accomplishments. Eventually, school success becomes life success. To the extent that the child has been successful in school, the adult is successful in educational attainment, occupational status, and income. To the extent that the child has failed in school, the adolescent, aided and abetted by like-minded peers, finds it reasonable to assault the school and the community through deviant behavior—demanding, in the final analysis, a degree of attention denied by all the conventional channels for approval (Schweinhart and Weikart 1980 p. 15).

Data were collected for 123 children from the time they were 3 years old to age 25. The total sample includes 65 control children and 58 experimental ones who attended a group preschool program weekday mornings and were visited along with their mothers at home 1½ hours a week at ages 3 and 4.

The results of a path analysis of the data are presented in Fig. 2.

Preschool education improves cognitive ability at school entry and influences the commitment to schooling. Cognitive ability at age 5 is the core of the model since it affects positively the commitment to schooling and school achievement, and reduces the probability of being assigned to special education classes. These three variables also predict the frequency of delinquency in the sense that commitment to schooling and fewer years in special education reduce delinquent offenses, while achievement alone gives rise to more delinquent offenses.

While the theoretical framework of Schweinhart and Weikart has generally been confirmed, they note that

> the direct relationship between commitment and preschool education suggests that the direct effects of preschool were motivational as well as cognitive. It was assumed that commitment to schooling began as a response to school success. The data suggest a slight reformulation: commitment began as a response to a cognitively stimulating preschool environment. (Schweinhart and Weikart 1980 p. 66)

One of the most interesting aspects of this study is its grounding in the application of role theory to education and especially to classroom events. As Schweinhart and Weikart hypothesize, when an individual comes into a new environment and interacts with it, he demonstrates a way of performing and, at the same time, he formulates a role and pattern of commitment which rapidly gives rise to social responses congruent with this role. By improving the cognitive ability of the children, preschool education helps these children to construct a role conducive to success and leads others (teacher, parents, and peers) to have and to communicate expectations which maintain and perhaps enhance children in this role. In this approach, motivation, performance, and social support are three facets of an experiential, dynamic interaction between the individual and the environment. As Schweinhart and Weikart (1980) have said:

> The person who is highly committed to schooling and who receives social reinforcement for a success-oriented student role is, of course, the one most likely to meet the objectives of schooling and does well in terms of school achievement. But it is equally true that the person who does well in terms of school achievement, all other things being equal, is most likely to become more committed to schooling and to receive social reinforcement for a success-oriented student role. (p. 12)

On the basis of data collected when the subjects were 19 years old (Berrueta-Clement et al. 1984), the High Scope team observed positive effects of preschool intervention on each category of criterion variables, namely, school success, social responsibility, and early socioeconomic status.

1.3 Contribution and Limits of the Longitudinal Evaluative Studies of Preschool's Effects

1.3.1 Consistency of the findings: The Head Start Synthesis Project. McKey et al. (1985) synthesized the findings of Head Start studies conducted between 1965 and 1984 and reinforced this consistency. Among these studies, 72 investigated gains in cognitive ability, 17 tested for socioemotional gains (self-esteem, social behavior, and achievement motivation), and 5 measured family impacts. Some studies also examined retention in grade and placement in special education classes.

As seen in Table 1, the immediate effect of Head Start on children's cognitive ability is positive.

However, this effect on cognitive ability does not persist.

> One year after Head Start, the differences between Head Start and non-Head Start children on achievement and school readiness tests continue to be in the educationally

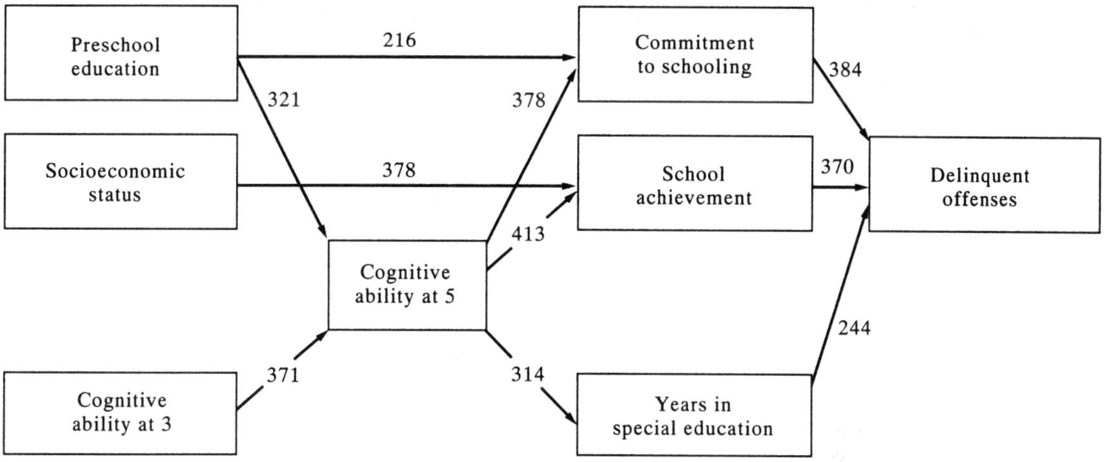

Figure 2
Causal model for the Perry preschool study
Source: Schweinhart and Weikart (1980)

Table 1
Effect of the Head Start intervention on children's cognitive ability (the values are effect sizes)

	Treatment/control studies	Pre-/post studies
IQ	0.59	0.43
Readiness	0.31	0.59
Achievement	0.54	0.37
Composite	0.52	0.48

Table 2
Summary of gender x program interaction according to scores

IQ		Achievement	
Boys	Girls	Boys	Girls
Montessori	Control	Montessori	Control
Control	Darcee	B–E	Darcee
Traditional	Traditional	Control	Traditional
B–E	B–E	Traditional	B–E
Darcee	Montessori	Darcee	Montessori

meaningful range, but the two groups score at about the same level on intelligence tests. By the end of the second year, there are no educationally meaningful differences on any of the measures. (McKey et al. 1985 p. 8)

Head Start also affected long-term school success of the children. Positive effects of Head Start on children's self-esteem (effect size = 0.17), achievement motivation (effect size = 0.22), social behavior (effect size = 0.35), and health and motor development were also found. Other findings include:

(a) Highly structured academic curricula produce larger immediate gains than traditional, cognitive, or Montessori programs. However, by the end of the third year after Head Start, the differences had disappeared.

(b) Treatment–control studies find that longer (6 to 8 hour) Head Start days are related to higher immediate cognitive effects than are shorter (2.5 to 5 hour) sessions.

(c) Children from Head Start classes with mixed proportion of minority children (70 to 90 %) show higher effects on achievement motivation than children from classes with a very high proportion (90 to 100%). This result was found at the end of the Head Start year and each year of the three following years.

1.3.2 Effects of early childhood intervention on primary school progress and performance in the developing countries.

(a) *Nutrition-related studies.* In the 1970s, academic interest in the relationship between malnutrition and behavioral development led to a series of nutrition-related interventions. The Guatemala INCAP Study and the Puebla Study (both in Mexico) involved only health surveillance and nutritional supplementation; the emphasis was placed on protein–energy supplementation with little or no attention on the deficit of vitamins and minerals. The Cali Study, the Bogota Study and the PORMESA Project (all in Columbia), the Indian Programme of Integrated Child Development Services and the Programa de Alimentacao do Preescolar (in Brazil) combined nutritional and educational interventions.

(b) *Preschool intervention studies.* Several evaluations of preschool programs which have operated in developing countries are reviewed even though they present design weaknesses, such as difficulties in identifying good matches for nonpreschool matching control groups, weak and poorly described psychometric measures, and a variety of sample follow-up problems.

(c) *Early childhood intervention.* Clearly early childhood intervention in developing countries can have positive effects, although many important questions remain about the kind of intervention, its persistence, and its relationship to primary education.

2. *Second Wave: Comparative Studies*

2.1 *The Head Start Planned Variation*

The objective of the Head Start Planned Variation (Rivlin and Timpane 1975) was to compare the cognitive, academic, and motivational development of children participating in 12 different programs. The results revealed that no program had a general impact that was superior or inferior to the others (Smith 1975). Models emphasizing the acquisition of academic skills did not produce greater general advantages over other programs, but favored more the learning of letters, numbers, and shapes. The High Scope Cognitive Curriculum model particularly influenced scores obtained on the Stanford–Binet IQ test. However, a number of methodological flaws have been attributed to the study. For example, the social and affective domains were neglected, largely due to the absence of valid measuring instruments; the tests used were too global to detect effects. As Rivlin and Timpane (1975) point out

> these [tests], however, are ill adapted to distinguishing among curricula with different emphases. Indeed, standardized tests are explicitly designed to give comparable measures of children's performance irrespective of what curriculum they have been exposed to, and hence are singularly ill suited for use as discrimators, among curricula. (p. 1)

Furthermore, it seems that model implementation varied considerably from one site to another and gains obtained in the sites most *faithful* to the intentions of the model were neutralized by the results from other sites. Although the models differed somewhat in the educational aims, they did not appear to differ greatly in what was taught or in their style of teaching.

2.2 *The Ypsilanti Preschool Curriculum Demonstration Project* (IPCD)

Weikart et al. (1978) compared the effects of three preschool programs: (a) the Bereiter–Engelman (B–E) program with strong academic emphasis; (b) a Piagetian-based model, high/scope cognitive curriculum; and (c) a traditional program (the unit-based curriculum). Forty-one 3-year old children, drawn from a population of economically disadvantaged and low IQ-score children (between 50 and 85) attended preschool for two years and received regular home visits. Noncurriculum variables were carefully controlled. Careful observation of classroom processes indicated that three distinct programs were implemented and that each program represented its curriculum model faithfully.

At the end of the first year of preschool, the average gain in IQ was 23 points. An unexpected finding was that "children in all three programs were quite similar to each other on cognitive-linguistic measures" (Weikart et al. 1978 p. 126). By the end of the second year of preschool, the gains had slightly dropped but children of the preacademic program did not drop as much as children of the other two programs and, thus, had significantly higher scores.

Follow up data revealed no differences between the three groups:

(a) IQ gains of the children of the three programs were maintained at the end of the fourth grade.

(b) Grade retention and special education placement rates were equally reduced for all experimental children compared to those who had no preschool.

Weikart et al. conclude that "The principal issue in early childhood education is not which curriculum to use but how to manage any curriculum to achieve positive results" (Weikart et al. 1978 p. 136). They assert that the primary role of the curriculum is mobilization of teachers' energy, rationalization for selecting children's activities, and a rational basis for teacher supervision. Furthermore, "Parents are more involved in educational activities with their children when the program goals are clearly articulated" (Weikart et al. 1978 p. 135).

2.3 *The Louisville Longitudinal Study of Four Preschool Curriculum Models*

Miller and her colleagues (Miller and Dyer 1975; Miller and Bizzell 1983a, 1983b) conducted a longitudinal comparative study which avoids most of the shortcomings of such studies.

Four curriculum models were compared: (a) Bereiter–Engelman (B–E), (b) Darcee program (D), (c) Montessori (M), and (d) a traditional Head Start (T) to which children were randomly assigned. A control group of children not attending any preschool program was included in follow up studies. At the end of the prekindergarten, 214 experimental children were in the sample. Observations by consultants showed that the programs were appropriately implemented. The greatest program variations were in the children's activities; no program differences in amount of time the teachers were out of contact with the children were found. Thus, the claim that differences in children's scores were attributable to program characteristics.

The Preschool Inventory (PSI) (Caldwell 1968) was administered eight weeks after preschool opening (PPK) and at the end of the year (EPK) and at the end of kindergarten (K). California Achievement Test scores were obtained from the school systems at the end of Grades 1 and 2. Stanford Achievement Test scores were available for children in Grades 4 to 8, and scores from the Comprehensive Test of Basic Skills were available for children in Grades 9 and 10. The STEP-Locator, a brief test of language and mathematics skills, was administered to children in Grades 9 and 10. Intelligence was measured with the Stanford–Binet at the beginning of the preschool experience, at the end, and in Grades 1, 2, and 8. The Wechsler Intelligence Scale was administered in 1977, and the Stanford–Binet Intelligence Test during alternate years.

The results indicate that the academic and IQ trends established by the end of kindergarten persisted into the 9th and 10th grades. They also indicate a persistent interaction between gender and program effects.

The Montessori model. IQ scores for the Montessori girls increased at the end of preschool and then dropped off radically. IQ scores for the Montessori boys were not lower in IQ at Grade 10 than at the end of preschool (see Fig. 3.1). Moreover, at the end of Grade 10, the Montessori boys were operating above national norms at the California achievement tests (see Fig. 3.2). The academic achievement of the Montessori girls was lower than that of the Montessori boys.

The Darcee program. The IQ scores of the Darcee boys were 15.3 points below the Grade 10 Montessori boys. Grade 10 Darcee girls scored higher than the Darcee boys (approximately 5 points). They also scored higher than the Montessori girls (approximately 10 points). Girls and boys also differed on the achievement test, with Darcee girls higher than Darcee boys and Montessori girls, lower than Montessori boys (see Figs. 3.3 and 3.4).

The Bereiter–Engelman model. B–E boys and girls reached quite similar scores for both tests (IQ and achievement) during the whole duration of the study. At Grade 10, the B–E boys scored higher than the Darcee, traditional, and control boys at the achievement test, but lower than the Montessori boys. The B–E girls scored lower than the Darcee and control girls, but higher than the Montessori and traditional girls (see Figs. 3.5 and 3.6).

The Traditional Head Start model. At Grade 10, IQ and achievement differences between boys and girls are weak. At Grade 10, traditional boys score lower on IQ than Montessori boys, but higher than B–E boys; Darcee boys do as well as the control boys. At the same grade, traditional girls score as well as Darcee and control girls but higher than B–E and Montessori girls.

At Grade 10, traditional and control boys are the same, but better than Darcee and worse than Montessori and B–E boys. Traditional girls do as well as Montessori and B–E girls but lower than control and Darcee girls (see Figs. 3.7–3.10).

The Grade 10 results are summarized by ranking the program according to the boys' and girls' scores on both lists, and shows a gender x program interaction (see Table 2).

The Montessori model is best for boys and worst for girls. The ranking for the boys on the achievement test is approximately the reverse of the one for girls. Moreover, girls without preschool education do at least as well as the girls with it. Considering the original random assignment and the absence of differential attrition, these findings cannot be attributed to chance alone.

3. *Third Wave of Studies: Quality of Life in the Preschool Settings*

Longitudinal studies of the first wave demonstrate that preschool education can have a beneficial effect on the development of children from low-income families but failed to indicate how it worked. Weikart suggested:

> It might be more fruitful for researchers to spend more time studying the teaching process and the learning experiences of the child through classroom observation rather than through delayed results on achievement tests. (cited in Beller 1973 p. 575)

3.1 The Oxford Preschool Research Project (OPRP)

The Oxford Preschool Research Project illustrates clearly the potential of this method of investigation (Bruner 1980). One hundred and twenty young children (60 of them $3\frac{1}{2}$–$4\frac{1}{2}$ years old and 60 of them $4\frac{1}{2}$–$5\frac{1}{2}$ years old) were observed in playgroups, nursery schools, and nursery classes (number of settings = 19) in England. The children's activities were noted during each 30 second period, for 20 minutes; each child was observed during 2 periods of 20 minutes. Each 30 second period of the child's activity was analyzed according to 12 different aspects:

(a) immediate task or activity;

(b) larger episode of which immediate task in part;

(c) cognitive complexity of task;

(d) cognitive complexity of larger episode;

(e) number of others present;

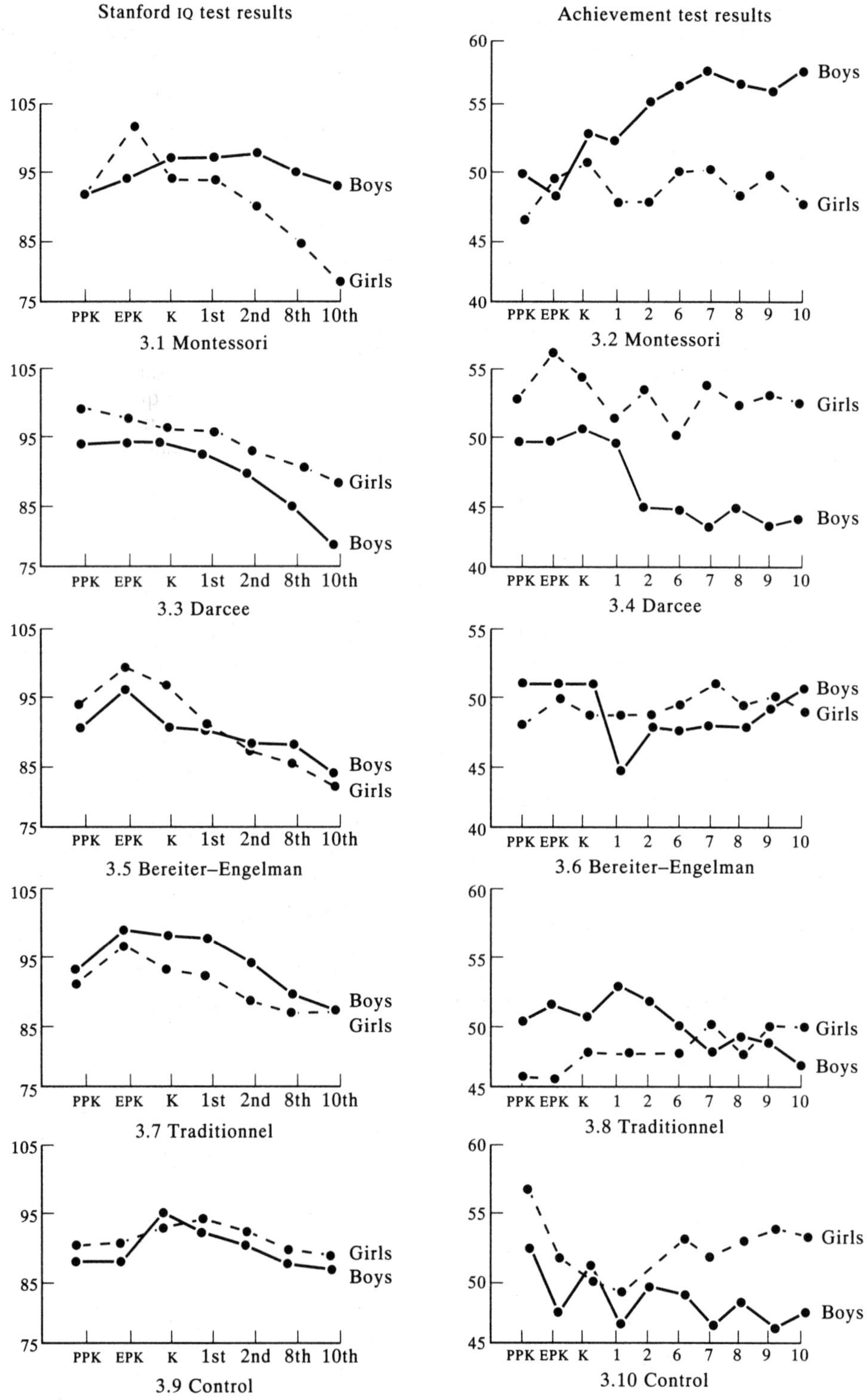

Figure 3
Academic and IQ trends and interaction between gender and program effects

(f) child interacting with others or parallel to them;

(g) status of others;

(h) adult presence active or passive;

(i) another activity embedded in or parallel to the main task;

(j) number of utterances;

(k) utterances connected or "one-off";

(l) who initiates utterances.

The data showed that children were nearly always preoccupied with materials that could produce clear goals with a means of achieving them, and logical feedback. Role-play led to relatively high levels of elaboration in activities, while unstructured activities led to little elaborate play. Moreover, children are much more likely to engage in complex activities in the company of another child and adult than they are alone.

Mutual conversation was rare, occurring in only 20 percent of observed cases; $\frac{2}{3}$ of these 20 percent occurred among children. Longer conversations occurred mainly in quiet corners as if conversation required intimacy. Situations where a child was less challenged to take part in elaborate activities fostered mutual conversation. The role of the adult was preponderant, but frequently managerial tasks interrupted dialogue.

The observational data differentiated between three kinds of institutions: playgroups were characterized by more adult-directed group activity than the others, possibly influenced by restricted space; nursery classes, always attached to primary schools, emphasized verbal activity and school readiness tasks; and nursery schools where emphasis was placed upon free expression gave rise to more "solo" activities and less elaborate play.

The Oxford Preschool Research Project shows that "children in the more structured settings generate more elaborated play than children in the less structured ones" (Bruner 1980 p. 21). It appears that where there are some prescribed activities, the children continue to perform in the same way as in the adult-directed situation. Adult–child ratio and group size are also important. The larger the adult–child ratio, the higher the proportion of time spent in activities which promote elaborate play and the more connected discourse there is. Small group size also seems to foster elaborate play and pretend play.

3.2 *The National Day Care Study*

The major objectives of the National Day Care Study were to determine the impact of caregiver–child ratios, group size, and other regulatory elements of care on its quality and cost (Ruopp et al. 1979 p. 10). Quality was determined from observations of interaction in the setting and from standardized tests of children.

Group size was related to the behavior of caregivers and children. Smaller group sizes are associated with higher gains on achievement. The smaller the groups the greater are the caregivers' tendencies to engage in interaction with children (questioning, responding, praising and comforting) instead of just observing them and interacting with other adults. Caregivers with relevant education provided better care and somewhat superior children's test performance than other caregivers.

3.3 *Inconsistencies in Childcare Research Findings*

Clark-Stewart (1987b) examines five studies of the relationship of childcare quality to child outcomes. Three of the five studies used the Early Childhood Environment Rating Scale (ECERS) as an index of quality. One study showed that ECERS scores positively related to social competence, intelligence, and language, while another found ECERS scores negatively related to social competence and language. Another study found the daycare version of the scale (DCHERS) positively related to children's intelligence and language in family daycare homes, and another showed no relationship between this measure of quality and intelligence and language in children between 2 and 5 years.

Similar inconsistencies were found as for the effects of such regulatory variables as adult–child ratio, group size, and characteristics of caregivers. Clarke-Stewart suggests that inconsistencies in the effects of global measures of program quality may be due to ambiguities in definitions of quality such that having high quality in one program element does not necessarily mean there will be high quality in any other element in any particular center (Clarke-Stewart 1987a p. 113).

4. *From the Process–Product Paradigm to an Ecological–Mediating Process Paradigm*

4.1 *The Search for Process–Product Relations*

In the last two decades, investigators have sought "direct links" between structural features (adult–child ratio, group size, space per child, equipment, and so on) or teacher classroom behavior and child development and achievement. Why are such relationships expected? According to Phillips and Howes (1987) describing a " mediating process paradigm":

> Adult-child ratio is considered an important quality indicator or the basis of assumptions that adult caregivers mediate children's contact with the social and physical world . . . the number of children with whom each caregiver can engage in a stimulating and sensitive fashion is obviously limited. With too many children to care for, the caregiver's interactions with each child are likely to become brief and cursory. (p. 5)

From this perspective, when correlations between some structural dimensions and adult or child behavior in the setting are reported, consistencies between research findings appear (see Phillips and Howes 1987 pp. 5–9). Similarly, Clarke-Stewart (1987a) finds consistent correlations between children's interactions with caregivers observed in the settings and child development measures. However, she notes that such interactions are not always included in the research in this field.

It may be argued that in some circumstances the quality of life in the setting is to be considered as an outcome in itself. Travers and Light (1982) argued in favor of this idea:

> In view of the fact that some programs, notably day care and preschool education, consume a significant portion of the child's waking life; a case can be made for considering the quality of life to be an outcome in itself . . .
>
> Quality of life and development are intertwined, patterns of behavior that indicate immediate engagement, stimulation, self-confidence, etc. on the part of the child are at least good bets to relate to long-term socioemotional growth. (p. 32)

4.2 Childcare in and out of the Home: The End of a Competition

Family and school have frequently been conceived as competitive educational spheres. Phillips and Howes (1987) point out that in the United States at least:

> Home-rearing (no regular use of other supplemental child care arrangements) has often been used as an implicit standard against which the use of child care has been compared. . . Alternatively, child care has frequently been studied as a separate socialization environment apart from children's homes. In reality, childrearing has become a collaborative endeavor with children moving back and forth—many on a daily basis—between their homes and child care. The effects of these two environments may be additive; they may compensate for each other; or some aspects of one may override aspects of the other in positive or negative ways. A full understanding of child development thus requires that both environments be examined. (p. 11)

In a study of regulatory characteristics of childcare centers and children's development Kontos (1987) found that family background variables predicted developmental outcomes, while structural characteristics of centers made virtually no contribution to developmental outcomes. Goelman and Pence (1982) reported that family variables superseded center quality variables in predicting child language outcomes in Canada, whereas quality variation in family daycare homes was a significant predictor of children's language development.

Similarly, Clarke-Stewart (1982) reported that associations between children's competence and childcare features such as group composition and caregiver characteristics, were substantially weakened when variance was removed. However, substantial effects of the quality of children's childcare centers remained in the Bermuda Study (McCartney 1984, Phillips et al. 1987) after the influence of the parents' childrearing values was statistically removed.

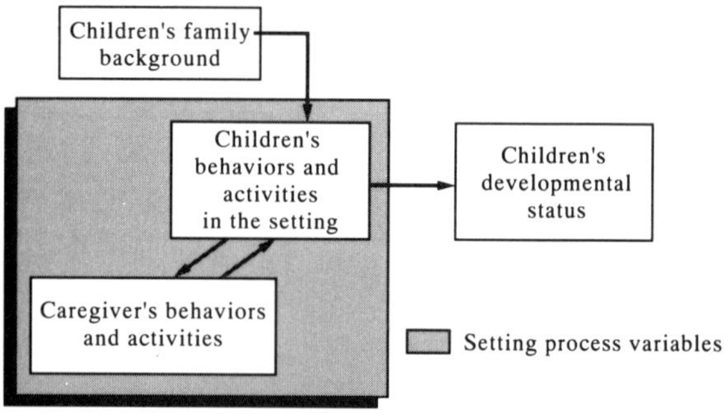

Figure 4
A model of the effects of family background and caregiver behavior on child outcomes

Howes and Olenick (1986) observed that families enrolling their children in low quality childcare had more complex and presumably more stressful lives than the families using higher quality care. Moreover, both parents and caregivers of the children in low quality centers were less involved and invested in assuring that their children complied with their requests. Analyses that incorporated both childcare and family influences were more predictive of several child outcomes (e.g., compliance in girls, task resistance in boys) than analyses that took into account only one set of factors.

A Swedish longitudinal study (Cochran 1977, Gunnerson 1978, Cochran and Robinson 1983) examined the interaction of structure and process variables in both in-home and out-of-home childcare settings. Children's developmental outcome measures are strongly influenced by the following interacting variables: (a) childcare structure variables (type of care), (b) childcare process variables (social interaction with caregivers and peers), (c) family process variables (social interaction with the mother), (d) family structure variables (maternal marital status), and (e) child gender. Cochran and Robinson (1983) concluded that while previous studies

> have tended to view day care as an independent, causal agent operating on the lives of young children . . . the day care experience is better conceptualized as an *intervening* variable (their emphasis) which mediates certain family types on the one hand (two working parents, single parent) and long-term developmental outcomes on the other. (p. 61)

Future studies should assume a mediator between family background and experience, on the one hand, and developmental or learning outcomes, on the other hand, as well as between caregivers' behaviors and developmental or learning outcomes. This is schematized in Fig. 4.

The study of Everson and his colleagues (Everson 1981, Everson et al. 1984) illustrates the recommended approach when they examined the mediating influence of mothers' positive or negative disposition to use childcare on toddlers' adjustment to childcare in both center and family daycare arrangements. After the children had been enrolled in childcare for five months, the results suggested that the congruence between maternal attitudes and use of childcare was a highly significant predictor of children's adjustment. Mothers who relied on childcare but were uncomfortable with it and mothers who felt comfortable with the use of childcare but were not using it (called "inconsistent mothers") had children who were more easily upset by a frustrating task, showed greater distress at maternal separation, and were less compliant with their mothers' requests while playing than children who had consistent mothers. The inconsistent mothers were also quicker to become angry and impatient with their children.

After 10 months in childcare, attitude-behavior consistency was no longer the issue. Attitude alone predicted child behaviors. Specifically, mothers who were positively disposed toward the use of childcare, compared to those who were negatively disposed, had children who were less cooperative with adults, were less compliant with their mothers, and displayed inferior approaches to a problem-solving task, regardless of whether they were in childcare or not. Everson et al. (1984 pp. 90–91) conclude that the "specific effects of daycare may depend in large measure on maternal attitudes" and other family characteristics.

5. Conclusion

Three waves of research on childcare and preschool education have been reviewed. The first wave focused on evaluating the effects of preschool education and was dominated by the American studies which showed that preschool intervention could have lasting positive effects. In this wave, early childhood intervention in the developing countries are also considered. In spite of methodological weaknesses, it is reasonable to conclude that they too are effective.

Considering the substantial effects of preschool intervention of children's development, and the multiple and complex factors that influence it in developed as well as developing countries, an interactive–ecological framework seems to be a promising perspective. The key issue is to determine how preschool intervention interacts with other influences in the child's social context.

The second wave of studies consists of comparative evaluation of the various kinds of programs. The findings have been inconclusive. A major weakness of these studies is that curriculum content, activities, materials, and teaching practices are typically confounded. Consequently, even if these evaluations had provided consistent findings, they would not have explained how a specific program achieves specific effects. Thus most of the contemporary third wave studies are seeking to determine what really happens in childcare and preschool settings.

Finally, the arguments in favor of a shift from the currently dominant process–product paradigm to an ecological–mediating process framework are presented.

See also: Evaluation of Preschool Programs; Assessment in Early Childhood; Early Childhood Interventions; Preschool Education: Worldwide Trends; Childcare, Economics of

References

Beller K E 1973 Research on organized programs of early education. In Travers R (ed.) 1973 *Second Handbook of Research on Teaching*. Rand McNally, Chicago, Illinois

Berrueta-Clement J R, Schweinhart L J, Barnett W S, Epstein A S, Weikart D P 1984 *Changed Lives. The Effects of the Perry Preschool Program on Youths Through Age 19*. Monographs of the High/Scope Educational Research Foundation, No. 8. High Scope Press, Ypsilanti, Michigan

Bronfenbrenner U 1974 *Is Early Intervention Effective ?* Office of Child Development, Washington, DC

Bruner J 1980 *Under Five in Britain*, Vol. 1. Oxford Preschool Research Project. Grant McIntyre, London

Caldwell B M 1968 *Preschool Inventory Experimental Edition: 1968 Administration Manual*. Education Testing Service, Princeton, New Jersey

Clarke-Stewart K A 1982 Predicting child development from child care forms and features: The Chicago Study. In Phillips D A (ed.) 1982 *Quality in Child Care: What Research Tells Us?* NAEYC, Washington, DC

Clarke-Stewart K A 1987a Daycare forms and features. In: Ainslie R C (ed.) 1987 *Quality Variations in Daycare*. Praeger, New York

Clarke-Stewart K A 1987b In search of consistencies in child care research. In: Phillips D A (ed.) 1987 *Quality in Child Care: What Research Tells Us?* NAEYC, Washington, DC

Cochran M M 1977 A comparison of group day and family childrearing patterns in Sweden. *Child Development* 48(2) 702–07

Cochran M M, Robinson J 1983 Day care, family circumstances and sex differences in children. In: Kilmer S (ed.) 1983 *Advances in Early Education and Day Care*. JAI Press, Greenwich, Connecticut

Everson M D 1981 The impact of day care on the attachment behavior of 12 to 24 month olds. Unpublished doctoral dissertation. Stanford University, Palo Alto, California

Everson M D, Sarnat L, Ambron S R 1984 Day care and early socialization: The role of maternal attitude. In: Ainslie R C (ed.) 1984 *Quality Variations in Daycare*. Praeger, New York

Goelman H, Pence A 1982 Effects of child care, family, and individual characteristic on children's language development: The Victoria Day Care Research Projects.

In: Phillips D A (ed.) 1982 *Quality in Child Care: What Research Tells Us?* NAEYC, Washington, D.C.
Gunnerson L 1978 Children in day care and family care in Sweden: A follow-up study. Unpublished Doctoral Dissertation, University of Michigan. Ann Arbor
Howes C, Olenick M 1986 Family and child care influences on toddlers compliance. *Child Dev.* 57(1): 202–16
Kontos S 1987 Day care quality, family background and children's development. Paper presented at the Biennial Meeting of the Society for Research in Child Development, Baltimore, April
Lazar I 1977 *The Persistence of Preschool Effects: Summary Report.* Cornell University, Ithaca, New York
Lazar I, Darlington R 1979 *Lasting Effects After Preschool. Summary Report.* US Department of Health, Education and Welfare, New York
McCartney K 1984 The effect of quality of day care environment on children's language development. *Dev. Psychol.* 20(2): 244–60.
McKey R H et al. 1985 *The Impact of Head Start on Children, Families and Communities.* CSR Incorporated, Washington, DC (DHHS No. 85–31193)
Miller L B, Dyer J 1975 Four preschool programs: Their dimensions and effects. *Monographs of the Society for Research in Child Development* 40, Nos. 5–6, Serial No. 162
Miller L, Bizzell R 1983a Long-term effects of four preschool programs: Ninth and tenth grade results. *Child Dev.* 55(4): 1570–87
Miller L, Bizzell R 1983b Long-term effects of four preschool programs: Sixth, seventh, and eighth grades. *Child Dev.* 54(3): 727–41.
Phillips D A, Howes C 1987 Indicators of quality in child care: Review of research. In: Phillips D A (ed.) 1987 *Quality in Child Care: What Research Tells Us?* NAEYC, Washington, DC
Phillips D A, Scarr S, McCartney K 1987 Dimension and effects of child care quality: The Bermuda Study. In Phillips D A (ed.) 1987 *Quality in Child Care: What Research Tells Us?* NAEYC, Washington, DC
Rivlin A M, Timpane P M 1975 Planned variation in education: An assessment. In: Rivlin A M, Timpane P M (eds.) 1975 *Planned Variation in Education: Should We Give Up or Try Harder?* The Brookings Institution, Washington, DC
Ruopp R, Travers J, Glantz F, Coelen C 1979 *Children at the Center: Summary Findings and Their Implications.* Final Report of the National Day Care Study, Vol 1. Office of Human Development Services, Department of Health, Education and Welfare, Washington, DC
Schweinhart L J, Weikart D P 1980 *Young Children Grow Up: The Effects of the Perry Preschool Program on Youths Through Age 15.* Monographs of the High/Scope Educational Research Foundation, No. 7. High/Scope Press, Ypsilanti, Michigan
Smith M S 1975 Evaluation findings in Head Start planned variation. In: Rivlin A M, Timpane P M (eds.) 1975 *Planned Variation in Education: Should we Give Up or Try Harder?* The Brookings Institution, Washington, DC
Travers J R, Light R J (eds.) 1982 *Learning for Experience: Evaluating Early Childhood Demonstration Programs.* (Panel on Outcome Measurement in Early Childhood Demonstration Programs. Committee on Child Development Research and Public Policy, Assembly of Behavioral and Social Sciences, National Research Council) National Academy Press, Washington, DC
Weikart D P, Epstein A S, Schweinhart L, Bond J T 1978 *The Ypsilanti Preschool Curriculum Demonstration Project.* Monographs of the High/Scope Educational Foundation, No. 4. High/Scope Press, Ypsilanti, Michigan

M. Crahay

Childcare, Economics of

As a result of the remarkable increase in women's labor force participation and women's participation in education and training in all Western industrialized countries, mothers no longer routinely care for their young children on a full-time basis. Arrangements for the care of infants and young children during the working or school hours of their parent(s) have now become matters of public policy. Economic issues include the supply and demand for childcare; its cost, quality, and external benefits; and alternative systems of finance, governance, and regulation.

Except for the United States, industrialized countries have developed extensive policies for dealing with the care of young children, including paid periods of maternal and parental leave (Kahn and Kamerman 1987). Bergman (1993) provided a full discussion of the French system. Kamerman (1991) provided a summary of policies and programs in an international context. The United States situation is of particular policy interest because numerous decisions have been debated at the national, state, and local levels.

1. Overview of the United States Childcare Market

The diversity of care options for preschool children is extraordinary. Children whose parent(s) are in school or in the labor force can be cared for informally or formally. Within the formal sector there is great variation in the auspices and ownership of care options. Moreover, within any given week, many parents often use combinations of types of care.

Informal care includes both paid and unpaid care: the child can accompany one or both parents to school or work; the parents can split their work and school time so that one of them is always available to care for the child in the child's own home (often referred to as "splitting shifts"); a relative (including an older sibling) can care for the child in the child's home or in the relative's home, either paid or unpaid; and a nonrelative (housekeeper, nanny, or au pair) can care for the child for pay in the child's own home, and either live in that home or not. Children also sometimes care for themselves; these are the so-called "latch-key children."

Formal care always involves payment and includes care in a family daycare home or in a childcare center.

Family daycare services are offered in the home of the child care-provider; in general 2 to 12 children of mixed ages are cared for in such homes (Hayes et al. 1990). According to the 1990 National Child Care Survey (National Association for the Education of Young Children (NAEYC 1991) there are an average of six children in regulated family day homes, and an average of three in nonregulated homes. Often, the provider cares for her or his own child as well as for other children.

A childcare center generally cares for a substantial number of children, who are grouped by age or developmental stage. The average number of children cared for ranges from 50 in Head Start programs to 91 in for-profit chains (NAEYC 1991). Centers may be public, private nonprofit, or private for-profit. Some centers are operated by employers, primarily for the children of their employees, and some are operated by school districts.

In the United States in 1988, almost two-thirds of children under the age of 5 whose mothers worked full-time were cared for in group care; about one-third (32.6 percent) in childcare centers, nursery schools, kindergartens, extended daycare or day camp; and about one-third (31.2 percent) in family daycare homes (Blau and Ferber 1992). The percentage of care provided by these two types of institutions increased greatly after the Second World War. For example, in 1958 less than 20 percent of children under 5 with full-time employed mothers were cared for in these two types of institutions (Hayes et al. 1990). The NAEYC (1991) study estimated that at the beginning of 1990 there were about 80,000 childcare centers serving about 4 million children, and about 118,000 regulated family daycare homes serving about 700,000 children. Estimates of unregulated family daycare homes ranged widely from 550,000 to 1.1 million (Hayes et al. 1990). The number of children served by unregulated family daycare homes was estimated to be about 5 million (Kahn and Kamerman 1987).

2. *The Market for Formal Care*

2.1 Supply

It is difficult to obtain precise estimates of the supply of childcare workers in the United States. Because many childcare workers, especially those who provide unregulated services in their own homes, do not report employment and income, it is likely that the Current Population Surveys underestimate the number of childcare workers (Blau 1992). The National Child Care Staffing Study, (Whitebrook et al. 1989) found that 97 percent of teachers and assistant teachers were female.

Relative to the female labor force as a whole, childcare workers are well-educated (NAEYC 1985). In the civilian labor force as a whole, less than half of all women have attended college, but Whitebrook et al. (1989) found that in their sample of childcare centers, more than half of assistant teachers and almost three-fourths of teachers had some college education. The NAEYC (1991) study found that among teachers in centers almost half (47 percent) had a four-year college degree, about 13 percent had a two-year college degree, about 12 percent had a Child Development Associate credential, and 15 percent had some college experience (NAEYC 1991).

Family daycare providers were found to be less well-educated than childcare center teachers and assistant teachers. Among United States parents who used family daycare facilities, less than half of those responding to a survey reported that their provider had childcare training (the survey had an 88 percent response rate). When providers were asked about their own training, only about two-thirds of regulated providers and one-third of unregulated providers said they had any training in child care (NAEYC 1991).

Relative to their education level, childcare workers were found to be poorly paid. The average hourly wage of teachers in childcare centers in the United States in 1990 was US$7.49; for providers in regulated family daycare homes, US$4.04; and for providers in unregulated homes, US$1.25 (NAEYC 1991). Moreover, the earnings structure was exceedingly flat: there was little wage variation by job level or by education. For example, the National Childcare Staffing study found that among those with some college education, aides were paid on average US$4.45 per hour, while teacher/directors were paid only about one dollar more (US$5.66) per hour. Among teachers, those with 12 years of schooling or less were paid US$4.74 per hour while those with a postcollege degree were paid only about three dollars per hour more (US$7.49) (Whitebrook et al. 1989).

A study of the determinants of earnings for childcare workers, using data from the Current Population Survey, found the surprising result that geographic location, race, and age were unrelated to earnings (Blau 1992). The result for geographic location was unexpected given the variation in fees by geographic area. The relationship between earnings and race needs further investigation.

The childcare market appears to be highly segregated by race. For example, the National Day Care Home Study found that 80 percent of children in family daycare centers were of the same race and ethnicity as their caregiver (Fosburg 1981). Given this segregation, it may be that there is an absence of the usual wage discrimination faced by minority workers, since, with all other factors held constant, female Black providers who cared for Black children appeared to be paid the same as female White providers who cared for White children.

Reasoning from a human capital framework, the absence of a significant relationship between earnings and age suggests that there may be little on-the-job learning in childcare. Alternatively, it may be that in the case of childcare workers, age is not a good proxy for experience: older workers in the field may not be any more experienced than younger workers.

The absence of a strong relationship between education and earnings for childcare workers was even more surprising. Among private household workers (including both nannies and family daycare providers) and among those who defined themselves as teachers (including teachers in childcare centers, nursery school teachers and kindergarten teachers), there was no significant relationship between education and earnings; however, for staff members in childcare centers who did not designate themselves as teachers (assistant teachers, aides, etc.) the wage rate was significantly related to education. Blau (1992) suggested that while teachers used their higher education to enter the more highly paid sector of the childcare market, once they did so their wage rate was not related to their education level.

Not only have wages been low among childcare workers, but benefits have also been minimal. In the National Childcare Staffing sample, even among full-time staff, only about 40 percent had employment-related health insurance and only about 20 percent had retirement benefits. Moreover, those earning the lowest wages had the poorest benefits packages (Whitebrook et al. 1989).

Partly as a consequence of low wages and poor benefits, turnover among childcare workers has been very high, a worrisome finding since continuity of care is an important element of childcare quality and children's well-being (Hayes et al. 1990). Moreover, high turnover increases the level of stress in the work environment and negatively affects the job performance and quality of care provided by remaining staff (Whitebrook et al. 1989, Strober et al. 1989). While the average turnover rate for all occupations is about 20 percent (Hayes et al. 1990), the estimates of turnover rates for childcare workers in centers ranged between 25 percent (NAEYC 1991) and 41 percent (Whitebrook et al. 1989).

The elasticity of the supply of childcare workers has been estimated by looking at the pattern of real earnings over time. Blau (1992) concluded that because real earnings remained constant over the period 1976–86, despite increases in government subsidies and regulation, the supply of childcare workers has been relatively elastic. Walker (1992), looking specifically at the elasticity of supply of family daycare providers, found that unlicensed providers had less attachment to the labor market than their licensed counterparts; they had less training, less experience, cared for fewer children per establishment, and were less involved in marketing their services.

The matter of supply elasticity deserves further research. If the elasticity of supply is indeed high, government attempts to improve quality of services by mandating higher educational requirements and requiring licensure could result in fewer childcare slots, and especially family daycare slots, as providers respond to these regulations and requirements by leaving the field altogether. The absence of a payoff to education among childcare workers also suggests that increased educational requirements may drive providers out of the market.

2.2 Demand for Childcare

Two key issues on the demand side of the market are the responsiveness of parental demand to changes in price and the effect of the availability and price of childcare on mothers' decisions to seek employment.

The price elasticity of the demand for childcare and the effect of price of childcare on mothers' employment decisions vary with the age of the child, in part because childcare costs are higher for younger children (Leibowitz et al. 1992), and with the marital status of the mother—single mothers are more responsive to changes in price than are married mothers (Michalopoulos et al. 1992).

Price has an important (negative) effect on parents' choice of type of care (Hofferth and Wissoker 1992). It also has a large and significant negative effect on mothers' labor supply, although researchers disagree on its size (Ribar 1992, Connelly 1991, Michalopoulos et al. 1992).

About one-fourth of mothers aged 21–29 who were not in the United States labor force in 1988 cited childcare problems as the major reason for their nonparticipation. Among poor women, the percentage was about one-third (Cattan 1991). Connelly's estimates suggest that universal no-cost childcare in the United States would cause an increase of about 10 percentage points in women's labor force participation (Connelly 1991 p. 110).

In Sweden, research on the price elasticity of demand for childcare suggests that if the price of care were to fall (as a result of an increased subsidy), the effect on labor force participation would be small. Most of the effect would consist of mothers moving from private to public care (Gustafsson and Stafford 1992).

The income elasticity of demand for childcare is complex. An increase in family income that comes from wife's own earnings has a positive effect on labor force participation, but does not significantly increase childcare expenditures. On the other hand, increases in family income derived from husband's earnings or nonwage sources decreases wives' labor force participation but increases expenditures on center care (but not on care by a nanny or relatives) (Hofferth and Wissoker 1992).

2.3 Cost of Childcare

Childcare is labor-intensive, with personnel costs accounting for between 50 and 80 percent of childcare centers' budgets (Willer 1987). Kagan and Glennon (1982) found that nonprofit centers spent about 73 percent of their budgets on wages, while profit centers spent about 63 percent. Since young children require a great deal of individual attention, especially if they are in childcare all day, quality care requires relatively low child–staff ratios. As a result, even though childcare providers receive low pay, childcare is expensive.

The cost of care ranges widely, by region of a country, age of child, and auspices of ownership. In 1990, average center fees in the United States ranged from US \$1.29 per hour in the South to US \$2.18 per hour in the Northeast. Average fees for regulated family daycare ranged from US \$1.32 per hour in the South to US \$2.02 per hour in the Northeast. Average fees in unregulated family daycare homes ranged from US \$0.89 per hour in the South to US \$1.83 per hour in the Midwest and Northeast (NAEYC 1991).

Among employed mothers with a child under 5, childcare costs represent about 10 percent of family income, about what the average family allocates to food expenditures (Hayes et al. 1990). For lower-income families, the fraction is even higher: in 1990, for those in families with an income less than US \$15,000 per year, childcare costs were almost one-fourth (23 %) of income. For those in families with income between US \$15,000 and US \$25,000, childcare costs were 12 percent of family income (NAEYC 1991).

Infant care is even more expensive: The National Childcare Staffing Study in the United States found that in 1988 in 227 centers in the five metropolitan areas surveyed, full-time infant care fees ranged from US \$62.00 to US \$150 per week (Whitebrook et al. 1989).

2.4 Quality of Care

Child development experts agree that the primary ingredients of quality care are caregivers who interact with children frequently and responsively (Hayes et al. 1990). Certain structural arrangements promote such interactions: small group size, low child–adult ratios, child-related training for the caregiver, caregiver stability and continuity, hygienic physical care and food preparation, safe and attractive physical space, and a program that promotes children's emotional, social, and cognitive growth (Hayes et al. 1990). The effects on quality of parental involvement, caregiver autonomy, overall size of the facility, and multicultural curricula are still being studied (Hayes et al. 1990).

Many children in United States family daycare homes and childcare centers do not receive quality care because they are in programs that have high child–adult ratios and/or caregivers without training in group care of children. Although almost all states regulate child–staff ratios in centers, the stringency of their requirements varies greatly, from 6:1 for 3-year olds to 25:1 for 5-year olds. For children cared for in centers, the child–staff ratio for those under one year old is on average about 4:1; for those aged one to three, about 6–8:1; and for those aged three to five, about 10:1. For children up to 5 years old cared for in family daycare homes (both regulated and unregulated), the child–staff ratio is about 4:1 (NAEYC 1991).

Only 14 states in the United States require that family daycare providers have training in group care of children. Only 28 states specify educational requirements for teachers in centers, and only eight states have such requirements for teacher assistants (aides) (Hayes et al. 1990). Even where states have stringent requirements, because the turnover rate among childcare workers has been so high, and because centers have had difficulty finding adequately educated workers, teachers and teacher aides who do not have requisite training have often been hired on an "emergency" basis (Strober et al. 1989).

The evidence on the relationship between the cost of care and its quality is mixed (Hayes et al. 1990, Hofferth and Wissoker 1992, Kisker and Maynard 1991). In some instances high-quality care is relatively low cost; low-paid teachers in effect subsidize the high-quality care. However, over time, these teachers tend to leave, contributing to discontinuity of teacher–child relationships.

Price appears to have a stronger effect on parental choice than does quality. However, Hofferth and Wissoker (1992) found that, given price, parents were more likely to choose a higher-quality center (as measured by child–staff ratio.) Others found that parents trade off quality attributes from a child-development point of view for attributes such as convenience of location or hours of operation (Blau 1991).

Some argue that parents are often poorly informed about what constitutes good quality care from a child-development point of view (Blau 1991) and cannot (or do not) seek information about quality (Hayes et al. 1990). Others (Hofferth and Wissoker 1992) have suggested that even when parents choose family daycare, they may be better informed about quality than researchers think.

3. Policy Issues

The major policy issue in childcare concerns government intervention: should governments intervene in childcare markets, and if so, how?

In 1988 in the United States about \$16 billion were spent on childcare by parents, other private sources, and government. The federal government spent about US \$7 billion, slightly more than half of that through the dependent care tax credit. The states spent approximately US \$500 million (Hayes et al. 1990). For purposes of comparison, it is useful to note that if all children under 6 years old were in full-time paid care, all children 6–14 years old were in paid care during non school hours, and all care measured up to quality standards that promoted emotional, social, and cognitive development (likely to cost about US $4,000 per year per preschooler and US $2000 per year per school-age child) the total cost of care would be US $126 billion (Hayes et al. 1990).

There are two economic justifications for increased government subsidization of childcare: increased efficiency and increased equity. The increased efficiency argument is that there is currently underinvestment in childcare, that parents spend too little on quality childcare, and that the negative effects of this underinvestment accrue not only to children and parents but also to society as a whole. This argument suggests that childcare has external benefits and that the populace as a whole has an interest (or should have an interest) in ensuring that young children whose parent(s) work receive high-quality childcare (Strober 1975).

External benefits of childcare include: enhanced social, emotional, and cognitive learning for young children which would reduce public social and educational expenditures for remediation later in childhood and in adulthood; improved ability for women to plan their education and employment with the expectation that market work can realistically be a permanent feature of their adult lives, even if they choose to have children; and increased productivity for employers as they experience decreases in employee turnover and absenteeism (Strober 1975).

With respect to equity, since children who come from families where there is economic and psychological stress are more often enrolled in low-quality childcare than are other children (Hayes et al. 1990), subsidy of childcare for these children has been seen as righting an existing inequality.

Because childcare produces private as well as social benefits, an economic case can be made for cost sharing between the private and public sectors. Moreover, since employers are one of the beneficiaries of a high-quality, reliable childcare system, it is sensible to require that they pay part of the costs, either through the provision of direct services or through taxation.

Government subsidization of childcare may take one of four forms: subsidies to parents for childcare; subsidies to parents for parental leave to care for their own children; subsidies to providers, including tuition benefits for their own training and assistance with liability insurance; and subsidies for the infrastructure of the childcare system, including the improvement of provider training facilities and information networks for parents and providers.

The costs and benefits of each of these alternatives need to be studied. Each will have different effects on quality of care and different external benefits. For example, existing evidence does not suggest that subsidization of childcare on the demand side would lead parents to purchase higher-quality care. In addition, each alternative needs to be considered in conjunction with possible more stringent state regulation of staff–child ratios, group and facility size, and caregiver training. Decisions also need to be made about the levels of government that should collect taxes and provide subsidies (Yeager and Strober 1992).

Questions concerning organization and productivity of resources also need attention. For example, care in Swedish childcare centers was found to be twice the cost of such care in the other Nordic countries, in part because Swedish centers operated for longer hours, even though few children attended during early morning and evening hours (Jansson and Strömquist 1988). The Swedish authors questioned the productivity implications of these organizational arrangements.

There are other important questions. Could costs be reduced without compromising quality if childcare centers were combined with family daycare homes in integrated systems (Strober 1975)? Should states and localities be encouraged to place childcare systems under the aegis of existing school boards? What should be the role of employer-sponsored care in the larger childcare system? How can sick children best be cared for? Finally, what should be the role of parents in the governance of childcare systems?

See also: Childcare and Preschool Effects; Childcare Policies and Programs: International Overview; Preschool Education: Worldwide Trends

References

Bergmann B B 1993 The French welfare system: An excellent system we could adapt and afford. In: Wilson W J (ed.) 1993 *Sociology and the Public Agenda*. Sage, Los Angeles, California

Blau D M 1991 Introduction. In: Blau D M (ed.) 1991 *The Economics of Child Care*. Russell Sage Foundation, New York

Blau D M 1992 The child care labor market. *J. Hum. Resources* 27(1): 9–39

Blau F D, Ferber M A 1992 *The Economics of Women, Men and Work*. Prentice-Hall, Englewood Cliffs, New Jersey

Cattan P 1991 Child care problems: An obstacle to work. *Month. Lab. Rev.* 114(10): 3–9

Connelly R 1991 The importance of child care costs to women's decisionmaking. In: Blau D M (ed.) 1991 *The Economics of Child Care*. Russell Sage Foundation, New York

Fosburg S 1981 *Family Day Care in the United States: Summary of Findings*. DHHS Pub. No. 80–30382. US Department of Health and Human Services, Washington, DC

Gustafsson S, Stafford F 1992 Child care subsidies and labor supply in Sweden. *J. Hum. Resources* 27(1): 204–30

Hayes C D, Palmer J L, Zaslow M J (eds.) 1990 *Who Cares for America's Children?: Child Care Policy for the 1990s*. National Academy Press, Washington, DC

Hofferth S L, Wissoker D A 1992 Price, quality and income in child care choice. *J. Hum. Resources* 27(1): 70–112

Jansson T, Strömquist S 1988 *Child Care in the Nordic*

Countries: Costs, Quality, Management. The Swedish Agency for Administrative Development, Stockholm
Kagan S, Glennon T 1982 Considering proprietary child care. In: Zigler E, Gordon E (eds.) 1982 *Day Care: Scientific and Social Policy Issues.* Auburn House, Boston, Massachusetts
Kahn A J, Kamerman S B 1987 *Child Care: Facing the Hard Choices.* Greenwood Press, New Haven, Connecticut
Kamerman S B 1991 Child care policies and programs: An international overview. *J. Soc. Issues* 47(2): 179–96
Kisker E, Maynard R 1991 Quality, cost, and parental cost of child care. In: Blau D M (ed.) 1991 *The Economics of Child Care.* Russell Sage Foundation, New York
Leibowitz A, Klerman J A, Waite L J 1992 Employment of new mothers and child care choice: Differences by children's age. *J. Hum. Resources* 27(1): 112–33
Michalopoulos C, Robins P K, Garfinkel I 1992 A structural model of labor supply and child care demand. *J. Hum. Resources* 27(1): 166–203
National Association for the Education of Young Children (NAEYC) 1985 *In Whose Hands?: A Demographic Fact Sheet on Child Care Providers.* National Association for the Education of Young Children, Washington, DC
National Association for the Education of Young Children (NAEYC); Administration on Children, Youth and Families of the US Department of Health and Human Services; Office of Policy Planning of the US Department of Education 1991 *The Demand and Supply of Child Care in 1990: Joint Findings from The National Child Care Survey, 1990 and A Profile of Child Care Settings.* National Association for the Education of Young Children, Washington, DC
Ribar D C 1992 Child care and the labor supply of married women: Reduced form evidence. *J. Hum. Resources* 27(1): 134–65
Strober M H 1975 Formal extrafamily child care: Some economic observations. In: Lloyd C B (ed.) 1975 *Sex, Discrimination, and the Division of Labor.* Columbia University Press, New York
Strober M H, Gerlach-Downie S, Yeager K E 1989 Child care centers as workplaces. Paper presented to Annual Meeting of the American Educational Research Association, Boston, Massachusetts
Walker J R 1992 New evidence on the supply of child care: A statistical portrait of family providers and an analysis of their fees. *J. Hum. Resources* 27(1) 40–69
Whitebrook M, Howes C, Phillips D 1989 *Who Cares?: Child Care Teachers and the Quality of Care in America.* Child Care Employee Project, Oakland, California
Willer B 1987 *The Growing Crisis in Child Care: Quality, Compensation and Affordability in Early Childhood Programs.* National Association for the Education of Young Children, Washington, DC
Yeager K E, Strober M H 1992 Financing child care through local taxes: One city's bold attempt. *Journal of Family Issues*

Further Reading

Hartmann H, Pearce D 1989 *High Skill and Low Pay: The Economics of Child Care Work.* Institute for Women's Policy Research, Washington, DC
Spalter-Roth R, Hartmann H 1988 *Unnecessary Losses: Costs to Americans of the Lack of Family and Medical Leave: Executive Summary.* Institute for Women's Policy Research, Washington, DC

M. H. Strober

Childcare Policies and Programs: International Overview

This entry examines the care of preschool-aged children: those under the age at which compulsory schooling begins (5, 6, or 7 years). The primary emphasis is on developments in the advanced, industrialized countries. Occasional mention is made of developing countries. All forms of out-of-home nonrelative childcare services are covered, including preschools, daycare centers, family-type daycare homes, as well as maternity and parental leave policies.

1. Terms, Concepts, and Focus

Childcare services internationally include a wide range of part- and full-day programs under education, health, and social welfare auspices, funded and delivered in a variety of ways in both the public and private sectors. These programs include: preschools (kindergartens, prekindergartens, compensatory education programs, and nursery schools); daycare centers; family-type daycare homes (both regulated and unregulated); and before- and after-school programs. The major national differences are related to: the extensiveness of the public sector role; the predominance of the education, health, or social welfare system in delivering the services; the proportion of children of different ages served by these programs; whether services are limited to the children of working mothers; and the quality of the care provided.

Childcare policies include the whole range of government actions designed to influence the supply and/or demand for childcare and the quality of care provided. These activities include: direct delivery of childcare services; direct and indirect financial subsidies to private providers of care, such as grants, contracts, and tax incentives; financial subsidies to parents/consumers, both direct and indirect, such as grants and tax benefits to permit or facilitate access to services, or to permit parents to remain at home (and stop working) without loss of income; and the establishment and enforcement of regulations. These policies are discussed only insofar as they specifically affect the pattern of childcare service delivery in different countries.

The changing roles of women in the home and the substantial growth in the female labor force have clearly had an impact on the supply of childcare services in different countries. Although the countries with the most generous childcare policies and extensive coverage tend to have a high rate of female participation in the labor force, several

Table 1
Labour force participation rates for married and single Women with children under 18 and childcare coverage rates

Country	Date	% of mothers in labor force		% of children in childcare full- and part-day	
		Married	Single	0–3 years	3–5 years
United Kingdom	1988	59	52	2	43[a]
Canada	1988	67	64	12	31[b]
Denmark	1988	87	87	44	85
Federal Republic of Germany	1986	48	70	2	80
France	1988	66	85	24	95
Hungary	1988	89	89	12[c]	86
Italy	1986	44	45	5	90
Sweden	1988	89	89	73[a]	
United States	1988	65	65	20	70[e]

Source: Data assembled by author from varied sources. Data for Sweden are for women with children under 16. Childcare data are largely from the mid-1980s.
a These data are for children aged 3–4, since compulsory school begins at age 5 b These data are for children whose mothers work or are in education at least 20 hours per week c Most Hungarian working women with children under age 3 are at home on leave, receiving a cash child-rearing grant d These data are for all children aged 1–6; compulsory school begins at age 7. The data include part- and full-day programs. The rate for full-day programs is 55 percent e estimate 1984–85; largely part-day programs.

countries with comparable policies and equal (or higher) rates of coverage have a lower proportion of women in the workforce (see Table 1). Clearly, those countries are responding to other concerns.

The major childcare policy and program issues currently debated internationally relate to the supply of services, and their cost and quality. Data on the proportion of preschool-aged children enrolled in the programs are provided for a sample of countries in Table 1.

The objective of this entry is to:

(a) identify and describe the policies that European countries have adopted regarding childcare for children from 2½ or 3 years to the age of primary school entry, and discuss cases where there still remains some debate, particularly on the quality of care provided;

(b) identify and describe the policy choices that Europe has largely made with regard to infant care;

(c) discuss toddler care, where national policies are still unsettled, and where the European childcare policy debate is now focused.

In Europe, policy diversity with regard to toddler care is extensive—even greater than in the United States and Canada, for example. The alternative policy strategies now being debated and/or experimented with reflect various priorities including: encouraging higher birthrates; increasing the female labor force; preparing children for preschools and primary school; enhancing gender equity; and reducing poverty. The policy options include various types of out-of-home childcare and preschool programs, as well as child rearing and parenting allowances.

While the focus in this entry is on childcare policies, these can be fully understood only in the context of the array of family and social policies in place in particular countries, including the cash benefits that support parenting, child rearing, family income, health insurance coverage, and so forth. Given the limitations of space, however, such policies are not addressed (Kamerman and Kahn 1989a, 1989b, 1991). Finally, although the focus is primarily on Europe, illustrations are also provided from Canada and other countries.

2. *Care for Children: Age 3 to Compulsory School Entry*

Universal preschool for children from 2½ or 3 years of age to 5, 6, or 7, depending on the age when compulsory schooling begins, has clearly emerged as the policy choice of the advanced industrialized countries. These programs are viewed as "good" for all children—in terms of child development and in order to prepare children for primary school—regardless of mothers' or parents' labor force status, family income, cultural background, or capacities as parents. Almost all children within the preschool age group participate in these programs on a voluntary basis. The programs are all heavily subsidized, operate largely within the public sector, are free or charge income-related fees, and cover, at least, the normal school day.

Throughout Europe these preschool programs are thought to be an essential component of general child and family policy, and of childcare policy in particular. A study prepared for the European Community (see Moss 1988) concluded that there is almost universal demand among parents of children of this age for preschool programs. Wherever preschool programs are available, places are readily taken up. The European childcare policy goal is to establish preschool as a legal "right" or entitlement and make it as accessible and available as primary school. Several countries have already achieved this goal and many others are rapidly approaching it.

These preschools are operated largely under educational auspices as part of the public education system or are publicly subsidized in the private nonprofit sector. The programs cover the normal school day and year, and provide more or less enriched and developmentally appropriate curricula, depending on the country. They are free and voluntary, and children participate to the extent that places are available.

There are two other childcare "models," which are less common: (a) a Scandinavian model characterized by a free-standing, autonomous, childcare program (not part of the educational system), most developed in Denmark, Finland, and Sweden, for all children under primary school age, designed to serve the children of working parents; and (b) a dual system in the United Kingdom (and Anglo–American countries) of social welfare daycare for neglected and/or abused and/or deprived children, and part-day, educational, nursery school for children from the middle and upper classes. This latter model is in flux. For example, the United States has expanded its public school-based preschool programs to include poor and handicapped children, and to provide compensatory education for some as well.

The coverage or enrollment pattern in most countries with a preschool program is fairly similar: full coverage for 4- and 5-year olds, and nearly that for children aged 2½ and 3 years. Thus, the French *écoles maternelles* serve almost all the 3-, 4-, and 5-year olds, and almost half of the 2-year olds, mainly those over 2½ years. The Belgian and Italian pattern is much like the French. Germany has somewhat lower rates, as do the Eastern European countries, but 75–85 percent of the cohort participate in preschool programs in these countries.

Coverage rates in Denmark are among the highest in Europe and extend over a full working day; rates in Finland and Sweden are slightly lower, but coverage is also for a full working day, rather than a school day. Coverage in The United Kingdom is inconsistently counted, though is at best modest, and generally described as very inadequate.

France, Belgium, and Italy are among the countries with the most extensive preschool programs in the world. The French *école maternelle* provides an excellent illustration of the dominant preschool model (Kamerman and Kahn 1981). It is a publicly financed program operated as an integral part of the French education system. The local facilities may be situated next to or in a primary school, but are often free-standing, completely separate structures.

All children are eligible to participate from the age of 2, although there are usually not enough places for all the 2-year olds whose parents want them enrolled. The program clearly provides childcare to the children of working parents, but participation is by no means limited to these children. Only where there is a shortage of places for 2-year olds do the children of working mothers get preference.

The program is educational, and stresses cognitive development within the framework of a developmentally appropriate curriculum. The hours follow the pattern of the normal school day, generally 8.30 a.m. to 4.30 p.m. Lunch is available at school, and many preschools (and primary schools) also have after-school programs as well.

The basic preschool program is free; parents pay income-related fees only for lunch and for the after-school program. On Wednesday, when French schools are closed (they are open for a half day on Saturdays), there are other programs available on a fee-paying basis.

Although the French regard these programs highly, group size and staff–child ratios would not satisfy American child development experts. Groups are large: as many as 25–30 (or more) 4-year olds in a group with one teacher (and sometimes an assistant). Nonetheless, the programs are enormously popular and viewed as an essential socialization experience to prepare children for school and to expose them to a valuable opportunity for peer play, growth, and development. French research has found that children who do not participate in these programs are likely to be disadvantaged when they begin school (Kamerman and Kahn 1981).

Coverage rates in France are extraordinarily high. Despite the fact that only about 60 percent of the mothers of children aged 3–5 are in the labor force, more than 95 percent of the children of this age participate in these programs (Moss 1988, 1990; Ergas 1990). Almost half of all 2-year olds are enrolled, and the waiting list for this age group is long. Although parents may choose to have their younger children participate only part of the day, most children, including 2-year olds, are enrolled for the full day.

The Belgian pattern is very similar, with comparable coverage rates for 3–5-year olds and children entering programs at age 2½ (Olmsted and Weikart 1989). The school day is slightly shorter, from 9.30 a.m. to 3.30 p.m., but after-school programs are increasingly available. Although parents may opt for a part-day program, most children participate for a full day.

The Italian *scuola materna* is similar, but operated under more diversified auspices (Moss 1990, Olmsted and Weikart 1989, Saraceno 1984). Although less than half of all women with children aged 3–5 are in the workforce, almost 90 percent of children of this age are in preschools. About two-thirds of these programs (in particular those in the north, which serve about 90% of the children there) are open for a full school day (8.30 a.m.–3.30 or 4.30 p.m.) or longer.

Despite a relatively low proportion of women with preschool-aged children in the labor force, German policy mandates coverage for at least 75 percent of all 3–5-year olds in preschool programs; by the end of the 1980s coverage was about 80 percent (Kamerman and Kahn 1991, Olmsted and Weikart 1989). These are largely part-day programs, as are German primary schools, and operate from 8.00 a.m. to 1.00 p.m.; about one-fifth cover a longer school day. Like primary schools, these programs are under the aegis of state and local governments rather than the national government. Ninety percent of the costs are subsidized equally by the state, region, and local governments; the remaining 10 percent are covered by parents' fees.

Many other countries have similar patterns of universal, or almost universal, preschool coverage for children aged 3 and older, including eastern European countries such as Hungary, and the Czech and Slovak Republics, and Israel, where compulsory school begins at age 5. Even some less developed countries, such as Hong Kong, are also heading in this direction.

Other countries are moving increasingly toward universal preschool for 4-year olds, just as they moved earlier toward kindergarten for 5-year olds. Thus, countries as diverse as Japan and the Netherlands now have extensive programs for 4- and 5-year olds, and the Netherlands is also expanding its coverage of 3-year olds. Among the less developed countries, although coverage rates are much lower than in the industrialized countries, preschool education for 3–5 or 6-year olds is increasingly evident (Olmsted and Weikart 1989).

Unlike the preschool pattern which dominates most of Europe, childcare in Denmark, Finland, and Sweden is a separate, free-standing, autonomous institution, under social welfare auspices. These programs serve all eligible children under the age of 7, when compulsory schooling begins. Given the parenting leave policies of these countries (see below), this means that the programs cover children from about 1 year of age. Swedish child development research indicates the short- and long-term positive consequences of high-quality child care for very young children.

In Denmark, more than 75 percent of women with children of preschool age work, but demand for childcare services still exceeds supply. Coverage rates for the Danish preschool program are about 85 percent, with 60 percent of children in programs that cover the full working day, and the remainder in programs covering either all or part of the school day. Both the quantity and quality of these programs far surpass those of programs in any of the other countries in the European Community: staff–child ratios are far higher, the groups much smaller, and quality is better regulated.

Childcare services in Sweden (as in Denmark) offer the highest quality of out-of-home care available anywhere. Regulations covering group size, staff–child ratios, and caregiver qualifications are based on extensive research, are rigorously set and enforced, and compare favorably with the views of experts in the United States on high-quality care (Hayes et al. 1990, Ruopp 1979). These programs are all heavily subsidized, but parents do pay income-related fees, usually equal to less than 10 percent of the average female wage (Kamerman and Kahn 1981).

Swedish programming stresses sibling (age-integrated) groups, in contrast to the age-segregated groups that exist in the preschool programs in most other countries. Thus, children aged 2 (or $2\frac{1}{2}$) to 6 years may be placed in the same group, although special age-appropriate activities are also incorporated into the curriculum.

Although these are universal programs, and all children are eligible, priority is given to the children of working parents, especially single mothers, and the children of immigrants. Since about 80 percent of the mothers of children under the age of 7 are in the workforce, the demand for these services is still well beyond the supply.

About 60 percent of children between the ages of 1 and 7 years were in municipal (public) childcare programs in Sweden in the mid-1980s, and another 13 percent in private care. Childcare services expanded enormously in the 1960s and 1970s with growth in female labor force and increasing concern for the well-being of children during times of rapid social change. Economic constraints precluded the full realization of the childcare service goals planned in the 1970s, but the programs grew, nonetheless. Currently, the objective is to extend parental leave to 18 months (see below) and to assure all children aged 18 months and older a place in a subsidized childcare program. Full implementation of this commitment has been deferred, but the expectation remains that within the next few years this objective will be met. Finland, which has stressed as its priority an expansion of the supply of care for children aged 1 and 2 years, has announced that by 1995 all children aged 3–7 years, whose parents wish them to participate, will have a place in a subsidized preschool.

By 1990, the movement toward universal preschool for children from the age of $2\frac{1}{2}$ or 3 years until they enter primary school had largely been accomplished in most of Europe. The countries that have not yet achieved this goal expect to achieve it soon. The combined pressure from the educational and child development side, as well as the demand for services to meet the needs of working parents, have made these programs an integral part of social policy generally, and provided a broad-based political constituency in support. Most European programs cover at least the normal school day and year, and are thus longer than similar programs in the United States. In countries where the school day is short, if there is interest in meeting the needs of working parents, the task for the 1990s will be to extend the school day or provide supplementary childcare programs. Nonetheless, existing programs go a long way toward providing childcare while parents work, but within a framework in which mothers' employment status is largely irrelevant.

3. *Care for Children Under 3 Years of Age*

This is the major international childcare focus for the 1990s. Care for children under 3 years of age increasingly involves some combination of parenting or child-rearing leave policies, income support policies, and childcare services. Almost all the advanced industrialized countries provide paid maternity or parenting leave to permit working women to recover physically from childbirth and to enable the family to adapt to a new baby. Some countries provide more extensive paid and job-protected leave as a form of infant—and even toddler—care. These leave policies vary in terms of duration, the proportion of the wage replaced, their availability to fathers as well as mothers, and whether any part of the leave is mandatory for mothers. There is no advanced industrialized country except for the United States without such a national policy. The policy diversity that exists has to do largely with care of 1–2-year olds, not with the care of babies. For "toddlers," some countries stress childcare services; others stress cash benefits to permit at-home parental care; and others offer a menu of options.

3.1 Infant Care: Maternity and/or Parenting Leave

The first component of most infant/toddler care policy packages addresses the needs of infants and their employed parents at the time the child is born and immediately thereafter.

Maternity and/or parenting policies for working parents include paid, job-protected leave and the continuity of health insurance benefits or medical care, often supplemented by additional unpaid, job-protected leave (see Table 2). These policies are designed to assure babies a good start in life and to protect maternal health while maintaining family income. More than 100 countries around the world have such leave policies, including all those in Europe, Canada, Israel, Japan, Singapore, and many developing countries. At least two to three months of paid maternal/parental care is assured an infant, and often as much as six months or longer in European countries.

The availability of maternity and parenting policies is not just a function of high labor force participation rates. Although among those countries with high rates only the United States is without national statutory policies, many countries with far lower participation rates have enacted such laws.

One result of these leave policies, of course, is that out-of-home infant care (care for children under the age of 1) is not an issue in many European countries. Even in countries with very high labor force participation rates among women with children under 3 years, such as Denmark, Finland, and Sweden (75% or higher: far higher than in the United States), very few children under the age of 1 are in care. Since virtually all working women who give birth are covered by leave policies, the child is at home for a good part of its first year, cared for by at least one of its parents. The length of maternity or parenting leave determines when childcare services are needed; and for those in countries with shorter leave policies, infant care services are essential.

In most countries, the benefit that is provided to protect the family against loss of income following childbirth is equal to 100 percent of the mother's or parents' insured wage (the maximum wage covered under social insurance), 90 percent (that wage less social insurance contributions), or a portion of the insured wage (60, 75, or 80%). And, in most countries (but not Canada, Finland, or Sweden) the benefit is tax-free.

All the benefits are financed as either a contributory or noncontributory social insurance benefit. In several countries the employer and the government jointly bear most or all of the total cost, while in others, such as Canada, the employee also contributes. A country's health insurance system (including the paid sick leave program) is the system most likely to carry administrative responsibility for maternity benefits. Israel, however, views this as an independent social insurance benefit; the United Kingdom mandates payments by the employer but provides reimbursement; and Canada and Austria deliver the benefit through the unemployment insurance system. The particular system employed is as much an artifact of the governmental structure of a country as it is of earlier history and ideology.

Traditional maternity policy stems from late nineteenth- and early twentieth-century legislation designed initially to protect the health of pregnant working women, new mothers, and their infants. Only since the 1960s has the goal of protecting employment and labor force attachment become more important.

A second model is based on the importance of parenting, and involving fathers as well as mothers in caring for new babies. A parent insurance benefit provides protection to the new mother before birth, and for 6–12 weeks after birth, but then permits fathers to share equally or partially in the remainder of the entitlement to the post-childbirth leave. Like

Table 2
Paid maternity/parenting leave provisions in selected western countries

Country	Date	Length of leave	Available to fathers	Supplementary benefits
Benefit level at 100% earnings[a]				
Norway	1988	18 wks.	Yes	Yes
Austria	1991	16 wks. + 10 mon. at lower level[b]		Yes[b]
Federal Republic of Germany	1992	14 wks.[c]	Yes	2 yrs. at flat rate[c]
Portugal	1984	3 mon.		Yes
Netherlands	1984	12 wks.		
Sweden	1991	12 mon. + 3 mon. at flat rate[d]	Yes	up to 3 more months; 6 hr. wrk. day, until child is 8
Benefit level at 90% of earnings				
Denmark	1991	24 wks.	Yes	Yes
France	1991	16 wks.[c]		up to 2 yrs.
United Kingdom	1990	6 wks. + 12 wks. at flat rate		Yes Unpaid maternity leave
Benefit level at 80% of earnings				
Finland	1991	$10\frac{1}{2}$ mon.[d]	Yes	2 yrs. at flat rate
Italy	1984	5 mon.		6 months at lower rate
Belgium	1984	14 wks.		
Ireland	1984	14 wks.		
Benefit level at 75% of earnings				
Spain	1984	14 wks.		
Israel	1984	12 wks.		
Benefit level at 60% of earnings				
Canada	1987	25 wks.[d]	Yes	
Benefit level at 50% of earnings				
Greece	1984	12 wks.		

a Up to maximum covered under Social Security b Plus 2 years for low-income single mothers if they cannot find childcare c The last 9 months are available on an income-tested basis d The benefit is taxable

maternity leave, parenting leave includes job, seniority, and benefit protection.

The prototypical illustration for this parent insurance model is Sweden. Sweden provides an 18-month, job-protected leave from work that both parents can share, a cash benefit covering 90 percent of the wages of the parent on leave for one year, and a small flat-rate benefit for an additional three months. The benefit and leave can be used to cover part-time work as well, and thus extend beyond the 18 months. It is expected that within the next few years the cash benefit will cover the full 18 months of permitted leave. All Swedish working mothers take advantage of the policy and about 85 percent return to work by the end of the leave, or by the time their child reaches the first birthday. In 1987, 25 percent of eligible fathers took at least some part of the leave, in addition to the two weeks paid leave all fathers are entitled to at the time of childbirth.

Maternity and parenting benefits are a basic entitlement for all working women—and some working men—in almost all advanced industrialized countries. They constitute modest social policies, but proponents argue that if the goal is to assure children a good start in life, they are an essential part of any country's childcare policy; and, if a second goal is to constrain the demand for infant care services, the duration of the paid leave is equally important, especially in countries with high labor force participation rates by women with very young children.

3.2 Toddler Care: Parenting Benefits and Childcare Services

A critical issue in much of Europe is childcare for children from about 1–$2\frac{1}{2}$ years of age (Moss 1988, 1990; Ergas 1987; EEC 1984; Kamerman and Kahn 1981, 1991). Until recently, expanding the supply of services was the most important childcare policy for this age group.

Currently, the international policy picture is in flux, as European countries experiment with different patterns: extending paid and job-protected leave until children are $1\frac{1}{2}$, 2, or 3 years old; providing cash benefits that support parents who choose to care for their very young children at home; targeting policies on low-income parents or employed parents; expanding the supply of childcare services for the children of working parents. Some countries have chosen a particular policy, others have selected a more diversified policy with a "menu" of options.

The countries that have established extended parental or child-rearing leave appear to have been motivated by some combination of factors, including: low birthrates, labor market shortages, high costs of infant and toddler care, child development concerns, and so forth.

Several countries, including Austria, the Czeck and Slovak Republics, Finland, France, Germany, Hungary, and Sweden are now providing either extended, job-protected paid leave or child-related cash benefits designed to make it possible for some mothers (or parents) of very young children to remain at home for longer periods than the paid parenting/infant care leave allows (Kamerman and Kahn 1981, 1991). For the most part, these are recent developments, and noted here as interesting alternatives to the more prevalent pattern of providing childcare services.

The countries that have expanded their toddler care services have done so largely in response to increases in labor force participation rates of women with very young children. Some countries are also responding to growing pressures for enhancing school (and preschool) readiness.

In contrast to the preschool programs described earlier, the delivery system for toddler care is highly diversified. Family daycare homes and group daycare centers both exist but there are not enough of either. In Denmark and Sweden public subsidies are also provided to permit three or four families to share the costs of a caregiver, who provides the care in the home of one of the families. In France and Finland, a subsidy is available to help pay for in-home care.

In contrast to maternity/parenting benefits (which are already universal in Europe) and preschool programs (which are universal in some countries and approaching that goal in others), provision of childcare services for 1–2-year olds is limited at best. Coverage rates range widely from less than 10 percent in most countries to 20 percent in the United States (largely in family daycare), 33 percent in France, and more than 50 percent in Denmark, (divided equally between group and family daycare) (see Table 1). In Britain, there is practically no care for children under 2, and that provided is for protective purposes only, not for the children of working parents.

In the countries in which preschool programs are part of the education system, programs serving children under 3 years are often under health ministry auspices. However, in a few countries, for example, Spain and Italy, they may also be under education auspices. As already indicated, the Scandinavian model constitutes an autonomous childcare program for all children under compulsory school age, including toddlers, and is administered under social welfare auspices.

Extensive public subsidies are provided for toddler care but, unlike the preschool programs, they are neither free nor universal. Parents pay income-related fees that cover between 10 and 50 percent of program costs, depending on the country. Only in France do payroll contributions by employers help to finance these programs. Fees often do not vary much between group programs and publicly sponsored family daycare.

Regardless of the program type, these services for very young children are designed primarily to provide care for the children of working parents. Eligibility is limited to these children, and to children with special social or psychological needs. Priority cases for acceptance include the children of working parents, in particular those from single-parent families; children in low-income families; children in need of protective or compensatory programs; immigrant children; and sometimes, in some countries such as Sweden and Italy, physically handicapped children.

The infant toddler group programs do not have consistent or uniform curricula and the family daycare programs have even less (Moss 1988). Programs usually operate 10–12 hours per day, and are often open from 6.30 a.m. in the morning to 6.30 p.m. in the evening. Children usually attend a full day. In some countries, such as Denmark and Sweden, where mothers are likely to work part-time, children may be in care only part of the day. In southern Europe these programs usually close for about one month during the summer, but elsewhere they are open all year. Although age of entry is often closely linked to the length of maternity/parenting leave, new places are often available only in September, when the older children leave the program to enter the preschool program. Shortages exist everywhere; no country describes an adequate supply of services for this age group (Moss 1988, 1990).

The dominant program for this age group is family daycare, often because the supply of places in group facilities is so limited, and not necessarily because parents prefer this type of care (Moss 1988, 1990). In contrast to the United States, much of family daycare in countries such as Denmark, Finland, France, Germany, and Sweden is under public sponsorship, with providers often recruited, trained, supervised, and even paid by municipal childcare administrators or local social agency administrators and staff. A significant group of private providers exists as well in many countries.

Finland is the only country that has made expanded coverage for children under 3 years the primary goal of its childcare policy, and it has done this in the context of a dual policy thrust: providing parents with a choice between a subsidized place in a childcare program or a cash benefit to support parenting at home. The government has announced that there are now sufficient places in municipal (public) family daycare or group care facilities to care for all the children whose parents want them in out-of-home care. Current estimates suggest that there is adequate public childcare coverage for about 45 percent of children under 3 years, and that another 10 percent are cared for in their own home by a caregiver whose salary is partially subsidized by the government. This definition of "adequate coverage" is based on the premise that the remainder of the cohort (45%) use parenting leave to cover care.

4. Conclusion

All the European countries have acknowledged the importance and value of preschool programs for 3–6-year olds, whether or not mothers are working, for socialization and educational reasons, as well as the role these services play in caring for children while their parents work. These programs are increasingly universal and free, and, even if voluntary, they are used by all children whose parents can obtain a place. Even those countries that have established an autonomous childcare program separate from the education system are aiming toward universal coverage. All the countries stress age and developmentally appropriate programming. The programs are publicly funded and often publicly operated. Variations in quality (group size; staff–child ratios; staff qualifications) are the most dramatic variable between countries, as more and more countries strive to expand supply to cover the whole cohort.

Almost all the industrialized countries (other than the United States) and many developing countries have recognized the necessity of establishing maternity/parenting policies that permit working parents some time off after childbirth to recover physically and to adapt to parenting and to a new baby without losing employment or income. Most Western countries now include adoptive as well as natural parents in their policies. The only differences among the countries have to do with the length of leave, the level of benefit, and whether benefits are available to fathers as well as mothers. In effect, infant care in many countries is once again becoming parental care, with the society protecting family income against the loss of earnings when a parent withdraws from the labor force to stay at home. The absence of parental care during infancy may be the next social risk that social policy will protect against.

There is a growing trend in Europe to extend parenting leave in some form, so as to make it possible for one parent to remain at home until a child is 1½-, 2-, or 3-years old (Kamerman and Kahn 1991). At the same time, there is a continued recognition of the importance of expanding the supply of childcare services for toddler-aged children, together with concern with the quality and, even more, with the cost of these programs. Indeed, this may be why some countries are exploring alternative policies or policy options. Coverage is nowhere near adequate in any country, and only Sweden and Finland have announced any significant commitment to expanding these services. With the exception of the United States, there are no proprietary childcare programs in any advanced industrialized countries except for a few in the United Kingdom—the country with the least adequate childcare provision of any of the major European countries. Nor, again in contrast to the United States, is employer sponsorship viewed as having major significance, or being the way to achieve needed coverage—despite an earlier history of such sponsorship, especially in Italy and elsewhere.

Increasingly, childcare, preschool, and early childhood education is viewed as a public responsibility and as an entitlement for children. Although some countries have introduced childcare programs to facilitate women's employment, others stress the child development consequences of these policies and programs, and still others view these policies as strategies for ensuring that women are willing to have children and that children are better prepared for formal schooling. Regardless, all these countries are prepared to invest heavily in these policies, and to continue to do so.

See also: Preschool Education: Worldwide Trends; Preschool Education, History of; Childcare and Preschool Effects; Early Childhood Interventions

References

Commission of the European Communities 1984, *Day-Care Facilities and Services for Children Under the Age of Three in the European Community*. Commission of the European Communities, Luxembourg

Ergas Y 1990 Child care policies in comparative perspective: An introductory discussion. (Prepared for the Conference of National Experts on Lone Parents: The Economic Challenge of Changing Family Structures, December 15–17, 1987.) In: Duskin E (ed.) 1990 *Lone Parent Families: The Economic Challenge*. OECD Social Policy Studies No. 8. OECD, Paris

Hayes C D, Palmer J L, Zaslow M J (eds.) 1990 *Who Cares for America's Children? Child Care Policy for the 1990s*. National Academy Press, Washington, DC

Kamerman S B, Kahn A J 1981 *Child Care, Family Benefits and Working Parents: A Study in Comparative Policy*. Columbia University Press, New York

Kamerman S B, Kahn A J 1989a The possibilities for child and family policy: A cross-national perspective. In: Macchiarola F J, Gartner A (eds.) 1989 *Caring for America's Children*. The Academy of Political Science, New York

Kamerman S B, Kahn A J 1989b Family policy: Has the United States learned from Europe? In: Hula R, Anderson E (eds.) 1989 Symposium on Family Policy, *Policy Studies Review*

Kamerman S B, Kahn A J (eds.) 1991 *Child Care, Parental Leave, and the Under 3s: Policy Innovation in Europe*. Auburn House, New York

Moss P (coordinator) 1988 *Childcare and equality of opportunity: Consolidated report to the European Commission*. Prepared for the Commission of the European Community, London
Moss P 1990 *Childcare in the European Communities 1985–1990*. Commission of the European Communities, European Commission Childcare Network, Brussels
Olmsted P P, Weikart D P (eds.) 1989 *How Nations Serve Young Children: Profiles of Child Care and Education in 14 Countries*. High/Scope Press, Ypsilanti, Michigan
Ruopp R, Travers J, Glantz F, Coelen C 1979 *Children at the Center: Final Report of the National Day Care Study*. Abt Associates, Cambridge, Massachusetts
Saraceno C 1984 The Social Construction of Childhood: Child Care and Education Policies in Italy and the United States. *Soc. Prob.* 31(3): 351–63

Further Reading

Kamerman S B 1988 Maternity and parenting benefits: An international overview. In: Zigler E, Frank M (eds.) 1988 *The Parental Leave Crisis: Toward a National Policy*. Yale University Press, New Haven, Connecticut
Langsted O, Sommer D in press Changing socialization patterns, child care policies and programs in contemporary Denmark. In: Cochran M (ed.) in press *International Handbook of Daycare Policies and Programs*. Greenwood Press, Westport, Connecticut

S. B. Kamerman

Childhood

In this entry, important changes that occur during childhood are examined. Included in the survey are changes in: (a) physical growth; (b) social and emotional development; (c) language; and (d) cognition.

Childhood begins when infancy ends, and this, for the purposes of this entry, is with the advent of children's first two-word sentences, usually between the ages of 16 and 20 months. The word "infancy" derives from the Latin and translates roughly as "without language," or more literally, "no speech." Childhood is followed by adolescence, and the onset of puberty is used here as the endpoint of childhood. Thus, the period of childhood to be reviewed here ranges from the beginning of true productive language, at approximately 18 months, to the beginning of puberty, at about 12 or 13 years.

1. Physical and Motor Development

Different organs and physical systems develop at different rates. The head and the central nervous system grow most rapidly during the neonatal and early childhood periods, with the head and brain reaching about 90 percent of their adult size by age 5. The reproductive system grows the slowest, with sexual maturity being achieved at puberty. Although adolescence begins with the enlargement of the reproductive organs, there is a one- to two-year period of low fertility in both boys and girls, thus extending the period humans spend as nonreproductive (Tanner 1978).

Generally, boys and girls grow taller at about the same rate until approximately 11 to 12 years of age. During this same time, girls have a growth spurt for approximately two years that gives them a temporary height and strength advantage over boys. Thereafter, boys grow more rapidly than girls until about age 14 or 15, at which time children are practically fully grown (Tanner 1978).

By early childhood, children are walking, although the toddling 2-year old lacks the gross-motor skills of older children and adolescents. Children's gross-motor skills are refined over the preschool years, with children walking and running in a way that is qualitatively similar to adults by age 6. Fine-motor skills develop gradually over the preschool years. For example, children are not able to copy accurately a visual design until about 5 years of age, with substantial improvements in drawing skills still developing over the school years (Goodenough 1926). Such fine-motor skills are important in technological societies for writing and for many activities in traditional societies, such as weaving.

2. Social and Emotional Development

2.1 Parents' Influence on Children's Behavior

Social development of children follows a general pattern from home/self-centered to external/other-centered behavior. As children grow more physically capable, they become increasingly independent of their parents and experience the broader world outside of their homes. Contemporary behavioral genetics theories hold that genetic factors (a child's genotype) become increasingly influential with age in determining what environments children will experience, thus affecting greatly their social and intellectual development. In other words, with increasing age, children actively choose which activities they engage in, with these choices being heavily influenced by genetically determined dispositions (Scarr 1992).

However, children's relationships with their parents continue to influence their behavior outside the home. For example, emotional relationships between children and their parents tend to be stable from late infancy through childhood, with securely attached infants becoming securely attached children (Main et al. 1985). Moreover, quality of attachment in infancy (secure, insecure, or disorganized) has been found to be related to later social and intellectual development, with children who were rated as securely attached as infants or toddlers developing a better self-image, being more effective problem solvers, and being better liked by peers than children who were insecurely attached (e.g., Cohn 1990).

Parenting style also affects children's behavior. The children of authoritarian parents, who establish firm rules and frequently enforce them by use of physical punishment, often tend to be withdrawn, discontented, aggressive, and distrustful of others. Children of permissive parents, who generally exert little control over their children, often lack self-reliance, self-control, and explorative tendencies. Children of authoritative parents, who set clear standards and enforce rules with warmth and explanations, often are independent, socially responsive, self-controlled, explorative, and self-reliant (Baumrind 1967).

2.2 Development of Peer Relations

During the preschool years (ages 2 to 5), children's social interaction with peers increases substantially. As their interaction increases, so also do conflicts. Preschoolers who are friends fight with one another just as much as preschoolers who are only acquaintances. Conflicts are less intense between friends than between nonfriends and are more likely to result in nearly equal outcomes for the involved children (Hartup et al. 1988).

Many preschoolers take part in parallel play, two or more children playing near each other, possibly involved in similar activities but not engaged in mutual, or cooperative play. This semisocial parallel play may be a precursor to more social forms of interaction and truly cooperative play, which increases over early childhood as children become more able to take the perspective of others.

Throughout childhood, children segregate themselves into same-sex groups for play and other social activities; this same-sex segregation is universal and increases during the early school years (Maccoby and Jacklin 1987). Boys and girls play differently, with boys engaging in more rough-and-tumble play and centering their interactions on movable toys, whereas girls tend to engage in dramatic play and table activities. During the preschool years, and through adolescence, girls are more apt to play in smaller groups than boys.

Dominance hierarchies, or "pecking orders," in children's groups are established as a result of children testing each other in games and activities that produce clear winners and losers. Dominance hierarchies serve to reduce antagonism within the group, distribute scarce resources, and focus division of labor. Younger children are more apt to establish dominance hierarchies based upon their physical abilities to control other children. As children grow older, and most especially at puberty, other factors such as sexual maturity tend to become important in the establishment of a dominant position in the peer group (see Shaffer 1988).

2.3 Prosocial Behavior

The development of prosocial behavior, behavior that is intended to benefit others, is based on the development of empathy. Beginning at about age 2, children begin to understand that others have needs and feelings that are different from their own. Their empathic abilities improve as they become less egocentric (that is, less self-centered in their perspective-taking abilities) and as their role-taking abilities improve. By about age 11, children have developed a capacity for empathy with another person's life experience rather than simply with a single event in the person's life.

Sharing is seen in toddlers, but is more common in older children. Older preschool children are more prone to try to "help," such as assisting a parent or other adult accomplish some task. These forms of prosocial behavior increase over the school years to about 9 years of age when "helping" activities seem to level off (see Shaffer 1988).

2.4 Aggression in Children

Aggression is not limited to one gender or one age group of children, although boys, on average, are physically more aggressive than girls. The frequency and nature of aggressive behavior change with age. Aggressive behavior is common among young preschoolers, but decreases in frequency from ages 2 through 5. Levels of aggression are fairly stable over childhood, with aggressive toddlers becoming aggressive school age children (Cummings et al. 1989).

2.5 Development of the Self

The development of the concept of the self is very important for social development. About 75 percent of children show some form of self-recognition (such as recognizing themselves in the mirror) by the age of 18–24 months. Late in their second year, children begin using pronouns in their language (*I, me, my*, and *mine*) that indicate a differentiation between themselves and others (Lewis and Brooks-Gunn 1979).

Initially, children's verbal references distinguishing themselves from others are centered on physical characteristics ("I'm stronger," "I'm bigger"). Only when children approach adolescence do they begin making more psychological, or abstract, references distinguishing themselves from others ("I'm happy," "I'm smart") (Montemayor and Eisen 1977).

3. Language Development

Beginning with their first combination of words into simple sentences at about 18 months, children's utterances become longer and more complex. Over the preschool years, children of all cultures learn the grammatical rules of their language, often applying them when not appropriate. This is reflected by overregularization, in which children use rules in situations where they do not apply (e.g., in English, saying "goed," "runned," or "mouses"). Children's syntax (the grammatical structure of their sentences) increasingly comes to resemble that of adults in their culture, as reflected by their formation of language constructions such as negatives, questions, and the use of relational terms. At all ages, children's receptive language (i.e., what they can understand) is more advanced than their productive language (i.e., what they can produce). By age 5, children's language greatly resembles that of adults. Although the structure of children's language does increase in complexity over the school years (e.g., in English, use of passive tense, more consistent noun/verb agreement), the differences between the grammar used by 6- and 7-year olds and by adults are subtle and minor (de Villiers and de Villiers 1978).

The ability to learn a new language is greatest in early childhood and wanes until adolescence, when second-language learning often becomes especially difficult. Adolescents and adults who successfully learn the syntax of a second language rarely sound like native speakers but continue to have decided accents, unlike children, who can master both the syntax and phonology of a new language "like a native."

Semantics (the meaning of language terms) also develops markedly through childhood. The number of words children have in their productive vocabularies grows rapidly beginning at about 2 years of age, increasing to between 8,000 and 14,000 words by the first grade, with individual words becoming more elaboratively encoded and associations with other words in memory becoming stronger and more numerous (see Bjorklund 1989).

Over childhood, children learn to categorize word concepts into natural language categories, first acquiring concepts at a basic level (e.g., chairs, cars) before learning to categorize according to superordinate categories (e.g., furniture, vehicles).

Children's representations can be expressed in terms of scripts, which are a form of schematic organization, with real-world events arranged in terms of temporal and causal relations between components of the event (e.g., who did what to whom and when). Preschool children's attempts at remembering sequences of events are based on scripts. Moreover, parents help young children form narratives in remembering events by asking them questions that focus on the important things to remember about events, such as who was involved, what was done, where did it occur, and what was the sequence of acts (see Fivush and Hudson 1990).

4. Cognitive Development

4.1 Representation

Developing alongside language late in the second year of life are imagery, fantasy play, and the ability to delay, or defer imitation. Piaget (1962) proposed that the representations of young children were symbolic but intuitive and illogical (preoperational period), becoming logical at some stage between the ages of 5 and 7 years, although still tied to concrete objects (the stage of concrete operations). Beginning in early adolescence, children's thinking was described by Piaget as abstract, with "hypothetico-deductive reasoning" characterizing thought (formal operations).

Experiments by Flavell and his colleagues have shown the limits of symbolic representation in young children by investigating their knowledge about the distinction between appearance and reality (e.g., Flavell et al. 1986). For example, in some experiments, children watched as white milk was poured into a filtered glass to appear red, or they were shown objects that had uncharacteristic sounds or smells (e.g., socks that smelled like peanut butter). Questions to the children then focused on two areas: what the objects looked like, "how they look to your eyes right now"; and the actual identity of the objects, "how they really and truly are." Somewhat surprisingly, Flavell et al. (1986) reported that most 3-year olds could not solve these apparently simple problems, even with explicit training, causing the authors to conclude that 3-year olds did not have even a minimal understanding of the appearance–reality distinction. Flavell et al. (1986) speculated that 3-year olds are unable to represent an object in more than one form at a time (dual encoding) and so base their answers on either the appearance (the milk looks red, so it really and truly *is* red) or the actual identity (the rock-like sponge is a sponge, so it *looks* like a sponge) of an object. With age, children become more adept at dual encoding, although it is not until late childhood or early adolescence before truly abstract distinctions can be made between the appearance and the reality of things.

During childhood, children develop naive "theories" of how the world works, and these theories reflect, in part, their representational abilities. For example, they learn what is animate and what is not, and what characteristics are attributed to the living and the nonliving. Children aged 3 and 4 develop theories of number, learning the one-to-one correspondence between count words and objects counted, that the last word in a count series reflects the total number of objects in the set (cardinal principle), and that anything, tangible or intangible, can be counted (Gelman and Gallistel 1978).

4.2 Learning and Remembering

Although most learning and memory tasks are mastered more easily by older than by younger children, there are some exceptions, notably in implicit memory. Implicit memory refers to memory for information that the individual did not explicitly set out to learn but was acquired in the process of performing related cognitive activity. For example, implicit memory is reflected in tasks where subjects are asked to make decisions about the perceptual characteristics of words (e.g., CHERRY: "Does it have an H in it?" or "Is it written in lower-case letters?") and later, unexpectedly, asked to recall the words or to complete word fragments (che—y). Because subjects do not explicitly attend to the meaning of words, performance on these tasks, when compared to proper controls, reflects the amount of information people acquire implicitly. Unlike explicit, or intentional, memory tasks, there are no age differences in implicit memory over childhood, suggesting that the processes of implicit memory are fully functional in school-age children (Naito 1990).

Age differences are dramatic, however, for explicit learning and memory tasks, where children intentionally attempt to solve problems. One popular approach to studying children's problem-solving behavior has been to evaluate strategies, usually defined as goal-directed, effortful, cognitive operations that are potentially available to consciousness.

Children aged 2 and 3 will use simple strategies to solve problems, such as staring at the place where a toy was hidden before they are allowed to retrieve it. Young children fail to use more complex strategies spontaneously, such as rehearsing or grouping items by meaning in a memory test; however, they can often be trained to use such strategies with corresponding improvements in their performance, a phenomenon referred to as "production deficiency." Research has found that when children are just learning to use a strategy there is a phase when they spontaneously produce the strategy without enhancing their task performance. Miller (1990) has referred to this as a "utilization deficiency," and describes it as a transition phase between nonstrategy use and effective strategic behavior.

Young children usually require more explicit training before they benefit from a strategy than older children, although even preschoolers will use a strategy when provided with familiar materials and clear instructions. Young children behave strategically only under highly favorable tasks conditions; with age, children broaden the situations in which they will use effective strategies (see Bjorklund 1989).

Age differences in explicit learning and memory tasks have been attributed to many different factors. For example, with age, children process information more quickly and experience less interference from both external sources (e.g., task-irrelevant stimuli) and internal sources (e.g., task-irrelevant thoughts) (Harnishfeger and Bjorklund 1993). Also, older children typically have more world knowledge than younger children, with the knowledge advantage influencing how information is processed (see Bjorklund 1989).

A particularly effective demonstration of the effect of knowledge on children's cognitive performance comes from an experiment by Schneider et al. (1989). In their study, third-, fifth-, and seventh-grade children were classified as either experts or novices for the game of soccer, and further classified, within each expertise group, as high or low IQ. The children were then given a text comprehension test on a soccer-related story. Soccer experts, regardless of their level of IQ, performed better than soccer novices. In short, having detailed background knowledge for the story overrode the effect of IQ on text comprehension.

Young children's problem-solving is often done "out loud" or by using physical prompts, and only in later childhood becomes covert. For example, preschool children will initially solve simple addition problems by physically counting their fingers or other external markers. They later count or add out loud, and only at the age of 7 or 8 years begin to solve problems of arithmetic mentally. Berk (1986) reported that the amount of "private speech" (i.e., children talking to themselves) while solving arithmetic problems was positively related to intelligence at Grade 1 but not at Grade 3, demonstrating that brighter children internalize their problem-solving sooner than less bright children.

Another factor that develops gradually over childhood and influences children's problem-solving is metacognition, namely, the knowledge a person has of his or her cognitive skills and the ability to monitor task performance and make adjustments toward achieving a goal. Older children are more aware of both endogenous and exogenous factors that influence attention, communication, imitation, memory, and reading than younger children and are better at evaluating the effectiveness of their attempts at task performance (see Bjorklund 1989). Young children generally overestimate their performance on cognitive tasks, thinking that they will remember more items on a memory test or achieve more in school than they actually will (Stipek and MacIver 1989).

Children's poor metacognition is generally viewed as a detriment to effective cognition, and understandably so. However, because young children are out of touch with their actual cognitive and physical abilities, they are less apt to be discouraged by their low levels of performance and thus tend to persist at tasks and attempt new ones where a better informed child, with a more realistic assessment of his or her performance, may not. This, and other aspects of young children's immature cognitive abilities may actually be adaptive and should not be viewed as simply ineffective thinking that must be overcome by instructions (Bjorklund and Green 1992).

4.3 Culture, Schooling, and Cognitive Development

Humans have evolved certain cognitive abilities to deal with problems encountered over thousands of years, and it can be assumed that children worldwide possess the same basic neurological hardware for developing these cognitive skills. However, which skills develop and how they are expressed will vary with cultural experience. Different cultures will value and foster different cognitive skills. Cognition always occurs within a cultural context and can never be evaluated out of that context.

Perhaps the most dramatic differences in cognitive development are observed between children from schooled and nonschooled cultures. Children who attend school learn to divorce their thinking from specific contexts. They more readily classify information on the basis of abstract criteria, reason about things for which they have no prior knowledge, and use strategies to learn and remember information (Rogoff 1990). However, when given the proper contextual supports, unschooled children perform comparably to schooled children. For example, nonschooled children are much less apt to use memory strategies and thus they perform poorly on tasks in which they are asked to remember unrelated pieces of information (such as words). Performance differences disappear, however, when children are asked to remember contextually relevant information (Rogoff 1990).

5. *The Significance of Childhood*

Childhood in humans is longer than that of any other mammal. This extended childhood has great significance for the species. Humans, more than any other animal, depend on learning for survival. Moreover, human development cannot be understood out of the cultural context in which it occurs. Children require time to learn the complicated procedures and the social web of relationships at the center of all cultures, and the extended childhood provides the time needed to learn what must be learned. Humans are not the only species with complex social organization, but the variety of human cultures is far greater than that of any other species. The diversity of cultures in which any particular child may find himself or herself necessitates that learning be flexible. Unlike the social insects, children are not genetically programmed for certain social roles. Slow growth and prolonged childhood equips a person not only with time to learn the ways of their specific culture but also with mental and social flexibility, so that a given child can become a weaver, hunter, navigator, or computer programmer, depending on the cultural apprenticeship provided.

See also: Human Development, Stages in; Piaget's Theory of Human Development; Physical Growth and Development: Universal Changes and Individual Differences; Human Development: Research Methodology; Social Cognitive Theory of Human Development; Family, School, and Social Capital

References

Baumrind D 1967 Child care practices anteceding three patterns of preschool behavior. *Genet. Psychol. Monogr.* 75(1): 43–88

Berk L E 1986 Relationship of elementary school children's private speech to behavioral accompaniment to task, attention, and task performance. *Dev. Psychol.* 22(5): 671–80

Bjorklund D F 1989 *Children's Thinking: Developmental Function and Individual Differences.* Brooks/Cole, Pacific Grove, California

Bjorklund D F, Green B L 1992 The adaptive nature of cognitive immaturity. *Am. Psychol.* 47(1): 46–54

Cohn D A 1990 Child–mother attachment of six-year-olds and social competence at school. *Child Dev.* 61(1): 152–62

Cummings E M, Iannotti R J, Zahn-Waxler C 1989 Aggression between peers in early childhood: Individual continuity and developmental change. *Child Dev.* 60(4): 887–95

de Villiers J G, de Villiers P A 1978 *Language Acquisition.* Harvard University Press, Cambridge, Massachusetts

Fivush R, Hudson J A (eds.) 1990 *Knowing and Remembering in Young Children.* Cambridge University Press, Cambridge

Flavell J H, Green F L, Flavell E R 1986 The development of children's knowledge about the appearance–reality distinction. *Monographs of the Society for Research in Child Development* 51(1): 1–68

Gelman R, Gallistel C 1978 *The Child's Understanding of Number.* Harvard University Press, Cambridge, Massachusetts

Goodenough F L 1926 *The Measurement of Intelligence through Drawing.* Holt Publishing, Yonkers, New York

Harnishfeger K K, Bjorklund D F 1993 The ontogeny of inhibition mechanisms: A renewed approach to cognitive development. In: Howe M L, Pasnak R (eds.) 1993 *Emerging Themes in Cognitive Development. Vol. 1: Foundations.* Springer-Verlag, New York

Hartup W W, Laursen B, Stewart M I, Eastenson A 1988 Conflict and the friendship relations of young children. *Child Dev.* 59(6): 1590–1600

Lewis M, Brooks-Gunn J 1979 *Social Cognition and the Acquisition of Self.* Plenum Press, New York

Maccoby E E, Jacklin C N 1987 Gender segregation in childhood. In: Reese H W (ed.) 1987 *Advances in Child Development and Behavior,* Vol. 20. Academic Press, San Diego, California

Main M, Kaplan N, Cassidy J 1985 Security in infancy, childhood, and adulthood: A move to the level of representation. In: Bretherton I, Waters E (eds.) 1985 *Growing Points of Attachment Theory and Research.* University of Chicago Press, Chicago, Illinois

Miller P H 1990 The development of strategies of selective attention. In: Bjorklund D F (ed.) 1990 *Children's Strategies: Contemporary Views of Cognitive Development.* Erlbaum, Hillsdale, New Jersey

Montemayor R, Eisen M 1977 The development of self-conceptions from childhood to adolescence. *Dev. Psychol.* 13(4): 314–19

Naito M 1990 Repetition priming in children and adults: Age-related dissociation between implicit and explicit memory. *Journal of Experimental Child Psychology* 50(3): 462–84

Piaget J 1962 *Play, Dreams, and Imitation in Childhood.* Norton, New York

Rogoff B 1990 *Apprenticeship in Thinking: Cognitive Development in Social Context.* Oxford University Press, New York

Scarr S 1992 Developmental theories for the 1990s: Development and individual differences. *Child Dev.* 63(1): 1–19

Schneider W, Körkel J, Weinert F E 1989 Domain-specific knowledge and memory performance: A comparison of high- and low-aptitude children. *J. Educ. Psychol.* 81(3): 306–12

Shaffer D R 1988 *Social and Personality Development*, 2nd edn. Brooks/Cole, Pacific Grove, California

Stipek D, MacIver D 1989 Developmental change in children's assessment of intellectual competence. *Child Dev.* 60(3): 521–38

Tanner J M 1978 *Fetus into Man: Physical Growth from Conception to Maturity*. Harvard University Press, Cambridge, Massachusetts

D. F. Bjorklund; W. S. Cassel

Children and Youth at Risk

Throughout history, children have endured countless hardships. They have been exposed to cruel mistreatment, excessive and brutal varieties of work, as well as physical and emotional abuse. In fact, until relatively modern times, children were considered chattel and treated as such (Hart 1991). Although the twentieth century has experienced marked changes in attitudes toward children, even in 1990 a quarter of a million children died every week from preventable illnesses and malnutrition. A UNICEF report, entitled *The State of the World's Children 1990*, indicated that "in many countries, poverty, child malnutrition and ill health are advancing again after decades of steady retreat" (committee 1990 p. 128). According to the report, every new day witnesses 6,000 children dying of pneumonia, 7,000 children dying of diarrhoeal dehydration, and 8,000 children dying of measles, whooping cough, or tetanus (p. 130). These facts have led to considerable concern over the status of the world's children, and in 1989 the United Nations held a Convention on the Rights of the Child. The articles developed at the convention outlined basic, fundamental rights for the world's children and provided a focal point for international child advocacy. While the United States was not one of the initial 54 countries to sign the articles, United States educators have become increasingly concerned over at-risk children and are engaging in considerable discussion of the many relevant issues involving this population. This entry summarizes the discourse regarding children and youth in at-risk circumstances.

1. Background

Since 1980, shifting political, social, and economic forces have dramatically changed conditions for the world's children. A war in the Middle East, the fall of the Soviet Union, an end to statutory apartheid in South Africa, and other events have reshaped the global educational landscape and left children and youth in a variety of at-risk situations (Glenn 1992, Murphy 1992, New 1992, Rust 1992). Educational systems must respond to these changing circumstances if they are to address the unique, individual needs of these children.

The 1980s were a period of social change and educational upheaval in the United States. Public schools reverberated from the aftershocks created by the publication of *A Nation At Risk* (National Commission on Excellence in Education 1983). Soon after the publication of this report, school reform packages were introduced in many states. These packages included raising academic standards, increasing graduation requirements, and evaluating schools through statewide assessment. The expressed intent of the reform efforts was to produce students with the skills and knowledge that would allow them to be competitive with their counterparts from countries such as Germany and Japan in the modern, technological, and global workplace.

At some point during this decade of school reform, another movement gradually gathered momentum. At first only a few educators expressed concern over the possible negative consequences of reform efforts for some children. Soon, however, hardly a day passed without a headline proclaiming that not only schools, but children and youth in the United States were at risk—from increasing levels of poverty, homelessness, substance abuse, or youth violence. International comparisons began to include not only achievement test scores, but also such factors as infant mortality rates, maternal health indicators, and incidences of teenage pregnancy.

In spite of this sudden proliferation of information about at-risk children, many United States educators of the 1990s are seeking guidance in developing effective policies and implementing successful programs. Besides, the relevant issues encompass ethical, cultural, and political dimensions; many United States educators feel overwhelmed, paralyzed into inaction, and are asking the question: "What do we mean by a child being 'at risk'?"

2. Definitions of "At Risk"

Definitions of "at risk" must take into account the social, economic, and cultural environment of the particular child. The term "at risk" may refer to the stress experienced by a Turkish immigrant child in a Scandinavian country (Glenn 1992); it may refer to the adjustments demanded of a South African child in a postapartheid society (Murphy 1992); or it may refer to the low self-esteem and cultural devaluation experienced by an Alaskan Eskimo child (New 1992). The term "at risk" is necessarily culture bound, and in the broader sense, may refer to any child or youth whose own beliefs, values, or cultural norms conflict with the dominant culture's social and educational environment (Davis and McCaul 1990).

Not surprisingly then, most definitions of "at risk" in the literature tend to be broad and inclusive. For example, Catterall and Cota-Robles (1988) described three common conceptions of at risk: (a) children from poor families; (b) children with different cultural backgrounds or minorities; and (c) children from limited English-speaking families. Levin (cited in NSBA Monograph 1989) defined at-risk students as "those who lack the home and community resources to benefit from traditional schooling practices. Because of poverty, cultural obstacles, or linguistic differences, these children tend to have low academic achievement and high dropout rates. Such students are heavily concentrated among minority groups, immigrants, non-English speaking families, and economically disadvantaged populations" (p. 6).

Natriello et al. (1990) delineated four perspectives that underlie most common definitions of at risk: (a) culturally deprived/socially disadvantaged; (b) educationally deprived; (c) at risk according to indicators or predictors of educational difficulty; and (d) at risk as the general population of children and youth. The first perspective has its roots in the reform movements of the mid-1960s and emphasizes the relative disadvantage with which some students begin their public school experience. The disadvantage may entail some family "shortcomings" such as low socioeconomic status or lack of a stimulating environment. Proponents of this view stressed early childhood intervention in order to compensate for experiential deficits of early childhood. In addition, the funding for federal programs aimed at remedial education in the United States public schools, such as the federal Chapter 1 and Migrant Education programs, are based on this perspective. Chapter 1 funds are allocated to economically disadvantaged schools but, at the school level, any child with the potential to benefit from remedial instruction may be served by the program and receive individualized or small group instruction aimed at raising his or her educational attainment. The Migrant Education Program also provides small group or individualized instruction for the children of migrant agricultural workers.

The second perspective, that of the disadvantaged as "educationally deprived," focuses upon the school program and the social, cultural, or political factors contributing to educational deprivation. Proponents of this perspective argue that the cultural differences should not be viewed as cultural deficiencies and that proponents of the culturally deprived/socially disadvantaged perspective have thus inadvertently promoted prejudicial treatment of minority groups such as African Americans. Further, the cultural difference/deprivation perspective tends to "blame the victim" instead of focusing upon school reform and restructuring.

The third perspective utilizes the term "at risk" to refer to children who have certain characteristics which point to possible educational problems in the future. Hence, the presence of certain individual and/or environmental characteristics place a child at risk and may serve as a predictor of later educational outcomes such as low educational achievement, dropout behavior, or social problems in the school environment. Interventions are then tailored toward identified students. This approach resembles the special education process of identifying students and then providing them with specially designed instruction. Nevertheless, from this perspective, many students other than those with disabilities are now considered as at risk. For example, it is well-established that characteristics such as being male, being a member of an ethnic minority group, or being from a family of low socioeconomic status are correlated with higher rates of dropping out of school. While the future-orientation of this perspective allows for intervention strategies, labeling a student as at risk may lead to problems of stigmatizing students or creating lowered teacher expectations, particularly for children from minority groups.

The final perspective, that of youth in general being at risk, is the broadest and most encompassing. "This perspective essentially defines the entire population or at least the entire youth population as potentially disadvantaged. By not identifying any one segment of the population as being disadvantaged, this conceptualization of at risk places the whole burden of addressing the problems of disadvantaged youth on an examination of the institutions that are intended to support and develop young people" (Natriello et al. 1990 p. 11). This perspective also emphasizes the impact on the youth of the United States of social and demographic changes such as the rise in single-parent families, youth criminal activity, alcohol and drug use, sexually transmitted disease, and the increasing number of children living in poverty. It is a perspective that focuses upon the need for broad, national attitudinal and political changes as a precursor to addressing the problem of youth at risk.

Each of the perspectives outlined above has potential strengths and weaknesses in terms of its implied intervention strategies. The culturally deprived perspective, for example, suggests active early intervention to remediate experiential deficits. Clearly, many early intervention efforts with students determined to be at risk of educational failure—for example, the Headstart Program—have enjoyed considerable success. As noted by proponents of the educational deprivation perspective, however, there is an inherent danger in cultural deprivation approaches of assuming that culturally different is culturally deficient. Similarly, each perspective has an implicit intervention strategy with its accompanying strengths and weaknesses.

3. Circumstances of At-risk Students

As with definitions of at risk, a variety of theories and perspectives exist regarding the circumstances of children at risk. Further, the circumstances of at-risk children vary widely from culture to culture. Circumstances may vary from the stress experienced by a South American youth adjusting to Swedish society (Ehn 1990) to the abject poverty and starvation facing some children in South Africa (Murphy 1992). In the United States, considerable concern has arisen over the increasing number of children experiencing problems such as substance abuse, teenage pregnancy, alcohol or drug effects as babies, and youth violence. Nevertheless, five key indicators are commonly associated with educationally at-risk children: (a) living in an economically poor household; (b) having minority/racial group identity; (c) living in a single-parent family; (d) having a poorly educated mother; and (e) having a non-English-language background. All of these indicators are correlated with poor performance in school, although not always for commonly understood or agreed upon reasons. Moreover, the indicators are not independent, and children with several indicators are at the greatest risk of educational failure. In discussing these indicators, there is a clear danger of stereotyping and stigmatizing specific groups of children. Not all poor children, for example, are educationally disadvantaged, and neither are all minority children, nor all children living in single-parent households. Many students are survivors and manifest remarkable resilience. Further, the individual circumstances of children need to be taken into account—students may be at risk because their value systems may be in conflict with the established norm for the school or community. Their diversity from the norm may not be valued, respected, or tolerated; therefore, they too are at a high risk for poor overall adjustment to school. Nevertheless, each of the five key indicators cited above clearly is associated with low levels of educational achievement. These are discussed below.

3.1 Poverty

Children represent the largest and fastest growing group of the poor in the United States. It is estimated that there are more than 12.6 million poor children presently living in that country—nearly 20 percent of all children under the age of 18 (Children's Defense Fund 1990, Reed and Sautter 1990). More United States citizens are poor in the 1990s than before the War on Poverty was initiated in 1964, despite the fact that the official United States' poverty rate for all citizens in 1989 edged slightly downward to 13.1 percent. Nearly 40 million people of all ages live in families that fall below the official poverty line (US$7,704 for a family of two; US$9,435 for a family of three; and US$12,092 for a family of four). Again, 40 percent of this population are children (Hodgkinson 1991, Reed and Sautter 1990).

Further, in the United States of the 1990s, the younger a child is the greater are his or her chances of being poor. Of all children age 3 and under, over four million children, 23 percent are poor; nearly 22 percent of 3 to 5-year olds are poor; and more than 20 percent (over 4 million) of 6 to 11-year old children are poor. Very young children who live in poor households are especially vulnerable and face threats to their health, safety, and psychological development that can have long-term effects on their chances of becoming healthy, productive adults. In fact, poverty increases the risk of infant mortality. As Zill and Rogers (1988) pointed out, "when the U.S. infant mortality rate is compared with that of other industrialized countries, the United States ranks only seventeenth, behind countries like Japan, the Scandinavian countries, France, Australia, and Britain" (pp. 55–56).

3.2 Race/Ethnicity

Of all of the factors associated with educational disadvantage, racial/ethnic minority status probably is the most commonly cited. In particular, African American and Hispanic children and youth have traditionally performed less well than White children on various standardized academic achievement tests. For example, in the National Assessment of Educational Progress (NAEP), the reading, writing, and mathematics skills of African American and Hispanic children are substantially below those of White children at ages 9, 13, and 17 (Davis and McCaul 1991). Although some data exist which suggest that this academic performance gap between ethnic/racial minority youth and White youth may be narrowing, there continues to be a significant discrepancy between the groups. Further, because African American and Hispanic children are far more likely to drop out of school than are White children in the United States, the educational achievement gap between the two groups may be underestimated. Data from the October 1986 Current Population Survey indicated that 17.3 percent of African American respondents and 38.2 percent of Hispanic respondents aged 22 to 24 were neither enrolled in school nor high-school graduates, as compared with only 13.9 percent of White respondents within the same age group. In some inner cities the dropout rate for African American and Hispanic youth exceeds 60 percent (Natriello et al. 1990 p. 18).

3.3 Living in Single-parent Homes

Family structure in the 1990s United States is vastly different from what it was in the 1950s and 1960s. Hodgkinson (1991) reported that over one-third of all marriages performed in 1988 were second marriages for at least one partner. Divorce is more common than it was. Hodgkinson also estimated that over one-half of all new marriages in the 1990s will end in divorce and that 23 percent of all children born in this period will be born outside of marriage. Children living in single-parent households, estimated to be one in four children, are far more likely to be impoverished than children living in two-parent households. Among children who grew up in the 1970s, nearly three-quarters of those who spent at least some time in a single-parent family lived in poverty at least part of the time. More than one-third (37.8%) of these children spent at least 4 years of their first decade in poverty, and one in five (21.8%) lived in poverty for 7 or more of their first 10 years. Conversely, children living continuously in a two-parent, male-headed family have but a 20% chance of living in poverty for at least 1 year in their first 10, and only a 2% chance of being poor continuously from birth to age 10 (Natriello et al. 1990).

3.4 Educational Level of Mother

Children of poorly educated mothers (a) perform worse academically and (b) leave school earlier than children of better educated mothers. According to 1986 NAEP test results, children of poorly educated mothers scored lower than children of better educated mothers in both reading and mathematics at every age level measured, with the most pronounced difference occurring in mathematics. For example, of the third-grade children participating in the 1986 NAEP, only 46% of those whose mothers had not completed high school scored above the level of beginning skills and understanding on the mathematics proficiency test, while 73% of those children whose mothers were at least high-school graduates attained that level of mastery (Natriello et al. 1990). Maternal education is also related to the likelihood of dropping out of school. Barro and Kolstad's 1987 study found that children in families where the mother has not completed high school are two to three times more likely to drop out of high school themselves than are children in families where the mother has obtained more schooling (Barro and Kolstad 1987).

The educational level of the mother is especially important because it is the mother who usually is the primary caretaker in single-parent households. Many of these mothers either do not work or hold low-paying jobs. Clearly, children living in single-parent households are much more likely to be poor than children who live in two-parent families.

3.5 Limited English Proficiency

Students whose primary language is other than English (PLOTE) or who have limited English proficiency (LEP) are generally at a distinct disadvantage in United States public schools. These students not only often encounter academic barriers, but many are forced to deal with emotional and social obstacles too. For example, children with limited English proficiency are also more likely to drop out of school than are children from homes in which English is spoken exclusively. In a study reported in 1987, those students from homes where only a non-English language was spoken were more than twice as likely to drop out of high school as students from homes where English was the sole or primary language (Salganik and Celebuski 1987).

Further, ethnic and cultural customs of these students are often not understood by their peers and teachers. For example, children from some cultures tend to be more passive in group settings. Thus, a child's "lack of verbal responsiveness" could be misinterpreted by teachers as lack of interest or motivation. Likewise, children from other cultural backgrounds may manifest behaviors in the classroom or in the community which are perceived as being verbally or physically aggressive. In reality, these verbalizations and physical behaviors may not represent overt acts of defiance or disrespect but rather they may more accurately be reflective of cultural or subcultural norms.

4. Estimated Size of the Population

Despite the broad and imprecise nature of the available indicators of the educationally disadvantaged population, it is clear that substantial numbers and troubling proportions of United States' children may be classified as educationally at risk. A conservative estimate is that at least 40 percent of these children are at risk of failure in school on the basis of at least one of the five factors cited above. Other estimates indicate large percentages of United States children are at risk. A national study using a large, representative sample of youth indicated that 22 percent of eighth graders had one "risk factor" and 20 percent had two or more (Hafner et al. 1990). Another estimate indicated that approximately 33 percent of young children in the United States could be considered at risk before they even began formal schooling (Hodgkinson 1991). Demographic projections suggest that the birth rate is highest for populations that have traditionally suffered from poverty and low educational levels, thus suggesting that a greater percentage of students will be at risk in the near future.

5. Programming for Children in At-risk Circumstances

Traditionally, many children considered to be at risk of educational failure received services through the federal special and compensatory education programs. However, research on effective practices with many of these children at risk suggests that traditional approaches have not worked successfully. Neither retaining lower achieving students nor separating students for pull-out programs (the traditional approach employed in compensatory and special education programs) has demonstrated effectiveness. Moreover, pull-out programs have been criticized as stigmatizing (Lipsky and Gartner 1989, Slavin and Madden 1989, Stainback and Stainback 1985, Wang et al. 1988). A final criticism of pull-out programs is that the eligibility requirements for compensatory and special education have led to many at-risk students "falling through the cracks" of the two systems and thereby failing to receive needed services.

In determining what is effective programming with at-risk students, Slavin and Madden (1989) identified three broad categories for intervention: (a) prevention, (b) classroom change, and (c) remediation. With regard to the latter two categories, several attributes have been identified as characteristics of effective programs for at-risk students: comprehensiveness, intensity, flexibility, accessibility, and adaptability to specific student needs (Schorr 1989, Slavin and Madden 1989).

One of the more recent and promising reform approaches for at-risk students is that of accelerated schools. Proponents of accelerated schools argue that compensatory and remedial programs "institutionalize" students at risk as slow learners, thus reducing teacher expectations. They slow down the pace of instruction so that students at risk fall farther and farther behind. Teachers may fail to motivate students at risk, may not close the achievement gap between at-risk and mainstream students, and may not help students at risk to develop effective learning strategies. Four premises underlie these accelerated education projects: (a) high expectations and high status for the participants; (b) a specific deadline for closing the achievement gap of at-risk children; (c) a fast-paced curriculum that includes concepts, analysis, problem-solving, and interesting applications; and (d) the involvement of parents, the use of community resources, and the extensive use of parents and volunteers (Levin 1988).

At the secondary level, several authors (Hahn et al. 1987, Hamilton 1986) have suggested that schools need to individualize their instruction and curriculum for those students who are at risk of academic failure and who suffer from low self-esteem. Schools should, therefore, consider providing students with flexible options for completing their education. Some students, for example, may need a program of less concentration but a longer duration—a 5 or 6-year program with work-study options. Indeed, Hamilton (1986) argued that many at-risk students would benefit from more out-of-school experiences and more intensive work-related training. Community-based learning, he suggested, leads to enhanced positive attitudes as well as increased achievement for at-risk students.

In a related vein, Wehlage and Rutter (1986) offered three suggestions for schools interested in providing positive educational experiences for at-risk youth: (a) a sense of responsibility on the part of teachers and administrators toward the education of at-risk youth; (b) an effort to establish fair and respected discipline practices; and (c) a reconceptualization of schoolwork which allows at-risk students to achieve satisfaction and continue their schooling. Other research supports the notion that school climate and organization can substantially affect student engagement with schooling. Therefore, a school's atmosphere must emphasize positive teacher–student contact and support. Schools with considerable social disorganization, characterized by high truancy rates and substantial discipline problems, can work to change the school atmosphere by improving staff–administrator relationships and by instituting fair and consistent discipline policies. Establishing a positive ethos in which faculty and students share a sense of mission lessens student alienation as evidenced by absenteeism and dropout behavior. Further, schools that experience lower dropout rates are those in which face-to-face contact between students is the rule rather than the exception, in which there is an emphasis on academic pursuits, and in which the environment is safe and orderly. Teachers in these effective programs tend to see themselves as having a counseling role with students and encourage students toward trust relationships and social bonding with adults. Also there is some evidence that community support and involvement are key factors in establishing a positive school climate for at-risk youth. In addition, it was found that teacher commitment was a necessary ingredient for the effective education of at-risk youth (Bryk and Thum 1989).

6. Conclusion

The importance of establishing a positive school climate, characterized by teachers' active involvement and nurturing support of students, permeates the literature on children in at-risk circumstances. The same spirit infused the 1989 United Nations Convention at which the rights of the world's children were delineated. These included rights commonly afforded adults—freedom of movement, association, and belief—in addition to rights to nurturance, protection, and care (Hart 1991).

Clearly, these rights transcend the boundaries of individual classrooms and extend to the family, community, and society at large. Nevertheless, educators are in a unique position to recognize children's problems, advocate for solutions, and facilitate the provision of necessary services using resources from the school, family, and community. Further, research has indicated the value of formal education in enhancing the human capital of a nation (Husén and Tuijnman 1991). With the advent of a global economy and international interdependence, lifelong education becomes a primary consideration and educating children in at-risk circumstances has become not a luxury, but a necessity.

See also: Prereferral Intervention for Students with Special Needs; Social Skills; Behavioral Disorders: Emotional; Behavioral Disorders: Social

References

Barro S, Kolstad A 1987 *Who Drops Out of High School? Findings from High School and Beyond*. National Center for Education Statistics, US Department of Education, Washington, DC

Bryk A, Thum Y M 1989 The effects of high school organization on dropping out: An exploratory investigation. *Am. Educ. Res. J.* 26(3): 353–83

Catterall J, Cota-Robles E 1988 The educationally at-risk: What the numbers mean. In: Conference on Accelerating the Education of At-risk Students 1988 *Accelerating the Education of At-risk Students*. Center for Educational Research at Stanford University, Stanford, California

Children's Defense Fund Staff 1990 *Children 1990: A Report Card, Briefing Book, and Action Primer*. Children's Defense Fund, Washington, DC

Committee on Foreign Relations, United States Senate 1990 *State of the World's Children*. US Government Printing Office, Washington, DC

Davis W E, McCaul E J 1990 *At-risk Children and Youth: A Crisis in Our Schools and Society*. College of Education, University of Maine, Orono, Maine

Davis W E, McCaul E J 1991 *The Emerging Crisis: Current and Projected Status of Children in the United States*. Institute for the Study of At-risk Students, Orono, Maine

Ehn B 1990 The rhetoric of individualism and collectivism. In: Swedish Immigration Institute (ed.) 1990 *The Organization of Diversity in Sweden*. Invandraminnesarkivet, Helsingborg

Glenn C L 1992 Educating the children of immigrants. *Phi Del. Kap.* 73(5): 404–08

Hafner A, Ingels S, Schneider B, Stevenson D, Owings J A 1990 *National Educational Longitudinal Study of 1988: A Profile of the American Eighth Grader* National Center for Education Statistics, Washington, DC

Hahn A, Danzberger J, Lefkowitz B 1987 *Dropouts in America: Enough is Known for Action*. Institute for Educational Leadership, Washington, DC

Hamilton S F 1986 Raising standards and reducing dropout rates. In: Natriello G (ed.) 1986 *School Dropouts: Patterns and Policies*. Teachers College Press, New York

Hart S N 1991 From property to person status: Historical perspective on children's rights. *Am. Psychol.* 46(1): 53–9

Hodgkinson H L 1991 Reform versus reality. *Phi Del. Kap.* 73(1): 9–16

Husén T, Tuijnman A 1991 The contribution of formal schooling to the increase in intellectual capital. *Educ. Researcher* 20(7): 17–25

Levin H M 1988 *Accelerated Schools for At-risk Students*. Center for Policy Research Education, New Brunswick, New Jersey

Lipsky D K, Gartner A (eds.) 1989 *Beyond Separate Education: Quality Education for All*. Paul H Brookes, Baltimore, Maryland

Murphy J T 1992 Apartheid's legacy to Black children. *Phi Del. Kap.* 73(5): 367–74

National Commission on Excellence in Education 1983 *A Nation At Risk: The Imperative for Educational Reform*. US Department of Education, Washington, DC

National School Boards Association (NSBA) 1989 *An Equal Chance: Educating At-risk Children to Succeed*. NSBA, Alexandria, Virginia

Natriello G, McDill E L, Pallas A M 1990 *Schooling Disadvantaged Children: Racing Against Catastrophe*. Teachers College Press, New York

New D A 1992 Teaching in the Fourth World. *Phi Del. Kap.* 73(5): 396–98

Reed S, Sautter R C 1990 Children of poverty: The status of 12 million young Americans. *Phi Del. Kap.* 71(10): K1–K12

Rust V D 1992 Educational responses to reforms in East Germany, Czechoslovakia, and Poland. *Phi Del. Kap.* 73(5): 386–89

Salganik L, Celebuski C 1987 *Educational Attainment Study: Preliminary Tables*. Pelavin Associates, Washington, DC

Schorr L B 1989 *Within Our Reach: Breaking the Cycle of Disadvantage*. Doubleday & Co, New York

Slavin R E, Madden N A 1989 What works for students at risk: A research synthesis. *Educ. Leadership* 46(5): 4–13

Stainback W, Stainback S 1984 A rationale for the merger of special and regular education. *Excep. Child.* 51(2): 102–11

Wang M C, Reynolds M C, Walberg H J 1988 Integrating the children of the second system. *Phi Del. Kap.* 70(3): 248–51

Wehlage G, Rutter, R 1986 Dropping out: How much do schools contribute to the problem? In: Natriello G (ed.) 1986 *School Dropouts: Patterns and Policies*. Teachers College Press, New York

Zill N, Rogers C C 1988 Recent trends in the well-being of children in the United States and their implications for public policy. In: Cherlin A J (ed.) 1988 *The Changing American Family and Public Policy*. University Press of America, Washington, DC

Further Reading

Kozol J 1991 *Savage Inequities: Children in America's Schools*. Crown Publishing, New York

W. E. Davis; E. J. McCaul

Children and Youth With Special Needs, Diagnosis and Classification of

Assessment is the process of gathering information for purposes of making decisions on educational programs for certain children and youth. Diagnosis and classification are part of this decision-making process. Because special education services are not universally accessible, decisions on students' eligibility for special education services and type of appropriate service are part of the special education process. Teachers participate in making these diagnosis and classification decisions and these practices

Table 1
Diagnostic practices

Type	Nature of practices
AB	Describes relation between historical events or causes and current pupil characteristics or behavior without considering treatment or outcomes.
AC	Describes relation between historical events or causes and particular treatments and interventions without concern for effects.
AD	Describes relation between historical events or causes and outcomes without considering pupil or treatment differences.
ABC	Describes relation between interventions and historical events, causes, and student characteristics without considering outcomes.
ABCD	Treatments with predictable outcomes are prescribed based on historical information and student characteristics—complete model.
BC	Describes relation between student characteristics and particular treatments and interventions without concern for effects.
BCD	Describes relation between student characteristics, treatments, and outcomes without considering historical information.
CD	Describes relation between treatments and outcomes without concern for causes or student characteristics.
BD	Describes relation between characteristics and outcomes without considering historical information and interventions.

Source: Adapted from Cromwell R L, Blashfield R K, Strauss J S 1975 Criteria for classification systems. In Hobbs N (ed.) 1975 *Issues in the Classification of Children*. Jossey-Bass, San Francisco, California

are applicable across the existing categories of students with special needs.

1. Purposes of Diagnosis and Classification

Diagnostic decisions result in the classification of students with special education needs, but the ultimate purpose is improved instruction that results from altered intervention practices (McLoughlin and Lewis 1990, Salvia and Ysseldyke 1991, Ysseldyke et al. 1992). Cromwell et al. (1975) described four categories of information and their relations in diagnostic practices (see Table 1). Category A represents historical and/or etiological information—the precursors of observable behaviors and characteristics used in making diagnostic decisions. Category B is comprised of information from current assessments of an individual's behavior and characteristics—test scores, observations, and data from structured and unstructured interviews. Category C represents specific treatments and interventions and Category D contains information about outcomes of interventions. Diagnostic practices that include categories C and D are considered more accurate because they include treatment and evaluation information. Gathering information simply to classify and group individuals is useful in calling attention to new diagnostic categories. However, most professionals agree that the process of making diagnostic and classification decisions is justifiable largely on grounds that improved intervention will result.

2. Legal Considerations in Diagnosis and Classification

Rules and regulations established by education laws greatly influence special education. This is partially due to the dissatisfaction many parents and professionals experienced with early special education practices. For example, there was a time when a special education classification meant the end to normal educational experiences. Students in special classes lost contact with their regular class peers and often remained in special education for their entire school careers. Parents and professionals argued that such educational segregation of students with special needs was not sound pedagogy and legal action was required to ensure that practices changed. There was also a time when diagnostic decisions were grounded in the recommendations of a single teacher or on the results of a single test. Such ill-founded decision-making resulted in special class enrollments in which minority students were overrepresented. Parents and professionals protested against such insensate educational policy and legal action was mandated to ensure that these unsound practices changed.

In the 1990s, special education is a disabled student's right. In 1975, President Ford signed into law the Education for All Handicapped Children Act (Public Law 94–142). The law was reauthorized with the passage of the Individuals with Disabilities Education Act (IDEA) amendments in 1990. Written to improve services provided to individuals with disabilities, the law provided parents (and their children) with specific rights related to diagnosis and classification practices.

By law, students with disabilities and their families are guaranteed rights of due process. This means that these students and their families have the same rights as any other person. Educational diagnoses and classifications cannot be changed without the informed consent (e.g., written permission) of parent(s) or guardian(s). Parents are also entitled to independent assessments and impartial hearings when decisions about their children are being made.

Students with disabilities and their families are also entitled by law to protection in evaluation activities that are part of the educational experience. This means that students cannot be classified for special programs in an arbitrary and capricious manner. Students with disabilities and their families are entitled to have diagnostic decisions made about them using individually administered tests. It is assumed that these tests are appropriate for students with disabilities and that the decisions will be made in an unbiased fashion (e.g., without regard to ethnic, cultural, or racial characteristics).

School personnel by law must prepare an individualized education program (IEP) for every student enrolled in a special education program. Teachers must have clearly documented plans for how instructional time will be spent. The IEP is a written document that specifies educational plans and objectives and serves as a management tool for implementing recommendations derived during this stage of the diagnostic process. Again, the ultimate purpose of diagnosis and classification is improved educational experiences.

Students with disabilities must be educated in the least restrictive environment. The education of students with disabilities must parallel as much as possible the education of nondisabled students. Many students with disabilities are enrolled full-time in general education classes and receive only indirect services from special education personnel. Others leave their general education classes periodically to go to other classes for special education services (pull-out programs). Still others are enrolled primarily in special education classes but, to the maximum extent possible, attend general education classes for part of the school day. For example, a student might be enrolled in special education but attend a general education class for instruction in mathematics, music, art, or physical education.

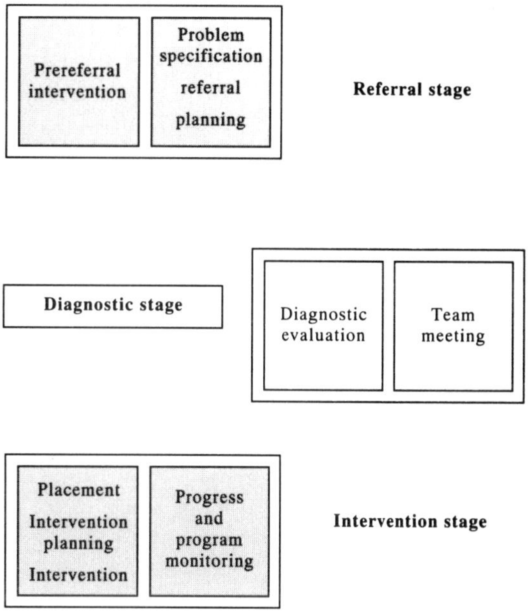

Figure 1
Steps in diagnostic process

3. *Models of Diagnosis and Classification*

Traditional models of diagnosis are test driven and focus on identifying problems in individuals. Within this model, the diagnostic process consists of several stages of decision-making.

During the referral stage, teachers identify problems and try interventions before deciding formally to refer a student. When these interventions fail, teachers refer the student for formal evaluation and participate in planning the diagnostic assessment (e.g., supply anecdotal records, complete checklists).

A diagnostic evaluation and team meeting take place during the diagnostic stage. The purpose of the diagnostic evaluation is to gather information on current levels of functioning in areas related to the suspected disability, classify the individual, and make a decision about the appropriateness of special education services. This evaluation must be conducted by personnel representing multidisciplinary perspectives (e.g., school psychologists, social workers, school nurses, speech and language pathologists, special education teachers, learning disabilities specialists, reading specialists, regular classroom teachers, principals, physicians, or parents). The written report typically includes the following information:

(a) the extent to which the student is eligible for special education (e.g., whether current classification criteria have been met);

(b) the basis for the decision (e.g., current levels of functioning);

(c) observed behavior supporting the diagnostic decision;

(d) relation of behavior to current levels of functioning;

(e) educationally relevant findings from other disciplines;

(f) other findings (e.g., environmental, cultural, or economic influences).

Following the written report, a team meeting is held to discuss the findings of the diagnostic eval-

Table 2
Curriculum-based decision-making model

Stages	Activities	Purpose
Problem identification	Observing and recording of student performance during instruction	Determining that a problem exists
Problem definition	Describing of discrepancies between expected and actual performance	Determining that discrepancies are important
Problem exploration	Identifying potential improvements and costs associated with them	Selecting a solution to be tested
Solution implementation	Implementing a solution and monitoring progress	Determining that solution should be continued or revised
Problem resolution	Identifying discrepancies between expected and actual performance	Determining that discrepancies are acceptable and special program may be discontinued

Source: Deno S L 1989 Curriculum-based measurement and special education services: A fundamental and direct relationship. In Shinn M R (ed.) 1989 *Curriculum-based Measurement: Assessing Special Students*. Guilford Press, New York

uation and plan interventions to meet the student's special learning needs. Typically parents, teachers, students, and representatives from agencies that participated in the diagnostic evaluation take part in this team meeting. Participants also discuss the content of the student's IEP at this meeting.

Arguing that special education exists because generalized education programs fail to educate a portion of the students assigned to them, Deno (1989) presented an alternative model for improving current diagnostic practices using curriculum-based methods of assessment. The steps in the curriculum-based measurement (CBM) decision-making model are illustrated in Table 2.

During the problem identification (screening/referral) step, observations and performance records are gathered in educationally relevant domains (e.g., basal readers, district-wide mathematics textbooks). Deciding if discrepancies between expected and actual performance are large enough to require special education is central to the problem definition (eligibility/classification) step. During the problem exploration (intervention planning) step, treatment alternatives, probable performance improvements, and associated costs are identified. In the solution implementation (progress monitoring) step, decisions are made about continuing or modifying interventions. During the problem resolution (program monitoring) step, differences between expected and actual performance are evaluated and decisions are made related to continuing an intervention program.

When using curriculum-based procedures to diagnose students with special needs, school district personnel develop local norms by identifying a representative sample of curriculum materials for each grade level, establishing a sampling plan, and training people to gather assessment information and summarize performances. After teams identify specific referral problems, gather assessment information, and determine if additional intervention is necessary, curriculum-based decision-making takes one of two general forms.

In single-step models, referred students are compared to local grade-level norms on appropriate curricular materials. In some districts, discrepancy ratios are calculated by dividing normative performance by referred student's performance and decisions are made based on local cutoff scores (e.g., −2.0 or greater discrepancy ratio). In other districts, percentile scores derived from local norms are used in establishing cutoff scores and making eligibility decisions (Shinn 1989).

In multiple-step models, teachers or parents first refer a student. Evidence is then collected illustrating performance outside the range of regular classroom peers. The performance of referred students is evaluated to determine if it is outside the range that can be accommodated in regular classrooms. This approach closely approximates the decision-making process described by Salvia and Ysseldyke (1991) and others (McLoughlin and Lewis 1990, Ysseldyke and Algozzine 1990).

4. Diagnostic Procedures

Teachers gather diagnostic information using tests, observations, and interviews; the three provide complementary information on a student (Ysseldyke and Algozzine 1990). Tests are sets of questions designed to provide information about an individual's knowledge of content; they vary by administration, content, and form. Observations are records of an individual's performance of a specified behavior; they vary by form, content, and count. Interviews are sets of questions about past life experiences, current performance, characteristics, or future plans. Interviews vary by administration, content, and form.

4.1 Application

School personnel answer the following questions

when conducting diagnostic evaluations and team meetings:

(a) What are the student's current levels of functioning?
(b) What multidisciplinary information is available?
(c) Does the student have an achievement discrepancy?
(d) Does the student have a disability?
(e) What goals, objectives, and placements are appropriate?
(f) What special education services should be provided?
(g) How will progress be monitored?

Formal and informal tests, observations, and interviews are used to gather this information during diagnostic evaluations for students suspected of having special learning needs (Hammill et al. 1989, McLoughlin and Lewis 1990, Salvia and Ysseldyke 1991). These measures may be administered to groups or individuals to provide information about most academic subjects as well as other areas of special learning needs. Some group-administered tests of intelligence include the Test of Cognitive Skills, the Otis-Lennon School Ability Test, and the Cognitive Abilities Test (McLoughlin and Lewis 1990, Salvia and Ysseldyke 1991). Popular individually administered intelligence tests include the Wechsler Intelligence Scale, for Children—Revised and the Stanford-Binet Intelligence Scale. Cognitive abilities are also measured as part of the Woodcock-Johnson Psychoeducational Battery and the Kaufman Assessment Battery for Children (McLoughlin and Lewis 1986, Salvia and Ysseldyke 1991). The Peabody Individual Achievement Test and the Wide Range Achievement Test are examples of popular achievement tests (McLoughlin and Lewis 1990, Salvia and Ysseldyke 1991). Names of these and other commonly used individual assessment devices are presented in Table 3.

5. *Issues in Diagnosis and Classification*

No area of special education has generated more critical analysis or controversy than diagnosis and classification. This is largely due to problems associated with defining disabilities, developing operational criteria for use in identifying students, and assigning labels to individuals as an indication of a diagnosis (Ysseldyke and Algozzine 1990).

Substantial variation exists across states and even across districts in the definitions and operational criteria used to make diagnostic decisions in special education. This flexibility, although regulated by the federal government, unfortunately encourages underidentification of students with some special needs, such as emotional disturbances. It also allows school personnel to avoid identification of students when it is expedient to do so. The situation also creates a problem for the student who qualifies for services in one locale, but who moves across state or even district lines and finds himself/herself not qualified for those same services in the new location.

Diagnosing and classifying students may also have adverse effects upon other school experiences by encouraging educators to:

(a) direct attention to supposed etiological factors that are either child specific or outside the school setting, thus alleviating educators of responsibility for instigating or exacerbating a child's difficulties;
(b) pursue causes of maladaptive child behavior in the realm of nonobservable, intrapsychic events, instead of analyzing student behavior in the context in which it is dysfunctional;
(c) cease to work toward solving problems as a result of discovering causal factors that are perceived as too deeply imbedded in the personality to respond to intervention;
(d) employ indirect interventions (e.g., nonbehavioral therapies) to change overt behavior patterns (e.g., aggression, withdrawal).

Although the process of diagnosing and classifying students seems to be grounded more in the need to secure monies for specific populations rather than to influence programming decisions, the impact of labeling students cannot be ignored. For example, research has demonstrated that educators have a more negative attitude toward students with behavior problems, as a group, than toward most other exceptionalities. It has also been shown that teachers have conceptions associated with different labels. The effects of these ideas remain even after the label has been removed or some conflicting or neutral information about the student has been provided. (International concerns emerge when tests developed in the United States are translated into foreign languages for use in other countries.)

5.1 *Diagnosis and Classification of Culturally Diverse Students*

Observation shows that diagnosis and classifications of special needs students have not measured up to acceptable standards when culturally diverse students are involved. It is assumed that teachers teach, judge, and evaluate students based on their personal perceptions, values and idiosyncrasies. If this supposition is correct, questions of accountability, psychological hazards, privacy invasion, and test bias must also be addressed. In addition, questions of

Table 3
Tests commonly used in diagnosis and classification

Cognitive Abilities and Intelligence
Cognitive Levels Test
Kaufman Assessment Battery for Children
Learning Potential Assessment Device
Peabody Picture Vocabulary Test—Revised
Stanford-Binet Intelligence Scale
Test of Nonverbal Intelligence
Wechsler Intelligence Scale for Children—Revised
Adaptive Behavior
AAMD Adaptive Behavior Scale
Scales of Independent Behavior
Vineland Adaptive Behavior Scales
Problem Behaviors
Behavior Rating Profile
Behavior Evaluation Scale
Behavior Problem Checklist—Revised
Burks' Behavior Rating Scale
Devereux Behavior Rating Scales
Walker Problem Behavior Identification
General School Achievement
BRIGANCE Diagnostic Comprehensive Inventory of Basic Skills
Kaufman Test of Educational Achievement
Peabody Individual Achievement Test
Wide Range Achievement Test
Reading Achievement
Diagnostic Reading Scales
Gray Oral Reading Tests
Stanford Diagnostic Reading Test
Woodcock Reading Mastery Tests
Mathematics Achievement
Diagnostic Test of Arithmetic Strategies
ENRIGHT Diagnostic Inventory of Basic Mathematics Skills
KeyMath Diagnostic Arithmetic Test
Test of Early Mathematics Ability
Language Abilities
Boehm Test of Basic Concepts
Diagnostic Spelling Test
Test of Language Development
Test of Written Language
Test of Written Spelling
Woodcock Language Proficiency Battery

appropriateness of assessment tools and procedures, accuracy of differential diagnosis, appropriateness of placement, and effectiveness of pedagogical strategies are important.

Many scholars (Obiakor 1991, Ogbu 1988, Salvia and Ysseldyke 1991, Samuda 1975, 1976, Ysseldyke and Algozzine 1990) agree that tests that produce consistent results may not measure what they purport to measure. Minority students are likely to differ as much as their norminority peers in test-taking skills (Minton and Schneider 1980). This makes it difficult to justify using methods and instruments that have been standardized to a middle-class, European–American sample. According to Samuda (1975), standardized tests "preserve the status quo" and relegate "Blacks and other minorities to an inferior position in the larger society" (p. 3). A logical extension is that tests and other assessment activities create labels and categories which have far-reaching social, economic, psychological, and educational implications. Samuda noted that tests lead to "mislabeling and poor learning environments that divert the education of Blacks and other minorities into a barely elementary and functional level" (p. 13).

Assessor bias is a critical factor, Dent (1976) and Johnson (1976, 1981) challenged assessors and teachers who failed to consider the culture of their students. The initial referral process must be properly investigated because of the cognitive, cultural, and learning styles that minority students bring into school programs. Cummins (1989) explained that "psychological assessment has served to legitimize the educational disabilities of minority students by locating the academic 'problems' within the students themselves" (p. 116). The endemic problem of looking "within" the student buttresses the theory of biological determinism that assumes that intelligence cannot be improved in spite of compensatory education programs. Gould (1981) remarked that biological determinism subscribes to the principle that "worth can be assigned to individuals and groups by measuring intelligence as a single quantity" (p. 20). This view was espoused by Goddard (1912), Hernstein (1971), and Jensen (1969), whose conclusions have particularly attracted the critical attention of many scholars (Obiakor 1991; Ogbu 1987, 1988, 1990; Rueda 1989). For example, Gelb et al. (1986) wrote:

> One cannot examine the relevant historical material without concluding that mental testers promoted eugenic and racist interests and that they sought to, and to some degree succeeded in, providing those interests with a mantle of scientific respectability. (p. 30)

5.1.1 The African Experience. In Africa, where the cultures are extremely diverse, there are no standardized tests or even educational programs designed with respect to cultural values, language symbols, and cognitive styles. In Nigeria, for example, there are problems with admitting exceptional individuals into school programs because of the lack of mandates. Educational programs are indiscriminately integrated without consideration for the specific needs of special students. Those students with serious integrative problems are admitted into residential programs and institutions; no systematic screening facility is available for exceptional children. As Ogbue (1975) pointed out, there is only one assessment center—the Child Guidance Center in Lagos. The lack of federal mandatory laws in special education has hindered efforts to identify instruments to assess the strengths and weaknesses of students. Classes are mainstreamed without consideration for the specific exceptionalities. In fact, severely disabled individuals are institutionalized and placed in residential settings. As Obiakor et al. (1991) explained:

> The borderline or at-risk cases are not easily identifiable which makes the whole idea of special education to be nonexistent in Nigeria. Most exceptional students are indiscriminately integrated into mainstream classes. It becomes a matter of "survival of the fittest" for these individuals. (p. 15)

In Nigeria, as in much of Africa, there are only a few poorly defined categories of special needs students. According to Ogbue (1975, 1981) the categories include (a) the blind and partially sighted, (b) the deaf and partially hearing, (c) the physically disabled, (d) the mentally retarded, (e) the hospitalized children, and (f) the gifted. The high illiteracy rate in Nigeria and other parts of Africa makes it difficult for citizens to be aware of their fundamental rights. Most educational programs are intensively politicized to the detriment of participants (Obiakor and Maltby 1989). Section 8 of the National Policy on Education (Federal Ministry of Education 1975), which was expected to ameliorate the plight of exceptional individuals, has not had the expected effect (Obiakor 1991). It is reasonable to conclude that diagnosis and classification in Nigeria have not materialized to instructional intervention.

5.1.2 Call for nontraditional focus. There is a lack of assessment tools that respond to all the needs of diversity in Africa and the United States. For example, there is the question of how assessment tools used by the Child Guidance Center in Lagos respond to Nigerian values, symbols, and styles. This same issue has been reiterated by minority group members in the United States. Samuda (1975) argued that:

> If it is our purpose to serve the mass of citizens and if it is our goal to use measurement to facilitate the education of the poor, of the minority student, and of the atypical individual, then we will need to expand our research endeavors. Psychometric technology must become the handmaiden of educational innovation in optimizing the individual's competence through qualitative analysis of achievement and weaknesses so as to point the way toward the modification of instruction matched to the individual needs of individual students. (pp. 156–57)

Samuda's statement suggests that assessment of culturally diverse students must respond to the needs of these students and their parents. The "shared enterprise" phenomenon must prevail as interaction is enhanced within the classroom setting. According to Duran (1989), "assessment will serve a more effective role if it is able to assist teachers and resource specialists in guiding the everyday instruction of pupils" (p. 158). Tests should lead to new learning. Culturally diverse students should be tested, trained, and retested to see if they have acquired new skills. The Midwestern National Origin Desegregation Assistance Center (1982) suggested (a) parental consent and involvement in psycho-educational assessment, (b) nonbiased assessment that considers culture, race, gender, and language, and (c) multidimensional assessment. Minton and Schneider (1980) concluded:

> We cannot limit ourselves to the identification of trait dimensions or typological classifications across individuals without also considering the characteristics of the environments within which individuals function. Nor can

we limit ourselves to an analysis of the environmental determinants of human differences without also considering the hereditary determinants. Finally, we have to ask ourselves what kind of society is most desirable for the expression of human diversity—for the opportunity for each of us to grow as individuals and at the same time not infringe on the rights of others to develop their own individuality. (p. 489)

6. Perspective on Diagnosis and Classification

Those who work with students with special learning needs use assessment information on a daily basis. Different types of tests are used to assess different skills, abilities, and characteristics of students. Intelligence tests measure various verbal and nonverbal abilities. Achievement tests measure performance in academic areas of instruction. Differences between performance scores on intelligence and achievement tests are the basis for deciding whether a student should be classified as learning disabled, mentally retarded, emotionally disturbed, or some other category. Observations of behavior and interviews are used to corroborate test results from diagnostic evaluations and support discussion presented at team meetings where professionals discuss placement issues of particular students.

While the diagnostic process appears straightforward, significant controversy continues to revolve around decision-making on the eligibility for special education for a student. The controversy is based largely on inconsistent use of diagnostic criteria. If states and local school districts are free to decide what tests, methods, and criteria can be used to assign students to classifications, decision-making will necessarily be varied. When decision-making is varied, the same student may be "learning disabled" in one school district and not in another. This apparent inconsistency can only cause problems for professionals trying to diagnose and serve students with special needs.

See also: Children and Youth with Special Needs, Education of; Disability Statistics

References

Cromwell R L, Blashfield R K, Strauss J S 1975 Criteria classification systems. In: Hobbs N (ed.) 1975 *Issues in The Classification of Children*. Jossey-Bass, San Francisco, California

Cummins J 1989 A theoretical framework for bilingual special education. *Excep. Child.* 56 (2): 111–19

Deno S L 1989 Curriculum-based measurement and special education services: A fundamental and direct relationship. In: Shinn M (ed.) 1989 *Curriculum-based Measurement: Assessing Special Children*. Guilford Press, New York

Dent H E 1976 Assessing Black children for mainstream placement. In: Jones R L (ed.) 1976 *Mainstreaming and the Minority Child*. Council for Exceptional Children, Reston, Virginia

Duran R P 1989 Assessment and instruction of at-risk Hispanic students. *Excep. Child.* 56(2): 154–58

Gelb S A, Allen G E, Futterman A, Mehler B 1986 Rewriting mental testing history: The view from the American psychologist. *Sage Race Relations Abstracts* 11(2): 18–31

Goddard H H 1912 *The Kallikak Family, a Study in the Heredity of Feeble-mindedness*. MacMillan, New York

Gould S J 1981 *The Mismeasurement of Man*. W W Norton & Company, New York

Hammill D D, Brown L, Bryant B R 1989 *A Consumer's Guide to Tests in Print*. Pro-Ed Austin, Texas

Hernstein R 1971 I. Q. *Atlantic Monthly* 43–64

Jensen A R 1969 How much can we boost IQ and scholastic achievement? *Harv. Educ. Rev.* 39: 1–123

Johnson J L 1976 Mainstreaming Black children. In: Jones R L (ed.) 1976 *Mainstreaming and the Minority Child*. Council for Exceptional Children, Reston, Virginia

Johnson J L 1981 Priorities for Black exceptional children in the 1980s. Paper presented at the Council for Exceptional Children (CEC) Topical Conference, New Orleans, Louisiana

McLoughlin J A, Lewis R B 1990 *Assessing Special Students*, 3rd edn. Macmillan Inc., New York

Midwestern National Origin Desegregation Assistance Center 1982 *Special Education for Exceptional Bilingual Students: A Handbook for Educators*. MNODAC, Milwaukee, Wisconsin

Minton H L, Schneider F W 1980 *Differential Psychology*. Waveland Press Inc., Prospect Heights, Illinois

Nigerian Federal Ministry of Education 1975 Section 8 of the National Policy on Education. Federal Ministry of Education, Lagos

Obiakor F E 1991 African–American quandaries in school programs. Paper presented at the General Meeting of the National Black Caucus of Special Educators, Council for Exceptional Children, Atlanta, Georgia

Obiakor F E, Aramburo D, Maltby G P, Davis E 1991 Comparison of special education in Nigeria and the United States. Paper presented at the 69th Annual International Convention of the Council for Exceptional Children (CEC), Atlanta, Georgia

Obiakor F E, Maltby G P 1989 *Pragmatism and Education in Africa: Handbook for Educators and Development Planners*. Kendall Hunt Publishing Co., Dubuque, Iowa

Ogbue R M 1975 *A Survey of Special Education Facilities in Nigeria*. Federal Ministry of Nigeria, Lagos, Nigeria

Ogbue R M 1981 Experiments in integration: The Nigerian experience. *Educafrica* 135–52

Ogbu J U 1987 *Types of Cultural Differences and Minority School Adjustment and Performance*. Distinguished Visiting Professor Lecture Series No. 1, New Mexico State University, Las Cruces, New Mexico

Ogbu J U 1988 Human intelligence testing: A cultural ecological perspective. *Nat. Forum* 68(2): 23–29

Ogbu J U 1990 Understanding diversity: Summary comments. *Educ. Urb. Soc.* 22(4): 425–29

Rueda R 1989 Defining mild disabilities with language-minority students. *Excep. Child.* 56(2): 121–28

Salvia J, Ysseldyke J E 1991 *Assessment in Special and Remedial Education*, 5th edn. Houghton Mifflin, Boston, Massachusetts

Samuda R J 1975 *Psychological Testing of American Minorities: Issues and Consequences*. Harper & Row Publishers, New York

Samuda R J 1976 Problems and issues in assessment of minority group children. In: Jones R L (ed.) 1976 *Mainstreaming and the Minority Child.* Council for Exceptional Children, Reston, Virginia
Shinn M R 1989 Identifying and defining academic problems: CBM screening and eligibility procedures. In: Shinn M (ed.) 1989 *Curriculum-based Measurement: Assessing Special Children.* Guilford Press, New York
Ysseldyke J E, Algozzine B, Thurlow M L 1992 *Critical Issues in Special and Remedial Education.* Houghton Mifflin, Boston, Massachusetts
Ysseldyke J E, Algozzine B 1990 *Introduction to Special Education*, 2nd edn. Houghton Mifflin, Boston, Massachusetts

Further Reading

Deno S L 1985 Curriculum-based measurement: The emerging alternative. *Excep. Child.* 52: 219–32
Deno S L 1986 Formative evaluation of individual programs: A new role for school psychologists. *School Psychology Review* 15(3): 358–74
Figueroa R A 1989 Psychological testing of linguistic minority students: Knowledge gaps and regulations. *Excep. Child.* 56(2): 145–52
Gickling E, Havertape J 1981 *Curriculum-based Assessment (CBA).* National School Psychology Inservice Training Network, Minneapolis, Minnesota
McLoughlin J A, Lewis R B 1986 *Assessing Special Students.* Merrill, Columbus, Ohio
Ysseldyke J E, Algozzine B 1984 *Introduction to Special Education.* Houghton Mifflin, Boston, Massachusetts

B. Algozzine; B. Wong; F. E. Obiakor

Children and Youth with Special Needs, Education of

The topics considered in this entry are generally related to fields such as history, policy development, administrative arrangements, personnel preparation, research, international activities, and major trends in the education of children and youth with special needs. For more detailed treatment of special education topics, see other entries under such headings as diagnosis and classification of children and youth with special needs or infant and preschool students with special needs and specific articles on such topics as 508031 or 508040. A complete story about education for disabled children and youth would tell mainly of neglect. The field of special education has developed only quite recently and unevenly in the various parts of the world. What is described here is mainly a positive story of developing efforts by educators to serve disabled students, but many disabled children are isolated and still lacking the special education they need.

1. Definitions

The specialized forms of education provided for disabled or handicapped children and youth comprise the field of special education. Sometimes special education is provided as a supplement to general or regular education; other times it totally replaces regular education.

Table 1
Students aged 6–21 enrolled in special education programs in the United States by category of disability 1988–89

Disability category	Number	Percentage
Learning disabled	1,998,422	47.7
Speech or language impaired	968,908	23.1
Mentally retarded	581,465	13.9
Emotionally disturbed	377,295	9.0
Multihandicapped	84,870	2.0
Hard of hearing and deaf	57,555	1.4
Orthopedically impaired	47,392	1.1
Other health impaired	50,349	1.2
Visually handicapped	22,743	0.5
Deaf blind	1,516	0.04
Total	4,190,515	100.0

Source: US Department of Education 1990 *Twelfth Annual Report to Congress on the Implementation of the Education of the Handicapped Act.* US Department of Education, Washington, DC

1.1 Disabilities

The term "handicapped" is often used interchangeably with other terms such as "disabled" or "impaired." A useful distinction is to use "impairments" in reference to direct defects or deficiencies of individual persons, such as torn ligaments or misshapen eyes. "Disabilities" refer to functions of the individual which are limited or distorted because of impairments; for example, the torn ligaments may cause inability of the individual to run or jump, the misshapen eyes may cause blurred vision. The term "handicapped" is used in a broader way to indicate a clear disadvantage in the person's life such as exclusion from employment, denial of entrance to a training program, or exclusion from certain forms of social life. The term "handicapped" encompasses social arrangements which operate to the disadvantage of disabled persons. Traditionally the term handicapped has been used in defining special education, but the term "disabled"—as defined here—might often be more appropriate.

1.2 Categories of Disability

The disabilities which lead to placement in special education programs vary greatly, both qualitatively and in degree. A common approach in delineating the disabilities of individuals and in organizing programs in the schools is to use a set of categories. Three special education categories which often receive attention are: students who are visually disabled, deaf, or mentally retarded. It should not be assumed that these categories are easily defined (*see Children and Youth with Special Needs, Diagnosis and Classification of*). Additional categories of special education are used in many places. In the United States, school districts throughout the nation are required to report enrollments in special education programs, using the categories listed in Table 1. In recent years an apparent trend is to make noncategorical approaches to special education, but few data are available to document this trend.

Also included in Table 1 are data showing the numbers and percentages of disabled students in the various categories for the school year 1988–89 (US Department of Education 1990). By far the largest category was learning disability (LD) in which about 48 percent of the special education students were enrolled. The LD category came into common use in the United States only in the 1960s and has grown very rapidly, though it is unused as a category in most of the world. In an important sense LD is not a distinct category; the methods for classifying students vary greatly from one school district to another. LD identifies a broad range of students who are not learning well in existing programs.

2. *Numbers of Disabled Children*

Attempting to define the numbers of children who need special education presents considerable difficulty. Care must be taken in considering any data that are presented since terminology and categorization vary considerably from country to country. Furthermore in some countries it is very difficult, even impossible, to obtain reliable and recent data. An estimated 10 percent of the world's children are disabled. Table 1 shows that in the United States 4.2 million children received special education in 1988–89. That is 9.4 percent of the total population of children and youth aged six to seventeen. Eighty percent of children live in developing countries and few receive special services of any kind (Hegarty 1990).

Despite the fact that it has been more than 40 years since the Universal Declaration of Human Rights asserted that "everyone has a right to education," many children in the world do not receive adequate education, including those who have disabilities. The text of the 1990 world Conference on Education for All, held in Thailand, pointed out that the following realities persist:

(a) More than 100 million children, including at least 60 million girls, have no access to primary schooling.

(b) More than 960 million adults, two-thirds of whom are women, are illiterate and functional illiteracy is a significant problem in industrialized and developing countries.

(c) More than one-third of the world's adults have no access to the printed knowledge, new skills, and technologies that could improve the quality of their lives and help them shape, and adapt to, social and cultural change.

(d) More than 100 million children and countless adults fail to complete basic education programs; millions more satisfy the attendance requirements but do not acquire essential knowledge and skills.

The contribution of special education, therefore, has to be considered against this background of international crisis with respect to education in general.

Probably the most helpful source of data with respect to special educational provision internationally arises out of a survey of 58 countries conducted in 1986–87 (UNESCO 1988b). The information provided by this survey illustrates the discrepancies in the level of progress among the various regions and countries. For example, 34 of the countries had fewer than one percent of pupils enrolled in special educational programs and 10 of these countries had special education available for less than one-tenth of one percent of pupils.

Precise figures for developing countries are particularly difficult to establish but the studies that are available confirm the disturbing scale of the problem. For example, Ross (1988) summarized data gathered from 13 countries in eastern and southern Africa indicating that virtually all these countries had special education enrollments for approximately 0.1 percent or fewer of the school age population. Such data led Hegarty (1990) to conclude: "The stark reality underlying these figures is that the great majority of children and young people with disabilities do not receive an appropriate education—if indeed they are offered any education. In many countries, less than one child in a hundred receives the special educational provision that s/he needs" (p. 4).

3. *Historical Developments*

3.1 *Early Developments*

It is possible to detect certain patterns in the historical development of special education across different countries. The pace of these developments varies from country to country. It is also important to note that the field of special education is of relatively recent origin. In its early stages the emphasis was on provision for children with distinct disabilities but with the expansion of public education, broader forms of special education have been introduced.

In the United Kingdom the first schools for the blind and deaf were founded toward the end of the eighteenth century. The first separate education provision for children with physical disabilities was made in 1851; before the middle of the nineteenth century so called mentally defective children were often placed in workhouses and infirmaries. Special provision for pupils with milder forms of disability came much later.

As with ordinary education, education for children with disabilities in many countries began with individual and charitable enterprise. Then the government intervened first to support voluntary efforts, and finally to create a national framework in which public and voluntary agencies could act in partnership to see that all children received a suitable education. In many developing countries such a national framework has still to be established (UNESCO 1988a).

3.2 Developments since 1960

Many current practices in special education have been developed since the early 1960s. This period has been marked by significant shifts in beliefs within the field and this process of change is still apparent in many parts of the world.

During the early part of that period there was a marked emphasis on making provision for children with particular disabilities. In many countries provision of special education depended on assessing a child with respect to a perceived handicapping category or condition. Thus, over the years, special education became a separate world catering to that small percentage of children perceived as disabled. Those involved in special education had relatively little contact with mainstream schools. This isolation was reinforced in some countries by the fact that many of the providers of special education were voluntary organizations and that some special schools were located in accommodations away from the community.

The emphasis changed in the later 1960s and early 1970s. A concern with equal opportunities in a number of Western countries heightened awareness of children in ordinary schools who were perceived as making unsatisfactory progress. Consequently there was a substantial growth in various forms of remedial education, including the establishment of special classes within or attached to mainstream schools.

3.3 Trends since the 1970s

Further changes occurred in the 1970s in several areas of the world, including the United States, Canada, Australia, and several Western European countries. New ideas emerged that challenged the basis of existing provisions for pupils having special educational needs. Adams (1986) summarized six trends that were particularly important. These were:

(a) a growing understanding that handicapping conditions are much more widely spread, more varied, and more complex than categorization systems based largely on medical criteria tended to indicate;

(b) greater awareness that not only does the incidence of handicap and the recognition of it alter over time as a result of medical, economic, and social changes, but also that the difficulties encountered by young people in their educational and general development are likely to arise as much from disadvantaged circumstances as from individual characteristics;

(c) more general acceptance of the fact that parents, however much in some cases they may be "part of the problem," not only have rights in relation to their children which must be respected but also have a unique and valuable contribution to make to their children's development which must be more effectively exploited by the professionals;

(d) a growing recognition of the value of early intervention to help children with special needs and of the need for continuing attention with regular review and appropriate modification of support programs to meet their changing needs;

(e) a better appreciation of the fact that there is no sharp divide between the "handicapped" and the "normal" but rather a range of individual needs across a continuum;

(f) wider understanding and acceptance of the fact that every young person has a right to as full, independent, and "normal" life as possible and that therefore the aim of the community in relation to young people with more severe difficulties must be as much integration as possible into mainstream school and community life.

3.4 National Legislation

As a result of these trends significant legislation to change the basis of special education was introduced in a number of countries. Possibly the most influential of these was Public Law 94–142, the Education for All Handicapped Children Act (1975), in the United States. This sought a legislative solution to educational inequities in that it was designed to redress the denial of rights to education of the handicapped (Yanok, 1986). The key provision was the requirement that public schools throughout the United States should provide appropriate education for every school-age handicapped child irrespective of the nature of the child's disability. More specifically the legislation mandated that all students with disabilities be provided with appropriate instruction in the least restrictive environment possible, which for most would be in the regular classroom. It also specified an elaborate set of procedures and timelines for referral, assessment, classification, and placement of students, and extended to students and parents certain constitutional rights and procedural safeguards (Skrtic 1991). In years following 1975, provisions of PL 94–142 were amended to extend the right to education to younger disabled children, mandatorily from age three and permissively from the moment of birth.

The United States legislation has subsequently inspired similar developments in other Western countries. For example, the 1981 Education Act in England and Wales sought to establish a new framework for children requiring special provision. Its main strategy was the introduction of the Statement of Special Educational Need, an extensive reporting procedure used to monitor the progress of individual pupils and, where necessary, provide them with additional resources. This legislation has broadly similar approaches to those required by the United States legislation.

Evidence of new legislation internationally is provided by a UNESCO survey (1988b). Two-thirds of the respondents in the survey (i.e., 38 out of 58 countries) made reference to new legislation under discussion or being introduced. This ranged from loosely formulated discussions of the need for various legislative developments to definite plans to introduce regulations governing specific aspects of educational provision.

4. Administrative Arrangements and Policies

Special education is provided through a variety of administrative arrangements. As noted above, in many parts of the world a first arrangement made for special education is in the form of specialized residential schools. This involves bringing disabled children together not only for schooling, but for a total living experience. For example, children who are blind may be collected from a whole province, state, or region for placement in a residential school where they live in dormitories and attend school, usually on campus. Sometimes the students remain in the residential school on a year-round basis; in other instances, they return to their homes for occasional weekends and for vacation periods. Residential schools are common for students who are blind, deaf, or mentally retarded; but the trend is downward for such placements in industrialized nations, especially for children who are mentally retarded (Zappolo et al 1990, Lakin et al 1982).

A second common type of arrangement is the specialized day school. In this case an entire school is staffed and equipped to serve a given category of students with disabilities, but it operates only during school hours. Students live at home or occasionally in foster homes or specialized community facilities. Usually this involves individualized arrangements to transport the students to and from the school. Such schools may employ physical and occupational therapists, remedial physical education teachers, speech therapists, nurses, and part-time medical physicians, in addition to specialized teachers.

Evidence from the UNESCO survey (1988b) indicates that the predominant form of provision for special education in many parts of the world is in separate special schools. Such schools often serve very limited numbers of children, leaving many children with disabilities with little or no education. These observations led the participants in UNESCO's consultation in special education (1988a) to make the following statement: "Given the size of the demand and the limited resources available, the education and training needs of the majority of disabled persons cannot be met by special schools and centres" (p. 15). Consequently, a way forward will require changes in both special and mainstream schools. Mainstream schools have to develop forms of organization and teaching that cater to greater pupil diversity; while those special schools that do exist must develop an outward looking stance and take on significantly new roles (Hegarty 1990).

Another arrangement is the special class. In this case an entire classroom, usually located in a regular school, is used to serve disabled children. For example, there may be a special class for children who are mentally retarded or learning disabled. By this arrangement, disabled pupils often attend the same school as the nondisabled children of their neighborhood. There may be some degree of mainstreaming or integration of the disabled and nondisabled students at the school; for example, in shared use of a lunchroom and playground, or perhaps more widely through other forms of integration. Usually enrollments in special classes are lower in number of students per class than in regular or general education classes. Limits in special class enrollments are often imposed by government rules or regulations in return for special financial subsidies to the program. Because special classes can be distributed widely geographically, less specialized transportation is needed than in special day school arrangements.

Still other arrangements include part-time specialized classes and resource rooms managed by teachers who provide part-time services to disabled pupils. A student might be enrolled in a general education class for most of the school day but go for part-time help each day, perhaps an hour or two, to the resource room. The resource room teacher offers intensive help in specific areas of need, such as remedial reading instruction. A student who is blind may go to a specialized resource room for limited periods of instruction in braille, mobility, and orientation. The resource room arrangement involves a degree of integration and has grown rapidly in recent years in some nations, most notably in the United States. Teachers who work in resource rooms may spend some of their work time in consultation with regular classroom teachers as a way of extending and coordinating programs for disabled students.

Some disabled students can be served while fully enrolled in regular education programs if they and/or their teachers are given extra help through contact

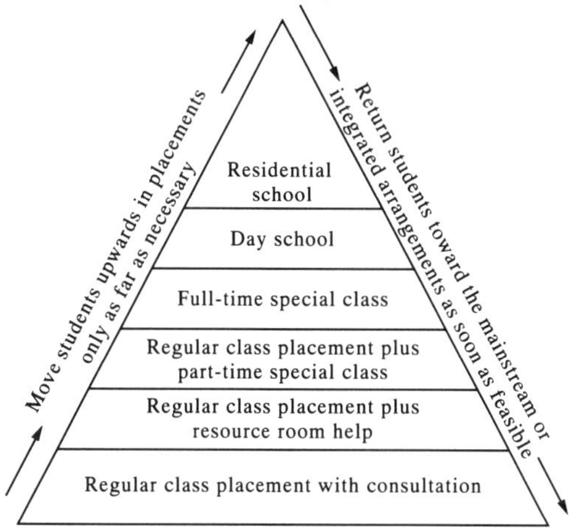

Figure 1
A continuum of special education arrangements

with itinerant specialists or consultants. Speech therapists often work on an itinerant basis, perhaps serving students in several schools. Students with speech and language problems may be called out of their regular classes for short periods of help each day or several times each week by the itinerant speech therapist. Similarly, itinerant teachers of braille and/or mobility and orientation may teach for brief periods in school hours pupils who are blind; others add help in afterschool and vacation periods in their special fields.

4.1 A Continuum of Placement Options

The full set of special education arrangements and policies concerning school placements for students with disabilities can be represented in chart form as in Figure 1 (Reynolds 1962). The continuum of placements is ordered according to the degree of separation or integration provided for disabled students. As one moves up the continuum, programs become more specialized, expensive, and segregated; at the top of the continuum, in residential schools, the student studies only with specialized teachers and lives only with other disabled students, most often with those who bear the same categorical labels.

The continuum is intended to convey the idea that most disabled students can be served in regular school placements, if supportive help is provided. To the side of the triangle, a policy is expressed to the effect that students should receive no more specialized placement than is required and that, if placed in a special education program, a goal should be to return pupils toward the mainstream as rapidly as is feasible.

In some industrialized nations, perhaps most notably in North America and Europe, there is criticism of the continuum idea for suggesting the possibility that any segregated form of special education, such as residential schools, is a suitable arrangement. Such critics assert that only fully integrated or mainstreamed arrangements of special education are acceptable (Meyer et al 1991, Taylor 1988).

4.2 The World-wide Movement for Integration

In many countries throughout the world integration is a central element in planning special education (e.g., Ainscow, 1990, Pijl and Meijer 1991, UNESCO 1988b). Such an emphasis seems sensible for Third World countries given the extent of the need and the inevitable limitations of available resources. It is also important to note that in many developing countries substantial "casual" integration of children with disabilities in ordinary schools occurs (Miles 1989).

In considering the current scene internationally with respect to integration there is again the problem of differences of definition. Pijl and Meijer (1991) use the term "integration" as a collective noun for all attempts to avoid a segregated and isolated education for pupils with disabilities. As a result of their survey of policies for integration in eight Western countries they suggest that its scope can range from the actual integration of regular and special schools (or classes) to measures for reducing the outflow of students from regular education to special education. Consequently it becomes very difficult to quantify the numbers of pupils with special needs who receive their education in integrated settings, particularly if the important distinction is made between social and curricular integration.

Developed countries are experiencing their own difficulties in establishing effective policies for integration. The existence of well established separate provision in special schools and classes creates complex policy dilemmas leading many countries to operate what Pijl and Meijer (1991) refer to as "two tracks." In other words, these countries have parallel, but separate, segregation and integration policies.

In some countries integration represents an aspiration for the future. In Germany, for example, while some pilot initiatives based on the idea of integration are underway, students who are declared eligible for special education must be placed in a special school; statistics for 1986 showed that 4.2 percent of all students between six and sixteen years of age were in separate schools for special education. On the other hand, Denmark and Norway have shown considerable progress in implementing the integration principle. Here the local community school is seen as the normal setting for pupils with special needs.

Discrepancies between stated policy and actual practice are evident in many countries. For example, Pijl and Meijer (1991) note that despite the fact that special schools were abolished in Italy in 1977 most of the so-called integrated pupils are "integrated outside the classroom." Often this means that they are taught by support teachers in separate classrooms. It is reported that the reasons for these problems in implementing a policy of integration are that regular school teachers still do not regard the teaching of pupils with special needs as their responsibility and are often not equipped (by training or materials) to do so.

A problem reported from a number of industrialized countries is that, despite national policies emphasizing integration, there is evidence of a significant increase in the proportions of pupils being categorized and given separate placements in order that their schools can earn additional resources (Ainscow 1991). As a result of her analysis of policies in Australia, the United Kingdom, Scandinavia, and the United States, Fulcher (1989) suggests that the increased bureaucracy that is often associated with special education and the inevitable struggles that go on for additional resources have the effect of escalating the proportion of school children labeled as disabled. As an illustration of this process she describes how in Victoria, Australia, 3,000 students in regular schools are now labelled as "integration children," a category of disability that did not exist prior to 1984.

Dissatisfaction with progress toward integration has caused demands for more radical changes in policy in a number of countries (Ainscow 1991). In the United States this has led to the Regular Education Initiative, a movement calling for the merger of special and regular education (Wang et al. 1986, Will 1986, Stainback and Stainback 1984b). A thorough critical analysis of this development and the heated debate that it has created in the United States is provided by Skrtic (1991).

5. *Classification*

A traditional first step in the practical operation of most special education programs is the identification of students as disabled and in need of specialized instruction. This usually involves the classification of students in accord with a prevailing system of categories in the state or other political entity. Such classification can result in a public and stigmatic labeling of the child. Severely disabled children are usually identified in preschool years, by parents in collaboration with physicians, and can be enrolled in special education programs at an early age. Early education programs are increasingly available for disabled children. In the case of milder disabilities, needs often are not clear until after the children have been enrolled in regular schools. Then teacher observations cause referrals for special study, classification, and possibly special placement.

5.1 Extending the Categories

A pervasive trend in classification practices is to enlarge or extend the inclusiveness of the categories. For example, programs initiated to serve students who are blind tend to be extended to serve those who are partially sighted. Programs first designed to serve students who are deaf tend gradually to include more who are hard of hearing. The category "mental retardation" tends, at first, to include only students with severe and obvious degrees of attenuation in cognitive abilities, but then expands to include those described as "educable" and perhaps "borderline." Speech therapists initially prepared to deal with speech and language disorders may later be expected to deal with problems of tongue thrust and eating. Programs organized to serve disabled pupils may later serve others who are judged to be "at risk" of becoming disabled. New categories of disability tend to emerge quite regularly in relatively affluent communities, as in the current proposals in the United States of programs for children born to AIDS-infected mothers, students with attention deficit disorders (with or without hyperactivity), and children born to heroin-addicted mothers.

The proliferation and extension of categories complicates the challenges of diagnosis, classification, and placement in special education and of program administration. This in turn has added to the criticism of programs, for ills such as disjointedness and proceduralism (Reynolds et al. 1987). Disjointedness refers to the problems of coherent administration of many separate programs within the schools, when each has its own rules, bureaucratic managers, advocacy system, funding arrangement, and accountability procedures. Proceduralism refers to the tendency for procedural norms and rules to assume primacy over substantive matters when details and paperwork require much time and energy.

5.2 Educational Classification

Presumably the classification and placement of students in special education programs should have enhancing effects on the instruction and learning of those who are classified. This proposes that classification in the schools should be related to distinctly educational decisions. Accordingly, a student is blind for educational purposes when instruction in braille reading methods is clearly indicated, in preference over clear print reading. Blindness thus may have a somewhat different meaning in the schools than in the medical clinic or in a social services office. Similarly, a pupil is deaf for educational purposes when special communications techniques not involving audition must be taught. A pupil is appropriately classified as mentally retarded in the schools only when a distinctive prescription for educational procedures is indicated for the child and when there is evidence that such a classification and placement is likely to have enhancing effects on the child's learning. This use of the mental retardation classification may not coincide fully with sociolegal classifications or approaches used in nonschool agencies.

Student classification and placement is often a problem because of failure to adhere to a strictly educational orientation. The problem is associated with the fact that a range of professionals, such as psychologists and physicians, are often involved in classification, some of them having little experience in school-related decisions. It appears that a trend toward wider use of curriculum-based assessment practices may be replacing diagnostic and classification procedures that have little relevance to instruction (Tucker 1985). A related development is the increasing use of noncategorical approaches to program organization (see *Mildly Handicapped Students: Noncategorical Approach*).

5.3 Labeling and Stigma

Some categorical classifications tend to result in a degree of public labeling of students. Terms such as "mentally retarded" and "emotionally disturbed" appear to be especially stigmatic. Some parents of children given such labels resent and resist the labels and occasionally use legal procedures to express their resistance. In the United States, a number of such legal cases have been pursued by parents, resulting in court-ordered revisions of classification and labeling practices (Larry P v Riles 1972). A further complication in such controversies is that stigmatic labels have been used more often for children of families that are in minority status on the basis of race, ethnicity, linguistic status, or socioeconomic level than for others. A study by a special panel of the US. National Academy of Science showed, for example, that children of African-American heritage were classified as mentally retarded at about three times the rate for the generality of pupils in American schools (Heller et al. 1982). Such a disproportion is considered by many to be biased and prejudicial.

Classification concerning mildly disabled pupils is controversial in many ways. Procedures tend to be unreliable and unrelated to needed instruction. Large discrepancies exist in use of categories in various political jurisdictions. These difficulties and inconsistencies are one cause for the belief held by significant numbers of educators that most mildly disabled pupils should be served in strengthened regular classes and schools and not be classified as disabled (Will 1986) (see *Children and Youth with Special Needs, Diagnosis and Classification of*).

6. Special Education Personnel

Often the earliest leadership in initiating special education programs in a country is provided by physicians. Correspondingly, earliest forms of special education are often conducted in hospitals, clinics, or other facilities separate from schools. Later, teachers and schools take increasing responsibility.

6.1 Teacher Preparation

In the most developed nations increasing numbers of special education teachers are prepared in colleges and universities in tracks that overlap with programs for preparation of regular class teachers. Much of the development of specialized teacher preparation in institutions of higher education has occurred since the Second World War. The rate of special education program development was very rapid in this same period and, even with the increasing number of teacher preparation programs, the number of specialized teachers available has always and virtually everywhere, lagged behind program developments and needs in the schools.

In the United States, for example, 84,000 specialized teachers of disabled students were employed in 1968–69; but it was estimated that an additional 237,000 special educators would have been required to completely serve disabled students aged five to seventeen (US Office of Education 1969). The number of colleges offering sequences of preservice preparation for special education teachers in the United States increased from a mere handful in the 1940s to about 350 in 1968. By 1988–89, the number of special education teachers employed in the United States increased to about 300,000; but at least 20 percent of them were judged to be underprepared for their work. The shortage of fully prepared specialized teachers is one cause of the increasing emphasis upon preparing regular teachers to accommodate disabled pupils in regular classrooms and increasing use of specialists in consultation with regular class teachers as an alternative to the direct instruction of disabled pupils by special educators.

The UNESCO survey (1988b) presents a gloomy picture with respect to the international scene in teacher preparation. Only a minority of the 58 countries reported coverage of disability issues in preservice training programs for all teachers. Inservice training opportunities for teachers in regular schools were similarly limited. A wide range of training opportunities was reported for teachers specializing in special education—a five-year course in a teachers college at one extreme, to on-the-job instruction offered on an ad hoc basis at the other. While it is difficult to generalize, it seems clear that the main thrust of training is directed at specialists who will work in segregated special schools. However, it can be argued that the vast majority of children with disabilities could be helped in mainstream schools by relatively minor adjustments to the teaching that is provided (Hegarty 1990). Thus an investment in the preservice preparation of teachers with respect to strategies for accommodating pupil diversity could bring about major improvements in the special education provision offered by schools.

6.2 Auxiliary Professional Staff

In addition to teachers, special education programs

involve a variety of other specialists such as psychologists, audiologists, social workers, physical therapists, ocupational therapists, and speech—language therapists who spend much of their time working with disabled students. In addition, a large number of paraprofessionals are employed in special education programs. Relatively little attention has been given to the preparation of paraprofessionals, but this is a likely area for increasing attention. Some paraprofessionals perform quite specialized functions, such as mediating communications between deaf and hearing persons. Such persons require specific skills and some vocational/technical schools are now offering the necessary training.

6.3 Burnout

Problems of supplying special education teachers are enlarged by relatively high rates of teacher "burnout" or withdrawal from the field. "Burnout" rates are especially high for teachers of students who are emotionally disturbed or mentally retarded. One proposal for addressing the "burnout" problem is to rotate special education teachers into regular classes for work with nondisabled pupils for a year or two after a period of service in special education. Better preservice preparation and stronger inservice supports for the special education teachers are also believed to be helpful.

6.4 Curricula for Specialized Teacher Preparation

Curricula for preparation of special education teachers who serve blind or deaf pupils involve some distinct elements, such as teaching braille in the case of blindness, or manual forms of communication in the case of the deaf. For most other categories of disability, general principles of instruction that apply in the instruction of nondisabled pupils appear to be important in special education as well; however, the disabled pupils probably need more intensive instructional help over longer periods of time and with more structure than do nondisabled pupils. Attention to individual differences among students is always important. Some curricular elements in special education teacher preparation which may require special emphasis are: understanding and working with families, methods for creating positive interdependencies among students (e.g., using cooperative groups of disabled and nondisabled pupils), individualized assessment practices, consultation, modifying curriculum and materials to meet individual needs, behavioral methods and direct instruction, teaching for self-regulation and strategic (metacognitive) behavior, teaching social skills, teaching basic literacy skills, and use of technology (including prostheses, computers, etc.) (see *Teacher Development*).

7. Research

The field of special education tends to rely heavily on psychologists and others from outside the field to conduct most of the relevant research. An exception to this observation is the subcategory of severe and profound mental retardation (or developmental disabilities) which has produced a good supply of long-term researchers (Meyer et al. 1991). This seems to be associated with the strong preference of researchers in this field for use of behavioral methods of analysis, instruction, and research. A second exception is in the field of language and speech disorders which has produced a significant number of career-oriented researchers. In both of these exceptional areas, major professional and scientific organizations exist which have provided publication outlets for research in the several fields.

7.1 Problems of Research

A number of practical difficulties make research in special education difficult. One such difficulty concerns cohort changes over time. For example, a large number of children became blind in the 1940s and early 1950s because of overconcentrated use of oxygen in incubators for infants with low birth weights. The cause was discovered in 1954 and the incidence rate for blindness decreased sharply in areas with good medical communications and services. A number of blind children appeared in the 1960s, many of them showing multiple disabilities, who had suffered German measles during an intrauterine period. Thus, the causes of blindness in children from each period were remarkably different. In many characteristics they vary markedly, not only individually but also as time cohorts.

A second difficulty concerns the increasing dispersal of disabled pupils. With the increased emphasis on an integration policy, it is becoming less common to find large numbers of disabled pupils in a single location. More of them attend regular schools in a highly dispersed way and under increasingly diverse circumstances. Doing research under such conditions involves more travel and time, more expense, and more difficulties in interpretation.

A third difficulty arises from unreliable classification practices, so that a researcher who wishes to study students with learning disabilities, for example, cannot be certain that the students found in one situation with that label bear much resemblance to students with the same label in other situations. The same difficulties offer complications for the researcher who wishes to do meta-analyses in special education; data on research subjects and other features of investigation are often lacking or ambiguous. Increasingly, the case is made that the field of special education needs a "marker variable" system to facilitate better communications among researchers and with practitioners. Use of more rigorous standards by editors of research journals in the field would also help to make clear the characteristics of subjects and other matters of research, thus facilitating meta-analyses and generalization of findings.

In addition to these practical difficulties it is possible to identify evidence of a growing theoretical discourse about the nature of research in the field of special education (Barton 1988, Stainback and Stainback 1984a). Specifically, researchers in a number of countries have drawn attention to the limitations of psychological perspectives that emphasize quantitative methodologies. Their analysis leads them to argue for a move towards a greater use of qualitative methods of inquiry. Stainback and Stainback (1984a) suggest that such a move could lead to the development of better-grounded theories and more attention being given to the social and educational relevance of research activities. It would also be welcomed, they argue, by teachers who would find this orientation less intimidating and more relevant to their day-to-day concerns.

7.2 Support for Research

Only rarely has significant support been provided for research on special education topics. The UNESCO survey found that approximately one-third of countries responding allocated separate national funds for research and development in special education. The research topics cited with greatest frequency were integration, early intervention, the organization of special education, the transition from school to adult life, and incidence surveys. The United States government launched a limited program of research in 1957 that has grown steadily in succeeding years. The program operates mainly on an extramural basis: the federal government gives grants and contracts to outside agencies such as universities, public schools, and state departments of education that compete for funds within priority areas targeted by federal officers. Even in the most prosperous environments, however, support for research is minimal.

7.3 Evaluation

The field of special education has so far failed to provide impressive data concerning merits of its programs. For example, efficacy studies concerning special classes for students who are mentally retarded have had equivocal outcomes, but reviewers uniformly find faults with the research methods and discount findings accordingly. However, more recent meta-analytic studies offer little more convincing evidence for the value of special educational programs. In a 1979 review of efficacy research, Semmel et al. concluded that the evidence does not show advantages for special education placements as compared with results when disabled students remain in regular school programs. A summary report by Dunn (1968) under the title "Special education for the mildly retarded: Is much of it justifiable?" was very negative about outcomes of some special education and caused a broad flow of criticism in the United States.

Broadly framed evaluation studies are very difficult to conduct with precision. In cases of severe disability, special education programs often represent the only opportunity available for education. Whether programs for mildly disabled pupils which involve separation from regular classes and schools are distinctly beneficial for students is a cause of widespread debate in the United States (Will 1986).

8. International Activities

Since the International Year of Disabled Persons (1981) there has been considerable international collaboration with respect to the development of special education policies and programs. Agencies such as UNESCO, UNICEF, and OECD have acted to encourage collaborative developments and many national agencies have invested resources to give them support. The world Declaration on Education for All that arose as a result of the 1990 conference in Jomtien, Thailand, gives further impetus to these efforts. In Article 3.5, it states: "The learning needs of the disabled demand special attention. Steps need to be taken to provide equal access to education to every category of disabled persons as an integral part of the education system."

This challenge is enormous, particularly in developing countries.

Preferred ways of conducting international efforts remain a matter of debate. For example, Miles (1989) questions the value of introducing Western models of special education into countries such as Pakistan and India. He suggests that the reasons they often do not seem to work are complex and include "conceptual blockage." He notes that Western special education is constructed on views of children and the purposes of schooling that may be largely alien to much of the population of the Indian subcontinent. Furthermore, he is critical of the work of advisers visiting Third World countries as part of what he characterizes as the "Western conceptual crusade" that seems to ignore the realities of Third World situations.

At the International Consultation on Special Education (UNESCO 1988a) participants reviewed and assessed international developments related to special education over the previous decade. They also made suggestions concerning the focus of actions to be taken. Conscious of the magnitude of the problems, and committed to the principles of normalization, integration, and participation, they recommended that the complementary approaches of community-based rehabilitation (CBR) and integrated education represented the most effective ways forward.

Community-based rehabilitation is being used by an increasing number of developing countries as a strategy to eliminate the constraints of institution-based rehabilitation. Its implementation in a particular context will depend to a large extent upon a country's strategies for socioeconomic development. Countries often start by setting up a CBR project in a selected district, which provides the basis for gaining national experience and expertise. This is followed by the launching of a wider program, possibly as part of a national plan. Werner (1987) provides an impressive manual of suggestions for setting up such initiatives in rural communities including examples of child-to-child activities. These are intended to encourage school-aged children to help their disabled peers. Approaches developed for use in Third World contexts mirror some of the techniques now being used to create inclusive schools in the West (e.g., Lipsky and Gartner 1989). Both emphasize collaboration, including cooperative learning approaches, as a means of utilizing existing resources for problem solving in educational contexts.

With respect to international efforts to encourage integrated education, a number of interesting initiatives exist. For example, Freeze and Rampaul (1991) describe a development project in Trinidad and Tobago involving the Ministry of Education, the University of Manitoba, and the Canadian International Development Agency. Their approach involves training administrators and teachers in a consultative–collaborative model for providing support to teachers in regular schools. As a result many schools have established resource programs resulting in the integration of previously segregated students.

The UNESCO project "Special Needs in the Classroom" aims to develop and disseminate ideas and materials that can be used by teacher educators to support teachers in mainstream schools (Ainscow 1990). The project materials have been developed through a process of international collaboration and are contained in a resource pack intended to be used as part of pre- and inservice staff development programs. Emphasis is placed on approaches to teaching whole classes that accommodate pupil diversity. During 1990 and 1991 the resource pack was tested in pilot projects by an international team in eight countries (Canada, Chile, India, Jordan, Kenya, Malta, Spain, and Zimbabwe). UNESCO intends to widen this project by using the existing resource team to mount regional initiatives throughout the world.

Additional assistance to the process of international collaboration is provided by a number of professional organizations. The division of International Special Education and Services of the Council for Exceptional Children (in Reston, Virginia, USA) serves as a catalyst for international sharing of promising practices, research, and technology. The International Association of Special Education, through its publications and biannual conferences, fulfills a similar role.

9. Problems and Issues

From this survey of international developments it is possible to draw out a number of important problems and issues that require urgent attention. While the field of special education has made much progress, an analysis of the scene around the world presents a disturbing picture. Hegarty (1990) states: "Those with disabilities, who ironically have the greatest need of education, are the least likely to receive it. This is true of developed and developing countries alike" (p. 2). In developed countries many pupils with disabilities, and others who fail to achieve satisfactory progress in school learning, are formally excluded from the mainstream education system or receive less favorable treatment within it than other children. On the other hand, in many developing countries the continuing struggle to achieve compulsory education for a majority of children takes precedence over meeting the needs of those with disabilities.

The UNESCO Consultation on Special Education (1988a) outlined a number of general obstacles to improvement. These are:

(a) inadequate perceptions and thus policy formation, which is linked to attitudes (cultural, religious, political, or ideological);

(b) rigid legislative and administrative provision, especially as related to characterization of disability and categorical allocation of resources often not matched to individual needs;

(c) the discrepancy between what exists and present knowledge of what should exist due to poor dissemination of knowledge.

(d) the fact that special education in some countries is still perceived as a charitable venture—a welfare program—and responsibility for special education is not always with educational authorities;

(e) administrative and professional separation that continues to divide the educational community into "special" and "regular" components isolated from each other.

As the international field of special education continues to move forward, there has emerged a new set of voices arguing for further reform. These voices reflect developments in different parts of the world. While inevitably they are not in full agreement with respect to their analysis and recommendations, they all adopt a critical perspective, seeking to question the field's theories and assumptions. Examples of writers sharing this perspective include in Australia, Fulcher (1989); in the United Kingdom, Tomlinson (1982); in New Zealand, Ballard (1990); and in the United States Skrtic (1991) and Reynolds et al. (1987). They all draw on theories from outside special education, such as sociology, politics, philosophy, and organizational analysis. Their work, and that of others adopting similar stances, offers a more radical analysis of the policy and practice of special education and points to new possibilities for reform.

One of their concerns is with the way pupils within schools come to be designated as having special needs. They see this as a social process that needs to be continually challenged. More specifically, they argue that the continued emphasis on explaining educational difficulties in terms of child-centered characteristics has the effect of preventing progress in the field. The argument is summed up by Dyson (1990) who states: "The fact remains that the education system as a whole, and the vast majority of institutions and teachers within it, are approaching the twenty-first century with a view of special needs the same as that with which their counterparts approached the present century. That view, for all its avowed concern for the individual child, promotes injustice on a massive scale. It demands to be changed" (pp. 60–61). This radical perspective leads to a reconceptualization of the special needs task (Ainscow 1991). This suggests that progress in the field is dependent upon a general recognition that difficulties experienced by pupils come about as a result of the way schools are organized and the forms of teaching that are provided. In other words, as Skrtic puts it, students with special needs are artifacts of the traditional curriculum.

The way forward must be to reform schools in ways that will make them respond positively to pupil diversity, seeing individual differences as something to be nurtured and celebrated. Within such a conceptualization, a consideration of difficulties experienced by pupils and teachers can provide an agenda for reform and insights as to how this might be accomplished. However, this kind of approach is only possible where there exists a respect for individuality and a culture of collaboration that encourages and supports problem-solving. Such cultures are likely to facilitate the learning of all pupils and, with them, the professional learning of all teachers. Ultimately, therefore, increasing equity is the key to improvements in schooling for all.

See also: Children and Youth with Special Needs, Diagnosis and Classification of; Integrated Services for Children and Youth with Special Needs; Mainstreaming

References

Adams F (ed.) 1986 *Special Education*, Councils and Education Press, Harlow

Ainscow M 1990 Special needs in the classroom: The development of a teacher education resourse pack. *International Journal of Special Education* 5(1): 13–20

Ainscow M (eds) 1991 *Effective Schools for All.* Paul H Brookes, Fulton, London

Ballard K D 1990 Special education in New Zealand: Disability, politics and empowerment. *International Journal of Disability, development and Education* 37(2): 109–24

Barton L 1988 Research practice: The need for alternative perspectives. In: Barton L (ed.) 1988 *The Politics of Special Education*. Falmer, Lewes

Dunn L 1968 Special education for the mildly retarded—Is much of it justifiable? *Excep. Child.* 35(1): 5–22

Dyson A 1990 Special educational needs and the concept of change. *Oxford Rev. of Educ.* 16(1): 55–66

Freeze D R, Rampaul W 1991 Consultative–collaborative resource teaching as a means of improving special education service delivery. In: Upton G (ed.) 1991 *Staff Training and Special Educational Needs*. Fulton, London

Fulcher G 1989 *Disabling Policies? A Comparative Approach to Education Policy and Disability* Falmer Lewes

Hegarty S 1990 *The Education of Children and Young People with Disabilities: Principles and Practice*. UNESCO, Paris

Heller K A, Holtzman W H, Messick S (eds.) 1982 *Placing Children in Special Education: A strategy for Equity.* National Academy Press, Washington, DC

Lakin K L, Krantz G C, Bruininks R H, Clumpner J L, Hill B K 1982 One hundred years of data on populations of public residential facilities for mentally retarded people. *Am. J. Mental Deficiency* 87(1): 1–8

Larry P v Riles 1972 495 Supp 926, US District Court for Northern District of California

Lipsky D K, Gartner A 1989 *Beyond Separate Education: Quality Education for All.* Paul H Brookes, Baltimore, Maryland

Meyer L, Peck C, Brown L (eds.) 1991 *Critical Issues in the Lives of People with Severe Disabilities.* Paul H Brookes, Baltimore, Maryland

Miles M 1989 The role of special education in information based rehabilitation. *International Journal of Special Education* 4(2): 111–18

Pijl S J, Meijer C J W 1991 Does intergration count for much? An analysis of the practices of integration in eight countries. *European Journal of Special Needs Education* 6(2): 100–11

Reynolds M C 1962 A framework for considering some issues in special education. *Except. Child.* 28(7): 367–70

Reynolds M C, Wang M C, Walberg H W 1987 The necessary restructuring of special and regular education. *Excep. Child.* 53(5): 391–98

Ross D H 1988 *Educating Handicapped Young People in Eastern and Southern Africa in 1981–88.* UNESCO, Paris

Semmel M I, Gottlieb J, Robinson N M 1979 Mainstreaming: Perspectives on educating handicapped children in the public schools. In: Berliner D C (ed.) 1979 *Review of Research in Education 7: 223–79.* American Educational Research Association, Washington, DC

Skrtic T M 1991 *Behind Special Education: A Critical Analysis of Professional Culture and School Organization.* Love, Denver, Colorado

Stainback S, Stainback W 1984a Broadening the research perspective in special education. *Excep. Child.* 50(5): 400–408

Stainback W, Stainback S 1984b A rationale for the merger of special and regular education. *Excep. Child.* 51: 102–111

Taylor S J 1988 Caught in the continuum: A critical analysis of the principles of the least restrictive environment.

Journal of the Association for Persons with Severe Handicaps 13(1): 41–53
Tomlinson S 1982 *A Sociology of Special Education*. Routledge, London
Tucker J A (ed.) 1985 Curriculum-based assessment. *Except. Child.* 52(3)
UNESCO 1988a UNESCO *Consultation on Special Education: Final Report*. UNESCO, Paris.
UNESCO 1988b *Review of the Present Situation in Special Education*. UNESCO, Paris.
US Office of Education 1969 *The Education Professions*. US Government Printing Office, Washington, DC
Wang M C, Reynolds M C, Walberg H J 1986 Rethinking special education. *Educ. Leadership* 44(1): 26–31
Werner D 1987 *Disabled Village Children*. The Hesperian Foundation, Palo Alto, California
Will M 1986 *Educating Students with Learning Problems—A Shared Responsibility*. US Department of Education, Washington, DC
Yanok, J 1986 Free appropriate public education for handicapped children: Congressional intent and judicial interpretation. *Remedial and Special Education* 72: 49–53
Zappolo A, Lakin K C, Hill B K 1990 Persons in institutions and special residential settings. In: Fitzgerald I, Thompson S (eds.) 1990 *Disability in the United States*. Springer, New York

Further Reading

Ainscow M 1989 *Special Education in Change*. Fulton Cambridge Institute of Education, London
British Journal of Special Education
Exceptional Children
International Journal of Special Education
Journal of Special Education
Scheerenberger R C 1983 *A History of Mental Retardation*. Paul H Brookes, Baltimore, Maryland
Special Children
Wang M C, Reynolds M C, Walberg H J 1987–91 *Handbook of Special Education: Research and Practice*. Pergamon, Oxford
Williams P 1991 *The Special Education Handbook*. Open University, Milton Keynes

M. C. Reynolds; M. Ainscrow

Children Caring for Children

Parents, children, and their communities strongly influence one another through a variety of styles and methods of personal and community interaction and care. In many societies, children have traditionally played a part in communal activities by concerning themselves with the social and intellectual development of other children through sibling care and informal peer instruction. More recently, concepts in sibling care with strong elements of role modeling have been reformulated in a broader approach under the rubric of the Child-to-Child program, which not only embraces educational and survival rationales, but also brings a more visible integration of school and community knowledge. This entry explores the main approaches to children caring for other children, and discusses the social and developmental contexts and situations in which the importance of Child-to-Child has evolved and contributed to the well-being of children in many developing countries.

The bulk of research on children caring for children comes from formal educational settings, and deals with helping behaviors such as peer tutoring and collaborative learning. Another strand of traditional research has examined the cultural and sociopsychological consequences of sibling care in different societies. However, there is little research data as yet on the type of caring behavior by children encompassed by Child-to-Child. While the processes of modernization and formal schooling initially tended to eliminate the need for children to care for other children, these same processes have, in many societies, resulted in the creation and continuation of conditions and contexts in which both sibling care and Child-to-Child are not only desirable, but essential.

1. Sibling Care

The responsibilities of siblings vary dramatically across cultures as a function of cultural differences in parent–child relationships. In general, industrialization, coupled with rapid political and economic changes, as well as the breakdown of many traditional ways of life, has devalued the contribution that children can make in seriously caring for other children. For example, in industrialized countries there is no expectation that children will contribute to feeding, bathing, and caring for the health of other children in the home. In less industrialized societies, however, siblings are expected to be important caregivers, and are accorded power appropriate to such roles. Older children look after siblings in the presence, and more often in the absence, of parents. They provide companionship, protection, and role models through direct instruction and play. They correct the language and behavior of the younger child. In societies where primary school pupils form the majority of those who are literate, children may be required to take their siblings to obtain services in modern institutions such as hospitals and immunization centers, a role which is critically important since the older children not only need to understand the instructions for the use of various technologies, but also have to explain those instructions to their parents.

Research on sibling relationships in the family has, unfortunately, tended to overemphasize negative aspects such as rivalry, competition, possible neglect of the younger child's needs, and the likelihood of passing on bad language, behaviors, and misinformation (Cooper and St John 1990). There is a paradoxical interplay between caring behavior and rivalry among children in the same family, and there is always the danger that the older child may present an unsuitable role model to the siblings. However, the broader framework in which serious sibling care is expected, developed, and provided emphasizes interdependency among all family members, responsibility to others, shared work and functions, and affiliation among the family members. Sibling care is seen not simply as a service to the younger child and the family, but also as an important social training experience to the older children in coping with present and future responsibilities.

2. *Child-to-Child Activities*

Many developing countries, with one third of their populations under the age of 15 years, face a challenge in meeting the needs of children. It had earlier been envisioned that schooling would quickly eliminate poverty, ignorance, and disease, leading to faster social and economic development. Unfortunately, schooling has neither been able to reach a large proportion of those who need it, nor achieved its promises for the largest part of the population. Children caring for children through Child-to-Child activities is a consequence of the inability of the educational and social service systems to make an overall impact in raising the quality of life for the majority of children living in rural and impoverished urban areas. Child-to-Child derives directly from the concept of primary health care (Morley and Lovel 1986), where the focus is on the way in which older children in a community can help to improve the health of younger ones. One solution is to mobilize the children themselves in helping to promote their own health and well-being.

Since 1975, the Child-to-Child program has mobilized teachers and health workers in some 70 countries to set up activities in schools; in informal educational institutions; in youth groups such as scouts, guides, and Red Cross clubs; in health centers; and on the streets. The power of children to spread health messages, ideas, and practices is being demonstrated in four ways: (a) through the modernized care they provide for younger brothers and sisters and other young children in the community; (b) through their influence upon other children in their age-group and community, especially those with less education and fewer opportunities than they have had; (c) through their influence as a group upon their own communities; and (d) through their influence as individuals upon their own families (Hawes 1988).

In approach and procedure, Child-to-Child is a broadening of the concepts and rationales of sibling care to a much more holistic approach, which increasingly addresses key variables such as feeding, nutrition, health, and physical care that affect the child's social and physical environment. Traditional sibling care is usually restricted to children in the same family and related households. The older children are not necessarily in school, and therefore rely on family and cultural knowledge of child rearing and care garnered through observation of parents. In contrast, the Child-to-Child program relies on school-based knowledge, at least initially.

The approach of Child-to-Child is to encourage children to understand various common health issues such as sanitation, water purification, accidents in rural environments, and basic nutrition and child feeding. This is achieved through teaching children more about health issues in their family and community; discussing the solutions to the identified health problems; encouraging children to take action as individuals and as a group to implement simple solutions; and evaluating how effective children's intervention has been in helping them plan how to do better the next time (Morley et al. 1987). It is understood that children cannot undertake and implement Child-to-Child activities without their teachers or other knowledgeable adults. Teachers must work with children in assembling and learning the knowledge that they are expected to pass on to other children.

There are many models for training children to participate as care givers (Somerset 1988). In the most structured programs, children referred to as "little teachers" are drawn from the elementary grades, and each chooses a younger child—a sibling, relative, or neighbor—to teach. The little teachers receive additional periods of instruction from the classroom teacher or Child-to-Child teacher each week, at the end of which the little teachers return home and teach the younger child the knowledge and skills they have acquired. Generally, the little teachers are largely left to develop their own methods, for it is assumed that effective transmission will take place spontaneously in the informal environment of the home or the neighborhood, provided the little teacher understands the material well. The little teachers help prepare the younger children for school entry, and, by so doing, enhance their own cognitive and affective growth. Therefore, the effort of the Child-to-Child teachers is directed towards developing their teaching skills (Somerset 1988). In many situations, however, such training is not recognized, and there has been no attempt to ascertain whether such training transcends typical rote learning, characteristic of the majority of classrooms in the developing world.

One of the consequences of desiring to arm children with accurate knowledge about community health has been the increasing tendency for Child-to-Child programs to bring together people from the education, health, nutrition, and environmental fields in order to introduce active learning in tackling environmental problems such as deforestation and urban pollution (Al Jarrash 1990). By integrating new approaches to learning, and consolidating literacy and numeracy, the Child-to-Child approach is helping to integrate health, nutrition, and environmental education more effectively into the school syllabus and across the curriculum.

There are, however, problems which limit the spread and effectiveness of Child-to-Child activities. As the ideas of Child-to-Child have been taken up, they have been adapted by different projects around the world, and have changed and developed. There has been little documentation of the ways in which local participants have translated the original ideas within new cultural and economic realities. Although some of the adaptations reaffirm the original notion that children can have influence with their friends and family working within the community, there is a tendency for these activities to become group-to-group rather than individual-to-individual. Many Child-to-Child activities are initiated with external funds which are not usually sustained. Increasingly, children lacking financial and material resources to work within communities and with individual children simply compose songs and poems and use radio and other media to spread health messages to an uncertain audience. There is a risk that children's group performances will be seen by the audiences simply as entertainment, and will therefore have little impact on their behavior. In Uganda, for example, UNICEF provided support to at least 10 rural schools in 1986 to initiate Child-to-Child activities, which included raising nursery seedlings and planning trees as a demonstration of what children can teach each other about protecting the environment. Within the following two years, tree-raising activities had ceased due to the failure of the children to raise additional funds to purchase either ready-to-plant tree seedlings or the plastic bags in which those seedlings are raised (Namuddu 1991).

3. *Innovative Programs Derived from Child-to-Child*

Allowing the needs of particular groups of children and youth to determine the nature of activities is a key factor in the success of Child-to-Child activities in different environments. In some communities, children who have dropped out of school, either because of receiving little learning or because of truancy, have become linked to school again through informal networks popularizing health and personal safety. In situations of war and political instability, orphaned children are cared for by primary school children from the community; forming foster relationships through activities such as storytelling, toy-making, playing, and watching films together. In other communities, children have been able to bring social services to handicapped children, and have assisted in giving support and adjustment to chronically ill children and youth. Other dimensions of activity emerging from the Child-to-Child concept expand the notion of children caring for children. They not only address the issues of academic help and the survival and development of children within a difficult and deteriorating socioeconomic environment, but also link these activities together in a more visible popularization of literacy, science, and technology (Young and Durston 1987).

3.1 Children Writing for Children

The persistence of high levels of illiteracy among large segments of the population in developing countries means that schools must improve their capacity to teach and consolidate reading and writing. Partly as a consequence of the desire to consolidate literacy, and parly because of the large quantities of information being amassed by children during Child-to-Child activities, a number of writing projects have emerged. These writing projects have five key characteristics which fit them into the concept of children caring for children: (a) the authors are children; (b) the target audience for the written texts is other children and youth, especially those who are out of school; (c) the texts are usually the product of research on a local problem, in areas such as health and the environment; (d) the main purpose of the writing is the instruction of other children; and (e) partnerships are formed between authors, readers, and the local community of adults in order to make the benefits of these activities widely visible and to preserve and legitimize indigenous knowledge (Namuddu 1991).

In many instances children have been encouraged to generate a continuous flow of language and numeracy materials for use by children in their own and other primary schools, thus enabling children to cope with the pernicious problem of the lack and inadequacy of locally relevant reading materials. Evidence from projects of this nature suggests that children come to feel that they have a responsibility for not only their own development and achievement, but also that of other children in the school.

3.2 Popularization of Science and Technology

Science has always been an important subject in the school curriculum. However, as economic and social conditions have deteriorated in many parts of the world, school systems have come under increasing stress and been unable to offer science as a practical subject. Within the Child-to-Child framework, ways have been sought to improve children's and the public's understanding of science either in or outside schools. The purpose has been to generate basic understanding by children and youth of science and the practical applications of technology meshed within local cultural and economic realities, using approaches generated and presided over by children (Savage 1992). Children have been responsible for many innovations. They have developed media that provide new ways to disseminate science to the public through drama, writing, film, and photography; planned, researched, written, produced, and distributed interactive publications about health, agriculture, and the environment; and helped to organize and participate in science camps and fairs. In the process, children have provided unusual opportunities for intervening and changing the way curriculum and learners are organized.

4. Conclusion

In conclusion, it is important to note that the concept of children caring for children is fluid, and evolving quickly as societies find themselves faced with the challenge of linking the work of schools to the task of uplifting the general standard of learning and living within the wider community. It is already evident in the early 1990s that children make an impact in the lives of communities through Child-to-Child and related activities. While there seems to have been a retreat from direct peer tutoring generally, children's indirect instruction of other children, youth, and even adults in areas such as practicing and consolidating literacy; popularizing science; and processing and using health, nutrition, agricultural and environmental technology is likely to increase, especially in developing countries.

See also: Childcare Policies and Programs: International Overview

References

Al Jarrash A 1990 *Child-to-Child 1990*. Institute of Education, London

Cooper C R, St John L 1990 Children helping children in the family: Developmental perspectives on sibling relationships. In: Foot C H, Morgan M, Shute R (eds.) 1990 *Children Helping Children*. Wiley, New York

Hawes H 1988 *Child-to-Child: Another Path to Learning*. UIE, UNESCO, Hamburg

Morley D, Lovel H 1986 *My Name is Today*. Macmillan, London

Morley D et al. 1987 *Mobilizing Education to Reinforce Health Care*. UNESCO, UNICEF, Paris

Namuddu K 1991 MINDSACROSS: *Primary School Pupils as Authors*. Kampala

Savage M 1992 Nourishing innovation in science education in Africa: The experience of the African Forum for Children's Literacy in Science and Technology. *Science, Technology and Development* 10(2): 246–64

Somerset H C A 1988 *Child-to-Child: A Survey 1987*. Institute of Education, London

Young B, Durston S 1987 *Primary Health Education*. Longman, London

K. Namuddu

Children's Literature

Children's literature includes the genres of realistic fiction, fantasy, poetry, biography, historical fiction, and nonfiction, as well as the picture book. Interest in books for children has continued to be strong since 1990, a trend reflected in the increased volume of publishing for children in many countries. Educators increasingly view children's literature as an important basis for reading and writing instruction and recognize that literature may significantly influence learning in other areas of the curriculum such as social studies, science, and art. The professional study of children's literature supports the trend toward literature throughout the curriculum, focusing on reading interests, reader response, historical research, and literary criticism. Teachers, librarians, and parents who are responsible for guiding children's reading recognize the importance of current information about reading interests, and that is reflected in the work of researchers from many countries. Information from studies of response to literature also plays a role in reading guidance. Research dealing with historical and critical features of children's literature provides a basis for examining trends over time as well as cross-national similarities and differences.

1. Reading Interests and Preferences

Contemporary studies of reading interests have focused on content factors and literary forms and devices as well as factors external to the text itself. Although such studies are useful guides to book selection, the results are not as clear as one might wish. For example, the category "animals" does not differentiate between a strong interest in informational books or a preference for realistic fiction about animals; nor does a category such as "make believe" reveal what elements of the genre actually appeal to children. Although the results should be taken as generalizations, interest studies are useful because they reveal trends over time and preferences of children at particular ages and in particular cultures.

Evidence from cross-national studies suggests that children from various countries show more similarity than difference in reading interests (Kirsch et al. 1976). In a comparison of preferences of children in the United Kingdom and United States, aged 7–10, Schofer (1981) found that adventure, animals, fantasy, hobbies, and travel were the most preferred categories for both boys and girls. There were some differences, however. Children in the United Kingdom preferred reading poetry to reading about people; United States children preferred reading about people.

In terms of factors external to text, students in middle grades and adolescence rely more on peers than on teachers and parents for reading guidance. Children in this age group are also more likely to choose books on the basis of favorite authors and are influenced by appearance factors such as the cover and content of the first page, length of the book, the illustrations, and the title (Burgess 1985, Wendelin and Zinck 1983).

1.1 United States

Broad-based studies suggest that the topics of strongest interest, across grade levels in the United States are animals, science, history, make-believe, mystery, and people (Chiu 1984). It appears that interest in history and science increases in intermediate grades and that interest in mystery and adventure is also strong at that level. By fourth grade, reading interests of boys and girls begin to diverge, with boys showing greater preference for nonfiction and girls for realistic fiction (Lynch-Brown 1977).

Preference for literary forms has changed somewhat over time. In the past, students preferred narrative material to informational books. During the 1970s, however, informational books began to have more appeal, especially for boys in upper grades and high school. The increase in publication of quality informational books may have influenced that trend.

There is some evidence that literary devices may influence reading interests. Students appear to prefer books with happy endings (Mendoza 1983) and episodic plots (Abrahamson and Shannon 1983). Adolescents prefer characters they believe are like themselves (Carter and Harris 1982) and there is some reason to believe that increased identification with a character produces more suspenseful reading (Jose and Brewer 1984). In studying preferences in poetry, Fisher and Natarella (1982) found that primary grade students responded to rhythm and rhyme in poetry and liked alliteration and onomatopoeia but disliked poems that rely on metaphor, simile, or personification.

1.2 India

A study reported by Brahma (1989) looked at the reading interests of children aged 8 to 11 enrolled in schools in India. Five hundred children from 200 primary schools in one district of India responded to a questionnaire about their reading preferences. In terms of subject matter, the preferred topics were science, lives of famous figures, lands and people, mythology, and animals and birds. The five forms of literature preferred by these students were stories, poetry, plays, comics, and novels. Essays, folk tales, encyclopedias, fairy tales, and picture dictionaries were the least liked forms. When students were asked about preference for format, 64 percent indicated a liking for colored illustrations and 36 percent for black and white illustrations. They reported that their most important sources for motivation were superiors, self, friends, and others' reading. Primary sources for book selection were teachers, librarians, guardians, and friends.

1.3 Australia

Hunt (1986) studied reading preferences by surveying children from three Australian schools who were enrolled in year seven. They were asked to identify favorite books, where they were obtained, favorite authors, and comics and magazines they enjoyed. Although reading patterns across the schools were similar, the library played a smaller role in choice of books in the school that had no regular library period. In another study, children in years three through six in New South Wales were asked about aspects of format that influenced book choices (Kirk 1986). Results indicated that cover illustrations were of consistent importance to most of the students, although illustrations appeared to be less important to older students than younger.

1.4 Scandinavia

Children's reading habits and preferences have been the subject of several studies in Scandinavia. Gjengset (1986) conducted a survey in which children between 10 and 11 years of age from four schools in Norway responded to a questionnaire. Results suggested that those children read more than their parents, they preferred series books, and listed reading as a "last choice" (lowest priority) activity when they were alone.

2. Response to Literature

Interest and response studies conducted with United States students suggest that treating reading interests and reader response as separate entities may not be realistic. Much research is related to both factors, since interest in a topic may strongly influence response to a book.

It is necessary to establish the context in which the treatment of children's literary responses has occurred. The driving force in the United States has been a work by Louise Rosenblatt (1983), originally published in 1938 as *Literature as Exploration*. A crucial aspect of Rosenblatt's work is the theory that reader and text function in a transaction in the interpretation of literature. Each reader brings to the printed page a personal background of interests and experiences that influence interpretation of the text. Rosenblatt's ideas about literary response went relatively unnoticed until the mid-1960s when the Dartmouth Conference was organized to bring together scholars from the United Kingdom and the United States for the purpose of discussing what ought to be the theoretical base for literature education in the common schools, beginning with the primary grades. Nevertheless, 10 years passed before reader response theory began to influence to any great extent the role of literature in the reading program.

The increased emphasis on reader response and teaching methods that may enhance response created international interest in the response patterns of students from different countries and from educational backgrounds that differed in the amount of emphasis placed on personal response, literary criticism, or interpretation of text. A study conducted by the International Association for the Evaluation of Educational Achievement was published as *Literature Education in Ten Countries* (Purves 1973). It revealed that the national curriculum in literature did indeed appear to influence the dominant response mode of high school students. It must be recognized, however, that these were responses to short stories that would not be termed children's literature but, more accurately, literature for young adults.

The growing interest in children's literature throughout the curriculum and especially in the reading/writing program, has led to the study of how classroom context and teacher strategies may influence reading preferences. This has lead to ethnographic studies of interaction between child and book (response) within a specified context, creating a tie between response and interest research. Hickman's (1981) classroom study of children's responses to literature represents an important link in that research trend.

Means of studying reader response have changed. Whereas early studies relied on written response, more recent research efforts have utilized interviews and classroom observations for data gathering (Hickman 1981, Galda 1983). The strong interest in literature-based reading programs in Canada has stimulated classroom-based research. McConaghy (1990) presented her observations of how children interact with literature to develop as readers and writers. The descriptive study revealed children's responses to specific books and illustrations through writing, talk, and drama. Considerable attention was given to the context in which the study was conducted and suggestions given for classroom organization and planning strategies to facilitate literacy learning. Attention was also given to the development of literacy within the home environment.

The interest in literature-centered reading instruction also grew in the United Kingdom over the 1970s and 1980s. Fry's (1985) study of how children view themselves as readers offers excerpts from interviews with six children ranging in age from 8 to 15. The children's comments reveal reasons for liking or disliking books and they also show sources of confusion as children try to make sense of a theme or a plot. Even in this small sample, there was a contrast in how the children viewed themselves as readers. Some wanted to keep their reading private; others enjoyed sharing it. Fry proposes a view of reading as active. He supports the importance of encouraging children to talk about what happens as they read so they will develop an awareness of themselves as readers.

A study of developmental differences by Cullinan et al. (1983) focused on children in Grades 4, 6, and 8 who were reading two novels. They found growth in content of story recall and in comprehension of metaphor and theme. Galda (1982), studying the responses of three fifth grade girls to two novels, noted distinct individual response styles, with one girl reading primarily for plot, one focusing on the central conflict and the main characters' reactions to the conflict, and the most mature reader focusing on characters' feelings, personalities, and motives rather than on the story events. Response appears to be influenced by characteristics of reader and text and also by the context of the reading.

3. Canadian Research

Professional treatment of children's literature in Canada reveals strong attention to Canadian publishing for children and includes French language as well as English language publications. The *Canadian Children's Literature* journal is a good source of information about book publishing and criticism in Canada. Each issue contains four or five articles and twenty or more reviews. Generally, the articles are analyses of the work of Canadian authors, poets, or illustrators; a critical analysis of one particular Canadian children's book; or historical treatment of a genre represented in Canadian publishing for children. French language reviews are included as well as English language reviews. The contents include a balance of research in the historical/critical mode and book reviews.

Other Canadian publications reveal attention to cross-national and multicultural matters in that country. Shlanka (1990) examined oriental stereotypes in Canadian picture books, concluding that books in the memoir format do the best job of giving information about Japanese and Chinese culture but that illustrations rarely show characters with personal uniqueness or strong female characters. Roy (1985) looked at the role of reading in the lives of children who had immigrated to Canada. She concluded that, although these children spoke a language other than English or French, they did not read in that language.

4. Australian Research

Publishing for children has advanced in Australia to the point where there is a sizable body of material available in that country. A number of Australian authors and illustrators are also well-known to children in other countries. Among them are Ivan Southall, Patricia Wrightson, and Mem Fox. The relative sophistication of publishing for children may have influenced the character of research reported since the early 1960s. An example is the attention to historical analysis of Australian children's books and discussion of trends over time. A good source for historical information is Niall (1984). The period of 1830 to 1890 is described as characterized by immigrant and settler's novels as well as novels that focused on "saving" the Aborigines and on temperance themes. During the period of 1890 to 1950, stories were more likely to be about family life, though hunting for gold also sometimes formed part of the plot. In the 1960s and 1970s, the dominant theme of Australian adventure stories was survival and, particularly, survival in the face of challenges from the land.

Research in children's literature reveals an interest

in several themes. Among them are an analysis of the portrayal of the Aborigine in Australian children's literature, including Aboriginal myths in the work of Wrightson. Murray (1991) examined the narrative, character, and fantastic elements in Wrightson's *The Nargun and the Stars* as they develop within the context of a bushland setting and Aboriginal mythology. He also analyzed the strengths of the novel and its place in Australian children's literature. White (1990) examined more broadly the portrayal of the Aboriginal in modern Australian children's books by analyzing 11 picture books published between 1985 and 1987 that include Aboriginal characters. The content analysis included settings, roles, and behavior of the Aborigines, and the point of view taken by the non-Aborigine authors. The conclusion was that newer books dealing with Aborigines show less prejudice toward them but that authors need to try harder to avoid stereotyping and present a more realistic view and understanding of the Aboriginal experience.

5. *Research in the United Kingdom*

The United Kingdom's tradition of publishing for children has a long history. Research reveals an interest in exploring the importance of Victorian children's literature as well as that of other historical periods.

Honig (1985) examines the portrayal of women in Victorian children's fantasy, presenting the thesis that Victorian literature provides a link between Victorian women and modern, more powerful fictional women. Four characters are identified that are repeatedly evident: mother, spinster, girl, and "magical woman" (as epitomized by powerful women in Victorian fiction).

The history of children's literature from the British tradition has been of interest to many scholars in the United States as well as the United Kingdom. Goldstone's (1984) study of didactic children's literature from the eighteenth century contributes yet another viewpoint on the subject. The study was based on five books from that period with secular themes. The books were apparently enjoyed by children, and were written by influential authors who thought of themselves as primarily writers of children's books. The study places children's literature within the context of relevant child-rearing practices of the time. Goldstone contends that children's views of their world influence their enjoyment of literature. In order to determine whether the books were actually read and enjoyed by children, she relied on eyewitness accounts which included statements by adults who had read the books as children and by children themselves, and also statistics regarding number of reprintings, lifespans of books, and so on. Finally, the books were reviewed critically on traditional criteria of style, theme, plot, and characterization. Goldstone's evaluation of the books takes into account the relationship to the culture that produced them. She notes that these authors freely pointed out the morals and purposes of their books in the prefaces and that they believed in the importance of early lessons.

6. *German Research*

German publications about children's literature reveal considerable interest in historical aspects of the genre. Moore (1987) analyzed the reading material available to German girls in the sixteenth and seventeenth centuries. In her introduction to the study, Moore points out that although information is available on popular authors of the time and the reading material they recommended, unfortunately, children's reactions to that literature have not been recorded. Therefore, the very important element of response is unaccounted for.

The study is of particular interest because Moore focuses on literature for girls. She recognizes that literature "for children" at that time may have referred only to books for boys and, therefore, includes such books only when they are clearly designated for both sexes or there is evidence that girls did read them. In order to establish the existence of literature for children prior to 1700, Moore relied on forewords and dedications which indicated the books were intended for children and produced lists of the genres represented, one for religious literature and one for secular literature. The secular literature included primers, classical literature, informational material, biographies, novels, books on manners, "how-to" books, and fables.

In a historical study from quite a different era, Kamenetsky (1986) presents a comprehensive account of the use and misuse of Nordic and German mythology and of contemporary literature in the education of the children of the Third Reich. She underscores the fact that many books were published during the early 1940s that clearly stated the didactic message of national socialism, and even the folk tales were edited and censored so as to remove alien influences that did not strongly portray the supposed original Nordic Germanic roots. Ultimately, children's literature in the Third Reich was intended as an educational tool; thus the literature needed no other justifications for its existence. Toll's (1986) study of children's literature with a national socialist theme also indicates the loss of an aesthetic focus and discusses the relationship of literature to education. She points out that from its beginning in the eighteenth century, children's literature has had an effect on the educational relationship between children and adults. However, she contends that the potential of children's literature was lost, and that literature lost its aesthetic quality from the treatment it was given by the national socialists. Insisting that aesthetics is a necessary condition for knowledge and insight to be imparted, she goes on to examine children's books about national socialism in order to explain her perspective.

Bernd (1980) presents an analysis of 135 books of fiction available in Germany between 1945 and 1978, arguing that the major content focus during the 1950s was the "flight from the East" and that persecution of the Jews did not emerge as a major topic until the 1960s. He found little attempt in these books to give readers a sense of the historical period.

German research in children's literature has also focused on contemporary social interest factors. A complex study by Wulfing (1986) examined old age and death in the Grimm tales and in children's books of the past several decades. Wulfing notes that the problems of old age and death were first seen in books for young people in 1970. With some exceptions, literature for children and young adults did not deal with the range of human lives until then, although a number of the Grimm tales have death as a major theme. Since 1976 a greater number of books for children and young adults have appeared in which the subject of death is treated.

7. Scandinavian Research

The Scandinavian countries have a long history of publishing for children and of research in children's literature. Sweden recently celebrated the 400th anniversary of publishing for children. Kareland (1991) presents a useful overview of those publishing efforts.

In a historical perspective on Norwegian publishing for children, Breen (1988) examined books published between 1968 and 1983, with particular emphasis on social and aesthetic trends that appeared to have influenced the content of children's books. The analysis identified a turning point in 1968 from aesthetic idealism to social criticism and another change in 1978 from social realism to fantasy, where the political messages came in the form of fantasy and lacked the didacticism of earlier books.

A number of Scandinavian researchers have studied the characteristics of literature produced by Scandinavian writers. Metcalf (1990) looked at the aspects of tall tale and spectacle in Astrid Lindgren's *Pippi Longstocking*. In a study of elements of the fantastic in Scandinavian children's literature, Svensen (1987) focuses on the interplay between real and unreal in fantasy, basing the discussion on writings by Scandinavian authors

In a study treating children's literature from a social perspective, Hene (1984) categorized books for girls and for boys as popular books or quality books. The books were then analyzed to determine how the characterization related to traditional sex role patterns, which the author found were equally evident in both popular and quality literature.

8. Conclusion

Children's literature research from the countries surveyed in this entry reveals national trends, but also cross-national common concerns. Reading interest studies appear in publications from many countries, as do reader response studies, though the latter are particularly characteristic of United States research. Historical research and literary criticism appear frequently in publications from Germany, the United Kingdom, Canada, and Sweden. An emerging trend in several countries including Canada, the United Kingdom, and the United States is the study of response to literature within the elementary school curriculum. This research describes the field and comprises an important resource for the professional study of children's literature and its influence on young readers.

See also: Literature: Educational Programs; Reading, Learning and Instruction of; Reading Comprehension, Learning of

References

Abrahamson R F, Shannon P 1983 A plot structure analysis of favorite picture books. *Read. Teach.* 37 (1): 44–48

Bernd O 1980 The Nazi period in German children's books. *Janus Bifrons* 3: 124–41

Brahma D 1989 *Children's Literature and Education in India*. Deep and Deep, New Delhi

Breen E 1988 *Slik Skrev De: Verdi og virkelighet i barneboker, 1968–1983*. Ashehoug, Oslo

Burgess S A 1985 Reading but not literature: The childread survey. *School Library Journal* 31(5): 27–30

Carter B, Harris K 1982 What junior high students like in books. *J. Read.* 26(1): 42–46

Chiu L 1984 Children's attitudes toward reading and reading interests. *Percept. Mot. Skills* 58(3): 960–62

Cullinan B, Harwood K, Galda L 1983 The reader and the story: Comprehension and response. *J. Res. Dev. Educ.* 16(3): 29–38

Fisher C J, Natarella M A 1982 Young children's preferences in poetry: A national survey of first, second, and third graders. *Research in the Teaching of English* 16(4): 339–54

Fry D 1985 *Children Talk about Books: Seeing Themselves as Readers*. Open University Press, Milton Keynes

Galda L 1982 Assuming the spectator stance: An examination of the responses of three young readers. *Research in the Teaching of English* 16(1): 1–20

Galda L 1983 Research in response to literature. *J. Res. Dev. Educ.* 16(3): 1–7

Gjengset G T 1986 Children's reading habits, A preliminary project report. *Scand. Publ. Lib. Q.* 19(3): 100–03.

Goldstone B P 1984 *Lessons to be Learned: A Study of Late Eighteenth Century English Didactic Children's Literature*. Peter Lang, New York

Hene B 1984 *"Den Dyrkade Lasse och stackers lilla Lotta": en syntaktisk-semantisk studie av personbeskrivande adjektiv och adverb i populara ungdomsbocker*. Almqvist and Wiksell International, Stockholm

Hickman J 1981 A new perspective on response to literature: Research in an elementary school setting. *Research in the Teaching of English* 15(4): 343–54

Honig E 1988 *Breaking the Angelic Image: Women Power in Victorian Children's Fantasy*. Greenwood Press, Westport, Connecticut
Hunt F 1986 Year 7 reading preferences in three Sydney schools. *Orana* 22(1): 39–46
Jose P E, Brewer S F 1984 Development of story liking: Character identification, suspense, and outcome resolution. *Dev. Psychol.* 20(5): 911–24.
Kamenetsky C 1986 *Children's Literature in Hitler's Germany: The Cultural Policy of National Socialism*. Ohio University Press, Athens, Ohio
Kareland L 1991 Mycket moral och lite underhalling den svenska barnboken 400 ar. *Abrakadabra* 2: 13–15
Kirk J 1986 Children's book choices: The influence of format. *Orana* 22(4): 180–84
Kirsch D, Pehrsson R, Robinson H A 1976 Expressed reading interests of young children: An international study. In: J E Merritt (ed.) 1976 *New Horizons in Reading*. International Reading Association, Newark, Delaware
Lynch-Brown C 1977 Procedures for determining children's book choices: Comparison and criticism. *Reading Horizons* 17(4): 245–50
McConaghy J 1990 *Children Learning through Literature: A Teacher Researcher Study*. Heinemann, Portsmouth, New Harryshire
Mendoza A 1983 Elementary school children's preference in literature. *Childhood Educ.* 59(3): 193–97
Metcalf E 1990 Tall tale and spectacle in Pippi Longstocking. *CLA Quarterly* 15(3): 130–35
Moore C N 1987 *The Maiden's Mirror: Reading Material for German Girls in the Sixteenth and Seventeenth Centuries*. Harrassowitz, Wiesbaden
Murray J 1991 Hurtling into freedom: Patricia Wrightson's "The Nargun and the Stars." *Papers: Explorations into Children's Literature* 2(2): 75–86
Niall B 1984 *Australia through the Looking-Glass: Children's Fiction 1830–1980*. Melbourne University Press, Carlton
Purves A C 1973 *Literature Education in Ten Countries: An Empirical Study*. Wiley, New York
Rosenblatt L 1983 *Literature as Exploration*, 4th edn. Modern Language Association of America, New York
Roy H 1985 Reading in the life of neo-Canadian children. *School Libraries in Canada* 5(4): 14–17
Schofer G 1981 Reading preferences of British and American elementary children. *Reading Improvement* 18(2): 127–31.
Shlanka D 1990 Oriental stereotypes in Canadian picture books. *Canadian Children's Literature* 60: 81–96
Svensen A 1987 Opening windows on to unreality: Some elements of the fantastic in Scandinavian children's literature. *International Review of Children's Literature and Librarianship* 2(1): 1–9
Toll C M 1986 *Asthetik im absiets: der padagogische gestus als prinzip der gestaltung von kinderliteratur: am biespiel von buchern zum thema nationalsozialismus*. P Lang, Frankfurt
Wendelin K H, Zinck R A 1983 How students make book choices. *Reading Horizon* 23: 84–88
White M 1990 The portrayal of the Aboriginal in modern Australian children's literature. *Papers: Explorations into Children's Literature* 1(2): 75–86
Wulfing I 1986 *Alter und tod in den grimmischen marchen und in Kinder- und Jugenbucher*. Verlag Murken-Altrogge, Herzogenrath

Further Reading

Martinez M, Roser N 1991 Children's responses to literature. In: Flood J et al. (eds.) 1991 *Handbook of Research on Teaching the English Language Arts*. Macmillan, New York
Monson D, Sebesta S 1991 Reading preferences. In: Flood J et al. (eds). 1991 *Handbook of Research on Teaching the English Language Arts*. Macmillan, New York
Westin B 1991 *Children's Literature in Sweden*. The Swedish Institute, Stockholm

D. L. Monson

Chile: System of Education

1. General Background

Chile has been an independent republic since the beginning of the nineteenth century. It extends along the southwestern coast of South America, stretching on average 4,300 kilometers north to south and only 180 kilometers east to west. It is very mountainous, with plains occupying only about 20 percent of the country, and it has extreme geographic contrasts: a desert covers about one-third of the territory in the north, and broken coasts with deep channels and fjords occupy another third of the country in the south. These features give rise to a very uneven distribution of population, with a concentration in the central zone, that has traditionally absorbed about 90 percent of the total number of inhabitants and also contains the most important agricultural, industrial, and cultural centers. The metropolitan region (where the capital Santiago is located) alone has 40 percent of the total number of the country's inhabitants.

The population is highly homogeneous in terms of its ethnic background and language. This is due to a successful process of integration of the native inhabitants with their Spanish conquerors beginning in the sixteenth century and, later on, with groups of immigrants of European origin.

The implications of these geographical characteristics for the educational system are felt in both administrative and curricular matters. The difficulties in communication and the isolation of the regions in both extremes of the country, as well as of those zones located in the mountains, make the administration of the system particularly complicated. As far as curricular aspects are concerned, the difficulty lies in the fact that the system has to reconcile the cultural unity of the nation with the diversity existing in the different regions.

The population of Chile has increased at a fast rate: it doubled in the 55 years between 1865 and 1920, and it doubled again in the following 40 years (1920–60). The growth was less marked between 1960 and 1990. During this period it increased from 8,900,000 to 13,200,000 and between 1982 and 1991 the average annual growth of the population was 1.8 percent. These 13 million people had a per capita

Gross National Product, (GNP) of US$1,770 in 1989. The annual growth rate of the GNP per capita was 0.3 percent in the period 1965 to 1989, and in 1989 the growth of the GNP was 10 percent. The export–import ratio of US$8,579 million: US$7,023 million was an additional indicator of the economic situation prevailing in the country in 1990. Due to migration from rural areas, the percentage of persons living in towns increased from 46.2 percent in 1920 to 82.2 percent in 1982.

Given that 30 percent of the population is aged under 15, economically active persons have represented between 30 and 35 percent of the total population in the 50 years to 1990, but their distribution in the different sectors of the Chilean economy varied substantially over this period. Whereas the percentage of individuals engaged in the secondary sector (industry) has remained fairly stable at around 20 percent, the tertiary sector (services) increased its share at the expense of agriculture and mining (the primary sector): it represented 35 percent in 1940, 65 percent in 1980, and 56 percent in 1990. The primary sector fluctuated between 43 and 22 percent in the same periods, with a 4 percent increase between 1980 and 1990 due to the substantial development that agriculture experienced in that decade.

The occupational structure of the population varied concomitantly, and while the percentage of professionals and technicians (9% in 1990), as well as manual workers, remained fairly stable, the proportion of salespersons and office employees grew from 14 percent in 1960 to 27 percent in 1980 and decreased to 24 percent in 1990. The percentage of fishermen, miners, and agricultural workers decreased from 29 percent in 1960 to 17 and 18 percent in 1980 and 1990 respectively.

From the point of view of the geographical distribution of economic activities, there were no important changes between the 1960s and 1990s. The metropolitan region continues to be the development center of the country; it has more than 40 percent of the workforce in the tertiary sector, which is the sector with the highest productivity. This excessive centralism has traditionally posed serious problems, since it has brought about not only a concentration of economic activities, but also disparities in per capita social investment, thus limiting the economic growth of many regions. A key element of the development strategy started in the 1970s was the regionalization of the country. A total of 12 regions plus the metropolitan area were designated in 1974, each with its own administrative system and also with autonomy in decision-making. These changes in the administration of the nation have been defined in accordance with the subsidiary role that the state adopted since the mid-1970s. In contrast to the period 1930–70 (which showed an increasing intervention of the state in the economy), in the early 1990s the role of the state was to carry out only those functions which cannot be performed by the private sector, either because of their nature or because of their interdependence with other functions. In 1991, the results of this strategy were just starting to become evident in terms of a better distribution of economic activities.

The stated objectives of this development strategy are to reach a steady economic growth and actively to seek equity through redistribution policies and mainly through increases in public social expenditure. Several factors have been identified as being important for the achievement of these goals and, among them, the improvement of human capital is considered essential. The new educational policies include changes in the regular system and also in adult education for the provision of vocational qualifications. Educational administration has become more decentralized.

2. *Politics and the Goals of the Education System*

In the twentieth century the political history of Chile has seen many changes, especially from 1970 to 1990. The long tradition of democratically elected governments acting in a presidential system was interrupted by brief periods of *de facto* governments in 1924–25 and 1931–32, and by an autocratic military regime in 1973 that lasted until 1990. Until the late 1930s, Chilean governments can be broadly defined as oligarchic. Between 1938 and 1952 the central–leftist tendencies dominated the political scene; after that time there were some independent and demo–Christian governments until the socialist and communist parties came to power in 1970. The socialist government lasted until 1973 and, following a 17-year military regime, a democratically elected president, supported by forces from the center–left, became the head of the Chilean government in 1990.

The concept of the state educating people (*estado docente*) has been important throughout the history of Chilean education, and is summarized by the motto of President Pedro Aguirre Cerda in the late 1930s: "To govern is to educate" ("*gobernar es educar*"). On the other hand, the educational bureaucracy constitutes a relevant part of the strong Chilean middle class.

Despite the political changes described, the main goals of the educational system have remained fairly stable since the 1920s. Traditionally, the state has emphasized equal opportunity of access to education for all citizens, mainly in order to lower the percentage of illiteracy (28.8% in 1940, 11.7% in 1970, and 5.4% in 1990) and to ensure that everyone completes at least primary education. At the beginning of the 1990s there were no important challenges as far as access to education was concerned, nor were there major dilemmas about the institutional organization of the sector. The core of the new educational policy is the quality of its internal processes and results, and the equity of the social distribution of them. The government is engaged in a midterm strategy aiming at the improvement of the quality and equity of Chilean education through a six-year program, to be financed with the cooperation of the World Bank, starting in 1991 (*Programa de Mejoramiento de la Calidad y Equidad de la Educación*—MECE). Additional objectives of this program are to broaden access to and improve the quality of preschool education and to evaluate institutional and curricular alternatives in order to reform secondary education through increasing its pertinence, quality, and equity.

3. The Formal System of Education

3.1 Primary, Secondary, and Tertiary Education

The structure of the regular educational system in 1990 was 6 years of voluntary preprimary schooling (ages 0 to 6), divided into three levels: nursery, middle level, and transition; 8 years of compulsory primary school, in which the first 4 years use a global methodology; 4 years of secondary school, with two branches—academic and vocational (which in 1990 included commercial, technical, industrial, agricultural, and maritime education) both branches having equal right of access to the university; and 3 to 7 years of higher education, which were (until 1980) the responsibility of Chile's eight universities. As well as these levels, which absorb the majority of the Chilean school population, there is special education and adult education.

A new structure was implemented during the 1980s. The main differences from the one previously described are found in the post-secondary alternatives offered, which are more varied and more appropriate to the needs of the labor market. Modifications in higher education have been put into practice since 1981. Universities are no longer the sole bodies offering professional training. Professional institutes and centers for technical training also do so, except for 16 courses (leading to traditional professions such as law, medicine, architecture, and engineering) which can only be taught by universities.

The number of students enrolled in the system increased steadily from 1940 to 1990, but more accelerated rates have occurred in different periods in the four levels defined. The largest increase in primary enrollment took place between 1960 and 1965; in secondary enrollment between 1965 and 1970; and at the university level between 1970 and 1975. The slight decrease in primary enrollment observed in the period 1975–90 is due mainly to a decreasing birth rate. Preprimary schooling (even if the number of children enrolled has increased from about 5,000 in 1940 to 220,396 in 1990) still absorbs only a limited proportion of the children aged 0 to 6 (12.7%)

The net and gross rates of schooling for the population aged between 7 and 14 are 91 percent and

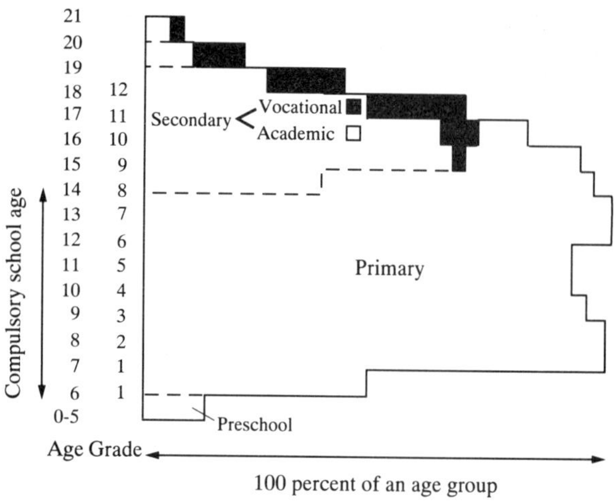

Figure 1
Chile: Structure of the formal education system

101 percent respectively, and the difference between these two percentages shows that average grade repeating is about 10 percent. Despite the fact that the criterion for promotion is attendance and not grades, 10 percent of first-grade students repeat, and this percentage is estimated to be higher in children belonging to families of low socioeconomic status. Grade repeating is also high in Grades 4 through 7. Although it is still a problem, grade repeating has decreased in the last 15 years, and in 1990 it was 7.8 and 12.4 percent in primary and secondary schools respectively. Permanent (vs. temporary) dropout in grades 1 to 7 fluctuates between 1.0 percent and 5.8 percent (in 1990, the figures were 2.29% for primary and 7.37% for secondary education). Despite the problems of grade repeating and dropout, an estimated 80 percent of the students entering school finish primary education, even if 20 percent of them graduate from this level after having repeated one or more grades. On average, for each student who finishes primary education (which is formally 8 years), 10.1 years of schooling are necessary. The following data about the average number of school years of the economically active population provide additional information regarding the increasing retentivity of the system: 1970–4.33; 1980–7.60; 1990–8.58. Figure 1 presents the structure of the system. The grade repetition is reflected in the diagram, especially in the increased enrollment in Grades 6, 7, and 8.

Educational opportunities for males and females have traditionally been equal in Chile. The proportion of boys was slightly higher in primary school (51% in 1990) and that of girls higher at the secondary level (51% in 1990), mainly in the academic track. At university, the situation (which was definitely more favorable for males in 1940, who then represented 75% of the total enrollment) has changed, and in 1990 only 56 percent of students were male.

In 1990, the total number of children enrolled in the lower levels of the system was 2,963,139, of which 7.4 percent were in preschool, 67 percent in primary, 15.7 percent in academic secondary, 8.6 percent in vocational secondary, and 1.3 percent in special education. Postsecondary education represents an additional enrollment of 249,482 students, of which 52.8 percent were at universities, 16 percent at professional institutes, and 31.2 percent at centers for technical training. The enrollment in adult education for the same year was 72,795, distributed among primary, technical, and academic and vocational secondary, the highest percentage being enrolled at the secondary level (54%).

Rural enrollment represented a total of 12.4 percent in 1990, with an unequal distribution among the different regions of the country: the extreme north (I, II, and III), the extreme south (XI and XII), the centre (V) and the metropolitan region having 8 percent or less, whereas in the more agricultural zones (Regions VI, VII, IX, and X) rural enrollment fluctuated between 25 and 28 percent.

Normally there are 30–33 weekly class periods of 45 minutes (40 minutes in Grades 1 to 4) in primary and 34–36 class periods a week in secondary school, the most common class size being 30–45 students.

3.2 Special Education

The main objective of special education is to rehabilitate children with learning difficulties in order to integrate them into the normal educational process, either permanently or transitorily, and thus to incorporate them in social life. It takes care of handicaps in learning, language, and vision, mental retardation, motor deficits, and specific learning disabilities. The detection of these cases is undertaken by specialists in special centers for diagnosis, which belong to the Ministry of Education. In 1990, a total of 31,746 children were enrolled in 336 special education units, 130 of which were located in the metropolitan region. About 84 percent of the children suffered from mental retardation, 10 percent from language problems, and 3.6 percent from hearing difficulties. The remainder had visual and motor problems. About 52.6 percent of these handicapped children go to municipal schools, 46.8 percent to private schools with fiscal subsidies, and less than 1 percent go to private schools. The Ministry of Education assigns a special subsidy for these children that is about 50 percent higher than for normal students. Handicapped children have special programs, mostly full-time, and most of them study in special education units since there are very few regular institutions that would accept them. Their transition to work is difficult in a country in which employment is still a problem.

3.3 Vocational, Technical, and Business Education

Vocational, technical, and business education is offered at both the secondary and tertiary levels. At the secondary level a total of 255,396 students were enrolled in 1990. This represents 35.5 percent of Chilean secondary-education students (47.7% women and 52.3% men). Vocational education can be municipal or private, with or without fiscal subsidy, the highest percentage of students (42%) attending private schools which are subsidized. Of the 255,396 students enrolled in this type of secondary education, 41.6 percent are in the commercial branch, 17.3 percent in the technical, 3.3 percent in the agricultural, and 1.3 percent in the maritime branch. Only students attending private vocational schools that have no subsidy from the state pay tuition; the rest is free. At the beginning of the 1990s, significant efforts were being made to bring vocational education close to the requirements of future employment, since traditionally both curricula and the available material resources in the schools did not correspond well to the needs of the labor market.

At the tertiary level, there are 82 professional institutes and 156 centres for technical training that offer different programs, lasting from 2 to 4 years; the former leading to a technical degree in different specialties, and the latter to several technical and professional degrees. Only two of the professional institutes receive a subsidy from the state; the rest are private, and financed by students or their families. In professional institutes, the highest percentages of students are enrolled in the areas of administration and commerce (24.6%) and education (20.7%). In centers for technical training, 47 percent are in administration and commerce, whereas 29.9 percent are in the area of technology. Both options described in tertiary education are less popular than universities for those students who finish secondary education, because job opportunities and social prestige are much higher—and have traditionally been so in Chile—for the latter type of education.

3.4 Adult and Nonformal Education

Adult education is habitually offered in evening or night courses which aim at providing primary or secondary education to people who are older than 16, who for diverse reasons (e.g., temporary dropout or early age of starting work), have not been able to study when they were of school age. Two different types of programs are offered for adults. One is at the primary level with a maximum of 300 hours (fundamental education) and offers an elementary training in some technical specialty. The second lasts between 600 and 800 hours, at the primary or secondary level, and aims at providing training that will enable the person to enter the labor market with a technical specialty (elementary technical education for adults). Of the total of 72,795 persons enrolled in adult education in 1990, 21.7 percent was in primary, 1.5 percent in technical, 38.7 percent in academic secondary, 15.1 percent in vocational secondary, and 23.0 percent in a special two-year academic program. The majority of adults go to municipal schools which are free.

In nonformal education, action has been rather limited in scope and also tends to be irregular. Universities have contributed through their special community extension programs, among which orchestras, ballet corps, choirs, theater groups, television channels, and radio stations deserve special mention in addition to the many courses on subjects of general cultural interest which the universities habitually offer.

The Ministry of Education provides nonformal education both for school children and for adults. For children, provision is mainly through the Department for Out-of-School Education (*Departamento de Educación Extraescolar*).

Nonformal education is perceived as a basic element in the development of children, adolescents, and adults. It complements the function of the school. It attempts to integrate the family and the community through an adequate utilization of their free time by means of group activities (clubs, brigades, academies). The Department for Out-of-School Education has defined five areas of action: culture–arts, science–technology, sports–recreation, environmental education, and social participation and integration (e.g., discussions on topics such as peace, human rights, etc.). Specific events organized by this department include literary, scientific, and artistic contests; fairs; sports events; and drama and folklore festivals. These are run both at the national and the international levels. The Department also trains specialists in out-of-school education, offering seminars and distance courses to teachers. Some examples of activities organized by this department in 1990 were the national contest of Chilean folk dance, with 120,000 students from primary and secondary education participating; a national contest on "*Pacifico Mare Nostrum 2000*" for primary-school students with 2,500 works presented; a national contest of needlework, with 2,520 pieces exhibited; a scientific–technological fair in which 18,450 students took part; and a national sports event, which had 400,000 primary- and secondary-school students participating. Most of the events are organized by the Ministry of Education in cooperation with either private or public institutions. Teachers coordinate activities at the school level; at the central level there are supervisors for these activities in communes and in provincial departments. Programs for adults have been implemented only to a very limited extent.

4. *Administrative and Supervisory Structure and Operation*

Since the beginning of the 1980s, the administration and supervision of the Chilean education system has undergone drastic changes. The consolidation of the new administrative structure of the country had strengthened the functions of the mayor and municipalities. The administration of public schools, which had traditionally been in the hands of the Ministry of Education, was given to the municipalities and into private hands. In 1990, of the total number of schools (15,325), 64 percent were municipal, 28 percent were private with a fiscal subsidy, and 8 percent were private without any public subsidy, the percentage of primary municipal units being the highest (68 percent).

The Ministry of Education is responsible for the technical and pedagogical aspects of the educational process, that is, for establishing educational policies; for producing technical norms; and for supervising, orienting, and evaluating public and private education through its specialized departments. These are the subsecretaryship of education, and several technical divisions, such as the divisions for general education, for planning and budgeting, for personnel, and for higher education. Within each region, the Ministry has delegated its functions of planning and supervision to the regional secretaries of the Ministry of Education. Regional secretaries coordinate their action with the Ministry and the provincial departments (40 in total) which work with schools through teams of supervisors. Thus, certain powers are delegated from the regional level to the provincial level and in turn to the community and school levels.

Responsibility for the administration of primary and secondary public schools lies with the municipal authority. Schools are responsible for carrying out the teaching–learning process. School principals have certain responsibilities for the administration of personnel and the curriculum. They may, for example, adapt the curriculum according to the characteristics and needs of the students.

5. *Educational Finance*

The resources invested in public education come mainly from the central government (the state budget), from regional and community organs, from grants from the private sector, and from income originating in the schools themselves. Private schools are supported by student fees and by government subsidies when the schools are free. Contributions from municipalities and private bodies have increased with the transfer of responsibility for schools to these bodies. Self-financing has become particularly important in higher education, and several legal acts decreed in the 1980s gradually diminished the contribution of the state to higher education. The proportion of the state budget devoted to education was 15.95 percent in 1990, (17% in 1940, 12% in 1955, 21% in 1970 and 15% in 1985). As a percentage of GNP, the allocation has been between 2.0 and 4.1 percent over the 10 years up to 1991. The allocation of the budget among the various levels in the system was as follows in 1990: 7.5 percent for preprimary, 51.7 percent for primary, 10.7 percent for academic secondary, 8.1 percent for vocational secondary, and 20.7 percent for higher education. The high priority given to education is demonstrated by an increase of approximately 13 percent in the budget of 1991 as compared with 1990, which has been devoted mainly to increasing the salaries of the teachers and to supporting the poorest schools in the country.

It is important to stress that besides fiscal subsidies to municipal and some private schools, amounting (in 1990) to US$12 and US$14 a month per student in primary and secondary education respectively, there are several additional forms of financial assistance that the state gives to students, mainly in preschool and primary education. This consists of food (approximately 1,200,000 meals a day in 1990), textbooks (4,523,938 distributed in 1990), and special summer programs (918 schools participated in 1990). Information about private resources devoted to education (which mainly refers to private schools financed entirely by families) is difficult to obtain and no available statistics exist.

6. *Supplying Personnel for the Education System*

Teacher training has always been given great emphasis in Chile. The first public institution created for preparing teachers for secondary education (the *Instituto Pedagógico*) was founded in 1889 and was part of the Faculty of Philosophy and Humanities of the University of Chile. From then until 1980, the training of secondary-school teachers was entirely in the hands of the universities and was regarded as postsecondary education. This training lasted five years, during which time prospective teachers studied general subjects, but specialized in one or two specific disciplines which they would later teach and in which they received special pedagogical training.

Primary teachers, on the other hand, were trained in normal schools until 1966, and afterwards (1967–80) in the existing universities. They are now trained in universities and also in some professional institutes. Normal schools belonged to the vocational branch of secondary education, and primary teachers received their professional training in parallel with secondary schooling. Preschool teachers and teachers for handicapped children were trained at the universities until 1980. From 1981, other institutions of postsecondary education as well as universities, prepare teachers for all levels of the system. Gradually, following a legal change introduced in 1990, universities will again be the only institutions which carry out teacher training.

In 1990, there were 134,389 persons working in the different levels of the system. About 89 percent were teachers and the rest were in administrative or technical positions. Of these 134,389 persons, 6 percent were in preprimary education, 2 percent in special education, 57 percent in primary, and 35 percent in secondary education. There is, in general, no shortage of teachers, and the teaching functions are performed to a large extent by qualified people. In 1990, for example, 98 percent of primary teachers and 92 percent of teachers in secondary schools had a degree in education. The distribution of qualified personnel is still uneven and some provinces, mainly in rural areas, are at a disadvantage in this respect. In general, there are more women than men teachers. In primary and secondary education, 75 and 55 percent respectively of teachers were women.

Inservice training for educational personnel is provided through staff-development programs, workshops, and seminars by many institutions. These are mainly universities, and coordinated by the Center for Inservice Training, Experimentation, and Educational Research of the Ministry of Education. Inservice training is considered to be so important that each teacher in municipal and subsidized schools receives a bonus in order to pay for the training he or she considers necessary. There is a wide selection of such courses for teachers. Increases in salaries are an additional stimulus for teacher training in Chile, both in public and private schools.

7. *Curriculum Development and Teaching Methodology*

The main curriculum reform took place between 1966 and 1970. The old curriculum was strongly content-oriented. In the new curriculum, the number of subjects was reduced and emphasis was placed upon student behavior and skills. The new programs included alternative content, types of activity, and evaluation procedures. These alternatives give teachers more freedom to carry out the teaching–learning process in accordance with the characteristics of their students.

In primary education, there is one uniform, nationwide curriculum developed by the Ministry of Education, starting with global activities in Grades 1 to 4, and gradually becoming more subject-centered. The curriculum for secondary education is nationwide as are the syllabuses of studies for the different subjects which contain general and specific learning objectives, the content being organized into units which contain a recommended bibliography. Vocational tracks have different curricula which initially are largely the same, as in the academic branch (70% of subjects), and later become more differentiated.

In academic secondary education, the curriculum included common subjects for grades 9 and 10 (Spanish, world history and general geography, mathematics, natural sciences, foreign language, arts, physical education, religion [optional]) and a homeroom period. In Grades 11 and 12, there were also 8 common subjects, plus a set of electives which represented about 30 percent of the total number of weekly periods. The teaching of foreign languages starts with one (usually English) in the first cycle of primary, continues with two (English and French in most of the schools) in the second cycle, and then with one (mostly English again) in secondary education. Primary schools that do not have the necessary resources may be exempted from teaching foreign languages.

Since 1967, the Center for Inservice Training, Experimentation, and Educational Research of the Ministry of Education has had major responsibility for the planning and implementation of school curricula. In accordance with the *Ley Orgánica Constitucional de Enseñanza,* there is a council constituted of outstanding representatives of the academic community (*Consejo Superior de Educación*) which has to analyze and give its approval to the fundamental objectives for each grade-level of both primary and secondary education, and also to the minimum obligatory content that will facilitate the achievement of those objectives. Once the Ministry of Education has formally established them, the schools are free to define the curricula and syllabuses they consider adequate to comply with the objectives and content determined by the Ministry. The Ministry of Education has then to accept these curricula, proposing changes if necessary, and has to prepare a common nationwide curriculum for those schools that do not have their own. This has to be approved by the Higher Council for Education (*Consejo Superior de Educación*).

Textbooks are produced by private companies and schools select those they prefer. Every year the Ministry of Education buys several million textbooks and distributes them to public schools. The Ministry also prepares audio-visual materials which schools can buy at very competitive prices. This is also the case for methodological guides for teachers.

The Ministry of Education carries out its functions of orientation and supervision of the implementation of the curriculum through specially trained supervisors who belong to the provincial departments of education.

The main problem in the areas of curriculum and teaching methods is the emphasis placed on lower mental processes and traditional teaching methods in schools. This has produced an important gap between what goes on in schools and the demands and stimuluses of life outside the schools; students thus perceive the curriculum as not being relevant, particularly at the secondary level.

8. The System of Examinations, Promotions, and Certifications

The decision as to whether a student is to be promoted lies with teachers and is based normally upon the performance of students in different types of tasks which test learning objectives in specific subject fields. No special examinations exist in order to pass from one level of the system to another, except for a nationwide examination that is held to select candidates for subsidized universities. The admission rate in 1990 was approximately 1:1.6 for these universities, which is very favorable compared with the situation prevailing in the 1970s and mid-1980s. It is due to the expansion of the private sector of higher education. The examination consists of a battery of tests, including an aptitude test (verbal and mathematical reasoning) and several achievement tests which the student takes according to the subjects to be studied. The tests are administered throughout the country on common dates, and more than 90 percent of the students finishing secondary education take them. Universities then select their students from among those candidates who obtained the highest scores in the tests and had the best average marks in secondary education. This system for selecting university students has been in existence since 1967.

9. Educational Assessment, Evaluation, and Research

Since 1988, and having as an antecedent a program for evaluating school outcomes (*Programa de Evaluación de Rendimiento*—PER, 1982–84), the Ministry of Education administers a nationwide examination alternatively to all students in Grades 4 and 8 (*Sistema de Medición de Calidad de la Educación*—SIMCE) in order to have a yearly diagnosis of the results of the educational process in terms of objectives attained. The system is based on the administration of multiple-choice tests in Spanish and mathematics to all children, and in history and geography and natural science to a sample of them. It also measures certain features of the personal development of students and some indicators of acceptance of the work of the school by students, parents, and teachers; and provides information on some indicators of school efficiency, such as pass/fail rates, the number of years studied, and the number of dropouts. The percentage of achievement in each one of the objectives measured is reported to every school in the country, by class, and schools can also evaluate their relative position by comparing their results to national outcomes, and to results obtained by similar schools which are also given to them. Recommendations are provided to schools to help them improve their education on the basis of the results attained, and schools use the information and the recommendations for the improvement of the teaching–learning process. The results obtained by schools have served as a basis for selecting the 900 lowest achieving schools located in poverty areas in order to provide them with material and human support to improve the quality of the education they offer.

Educational research may be traced back to the beginning of the twentieth century in Chile and has had continuous development. However, its importance in decision-making has been limited and only a few educational policies have been based upon the results of research. These have included coordinated efforts to reduce grade repeating, the provision of textbooks to primary schools, and the implementation of the entrance examination to Chilean universities.

From 1950 onwards, several public and private research institutions were created. Their work was to have an impact upon the reforms introduced in education after 1960. Among them, two at the University of Chile stood out: the Institute for Education and the Institute for Statistical Research. At the Ministry of Education, the main research organism was the Center for Inservice Training, Experimentation, and Educational Research founded in 1967. Among private institutions the main one was the Center for Educational Research and Development (CIDE), created in 1965 and initially connected with the Catholic University. Educational research was given high priority in the 1960s since its importance in deciding and evaluating the changes that were taking place in education was widely recognized. During this period, the tendency was mainly to study educational achievement and the variables associated with it, the flow of students through the different levels of the system, and descriptive statistics of the psychological and sociological characteristics of students.

During the 1970s, educational research became a more common activity in those universities having faculties of education, and since the late 1970s many nongovernmental organizations have also had an important role in educational research. The interest in determinants of achievement continued, but, in addition, emphasis was placed on dropout, language development, and the relationship between education and different elements in the social context.

At the beginning of the 1980s the main research issues were achievement, preschool education, nonformal educational programs, teacher training, and higher education. Starting in the late 1980s school processes have received great attention, with emphasis on qualitative–ethnographic methods. The topics that were most popular with researchers (according to the number of papers presented at the educational researchers' meeting held in 1991) were teaching–learning strategies (28); curricular experiences (25); family, community, and school (25); higher education (23); teacher training and development; and early primary education (20). Within the framework of the program for improving the quality and equity of education at the secondary level, the Ministry of Education has defined a number of research projects aiming at providing an information basis for restructuring secondary education according to the needs of Chilean society in the areas of curriculum, socialization and pedagogical practices, measurement of quality, internal and external efficiency, and teacher training. These projects will be financed with the cooperation of the World Bank.

At the national level, there is a National Commission for Scientific and Technological Research which finances research projects in all disciplines and which is the main institution for financing research in Chile.

The Ministry of Education collects and regularly publishes information on several important educational indicators such as school retentivity for children and adults, coverage, attendance, pedagogical retardation, quality of education (achievement of academic objectives), enrollments, human and financial resources, nonformal education, and illiteracy.

10. Major Reforms in the 1980s and 1990s

The decentralization of educational administration and changes in the role that the state had traditionally played in education had important consequences, and the consolidation of the new administration is still in progress. The major reforms expected for the 1990s will be oriented towards improving the quality and equity of Chilean education, mainly through participation, decentralization, efficiency, and open design to allow schools to develop their own educational initiatives. The first steps toward a reform of secondary education were taken in 1991 in order to make this level of the system more meaningful and more adjusted to the needs of society. The reforms of secondary education will be based on research data which will provide the basis for specific actions to be taken in the near future.

11. Major Problems for the Year 2000

Since the 1960s major efforts have been devoted to the quantitative expansion of the system, and increases in enrollment rates have been substantial. Efforts will have to be made in the 1990s to increase enrollments, not only in primary education but also in preschool and secondary education.

The major concern, both at the time of writing and in the near future, is the quality and equity of education. Many studies show serious discrepancies between the intended curriculum and the levels of student achievement and, particularly, in the equity of the social distribution of the quality of the educational process. The changes in the structure of the system and in the administration of the schools have begun implementation since the beginning of the

1980s. The curricular changes that are being studied and the efforts that are being made to enhance teacher participation in those curricular changes have as their ultimate goal the improvement of both the quantitative and qualitative problems. Yet education cannot be isolated from the whole social context, and its growth will therefore depend to a large extent on the development that takes place in the other subsystems of Chilean society.

Bibliography

Diario Oficial de la República de Chile, Santiago, 10 de Marzo de 1990, Ministerio de Educación Pública, Ley No 18,962, *Ley Orgánica Constitucional de Enseñanza*. Empresa Periodística "La Nación." Santiago

Fondo Monetario Internacional 1991 *Estadísticas Financieras Internacionales. Anuario 1991*. Publication Services IMS, Washington, DC

Lemaitre M J (ed.) 1990 *La Educación Superior en Chile: Un sistema en Transición*. Corporación de Promoción Universitaria, Santiago

Ministerio de Economía, Fomento y Reconstrucción, Instituto Nacional de Estadísticas 1991 *Compendio estadístico 1991*. Imprenta INE, Santiago

Ministerio de Economía, Fomento y Reconstrucción, Instituto Nacional de Estadísticas 1991 *Encuesta Nacional del Empleo 1991 (Octubre - Diciembre, total del país)*. Imprenta INE, Santiago

Ministerio de Educación Pública 1981 *La Educación en Chile 1979–1980*. Informe de Chile a la 38ª reunión de la Conferencia Internacional de Educación. Ginebra 10–19 de noviembre, 1981. Oficina de Relaciones Internacionales, Santiago

Ministerio de Educación Pública 1991, 1989 *Revista de Educación* No. 79, (2nd edn. 1989), No. 94 (1982). Centro de Perfeccionamiento, Experimentación e Investigaciones Pedagógicas, Santiago

Ministerio de Educación Pública 1990 Compendio de Información Estadística 1990. Departamento de Estadística, División de Planificación y Presupuesto, Ministerio de Educación, Santiago

Ministerio de Educación Pública, División de Educación General, Departamento de Educación Extraescolar, 1991 *Documento de Trabajo: La Educación Extraescolar*. Ministerio de Educación, Santiago

Ministerio de Educación Pública 1991 *Resúmenes de los trabajos presentados al XI Encuentro Nacional de Investigadores en Educación*. Perfeccionamiento, Experimentación e Investigaciones Pedagógicas Serie de Estudios No. 226. Santiago

Ministerio de Educación Pública 1991 *Revista de Educación: Orientaciones Básicas, Objetivos y Componentes del Programa MECE*. Documento de difusión, Agosto 1991. Centro de Perfeccionamiento, Experimentación e Investigaciones Pedagógicas, Santiago

Schiefelbein E 1976 *Diagnóstico del sistema educacional chileno en 1970*. Universidad de Chile, Departamento de Economía, Santiago

Schiefelbein E, Grossi M C 1981 Antecedentes para un análisis de la eficiencia de la educación media en Chile. Corporación de Promoción Universitaria, Documento de Trabajo No. 229, Santiago

Schiefelbein E, Heikkinen S 1991 Chile—*Acceso, Permanencia, Repetición y Eficiencia en la Educación Básica*. Documento de Trabajo UNESCO-OREALC, 18 de abril de 1991.

World Bank 1991 *World Development Report 1991: The Challenge of Development*. Oxford University Press, Oxford

C. Rodríguez

China, People's Republic of: Adult Education

The aim of this entry is to give an introduction to adult education and training in the People's Republic of China. The following aspects are discussed: the concepts and principles of adult education in China, the history of adult education, the functions of adult education, the systems and forms of adult education, and the administration of adult education. Major policies are described and a perspective on research on adult education in China is given.

1. Concepts and Principles

Adults make up 60 percent of China's vast population. They occupy a significant position in society as builders of the nation and as a force of social and economic development. The education and training of the workers, farmers, administrative cadres, and science and technology personnel that make up the labor force is therefore an important and recognized part of China's education policy. Given this acknowledgment, China has strived to improve the ideological, moral, technical, and cultural quality of the whole labor force and whole nation by providing extensive educational services for all adults.

The worker–peasant alliance forms the foundation of the People's Republic of China. Instead of "adult education" the term "worker–peasant education" was used from 1949 to 1981. Since the people who receive adult education study mainly during their spare time, such education has also been referred to as "spare-time education." As a consequence of the enormous expansion and diversification of such education it is now formally called adult education.

Since China adopted a policy of reform and has opened up to the outside world, its adult education has developed in accordance with the guiding principles of democratic and lifelong education.

2. Brief History of Adult Education in China

Adult education has a long history in China. The great thinker and educator Confucius (551–479 BC) advocated that "education should not be selective," thus expanding the range of receivers of education to include not only the nobility but also the common people. Later, distinguished scholars such as

Mohcius, Mencius, Jian Kuang, Wang Chong, Han Yu and Zhu Xi further developed the principles of establishing a democratic, mass education system based on lifelong education (see 501010). The ideas contributed by these scholars—for example, "teaching and learning promoting and enhancing each other," "elicitation and inducement," "teaching in accordance with student aptitude," and "teaching and advancing step by step"—have greatly enriched the content and practice of both schooling and adult education in China.

Systematic and organized adult education began to emerge in China at the turn of the twentieth century. For instance, in the last years of the Qing dynasty, supplementary education was organized for the aged and those deprived of education. The plan for elementary literacy schools was formulated and implemented at that time. After the revolution in 1911, a social education department was set up in the Ministry of Education of the provisional government in Nanking (now Nanjing) to promote adult education. During the time of the Republic of China several experiments involving adult education were conducted in various places and under different names (such as popular education, common people education, social education, and mass education) and with different contents (such as character-learning education, supplementary education, vocational education, citizen education, and science, literature, and arts education, etc.). From 1927 to 1949, at the revolutionary bases and in the liberated areas under the leadership of the Chinese Communist Party, adult education mainly for peasants, soldiers, and worker–peasant cadres was carried out, thus forming a mass education movement in the service of the revolutionary war.

The People's Republic of China was founded in 1949 to meet the needs of restoring and developing the national economy and building a new social system. The Common Program of 1949, which served as a constitution before the Constitution of the People's Republic of China was promulgated in 1954, explicitly stated that "Spare-time education for the laborers and in-service personnel should be strengthened." In 1950 the Government Administration Council (now the State Council) issued a decree making worker–peasant education the focal point of the country's education work. Also in 1950, the Central People's Government issued the call "to develop literacy education and progressively decrease illiteracy." The urgency and immensity of this task was clear, since it was established that 80 percent of the total population were illiterate.

Great strides were made in the development of adult education from 1949 to 1966. However, during the tumultuous period of the so-called "cultural revolution" from 1966 to 1976, adult education was not in a position to build on its initial foundation. It was not until after 1976 that China's adult education was restored. Since 1978, when China entered the new stage of modernization, adult education has developed vigorously. In 1987 the Chinese government reaffirmed the significant position of adult education and in-service training in the country's education cause, stating that adult education "is the indispensable condition for achieving social and economic development and scientific and technological progress."

3. Functions of Adult Education

By 1990 China had 130 million workers and cadres, over 400 million farmers under the age of 45, and 90 million aged people. Faced with such a vast target population, China's adult education had the following formal tasks:

(a) to provide those who either are in service or need to transfer to new posts, or are seeking an occupation, with the necessary cultural and professional knowledge, skills, and practical ability;

(b) to provide literacy education to the illiterate;

(c) to provide those who have had a regular schooling with either elementary or higher education according to their level and needs, and to grant diplomas to those who qualify;

(d) to provide the professional, technical, and management personnel who have received a higher education with continuing education so as to expand their knowledge and improve their ability;

(e) to provide education in a variety of subjects ranging from law and engineering to hygiene, old-age health protection, home economics, fine arts and calligraphy, and gastronomy and horticulture, to people from all ages and walks of life in order to enable them to live a culturally rich and healthy life based on scientific principles.

4. Systems and Forms of Adult Education

A new organization for adult education has been implemented in China. This organization is characterized by a multichannel, multiform and multisystem approach to adult education provision. It has been set up with the explicit aim of mobilizing the entire adult population to participate in programs specifically designed to meet the needs of the society.

China has two adult education systems: one for degree education and another for nondegree education. The former includes undergraduate college education, vocational junior college education, secondary vocational education, and middle school education. The latter includes literacy education, the training of practical agricultural techniques, on-the-job training, single-course certificate training, and continuing vocational education.

Authorities responsible for adult education include the ministries and commissions under the State Council, the education administrative departments of the provinces, autonomous regions and municipalities which are directly under the State Council, and the ministries in charge of industry, construction, mining, railway and transportation, agriculture and forestry, environmental protection, and so forth.

Adult education is also offered by factories, enterprises, and county and township governments. Trade unions, the organizations of the Communist Youth League and the Women's Federations, in collaboration with local education administrative departments, have set up training schools and other relevant institutions. Social and mass organizations, academic institutions, collective economic enterprises, and individual citizens also organize adult education in various forms.

Adult basic and secondary education is provided by adult secondary vocational schools, secondary vocational classes for workers set up in ordinary secondary schools, adult middle schools, adult technical training schools, peasants' cultural and technical schools and agricultural radio and television schools. Self-study secondary and vocational education examinations are also organized.

The different forms of adult higher education include radio and television universities, colleges for workers and peasants, management personnel institutes, educational administration institutes, adult education institutions in conventional universities and colleges (night schools, correspondence schools, teacher-training courses, etc.), correspondence institutes, distance education, and self-study higher education.

The above-mentioned institutions use different methods in reaching and teaching the adult learners. These include full-time classroom teaching, guided self-study in distance education by means of printed materials and sound and video recordings, and spare-time learning. They offer courses in many subjects, according to their own conditions and the needs of the society and learners. Adult education for farmers is a good example. Because of structural adjustment in the agricultural sector, the focus of adult education in rural areas has shifted from character-learning and reading and writing to practical courses in agriculture, forestry, animal husbandry, side-line production, fishery, small-scale industry, commerce and transportation, and service trades, which the peasants need in order to increase production.

5. *Achievements of Adult Education in China*

Adult education in China has developed rapidly and is reaching a very significant part of the adult population. From 1978 to 1990 some 42,494,000 illiterate people learned to read and write, bringing the total number of illiterate turned literate since 1949 to 170 million. From 1986 to 1990, some six million people took part in literacy classes each year, and the number of illiterate decreased at a rate of three million annually. However, census data show that there were still 180 million illiterate people in China in 1990. This indicates that China has still much to do in eradicating illiteracy.

From 1986 to 1990 an estimated 170 million peasants in rural areas took part in different forms of adult education of a cultural and technical nature. The volume of vocational training received by staff and workers in industry has increased rapidly since the mid-1980s. Training was received by 110 million workers and staff in 1990, while the comparable figure for 1986 was 32.4 million.

A total of 3,639,800 people graduated from adult higher education institutions from 1980 to 1990. An additional 520,000 adults obtained higher education graduation diplomas through self-study, and another 86,000 received secondary vocational school diplomas. From 1986 to 1990, 6,649,100 adults graduated from adult middle schools, and 69 million people obtained certificates from elementary schools for adults. In 1990, the numbers of on-campus students in adult elementary, secondary, and higher education were 22.8 million, 15.3 million, and 1.7 million respectively.

6. *Administration of Adult Education*

China's adult education is under the central supervision of the State Education Commission, the Adult Education Department of which is in charge of routine administration. In the ministries and commissions residing under the State Council, there are special sections in charge of adult education and the in-service training of their own personnel. In the provinces, autonomous regions, counties, municipalities, and townships there are administrative units in charge of adult education.

Nongovernmental organizations such as the All China Trade Union, the All China Federation of Women, and the Communist Youth League Central Committee have the task of guaranteeing and promoting provision, and encouraging staff and workers, women, and youth to engage in learning activities. The China Association for Science and Technology is responsible for providing adult learners with education and training in basic and applied science and technology.

Another important partner of the State Education Commission is the China Association for Adult Education. Founded in 1981, the Association has become a national platform for the promotion, organization, and coordination of adult education activities in the country. It collaborates with other organizations such as the China Association of Staff and Workers' Education and the China Association for Continuing Engineering Education, and provides consultation and advice to affiliated research institutions specializing in literacy work, adult higher education, industrial training, and rural adult education. The China Association for Adult Education became a member organization of the International Council of Adult Education (ICAE) in 1983 and of the Asian and South Pacific Bureau of Adult Education (ASPBAE) in 1988 (see *Interchange in Adult Education: North-South Dialogue; Nongovernmental Organizations: Adult Education; Professional Associations for Adult Education*).

7. Policy of Adult Education in China

Article 19 of the Constitution of the People's Republic of China stipulates: "The state develops all kinds of educational facilities, eradicates illiteracy, gives political, cultural, scientific, technical and vocational education to workers . . . and encourages people to become useful persons through self-study." In accordance with the Constitution, the responsible councils, ministries, and administrative agencies have issued various documents stating the principles and policies that guide the organization, financing, and provision of adult education in the country. Since 1987, when a new budget was created for national expenditure on adult education, increased attention has been given to tasks such as the expansion and improvement of training systems and the establishment of assessment procedures for the certification of knowledge, skills, and competences acquired on the job and through the provision of continuing education and further training of the labor force.

8. Research on Adult Education in China

The number of research studies on the theory and practice of adult education and training increased at an unprecedented rate during the 1980s. This reflects the increased attention given to the development of adult education in a developing country with a population of over 11.3 hundred million people, of which some 678 million are adults. Adult education in China is highly diversified, and the multichannel, multisystem, and multiform approach to its development makes it imperative that research be carried out in order to achieve clarity and monitor developments. There is a great need for studies collecting information that make it possible to systematize the experience so far gained. The focus is mostly on applied research serving the different needs of practitioners and institutions that deliver adult education and training, although high priority is also given to theoretical research studies on questions of policy and strategy that serve the needs of decision makers and reform planners.

The research work on adult education is being coordinated and supervised by the National Steering Group for Education Science Programs. Fields and topics for research are suggested through consultation with various administrative departments, theoretical research institutions, and the organizations and institutions that provide adult education and training. Topics that have been identified as national priorities are research on relations between rural technical education and rural economic development, research on literacy and post literacy education, research on continuing vocational education and on-the-job training in enterprises, research on schools run by the various mass organizations, research on diversified patterns of postsecondary education, and research on new information technologies in distance education.

See also: China, People's Republic of: System of Education; Russia (Soviet Union): Adult Education

References

Central People's Government of China 1949–1981 *Yearbook of Education in China* (annual). Chinese Encyclopaedia Publishing House, Beijing

Central People's Government of China 1991 *Education Statistics Yearbook of China 1990*. People's Education Publishing House, Beijing

State Education Commission 1985 *Chinese Encyclopaedia*. Special volume on education in China. Chinese Encyclopaedia Publishing House, Beijing

State Education Commission 1988 *Post-secondary Education in China: Present State and Trends*. Third Department of Higher Education, State Education Commission, Beijing

State Education Commission 1990a. *Literacy in China*. Adult Education Department of State Education Commission, Beijing and China Association for Adult Education, Beijing. People's Education Publishing House, Beijing

State Education Commission 1990b *Collected Research Works on China's Post-senior Middle School Education*. Staff and Workers' Education Publishing House, Beijing

Further Reading

Colletta N J 1982 *Worker-Peasant Education in the People's Republic of China*. World Bank Staff Working Paper, No. 527. The World Bank, Washington, DC

Wang J, Colletta N 1991 Chinese adult education in transition. In: Epstein I (ed.) 1991 *Chinese Education: Problems, Policies and Prospects*. Garland Publishing, London

Yu B, Xu H Y 1988 *Adult Higher Education: A Case Study of the Workers' Colleges in the People's Republic of China*. International Institute for Educational Planning, UNESCO, Paris

Ming Chuan Dong

China, People's Republic of: System of Education

1. General Background

China is one of the largest countries in the world, with a total land area of approximately 9.6 million square kilometers accounting for 6.5 percent of the global land area.

In 1990, the total population of China (including Taiwan) reached 1.16 billion. With 540 million in 1949, the present figure represents a net increase of 620 million and an average annual growth rate of 1.87 percent. Since the 1970s, the birthrate has dropped from 35 per thousand to 20 per thousand in the early 1990s, and the natural growth rate has also declined from 25 per thousand to about 15 per thousand due to the family planning policy. The urban population in mainland China constitutes 26 percent of the total, while the rural population makes up the remaining 74 percent.

As a multinational country, China is comprised of 56 nationalities. The Han nationality accounts for 92 percent of the total population, and the other 55 national minorities together represent the remaining 8 percent. The Han people have their own spoken and written language, which is the most common and widely used language in China. Most of the other 55 national minorities have their own languages, but 34 of them did not have written forms prior to 1949. Since 1949 the relevant government departments have assisted ten national minorities in creating and standardizing the written forms of their languages. The Chinese government has stipulated that in the national minority region, classes should be conducted in the national language so long as the written form of the language exists, and that national pupils should master their own languages while also learning the Chinese language.

China is traditionally an agricultural nation. In 1952, agricultural workers constituted 83.5% percent of the total social labor force in the country, industrial workers accounted for 7.4 percent, and workers in the service sector for 9.1 percent. With the development that has occurred since the early 1950s, the value of fixed industrial capital assets has increased 50-fold, and an independent comprehensive industrial system has been established. Great progress has also been made in agricultural production. By 1989, the proportion of the agricultural labor force had fallen to 60.2 percent, while the industrial and service sectors had risen to 21.9 and 17.9 percent respectively.

The economic system of China is a socialist market economy based on public ownership. The state organizations of the People's Republic of China include: organs of state power—the National People's Congress and local people's congresses at various levels; state administrative organs—the State Council and various levels of people's governments; the state judicial organs—the people's courts; and the state law supervision organs—the people's procuratorates. In the early 1980s, the Chinese government formulated a three-phased economic development strategy for China's socialist modernization: the first phase aims to double the 1980 Gross National Product (GNP) and to solve the problem of providing food and clothing for the people; the second phase aims to quadruple the 1980 GNP by the end of the century and to raise the standard of living of the Chinese people to a comfortable level; and the third phase aims basically to realize modernization by the middle of the next century, with per capita GNP reaching the level of a medium-developed country.

2. Politics and the Goals of the Education System

Since the 1980s, the Chinese government has established, on the basis of sound analysis of China's national condition, the fundamental principle of undertaking economic construction as the central task, while upholding the four cardinal principles (i.e., socialism through the proletariat dictatorship, the leadership of the Communist Party, and adherence to Marxism–Leninism and the ideology of Mao Zedong) and maintaining the policy of reform and opening China to the outside world. The 1985 Communist Party of China (CPC) Central Committee Decision on the Reform of Educational Structure explicitly stated that "education must serve the purpose of socialist construction and socialist construction must rely on education." This document set out the correct relationship between education and economic development, and called for economic development to rely on the advancement of science and technology and the improvement of the quality of the labor force.

The guiding principle of Chinese education is that education must serve the cause of socialist modernization and be integrated with practical work in order to ensure the all-round moral, intellectual, and physical development of the builders of socialism and their successors.

The general objective for the development of Chinese education is to establish, by the end of the century, the basic framework of an educational system which is well-adapted to the needs of the socialist modernization drive, geared to the requirements of the twenty-first century, and which bears distinct Chinese characteristics.

3. The Formal System of Education

3.1 Primary, Secondary, and Tertiary Education

Figure 1 presents the structure of the education system. Education in China comprises four sectors: basic education (BE), technical and vocational education (TAVE), higher education (HE), and adult edu-

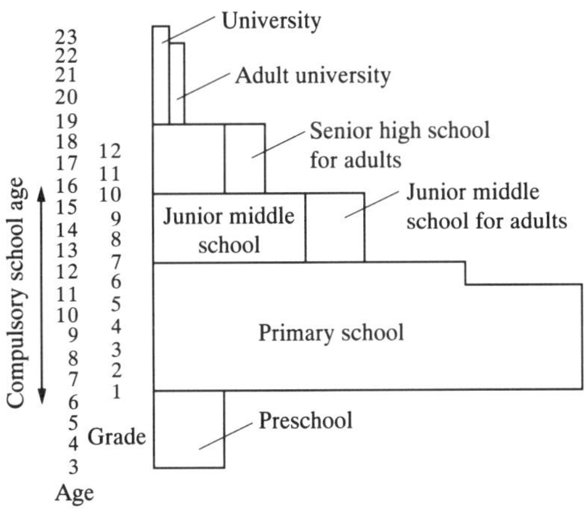

Figure 1
People's Republic of China: Structure of the formal education system

cation (AE). BE covers preschool, formal primary, and secondary education; TAVE is carried out mainly in specialized secondary schools, skilled worker schools, secondary vocational schools, and the advanced technical and vocational colleges; HE essentially refers to the education of regular higher education institutions; and AE offers literacy programs, various types of school instruction, and other forms of education which are targeted at adults.

The lengths of education at different levels and types of institutions are set as follows: kindergarten admits preschool children (age 3 or older); primary schools, lasting 5 or 6 years, enroll children at the age of 6; and secondary education consists of lower-middle school and upper-middle school, the former is for 3 or 4 years and the latter 3 years. In 1986, the National People's Congress adopted the Compulsory Education Act, which stipulates that a total of nine years of education should be made compulsory, covering primary and lower-secondary levels. Specialized secondary schools admit lower-middle school leavers normally for a four-year study program. The undergraduate courses of higher education institutions are mostly of four years' duration, medical and some engineering courses last five years, and a few medical universities even offer six-year courses. College diploma courses normally last 2 or 3 years. Graduate studies may be divided into master's degree courses and doctoral studies, with the former lasting 2.5 to 3 years and the latter usually 3 years.

In 1990, the enrollment of primary school-aged children reached 97.8 percent and the proportion of primary school leavers who proceed to lower-middle schools stood at 77.8 percent. In China, there are 766,000 primary schools with a total enrollment of 122.41 million pupils; 72,000 lower-middle schools with 38.69 million pupils; 16,000 upper-middle schools with 7.17 million students; and 1,075 regular higher education institutions with 2.15 million students.

3.2 Preschool Education

The development of preschool education in China has always been guided by the principle of reliance on the efforts of the public and local community. Apart from the endeavors of local governments, preschool education is mainly provided by various departments, work units, and social organizations within the framework of relevant laws and regulations of the state. Preschool education is mostly full-time. The training of children in the kindergartens is conducted through games, sports, classroom activities, observation, physical work projects, and daily activities. In 1990, there were over 170,000 kindergartens nationwide with an enrollment of 19.72 million children.

3.3 Special Education

The provision of special education has expanded substantially since the founding of the People's Republic. The number of special schools for the blind, deaf and mute, and the mentally retarded has grown from 42 before 1949 to 746, with the pupil population increasing from 2,000 to 72,000. Since the 1980s, a total of over 5,000 handicapped youths have entered higher education institutions.

3.4 Vocational and Technical Education

The rapid development of Technical and Vocational Education (TAVE) since the 1980s is an important indication that Chinese education is being further geared to serving the modernization process. In 1990, the total student population in the various types of technical and vocational schools all over the country reached 6.048 million, representing a fourfold increase in the 1979 figure. TAVE enrollment now accounts for 45.7 percent of the total enrollment at the upper-secondary level. Specialized secondary schools are run by the relevant ministries of the State Council and professional organizations. The purpose of these schools is to train middle-level technicians and line managers for the economic sectors. Skilled worker schools are run by local professional organizations and enterprises to train elementary – and middle-level skilled workers. The state guarantees employment for graduates from these two types of schools. Vocational schools include vocational middle schools and agricultural schools, which are run by local education authorities to supply elementary – and middle-level technicians and managerial personnel as well as the future labor force. Students in these schools are not guaranteed employment when they complete their studies. They may seek employment by their own efforts through a competitive selection process, and they may also try to undertake further study in their own discipline.

Funding for TAVE comes mainly from the state budget allocations (including the central budget and the local budgets) for the operation of various types of public schools and assistance to community-run institutions. At the same time, industrial enterprises, public establishments, organizations, individuals, and various social sectors are encouraged to raise funds to run such educational establishments.

3.5 Adult and Nonformal Education

Adult education is an important component of the Chinese education system. Its main purpose is to raise the quality of inservice personnel and contribute directly to socioeconomic development. As far as its forms are concerned, the provision of adult higher education in China includes radio and television universities, advanced staff development colleges, farmers' colleges, and the higher education self-study examination system. Elementary and secondary adult education provision includes specialized secondary schools or classes for adults and adult technical training schools. In 1990, there were 1,321 adult institutions of higher education in China with an enrollment of 1.56 million students, in addition to 58,501 secondary adult schools with 15.29 million students and 258,134 elementary adult schools with 22.82 million students. These adult education establishments have designed different modes of study to meet the needs of adult learners—for instance, classroom instruction, the provision of audio-visual materials and textbooks to assist distance learning, full-time and part-time studies, or sparetime studies. Although funding for an adult education program is primarily the responsibility of the organization that runs the program, the school may also charge students a small fee.

The Chinese government attaches great importance to literacy education. Since the founding of the People's Republic, a total of 169 million people have learned to read and write through literacy programs. From 1978 to 1990, 42.5 million illiterate people have benefited from the programs, with another 5.6 million people currently undertaking literacy study in China. It is estimated that over 50 percent of the countries all over the country have all but eliminated illiteracy.

4. Administrative and Supervisory Structure and Operation

The basic pattern of educational management system in China is that education authorities are established at the central, provincial (including autonomous regions and metropolitan municipalities), municipal (or prefectural), and the county levels to take the responsibility of national and local education administration. The departments of planning, finance, labor, and personnel of governments at all levels assist the education authorities in formulating educational development plans, budgets, and the basic personnel and salary systems. The State Education Commission (SEDC) is a professional organization of the State Council with overall responsibility for the administration of education throughout the country. In 1985, the Chinese government decided to delegate responsibility for basic education to local authorities and implement a system of management by various departments for education. The rural township governments are thus charged with part of the responsibility for local education provision.

Educational inspection in China is a system under which the higher government authorities undertake to monitor, inspect, evaluate, and provide guidance for the educational work of the lower-level people's governments, the education authorities, and schools (lower-secondary, upper-secondary, teacher-training schools, and vocational middle schools, in particular). Its purpose is to supervise the implementation of the laws and decrees, guiding principles, and policies governing education provision, and to ensure the realization of educational goals and the improvement of educational quality. An inspection network has been established.

5. Educational Finance

State financial allocation is the main source of educational funding in China. State financial allocation includes both central government allocation and fundings by local governments. Generally speaking, local financial allocations are spent on the educational provisions run and managed by local governments, whereas the central government finance is mainly used to support the institutions under various central government ministries and as special grants for specific national education development projects. In addition, considerable efforts are made by the people's governments at all levels to raise education funds through all possible channels. These include the education surcharge levied by government authorities, expenditures incurred by industrial enterprises for educational purposes, funds raised and donated by local communities, revenues generated through social services and work–study programs which are spent on improving the conditions for education, and incomes from tuition and other miscellaneous fees. In 1990, state finance provided a total expenditure of 43.3 billion Renminbi yuan (RMB yuan) on education, which accounts for 13.1 percent of the state revenue for that year; other educational funds and revenues amounted to about 11.6 billion RMB yuan. The state budget for education in 1991 was 115 RMB yuan per student at primary level and 255 RMB yuan per student at secondary level. Since 1981, China has been actively utilizing the World Bank loans for educational development.

6. Supplying Personnel for the Education System

In 1990, China had a total of 13.45 million teaching, administrative, and support staff in educational institutions of various kinds and at all levels—10.37 million of which were full-time teachers. This includes 5.58 million full-time primary school teachers, 3.63 million mainstream secondary school teachers, and 394,500 faculty members in regular higher education institutions. In comparison with 1980, the total number of employees in the school system has increased by 1.91 million; full-time teachers increased by 1.04 million. Thus, the size of the teaching force in China is sufficiently large and the primary task for the future is to raise its ideological and professional quality and optimize its structure.

To ensure the quality and standards of education and teaching, the state has laid down relevant academic qualification requirements and criteria for professional certificate assessment for primary and secondary school teachers. The state encourages teachers to upgrade their educational and professional levels through further training. There are two types of training provisions: full-time training and inservice training which are mainly provided by education colleges, teacher-training colleges, undergraduate or diploma teacher education courses run by higher education institutions, televized universities and teacher-training colleges, and correspondence schools. Such training may also be conducted through workshops and seminars on teaching materials and methodology. Teachers may also participate in the National Higher Education Self-Study Examination. Inservice training of teachers of higher education institutions is conducted through either the Senior Visiting Scholars Program or the Advanced Teacher Training Course. In addition, there are interuniversity exchanges of teachers for training purposes. The government and institutions provide the necessary conditions for the training of teachers. Those who participate in training programs are paid in full during the training period and the costs for training are met by the state. The state recognizes the qualifications of the teachers after they have satisfactorily completed their training. Appropriate status will also be given to these teachers.

The Chinese government has adopted a series of positive and effective measures to stabilize the teaching force and to improve its quality. These measures include the following:

(a) Raising the economic status of teachers and improving their working conditions. The salary of teachers has been raised on several occasions in recent years. Primary and secondary school teachers are paid an additional allowance for their years of service. The salary scale for teachers is 10 percent higher than that of other public services. Teachers with 30 years of service are entitled to full pay after retirement in some provinces and municipalities.

(b) Setting up honors and reward systems for teachers. September 10 has been designated Teacher's Day. A National Fund for Kindergarten, Primary, and Secondary School Teachers has been established to reward those teachers who have made outstanding contributions.

(c) Establishing a tenure system in primary and secondary schools. Primary and secondary school teachers are included in the professional post system. They are thus entitled to the same salary scale as other professionals.

(d) Encouraging talented secondary school leavers to enter teacher education institutions so as to ensure the quality of the student intake of these institutions. Teaching practice is to be enhanced in order to raise the quality of teacher education.

(e) Introducing the professional certificate system for primary and secondary school teachers. It is estimated that a total of 1.62 million primary and secondary school teachers took part in the qualification examination between 1986 and 1990.

The overall quality of the teaching force is constantly improving as the state attaches greater importance to, and has effectively strengthened, teacher education and teacher-training programs.

7. Curriculum Development

In order to improve the quality of the whole national effort and ensure the effectiveness of basic education, the State Education Commission (SEDC) has formed expert groups and formulated curricula guidelines for the country's primary and secondary schools. In view of the huge regional socioeconomic disparity, SEDC permits the flexible implementation of the guidelines by the provinces, autonomous regions, and the metropolitan municipalities. Necessary adaptation can be made as appropriate to local conditions, provided that the basic requirements of the curricula are met. There are two versions of the six-year primary school curriculum: one for the urban schools and the other for rural schools. It offers ten subjects including moral studies, Chinese, and mathematics. The urban schools should, in addition, provide sports activities for Grade 1 and Grade 2 pupils, while rural schools should add provisions of agricultural studies for Grade 6 pupils. The five-year primary schools do not offer sports. The middle school provides 13 compulsory subjects, including moral education and politics, Chinese, mathematics, and a foreign language. The upper-middle school is required to offer optional subjects, the contents of which are determined in accordance with the wishes of the pupils, social needs, and the conditions of specific schools. English is the most common foreign language, although some schools also offer Japanese, Russian, French, German, and Spanish. The syllabus teaching materials for each subject are all developed by subject experts according to the requirements of the curriculum and are approved by the Primary and Secondary School Teaching Materials Board of SEDC.

As far as higher education institutions are concerned, SEDC laid down the basic requirements and principles for course designs. The institutions are responsible for the formulation of their curricula and syllabuses in line with SEDC requirements and in accordance with social demand, as well as their own conditions. As a general pattern, higher education institutions offer optional courses in addition to compulsory subjects. The development of standard textbooks for higher education institutions must be approved by specific subject committees organized by SEDC.

8. The System of Examinations, Promotions, and Certifications

Primary and secondary schools administer four types of examinations: term examinations (TE), school year examinations (STE), completion examinations (CE), and entrance examinations (EE). In primary schools, TEs, STEs, and CEs are all confined to the subjects of Chinese and mathematics. The entrance examination to the lower-middle school is being phased out. The upper-middle school EE is of a selective nature and is usually combined with the middle school CE. The upper-middle school CE is independent of the higher education EE. The former is a qualifying examination and the latter a selective one. The higher education EE is a common national examination with separate provisions for liberal arts candidates and science candidates. Successful CE examinees of primary and secondary schools are awarded completion certificates, whereas university students will be awarded the completion certificate and a degree after passing various examinations and assessments.

9. Educational Evaluation and Research

Educational evaluation is an important form of supervision of the performance of schools and institutions. Since the 1980s, educational evaluation has been given due emphasis and has experienced rapid development. In higher education institutions and specialized secondary schools, assessment mainly consists of qualification evaluation, standard evaluation, and excellence evaluation. At the primary and secondary levels, the evaluation normally covers the aspects of purpose, school management, educational quality, and school conditions. Educational evaluations are normally conducted by local governments and the educational authorities.

With regard to educational research, a multilevel research network has been established with over 10,000 full-time research personnel in the country. Research funding is provided by the state and the local authorities through special funds and projects. Apart from basic educational theories, the topics of educational research are mostly concerned with the changes and development of Chinese education as well as educational and teaching practices. Research results can thus directly serve both educational policy-making and the educational reform process.

In the early 1990s, the key research topics were as follows: the relationship between rural educational development and the advancement of rural society; the main issues concerning the theory and practice of ethnic minority education in China; the theory and practice of the integration of education with productive labor; the theory and practice of Chinese educational legislation; the reform of teacher education and the building of the teaching force; the reform of primary and secondary school curriculum and teaching materials; the reform of teaching methods and the examination system; literacy education in China, and so on.

10. Major Reforms in the 1980s and 1990s

Since the early 1980s, the Chinese government has undertaken a series of effective educational reforms. These include:

(a) The adjustment of the educational structure. In 1980, secondary education in China consisted primarily of mainstream secondary schools, and the proportion of pupils in secondary technical and vocational schools accounted for only 19 percent of the total enrollment at the upper-secondary level. Following the adjustment, this proportion had increased to 46 percent by 1990. Progress was also made in the reform of the structure of higher education. In terms of the structure of subject areas, the disciplines with the greatest social demand were rapidly expanded. Between 1978 and 1990, the number of full-time students in finance and economics, politics and law, and liberal arts disciplines increased by 12, 32, and 2.2 times respectively. A large number of new and interdisciplinary subject areas were developed. With regard to the structure of program levels, the development of diploma education was accelerated. By 1990, the number of higher diploma institutions had grown to 455, accounting for 42.6 percent of the total number of higher education institutions, with an enrollment of 743,000 students representing 36 percent of the total student population in higher education. The ratio of graduate, undergraduate, and diploma students had been adjusted from 0.7:100:24 in 1949 to 7:100:56 in 1990, illustrating a rationalization of the structure of higher education.

(b) Change of the management system. A new decentralized management system was established, with local authorities being given the responsibility for basic education. With regard to the provision of education, the traditional mode—according to which the government assumed full responsibility—decreased and provisions by enterprises and social communities expanded substantially. In addition, the degree of institutional autonomy was extended. This change was marked by great success, particularly in the rural areas. In the early 1990s, efforts are being made to improve the macrocontrol and internal management systems of institutions.

(c) Comprehensive reform of education. Since 1987, SEDC has launched pilot projects in the comprehensive reform of education in 15 municipalities and 116 counties. The main contents of the urban comprehensive reform were: to enhance the overall coordination of economy, science and technology, and education (including all levels and types) by the government; to change the admission and job assignment system of the specialized secondary schools and the skilled worker schools, with corresponding reforms of the labor personnel system; to improve the overall structure of urban education; and to promote the diversification of upper-secondary education. The main contents of the rural comprehensive reform of education included: the overall coordination and integration of agriculture, science and technology, and education: and the overall management of BE, TAVE, and AE, so as to facilitate coordinated socioeconomic and educational development.

11. Major Problems for the Year 2000

The main problems of Chinese education are as follows: a degree of irrationality in the educational structure (e.g., TAVE is not adequately developed); insufficient investment in education and poor school conditions; educational principles, contents, and methodology are out of touch with social reality to varying degrees; and the efficiency of the system is less than ideal. Thus, in general terms, the Chinese education system is not yet well-adapted to the needs of the national socialist development program.

The Chinese government has formulated a Ten-Year Program and the Eighth Five-Year Plan for educational development. It may be anticipated that, by the end of the century, the educational structure in China will become more rational, the education quality will be substantially improved, the force of specialized personnel will be expanded, and the quality and standard of the labor force and professionals will be further improved. The educational system will largely meet the needs of state economic and social development.

Bibliography

Liu Huozi (ed.) 1990 *Chinese Encyclopaedia*. Chinese Encyclopaedia Press, Beijing

Li Jian (ed.) 1989 *Chinese Education Yearbook*. People's Education Press, Beijing

People's Republic of China 1985 *The Central Government's Decision on Educational Reform*. Government Office, Beijing

People's Republic of China 1986 *The Compulsory Education Act*. Government Office, Beijing

Xue Muqiao (ed.) 1990 *Chinese Economic Yearbook*. Chinese Statistics Press, Beijing

Teng Teng

China, People's Republic of: Vocationalizing Education

Vocational and technical (VT) education in China has experienced significant shifts in its development since the founding of the People's Republic of China in 1949. In the 1980s, the Chinese government launched a major vocationalization effort which drastically changed the structure of education, especially at the upper secondary level. In the early 1990s, Chinese VT education is a diversified delivery system characterized by unevenness in development across regions and modes of delivery. Vocational changes in education are reflective of larger economic, social, and political changes in the country (Tsang 1991). This entry analyzes the contents, rationale, and implementation of the vocationalization effort in the 1980s. The analysis relates this effort to vocationalization shifts in previous periods, to changing government perspectives of national development, and to the international experience of vocationalization of education.

1. Vocationalizing Education in the 1980s

A major effort to reform education in China was announced by the Chinese government in May 1985. There were three key components in the reform proposal: (a) decentralization in the administration and financing of basic education and the implementation of nine-year compulsory education; (b) structural change in secondary education and the development of VT education; and (c) reform in student admission and allocation of graduates in higher education as well as increased operational autonomy for institutions of higher education. The reform was aimed at addressing the problems of structural weakness and administrative rigidity in education (People's Press 1985).

1.1 Contents and Rationale

The Chinese government saw the predominance of general education at the upper secondary level as a major structural weakness in education and the development of VT education was the solution to this structural problem. The reform called for changing the monolithic structure in upper secondary education in the late 1970s to an equal mix of general education and VT education by about 1990. It also encouraged the development of postsecondary VT institutes and colleges as well as the capacity to provide short-term vocational and technical training. Given the goal of nine-year compulsory basic education, educational streaming would take place after lower secondary education. Graduates from lower secondary schools could apply for admission to upper secondary general schools or VT schools, and graduates of upper secondary schools could apply for admission to regular universities or post secondary VT institutes and colleges. Graduates who failed to get into these institutions could receive some short-term VT training before employment.

In the 1985 reform pronouncement, the focus of the development of VT education was at the upper secondary level. There are three types of VT schools at this level in China: upper secondary vocational schools run by education bureaucracies, skilled workers schools run by the Ministry of Labor and its local bureaucracies, and secondary specialized schools which consist of teacher training schools run by educational bureaucracies and secondary technical schools run by noneducation ministries, departments, and enterprises. The rapid vocationalization of upper-secondary education could be accomplished by a combination of four strategies: the conversion of some upper secondary general schools (run by education bureaucracies) into upper secondary vocational schools, the addition of vocational classes in some upper secondary general schools, building new upper secondary vocational schools, and increasing enrollment in existing skilled workers schools and secondary technical schools.

The official rationale for the vocationalization of upper secondary education was articulated primarily in economic terms. With the promulgation of modernization policies in the Third Plenary Session of the Eleventh Congress in 1978, a large-scale industrialization program was launched in the late 1970s. By the early 1980s, there were serious shortages of skilled workers, semiskilled workers, and middle-level technicians. Such shortages were attributed to the predominance of general education at the secondary level.

The development of secondary VT education would meet the needs for middle-level technical personnel and skilled workers. In addition, economic reform also resulted in increased attention to economic efficiency. In the early 1980s, workers recruited from upper secondary general schools were reported to lack the technical skills and the psychological preparation for work in the factory. By contrast, VT education was expected to provide a better technical and psychological preparation for industrial work than general education; graduates from VT education would presumably be more productive than general education graduates in such work. Vocationalization of upper secondary education would contribute to increased efficiency in educational investment.

Though not highlighted by government officials, educational streaming at the upper secondary level was also a factor. Because of the focus of upper secondary schools on college preparation and the low transition rate (about 4% in 1980) between upper secondary education and higher education, there was tremendous academic pressure at the secondary higher education junction. Students and teachers were caught up in learning and teaching for examination and for higher promotion rates up the education ladder. The structural reform was aimed at putting half of the students at the upper secondary level into VT schools, and subsequently to work, and thus alleviating the transitional pressure and its negative effects on teaching and learning at lower levels of education.

1.2 Historical Significance

The historical significance of the 1985 vocationalization plan can be better understood by tracing the development of VT education in China since 1949. Before 1985, development in secondary education in China can be divided into three periods: 1949–65, 1966–76, and the post-1976 period (China Education Yearbook Editorial Board 1984).

Soon after the founding of the People's Republic in 1949, the emphasis at the secondary level was on general education, first in expanding the scope of general education and then on improving its quality. Though there was some fluctuation in quantitative targets, overall there was very significant achievement in terms of access to secondary general education during 1949–65. In 1949, there were 0.83 million students in lower secondary general education and 0.21 million students in upper secondary general education; by 1965, the corresponding enrollments were 8.0 million and 1.3 million respectively.

At the same time, VT education increased significantly in size and in type. Secondary specialized schools were the first VT schools to appear and could be traced to education institutions that existed prior to 1949. Among these schools, secondary teacher training schools prepared teachers for primary schools and kindergartens. Secondary technical schools prepared middle-level cadres for various ministries and departments. Secondary specialized schools enrolled students at both the lower secondary level and upper secondary level; but over time there was a shift in expansion towards the upper secondary level. Skilled workers schools began to emerge in the early 1950s, following the Soviet model of VT education. They enrolled students at the upper secondary level and prepared middle-level skilled workers. Secondary vocational schools consisted of two kinds: agricultural schools in rural areas that were first established in 1958 at the lower secondary level, and vocational schools in urban areas that first appeared in 1963 and enrolled students at both levels. Secondary vocational schools expanded much more rapidly than the other types of VT schools; they were less well financed and were of lower quality.

Secondary education became increasingly vocationalized during the 1949–65 period. In 1949, VT education accounted for 13 percent and 35 percent of total enrollment at the lower secondary level and upper secondary level respectively; by 1965, the ratio had increased to 31 percent and 52 percent respectively. In 1965, China had a diversified secondary education structure. There were 5.1 million students enrolled in VT education; 3.7 million (or 72%) of these students were in lower secondary VT schools and 99 percent of these 3.7 million students were found in lower secondary vocational schools.

Education was at the center of the social upheaval of the Cultural Revolution period of 1966–76. Being accused of promoting social differentiation and elitism, the diversified structure was drastically homogenized during this period. The VT schools were converted into secondary general schools; and new secondary general schools proliferated throughout the country. At the same time, many secondary technical schools and skilled workers schools were either consolidated, closed down, or turned into factories. By 1976, lower secondary education was wholly devoted to general education, and only one percent of the students at the upper secondary level were enrolled in some type of VT school. Secondary education had became a monolithic structure.

The structural reform of 1985 was the climax of a series of small-scale and experimental efforts undertaken by the Chinese government since 1978 to "revocationalize" secondary education. The recovery of the different types of VT schools in the early 1980s was rather uneven in different parts of the country, and was particularly slow for secondary vocational schools. The official pronouncement in 1985 was intended to provide a strong push for the development of VT education.

Thus the 1985 reform was aimed at a complete reversal of the national policy on secondary education during the period of the Cultural Revolution. It supported and called for a return to the diversified structure that existed in secondary education in 1965. The vocationalization effort in the 1980s, however, was directed primarily at upper secondary education while the vocationalization effort before 1966 was mostly focused on lower secondary education.

1.3 Implementation

In the early 1980s, the government experimented with a number of strategies to promote the development of VT education which were implemented on a large scale after 1985. The first strategy was to stimulate the demand for VT education by enhancing the employment prospects of its graduates. The government stipulated that VT education graduates be given more favorable consideration than general education graduates in the hiring and promotion practices in state enterprises and bureaucracies. It also established a policy of "training before employment" by which job openings in state enterprises and bureaucracies are accessible to those with the required education and training qualifications; and jobs in industry often require VT education or training. This policy is aimed at discouraging the informal practice in the Chinese workplace whereby a son or daughter inherits the position left vacant by a retiring parent.

Second, a decentralization approach is adopted in which the local government (city and county) has the primary responsibility in the development of VT education. It is meant to encourage the diversification of modes of delivery, to broaden the financing base, and to promote VT education development in accordance with varying local needs. Third, the media and the machinery of the Chinese Communist Party are used to raise the awareness of local decision makers about the importance of VT education. Fourth, each state bureaucracy or enterprise that operates VT schools is responsible for staffing its schools, and provincial governments are encouraged to establish VT teacher training colleges to provide a stable source of teachers for VT schools. Finally, career education was experimented with in urban areas to improve the selection of students to VT schools.

There were dramatic quantitative changes in upper secondary education in the 1980s. Between 1980 and 1989, enrollment in general education schools decreased from 9.7 million students to 7.2 million students (−26%), enrollment in secondary vocational schools increased from 0.32 million to 2.4 million (+641%), enrollment in secondary technical schools increased from 0.76 million to 1.5 million (+96%), enrollment in skilled workers school increased from 0.70 million to 1.3 million (+81%), and enrollment in secondary teacher training schools increased from 0.28 million to 0.69 million (+143%). As in the pre-1966 period, most of the VT education students were located in secondary vocational schools. The proportion of all upper-secondary students in VT schools increased from 19 percent in 1980 to 43 percent in 1988 and to 48 percent in 1990. The government had essentially achieved its quantitative target for vocationalization.

Despite this quantitative achievement, the vocationalization effort has significant problems, the most obvious of which is the poor quality of secondary vocational schools. These schools have a shortage of qualified teachers, as well as substandard equipment and other facilities. Due to a lack of required resources, the rapid conversion of upper secondary general schools into upper secondary vocational schools often results in a change in the name of a school only; not much has actually taken place within the school. Local educational decision makers have concentrated on the quantitative development of VT education to show that they have understood the importance of VT education and to comply with the quantitative target of the central government.

Some secondary vocational schools actually closed down at the end of the 1980s and beginning of the 1990s because of poor quality, inadequate funding, and difficulty in obtaining employment for their graduates. Other secondary vocational schools stayed alive by reverting to a general curriculum in the first two years and providing vocational training only in the third year; the first two years are funded by a local education bureaucracy and the third year by a sponsoring production unit. These schools are still called vocational schools despite their having a mostly general curriculum. Secondary technical schools and skilled workers schools have had fewer problems because they are much better funded and have stronger linkages to production departments and enterprises.

Beside the problem of low quality, the lack of coordination among local government bureaucracies results in duplication in VT education programs, an overall mismatch in the supply of and demand for training, and VT schools of suboptimal size and high unit costs.

2. *Vocationalizing Education and National Development*

The vocationalizing effort in the 1980s is significant in the history of Chinese education not only because of its scale and complexities, but also because it reflects fundamental changes in the ruling Chinese Communist Party's perspective on education and national development. In fact, the 1985 reform is the most recent episode in a cycle of changes in education which has oscillated between "redness" and "expertise" since the late 1950s; vocationalization has been caught up in continuing social and political conflicts between two factions within the Party (Tsang 1991). The two factions are often labelled the Radicals and Moderates by outside observers of Chinese politics. The Radicals believe that socialist development is achieved by transforming the social relations of production through continuing class struggles and revolution. The development process is characterized by mass participation in all aspects of social life. People are to be inculcated with communist ideals (redness) through political campaigns and other educational means. The Moderates believe that socialist development is achieved by first transforming the forces of production; the development process is economic and technical in nature and is characterized by the employment of a skilled labor force (expertise) and the application of science and technology to production.

The Party had a unified policy of national reconstruction in the early 1950s. In 1958, the Radicals (led by Mao Zedong) tried to push China into the accelerated development ("great leap forward") through the "mass line" approach. Education was politicized. The economic failure under the Radicals led to the rise in power of the Moderates in the early 1960s. The Moderates introduced individual incentives in economic production and emphasized expertise through education. The structure of education became more diversified. The Radicals launched the Cultural Revolution in 1966 and recaptured political power from the Moderates. Redness through education was again in vogue, and VT education was almost completely eliminated because it was seen as emphasizing technical skills and contributing to social differentiation. The death of Mao in 1976 and the intervention of the military resulted in the return of Moderates to power, and modernization policies consistent with the developmental approach of the Moderates were launched in the late 1970s. Expertise was again emphasized, and a diversified education system was expected to produce different levels and types of skilled personnel for a differentiated workplace. Secondary VT education began to recover in the early 1980s to train middle-level technical personnel.

The vocationalization experience shows that educational change is part and parcel of larger social and political conflicts within the state in China, as it is in other countries (Carnoy and Levin 1985, Carnoy and Samoff 1990).

3. *Chinese Vocationalization in International Perspective*

The Chinese vocationalization effort in the 1980s was unquestionably the largest and most complex among all nations in recent years; and it runs against the thinking of policy analysts in international development organizations (Middleton et al. 1991). It is instructive to examine the rationale and empirical basis of the Chinese effort against the background of international experience in this area.

For many years in other countries, the development of VT education has been supported on the basis of a number of assumptions: VT education graduates are more productive than general education graduates, VT education is a more efficient form of investment than general education, VT education is a solution to unemployment for noncollege bound youth, and VT education facilitates the transition between school and work and reduces the social demand for higher education.

The formulation of the vocationalization policy in the early 1980s in China was not based on empirical evidence but rather on a belief in the productivity advantage of VT education over general education. The findings of productivity studies in other countries are mixed, with no consistent and convincing evidence in favor of VT education (Min and Tsang 1990).

Similarly, there was no empirical evidence of higher rates of return to VT education in China. Rates of return studies in other countries generally show that general education has a higher rate of return than VT education (Psacharopoulos 1986). Rates of return depend on the ratio of benefits (higher productivity) to costs, and VT education is more costly than general education in China as well as in other countries (Tsang 1988). The quantitative target of an equal mix of the two types of education simply represents a return to the education structure in 1965, with a focus on upper secondary education instead of lower secondary education. It has no economic basis in terms of an analysis of rates of return or the demand for skill in the changing Chinese economy.

The fallacy of VT education as a solution to youth unemployment was documented years ago (Foster 1965), and is recognized by Chinese decision makers. In China, VT education is not posed as a solution to youth unemployment; instead employment policies are manipulated to support VT education. The Chinese government has been successful in manipulating employment practices, controlling wage differentions between workers of different educational qualifications, and limiting the size of higher education. The social pressure to expand higher education has been reduced during the 1980s. To the extent that VT education may be a less efficient investment than general education, such practices can be inconsistent with the move toward a market-oriented economy in China. Few governments can implement such measures without adverse political consequences.

In short, although the Chinese vocationalization effort was justified in largely economic terms, there is actually little empirical support for the economic assumptions; the social streaming objective of the effort is more significant than what has been officially admitted.

4. Rethinking Vocationalization Policies

Improving the quality of VT education is the focus of education decision-makers in China for the first half of the 1990s. Assuming the continuation of the modernization approach to national development, the discussion in the above section still raises serious questions about vocationalization policies in China. These questions include: What is the appropriate scale of VT education? How should vocational training be provided? What are the implications of a market-oriented economy for VT education and training?

The government's quantitative target of an equal mix of VT education and general education at the upper secondary level has no economic basis. Experience has cast doubt about the scale of VT education, especially that of secondary vocational schools. There are reports of overproduction of graduates from these schools, and some schools have either closed down or turned away from a traditional vocational curriculum. The scale of VT education should be driven by skill demand factors instead.

Experience from other countries shows that VT institutions that have close linkages to enterprises or firms are more successful in terms of the quality of skill training, placement of graduates, and responsiveness to changing skill demand. This finding is consistent with the observation in China that secondary technical schools and skilled workers schools perform much better than secondary vocational schools. The rapid development of secondary vocational schools as the dominant mode of delivery in the 1980s is very problematic indeed. Additional resources to raise the quality of these schools may be more efficiently used elsewhere.

Among other things, the move toward a market economy requires policies that encourage flexibility in skill training, responsiveness to changing production conditions, and efficiency in education and economic production. The government's policies regarding the promotion of a vocational curriculum, the use of costly school-based vocational education, training before employment, and manipulation of hiring and promotion practices should be reexamined in light of the market requirements.

Finally, there will be continued interest among Chinese decision makers in employing a diversified education structure for social streaming in the 1990s. The challenge is to strike a proper balance between the economic and social roles of education in national development.

See also: Vocationalism: Theoretical Assumptions; Vocational Education and Training: Anglo-German Comparisons; Vocational Education and Training: Improving Cost-effectiveness in Developing Nations; Primary School Agriculture in Sub-Saharan Africa; Planning for Vocational Education and Training; Education and Productive Work; Technical-Vocational Education: Comparative and International Studies; Returns to Vocational Education in Developing Nations; Vocational Education and Productivity

References

Carnoy M, Samoff J 1990 *Education and Social Transition*

in the Third World. Princeton University Press, Princeton, New Jersey

Carnoy M, Levin H 1985 *Schooling and Work in the Democratic State.* Stanford University Press Stanford, California

China Education Yearbook Editorial Board 1984 *China Education Yearbook, 1949–1981.* China Education Yearbook Editorial Board, Beijing, China

Foster P 1965 The vocational school fallacy in development planning. In: Anderson C, Bowman M (eds.) 1965 *Education and Economic Development.* Aldine, Chicago, Illinois

Middleton J, Ziderman A, Van Adams A 1991 *Vocational and Technical Education and Training.* World Bank, Washington, DC

Min W, Tsang M 1990 Vocational education and productivity: A case study of the Beijing General Auto Industry Company. *Eco. Educ. Rev.* 9(4): 351–64

People's Press 1985 *Document on the Reform of the Educational System.* 1–18. People's Press, Beijing, China

Psacharopoulos G 1987 To vocationalize or not to vocationalize? That is the curriculum question. *Int. Rev. Educ.* 33(2): 187–211

Tsang M 1991 The structural reform of secondary education in China. *J. Educ. Admin.* 29(4): 65–83

Further Reading

Dougherty C 1990 Unit costs and economies of scale in vocational and technical education: Evidence from the People's Republic of China. *Econ. Educ. Rev.* 9(4): 389–94

Hu S, Seifman E (eds.) 1976 *Towards a New World Outlook: A Documentary History of Education in the People's Republic of China, 1949–1976.* AMS Press, New York

Montaperto R, Henderson J (eds.) 1980 *China's Schools in Flux.* M E Sharpe, White Plains, New York

Psacharopoulos G, Loxley W 1985 *Diversified Secondary Education and Development: Evidence from Colombia and Tanzania.* Johns Hopkins University Press, Baltimore, Maryland

Townsend J 1980 *Politics in China,* 2nd Ed. Little, Brown, Boston, Massachusetts

Tsang M 1988 *The Costs of Vocational Training.* Population and Human Resources Department, World Bank, Washington, DC

M. C. Tsang

Christian Theory of Human Nature and Development

The task of extracting a theory of human nature and development from Christian doctrine requires at the outset several methodological decisions. First is the question of what properly constitutes Christian doctrine for such an undertaking. While it is obvious that the Bible is the basic source of Christian belief, there is the problem of which version of the Bible should be used, since different Christian denominations subscribe to separate versions whose contents are not entirely the same. A second question concerns what writings—if any—beyond the Bible can also qualify as doctrine for this purpose. Can interpretations of Biblical passages written by religious scholars in recent centuries qualify? If so, what criteria should be used to separate authentic interpretations from false or doubtful ones? A third issue is that of literal versus symbolic meanings. For example, in Genesis, the first book of the Bible, a description of the origins of the earth and its inhabitants states that the Lord created the universe and all living things in six days, then rested on the seventh. Is this passage to be interpreted literally as meaning six 24-hour days, or is the term *day* meant to symbolize eons of time and not a 24-hour period? And if certain words are to be regarded as symbols, or if described incidents are to be interpreted as parables that signify broader meanings, how is such interpretation to be validated? In short, who is competent to decide which words are symbolic and what meanings they intend?

For the purpose of this entry, the forgoing three issues have been settled in the following manner. First, the Bible translation authorized by King James I of England in the year 1611 has been used for the present enterprise because it continues to be the most widely adopted version in the English-speaking world. As for other sources of Christian theory besides the Bible, extensions or interpretations of basic doctrine have been accepted which have been written since early Christian days if such extensions have been regarded in recent times as authoritative by one or more of the major Christian sects. Likewise, interpretations of symbolism or parables are included if they have been regarded as valid by one or more of the major sects.

It should be apparent that when such a set of ground rules is adopted, the resulting theory cannot be considered *the* Christian model of human nature and development, but rather must be viewed only as one version of Christian theory, which may even include some variations among its subparts. In recognition of this fact, at several points in the following account opposing beliefs are identified that different Christian denominations may hold regarding a given issue.

It should be recognized at the start that the aspect of human life on which Christian theory focuses is that of moral development, meaning the growth of an individual's relationship to a Supreme Being and to fellow humans. Christian theory gives little or no attention to physical growth or to cognitive development, except as cognition may relate to moral behavior.

The topics to be inspected include: (a) personality structure and its origin, (b) the original moral nature of the child, (c) the goals of development, (d) the length of development, (e) stages of development, (f) influences on development, (g) sources of evidence, and (h) implications of the theory for child rearing and education. (Throughout the review, quotations from the Bible are cited in terms of the particular Biblical book's name, chapter number, and verse number in the King James version—for instance: Hebrews 4:12.)

1. Personality Structure and its Origin

The most basic components of human nature, as reflected in scripture from both the Old and New Testaments of the Bible, are the physical and the immaterial, that is, body and soul. This bipartite division is initially described in Genesis (2:7) with the creation of the first man: "And Jehovah God formed man of the dust of the ground, and breathed into his nostrils the breath of life; and man became a living soul." The two aspects are recognized again at the time of death: "Then shall the dust return to the earth as it was, and the spirit shall return unto God who gave it" (Ecclesiastes 12:7).

However, Christian interpretations of human nature often go beyond the bipartite concept to propose additional components of the human's immaterial portion, the portion which, for convenience of discussion, will be referred to as personality. One question theologians have long debated is whether soul and spirit are merely different words for the same entity. Or are soul and spirit separate components of the personality, as suggested in such phrases as "your whole spirit and soul and body be preserved" (1 Thessalonians 5:23)? In pursuing this issue, advocates on both sides of the question have argued their positions without being able to adduce sufficient unequivocal scripture or empirical psychological evidence to convince the other side of the validity of their position, so that the matter still remains unsettled in the early 1990s. A further problem has been that of determining if spirit and soul are identical to, or different from, heart or mind as in the passage "thou shalt love the Lord thy God with all thy heart, and with all thy soul, and with all thy mind" (Mark 12:30).

The debate about the composition of personality has become even more complex over the centuries as Christian scholars have proposed further divisions of the nonphysical self. By the twentieth century these divisions had emerged as faculties of the mind, with the term faculty meaning a power, capacity, function, or trait of personality. For several centuries past, this faculty psychology has provided the generally accepted view of personality structure for large numbers of Christian theologians and it continues to do so in the late twentieth century. Typical faculties within Christian conceptions of personality are intellect, sensibility, will, and conscience.

> Intellect is the soul knowing; sensibility is the soul feeling (desires, affections); will is the soul choosing (end or means) . . .. Man has intellect or reason, to discern the difference between right and wrong; sensibility, to be moved by each of these; free will, to do the one or the other . . .. But in connection with these faculties there is a sort of activity which involves them all, and without which there can be no moral action, namely, the activity of conscience. (Strong 1907 pp. 497, 505)

However, these four are not the only powers or divisions of mental activity. Theologians also speak of such faculties as judgment, intuition, memory, imagination, and others. Although Christian scholars may disagree on the exact number and types of faculties, their discussions of human nature reflect a conviction that personality is indeed composed of traits or faculties that operate within the soul, or along with the soul, to make up the nonmaterial individual.

A key element of doctrine for most Christian sects has been the belief that the chief distinction between humans and other living things is in the soul, which only humans have, and it is the soul that gives them a God-like character that makes them supreme among beings. ("And God said, let us make man in our image, after our likeness . . . [to] have dominion over the fish of the sea, and over the fowl of the air, and over the cattle, and over all the earth . . ." Genesis 1:26.) Or, as an alternative interpretation, plants and animals are credited with immaterial characteristics that can be labeled soul, but the types of souls they possess are not identical to the human soul. From such a perspective, the human soul is a unitary object; but like God himself, it forms a trinity consisting of a vegetative soul, a sensible soul, and a rational soul. The vegetative soul has the powers of nourishing and propagating, two characteristics that people share with the earth's plant life. The sensible soul has not only powers of nourishing and propagating but also additional equipment possessed by animals—external senses as well as an internal common sense and such faculties as imagination and memory, emotions, and the musculature (sinews) that makes locomotion possible. But it is the rational soul, the highest in the trinity, that contains all the powers of the other two, plus the faculties of reason and will and conscience that make humankind more Godly than the beasts.

1.1 The Origin of the Soul

The matter of how and when the soul of the individual person originates is an issue not only of theoretical significance but of practical importance as well. Three main theories about the soul's origin, disputed over the centuries, continue to be debated in the late twentieth century.

First is the pre-existence theory, the belief that every person's soul existed in the mind of God prior to the creation of the individual's body. Such a theory is proposed to account for what are assumed to be people's intuitive ideas—their sense of space, time, causality, right, and God—with which, ostensibly, they are born. It is reasoned that since these ideas are innate and not the result of experience in the world, they must have existed in a soul or mind prior to the individual's conception and birth.

Second is the creation theory, the proposal that the soul of each human is immediately created by God and joined to the body at conception or at birth, or at some time between the two. The creation theory has been advocated by most Roman Catholic and Reformed theologians who support their belief by "referring to God as the Creator of the human spirit, together with the fact that there is a marked individuality in the child, which cannot be explained as a mere reproduction of the qualities existing in the parents" (Strong 1907 p. 491). In late twentieth-century disputes about the practice of abortion, supporters of the creation theory propose that aborting the normal development process of the unborn baby is an act of murder if the abortion is performed after the soul has been entered into the fetus by God. The question of when between conception and birth the soul is created by God becomes, therefore, an issue of great import to those who subscribe to a creationist view.

Third is traducian theory, a prevailing view of many followers of Martin Luther. From the traducian viewpoint, the human race began with God's creating Adam and Eve—creating them body and soul—and from that original pair all subsequent humans have inherited their characteristics, both material and immaterial. Advocates of the traducian position contend that the scriptural evidence of God's final creative act appears in Genesis (2:1–3): "Thus the heavens and the earth were finished, and all the host of them. And on the seventh day God ended his work which he had made . . . And God blessed the seventh day, and sanctified it: because that in it he had rested from all his work which God created . . ." If this was indeed the last of God's creative acts, then individual souls must have been inherited from one generation to the next over the centuries rather than each soul being created anew by God prior to the birth of every new infant.

Nevertheless, while Christian theorists may disagree on the origin of the soul and on exactly what faculties or traits compose the soul, all agree that the key element of human personality is a soul or spirit, which represents God's essence and thereby differentiates humans from other living things.

2. *The Child's Original Moral Nature*

Intimately linked to notions of the origin of the soul is the issue of whether the newborn is moral (naturally inclined to perform morally correct acts), is immoral (inclined to do evil), or amoral (neutral, that is, inclined neither to good nor to evil acts).

The dominant position on this issue in most Christian sects is that children are naturally inclined to evil. One rationale for such belief is that the original sin committed by Adam and Eve has been transmitted through the souls of everyone born since their time. This conviction derives logically from the traducian theory and has been reflected in such educational material as the New England Primer, which served as the chief primary-school reading textbook in North America from the late seventeenth century through the mid-nineteenth century. To teach children the first letter of the alphabet, the primer used the phrase "A = In *A*dam's fall, we sinned all" (*New England Primer* 1836 p. 11).

Even Christians who do not subscribe literally to the inheritance of original sin still typically see humans inclined toward immoral behavior.

> In the sight of God his Judge, man is a sinner . . . This is not a condition to which God has fatally condemned mankind, but a perversion of the nature and destiny of man as God created him for which man himself is responsible. It is a misuse of the great powers with which God has endowed man, so that he oppresses his fellows instead of loving and serving them, is inwardly at war with himself, and becomes the slave of those natural and temporal forces he was meant to dominate. So long as man remains impenitently in this condition, he remains under the condemnation of God his Judge. (Dunstan 1961 p. 208)

3. *The Goals of Development*

The goals of human development in Christian theory can be divided into the ultimate and the intermediate. The ultimate goal is to achieve life everlasting in the company of God and Christ in Heaven. The intermediate goal is to do God's will in one's daily life on earth. The behaviors that represent God's will have been defined in the Old Testament of the Bible mainly in the form of specific commandments and proverbs, often illustrated with examples from people's lives. Most prominent of these are the 10 commandments that warn against such acts as killing, stealing, telling lies, committing adultery, coveting others' possessions, worshipping idols, misusing God's name, failing to respect one's parents, and improperly conducting religious rites (Exodus 20:4–26). God's will is reinterpreted by Christ in the New Testament in the form of more general principles of conduct, the chief of which are to love God and all mankind.

> And thou shalt love the Lord thy God with all thy heart, and with all thy soul, and with all thy mind, and with all thy strength: this is the first commandment. And the second is . . . thou shalt love thy neighbor as thyself. (Mark 12:30–31)

The principle of treating others with love is illustrated with examples in the accounts of Christ's life and with suggestions in subsequent books, most of which consist of letters sent by the apostle Paul to various groups of Christian adherents.

Hence, according to Christian theory, human development can be judged satisfactory when the individual's behavior increasingly matches the behavior described in God's commandments. Or stated differently, because the term sin identifies all behaviors contrary to God's will, human development is progressing satisfactorily when a person increasingly avoids sin.

However, Christian theologians disagree on the question of the connection between: (a) the intermediate goals of abiding by God's commandments; and (b) the ultimate goal of the soul's ascending to Heaven after the death of the body. The question is: will a person earn an after-life of everlasting joy in Heaven by having faithfully followed God's commandments while on earth, or earn an after-life of misery in Hell by having lived an earthly life of sin? Or is the soul's destiny after death dependent simply on God's inclination or grace, regardless of one's conduct during the years on earth? Can people who have lived sinful lives attain a Heavenly after-life by, at the time of death, confessing their sins and accepting Christ as their savior? While some Christians would answer yes and others no to such queries, all Christians endorse the belief that humans are obligated to follow the Lord's commandments, and child-raising and educational practices are directed toward such an end.

4. *The Length of Development*

Defining the length of life and of development from a Christian perspective requires that the material being—the body—be considered separately from the nonmaterial—the soul or spirit. For the body, the beginning of both life and development occurs with conception, with the joining of the sperm and egg, and the end comes with physical death as the heart stops beating. For the soul, life is far longer, although the length of development may be the same as for the body. The decision about when the life of the soul starts depends upon which theory of the soul's origin is adopted. To people who subscribe to either the pre-existence or traducian theory, the soul originates at the time of conception, when the sperm and ovum merge. To those who subscribe to the creationist theory, the soul originates at whatever time between conception and birth God places the individual soul in the fetus. It is not clear in Christian doctrine whether the soul achieves any prenatal development, so the beginning of development of the soul appears indeterminate. However, it is clear that from birth until physical death the soul develops; that is, it changes with experience and knowledge. One of the key tenets of Christian belief is that the life of the soul does not end with physical death but continues on through everlasting time. Hence, the life of the soul extends from the prenatal period into eternity. It is unclear, however, whether any development of the soul occurs after physical death. In the view of Jonathan Edwards, a seventeenth-century American Protestant theologian, "An unbodied spirit may be as capable of love and hatred, joy and sorrow, hope or fear, or other affections, as one that is united to a body" (Simonson 1970 p. 163), but the question of whether such an ostensibly sensate soul experiences any development while in its unbodied state following physical death is left unsettled.

5. *Stages of Development*

For present purposes, a stage of development is considered to be a period of life which is marked by characteristics that differ from those of other periods. Passage from one stage to another is often indicated by a society's assigning responsibilities and rights not expected at an earlier stage. Sometimes passage is also signified by a formal ceremony.

In view of this definition, there appear to be at least five stages of development in Christian theory—the prebaptismal, the postbaptismal childhood stage, the age of reason, the years of marriage, and the postmortem period.

In most Christian denominations the prebaptismal stage consists of the 9-month prenatal period as well as the early days or early months of infancy until the baby is baptized. During the baptism ceremony, the child is officially assigned the name that he or she will bear throughout life, and the ceremony shows the world that the parents dedicate the child to a Christian life. People who have not been baptized in infancy may be baptized at any later time in life.

During the postbaptismal period of childhood, which typically extends from infancy until around puberty, children are expected to gradually learn how to be good Christians. However, during this first decade of life, children are considered too immature to fully understand Christian doctrine or the consequences of their behavior, so they are not held responsible for moral decisions. But around the time of puberty, they are thought to reach the age of reason and thus become capable of comprehending more completely the significance of Christian commitment. They are now considered to be accountable for their moral decisions and behavior. This passing from the state of irresponsible childhood into the fellowship of responsible, mature Christians is signified by a formal ceremony conducted before the church congregation. The ceremony in the Catholic church is the confirmation rite, and in most Protestant denominations it is the ritual of accepting the youth as a full church member with the right to partake of holy communion. During the period immediately preceding the ceremony, the youth usually engages in intensive study of key elements of church doctrine to help ensure that he or she enters the new stage of life with a truly enlightened Christian commitment.

Entrance to the next stage, which traditionally

occurs in early adulthood, is signified by a marriage ceremony during which the bride and groom publicly pledge to respect, love, and protect each other, forsaking all other potential mates "until death do us part." An important facet of marriage is that of achieving parenthood.

The final stage of development begins with death. Whereas physical death means the end of the corporeal self, for the soul it signifies the onset of life hereafter. Although there may be no change in the soul's condition during the after-life, passage into the final stage is itself a developmental change. A person's entering this last stage is marked by a funeral ceremony in which the soul of the departed is entrusted to the care of the Lord.

In certain versions of Christian theory an additional stage, or perhaps substage, during the period of adulthood is postulated. It is that of the born-again Christian, a condition achieved when an adult experiences a spiritual reawakening, a revival of Christian insight and commitment, with the spiritual rebirth often occurring during the conduct of a religious ceremony.

6. *Influences on Development*

The four varieties of influence that shape development in Christian theory are heredity, the environment, supernatural acts, and human will.

Heredity, as set by the genes contributed by the two parents at the time of conception, determines the general structure of the human body and the basic pace of its growth throughout life. This is true in all forms of Christian theory. And as noted earlier, in the opinion of Christians who subscribe to either a pre-existence or traducian belief in the origin of the soul, heredity also accounts for the condition of the human soul at the time of birth.

Environmental forces significantly affect the development of the body through nutrition, exercise, illness, and accident. The environment also strongly influences the contents of the soul or mind through the direct instruction of parents and educators, through the examples set by parents and by companions, and through the way life is portrayed in mass communication and entertainment media.

As for supernatural acts, the primary sources of these are God and Satan. Satan, or the Devil, constantly urges the individual to adopt sinful ways, to behave contrary to God's directives. To combat Satan's influence, God is always available as a guide and supporter for people in moments of indecision, of spiritual weakness, and of temptation. God's guidance and strength may be sought directly through prayer and through reading passages of holy scripture, or sought indirectly through consulting a priest or pastor. Not only do Christians believe God serves as adviser and spiritual supporter, but also that he can intervene to change either the individual or the environment so as to cause an event to turn out as the individual has hoped it would. This conviction that God at any moment can manipulate events to effect a particular outcome is suggested in many passages of the Bible. A familiar example is Psalm 23, which reflects the faith that both the individual's behavior and the influence of environmental elements—such as one's enemies—can be controlled by God on any occasion.

> The Lord is my shepherd . . . He maketh me to lie down in green pastures; he leadeth me beside the still waters.
> He . . . leadeth me in the paths of righteousness for his name's sake. Yea, though I walk through the valley of the shadow of death, I will fear no evil; for thou art with me . . . Thou preparest a table before me in the presence of mine enemies . . .

A passage from the oft-repeated Lord's prayer (Matthew 6:11,13) reflects this same belief in God's ability to fashion events that influence the individual's development: "Give us this day our daily bread . . . And lead us not into temptation, but deliver us from evil."

The fourth force affecting development is human will or intention. In contrast to a belief in complete determinism, which holds that a person's development is entirely the result of hereditary and environmental factors that are beyond the control of the individual, Christian doctrine suggests that humans have a free will which permits them to make decisions about how to behave. Hence, people's conscious intentions and determination play an important part in deciding the direction their lives take. Expressing one common view of will within Christian doctrine, Strong (1907 p. 509) has proposed that:

> Man is responsible for all effects of will, as well as for will itself; for voluntary affections, as well as for voluntary acts; for the intellectual views into which will has entered, as well as for the acts of will by which these views have been formed in the past or are maintained in the present.

In summary, then, from conception until death, human development results from the interaction of forces of heredity, environment, God and Satan, and the individual's own will or determination.

7. *Sources of Evidence and Investigative Methodology*

To answer questions about sources of evidence and types of investigative methods used for generating and supporting Christian theory, it is useful to adopt Dunstan's (1961) three categories of Christians—conservatives, liberals, and mainstream Christians. The categories cut across denominational lines, so that conservatives, liberals, and mainstreamers are found within nearly all large Christian sects—Roman Catholic, Presbyterian, Lutheran, Baptist, Anglican, and others.

Conservatives, who sometimes refer to themselves as evangelical Christians, base their beliefs about human nature and development on the literal word of the Bible. If a theory derived from modern-day science is in conflict with Bible scripture, then there is no question that the scientific theory is false. A case in point is the conflict between: (a) the description of the creation of animal life and of human life in the Bible (Genesis 2:7–22), and (b) Charles Darwin's theory that humans have evolved over time from simple forms of animal life. In the view of conservatives, no matter what evidence Darwinian evolutionists present in support of their case, Darwin's theory could not possibly be true because it deviates from the Biblical version of creation.

To conservatives, the truth about any phenomenon is not discovered by humans through their own cleverness or the investigative techniques they devise. Rather, truth is revealed to mankind by God in messages sent through specially chosen people, such as Moses, David, and Solomon among the compilers of the Old Testament of the Bible, and such followers of Christ as Matthew, Mark, Luke, John, and Paul for the New Testament. Since earliest Christian times there have also been other people credited with being authentic recipients of divine revelations. These have included Christian saints, the popes of the Catholic church, and such individuals in Protestant denominations as Martin Luther (1483–1546), John Calvin (1509–1564), John Knox (1505–1572), Joseph Smith (1805–1844) as founder of the Mormon Church, and Mary Baker Eddy (1821–1910) as founder of the Christian Science Church.

At the opposite end of the philosophical spectrum from the conservatives are Christian liberals who do not regard the Bible as the literal, infallible word of God. Rather, they consider the Bible to be an inspired record of a people's search for the truth about the nature and origins of the universe, in particular a search for the truth about how a person can most satisfactorily interact with other people, with God, and with the nonhuman world so as to achieve a feeling of contentment and self-worth. Typical liberals subscribe to the principles of living as exemplified in the teachings and actions of Jesus Christ. They regard Christ as certainly the best and most godly of men if not literally the special Son of God.

In regard to methods for learning the truth about human nature and development, liberals do not depend on the authority of any scripture or any individual, past or present, even if that individual is labeled a saint or holds high church office. Liberals believe in giving any "authority" a fair hearing, but they then weigh the authority's evidence and line of reasoning against competing proposals and thereupon draw conclusions that seem logically convincing. A typical liberal contends that:

> Religion is devoted and loyal commitment to the best that reason and insight can discover. The liberal understands what loyalty to the best means as the authoritarian never can . . .. God has to talk our language if we are to understand him, and if we don't understand him I see no use in talking either with him or about him . . . Every sense experience, value experience, or experience of God must be put through the critical mill, . . . in a good sense rationalized, before it can take its place in the reasonable stream of thought. (Bixler in Dunstan 1961 pp. 197–98)

In effect, liberals welcome scientific inquiry and seek to accommodate differences between scientific theory and Christian scripture by determining which is the more reasonable or by proposing a line of reasoning that links the two compatibly. Thus, liberals can accept both a Darwinian view of the evolution of humans and a Biblical description of creation by reasoning that the Biblical version is a poetic estimate rather than a literal depiction of what occurred.

Between the conservative and liberal viewpoints are the convictions of mainstream Christians, who believe that humans, like other mortal and finite creatures of God, fit into the order of nature. But humans are special in the sense that they are responsible beings that are:

> capable of personal confrontation with God, and conscious "response" to God. In this basic fact, man's "chief end" is already indicated; he is made for fellowship with God. In the sight of God his Judge, man is a sinner . . . This is not a condition to which God has fatally condemned mankind, but a perversion of the nature and destiny of man as God created him, for which man himself is responsible . . . There is thus a considerable agreement among Christians concerning the position of man in God's world, the fact that he tends tragically to miss his high calling, and the centrality of sin among the imprisoning forces from which he needs deliverance, if he is to be restored to his true destiny. (Hodgson 1938 p. 224)

As for the proper means of learning about human nature, mainstream Christians subscribe neither to the conservative's accepting the literal statements of the Bible as infallible nor to the liberal's questioning or reinterpreting scripture that conflicts with logical conclusions drawn from evidence gathered by ostensibly scientific methods. Instead, mainstream Christians believe that while the exact phrasing of tenets and incidents in the Gospel should not be considered the literal Word of God, "any teaching that clearly contradicts the Biblical positions cannot be accepted as Christian" (Richardson and Schweitzer 1951 p. 243).

In summary, although differences exist among Christians about the proper status of the Bible as a source of evidence, on the most central issues regarding human nature and development most Christians hold that the Biblical version is paramount and thus takes precedence over opposing views.

8. Educational and Child-rearing Implications

Suggestions about goals and instructional methods in education and child raising can be derived from the views of human development reflected in both the contents and the form of the Bible. The following examples demonstrate how the process of extracting implications can be carried out.

First is the question of who should set the goals of instruction. From a Christian view, because children by their nature are inclined to sinful acts, they should not be the ones to determine the objectives of child rearing or schooling. Rather, the aims should be set by adults who are no longer "childish" but who have advanced well into the age of reason and who know well the teachings of the Lord. As the apostle Paul wrote to members of the church at Corinth (1 Corinthians 13:11):

> When I was a child, I spake as a child, I understood as a child, I thought as a child: but when I became a man, I put away childish things.

The central goal of Christian education in both home and school is to teach the nature of God and his commandments so the learners will understand the consequences of a sinful life in contrast to a virtuous life and will be motivated to adopt the virtuous and avoid the sinful. Consequently, a major portion of educational programs and child care should focus on understanding God's will and on living by Christian principles.

> It cannot . . . be desirable or advantageous that religion should be excluded from the school. On the contrary, it ought there to be one of the chief agencies for moulding the young life to all that is true and virtuous and holy . . . Therefore, the school, which principally gives the knowledge fitting for practical life, ought to be pre-eminently under the holy influence of religion. (Brantl 1961 p. 202)

The form of the Bible's contents can serve as a model for teaching methods, since the contents illustrate a variety of instructional approaches. The Bible teaches its lessons through descriptions of historical events, proverbs, songs (psalms), parables that point out moral precepts, letters of consolation and instruction, and the direct preaching of moral principles. All of these methods appeal to the intellect, to cognition rather than simply to the emotions, thus implying that people can learn through an appeal to reason to overcome sinful tendencies and follow the path traced in the Lord's word. The inclusion of these different instructional approaches in the Bible may imply that different people have different learning styles, so that teachers can profitably use a diversity of instructional methods in order to succeed with as wide a variety of learners as possible. Another possible implication of the variety of approaches is that different instructional techniques can reinforce each other, so that when a teacher uses a variety of approaches with a particular learner, the cumulative effect of the several methods can be greater than that of a single method alone.

Finally, the question of how to motivate people to learn should be considered. Many passages of the Bible reflect the assumption that people can be motivated both by promises of reward and by threats of punishment. This assumption also includes the belief that people are motivated not only by promises of immediate consequences. Instead, the promise of distant consequences—such as during life-after-death—will motivate learning and behavior as well if the expected rewards are sufficiently magnificent or the expected punishments sufficiently devastating. In promising a distant consequence, Jesus told the multitude in his sermon on the mount, "Rejoice, and be exceeding glad: for great is your reward in heaven" (Matthew 5:12). He later assured his disciples that "In my Father's house are many mansions . . . I go to prepare a place for you" (John 14:2). The psalmist, addressing God, acknowledged that "at Thy right hand there are pleasures for evermore" (Psalms 16:11). "Again, the kingdom of heaven is like unto a treasure hid in a field" (Matthew 13:44); and faithful Christians, after death, "shall hunger no more, neither thirst any more . . . and God shall wipe away all tears from their eyes" (Revelation 7:16–17).

Frequent mention is also made of punishments to be suffered by sinners, either immediately or in life-after-death. Immediate punishments to be meted out by society for specific sins include banishment from the community, depriving the sinner of possessions, and death by stoning, burning, hanging, beheading, and crucifying. Then after death "the wicked shall perish; . . . as the fat of lambs, . . . into smoke shall they consume away" (Psalms 37:20), while other sinners "shall go away into everlasting punishment: but the righteous into life eternal" (Matthew 25:46).

In such ways the contents and form of holy scriptures can be interpreted as implying concepts of human development that suggest applications to educational practice.

See also: Socialization; Cross-cultural Study of Education; Human Development: Cultural and Religious Concepts

References

Brantl G 1961 *Catholicism*. Braziller, New York
Dunstan J L 1961 *Protestantism*. Braziller, New York
Hodgson L (ed.) 1938 *The Second World Conference on Faith and Order*. Macmillan, New York
Massachusetts Sabbath School Society 1836 *New England Primer: Or an Easy and Pleasant Guide to the Art of Reading*. Boston, Massachusetts
Richardson A, Schweitzer W (eds.) 1951 *Biblical Authority for Today*. SCM Press, London
Simonson H P (ed.) 1970 *Selected Writings of Jonathan Edwards*. Ungar, New York
Strong A H 1907 *Systematic Theology: A Compendium and*

Common-place Book Designed for the Use of Theological Students. Judson, Valley Forge, Pennsylvania

Further Reading

Berkouwer G C 1962 *Man: The Image of God*. Eerdmans, Grand Rapids, Michigan
Chafer L S 1947 *Systematic Theology*, Vol. 2. Dallas Seminary Press, Dallas, Texas
Darwin C 1964 *On the Origin of the Species*. Harvard University Press, Cambridge, Massachusetts
Schofield C I (ed.) 1967 *Holy Bible: Authorized King James Version: The New Schofield Bible*. Oxford University Press, New York

R. M. Thomas

Civic Education

Civic education is broadly concerned with the development of citizenship or civic competence by conveying the unique meaning, obligation, and virtue of citizenship in a particular society or the acquisition of values, dispositions, and skills appropriate to that society. Civic education includes both explicit and implicit aims, which may be conveyed through statements of educational goals, curriculum guidelines, textbook content, and teacher lessons; through explicit routines and rituals, such as student recitation of nationalistic pledges; and through explicit and implicit teaching practices, such as engaging students in community service or encouraging group cooperation and discussion.

1. Regional and National Differences

Civic education varies by region and country. Some countries, especially those involved in political or ideological conflict with neighboring countries or those faced with internal divisions, emphasize nationalism and traditional culture. Other countries interpret civic education as primarily religious and moral education. In the West, various conceptions of civic education exist. Some envision civic education as a means of promoting patriotism and national pride. Others promote civic education as a means of instilling in students a range of values that will motivate "and enable them to play their parts as informed, responsible, committed, and effective members of a modern democratic system" (Butts 1980). Still others locate civic education within an examination of conflicts over power, reflected, for example, in the goal of developing an educational climate and school structure that promote a revitalized civic culture in which students and teachers examine "the nature of meaningful self-development in relation to a larger whole (the society), as well as the nature of the relationship between the individual and society, between individual power and collective power" (Pratte 1988 p. 5)

1.1 Western Europe and Australia

How various Western European countries conceptualize civic education reflects some of the central conflicts over civic education. The Conservative governments in the United Kingdom in the 1980s and 1990s emphasized the teaching of respect for tradition, distrust of governmental solutions, and the United Kingdom's separateness from Europe (Lister 1991). Civic education in the United Kingdom can be contrasted with that in the former West Germany, which was oriented not toward distrust of governmental solutions but "social problems that the government is expected to solve" and not toward separation from Europe but a national history embedded within an European context (Torney-Purta 1991 p.598).

Another difference is exemplified by Sweden which, with its highly centralized school system, has a national curriculum that explicitly provides the civic values teachers are obliged to teach: tolerance, equal rights, gender equity, and respect for truth, justice, and human dignity. These values are taught not through traditional lecture methods but by teachers leading student discussions on local school problems as well as those of national scope (National Swedish Board of Education 1980).

Postindustrialist nations in Western Europe, along with Australia and the United States, face changing notions of the relationship between the individual and the state. Postmodernist culture characterizes the individual as a consumer rather than as a producer. The media present a fragmented view of the world. Postmodernism also challenges traditional assumptions about rationality, progress, individual autonomy, and the unified self (Wexler 1987) and threatens "the possibilities of a discourse of morality and connected political action, for both require some recognition of common interests and values derived from shared past experiences" (Gilbert 1992 p.55).

Responses to postmodernism vary. Some, such as that of Heater (1990), recognize the difficulty of claiming continued allegiance to the nation-state and propose, instead, that citizenship be applied at various geopolitical levels. Citizenship would emphasize social reciprocity and common interests within the conflicting demands of state and national citizenship. Others are less hopeful regarding citizenship in a postmodern society. Wexler (1990), for example, calls for a new form of citizenship based on collective identities (such as those embodied in the women's movement) but warns that the idea of citizenship can be coopted by the mass media.

Gilbert (1992) provides a possible resolution of the dilemma of choosing between the potential relativism of postmodernism and the social and moral grand narratives of traditional conceptions of citizenship. He agrees with the view that society is becoming increasingly fragmented and diverse and that citizenship is more contingent and contested than has traditionally been formulated. He proposes, therefore, that there can be no single approach to civic education, stating:

> Rather than seek a common symbol of local, national or world community as an embodiment of virtue, the focus must be on the concrete and experiential manifestation of the achievements of past struggles—the entitlements which attach to the status of citizen in the democratic state. These entitlements include civil and political rights, but also the social or welfare rights to certain material standards of living. (Gilbert 1992 p.63)

1.2 Eastern Europe and the Former Soviet Union

In Eastern Europe and in the nations and states that once belonged to the Soviet Union, curriculum textbooks have changed from an ideological and discursive emphasis on instilling rigid stereotypes and allegiance to the state to emphasizing democracy, tolerance, the individual, and democratic socialization (Fritzsche 1990).

1.3 Asia, Africa, and Latin America

While in the West civic education emphasizes instruction in the values guiding the relation of individuals to the state and polity, in much of Asia and the developing world the stress is on interpersonal or moral values. In east Asia the Confucian tradition provides clear legitimation for schools to assume an active role in moral education. Asian countries rely on education to teach a code of behavior for everyday life along with loyalty to the state (Cummings et al. 1988)

The Asian emphasis on moral education and on how it is taught has undergone changes in each country, in part as a response to changes in the country's politics. In South Korea, especially since the end of the Korean War in 1953, the state has used civic or values education to teach the traditional culture of Korea, nationalism, and anticommunism. Such goals have been contested by intellectuals who "have charged that the aim is to instill passive subordination to the dominant ideology rather than to cultivate personal autonomy" (Suh 1988 p.93).

The People's Republic of China, in 1979, moved away from emphasizing equality and redistribution and toward hierarchical values. During the latter part of the 1980s, schools, especially primary grade schools, offered courses on communist ideology and morality, emphasizing "correct attitudes towards hard labor," "thrift," and "the ability to distinguish between right and wrong" (Meyer 1988 p.127).

In Japan moral education was emphasized before the Second World War, abolished under the Allied occupation (1945–52), but later reintroduced by conservatives. Japanese educators, in the most industrialized of the Asian countries, are firmly committed to transmitting a core of moral and civic values through the school (see Cummings et. al. 1988). Through civic education "students learn about modern society and democracy, organization and management of democratic government" and "the economic and industrial structure of our society" (Tomoda 1988 p.84).

In sub-Saharan Africa educational ministries have identified national development goals for social studies, including building a national consensus, addressing environmental problems, and developing problem-solving skills. Here civic education is used to promote national development, social harmony, and self-reliance as means of overcoming the lack of political cohesion and supporting social solidarity (Barth 1989, Cummings et al. 1988); because civic education and social studies have only replaced the emphasis on history and geography in schools comparatively recently, however, the curriculum tends to be unorganized and to rely on textbooks and the preparation for national examinations inherited from the colonial period. Merryfield and Muyanda-Mitebi (1991) have suggested that the examination emphasis on factual recall undermines the aims of changing social attitudes and skills.

The diversity of goals for civic education in Latin American countries reflects the diverse political agendas throughout the world. Latin American countries that are strongly influenced by their Western European colonizing countries share the goals of those countries. Countries controlled by military dictatorships, like other authoritarian nations, use civic education to teach obedience to the state. Finally, emerging democracies contend with some of the same issues regarding civic education as the United States (Cummings et al. 1988).

2. The Implicit Curriculum

In evaluating the consequences these different approaches to civic education have on the values that students hold, research by Torney et al. provides evidence that "the content of the formal curriculum is only effective in instilling values if the classroom and school provide an appropriate reinforcement of those values. That is, students learn as much or more from what they experience and from the models that they see than as from what is told them" (Torney et al. 1975 p.37). When students participate in classroom discussions and are encouraged to express their opinions, they are more politically knowledgeable and interested, and less authoritarian. On the other hand, students who are taught through an emphasis on lectures and patriotic rituals tend to be more authoritarian and less knowledgeable about politics. The stress on patriotism may actually harm support for civil liberties (Torney-Purta 1986).

3. Issues in the West

Debates about civic education in the United States

have reflected, as in Western European countries, differences over whether civic education should emphasize a narrow range of values, such as patriotism and nationalism, or a wider range of values, such as Butts's decalogue (1980). There has also been debate about whether teaching should emphasize the transmission of certain facts or should emphasize learning through process. This debate has intensified during the twentieth century as agreement declined over what moral and religious values were to be transmitted in schools and debates increased about what to teach in civic education and how to teach it. During the Great Depression of the 1930s, for example, explicit differences arose in the United States over whether schooling was to prepare students for the existing social order or for a more democratic and cooperative one.

Underlying many of the debates in civic education has been a constant conflict over what values should be taught (Shaver and Knight 1986). For example, one response to the increasing racial and ethnic diversity in the United States has been to emphasize the teaching of facts in a core curriculum. Finn (1988) has criticized social studies educators for allegedly favoring teaching that reflects decision-making and neglects the teaching of social studies facts. While Finn claims to reflect the dominant view of the public, proposals similar to that of Butts reflect the dominant view of social studies educators. Butts proposes that if students are to fulfill their obligations and rights as United States citizens, they must develop the ability to make careful judgments, based on a reasoned historical perspective and a meaningful conception of the basic democratic values underlying citizenship. He has proposed 12 core civic values—6 obligations and 6 rights of citizenship—which are fundamental to the theory and practice of democratic citizenship. A curriculum developed by the Center for Civic Education and the Council for the Advancement of Citizenship, and known as CIVITAS, reflects many of Butts's ideas, including a list of civic dispositions and civic commitments (Center for Civic Education 1991).

In contrast to Butts, Pratte (1988), Englund (1986), Engle and Ochoa (1988), Beane (1990), and Shaver and Knight (1986) take a more problematic and holistic view of civic education. Pratte claims that Butts ignores the intricate connections among economics, power, and morality and short-circuits what is needed: "a wide ranging, public discussion of (1) what a feasible and moral human flourishing could look like in the future and (2) which virtues and values really are basic to living well and which are changeable" (Pratte 1988 p.5). Therefore Pratte proposes that civic education should consider both the nature of meaningful self-development in relation to the larger society, "as well as to the nature of the relationship between the individual and society, between individual power and collective power" (p.11).

Pratte also raises the importance of examining how the hidden curriculum influences the learning of civic values. He defines the hidden curriculum as "all the experience, both planned and unplanned, that learners have under the auspices of the school." He recommends that schools become vital civic institutions to a greater extent. Rather than exhorting students to patriotism, a focus is required on how political and social justice as well as a sense of moral decency might be achieved. Following analyses of schools as discursive communities, he encourages teachers to:

> make their classrooms into miniature public spheres where the discourse of democracy can be debated and where the issues that arise in such a context can be collectively and seriously evaluated. In short, teachers and students can investigate historically how the nation–society was formed, how institutions helped shape its interest and vice versa, the techniques of power and their political usefulness, and the economic advantages derived from them for particular individuals and groups.

Pratte also diverges from Finn in desiring not to develop a common culture but to reduce ethnocentrism in the point of view that one way of life is to be preferred over another and to appreciate that there is no one correct solution to the task of developing a curriculum to promote civic virtue. (Pratte 1988).

Englund (1986), like Pratte, in examining the evolution of civic education in Sweden, proposes that schools move away from the pre-established standards implied in scientific–rational views of the state and instead create public discussions and seek to develop reasonable citizens who discharge their civic purposes.

While academics and policymakers debate the goals and methods of civic education, the textbook may be the best indicator of what actually occurs in classrooms. In the United States, textbooks reflect national curriculum patterns. At the elementary level textbooks and teachers' guides "are filled with statements about civic traditions, norms, patriotic ritual, conformity to rules and laws, and other facets of dutiful behavior. Prescriptions about good citizenship are emphasized to a point of redundancy" (Patrick and Hoge 1991 p.429) Secondary school textbooks are "largely compendiums of information about institutions of American government, political processes, and the rights and responsibilities of citizenship" (p.429). Common criticisms of civic content in elementary textbooks have claimed that they are too supportive of the status quo and deficient in treatments of democratic values. Secondary school textbooks have been criticized for their "dull presentation of subject matter, covering too much information, avoiding in-depth discussion of important events and ideas, and glossing over or omitting controversial topics, and failing to emphasize the crucial role of citizen participation in a democracy" (Patrick and Hoge 1991 p.430).

Some American school districts have begun to implement the proposals of Butts and Pratte. Both the Montgomery County School District (Baltimore, Maryland) and the Rochester City School District (New York) have developed lists of rights and responsibilities that are to be promoted in the school district. The Rochester City School District has expanded Butt's list of 12 civic values to 20 and has emphasized, like Pratte, the aim of developing discursive civic communities both in and beyond the classroom and among students, parents, administrators, and teachers.

See also: Educational Achievement: Comparative Studies; Attitudes and Values, Acquiring; Attitudes, Measurement of; Critical Thinking: Philosophical Issues; Political Socialization and Education

References

Barth J 1989 Botswana social studies: Citizenship and nation building. *Int. J. Soc. Ed.* 4(2): 53–59

Beane J 1990 *Affect in the Curriculum: Toward Democracy, Dignity, and Diversity*. Teachers College Press, New York

Butts R F 1980 *The Revival of Civic Learning: A Rationale for Citizenship Education in American Schools*. Phi Delta Kappan Educational Foundation, Bloomington, Indiana

Center for Civic Education 1991 *CIVITAS: A Framework for Civic Education*. Center for Civic Education, Calabasas, California

Cummings W, Gopinathan S, Tomada Y (eds.) 1988 The revival of values education. In: Cummings W, Gopinathan S, Tomada Y (eds.) 1988 *The Revival of Values Education in Asia and the West*. Pergamon Press, Oxford

Engle S, Ochoa A 1988 *Education for Democratic Citizenship*. Teachers College Press, New York

Englund T 1986 *Curriculum as a Political Problem: Changing Educational Conceptions, with Special Reference to Citizenship Education*. Almqvist and Wiksell, Stockholm

Finn C 1988 Among the educationaloids: The social studies debacle. *American Spectator* 21(5): 35–36

Fritzsche K P 1990 In search of a new language: Textbooks in the GDR. Paper presented at the Annual Scientific Meeting of the ISPP, Washington, DC

Gilbert R 1992 Citizenship, education and postmodernity. *Br. J. Sociol Ed.* 13(1): 51–68

Harber C 1991 International contexts for political education. *Educ. Rev.* 43(3): 245–55

Heater D 1990 *Citizenship: The Civic Ideal in World History, Politics, and Education*. Longman, London

Lister I 1991 Research on social studies and citizenship education in England. In: Shaver J (ed.) 1991 *Handbook of Research on Social Studies Teaching and Learning*. Macmillan, New York

Merryfield M, Muyanda-Mutebi P 1991 Research on social studies in Africa. In: Shaver J (ed.) 1991 *Handbook of Research on Social Studies Teaching and Learning*. Macmillan, New York

Meyer J 1988 A subtle and silent transformation: Moral education in Taiwan and the People's Republic of China. In: Cummings W, Gopinathan S, Tomoda Y (eds.) 1988 *The Revival of Values Education in Asia and the West*. Pergamon Press, Oxford

National Swedish Board of Education 1980 *The 1980 Compulsory School Curriculum*. National Swedish Board of Education, Stockholm

Patrick J, Hoge J 1991 Teaching government, civics, and law. In: Shaver J (ed.) 1991 *The Handbook of Research on Social Studies Teaching and Learning*. Macmillan, New York

Pratte R 1988 *The Civic Imperative: Examining the Need for Civic Education*. Teachers College Press, New York

Shaver J, Knight R 1986 Civics and government in citizenship education. In: Wronski S, Bragshaw D (eds.) 1986 *Social Studies and Social Sciences: A Fifty-Year Perspective*. National Council for the Social Studies, Washington, DC

Suh S 1988 Ideologies in Korea's morals and social studies texts: A content analysis. In: Cummings W, Gopinathan S, Tomada Y (eds.) 1988 *The Revival of Values Education in Asia and the West*. Pergamon Press, Oxford

Tomoda Y 1988 Politics and moral education in Japan. In: Cummings W, Gopinathan S, Tomada Y (eds.) 1988 *The Revival of Values Education in Asia and the West*. Pergamon Press, Oxford

Torney J, Oppenheim N, Farner R F 1975 *Civic Education in Ten Countries: An Empirical Study*. Wiley, New York

Torney-Purta J, Schwille J 1986 Civic values learned in school: Policy and practice in industrialized nations. *Comp. Educ. Rev.* 30(1): 30–49

Torney-Purta J 1991 Cross-national research in social studies. In: Shaver J (ed.) 1991 *Handbook of Research on Social Studies Teaching and Learning*. Macmillan, New York

Wexler P 1987 *Social Analysis of Education: After the New Sociology*. Routledge and Kegan Paul, London

Wexler P 1990 Citizenship in the semiotic society. In: Turner B (ed.) 1990 *Theories of Modernity and Postmodernity*. Sage, London

D. Hursh

Class Size

The question "Are smaller classes better than larger classes?" continues to be debated among teachers and administrators, and in the research community. In the years since the first edition of the *International Encyclopedia of Education* (Husén and Postlethwaite 1985) was published, a great deal of writing and some excellent research on the topic has appeared. Proponents of small classes argue that both teacher morale and the amount of attention to individual pupils are increased. The ultimate result—and the ultimate criterion by which small classes would be evaluated—is improved achievement on the part of all students or of particular subgroups. When research does indicate the superiority of smaller classes, however, cost considerations and tradition often stand as barriers to any meaningful change in practice. Thus it is clear that the issue of optimal class size does not stand by itself but is enmeshed in a complex of additional issues.

Unfortunately, the empirical research is confounded by lack of agreement about how the basic construct—class size—should be measured. Some analyses use measures such as student–teacher ratio or student–professional staff ratio for a school or larger unit (e.g., country). These measures are less than useful for understanding interactions between teachers and students in a classroom (see Odden 1990). They do not indicate the actual number of students in any given class setting and may mask tremendous variation from one class to another or one school subject to another. Even the number of students on a class roster may not represent the number actually present on a given day or the number engaged in learning activities. Thus, while in-class measures are better than student–staff ratios for understanding educational process, a refined understanding of the connotations of "class size" is still needed.

1. The Glass–Smith Meta-analysis and its Aftermath

Almost without exception, studies of the relationship of class size to academic and behavioral outcomes cite the classic *Meta-analysis of Research on the Relationship of Class Size and Achievement* (Glass and Smith 1978). The authors collected and summarized nearly 80 studies of the relationship of class size and academic performance that yielded over 700 class-size comparisons on data from nearly 900,000 pupils. The two primary conclusions to be drawn from their massive review were: "That reduced class size can be expected to produce increased academic achievement" (p. iv), and "The major benefits from reduced class-size are obtained as size is reduced below 20 pupils" (p. v).

Other summaries of the research have followed, most notably the extensive work by Robinson and Wittebols (1986). Their conclusions partially contradict and clearly qualify the earlier findings of Glass and Smith:

> Existing research findings do not support the contention that smaller classes will of themselves result in greater academic achievement . . . There is research evidence that small classes are important to increased pupil achievement in reading and mathematics in the early primary grades . . . There is evidence that pupils with lower academic abilities tend to benefit more from smaller classes than do pupils with average ability. (pp. 18–19)

Robinson and Wittebols emphasize that small classes may not benefit all groups of students equally, an important consideration in all class size research. Unfortunately, their review failed to distinguish the best designed studies from those using the poorest methodology, and thus their conclusions must be viewed with a degree of skepticism.

2. Approaches to the Study of Class Size

Research on class size has been conducted at different grade levels, in numerous school subjects, and employing a variety of analytic techniques. Unfortunately, there are almost as many disparate findings as there are individual studies. Three general approaches to the study of class size—the ecological approach, the cost-related approach, and the classroom-focus approach—are described below.

2.1 Ecological Approach

The ecological approach involves the study of class size in historical or geopolitical perspective. For example, Tomlinson (1988) tabulated the median number of pupils per class in the United States from 1960 to 1984. The numbers decreased regularly during this period from 30 to 24 in the elementary grades and from 27 to 22 in secondary schools. Tomlinson also summarized research showing that there was a decline during the same period "on virtually all standardized tests of academic aptitude and achievement, in all grades, among many different strata of students, in many subjects, and in every region" (p. 23). Student–teacher ratios decreased between 1965 and 1985 in other countries as well, declining by approximately 11 percent in "low" and "lower middle" income countries and by about 19 percent in "upper middle" income countries (Lockheed and Verspoor 1991). Test data were not available to document an association with student performance, however.

The implication that might be drawn from the trend in the United States is that large classes are superior or that, at least, small classes are not. Other explanations for declining performance are equally plausible, however. Among them, the 1960s and 1970s saw dramatic changes in the nature of the school-aged population. Specifically the proportion of minorities entering United States schools increased substantially. It is equally if not more likely that this factor as well as a multitude of institutional and cultural changes that occurred during these decades are responsible for the decline in test scores.

The studies reported by the International Association for the Evaluation of Educational Achievement (IEA) also permit ecological comparisons, but among countries rather than over time. The Second International Study of Achievement in Mathematics (McKnight et al. 1987) found great variation in the average size of mathematics classes in the 13-year-old population among 18 countries, from 19 to 20 students in Belgium, Sweden, and Luxembourg, to 41 to 44 in Japan, Hong Kong, Thailand, and Swaziland. At the same time, Belgium, Japan, and Hong Kong were among the top half of the countries in mean mathematics achievement, while Sweden, Luxembourg, and Swaziland were in the lower half. In general, there is no clear association of average class size with mathematics performance at the national level, a finding that is repeated for each age group studied and on most subtests.

The same conclusion can be drawn from the Second International Study of Achievement in Science (Postlethwaite and Wiley 1991). At the 10-year-old level, Hong Kong, Japan, the Philippines, and South Korea had the largest average class sizes, while Finland and Hungary were among countries with the smallest. However, Japan, Finland, Hungary, and South Korea were found to have achievement scores that were high in the cross-national rankings at this age level while the Philippines was among the lowest.

The ecological approach to studying class size leaves many questions unresolved. When units of measurement as large as countries are characterized by a single average, a plethora of other important effects is camouflaged. National differences in such factors as educational expenditures, educational goals, teacher preparation practices, and student characteristics, may contribute both to the average class size in a country and to the average achievement level. Further, class size often varies substantially within a country. At the extreme, the IEA Classroom Environment Study (Anderson et al. 1989) indicated that Thailand had class sizes from 17 to 57 pupils. Even a relatively homogeneous region, Canada (Quebec), ranged in class size from 24 to 33 pupils. Large achievement differences within countries are also the rule rather than the exception. For example, in the Second IEA Science Study, Japan scored well on subtests in biology and physics, and relatively poor on the chemistry subtest at the 10-year-old level. Thus, associations across countries obscure the true impact of class size on the individuals within a school.

2.2 Cost-related Approach

Cost-effectiveness analysis examines both costs and consequences in considering alternatives for decision-making. In educational applications, outcomes are typically assessed in terms of school attainment. Cost-effectiveness ratios are characteristically based upon the average effect and cost per student.

Levin (1988) reviewed the comparison of costs and effects among four strategies for educational improvement: cross-age tutoring, computer-assisted instruction, lengthening the school day, and reducing class size. Data on class size were taken from 14 evaluations collected in previous research. Costs were estimated using the "ingredients approach" which involved the identification of ingredients of each intervention and their respective values, and determination of the overall cost of implementation. For example, the ingredients needed to reduce class size include personnel, facilities, and equipment. While the projected annual cost per student of reducing class size by five students was not found to be as great as either lengthening the school day or use of computer-assisted instruction, larger reductions in class size become quite expensive. The estimated annual costs per student, per subject in school were \$45US, \$63US, \$94US, and \$201US, respectively, for reductions in class size from 35 to 30 students, 30 to 25 students, 25 to 20 students, and 35 to 20 students. From a cost-effectiveness perspective, reducing class size was found to be especially inefficient for increasing reading achievement. Peer tutoring, in contrast, was more cost-effective.

A second cost-related perspective on class size research is the production function approach. Relying heavily on multiple regression analysis, this quantitative approach directly relates a series of inputs, or cost factors, to an output. As applied to the analysis of class size, the output of the educational process is assumed to be student achievement. The selected inputs include indicators of instructional expenditures such as teacher experience, teacher education, and class size or student–teacher ratio. These instructional expenditures, in turn, make up approximately two-thirds of total school expenditures. Holding constant family background and other inputs, partial regression coefficients are considered to be estimates of the effects of the inputs on achievement.

Hanushek (1986) reviewed 147 studies that used the educational production function approach to examine these three expenditure parameters (i.e., inputs). Of the 147 studies reviewed, 112 provided information on the relationship between student–teacher ratio and student achievement. Only nine showed a significant relationship in the expected positive direction. Hanushek (1986) concluded, "There is little apparent merit for schools to pursue their ubiquitous quest for lowered class sizes" (p. 1167). Teacher experience and education failed to have the expected positive effect on student achievement as well, leading to the conclusion that there is no strong or systematic relationship between school expenditures and student achievement. In particular, reducing class size does not appear to be an economically efficient strategy for increasing school performance.

2.3 Classroom-focus Research

Classroom-focus investigations include both experimental and nonexperimental studies directed toward answering the primary questions: Are small classes superior to large classes in terms of academic and/or affective outcomes? If small classes are better, do they benefit particular groups of students identified by characteristics such as ability, age, race, or enrollment in specific courses? And finally, what aspects of classroom process are affected when regular-sized classes are reduced to smaller numbers of students?

A careful evaluation of research on class size was conducted by Slavin (1989). Rather than undertake a comprehensive integration of studies, Slavin reviewed only those that met three important criteria, as follows: (a) The studies were of nontrivial duration, that is, lasted a minimum of one year. Unfortunately, much research has been of limited duration (e.g., 30 minutes) and cannot reveal the impact of policy decisions to reduce class size for an entire school year, even if it is only at one grade or for one subject area. (b) Only substantial reductions in class size were examined, so that larger classes were compared to classes that were at least 30 percent smaller and had 20 students or fewer. This limited the selection of studies to those that are typical of public school classes in the United States and that involve a "real" reduction in the number of students in the classroom. (c) The studies involved random assignment of youngsters to class sizes or, as an alternative, "matching" to assure that the class groups were equivalent initially. Thus the studies had high internal validity.

Of all the research summarized by Glass and Smith (1978) as well as more recent work, Slavin identified only eight studies that met these criteria. From these studies, Slavin concluded that substantial reductions in class size have a positive effect on student achievement, but that the effect is small; the median effect size for the eight studies was approximately one-eighth of a standard deviation. In addition, the effect was not cumulative and even disappeared in later years. Finally, while teachers may change their behaviors in small classes, the changes are so slight that they are unlikely to make important differences in student achievement.

Slavin's conclusions are consistent with those of Glass and Smith (1978) and with the concept of a class-size threshold. Small reductions in class size are accompanied by little or no academic improvement. Larger reductions, however, result in modest achievement gains in the early school years. The Project STAR results described in Sect. 3 below add further support to this finding.

In contrast, research on the secondary school years is very mixed. Robinson and Wittebols (1986) reviewed 22 studies in the United States that related class size to student achievement in Grades 9 to 12. Ten of the 22 studies involved classes with more than 45 students, and only five studies involved classes of fewer than 22 students. Very few studies favored either smaller or larger classes, and many showed no significant differences in achievement between small and large classes. The diversity of the evidence about class size at the secondary level does not yield any generalizable findings.

The classroom processes that distinguish small from large classes have proven to be remarkably elusive. Finn and Achilles (1990) proposed three process dimensions that may be affected: (a) With fewer students in the class, teachers may be more enthusiastic, which may in turn impact on students' motivation to learn. (b) Fewer students per teacher could result in increased student–teacher interaction and more individualized instruction. (c) Students in smaller classes may be more compelled to attend to, and participate in, learning activities.

A well-designed study that focused on processes such as these was conducted in Toronto (Shapson et al. 1980). Teachers and students in 62 Grade four classes were randomly assigned to four class sizes: 16, 23, 30, or 37. Measures were taken during and at the end of the school year. In Grade five, the students and teachers were again assigned at random and were followed for a second year. In addition to achievement measures, repeated ratings of the classrooms were made by trained observers. The rating scales included measures of teacher–student interaction, student participation, student satisfaction, method of instruction, subject emphasis, physical conditions, use of educational aids, classroom atmosphere, and four indicators of the quality of classroom activity. Additional questionnaires were administered to the students and to the teachers.

The analysis of the data was exemplary, but the findings were mixed with most being negative. Teachers initially expected smaller classes to facilitate more individualized programs and stated later that their expectations were confirmed. They generally had more positive attitudes in the smaller classes and were pleased with the ease of managing and teaching in the small class setting. However:

> The observation of classroom process variables revealed very few effects of class size. Class size did not affect the amount of time teachers spent talking about course content or classroom routines. Nor did it affect the choice of audience for teachers' verbal interactions; that is, when they changed class sizes, teachers did not alter the proportion of their time spent interacting with the whole class, with groups, or with individual pupils, (Shapson et al. 1980 pp. 149–50)

Further, no differences were found in pupil satisfaction or affective measures, and no differences were found for most teacher activities, subject emphasis, classroom atmosphere, or the quality measures. Shapson et al. (1980) also found only minor differences in academic achievement, but this might be expected given the lack of process effects. This study is a clear illustration of the difficulty encountered in trying to understand how classes as distinct as those with 16 and 37 pupils differ operationally.

3. *A Major Classroom-focus Study: Project* STAR

Project STAR (Student–Teacher Achievement Ratio), the largest controlled study of the effects of reduced class size, was conducted in 76 elementary schools in the state of Tennessee from 1985 to 1989. Within each school, children entering kindergarten were assigned at random to one of three class sizes:

small, with an enrollment range of 13–17 pupils; regular, with an enrollment of 22–25 pupils; or regular, with a teacher aide. Teachers were also assigned at random to the class groups. The within-school design was particularly effective in controlling for differences among school settings including, but not limited to, the socioeconomic status of the student body, per-student expenditures, and the manner in which schools are administered.

Every class remained the same type—small, regular, or regular with an aide—for four years, until the students were in Grade three. A new teacher was assigned at random to the class each year. Standardized achievement tests were administered to all participating students at the end of each school year. Also, curriculum-based tests reflecting the State's instructional objectives in reading and mathematics were administered at the end of Grades one, two, and three. In all, over 6,000 youngsters in more than 300 classrooms participated in the four-year longitudinal study. The results of the study are reported in Finn and Achilles (1990) and Word et al. (1990), and are summarized in the Fall 1989 issue of *The Peabody Journal of Education*.

Cross-sectional analysis at each grade level found statistically significant advantages for youngsters in the small classes on every achievement scale each year. When the means on the standardized tests were converted to percentiles, the small-class advantage ranged from 6.2 to 10.3 percentile points in reading and from 4.9 to 11.3 percentile points in mathematics; these correspond to average "effect sizes" of 0.23σ in reading and 0.21σ in mathematics. Mastery rates on the curriculum-based tests were between 7.2 percent and 11.5 percent higher in small classes in reading, and between 6.3 and 6.7 percent higher in mathematics.

It is noteworthy that these effects were realized on a large scale for four years without any special training or policy changes to assist teachers in the small-class setting. They provide the most definitive evidence to date of the benefits of small classes in the elementary grades. The effects of a full-time teacher aide, in contrast, were mostly nonsignificant.

Other findings from Project STAR are also informative. First, each year, some of the "interactions" of class size with race were statistically significant. In each instance, minorities—whose overall achievement levels are below those of nonminority students—benefitted significantly more from small classes than their nonminority peers. The small-class advantage for minorities was greater than that for nonminority students in 18 of 20 comparisons. There is a strong suggestion that smaller classes are helpful especially for students who would otherwise be expected to perform most poorly.

Second, a longitudinal analysis of the Project STAR data indicated that the initial benefit to small classes occurred in the first year of the study (kindergarten). The small class advantage increased significantly in Grade one but only in reading. After that, small classes maintained a constant performance advantage over regular sized classes that neither increased nor decreased significantly for the duration of the study.

A follow-up component to the study was conducted in Grade four, once all students were returned to regular sized classes. Students who had attended small classes during the preceding years continued to score significantly above their classmates on all achievement tests. The effect sizes were not as great as they had been during the experimental years, however, indicating that the benefit may be diminishing. Grade four teachers also rated a sample of students on a 29-item "student participation questionnaire." Students who had been in small classes during the preceding years displayed significantly more effort to learn in the classroom, took more initiative in learning activities, and exhibited less nonparticipatory or disruptive behavior than their peers.

Other large-scale demonstration projects have been undertaken including Indiana's Project PRIME TIME (Center for School Assessment 1986). To date, however, Tennessee's Project STAR remains the only large-scale study that employed a full set of sound scientific principles.

4. Alternatives and Conclusion

While some gains are associated with reducing class size, small classes are not without their costs and practical difficulties, and many regard them as inefficient and counterproductive. A policy of having small classes may encourage schools to hire less qualified teachers, and result in increased expenditures and only trivial benefits for student achievement (Tomlinson 1989). Not counting the expense of additional classrooms, Tomlinson (1988) estimated that the cost of reducing average class size in the United States in 1986 from 24 to 23 students would require approximately 73,000 additional teachers and US\$5 billion. To reduce to 15 students, the "optimum" number, would cost almost US\$69 billion and require an additional one million teachers. In an effort to save US\$26.2 million, one state actually proposed increasing class size from 24 to 25 students in Grades one to four, and from 27 to 29 students in Grades five to twelve.

Odden (1990) explored whether the effect of reducing class size on student achievement could be achieved with other lower-cost policy alternatives, or whether larger effects could be produced through other interventions at the same cost. After reviewing a number of alternatives, he concluded that particular uses of small classes are worthwhile, especially in kindergarten to Grade three. He recommends reducing class size in classes with students achieving below grade level to allow for individual or small-group tutoring, and combining individual tutoring with classes reduced to 15 students for language arts/reading instruction.

Odden (1990) proposed further that these two strategies for implementing small classes be coupled with a "larger, comprehensive set of strategies, with class size reduction used sparingly and strategically" (p. 223). These include interventions shown to be especially effective for low-income, ethnic, and language minority students; that is, early childhood education for three- and four-year-olds, extended day kindergarten, computer-assisted instruction, cooperative learning, and peer or volunteer tutoring. Most of these have been shown to improve student achievement by at least 0.5σ. Systematic comparisons of these strategies for affecting learning outcomes have been made by Levin (1988) and Slavin (1989).

It is remarkable that, after all the years of research and debate over the issue of class size, more questions remain unanswered than resolved. Within the limited domain of classroom-focus studies, the effects of small classes in the upper grades or particular school subjects have not been explored systematically, and the processes that distinguish small classes in elementary grades are not clear. The potential for substantial gains if teachers are encouraged or trained to adapt instruction to a small-class setting has not been examined at all.

In the broader perspective, the question "are small classes worth the investment?" remains unclear, primarily because educators are unable to attach a value to a given increment in learning in one subject area or many. The worth of improved teacher attitudes and morale is all the more difficult to assess. Given these limitations, the extreme view advanced by Hanushek (1986) is understandable: "Stop requiring and paying for things that do not matter" (p. 1167). On the other hand, strong sentiment and some solid evidence indicates that benefits can be effected in reduced-size classes. That these will not be realized if the status quo is maintained is indisputable.

See also: Teacher Managerial Behaviors; Seating Arrangements in Classrooms; Classrooms: Grouping of Students; Quality of Education in Developing Nations: Policies for Improving

References

Anderson L W, Ryan D W, Shapiro B J (eds.) 1989 *The IEA Classroom Environment Study*. Pergamon Press, Oxford

Center for School Assessment 1986 *The Relationship Between Class Size and Achievement for First Grade Students in Indiana (PRIME TIME Report)*. Indiana Department of Education, Indianapolis, Indiana

Finn J D, Achilles C M 1990 Answers and questions about class size: A statewide experiment. *Am. Educ. Res. J.* 27 (3): 557–77

Glass G V, Smith M L 1978 *Meta-Analysis of Research on the Relationship of Class Size and Achievement*. Far West Laboratory for Educational Research and Development, San Francisco, California

Hanushek E A 1986 The economics of schooling: Production and efficiency in public schools. *J. Econ. Lit.* 24 (3): 1141–77

Husén T, Postlethwaite T N (eds.) 1985 *The International Encyclopedia of Education*, 1st edn. Pergamon Press, Oxford

Levin H M 1988 Cost-effectiveness and educational policy. *Educ. Eval. Policy Anal.* 10: 51–69

Lockheed M E, Verspoor A M 1991 *Improving Primary Education in Developing Countries*. Oxford University Press, Oxford

McKnight C C et al. 1987 *The Underachieving Curriculum: Assessing U.S. School Mathematics From an International Perspective*. Stipes, Champaign, Illinois

Odden A 1990 Class size and student achievement: Research based policy alternatives. *Educ. Eval. Policy Anal.* 12 (2): 213–27

Peabody Journal of Education 1989 Vol. 6, Fall (entire issue)

Postlethwaite T N, Wiley D E 1991 *Science Achievement in Twenty-Three Countries*. Pergamon Press, Oxford

Robinson G E, Wittebols J H 1986 *Class Size Research: A Related Cluster Analysis for Decision Making*. Educational Research Service, Arlington, Virginia

Shapson S M, Wright E N, Eason G, Fitzgerald J 1980 An experimental study of the effects of class size. *Am. Educ. Res. J.* 17 (2): 141–52

Slavin R E 1989 Achievement effects of substantial reduction in class size. In: Slavin R E (ed.) 1989 *School and Classroom Organization*. Erlbaum, Hillsdale, New Jersey

Tomlinson T M 1988 *Class Size and Public Policy: Politics and Panaceas*. US Department of Education, Washington, DC

Tomlinson T M 1989 Class size and public policy: Politics and panaceas. *Educ. Policy* 3: 261–73

Word E et al. 1990 *Student/Teacher Achievement Ratio (STAR): Tennessee's K-3 Class Size Study*. Final summary report 1985–90. Tennessee Department of Education, Nashville, Tennessee

J. D. Finn; K. E. Voelkl

Classical Sociological Theories of Education

This entry will focus on the sociological writings about education by the three founding fathers of sociology, Durkheim, Marx, and Weber, and will briefly discuss four other important writers, Spencer, Mannheim, Veblen, and Znaniecki. These early sociologists continue to influence contemporary thought through the main sociological theoretical traditions of functionalism, conflict theory, interpretive sociology, and critical theory.

1. Education in Social and Political Theory

From the time philosophers and social thinkers began to consider the major questions of society, education has been a part of their concern, particularly in relation to social and political matters. Often references were made to education in the broadest sense, including forms of socialization, as in Plato's *Republic*, Aristotle's *Politics*, and Adam Smith's *The Wealth of Nations*. In some cases, references to education and learning pertained to the writer's own education, as in Augustine's *Confessions* or Descartes's *Discourse*. In many instances, education was the central focus of the treatises themselves, as in Augustine's *Concerning the Teacher*, Milton's *Of Education*, Locke's *Some Thoughts Concerning Education*, Comenius's *The Great Didactic*, and Rousseau's *Emile* (see Adler and Gorman 1952). The nineteenth century produced educational writings such as Newman's *The Idea of a University*, Arnold's *Culture and Anarchy*, and Spencer's *Education: Intellectual, Moral and Physical*, while the twentieth century produced the writings of Russell, Dewey, and Whitehead.

These early classical works of social and political thought usually related the notion of education to teaching and learning, the cultivation of character (in particular the acquisition of values such as virtue and truth) and habits of the mind, and, above all, the exercise of citizenship. These concerns were both pedagogical and sociological, and in many respects the understanding of education can be traced back to these early writers.

2. Emile Durkheim and the Origins of the Sociology of Education

Modern sociology of education had its formal beginnings in the writings of Emile Durkheim, who seems to have been one of the first to have systematically examined the relationship between education and society. This is not to say that earlier social philosophers ignored the social context of education. Nothing could be further from the truth, as any history of educational thought makes patently clear. Much of this earlier concern, however, focused on the social and moral development of the child, as did Rousseau, for example. It was the sociologists, however, who began to explore the social link between education and society, particularly in terms of education's role in social integration, social cohesion, social conflict, and social inequality. Durkheim, as a teacher of teachers, was preoccupied with some of these aspects of education's link with society.

Emile Durkheim (1858–1917) was born in the Alsace-Lorraine region of France into a Jewish rabbinical family. He attended the best of the Parisian schools, leading to entry to the Ecole normale supérieure, the training ground for the French elite, and there he prepared for a teaching career and also embarked on doctoral studies. Durkheim spent a number of years teaching in French *lycées*, spent a year on scholarship in Germany, and in 1887 was appointed to the University of Bordeaux, where he taught social science and pedagogy. In 1902 he transferred to the Sorbonne, where he was appointed Professor of Pedagogy in 1906, and to the Chair of Pedagogy and Sociology in 1912. He remained there for the rest of his life.

Through his main sociological works, *The Division of Labor in Society* (1893), *The Rules of Sociological Method* (1895), *Suicide* (1897), and *The Elementary Forms of Religious Life* (1915), Durkheim not only firmly established sociology as a legitimate academic discipline, but also laid the foundation for a sociological perspective which continues to influence contemporary sociological theory and research.

Durkheim's primary sociological preoccupation was the study of social solidarity and social order. Although not sympathetic to revolutionary Marxism, Durkheim was aware of conflict and inequality in industrial society, and believed that reform was possible by means of new forms of occupational associations and social cohesion. Although Durkheim was basically a functionalist in his analysis of major social institutions (like the division of labor and religion), his sociology is much more complex. His functionalism has caused him to be regarded, until recently, as a conservative (Nisbet 1965) when in fact he held left-wing political views and was not solely concerned with the conservative forces in society (see, for example, Pearce 1989).

2.1 Durkheim, Sociological Functionalism, and Education

Put simply, functionalism is a type of social theory which explains a social phenomenon in terms of its contribution to the operations of a larger social phenomenon, institution, or society. A pattern of behavior is said to be "functional" when it can be explained in terms of its beneficial effects on the integration or survival of the larger society; it is said to be "dysfunctional" when it exercises negative effects on the integration or survival of a society. Various functionalist arguments have become common in the sociological literature, for example, in terms of manifest and latent functions, system maintenance or stability, and the satisfaction of basic societal needs or prerequisites for the survival of society.

The origins of functionalism are usually traced to the notion of society compared to a biological organism, seen as a system made up of many interdependent parts. Some have argued that its first impetus and use came from the early sociologists Auguste Comte and Herbert Spencer, since they tended to take a more holistic and biological view of society. However, the dominance of functionalism owes much more to Emile Durkheim (although Durkheim never used the term "functionalism"). In his work *The Rules of Sociological Method* Durkheim commented: "When, then, the explanation of a social phenomenon is undertaken, we must seek separately the efficient cause which produces it and the function it fulfils" (Durkheim 1964 p. 95).

For Durkheim, the importance of a focus on function is that it represents a methodology for the analysis of what he called "social facts," that is, patterns of behavior in society which exercise external constraints on individual behavior. The importance of a functional approach is thus evident in his argument that "to explain a social fact it is not enough to show the cause on which it depends; we must also, at least in most cases, show its function in the establishment of social order" (p. 97).

It is important, however, to appreciate that Durkheim was not wholly deterministic in his view of the force of social facts. Liberty and freedom, for Durkheim, were not inhibited by "social facts." As he saw it, "Liberty is the daughter of authority properly understood. For to be free is not to do what one pleases; it is to be master of oneself, it is to know how to act with reason and to do one's duty" (pp. 89–90). In this context, one can understand Durkheim's opposition to those such as the Epicureans and Montaigne who saw education as pleasure. For Durkheim, education was the mechanism through which the child learned to exercise strong control and restraint in order to become an "ideal adult" and thus ensure the survival of a differentiated society. In such a society, dominated by the ideals of moral individualism, conformity must "not amount to passive resignation, but to enlightened allegiance" (Durkheim 1961 p. 115).

From these principles, it is clear that Durkheim's functionalist sociology and his understanding of education in society have exercised considerable influence on much of twentieth-century educational theory and research. The development of the functionalist view of society in sociology, particularly through the work of Talcott Parsons and Robert Merton, was important for the study of how the young are integrated into adult society. Socialization generally, and the family and school in particular, became essential components of modern functionalist analysis of schooling and of society. (see *Contemporary Sociological Theories of Education; Socialization*).

2.2 Durkheim on Education and Society

The earliest of Durkheim's educational writings, *Education and Sociology* (1922) and *Moral Education* (1925), were published posthumously, and for decades were taken to represent the corpus of Durkheim's theory of education and society. However, with the growing awareness of his work following the publication of a series of later lectures given between 1904–05 and 1914, *The Evolution of Educational Thought: Lectures on the Formation and Development of Secondary Education in France*, Durkheim's sociology of education has become the focus of renewed interest. In France, Cherkaoui (1976, 1981) has argued that a different Durkheim is found in this volume: not one of consensus, order, equilibrium, and functionalism, but rather one of struggle and ideological conflict. Fenton (1984) comments that there remains much of value to be found in a closer analysis of Durkheim's sociology of education.

In *Education and Sociology* Durkheim put forward his broadest interpretation of the link between education and society. It is an eminently functionalist interpretation. Durkheim reserved the term "education" to mean the influence exercised by adult generations on those not yet ready for social life, in other words, the methodological socialization of the young. Every society, according to Durkheim, has adapted education to conform to its values and goals. This is why, he argued, educational systems have displayed such variety both across societies and in the same societies over time. For Durkheim, it was unthinkable that education could function differently: "Of what use is it to imagine a kind of education that would be fatal for the society that put it into practice?" (Durkheim 1956 p. 64).

Durkheim, then, saw education and society as inextricably linked, the former as an element in the latter's overall structure. Furthermore, Durkheim argued that the educational system contributes to the survival of society: "Education is, then, only the means by which society prepares, within the children, the essential conditions of its very existence" (p. 71). In this respect, Durkheim admired great educational thinkers such as Comenius, Rousseau and Condorcet, because they saw education as oriented to the external world, to the needs of society, and in this sense they took a utilitarian perspective. He was less impressed with Montaigne, Erasmus, and the Jesuits, because they were too humanistic, antiscience, and other-wordly in their educational goals. Thus Durkheim maintained that every society has its own "ideal of man, of what he should be, as much from the intellectual point of view as the physical and moral" (p. 70). This ideal included religious and moral priorities, national traditions, and group consciousness (or what he called a "conscience collective"). In other words, the function of education is to produce "ideal adults" for society (Fauconnet 1923).

2.3 Durkheim and Moral Education

It is precisely in this context that one can understand Durkheim's observation that all education is moral education, for the notion of morality lay at the heart of his theory of society. Durkheim regarded morality as the set of duties and obligations which influences the behavior of individuals. Although earlier notions of morality were linked with religious beliefs, Durkheim contended that modern industrial society requires a secular morality, one resting on reason. The future of a cohesive society rests on the maintenance of a moral code of social obligations and duties which benefit the individual as well as society. "In a word," he argued in his Sorbonne lectures of 1902–03, "we must discover the rational substitutes for those religious notions that for a long time have served as the vehicle for the most essential moral ideas" (Durkheim 1961 p. 9).

For Durkheim, then, formal or systematic education lay at the center of his larger concern for the creation and maintenance of consensus and solidarity in an increasingly differentiated, specialized, and heterogeneous industrial society. Furthermore, Durkheim's personal commitment, as well as his view of academic sociology, was that it should be used to "help us determine the way in which we ought to orient our conduct" (cited in Wilson 1961 p. ix). Given his concern for the practical uses of basic research, Durkheim therefore constructed a theory of educational practice which included what he considered the three basic elements of morality: discipline, attachment to social groups, and autonomy. Durkheim believed that discipline was essential to ensure consistency and regularity of conduct, as well as a sense of authority which would serve to evoke both the desired responses and restraints in human behavior. This moral discipline is relevant only insofar as it is oriented to a particular group or society. Thus Durkheim argued that moral behavior requires an attachment (or belonging) to a social group. Finally, Durkheim did not believe that moral behavior could be coerced or forced behavior. In other words, the individual must freely choose to behave in a manner which reflects obligation and responsibility toward society as a whole. Durkheim, even in his concern for the integration of the larger society, wished to preserve individual and self-determined behavior.

2.4 Durkheim, Conflict, and Education

In two works, *Professional Ethics and Civic Morals* (1957) and *The Evolution of Educational Thought* (1977), Durkheim dispels the notion that his sociology is purely conservative and functionalist.

In the former, Durkheim recognized the need for social change in the France of his day. As a nonrevolutionary socialist, Durkheim was concerned that the goals of the French Revolution (liberty, equality, and fraternity) had not been achieved. Durkheim observed that the economic structure of modern society was changing: "There has been talk, and not without reason, of societies becoming mainly industrial" (1957 p. 11). Furthermore, Durkheim was mistrustful of the self-interest with which individuals carried out their economic activities. He recognized the possibility of continual conflict between members of economic groups and argued that stability and order constituted a "moral task." As he wrote: "It is therefore extremely important that economic life should be regulated, should have its moral standards raised, so that the conflicts that disturb it have an end" (p. 12). For Durkheim, this moral regulation could only come about through the formation of organizational groups which would foster a moral code of behavior which would protect the rights of individuals and groups. Durkheim saw education as one of the professional activities connected with the state which required regulation. Therefore, while Durkheim saw the functional importance of education in terms of its production of the "ideal adult" and moral consensus in society, he was also aware that education was an occupation (a profession) within which self-interest and conflict were endemic, and, furthermore, that conflict between education and the state could be expected.

This Janus-faced view of education is most apparent in *The Evolution of Educational Thought*. In this important analysis Durkheim was concerned with historical struggle and ideological conflict. As with the rest of society, Durkheim believed that the struggle over educational ideas (and as he calls it here, the production of "the man of his times") has always existed, and explains the forms of education found in France in the first part of the twentieth century. For Durkheim, the history of education was in reality the history of secondary education, and this secondary education had its origins in the cathedral and cloister schools of the pre-Carolingian period. Because these schools incorporated the church's need both to perpetuate its teachings (through the training of priests) and to preach and convert, they contained both sacred and profane elements, or what Durkheim called "the germ of that great struggle" (1977 p. 26). In this sweeping sociological and historical analysis of French education, Durkheim wove a convincing argument that it was conflict, rather than consensus, out of which French secondary education originated and developed. From the beginning, even though the influence of the church prevailed, education was hierarchically structured, starting with parish schools on the bottom, equivalent to elementary schools, then the cathedral schools, and finally the elite Ecole du Palais at the top (Durkheim 1977).

Thus for Durkheim there were two main struggles in the development of French education: that between the sacred and the profane, and that between the various social groups in their access to and participation in schooling.

Ultimately, however, Durkheim never lost his conviction that a strong society required a strong educational system, and the "ideal adult" was a person who was integrated and committed to the goals of the society as a whole. Toward the end of his life Durkheim lamented the weak moral integration of French society during the First World War. The solution rested in the school, through which the moral fiber of France was to be reawakened. Thus the future French school should inculcate "respect for legitimate authority," the "joys of acting in conjunction with others" in accordance with a law common to all, and a school discipline which would appear to children as "something good and sacred." In this way, Durkheim argued, "when they are men, they will accept spontaneously and consciously that social discipline which cannot be weakened without endangering the community" (Durkheim 1977 pp. 160–61).

Durkheim's belief that the moral fabric of a society rested on its educational system is one that survives in much of modern educational thought. In spite of the instrumental (vocational) aspects of education which have dominated much debate in the 1980s and 1990s over the functions of education, the concern with moral aspects of education survive. The belief in the "ideal adult" is as prevalent in the 1990s as it was in Durkheim's day. However, what has been lost among many modern educational functionalists is the awareness that the notion of the "ideal adult" is the product of competing (and conflicting) beliefs and interests in society as a whole.

3. *Karl Marx and Education as Conflict*

In many respects, the Marxist view of schooling, and particularly of school processes, shares much with its functionalist counterpart. Like functionalism, Marxist and neo-Marxist theories focus primarily on structural aspects of society in order to understand what is happening within society and its institutions. Underlying the Marxist theory is the added conviction that social structure and social processes can be explained in terms of the economic base of society. Both the superstructure of society (social institutions such as political, religious and military institutions) and "forms of consciousness" (ideas and knowledge) are ultimately to be understood in terms of the dominant mode of economic production (for example, feudalism, capitalism, or communism) and the relation of individuals and groups of individuals to that mode of production.

3.1 Marx's Writings on Education

While Karl Marx (1818–83) never made any systematic reference to education as part of the capitalist class system which he saw as dominating Western industrial societies, the importance of education is nevertheless implicit in his theory. Comments about education and schooling are scattered throughout Marx's writings. For example, an examination of the volumes of the collected works of Marx and Engels reveals many substantial discussions of education and schooling (Cleverly 1985). For the most part these comments are in the context of other, more central features of his theory of society, particularly those of class struggle and alienation. Marx apparently held education in high regard. It was rather the content of education and the way its facilities were distributed and used in industrializing societies of the late nineteenth century that concerned him.

Marx's early writings about education are almost functionalist, for he regarded education as an important agent for the socialization of the young into the roles they would assume as adults. Indeed, Marx regarded the outside world as a wider classroom than the narrower classroom of the school, but he also recognized the specific functions of formal education. In 1842, writing in the *Kölnische Zeitung*, Marx commented that through education the state converts "the aims of the individual into general aims, crude instinct into moral inclination, natural independence into spiritual freedom, by the individual finding his good in the life of the whole, and the whole in the frame of mind of the individual" (Marx 1842 p. 193).

Both Marx and his colleague, Frederick Engels, advocated education for all. Even more, they regarded the general education of children to be the responsibility of the state and an essential factor for the attainment of "practical communism." However, the main concern of Marx was with the type of education working-class youth received. It was in this context that he regarded education in capitalist societies as a tool which the ruling class, the bourgeoisie, used to their advantage. According to Marx, the bourgeoisie regarded the education of the workers as a form of "indoctrination with bourgeois principles, and that . . . the bourgeois class neither has the means, nor if it had them would it use them, to offer the people a real education" (Marx 1847 p. 427).

One of Marx's main concerns was the monopoly which the ruling class had on education, and by which it created a working class which was useful for it. The ruling class, through education, became noble, wise, and articulate, while the working class was kept silent and inarticulate. Thus Marx gradually began to understand the educational system of the capitalist industrial period as a means of perpetuating the advantaged position of the ruling class and the disadvantaged position of the working class.

3.2 Marx and Contemporary Theories of Education

Marx and Engels never fully integrated their views on education into their theory of capitalism and the transition of capitalist to socialist and communist societies. Nor did they clearly develop a model of an educational system which would not act as a tool for the ruling class. This was left to later generations of Marxists and neo-Marxists, particularly in the 1960s and 1970s, when Marxist sociology was in the ascendant in the discipline. It was during this period that socialist and liberation pedagogies, as alternatives to capitalist education, were developed among Western Marxists (see, for example, Norton and Ollman 1978). Furthermore, two identifiable Marxist sociological traditions emerged, each with relevance for education: the structuralists and the voluntarists.

Structural Marxists argue that patterns of social behavior are "determined" by the structures of society, especially the economic structure. In the 1960s and early 1970s, the person most responsible for developing this view was Althusser (1972). Althusser argued that in capitalist societies most social institutions, such as religion, education, and the military, serve the interests of the state. In turn, the state is controlled by the ruling capitalist class. In a capitalist system an important component is the reproduction of labor power and the reproduction of the conditions of production, that is, the reproduction of the relations of production. Althusser's application of his perspective to schooling is particularly important in this regard.

According to Althusser, capitalist state apparatuses such as schools operate through "ideological" means rather than repressive means or force. In this respect, schools serve to maintain the status quo not by force (as might the police or the military) but through nonphysical means. Thus through the inculcation of the ruling class ideology, schools "will provide for the domination of the ruling class 'in words' " (Althusser 1972 p. 245–46).

The significant aspect of Althusser's Marxist interpretation of the educational system is that it functions in a "deterministic" manner. Althusser argued that human behavior is determined by the structures and processes of society, and in this context he represents "scientific Marxism," which regards schools as a tool or apparatus of the ruling class through which the "means of production" and the "relations of production" are maintained. Further developments of education as an agent of social reproduction are found in the writings of Bourdieu in France and Bowles and Gintis in the United States (see *Reproduction Theory; Contemporary Sociological Theories of Education*).

An alternate "humanistic" form of neo-Marxism with respect to schools and school processes is exemplified by the ideas of Gramsci (1891–1937). Writing during Italy's Fascist period, Gramsci argued that subjective factors, such as beliefs, values, aspirations, and culture in general, could not be ignored in trying to understand capitalism and human behavior. Thus Gramsci contended that schools do not simply reflect the dominance of the ruling class (as Althusser argued), but can be instruments of general social change and, in particular, instruments for overthrowing the dominance of the capitalist system (see Entwistle 1979). In this respect, Gramsci's "voluntarist" theory is closely related to the views of the Frankfurt School of sociology, which argued that the transformation from capitalism to socialism could be accomplished through nonrevolutionary means, primarily through the development of "critical consciousness" or "awareness" which would lead to emancipation from capitalist oppression. Represented by the writings of Habermas, Marcuse, and others, the members of the Frankfurt School have tended to oppose positivism and quantitative research and endorse social criticism and social transformation. Although the writings of these latter so-called "critical theorists" do not fall into a tidy homogeneous category, they have exerted an influence on the sociological study of education, which has resulted in critiques of the process of schooling in capitalist societies (see *Critical Theory and Education*).

4. Max Weber and Education

Max Weber (1864–1920), a German sociologist who is often regarded as the third of the founding fathers of modern sociology, never wrote a specific treatise about education. Nevertheless, his concerns regarding the changes taking place in Germany and Europe during the nineteenth century resulted in an approach to sociological analysis which has had an important impact on contemporary sociology of education.

Weber is best known for his rejection of Marx's historical materialism, the class struggle, and the notion that working-class domination was the desired end-state of conflicts in Western society. The topics addressed by Weber in his sociological writings were wide ranging, including the increasing rationalization and bureaucratization of modern society, value freedom in the social sciences, and the subjective meaningfulness of human action. Because of the breadth of his inquiries, and the absence of a unified integrated theory of society, Weber's influence on modern sociology of education has tended to be indirect and multistranded. The three most relevant areas of impact derive from Weber's understanding of conflict in society and his multifactor interpretation of social stratification, from his concern with the subjective nature of human action, and from his concern with value freedom.

4.1 Weber, Credentialism, and Social Exclusion

Weber's rejection of Marx's economic determinism and the latter's belief in the inevitability of proletarian dominance of the class struggle in Western capitalist society led Weber to adopt a more complex threefold conceptualization of the conflict base in society: property ownership (class), cultural position in society (status), and differences in power derived from cultural and organizational position in society (power). While Marx saw one form of conflict dominating society (class), Weber saw conflict emerging from all three dimensions. Furthermore, Weber saw social groups in a constant state of struggle to preserve their control over one or more of these dimensions and thereby "exclude" access to them by nongroup members. One way of exercising this control was through the use of knowledge credentials which certified claim or access. Thus for Weber, knowledge, and the proof of possessing that knowledge (credentials), was a major mechanism for the struggles between groups in society.

4.2 Weber and the Subjective Meaning of Human Action

One of Weber's contributions to sociology was his notion of *verstehen*, that is, the observation and theoretical interpretation of the subjective "states of mind" of actors (Parsons 1947). For Weber, sociology could be defined as a "science which attempts the interpretive understanding of social action in order thereby to arrive at a causal explanation of its course and effects" (Weber 1964 p. 88). Most importantly, social action, in turn, includes "all human behaviour when and in so far as the acting individual attaches a subjective meaning to it" (Weber 1964 p. 88). Although the notion of subjective meaning for Weber was not straightforward, the essential component of *verstehen*, and interpretive sociology, is that subjective meanings must be differentiated from "objectively 'correct'" meanings, or from truth in a metaphysical sense.

From this approach to the study of human behavior, a strong tradition of an interpretive sociology of education has developed since the late 1960s. The study of the meaning of the classroom experience through the eyes of teachers and students, and the implications of these meanings, stem directly from Weber's preoccupation with social action as he defined it. Teacher expectations and the process and implications of labeling have been a focal point of sociological study of education based on a Weberian perspective. Although Weber himself never applied this perspective to schooling, it remains an important and rich tradition in the sociology of education (see *Sociology of Teaching; School and Classroom Dynamics*).

4.3 Weber and Bureaucracy

The study of schools as organizations owes much to Weber's concern with the increasing bureaucratization of modern society. This process of bureaucratization is linked to what Weber saw as changing forms of legitimate authority, namely, the traditional, the charismatic, and the rational. Whereas traditional authority is based on belief in the "sanctity" of tradition, and charismatic authority on the devotion to unique characteristics of a specific person, rational authority rests on the believed legality of rules and the rights of those in positions to issue commands.

Weber saw rational authority as emerging from a new form of organizational structure which he called "the bureaucracy." Modern bureaucracy empowers persons in legitimate positions with an authority of office. The main characteristics of bureaucracy are: (a) a division of labor which includes obligations and tasks, (b) an elaborate system of rules and regulations which governs behavior, (c) a hierarchical structure with clear lines of authority, (d) an impersonal and detached approach in dealing with others, (e) a system of record keeping, (f) an administrative staff who do not "own" the organization, and (g) a career structure within the organization (Weber 1964).

Weber's writings on types of authority and bureaucracy have become a central subdiscipline within sociology. However, this same focus has influenced much research into the organization of schools, and the roles and functions of principals and teachers, and the interactions between them. The extent to which teachers are seen as professionals in their own right or as officers of an organization has a direct link with Weber's arguments about bureaucracy. In addition, the study of mobility within the educational system is often analyzed in the context of bureaucratic career structures. Finally, the extent to which the chain of command from central educational authorities, through school principals or head teachers to classroom teachers, is "loosely" or "tightly" coupled is directly related to Weber's notion of bureaucracy (see *Loose Coupling and Educational Systems*).

4.4 Some Applications of Weberian Sociology to the Study of Schools

It has been suggested that one of the reasons why Weber has been relatively neglected by sociologists of education has been the fact that he never developed a unified theory of society. In this respect, Durkheim and Marx have been more utilized (King 1980), although it has been argued that much of what has been labeled as Marxist sociology of education is, in reality, closer to a Weberian perspective. In spite of the fact that there has been no attempt to develop a distinctive Weberian sociology of education, examples of a Weberian approach are numerous.

In the United States, Collins (1971, 1979) contended that a Weberian model of conflict, using the concepts of class, status, and power, provides a plausible explanation for the link between education and occupations. Collins demonstrated that employers use educational qualifications as indicators of characteristics which they consider most important for their jobs. Collins argued that the conflicts over education are more a manifestation of conflict between status groups and less a factor of class struggle. Thus for Collins, "the main activity of schools is to teach particular status cultures, both in and outside the classroom" (1971 p. 1010). It is the conflict between status groups which motivates group members to establish barriers against those outside the group: "the interests of the members in wealth, power, and prestige motivate them to institute strong collective controls over insiders and to seek monopolistic sanctions against outsiders" (1979 p. 135). Collins argued that it is therefore not surprising that "educational credentials are most heavily emphasized within organizations stressing normative control—that is, cultural socialization—and in the large national bureaucracies; nor is it surprising that these are stronger determinants than technological change" (1979 p. 48).

A similar observation was made by Murphy (1977, 1982) in his studies of Canadian education. Murphy supported the Weberian notion of education as a mechanism of "closure" whereby the interests of particular status groups are protected. In this respect he regarded schools as more autonomous than the Marxist theories have postulated.

In Australia, Etzioni-Halevy (1987) argued that inequalities in Australian education are better interpreted from a Weberian rather than Marxist perspective. Using data from the Australian census, she demonstrated that status and cultural variables differentiate better between various measures of educational resources and attainments than Marxist economic variables.

Finally, an example from the United Kingdom of a Weberian influence on education is found in Archer's (1979) analysis of the expansion of the educational systems of the United Kingdom, Denmark, France, and Russia. Archer's study is based largely on a Weberian interpretation of educational change as a result of purposeful action or, in Weber's terminology, the subjective meanings of action. At the same time, while critical of the structural or determinist interpretations of education (for example, derived from Durkheimian and Marxist perspectives), Archer recognized the need to understand purposeful change within a structural context. In this respect, by emphasizing both micro and macro perspectives, she foreshadowed much of the sociological debate of the 1980s and 1990s over agency and structure as explanations of human behavior. Thus she argued that educational change in these countries profoundly affected the behaviors of individuals, but within a structural context.

5. Other Social Theories of Education: Spencer, Mannheim, Veblen, and Znaniecki

Although most contemporary sociological theories of education can be traced back to one of the three founding fathers, there were others who were in part contemporaries, and who also made contributions to the development of the sociological study of education. Four sociologists, who might be considered among the "classics," and whose work continues to influence contemporary educational theory and research, merit attention, namely Herbert Spencer, Karl Mannheim, Thorstein Veblen, and Florian Znaniecki.

5.1 Herbert Spencer: Social Darwinism and Education

Herbert Spencer (1820–1903), along with Auguste Compte, has been called one of the two great systematic sociologists of the nineteenth century (Peel 1971). In contrast to Marx, Weber, and Durkheim, Spencer was systematic in his attempt to develop a unified sociology. Spencer was a social evolutionist who believed that society was like an organism which passed through stages of development. Because of this, he argued against social or state intervention and espoused a *laissez-faire* approach to dealing with social problems. Spencer is best known for his *Principles of Sociology* which had a profound effect on social thought in the United States during the late nineteenth century, and was largely responsible for the dominance of what was known as Social Darwinism.

Spencer was also one of the few nineteenth-century sociologists who wrote specifically about education, in particular a work called *Education: Intellectual, Moral and Physical* (1861). As an evolutionist, Spencer regarded education in much the same way as he did other social institutions, that is, as a mechanism to promote the beneficial evolution of society. Thus Spencer did not believe in universal primary (or secondary) education. Nor did he believe that the state should be involved in education. Spencer championed a *laissez-faire* policy regarding all activities of the state (Peel 1971).

Spencer's treatise on education was focused on the value of different kinds of knowledge. Spencer was critical of the education in schools and universities in the United Kingdom in the nineteenth century. He believed that most education was useless in that it was oriented to "bring applause" from others rather than to have any practical value to the individual or society (Spencer 1949). Although he did not promote intervention in the development of school curricula, Spencer favored science education over other subjects, as he saw it as more beneficial for the individual and for the development of society as a whole: "the study of surrounding phenomena is immensely superior to the study of grammar and lexicons" (Spencer 1949).

Although Spencer's influence today hardly compares to that of Durkheim, Marx, or Weber, his *laissez-faire* approach to education parallels much of contemporary debate about privatization of schooling, streaming, and the importance of vocational over academic curricula.

5.2 Karl Mannheim: Education for Social Reconstruction

Karl Mannheim (1893–1947) was a German-born sociologist who spent much of his professional life in the United Kingdom. He is known for his work on ideology and irrationalism. Like Spencer before him, Mannheim also wrote a treatise on education in which many of his ideas are found (Mannheim and Stewart 1969). In this regard, Mannheim is perhaps most well-known for his work on the social context of knowledge, or what is known as the sociology of knowledge (*Ideology and Utopia* [1936] 1962). In this work he argued that education is a "living struggle, a replica, on a small scale of conflicting purposes and tendencies which rage in society at large" (p. 156). Thus for Mannheim, there are two kinds of educated persons, those who participate directly in the production of knowledge, and others who simply absorb the dominant world-view (*Weltanschauung*) of their particular social group, and act within it without question. In many ways, this approach to education was a precursor to the "new" sociology of education which emerged in the late 1960s, and within it, the sociology of the curriculum, in which definitions of legitimate school knowledge, by whom, and for whom, became central questions (Young 1971, Saha 1978, Sharp 1980).

5.2.1 Education as a tool. Mannheim considered education to be one of the social techniques, a general category of methods for influencing human behavior so that it fits into the prevailing patterns of social intention and organization. He saw this technique of education as an instrument of social reconstruction. Mannheim was much influenced by American education, which, under the influence of John Dewey's pragmatism, placed less emphasis on the conservative social function of education and more on the part it had to play in social change. Mannheim, more than the other classical theorists, visualized education as an essential tool for the social reconstruction of mass society which he saw as composed of disconnected groups of atomized individuals with no social ties.

5.2.2 Education as process. Mannheim's formal treatise on the sociology of education, which was published posthumously from his lecture notes (Mannheim and Stewart 1969), reflects his ongoing concern with education as a broad social process, that is, the reflection of a society's social and philosophical values. He made the distinction between the "school in society" and the "school and society" in an effort to emphasize the existence of what he called the "educative society." Mannheim's primary concern with knowledge and ways of knowing meant that he directed attention not only to formal education and schooling, but also to other educative processes. Thus, being influenced by Cooley and Mead, he focused on the impact of primary groups on the educative process, and because he was also influenced by Waller (1965), he attempted an analysis of classroom interaction, all consistent with his own overarching concern with ideology and the social context of knowledge and knowledge transmission.

Although he was more of a "new generation" classical sociologist, Mannheim has indirectly exercised an impact on thinking about education by and large through his writings about ideology and knowledge, and his sociology of knowledge. Late-twentieth-century sociologists of education who take a sociology of knowledge perspective or who see the curriculum as negotiated knowledge are followers, in some degree, of the pioneering work of Mannheim in this area.

5.3 Thorstein Veblen: Education and the Leisured Classes

Thorstein Veblen (1857–1929) was a United States sociologist and economist, sometimes labeled as a technological evolutionist, who was primarily concerned with the leisured classes and the industrial classes. Veblen was particularly critical of the leisured classes which were unproductive but privileged, and the industrial classes which were productive. Because honor and prestige are related to the possession of wealth and material goods, Veblen used the phrase "conspicuous consumption" to argue that even the lowest classes consume goods in order to indicate or increase their social position in society (Veblen 1970).

Although not a specialist on education, Veblen did consider the manner in which the various classes experienced education, and he was particularly concerned with the influence of business on higher education (Veblen 1957). With respect to the latter, Veblen saw United States universities in the early twentieth century as in a process of transition, from institutions of liberal education and intellectual curiosity, to institutions which reflect the interests of business and industry.

Veblen considered education to be the site where the contradictions of the classes were resolved. In this respect, his interpretation of education foreshadowed much of neo-Marxist thinking in the 1970s and 1980s. The children of the industrial classes received an education which prepared them for their future work roles in industry, while the children of the leisured classes were educated in a way that prepared them for a life-style of leisure.

Veblen's impact on subsequent sociological approaches to the study of education has not been as direct as that of Durkheim, Weber, or Marx. There is no Veblen theory or perspective about education, either at the individual or societal level. Nevertheless, current neo-Marxist research mirrors much of Veblen's thought about the class structure and its relation to education. Furthermore, his writings on both school education and higher learning bear a strong resemblance to contemporary reproduction theory. Although not as influential as the three major classical sociologists in the study of education, it is nevertheless appropriate to include Veblen as an intellectual precursor of some important aspects of contemporary sociological thought about education.

5.4 Florian Znaniecki: The Role of Educating Institutions

Florian Znaniecki (1882–1958) was a philosopher

turned sociologist whose career spanned two countries, his native Poland and the United States. He rose to prominence first in Poland as a philosopher through the publication of two works (*The Problem of Values in Philosophy* 1910; *Humanism and Knowledge* 1912) that foreshadowed the dual focuses of his subsequent sociological inquiries: the significance of values rather than actions for heuristic purposes, and the notion of the "humanistic coefficient" representing his conviction that any student of cultural life can only understand the data he or she observes if one takes into account the experiences of the human agent. These methodological insights served as Znaniecki's original contribution in the monumental two-volume study in empirical sociology written jointly with W I Thomas, *The Polish Peasant in Europe and America* (1927) and in his own masterpiece published shortly after he was forced to seek refuge in the United States during the Second World War, *The Social Role of the Man of Knowledge* (Znaniecki 1965).

The latter work, and especially its chapter titled "Schools and Scholars as Bearers of Absolute Truth," together with the two-volume *Socjologia wychowania* (*Sociology of Education*) (Znaniecki 1928, 1930), published 10 years earlier, provide a comprehensive and fully integrated theory of education as a social process. Writing in the mid-1920s and restating his position in 1940, Znaniecki attempted to treat the entire sociological question of education with its methodological and educational foundations as a branch of sociology. In a manner comparable to Durkheim's work, Znaniecki traced the development of the sociological functions of the family, teacher, and school as components of the "educating institutions in society." Where he departed from Durkheim's argument was in pinpointing the modern phenomenon of the growing isolation of these institutions from the broader social context, and the resulting threat to their educational functioning. Znaniecki's analysis of contradictions in educational goals and tasks among diverse ideological and political groupings, and the impact of these contradictions on the educating institutions, is paralleled by his treatment of the process of socialization to which the "educand" is subject. The conjunction between the two sides of the problematic (or feedback) has anticipated and prepared the theoretical basis for the subsequent proliferation of studies of the mechanisms and phases of the socialization process not only in the school but through the life course of the individual.

Thus, already in the interwar period in Poland, and later at Columbia and the University of Illinois, Znaniecki was addressing problems which only later came to prominence: the links between the school and its environment; the recognition of the functioning of the family within the overall system of socialization; the recognition of the importance of the local community within the educational environment; and the role of the peer group in the process of socialization. Znaniecki's insights are not only convincing at a theoretical level, but also still amazingly apt and influential, more than half a century after their initial appearance in Poland.

6. Conclusion

The concern of sociology with aspects of education, taken broadly, is as old as sociology itself. However, in classical sociological discourse there is a degree of "tension" between pedagogy and moral education, between education as practice and education as an instrument of social cohesion and social stability. In this sense, education in much of the writings of these early sociologists includes activities of all social institutions—the family, the church, schools, and (perhaps in Marx) the state—which socialize individuals of all ages. This particular tension was resolved to some extent by Mannheim in his view of education as a technique, a tool of social reconstruction, and a tool of social engineering. In another sense, this tension also manifested itself in views of education as part of the dynamic of both social stability and social change, particularly in the writing of Durkheim.

The influence of these early writers, particularly Durkheim, Marx, and Weber, continues to exercise direct impact on current interpretations of education. To a lesser extent, and in different countries and schools of thought, Spencer, Mannheim, Veblen, and Znaniecki have also left behind intellectual legacies which can be detected in much of current sociology of education. Although none of these writers, except perhaps Durkheim, developed a coherent social theory of education, coherent theories have been developed from the corpus of their work. It is likely that the influence of the classical sociological theorists on social interpretations of education will continue.

See also: Critical Theory and Education; Contemporary Sociological Theories of Education; Reproduction Theory; Resistance Theory; Marxism and Educational Thought

References

Adler M J, Gorman W 1952 Education. In: Adler M J, Gorman W (eds.) 1952 *The Great Ideas. A Syntopicon of Great Books of the Western World.* Encyclopedia Brittanica, Chicago, Illinois

Althusser L 1972 Ideology and ideological state apparatuses. In: Cosin B R (ed.) 1972 *Education, Structure and Society.* Penguin, Harmondsworth

Archer M S 1979 *Social Origins of Educational Systems.* Sage Publications, London

Cherkaoui M 1976 Socialisation et conflict: les systemes educatifs et leur histoire selon Durkheim. *Revue Francaise de Sociologie* 17(2): 197–212

Cherkaoui M 1981 Consensus or conflict? Return to Durkheim's proteiform theory. *Theory and Society* 10(1): 127–38

Cleverly C 1985 Marx-Engels on education: Some lesser and better known writings. In: Maddock J, Hindson C (eds.) 1985 *Quality and Equality in Education*. Proc. 13th Annual Conf. Australian and New Zealand Comparative and International Education Society. Flinders University of South Australia, Bedford Park
Collins R 1971 Functional and conflict theories of educational stratification. *Am. Sociol. Rev.* 36(6): 1002–19
Collins R 1979 *The Credential Society: An Historical Sociology of Education and Stratification*. Academic Press, New York
Durkheim E 1956 (1st edn. 1922) *Education and Sociology*. Free Press, Glencoe, New York
Durkheim E 1957 *Professional Ethics and Civic Morals*. Routledge and Kegan Paul, London
Durkheim E 1961 (1st edn. 1925) *Moral Education*. Free Press, Glencoe, New York
Durkheim E 1964 (1st edn. 1895) *The Rules of Sociological Method*. Free Press, Glencoe, New York
Durkheim E 1977 (1st edn. 1938) *The Evolution of Educational Thought: Lectures on the Formation and Development of Secondary Education in France*. Routledge and Kegan Paul, London
Entwistle H 1979 *Antonio Gramsci*. Routledge and Kegan Paul, London
Etzioni-Halevy E 1987 Inequalities in Australian education: A neo-Weberian perspective. *Australian and New Zealand Journal of Sociology* 23(2): 199–216
Fauconnet P 1923 The pedagogical work of Emile Durkheim. *Am. J. Sociol.* 28(5): 529–53
Fenton S 1984 *Durkheim and Modern Sociology*. Cambridge University Press, Cambridge
King R 1980 Weberian perspectives and the study of education. *Br. J. Sociol. Educ.* 1(1): 7–23
Mannheim K, Stewart W A C 1969 *An Introduction to the Sociology of Education*. Routledge and Kegan Paul, London
Marx K 1842 Leading article in no. 179 of *Kölnische Zeitung*. In: 1987 *Karl Marx Frederick Engels: Collected Works*, Vol. 1. Lawrence & Wishart, London
Marx K 1847 Wages. In: 1987 *Karl Marx Frederick Engels: Collected Works*, Vol. 6. Lawrence & Wishart, London
Nisbet R A 1965 *Emile Durkheim*. Prentice-Hall, Englewood Cliffs, New Jersey
Norton T M, Ollman B (eds.) 1978 *Studies in Socialist Pedagogy*. Monthly Review Press, New York
Parsons T 1947 Footnote 2. In: Weber M 1947
Pearce F 1989 *The Radical Durkheim*. Unwin Hyman, London
Peel J D Y 1971 *Herbert Spencer: The Evolution of a Sociologist*. Heinemann Educational, London
Saha L J 1978 The "new" sociology of education and the study of learning environments: Prospects and problems. *Acta Sociol.* 21(1): 47–63
Sharp R 1980 *Knowledge, Ideology and the Politics of Schooling: Towards a Marxist Analysis of Education*. Routledge and Kegan Paul, London
Spencer H 1949 *Education: Intellectual, Moral and Physical*. Hurst, New York
Thomas W I, Znaniecki F 1927 *The Polish Peasant in Europe and America*, 2nd edn., 2 Vols. Alfred A Knopf, New York
Veblen T 1957 *The Higher Learning in America*. Academic Reprints, Stanford, California
Veblen T 1970 *The Theory of the Leisure Class: An Economic Study of Institutions*. Allen and Unwin, London
Waller W 1965 *The Sociology of Teaching*. Wiley, New York
Weber M 1947 *The Theory of Social and Economic Organization*. The Free Press, New York
Wilson E K 1961 Editor's introduction. In: Durkheim E 1961 *Moral Education*. Free Press, Glencoe, New York
Young M F D 1971 An approach to the study of curricula as socially organized knowledge. In: Young M F D (ed.) 1971 *Knowledge and Control: New Directions for the Sociology of Education*. Collier-Macmillan, London
Znaniecki F 1928 1930 *Socjologia wychowania*, Vol I, II. The Ministry of Education of Poland, Warsaw
Znaniecki F 1965 *The Social Role of the Man of Knowledge*. Octagon Books, New York

Further Reading

Blackledge D, Hunt B 1985 *Sociological Interpretations of Education*. Croom Helm, London
Liston D P 1988 *Capitalist Schools: Explanation and Ethics in Radical Studies of Schooling*. Routledge, London
Lukes S 1975 *Emile Durkheim, His Life and Work: A Historical and Critical Study*. Penguin, Harmondsworth
Mannheim K 1940 *Man and Society in an Age of Social Reconstruction*. Routledge and Kegan Paul, London
Mannheim K 1943 *Diagnosis of Our Time*. Kegan Paul, London
Murphy R 1979 *Sociological Theories of Education*. McGraw-Hill Ryerson, Toronto
Sarup M 1978 *Marxism and Education*. Routledge and Kegan Paul, London
Weber M 1958 The "rationalization" of education and training. In: Gerth H H, Mills C W (eds.) 1958 *From Max Weber: Essays in Sociology*. Oxford University Press, New York
Weber M 1968 Bureaucracy and education. In: Roth G, Wittich C (eds.) 1978 *Max Weber: Economy and Society*. University of California Press, Berkeley, California

L. J. Saha; J. Zubrzycki

Classical Test Theory

After a brief statement about measurement theory, this entry describes "weak true score theory," its implications and difficulties in practice. This section is followed by short statements on guessing in multiple choice tests, item homogeneity and "ordinal true score theory." The problems of weak true score theory gave rise to the development of "strong true score theory", which is described in detail. Finally there is a short section on the future of true score theory.

Although measurements of different kinds, such as educational and psychological, have been used for many centuries in different cultures, it is only in this century that theories of measurement have been developed. This fact raises the question of the role of theory when so much practical application has existed without it. One answer could be that although theory had not been enunciated it was implicit in practice: for example, the need for accurate standards of measurement became evident when subjective methods of marking essay examinations were found to be unreliable.

In mathematics, the need for an axiomatic approach became widely recognized in the late nineteenth century, and was also prevalent in the sciences in relation to physical measurement. Campbell's influential book on the theory of measurement was a result of this movement (see Campbell 1957). The practices of measurement could now be evaluated in terms of this theory.

Twenty-three years after the first publication of Campbell's book in 1917, a committee of the British Association for the Advancement of Science concluded that measurement in education and psychology was not of the same kind as physical measurement, in that the combining condition for physical measurement had no parallel in those disciplines (see Ferguson et al. 1940). In the early 1960s extensions of physical measurement to conjoint measurement axioms and theory were explicitly stated by Luce and Tukey (1964) and implicit in the work of Rasch (1980). Whereas physical measurement theory refers to a common attribute, say weight, of a certain class of objects, "conjoint measurement" refers to two classes of objects for which the interaction between one member of each class can be quantified in some way so that certain axioms are satisfied. Conjoint measurement could apply to educational and psychological measurement (see *Measurement in Educational Research*).

Weak true score theory can be seen as an application of the theory of errors in physical measurement without consideration of the question of whether or not this theory is applicable to test data. The most complete statement of weak true score theory was given by Gulliksen (1950). Strong true score theory is based on axioms which have been shown empirically to be more applicable to objective tests than those of weak true score theory. This stronger theory was published by Keats and Lord (1962), Keats (1964a, 1964b), and Lord (1965).

1. Weak True Score Theory

The assumptions of weak true score theory include the assumption of linear independence and the assumption that the observed quantity, the raw score, can be decomposed into two additive components: the true score and the error score. The assumption of linear independence asserts that repeated estimates of true score for the same person are not linearly correlated, which implies that true score and error score are not linearly correlated. From these assumptions it is possible to show that: (a) the variance of raw scores is equal to the variance of true scores plus the variance of error scores; (b) the correlation between two sets of raw scores from parallel tests, or the reliability of the tests over the population, is equal to the ratio of the variance of true scores to the variance of raw scores; and (c) if a test of reliability R is increased or decreased in length by a proportion k of its original number of items, the reliability of the new test will equal $kR/[1 + (k - 1)R]$ which is known as the Spearman–Brown formula.

In order to estimate a true score range from a raw score it is necessary to assume that error variance is constant over raw score and that the regression of true score on raw score is linear. The first of these assumptions has been shown to be untrue in practice by Keats (1957), among others, while the latter assumption has broad implications, as will be shown below, and also may not be true in practice. Given these two assumptions, the formula proposed by Kelley (1947) would appear to be the most appropriate. This formula may be written as:

$$\begin{aligned} Est[T] &= R_{x \cdot x} \cdot X + [1 - R_{x \cdot x}]M(X) \\ &= M(X) + R_{x \cdot x} \cdot [X - M(X)] \end{aligned}$$

where $Est[T]$ is the estimate of true score; $R_{x \cdot x \cdot}$ is the reliability of the raw score, X; and $M(X)$ is the mean of X, which is of course equal to $M(T)$, the mean of T, since it is assumed that the mean of the error scores is zero.

The "reliability" of the raw score may be estimated in several different ways. It has been defined as the ratio of true score variance to raw score variance, which may be shown to be equal to the correlation between two tests of the same length and measuring the same characteristic. Thus, the correlation between scores on parallel tests provides a direct measure, but there is the problem of defining parallel tests. This problem may be tackled by matching tests item by item in terms of the difficulty and discriminating power of corresponding items. If the results of only one testing are available, two parallel tests of half the length can be formed by matching items and randomly allocating one of each pair to each of the parallel halves. The correlation between the two halves (r) is not a measure of the reliability of the total test (R), which is twice as long, but the Spearman–Brown formula $R = 2r/(1 + r)$ relates these two quantities. This formula generalizes to the formula $R = kr/([1 + k - 1]r)$ given above (see *Reliability in Educational and Psychological Measurement*).

Other estimates of reliability may be obtained using the Kuder–Richardson formula 20 ($KR20$) and:

$$KR20 = \frac{n}{n-1}\left\{1 - \frac{nM(p)M(q) - n\,\mathrm{Var}(p)}{\mathrm{Var}(x)}\right\}$$

where n is the number of items, $M(p)$ is the mean of the item difficulties, $M(q) = 1 - M(p)$, $\mathrm{Var}(p)$ is the variance of p, and $\mathrm{Var}(X)$ is the variance of raw scores.

In addition: $Alpha = n[1 - Sum\,\mathrm{Var}(i)/\mathrm{Var}(X)]/(n - 1)$ where $\mathrm{Var}(i)$, $i = 1 \ldots\ldots n$, is the variance within each of the n components. With only two possible scores within each component, *Alpha* is equal to *KR*20. However, *Alpha* assumes that the three or more item scores form an equal interval scale and this assumption is unlikely to be true in practice. Keats (1951) showed that *KR*20 is uniquely related to the "concordance coefficient w" (Kendall and Gibbons 1990) and is thus a measure of the extent to which items order subjects in the same way. This relationship suggests a different method of scoring polytomous items using the mean rank of subjects giving each of the alternatives. With dichotomous items this leads to a linear transformation of the sum of item scores (Keats 1951) but this is not the case with three or more alternatives in each item. With three or more alternatives scored in the way suggested here, the coefficient W can be calculated and transformed into a generalization of *KR*20, which is different from coefficient alpha as usually calculated.

The other important concept arising from weak true score theory is that of "validity." In its simplest and most practical form this concept refers to the extent to which a test predicts future performance in a given situation. This is known as "predictive validity." Other types of validity include "face validity," which relates to the validity of the test as perceived by the person tested, and could therefore affect the motivation of that person.

"Construct validity" is usually defined by factor-analytic methods and relates to the extent to which the test measures a more general construct defined by a group of similar tests. "Content validity" is based on expert opinion. For practical purposes, predictive validity is the most important but should be determined for each applied situation. In this sense, tests are not generally valid but may be valid for a number of different situations (see *Validity*).

When it is proposed to use tests to replace complicated and expensive physiological examinations it is also important to show that the tests have "concurrent validity" in that they agree with the results of physiological examinations carried out at the same time. Because many forms of validity are based on correlation coefficients it is important to remember that the value obtained depends upon the variance of the group on the measures used to establish this validity. In general, validity also depends on reliability and can be shown to increase as reliability is increased, which is achieved by adding to the test further items measuring the same attribute.

One of the embarrassments of weak true score theory arises from the paradox that the more internally consistent a test is beyond a certain point, the lower is the correlation between raw score and true score. The paradox arises because the relationship between raw score and true score can become nonlinear at high levels of internal consistency.

This kind of embarrassment has led to the seeking of more satisfactory theories. The concept of reliability itself has been criticized on the grounds that its value is affected by restricting or expanding the range of true scores in the sample. What has less often been noted is that average error variance, and so the reliability measure, is also affected by the skewness of the raw score distribution. Thus the usefulness of the reliability coefficient can be questioned unless steps are taken to control these two factors. The concept of reliability has also been criticized on the grounds that it is an index that is applied to the whole test. Under "Item Response Theory" it is claimed that the information function for a test or even an item should be used instead of a single reliability coefficient (see *Item Response Theory*).

Weak true score theory leads naturally to the adoption of "standard scores" with a prescribed mean and standard deviation as the derived score to be used in practice. This approach, although widely followed, has some disadvantages. First, the standard score is often interpreted in terms of the normal distribution, so that a standard score of one standard deviation above the mean is taken to correspond to the 84th percentile of the population. The fact that test scores are not necessarily normally distributed (Keats 1951) shows that this interpretation is not valid.

To overcome this difficulty some test constructors proceed from the percentiles in the standardization sample directly to "normalized scores" with fixed mean and standard deviation, usually taken as 100 and 15 respectively. It would seem preferable to proceed from the estimated population percentiles to the normalized scores, but this practice is rarely followed (see ACER 1951 for an example of this method). Population percentiles can be estimated under the conditions of strong true score theory described below.

Another disadvantage of the approach of using standard scores for an age group as the derived score is that it precludes the possibility of measuring growth. This applies whether or not the derived scores have been normalized. The overall growth of ability within a population has been ironed out by setting the mean of each age group at 100. Bayley (1955) discussed this problem and attempted to solve it by ad hoc methods. This problem can be overcome by defining a latent ability variable which is on the same scale at all age levels.

A procedure which also derives readily from weak true score theory with the assumption of linear regression of true score on raw score is that of "linear equating." There are various methods of collecting and analyzing data with a view to equating the derived scores on two parallel tests. These methods are summarized by Angoff (1988) (see *Tests, Equating of*).

It should be noted that if derived scores are obtained by normalizing through percentiles, then the appropriate method of equating is through estimates of population percentiles obtained by using methods described below under strong true score theory.

Another way of defining a derived score or "intelligence quotient" (IQ) stems from Binet and Simon (1916). A mean score by chronological age (CA) curve is defined empirically for the age range over which the test can be used. A person's score can be converted to a "mental age" (MA) by means of the graph, and thence to an IQ from the formula IQ = 100MA/CA. Mental age can also be estimated by defining a basal age in terms of items appropriate for each age level as the highest age at which a person succeeds on all of the items plus two months for each item passed beyond this age.

This approach, using the concept of mental age, has been questioned by Thurstone (1926) on the grounds that it can not be applied to people whose ability is above the adult average, and that the wrong regression line is used. The correct regression would be that of age on score rather than score on age. For these and other reasons this method has become less frequently used in practice. However, there are ways of meeting these criticisms and so preserving this approach, which has proved to be very useful for studying cognitive growth.

2. *Guessing in Multiple Choice Questions*

While true score theory can be applied to various types of testing and examination, the applications have been mainly in the area of objective testing of the multiple choice kind. In this type of testing the question arises as to the extent to which the subject can give the correct response by randomly guessing from a small number of alternatives—usually four or five, but sometimes as few as two, as in true-false questions.

The first suggestion for adjusting the number correct score (X) for guessing was referred to as formula scoring, which produced an adjusted score (X') by means of the formula:

$$X' = X - W/(N - 1)$$

where W is the number of wrong answers given and N is the number of alternatives. However, the assumptions of formula scoring have been found to be untenable (Hutchinson 1986) (see *Multiple Choice Tests, Guessing in*).

The guessing phenomenon was studied by Brownless and Keats (1958) using a method of repeated testing in which subjects were given a test in the standard way and then, without notice, were given the same test one week later. From data for two tests with five alternatives they found that the effective number of alternatives was 3.6 and 3.5.

Thus, to use five as the basis for inferring the probability of a correct response by guessing for all subjects would not be valid. The extent of guessing was much smaller on the verbal test than on the nonverbal test, but there was evidence that learning was greater on the nonverbal test while memory effects were smaller for that test.

In the case of three-parameter item response theories, a pseudo-guessing parameter (c) is introduced, which may be different for different items but is assumed to be the same for all subjects independent of their abilities. Using the model of Brownless and Keats (1958), which Wilcox (1982) has described as the first "state"—as opposed to trait—model of cognitive performance, it is possible to test the assumption that the effective number of alternatives is the same for all subjects, independent of their ability as measured by raw score. Keats and Munro (1992) report a study using this procedure with 755 subjects. The correlation between the average effective number of alternatives for each subject and score on the first testing was −0.53 and −0.43 for space rotations and mechanical reasoning tests respectively. The conclusion is that the effective number of alternatives, and so the probability of success by guessing, is significantly correlated to the ability of the subject.

To conclude this discussion of guessing, it should be noted that the inclusion of a term for guessing in the Rasch model as proposed by Keats (1974) destroys the consistency property of that model as shown by Colonius (1977).

Finally, de Gruijter and van der Kamp (1984 p. 177) have reported results that show that including the pseudo-guessing parameter in three-parameter models makes the difficulty and discriminating power parameters not comparable between items, and so makes them meaningless. Furthermore, although the pseudo-guessing parameter should theoretically always be greater than $1/N$, in practice estimates of this parameter are mostly less than this value. Keats and Munro (1992) provide a possible explanation for this finding.

In short, the problem of guessing has never been solved in either true score theory or item response theory. In the latter case the admission of such a phenomenon is contrary to the assumption that correct responses are due solely to the ability parameter. There is a strong argument for using only constructed response questions in situations such as tailored testing in which some form of latent trait or item response theory is essential.

3. *Item Homogeneity*

Before proceeding to the discussion of strong true score theory it is important to note a concept which was variously called unidimensionality, "item homogeneity", "local independence," and factorial purity, and was also variously quantified. Factor analysis was suggested by McDonald (1985) as a satisfactory method of testing for homogeneity.

Lord (1952) showed that such analysis could also

be a test for local independence on the assumption that ability was normally distributed and that the item response curve was the cumulative normal distribution which implied the use of tetrachoric correlations. Local independence can be tested directly by considering the relationship between pairs of items for subjects at the same score level.

Item homogeneity can be thought of as an important adjunct to weak true score theory in that it provides a way of testing whether or not a collection of items constitutes a measure of a single homogeneous variable. However, it is assumed by strong true score theory based on the binomial error model, and is an essential assumption in latent trait theory and item response theory. A minor variation of the assumption is also used by Cliff (1989) in his "ordinal true score theory" discussed below.

4. *Ordinal True Score Theory*

Keats (1951) showed that raw score was linearly related to the sum of the orderings of subjects by each of the items and, as such, could form the basis for obtaining a best estimate of the true order in a sense associated with least squares (Kendall and Gibbons 1990).

These observations have suggested an ordinal true score theory of the kind proposed by Cliff (1989). He defined local independence of rankings by any pair of items in terms of the probability of their being in agreement on the ordering of subjects, and this is independent of whether or not either is in agreement with the true ordering. He showed that this was equivalent to requiring that the partial rank order correlation between the two items, given the true ordering, was zero, as measured by Kendall's partial tau (Kendall and Gibbons 1990). The similarity between this definition and the usual one for local independence is evident. He defined a true rank order without ties and, in addition to assuming local independence as defined for rankings, he also assumed the proportional distribution of subjects tied on one item between those correctly and incorrectly ordered on the other. He then showed that many of the characteristics of reliability coefficients found in weak true score theory could be demonstrated in ordinal true score theory without having to assume interval scale properties, or define them in terms of conjoint measurement.

While Cliff's criticism of two- and three-parameter item response theory—that neither can form the basis of an interval scale—is sound, his only objection to the Rasch theory is on practical grounds, which may well apply in some form to ordinal true score theory. However, applications which require only an ordinal scale could well be based on this ordinal theory.

The major contribution of this work is to show that it is not necessary to assume interval scale properties to derive a theory which both yields many of the results of weak true score theory and does not seem to have some of the embarrassing paradoxes of weak true score theory.

5. *Strong True Score Theory*

The weaknesses of weak true score theory arise from the fact that estimates of true score cannot be obtained without making further assumptions about the constancy of error variance at different raw score levels and the linearity of the regression of true score on raw score. The variation of error variance with raw score was reported by Keats (1957) who suggested the formula:

$$\text{Error Variance} = x(n - x)/(n - 1)$$

where x represents raw score and n the number of items in the test. Thus error variance is equal to the estimated variance of a binomial distribution.

This model became known as the binomial error model, because the distribution of errors was binomial. It fitted published data relating error variance to raw score values. The binomial error model forms the basis of the only strong true score theory that has been thoroughly explored (see Keats and Lord 1962, Keats 1964a, 1964b). The general form of the theory may be stated as:

$$g(x) = \int_{-\infty}^{\infty} \binom{n}{x} p^x (1 - p)^{(n-x)} f(p)\, dp$$

where $g(x)$ represents the frequency distribution of raw scores, p represents the probability of a correct response or relative true score ranging from 0 to 1, and $f(p)$ represents the frequency distribution of relative true scores. Keats and Lord (1962) showed that:

$$\begin{aligned} g(x + 1)\,[1 - \text{Mean}(p/x + 1)] \\ = (n - x)\,\text{Mean}(p/x) g(x)/(x + 1) \end{aligned}$$

which related terms in the frequency distribution of raw scores to the regression of relative true score on raw score, which may or may not be linear.

In the case of linear regression of true score on raw score Keats and Lord (1962) have shown that the frequency distribution of raw scores is the negative hypergeometric distribution. Keats (1951) as well as Keats and Lord (1962) showed that this distribution gave a good representation of observed raw score distributions. In this special case the relative true scores are distributed according to the Beta function as the simplest possible case.

However, it is not necessary to assume linearity, as Keats (1964a) has shown that nonlinear regressions represented by orthogonal polynomials leads to natural generalizations of the hypergeometric distribution. From the bivariate distribution of raw score and relative true score, which can be generated numerically by methods described by Keats (1964a) and Keats and Lord (1962), the range of true scores corresponding to a given raw score can be estimated. Thus strong true score theory meets the two criticisms raised against weak true score theory if the generalized form of the hypergeometric distribution is used. This generalized form may be written as:

$$g(x) = [(-n)_x(a_1)_x(a_z)_x \ldots]/[(b_1)_x(b_z)_x \ldots x!]$$

where

$$(a_1)_x = a_1(a_1 + 1)\,(a_1 + 2) \ldots\ldots\ldots (a_1 + x - 1)$$

and a_1 and b_1 are constants of the linear regression of relative true score on raw score, and a_2 and b_2 are constants from the orthogonal parabolic component of regression and so on for cubic, quartic, and so forth, orthogonal components.

Another form of generalization of the beta binomial model which depends on linear regression of true score on raw score was proposed by Lord (1965). Instead of relaxing the linear regression assumption as in the case of generalized hypergeometric distribution, this proposal approximates the generalized binomial distribution and adds parameters a and b to the beta distribution such that $o < a < p < b < 1$, so that relative true score has a reduced range.

The first of these is introduced to take some account of differences in item difficulty and the second is to allow for guessing and fatigue, reducing the possible range of true score. While this form of strong true score theory produces a reduced chi-square value when fitting the raw score distribution, even to the extent of producing chi-square values which are significantly too small, it does not account for nonlinear regression of true score on raw score.

Although the complete form of the strong true score theory has been in the literature since 1964 it has never been included in standard texts, which seem to prefer the special form of the beta-binomial model which assumes linear regression of true score on raw score (see Lord and Novick 1968, de Gruijter and van der Kamp 1984). They do not provide methods for testing this assumption and, if significant curvilinearity is found, incorporating the degree of this curvilinearity into the model. In this respect the beta-binomial model, whether defined by two or up to six parameters, is not an improvement on weak true score theory but the "generalized negative hypergeometric model" is.

Given that the generalized hypergeometric distribution can produce theoretical frequencies which, when compared with observed frequencies at each score level, yield a total chi-square value close to the degrees of freedom, it is possible to generate percentiles that estimate the population percentiles. The aim is not to reduce the chi-square value to as low a figure as possible by adding further parameters because, if successful, this will simply preserve the sampling fluctuations in the data, and one might just as well use the sample percentiles. The estimates of the population percentiles can be used to produce normalized derived scores or to equate tests through percentiles.

Other ways of producing normalized derived scores have been suggested. In view of the binomial error model it is tempting to use the arc–sin transformation to stabilize the approximate error variance at each score level and produce a more nearly normal distribution, and this has been suggested with or without minor changes. Ikeda (1989), among others, has suggested the logit transformation, or a variation of this, as a means of obtaining a normalized derived score with constant error variance at each level. He was interested in producing a method which teachers could use without major calculations, and produced some impressive results.

Perhaps the most remarkable characteristic of the strong true score theory is its robustness. Keats (1964b) reported that, of eleven tests and data from samples ranging from 1,000 to 11,000 cases, two tests showed nonsignificant chi-square values for linear regression and three showed nonsignificant values for quadratic regression. Of the remaining six, four showed significance at the 5 percent level and only two showed significance beyond the 1 percent level. Cubic and higher order curvilinear regressions were not examined. Ikeda (1989) reported even more remarkable data for seven samples in the range 320,000–350,000 cases. Using only the assumption of linear regression of true score on raw score, four of the seven samples yielded chi-square values close to the degrees of freedom. Unfortunately the remaining three samples were not checked for quadratic or higher order regression. It should be noted that with such large samples, cluster sampling methods would have to be used and these would have the effect of reducing the effective number of degrees of freedom.

What makes this robustness of strong true score theory so remarkable is the fact that the theory leads to a representation of the frequency distribution of raw scores without taking into account the difficulties of the individual items. In other words, the theory assumes that the difficulties of items are equal, a possibility discussed by Keats (1967) in terms of combining individuals' performances.

On the other hand Lord (1965), in his presentation of a form of strong true score theory, weakened the assumption of equal item difficulty slightly and incorporated further parameters restricting the range of true scores. With these changes he was able to improve the goodness of fit to the observed frequency distribution to the extent that the chi-square value became significantly too small, and sampling fluctuations in the observed distribution were incorporated in the theoretical distribution. Such a result can hardly be thought of as desirable in practice or theory.

The concept of "item difficulty" used in most test theories is an average across subjects, and as such does not necessarily apply to any particular person. If a person gives the incorrect response to a question, it can be concluded that the question was too difficult for the person, without any implication as to its difficulty for a group of people. The difficulty of the test for the person is reflected in the person's score, which may be compared to another person's score to decide which has the greater ability in the field tested. In item response theories that use two or more item parameters, one item may appear more difficult than another for low scorers but easier than the same item for high scorers. This incongruity is avoided by the Rasch theorists who insist that items should be equal in discriminating power.

As stated earlier the binomial error aspect of strong true score theory shows that error variance is related to raw score by the formula:

$$\text{error variance} = x(n - x)/(n - 1).$$

Thus error variance depends only on the raw score and number of items in the test. If this quantity is averaged over a given sample of subjects it is possible to derive the formula for $KR21$ from the average error variance.

Once again the model behaves as if all items are of the same difficulty, but in this case there is a simple correction that can be made by defining $k = (1 - KR20)/(1 - KR21)$, where $0 < k \leq 1$ and:

$$\text{error variance} = kx(n - x)/(n - 1).$$

Keats (1957) showed that this formula gives a good representation of the graph of error variance against raw score for tests with moderate spread of item difficulty. Thus error variance is defined independently of reliability apart from the correction term, which should remain fairly constant across samples. However, average error variance and reliability will depend on the distribution of scores in the sample and so can hardly be considered as constant characteristics of the test.

In summary it can be said that strong true score theory based on generalized hypergeometric distributions derived from the binomial error model as shown here is complete in that the regression of true score on raw score, linear or nonlinear, leads to estimates of true scores for each raw score. Furthermore the bivariate distribution of true scores and raw scores can be estimated, and leads to confidence limits for the estimates of true score.

The assumptions of weak true score theory needed to obtain estimates of true score and confidence intervals for these include the assumption of linear regression of true score on raw score and constancy of error variance over raw scores, and normal distribution of true scores has been shown to be untenable in empirical data as well as in theory. As a consequence of these findings the concept of reliability as usually defined is practically useless as a basis for estimating true score and its confidence limits (de Gruijter and van der Kamp 1984 pp. 53–57).

A further criticism of weak true score theory in general arises from the factor analytic approach to test theory developed by McDonald (1985). He makes the point that raw score could be composed of general factor score, specific factor score, and error score, and shows that from this point of view certain formulas for reliability such as alpha and $KR(20)$ are biased downwards, unless the variance of specific factor scores is zero.

However, this approach usually assumes linear relationships between factor scores and raw scores and homoscedasticity which are assumed by weak true score theory, and have been shown to be untenable. Moreover, there seems to be no empirical evidence of the extent to which specific score variance is important. As McDonald (1985 pp. 215–16) concedes, and has been noted above, the reliability coefficient is of doubtful value. Whether it would be possible to develop a form of factor analysis which would be compatible with strong true score theory has yet to be established.

6. *Future Use of the Strong True Score Theory*

At the practical level, an atheoretical approach to testing will undoubtedly continue (with all its inefficiencies) as will weak true score theory, with its emphasis on item selection in terms of difficulty and discriminating power and on reliability coefficients which are often meaningless figures. As far as strong true score theory is concerned, it will be noted that this was formulated in the early 1960s at a time when the theory of conjoint measurement was also developing.

The practicability of using latent trait theory was increasing because of the availability of computers of greater speed and capacity. Thus, developments in latent trait theory, or item response theory as it has been called more recently, have been very rapid in the past 25 years. However, with its problems of unmet assumptions and uninterpretable parameters, as well as estimation difficulties noted above, the three- and two-parameter models may become less popular in future. This could well lead to a resurgence of interest in strong true score theory and an extension of its use in practice. The development of computers makes solving for the parameters of strong true score theory easy, and so its use in estimating true score and its confidence range, establishing norms, and equating tests is likely to increase.

See also: Measurement in Educational Research; Rasch Measurement, Theory of; Multiple Choice Tests, Guessing in; Scaling Methods

References

Angoff W H 1988 *Scales, Norms and Equivalent Scores*. Educational Testing Service, Princeton, New Jersey

Australian Council for Educational Research (ACER) 1951 ACER Intermediate Test D. Australian Council for Educational Research, Melbourne

Bayley N 1955 On the growth of intelligence. *Am. Psychol.* 10: 805–18

Binet A, Simon T 1916 *The Development of Intelligence in Children*. LLoyd M Dunn, Honolulu

Brownless V, Keats J A 1958 A re-test method of studying partial knowledge and other factors influencing item response. *Psychometri.* 23(1): 67–73

Campbell N R 1957 *Foundations of Science* (formerly *Physics: The Elements*). Dover Publications, New York

Cliff N 1989 Ordinal consistency and ordinal true scores. *Psychometri.* 54(1): 75–91

Colonius H 1977 On Keats' generalization of the Rasch model. *Psychometri.* 42: 443–45

De Gruijter D N M, van der Kamp L J T 1984 *Statistical Models in Psychological and Educational Testing*. Publication Service, Amsterdam

Ferguson A, Meyers C S, Bartlett R J 1940 Quantitative estimation of sensory events. Final report. *Advancement of Science* 2: 331–49

Gulliksen H 1950 *Theory of Mental Tests*. Wiley, New York

Hutchinson T P 1986 Evidence about partial information from an answer-until-correct administration of a test of spatial reasoning. *Contemp. Educ. Psychol.* 11: 264–75

Ikeda H 1989 Applicability of logit transformation to test score. In: Keats J A, Taft R, Heath R A, Lovibond S H (eds.) 1989 *Mathematical and Theoretical Systems*. Proc. 24th Int. Congress of Psychology of the International Union of Psychological Science. North Holland, Amsterdam

Keats J A 1951 *A Statistical Theory of Objective Test Scores*. Australian Council for Educational Research, Melbourne

Keats J A 1957 Estimation of error variances of test scores. *Psychometri.* 22: 29–41

Keats J A 1964a Some generalizations of a theoretical distribution of mental test scores. *Psychometri.* 29: 215–31

Keats J A 1964b Survey of test score data with respect to curvilinear relationships. *Psychol. Rep.* 15: 871–74

Keats J A 1967 Test theory. *Annu. Rev. Psychol.* 18: 217–38

Keats J A 1974 Applications of projective transformations to test theory. *Psychometri.* 39(3): 359–60

Keats J A, Lord F M 1962 A theoretical distribution of mental test scores. *Psychometrika* 27: 59–72

Keats J A, Munro D 1992 The use of the test-retest method to study guessing, partial knowledge, learning and memory in performance on multiple choice tests. *Bulletin of the International Test Commission*

Kelley T L 1947 *Fundamentals of Statistics*. Cambridge University Press, Cambridge

Kendall M G, Gibbons J D 1990 *Rank Correlation Methods*, 5th edn. Edwin Arnold, London

Lord F M 1952 *A Theory of Test Scores*. Psychometric Monographs No. 7. University of Chicago Press, Chicago, Illinois

Lord F M 1965 A strong true score theory, with applications. *Psychometri.* 30: 239–70

Lord F M, Novick M R 1968 *Statistical Theories of Mental Test Scores*. Addison-Wesley, Reading, Massachusetts

Luce R D, Tukey J W 1964 Simultaneous conjoint measurement: A new type of fundamental measurement. *J. Math. Psy.* 1: 1–27

McDonald R P 1985 *Factor Analysis and Related Methods*. Erlbaum, Hillsdale, New Jersey

Rasch G 1980 *Probabilistic Models for Some Intelligence and Attainment Tests*. University of Chicago Press, Chicago, Illinois

Thurstone L L 1926 The mental age concept. *Psychol. Rev.* 33: 268–78

Wilcox R R 1982 Some empirical and theoretical results on an answer-until-correct scoring procedure. *Br. J. Math. S.* 35: 57–70

J. A. Keats

Classroom Assessment

Classroom assessment is the process teachers use when they collect, synthesize, and interpret information to aid them in decision-making. When classroom assessment is viewed from teachers' decision-making perspectives, rather than as the application of particular evidence-gathering techniques, its dimensions are greatly broadened. Both the number of viable assessment purposes and useful information-gathering techniques expand considerably.

The genesis of the teacher-centered view of classroom assessment can be traced over years of close examination of teachers' classroom responsibilities and the decisions needed to carry them out. Teachers' classroom lives have been reported on by Jackson (1990), Lortie (1975), and Bullough (1989). Teachers' thought processes have been studied and described by Calderhead (1987), Clark and Peterson (1986), Elbaz (1991), Feiman-Nemser and Floden (1986), and Schon (1983). General collections on teachers and teaching are also available (Anderson 1989, Wittrock 1986).

A synthesis of this body of research leads to four generalizations that provide a useful perspective for considering the nature and dimensions of classroom assessment. First, classrooms are both social and academic environments. To survive and succeed in classrooms, teachers must know their pupils' social, personal, and emotional characteristics as well as their academic ones. Second, the classroom is an ad hoc, informal, experiential, person-centered environment which calls for constant teacher decision-making. Third, most of the decisions that confront teachers are immediate, practical ones that involve particular students and contexts. Classroom decision-making must invariably take into account the unique qualities of the students and situations involved, thereby requiring teachers to rely on their tacit, practical knowledge of students and the classroom context. Fourth, teachers are both assessors and participants in the classroom society, which has implications for their objectivity in collecting and interpreting assessment information.

Although the general, overriding purpose of classroom assessment is to help teachers make decisions, there are many different decisions and decision contexts that define the nature of classroom assessment. General categorizations of teachers' classroom decisions have been identified. One such organizational schema is based on social/personal, instructional, and bureaucratic teacher decisions (Airasian 1991a), while another classifies decisions in terms of whether they occur before, during, or after instruction (American Federation of Teachers National Council on Measurement in Education National Education Association 1990). While there is a great deal of overlap between these two schemata, the categorization based on assessments made before, during, and after instruction will be used in this review.

1. *Assessment Before Instruction*

Before instruction can begin, teachers must address two assessment needs: (a) learning about their pupils' characteristics, needs, and abilities, and (b) planning their instruction.

1.1 Learning Pupil Characteristics

Before teachers can organize their pupils into classroom societies that are characterized by communication, order, and common goals, they must learn about their pupils' unique strengths, weaknesses, and personalities. This process of "sizing up" others, which occurs in all social settings, is used to form perceptions and expectations that can be used to establish rapport and guide future interactions. Because classrooms are interactive social and academic settings, they require teachers to assess and make decisions about their students' personal, social, and academic characteristics. These decisions produce the perceptions, expectations, interaction patterns, and practical knowledge which teachers rely upon when interacting with, managing, planning for, or instructing students (Feiman-Nemser and Floden 1986, Elbaz 1991).

Many kinds of information are used to inform these "sizing up" decisions, including formal academic pretests in the subject matter, hearsay evidence, students' modes of dress, their friends, and siblings' past performance. Teachers collect this information primarily through naturalistic observation. By the end of a week or two, most classroom teachers can provide detailed descriptions of each student's personal, social, and academic strengths and weaknesses. These initial, tacit perceptions, which remain quite stable over the school year, guide teachers' future academic and social interactions with students.

In spite of their inevitability and the trust teachers place in them, these initial perceptions and expectations often have limited validity and reliability (Airasian 1991a). Much of the evidence that teachers use to inform these decisions at the beginning of the year is based upon spontaneous, informal observations which are rarely uniform across either pupils or occurrences. Moreover, the judgments teachers make about students often have little to do with the evidence they observed as, for example, when teachers commonly rely on observations of students' mode of dress, peer group membership, in-class posture, or homework neatness to judge their abilities or motivation. Finally, these initial decisions about pupils' characteristics are, of necessity, made quickly and often on the basis of small samples of behavior, leading to concern about the reliability of the assessment evidence. This concern is especially warranted since the first few days of school often elicit atypical student behavior.

1.2 Planning Instruction

The processes of planning and delivering instruction are important for classroom teachers, partly because they occupy a great deal of their time but mainly because they provide teachers with their chief source of professional satisfaction (Lortie 1975). When teachers plan instruction, they consider information both about student characteristics (such as ability levels, work habits, and readiness) and instructional resources (such as materials, time, space, equipment, and prior teaching experience in the subject area). A synthesis of this information results in a plan which outlines the nature of the instructional activities and goals that will be implemented with students. The primary motive for planning is to help teachers gain control over the instructional process by reducing their uncertainty and anxiety about teaching, reviewing the material to be presented, and identifying ways to get instruction started (Clark and Peterson 1986).

Among the materials teachers consider when planning instruction, none is more important than the textbook, or, more appropriately, the instructional package that is used in a subject area. In most classrooms at most grade levels, the traditional textbook has been replaced by an instructional package, which supplements the textbook with additional instructional and assessment resources such as educational objectives, daily lesson plans, chapter and unit reviews, chapter tests, practice worksheets, motivational activities, follow-up exercises, and so on. The instructional package could conceivably provide all the resources teachers need to plan, carry out, and assess instruction, and studies have shown that a large portion of the elementary school student's learning time and the teacher's instructional time, up to 75 percent, is focused on textbook use (Stodolsky 1988). This heavy reliance on packaged instructional plans and activities is understandable when one considers that many teachers must prepare many daily lesson plans.

Although the instructional package provides virtually all the resources needed to prepare, conduct, and assess a lesson, teachers should determine the appropriateness of these materials for their own particular settings and groups of pupils. Textbooks or instructional packages are intended to have applicability across a range of schools, teachers, and classes. They are not tailored to meet the unique needs and readiness of every group of users. It is, therefore, the responsibility of classroom teachers to assess the appropriateness of the instructional package for their own students and classroom contexts, using criteria such as clarity, comprehensiveness, pertinence, and pupil readiness (Airasian 1991a, Brophy and Alleman 1991). Regardless of whether teachers develop lesson plans from scratch or select them from an instructional package, they have a responsibility to collect and examine assessment information both about students' needs, abilities, and work habits and the instructional materials in order to decide which instructional plan is most appropriate.

Thus, even before instruction begins, teachers must carry out considerable assessment and decision-making. They must learn enough about their students' academic and personal characteristics to feel sufficiently familiar with them to create a classroom social setting that encourages communication, order, and learning. Once the classroom society is organized, teachers begin the task of planning their instruction, a task they will repeat daily throughout the school year. In carrying out their planning, teachers consider and meld information about their students and instructional resources into an appropriate plan for instruction.

2. *Assessment During Instruction*

During instruction, teachers perform two activities. They implement the instructional plans developed or selected during the planning period, and they assess and make decisions about the success of the plan's implementation. As might be expected given the dynamic nature of instruction, teachers rely heavily upon informal observations and questions to collect evidence for their decisions. They focus on pupils' facial expressions, posture, participation, eye contact, deportment, and questions asked or answered to indicate how a lesson is going. They refer to the necessity of "reading" their audience to help them make decisions while teaching (Clark and Peterson 1986, Jackson 1990).

The information teachers collect is used to make decisions about the curriculum, student learning, and class management. Curriculum decisions involve the appropriateness of materials, educational objectives, and activities, as well as the adequacy of their presentation to students. Learning decisions concern whether students understand or follow the main points of instruction. Management decisions monitor whether the students are paying attention or whether they need to be refocused on the lesson.

Assessments during instruction are formative. Their purpose is to monitor and, if necessary, remediate the instructional process. This largely informal approach to assessment during instruction creates two potential problems for the resulting decisions (Airasian 1991a). First, classroom teachers may lack objectivity when assessing the adequacy of their teaching and its effects on student learning. Because teachers derive their main professional satisfactions from their instructional successes, it may be hard for them to observe and judge objectively. Every time a favorable judgment about instruction or learning is made, teachers are, in part, rewarding themselves.

Second, the incompleteness of the indicators teachers use in making assessments during instruction also creates a problem. Because instruction is an activity-based, interactive process, it is logical for teachers to focus their assessments on the process itself and students' immediate reactions to it. Such a focus, however, ignores the results of the process on student learning. The fact that students are responsive, attentive, or involved does not necessarily mean that they are learning, although this is a conclusion many teachers make. To increase the validity of assessments made during instruction, information should be collected not only about student reactions to the process, but also about their learning from it. Oral questioning and written assignments (including homework) are the most feasible techniques to utilize in these assessments.

3. *Assessment After Instruction*

Assessment carried out after the completion of instruction is usually designed to inform decisions about grading, placing, or promoting pupils. Postinstructional assessments focus on summative, bureaucratic decisions that teachers are required to make by virtue of their official positions within the school organization. The preponderance of these decisions are related to assessing students' attainment of the content, skills, and behaviors they were taught during instruction.

Postinstructional assessments lead to decisions that are both public and important. They are recorded in school files, sent home in periodic school reports, and discussed by students, parents, and teachers. They reflect important summative judgments about pupils that can affect their immediate opportunities, future educational placements, and, in some cases, life chances. For these reasons, assessment procedures used to gather evidence about pupil achievement after instruction is completed rely heavily on formal techniques that produce "hard," usually numerical, evidence of performance. This emphasis differs from the reliance on less formal, non-recorded, often impressionistic evidence for most assessments conducted before and during instruction.

Two features of assessments made after the completion of instruction are noteworthy. First, such postinstructional assessments often become the basis for subsequent planning decisions. There is, then, a cycle that unites assessment decisions made before, during, and after instruction. Second, the usefulness of postinstructional, summative assessments of achievement is dependent upon many of the assessments teachers make before and during instruction. To insure valid interpretations and decisions about pupil achievement after instruction, it is necessary that before and during instruction teachers know their students' status and needs, plan instructional activities and outcomes appropriate to these, provide effective instruction, construct or select assessment procedures that assess what their students have been taught, score performance objectively, and assign grades or marks fairly. If there are gaps or inadequacies in one or more of these prerequisite steps, the validity of postinstruction assessments and decisions will likely be diminished.

The primary goal in assessing learning after the completion of instruction is to insure that students are given a fair opportunity to demonstrate how much they have learned from the instruction they were given. A range of formal assessment techniques can be used to attain this goal. These techniques, which are the primary focus of traditional courses and textbooks in educational measurement (Airasian 1991b), include teacher-made or textbook-supplied paper-and-pencil tests, performance assessments, and standardized tests. General discussions of assessment topics such as writing test items, observing and rating performance, test scoring, grading and marking, and test administration can be found in many textbooks. It is known that very few classroom teachers have had formal training in these or the other assessment areas described here (Schafer and Lissitz 1987).

The most commonly used postinstructional assessment technique is the teacher-made or textbook-supplied paper-and-pencil achievement test administered at the end of instruction on a unit or chapter of text. Most teacher-made and textbook-supplied tests tend to focus assessment on lower level rote learning, primarily because these are the kinds of behaviors for which it is easiest to construct test items. Although the ready availability of textbook-supplied tests makes them a convenient source of assessment material, these tests should be examined in terms of their appropriateness to teachers' particular classroom objectives and instructional emphases. In general, the more teachers deviate from the textbook during instruction, the less valid a textbook-supplied test is likely to be.

Many classroom achievements are not suitably assessed by paper-and-pencil tests. For example, such methods are not useful for assessing performances such as using a microscope, oral reading or speaking, cutting with scissors, bouncing a ball, or cooperating in group activities. These behaviors are best assessed by formally observing and rating students as they perform them (Burstall 1986). Although much of the assessment that teachers carry out before and during instruction also gathers evidence through teachers' observations of students' performance, these observations are primarily informal, unplanned, and spontaneous, in contrast to the formal, planned observations used to assess achievement after instruction. The use of formal performance assessments is being encouraged to replace perceived overreliance on paper-and-pencil tests in assessing students' learning (National Commission on Testing and Public Policy 1990).

Standardized tests are the third type of formal assessment used to inform postinstructional decisions about students. A standardized test is one which is designed to be used in many different locations and to be administered, scored, and interpreted in the same way no matter when or where it is administered. Most standardized tests provide information about how a given pupil achieved in comparison to his or her peers nationwide. Although the results of these tests are not very influential in teachers' overall assessment repertoire or decision-making, parents, students, and school administrators do take them seriously.

In sum, there are three general domains of assessment: those that occur before, during, and after instruction. Assessments in these domains differ in terms of timing, purpose, evidence-gathering techniques, formality, and record-keeping. All have consequences for student learning and classroom interaction. Taken together, they reflect the richness, complexity, and importance of teachers' classroom assessment activities.

4. *Interpreting Classroom Assessments*

Before assessment evidence of any kind can be used in decision-making, teachers must interpret it. Interpretation is a subjective process calling for teachers' judgments, and in classrooms, interpretations are heavily influenced by both the sizing-up decisions teachers make of their pupils and teachers' personal theories about children, schools, and learning. Within this framework, a few guidelines can be stated to improve teachers' interpretations and decision-making (Airasian 1991a). First, assessment information describes students' learned behaviors and present status. Teachers should not interpret assessment information as representing the fixed "potential" or "capacity" of their students or the way the students necessarily will perform in the future.

Second, all assessment evidence contains some error or imprecision and thus should be interpreted as providing an estimate, not an exact indication, of pupil characteristics or learning. Some assessment error is random and uncontrollable, while other error is related to factors such as teacher bias or inadequate sampling of students' behaviors. Rarely should small differences in students' assessed performance be interpreted as representing significant or meaningful differences.

Third, a single assessment is a poor basis for making important decisions such as grading or promotion. Multiple sources of evidence provide a more valid and reliable indication than single assessments, especially when the decision to be made has significant import for the student. Corroboration of any single source of assessment information is desirable.

Fourth, assessments describe performance; they do not explain it. Assessment that identifies how a student did on a mathematics test or how a learning activity was received by students cannot itself explain why the student and class reacted as they did. To explain assessment results generally requires the collection of additional evidence.

These guidelines suggest the following teacher behaviors in interpreting assessment information: base interpretations on multiple sources of evidence; recognize the range of cultural and educational factors that can influence a student's performance; consider contextual factors which might provide alternative explanations for students' performance; and recognize that any single assessment provides an estimate of performance that can alter with changes in the student or classroom environment.

5. *Ethical Aspects of Classroom Assessment*

Teaching is both a practical and moral undertaking. Classroom teachers are professionals who have great autonomy in their classrooms, who possess knowledge their students do not, and who are permitted to make decisions that affect their students' lives. As a consequence, teachers, like other professionals, have ethical responsibilities to their students (Fenstermacher 1990). In the areas of assessment and decision-making, teachers' ethical responsibilities include both the collection and appropriate use of assessment information. Consequently, teachers are responsible for demonstrating behaviors such as respect for student diversity, fairness in grading and judging students, collecting the best evidence possible on which to base decisions, interpreting evidence correctly, and respecting students' privacy.

See also: Teacher Planning, Approaches to; Teaching, Student Evaluation of

References

Airasian P W 1991a *Classroom Assessment*. McGraw-Hill, New York

Airasian P W 1991b Perspectives on measurement instruction. Educ. Meas.: *Issues Pract.* 10(1): 13–16

American Federation of Teachers National Council on Measurement in Education National Education Association 1990 Standards for teacher competence in educational assessment of students. *Educ. Meas.: Issues Pract.* 9(4): 30–32

Anderson L W 1989 *The Effective Teacher*. McGraw Hill, New York

Brophy J E, Alleman J 1991 Activities as instructional tools: A framework for analysis and evaluation. *Educ. Res.* 20(4): 9–23

Bullough R 1989 *First-Year Teacher. A Case Study*. Teachers College Press, New York

Burstall C 1986 Innovative forms of assessment: A United Kingdom Perspective. *Educ. Meas.*: *Issues Pract.* 5(1): 17–22

Calderhead J (ed.) 1987 *Exploring Teachers' Thinking*. Cassel, London

Clark C M, Peterson P L 1986 Teachers' thought processes. In: Wittrock M C (ed.) 1986

Elbaz F 1991 Research on teachers' knowledge: The evolution of discourse. *J. Curric. Stud.* 23(1): 1–19

Feiman-Nemser S, Floden R E 1986 The cultures of teaching. In: Wittrock M C (ed.) 1986

Fenstermacher G D 1990 Some moral considerations in teaching as a profession. In: Goodlad J L, Soder R, and Sirotnik K A (eds.) 1990 *The Moral Dimensions of Teaching*. Jossey-Bass, San Francisco, California

Jackson P W 1990 *Life in Classrooms*, 2nd edn. Teachers College Press, New York

Lortie D C 1975 *Schoolteacher. A Sociological Study*. University of Chicago Press, Chicago, Illinois

National Commission on Testing and Public Policy 1990 *From Gatekeeper to Gateway: Transforming Testing in America*. Boston College, Chestnut Hill, Massachusetts

Schafer W D, Lissitz R W 1987 Measurement training for school personnel: Recommendations and reality. *J. Teach. Educ.* 38(3): 57–63

Schon D A 1983 *The Reflective Practitioner. How Professionals Think in Action*. Basic Books, New York

Stodolsky S S 1988 *The Subject Matters. Classroom Activity in Math and Social Studies*. University of Chicago Press, Chicago, Illinois

Wittrock M C (ed.) 1986 *Handbook of Research on Teaching*. Macmillan, New York

P. W. Airasian

Classroom Culture and Social Organization, Anthropological Study of

The classroom, once considered a mediating variable in studies correlating instruction with student learning, has emerged as the subject of research in its own right. The classroom's language, culture, and social organization interest an interdisciplinary group of educators and researchers. While educational anthropologists cannot lay exclusive claim to the study of classrooms, a large number of them conduct research there. Anthropologists view classrooms as cultural settings. These settings are of interest because of the social and academic learning which takes place within them and because they are gatekeeping sites where students are publicly evaluated. Additionally, classrooms are apt settings for basic and methodological research on the acquisition of cultural knowledge because they are bounded and offer access to recurrent patterns in language and activity. Classrooms are interesting for what they can teach about the transmission and, in some cases, the transformation of social beliefs, values, and practices, and for what they reveal about the process of social stratification.

Anthropologists' studies of classroom culture, communication, and social order inform three important educational issues: (a) the social structuring processes of the school; (b) the role of classroom discourse in students' learning of reasoning and problem-solving; and (c) the persistence of school failure among youngsters from particular social and ethnic groups. This entry briefly reviews the anthropological study of classrooms, giving examples of research on these three issues.

1. An Anthropological Approach to the Study of Classrooms

A shift in the 1970s from research focused on the outcomes of instruction to studies describing the teaching process led to a generation of research on the classroom as a cultural setting. Dunkin and Biddle (1974) argued that "contextual variables" (e.g., the influence of the school, community, and classroom on teaching and learning) and "process variables" (e.g., the dynamics of communication during instruction) needed to be studied closely if school learning was to be understood. While this was largely a call to educational psychologists to modify their theories and methods, it resonated with the aims and methods of educational anthropologists.

1.1 The Cultural Lens

Anthropologists contribute a cultural lens through which to view classroom language, activity, and social relations. Culture is commonly thought of as the customs, practices, and traditions of a social group. While these are all part of culture, in a more general sense, according to Spradley and McCurdy (1972), culture is "the knowledge people use to generate and interpret behavior" (p. 8). Culture can be thought of as the knowledge of shared rules for behaving and interpreting the behavior of others. It is from this definition of culture that researchers interested in social life and communication in classrooms typically begin.

Viewing the language and activity of the classroom in cultural terms, anthropologists use a variety of ethnographic methods to discover and describe the behavior and sense-making of teachers and pupils. In Spradley and McCurdy's terms, their goal is not "an objective description of people and their behavior from the observer's viewpoint," but a representation of "the knowledge a group of people has learned and is using to organize their behavior" (p. 9). The criterion for an ethnographically adequate account therefore is, according to Frake, not "to state what somebody did but to specify the conditions under which it is culturally appropriate to anticipate that he, or another person occupying his role, will render an equivalent performance" (Frake 1980 p. 145).

Shared knowledge of behavior and sense-making enables participants to navigate social life's uncertainty and complexity. Nowhere is the acquisition of such shared knowledge more visible than in the process of learning how to go to school. The cultural knowledge required by students to participate appropriately in the classroom is of great interest to educational anthropologists. That knowledge is acquired largely in use and typically held "in common with others and in common with others to be taken for granted" (Garfinkel paraphrased in Cook-Gumperz 1975 p. 138). Thus, when educational anthropologists study classrooms, they tend to ask what seem like obvious questions about the shared cultural knowledge that organizes participation and practice. Among them are the following which have been paraphrased from Erickson (1986).

(a) What is happening in the social action taking place in this particular setting?

(b) What do these actions mean to those involved in them and at the moment they are taking place?

(c) How are the happenings organized in patterns of social relations and learned cultural principles for the conduct of everyday life?

(d) How is what is happening in the classroom related to other happenings at other system levels within the school and outside it?

(e) How do the ways everyday life is organized in the classroom compare to other ways of organizing life in a wide range of settings and at other times?

Such questions demonstrate educational anthropologists' concern for local meanings, but they also acknowledge that classrooms are embedded in the institution of schooling and in the wider society. In addition, they recognize that life and learning inside the classroom may bear little resemblance to life and learning elsewhere in a student's life. Despite this lack of resemblance, however, classrooms are places where students construct, in their discourse with teachers and one another, institutional biographies which follow them through school and help to shape their life chances. For this reason, anthropologists are extremely interested in the structuring practices of schools and classrooms, and the means by which some students succeed and others fail.

1.2 Theory and Methods

Anthropologists adapt the data collection methods and interpretive processes of ethnography to study classrooms. They spend extended periods of time inside the classroom as participant observers, collect and analyze field notes, interview teachers and pupils, and catalog documentary and historical information about the setting. This work is often supplemented with study of the wider school community, the neighborhood, or the family life of students. Researchers collect audiovisual records of important classroom events such as lessons, teacher–student conferences, or group work. These records are typically used for transcription and analysis of discourse and nonverbal behavior. They may also be shared with participating teachers and pupils in an attempt to elicit their interpretations. In addition, teachers often participate in anthropological studies of classrooms, either as key informants or as co-investigators.

When studies of school and classroom social organization are undertaken in their own society, anthropologists must work to "make the familiar strange" (Erickson 1986). This is done in several ways.

(a) Cross-cultural or cross-site comparisons help researchers identify alternative ways of organizing talk and learning activities.

(b) Close analysis of classroom discourse patterns, use of space, and nonverbal behavior helps researchers suspend their initial interpretations and look closely at the sociolinguistic resources used by participants to behave sensibly together.

(c) Studying breaches in the normal order of the classroom sheds light on its implicit structuring. These breaches can occur when students fail at, or resist accomplishing, school tasks or when novices or other newcomers behave in ways deemed inappropriate by insiders. In these instances, participants are likely to make explicit their understandings of "who we are and what we are doing" in the classroom.

(d) Examining the history and politics of schooling in a society can help researchers see how the classroom social order developed, whose interests are served by that order, and why students may or may not comply with it.

The field of sociolinguistics dominates theory and method in the study of classroom culture and social life (Gumperz 1976). Also called "the ethnography of communication" (Hymes 1974), this approach merges linguistic and social analysis and stresses the study of language in the actual contexts of its use. There are several reasons why language is stressed in the anthropological study of classrooms. First, classrooms are language-saturated environments where social norms and practices are accessible to researchers in the many linguistic transactions of their members. Second, analysis of classroom discourse permits researchers and practitioners alike to track the teaching and learning of reasoning inside classrooms. Third, there is widespread interest among researchers and policymakers in classrooms as places where social stratification occurs through speech and text-related transactions of learners and teachers.

2. School Structuring and Classroom Social Organization

Sarason (1982) initially applied the concept of culture to the problem of educational change within schools and classrooms. He argued that tacitly held cultural norms and practices make everyday life sensible and meaningful, in schools and elsewhere. For this reason, the thought that classroom or school life might be organized differently is, in his words, "a nearly impossible one for most people because it confronts them with the necessity of changing their thinking, then changing their actions, and finally changing the overall structure of the setting" (p. 13). The cultural knowledge of which Sarason speaks resides deeply in the thought, action, and social identities of participants. It is taken for granted by teachers, who themselves have spent many years learning it as pupils, and it is largely taught to pupils implicitly in the activities of academic instruction and assessment.

2.1 Findings of Research on the Structure of Classroom Talk and Activity

Research on the social structuring of classrooms is of broad concern. Anthropologists share with practitioners and policymakers an interest in these structures as they influence pedagogy and the academic curriculum and as they create a so-called "hidden curriculum," teaching students how to work in conditions of "crowds, praise, and power" (Jackson 1968). What ethnographers find as they analyze classrooms is a persistent pattern in their organization of talk and activity that is shared across nations. This pattern involves the teacher, as both the social and academic authority, holding the right to determine conversational topics and turns. Classroom discourse about academic subjects is decontextualized in the sense that it is often about knowledge unconnected to authentic contexts of its development and use. Teacher and students typically talk about knowledge in lessons. These are instructional conversations characterized by three-part turns consisting of a "teacher initiation" (usually by asking a known-answer question), "student response" (including the bidding for turns to answer), and a "teacher evaluation," or I-R-E (Mehan 1979). The I-R-E structure refers to the ritualized, sequential dimension of lesson talk. Cazden (1988) points out that, like invariant sequences in other cultural events such as the order of courses in a dinner, the I-R-E is invariant in the central social and academic event of the classroom.

Discourse both embodies the structure and authority relations of schooling and routinely recreates them. While participants have choices about what to say within the three-part turn sequence for lesson talk, classroom ethnographers have found that those choices are constrained by such situational circumstances as crowding, time press, public formal assessment, and predetermined curricular objectives. These elements combine to produce ways of speaking peculiar to the classroom and to the teacher's occupational role, what Cazden (1988 p. 159) calls "teacher register."

Students assessed by the teacher to be behaving in socially and academically appropriate ways are engaged by the teacher in learning-oriented conversation. Other students, assessed negatively, often adapt to that assessment with passivity or resistance to teacher talk. Classroom activity is characterized by the completion of brief, discrete tasks and the answering of questions testing mastery and compliance (Perrenoud 1988). Thus classroom discourse constructs and is constructed by norms for appropriateness that circumscribe both what counts as academic knowledge in classrooms and who is thought to be a knower.

The I-R-E discourse pattern has been identified in countries including the United Kingdom, France, Austria, the United States, Australia, and Papua New Guinea (Schratz and Mehan 1990), the Philippines (Campbell 1989), and Peru (Hornberger 1987). Borrowing from linguistics, Cazden (1988) calls this pattern the "unmarked" form or, in computer terms, the "'default' pattern—what happens unless deliberate action is taken to achieve some alternative" (p. 53). Despite both differences and some shared professional values across nations, these patterns of classroom discourse appear in many settings. While further research is needed to understand why this way of teaching and organizing classrooms is so pervasive, research is also needed to characterize teachers and students attempting alternate ways of communicating with one another about knowledge (see Sect. 3).

2.2 Strengths and Limitations of Ethnographic Research on Classroom Discourse

Analyses of classroom discourse are limited for several important reasons. First, descriptions of the "default" mode, no matter how precise, can lack a vision of alternatives. In fact, such descriptions may unintentionally reify ordinary practice by presenting a picture of classroom culture as inevitably scripted rather than as socially constructed and therefore open to change. Second, these accounts do not easily move to levels of cultural and social description outside the school and classroom which would reveal, in Anderson's words, "the broader social forces that inform the lives of social actors in specific settings" (1989 p. 262). Thus, they document the dynamics of student success and failure within classrooms; their emphasis on teacher and student sense-making tends "to direct the attention of policymakers toward personal change without structural change" (Ogbu 1981 p. 13 cited in Anderson 1989 p. 262). Third, some anthropologists argue that when classroom ethnographers focus on the microprocesses of classroom interaction, they risk missing holistic cultural description and are best thought of as contributing method rather than theory to the anthropologist's armamentarium (Chilcott 1992).

These limitations notwithstanding, ethnographic accounts of classroom culture and communication contribute greatly to our understanding of the inner workings of school and the experience of teachers and learners. They shed light on the immediate contextual factors which shape both students' opportunity to learn and their emerging social identities. They also offer a means to examine at close range efforts to improve not only classroom instruction, but students' life chances by means of educational reform. Finally, they contribute to the curriculum for teacher education, helping practitioners become more aware of culturally patterned classroom practices so that they can assess their effects and work to improve them.

3. Classroom Ethnography and Students' Learning of Reasoning and Problem-solving

The interests of anthropologists, sociolinguists, psychologists, and educators converge in the study of what Erickson calls "taught cognitive learning," or "studies of deliberate teaching and learning of cognitive subject matter" in the classroom (1982 p. 150). Informed by theories of cognitive development of the Soviet psychologist Vygotsky (1978), this research examines communication in both traditional lessons and in innovative instructional arrangements where the default mode of classroom discourse is deliberately modified (Cazden 1988, Trueba and Delgado-Gaitan 1988, Tharp and Gallimore 1989). Such innovative arrangements include teacher–student conferences, peer tutoring, interactive technology, and computer networking.

3.1 Findings of Classroom Ethnographic Research on the Learning of Reasoning and Problem-solving

To study taught cognitive learning, ethnographers look closely at communication within classroom groups, but they also research the individual learner's understandings and the interweaving of the social and the academic. They track intellectual change as a function of the sociolinguistic processes they observe, often doing this from the starting point of a particular school subject. Rosaen (1987), for example, studied the social construction of historical literacy in a Montessori school. Collecting field notes, videotapes, interviews, and student work samples, she traced event structure, academic content, classroom interaction, and teacher and student thinking during a two-month unit on American history. She found that changes in social participation among the students were entwined with changes in the nature and content of their learning of history.

Classroom-based work is augmented by cross-cultural research, contrasting learning at school with learning in other parts of a youngster's life. Such analysis offers alternative ways to view the acquisition of higher order thinking in academic and non-academic, and Western and non-Western contexts. Scollon (1988), for example, contrasts literacy practices in Western European-style schooling with those among Athabaskan natives in Alaska. He finds that literacy is construed, practiced, and learned differently in settings where text is viewed as authoritative and students are seen as responsible to master its contents, than it is in settings where texts are traditionally oral and jointly constructed by participants. In related research, Heath (1983) contrasted children's text-based interactions with adults in three communities in the Piedmont Carolinas with school-based literacy events. These contrasts demonstrated the effects on children's school performance of different background knowledge about literacy. Ethnographers also studied social participation by Hawaiian children in "talk story" events within their community for insight into the ways the children participated in school reading groups. On that basis, reading instruction was modified to enhance students' participation in comprehension discussions by drawing on the conversational resources they bring from "talk story" to school literacy events (Au and Mason 1981).

These comparative studies demonstrate different ways of transacting about knowledge: different "literacies" (Gee 1989) operant in the school and non-school lives of students. Fundamental to this work is the idea that thinking, or "inner speech," begins as "social speech" (Vygotsky 1978). Learning involves the creating of thought by the internalization and transformation of information acquired in talk and activity with more experienced members of the culture. This way of thinking about teaching and learning suggests vivid alternatives to the dominant discourse pattern in classrooms. For this reason, the ethnographic study of taught cognitive learning frequently tracks attempts to reform classroom discourse so that it is more likely to provide conversational support for the novices' thinking.

3.2 Strengths and Limitations of Classroom Research on the Learning of Reasoning and Problem-solving

United States classroom ethnographers stress the ways that language and activity help to structure classroom social life and authority relations. To this extent, they have tended to dwell on the classroom's "hidden", normative curriculum and have only recently turned to linking their research to the teaching and learning of academic subject matter. Their counterparts in the United Kingdom, in contrast, have taken the lead in studying classroom culture and communication as they affect the possibilities for academic learning and focused, in Barnes's words, on how teachers and students move "from communication to curriculum" (1976 p. 14). This is an area for expansion of research, both cross-nationally and across the range of academic subjects.

4. Classroom Ethnography and the Study of School Failure

Perhaps the most provocative classroom research undertaken by educational anthropologists concerns differential treatment and access to knowledge among youngsters from racial, ethnic, or language minority populations. This work is interesting for its history, its contributions to policy and practice, and for ongoing debates about its explanatory power. It is a promising site for further research (see Jacob and Jordan 1987 for a summary).

4.1 Initial Studies of Differential Treatment and Access to Knowledge

In a brief history, Foley argues that the 1960s saw educational anthropologists in the United States enter "policy debates about the high rates of academic failure among some ethnic minorities" in their country (1991 pp. 61–62). Prevailing psychological accounts of school failure to this point had argued that children raised in poverty or in nonmainstream families suffered a "cultural deprivation" that hampered their ability to learn in school. However, research on language and culture in the United States and the United Kingdom contradicted this explanation with the discovery that:

(a) the grammars of languages or of dialects of a given language manifest equivalent systematic complexity;

(b) there are, in fact, few linguistic differences among the various dialects of English sufficient to prevent comprehension among speakers of different dialects;

(c) differences in native language or culture do not imply, or in themselves create, differences in cognitive ability.

These findings presented a picture of school children as more cognitively and linguistically comparable than might be expected from their vast differences in school achievement. Viewed in this light, school failure appeared to educational anthropologists to be not simply a matter of dialectal intereference or cognitive deficiency.

4.2 Findings of Classroom Ethnographic Research on Minority School Failure

School difficulty, especially among children culturally different from their classmates or teachers, underscored for United States researchers in the 1970s and 1980s the need to investigate the dynamics of those social performances by which all children are called to demonstrate intellectual competence to their teachers. As has been previously reviewed, this research illuminated patterns of classroom discourse sustaining and sustained by school's academic curriculum and by its "hidden curriculum" of normative socialization. In addition, particularly in studies comparing learning at home and at school, the strictures of classroom participation seemed especially to disadvantage youngsters who did not have home-learning experiences bearing a "family resemblance" to those in the classroom.

Three kinds of explanations for the classroom-based problems experienced by students from diverse cultural backgrounds were offered by this early work of Erickson and Mohatt (1982), McDermott and Gospodinoff (1979), and Michaels (1981).

(a) Mismatches between situationally appropriate strategies for participation at home and at school led students to misapply strategies acquired at home to participation in school speech events.

(b) Teachers failed to value the different communication and learning styles of diverse pupils and misassessed inappropriate classroom behavior as unwillingness or unreadiness to learn.

(c) Instructional "uptake" was minimal or not supportive of the higher order thinking of youngsters who did not respond to teacher elicitations in school-appropriate ways.

Comparative studies of minority children's communication at home and at school have proliferated since the late 1970s. They typically involve extensive participant observation in both settings and close analysis of recorded speech and nonverbal communication within them. Philips (1983), for example, investigated "participant structures," or culturally learned patterns of conversational rights and obligations at home on the Warm Springs Indian reservation and at school. She found differences in the ways American Indian children were expected to participate at home and in school lessons, and traced the school difficulties of the children she studied to differences in culturally based, tacit ways of getting along with peers and learning from adults.

Like her contemporaries, Philips was identifying conflicts between two systems of child socialization in systems where the norms regulating practice remain largely unspoken. Researchers in this tradition argued that miscommunication and cultural conflict could result, initially, in pupil misassessment and differential instructional treatment. Gradually, students would experience significant differences in their opportunity to learn, would compile negative institutional biographies, and ultimately would be alienated from formal education. To redress these problems, it was argued, changes were needed in educational policy and practice so that schools could become places where culturally different students and their teachers could achieve some common ground for learning. However, researchers differed on the means to this end. While some called for teachers to teach in ways more congruent with children's home cultures and languages, others called for direct teaching of mainstream norms for school talk and activity to children from diverse cultural and linguistic backgrounds. This debate has especially penetrated discussions of educational research and policy in bilingual education.

4.3 Strengths and Limitations of Classroom Ethnographic Research on School Failure

Explanations of minority school failure based on cultural discontinuity have been alternately lauded and criticized for their focus on the microprocesses of classroom interaction and for their identification of teacher behavior as a key area for reform. On the one hand, this research has had powerful and immediate applications in both continuing and preservice education. It has been a source of insight for teachers about the narrowness of status quo classroom discourse, the reality of cultural practices among students, and the power of an inquiring stance toward pupils and their families (Cazden and Mehan 1989, Florio-Ruane 1989).

However, as was mentioned above, solutions at the instructional level are varied and often in conflict. In addition, substantial criticism of this research has been led by Ogbu (1981) for several key reasons. He argues that its focus on the construction of inequality in the face-to-face communication of classrooms neglects examination of the historical, political, and economic realities accounting for school failure. Calling for more general cultural description and analysis, Ogbu asserts that ethnographers should be asking both "transactional and structural questions" (1981 p. 4). Of particular relevance to Ogbu's critique is his claim that the argument of cultural discontinuity in school failure cannot account for the school success of students from many immigrant groups. The account of school failure he advances more broadly contrasts the experiences of immigrant groups entering the United States voluntarily as compared to those who, as "involuntary immigrants," are subject to racism, job ceilings, and diminished expectations. Ogbu's analysis moves the locus for reform from the individual teacher, or even from school systems, to the society at large.

5. Future Directions

The debate about framing a theoretically adequate account of school failure continues and is a productive source of discussion among educational anthropologists. It challenges those who would describe classroom culture and communication to ask difficult new questions. For some, these questions involve linking face-to-face communication with the acquisition and display of cultural capital. Others seek to understand the processes by which disenfranchised students actively resist success in school and its classroom speech events. Still others wonder if school failure is the appropriate focus for what might be better thought of as research on the nature and limits of institutions. Others remain committed to reforming classroom discourse, but with a sense that what teachers and students bring to that discourse is far more than preconceptions about how to participate. In general, the ends of both anthropological theory and educational practice seem to require greater movement among previously isolated units and levels of analysis; more attention to cross-national teaching and classroom comparisons; and improved dialogue among those who have a stake in classroom research and the policies and practices it informs.

See also: School Culture and Peer Groups; School and Classroom Dynamics; Classroom Environments; Group Dynamics

References

Anderson G 1989 Critical ethnography in education: Origins, current status, and new directions. *Rev. Educ. Res.* 59 (3): 249–70

Au K, Mason J 1981 Social organizational factors in learning to read: The balance of rights hypothesis. *Read. Res. Q.* 17(1): 115–52

Barnes D 1976 *From Communication to Curriculum*. Penguin, Harmondsworth

Campbell D 1989 Teaching as discourse: The social construction of a mathematics lesson. In: Emihovich C (ed.) 1989 *Locating Learning: Ethnographic Perspectives on Classroom Research*. Ablex, Norwood, New Jersey

Cazden C B 1988 *Classroom Discourse: The Language of Teaching and Learning*. Heinemann, Portsmouth

Cazden C B, Mehan H 1989 Principles from sociology and anthropology: Context, code, classroom and culture. In: Reynolds M (ed.) 1989 *Knowledge Base for the Beginning Teacher*. Pergamon Press, Oxford

Chilcott J 1992 Some contributions of anthropology to professional education. *Educ. Researcher* 21 (2): 31–35

Cook-Gumperz J 1975 The child as practical reasoner. In: Sanches M, Blount B G (eds.) 1975 *Socio-cultural Dimensions of Language Use*. Academic Press, New York

Dunkin M J, Biddle B J 1974 *The Study of Teaching*. Holt, Rinehart and Winston, New York

Erickson F 1982 Taught cognitive learning in its immediate environments: A neglected topic in the anthropology of education. *Anthropol. Educ. Q.* 13(2): 149–80

Erickson F 1986 Qualitative methods in research on teaching. In: Wittrock M C (ed.) 1986 *Handbook of Research on Teaching*, 3rd edn. Macmillan, New York

Erickson F, Mohatt G 1982 Cultural organization of participant structures in two classrooms of Indian students. In: Spindler G D (ed.) 1982 *Doing the Ethnography of Schooling: Educational Anthropology in Action*. Holt, Rinehart and Winston, New York

Florio-Ruane S 1989 Social organization of classes and schools. In: Reynolds M (ed.) 1989 *Knowledge Base for the Beginning Teacher*. Pergamon Press, Oxford

Foley D E 1991 Reconsidering anthropological explanations of ethnic school failure. *Anthropol. Educ. Q.* 22(1):60–86

Frake C O 1980 A structural description of Subanun "religious behavior." In: Frake C O (ed.) 1980 *Language and Cultural Description: Essays*. Stanford University Press, Stanford, California

Garfinkel H 1967 *Studies in Ethnomethodology*. Prentice-Hall, New York

Gee J 1989 *What is Literacy?* Technical Report No. 2. The Literacies Institute, Educational Development Center, Inc., Newton, Massachusetts

Gumperz J 1976 Language, communication, and public negotiation. In: Sanday P (ed.) 1976 *Anthropology and the Public Interest: Fieldwork and Theory*. Academic Press, New York

Heath S B 1983 *Ways with words: Language, Life and Work in Communities and Classrooms*. Cambridge University Press, Cambridge

Hornberger N H 1987 Schooltime, classtime, and academic learning time in rural highland Puno, Peru. *Anthropol. Educ. Q.* 18(3): 207–21

Hymes D 1974 *Foundations in Sociolinguistics: An Ethnographic Approach*. University of Pennsylvania Press, Philadelphia, Pennsylvania

Jackson P W 1968 *Life in Classrooms*. Holt, Rinehart and Winston, New York

Jacob E, Jordan C (eds.) 1987 Explaining the school performance of minority students. *Anthropol. Educ. Q.* (special issue) 18(4)

McDermott R, Gospodinoff K 1979 Social contexts for ethnic borders and school failure. In: Wolfgang A (ed.) 1979 *Nonverbal Behavior: Applications and Cultural Implications*. Academic Press, New York

Mehan H 1979 *Learning Lessons: Social Organization in Classrooms*. Harvard University Press, Cambridge, Massachusetts

Michaels S 1981 "Sharing time": Children's narrative styles and differential access to literacy. *Lang. Soc.* 10: 423–42

Ogbu J 1981 School ethnography: A multilevel approach. *Anthropol. Educ. Q.* 12(1): 3–29

Perrenoud P 1988 Nouvelles didactiques et strategies d'élèves face au travail scolaire. In: Perrenoud P, Montandon C (eds.) 1989 *Qui maitrise L'école? Politiques*

d'institutions et pratiques des acteurs. Editions Realities Sociales, Lausanne
Philips S 1983 *The Invisible Culture: Communication in Classroom and Community on the Warm Springs Reservation*. Longman, New York
Rosaen C 1987 Children as researchers: A descriptive study of intentions, interpretations, and social interaction in an elementary classroom. Unpublished doctoral dissertation. Michigan State University, East Lansing, Michigan
Sarason S 1982 *The Culture of the School and the Problem of Change*. Allyn and Bacon, Boston, Massachusetts
Schratz M, Mehan H 1990 Gulliver travels into a math class in search of alternative discourse in teaching and learning. Paper presented at annual meeting of The American Educational Research Association, Boston, Massachusetts
Scollon R 1988 Storytelling, reading, and the micropolitics of literacy. In: Readance J E, Baldwin R S (eds.) 1988 *Dialogues in Literacy: 37th Yearbook of the National Reading Conference*. National Reading Conference, Chicago, Illinois
Spradey J P, McCurdy D W 1972 *The Cultural Experience: Ethnography in Complex Society*. SRA, Chicago, Illinois
Tharp R, Gallimore R 1989 Rousing schools to life. *Am. Educ.* 13: 20–25; 46–52
Trueba H T, Delgado-Gaitan C (eds.) 1988 *School and Society: Learning Content through Culture*. Praeger, New York
Vygotsky L 1978 *Mind in Society: The Development of Higher Psychological Processes*. Harvard University Press, Cambridge, Massachusetts

S. Florio-Ruane

Classroom Discussion

Through discussion, people join with others to form answers to their questions about what to think and how to act. Discussion is also used to educate children. While discussion is an ancient and essential educative activity, it is rarely practiced in schools. The principal things to learn about discussion are its nature, conduct, and rationale. What is it? How does one do it? Why use it?

1. Nature of Discussion

Discussion is a particular kind of back-and-forth talk wherein group members examine and resolve together some question at issue for them; something they need to understand, appreciate, or decide. It is free and open communal address with mutual exchange and response, as discussants join in thinking and forming together their own ideas, sentiments, and solutions. This is not a common form of discourse in society or in schools. Other contrary forms of discourse are much preferred socially and much more practiced scholastically.

1.1 Terminology

Educators, like most people, use the term discussion in two ways: as a rubric covering all manner of back-and-forth talk or interaction; and as a designator of one distinct form of back-and-forth talk. As a rubric, "discussion" covers talk which is also termed "conversation," "bull session," "debate," "argument," or "recitation." The term is stretched to include interview, negotiation, and even lecture ("I will now discuss . . ."). Each of these varieties of talk is denominated by a specific term in addition to the umbrella term of discussion. The second usage of "discussion," is to designate a particular kind of back-and-forth talk. Thus, for example, in the first case talk that is called conversation can also be called discussion. In the second case, there is talk that is called only discussion, there being no other term available by which to call it.

This entry treats discussion in the second usage, a specified form of back-and-forth talk that has no other name and which, accordingly, must be understood from the start not to include recitation, debate, bull session, and the rest. These terms are commonly confused in education and there is no point in trying to define them away by stipulation. The point is to keep clear the thing to which reference is being made. On that score it is easy to distinguish discussion from other forms of interaction in terms of the particular characteristics of talk in discussion, the preconditions of its use, and the intentions of the participants (detailed in Dillon 1988a, c, in press). On a loftier plane, the concept of discussion can be finely delineated (Bridges 1979, Paterson 1970), but less readily seen, touched, or felt. In practice, observers and participants such as students can readily tell when they are in a discussion or when the interaction is something else.

Discussion can be characterized as a form of group interaction wherein members join together in answering a question of common concern, exchanging and examining different views to enhance their understanding, appreciation, or judgment of the matter at issue. Since it is their question and they need a good answer, they want to hear divergent views and are willing to change their view for a better one if it stands up to group scrutiny. These and like sentiments inform the distinctive talk in discussion and make it plainly different from the talk in right-answer recitation, opinion-venting bull sessions, position-defending and victory-seeking debates and arguments, and the aimless wandering and insouciant chatter of conversation. These, rather than discussion, are the predominant forms of interactive talk in classrooms.

1.2 Usage

Discussion is hardly ever heard in classrooms. Teachers may well say that they use discussion a lot, but their self-reports are demonstrably unreliable.

Whereas a high-school English teacher reported discussion to be her most preferred method of teaching, used at least three or four times a week—with recitation specifically her next preference—observation revealed that she used discussion 5 percent of the time and recitation 45 percent (Conner and Chalmers-Neubauer 1989). Although two dozen middle school teachers of various subjects reported using discussion, moreover defining it by contrast to related forms of talk, only seven of them could be observed using discussion; the others used recitation and lecture with question–answer (Alvermann et al. 1990).

Extensive observations of 1,000 elementary and secondary classrooms across the United States have revealed that discussion (i.e., undifferentiated back-and-forth talk) could probably be seen only 4 to 7 percent of the time (Goodlad 1984). Intensive observations of three dozen fifth-grade mathematics and social science classrooms in a United States city have revealed discussion—by specific contrast to recitation, also observed—being used in no more than 3 percent of the instructional episodes (Stodolsky et al. 1981).

1.3 Tradition

No one knows the history of discussion. The tradition is fragile and impossible to trace in any direct or developmental line. Its greatest sources can be savored, however, for they are invoked to sustain modern efforts at discussion.

These earliest sources of discussion start with Socrates in fifth-century BC Greece, in his dialogues as recounted by Plato and Xenophon, as well as the deliberations by Athenians of Socrates' time, recounted in the histories of Thucydides and Xenophon, and in the orations of Demosthenes. Later sources are found in first-century AD Rome and the *Discourses* of Musonius Rufus, and in twelfth-century Paris with the dialectician Peter Abelard in his *Sic et Non*.

The rest of the tradition comes in the main through England and liberal political theory. Francis Bacon in the sixteenth century is significant, less for his famous writings on scientific method than for his quiet practices of deliberation in nascent parliamentary committees. Even more important are John Stuart Mill's manifesto *On Liberty* in 1859, and John Dewey's corpus of writing on group participation in democratic society, as in *Democracy and Education* in 1916.

In the 1930s courses and textbooks on discussion and its practice throughout entire curricula appeared in select United States universities. The Second World War era in the United States and Anglo-Saxon countries saw a vast and intensified aspiration toward discussion as a means of democratic decision-making, or at least involvement, poignantly revealed in books such as *Democracy through Discussion* (Lasker 1949), in innumerable discussion groups, in radio and television panels, in all manner of citizen and community organizations, in book clubs, unions, industry, religion, police, and social work, psychotherapy, and adult education.

Nothing much is known to have happened regarding discussion in schools. However, the intellectual and moral tradition of discussion has been given contemporary impulse by Bridges (1979) in his *Education, Democracy and Discussion*. The background to Bridges' argument takes in the whole of English liberal political democracy, and Dewey as well, with epistemological grounds stretching clearly all the way back to Socrates. Haroutunian-Gordon's (1991) study, *Turning the Soul*, makes a connection between today's United States inner-city schools and Plato, if not Socrates, via teenage discussion of a play by Shakespeare. The field of education continues in this tradition through group efforts to spread discussion among Scottish schools (Francis 1986); through multidisciplinary efforts by United States, Canadian, United Kingdom, and German scholars to understand discussion together (Dillon 1988b); through efforts by Dutch, French, English, Australian, and United States colleagues to understand group deliberation (Dillon 1993); through anthologies of theory, research, and practice of discussion (Wilen 1990); and through teacher manuals or textbooks on discussion in classrooms (Dillon in press).

2. Conduct of Discussion

For a group to engage in discussion, the members must have some topic at issue and they must be disposed to discuss it. Given these two elemental conditions, students of any age can discuss any subject matter in school. They need only a willing teacher to help them do it.

2.1 Subject Matters

The requirement of an issue, or a topic in question, is widely mistaken to exempt from discussion "hard" subject matters like mathematics and science, together with facts in all subjects, including "soft" ones like literature and social studies. However, there are controversial issues in the hard as in the soft subjects, and issues other than controversial ones in all subjects. Moreover, any topic at all can come to issue, including a matter of fact.

In education, one of the grounds for discussing facts and other matters in any subject is that students need to learn and to use them. Students have to identify them, assess, know, and understand them, apply, modify, articulate and communicate them. Students also need to learn the processes surrounding these matters; discerning the fruitful problem formulation, the relevant principle, the apt method, the pertinent data, the alternative solution, the sound conclusion, and the suitable application, not to mention the moral, ethical, and social concerns respecting these. All of these considerations apply not just to the familiar areas such as social studies, but also to the supposedly undiscussable subjects of mathematics (Hoyles 1985), biology (Dreyfus and Lieberman 1981), chemistry (Fasching and Erickson 1985), and genetics (Hendrix et al. (1983).

2.2 Dispositions

Once having a topic at issue the group must further be disposed to discuss it. This disposition comes down to little more than a basic willingness to discuss: a willingness to talk the issue over with others, to listen to other views, to change one's own view, and to form together a better understanding, judgment, or decision in response to the question at hand. Such willingness embraces as a matter of course a number of sentiments including open-mindedness, reasonableness, truthfulness, and respect for other persons (detailed in Bridges 1979). People do not need virtues and excellences in order to discuss, however; all they need is the basic willingness to discuss. Without this basic disposition people cannot engage in discussion; to the extent that they enjoy this disposition, they will engage in discussion.

Skills are also evident in discussion (particularly communication and social skills) as are intelligence, experience, knowledge, and wisdom. Well-developed skills and high accomplishments are required for a highly developed discussion, but they are not essential requirements for discussion. The youngest children in school can talk and listen to one another, can wonder, think, and work together. Far from being a prerequisite for discussion, skills and accomplishments can be developed through discussion.

2.3 Pedagogy

It is the students who discuss. Accordingly, the teacher's actions must be those that help the students to discuss. The pedagogy of discussion is distinct in behavior and spirit from that of other types of lessons such as recitation.

To lead a classroom discussion the teacher needs to possess fundamental dispositions—intellectual, moral, and democratic sentiments if not commitments—which appear to be unusual and even contrary to predominant pedagogical practices. At very least the teacher has to show a basic willingness to have the class discuss and an aspiration to help it discuss. The teacher's approach in discussion is far less didactic, directive, controlling, and instructional than in the normal teaching situation. It is more suited to a moderator, facilitator, and exemplifier of discussion, who is able to discourage efforts and tendencies that work against discussion.

A teacher's role as discussion leader involves an additional service: helping the students to learn how to discuss at the same time as helping them to discuss the topic in question. It is a hard task, and achieving it is one of the accomplishments of teaching. Yet no teacher is required to be an excellent discussion leader. Willing teachers are only being asked to conduct discussion: to join with students in the basic activity, to do it as well as they can, and to try to do a bit better next time. The discussion they hold may be elementary, but elementary discussions are no less discussion than the most sophisticated ones.

So disposed, the teacher's first act is to prepare the question for discussion. The teacher conceives and carefully formulates the question. He or she then outlines the related and subsidiary questions likely to arise in the course of discussing this question. In the classroom the teacher's first act is to present the question, writing it on the board, and telling the class essential points about it, such as why it is a question for this class now and what its terms mean. Presentation of the question takes two minutes, and it is the sole question the teacher will pose during the class hour. Having posed it, the teacher falls silent to allow the students to begin addressing the question.

As students speak, the teacher acts to maintain and to model discussion, by attentively listening and responding to contributions. Rather than asking questions, the teacher uses a range of nonquestion moves: various statements, signals, silences, and student questions (detailed in Dillon 1988c, in press). These prove to enhance discussion processes, whereas teacher questions foil discussion and turn it into some other group talk (Dillon 1985, 1990).

Toward the end of the lesson, or at suitable midpoints, the teacher helps by summarizing the discussion and stating the question that now seems to face the class. As the students gain experience with discussion the teacher helps them to work out the summaries and questions. A new question may then serve for subsequent class activity, the next reading or presentation, or continuing discussion. In that way the question for discussion arises out of the students' previous engagement with the subject matter and gives force and sense to both the ongoing and upcoming engagement.

3. Rationale

Only a conviction of its goodness and centrality as an educative activity would encourage the use of discussion, while powerful pragmatic forces frustrate the move and sometimes even the very idea of its attempt. Of the many things that discourage the use of discussion, only a very few attach to discussion itself. The majority reflect on other matters such as the incapacity of teachers and the antipathy of systemic conditions.

3.1 Reasons Against the Use of Discussion

Discussion has to be learned and both students and teachers must take a long time to learn it. It is time-consuming, uncertain of outcome, and difficult to conduct. Furthermore, critics of discussion claim that it does not cover subject matter content or convey information, it is neither efficient nor effective in producing results, and it is not a step-by-step procedure that can be trained, implemented, and evaluated by checklist.

The incapacity of teachers to engage in discussions consists of a lack of experience and know-how, but above all a lack of disposition to hold discussions in their classes. Teachers might not have a strong sentiment of inquiry, interest in student thinking, trust of group process, nor indeed democratic attitudes generally and in particular toward knowledge and authority. They may be worried about the waste of time in discussion (of "not getting anywhere"), the curriculum material not being covered, the topic not being closed, the immaturity and incorrectness of student opinion, the rise of conflict and emotion, the loss of authority and control over the whole process. They may be left with the debilitating sense that they do not even seem to be teaching when using discussion. These are powerful reasons against using discussion.

Even more powerful are systemic conditions in school and society, in which not much discussion can be seen nor much room where it might fit in. Predominant features of schooling offer no support of efforts to discuss, and moreover they actively support practices contrary to discussion. Social norms and practices make discussion foreign to everyday life and experience as well as to education. These norms and practices emphasize individual over group, privacy of thought and pursuit over public participation, authority instead of inquiry, and policy over community as source of knowledge and decision. The pattern of discourse is chatter, conversation, assertion, persuasion, and deception, by contrast to disciplined concert of reason, analysis, and evidence. An entire mind-set regards the essence of things to be their effectiveness or payoff in results, products, and outcomes. In face of systemic antipathies all around, discussion understandably keeps a low profile.

3.2 Reasons for the Use of Discussion

Through discussion things are learned and processes enhanced. Students acquire the subject matter in question, gain greater knowledge and understanding, and are able to make judgments regarding it. Through discussion, students also learn how to discuss. Above all they learn democratic attitudes and behaviors, such as befit group deliberation in a democratic polity and intellectual inquiry in a free society of thought and action. Thus, the considerations in favor of discussion count not just products but also processes, and not just intellectual processes but also attitudinal and behavioral ones. Discussion enhances cognitive, affective, and communicative processes as well as the group's collaborative, constructive, and deliberative powers.

Yet none of these considerations is primary. All of them might be construed to refer to discussion in its instrumentality, as if it were a technique competing with others in the gimmickry of efficient production of outcomes. Discussion is a fundamental educative activity in itself. People discuss for community and inquiry in the lived moment as well as for participation with others in communal reflection, discovery, and decision. This is the ancient usage of discussion, which inspires people to discover together through discussion what is right and true and then to act on it.

4. Conclusion

Rather than demonstrate or vindicate discussion by its outcomes or effectiveness, researchers might better describe and promote its good use. Studies might describe not just the processes of discussion, but also the conditions of its use and success. Knowledge is needed of what discussion looks like when it is going well in a classroom and when it is not. Thoughtful writings that exhort, persuade, and provide motivation to action, to the right use of discussion, and to perseverance in its practice are also needed.

For willing practitioners, the one recommendation is to practice discussion. Through study, observation, participation, and reflection practitioners can learn much about discussion. Thereafter, it is a matter of long and faithful trying.

See also: Group Dynamics

References

Alvermann D E, O'Brien D G, Dillon D R 1990 What teachers do when they say they're having discussions of content area reading assignments. *Read. Res. Q.* 25: 296–322

Bridges D 1979 *Education, Democracy and Discussion*. NFER, Slough

Conner J, Chalmers-Neubauer I 1989 Mrs Schuster adopts discussion. *English Education* 21: 30–38

Dillon J T 1985 Using questions to foil discussion. *Teaching and Teacher Education* 1: 109–21

Dillon J T 1988a Discussion vs. recitation. *Tennessee Educational Leadership* 15: 52–64

Dillon J T (ed.) 1988b *Questioning and Discussion: A Multidisciplinary Study*. Ablex, Norwood, New Jersey

Dillon J T 1988c *Questioning and Teaching: A Manual of Practice*. Croom Helm, London

Dillon J T 1990 *The Practice of Questioning*. Routledge, London

Dillon J T (ed.) in press *Deliberation in Education and Society*. Ablex, Norwood, New Jersey

Dillon J T in press *Using Discussion in Classrooms*. Open University Press, Buckingham

Dreyfus A, Lieberman R 1981 Perceptions, expectations and interactions: The essential ingredients for a genuine classroom discussion. *Journal of Biological Education* 15(2): 153–57

Fasching J, Erickson B 1985 Group discussions in the

chemistry classroom and the problem-solving skills of students. *Journal of Chemical Education* 62(10): 842–46
Francis E 1986 *Learning to Discuss*. Scottish Curriculum Development Service, Edinburgh
Goodlad J T 1984 *A Place Called School*. McGraw-Hill, New York
Haroutunian-Gordon S 1991 *Turning the Soul: Teaching Through Conversation in the High School*. University of Chicago, Chicago, Illinois
Hendrix J, Mertens T, Smith J 1983 Facilitating effective small group discussions of controversial issues. *Journal of College Science Teaching* 13: 21–25
Hoyles C 1985 What is the point of group discussion in mathematics? *Educ. Stud. Math.* 16(2): 205–14
Lasker B 1949 *Democracy through Discussion*. Wilson, New York
Paterson R K 1970 The concept of discussion: A philosophical approach. *Stud. Adult Educ.* 2(1): 28–50
Stodolsky S, Ferguson T, Wimpelberg K 1981 The recitation persists, but what does it look like? *J Curric. Stud.* 13(2): 121–30
Wilen W (ed.) 1990 *Teaching and Learning through Discussion: The Theory, Research and Practice of the Discussion Method*. Thomas, Springfield, Illinois

J. T. Dillon

Classroom Environments

The environment, climate, atmosphere, tone, ethos, or ambience of a classroom is believed to exert a powerful influence on student behavior, attitudes, and achievement. Although classroom environment is a somewhat subtle concept, remarkable progress has been made over the last quarter of the twentieth century in its conceptualization and assessment, which has led to an increased understanding of its determinants and effects.

1. An Historical Perspective on the Assessment of Classroom Environments

Murray (1938) introduced the term "alpha press" to describe the environment as assessed by a detached observer and "beta press" to describe the environment as perceived by those who inhabit it. Over the years, both observational instruments and questionnaires have been used to study the classroom environment.

Several structured observation schedules for coding classroom communication and events have been reviewed by Rosenshine and Stevens (1986) and Good and Brophy (1991). One of the most widely-known is Flander's Interaction Analysis System (FIAS) which records classroom behavior at three-second intervals using 10 categories (e.g., praising and encouraging, asking questions, student-initiated talk). Medley and Mitzel constructed an omnibus instrument called OSCAR (Observation Schedule And Record) which includes 14 categories (e.g., pupil leadership activities, manifest teacher hostility, emotional climate, verbal emphasis, and social organization). Other systematic observation schemes are the Emmer Observation System, the Brophy–Good Dyadic Interaction System, and Blumenfeld and Miller's method of coding vocabulary (Good and Brophy 1991).

Since the 1970s, numerous questionnaires have been developed to assess student perceptions of their classroom environments (Fraser 1986; Fraser and Walberg 1991). Advantages claimed for questionnaires are that they can be more economical than classroom observation techniques; they are based on students' experiences over many lessons; they involve the pooled judgments of all students in a class; they can be more important than observed behaviors because they are the determinants of student behavior; and they have been found to account for more variance in student learning outcomes than have directly observed variables.

One of the most widely used questionnaires, the Learning Environment Inventory, was developed as part of the research and evaluation activities of Harvard Project Physics (Welch and Walberg 1972). About the same time, Moos began developing numerous social climate scales which ultimately resulted in the development of the well-known Classroom Environment Scale (Moos and Trickett 1987). Both of these questionnaires built upon the theoretical, conceptual, and measurement foundations laid by pioneers such as Lewin (1936), Murray (1938), and their followers (e.g., Stern 1970). Furthermore, research using these instruments was influenced by prior studies using structured observation instruments.

A more recent approach to studying educational environments involves the application of techniques of naturalistic inquiry, ethnography, and case study. In the early 1990s there is a growing acceptance of a combination of qualitative and quantitative methods (based on observation or student perceptions) in the study of classroom environment (Fraser and Tobin 1991).

2. A Summary of Questionnaires for Assessing Classroom Environments

Table 1 summarizes several questionnaires commonly used to assess student perceptions of classroom learning environment. Each questionnaire is suitable for convenient group administration, can be scored either by hand or computer, and has been shown to be reliable in extensive field trials. All questionnaires include multiple variables or scales. For example, the My Class Inventory contains five scales: cohesiveness, friction, satisfaction, difficulty, and competitiveness. A distinctive feature of most of these instruments is that, in addition to a form that measures perceptions of actual classroom environment, there is another form to measure perceptions of preferred classroom environment. The preferred forms are concerned with goals and value orien-

Table 1
Overview of scales contained in seven classroom environment instruments (LEI, CES, ICEQ, MCI, CUCEI, SLEI, and QTI)

Instrument	Level	Items per scale	Scale classified according to Moos's Scheme: Relationship dimensions	Personal development dimensions	System maintenance and change dimensions
Learning Environment Inventory (LEI)	secondary	7	cohesiveness friction favoritism cliqueness satisfaction apathy	speed difficulty competitiveness	diversity formality material environment goal direction disorganization democracy
Classroom Environment Scale (CES)	secondary	10	involvement affiliation teacher support	task orientation competition	order and organization rule clarity teacher control innovation
Individualised Classroom Environment Questionnaire (ICEQ)	secondary	10	personalization participation	independence investigation	differentiation
My class Inventory (MCI)	elementary	6–9	cohesiveness friction satisfaction	difficulty competitiveness	
College and University Classroom Environment Inventory (CUCEI)	higher education	7	personalization involvement student cohesiveness satisfaction	task orientation	innovation individualization
Science Laboratory Environment Inventory (SLEI)	upper secondary higher education	7	student cohesiveness	open-endedness integration	rule clarity material environment
Questionnaire on Teacher Interaction (QTI)	secondary elementary	8-10	helpful/friendly understanding dissatisfied admonishing		leadership student responsibility and freedom uncertain strict

tations and measure perceptions of the ideal classroom environment.

Table 1 includes the name of each scale contained in each instrument, the school level (elementary, secondary, or higher education) for which each instrument is suited, the number of items contained in each scale, and the classification of each scale according to Moos's (1974) scheme for classifying human environments. Moos's three basic dimensions are: Relationship (which identify the nature and intensity of personal relationships within the environment and assess the extent to which people are involved in the environment and support and help each other); Personal Development (which assess basic directions along which personal growth and self-enhancement tend to occur); and System Maintenance and System Change (which involve the extent to which the environment is orderly, clear in expectations, maintains control, and is responsive to change).

As mentioned above, the development of the Learning Environment Inventory (LEI) began in the late 1960s in conjunction with the evaluation and research on Harvard Project Physics (Fraser et al. 1982). The LEI contains 105 statements (seven per scale) with response alternatives of "Strongly Disagree," "Disagree," "Agree," and "Strongly Agree." The scoring direction (or polarity) is reversed for some items. A typical item contained in the "Cohesiveness" scale is: "All students know each other very well."

The Classroom Environment Scale (CES) grew out

of a comprehensive program of research involving perceptual measures of a variety of human environments including psychiatric hospitals, prisons, university residences, and work milieus (Moos 1974). Moos and Trickett's (1987) final version contains nine scales with 10 true–false items in each scale. Published materials include a test manual, a questionnaire, an answer sheet, and a transparent hand scoring key. A typical item in the CES is: "The teacher takes a personal interest in the students" (Teacher Support).

The Individualized Classroom Environment Questionnaire (ICEQ) differs from other classroom environment scales in that it assesses those dimensions which distinguish individualized classrooms from conventional ones. The final published version (Fraser 1990) contains 50 items with an equal number of items belonging to each of the five scales. Each item is responded to on a five-point scale with the alternatives of "Almost Never," "Seldom," "Sometimes," "Often," and "Very Often." A typical item is: "Different students use different books, equipment, and materials" (Differentiation). The published form consists of a handbook and test master sets from which unlimited numbers of copies of the questionnaires and response sheets may be made.

The LEI has been simplified to form the My Class Inventory (MCI) which is suitable for children in the 8–12 years age range (Fraser et al. 1982) and students in the junior high school, especially those who might experience reading difficulties with the LEI. The MCI differs from the LEI in four ways. First, in order to minimize fatigue among younger children, the MCI contains only five of the LEI's original 15 scales. Second, item wording has been simplified to enhance readability. Third, the LEI's four-point response format has been reduced to a two-point (Yes–No) response format. Fourth, students answer on the questionnaire itself instead of on a separate response sheet to avoid errors in transferring responses from one place to another. The final form contains 38 items. A typical item is: "Children are always fighting with each other" (Friction).

The College and University Classroom Environment Inventory (CUCEI) was developed for small classes (but not for lectures or laboratory classes) (Fraser and Treagust 1986) as a result of the fact that little work had been done in higher education classrooms parallel to the traditions of classroom environment research at the secondary and elementary school levels. The final form of the CUCEI contains seven-item scales. Each item has four responses ("Strongly Agree," "Agree," "Disagree," "Strongly Disagree") and polarity is reversed for approximately half the items. A typical item is: "Activities in this class are clearly and carefully planned" (Task Orientation).

An instrument specifically suited to assessing the environment of science laboratory classes at the senior high school or higher education levels was developed (Fraser et al. 1992) as a result of the critical importance and uniqueness of laboratory settings in science education. The Science Laboratory Environment Inventory (SLEI) has five scales and the response alternatives for each item are "Almost Never," "Seldom," "Sometimes," "Often," and "Very Often." A typical item includes: "We know the results that we are supposed to get before we commence a laboratory activity" (Open-endedness). A noteworthy feature of the validation procedures employed is that the SLEI was field tested simultaneously in six countries (the US, Canada, England, Israel, Australia, and Nigeria).

In the Netherlands a learning environment questionnaire was developed to enable teacher educators to give preservice and inservice teachers advice about the nature and quality of the interaction between teachers and students (Wubbels and Levy in press). Drawing upon a theoretical model of proximity (Cooperation–Opposition) and influence (Dominance–Submission), the Questionnaire of Teacher Interaction (QTI) was developed to assess eight scales: Leadership, Helpful/Friendly, Understanding, Student Responsibility and Freedom, Uncertain, Dissatisfied, Admonishing, and Strict Behavior. The QTI has 77 items altogether (approximately 10 per scale), and each item is responded to on a 5-point scale ranging from Never to Always. A typical item is "she or he gets angry" (Admonishing behavior). The validity and reliability of the QTI have been established for secondary school students in the Netherlands, the United States, and Australia (Wubbels and Levy in press).

3. Classroom Environment Research

The strongest tradition in classroom environment research in several countries has involved investigation of associations between students' cognitive and affective learning outcomes and their perceptions of their classroom environments (Fraser in press). Numerous studies have shown that student perceptions account for appreciable amounts of variance in learning outcomes often beyond that which can be attributed to student background characteristics. For example, better student achievement on a variety of outcome measures was found consistently in classes perceived as having greater cohesiveness and goal direction, and less disorganization and friction (Haertel et al. 1981)

Classroom environment measures were employed as dependent variables in curriculum evaluation studies, investigations of differences between student and teacher perceptions of classroom environment and studies involving other independent variables (e.g. different subject matters). The significance of curriculum evaluation studies is that classroom environment differed markedly between curricula, even when various achievement outcome measures showed negligible differences. Research involving teachers and students informs educators that teachers are likely to perceive the classroom environment more favorably than their students in the same classrooms. Research studies involving the use of classroom environment as a criterion variable have identified how the classroom environment varies with such factors as teacher personality, class size, grade level, subject matter, the nature of the school-level environment, and the type of school (see *Student Perceptions of Classrooms*).

4. Practical Uses of Classroom Environment Information

Knowledge of student perceptions can be employed as a basis for reflection upon, discussion of, and systematic attempts to improve classroom environments. For example, Fraser and Fisher's (1986) attempt to improve classroom environments made use of the CES with a class of 22 Grade 9 boys and girls of mixed ability studying science at a government school in Tasmania. The procedure incorporated five fundamental steps.

First, the actual and preferred forms of the CES were administered to all students in the class. Second, the teacher was provided with profiles representing the class means of students' actual and preferred environment scores. Third, the teacher engaged in private reflection and informal discussion about the profiles in order to provide a basis for a decision about whether an attempt would be made to change the environment in terms of some of the CES's dimensions. In fact, the teacher decided to introduce an intervention aimed at increasing the levels of teacher support and order and organization in the classroom. Fourth, the teacher used the intervention for approximately two months. For example, enhancing teacher support involved the teacher moving around the class more to mix with students, providing assistance to students and talking with them more than previously. Fifth, the actual form of the scales was readministered at the end of the intervention to see whether students were perceiving their classroom environment differently from before.

The results showed that some change in student perceptions occurred during the time of the intervention. Pretest–posttest differences were statistically significant only for teacher support, task orientation, and order and organization. These findings are noteworthy because two of the dimensions on which appreciable changes were recorded were those on which the teacher had attempted to promote change. Also, there appears to be a side effect in that the intervention could have resulted in the classroom becoming more task oriented than the students would have preferred. Overall, this case study suggests the potential usefulness of teachers employing classroom environment instruments to provide meaningful information about their classrooms and a tangible basis to guide improvements in classroom environments.

5. Future Research

Assessment involving students' perceptions of classrooms can involve either individual students' perceptions or the intersubjective perceptions of all students in the same class. This distinction in past classroom environment research has often been important when choosing an appropriate unit of statistical analysis (e.g., individual student scores or class mean scores; see Fraser 1986). The advances in multilevel analysis mean that more sophisticated techniques are available for analyzing the typical data (e.g., with students nested within classes) found in much research on classroom environments (see *Multilevel Analysis*).

Although only limited progress has been made toward the desirable goal of combining quantitative and qualitative methods within the same study, the fruitfulness of this objective is illustrated in several studies (Tobin et al. 1990, Fraser and Tobin 1991). For example, in a study of higher-level cognitive learning, six researchers intensively studied the Grade 10 science classes of two teachers over a 10-week period (Tobin et al. 1990). Each lesson was observed by several researchers, interviewing of students and teachers took place on a daily basis, and students' written work was examined. The study also involved quantitative information from questionnaires assessing student perceptions of their classroom environments. An important finding was that students' perceptions of the environment within each classroom were consistent with the observers' field records of the patterns of learning activities and engagements in each classroom. For example, the high level of personalization perceived in one teacher's classroom matched the large proportion of time that she spent in small-group activities during which she constantly moved about the classroom interacting with students.

6. Conclusion

Positive classroom environments are generally assumed to be educationally desirable ends in their own right. Moreover, comprehensive evidence from past research establishes that classroom environments have a potent influence on how well students achieve a range of desired educational outcomes. Consequently, educators need not feel that they must choose between striving to achieve constructive classroom environments and attempting to enhance student achievement of cognitive and affective aims. Rather, constructive educational climates can be viewed both as means to valuable ends and as worthy ends in themselves.

See also: Descriptive Scales for Measuring Educational Climate; School and Classroom Dynamics; Class Size; Group Dynamics

References

Fraser B J 1986 *Classroom Environment*. Croom Helm, London

Fraser B J 1990 *Individualized Classroom Environment Questionnaire*. Australian Council for Educational Research, Melbourne

Fraser B J 1993 Classroom and school climate. In: Gabel D (ed.) 1993 *Handbook of Research on Science Teaching and Learning*. Macmillan, New York

Fraser B J, Anderson G J, Walberg H J 1982 *Assessment of Learning Environments: Manual for Learning Environment Inventory (LEI) and My Class Inventory (MCI)* (3rd version). Western Australian Institute of Technology, Perth

Fraser B J, Fisher D L 1986 Using short forms of classroom climate instruments to assess and improve classroom psychosocial environment. *J. Res. Sci. Teach.* 5: 387–413

Fraser B J, Treagust D F 1986 Validity and use of an instrument for assessing classroom psychosocial environment in higher education. *High. Educ.* 15: 37–57

Fraser B J, Tobin K 1991 Combining qualitative and quantitative methods in classroom environment research. In: Fraser B J, Walberg H J (eds.) 1991 *Educational Environments: Evaluation, Antecedents and Consequences*. Pergamon Press, Oxford

Fraser B J, Walberg H J (eds.) 1991 *Educational Environments: Evaluation, Antecedents and Consequences*. Pergamon Press, Oxford

Fraser B J, Giddings G J, McRobbie C J 1992 Science laboratory classroom environments at schools and universities: A cross-national study. Paper presented at the annual meeting of the National Association for Research in Science Teaching, Boston, Massachusetts

Good T L, Brophy J 1991 *Looking in Classrooms*, 5th edn. Harper Collins, New York

Haertel G D, Walberg H J, Haertel E H 1981 Socio-psychological environments and learning: A quantitative synthesis. *Br. Educ. Res. J.* 7: 27–36

Lewin K 1936 *Principles of Topological Psychology*. McGraw, New York

Moos R H 1974 *The Social Climate Scales: An Overview*. Consulting Psychologists Press, Palo Alto, California

Moos R H, Trickett E J 1987 *Classroom Environment Scale Manual*, 2nd. edn. Consulting Psychologists Press, Palo Alto, California

Murray H A 1938 *Explorations in Personality*. Oxford University Press, New York

Rosenshine B, Stevens R 1986 Teaching functions. In: Wittrock M C (ed.) 1986 *Handbook of Research on Teaching*, 3rd. edn. Macmillan, New York

Stern G G 1970 *People in Context: Measuring Person-Environment Congruence in Education and Industry*. Wiley, New York

Tobin K, Kahle J B, Fraser B J (eds.) 1990 *Windows into Science Classrooms: Problems Associated with Higher-Level Cognitive Learning*. Falmer Press, London

Welch W W, Walberg H J 1972 A national experiment in curriculum evaluation. *Am. Educ. Res. J.* 9: 373–83

Wubbels T, Levy J (eds.) in press. *Do You Know How You Look? Interpersonal Reationships in Education*. Falmer Press, London

B. J. Fraser

Classroom Observation

Structured observation, as used to monitor classroom events, requires an observer to assign such events to previously defined categories. These events may be recorded by mechanical means (e.g., film, audiotape, or videotape) and subsequently coded, or the observer can simultaneously record and code the events while present in the classroom. The three stages of the process therefore involve: (a) the recording of events in a systematic manner as they happen, (b) the coding of these events into prespecified categories, and (c) subsequent analysis of the events to give descriptions of teacher–pupil interaction.

Structured observation is also referred to as systematic observation or more particularly as interaction analysis, although the latter term is more typically applied to observation systems derived from the Flanders Interaction Analysis Category System (FIAC). According to Flanders (1964), interaction analysis is a "specialised research procedure that provides information about only a few of the many aspects of teaching and which analyses the content-free characteristics of verbal communication" (p. 198). Since, structured observation techniques have also been used to monitor nonverbal behaviors, Flanders's definition of the methodology is now seen to be too restrictive.

1. The Origins of Structured Observation

The origin of these observational techniques arose, in part, from the creation of the Committee of Child Development by the American National Research Council at the beginning of the 1920s. This committee sponsored research into teaching methods in nursery schools and kindergartens. Researchers found it necessary to observe these infants and record their behavior "as it happened." Initially, observers prepared diaries or narrative logs of the activities observed, but the sheer volume of descriptive material collected made the task a very arduous one. Olson (1929) introduced the notion of time sampling, whereby certain categories of behaviors were recorded at specified fixed intervals of time. An essential distinction used to classify behaviors by workers in the child development movement was that between direct teaching, where pupils were told what to do, and indirect teaching, where pupils were consulted and decisions reached by means of discussion and consensus.

By the early 1970s, an anthology of United States observation systems listed 92 instruments (Simon and Boyer 1970), the majority of which were derived from FIAC (Rosenshine and Furst 1973). The Flanders system has been widely criticized, however, for its limited applicability in that it was originally designed for relatively static classrooms where teachers stood in front of pupils who were arranged before them in rows while working on the same subject matter (Hamilton and Delamont 1974). With the increase of "open" or informal approaches to classroom organization, a greater variety of observational methods have been developed. In the 1980s, for example, a review of United Kingdom observation studies (Galton 1979) identified only two systems derived from FIAC. Most of this research had been carried out at the primary stage of schooling where informal approaches are more likely to be found. More recent discussion of the different methodologies can be found in Croll (1986) and Anderson and Burns (1989).

2. Characteristics of Structured Observation

Structured observation involves low-inference measurement (Rosenshine 1970) which requires the development of unambiguous criteria for assigning the various events into categories. Provided that the criteria are sufficiently explicit to be shared by different people, then different observers should arrive at identical descriptions of the same events. Thus an important requirement of a successful systematic observation system is high interobserver agreement.

Although the choice of categories and the definition of the criteria may be highly subjective, reflecting the values of those who construct the system, the technique itself is objective in the sense that the criteria used to describe classroom life are clearly defined. Thus, when the system is used correctly it is unaffected by the personal biases of individual observers. This is in sharp contrast to ethnographic methods where the researcher, although sometimes claiming to take a total view of the classroom before gradually focusing on the more meaningful features (Hamilton and Delamont 1974), in practice can only offer a partial view because the criteria governing the selection are rarely available for consideration by others.

While Anderson and Burns (1989) contrast a number of approaches based upon different theoretical perspectives, most modern observation schedules are, in practice, combinations of category and sign systems (Croll 1986). The selection of behaviors for use in a sign system is dependent upon those which are thought to be most useful for the particular research purpose. In classroom research, such variables are usually selected because they are thought to be related to learning outcomes or to systematic differences between teachers and their pupils.

3. Data Collection

Galton (1987) lists a number of ways in which a permanent record of classroom events can be obtained, thereby enabling an observer to conduct a subsequent analysis under less pressurized circumstances than those that exist under conditions of live recording. The two most frequently used approaches involve tape and video recorders. There are advantages and disadvantages to such methods.

The availability of relatively cheap hand-held video recorders has increased the popularity of using this method to record classroom events. The method's main advantage is that it supplies permanent visual and sound records which can be played and replayed and then edited. Thus the likelihood of observer agreement during subsequent analysis is increased. Set against this advantage is the highly selective representation of the camera which does not inform the viewer of what is going on in other parts of the classroom. For example, a category such as *target pupil is interested in another pupil's work* would be difficult to code using a video recorder, since the viewer would be uncertain whether the pupil was looking elsewhere in the classroom at what was happening between the teacher and another pupil or whether the pupil was totally distracted.

In an attempt to overcome such difficulties two cameras are sometimes used, one focused on the teacher or pupil and the other using a wide-angle lens to provide a general view of the classroom. Such arrangements, however, can be potential sources of distraction for both pupils and teachers so that what is gained in reliability may be lost in validity.

Another method of producing visual cues is to use stop-frame photography with synchronized sound (Adleman and Walker 1974). The flexibility of such a system has been greatly increased by the use of radio microphones which allow the teacher to move freely around the classroom and reduce the problem of background noise (Bennett 1985). However, the process of transcribing the permanent record from a recording can be very tedious and time-consuming.

It is estimated that to transcribe one hour of audiotape takes nearly a week of an efficient typist's time. Research involving a large number of teachers will, therefore, tend to favor direct observation methods because of the costs of transcribing and processing the data. More importantly, when an observer records events "as they happen," the presence of the observer in the classroom over a period of time has the advantage of enabling him or her to appreciate the shared understanding which exists between pupils and teacher so that certain behaviors can more easily be interpreted. This understanding is particularly important when the investigation concerns aspects of teacher–pupil relationships where private jokes (see Adleman and Walker 1975) are a common feature.

The general view is that it is preferable, at least in the early stages of an investigation, to make use of permanent records only when the focus of interest is in the children's language. Detailed descriptions of the methodology involved in such studies are provided by Edwards and Westgate (1987).

4. *Training Observers*

According to Flanders (1967), one of the main problems of training observers in the use of systematic observation is "converting men into machines" (p. 158). The usual training technique is to concentrate on a few categories at a time using a teach–test and feedback–reteach cycle. Details of the process are given by Jasman (1980).

Anderson and Burns (1989) provide a number of suggestions for a comprehensive training program. They draw attention, in particular, to the advantage of systematic observation in not requiring highly qualified, experienced observers because the training tends to be more rigorous. The method is, therefore, eminently suitable when employing teachers, who often have greater credibility with colleagues in school.

Usually audiotape and videotape recordings are used to introduce the observer to the problems of classifying particular categories and at the end of a training session another tape can be used to test if the observers can achieve acceptable levels of agreement. It is important to provide simple examples initially, with the guarantee that most observers will obtain total mastery, since observers who fail to identify behaviors correctly during training can often develop hostile reactions to the observation instrument. It is also useful to provide observers with experience of coding under classroom conditions as soon as possible. As stated earlier, it is often difficult to identify the context in which a behavior takes place on videotape which in turn means that the decision about the use of a particular category is not as clear-cut as the trainer might wish.

Once the initial training has been completed, it is important to build into any observation study refresher periods in which the observers go over the categories and check their reliability. These periods protect against what is termed "observer drift," which occurs when observers, who have come to accept criteria which do not conform to their own view of a particular behavior, gradually modify the category definitions over time to fit their own view.

5. *Reliability and Validity*

Most studies use only observer agreement as a test of reliability. The simplest measure of agreement is the percentage of occasions on which a pair of observers agree. However, this does not allow for the fact that two observers who were coding categories at random would still code the same categories on certain occasions by chance. The Scott (1955) coefficient corrects for this chance effect and is a more rigorous test of reliability. A weakness of this method, however, is that it does not permit study of observer agreement in research using a number of teachers. Medley and Mitzel (1963) offer several designs, based upon analysis of variance, in which each teacher is visited on one occasion by two observers, with the pairing of observers organized so that different observers are paired on each visit. Such a design also allows the teacher stability coefficient to be estimated.

Croll (1986) argues that *absolute agreement*, where the individual coding decisions of the observer are correlated, is preferable to *marginal agreement*, where only the total frequency of each category is compared irrespective of how an observer arrived at this total. Some systems, however, notably those which use broad sampling procedures, prevent any calculation of absolute agreement in the manner recommended by Croll. Croll (1986) also warns against including within a reliability coefficient a number of categories which are described as part of a single variable, but which are not mutually exclusive. If multiple categories can be coded simultaneously, they should be treated as separate variables with separate coefficients (Harrop 1979).

If an observation instrument is to be used by researchers other than those who developed the instrument, then the question of interinvestigator agreement arises, since each group may achieve high levels of observer agreement but interpret the categories differently (Rosenshine and Furst 1973). Anderson and Burns (1989) argue that in certain cases objectivity, expressed as observer agreement, is less important than the question of objectivity viewed as a measure of observer detachment. In some cases differences between observers mask real differences in interpretation and need to be investigated. However, in most cases of structured observation, differences between observers are regarded as error. Some developers of observation systems provide videotape examples already coded so that new users can check their degree of agreement with the developers on a trial tape (Eggleston et al. 1975).

Many researchers concern themselves only with the face validity of the observation instrument, assuming that the definition of the categories is so clear-cut that validity may be assumed providing observer agreement is high. The more complex the observation instrument, however, the less advisable it is to take this face validity for granted. In this case a number of alternative procedures can be employed.

When cluster analysis is used to create a typology of teaching styles or pupil types, observers can be asked to write descriptive accounts (mini case studies) of the teachers and the appropriate pupils. These accounts can then be cross-referenced with the descriptions derived from the clusters. Such descriptions can also be fed back to the observed teachers who can be asked to identify their own particular style or recognize particular types of pupils present in their classrooms.

Where two different observation systems exist having a similar focus, they can be used in the same classroom to compare and contrast results. While this type of cross-validation is recommended by Rosenshine and Furst (1973), only a few studies have attempted this task. In the ORACLE study, however, both the teacher and the pupils were observed using two instruments and the asymmetry of classroom behavior from both the teachers' and pupils' perspective was contrasted (Galton et al. 1980). The same study also made it possible to compare and contrast the "real curriculum" as perceived through both the teachers' and the pupils' activity.

Anderson and Burns (1989) argue that in some contexts, notably the study of different subject matter, it may be more important to investigate the inconsistencies across classrooms rather than seeking to submerge or eliminate these differences. They argue that inconsistencies across occasions are more problematic than inconsistencies across classrooms because of the limited amount of data collected.

Anderson and Burns (1989) conclude that one of the most important tests of validity is the reception of the evidence by teachers. In this regard Anderson and Burns (1984) quote claims that teachers often remarked, after the presentation of the research findings, "You've been in my classrooms." Similar responses have been found in United Kingdom classrooms with respect to reports of research from the ORACLE and PRISMS studies (Galton et al. 1980, Galton and Patrick 1989).

6. *Coding and Analysis*

In any observation system, discrete analytic units must be used in order to code the behaviors. The simplest division is based on some form of time sampling, where the time unit may vary from three seconds, as used by Flanders, to five minutes as used in Medley and Mitzel's (1958) OSCAR schedule. Every system has its own ground rules which differentiate between the beginning and the end of successive time units and which deal with the problem of behaviors which overlap from one unit to the next. It is important to choose time units so that observed behaviors do not regularly overlap into the next unit since, when this happens, it is found that the degree of agreement between observers decreases rapidly. Observer agreement is also improved when a steady rhythm of recording can be maintained.

Various methods exist for recording behavior and these are discussed in some detail by Croll (1986). These include event sampling (which records a particular event whenever it occurs), instantaneous time sampling (where only events occurring at a particular pretimed interval are recorded), scanning (where the number of individuals within a class who are engaged in a particular activity is recorded at pre-timed intervals), and continuous recording (where an ongoing record is made and the exact time in which a change in activity takes place noted). Finally, there exists a little-used method, one–zero time sampling, where only the first occurrence of a particular event within a given time interval is recorded.

With time sampling methods the extent to which the sample of behavior recorded is representative of the total behavior that occurred during a lesson is clearly dependent on the length of the interval between recordings. If the period is too short, the observers are likely to make mistakes; if the time interval is too long, they may record the behavior accurately but underestimate its overall frequency.

Consequently, when difficult and complex decisions have to be made by the observer, some researchers have preferred to use one–zero time sampling procedure, where the observer records the behavior only once as it occurs within a given time unit. If the time interval is short, then one–zero time sampling approximates to continuous recording of a classroom activity. With longer time intervals—for example, five minute units as used by Eggleston et al. (1975)—only the minimum frequency of occurrence is recorded. Such data, therefore, cannot be used to estimate the overall occurrence of individual categories within the classroom.

Criticisms of one–zero time sampling by Croll (1986) and Dunkerton (1981) are essentially correct in arguing that such systems are unsatisfactory in describing general aspects of classroom behavior. However, in cases where behaviors which discriminate among teachers are very infrequent, as for example in science lessons where it was rare to find teachers encouraging pupils to hypothesize (Eggleston et al. 1975), the method has some advantages in that it discriminates among teachers while, at the same time, allowing the observer sufficient time to recognize and code these infrequent complex interactions.

Critics of this type of coding system have been distracted from its prime purpose because such schedules still retain a number of frequently used categories. The presence of such categories is, however, irrelevant to the purpose for which the schedule is designed. Commonly occurring categories are included primarily to aid reliability, since observers who are not able to code continuously tend to become anxious, with the result that their concentration and reliability decreases. Such systems do, however, have very limited application. They are only preferable in cases where the complexity and variety of behaviors within the observation system require that the observer be given time to reach decisions in more difficult coding areas.

The simplest approaches to analysis operate at a descriptive level and are concerned with an estimation of either the frequency of occurrence of different events or the proportions of time taken up by different activities. The latter analysis is usually the product of time sampling systems.

More sophisticated schedules can be developed which allow the exact moment in time when a particular event occurs to be determined. Time sampling systems, provided the interval is very short, can also be used to determine the sequence of events taking place, since the observer is, in effect, recording a change of category rather than sampling a behavior within a defined period.

Recording a new behavior every time a different category is used employs the use of what are termed "naturalistic units." Here the problem for the researcher is to define a set of rules which will identify the unit of classroom transaction which can be coded under a particular category. Smith and Meux (1962) defined these natural units as "episodes" and "monologues," where an episode involved more than one speaker and a monologue identified a solo performance. The ground rules for identifying the nature of the transaction, however, make it difficult, if not impossible, for an observer to use such a system live in a classroom. For this reason, naturalistic units are most frequently used for the analysis of transcribed recordings. Observers can play and replay recordings until general agreement is obtained on the classification of each transaction.

When naturalistic units are used, the total number of episodes represents the total recorded behavior, since one tally only is made for each episode. In such a case, some record of the sequence of events can be obtained, but the most usual practice is to count the number of recorded tallies for each category and to divide this number by the total number of analytic units observed. With naturalistic units, this ratio closely represents the proportion of the total behavior occurring in a particular category. With longer time units, when a point–time sampling procedure is used, the ratio of the sum of tallies in a particular category compared to the total number of tallies recorded can again be interpreted as a proportion of total behavior.

One–zero time sampling methods in which frequently occurring events may only be coded once during a time unit can give no absolute value for the frequency of the particular behavior. Instead, an estimate of the minimum frequency of occurrence is obtained by dividing the total number of tallies obtained for a category by the total number of observation units.

The simplest analytic approach is that of Flanders (1964). Using a 10×10 matrix, the position of each subsequent event can be coded relative to the preceding interaction. Attempts to extend these procedures beyond the two category model have not been successful. For this reason Croll (1986) suggests the use of developmental profiles.

Anderson and Burns (1989) raise a number of important issues involved in the analysis of quantifiable data such as those obtained from structured observation, specifically the procedures for data aggregation and data reduction and the methods used to establish relationships between different variables. Croll (1986) also discusses a number of multivariate analyses which can be used to interpret observational data, including the use of multiple regression and the analysis of covariance in conducting analysis of the relationships between the observation processes and classroom products such as standardized tests.

With transcribed accounts of lessons, either from videotape or audiotape, greater attention can be paid to the sequential character of exchanges between teacher and pupils. Once suitable units of transcript have been identified, then different patterns in the sequence of these units can be observed. Unfortunately, researchers have tended to use different units for this analysis. The "episode" developed by Smith and Meux (1962) became the "incident" in Nuthall and Lawrence's (1965) study, while others have defined "pedagogical moves" (Bellack et al. 1966). Comparison between different studies is therefore difficult and although it is attractive to believe that effective teaching will eventually be explained in terms of sequential behavior rather than simple frequency units, there has been little progress in this direction since the early 1970s.

7. General Conclusions

In spite of these difficulties, there remains a continued interest in the collection of systematic observational data. Reviews of research on teaching in the United States list a large number of studies which have been carried out since the publication of Rosenshine's review (Rosenshine and Furst 1973). According to Brophy and Good (1986), there is now firm evidence about the most effective teaching strategies for improving pupil performance when measured on standardized tests of reading, language, and mathematical computation. Similar evidence has emerged from studies in the United Kingdom (Galton 1989), although Rosenshine warns that the more complex the intellectual activity the less likely are these direct instructional procedures to be effective. Subsequently (e.g., Galton and Patrick 1990), observational research has concentrated less on teaching behaviors and has instead examined aspects of the curriculum, supporting the view of Anderson and Burns (1989) that the instructional task, particularly the nature of its subject matter, largely determines the frequency and type of teacher–student interaction.

For the future, research is likely to concentrate on two major areas. The first of these concerns itself with models of teacher development. A large amount of research in the 1990s has concentrated on establishing differences between novice and expert teachers (Berliner 1992). However, little information exists about the intervening stages of development. As a consequence, the design and use of structured observation systems which will discriminate between these different stages is likely to assume greater importance. Second, the political attention given to reward systems for teachers based upon related performance criteria means that structured observation systems will increasingly play a part in both systems of appraisal and in school inspection to the neglect of more important issues concerning pupil learning strategies.

References

Adelman C, Walker R 1974 Stop-frame cinematography with synchronized sound: A technique for recording in school classrooms. *Journal of the Society of Motion and Picture and Television Engineering* 83: 189–91

Adelman C, Walker R 1975 *A Guide to Classroom Observation*. Routledge, London

Anderson L, Burns R 1989 *Research in Classrooms*. Pergamon Press, Oxford

Bellack A A, Hyman R T, Smith F L, Kliebard H M 1966 *The Language of the Classroom*. Teachers College Press, Columbia University, New York

Bennett N 1985 Interaction and achievement in classroom groups. In: Bennett N, Deforges C (eds.) 1985 *Recent Advances in Classroom Research* monograph No 2, *British Journal of Educational Psychology*. Scottish Academic Press, Edinburgh

Berliner D 1992 Some characteristics of experts in the pedagogical domain. In: Oser F, Dick A, Patry J (eds.) 1992 *Effective and Responsible Teaching: The New Synthesis*. Jossey-Bass, San Francisco, California

Brophy J, Good T 1986 Teacher behaviour and student achievement. In: Wittrock M (ed.) 1986 *Handbook of Research on Teaching*, 3rd edn. Macmillan, New York

Croll P 1986 *Systematic Classroom Observation*. Falmer Press, London

Dunkerton J 1981 Should classroom observation be quantitative? *Educ. Res.* 23: 144–51

Edwards T, Westgate D 1987 *Investigating Classroom Talk*. Falmer Press, London

Eggleston J F, Galton M J, Jones M E 1975 *A Science Teaching Observation Schedule*. Macmillan, London

Flanders N A 1964 Some relationships among teacher influence, pupil attitudes and achievement. In: Biddle B J, Ellena W J (eds.) 1964 *Contemporary Research on Teacher Effectiveness*. Holt, Rinehart, and Winston, New York

Flanders N A 1967 Problems of observer training and reliability. In: Amidon E J, Hough J E (eds.) 1967 *Interaction Analysis: Theory, Research and Applications*. Addison-Wesley, Reading, Massachusetts

Galton M 1979 Systematic classroom observation: British research *Educ. Res.* 21: 109–15

Galton M 1987 An ORACLE chronicle: A decade of classroom research. *Teaching and Teacher Education* 3(4): 229–312

Galton M 1989 *Teaching in the Primary School*. David Fulton, London

Galton M, Patrick H (eds.) 1990 *Curriculum Provision in the Small Primary School*. Routledge, London

Galton M, Simon B, Croll P 1980 *Inside the Primary Classroom*. Routledge and Kegan Paul, London

Hamilton D, Delamont S 1974 Classroom research: A cautionary tale. *Res. Educ.* 11: 1–15

Harrop L 1990 Unreliability of classroom observation. *Educ. Res.* 21(3): 207–11

Jasman A 1980 Training observers in the use of systematic observation techniques. In: Galton M, Simon B, Croll P 1980

Medley D M, Mitzel H E 1958 A technique for measuring classroom behavior. *J. Educ. Psychol.* 49: 86–93

Medley D M, Mitzel H E 1963 Measuring classroom behavior by systematic observation. In: Gage N L (ed.) 1963 *Handbook of Research on Research on Teaching: A Project of the American Educational Research Association*. Rand McNally, Chicago, Illinois

Nuthall G A, Lawrence P J 1965 *Thinking in the Classroom: The Development of a Method of Analysis*. New Zealand Council for Educational Research, Wellington

Olson W C 1929 *The Measurement of Nervous Habits in Normal Children*. University of Minnesota Press, Minneapolis, Minnesota

Rosenshine B 1970 Evaluation of classroom instruction. *Rev. Educ. Res.* 40: 279–300

Rosenshine B, Furst N 1973 The use of direct observation to study teaching. In: Travers R M W (ed.) 1973 *Second Handbook of Research on Teaching: A Project of the American Educational Research Association*. Rand McNally, Chicago, Illinois

Scott W A 1955 Reliability of content analysis: The case of nominal coding. *Public Opinion Questionnaire* 19: 321–25

Simon A, Boyer E G (eds.) 1974 *Mirrors for Behavior: An Anthology of Classroom Observation Instruments*. Research for Better Schools, Philadelphia, Pennsylvania

Smith B O, Meux M 1962 *A Study of the Logic of Teaching*. Bureau of Educational Research, University of Illinois, Urbana, Illinois

M. Galton

Classroom Rules and Routines

Some of the most fundamental decisions for classroom teachers are concerned with organizing and managing academic tasks and activities and controlling student behavior. Solving the problem of order in classrooms (Doyle 1986) has much to do with developing a workable set of rules and routines and teaching these to students (Emmer et al. 1980, Evertson and Emmer 1982). Rules and routines function to support and frame learning in classroom settings in much the same way that laws and directions guide behavior in the larger society. "Both policy-directed and descriptive studies indicate that life in classrooms begins with the creation of a work system and the setting of rules and procedures to hold the system in place, and that a considerable amount of energy is devoted to this process" (Doyle 1986 p. 413). While this process may seem common sense to most educators, research from different perspectives on how rules and routines function in classrooms has revealed considerable complexity.

This entry will examine research perspectives on this crucial aspect of classroom life, beginning by establishing what is meant by the terms "rules" and "routines." It will discuss briefly how rules and routines function to support or constrain learning in classrooms from three research perspectives: process-product/behaviorals, ethnographic/interpretive, and systems communication. How rules and routines are established, and how they function in classrooms will be examined.

An additional key issue has to do with consequences for noncompliance with established rules and routines and how these relate to various behavioral intervention strategies designed to regain compliance. While this issue is at the heart of many school discipline programs, it is beyond the scope of this entry. However, Emmer and Aussiker (1990) have written a critical review of research related to the effectiveness of several commonly used disciplinary intervention systems.

1. What Are Rules and Routines?

The first step in understanding rules and routines is to define them. While in the literature the two terms are often used interchangeably, it is useful for both researchers and practitioners to distinguish between them. A third term, "procedures," is frequently used synonymously with "routines." The distinction between the two terms is subtle, and for the purposes of this entry, "routines" will be assumed to include procedures.

Rules and routines can be distinguished from each other by content and scope. For example, in a grocery store, it is a stated rule that one must pay for all goods which leave the store. It is a stated routine, or procedure, that to pay for goods, the purchaser stands in a particular line. Similar layers of rules and routines are apparent in classrooms, although the universality of a rule such as paying for goods is rare in classrooms, where even such widespread standards as "Raise your hand before speaking" have frequent exceptions.

Simply stated, rules are general norms for expected behavior. Thus, they govern the moral and ethical life of the classroom, and tend to be stated in global terms: "Show respect for yourself and others," or "Come to class prepared to learn." Rules are the class values underpinning all classroom activity. Routines, in contrast, are procedures for accomplishing particular classroom tasks; they are the "how-to's" for day-to-day functioning within the value system provided by the rules. Routines govern physical relationships, space, and materials, and tend to be very specific: "If you need help, raise your hand." "Use the pencil sharpener only before the bell rings." Rules can be distilled down into a few guiding principles for the classroom, while routines are much more numerous.

Clearly there is overlap between rules and routines as they have been defined here. While rules may sound universally applicable, ethnographic studies such as that of Hargreaves et al. (1975) indicate that, in practice, the rules "in play" at various points in a lesson may differ greatly, making them much more situational, and hence more like routines. The notion that only rules carry the values of the classroom is also overly simplistic; clearly the routines which are enacted and enforced communicate who or what is important at any one time. This point will be further elaborated in the section on ethnographic studies below.

The importance of routines to the effective functioning of classrooms has been discussed from a cognitive psychology perspective by Leinhardt (1987), building on the findings of Evertson and Emmer (1982, see also Emmer et al. 1980). Leinhardt et al. contrast rules with routines by defining rules as limits to behavior, while routines are systems of exchanges that are set up to accomplish tasks and allow instruction to take place. The "small cooperative scripts of behavior" (p. 135) which are routines serve to reduce unnecessary cognitive demands on teachers and students by developing certain frequent tasks into schemata, thus making them automatic. Teacher planning and instruction are facilitated by these schemata: "The instruction to 'pass your papers in' results in all actors understanding the expected actions and executing them in a routine way" (p. 138).

Leinhardt et al. describe three types of routines: management routines, support routines, and exchange routines. Management routines include housekeeping, discipline, maintenance, and people-moving tasks. One example of a management routine is "how to line up for lunch." Support routines define and specify the behaviors and actions necessary for a learning–teaching exchange to take place, for example, "how to pass in papers." Exchange routines specify the interactive behaviors that permit the teaching–learning exchange to occur. They govern the language contacts between teachers and students—for example, routines for choral responses.

Rules and routines are not always stated or taught explicitly by teachers. In their study of deviance in classrooms, Hargreaves et al. (1975) identified rules and routines in order to document deviance from them. They found identification to be a complex task because teachers and students could not consistently verbalize the rules and routines of the classroom, even though most participants seemed to be functionally fluent in their applications and to share an understanding of why sanctions were applied in certain situations. Thus, generally speaking, rules and routines were public knowledge. Observations of classrooms and interviews with teachers and students revealed a complex set of norms and expectations which were highly context-dependent and which shifted not only from setting to setting, but from activity to activity within each setting.

Using the term "rules" as an umbrella encompassing both rules and routines, Hargreaves et al. identified three levels of rules which operate in a school. The first category, institutional rules, govern behavior in public places, such as hallways, cafeteria, and playground. When asked about "the school rules," these are the rules teachers and students were likely to recite. The second category, "situational rules," apply only in particular locations, such as in assembly or in classrooms. Situational rules supplement institutional rules in some settings. The last category was "personal rules," which are rules unique to a single teacher. One teacher in this study, for example, required students to stand when a visitor entered the classroom. Under a previous headmaster, this had been an institutional rule, but it had since fallen into disuse by everyone except the one teacher, becoming one of her personal rules. Students who moved from classroom to classroom thus had the task of interpreting and acting on different teachers' personal rules as well as the academic demands of the classroom.

Hargreaves et al. (1975) grouped classroom rules, which are situational and personal, under five themes. Generally, rules govern areas of teacher and student talk, movement, time, teacher–student relationships, and student–student relationships. The five themes overlap heavily in practice, with most rules covering more than one area and the placement of rules into categories dependent on the context in which the rule is invoked. For example, a teacher issuing a reprimand to two students talking could be interpreted as a "student–student relationship" rule if the issue is one student disrupting another's work, or as a "talk" rule, indicating that talk is prohibited during this part of the lesson.

Rules and routines may be formal (stated, taught, and practiced), or informal (unstated, but expected and understood by participants). The two types of rules and routines have typically been studied through the lenses of different research perspectives (Everton and Smylie 1987). Research in the behavioral psychological tradition has examined the planning, teaching, and effectiveness of formal, stated rules. Many rules and routines, however, are part of students' and teachers' tacit knowledge of classrooms (e.g., "Must I raise my hand in this particular discussion?" "Need I head my rough draft in the same way as my final draft?"). Ethnographic/interpretive research is more likely to address the evolution of such rules and routines. Informal rules and routines are highly context-dependent and their identification frequently requires prolonged observation of the classroom culture and microlevel analysis of classroom activity and communication.

2. *Rules and Routines from a Behavioral Psychological Perspective*

The focus of process–product/behavioral research on rules and routines has been on rules constructed *a priori* and implemented to structure the learning environment, manage resources, and control student attention and behavior. Of primary concern has been the form of rules and routines. Using research which demonstrates that productive use of class time correlates with higher student achievement as their rationale, process–product researchers have examined how effective use of rules and routines contributes to effective use of class time. "The opportunities for teachers to devote significant portions of class time in productive ways is determined in large part by the rules and routines teachers implement to structure and maintain their classroom environment" (Evertson and Smylie 1987 p. 358). Smooth and efficient routines for transitions, paperwork, and similar classroom events provide more time for academic work in the classroom.

More effective classroom managers devote significant amounts of time to teaching rules and routines at the beginning of the year, particularly in elementary classrooms but also in secondary classrooms (Emmer et al. 1980, Evertson and Emmer 1982, Leinhardt et al. 1987). Successful managers spent much of the first days of school actively teaching routines which would be used throughout the coming year. Content lessons during these first two days served as vehicles for conveying appropriate routines.

3. *Rules and Routines from an Ethnographic/Interpretive Perspective*

Process–product/behavioral research provides essential information about what practices for rules and routines are associated with student task engagement and achievement. Ethnographic/interpretive research on classroom communication, which focuses on much smaller samples (often only one classroom) in much greater detail, provides information about how rules and routines function in particular classrooms. While process–product research asks questions such as, "What rules and routines are associated with success?," ethnographic/interpretive research asks questions such as, "How do rules and routines function in this classroom? For whom, and for what purposes?"

Classroom communication researchers conceive of all classroom interaction as rule-governed (Green 1983). The focus of the research is on the functional rules and expectations that govern communicative interaction in the classroom. These rules are mutually constructed by teachers and students and constantly evolve during interactions, shifting and changing according to task or lesson phase. The rules, however, do not strictly limit classroom communication; instead, they provide a framework within which teachers and students improvise (Erickson 1982).

Studies about classroom communication—verbal and nonverbal ways that norms, rules, and expectations are signaled—show how both students and teachers actively mediate and construct the learning environment (see Erickson 1986 and Green and Smith 1983 for reviews). Studies identify what students need to understand in order to participate in lessons and how teachers orchestrate that participation. Some ritualistic activities, such as passing out papers, require little understanding. However, nonritualistic activities require students to "read" the requirements correctly or risk negative evaluations of their behavior and abilities (Green and Harker 1982). A close look at how class activities evolve reveals the need for a system of rules and routines that is visible, established, monitored, modified, refined, and reestablished.

Rules and routines thus take on broader meanings from the ethnographic/interpretive perspective. In this body of work, their definitions are extended to include spoken and unspoken norms for participation, often at a micro level of classroom interaction. For example, the routines of a classroom are assumed to include not only the expectation that students will raise their hands to request assistance, but also the subtle shifts in teacher and student behavior that signal when hand-raising is appropriate, whose hands will be recognized, and when calling out is the actual expected behavior.

Hargreaves et al. (1975) identified rules and routines as context-dependent within an individual class period or lesson. In the classes they observed, different rules were in play during each of five phases of a class session: entry, settling down/ preparation, the lesson proper, cleaning up, and exit. For example, students were allowed to chat during the entry and settling down phases, but not during the lesson proper. Such differences have been consistently found by researchers; ecological studies, in fact, use such shifts in "rules of appropriateness" (Erickson and Shultz 1981) to divide a lesson chronicle into segments (Doyle 1986). These differences were not explicitly stated by the teacher in the classrooms Hargreaves et al. observed; rather, they were unspoken norms which seemed to be an expectation of classroom life shared by teachers and students. By identifying unspoken expectations, such research points out how misunderstandings and miscommunications can occur, and helps to explain the process–product finding that time spent at the beginning of the year making classroom rules and routines explicit is crucial to effective management.

Numerous studies of classroom communication have examined the rules in play in particular classroom activity settings, with the emphasis on demands for social participation. For example, Wallat and Green (1979) have examined group interactions in a kindergarten class, including the cues which signal participation structures. As an example, Wallat and Green describe the norms for participation in "sharing time." The stated rule is that only one person may speak at a time. However, through nonverbal communication with the teacher (such as eye contact) and through verbal gestures (such as staying on-topic), a child could successfully negotiate an out-of-turn comment. Thus, the rules in play at any time are dependent on context, and are constructed in an ongoing process of interaction between teacher and students. Furthermore, Wallat and Green emphasize the importance of unspoken rules and routines, noting that, to an outsider, it may appear that a teacher is not making his or her expectations clear, when in fact both teacher and students may understand the verbal and nonverbal signals being given.

Ethnographic/interpretive research also provides information about why it is important to look beneath the surface of student behavior to determine how the rules in play are functioning. An overemphasis on following rules and routines can mask how they support or constrain what students are learning. Students may follow rules without taking the further step of engaging in substantive content. Their behavior is mere "procedural display" or "mock participation" (Bloome et al. 1989). In such cases, the "doing" of the routine replaces making sense of the content as a definition of learning.

4. Systems Communication, Rules, and Routines

Wubbels et al. (1988) describe a third approach which can be applied to an understanding of rules and routines: the systems communication approach to classroom interaction. They distinguish systems communication from other studies of classroom communication because of the former's emphasis on the long-term development of routine and ritual rather than on the generally short interaction units addressed by sociolinguists. From the systems communication perspective, routines develop over time as a part of the process by which teachers and students try to define what kind of relationship they have. Routines or rituals are thus the stabilized interaction patterns which develop in a classroom over time.

In a further explication of the same body of work, Creton et al. (1989) describe the circular effects of teacher and student behavior. As each participant acts, his or her behavior informs the action of the other participant, which in turn informs the behavior of the first participant. Thus, as routines develop and progress, it is impossible to distinguish cause and effect, and events which could appear isolated are actually shown to be connected. Dysfunctional routines develop as well as functional ones, and the issue for teachers, rather than assigning blame, is to acknowledge and act on their own contributions to dysfunctional routines. For example, the teacher in Creton et al.'s study had severe behavior problems in her classroom. Early in the year, she blamed the inappropriate behavior on students, and responded with punitive measures which seemed unfair to students and further contributed to their misbehavior, which they blamed on the teacher. As long as teacher and students continued to blame each other, they were locked into a dysfunctional system of routines which led to ongoing escalations in misbehavior and punishment. When given information about the routine which had developed, the teacher was able to break her part of the system, in this case by seeking positive student accomplishments rather than negative ones. Over time, as actions within this new system reinforced each other, more functional routines developed. Leinhardt et al. (1987) also documented dysfunctional routines which developed in two of the elementary school classrooms they observed.

5. Conclusion

While studies from both the ethnographic/interpretive and the process–product/behavioral traditions point to the importance of understanding rules and routines as a guide to understanding classroom functioning, they also point to the danger of focusing on rules and routines to the exclusion of the substance of the lesson. A focus on the doing rather than the meaning allows observers, teachers, and students to see procedural display as a desirable outcome, when in fact little or no actual learning may be taking place. Rules and routines can support instruction, but it is an error to focus solely on them rather than looking at the kinds of teaching and learning that they support. As Doyle (1986) has pointed out, there is a gap in the literature between research on the problem of order in classrooms, including the roles of rules and routines, and research on the problem of learning. This is a gap which must be bridged in order for either body of work to be meaningful.

See also: Discipline in Schools; Hermeneutics; Teacher Managerial Behaviors

References

Bloome D, Puro P, Theodorou E 1989 Procedural display and classroom lessons. *Curric. Inq.* 19(3): 265–91

Creton H A, Wubbels T, Hooymayers H P 1989 Escalated disorderly situations in the classroom and the improvement of these situations. *Teaching and Teacher Education* 5(3): 205–15

Doyle W 1986 Classroom organization and management. In: Wittrock M C (ed.) 1986 *Handbook of Research on Teaching*. Macmillan, New York

Emmer E T, Aussiker A 1990 School and classroom discipline programs: How well do they work? In: Moles O C (ed.) 1990 *Student Discipline Strategies*. State University of New York Press, Albany, New York

Emmer E T, Evertson C M, Anderson, L M 1980 Effective classroom management at the beginning of the school year. *Elem. Sch. J.* 80(5): 219–31

Erickson F 1982 Classroom discourse as improvisation: Relationships between academic task structure and social participation structure in lessons. In: Wilkinson L C (ed.) 1982 *Communicating in the classroom*. Academic Press, New York

Erickson F 1986 Qualitative methods in research on teaching. In: Wittrock M C (ed.) 1986 *Handbook of Research on Teaching*. Macmillan, New York

Erickson F, Shultz J 1981 When is a context? Some issues and methods in the analysis of social competence. In: Green J L, Wallat C (eds.) 1981 *Ethnography and Language in Educational Settings*. Ablex, Norwood, New Jersey

Evertson C M, Emmer E T 1982 Effective management at the beginning of the school year in junior high classes. *J. Educ. Psychol.* 74(4): 485–98

Evertson C M, Smylie M A 1987 Research on teaching and classroom processes: Views from two perspectives. In: Glover J A, Ronning R R (eds.) 1987 *Historical Foundations of Educational Psychology*. Plenum Press, New York

Green J L 1983 Research on teaching as a linguistic process: A state of the art. In: Gordon E W (ed.) 1983 *Review of Research in Education*, Vol. 10. American Educational Research Association, Washington DC 151–252

Green J L, Harker J O 1982 Gaining access to learning: Conversational, social, and cognitive demands of group participation. In: Wilkinson L C (ed.) 1982 *Communicating in The Classrooms*. Academic Press, New York

Green J L, Smith D 1983 Teaching and learning: A linguistic perspective. *Elem. Sch. J.* 83(4): 353–91

Hargreaves D H, Hester S K, Mellor F J 1975 *Deviance in Classrooms*. Routledge and Kegan Paul, London

Leinhardt G, Weidman C, Hammond K M 1987 Introduction and integration of classroom routines by expert teachers. *Curric. Inq.* 17(2): 135–76

Wallat C, Green J L 1979 Social rules and communicative contexts in kindergarten. *Theory Pract.* 18(4): 275–84

Wubbels T, Creton H A, Holvast A 1988 Undesirable classroom situations: A systems communication perspective. *Interchange* 19(2): 25–40

Further Reading

Bossert S T 1979 *Tasks and Social Relationships in Classrooms*. Cambridge University Press, Cambridge

Emmer E T, Evertson C M, Clements B S, Worsham M E 1994 *Classroom Management for Secondary Teachers*, 3rd edn. Allyn and Bacon, Boston, Massachusetts

Evertson C M, Emmer E T, Clements B S, Worsham M E 1994 *Classroom Management for Elementary Teachers*, 3rd edn. Allyn and Bacon, Boston, Massachusetts

C. M. Evertson

Classrooms: Grouping of Students

The issue of how students can best be organized for instruction in classrooms has stimulated much theoretical and ideological debate. This entry addresses cross-national differences in the social organization of schools and classrooms; briefly describes the trends in the historical literature; examines the findings from the more recent case study and survey literatures pertaining to elementary, middle, and secondary schooling; and speculates about future patterns of social organization.

1. *Cross-national Differences*

Because of national differences in historical experiences, schools in different countries serve such varied functions as education for the masses, entrance into the labor force, formation of governing and social elites, and inculcation of moral values. Consequently, different kinds of schools have developed in different nations, with different boundary lines drawn between levels of schooling. There also are differences within levels in how aggregates of students are grouped for instruction.

Educational systems in all societies deal with issues of how students can best be grouped together to profit from instruction and arrive at varying solutions to this problem depending on social and historical circumstances. "Streaming" in the lower schools in the United Kingdom, for example, represents an approach similar to some forms of ability grouping in schools in the United States. In both countries, teachers tend to group students within classes on the basis of ability (Jackson 1964). However, private schools attended by the socially elite provide a form of stratification that is more prominent in the United Kingdom than in the United States. Differentiation in the United Kingdom as well as in continental Europe occurs as well through the development of different types of schools, particularly at the secondary level (Hamilton 1987, Kerckhoff 1986).

Japan represents a major exception in this pervasive tendency to group elementary school students on the basis of ability for instruction (Cummings 1980). Japanese schools do, however, confront the problems of diversity by different means such as a slow instructional pace, out-of-school tutoring, and parental involvement through home instruction (Mason et al. 1989). This early whole-class instruction in elementary schools is, however, followed by instruction in differentiated secondary schools (Kariya and Rosenbaum 1987).

In general, where secondary schools are distinguished by type and ability (as in Japan, the United Kingdom, and the European continent), the curriculum is not highly differentiated within schools. In contrast, where high schools are of the comprehensive type serving highly diverse student populations (as in the United States and, to a lesser extent, in the United Kingdom), tracking and curriculum differentiation prevail (Oakes et al. 1992). Trends similar to those in the United Kingdom are reported for Israel (Shavit and Williams 1985).

2. *Traditional Studies Assessing the Effectiveness of Ability Grouping*

An assumption underlying an ability grouping strategy is that the content of instruction needs to be matched to the prior knowledge of students for them to realize optimal learning. The validity of this assumption has been questioned. Traditionally, researchers have been concerned mainly with two questions: (a) Are more homogeneous groups of learners created through grouping? and (b) Do students grouped by ability learn more than comparable students in more heterogeneous groups?

The literature contains two major waves of reviews, one in the early 1930s and another in the 1960s. With respect to group homogeneity, educational researchers in the 1930s found that student performance in one area was not highly related to that in another, and that classes formed to be high and low in achievement were, in fact, highly overlapping in distribution. More recent appraisals continue to reveal significant overlap among groups, with less overlap among ability groups for reading instruction at the primary level than in intermediate grades (Barr and Dreeben 1991).

The reviewers of both periods criticize the adequacy of the quasi-experimental studies that had been undertaken and emphasize the equivocal and inconsistent results from study to study. Yet these two groups of reviewers differ in their conclusions even though they are based, for the most part, on the same evidence. A substantial number of the early reviewers concluded, for example, that ability grouping benefited "slow" students. Many from the second wave, in contrast, discerned a tendency for high achievers in homogeneous groups to learn more than comparable students in heterogeneous groups, but for low achievers to do less well in homogeneous than heterogeneous groups (Barr and Dreeben 1991).

The findings from this quasi-experimental literature have been summarized using approaches such as meta-analysis (see, e.g., Slavin 1990). Still the main point in thinking about the traditional literature on grouping is its inconclusiveness. Ability grouping has not been shown to be clearly advantageous. Moreover, why one should expect more than inconsistent results is interesting. A social arrangement, of itself, does not lead directly to learning outcomes; rather, it is the instructional activities that students experience that influence what they learn and how they feel about it.

3. Descriptions of How Ability Grouping Schemes Work

Research in the 1980s and 1990s examines grouping in more broadly conceived ways, focusing on the instruction that students in different ability groups receive. It has become clear that membership in an ability group or track does not mean the same thing in different schools or even in the same school. The educational experiences of students vary markedly across tracks or groups, depending on the level and quality of the curricular materials used, the capabilities of teachers, and the aggregate characteristics of students from class to class. Reviews of this literature focus mainly on the results from case studies and surveys (Barr and Dreeben 1991, Oakes et al. 1992).

Concern with equality spawned several lines of inquiry, some going beyond narrow ideological concerns and leading to conceptualizations of ability grouping as part of the social systems of schools and classrooms. Some of the more interesting research of the 1970s and 1980s stems from concern with the mechanisms, such as curriculum differentiation and instructional quality, through which social background might influence education and life changes (Alexander and Cook 1982). Barr et al. (1983), for example, argue that the rate of curricular presentation is responsive to group ability, and it, in turn, influences the learning of students (for similar formulations, see Rowan and Miracle 1983, Sørenson and Hallinan 1986).

Along somewhat different lines, Cohen (1986) considers how individualized versus more traditional forms of teaching influence classroom authority, friendship among students, the attribution of status, and collaboration among teachers. She and her associates argue that traditional forms of instruction (restricted curricular tasks, ability grouping, and comparative grading) serve as the occasion for attributing low status to low achievers, thereby depressing their interaction and learning (see also Bossert 1979).

Explanations based on case studies of classrooms and schools tend to focus on the quality of instructional interaction, the perceptions and attitudes of participants, and their interpretations of events. Rather than positing linear models of events, these researchers describe the intentions of participants and the constellations of factors that characterize the instructional experiences of low and high achieving groups and classes (Rist 1970, Schwartz 1981).

Survey studies which explore the mechanism intervening between group structure and learning and rich case study descriptions of classroom events, in combination, yield evidence on how ability grouping works (Gamoran and Berends 1987). Some of the main issues addressed include the nature of organization patterns, placement of students in groups or tracks, stability of grouping schemes, curriculum differentiation, instructional interaction in groups and classes, and student outcomes.

3.1 Organizational Patterns

Although grouping in elementary schools is often described in terms of the types of ability grouping within and between classes, the experiences of students typically involve a mixture of total class, ability group, and individual experiences. Ability groups are frequently organized for reading instruction, sometimes for mathematics instruction, and rarely for social studies and science instruction. Although the percentage of time students spend in heterogeneous groups (cooperative groups, partnerships, writing workshops) has been minimal, the United States case study literature suggests an increase.

United States secondary schools vary in the extent to which they are tracked internally—some with most students enrolled in a single level, others with a fairly rigid three-track system, and still others with a more flexible system of levels. Schools seem to be moving away from more rigid forms of tracking toward systems of enrollment based on student course selection. Yet, even then, various mechanisms preserve the reality of tracks, as indicated by the high overlap among students taking honors courses and those taking remedial classes (Oakes et al. 1992).

3.2 Placement of Students in Ability Groups

Elementary students are sometimes placed into classes on the basis of ability; they are often also grouped within classes. Placing students in classes and tracks is typically an administrative matter, whereas forming groups in classes represents an interactive decision in which teachers derive a grouping pattern in response to the characteristics of students. Several investigators have examined how teachers form ability groups. Barr et al. (1983) found, for example, that the number of low-ability children in a class influenced the number and relative size of the reading groups formed. It has been argued that teachers assign students to groups using such characteristics as their cleanliness and nonagressiveness (Rist 1970), but others have found teachers to be less strongly influenced by social class or racial characteristics than achievement-related considerations (Haller 1985, Sørensen and Hallinan 1984).

While placement in high-school courses is responsive to student preferences, other criteria such as test scores, prior placement, and advisor recommendations have a bearing (Oakes et al. 1992). In particular, studies of high-school tracking show that middle-school choices by students in such areas as foreign language or algebra or their ability group placement may determine future track or school placements (Rosenbaum 1976).

Case studies of secondary students in the United

States suggest that those of lower social status and those speaking English as a second language are given placement information biased toward lower track placements. Although it is difficult to assess the extent to which background experiences confound ability measures, the weight of the evidence from survey studies supports the view that the direct effects of student ability and prior achievement are more important than those of social status (Gamoran and Berends 1987).

3.3 Stability of Groups and Track Assignments

The assertion is repeatedly made that ability groups, once established, are highly stable. Observational evidence, however, suggests some mobility between ability groups within classes, in the range from 20 to 35 percent in Grades 1 to 3, and from 10 to 25 percent in Grades 4 to 7. Teachers show different patterns of group changes; more effective teachers tend to move more students up than down (Barr et al. 1983).

There has been relatively little documentation of the stability of ability group membership from year to year. Gamoran (1989) reports a high degree of stability from first to second grade, particularly in schools where second grade placement was based on first grade basal placement; in some schools, however, groups were reformed on the basis of standardized test results. Similarly, researchers in the United Kingdom report little change in stream membership during the primary years (Barker-Lunn 1970).

Stability of track placement in secondary schools appears to be higher when track systems are more rigidly adhered to than when students have greater discretion in course selection. Further, the stability of track membership is influenced by the extent to which middle school course choices determine future course placements (Oakes et al. 1992).

3.4 Curriculum Differentiation

Case studies in elementary and high schools have examined the academic task characteristics of low and high groups. With respect to the curriculum, low group members typically cover less material, complete simpler assignments, and perform more drill and skill work than students in higher achieving groups (Allington 1983, Barr and Dreeben 1991). While content differences have been emphasized, these differences may be of minor significance in relation to the similarities in curriculum that characterize elementary school instruction in the United States. Most children in a school use the same reading and mathematics textbooks and workbook materials, and although groups may proceed at somewhat different paces through the materials, the curricular tasks are essentially the same (Barr 1992).

At the secondary level, students in the United States are allowed considerable choice, with a balance between elective courses and those required for graduation. Courses, however, vary considerably in their demand. Typically, lower level courses have different syllabuses and easier textbooks, with fewer, less demanding topics and more concrete illustrations than higher level courses. Emphasis on basic skills and more superficial treatment of course concepts characterize lower level courses in contrast to more engaging and authentic assignments in higher level courses. Less of the text is covered in lower level classes. Moreover, lower level students have fewer academic course choices, particularly in the areas of mathematics and science (Gamoran and Berends 1987).

3.5 Instructional Interaction

Case studies have also revealed the nature of the interaction during instruction. In elementary schools, low reading group members tend to experience a greater number of intrusions and less time-on-task than do students in higher achieving groups. Lower group members read orally more often, focus on smaller units of print and have decoding rather than meaning emphasized, are asked more questions that require recall of information rather than reasoning, receive different prompts from teachers, and are provided with more structure through the provision of advanced organizers for lessons than their higher group peers. While some instructional researchers also claim that low group members receive less instructional time, others have not found differential time allocations (Allington 1983, Barr and Dreeben 1991).

Findings are similar in middle and high school classes. Low-level class members experience less problem-solving and answer more questions with prespecified answers, and they have less influence on the nature of their assignments than their peers in higher level courses. There is a greater emphasis on control and management issues, and students in lower level classes are less involved in discussion and initiate fewer questions than those in higher level classes (Oakes et al. 1992).

Interpretive studies at the secondary level link the instructional treatment of students to teacher assumptions about the potential learning of their students. Because they are perceived as being unwilling or incapable of completing academic work, they are given simplified tasks and they learn correspondingly little. Similarly, it is typically concluded on the basis of the elementary school evidence that low-ability group members are being treated unfairly and that their instruction is causing them to achieve poorly (Allington 1983). It is assumed that low group members would learn more if they participated in more challenging instruction. But before it can be concluded that this assumption is valid, low groups and classes need to receive and respond positively to the same kind of instruction that their higher achieving peers receive.

3.6 Student Outcomes

Friendship choices and attitudes toward school are also associated with group and track placement. Group membership increasingly determines friendship choices as the year progresses in elementary, middle, and secondary schools (Hallinan and Sørenson 1985). Students in high groups or tracks have more favorable attitudes toward school than do their peers in lower groups or tracks (Rosenbaum 1976, Schwartz 1981).

Results from elementary school studies show differences in learning related to ability group placement. This research, however, goes beyond earlier studies by linking these differences to curricular coverage and instructional time (Barr and Dreeben 1991, Oakes et al. 1992). At the secondary level, track location influences achievement (basic cognitive skills and subject matter knowledge), though the evidence is mixed. However, as evidence accumulates and research designs become more sophisticated, there is increasing reason to believe that patterns of course-taking related to track location contribute to academic achievement. Further, the evidence generally indicates that track location influences aspiration for education beyond high school as well as the actual attainment of it (Alexander and Cook 1982).

4. Changing Existing Patterns

Changes in established grouping practices seem to be less influenced by the empirical literature than by prevailing views. Important among these is concern with equality, and the *de facto* segregation that may result from ability grouping. In the United States, well-articulated ideological positions identify tracking as a practice that violates the principle of equal educational opportunity (Oakes 1985, Rosenbaum 1976). Also important, a shift has occurred from behavioristic perspectives on learning to those emphasizing its social constructive nature. These perspectives challenge the basic assumption of ability groups by asserting that what is to be learned cannot be easily fractured into hierarchically ordered pieces that correspond to measures of student ability. These changes in perspective have led to a greater variety of grouping procedures, and researchers have begun to describe these alternatives and their effectiveness.

Studies of alternatives to traditional ability grouping include classroom studies of cooperative group work, heterogeneous grouping, and total class instruction. Elementary students instructed in heterogeneously composed small groups have been shown to learn as well as those in ability groups in primary reading and intermediate level mathematics (Barr and Dreeben 1991). Generally, in studies where cooperative peer groupwork takes the place of seatwork, student achievement is often enhanced; it is usually not negatively affected by diverse grouping arrangements (Slavin 1989).

Total class instruction has long been a favored method in intermediate grades and secondary schools when students are grouped into classes on the basis of ability. Studies have suggested the effectiveness of primary and intermediate total class instruction with heterogeneous groups. With the total class instruction, small group work may be needed to support the learning of children making slow progress (Barr and Dreeben 1991).

Further research can be expected to provide additional evidence on the advantages and limitations of alternative grouping arrangements. While most existing studies involve individual classroom cases, researchers are also beginning to examine the consequences of school, district, and statewide change in grouping arrangements. This emerging literature reveals the political volatility of the change process and the number of related curricular, instructional, and professional development issues that must be considered (see, e.g., Anderson and Barr 1990).

See also: Ability Grouping and Tracking in Schools; Stratification in Educational Systems; Student Diversity and Classroom Teaching

References

Alexander K L, Cook M A 1982 Curricula and coursework: A surprise ending to a familiar story. *Am. Soc. Rev.* 47: 626–40

Allington R 1983 The reading instruction provided readers of differing reading abilities. *Elem. Sch. J.* 83: 548–59

Anderson C, Barr R 1990 Modifying values and behaviors about tracking: A case study. In: Page R, Valli L (eds.) 1990 *Curriculum Differentiation: Interpretive Studies in US Secondary Schools.* State University of New York Press, Albany, New York

Barker-Lunn J C 1970 *Streaming in the Primary Schools.* National Foundation for Educational Research in England and Wales, London

Barr R 1992 Teachers, materials, and group composition in literacy instruction. In: Dreher M J, Slater W H (eds.) 1992 *Elementary School Literacy: Critical Issues.* Christopher-Gordon, Norwood, Massachusetts

Barr R, Dreeben R 1991 Grouping students for reading instruction. In: Barr R, Kamil M, Mosenthal P, Pearson P D (eds.) 1991 *Handbook of Reading Research*, Vol. 2. Longman, New York

Barr R, Dreeben R, Wiratchai N 1983 *How Schools Work.* University of Chicago Press, Chicago, Illinois

Bossert S T 1979 *Tasks and Social Relationships in Classrooms.* Cambridge University Press, New York

Cohen E G 1986 On the sociology of the classroom. In: Hannaway J, Lockhead M E (eds.) 1986 *The Contribution of the Social Sciences to Educational Policy and Practice 1965–1985. McCutchan, Berkeley, California*

Cummings W K 1980 Education and Equality in Japan. Princeton University Press, Princeton, New Jersey

Gamoran A 1989 Rank, performance, and mobility in elementary school grouping. *Soc. Q.* 30(1): 109–23

Gamoran A, Berends M 1987 The effects of stratification in

secondary schools: Synthesis of survey and ethnographic research. *Rev. Educ. Res.* 57: 415–35
Haller E J 1985 Pupil race and elementary school ability grouping: Are teachers biased against black children? *Am. Educ. Res. J.* 22(4): 465–83
Hallinan M T, Sørensen A B 1985 Ability grouping and student friendships. *Am. Educ. Res. J.* 22(4): 485–99
Hamilton S F 1987 Apprenticeship as a transition to adulthood in West Germany. *Am. J. Educ.* 95(2): 314–45
Jackson B 1964 *Streaming.* Routledge and Kegan Paul, London
Kariya T, Rosenbaum J E 1987 Self-selection in Japanese junior high schools: A longitudinal study of students' educational plans. *Sociol. Educ.* 60(3): 168–80
Kerckhoff A C 1986 Effects of ability grouping in British secondary schools. *Am. Soc. Rev.* 51(6): 842–58
Mason J M et al. 1989 Learning to read in Japan. *J. Curric. Stud.* 21(5): 389–407
Oakes J 1985 *Keeping Track: How Schools Structure Inequality.* Yale University Press, New Haven, Connecticut
Oakes J, Gamoran A, Page R N 1992 Curriculum differentiation: Opportunities, outcomes, and meanings. In: Jackson P W (ed.) 1992 *Handbook of Research on Curriculum.* Macmillan, New York
Rist R 1970 Student social class and teacher expectations: The self-fulfilling prophecy in ghetto education. *Harv. Educ. Rev.* 40(3): 411–51
Rosenbaum J E 1976 *Making Inequality: The Hidden Curriculum of High School Tracking.* Wiley, New York
Rowan B, Miracle A W 1983 Systems of ability grouping and the stratification of achievement in elementary schools. *Sociol. Educ.* 56(3): 133–44
Schwartz F 1981 Supporting or subverting learning: Peer patterns in four tracked schools. *Anthropol. Educ. Q.* 12(2): 99–120
Shavit Y, Williams R 1985 Ability grouping and contextual determinants of educational expectations in Israel. *Am. Soc. Rev.* 50(1): 62–73
Slavin R E 1989 *Cooperative Learning: Theory, Research, and Practice.* Prentice-Hall, Englewood Cliffs, New Jersey
Slavin R E 1990 Achievement effects in ability grouping in secondary schools: A best evidence synthesis. *Rev. Educ. Res.* 60(3): 471–99
Sørenson A B, Hallinan M 1984 Effects of race on assignment to ability groups. In: Peterson P L, Wilkinson C, Hallinan M (eds.) 1984 *The Social Context of Instruction.* Academic Press, San Diego
Sørenson A B, Hallinan M T 1986 Effects of ability grouping on growth in academic achievement. *Am. Educ. Res. J.* 23(4): 519–42

Further Reading

Svensson N E 1962 *Ability Grouping and Scholastic Achievement.* Almqvist and Wiksell, Stockholm
Yates A (ed.) 1966 *Grouping in Education.* Almqvist and Wiksell, Stockholm

R. Barr

Cluster Analysis

One of the most basic abilities of living creatures involves the grouping of similar objects, individuals, and so on, to produce a classification. Prehistoric people, for example, must have been able to recognize that many individual objects shared certain properties such as being edible, or poisonous, or ferocious, and so on. The idea of sorting similar things into categories is clearly a primitive one since classification, in the widest sense, is necessary for the development of language, which consists of words which help in the recognition and discussion of the different types of events, objects, and people encountered. Each noun in a language, for example, is a label used to describe a class of things which have striking features in common. So animals are named as cats, dogs, horses, and so on, and such a name collects individuals into groups. Naming is classifying.

As well as being a basic human conceptual activity, classification is also fundamental in most branches of science, since it involves two basic scientific functions: (a) the description of objects of interest or those under investigation, and (b) the establishment of general laws or theories by means of which particular events may be explained or predicted. Some areas where classification has played an important role are biology, where attempts at the classification of living organisms date from the time of Aristotle, and were a necessary prerequisite to the development of the evolutionary theories of Darwin; chemistry, where the classification of the elements in Mendeleyev's periodic table had a profound influence on uncovering the structure of the atom; and medicine, where a satisfactory classification of diseases is needed prior to investigating etiology and developing treatments. In education, researchers are often interested in producing classifications of both teachers and pupils.

1. Numerical Classification Techniques

Numerical methods for classification have been developed largely since the 1960s, this development clearly paralleling that of the electronic computer, a machine necessary to undertake the prodigious amounts of arithmetic generally associated with such techniques. Most of these methods operate either directly on a matrix of scores on a number of variables for each of the objects or individuals to be classified, or on a matrix of distance or similarities usually derived from the raw data matrix.

Many clustering methods are now available and can be used routinely via their implementation in standard software packages such as BMDP, SAS, or SPSS, or in other more specialized packages such as CLUSTAN, GENSTAT, and S-PLUS. The most commonly used methods can be grouped broadly into three classes, "agglomerative hierarchical," "K-means iterative reallocation," and "mixtures." It is important to remember however, that in some situa-

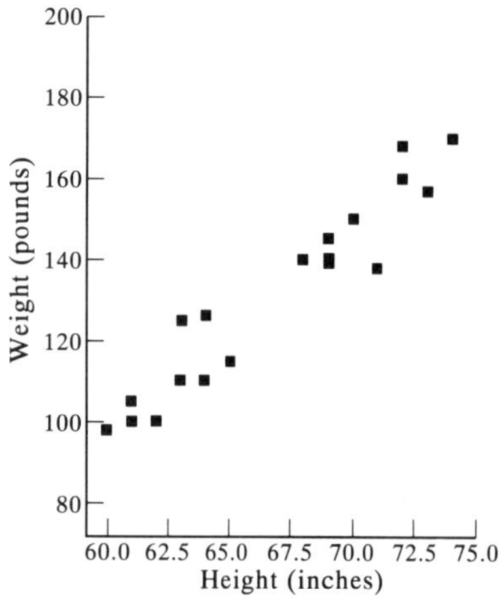

Figure 1
Scattergram of height versus weight

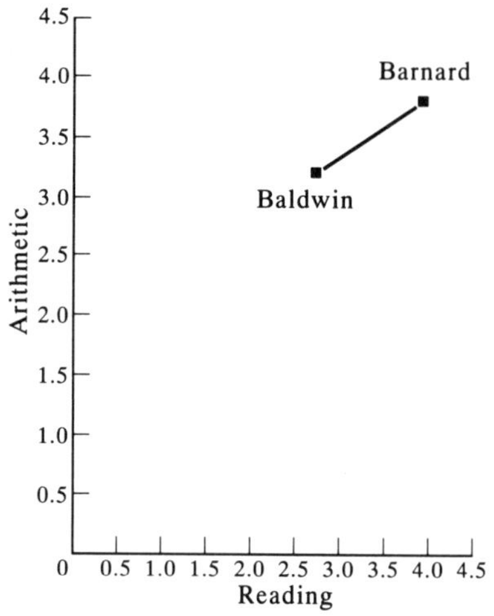

Euclidean distance = $[(2.7 - 3.9)^2 + (3.2 - 3.8)^2]^{0.5} = 1.33$

Figure 2
Euclidean distance in two dimensions

tions, simple graphical approaches may often be sufficient to identify groups or clusters. Suppose, for example, a number of individuals have had their height and weight recorded. A scattergram of such a data set is shown in Fig. 1. Two distinct "clusters" of points are clearly visible. In one sense the aim of most clustering techniques is to imitate and automate the process that the human observer does so well when the data involve only two variables, and extend it to the more common situation where more than two variable values are recorded on each of the objects or individuals under investigation. A description of several other graphical methods which might be helpful in a clustering context is given in Everitt (1993).

A point which should be noted before proceeding is that clustering is concerned with classifying previously unclassified material. At the start of the investigation, the number and composition of the classes is unknown. It is this that differentiates the techniques of cluster analysis from those of discrimination where groups are known *a priori*. Such methods are described in Everitt and Dunn (1992).

2. Distance and Similarity Measures

The raw data for clustering is usually a set of scores for a number of individuals or objects. An example is given in Table 1. These data consist of achievement test scores on reading and arithmetic for children in the fourth and sixth grades of 25 schools. Here the interest in clustering the schools might be to identify different levels of performance, and to assess similarities and differences in the patterns of change from fourth to sixth grade.

Many, though not all, methods of cluster analysis operate not directly on the profile of variable values of each object or individual, but on a matrix of interindividual distance or similarity values derived from these. The most commonly used distance measure, for example, is Euclidean. This measure is illustrated in Fig. 2 for the fourth grade scores of the first two schools in Table 1.

Table 1
Achievement test scores for twenty-five schools[a]

	Fourth Grade		Sixth Grade	
SCHOOL	Reading	Arithmetic	Reading	Arithmetic
Baldwin	2.7	3.2	4.5	4.8
Barnard	3.9	3.8	5.9	6.2
Beecher	4.8	4.1	6.8	5.5
Brennan	3.1	3.5	4.3	4.6
Clinton	3.4	3.7	5.1	5.6
Conte	3.1	3.4	4.1	4.7
Davis	4.6	4.4	6.6	6.1
Day	3.1	3.3	4.0	4.9
Dwight	3.8	3.7	4.7	4.9
Edgewood	5.2	4.9	8.2	6.9
Edwards	3.9	3.8	5.2	5.4
Hale	4.1	4.0	5.6	5.6
Hooker	5.7	5.1	7.0	6.3
Ivy	3.0	3.2	4.5	5.0
Kimberley	2.9	3.3	4.5	5.1
Lincoln	3.4	3.3	4.4	5.0
Lovell	4.0	4.2	5.2	5.4
Prince	3.0	3.0	4.6	5.0
Ross	4.0	4.1	5.9	5.8
Scranton	3.0	3.2	4.4	5.1
Sherman	3.6	3.6	5.3	5.4
Truman	3.1	3.2	4.6	5.0
West Hills	3.2	3.3	5.4	5.3
Winchester	3.0	3.4	4.2	4.7
Woodward	3.8	4.0	6.9	6.7

a Data used with permission from Hartigan (1975)

Table 2
Euclidean distances for first five schools in Table 1[a]

		1	2	3	4	5
	1	0.00				
	2	2.39	0.00			
D =	3	3.32	1.48	0.00		
	4	0.57	2.42	3.21	0.00	
	5	1.32	1.12	2.24	1.33	0.00

a Only the lower triangular part of this matrix is given since it is 'symmetric'

Table 3
Binary variables observed on abused children

Child	Variable			
	1	2	3	4
1	0	1	0	1
2	0	1	1	1
3	1	0	1	1
4	0	0	0	0
5	1	1	1	0

Variable 1: Academic performance: below average (0), above average (1)
Variable 2: Child still living with perpetrator: no (0), yes (1)
Variable 3: Age at time of abuse: $\leqslant 4(0)$, $> 4(1)$
Variable 4: Social class: I or II (0), III or IV (1)

When more than two variable values are involved the Euclidean distance between two individuals, *i* and *j* is given by

$$d_{ij} = \sqrt{\sum_{k=1}^{p} (x_{ik} - x_{jk})^2} \quad (1)$$

where p is the number of variables and x_{ik} and x_{ij}, $k = 1,2 \ldots, p$ are the variable values for the two individuals concerned.

The Euclidean distance matrix for the first five schools in Table 1 is shown in Table 2. Problems with use of the Euclidean distance measure, particularly the scaling of the variables, are discussed in Everitt (1993).

Also familiar in a clustering context are measures of similarity, particularly those for dichotomous, binary variables. To illustrate, consider Table 3 which shows four such variables recorded for five 15-year olds who had been subjected to sexual abuse as young children. Interest in clustering such data might center on determining groups of abused children with different outcome patterns.

An intuitively sensible index of the similarity between two children would be the number of variables on which they were given the same score. In general, however, similarities are scaled to be between zero and one, so an appropriate index would be simply number of matches divided by number of variables. This index will take the value zero for two

Table 4
Matching coefficient for data in Table 3

		1	2	3	4	5
	1	1.00				
	2	0.75	1.00			
S =	3	0.25	0.50	1.00		
	4	0.50	0.25	0.25	1.00	
	5	0.25	0.50	0.50	0.25	1.00

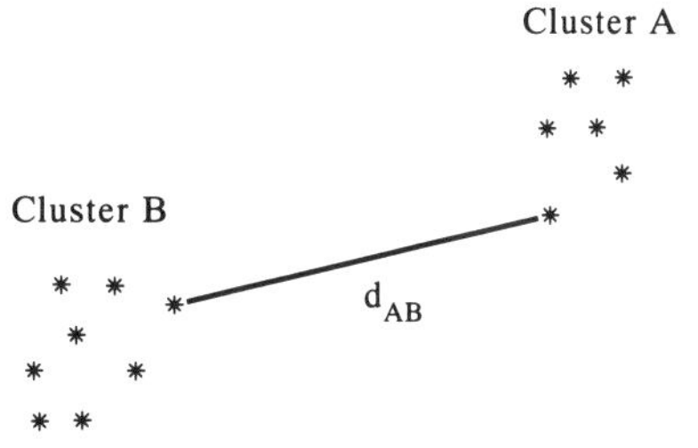

Figure 3
Single linkage distance

children who do not match on a single variable and one for two children who have an identical set of scores. For the data in Table 3, this matching coefficient for each pair of children is shown in Table 4. Many other such coefficients are discussed in Everitt (1993).

3. Agglomerative Hierarchical Clustering Methods

Members of this class of clustering technique are perhaps the most widely used in practice. All operate in essentially the same way, building up clusters by combining one or more individuals at a time, beginning at the stage of separate individuals and ending at the stage where all individuals are combined into a single group. The whole series of steps is conveniently described by means of a diagram known as a "dendrogram," examples of which are given below. Each intermediate stage in the procedure corresponds to a partition of the individuals into a particular number of groups or clusters; choosing the most appropriate or "best" number of groups for a set of data is usually a difficult problem (see Everitt 1979).

A variety of agglomerative hierarchical techniques exist because of the different ways of defining distance (or similarity) between a single individual and a group, or between two groups. This intergroup distance could, for example, be taken as the distance between the closest pair of individuals, one from each group (see Fig. 3) leading to "single linkage" clustering. An alternative is to use the opposite of this, that is, to take the intergroup distance as that between the most remote pair of individuals (see Fig.

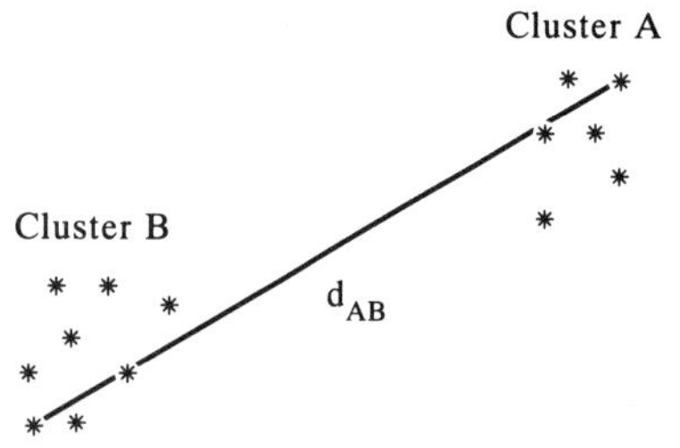

Figure 4
Complete linkage distance

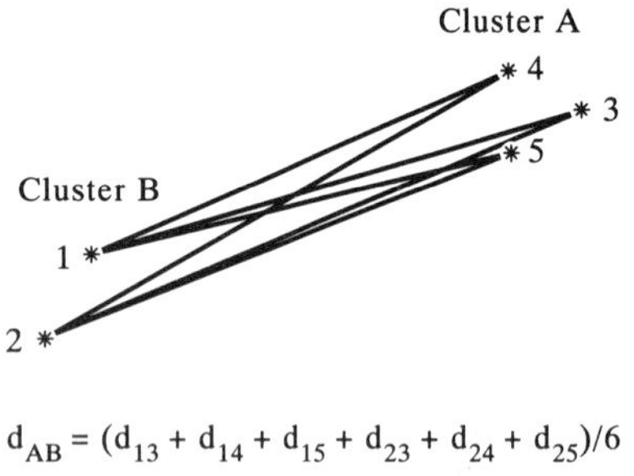

Figure 5
Group average distance

4), giving "complete linkage" clustering. Each of these uses only a single interindividual distance measure to define the intergroup measure. A method using all the distances between members of the two groups is "group average," illustrated in Fig. 5.

To describe the operation of an agglomerative hierarchical clustering method, single linkage will be applied to the first five schools in Table 1 using the Euclidean distance matrix shown in Table 2. Initially there are five clusters each containing a single school. The first step is to combine the closest pair of schools. From Table 2 this is seen to be schools 1 and 4. The distance between each of schools 2, 3, and 5 and the two school cluster [1, 4] must now be calculated. The single linkage distance between school 2 and the pair [1, 4] is found as follows:

$$d_{2,[4]} = \min[d_{1,2}, d_{2,4}] = d_{12} = 2.39 \qquad (2)$$

After these new distances are calculated, the smallest value is again used to decide which fusion should take place. Here this involves schools 2 and 5. At this stage there are three clusters, containing schools [1, 4],[3], [2, 5]. The next stage involves the combination of individual 3 with the [2, 5] cluster and the final stage the fusion of clusters [1, 4] and [2, 3, 5]. The corresponding dendrogram is shown in Fig. 6. Figs. 7 and 8 show the corresponding dendrograms for complete linkage and group average clustering.

The dendrogram from applying complete linkage to all 25 schools is shown in Fig. 9. Details of the three-group solution given by this method are shown in Table 5.

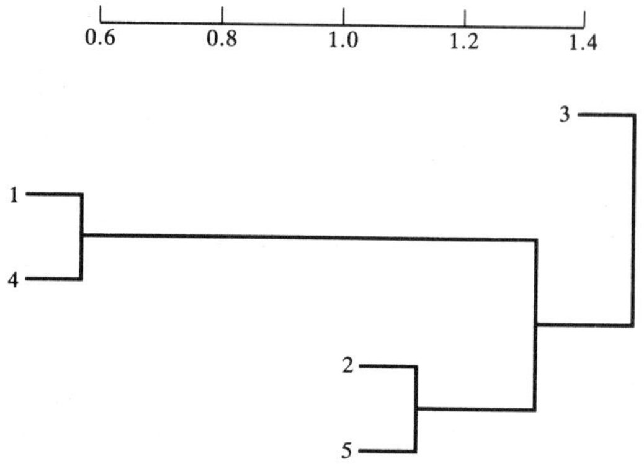

Figure 6
Single linkage dendogram for distances in Table 2

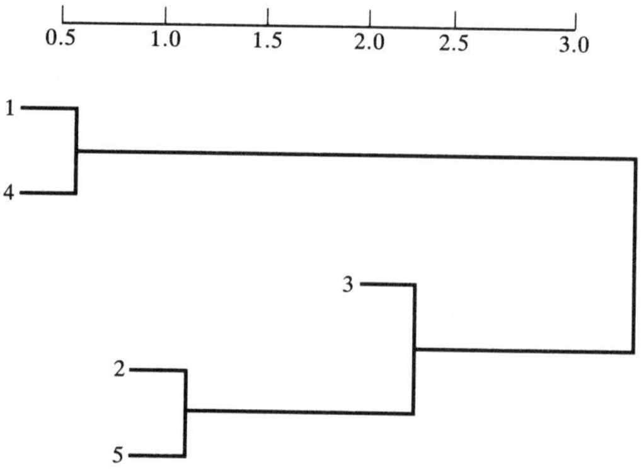

Figure 7
Complete linkage dendogram for distances in Table 2

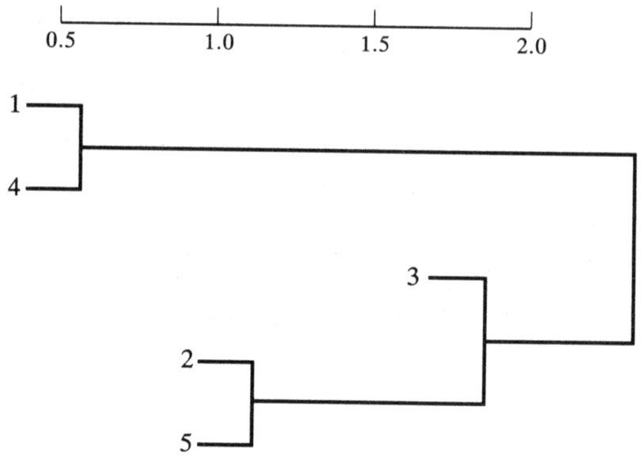

Figure 8
Group average dendogram for distances in Table 2.

4. *K-means Iterative Reallocation Methods*

Methods in this class operate by attempting to pro-

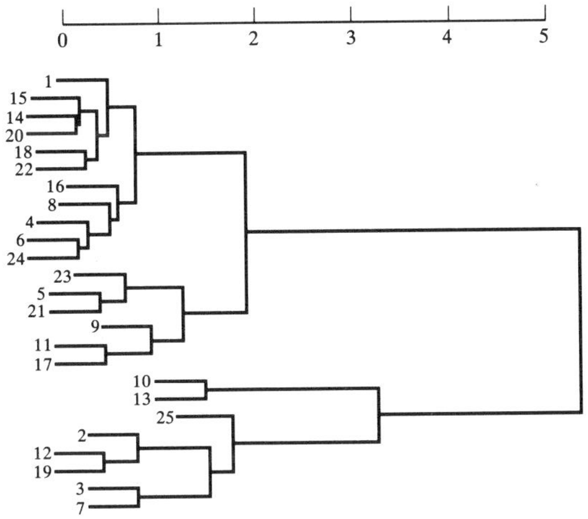

Figure 9
Complete linkage dendogram for Euclidean distances between all schools in Table 1

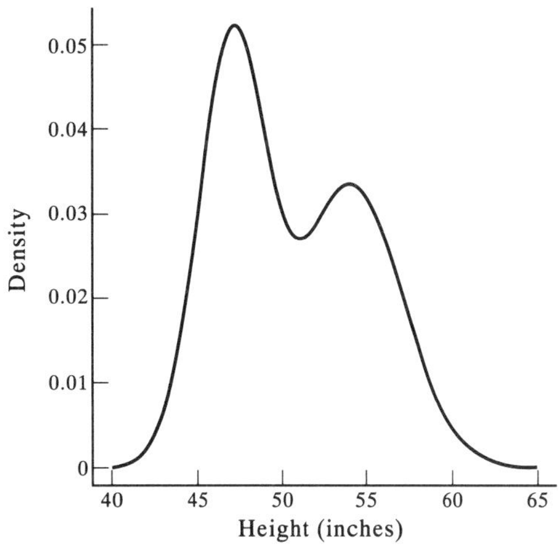

Figure 10
Density function for the heights of school children

Table 5
Three-group solution given by complete linkage clustering on data in Table 1

	Means			
Group	G4A	G4R	G6A	G6R
1	3.25	3.43	4.65	5.05
2	4.20	4.07	6.28	5.98
3	5.45	5.00	7.60	6.60

Schools in each group:
Group 1: 1, 4, 5, 6, 8, 9, 11, 14, 15, 16, 17, 18, 20, 21, 22, 23, 24
Group 2: 2, 3, 7, 12, 19, 25
Group 3: 10, 13

duce a partition of the individuals or objects into a given number of clusters so as to optimize some index measuring the internal homogeneity of the clusters. One such index, for example, might be the average within cluster distance between individuals. Given the number of groups it appears to be a relatively straightforward task to identify the partition which minimizes this index: simply consider every partition into the requisite number of groups, calculate the index for each, and select the appropriate one. Unfortunately the number of partitions is very large; with 19 individuals and 8 groups, for example, there are 1,709,751, 003,480 distinct partitions. Complete enumeration is clearly out of the question even with the very fastest computers now available. Some restriction is obviously required to reduce drastically the possible partitions that need to be considered. The strategy generally adopted is to begin with some initial, relatively arbitrary partition into the required number of groups, and then consider individuals for re-allocation from their own to some other group, such re-allocation being made if it improves the particular criterion value being used. The process continues until no re-allocation causes further improvement. Such "hill-climbing" algorithms are described in more detail in Everitt (1993).

As with hierarchical techniques, a difficult problem is that of deciding on the number of groups appropriate for the data. Some ad hoc procedures are described in Dubes and Jain (1979), and a detailed investigation of the number of groups problem is undertaken by Milligan and Cooper (1985).

Iterative relocation methods were used by Bennett (1976) and Galton et al. (1980) to delineate both teacher and pupil types.

5. *Mixture Method*

Most cluster analysis methods are essentially nonstatistical in the sense that they have no associated distribution theory or significance tests; consequently it is often difficult to know how much confidence to place in any clusters found, and generally impossible to relate from sample to population. For many investigators involved in an initial exploration of their data, this may present no real difficulties. Attempts have been made, however, to develop a more acceptable statistical approach to the clustering problem, using what are generally known as *finite mixture distributions* (see Everitt and Hand 1981). Consider, for example, a set of data consisting of the heights of a number of school children of a particular age. The frequency distribution of such a data set might look like Fig. 10, and might be described by the sum of two normal distributions with different means and possibly different variances. Here the component distributions are likely to correspond to those well-known clusters "boys" and "girls." The idea can be extended to more than a single variable using

Table 6
Two-Class parameter estimates for teacher data[a]

	Class 1	Class 2
1. Students have choice in where to sit	22	43
2. Students sit in groups of three or more	60	87
3. Students allocated to seating by ability	35	23
4. Students stay in same seats for most of day	91	63
5. Students not allowed freedom of movement in classroom	97	54
6. Students not allowed to talk freely	89	48
7. Students expected to ask permission to leave room	97	76
8. Students expected to be quiet	82	42
9. Monitors appointed for special jobs	85	67
10. Students taken out of school regularly	32	60
11. Timetable used for organizing work	90	66
12. Use own materials rather than textbooks	19	49
13. Students expected to know tables by heart	92	76
14. Students asked to find own reference material	29	37
15. Students given homework regularly	35	22
16. Teacher talks to whole class	71	44
17. Students work in groups on teacher tasks	29	42
18. Students work in groups on work of their own choice	14	46
19. Students work individually on teacher tasks	55	37
20. Students work individually on work of their own choice	28	50
21. Explore concepts in number work	18	55
22. Encourage fluency in written English even if inaccurate	87	94
23. Students work marked or graded	43	14
24. Spelling and grammatical errors corrected	84	68
25. Stars given to students who produce best work	57	29
26. Arithmetic test given at least once a week	59	38
27. Spelling test given at least once a week	73	51
28. End of term tests given	66	44
29. Many students who create discipline problems	09	09
30. Verbal reproof sufficient	97	95
31. Discipline: extra work given	70	53
32. Smack	65	42
33. Withdrawal of privileges	86	77
34. Send to head teacher	24	17
35. Send out of room	19	15
36. Emphasis on separate subject teaching	85	50
37. Emphasis on aesthetic subject teaching	55	63
38. Emphasis on integrated subject teaching	22	65
Estimated proportion of teachers in each class	0.538	0.462

a Decimal point omitted from class probabilities

"multivariate normal distributions" and to more than simply the two-cluster situation.

An analogous mixture model for categorical (usually) binary variables is the basis of a technique generally known as "latent class analysis." Here a number of clusters or latent classes are assumed present in the data, within which the observed categorical variables are independent. The observed associations between the variables are generated by the presence of the classes. (Compare the factor analysis model for continuous data.) Details of the model are given in Everitt and Dunn (1992). The method has found wide use in education and a number of interesting applications are to be found in the papers by Macready and Dayton (1977, 1980) and Dayton and Macready (1980). A particularly important and influential study was that of Aitkin et al. (1981) into teaching styles and pupil progress using data originally collected and analyzed by Bennett (1976). One part of the investigation involved applying latent class analysis to 468 teachers each described in terms of 38 binary items relating to teaching style. Two and three class models were considered. The results for two classes are shown in Table 6, each class being characterized by a set of 38 estimated response probabilities, that is, the probabilities of responding "yes" to each of the 38 binary items. An obvious interpretation of the two classes is that they represent essentially "formal" and "informal" teaching styles.

6. *Evaluating and Interpreting Results*

There are many problems associated with using clustering techniques in practice. Some have already been mentioned: choosing the number of clusters, the lack of any inferential framework, and the lack of a satisfactory definition of exactly what constitutes a cluster. Others concern the appropriate scaling of variables and how to use both quantitative and qualitative variables in the same analysis. Perhaps of overriding importance is the question of how to evaluate the results of clustering in terms of the stability, validity, and in particular, the usefulness of the clusters found. The latter issue is clearly demonstrated in the following quotation from Needham (1965) discussing the classification of human beings into men and women.

> The usefulness of this classification does not begin and end with all that can, in one sense be strictly inferred from it—namely a statement about sexual organs. It is a very useful classification because classing a person as man or woman conveys a great deal more information about probable relative size, strength, certain types of dexterity and so on. When a statement is made that persons in class *man* are more suited than persons in class *woman* for certain tasks and conversely, then only incidentally is it a remark about sex, the primary concern being with strength, endurance etc. The point is that it has been possible to use a classification of persons which conveys information on many properties. On the contrary a classification of persons into those with hair on their forearms between 3/16 inch and 1/4 inch long and those without, though it may have some particular use, is certainly of no general use, for imputing membership in the former class to a person conveys information on this property alone. Put another way there are no known properties which divide a set of people in a similar manner. (Needham 1965 p. 347)

Clearly a number of questions need to be asked and satisfactorily answered before any given solution can be offered as a reasonable and useful system of classification. Do the members of different groups differ substantially on variables other than those used in deriving them? Do essentially the same groups emerge when a new sample of similar individual is clustered? Are the clusters predictive of outcome, or reaction to treatment? Consideration of such questions may help to curb overenthusiastic researchers making inappropriate claims for the clusters they find.

In summary, the methods of cluster analysis are potentially very useful, but they require care in their application if misleading solutions are to be avoided. Researchers should remember the essential "exploratory" nature of the techniques.

See also: Multivariate Analysis; Scaling Methods

References

Aitkin M, Bennett S N, Hesketh J 1981 Teaching styles and pupil progress: A re-analysis. *Brit. J. Educ. Psychol.* 51(2): 170–86

Bennett N 1976 *Teaching Styles and Pupil Progress*. Open Books, London

Dayton C M, Macready G B 1980 A scaling model with response errors and intrinsically unscalable respondents. *Psychometri.* 45(3): 343–56

Dubes R, Jain A K 1979 Validity studies in clustering methodologies. *Pattern Recognition* 11(4): 235–54

Everitt B S 1979 Unresolved problems in cluster analysis. *Biometrics* 35(1): 169–81

Everitt B S 1993 *Cluster Analysis*, 3rd edn. Edward Arnold, Sevenoaks

Everitt B S 1992 Examining multivariate data graphically. *Journal of the Royal Statistical Society*, Series A

Everitt B S, Hand D J 1981 *Finite Mixture Distributions*. Chapman and Hall, London

Everitt B S, Dunn G 1992 *Applied Multivariate Data Analysis*. Edward Arnold, Sevenoaks

Galton M, Simon B, Croll P 1980 *Inside the Primary Classroom*. Routledge, London

Hartigan J A 1975 *Clustering Algorithms*. Wiley, New York

Macready G B, Dayton C M 1977 The use of probabilistic models in the assessment of mastery. *J. Educ. Stat.* 2(2): 99–120

Macready G B, Dayton C M 1980 The nature and use of state mastery models. *App. Psychol. Meas.* 4(4): 493–516

Milligan G, Cooper M 1985 An examination of procedures for determining the number of clusters in a data set. *Psychometri.* 50: 159–79

Needham R M 1965 Computer methods for classification and grouping. In: Hymes D (ed.) 1965 *The Use of Computers in Anthropology*. Mouton, The Hague

B. S. Everitt

Coeducation versus Single-sex Schooling

Single-sex education refers to three types of schooling, classified according to the gender composition of the school, classroom, and teaching staff. The purest type of single-sex education is where the entire student body of the school and the teachers are the same sex. Examples are Roman Catholic convent education for girls, or traditional, elite boarding schools for boys. The next type of single-sex configuration includes a mixed-sex teaching staff. Most single-sex schools are of this type. A third type of single-sex education occurs when school buildings are coeducational, but all instruction occurs in gender segregated classes. This form of instruction is common in many coeducational schools in the Third World, particularly in Asia.

1. Historical Trends with Respect to Single-sex Education

In the United States, a movement away from single-sex education at both the secondary and post-secondary levels was experienced in the 1960s and 1970s. These developments were motivated by both social and economic considerations. Single-sex education was viewed as a barrier to successful adolescent cross-sex socialization, and the declining demand for single-sex education led to institutions either closing or converting to coeducation in order to stabilize enrollments (Astin 1977). This trend occurred at precisely the time that research on American postsecondary institutions was beginning to document positive effects—especially for young women—for single-sex education on students' academic and occupational achievement pattern, self-image, and career choice (Astin 1977, Furniss and Graham 1974, Oates and Williamson 1978, Tidball and Kistiakowsky 1976). In countries where education systems are still expanding, as in many developing countries, coeducation is also advocated for economic reasons. The cost of providing parallel single-sex education is seen to outweigh possible benefits, except in countries such as Saudi Arabia, where coeducation is culturally unacceptable.

2. *Effects of Single-sex Education*

Provision of single-sex education is of interest for two reasons, both related to the education of women. First, where female participation in schooling is low, as in much of the Third World, single-sex education enhances the probability of female school participation. Second, where female school performance is depressed in comparison with male performance, single-sex schools boost female achievement and enhance female academic attitudes and self-esteem.

Most research on single-sex education has examined its effects on student attitudes and achievement only, and has not addressed its effects on increasing participation. With the exception of a few studies, research on single-sex education is limited to: (a) studies at the tertiary level in the United States, and (b) studies at the secondary level in the United States and other developed Western countries. Only very few studies have examined single-sex education in developing countries.

2.1 Tertiary Education in Developed Countries

Summarizing the results of a large longitudinal study of more than 200,000 students in over 300 colleges, Astin concluded that, "Single-sex colleges show a pattern of effects that is almost universally positive" with respect to a large array of academic and preprofessional outcomes (Astin 1977 p. 41): the effects of single-sex schooling were generally stronger for women than men. Astin speculated that such effects were probably due to the more circumscribed heterosexual activity and to a greater sense of identification and communal feeling when both students and faculty are predominantly of the same sex. Other studies have found that undergraduate education in a women's college, particularly highly selective private sector schools, is a major explanatory factor for women's career achievement patterns (Graham 1970, Oates and Williamson 1978, Tidball 1980, Tidball and Kistiakowsky 1976).

2.2 Secondary Education in Developed Countries

Most research comparing single-sex with coeducational schooling has been conducted in secondary schools in developed Western countries. The focus has been more on students' attitudes about the social and psychological environments of their schools than on academic attitudes and behaviors, and most studies have not measured achievement differences between students attending the two school types.

Whereas single-sex schools, especially those for girls, were considered to emphasize control and discipline to a greater extent, coeducational schools were found to have a more relaxed and friendlier atmosphere. However, there is some disagreement about actual academic emphasis between the two school types, with some researchers finding girls' schools to evidence a more academic orientation, and other studies finding no positive relationship between single-sex status and academic orientation. Finn (1980) reported on a cross-national study, using 1970 data from the International Association for the Evaluation of Educational Achievement (IEA) of attitudes and achievement in science and reading among 14-year olds in both single-sex and coeducational schools in the United States and the United Kingdom. While no differences were found between coeducational and a small sample of single-sex schools in the United States ($n = 8$), noticeable effects appeared in the British sample, which included 47 single-sex schools. Girls in coeducational schools in the United Kingdom showed a decline in science and vocabulary relative to male peers, while girls in single-sex schools excelled in reading and science.

Two studies in the 1980s have focused on large, randomly selected, samples of United States Roman Catholic secondary schools. Lee and Bryk (1986) examined 75 Roman Catholic schools from the High School and Beyond study, which included longitudinal information on student background, attitudes, behaviors, and achievement. Whether concerning academic achievement, achievement gains, educational aspirations, locus of control, sex-role stereotyping, or attitudes and behaviors related to academic study, results indicated that single-sex schools delivered specific advantages, especially to their female students. All analyses included considerable adjustment for student background and contextual differences between schools. Riordan (1985) compared White students in public schools with Roman Catholic single-sex and coeducational school students, using 1972 National Longitudinal Study data, and controlling for students' social class and census region. Positive effects were found for achievement in single-sex schools, particularly for girls.

The relation between sex-stereotyped attitudes and behaviors and United States sex-segregated education has received some research attention. Girls in girls' schools were found to have less stereotypic views of women's role than their coeducational counterparts, and showed a decrease in sex-role stereotyping over the last two years of high school (Lee and Bryk 1986). Girls in single-sex Roman Catholic high schools in suburban Chicago held less stereotypic views of scientific professions than did a comparable group of public school girls. High school girls in single-sex schools had a significantly higher interest level in the feminist movement than their coeducational female counterparts. Fear of success was greater among girls in a coeducational than all-girls New York Jewish high school, with fear of success even less for girls who had also attended a single-sex elementary school. Adolescent female participation rates and leadership behavior in a laboratory game-playing situation increased when preceded by game experience in a single-sex condition. Positive effects of single-sex grouping in both the cognitive and affective domains have also been found for girls in the first grade. No significant single-sex effects for boys were reported in any of these studies.

2.3 Developing Countries

Research on the comparative effects of sex-segregated and coeducational schooling in developing countries is scarce, although single-sex education is somewhat more common in those countries than in developed countries. One study compares the relative advantages of the two types of school grouping on male and female eighth-graders in Thailand, using longitudinal data on mathematics achievement before and after eighth-grade (Jimenez and Lockheed 1989). These researchers found that single-sex schools were more effective for female students, whereas coeducational schools were more effective for male students. The longtitudinal nature of the data and the econometric two-stage modeling of choice into school and effects of school on achievement make these findings particularly strong.

A second study from a developing country analyzes the effectiveness of single-sex and coeducational schools with respect to student mathematics achievement and gender-stereotypic attitudes toward mathematics, for secondary students in government-owned schools in Nigeria (Lee and Lockheed 1990). After controlling for student background, student attitudes, and teacher characteristics and practices, single-sex schools were found to have a positive effect for female students, but a negative effect for male students, with an effect size of approximately one tenth of a standard deviation in both cases.

3. Utility of Single-sex Education for Girls in Developing Countries

Women's education in developing countries is of interest to policymakers because of its important contribution to national economic development directly through increased productivity and indirectly through lowered fertility, increased child health and nutrition, and increased child school participation. In most developing countries, however, female participation in education lags well behind male participation, with fewer females than males entering, remaining in, or completing every level of schooling. The situation is most acute in the nonindustrialized countries of East Africa, South Asia, and Southern Europe. Moreover, female participation rates in the lowest income countries decline precipitously between primary and secondary educational levels. Explanations for this decline emphasize the role that female maturation, marriage, and anitcipated marriage plays in family decisions to remove girls from (largely coeducational) schooling. Single-sex secondary education, therefore, could not only facilitate female achievement, but could also promote greater female participation in schooling where the physical safety of adolescents is an issue.

4. Schooling Factors Affecting Participation

Previous policy research on female participation has touched on single-sex education only lightly. Instead, studies seeking to understand differences in male and female school participation rates have concentrated on household economic decision-making and the opportunity costs of child schooling, particularly in rural farm households. This research has emphasized: (a) the role that the demand for female child labor plays in determining school participation, and (b) the absence of anticipated returns to the family for investment in female education. Policy efforts to increase female school participation in developing countries have therefore sought to lower the direct and indirect costs to families. Projects have subsidized families' out-of-pocket expenses for such things as schools fees, uniforms, textbooks, and other materials, and have tried to reduce the opportunity costs incurred by loss of child labor by such strategies as changing the school calendar to coincide with agricultural schedules, modifying the designs of primary schools to include preschools where students' childcare responsibilities could be met, and building more schools—particularly girls' schools—located in closer proximity to children's homes.

Of these approaches, school availability has been most studied for impact. Policy interventions have not been designed to increase the particular within school factors which might be differentially more facilitating for girls, nor has school effects research in developing countries consciously searched for such factors. Instead, school effects research has focused on inputs having uniform effects on achievement of both girls and boys, and the issue of differentiating effects has been limited to identifying factors that increase female participation in school: the presence of a (female) school, distance to school, and school safety.

4.1 Presence of a School

The actual presence or availability of schools is, of course, a major determinant of whether or not a child attends school. For example, the presence of primary schools has been found to increase the probability of children's school attendance and to increase the number of years of attained schooling in Indonesia and Brazil. However, village-level school availability was found to have no effect on primary school participation in Nepal. In many developing countries, schooling is available for the overwhelming majority of primary school-age children, including girls. On the other hand, in 1983 there were still at least 30 countries in which fewer than 80 percent of the primary school-age population had access to primary school places, and over 35 countries for which this was the case for girls. At the secondary level, access is restricted for both girls and boys, with only 31 percent of children aged 12 to 17 enrolled in the lowest income countries.

4.2 Distance to School

The distance between the child's home and the nearest appropriate school is also an important factor for participation, and distance to school has been found to be negatively associated with female school enrollment in Egypt, Philippines, Nepal, and Thailand. In all cases, children residing further from school were less likely to enroll in school than children living closer to school. Once enrolled, children living further from school were more likely to drop out than children living closer. Finally, children living further from school completed fewer years of schooling than children living closer to school; this was found in studies in Egypt, Philippines, and Thailand, but not in Nepal, principally because distances were, on average, quite short.

4.3 Safety within Schools

While school availability is certainly important for participation, the safety of students—particularly girls—within schools is emerging as a determinant of participation. There is little empirical evidence regarding unsafe schools, but anecdotal evidence abounds. For example, Deble (1980 p. 89) notes that "many people still hesitate to trust the school where girls are concerned." Lycette (1986) cites a survey of rural households in India that found about one-fifth of girls were withdrawn from school at the onset of puberty, often because parents felt it was dangerous for an unmarried girl to appear in public. The danger is, not surprisingly, sexual in nature. For example, a study of factors affecting repetition and dropout in Papua New Guinea identified "rape and [sexual] coercion" as a major fear of parents about sending daughters to school. Furthermore, "about 75 percent of parents interviewed indicated a preference for sending their daughters to a mission school," since "mission schools generally provided closer supervision of both pupils and teachers, and more stringent punishment for misdemeanors—lessening the likelihood of sexual involvement" (Yeoman 1985 p. 24).

See also: Sex Differences and Educational Outcomes; Sex Differences in Behavior and Behavioral Development; Individual Differences and Instruction

References

Astin A W 1977 *Four Critical Years: Effects of College on Beliefs, Attitudes, and Knowledge*. Jossey-Bass, San Francisco, California

Deble I 1980 *The School Education of Girls*. UNESCO, Paris

Finn J D 1980 Sex differences in educational outcomes: A cross-national study. *Sex Roles* 6(1): 9–26

Furniss W T, Graham P A (eds.) 1974 *Women in Higher Education*. American Council on Education, Washington, DC

Graham P A 1970 Women in academe. *Science* 169(3952): 1284–90

Jimenez E, Lockheed M E 1989 Enhancing girls' learning through single-sex education: Evidence and a Policy Conundrum. *Educ Eval. Policy Anal.* 11(2): 117–42

Lee V E, Bryk A S 1986 Effects of single-sex secondary schools on student achievement and attitudes. *J. Educ. Psychol.* 78(5): 381–95

Lee V E, Lockheed M E 1990 The effects of single-sex schooling on student achievement and attitudes in Nigeria. *Comp. Educ. Rev.* 34(2): 209–31

Lycette M A 1986 *Improving Basic Educational Opportunities for Women in Developing Countries*. International Center for Research on Women, Washington, DC

Oates M J, Williamson S 1978 Women's colleges and women achievers. *Signs: J. Women Culture Soc.* 3(4): 795–806

Riordan C 1985 Public and Catholic schooling: The effects of gender context policy. *Am. J. Educ.* 93(4): 518–40

Tidball M E 1980 Women's colleges and women achievers revisited. *Signs: J. Women Culture Soc.* 5(3): 504–17

Tidball M E, Kistiakowsky V 1976 Baccalaureate origins of American scientists and scholars. *Science* 193(4254): 646–52

Yeoman L 1985 Universal primary education: Factors affecting enrolment and retention of girls in Papau New Guinea community schools. Paper presented at the UNESCO Regional Review Meeting, Bangkok

Further Reading

Carpenter P, Hayden M 1987 Girls' academic achievements: Single-sex versus coeducational schools in Australia. *Sociol. Educ.* 60(3): 156–67

Dale R R 1974 *Mixed or Single-sex School? Vol. III: Attainment, Attitudes and Overview*. Routledge and Kegan Paul, London

M. E. Lockheed; V. E. Lee

Cognition and Learning

What does it mean to know something? How do people use what they know? How do they learn it? Answers to these questions—central to a broadly defined field of cognitive research—will deeply influence choices about what is taught, how classrooms and other environments for learning are organized, and what is expected for educational institutions. This entry examines the implications of three major themes in cognitive theory. It begins with constructivism, a point of broad consensus among cognitive researchers with profound and still unresolved implications for what and how to teach. It turns next to recent conceptions of learning and cognitive change, considering especially how learning abilities arise, whether and how they can be taught. Finally, there is a discussion of the idea that thinking may need to be understood not just as an individual act but also as a process that is distributed among people and between people and tools.

1. Constructivist Dilemmas

Students of cognition generally agree on the *constructive* character of learning. The theoretical framing varies—from Piaget (1970) to Vygotsky (1978), from social discourse to schema theory, from symbolic processing to situated cognition—but virtually all concur that learners are the builders of their own knowledge. The implications of the constructivist turn for education are profound. Put most simply, teaching cannot be construed as putting information into students' heads. Rather it must be construed as arranging for students to construct knowledge for themselves.

For many years, particularly under the influence of Piagetian interpretations of cognitive development, constructivism was taken to mean that there should be no "didactic" teaching. Instead it was proposed that educators should arrange rich exploratory environments for children. In such environments, students would discover or invent knowledge for themselves. It is now known that arranging for students to construct their own knowledge is a far more complex matter, filled with challenges that derive from the nature of expertise and learning.

1.1 Thinking and Learning are Knowledge-dependent

Cognitive research has focused heavily on mapping the nature of problem-solving and the knowledge that supports it. From chess-playing to radiology, and in every school curriculum subject that has been researched, it has been discovered that good thinkers and problem-solvers possess large amounts of problem-specific knowledge (Glaser 1984). Experts call on that knowledge (more heavily than on general cognitive capabilities) to produce skilled, efficient performance. Nevertheless, it appears that educators cannot build expertise by having their students memorize experts' knowledge. Such a method of learning appears to produce "inert" knowledge, which is unlikely to be usable in complex performances. Instead, expert knowledge must be constructed by each individual.

But therein lies a dilemma, for what people are able to construct in the way of new knowledge is itself heavily dependent on what they already know. People need organizing schemas in order to understand and retain new information. The richer and more appropriate to the new knowledge these schemas are, the faster and more fully the new ideas will be assimilated. Research in several subject matters shows that students have substantial knowledge when they enter school, but that this knowledge is rarely built upon while they are there. Moreover, informally acquired knowledge is as likely to interfere with school learning (as in the case of scientific "misconceptions") as to enhance it. Recognition of this problem has begun to produce theory-driven experimentation on how to use and adapt to students' knowledge. Such research is necessarily subject-matter specific, and the way in which old and new knowledge interact apparently varies substantially among subjects and even specific concepts.

1.2 Expert Learners are Strategic Knowledge Constructors

Knowledge is undoubtedly more influential for future learning than "general learning skills." Nevertheless, successful learners also apply certain generic strategies more often and more effectively than those who are less successful (e.g., Chi et al. 1989). These strategies have been studied under many labels, all pointing to the importance of self-conscious management of one's own learning and thinking processes (e.g., Brown et al. 1983). A good deal is now known about what these strategies are, but very little about how to teach them effectively. Efforts to teach metacognitive skills and other deliberate learning strategies directly have been disappointing. The taught skills often do not "stick," are not applied independently by students, or take a brittle form that does not seem to enhance other learning, even when the new strategies themselves are performed to specification. A repeated finding is that strategies directly taught to students tend not to be spontaneously used under conditions different from those in which they were initially practiced.

1.3 Cognitive Equity: The "Rich Get Richer" Problem

Those already rich in knowledge and in school-valued learning strategies are most likely to benefit from the new opportunities for learning offered in school. Their informally acquired knowledge of concepts relevant to school subject matters gives them a head start on the formal curriculum. Their habits of language, questioning, and elaboration allow them to understand what is wanted and to engage easily in what school asks of them. As long as cognitive research focuses mainly on these "already rich" students, it will fail to provide a foundation for educating the diverse student bodies now in many schools.

Although there exists a long history in psychology of attending to *individual* differences in cognition, a new challenge for cognitive research is to attend to *cultural* differences in cognition. Substantial evidence indicates that some students' cultural knowledge and habits differ significantly from those expected at school and that these differences can limit their *de facto* opportunity to learn in school (Laboratory of Comparative Human Cognition 1983). Until now, however, those who have led the most influential cognitive research programs on school subject-matter learning generally have not attended to group and cultural differences in knowledge and learning; whereas those who have concentrated on such differences—coming often from anthropological, linguistic, and sociological rather than psychological research traditions—have not attended deeply to the content of learning or to the details of the cognitive processes involved. The result has been two largely independent bodies of research knowledge.

The two lines of research are now beginning to converge, most often in the context of instructional development programs in which researchers and teachers jointly assume responsibility for entire programs of teaching and learning (e.g., Brown and Campione 1990). One issue is how to develop general learning habits among students who do not bring them to school on their own: Is it by engaging students in metacognitive processes of analyzing school tasks to see where their own knowledge might apply? Is it by changing the classroom environment to provide a better match to students' out-of-school learning habits? Is self-attribution in learning important? How does it interact with specific forms of knowledge and learning strategy?

Another approach has concentrated on identifying the knowledge that apparently underprepared students do have. Some surprises are emerging. For example, research on the entering mathematics knowledge of various groups of poor children has shown they have most of the basic understanding that more favored students have. Furthermore, some instructional experiments suggest that, contrary to older theories in which prerequisites supposedly needed to be firmly in place before more complex problems were posed, it now seems possible to overcome weak preparation by engaging children in intellectually challenging problem-solving while providing supporting "scaffolding" (e.g., Resnick et al. 1992).

1.4 Knowledge Construction is Time-consuming

The personal mental elaboration necessary for successful learning takes time, much more time than is typically allowed for the study of any topic in the school curriculum. This means that efforts to "cover" an extensive body of knowledge are bound to fail to produce significant learning. In response to this understanding, several leading thinkers have been promoting a philosophy of "less is more." Their idea is that learning a few important ideas and concepts well is more educationally powerful than is a curriculum of extensive but superficial exposure. This has begun to engender a research agenda concerned with identifying powerful, generative concepts—the ones to include in the "less" curriculum—and with figuring out how to teach them so that they are, in fact, generative. This research on the generative curriculum is being pursued subject matter by subject matter, most often in collaborative teams that include cognitive researchers and subject matter experts.

2. Learning and Cognitive Change

From about 1960 to the mid-1980s, cognitive research was concerned primarily with the nature of knowledge and skill, and only peripherally with its acquisition. Cognitive science was, in other words, a science more of knowing than of learning. What was learned about the nature of knowing and about the differences between experts and novices has been extremely valuable in helping to map what is to be learned in ways that reflect the complexity of human thought. But that research did not show how people became expert, much less how others could help them do so, which is, of course, the central problem for education. For the most part, efforts to teach difficult concepts with more directness and clarity, or to train students in the metacognitive or problem-solving strategies that characterize expert thinking, have not worked. Students practiced what they were taught but did not seem to learn when or how to apply the new ideas or skills. On the other hand, in relatively unstructured "discovery" or "exposure" programs, the "rich get richer" phenomenon was encountered repeatedly: that is, initially strong students often prospered, but the weaker ones did not and sometimes even lost ground when compared with students taught in more traditional supervised practice and memorization approaches. None of this is surprising from the constructivist perspective. Nevertheless, it has been disappointing to find that studies on cognitive expertise did not translate directly into successful instruction.

In the second half of the 1980s, the earlier interest of a few cognitive scientists in learning processes began to spread to more of the cognitive research community. The new focus is on learning as cognitive change. There is little orthodoxy in the new cognitive learning research. Various approaches and methodologies are being developed. They range from intensive microgenetic analyses of individuals' conceptual learning to connectionist-inspired research on skill and knowledge change to analyses of biological constraints on conceptual development. Analytic and descriptive methods coexist with classical experiments. Various kinds of formal modeling—rule-based and connectionist—are used. Instructional interventions play a role as a research tool.

2.1 New Conceptions of Transfer

A century or so of research on transfer from school to out-of-school learning, or even between school subject matters, has produced disappointing results. There has not been much evidence that what is learned in one setting is spontaneously or easily "applied" in another. Some studies (e.g., Nisbett et al. 1987) suggest that a reconceptualization of the Thorndikian "common elements" theory of transfer to focus on higher level rules of reasoning, together with direct instruction in how to apply those rules in apparently disparate situations, may produce substantial generalization. An alternative view revives a neglected concept of transfer as a process of learning in specific domains rather than as a direct application of what has already been learned. In these interpretations (e.g., Brown 1990, Greeno et al. 1992, Resnick in press), the search is not for how knowledge or skill is transported "whole" from one setting to another, but for how learning and performance in one setting prepare one to learn the rules, habits, and knowledge appropriate to a new setting.

2.2 Intentional Learning and Habits of Mind

Although direct training of learning strategies has had limited success in actual practice, there is a broader conceptualization of learning strategies that, in early experiments, looks promising. According to this view, learning skill is construed as a set of habits: of questioning, of elaboration, of exerting deliberate personal effort to understand and to communicate to others. In this conception, emphasis on specific learning strategies gives way to a broad emphasis on putting the management of learning in the hands of learners themselves (e.g., Bereiter and Scardamalia 1989). There are several established research traditions that inform this conception: personality theories suggest that self-concepts are at stake; social psychology offers elaborated theories of attribution by which people explain success and failure and thereby direct their future energies; child development tells us how children are socialized into characteristic roles and ways of behaving. The suggestion is that cognitive habits and ways of behaving might be shaped in ways that are analogous to the ways in which other personal traits are developed. This conception is engendering research on how to create environments for learning that will promote the habits of active mental elaboration and self-management associated with effective learning.

3. Distributed Cognition

Cognitive research has begun to move out of the laboratory and toward a concern with more naturalistic learning environments. Cognitive scientists are beginning to study learning in all kinds of situations, from the workplace to sports teams to museums and scouting groups. This research carries forward many elements of older traditions of human factors research, but it is much broader in scope and orientation, including ethnographic, ethnomethodological, and cultural psychology traditions. A theory of cognitive situations is beginning to emerge that takes the *distributed* nature of cognition as a starting point (Brown et al. 1989, Pea 1993, Resnick 1987). In these theories, cognition is assumed to be shared both with other individuals and with tools and artifacts. This means that thinking is situated in a particular context of intentions, social partners, and tools.

3.1 Tools and Artifacts as Partners in Cognitive Activity

Studies of cognitive performance in complex work situations show that thinking is both enabled and constrained by tools and artifacts that share the load with human beings. In navigation, for example, measuring instruments, charts and graphs, and specialized computational tools embody some of the knowledge that is needed for deciding where to steer a ship. These tools extend human intelligence, enabling people to perceive and think in ways they could not manage unassisted. At the same time, the tools constrain thinking, forcing performances that accord with the theories of measurement that are built into the tools. Not only physical tools but also culturally established conventions for reasoning, such as those built into the practice of science and scientific reporting, function both to extend human cognitive capacity and to limit individuals' likelihood of imagining solutions that fall far outside the norms of a profession.

3.2 Social Partners in Cognition

Cognition also can be socially distributed, that is, shared across several individuals (Levine et al. 1993, Resnick et al. 1991). Two aspects of socially distributed cognition are of great potential significance for instruction and teaching. The first is learning via interaction: the idea that learning is a matter of internalizing processes initially practiced in interaction with others. This formulation is derived from Vygotsky (1978) and from Mead (1967). It suggests that interacting with others—for example, to solve a mathematics problem, to manage a complex piece of machinery, or to read and interpret a text—is the foundation for eventually being able to perform these tasks on one's own. This suggests that a crucial part of the educator's job is carefully to design interactions that promote the internalization of particular strategies, forms of reasoning, and conceptual stances (Rogoff 1990).

The second theme of importance to education is learning to interact. Outside the classroom, most intellectual work is done in direct interaction with others. In these situations—on the job, in civic life, inside families—one's cognitive competence is judged not only by what one knows, but also by how smoothly one uses this knowledge in joint activity with others. Employers increasingly count on schools to develop these cognitive interaction competencies in students. A new community of scholars with diverse backgrounds—in cognitive science, social psychology, linguistics, anthropology, and sociology—is beginning to assemble a body of data and theory on shared discourse and interactive cognition. A feature of this work is the attention paid to cultural variations in discourse and cognition, variations influenced both by the organizations and institutions in which people function and by the personal and familial habits of interaction that individuals bring with them.

See also: Constructivism and Learning; Expert Level of Understanding; Culture and Learning; Learning Environments; Metacognition; Transfer of Learning; Cognitive Development: Overview; Cognitive Development: Information-processing Approach; Cognitive Styles and Learning

References

Bereiter C, Scardamalia M 1989 Intentional learning as a goal of instruction. In: Resnick L B (ed.) 1989 *Knowing, Learning, and Instruction: Essays in Honor of Robert Glaser.* Erlbaum, Hillsdale, New Jersey

Brown A L 1990 Domain-specific principles affect learning and transfer in children. *Cognit. Sci.* 14(1): 107–33

Brown A L, Bransford J D, Ferrara R A, Campione J C 1983 Learning, remembering, and understanding. In: Flavell J H, Markman E M (eds.) 1983 *Mussen's Handbook of Child Psychology*, 4th edn., Vol. 3 . Wiley, New York

Brown A L, Campione J C 1990 Communities of learning and thinking, or a context by any other name. *Contributions to Human Development* 21:108–26

Brown J S, Collins A, Duguid P 1989 Situated cognition and the culture of learning. *Educ. Researcher* 18(1):32–42

Chi M T H, Bassok M, Lewis M W, Reimann P, Glaser R 1989 Self-explanations: How students study and use examples in learning to solve problems. *Cognit. Sci.* 13:(2)145–82

Glaser R 1984 Education and thinking: The role of knowledge. *Am. Psychol.* 39(2): 93–104

Greeno J G, Smith D R, Moore J L 1992 Transfer of situated learning. In: Detterman D, Sternberg R J (eds.) 1992 *Transfer on Trial: Intelligence, Cognition, and Instruction.* Ablex, Norwood, New Jersey

Laboratory of Comparative Human Cognition 1983 Culture and cognitive development. In: Kessen W (ed.) 1983 *Mussen's Handbook of Child Psychology*, 4th edn., Vol. 1. Wiley, New York

Levine J M, Resnick L B, Higgins E T 1993 Social foundations of cognition. *Annu. Rev. Psychol.* 44:585–612

Mead G H 1967 *Mind, Self, and Society from the Standpoint of a Social Behaviorist.* University of Chicago Press, Chicago, Illinois

Nisbett R E, Fong G T, Lehman D R, Cheng P W 1987 Teaching reasoning. *Science* 238: 625–31

Pea R W 1993 Practices of distributed intelligence and designs for education. In: Salomon G (ed.) 1993 *Distributed Cognitions: Psychological and Educational Considerations.* Cambridge University Press, New York

Piaget J 1970 *L'epistemologie genetique.* Presses Universitaires de France, Paris

Resnick L B 1987 The 1987 Presidential Address: Learning in school and out. *Educ. Researcher* 16(9): 13–20

Resnick L B in press Situated rationalism: Biological and social preparation for learning. In: Hirschfeld L, Gelman S (eds.) in press *Cultural Knowledge and Domain Specificity.* Cambridge University Press, Cambridge

Resnick L B, Bill V, Lesgold S 1992 Developing thinking abilities in arithmetic class. In: Demetriou A, Shayer M, Efklides A (eds.) 1992 *Neo-Piagetian Theories of Cognitive Development: Implications and Applications for Education.* Routledge, London

Resnick L B, Levine J M, Teasley S D (eds.) 1991 *Perspectives on Socially Shared Cognition.* American Psychological Association, Washington, DC

Rogoff B 1990 *Apprenticeship in Thinking: Cognitive Development in Social Context.* Oxford University Press, New York

Vygotsky L S 1978 *Mind in Society: The Development of Higher Psychological Processes.* Harvard University Press, Cambridge, Massachusetts

L. B. Resnick; A. Collins

Cognitive Development and the Acquisition of Expertise

Are children less competent than adults in the abilities of thinking and problem-solving primarily because they lack rich experience and knowledge, or primarily because their basic processes of storing and retrieving information and/or general problem-solving and reasoning skills are inferior? Are cognitive differences between adults and children similar to expert–novice differences? Is the process of cognitive development analogous to that of gaining expertise? To address these questions, this entry, after briefly reviewing research on expertise, examines the relationship between cognitive development and the acquisition of expertise, and attempts to derive a few educational implications.

1. Research on Expertise

Typical studies on expertise follow three steps: (a) identifying experts who reveal outstanding performance on a criterion task; (b) analyzing how they perform on a set of variants of the criterion task, often in comparison with novices or intermediates; and (c) proposing and examining learning mechanisms for their performances. The first step can easily be implemented in any domain where an external system of evaluation or qualification exists. For example, expert chess or tennis players can be identified by their success at tournaments, or by the high ratings they attain through an acknowledged organization of players. Experts can also be identified by their outstanding performance on an experimental task that has been administered to a large number of people, as in the case of memory experts (e.g., how many digits can be repeated immediately after presentation). Yet another method is to select experts according to their status (e.g., to accept university professors in physics as experts in physics).

The second step involves using outcome measures such as the percentage correct for solving different kinds of tasks or the time needed for solution. Ideally, in order to help provide exact characterizations of experts' strength, some of the variant tasks should reveal marked differences between experts and novices or intermediates, whereas others should show only negligible or even reversed differences. An early successful example of this is provided by Chase and Simon (1973), who demonstrated that the more accurately certain chessboard positions (taken from actual games and presented for a short period of time) were recalled the greater the expertise of the player, although the difference disappeared for random board positions. Even stronger evidence for the effect of expertise on the memory of relevant pieces of information was obtained by Chi's (1978) study which showed better memory of board positions by children already experienced in playing chess, who averaged 10 years of age, than by novice graduate students.

Outcome measures are not sufficient to illuminate the cognitive processes involved in experts' task performance. Therefore, protocol analysis (typically of subjects' utterances while performing the task under instructions of "thinking aloud") is often undertaken in this step. Through the use of protocol analysis, De Groot's (1965) pioneering work showed that chess masters could pick out good candidate moves without extensive search. Other verbal techniques (e.g., asking for justifications) and nonverbal techniques (e.g., classification, solving the target task with an additional task or constraint) are also used.

The third step is to give an explanation for the outstanding performance of experts in terms of acquisition or learning. As with expertise in the real world, most studies can only propose models of gaining expertise from the comparison of subjects differing in the extent of mastery, because observing the actual process involved takes a long time. Many such explanations take the formation of chunks, namely, higher-order units that often serve as conditions for specific actions as critical. Perceptual chunks allow chess experts to choose a good move without extensive search. Similar but more abstract problem schemas enable physics experts to solve a variety of physics problems without relying on weak heuristics. As for expertise in the laboratory, in very small, artificial domains like digit memory or the Tower of Hanoi puzzle, proposed mechanisms can be examined by the observation and fine-grained analysis of the process of gaining expertise, for example, by describing how a rich repertoire of strategies is accumulated (Anzai 1987).

An important contribution to the understanding of human competence presented by investigators of expertise is the innovative view of individual differences (e.g., Chi et al. 1982). These researchers attribute the outstanding performance of experts primarily to what has been acquired, that is, to a well-organized body of domain-specific knowledge and skill, rather than IQ or genetically given talents. Another contribution is their demonstration that knowledge acquisition and problem-solving are mutually facilitative, that is, knowledge acquired through problem-solving tends to enhance later problem-solving.

However, it must be pointed out that there are inadequacies in studies on expertise undertaken thus far: They have failed to consider sociocultural contexts of gaining expertise (Brown et al. 1989); have ignored qualitative changes in the acquisition process, treating expertise as if it were linearly incremental (Carey 1985); and have often neglected the fact that there are different courses of expertise as well as different types of experts (Hatano and Inagaki 1986).

2. Commonalities and Differences Between Cognitive Development and Gaining Expertise

Is the process of acquiring expertise described above similar to that of cognitive development? Are studies on expertise informative for investigators of cognitive development? Answers to these questions vary even among leading cognitive developmentalists. Some give affirmative answers and argue that developmental or adult–child differences are similar to expert–novice differences, because children are "universal novices" (e.g., Brown and DeLoache 1978). This implies that adults and children differ primarily in the amount of their knowledge; in other words, what develops is domain-specific knowledge. Moreover, they take the acquisition of knowledge through repeated experiences of problem-solving as most important in cognitive development.

Others offer negative answers. They assert that the characterization of the child in this way oversimplifies what develops (Keil 1989), and hence that many models of novice–experts shifts have little relevance for cognitive development.

The two research traditions, one on expertise and the other on cognitive development, started with studies of very different sorts of phenomena (playing chess in the former and solving problems of a logicomathematical nature in the latter), and therefore their typical studies have been very different. Moreover, the process of cognitive development surely involves something more than the acquisition of expertise in narrow and artificial domains like chess. However, it can still be asserted that the process of cognitive development is similar to that of gaining expertise, and that theories as well as data on expertise are informative for understanding cognitive development for the following reasons: (a) both processes are conceptualized primarily in terms of the acquisition of knowledge available in the society; and (b) some similar phenomena, for example, the acquisition of naive theories, have recently been studied in the two streams. The differences between them lie in their characterizations of the acquisition of knowledge, and are often matters of emphasis on one point over another.

Below, five frequently mentioned characterizations of knowledge acquisitions are offered. For each, it will be investigated whether and how these characteristics are shared by accounts of the processes of gaining expertise and of cognitive development; that is, the extent to which adult novices and children acquire a body of knowledge in similar ways.

2.1 Knowledge is Constructed

Human beings are active agents in information processing and action, and often construct knowledge as a by-product of their problem-solving or comprehension activity. However, the claim that knowledge is acquired by construction does not deny that knowledge is to some extent transmitted, as in the case of a recipe or a manual of instructions. Because the transmission of knowledge usually relies on verbal communication, adult novices seem to acquire knowledge by transmission, whereas children almost always do so by construction.

However, transmission cannot be perfect, because human language is able to describe only part of the target knowledge, involves some ambiguity, and allows for different interpretations, especially when the sender and receiver do not share much common knowledge. More importantly, active agents, whether adults or children, often try to interpret and enrich what is transmitted, that is, to supplement it by construction. Therefore the difference between adult novices and children with regard to the construction of knowledge is a matter of degree; they do not seem qualitatively or fundamentally different.

2.2 Knowledge Acquisition Involves Restructuring

The process of knowledge acquisition involves restructuring as well as enrichment. Studies on cognitive development have been concerned with conceptual change, a radical form of restructuring, and have found that some of the concepts found in children cannot readily be translated into adult "vocabulary" (Carey 1988). In contrast, studies on expertise have demonstrated that knowledge becomes richer and better organized as students gain expertise, but have often neglected restructuring or reorganization of knowledge.

However, in principle, reorganization of knowledge may take place in adults as they go through the process of gaining expertise. For example, constituent pieces of knowledge, and/or concepts included, may change (e.g., naive misconceptions may be replaced by scientific conceptions). Thus differences between cognitive development and expertise are more apparent than real with regard to restructuring of knowledge.

2.3 Process of Knowledge Acquisition is Constrained

Knowledge acquisition can concisely be described as the process of constructing and reorganizing knowledge under a variety of constraints. Here the term "constraints" refers to conditions that facilitate the process of acquisition as well as restrict its possible range. The process of knowledge construction and restructuring is constrained both internally (by cognitive constraints) and externally (by sociocultural constraints). The former includes innate tendencies and acquired pieces of knowledge. Young children are more competent than previously believed (Gelman 1979), because, due to innate constraints, they can learn quickly and solve problems in several specific areas, for example, naive physics, psychology, and biology (Wellman and Gelman 1992). In addition, children exhibit more advanced modes of reasoning in a domain where they possess fairly rich acquired knowledge and can use it. Domain-specific knowledge can help problem-solvers to represent aptly a given problem so that they can readily handle it.

Although those who investigate expertise emphasize the role of acquired knowledge, and those who investigate cognitive development take innate tendencies to be more critical, it can reasonably be assumed that both types of internal constraints apply to both expertise and cognitive development. In other words, the two processes do not seem very different in terms of cognitive constraints.

Sociocultural constraints can be divided into cultural constraints such as shared artifacts (e.g., tools, social organizations, symbols, beliefs) and social constraints such as behavior of other people, interactions with them, and social contexts created by them. These constraints serve to eliminate a great number of possible hypotheses and interpretations in advance, so that it is usually easy for people, including children, to find what they should do in everyday situations.

2.4 Knowledge Acquisition is Usually Domain-specific

Recent cognitive studies have demonstrated that individual competence varies considerably from domain to domain. Investigators of expertise, as pointed out above, have asserted that the most critical determinant of problem-solving competence is not general intelligence but the relevant domain-specific knowledge and also that people accumulate knowledge only in the domain within which they solve problems repeatedly. In research on cognitive development, Piaget's stage theory, which assumed that subject's competence depended on their logicomathematical structures applicable across domains, has been challenged or even rejected by many investigators. Thus investigators in the two research streams apparently agree that knowledge is usually acquired separately for each domain.

However, there exist a few differences in interpreting this characterization. First, the notion of domain is not the same in the two traditions: whereas it denotes a narrow, often artificially defined range of an activity in the expertise tradition, in the cognitive development tradition it typically refers to a body of knowledge representing some aspect of the world. Second, the expertise tradition emphasizes the self-contained nature of a domain, whereas the cognitive development tradition supposes that analogical transfer of knowledge or skill across domains is not only possible but also occurs quite often. Third, cognitive developmentalists stress that some domain-general skills (e.g., literacy and measurement or quantification as well as general reasoning and metacognitive skills) are used in the acquisition of domain-specific knowledge, and that adult novices and children differ markedly in their repertoire of domain-general skills and in how promptly they can retrieve them. Fourth, many cognitive developmentalists believe that the course and process of development vary from domain to domain, because each domain is expected to embody a different set of innate constraints (Carey and Gelman, 1991). These differences between the two research streams probably reflect the corresponding differences between adult novices and children.

2.5 Knowledge Acquisition is Situated in Contexts

Human knowledge acquisition is conceptualized as a process of representing experiences with an object, event, conceptual entity, or the like, so that the resulting representation (i.e., knowledge) can readily be used in future problem-solving and understanding. As such, it is situated in and influenced by various features of contexts. Acquired knowledge is also situated in the sense that it reflects the history of its acquisition and use, including associations with contexts. Although textbooks of a given domain summarize a body of knowledge as a set of propositions, the knowledge which individuals "possess" in their heads includes representations of a more personal, concrete nature.

However, as humans gain expertise, knowledge underlying their performances becomes decontextualized (or "desituated") in the sense that it is no longer inextricably associated with the situation in which it was originally acquired. The problem-solving competence of experts is no longer context-bound in the same sense as that of novices; they are able to achieve their goals across contexts, and to solve various novel problems in the domain.

A debatable point here is whether cognition and knowledge of an adult who is a local novice and those of a child who is a universal novice are situated to the same extent. Adults may have an advantage in this point because of their more efficient and solid basic processes, for example, ability to verbalize and grasp rules more firmly, larger working memory capacity, and proficiency in performing operations.

3. Educational Implications

The implications for educating children that can be derived from the preceding discussion are summarized below:

(a) If cognitive development is taken as a form of acquisition of expertise, it suggests the possibility of a more flexible choice of subject-matter content. Educators can choose any content insofar as children are deeply involved in it and recognize the significance of learning it. This is because theories of expertise do not give priority to the age of students (or the total amount of general experience, logicomathematical structure, or anything that is closely correlated with age), and assume that learning becomes easier, irrespective of age, as students accumulate relevant pieces of knowledge, which work as internal constraints.

(b) If cognitive development is approximated by the acquisition of expertise, this suggests that educators use students' prior knowledge as a constraint. Although the body of their acquired domain-specific knowledge is internal and not directly subject to educators' control, modifying it prior to the target lesson is often not too difficult. Theories of expertise indicate that acquired rich and well-organized knowledge in a specific domain enables students both to acquire new pieces of knowledge easily and to reason in advanced modes.

(c) Although the view of cognitive development which regards it as the acquisition of expertise has advantages such as those mentioned above, educators should pay due attention to those aspects of cognitive development that cannot be grasped by expert–novice shift models. For example, they should consider what students possess prior to formal instruction, more specifically, their informal knowledge that may be used as a source for analogical learning of school subjects, and weak heuristics that can be relied on in the beginning phases of instructed learning. Children's competence should not be underrated, as suggested by investigators of expertise, but neither should the magnitude of labor and time needed for cognitive growth be underestimated.

See also: Cognitive Development: Overview; Cognitive Development: Information-processing Approach; Cognitive Styles and Learning

References

Anzai Y 1987 Doing, understanding, and learning in problem solving. In: Klahr D, Langley P, Neches R (eds.) 1987 *Production System Models of Learning and Development*. MIT Press, Cambridge, Massachusetts

Brown A L, DeLoache J S 1978 Skills, plans and self-regulation. In: Siegler R S (ed.) 1978 *Children's Thinking: What Develops?* Erlbaum, Hillsdale, New Jersey

Brown J S, Collins A, Duguid P 1989 Situated cognition and the culture of learning. *Educ. Researcher* 18: 32–42

Carey S 1985 *Conceptual Change in Childhood*. MIT Press, Cambridge, Massachusetts

Carey S 1988 Conceptual differences between children and adults. *Mind and Language* 3: 167–81

Carey S, Gelman R (eds.) 1991 *The Epigenesis of Mind: Essays on Biology and Cognition*. Erlbaum, Hillsdale, New Jersey

Chase W G, Simon H A 1973 The mind's eye in chess. In: Chase W G (ed.) 1973 *Visual Information Processing*. Academic Press, New York

Chi M T H 1978 Knowledge structures and memory development. In: Siegler R S (ed.) 1978 *Children's Thinking: What Develops?* Erlbaum, Hillsdale, New Jersey

Chi M T H, Glaser R, Rees E 1982 Expertise in problem solving. In: Sternberg R (ed.) 1982 *Advances in the Psychology of Human Intelligence*, Vol. 1. Erlbaum, Hillsdale, New Jersey

De Groot A D 1965 *Thought and Choice in Chess*. Mouton, The Hague

Gelman R 1979 Preschool thought. *Am. Psychol.* 34(10): 900–05

Hatano G, Inagaki K 1986 Two courses of expertise. In: Stevenson H, Azuma H, Hakuta K (eds.) 1986 *Child Development and Education in Japan*. Freeman, New York

Keil F C 1989 *Concepts, Kinds, and Cognitive Development*. MIT Press, Cambridge, Massachusetts

Wellman H M, Gelman S A 1992 Cognitive development: Foundational theories of core domains. *Annu. Rev. Psychol.* 43: 337–75

Further Reading

Chi M T H, Glaser R, Farr M J (eds.) 1988 *The Nature of Expertise*. Erlbaum, Hillsdale, New Jersey

Ericsson K A, Smith J (eds.) 1991 *Toward a General Theory of Expertise: Prospects and Limits*. Cambridge University Press, Cambridge

Osherson D N, Smith E E (eds.) 1990 *An Invitation to Cognitive Science. Vol. 3: Thinking*. MIT Press, Cambridge, Massachusetts

G. Hatano

Cognitive Development: Individual Differences

Mainstream cognitive development research is based on a universalistic model of the ontogenesis of mental abilities and intellectual competencies. It is assumed "that cognitive changes during childhood have a specific set of formal 'morphogenetic' properties that presumably stem from the biological–maturational growth process underlying these changes. Thus, childhood cognitive modifications are largely inevitable, momentous, directional, uniform, and irreversible." (Flavell 1970 p. 247).

Consistent with this conceptual orientation, most theories of cognitive development can be characterized by four typical features. Specifically, more or less similar to the Piagetian approach, these theories are:

(a) universal: theories intended as valid for all humans,

(b) general: theories addressed, in principle, to the development of all cognitive functions and phenomena,

(c) structural: theories that, in principle, pertain only to changes in basic cognitive competencies and generally ignore the acquisition of knowledge and skills that can or must be learned as a consequence of attaining a particular developmental level, and

(d) naturalistic–descriptive: theories that attempt to encompass those developmental processes that cannot be produced by environmental conditions, although they can be modified.

The dominance of universal and general theories of development since the scientific beginnings of developmental psychology in the nineteenth century has led to a persistent lack of descriptions and explanations of individual differences in cognitive development. Although intra- and interindividual differences in cognitive development have been addressed in educationally directed research since the scientific beginnings of psychology, they have generally played a marginal role in theory construction. This one-sided orientation is also one important reason why developmental psychology has been less important for educational theory and practice than it could be, given its scientific potential.

The situation is changing in dramatic ways. Comprehensive and diverse efforts to study both universal changes and individual differences systematically began only in the 1970s. Nonetheless,

> the research evidence is clear: many studies have documented that cognitive development demonstrates some general stage-like properties and some consistency across domains. At the same time, research also shows that environmental and organismic factors have powerful effects on levels, and individual differences in development seem to be common. Different children show different developmental patterns as a function of both environmental and organismic factors. (Fischer and Silvern 1985 p. 624)

Different approaches for conceptualizing individual differences in cognitive development are described below, followed by a brief review of the influence of genetic and environmental factors on the emergence, stability, and change in cognitive differences. Finally, some conclusions concerning the necessity of matching instruction to individual differences in cognitive development will be drawn.

1. Conceptualization of Individual Differences in Cognitive Development

If one observes a large number of children over a long enough period of time, several types of differences in cognitive dispositions and performances can be ascertained.

First, there are some developmental differences that are not stable. For example, particular linguistic competence criteria are achieved by some young children sooner than others, but these differences do not necessarily have an effect on later language achievement in childhood or adulthood (individual differences in developmental rate).

Second, one can observe individual differences in intellectual abilities in early and middle childhood (e.g., in nonverbal reasoning, inductive and deductive thinking, spatial reasoning) that remain relatively stable over long periods of life and that can only marginally be influenced by variations in education or by intensive training (stable individual differences in cognitive capabilities).

Third, there are great individual differences in knowledge and skills among children, adolescents, and adults with comparable intellectual abilities. For example, whereas some individuals have specialized expertise in chess, others have equally good knowledge of biology, and yet others have exceptional computer skills. These differences, and changes in such differences throughout life, are primarily dependent on the quantity and quality of content-specific learning (individual differences in domain-specific knowledge).

1.1 Individual Differences in Developmental Rate

The empirical fact that the cognitive development of individuals can be faster or slower than the mean development of their age group is common knowledge, and has been replicated in countless scientific studies. Motor development in infancy, language development in early childhood, and logical thinking in schoolchildren are well-known examples.

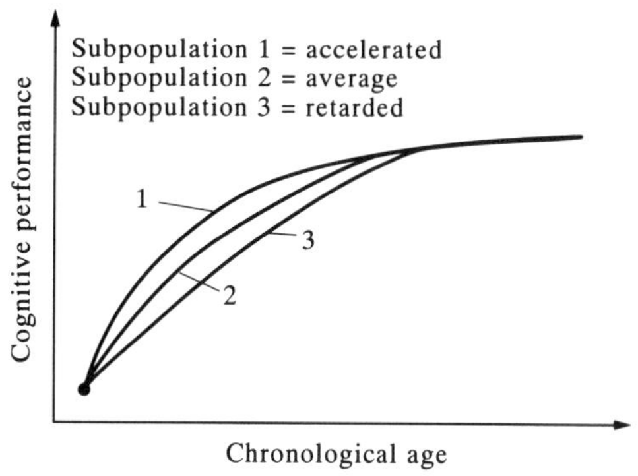

Figure 1
Rate differences in cognitive development with no predictive value

What is scientifically interesting is not so much the existence of such phenomena, but rather the question of the causes, stability, and long-term consequences of individual variability in developmental rate. However, the theory-based knowledge about causes, stability, and consequences of such differences still remains unsatisfactory.

Nonetheless there is sufficient empirical evidence to suggest that genetic (e.g., from mentally retarded and gifted populations), organismic (e.g., prematurity), and environmental conditions (e.g., severe sensory deprivation) can have considerable influence on the emergence and stability of developmental differences. When a developmental difference is classified according to the extent to which it deviates from the norm, its persistence, and its long-term consequences, it is possible to differentiate two types of differences in developmental rate.

The first type includes variations in the rate at which particular competencies and performances are attained that are more or less specific, within the range of broadly defined population norms, and not predictive of later cognitive development. As is seen in Fig. 1, for example, moderate interindividual age differences in the acquisition of particular motor, linguistic, and intellectual skills can be observed, but they are not correlated with later performance differences in these individuals. Compensatory education for this type of retarded development is thus not necessary.

A particular variant of such nonpredictive, unstable developmental differences are those that Piaget called horizontal *décalages* in his stage model of cognitive development. This refers to the fact that

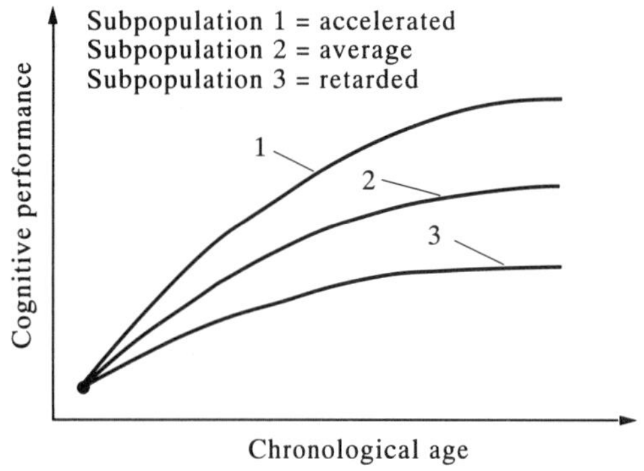

Figure 2
Rate differences in cognitive development with predictive value

children often display a cognitive operation of a lower structural level in unfamiliar contexts, although they have acquired the general competence of a higher level. In other words, "cognitive structures are consolidated and integrated through generalized use. The entire cognitive system is consequently distinguished by increasing invariability and stability" (Edelstein et al. 1990 p. 528). Temporary intra-individual variability in cognitive performance level thus has no special significance. However, despite Piaget's skepticism concerning attempts to systematically facilitate development through instruction, practice with variable content-related contexts designed to overcome horizontal *décalage* in the structural level of cognitive development nonetheless seems effective and useful (Aebli 1970).

The second type of variations in the rate at which particular competence and performance criteria can be achieved are severe, more or less general, and are predictive of later cognitive development (see Fig. 2).

For differences in developmental rate that lie outside of broadly defined population norms (means above or below two standard deviations) and that concern more general cognitive functions (e.g., intellectual abilities, severe language disorders), it must be assumed that there is a significant correlation between the developmental tempo and the maximum achievable developmental level. This means that early and massive delays in cognitive development frequently indicate large and persistent handicaps in cognitive competencies and, complementarily, that early and massive accelerations in cognitive development frequently indicate giftedness with related educational opportunities. There are empirical suggestions that both very delayed and very accelerated developmental rates reflect not only quantitative differences, but usually also qualitative differences in the development of information processing capabilities. This has been shown both for mentally retarded (Weiss et al. 1986) and for highly gifted individuals (Waldmann and Weinert 1990).

As noted above, despite some similarities in their behavioral manifestations, the two types of differences in developmental rate are fundamentally different. Whereas the first type primarily refers to transitory acceleration or retardation within a "normal" developmental range, the second type refers to developmental differences that are early and significant indicators of stable individual differences in cognitive abilities.

1.2 Individual Differences in Cognitive Capabilities

Since Binet and Simon's (1905) pioneering work, it has been assumed that the rate of intellectual development in childhood allows a valid prognosis of adult intelligence. This hypothesis has been generally supported from the eighth year of life by the demonstration of an increase in the stability of performance differences on unfamiliar and complex intelligence test tasks with increasing chronological age. This has provided an important theoretical basis for the psychometric approach to the differential description of cognitive development and for the construction of intelligence tests for children.

Originally the measure used to characterize the level of intellectual development was "mental age." This was based on the observation that intelligence test performance regularly improved over childhood and adolescence. One can determine the mean standardized intellectual performance level achieved at each age level, and use this empirical norm to judge whether an individual is accelerated, retarded, or normal in development. In the last case, chronological age and mental age are identical.

Although this measurement technique was adopted and used with enthusiasm in Europe and North America, it was also criticized. For example, a delay or acceleration of two mental age years in a 4-year old clearly means something completely different from the same delay or acceleration in a 10-year old. Stern (1911) therefore proposed the intelligence quotient (IQ) as a relatively stable measurement. This measure has been primarily calculated by dividing the mental age by chronological age and multiplying the result by 100. An individual with an age-typical intelligence level would thus have an IQ of 100. The range of interindividual variability in developmental and ability differences is from about 40 to 160; IQs under 70 are frequently interpreted as an indication of mental retardation and IQs over 130 are frequently interpreted as an indication of giftedness.

Throughout the twentieth century, the methods for measuring intelligence have been greatly improved, the reliability of the testing procedure has increased, and the underlying psychological and statistical models have become extremely sophisticated. Psychometric methods are presently useful tools for measuring individual differences in intellectual development and cognitive abilities, despite continuing theoretical and pragmatic critiques, some of which are justified, and some not.

It is important to note that although the intelligence quotient is very useful, it is in principle a highly aggregated and global measure of intellectual ability that reflects a variety of abilities, knowledge, and skills. More specifically, as both everyday experience and many empirical studies have shown, the IQ masks intra-individual differences in cognitive abilities. This shortcoming has led to the development of models of multiple intelligence. For example, Thurstone (1938) differentiated the following types of primary mental abilities that are relatively independent in strength: verbal understanding, verbal fluency, memory, inductive and deductive reasoning, spatial visualization, and mathematical aptitudes. Similar classifications of cognitive abilities are also included in more modern theories of intelligence (Sternberg 1985).

1.3 Individual Differences in Content-specific Knowledge

The focus on the study of cognitive functions and formal skills in the psychometric approach led to a preference for tests that can be solved with a combination of everyday knowledge and logical reasoning. This meant that the importance of content-specific knowledge for the quality of intellectual performance was not considered in developmental and differential psychology. This began to change in the 1970s because of input from cognitive psychology. Investigations of behavior and performance on difficult tasks from different content areas (e.g., chess, physics, medicine, social sciences) showed that high intellectual ability cannot compensate for a lack of content-specific knowledge. This knowledge refers not only to the amount of information about a specific content area, but also to its organization (e.g., unorganized vs. hierarchically organized), its mental representation (e.g., iconic, verbal-declarative, procedural) and its accessibility across situational variations.

The extraordinary importance of content-specific knowledge for productive thinking has been especially vividly demonstrated by the expert–novice paradigm. If one compares people similar in intelligence but differing in content-specific knowledge on problem-solving tasks, those who possess extensive knowledge (experts) outperform novices in all regards (Ericsson and Crutcher 1990). Superior performance by experts is only found for tasks for which content-specific knowledge is available and necessary. For example, chess masters show extraordinarily good memory for complex chess configurations, but show only average performance for random chess configurations or for material irrelevant to chess knowledge.

The expert–novice paradigm has also been successfully applied in developmental studies (Carey 1984, Chi 1978). It has been shown that the typical performance superiority of older versus younger children arises not only from their advanced cognitive developmental level, but is also related to age-typical differences in knowledge. For example, if a comparison is made of the performance of younger experts and older novices, the younger children with more expert knowledge show superior performance. Although children acquire a large storehouse of culturally and socially shared knowledge over the course of development, there are nonetheless relatively early intra- and interindividual differences in content-specific knowledge that increase with increasing age, and that contribute significantly to variations in cognitive performance.

2. Determinants of Individual Differences in the Development of Cognitive Competencies

The relative contribution of inherited factors and environmental conditions to the development of individual differences in cognitive abilities is a controversial theme in scientific psychology. Nevertheless, a review of the results from studies of identical twins and adopted children leads to the relatively unambiguous inference that at least half or somewhat more of the variance in IQ in industrial countries is determined by genetic differences. Such a statement of course also means that close to half of the variance in IQ is not genetically determined (Plomin 1990). This conclusion has frequently led to misunderstanding and false interpretations in public opinion. Bouchard and his colleagues have phrased the fundamental problem in the following way:

> The proximal cause of most psychological variance probably involves learning through experience, just as radical environmentalists have always believed. The effective experiences, however, to an important extent are self-selected, and that selection is guided by the steady pressure of the genome (a more distal cause) (Bouchard et al. 1990 p. 227).

The genetic determination of cognitive competencies is larger for variations in IQ and primary mental abilities than for interindividual differences in knowledge, skills, and school achievement (Plomin 1990, Scarr 1992). However, this does not mean that all students can acquire the same quantity and quality of knowledge, given that they are equally motivated and invest the necessary time in learning. Although many social scientists appear to believe in such an educational utopia (Ericsson and Crutcher 1990), empirical studies show that: (a) more intelligent students can acquire and process more new information than less intelligent students, even with equivalent prerequisite knowledge; (b) students with higher learning prerequisites achieve better performance outcomes with the same learning time, or require less learning time to achieve the same performance outcomes (Slavin 1987); and (c) there are greater possibilities for compensating for lower abilities (above a minimal threshold) by increased learning effort in the acquisition of knowledge and skills than in the acquisition of formal cognitive operations (Blagg 1991).

In addition to genetic differences, environmental conditions also play a substantial role in the emergence of and change in individual differences in cognitive development. Important environmental conditions are the influence of the cultural–historical context, the family, the school (Weinert 1989), and work-related activities. In contrast to many skeptical claims, recent studies show that the school plays an especially important role in the development of cognitive competencies and in the emergence of individual differences:

> Of course, schooling is not the complete story in the formation and maintenance of IQ-scores and IQ-related cognitive processes. . . .. Children differ in IQ and cognitive processes prior to entering school, and within a given classroom there are sizeable individual differences despite an equivalence of schooling. . . Thus, the conclusion seems fairly clear: Even though many factors are responsible for individual and group differences in the intellectual development of children, schooling emerges as an extremely important source of variance, notwithstanding historical and contemporary claims to the contrary. (Ceci 1991 p. 719).

3. Conclusion

Psychological models for describing, explaining, and changing individual differences in cognitive development have direct importance for instructional theories and educational practice. If educational goals are to provide motivating challenges for students, they must represent realistic discrepancies from the current level of cognitive performance (dispositions). If teachers want to facilitate students' learning, they must consider individual learning prerequisites. If remedial instruction is to help students overcome learning difficulties, individual differences in general skills, content-specific knowledge and information processing skills must be considered.

The prerequisites for appropriately using psychological models to solve educational problems are the availability of standardized aptitude, learning, and achievement tests, teachers with the professional skills to construct informal tests, and instructors and students who can intuitively diagnose (or self-diagnose) learning progress and learning difficulties. It is empirically certain that a combination of such diagnostic competencies and effective instructional skills is a necessary and favorable precondition for successful teaching (Helmke and Schrader 1987).

Instructional strategies that take account of individual differences in cognitive development include adaptive teaching, individualized instruction, ability grouping, teaching for mastery learning, aptitude–treatment–interaction, and training programs to enhance students' cognitive skills, as well as their self-instructional skills (Corno and Snow 1986, Slavin 1987).

See also: Cognitive Development: Overview; Cognitive Modifiability

References

Aebli H 1970 Piaget—and beyond. *Interchange* 1: 12–24
Binet A, Simon T 1905 Application des méthodes nouvelles au diagnostic du niveau intellectuelle chez des enfants normaux et anormaux d'hospice et d'école primaire. *Année Psychol.* 11: 245–336
Blagg N 1991 *Can We Teach Intelligence?* Erlbaum, Hillsdale, New Jersey
Bouchard T J Jr, Lykken D T, McGue M, Segal N L, Tellegen A 1990 Sources of human psychological differences: The Minnesota study of twins reared apart. *Science* 250: 223–28
Carey S 1984 Cognitive development. The descriptive problem. In: Gazzaniga M S (ed.) 1984 *Handbook of Cognitive Neuroscience*. Freeman, New York
Ceci S J 1991 How much does schooling influence general intelligence and its cognitive components? A reassessment of the evidence. *Dev. Psychol.* 27: 703–22
Chi M T H 1978 Knowledge structure and memory development. In: Siegler R (ed.) 1978 *Children's Thinking: What Develops?* Erlbaum, Hillsdale, New Jersey
Corno L, Snow R E 1986 Adapting teaching to individual differences among learners. In: Wittrock M C (ed.) 1986 *Handbook of Research on Teaching*, Vol. 3. Macmillan, New York
Edelstein W, Keller M, Schröder E 1990 Child development and social structure: A longitudinal study on individual differences. In: Baltes P B, Featherman D L, Lerner R M (eds.) 1990 *Life-span Development and Behavior*, Vol. 10. Erlbaum, Hillsdale, New Jersey
Ericsson K A, Crutcher R J 1990 The nature of exceptional performance. In: Baltes P B, Featherman D L, Lerner R M (eds.) 1990 *Life-span Development and Behavior*, Vol. 10. Erlbaum, Hillsdale, New Jersey
Fischer K W, Silvern L 1985 Stages and individual differences in cognitive development. *Annu. Rev. Psychol.* 36: 613–48
Flavell J 1970 Cognitive change in adulthood. In: Goulet R, Baltes P B (eds.) 1970 *Life-span Developmental Psychology: Research and Theory*. Academic Press, New York
Helmke A, Schrader F W 1987 Interactional effects of instructional quality and teacher judgement accuracy on achievement. *Teaching and Teacher Education* 3: 91–98
Plomin R 1990 *Nature and Nurture*. Brooks/Cole, Pacific Grove, California
Scarr S 1992 Developmental theories for the 1990s: Development and individual difference. *Child Dev.* 63: 1–19
Slavin R E 1987 Mastery learning reconsidered. *Rev. Educ. Res.* 56: 175–213
Stern W 1911 *Intelligenzproblem und Schule*. Teubner, Leipzig
Sternberg R J 1985 *Beyond IQ: A Triarchic Theory of Human Intelligence*. Cambridge University Press, Cambridge

Thurstone L L 1938 *Primary Mental Abilities*. University of Chicago Press, Chicago, Illinois

Waldmann M, Weinert F E 1990 *Intelligenz und Denken—Perspektiven der Hochbegabungsforschung*. Verlag für Psychologie, Göttingen

Weinert F E (ed.) 1989 The relation between education and development. *Int. J. Educ. Res.* 13: 827–948

Weiss B, Weisz J R, Bromfield R 1986 Performance of retarded and nonretarded persons on information processing tasks: Tests of the similar structure hypotheses. *Psych. Bull.* 100: 157–75

Further Reading

Ackerman P L, Sternberg R J, Glaser R (eds.) 1989 *Learning and Individual Differences*. Freeman, New York

F. E. Weinert

Cognitive Development: Information-processing Approach

The modern study of cognitive development is dominated by the information-processing perspective, which draws heavily on an analogy with computer operations to explain the development of mental activities. Information processing is not a unified theory but instead denotes a collection of concepts that provides a unique lens with which to view cognitive development. This entry begins with a description of some of the core assumptions of this approach, then illustrates how the approach has been used to understand human development, and finally examines differences between the information-processing model and other models of development.

1. Core Assumptions

At the core of information-processing research is a shared view of how psychological activities are best understood. Generally, information-processing psychologists seek to understand relations between observable stimuli (input) and observable responses (output) by describing activities that intervene between input and output. They typically proceed by devising models of cognition in specific domains on the assumption that these models will converge in a way that reveals general principles of cognition. The components of these models consist of internal representations of information and of processes that operate on these representations. A complete model of cognition for a particular task or domain would include specific mechanisms for all cognitive activities that underlie performance, including perceptual mechanisms for encoding information, processes for manipulating and storing information, processes for selecting and retrieving stored information, and processes that decide among alternative actions. The resulting model would characterize cognition in individuals at a particular age. Extended to the problem of development, information-processing psychologists have the following additional goals: (a) describing features of information processing that are associated with different ages; (b) identifying properties of the information-processing system that both enable and constrain change.

This general account of the information-processing approach actually includes a number of individual assumptions that need to be stated explicitly, as they define a commonly shared, if minimal, view of this perspective.

The first assumption is that cognitive phenomena can be described and explained in terms of mental processes and representations that intervene between observable stimuli and responses. Information processing is primarily an approach to understanding cognition, defined broadly as psychological acts of knowing. Information-processing theorists assume that information is represented internally and manipulated by mental processes. The aim of research is to determine how information is represented and organized, and to identify the specific processes used in achieving particular cognitive aims. This account of human thought in terms of internal codes and processes is the essence of the computer metaphor that forms the core of the information-processing approach. Humans and computers engage in many similar activities: they must interpret symbolic information, perform operations on the interpreted information, and emit a response. Thus humans, like computers, can be considered as symbol manipulators (Newell et al. 1958).

A second assumption is that a relatively small number of elementary processes underlie all cognitive activity. Information-processing psychologists contend that acts of knowing can be decomposed into distinct, component processes. In turn, these components can also be decomposed, a process that can, in principle, be repeated until a set of fundamental cognitive operations has been identified. This organization means that most cognitive phenomena can be analyzed at many levels. For example, reading might be considered as a single process at one level of analysis, but at another it might be viewed in terms of such components as decoding and comprehension. These components might then themselves be decomposed into even more fine-grained operations, such as specific memory-manipulation processes (Kail and Bisanz 1992).

A third assumption is that individual processes operate in concert. The fundamental operations of a computer become useful only when they are combined with other operations to form routines that may, in turn, be combined with other routines to form higher-order programs. According to the information-processing view, the same is true of human cognition. A critical goal of psychological research is to understand how fundamental processes are combined and organized to produce performance on different tasks. Moreover, it is generally assumed that higher levels of organization may have emergent properties that are qualitatively different from the properties of lower-level operations (Palmer and Kimchee 1986).

It should be noted that, although the second assumption emphasizes the need to identify microscopic components of cognition, the third assumption makes it clear that reductionism of this sort is not the sole aim of research. Instead, identifying fundamental processes *and* determining their organization in performance in particular domains are both essential goals (Kail and Bisanz 1982).

A fourth and final assumption is that cognitive development occurs by means of self-modification. In information-processing theories, thinking is to be understood through an account of the representation of information and of the processes that manipulate this information. These accounts focus on internal factors rather than external, environmental factors such as reward or punishment. In like manner, when information-processing psychologists seek to explain how thinking changes with development, they focus on internal factors. The mechanisms that underlie development are thought to be internal to the system itself, rather than imposed by the environment; hence developmental change is construed as self-modification. This orientation does not deny the importance of environmental events for cognitive change, but simply claims that "whatever the form of the external environment, the information-processing system itself must ultimately encode, store, index and process that environment" (Klahr 1989 p.138).

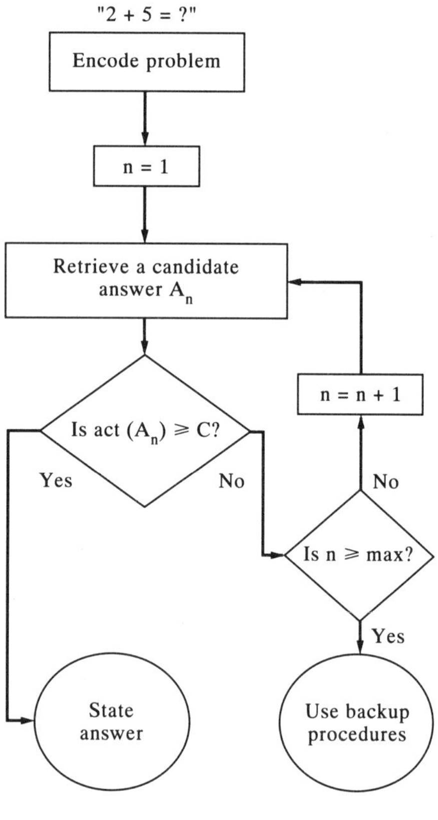

Figure 1
Simplified model of mental arithmetic processes[a]

Source: Kail and Bisanz (1992), after Siegler and Shrager (1984)
a The number of retrieval attempts is indexed by n, and *max* represents an upper limit on this number. $Act(A_n)$ refers to the activation level of the candidate answer retrieved on attempt n, and C refers to the confidence criterion for accepting a retrieved answer

2. Analyses of Developmental Change

The assumptions described in Sect. 1 have provided the basis for information-processing analysis of developmental change in a number of domains, including perception, problem-solving, language, motor control, and social cognition. This section begins with an example of an information-processing approach in a particular domain, then describes some general mechanisms of developmental change.

2.1 An Illustrative Example: Information-processing Analysis of the Development of Arithmetic Skills

In many societies mastering arithmetic skills is an important objective in the early years of schooling. The processes underlying acquisition of these skills have been described in a number of information-processing theories; work by Siegler and his colleagues is representative (Siegler and Shrager 1984, Siegler and Jenkins 1989). Siegler's account of the steps involved in solving a simple addition problem is illustrated in Fig. 1. A child or adult begins by encoding the problem and then attempting to retrieve an answer directly from a knowledge base consisting of stored facts. These facts are represented mentally in terms of associations between problems (e.g., what is 2 + 5?) and candidate answers (6, 7, 8, etc.), associations that vary in strength. If the associative strength between the retrieved answer and the problem ($Act\ [A_n]$) exceeds a preset confidence criterion (C), then the answer is stated. If this associative strength does not exceed the confidence criterion, then retrieval is attempted again. This retrieval cycle is repeated until an answer is retrieved that has an associative strength exceeding the confidence criterion or the number of retrieval attempts exceeds a preset limit (*max*). In the latter case, retrieval is abandoned and an answer is generated using a backup procedure such as counting on one's fingers or counting mentally.

The general process illustrated in Fig. 1 does not

change with age. However, a problem becomes more strongly associated with the correct answer through repeated exposure. In other words, children's answers to problems are frequently confirmed or disconfirmed by parents, teachers, peers, or self-discovery. The associative strength between a problem and an answer increases every time the child responds with that answer. Frequency of exposure to arithmetic problems is moderately correlated with age, which means that correct answers gradually increase in associative strength as children get older.

Of course, children do not experience all simple addition problems equally often. Problems with smaller addends are presented by parents and in textbooks more often than problems with larger addends (Hamann and Ashcraft 1986). Consequently, answers to problems with small addends develop associative strength more rapidly, which means that a child may well use retrieval for these problems while at the same time using backup strategies for problems with larger addends.

Siegler's work exemplifies the information-processing perspective in many ways. Observed behaviors—in this case, the speed and accuracy with which children answer addition problems—are explained in terms of a relatively small set of processes that operate in certain ways on internal representations of knowledge. The processes are represented by the retrieval cycle shown in Fig. 1 and knowledge of arithmetic facts is represented by the associative strengths that are acquired as children develop. Performance is determined by the interaction of these processes and knowledge representations as the child is attempting to solve a problem. The environment, and particularly the frequency with which a child experiences certain types of problems, has an important influence on development, but this influence is mediated by the way in which information is processed.

2.2 *Mechanisms of Development*

Many developmental psychologists view human development as a series of discrete states connected by transitions. This view has led to two primary goals for research: (a) to describe each developmental state precisely; (b) to explain transitions from one developmental state to the next. Information-processing analyses of the sort typified by Siegler's work have yielded much evidence pertinent to both of these goals. Hypotheses about specific mechanisms are still somewhat speculative, but some consensus is beginning to emerge about the general functions and characteristics of developmental mechanisms. The remainder of this section focuses on mechanisms of development suggested by the information-processing approach.

2.2.1 Change in procedures and rules. As children develop, their approaches to problems become more sophisticated and more efficient. For example, when reasoning about scientific concepts, adolescents typically use more sophisticated rules than children. In like manner, when trying to remember information, adolescents use more powerful mnemonics than do younger children. These insights about cognitive development are not unique to the information-processing view. The important contribution of the information-processing perspective has been to explain the transition toward more sophisticated and efficient procedures. In Siegler's work, for example, exposure to addition problems gradually increases associative strength, ultimately to the point where the correct answer exceeds the confidence criterion; the result is that answers are no longer calculated (using backup strategies such as counting) but are retrieved instead.

Another method by which more advanced procedures may emerge is through generalization. Consider the following, simplified example. Suppose that children just learning to add sometimes use the following rule:

> Rule 1: *If* the goal is to add (1 + 2), *then* count 1 finger, followed by 2 fingers, and say the result.

Suppose that children also have the rule:

> Rule 2: *If* the goal is to add (3 + 4), *then* count 3 fingers, followed by 4 fingers, and say the result.

A generalized version of these results would replace the constants—(2 + 3) and (3 + 4)—with variables, producing a new, generalized rule:

> Rule 3: *If* the goal is to add two numbers, m and n, *then* count m fingers, followed by n fingers, and say the result.

Generalization is thought to occur because new rules are compared to existing rules. If a new rule differs from an existing rule only in the constants included in the conditions, then a more general rule is created by replacing the constants with variables (Anderson 1983).

Of course, children sometimes learn rules that are too general and they must learn appropriate boundary conditions. "Discrimination" refers to the process by which more specific conditions are associated with rules. Continuing the examples with simple addition, children might attempt to apply Rule 3 to problems such as 8 + 11 and 6 + 7. Upon discovering that they lack enough fingers for these problems, the situations associated with successful use of Rule 3 are compared with those associated with unsuccessful use. The result is a narrowing of the conditions that elicit Rule 3:

> Rule 4: *If* the goal is to add two numbers, m and n, each of which is 5 or less, *then* count m fingers, followed by n fingers, and say the result.

Changes such as generalization and discrimination require self-modification processes that examine existing rules and their output, examine the adequacy of the outputs, and modify existing rules. Most information-processing theorists assume that the human cognitive system comes equipped with many or most of the basic processes for self-modification, although the precise nature of these processes remains primarily a matter of speculation (Kail and Bisanz 1982).

2.2.2 Development caused by change in mental effort. All people are limited in the amount of mental activity they can perform at one time. People can usually concentrate their efforts on one or two activities; if they try to do more, performance deteriorates rapidly. This limit on mental activity has been referred to as a limitation in processing resources or mental effort. Common to both terms is the idea that most intellectual tasks require effort and that all individuals are limited in the effort available to them.

Applied to development, the resources available for mental activity may simply increase with age. Adolescents may have more processing resources than children, who have more resources than preschoolers and infants. Just as additional random-access memory allows a computer to run more complex software, a gradual age-related increase in processing resources may be responsible for developmental change in the complexity of thought.

Processing resources may be implicated in developmental change in a second way. As individuals acquire more experience on a particular task, fewer resources may be required for successful performance. Performance may become so refined that ultimately the task is performed without effort. Automatization has occurred when a process can be performed without using processing resources at all. For example, beginning drivers are instructed to avoid talking with passengers and listening to the radio; both activities would take resources needed for driving. However, with more experience behind the wheel, fewer resources are needed for safe driving, so drivers can converse while maintaining the same level of driving skill.

Applied to development, children are seen as "universal novices." Whatever the task, their experience is limited compared with that of adults. With age, children gain greater experience, so that processing requires fewer resources. Thus, although the total amount of resources may not change with age, greater experience means that children gradually have more resources available for allocation to novel or particularly challenging tasks.

2.2.3 Increased speed of processing. As children develop, they complete most mental processes more rapidly. A useful rule of thumb is that 4- and 5-year olds will respond three times as slowly as adults; 8-year olds will respond twice as slowly. These age differences apparently reflect a global mechanism that limits the speed with which children and adolescents can execute cognitive processes (Kail 1991). The impact of this global mechanism on the speed of mental processing is most evident on tasks where the response speed is measured, but is not limited to them. On the contrary, speed of processing may play a role whenever a specified number of actions must be completed in a fixed period of time. Thus, for any task where children must answer in a specified period, age differences in performance may be due to the fact that younger children could not complete all of the processes responsible for successful task performance in the time allotted.

3. Comparison with Other Approaches

Further insights into the nature of the information-processing framework come from comparisons with two other major theoretical approaches—Piaget's theory and the contextual viewpoint. These approaches are examined in detail elsewhere (see *Piaget's Theory of Human Development*), but a brief description here will set the stage for comparisons with information processing.

The Piagetian approach emphasizes general theoretical principles that govern intellectual growth and change. Intellectual growth is described as a set of states that are qualitatively different, reflecting major changes in cognitive structure. Performance on individual tasks is of interest only insofar as it sheds light on general principles of cognitive development.

The contextual approach emphasizes that human development is inseparable from the environmental contexts in which a child develops. That is, theories cannot consider development in a vacuum but must instead examine it in the multiple interactive contexts in which it occurs, including institutions (e.g., families and schools), culture, and history. In Rogoff's words, "the individual child, social partners, and the cultural milieu [are] inseparable contributors to the ongoing activities in which child development takes place." (Rogoff 1990 p. 18)

When contextual theory is the reference point, information-processing and Piagetian theory have many similarities. Unlike contextual theory, both information-processing and Piagetian theory focus primarily on an individual's mental development. Both approaches agree that the outward manifestations of cognition may depend strongly on context but that the underlying developmental principles should be relatively unaffected by contextual variation. In Piagetian theory, for example, the functional invariants (adaptation, organization) are thought to be invariant across cultures. Similarly, information-processing theories hold that mental processes can be understood in terms of organized sets of basic processes regardless of the specific context in which children develop. Furthermore, although Piagetian and information-processing psychologists would agree that cultural context (at many different levels) can have a profound impact on cognitive development, the impact is always mediated by the developing individual's mental structures.

Although the Piagetian and information-processing frameworks emphasize the primacy of individual mental development, their approaches differ considerably. The remainder of this section focuses on two related issues that illustrate differences in these approaches.

3.1 Homogeneity of Mind

Traditional stage theories of development, such as Piaget's, are often criticized for their monolithic approach to the phenomenon. In other words, at each stage in development, a unified mental structure—a homogeneous mind—is presumed to be responsible for all cognition, which leads to the prediction of considerable consistency in performance across tasks. This viewpoint is unable to account for the fact that children sometimes solve tasks successfully at younger ages than those expected by Piaget's theory or that performance on some tasks improves more rapidly with age than performance on other tasks that are equally demanding.

Information-processing theories adopt a less homogeneous approach to the mind. The transition mechanisms described above—increased processing resources, increased processing speed, and more frequent automatization—are not mutually exclusive; all could be involved in development. Combined, they yield a steady age-related increase in cognitive skill. However, unlike Piaget's concept of disequilibrium, the process of change is continuous. There are no abrupt or qualitative changes in development. Instead, increased resources, automatization, and processing speed result in constant but gradual cognitive change. In addition, they allow for variations across tasks because a child's performance may be automatic on some tasks but not on others. This approach even allows for variation on different versions of the same task: in Siegler's model, for example, a child should solve familiar addition problems with retrieval but less familiar problems by counting.

3.2 Task Specificity

Piaget's theory "has been concerned with pervasive, abstract structures that apply to a broad range of tasks . . . and to long-term temporal phenomena in the form of structural change . . .. A task is only of interest insofar as it does require a certain concept for its solution" (Breslow 1981 p. 348). Thus, the emphasis is on general principles of development which are wide ranging and not specific to particular tasks. In contrast, information-processing psychologists argue that cognitive structures cannot be studied independently of specific tasks or domains. Most methods for studying cognition require that inferences be made from performance on specific behavioral tasks. Consequently, understanding of cognitive development is necessarily linked to an understanding of performance on cognitive tasks of interest.

This orientation does not mean that information-processing theories have no general components. Modern information-processing theories often include such general components because detailed analyses of separate tasks have pointed to common components of performance (Kail 1991).

4. Conclusion

Information-processing approaches have led to greater understanding in many domains of cognitive development. These advances have begun to converge on a number of conclusions concerning the nature of cognitive–developmental change in infancy, childhood, and adolescence, and the mechanisms responsible for this change. The view that emerges from the approach is one that combines Piaget's search for general principles of development with an appreciation for the importance of the acquisition of skill in particular domains.

See also: Cognitive Development: Overview; Cognitive Development: Individual Differences; Cognition and Learning

References

Anderson J R 1983 *The Architecture of Cognition*. Harvard University Press, Cambridge, Massachusetts

Breslow L 1981 Reevaluation of the literature on the development of transitive inferences. *Psych. Bull.* 89(2): 325–51

Hamann M S, Ashcraft M H 1986 Textbook presentations of the basic arithmetic facts. *Cognition and Instruction* 3: 173–92

Kail R 1991 Development of processing speed in childhood and adolescence. In: Reese H W (ed.) 1991 *Advances in Child Development and Behavior*, Vol. 23. Academic Press, San Diego, California

Kail R, Bisanz J 1982 Information processing and cognitive development. In: Reese H W (ed.) 1982 *Advances in Child Development and Behavior*, Vol. 17. Academic Press, New York

Kail R, Bisanz J 1992 The information-processing perspective on cognitive development in childhood and adolescence. In: Sternberg R J, Berg C A (eds.) 1992 *Intellectual Development*. Cambridge University Press, Cambridge, Massachusetts

Klahr D 1989 Information-processing perspectives. In: Vasta R (ed.) 1989 *Annals of Child Development*, Vol. 6. JAI Press, Greenwich, Connecticut

Newell A, Shaw J G, Simon H A 1958 Elements of a theory of human problem solving. *Psychol. Rev.* 65: 151–66

Palmer S E, Kimchee R 1986 The information-processing approach to cognition. In: Knapp T J, Robertson L C (eds.) 1986 *Approaches to Cognition: Contrasts and Controversies*. Erlbaum, Hillsdale, New Jersey

Rogoff B 1990 *Apprenticeship in Thinking: Cognitive*

Development in Social Context. Oxford University Press, New York
Siegler R S, Jenkins E 1989 *How Children Discover New Strategies*. Erlbaum, Hillsdale, New Jersey
Siegler R S, Shrager J 1984 Strategy choices in addition and subtraction: How do children know what to do? In: Sophian C (ed.) 1984 *Origins of Cognitive Skills*. Erlbaum, Hillsdale, New Jersey

Further Reading

Bjorklund D (ed.) 1990 *Children's Strategies: Contemporary Views of Cognitive Development*. Erlbaum, Hillsdale, New Jersey
Klahr D, Langley P, Neches R (eds.) 1987 *Production System Models of Learning and Development*. MIT Press, Cambridge, Massachusetts
Siegler R S 1983 Information processing approaches to development. In: Mussen P H (ed.) 1983 *Carmichael's Manual of Child Psychology*. Wiley, New York
Sternberg R J, Berg C A 1992 (eds.) *Intellectual Development*. Cambridge University Press, Cambridge

R. Kail

Cognitive Development: Overview

Cognitive development has traditionally been understood as the study of how cognition develops, where cognition is conceived of as one part within the tripartite division of the mind into cognition, conation, and affection. The field has been dominated since its inception by Piaget's theory. However, growing dissatisfaction with Piaget's methods, in particular by Anglo-American experimentalists, led to increasing assimilation of the field to the information-processing paradigm of cognitive psychology. This brought about great improvements in experimental control for alternative determinants of children's performance on Piagetian tasks, for example, memory limitations and communication problems between experimenter and child (Donaldson 1978). It also brought clearer formulation of and greater precision in identifying the mental structures underlying children's problem-solving strategies. Also, disenchantment with the deductive intractability of Piaget's fundamental developmental concepts (e.g., assimilation and accommodation) led to attempts to make these notions more precise within computer models of cognitive change (Klahr 1984).

Despite these advances Piaget remains influential in the early 1990s in at least two respects. Most cognitive developmentalists are still investigating the developmental phenomena that Piaget discovered, and the deeper problems that he raised remain unsolved. Although becoming a subdiscipline of cognitive psychology brought better methods and better conceptual tools for studying cognition, it did not provide a cogent alternative to Piaget in accounting for development. The reason for this failure is related to the foundational problems of cognitive science at large, which are under debate by philosophers of mind and cognitive scientists, and which are fueled by controversy between the traditional symbolic account of cognition and the new connectionist paradigm.

1. Concept Acquisition

One of the most serious problems of cognitive science in the late twentieth century is the inability to explain how concepts can be acquired. An important theoretical approach to solving some of these problems is the idea that the mind is like a computer program. This is the governing idea behind Fodor's (1975) proposal of a "language of thought." Of course, the proposal is not that human thoughts are exactly like language but that they share some of the critical properties of languages. One of these properties is *compositionality*, by which the meaning of complex expressions (sentences) are systematically related to the meaning of its component expressions (e.g., words). This is a crucial property because without it, it is difficult to see how people could know the meaning of an infinite variety of sentences. Compositionality explains this because it is necessary to learn only the meaning of a finite set of words and rules of composition and with that the meaning of all possible, meaningful sentences can be constructed.

This approach is now known as the "classical view," in which a set of basic symbolic expressions are combined into new and complex expressions. There is a severe developmental limitation inherent in this view because it can account for knowledge change only in terms of a change in combinations of basic, preformed expressions. In other words, learning is conceived as the formation of mental sentences out of a given mental vocabulary (basic concepts). Since the starting point is a given vocabulary, traditional cognitive science finds it difficult to explain where that basic vocabulary comes from. The traditional empiricist answer to this, as demonstrated in the concept formation experiments pioneered by Ach (1925) and known to developmental psychologists through Vygotsky (1965), is that concepts (corresponding to all the words in a dictionary) can be decomposed into perceptual features. However, attempts to flesh out this theory (e.g., Miller and Johnson-Laird 1976) and to design concept-learning computer programs were largely unconvincing (e.g., Winston 1975). Fodor explains that lack of success.

Fodor (1981) argued that because attempts to give definitions have persistently met with failure for the vast majority of words to be found in the dictionary, all these words must reflect basic concepts; that is, concepts that cannot be reduced to a much smaller set of just a few basic perceptual concepts. Furthermore, since there is no conceivable explanation within the framework of cognitive science of how basic concepts could be acquired, he concludes that they must be innately given. Experience is required only in order to trigger these preformed concepts.

These are not philosophers' esoteric ideas. Rather they bring into the open the tacit assumptions underlying most post-Piagetian research in cognitive development. This research, therefore, stands in this respect in contrast to Piaget's theory which is centrally based on the emergence of new concepts through the organism's interaction with its environment. Take Piaget and Inhelder's (1974) conservation experiments. For Piaget, the ability to conserve quantity over changing perceptual appearances signals the construction of a genuinely new form (concept) of quantity out of an older, more primitive one. There has been much research on this topic but without providing an alternative explanation of how these conceptual changes occur. Rather, the more outstanding research results are based on smarter, more child-adequate methods, so that one could demonstrate earlier correct performance on conservation tasks than described by Piaget. But these results leave open the question as to when these concepts are acquired. The implicit message, though, is that smarter experimenters will devise even smarter experiments to demonstrate understanding of quantity invariance at ever younger ages until the neonate stage is reached. In a word, this research tradition tacitly assumes that knowledge is really innately specified.

Moreover, the main theoretical proposals for the observed improvement with age on Piaget's original tasks have—as far as concepts are concerned—a nativist flavor, since these theories are silent on the origin of concepts. The existence of requisite concepts seems to be tacitly assumed and the young child's failure on diagnostic tasks is purported to be explained in terms of an inability to apply these concepts due to insufficient memory or information-processing limitations (Pascual-Leone 1970, Case 1978). Thus it seems ironic that Pascual-Leone and Case describe their theories as "neo-Piagetian," when from the point of view of conceptual development which is close to the heart of Piagetian theory, they would be better described as "anti-Piagetian." Few researchers in this tradition have recognized this nativist implication of their research enterprise. Only more recently have infancy researchers, who have been able to demonstrate quite remarkable cognitive abilities at very early ages, argued for innateness of at least the very basic conceptual framework (Spelke 1990).

So Fodor (1981) seems to be right about cognitive development as practiced within late-twentieth-century cognitive science: it assumes—in most cases tacitly—the pre-existence of concepts. But does this mean that Fodor's nativist claim about concept acquisition is right, or is his claim rather an indication of a flaw in the theoretical basis of cognitive science as currently practiced? Fortunately, as Samet (1986) points out, empiricists (who want to grant experience more of a role in concept acquisition) have several defences against Fodor's argument. In particular, they can deny that concept acquisition is through "learning" in the specific sense used by Fodor as rational change through testing hypotheses. Instead, it could proceed by nonrational, physical changes. Fodor considered that possibility but only in the absurd-sounding instance of being knocked on one's head. There is, however, a very popular and certainly less absurd alternative of a nonrational, physical change: connectionist learning (see Rumelhart et al. 1988, McClelland et al. 1986).

Since connectionist models give hope for genuine concept formation they might soon play an important role in cognitive development. Enthusiasm must, however, remain guarded. It is necessary to ask whether what connectionists call concepts really are concepts. For Fodor one essential feature of concepts is that they provide the basic vocabulary in a compositional symbolic system (language of thought). Fodor and Pylyshyn (1988) have argued that connectionism is not compositional and, hence, falls short of the conceptual abilities of the human mind. Connectionists have responded to this challenge. Van Gelder (1990) argues that Fodor and Pylyshyn's argument applies only to a certain version of compositionality but not to a more abstract conception of it. So, the dispute continues and it is too early to make predictions about the eventual success of connectionist theory. Consequently it is also too early to talk in terms of the educational implications of this newly opening research area.

2. *Children's Theories*

Connectionism may eventually only be part of an explanation of how genuine conceptual change can occur, because the concepts acquired in the connectionist models' nets reflect only statistical regularities across input patterns. In philosophy of science it has become clear that scientific concepts cannot be reduced to logical combinations of perceptual categories. The same also seems to be true for our everyday concepts. Although infants may initially base their concepts solely on perceptual similarity (Keil 1989), they soon transcend that stage and base their concepts on causal relations (Carey 1985b). When based on causal relations concepts are usually considered to be theoretical terms in a (causal) theory.

Carey (1985b) explored how children's biological concepts, such as "living thing," "animal," "baby," and so on, change as a function of children's growing understanding of how the body works. For instance, young children of 4 to 7 years have an essentially behavioral theory of internal organs (lungs are for breathing). Later, by about 10 years, they understand that organs interact for the purpose of maintaining life (metabolism). The important point is that this growth in their biological theory prompts a change in their concepts in this domain. For instance, younger children do not have a concept of "living thing" as it is usually understood. They only consider animals as "alive" in distinction to inanimate objects. Plants are, therefore, grouped with inanimate objects because on a "behavioral theory" they are more similar in distinction to animals. By age 10 this changes, because by this stage children have the theoretical prerequisite for understanding that plants and animals share the essential necessity of life sustenance.

Keil (1989) provides evidence for this view of conceptual change being tied to theory change in terms of a shift from characteristic to defining features which occurs for all domains of knowledge. For instance, kindergarten children will judge "a man of daddy's age who visits often and brings presents but is not related to your father or mother" to be an uncle but deny that status to "a 2-year old brother of your mother." From about age 7 onwards most children make the opposite judgment.

Keil interprets this shift as a consequence of the child's acquisition of the appropriate theory of kinship. In other words, the younger children pin down their concept of uncle on the surface similarities of all the typical instances of uncles that they have encountered, whereas the older children embed their concept in a theory of family relationships. In support of this interpretation, Keil reports that the shift is observed at about the same age for concepts that belong to the same theoretical domain but at different times for different domains, for example, for cooking terms the shift occurs well after the age of 9 years.

Carey (1985a) pointed out that the "theory view" of cognitive development provides an interesting compromise between two extreme views about the generality of developmental constraints. There is, on the one hand, Piaget's theory that postulates the development of completely overarching logical constraints on what children at a particular developmental stage can learn. These constraints pertain to any domain of knowledge. Unfortunately for Piagetian theory, the correlations between tasks from different domains do not bear out this prediction (e.g., Brainerd 1978). The opposite view is that children can develop any level of expertise within a particular domain if they are given enough time and opportunity to practice the relevant skills. This is exemplified in Chi's (1978) research with young chess experts. It demonstrates that there is not a uniform increase in memory capacity with age. Rather, memory depends on level of expertise, as 10-year old chess experts have a considerably better memory for chess positions, but not for other spatial patterns, than mediocre adult players.

Carey (1985a) emphasizes that the "theory view" cautions against interpreting such results to mean that children at any age can become experts in any field if they just spend enough time and effort on it. The reason for this caution is that a domain like chess is not independent from other bodies of knowledge. Each domain is based on a groundwork of more general theories. Thus there is a clear educational implication. Contrary to what Piaget's (1971) theory suggests, one can do more than wait until the child matures and reaches formal operations before he or she can become a chess master. Training on any task, whatever the domain, should be valuable at any age. However, one must not forget that for training to be successful it has to build from the bottom up and so, depending on how extensive the groundwork is before the target domain is reached, there may be a practical limit as to when a child can become a chess expert even under optimal conditions. Chess expertise is just the tip of a large iceberg of hidden knowledge, because chess is not just the moving of pieces around a board according to certain rules. To even understand the point of it children have to be able to appreciate the interpersonal motivation of the players for moving the pieces. That is, they need the foundation of what is called a "theory of mind" (Perner 1991). For instance, children need to appreciate that both their opponents and themselves want to win and that their opponents may sometimes not realize the implication of a move, and so on.

People take all this required social background knowledge for granted by the time they start to learn chess, and so are not aware that it was a necessary prerequisite for playing chess. It is well-known, however, that it takes some years before young children develop their theory of mind to the level at which they can appreciate the point of competitive games (Sodian 1991). Thus a naïve approach to training may be actually harmful because premature preoccupation with chessboards may not be a good way of acquiring the prerequisite theory of mind. Putting pressure on a 1-year old to play with chess pieces may be quite counterproductive and have a quite different effect than it would have for a 6-year old who is already endowed with the necessary understanding of the opponent's mind.

All this, however, does not mean that one simply has to wait for a "theory of mind" to mature, as Leslie (1987) seems to imply. Training a theory of mind may not be an easy thing to do but there is suggestive evidence that under, as it were, permanent training conditions in conducive family conditions substantial gains can be obtained. Perner et al. (1992) found that children with two siblings achieve a particular level of performance on theory-of-mind tasks almost one year earlier than children without siblings, and Dunn et al. (1991) found that 2-year old children who show certain interaction patterns with their mothers concerning their siblings tend to do better on theory-of-mind tasks a year later.

So, to follow through with the logic of the "theory view" on the hypothetical chess training example, it appears that in principle one could produce younger and younger chess experts, but because at increasingly younger ages more and more prerequisite theories need to be built up there are severe practical limits as to what could possibly be achieved at a very young age.

3. Consciousness and the Distinction between Implicit and Explicit Knowledge

Since the 1980s there has been greater critical comment that cognitive psychology needs an account of the difference between unconscious and conscious and of related distinctions like that between *knowing how* (to do something) and *knowing that* (something is the case), procedural and declarative, inaccessible and accessible, which different theorists relate in different ways.

In the developmental literature it is primarily Karmiloff-Smith (1992) who has drawn attention to these distinctions. In an example from language development (1991), she points out that by 5 years children are competent users and interpreters of the articles "a" and "the." Their knowledge about the use of these articles is, however, purely implicit because this knowledge is entirely embedded in the procedures by which children produce and interpret articles. After the age of 5, children acquire a more explicit understanding of the conditions of use as indicated by their spontaneous corrections. This means that their knowledge cannot be purely implicit, embedded in their procedures of use, because for corrections to occur there must be explicit knowledge about the correct use by which to measure the performance of the currently executed procedure. Around 9 or 10 years, children have an even more explicit understanding, in fact, they have elaborate theories about the conditions of use. Their knowledge about these conditions is explicit in the strongest sense of being conscious and verbally expressible.

Mandler (1983) used the distinction between implicit and explicit mental representation to bring Piaget's distinction between sensorimotor intelligence and "mental representation" in line with terminology in cognitive science. More recently the distinction has found another application in an intriguing finding by Goldin-Meadow and her colleagues (e.g., Goldin-Meadow et al. 1992). They investigated the transitional phase in coming to understand Piagetian conservation tasks. Nonconservers say that when liquid is poured from a wider bowl into a thinner beaker it becomes more, because the column of the liquid in the thinner beaker is higher than in the original bowl. Conservers understand that the amount of liquid stays the same and they can justify this in view of the increase in level in the thin beaker by pointing out that this increase is compensated for by a decrease in width. What Goldin-Meadow and her colleagues discovered was that for a few months before they become conservers, nonconservers, who fail to take width of the containers into account in their judgment of quantity and show no sign of awareness of its relevance in their verbal justifications, nevertheless start to gesture about width with their hands. It seems as if their gestures express some implicit knowledge of its relevance.

Admittedly the understanding of the nature of the distinction between implicit and explicit knowledge is far from perfect. But until the early 1980s it was still heresy in some circles to think that there was implicit, unconscious knowledge. By the early 1990s it has become an intensively researched field.

Research on implicit learning is probably of most relevance to developmental concerns because it aims at finding the basic mechanism by which implicit knowledge is acquired. This has been studied in two paradigms. Broadbent (1991) adopted a paradigm for studying complicated systems interactions to demonstrate that people can learn to control such a system without any explicit, conscious knowledge of the rules which they must be using to achieve their level of performance.

Reber (1989) studied implicit knowledge of artificial grammars. Subjects were given a list of letter strings (which had been generated by some grammar) to memorize. By letting them later sort new strings according to whether they thought they belonged to the old set or not, Reber was able to demonstrate that subjects must have abstracted the structure of the grammar, and yet his subjects were unable to describe the basis of their judgments with any degree of accuracy (i.e., no conscious, explicit awareness). The theoretical framework that grew out of this work on implicit learning of artificial grammars has been used to explain the language learning problems of dysphasic children (Weinert 1991).

The area with perhaps the most intense focus on the implicit–explicit distinction is research on memory. This also offers promising links with developmental research. For instance, Tulving (1985) proposed a threefold distinction of levels of consciousness and types of memory. Implicit or procedural memory involves no consciousness of knowing (anoetic consciousness). A paradigm example is priming experiments, for example, presentation of the word "butter" increases the probability that the word fragment "b–t–er" is completed as "butter" rather than "bitter," "butler," or "bother," without any awareness (inability to recognize or recall) that the word "butter" had been presented. The effect of presenting "butter" can be explained as an effect on the procedures that are later used in thinking of a suitable completion of the word fragment, but no explicit representation that the word "butter" had been encountered is formed. Infants' memory may be predominantly of this kind (Mandler 1983).

Tulving's second level of consciousness relates to semantic memory, which involves awareness that one knows (noetic consciousness), for example, that the word "butter" was part of a list of words. Tulving, however, distinguishes this level of consciousness from a further level of autonoetic consciousness which is required for true remembering which is accompanied by the recollective experience that, for example, one knows that "butter" was on the word list because one has experienced it being there.

Perner (1991) argued that if recollective experiences are based on the understanding that one knows something because one has experienced it then children should not have this type of memory until they can understand the origin of their knowledge. Theory of mind research indicates that children cannot do this before the age of about 4 years. And indeed, Perner (1992) reports a correlation between children's free recall (an indicator of episodic memory) and their ability to distinguish knowledge from lucky guesses and their understanding that senses inform about particular properties only (e.g., the eyes about color, lifting by hand about weight).

This finding illustrates the wider role that research on children's theories of mind will play in explaining how children come to reflect on their own knowledge, how they can make their implicit knowledge explicit and accessible to consciousness. Although theory-of-mind research focused initially on children's difficulty in understanding other people's minds, as it partly grew out of the Piagetian research on perspective taking, it has since become increasingly clear that there is as much for children to learn about their own minds.

The educational implications of this research can potentially be quite significant. By finding systematic ways to foster children's theory of mind there would be a way to increase their understanding of their own minds with beneficial effects on, for example, their episodic memory and, perhaps most significant, on their ability to gain self-control. As Perner (1991) speculated, the ability to conceptualize their own desires and intentions ought to be a first step towards children's ability to gain control over these internal states.

See also: Cognitive Development: Individual Differences

References

Ach N 1925 *Über die Begriffsbildung: Eine experimentelle Untersuchung zur Psychologie und Philosophie und Pädagogie*. Cälvor, Göttingen

Brainerd C J 1978 *Piaget's Theory of Intelligence*. Prentice-Hall, Englewood Cliffs, New Jersey

Broadbent D E 1991 Recall, recognition, and implicit knowledge. In: Kessen W, Ortony A, Craik F I M (eds.) 1991 *Memories, Thoughts, and Emotions: Essays in Honor of George Mandler*. Erlbaum, Hillsdale, New Jersey

Carey S (1985a) Are children fundamentally different kinds of thinkers and learners than adults? In: Chipman S F, Segal J W, Glaser R (eds.) 1985 *Thinking and Learning Skills*, Vol. 2. Erlbaum, Hillsdale, New Jersey

Carey S 1985b *Conceptual Change in Childhood*. MIT Press, Cambridge, Massachusetts

Case R 1978 Intellectual development from birth to adulthood: A neo-Piagetian interpretation. In: Siegler R S (ed.) 1978 *Children's Thinking: What Develops?* Erlbaum, Hillsdale, New Jersey

Chi M T H 1978 Knowledge structures and memory development. In: Siegler R S (ed.) 1978 *Children's Thinking: What Develops?* Erlbaum, Hillsdale, New Jersey

Donaldson M 1978 *Children's Minds*. Fontana, London

Dunn J, Brown J, Slomkowski C, Tesla C, Youngblade L 1991 Young children's understanding of other people's feelings and beliefs: Individual differences and their antecedents. *Child Dev.* 62(6): 1352–66

Fodor J A 1975 *The Language of Thought*. Harvard University Press, Cambridge, Massachusetts

Fodor J A 1981 The present status of the innateness controversy. In: Fodor J A 1981 *Representations*. Harvester Press, Brighton

Fodor J A, Pylyshyn Z W 1988 Connectionism and cognitive architecture: A critical analysis. *Cog.* 28 (1–2): 3–71

Goldin-Meadow S, Alibali M W, Church R B 1992 Transition in concept acquisition: Using the hand to read the mind. Unpublished manuscript, University of Chicago, Chicago, Illinois

Karmiloff-Smith A 1991 Beyond modularity: Innate constraints and developmental change. In: Carey S, Gelman R (eds.) 1991 *The Epigenesis of Mind*. Erlbaum, Hillsdale, New Jersey

Karmiloff-Smith A 1992 *Beyond Modularity: A Developmental Perspective on Cognitive Science*. MIT Press, Cambridge, Massachusetts

Keil F C 1989 *Concepts, Kinds, and Cognitive Development*. MIT Press, Cambridge, Massachusetts

Klahr D 1984 Transition processes in quantitative development. In: Sternberg R J (ed.) 1984 *Mechanisms of Cognitive Development*. W H Freeman, New York

Leslie A M 1987 Pretense and representation: The origins of "Theory of Mind." *Psychol. Rev.* 94(4): 412–26

Mandler J M 1983 Representation. In: Flavell J H, Markman E M (eds.) 1983 *Manual of Child Psychology. Vol 3: Cognitive Development*. Wiley, New York

McClelland J L, Rumelhart D E, the PDP Research Group 1986 *Parallel Distributed Processing: Explorations in the Microstructure of Cognition, Vol. 2: Psychological and Biological Models*. MIT Press, Cambridge, Massachusetts

Miller G A, Johnson-Laird P N 1976 *Language and Perception*. Cambridge University Press, Cambridge

Pascual-Leone J 1970 A mathematical model for the transition rule in Piaget's developmental stages. *Acta Psychol.* 32(4): 301–45

Perner J 1991 *Understanding the Representational Mind*. MIT Press, Cambridge, Massachusetts

Perner J 1992 Episodic memory and autonoetic consciousness: Developmental evidence and a theory of

childhood amnesia. Unpublished manuscript, University of Sussex, Brighton
Perner J, Leekam S R, Ruffman T 1992 Theory of mind is contagious; you catch it from your sibs. Unpublished manuscript, University of Sussex, Brighton
Piaget J 1971 *Biology and Knowledge*. University of Chicago Press, Chicago, Illinois
Piaget J, Inhelder B 1974 The child's construction of quantities: Conservation and atomism. Basic Books, New York
Reber A 1989 Implicit learning and tacit knowledge. *J. Exp. Psychol. Gen.* 118(3): 219–35
Rumelhart D E, McClelland J L, the PDP Research Group 1988 *Parallel Distributed Processing: Explorations in the Microstructure of Cognition, Vol. 1: Foundations*. MIT Press, Cambridge, Massachusetts
Samet J 1986 Troubles with Fodor's nativism. *Midwest Studies of Philosophy* 10: 575–94
Sodian B 1991 The development of deception in young children. *British Journal of Developmental Psychology* 9(1): 173–88
Spelke E S 1990 Principles of object perception. *Cognit. Sci.* 14(1): 29–56
Tulving E 1985 Memory and consciousness. *Canadian Psychology* 26(1): 1–12
Van Gelder T 1990 Compositionality: A connectionist variation on a classical theme. *Cognit. Sci.* 14(3): 355–84
Vygotsky L S 1965 *Thought and Language*. MIT Press, Cambridge, Massachusetts
Weinert S 1991 *Spracherwerb und implizites Lernen*. Hans Huber, Bern
Winston P H 1975 Learning structural descriptions from examples. In: Winston P H (ed.) 1975 *The Psychology of Computer Vision*. McGraw-Hill, New York

J. Perner

Cognitive Modifiability

Cognitive modifiability refers to the ability to use generalizable cognitive operations to modify one's own cognitive structures. It is based on the notion that the amount and nature of intelligent behavior displayed by an individual can change in fundamental ways regardless of etiology, age, or severity of condition. Cognitive modifiability implies that the rate, amount, and type of learning that a person is capable of can be altered through assisted acquisition of generalizable cognitive operations.

Interest in cognitive modifiability arises from the long-standing debate about whether intelligence is primarily influenced by hereditary factors, environmental factors, or an interaction of both. While it is now generally accepted that intelligence is influenced by both heredity and the environment, questions regarding the nature of intelligence, how best to measure intelligence, and whether or to what extent it can be modified continue to be the subject of much debate and discussion. Intelligent behavior likely requires two components: native ability, which is largely genetically determined, and cognitive functions, which are entirely acquired. Cognitive functions include learned cognitive operations, principles, processes, and strategies as well as "non-intellective" factors such as attitudes, beliefs, and motivational orientation. The focus of research on cognitive modifiability has been on the modifiability of cognitive functions. Cognitive modifiability is in contrast to notions of fixed ability in which it is believed that little can be done to change significantly an individual's intelligence and hence, the environment is adapted to meet the needs of the individual.

Contributions to theory and research on cognitive modifiability have been international in scope. Educators and psychologists in Switzerland, Russia, Israel, the United States, Canada, the Netherlands, South Africa, Australia, New Zealand, France, Spain, the United Kingdom, and Venezuela have contributed to the development of theories and programs. Application of cognitive education approaches has been worldwide.

1. Theorists

The term "cognitive modifiability" appears to have been coined by Reuven Feuerstein, whose theory of structural cognitive modifiability has been the basis of many educational applications to promote higher level thinking. Other theorists have also contributed to current understanding of the concept of cognitive modifiability, in particular, Jean Piaget and Lev Vygotsky.

1.1 Jean Piaget

Piaget, a Swiss psychologist, wrote extensively about cognitive modifiability in relation to the developmental process. His theories regarding intellectual development had a major influence on educational practice in the 1960s and 1970s and gave rise to extensive research and educational programs. Neo-Piagetians have continued to refine and develop his theories.

Piaget (1952) proposed that intellectual development proceeds through qualitatively different stages, each stage characterized by particular patterns of thought. He suggested the process of equilibration, that is, a balance between the assimilation of new information to cognitive schemes (i.e., organized patterns of thinking) and accommodation by the learner to that information, as a means of resolving cognitive conflict. Cognitive conflict promotes the growth of personal logic systems by confrontation between new and stored knowledge. Piaget believed that children's understanding, learning, and subsequent development is a function of their own activity which, in turn, is based on prior knowledge.

Many research investigations have focused upon Piaget's theories. Studies have found that children can be taught strategies and processes that promote intellectual development, but the general stages proposed by Piaget have not been supported by later research (Case 1985). Moreover, the mechanism of equilibration is considered vague. Nevertheless, the hierarchical and structural aspects of development have been confirmed (Paour 1990) and Piaget's theories continue to have a profound impact on educational practice.

1.2 Lev Vygotsky

Another theorist who has had a major influence on notions of cognitive modifiability was the Russian psychologist, Vygotsky. Vygotsky's ideas have given rise to extensive research and developments in the area of assessment of learning potential (Brown and Ferrara 1985).

Vygotsky believed that all psychological processes are originally encountered within a social context. Children first experience cognitive activities such as problem-solving in the presence of significant others. They gradually begin to share in the cognitive activity and to internalize such functions until, eventually, cognitive work can be performed independently. The process of internalization is gradual, proceeding developmentally from other-regulation to self-regulation. Vygotsky saw imitation as an important process in this development; however, he suggested that children are limited in what they can imitate at any point in development. He suggested that "the child can imitate only that which lies within the zone of his own intellectual potential" (1986 p. 204). Implicit within this theory of cognitive development (Vygotsky 1978) is the concept of a zone of proximal development (ZPD), defined as: "the distance between the actual developmental level as determined by individual problem-solving and the level of potential development as determined through problem-solving under adult guidance or in collaboration with more capable peers" (p.86).

Vygotsky saw the ZPD as a way of understanding the kinds of psychological processes that children would be capable of in the next phase of development and used the analysis of the ZPD to identify the type of instruction needed to realize this potential. He considered the ZPD to be an index of learning potential. For example, for one child, the zone may be quite narrow, indicating that the child is not yet ready to perform at a more advanced level than that indicated by unaided performance. For another child, or for the same child in a different task domain, the zone might be quite broad, indicating a readiness to perform at a higher level. Vygotsky's theory of ZPD has been a major impetus in the development of dynamic assessment procedures, discussed below.

1.3 Reuven Feuerstein

An Israeli clinical psychologist, Feuerstein, who studied with Piaget and his colleague, André Rey, has developed an assessment approach (Feuerstein et al. 1979) and an intervention program (Feuerstein 1980) based on theories of structural cognitive modifiability and mediated learning experience.

The theory of structural cognitive modifiability assumes that human beings have the unique capacity to modify their cognitive functioning in response to changing demands across the life-span. This modifiability can occur irrespective of variables such as age, etiology, and severity of condition, which are often considered barriers to change. Structural changes affect the way in which an individual interacts with, understands, and responds to sources of information. It is a change that is enduring, generalizable, and affects the future course of development.

Structural cognitive modifiability is brought about through direct encounters with stimuli much as Piaget describes, and through interaction with others. It is a particular mode of interaction, the mediated learning experience (MLE), that Feuerstein considers critical to the development of efficient cognitive functions. Feuerstein and his colleagues suggest that mediated learning experiences, intentional acts upon the part of a mediator, are the key to understanding why two children of similar age and etiology may develop very differently. They believe that a child must receive adequate MLE for normal cognitive development to occur. A lack of MLEs, either because they were not provided by the parent or because the child was unable to accept the type of MLE offered, is believed to lead to inadequate cognitive development and inefficient cognitive functioning.

Twelve characteristics of MLE have been described (Feuerstein et al. 1988). Of these, three must always be present for an interaction to be considered an MLE: intentionality and reciprocity, transcendence (i.e; generalization beyond the immediate event), and mediation of meaning. A mediated interaction is done with the intent to change the child's functioning in some way; to learn a generalizable cognitive operation, rule or strategy, that can be applied in appropriate situations with understanding. The interaction must also be reciprocated on the part of the child. It is not sufficient for an adult to focus a child's attention on an object, for example. The child must indicate some response to this effort. The goal of a mediated interaction is also to go beyond the immediate situation to an application of what is learned to other situations. Mediation of meaning refers to the "why" or "what for" of an interaction. In a mediated learning interaction the reasons for why something is happening are made explicit, either verbally or nonverbally through affect, body language, verbal communication, and the like.

The belief that human beings are modifiable and that the provision of MLE at any time in the life-span can lead to the development of efficient cognitive functions underlies many cognitive education programs and has also influenced assessment of people exhibiting learning difficulties. These will be discussed below.

2. Educational Applications

Theories and research related to cognitive modifiability have given rise to educational applications in three main areas; assessment, educational programs, and parent training programs.

2.1 Assessment

Beliefs about cognitive modifiability have brought about assessment approaches, which have the goal of assessing the amount and type of intervention necessary to produce change. "Dynamic assessment" is the term used to describe a variety of techniques, based primarily on the theories of Vygotsky and Feuerstein, that are used to assess cognitive change. Dynamic assessment approaches have gained in popularity with the publication of a text on the learning potential assessment device (Feuerstein et al. 1979) and with the research of Brown and Campione (Brown and Ferrara 1985) based on Vygotsky's theory of the zone of proximal development.

Essentially, dynamic assessment refers to an approach, often a test–teach–test design, in which the examiner teaches cognitive operations and strategies or provides feedback with the intent of observing the effect of this intervention on subsequent performance. Dynamic assessment is designed to go beyond the goal of simply describing the learner's difficulties and matching appropriate instruction to a goal of promoting structural changes in the course of assessment. One of the goals of dynamic assessment is to gain a clear understanding of the amount and type of input needed to modify cognitive functions.

Dynamic assessment approaches have been found to be particularly useful with populations for whom standardized testing results are questionable. Results from dynamic assessment help clarify why an individual is encountering difficulties and the type of intervention needed to remediate those difficulties.

The research, in general, has found that gains in cognitive functioning during dynamic assessment are not simply due to practice. Provision of elaborated feedback and mediational interventions significantly improve performance on tests. It has also been found that subjects with low initial performance levels make unanticipated gains in performance and that post-performance levels relate to parents' mediational ratings. Lidz (1991) reviews current dynamic assessment models and research.

2.2 Educational Programs

In the decade of the 1980s there was a great increase in programs that focused on teaching thinking. Many of these programs have come about because of the concern that children are not learning to think and reason in schools, while society increasingly demands high levels of thinking. Other programs have been developed based on the theories of Piaget, Vygotsky, and Feuerstein with the primary goal of teaching systematic thinking so that cognitive functions will become more efficient and children will benefit more from their experience. It is the latter programs that are discussed here. Costa (1991) provides a good overview of cognitive education programs.

A key variable in the educational programs that promote cognitive modifiability is a focus on the learning of process ("how") rather than content ("what"). Children are taught operations, principles, and strategies for learning as well as a metacognitive awareness (i.e., understanding their own thinking processes) so that they can become active, independent learners. The development of intrinsic motivation (i.e., rewards from the learning itself, as opposed to extrinsic motivation), is an important goal of these programs. Elaborated feedback concerning what the child has done well, what processes were helpful, and how these processes make a difference is considered important for learning and for developing intrinsic motivation. An understanding of and belief about this theoretical orientation by teachers is considered to be the key to effective implementation of cognitive education programs.

Several cognitive education programs have been developed based, in part, on Feuerstein's theoretical orientation. Instrumental Enrichment (Feuerstein 1980) has been implemented in many countries with many different populations. It has been used with Native American and Canadian children, gifted underachieving children in South Africa, deaf children in the United States and New Zealand, and low functioning adolescents in Israel, France, United Kingdom, United States, Canada, and many other countries. Several reviews of research on this program are available (Blagg 1991).

The COGNET (Greenberg 1990) program is also designed to be used with children from kindergarten through Grade 12. It is based on Feuerstein's theory of MLE. The COGNET instructional model assists teachers to analyze the types of teacher–student interactions in order to improve the quality of MLE provided. Children learn ten "building blocks of thinking" and eight "tools of independent learning" in personally relevant situations in the classroom. Cooperative learning and computer activities are used by COGNET teachers to facilitate learning. This program has been evaluated in the United States and is now being used in other countries (e.g., Belgium, the Netherlands).

A program for the cognitive education of preschool children, Bright Start: Cognitive Curriculum for Young Children (Haywood et al. 1992; for a brief description see Costa 1991 Vol. 2) is based on the theories of Feuerstein, Haywood, Piaget, and Vygotsky. Preventive rather than remedial, its primary goal is to equip young children with the cognitive tools that they will need for learning the academic and social content of the primary grades, and to do so before the children have been exposed to the failure that they often encounter because they lack such tools. Other goals are to enhance the development of intrinsic motivation, to remediate already deficient cognitive processes, and to prevent inappropriate placement in special education classes. Available in prepublication form since 1984, Bright Start has been implemented in the United States, Canada, France, Belgium, Israel, Mexico, and Switzerland, and is available in English, French, Spanish, Dutch, and Hebrew versions. This program relies heavily on the mediational teaching style based on Feuertein (1980) and elaborated by these authors. Seven curriculum "units" focus on: self regulation, quantitative relations, comparison, classification, role-taking, seriation, and identification by distinctive features. In addition, it has a cognitive-mediational system of behavior management and a program for parent participation. Evaluation studies done in the United States, Canada, Belgium, and Israel suggest that the program is associated with gains in cognitive modifiability, verbal elaboration, metacognitive process orientation, intelligence, and intrinsic motivation, and may be associated with reduced likelihood of special education placement.

2.3 Parent Programs

There have been many early intervention programs designed to enhance cognitive development of young children. A program that has focused specifically upon training parental mediational behaviors is the More Intelligent and Sensitive Child (MISC) intervention (Klein and Hundeide 1989). A major thrust of the MISC intervention is to enhance the quality of adult–child interaction and consequently to improve the child's cognitive modifiability, through an effect on the need system, that is, the need to focus clearly, to seek novelty, and to associate, contrast, or examine things logically. The MISC is based on a careful preintervention and on an ongoing focus on the close interconnectedness of emotional and cognitive development. It takes into account cultural psychosocial variables relating to questions such as: the parents' goals for the child, how they view their child as compared to others, what they see as their role, what they consider as good parenting, and how much effect they believe they can have on their child's development. The MISC approach advocates the establishment of a positive affective parent–child communication cycle. It helps parents identify and increase particular mediational behaviors already in their repertoire and to learn others. The program is based upon Feuerstein's theories of structural cognitive modifiability and mediated learning experience (Feuerstein 1980) and upon empirical data, gathered by Klein and her colleagues suggesting that specific characteristics of adult interaction with children, namely mediational behaviors, affect children's predisposition to learn from new experiences. MISC has been implemented in Norway, Sweden, Portugal, Ethiopia, Sri Lanka, Zimbabwe, Indonesia, Israel, and the United States.

2.4 Publications and Association

Interest in cognitive modifiability has been increasing as evidenced by new publications in this area. There are two new journals, *International Journal of Cognitive Education and Mediated Learning* and *The International Journal of Dynamic Assessment and Instruction*, in the area of cognitive modifiability. There is also a new association, The International Association for Cognitive Education, to promote cognitive approaches and provide a forum for exchange of research and practical applications (Price 1989).

See also: Cognitive Development: Overview; Cognitive Development: Individual Differences

References

Blagg N 1991 *Can we Teach Intelligence? A Comprehensive Evaluation of Feuerstein's Instrumental Enrichment Program*. Erlbaum, Hillsdale,

Brown A L & Ferrara R A 1985 Diagnosing zones of proximal development. In: Wersch J (ed.) 1985 *Culture Communication and Cognition: Vygotskian Perspectives*. Cambridge University Press, Cambridge, Massachusetts

Case R 1985 *Intellectual Development: Birth to Adulthood*. Academic Press, Orlando

Costa A L 1991 *Developing Minds, 2nd Edn*. Association for Supervision and Curriculum Development, Alexandria, Virginia

Feuerstein R 1980 *Instrumental Enrichment*. University Park Press, Baltimore, Maryland

Feuerstein R, Rand Y, Hoffman M 1979 *The Dynamic Assessment of Retarded Performers*. University Park Press, Baltimore, Maryland

Feuerstein R, Rand Y, Rynders J E 1988 *Don't Accept Me as I Am: Helping "Retarded" People to Excel*. Plenum, New York

Greenberg K H 1990 Combining Research and theoretical application: The Cognet project *International Journal of Cognitive Education and Mediated Learning* 1(3): 237–44

Haywood H C, Brooks P, Burns S 1992 *Bright Start: Cognitive Curriculum for Young Children*. Charlesbridge, Watertown, Massachusetts

Klein P S, Hundeide K 1989 *Training Manual for the MISC (More Intelligent and Sensitive Child) Program*. UNICEF, Sri Lanka

Lidz C 1991 *Practitioner's Guide to Dynamic Assessment*. Guilford Press, New York

Paour J L 1990 Piagetian constructivism and the concept of mediated learning experience. *Eur. J. Psycho. Educ.* 5(2): 177–90

Piaget J 1952 *The Origins of Intelligence in Children*. International Universities Press, New York

Price M (ed.) 1989 *Cognitive Education: A Publication of the International Association for Cognitive Education* The Learning Center, Calgary

Vygotsky L S 1978 *Mind in Society: The Development of High Psychological Processes*. Harvard University Press, Cambridge, Massachusetts

Vygotsky L S 1986 Thinking and speech. In: Vygotsky L

S *Collected Works: Problems of General psychology*, Vol. 1. Plenum, New York

M. Samuels; P. Klein; H. C. Haywood

Cognitive Strategy Instruction: Special Education

"Cognitive strategy instruction" refers to instruction that is designed to increase the learner's ability to regulate and monitor his or her own learning activity. There are three types of knowledge generally regarded as essential to self-regulation: (a) knowledge of strategies, or effortful and deliberate activities engaged in for the purpose of accomplishing learning tasks; (b) metacognitive knowledge, or knowledge of one's own learner characteristics as well as knowledge of the task demands, that enables the learner to select, employ, evaluate, and modify strategy use; and (c) real world knowledge. Special educators have been particularly intrigued by cognitive strategy instruction as a response to descriptive research documenting the failure of students experiencing learning difficulties to display the knowledge, beliefs, and behaviors that characterize self-regulated learners (Meltzer et al. 1989).

This entry begins with some historical information regarding cognitive strategy instruction. This is followed by a summary of models of strategy instruction that have attained some prominence in special education (drawn from the reading literature). The entry concludes by identifying enduring issues regarding cognitive strategy instruction.

1. Historical Perspective

Research on cognitive strategy instruction has burgeoned since the 1970s when cognitive psychologists began intensive inquiry into human thought processes. Special educators embraced this model partly because of the disillusionment they were experiencing regarding two other prominent approaches to the instruction of special education students. The first approach—suggested by the underlying ability deficit model—was to teach processes that were assumed to underlie successful academic achievement; for example, auditory memory or visual perception. This orientation failed to muster support because of its limited usefulness when planning and delivering instruction; when students did demonstrate improvement with the underlying process, this improvement was not reflected in academic performance (Wong 1992). The second approach was the use of operant procedures to modify both social and academic behavior; for example, students would be praised and rewarded for fluency and accuracy in decoding and comprehension. Typically, operant procedures of this nature failed to improve the targeted behavior, or, when improvement was discerned there was little evidence of maintenance of the improvement or generalization to situations different from the one in which the behavior was modified.

In contrast to either of these approaches, a cognitive strategy approach is rooted in theoretical analyses of the task at hand to determine the component skills or procedures underlying successful completion of the designated task, as well as observations of the activity of skilled learners engaged in the academic task of interest. For example, Bereiter and Bird (1985) observed skilled readers who engaged in thinking aloud while reading as a means of sharing the kinds of cognitive activity in which they were engaged. The protocols of these "think alouds" revealed that skillful readers paraphrased as they read, reread for clarification, and predicted in advance of reading. These kinds of observations, in turn, informed the design of strategy instruction programs. For example, reciprocal teaching instruction to improve reading comprehension employs several of the strategies observed with skillful readers in the Bereiter and Bird study. Similarly, in writing, Flower and Hayes (1980) developed a model of writing instruction, informed by the think aloud protocols of skillful writers, which has been successfully employed in the writing instruction work that Englert and her colleagues (Englert and Mariage 1991, Englert et al. 1991); Harris and Graham and their colleagues (Harris and Graham 1985, Graham and Harris 1989) and Wong et al. (1989) have conducted with special education students.

Since the early 1970s, a number of instructional approaches have been designed to teach students problem-solving strategies. These approaches differ in terms of the knowledge and skills that are targeted for instruction, and reflect different assumptions about the role of knowledge and the cognitive processes involved in thinking and problem-solving. Two large categories of approaches will be described: (a) general approaches to enhance thinking and problem-solving independently of academic content, and (b) domain-specific approaches.

A complete review of general thinking-skills approaches that have been developed to teach students a set of thinking skills independent of specific content has been conducted by Nickerson et al. (1984). Generally, this instruction is designed to promote students' general metacognitive and self-monitoring knowledge and skills such as defining the problem goals, identifying relevant facts, and developing a plan to solve the problem. These approaches are based upon two assumptions: (a) that there are general metacognitive skills that can be applied across a wide range of tasks; and (b) that in contrast to good problem-solvers, poor problem-solvers demonstrate a passive approach to problem-solving in which they do not seem to be consciously aware of and use self-monitoring processes (Bloom and Broder 1950). Examples of this approach include: a program developed by Feuerstein et al. (1980) entitled *Instrumental Enrichment*; Whimbey and Lochhead's (1991) program, *Problem Solving and Comprehension*, and The Philosophy for Children Program (Lipman et al. 1980). Data to support the relative effectiveness of these programs are sparse, despite their widespread adoption. Data which do exist suggest that while participants in these programs demonstrate improvement on the kinds of problems encountered in the problem-solving curricula, these improvements do not, in turn, enhance academic achievement.

Alternative models of strategy instruction are domain-specific. The domain-specific nature of strategy use is largely based on research in developmental and cognitive psychology that has demonstrated the importance of examining the ways in which strategies and knowledge interact to enhance problem-solving performance. For example, developmental studies in the area of memory (Chi 1978), examining the role of knowledge on recall performance, have demonstrated that an individual's knowledge influences recall performance as well as the strategies that are employed. Studies conducted to compare the performance of experts and novices within particular domains such as physics (Larkin et al. 1980, Linn 1985), have provided further evidence of the powerful effect that knowledge, not simply the quantity but also the qualitative organization of that knowledge (Chi and Koeske 1983), has on problem-solving performance.

Domain-specific strategy instruction has been a thriving enterprise in special education research since the early 1980s. The reader is referred to the special series of *Journal of Learning Disabilities* (1992) for a representative review of strategy instruction interventions across domains (mathematics, composition, reading). The next section of this entry considers the instructional implications of this research by characterizing and evaluating an array of strategy instruction models that have been implemented with special needs populations in reading.

2. Models of Domain-specific Strategy Instruction in Reading

A considerable amount of the research on cognitive strategy instruction in special education has concentrated on reading, due to the central role reading plays across the curriculum. While reading activities are fundamental, they are differentially employed by students, prompting research efforts to understand these differences in order to develop instructional models to promote greater strategy use across students. The following discussion focuses on six different models of cognitive strategy instruction within the area of reading and these models are used to examine such issues as the role of the teacher and student in strategy instruction, the nature of the context of instruction, and the outcomes of instruction.

2.1 Direct Instruction

Direct instruction is an approach in which the steps of selected strategies are presented by the teacher in a sequential fashion, generally determined through task analysis. Students practice these steps as the teacher provides and eventually fades prompts. A hallmark of direct instruction is the active and directive role assumed by the teacher, who maintains control of the pace, sequence, and content of the lesson.

The effects of direct instruction have been investigated with general and special education students learning an array of comprehension strategies, such as identifying the main idea (Baumann 1984), understanding anaphoric relationships (Baumann 1986), critical reading (Darch and Kameenui 1987, Patching et al. 1983), and study skills (Adams et al. 1982). Typically, the effectiveness of direct instruction approaches has been investigated by comparing them to traditional basal reading instruction methods. The outcomes of these studies suggest that direct instruction is an effective means for teaching specific comprehension strategies to both low and normally achieving students. What is less clear from these studies is the extent to which these students' ability to understand and recall text has been enhanced as a consequence of direct instruction of particular strategies. In part, the results are inconclusive as a function of the measures selected. Those studies that have included measures to evaluate students' generalization beyond the targeted strategies suggest that improvement is typically limited to the specific strategies that were taught; students who have demonstrated mastery of the targeted strategies have neither concurrently demonstrated improvement in their ability to comprehend text nor displayed the flexibility necessary to use the targeted strategies in novel contexts. In other words, the problem of inert knowledge appears prevalent in examining the results of direct instruction.

2.2 Cognitive Behavior Modification

Cognitive behaviour modification (CBM) has been used to refer to a broad array of self-instructional programs. Traditional CBM programs are based upon the hypothesis that students can learn to regulate their own performance by means of internalizing a prescribed set of monitoring statements before, during, and after performing a task. The statements, which are developed based upon task analyses, typically assist the student in defining the task, directing attention, reinforcing performance, and coping with difficulties.

The development of CBM has been informed by

several different theories of learning including social learning theory and social constructivism, as well as research in the area of verbal mediation (Meichenbaum 1985). Social learning theory emphasized the importance of students' cognitions in facilitating self-control, which directed researchers' attention away from overt behaviors to the ways in which students were mediating those behaviors. Verbal mediation research was informative regarding the importance of teaching individuals to produce and use mediating statements to enhance task comprehension, as well as task completion. A third influence is social constructivist theory, represented by the writings of Vygotsky (1978) and Luria (1976). They were interested in the role of social interactions in cognitive development and the shift of psychological functions from the interpersonal to intrapersonal levels. Luria proposed that this shift occurred in three phases. First, an adult (or more capable person) verbally controls the child's (or a less capable person's) behavior. Second, the child begins to direct his or her own behavior by overt speech. Gradually over time, this speech becomes internalized thus enabling the child to control his or her own behavior.

Within reading, CBM has been used as a means for enhancing students' study skills (Dansereau et al. 1979) and their ability to detect errors in reading passages (Miller et al. 1987). Research indicates that CBM is an effective means of strategy instruction, particularly for above-average learners. This research has, however, not addressed the following matters: flexibility of strategy use, generalized use of instructed strategies, and changes in reading awareness and attitudes following instruction. Similar to direct instruction, CBM represents strategies as a series of discrete steps, selected and modeled by the teacher with no occasion to evaluate the students' representation of reading activity. Furthermore, there is variability across the CBM studies in terms of the focus on the processes of reading (e.g., how one determines the main idea vs. detail and how one reads for understanding). Finally, Diaz and Berk (1992) critique self-instructional approaches, such as those used in CBM, that were inspired by Vygotskian theories regarding the development of verbal self-regulation. They suggest that the limited success of many of these programs is actually consistent with Vygotsky's theory since they are based upon erroneous assumptions regarding the development of private speech. For example, some approaches are based upon the assumption that children with learning and behavior problems emit less private speech than their normally achieving peers. Yet empirical evidence indicates that this is not the case (Berk and Potts 1991, Copeland 1979, Berk and Landau 1991, Harris 1986). A second erroneous assumption is that simply modeling and asking children to repeat a prescribed set of verbalized instructions will lead children to engage in more spontaneous private speech. Padilla and Diaz (1986) found that adult modeling had no impact on children's private speech or task performance. The authors indicate that modeling does not reflect the kinds of dynamic social interactions that are critical in fostering the emergence of children's spontaneous private speech and the development of self-regulation. Successful interventions that are consistent with Vygotsky's theory are characterized by highly interactive communications among the adult and child in which the child assumes an active role in the problem-solving process. The adult constantly evaluates the child's current level of competence and provides support accordingly. Socially mediated interactions are characterized by a two-way process of appropriation on the part of adult and child (Litowitz 1990), in contrast to modeling which involves little or no reciprocity between the two parties.

2.3 The Strategies Intervention Model

The strategies intervention model, developed at the University of Kansas Institute for Research in Learning Disabilities, has emerged from an extensive research program that investigated the academic performance of students who were identified as either learning disabled or low achieving (Deshler and Schumaker 1986, Lenz et al. 1989). As in direct instruction and cognitive behavior modification, the strategies are taught as a series of steps. Unlike the other models, the strategies intervention model comprises two phases of instruction. In the acquisition phase, students are taught to apply the strategy in a supported setting. In the generalization phase, students learn to apply the strategy in the general education setting. The strategies intervention model is also distinguished by the fact that instruction is preceded by assessment regarding the students' current strategy use in specific contexts. Thereafter, the instructional steps are quite comparable to those used in direct instruction and cognitive behavior modification: modeling and verbal rehearsal of the steps of the strategy, and guided practice and feedback with materials controlled for complexity, length, and difficulty, with the use of mastery criteria to determine when the student can proceed to more difficult materials. Investigations indicate that sustained instruction is successful in improving strategy use, as well as content learning.

2.4 Direct Explanation

Direct explanation (Duffy et al. 1986, 1987) is distinguished from the previous models in several respects. It is an approach in which skills are recast as strategies that serve as tools for understanding text. To make this explicit to students, teachers provide: (a) declarative knowledge (i.e., inform the student about the name of the strategy, the purpose for which it could be useful, and steps in deploying the strategy); (b) procedural knowledge (i.e., teach the students how to use the strategy); and (c) conditional knowledge (i.e., inform the students about when the strategy would be appropriately used). In an effort to teach the skills as tools, the teachers "talk aloud" about the mental processes they use when experiencing difficulty understanding text, the way in which application of the skill can increase comprehension, and the mental steps that should be taken to use the skills strategically. At this point, the steps correspond quite well with those of the learning strategies intervention model, including the use of modeling, guided practice, and independent practice.

Investigations of direct explanation have been conducted by third- and fifth-grade teachers working with their lowest groups of readers. Students in the direct explanation condition showed significantly greater procedural and conditional knowledge of the strategies. In addition, metacognitive interviews indicated greater awareness on the part of the experimental students regarding the strategic nature of reading. The results of reading achievement measures have been somewhat mixed, with experimental students scoring significantly higher on the word study subtest of a reading achievement test, but not on the comprehension subtest of this measure.

2.5 Informed Strategies for Learning

Informed strategies for learning (ISL) is a curricular approach to strategy instruction that was designed to enhance students' reading comprehension (Paris and Oka 1986). It consists of 20 modules addressing 4 comprehension processes: planning for reading, identifying meaning, reasoning while reading, and monitoring comprehension. Each module includes 3 lessons that focus on a specific strategy (e.g., finding the main idea). These lessons inform students about the usefulness of the strategy, provide metaphors to help students understand the strategy, and offer guided practice, as well as opportunities to apply the strategies to a variety of texts (e.g., science and social studies).

Informed strategies for learning is distinguished from the models of cognitive strategy instruction previously described since it includes an additional component, group dialogues. The purpose of these dialogues is to provide opportunities for teachers and students to discuss their thoughts and feelings about the strategies, and their usefulness, with particular attention paid to personal aspects of strategy use. Although the effectiveness of ISL has been determined with regard to increasing students' awareness of strategies and strategy use, the effects of ISL on reading comprehension with poor readers has been less encouraging.

2.6 Reciprocal Teaching

Reciprocal teaching (Brown and Palincsar 1989, Palincsar and Brown 1984, 1988) features the instruction of four strategies that are taught and practiced as a set of complementary activities to be used flexibly as the text, the needs of the reader, and the demands of the text suggest. In contrast to the previous methods, reciprocal teaching (RT) places less emphasis on teacher explanation or mastery of discrete strategies and greater emphasis on the collaboration of teachers and students to use specific strategies to render the text meaningful.

In RT, teachers and students take turns leading a dialogue about the meaning of the text with which they are working. The discussion focuses on generating questions from the text, summarizing the text, clarifying portions that impair understanding, and predicting upcoming content based on clues that are provided by the content and structure of the text. When these dialogues begin, the teacher assumes principal responsibility for leading and sustaining the discussion, modeling skilled use of the strategies for the purpose of understanding the content. Even from the first day of instruction, however, the children are encouraged to participate in the discussion by generating their own questions, elaborating upon or revising the summary, or suggesting additional predictions. The teacher enables the participation of each student in the dialogue through the use of specific feedback, additional explanation, and modeling.

Investigations of RT have been conducted with at-risk students in the primary grades (as listening comprehension instruction) and with remedial readers in middle school. At both levels, RT has significantly increased students' ability to use the targeted strategies and to attain higher scores on standardized and criterion-referenced comprehension measures. In addition, these gains have been demonstrated to maintain over time and to generalize beyond the experimental setting. Reciprocal Teaching research has not assessed students' conceptions of reading activity or changes in those conceptions with instruction. In addition, the highly interactive nature of RT renders it a difficult model to implement for teachers who are more accustomed to "directive teaching".

3. Challenges of Effectively Implementing Cognitive Strategy Instruction

While there are now a number of models of strategy instruction that have been implemented with special education students, with varying degrees of success, there are still numerous challenges confronting the teacher and researcher concerned with teaching for self-regulation. Some of these challenges are considered below.

3.1 Responding to the Social Context of Education

Alvermann (1992) discusses the importance of engaging in strategy instruction that is culturally sensitive with respect to the norms and values of nonmainstream cultures. Typically, there has been little attention paid to this issue in strategy instruction research. Yet cultural variables may help to explain the differential effects of strategy instruction. Research efforts have been directed toward identifying possible discontinuities between students' native cultures and the school cultures with respect to a number of instructional variables (e.g., discourse modes, participation structures, objectives, and content) that might account for the low academic achievement of some minority groups. This has led to the development of several model programs that are congruent with students' native culture in homogeneous communities (Au 1980, Jordan 1984, 1985). However, additional research is needed since there are still many unanswered questions about how to implement culturally sensitive instruction in culturally diverse communities (Tharp 1989).

Alvermann indicates that for some students, the objectives of strategy instruction may be incongruous with those of their native culture. For example, a commonly identified purpose of this form of instruction is to ensure that each individual can function independently of the teacher. Yet this instructional goal may not be congruent with the values of some cultures that encourage greater interdependence among group members. Alvermann suggests that students who understand the purpose of instruction may value and accept the instructional approach. In culturally diverse classrooms it is important to strike a balance so that one group is not consistently required to compromise its values.

Another possible source of cultural conflict is the nature of instruction. For example, in one replication study of reciprocal teaching, Gaber (1987) raised questions about whether students' lack of participation might be due to cultural differences between their natural discourse modes and the targeted form of discourse. Native Canadian adults, whom Gaber identified as functionally illiterate, were taught to engage in the reciprocal teaching dialogues. While most participants achieved criterion performance on the comprehension assessments, they did not engage in the dialogues among themselves when the teacher was absent from the group. For these students the form of instruction may have been discrepant with their cultural practices, raising questions about whether this form of instruction is appropriate for this particular group.

Another possible reason for the Canadian students' limited participation is their failure to internalize the strategies to the extent that they were able to function independently of the teacher. They might need additional time and teacher support before they become proficient at engaging in the dialogues independently. These issues underscore some of the complexities involved in conducting effective strategy instruction (Duffy and Roehler 1989), as well as emphasizing the way in which knowledge is socially constructed. More effective approaches do not consist of neatly packed instructional programs. Instead, they require skillful instruction in which the teacher mediates the learning of individual students by adjusting the demands of the task in relationship to the students' current knowledge and level of competence. The teachers' role as mediator is an extremely demanding one that requires considerable knowledge regarding development, the use of language in instruction, assessment, and domain knowledge. Duffy and Roehler (1989) suggest that teachers need instructional programs that provide structure and guidance to support the constant decision-making process that is an essential component of effective strategy instruction. This support might be in the form of metascripts (Gallimore and Tharp 1983) or general guidelines that enhance teachers' ability to teach in a responsive and flexible manner.

3.2 The Pursuit of Higher Order Literacies

The question regarding the generality versus domain-specificity of the thinking and problem-solving skills that should constitute the core of curricula continues to be a pressing one. Considerable research is needed to identify those thinking skills that will promote understanding across domains and will have applicability to daily life. One approach to this question is pursued by Perkins and his colleagues (Perkins and Simmons 1988) who examine the teaching of "epistemic forms," which are basic conceptual structures that provide useful ways of organizing knowledge and promoting conceptual understanding. Examples of epistemic forms include "comparison/contrast" and "form fits function." This pursuit will be particularly important when considering the needs of special education students who have, historically, been disenfranchised from the pursuit of higher-order literacy (cf. McGill-Franzen and Allington 1992).

3.3 The Relationship Between Motivation and Strategy Use

Current models of motivation provide a more complete picture of individual and situational variables that account for the learned helplessness approach that characterizes the achievement behavior of many special education students. Dweck and her colleagues developed a social-cognitive model that explains how two factors—students' goal orientation and perceived ability—interact to influence students' patterns of behavior, cognition, and affect (Dweck and Leggett 1988). Two common goal orientations reflect the different concerns or purposes of students:

(a) a task orientation reflects a concern with increasing one's understanding and skills; and (b) an ego orientation reflects concern with obtaining favorable ability evaluations and avoiding negative ones. These goal orientations in combination with students' perceived ability level influence students' response to challenging tasks. Performance-oriented students with low ability perceptions typically exhibit a helpless pattern that is characterized by the avoidance of challenge, decreased effort, and decrements in performance. This contrasts with task-focused students who seek challenging tasks, and maintain effective striving when confronted with difficult tasks.

One striking difference that has been observed between task-focused and helpless students is their use of effective problem-solving strategies. In one study, both groups employed effective problem-solving strategies to solve one set of tasks (Diener and Dweck 1978). However, when presented with more challenging tasks, helpless children employed less effective strategies than task-focused children. Additional studies have demonstrated a relationship between students' goal orientations and their valuing and use of effective learning strategies (Nolen 1988, Ames and Archer 1988, Pintrich and DeGroot 1990).

Since a task orientation is more conducive to fostering adaptive problem-solving among students, research has focused on identifying factors that influence the goals students are likely to adopt, including: classroom practices (Epstein 1989, Ames 1992), students' perceptions of classroom goals (Ames and Archer 1988), beliefs about the nature of ability and intelligence (Nicholls 1984, Dweck and Leggett 1988), and valuing of the task. Research indicates that students' goal orientation is not a stable trait but varies across domains and tasks depending upon how important the domain or task is to the student (Ames in press). Other researchers (Maehr and Midgely 1990) have designed interventions to help teachers implement instructional practices that foster a mastery approach to learning that focuses on areas including evaluation, tasks, rewards, and grouping. Results indicate that the children who are most likely to benefit from an enhanced mastery climate are children who are at risk for academic difficulty (Ames in press).

One approach that has been effective in addressing student motivation is combining attributional retraining with strategy instruction (Borkowksi et al. 1988). Current models of motivation suggest that in addition to addressing the maladaptive attributional styles of special education students through attributional retraining, it is important to attend to other individual and classroom variables that influence student performance.

3.4 Restructuring Assessment Practices

It is difficult to overestimate the importance of designing assessment practices in such a manner that they are more closely aligned with instructional goals; in this instance assessment strategies must be consistent with strategic approaches to teaching and learning (Valencia and Pearson 1987). Traditional assessment practices have generally focused on measuring in static ways the outcomes of learning as opposed to the dynamic processes of learning. A movement toward portfolio assessment that is occurring concurrently with the movement toward teaching for self-regulation may advance this agenda (Gifford and O'Connor 1992). In portfolio assessment, there is an emphasis on student and teacher reflection on the learning process as well as the resulting products. Student performance is studied over time, in multiple contexts, with the use of on-line measures, and in a manner that solicits student self-evaluation.

3.5 Supporting Teachers in Instructional Change

The demands of teaching for self-regulation are considerable, suggesting the need to determine ways in which teachers can be supported in their efforts to teach general as well as domain-specific problem-solving activity. Ongoing efforts such as those by Gaskins and Elliot (1991) support the need to: (a) involve faculty in selecting and formulating strategy instruction approaches; (b) provide opportunities to voice the concerns, difficulties, and successes that teachers are experiencing during implementation efforts; (c) support instructional chaining such as peer coaching and peer collaboration; (d) align instructional objectives with assessment; and (e) recognize that change takes time. Based upon their efforts to implement change, Gaskins and Elliot recommend that instructional innovation be phased in over a period of three to five years.

See also: Cognitive Development: Individual Differences; Learning Strategic and Learning to Learn; Learning Strategies, Teaching and Testing

References

Adams A, Carine D, Gersten R 1982 Instructional strategies for studying content area texts in the intermediate grades. *Read. Res. Q.* 18(1): 27–55

Alvermann D 1992 The influence of sociocultural factors on cognitive strategy instruction: A review of the research. Paper presented at the annual meeting of the American Educational Research Association, San Francisco, California

Ames C 1992 Classrooms: Goals, structures, and student motivation. *J. Educ. Psychol.* 84(3): 261–71

Ames C, Archer J 1988 Achievement goals in the classroom: Student learning strategies and motivation processes. *J. Educ. Psychol.* 80(3): 260–67

Au K H 1980 Participation structures in a reading lesson with Hawaiian children: Analysis of a cultural appropriate instructional event. *Anthropol. Educ. Q.* 11(2): 91–115

Baumann J F 1984 The effectiveness of a direct instruction paradigm for teaching main idea comprehension. *Read. Res. Q.* 20(1): 93–115

Baumann J F 1986 Teaching third-grade students to comprehend anaphoric relationships: The application of a direct instruction model. *Read. Res. Q.* 21(1): 70–90
Bereiter C, Bird M 1985 Use of thinking aloud in identification and teaching of reading comprehension strategies. *Cognition and Instruction* 2(2): 131–56
Berk L E, Landau S 1991. Setting effects on the private speech of learning disabled and normal children. Paper presented at the biennial meeting of the Society for Research in Child Development, Seattle, Washington
Berk L E, Potts M 1991 Developmental and functional significance of private speech among attention-deficit hyperactivity disordered and normal boys. *J. Abnorm. Child Psychol.* 19(3): 357–77
Bloom B S, Broder L J 1950 *Problem-solving Processes of College Students: An Exploratory Investigation.* University of Chicago Press, Chicago, Illinois
Borkowski J G, Weyhing R S, Carr M 1988 Effects of attributional retraining on strategy-based reading comprehension in learning-disabled students. *J. Educ. Psychol.* 80(1): 46–53
Brown A L, Palincsar A S 1989 Guided cooperative learning and individual knowledge acquisition. In: Resnick L (ed.) 1989 *Knowing and Learning: Issues for a Cognitive Psychology of Learning. Essays in Honor of Robert Glaser.* Erlbaum, Hillsdale, New Jersey
Chi M T H 1978 Knowledge structures and memory development. In: Siegler R S (ed.) 1978 *Children's Thinking: What Develops*? Erlbaum, Hillsdale, New Jersey
Chi M T H, Koeske R D 1983 Network representation of a child's dinosaur knowledge. *Dev. Psychol.* 19(1): 29–39
Copeland A P 1979 Types of private speech produced by hyperactive and nonhyperactive boys. *J. Abnorm. Child Psychol.* 7(1): 169–77
Dansereau D F et al. 1979 Development and evaluation of a learning strategy training program. *J. Educ. Psychol.* 71(1): 64–73
Darch C, Kameenui E J 1987 Teaching LD students critical reading skills: A systematic replication. *Learning Disability Quarterly* 10(2): 82–91
Deshler D D, Schumaker J B 1986 Learning strategies: An instructional alternative for low-achieving adolescents. *Excep. Child.* 52(6): 583–90
Diaz R M, Berk L E 1992 Misguided assumptions of self-instructional training. Paper presented at the annual meeting of the American Educational Research Association, San Francisco, California
Diener C I, Dweck C S 1978 An analysis of learned helplessness: Continuous changes in performance, strategy, and achievement cognitions following failure. *J. Pers. Soc. Psychol.* 36(5): 451–62
Duffy G G, Roehler L R 1989 Why strategy instruction is so difficult and what we need to do about it. In: McCormick C B, Miller G E, Pressley M (eds.) 1989 *Cognitive Strategy Research: From Basic Research to Educational Applications.* Springer-Verlag, New York
Duffy G G et al. 1986 The relationship between explicit verbal explanations during reading skill instruction and student awareness and achievement: A study of reading teacher effects. *Read. Res. Q.* 21(3): 237–52
Duffy G G et al. 1987 Effects of explaining the reasoning associated with using reading strategies. *Read. Res. Q.* 22:(3) 347–68
Dweck C S, Leggett E L 1988 A social cognitive approach to motivation and personality. *Psychol. Rev.* 95(2): 256–73
Englert C S, Mariage T V 1991 Shared understandings: Structuring the writing experience through dialogue. *J. Learn. Disabil.* 24 (6): 330–42
Englert C S, Raphael T M, Anderson L M, Anthony H M 1991 Making strategies and self-talk visible: Writing instruction in regular and special education classrooms. *Am. Educ. Res. J.* 28 (2): 337–72
Epstein J 1989 Family structures and student motivation: A developmental perspective. In: Ames C, Ames R (eds.) 1989 *Research on Motivation in Education*, Vol 3. Academic Press, New York
Feuerstein R, Rand Y, Hoffman M B, Miller R 1980 *Instrumental Enrichment: An Intervention Program for Cognitive Modifiability.* University Park Press, Baltimore, Maryland
Flower L, Hayes J R 1980 The dynamics of composing: Making plans and juggling constraints. In: Gregg L W, Steinberg E R (eds.) 1980 *Cognitive Processes in Writing.* Erlbaum, Hillsdale, New Jersey
Gaber D 1987 The use of reciprocal teaching method to improve the reading comprehension of functionally illiterate adults. Paper presented at the annual meeting of the National Reading Conference, Petersburg, Florida
Gallimore R, Tharp R G 1983 *The Regulatory Functions of Teacher Questions: A Microanalysis of Reading Comprehension Lessons.* Kamehameha Educational Research Institute, The Kamehameha Schools, Honolulu, Hawaii
Gaskins I, Elliot T 1991 *Implementing Cognitive Strategy Training in a School Setting. A How-to Manual for Teachers.* Brookline Books
Gifford B, O'Connor M (eds.) 1992 *Changing Assessment: Alternative Views of Aptitude, Achievement, and Instruction.* Kluwer, Boston, Massachusetts
Graham S, Harris K R 1989 Components analysis of cognitive strategy instruction: Effects on learning disabled students' compositions and self-efficacy. *J. Educ. Psychol.* 81 (3): 353–61
Harris K R 1986 The effects of cognitive-behavior modification on the private speech and task performance during problem solving among learning-disabled and normally achieving children. *J. Abnorm. Child Psychol.* 14 (1): 63–76
Harris K R, Graham S 1985 Improving learning disabled students' composition skills: Self-control strategy training. *Learning Disabilities Quarterly* 8 (1): 27–36
Jordan C 1984 Cultural compatibility and the education of Hawaiian children: Implications for mainland educators. *Educ. Res. Q.* 8 (4): 59–71
Jordan C 1985 Translating culture: From ethnographic information to educational program. *Anthropol. Educ. Q.* 16 (2): 105–23
Journal of Learning Disabilities 1992 Vol. 25: 3–4 (special series)
Larkin J H, McDermott J, Simon D P, Simon H 1980 Expert and novice performance in solving physics problems. *Science* 208 (4450): 1335–42
Lenz B, Clark F L, Deshler D D, Schumaker J B 1989 *The Strategies Instructional Approach: A Training Package.* University of Kansas Institute for Research in Learning Disabilities, Lawrence, Kansas
Linn M C 1985 The cognitive consequences of pro-

gramming instruction in classrooms. *Educ. Researcher* 14: 14–16
Lipman M, Sharp A M, Oscanyan F S 1980 *Philosophy in the Classroom*, 2nd edn. Temple University Press, Philadelphia, Pennsylvania
Litowitz B E 1990 Deconstruction in the zone of proximal development. *The Quarterly Newsletter of the Laboratory of Comparative Human Cognition* 12(4)
Luria A R 1976 *Cognitive Development: Its Cultural and Social Foundations*. Harvard University Press, Cambridge, Massachusetts
Maehr M Midgely C 1990 Enhancing student motivation: A school-wide approach. Unpublished manuscript. University of Michigan, Ann Arbor, Michigan
McGill-Franzen A Allington R L 1992 The gridlock of low reading achievement: Perspectives on practice and policy. *Rem. Spec. Educ.* 12(3): 20–30
Meichenbaum D 1985 Teaching thinking: A cognitive-behavioral perspective. In: Chipman S F, Segal J W, Glaser R (eds.) 1985 *Thinking and Learning Skills: Vol. 2. Research and Open Questions*. Erlbaum, Hillsdale, New Jersey
Meltzer L J, Solomon B, Fenton R, Levine M D 1989 A developmental study of problem-solving strategies in children with and without learning difficulties. *Journal of Applied Developmental Psychology* 10(2): 171–93
Miller G E, Giovenco A, Rentiers K A 1987 Fostering comprehension monitoring in below average readers through self-instruction training. *J. Read. Behav.* 19(4): 379–93
Nicholls J G 1984 Achievement motivation: Conceptions of ability, subjective experience, task choice, and performance. *Psychol. Rev.* 91(3): 328–46
Nickerson R S, Perkins D N, Smith E E 1985 *The Teaching of Thinking*. Erlbaum, Hillsdale, New Jersey
Nolen S B 1988 Reasons for studying: Motivational orientations and study strategies. *Cognition and Instruction* 5(4): 269–87
Padilla K A, Diaz R M 1986 The training of self-regulatory private speech. Paper presented at the Conference of the Minority Biomedical Research Program, New Orleans, Louisiana
Palincsar A S, Brown A L 1984 Reciprocal teaching of comprehension-fostering and comprehension-monitoring activities. *Cognition and Instruction* 1(2): 117–75
Palincsar A S, Brown A L 1988 Teaching and practicing thinking skills to promote comprehension in the context of group problem solving. *Rem. Spec. Educ.* 9(1): 53–59
Paris S, Oke E 1986 Children's reading strategies, metacognition, and motivation. *Dev. Rev.* 6(1): 25–56
Patching W, Kameenui E, Carnin D, Gersten R, Colvin G 1983 Direct instruction in critical reading skills. *Read. Res. Q.* 18(4): 406–18
Perkins D, Simmons G 1988 Patterns of misunderstanding: An integrative model for science math, and programming. *Rev. Educ. Res.* 58(3) 303–26
Pintrich P, DeGroot E 1990 Motivational and self-regulated learning components of classroom academic performance. *J. Educ. Psychol.* 82(1): 33–40
Tharp R G 1989 Psychocultural variables and constants: Effects of teaching and learning in school. *Am. Psychol.* 44(2): 349–59
Valencia S, Pearson P D 1987 Reading assessment: Time for a change. *Read. Teach.* 40(8): 726–32
Vygotsky L S (1978) *Mind in Society: The Development of Higher Psychological Processes*. Harvard University Press, Cambridge, Massachusetts
Whimbey A, Lochhead J 1991 *Problem Solving and Comprehension*, 5th edn. Erlbaum, Hillsdale, New Jersey
Wong B Y, Wong R, Blenkinsop J 1989 Cognitive and metacognitive aspects of learning disabled adolescents' composing problems. *Learning Disability Quarterly* 12(4): 300–22
Wong B Y (ed.) 1992 *Contemporary Intervention Research in Learning Disabilities: An International Perspective*. Springer-Verlag, New York

Y. M. David; A. S. Palincsar

Cognitive Styles and Learning

Cognitive styles are usually conceptualized as characteristic modes of perceiving, remembering, thinking, and problem-solving, reflective of information-processing regularities that develop in congenial ways around underlying personality trends. They are inferred from consistent individual differences in ways of organizing and processing information and experience.

Describing cognitive styles as self-consistent regularities implies that to some degree they are both integrative and pervasive. Yet they are pervasive not just in the sense of individual consistencies cutting across activities *within* broad domains such as thinking or interpersonal functioning, but often also in the sense of cutting *across* broad domains. As an instance, the cognitive style of field independence versus field dependence embraces personal/social and not merely cognitive consistencies: the field-independent person is characterized as analytical, self-referent, and impersonal in orientation, the field-dependent person as global, socially sensitive, and interpersonal in orientation (Witkin and Goodenough 1981).

1. Historical Roots

The idea that different individuals have contrasting personalities that differentially influence their modes of cognition and behavioral expression can be traced back to ancient classifications of temperament and physique. The idea is more closely linked to early twentieth-century European notions of type, as exemplified by Jung's conception of extroverted versus introverted types and thinking versus feeling types.

More recently, three major research traditions have contributed directly to work on cognitive styles. The first was differential psychology, especially the factor analysis of perceptual and intellective task performance as exemplified by the studies of Thurstone and Cattell, both of whom uncovered factorial dimensions similar to field-independence. Indeed, the first succinct formulation of the cognitive-style thesis was provided by Thurstone (1944 p. 6): "The attitudes which the subject adopts spontaneously in making the perceptual judgments in these experiments reflect in some way the parameters that characterize him as a person."

The second tradition was psychoanalytic ego psychology, wherein cognitive styles were viewed as organizing and regulating variables in ego adaptation to the environment (Gardner et al. 1959). Within this tradition, Thurstone's notion of "perceptual attitudes" was generalized first to "cognitive attitudes" and then to "cognitive controls," which are adaptive regulatory mechanisms for coping with cognitive environmental demands. The even more general term "cognitive style," which stresses organizing as well as controlling functions, was first used by Gardner (1953).

The third research tradition was the experimental psychology of cognition, with an emphasis on regularities in information-processing. Within cognitive psychology, the Gestalt movement's focus on issues of form in cognition was particularly influential because it led cognitive-style theorists such as Witkin to view individual consistencies in the manner or form of perceiving and thinking as critical psychological phenomena.

Over time, cognitive styles have been characterized in a number of distinct but overlapping ways (Messick 1984). One way, as was seen, is to view cognitive styles as self-consistent characteristic modes of cognition. Another way views them as individual differences in structural properties of the cognitive system itself, such as degree of differentiation, of discrimination or articulation, and of hierarchic integration of cognitive units, which together comprise the style of cognitive complexity versus simplicity (Messick 1976). Another viewpoint conceives of styles as consistent intra-individual contrasts of abilities or of cognitive controls, as in converging versus diverging styles of thinking (Hudson 1968). Still other conceptions define cognitive styles as enduring preferences for different ways of conceptualizing and organizing the stimulus world; as preferred or habitual decision-making strategies; or, as differential preference (or facility) for processing different forms of information. As a final instance, cognitive styles are viewed as cognitive manifestations of underlying personality structures.

Since these various characterizations are overlapping rather than mutually exclusive, a core conceptualization is derived by playing down some features and emphasizing others in accord with empirical findings and theoretical rationales. This core conceptualization is best described by contrasting cognitive styles with intellective abilities and cognitive strategies so as to highlight their differential implications for learning.

2. *Cognitive Styles versus Abilities and Strategies*

In contrast with intellective abilities, which refer to the content and level of cognition (the questions of What? and How much?), cognitive styles refer to the manner or mode of cognition (the question of How?). Moreover, abilities are unipolar and value-directional (high amounts of ability are always preferable to low amounts and are uniformly more adaptive), while cognitive styles are typically bipolar and value-differentiated (each pole of a style dimension has different adaptive implications). Cognitive styles also differ from abilities in their breadth of coverage and pervasiveness of application. By and large, an ability is specific to a particular domain of content or function, such as verbal, numerical, or spatial ability or fluency and memory ability. A cognitive style, in contrast, cuts across domains of ability, personality, and interpersonal functioning.

In contrast with cognitive strategies, which refer to conscious decisions among alternative approaches as a function of task requirements and situational constraints, cognitive styles are spontaneously applied without conscious consideration or choice in a wide variety of situations having similar information-processing requirements. In comparison to styles, which tend to be stable and relatively pervasive across diverse areas, strategies are likely to be more amenable to change through instruction and training. Individuals may not only learn to use a variety of problem-solving and learning strategies that are consonant with their cognitive styles but, with effort, also learn to shift to less congenial strategies that are more effective for a particular task.

The bipolarity, pervasiveness, and value differentiation of cognitive styles are idealized properties of the core conceptualization. However, there is considerable variation in the extent to which these properties characterize particular cognitive styles in empirical research (Kogan 1983, Messick 1984). There is also controversy over whether some cognitive styles are value directional rather than value differentiated. In particular, although field-dependent persons may be interpersonally oriented as Witkin claimed, there is sparse evidence that such an orientation translates into interpersonal skill.

More generally, one might expect evidence of cross-situational generality and of value differentiation (i.e., optimal matches between styles and tasks) to be equivocal and complex. This follows because the critical match is not between the style and the task but between the style and the perception of the task and because task goals, and hence optimal strategies, vary both across people and for a given person over time. This raises the problem of the match between cognitive styles and learning tasks or contexts as well as the attendant need for stylistic flexibility in learning, which is addressed in Sect. 5.

3. *Cognitive Styles and Information Processing*

In addition to field independence versus field dependence and cognitive complexity versus simplicity, other cognitive styles having implications for learning include:

(a) reflection versus impulsivity, the tendency to evaluate alternative solution hypotheses versus the tendency to respond quickly with the first seemingly reasonable answer;

(b) focused scanning versus unfocused scanning or sharp-focus versus broad-focus scanning, a dimension of individual differences in the intensity and extensiveness of attention deployment;

(c) broad versus narrow categorizing, consistent preferences for broad inclusiveness as opposed to narrow exclusiveness in establishing the acceptable range for specified categories (also referred to as "category width" or "equivalence range");

(d) conceptualizing styles, individual consistencies in the utilization of particular kinds of stimulus properties and relationships as bases for forming concepts, such as the preferred use of thematic or functional relations among stimuli (thematic–relational conceptualizing) as opposed to the analysis of descriptive attributes (analytic–descriptive conceptualizing) or the inference of class membership (categorical–inferential conceptualizing);

(e) leveling versus sharpening, the tendency to minimize as opposed to exaggerate stimulus differences in memory and perception;

(f) converging versus diverging, an individual's relative reliance on convergent thinking (pointed toward logical conclusions and uniquely correct or conventionally best outcomes) as contrasted with divergent thinking (pointed toward variety, quantity, and originality of relevant output).

For further descriptions and references, see Kogan (1983) and Messick (1976, 1984). The two most widely studied cognitive styles, field independence versus field dependence and reflection versus impulsivity, continue to sustain vigorous research interest (Bertini et al. 1986, Globerson and Zelniker 1989, Wapner and Demick 1991).

These various cognitive styles can be distinguished from one another in a number of ways, but the most critical distinction relates styles to different phases of an input–output sequence of information-processing or problem-solving. For example, focused scanning versus unfocused scanning is implicated in information search, category width and conceptualizing styles in encoding, leveling versus sharpening in memory storage and retrieval, cognitive complexity versus simplicity in problem representation, field independence versus field dependence in problem-structuring and restructuring, converging versus diverging in hypothesis generation, and reflection versus impulsivity in strategy selection and decision-making. But such association is by no means one-to-one, because some cognitive styles appear to influence inforamtion-processing sequences at several points. As an instance, intensity and extensiveness of scanning affects information search of both external stimulus fields and internal fields of memory, meaning, and knowledge.

4. *Learning Styles and Orientations Toward Instruction*

Although acknowledged to be manifestations of cognitive styles and personality in learning and studying, a number of learning styles have been identified that are more closely tied to learning tasks than to underlying personality structures. (For references to research in this section, see Schmeck 1988.) In particular, three major learning styles or orientations have been delineated in different research programs. In Entwistle's (1981) program, the three learning styles are labeled "meaning," "reproducing," and "achieving" orientations. They entail, respectively, a search for personal understanding, memorization, and whatever is required to attain high grades. Students with a meaning orientation are intrinsically motivated, those with a reproducing orientation are externally motivated by fear of failure, while those with an achieving style are extrinsically motivated by hope for success. Three similar dimensions isolated by Biggs (1987) are labeled "internalizing," "utilizing," and "achieving" approaches.

In related research by Pask (1976), two learning strategies and associated learning styles have been exhibited by students who were asked to learn principles and procedures well enough to teach them back to others. One strategy is labeled "holist"; consistency in its use indicates a style of comprehension learning. Comprehension learners adopt a global task approach, have a wide range of attention, rely on analogies and illustrations, and tend to construct an overall concept before filling in details. The contrasting learning strategy is labeled "serialist" and the associated style is operation learning. Operation learners adopt a linear task approach and focus attention on operational details and sequential procedures. Students who flexibly employ both strategies are called "versatile" learners.

Similar distinctions have been made by Marton (Marton and Säljö 1976), emphasizing a conclusion-oriented deep-processing approach to learning as opposed to a description-oriented shallow-processing approach. In conclusion-oriented learning, the student's intention is to understand the material and a deep-processing approach is adopted that relates arguments to evidence and ideas to personal experience. In description-oriented learning the student's intention is to memorize the material, and a shallow-processing approach is adopted focusing on discrete facts and disconnected information learned by rote.

In the terms used by Biggs (1987), Entwistle (1981), and Pask (1976), individuals with a meaning or internalizing orientation tend to adopt a deep-processing approach or a holist strategy, or both; students with a reproducing or utilizing orientation tend to adopt a shallow-processing approach or a serialist strategy, or both; and, those with an achieving orientation employ any approach that leads to high grades, deep-processing if understanding is rewarded or shallow-processing if reproduction is rewarded. Biggs demurs on the latter point, however, holding that achieving students develop a shallow approach even under conditions that should foster deep processing.

Although these learning styles clearly reflect stylistic consistencies in learning, Entwistle prefers the term orientation to refer to this style-like consistency. This usage serves to highlight his belief that stylistic consistencies in learning are heavily influenced by the student's perception of the situation, mediated by his or her motives.

5. *Optimal Learning and the Problem of the Match*

Accumulating research evidence indicates that at least some cognitive styles variously influence how students learn, how teachers teach, how students and teachers interact, and how educational and vocational choices are made. For example, teachers and students who are similar in cognitive style tend to view each other with greater mutual esteem than do those who are dissimilar. They also tend to communicate more effectively, as if they were on the same wavelength.

Cognitive styles might thus provide a basis for tailoring the mode of presentation as well as the nature and degree of substantive structure to stylistic characteristics of learners. Student style and instructional mode would be matched so as to develop, compensate for, or capitalize upon student style for the optimization of subject-matter learning. Contrariwise, depending on the educational goals, students might be deliberately confronted with instructional demands that are uncongenial to their cognitive styles so as to stimulate growth and flexibility.

There is thus a continuing tension over the relative value of matching educational treatments to learner characteristics as opposed to mismatching them. Although matching may be facilitative when the aim is to enhance immediate subject-matter achievement, mismatching may be needed when the aim is to promote flexibility and creative thinking. Such trade-offs are the essence of the problem of the match between learner styles on the one hand and the methods and materials of instruction as well as the conditions of learning on the other.

In this connection, because each direction of a cognitive style dimension has adaptive value under different circumstances, attention can be given to the possibility of effectively utilizing the positive features of both poles—as in Pask's (1976) "versatile" learners who combine comprehension and operation learning, in Hudson's (1968) "all-rounders" or intellectual "labiles" who combine converging and diverging, and in the "bicognitive" development of both field independence and field sensitivity espoused by Ramírez and Castañeda (1974). In this regard, Entwistle (1981) stressed the advantages of systematically alternating learning conditions that foster complementary modes of thought. This suggests that an important educational goal should be to develop and enhance flexibility in modes of thinking, thereby reducing to some extent the restrictiveness and preemptiveness of habitual or stylistic thought.

See also: Abilities and Aptitudes; Individual Differences and Instruction; Intelligence, Learning, and Instruction; Learning Strategies and Learning to Learn

References

Bertini M, Pizzamiglio L, Wapner S 1986 *Field Dependence in Psychological Theory, Research, and Application.* Erlbaum, Hillsdale, New Jersey

Biggs J B 1987 *Student Approaches to Learning and Studying.* Australian Council for Educational Research, Hawthorn

Entwistle N 1981 *Styles of Learning and Teaching: An Integrated Outline of Educational Psychology for Students, Teachers, and Lecturers.* Wiley, New York

Gardner R W 1953 Cognitive styles in categorizing behavior. *J. Pers.* 22: 214–33

Gardner R W, Holzman P S, Klein G S, Linton H B, Spence D 1959 Cognitive control: A study of individual consistencies in cognitive behavior. *Psychol. Iss.* 1(4): 1–186

Globerson T, Zelniker T (eds.) 1989 *Cognitive Style and Cognitive Development.* Ablex, Norwood, New Jersey

Hudson L 1968 *Contrary Imaginations: A Psychological Study of the English Schoolboy.* Penguin, Harmondsworth

Kogan N 1983 Stylistic variation in childhood and adolescence: Creativity, metaphor, and cognitive style. In: Mussen P H, Flavell J H, Markman E M (eds.) 1983 *Handbook of Child Psychology. Vol. 3: Cognitive Development.* Wiley, New York

Marton F, Säljö R 1976 On qualitative differences in learning: I, Outcome and processes. *Br. J. Educ. Psychol.* 46(1): 4–11

Messick S 1976 Personality consistencies in cognition and creativity. In: Messick S (ed.) 1976 *Individuality in Learning: Implications of Cognitive Styles and Creativity*

for Human Development. Jossey-Bass, San Francisco, California
Messick S 1984 The nature of cognitive styles: Problems and promise in educational practice. *Educ. Psychol.* 19(2): 59–74
Pask G 1976 Styles and strategies of learning. *Br. J. Educ. Psychol.* 46(2): 128–48
Ramírez M, Castañeda A 1974 *Cultural Democracy, Bicognitive Development, and Education*. Academic Press, New York
Schmeck R R (ed.) 1988 *Learning Strategies and Learning Styles*. Plenum, New York
Thurstone L L 1944 *A Factorial Study of Perception*. University of Chicago Press, Chicago, Illinois
Wapner S, Demick J 1991 *Field Dependence–Independence: Cognitive Style Across the Life Span*. Erlbaum, Hillsdale, New Jersey
Witkin H A, Goodenough D R 1981 *Cognitive Styles: Essence and Origins—Field Dependence and Field Independence*. International Universities Press, New York

S. Messick

Colombia: System of Education

1. General Background

Colombia, located on the northwestern corner of South America, is the only country of the continent which borders on both the Atlantic and the Pacific Ocean. With a land area of 703,248 square kilometers, it is the fourth largest country in South America.

Colombia is made up of seven macroregions with different geographic, socioeconomic, and cultural characteristics which constitute peculiar environments for education. Variations in geographic conditions and in specific patterns of settlement of the population result in different degrees of educational opportunities as well as diverse kinds of available educational services.

According to the 1991 Constitution: "Colombia is a national state based on law, organized as a unitarian, decentralized republic, autonomous in its territory, democratic and pluralistic, founded on respect for human dignity and labor, on the solidarity of its population, and on the predominance of common interests" (Article 1). Since Independence in 1810, Colombia has been a republic with a centralized political organization that is now becoming decentralized in accordance with the new Constitution. In the past, education was the responsibility of the central government which defined policies and financed programs and projects. At the beginning of the 1990s responsibility shifted to regional and local governments for the implementation and financing of some programs and projects designed for their particular needs.

Colombia's population is made up of Whites of European origin, Blacks of African origin, Native Americans, *mestizos* (White and Native American), *mulatos* (White and Black), and *zambos* (Native American and Black). Populations of those with solely White, Black, or Native American roots are smaller than mixed groups.

Spanish is Colombia's predominant language; Native American groups tend to maintain their own language but use Spanish as a second language. Minor efforts have been made to develop educational materials in vernacular languages for the more isolated Native American groups.

According to the last national population census of 1985, Colombia had just over 30 million inhabitants, with a projected population of 33.6 million for 1991, 36.2 million for 1995, and 39.4 million for the year 2000. Since 1960, Colombia has undergone two significant demographic changes: urbanization and a decrease in population growth rates. The exponential rate of growth fell from 3.2 percent for the period 1964–73 to 2 percent for the period 1973–85. The rural population has fallen from 48 percent of the total population to 35 percent in 1985. This was due to such factors as expansion of educational opportunities, birth control campaigns, urbanization, and migration from rural to urban areas. These factors have been accelerated by political turmoil and by people's aspirations to improved living standards, particularly in large cities. For this reason, migration has led to higher growth rates for the four largest cities in the country—Bogotá, Medellín, Cali, and Barranquilla—than for other cities.

Urbanization and decreased rates of population growth have had a great influence on the distribution of educational opportunities and on improvements in the quality of education. Traditionally, considerations of educational opportunities involved two sectors of the population, rural and urban groups. Inadequate education for marginal groups in the so-called "poverty belts" in large cities has brought about the need to consider this new population sector. New educational content, materials, and strategies must be designed to meet their specific needs.

From an economic point of view, between 1958 and 1970 policies were aimed at promoting industrial development which would lead to the replacement of imports by home produced goods. Toward 1967, a period of growth began. It was fueled by increased foreign trade and new exchange and commercial policies. This growth declined by 1980 when an economic recession started. Between 1970 and 1974 the average growth of the Gross Domestic Product (GDP) was 6.1 percent, due to the increase of minor exports, world trade, and the dynamics of public and private investments. From 1974 to 1975, the GDP growth rate was only 2.3 percent; between 1981 and 1985 deterioration of the external sector led to recession, and the GDP increased only by 1.8 percent. Agricultural production in this period only increased by 1.3 percent compared to 4.3 percent for 1970–74 and 5.8 percent for 1975.

Before the 1950s the economy was based mainly on agricultural production and Colombia had one of the most underdeveloped educational structures in the world. By the 1960s, however, educational expectations had increased from 2 to 6 school years for Colombian children. This led to significant changes in the urban labor market and consequently in the distribution of income. Expectations of up to 9 years of basic education should be reached by the year 2000.

The National Socioeconomic Development Plan for 1990–94 calls for reinforcement of dynamic foreign trade; investment on physical infrastructure and on transportation and communications; a stimulus to private investments on agriculture, housing, and industry; and investments on human capital through formal and nonformal education for children, youths, and adults, and on scientific and technological research. By the end of the 1990s economic growth in Colombia is expected to reach an annual average rate of 5.35 percent.

The program for economic openness is designed to reorient the Colombian economy toward continuous and efficient growth, expanding production in order to increase employment, improving the quality and lowering the prices of goods and services. Since a strengthened society is a necessary complement to this process, educational needs become a significant factor in improving productive capacity. In addition, women's education is seen as a means to healthier children, and general education is considered a factor in greater social mobility, according to the National Development Plan for Education for 1990–94.

2. *Politics and the Goals of the Education System*

Colombia once had only two major political parties, Liberal and Conservative. Since 1970, however, factions have emerged from the traditional parties, affecting their internal stability, and new political parties have appeared, notably the Patriotic Union (UP) and the National Alliance M–19. The former has been associated with, and the latter is a direct descendent of, guerrilla movements that achieved integration into the system of constitutional democracy through negotiations with the government.

On the other hand, the political dynamics of the country have become increasingly more complex as guerrilla movements, organized within a national coordinating body, advance peace negotiations with the government. As negotiations continue, it is likely that other new parties will appear in the political arena.

Each party and guerrilla movement has different philosophical and ideological positions concerning the policies that will lead to national, regional, and local development. However, there appears to be a consensus regarding education as a human right and as an important ingredient for the improvement of personal and social conditions. Consequently, policies that tend toward the implementation of universal basic education are widely supported. Nevertheless, conceptions of the strategies, means, and instruments needed to achieve this goal are not shared. For example, according to some political groups responsibility for basic education should lie with the public sector; for other groups, it should be shared by public and private sectors and by the communities.

In the past, differences between the two traditional parties regarding their position on education concerned who should be educated, the content of education, and whether official or unofficial education should be emphasized. On these issues, however, the two traditional parties seem to have come together. Healthy rivalry between official and unofficial institutions, particularly in higher education, is expressly emphasized in the National Development Plan for Education for 1990–94.

Since 1970, politics have also influenced education directly as parties, guerrillas, and other nongovernmental organizations (NGOs) have imparted political education, particularly to the more deprived sectors of the population in rural areas and to marginal sectors in the large cities. This political education is related to strategies for community organization, consciousness-raising in relation to rights and duties, the assimilation of participatory strategies and means for participative planning, and the development and monitoring of programs and projects for community development.

The stress laid by the 1991 Constitution on the participation of the people strengthens an existing and growing practice and formalizes it through political, normative, and institutional channels. State governors and city mayors were formerly appointed by the President; the first elected mayors will conclude their first term at the beginning of 1992, while the first elected governors will begin their first term in January 1992.

In sum, politics has played, and will continue to play, a significant role in determining educational conceptions, values, expectations, and actions, beyond the role played by political parties. Some questions, however, remain; among them, to what extent political parties, guerrilla movements, and NGOs have contributed to social consciousness-raising and to self- and community-improvement, and what role will they continue to play in such processes, including education.

3. *The Formal System of Education*

3.1 *Primary, Secondary, and Tertiary Education*

Figure 1 outlines the structure of Colombia's formal

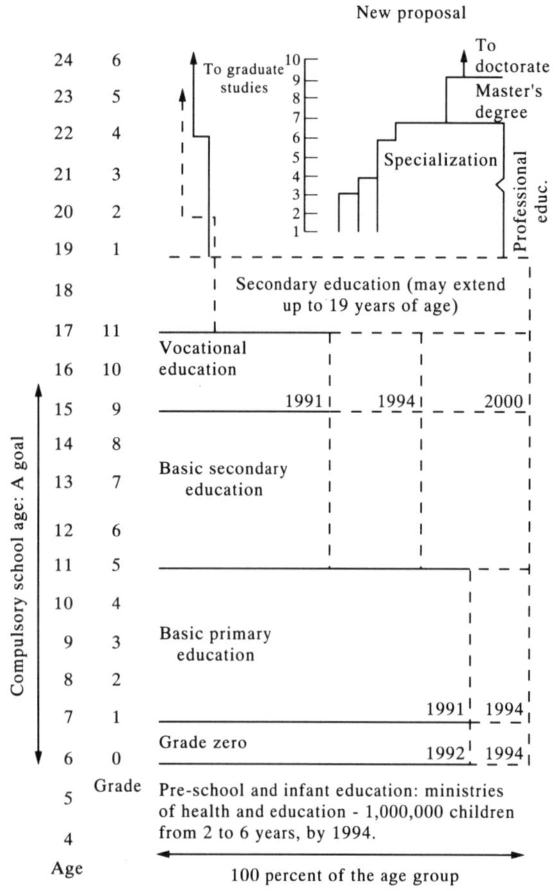

Figure 1
Colombia: Structure of the formal education system 1991

education system; key data will be presented for each level of education in text.

Education in Colombia is compulsory for children from 5 to 15 years of age; it comprises a minimum of one year of preschool education and nine of basic education, as stipulated in Article 67 of the 1991 Constitution.

Previous constitutions, as well as the present one, state that education, especially at the elementary level, is a public responsibility. The present Constitution, however, adds that some academic costs might be met by those who are able to pay them. In actual practice, education does involve a financial cost to the family, in tuition or a proportion of fees, books and other learning materials, uniforms, or contributions.

Educational services are offered in official and unofficial institutions; both types of institution implement the curriculum approved by the Ministry of Education.

The present structure of the educational system encompasses four levels: one to two years of preschool education, five years of elementary basic education, four of basic secondary education and two of vocational secondary education, and two to ten years of higher education. As will be shown later, some reforms are being introduced which particularly affect preschool, vocational secondary, and higher education. Figure 1 presents not only the system in 1991, but expected enrollments in 1994 and the year 2000.

Public institutions have always had a large coverage of elementary education in Colombia. Public education at the elementary level has experienced significant growth in the past; enrollment rose from only 0.5 million students in 1933 to 3.5 million in 1976. Unfortunately, in the last 15 years the annual rate of growth for enrollment has decreased to the point where, between 1980 and 1984, it dropped to zero, with a rise to 1 percent between 1984–89. At present, 4.2 million students are enrolled in elementary grades, but 16 percent of school-age children do not attend school.

One of the major problems in elementary education in the past was enrollment; at present the main problem is keeping the students in school. In the 1980s, more than 90 percent of school-age children enrolled in first grade, but 40 percent of them did not complete elementary education. One-third of overall enrollment is made up of overaged children repeating grades, especially first grade. Strategies devised to control this phenomenon have not been effective. In addition, school days are short and school years even shorter: effective time for learning at elementary schools is approximately 5 hours per day and 180 days per year.

The goals of expansion of enrollment and improvement in the quality of education in rural areas have been sought through the *Escuela Nueva* methodology, in which elements of nongraded schools are combined with personalized strategies and active student participation techniques. These methods have brought about a positive change in the role teachers play in the learning process. Schools have also become focal points for communities, which in turn become involved in school activities.

Average class size has ranged from 45.3 in 1968 to 39.1 in 1984; for 1991, it has been estimated at 30. The student–teacher ratio was 52 in 1933 for urban and rural schools, 34.8 and 37 respectively for 1964, and 30.4 and 28.4 for 1984. For 1991 this ratio has also been estimated at 30. In elementary graded schools it is frequently the case that there is one teacher per grade; consequently, class size and the ratio of students per teacher tend to be identical. However, some schools work two shifts, particularly in deprived urban areas. In rural areas, where the *Escuela Nueva* methodology is applied, several grades are taught in the same classroom and by the same teacher. Up to now, no information about the ratios for *Escuela Nueva* have been made available.

Secondary education includes grades 6 to 11. In 1990, more than 2.6 million students enrolled in secondary schools, 60 percent of them in public and 40 percent in private institutions. The annual growth rate for enrollment was 5 percent in 1983–84, but since 1985 it has been close to 2.2 percent.

Major problems found in secondary education include the low coverage of educational opportunity (only 46% of the target population, aged 12 to 17, is enrolled in schools, of which 58% correspond to large cities and 36% to rural areas) There is also the fact that the structures of basic elementary, basic secondary, and vocational secondary education in the public sector do not lead to an integrated educational process from first to eleventh grade, as is common in private institutions. This disparity leads to decreases in enrollment in the higher grades, particularly in the transition from fifth to sixth grade; during the latter there are also high levels of dropout. The lack of integration has an additional negative effect upon the quality of education due to changes in norms, teachers, methodologies, and environment. A further problem, low levels in the quality of education, is evidenced in the data collected through state examinations for entrance to institutions of higher education. These low levels are due, among other reasons, to the low quality of teacher training, an obsolete curriculum, lack of adequate materials, and insufficient time dedicated to actual academic work since public institutions work in up to three shifts (morning, afternoon, and evening) per school day.

The low coverage of secondary education (46%) and its poor quality have led the present government to consider secondary education a priority for 1991–94. Policies included in the National Development Plan for 1990–94 aim at the integration of public and private efforts, to achieve 100 percent coverage of the population aged 12–17 by the year 2000. It is expected that by 1995 coverage will reach 70 percent. A project to integrate elementary and secondary public institutions is underway; emphasis on general education will be reinforced with vocational options for Grades 10 and 11, and transfer of technical and technological education as part of higher educational levels.

Available data indicate that in 1989 there were 236 institutions of higher education, 30 percent of which were public and 70 percent private. Over two-thirds of the institutions are universities and the rest are for technical and technological education. Enrollments for the same year totaled 475,000; of these 42 percent attended public and 58 percent private institutions. At the same time, 78 percent of total enrollment was in the universities, 13 percent in technological institutions, and 8 percent in technical professional institutions.

Enrollment in graduate schools for 1989 was 9,904 students, of which 87 percent studied education, health sciences, economics, and social sciences; 7 percent were in engineering; 5 percent in mathematics and basic sciences; and 1 percent in agricultural sciences. Some 56 percent of enrolled students were in specialization programs (one year of study after a professional degree) and 44 percent in programs leading to a master's degree. Only 15 students were enrolled in doctoral programs; half of them were in theology and the rest in basic sciences.

The main problems found in Colombian higher education are, in order of importance: low quality levels, institutional dispersion in the system, and unequal distribution of financial support by the government. Some major causes of these problems are lack of planning, low levels of credibility due to fast expansion without the requisite infrastructure, and loss of national leadership on the part of the universities.

Policies for higher education for 1991–94 are oriented to strengthening undergraduate general education and de-emphasizing specialization at this stage, to reinforcing curriculum flexibility and restructuring teaching strategies in order to place more value on the work of students and to facilitate participation of teachers and students in research. Additionally, there are plans to promote the development of new master's and doctoral programs associated with research programs and projects.

3.2 Preschool Education

In the 1980s great emphasis was placed on educating children under 6 years of age. Between 1982–86 enrollment in preschool education increased by 26 percent, although official institutions covered only 7 percent of the target population. In the past, preschool education has been entirely the family's responsibility. At present, 80 percent of the target population of 4–5-year olds remains unassisted. However, the ministries of Health and Education have developed a joint care program, aimed at the most disadvantaged sectors of the populace, for integral attention to children under 5 in welfare homes established under the care of a community mother.

The Educational Development Plan for 1991–94 includes a program for the establishment of a "Grade Zero" in all public elementary schools for children under 6 in order to prepare them for first grade. Repetition of the first grade has been high, particularly in deprived sectors of the populace. In 1987, for instance, first-grade repetition reached 21.9 percent for rural areas and 14.1 percent for urban areas. Grade Zero is expected to increase the level of internal efficiency of the educational process.

3.3 Vocational, Technical, and Business Education

The last two years of secondary education, Grades 10 and 11, include vocational education; at the same time, some options in technical and business education are offered.

Vocational, technical, and business education in Colombia have three purposes: first, to respond to the aptitudes and preferences of secondary-school students; second, to allow them to apply their knowledge to practical problems related to life and production; and third, to train dropouts from the educational system and students interested in learning a trade and in joining the labor market. The first purpose is being met through Grades 10 and 11 of vocational secondary education; the second is considered a pedagogical element at all levels of education, and the third is a responsibility of public and private institutions established for this purpose.

The most important institution of this kind is the National Apprenticeship Service (SENA), under the Ministry of Labor. It runs several schools which offer vocational training in options related to the specific circumstances and perspectives of each geographical region. Private institutions for vocational training are supported mainly by religious communities.

Vocational secondary education offers a variety of options including programs in industrial, agricultural, and business education. The Colombian system also includes the options of academic preparation for higher education (particularly for careers related to humanities and natural and social sciences) and teacher training, which prepares teachers for basic elementary education. In 1958, 70 percent of students enrolled in the preparatory option were men and 30 percent were women. In 1980, distribution was 59 and 41 percent respectively. For the teacher-training option 43 percent of the enrollment was made up of men and 57 percent of women in 1958; by 1980, women made up 60 percent of enrollment and men 40 percent. By 1990 the percentage of men had decreased even further.

Business vocational education is, after the academic preparation option, the second most popular in terms of enrollment. In 1983, over 77 percent of enrollment corresponded to the preparatory option and 12 percent to business education, while the percentages for industrial, agricultural, teacher training, and social work were 3.98, 1.71, 3.77, and 1.46 respectively.

3.4 Adult and Nonformal Education

The rate of illiteracy in Colombia for the population over 10 years of age was over 38.5 percent in 1951. By 1985, it had decreased to 12.2 percent, but there are still 2.3 million illiterate adults. In 1991, the percentages were 23.4 for rural and 7.3 for urban areas. The more deprived area with regard to basic elementary education are the Atlantic and Pacific coasts. Literacy campaigns have been significant in the past; it has been difficult, however, to implement basic primary education as postliteracy programs for adults.

Major problems include lack of educational opportunities, inadequate curriculum, lack of special training for teachers to deal with adult learners, and lack of adequate materials. Unfortunately, provisions for 1991–94 do not include additional programs to improve educational conditions in adult and nonformal education. It is important to mention the contributions nongovernmental organizations have made to the development of programs of popular education through community development projects which include educational activities.

4. Administrative and Supervisory Structure and Operation

Traditionally, Colombia has had a centralized organizational structure for education; the reorganization of the educational system in 1968 and 1976 was aimed at decentralizing educational administration. National development plans formulated in the 1980s were oriented toward the growth of enrollment and the improvement of quality of educational opportunity through the implementation of projects that respond to regional characteristics and educational needs.

One strategy devised in 1982 in order to decentralize administration was educational mapping, which created local administrative units called "Nuclei for Educational Development." A nucleus is made up of communities that interrelate in social, economic, and cultural affairs. Several nuclei with similar characteristics make up an Educational District, the second-level administrative unit. A Secretariat of Education is the regional administrative entity in each of the politico-territorial units into which the country is divided. It constitutes a link between the region and the central units for educational administration. Until 1990 educational mapping had not been as successful as expected because it has failed to integrate with city governments.

Supervision has traditionally been an important element in the development of Colombian education. The first legal act to establish objectives and responsibilities for the work of national inspectors dates from 1936. Inspectors were to oversee the organization and operation of all public institutions of preschool, elementary, and complementary education, as well as public and private secondary schools. In 1949 inspection was organized by specialized subject areas and considered a link between the government and the people through the schools. In 1958 inspection was regarded as more of an academic than an administrative function, while in 1963 criteria for recognition and approval of curricula were established, and in 1970 a supervision manual, introducing the term and concept of "supervision," was published.

Lack of funds resulted in a decline in the importance of supervision for education development. It is likely that supervision as it now exists in Colombia will be abolished in the near future. Supervision as a function is becoming a responsibility of local and regional curriculum administrators such as academic vice-principals, pedagogical coordinators, and nuclei directors.

5. *Educational Finance*

In the 1970s and 1980s there has been a gradual increase in the percentage of the total national budget dedicated to education. In 1970, 13.6 percent of the budget was allocated to education; in 1975, it was 16.5 percent; and in 1980, it was 19 percent. In 1980, 37.69 percent of the educational budget was dedicated to elementary education, 21.1 percent to secondary education, and 22.1 percent to higher education.

Since 1971, Colombia has aimed at concentrating the financing of public education in the central government while decentralizing responsibility for the administration of the school system at the regional level. This policy was meant to empower the government to redress severe regional inequities in the distribution of educational expenditures and opportunities. As a result, by 1980 the central government financed 84 percent of expenditure in public education, as compared with 65 percent in 1970.

The government's financial effort to increase educational opportunities and to improve quality is based on Law 46 of 1971 (called "*Situado Fiscal*," or tax allowance) and Law 43 of 1975 (Law of Nationalization). The *Situado Fiscal* requires that at least 11.1 percent of the government's ordinary income be allocated to support elementary education. Nationalization requires that one-half of the sales tax returnable to departmental (state) capitals and the Special District of Bogotá be transferred to the Ministry of Education as financial assistance to secondary education.

At present, expenditure in education comprises public and private efforts; in the 1980s, they represented 5 percent of the GDP. The public sector contributed approximately 60 percent of total expenditure in education, as compared with 84 percent in 1980.

Programs and projects planned for 1991–94 will be financed as follows: 42 percent through the national budget, with the remaining 58 percent to be shared by municipalities, the private sector, and regional governments. National funds for investment in basic elementary education include part of a loan for projects tending to universalize elementary education.

Private institutions are financed by student tuition fees and contributions from private enterprise; in some cases, however, these schools receive some support from the government.

Public institutions of higher education charge tuition fees according to family or student income statements. Starting in 1992, tuition at public universities will be as expensive as at comparable private institutions. However, students will receive scholarships on the basis of scholastic achievement and financial needs. It is projected that in 10 years tuition will supply 33 percent of the money needed to run public universities. At present tuition represents 5 percent of the total income of these institutions.

In the 1950s, the Colombian Institute for Technical Studies Overseas (ICETEX) was created to help Colombians attend graduate school abroad. The Institute has served as a clearing house for scholarships and as a financial corporation for loans. From the 1960s, loans were also made available for professional studies, both in Colombia and overseas. ICETEX has retained both functions but its loan capacity does not meet increasing demands. Loans usually cover tuition, room and board, and books. Repayment starts after graduation, when the graduate enters the labor market, with a low rate of monthly interest. Policies for 1991–94 aim at creating new sources for loans; governmental banks will establish lines of credit for education for the benefit of students from low-income families.

6. *Supplying Personnel for the Education System*

Elementary and secondary education (basic and vocational) is imparted by 280,000 teachers. The public sector includes 200,000 of them, of which 120,000 teach in basic elementary schools and the rest in secondary. Private education employs 80,000 teachers, 62 percent of whom are in secondary schools.

Elementary-school teachers are trained in normal schools, a type of secondary school whose curriculum includes four years of general education and two years of specialized teacher training in all subjects taught in elementary school. In the 1980s special programs were established at universities to train elementary-school teachers. Some of these programs apply education-at-a-distance strategies, becoming inservice education programs. Data indicate that the educational level of teachers has increased. While in 1950 two-thirds of elementary-school teachers had little schooling beyond elementary level and the rest were graduates from normal schools, at present around 68 percent are graduates from normal schools, 17 percent from other types of secondary schools, and 15 percent from universities.

Secondary-school teachers usually receive university training at schools of education offering majors that correspond to the main subjects taught in high school. University-level teacher-training programs, like all higher education programs, are evaluated and supervised by the Colombian Institute for the Promotion of Higher Education (ICFES).

Data indicate that 21.51 percent of graduate programs are in education. However, a small fraction of teachers and educational administrators hold graduate degrees.

University faculties are made up of professionals from different fields of knowledge. Most universities grant some members of their staff paid study leaves to pursue graduate studies. Staff members are also encouraged to apply for scholarships to carry out graduate work. Some universities offer training programs on university teaching methods, especially for professors in the areas of engineering, health, and architecture.

Teachers at normal schools often supplement their income by teaching in adult education programs. In the 1980s, few undergraduate and graduate programs offered training for adult and nonformal education.

Foreseeable reforms for teacher training in basic education include abolishing normal schools, granting schools of education full responsibility for training elementary and secondary school teachers (Grades 6 to 9), and leaving the training of tenth- and eleventh-grade teachers in the hands of university schools of humanities, and natural and social sciences. Teachers for technical and technological education will be trained mainly by schools of engineering, architecture, and others as needed.

7. Curriculum Development and Teaching Methodology

Curriculum design and development have traditionally been the responsibility of the central government. There is a General Directorate for Curriculum Development within the Ministry of Education, with sections for curriculum design and development for basic elementary and secondary education (Grades 1 to 9) and vocational secondary education (Grades 10 and 11).

During the 1950s, the curriculum for elementary schools was different in urban and rural areas. By 1963, a new curriculum was designed, to give rural children access to knowledge formerly available only to children in urban areas. Consequently, a national curriculum was approved but implemented through traditional methodologies in which teacher and content were the center of the learning process. Later the *Escuela Nueva* methodology described above was developed.

In 1978, the Curriculum Renovation Program was launched. This new curriculum includes four basic areas: mathematics, natural sciences, social studies, and Spanish and literature. Other subjects such as art, physical education, vocational training, and religious education complement the curriculum.

Different teaching materials have been designed for rural and urban areas. At present, materials for urban schools are published according to specific standards defined by the Ministry of Education. These materials are distributed free of charge to all urban schools along with small libraries as programmed by the project for universalization of basic elementary education. Learning materials for *Escuela Nueva* are designed by a technical team at the Ministry of Education and their publication contracted with a private firm.

The curriculum for vocational secondary education is also designed at the Ministry of Education according to the different options offered at schools. In the 1980s a more flexible approach was implemented for the creation of new options: localities and regions are invited to present proposals for vocational secondary education programs to respond to their specific needs. This has resulted in the creation of such vocational training programs as theater, ballet, music, tourism, and recreation.

In the case of higher education, each program designs its own curriculum. Teams of specialized teachers with the assistance of a curriculum expert design study plans for each career. The resulting curriculum is evaluated at different administrative levels of the institution, which must approve it before it is sent to ICFES. Only after ICFES approval is the creation of a new program or the curriculum reform authorized.

Specialization in a professional field begins early in most undergraduate curricula. Students are allowed to register in some elective subjects, but usually few electives will count as credits for graduation.

As far as methodology is concerned, the present teaching methods for elementary education are geared toward individualized learning, promotion of team work, and encouragement for children to play the central role in the teaching–learning process. These developments have been made possible by the adoption of new learning materials in the case of *Escuela Nueva* and of the new curriculum at urban schools. Teaching methods at vocational secondary schools tend to be more traditional but they also assume different characteristics depending on the type of program involved. At the level of higher education, teaching methods are adapted to each specific field: methodologies that allow students to come in contact with real situations are being emphasized in fields like engineering, architecture, and education. Methodologies stressing research as a means for learning are also being implemented.

According to the National Development Plan for Education for 1991–94, work will continue on the design of a new curriculum for basic elementary eighth and ninth grades. The secondary-school curriculum will be reformed to meet the requirements of basic education with optional subjects for vocational education. Higher education will have a new structure: three years of general education, two or three years of professional education plus the option of an additional year for specialization, and from two to five years of graduate education in master's and doctoral programs.

8. *The System of Examinations, Promotions, and Certifications*

Evaluation of learning at the elementary level is somewhat flexible and is focused on the quality of learning processes and on the achievement of objectives. Tests, written work, and direct observation by the teacher are the tools used by teachers to collect information for evaluation. Reports to parents are issued four times a year.

In urban schools where new teaching methods and evaluation strategies are used, all children enrolled in a grade are expected to be promoted to the next with remedial learning activities when necessary. Despite the fact that teachers have been trained to apply automatic promotion, traditional examinations measuring rote learning are still administered in some schools.

The *Escuela Nueva* methodology is flexible with regard to student promotion from one grade to the next. Because students learn at their own pace, promotion is possible in one or more subjects or in the whole curriculum. Parents are periodically informed of their children's progress and learning problems. This is made possible by parents' permanent involvement in school activities, even in those related to the learning process.

In secondary schools, both basic and vocational, the evaluation process is more rigid. Students must take frequent quizzes and partial examinations. Parents receive grade reports four times during the school year. Grades for all periods are averaged to arrive at the final grade, which determines whether the student is promoted to the next grade. Norms regulating secondary-school evaluation are being revised.

Secondary-school graduates who wish to enter higher education institutions are required to take a state examination. Some public and private universities also require applicants who have scored sufficiently high marks in the state examination to take an additional entrance examination. Each university determines the score an applicant should achieve to enter a particular program. Each university has its own norms in relation to the evaluation of student learning, and for graduation and certification.

One of the most significant problems in the areas of evaluation, promotion, and certification is the disparity at the elementary level between schools and between urban and rural schools, as well as the insufficient training of teachers to conduct these tasks. In secondary schools, norms tend to be too rigid. For universities and other institutions of higher education, the fact that quality differs from one institution to the next may constitute an obstacle when students need to transfer between schools.

9. *Educational Assessment, Evaluation, and Research*

A national evaluation system is in the process of being developed. It is geared to continuous evaluation of growth and improvement through basic and elementary education. Instruments for the evaluation of scholastic achievement in mathematics, sciences, and Spanish and literature are being prepared.

Traditionally there has been a lack of approved strategies for educational assessment. Specific programs (such as *Escuela Nueva*, the National Institutes for Diversified Secondary Education, or the normal schools) have incorporated their own evaluation processes. Only in the case of *Escuela Nueva* are the results used to refine and improve the methodology in order to expand its application.

At the end of the 1980s, the Ministry of Education invited schools of education to evaluate, on a regional basis, the effect of automatic promotion on student achievement. Results have not yet been published.

The National Planning Department and the Educational Planning Office of the Ministry of Education habitually carry out research as input for policy-making. In addition, some research centers and universities have contracts to conduct studies. Basic statistics are issued by the National Statistics Department (DANE), but in education statistics are insufficient and not always reliable. Colombia is expected to have developed a reliable information system by 1995.

Research is mainly the responsibility of universities and nongovernmental research institutions. COLCIENCIAS, an institute associated with the National Planning Department, is responsible for promoting research at universities and research centers. A National Plan for Scientific and Technological Research is being implemented. Under it, research and graduate training are expected to become a significant input for socioeconomic development.

10. *Major Reforms in the 1980s and 1990s*

The major reforms implemented in elementary education have sought to effect improvements in the quality of education. Through the project for universalization of elementary education, for instance, all schools in the country were endowed with a small library, textbooks for children, inservice training for teachers, teaching aids, and certain elements of infrastructure for schools and classrooms.

The introduction of automatic promotion at urban elementary schools brought about changes in teaching methods and evaluation strategies which represent a significant advance. Expansion of educational opportunity and changes in methodology through *Escuela Nueva* have resulted in improvements in the quality of the educational process.

Teacher training and some technical and technological programs have increased coverage through education-at-a-distance strategies.

Goals for the 1990s include achieving 100 percent elementary school coverage for school-age children, increasing coverage for secondary education from 46 to 70 percent by 1995, promoting graduate studies as well as scientific and technological research at universities, reorienting research toward projects that have a bearing on socioeconomic development, creating a Grade Zero for children under 6 years of age, and reinforcing decentralization not only in the administration but also in the financing of education.

11. Major Problems for the Year 2000

Major challenges for the educational system in Colombia in the 1990s and into the next century include:

(a) to find sufficient resources to support the continuous expansion of elementary education as population grows, to increase expansion of secondary and higher education, to cope with rapidly growing financial deficits at public universities, to expand scientific and technological research due to costs of infrastructure, and to meet foreign debt commitments (several programs are financed with foreign loans.);

(b) to respond to the great cultural differences that arise from social, economic, and cultural inequalities among the population;

(c) to improve the training of educators and their working conditions;

(d) to strengthen coordination between literacy programs and nonformal educational activities;

(e) to implement a general system of evaluation in the whole country; and

(f) to establish a reliable system of information.

Bibliography

Constitución Política de Colombia 1991 Vigésima Edición. Editorial Tamis, Bogotá

ICFES 1990 *Calidad, Eficiencia, Equidad de la Educación Superiore Colombia, 1990. Seminario Permanente: Memorias,* Vols. I and II. Editorial Delfin Ltda., Bogotá

Presidencia de la República, Departamento Nacional de Planeación 1991 *La Revolución Pacífica: Plan de Desarrollo Económico y Social 1990–1994.* Impreandes, Bogotá

República de Colombia, Departamento Nacional de Planeación 1991a Plan de apertura educativa 1991–1994. Working paper (Documentos MEN-DNP-UDS-DEC-2518)

República de Colombia, Departamento Nacional de Planeación 1991b Plan de apertura educativa 1991–1994. Anexo Estadistico. Working paper (Documentos MEN-DNP-UDS-DEC-2518)

República de Colombia, Ministerio de Educación Nacional 1987 *La Planeación Educativa en Colombia 1950–1986,* Vols. I and II. Editorial MEN, Bogotá

República de Colombia, Ministerio de Educación Nacional 1988a *Análisis del Sector Educativo con Enfasis en sus Aspectos Administrativos y Financieros.* OSPE, Bogotá

República de Colombia, Ministerio de Educación Nacional 1988b *Un Siglo de Educación en Colombia 1886–1896.* Editorial MEN, Bogotá

Tirado Mejia A 1989 *Nueva Historia de Colombia. Vol. V: Economía, Café e Industria.* Editorial Planeta, Bogotá

J. Mora

Comenius and Education

John Amos Comenius or Jan Amos Komenský (1592–1670), Czech philosopher, theologian, and educational and social reformer, tried to contribute to the transformation of the structure of seventeenth-century European society into a peaceful and creative, harmonious community for all people.

1. Biographical Details

Comenius came from southeastern Moravia, a margravate within the lands of the Czech Crown. He was born on March 28, 1592. There is no direct evidence concerning his birthplace. His parents originated from the village of Komňa and settled in Brod (Uherský Brod) where they became wealthy burghers and owned a farm in a suburb of Brod. In 1604 they died and the orphan Jan then lived with his aunt in Strážnice in southern Moravia. When the troops of the anti-Habsburg Hungarian insurgent, István Bocskai, invaded Moravia and burned down Strážnice, 13-year-old Jan lost his temporary home with his aunt. He then lived in Nivnice with his guardians.

During his studies Jan signed himself as Nivnicensis or Nivanus, and in his notes (*Clamores Eliae*) from his old age, he was known as "Jan Segeš Nivnický. po otci zvaný Komenský" (after his father who was called Komenský). In a publication during his exile as a young man, he used the name "Hunnobrodensis," that is, from Uherský Brod. Since in those days names were taken not only from one's birthplace but also from one's place of residence, the uncertainty as to his real name remains. As an adult he adopted the surname "Komenský," Latinized "Comenius."

2. Religious Following and Exile

In Brod and Strážnice Comenius grew up in the milieu of the Unity of Brethren (*Unitas Fratrum*) a small Church within the Czech Reformation—to which his family belonged. It was the first European Reformation, founded at the beginning of the fifteenth century. The Czech Reformation was at first known as Hussitism (followers of Jan Huss). Even after 1534, when the radically socialist wing was defeated, the Reformation continued to develop until 1620 within *Utraquists* or the teaching of *Calixtines*. The *Unitas Fratrum* originated in the second half of the fifteenth century in eastern Bohemia and later spread to Moravia. An important tradition that later influenced Comenius, was created when the *Utraquists* and the *Unitas Fratrum* elaborated upon a mutually acceptable agreement—the "Czech Confession"—in 1575.

Comenius attended Brethren schools in Brod, Strážnice, and after some time, the secondary school in Přerov in central Moravia. There he gained a patron—the educated Moravian nobleman Charles the Elder of Žerotín, who also supported Jan's university studies from 1611 to 1614 in Herborn and Heidelberg where he attended higher schools of Calvinist orientation. Before his return home Comenius also visited the Netherlands for the first time.

In Přerov, Comenius worked as a teacher at the Brethren school and, after having been ordained as a preacher (minister) of the *Unitas Fratrum*, he began historical writings on ancient Moravia. He was also preparing an encyclopedia—*Theatrum Universitatie Rerum*—and developing his idea that the world is a school. His interest in social problems was shown in his *Letters to Heaven*.

His teaching and pastoral activity continued in Fulnek, in north-eastern Moravia, where he spent happy years with his young family and also engaged in full literary activity.

Until 1620 the Bohemian Estates struggled against the endeavors of the Austrian House of Habsburg to create a Central European despotic monarchy and to limit the rights of the Czech Crown. Events culminated in the so-called Czech War in the years 1618–20, the beginning of the Thirty Years War which lasted from 1618–48. This war affected not only the Czech nation, the majority of which were Protestants, but also Comenius personally as a representative of the *Unitas Fratrum*, which belonged to the anti-Habsburg camp. After the Catholic victory over the Protestants in 1620, he became an outcast in his own land and ultimately, in 1628, following the harshest of edicts against non-Catholics, he had to go into exile.

Comenius lost his family in the War (his wife Magdalena and two very young children) as well as his property. His library was burned down, and he had to leave Moravia to find asylum in eastern Bohemia, in Brandýs u. Orlice and in Bílá Třemešná, before he left the country.

3. Major Works

Comenius had already expressed many of his main ideas in works written before his exile in 1628. The pain of lost political, religious, and personal liberty was mixed with doubt, resignation, and fierce social criticism as he sought to escape from so many conflicts. He was always mobilizing his energy to help other people, and to seek spiritual balance and new security in life. The titles of his works reflect his experience, for instance, *The Mournful*, Books I and II, *On Orphanhood*, and *Centrum securitatis*. The most famous of them is *The Labyrinth of the World* and the *Paradise of the Heart* (see Comenius 1991), containing a description of both a corrupt society and his ideal of a peacefully cooperating Christian society. He also wrote about Czech poetry, popularized science for the people, carefully drew a map of Moravia, and finally entered upon his new theory of education that started with his Czech *Didactic*.

In exile Comenius found a second home at Leszno in Poland where the *Unitas Fratrum* had established a Czech congregation after the first unsuccessful insurrection against Ferdinand I of Habsburg in 1547. The Brethren lived there in tolerance with other denominations. During his first stay in Leszno from 1628 to 1641 Comenius was active on many fronts. He taught at the grammar school; elaborated upon his pansophic ideas in his *Prodromus pansophiae*, and defended them, finished both versions of his *Didactica*, in Czech and Latin; wrote religious, educational and historical publications for the *Unitas Fratrum*; developed practical humanitarian advice on how to treat people struck by the plague; and developed the first systematic theory of early childhood education ("School of Infancy"). He gained European fame through a new type of textbook, *Janua linguarum reserata*, in which his representation of the content of knowledge was based on man's relation to the whole world (i.e., nature, man, and God). He also combined factual knowledge with language instruction. In addition, he wrote successful school plays (*Diogenes Cynicus redivivus*) and published his School Regulations (*Leges gymnasii Lesnensis*).

From 1641 to 1642 Comenius was invited to England to reform schools and to found a pansophic college for scientific progress. His conception of education, connected to a broad social reform, was outlined in *Via lucis*, published in 1668, and also in shorter treatises. He was, no doubt, inspired by some ideas developed in England surrounding Cromwell's revolution. It was in England that he pursued the idea of the social significance of science and of every human activity.

Of several invitations (from France, the United States, and Sweden) Comenius decided to accept the one from Sweden, at that time at war with the Habsburgs. In Sweden Comenius hoped for some assistance for his nation. He wrote textbooks for Swedish Latin schools during his stay at Elbing, which was then under Swedish administration. However, he also developed thoughts about a universal social reform and began his greatest work—*The General Consultation of the Reform of Human Affairs*

(*De rerum humanarum emendatione consultatio catholica*) (Comenius 1966). He wrote it in seven parts: *Panegersia* (Comenius 1990), *Panaugia* (Comenius 1987), *Pansophia*, *Pampaedia* (Comenius 1986), *Panglottia* (Comenius 1989), *Panorthosia*, and *Pannuthesia*. This great work included: a concept of the universe (cosmos), and knowledge of it; a theory of lifelong education for everybody; a plan of a world language, common to all; universal reform of not only individuals but also of families, schools, states, and Churches; a plan of institutions for promoting the advancement of learning (*collegium lucis*); a plan for the realization of peaceful cooperation between nations (*dicasterium pacis*); and a plan for peace among Churches (*consistorium oecumenicum*).

4. Disillusionment and Travel

The end of the Thirty Years War brought disillusionment to Comenius' hopes for the liberation of his people, as the Czech lands remained in the power of the Habsburg regime. He expressed his grief over the fact that the *Unitas Fratrum* was dispersed in European countries, and was even disappearing, in his Czech publication, the *Testament of the Dying Mother Unity of Brethren*. However, he hoped for an awakening of his nation to labor for its spiritual and cultural development.

After the return to Leszno in 1648 his second wife died leaving several children behind. It was a relief for Comenius when his family were cared for by Jana Gajus, whom he married in 1649. Having been elected bishop of the *Unitas Fratrum* in 1632, he was overburdened with responsibilities and publishing books during his stay at Elbing. The most important of these books was *Novissima linguarum methodus* with a supplementary *Consultatio* (Comenius 1966)

In 1650 Comenius accepted an invitation to Hungary by the House of Rákóczi to reform the school in Sárospatak. During his journey there he visited Brethren congregations in Slovakia and met a positive response to his textbooks in schools. Supported by Duke Sigismond, he wrote theoretical treatises in Sárospatak on pansophic education, self-education, and national progress.

Comenius discovered that Hungarian youth were insufficiently prepared for secondary school studies and this led him to a further development of educational practice in the form of simple, swift, pleasant, and thorough learning and teaching by means of the illustrated *Orbis pictus* that became even more popular than *Janua linguarum*. In 150 small chapters he presented a knowledge of the world as he had done in *Janua*, but this time complemented by illustrations of things described in the text in Latin and one or two other languages. In Sárospatak, Comenius also developed the concept of interrelationships of all the factors of the educational process (*Schola pansophica*), and the interrelation between general and specific education which also included rest, recreation, and physical health.

Comenius' third stay in Leszno (1654–56) ended tragically. During the Swedish–Polish war in 1656, Leszno was destroyed by fire and Comenius lost all his property including precious manuscripts and books. He felt deeply disappointed to see the manifestation of hatred in Poland, a tolerant country where he had once found a new home in his exile. He described the disaster in his publication *Lesnae excidium*.

The final refuge for Comenius was Amsterdam in the Netherlands where, from 1652, he was kindly received by Laurentius de Geer, the son of his old protector, Louis de Geer, who had left the Netherlands for Sweden and had invited Comenius to come there. Apart from further educational writings; religious and philosophical polemics; writings for *Unitas Fratrum* and other exiles (e.g., *Kancionál*–A Hymn Book); historical writings on the Reformation; political treatises; and works defending peace, such as *Angelus pacis*; he protested against wars, disrespect toward men, and the editions of prophecies to which he ascribed political significance. At this time he carried out two great enterprises worthy of particular consideration: *Opera didactica omnia* (collected educational writings) (Comenius from 1969) published in 1657–58 and the manuscript of *Consultatio catholica* (Comenius 1966)

5. Educational Writings and Reform

Opera didactica omnia (ODO) (Comenius from 1969) contains four parts: pansophic–educational writings of Comenius from the first Leszno period; his works produced during his stay in Elbing; his writings from Sárospatak; and new treatises written after his arrival in Amsterdam. Each part begins with an important theoretical work: *Didactica magna, Novissima linguarum methodus, Schola pansophica*, and *Vita gyrus*.

Consultatio catholica (Comenius 1966) remained a body of work. The first two parts were saved from the Leszno fire and could therefore be published. Comenius also prepared selected parts from *Pansophia, Panorthosia* and *Pannuthesia*. However, they aroused sharp criticism from Samuel Maresius in Groningen. The polemic with him embittered the last two years of Comenius' life. However, owing to Maresius' apology a considerable part of Comenius' life's activity was described in *Continuatio admonitionis fraternae*. It is mainly the eight-part *Pansophia*, (also called *Pantaxia*), that remained unfinished. It contains a system of knowledge about the whole world: first, selected principles on which the world has been constructed (*Mundus possibilis*); and second, selected knowledge concerning things and phenomena in the world, all dealt with in seven "worlds" ("*mundus*") or stages. Comenius' concept begins with the world of God and evolves, via the world of angels, to the natural world (*Mundus materialis*); then is further explored through human creative activity in three human worlds (*Mundus artificialis, Mundus moralis* and *Mundus spiritualis*), which again move toward the eternal world. *Pansophia* describes and explains the position and tasks of man in general reforming terms. It is a final application of Comenian philosophy to didactics, education generally, and social reform.

Comenius drew inspiration from the ancient idea of *panharmonia*. He elaborated upon his pansophy so that it integrated not only all knowledge, but all human activities (i.e., individual, social, intellectual, emotional, and those of will and decision—moral and practical), so that they can be applied correctly to life.

Furthermore, pansophy provided a complex method, namely, a combination of analysis, synthesis, and syncrisis, the last being a special method of comparison (i.e., analogy) used in order to determine what is substantial and what is peripheral, and which interrelations of parts toward the whole and toward single parts play a significant role in universal knowledge. Adopting the Neo-Platonist concept of the whole as an organic unity, Comenius was not content with solving partial problems, such as language teaching only. From the concept of the reform of teaching Latin he moved into the reform of education in general: from the reform of Czech schooling to the improvement of education for all nations; and from the education of children to the education of adults and old people, in the "School of life" explained in *Pampaedia*.

Similarly, in his concept of *formatio hominis* (in both versions of his *Didactica*) Comenius developed the idea of *cultura universalis*, a complete culture of the whole of mankind. For this reason he could not separate any activity from other manifestations of man. That is why he disagreed with the separation of the investigation of nature (Bacon) or the investigation of the processes of the human mind (Descartes) from other manifestations of men. Comenius' considerations were based on the conception of man in his relations to the whole world (i.e., nature, man, and God). His idea was to make schools, and then the whole of life, a workshop of humanity. He understood the development of mankind as a stockpiling of experience in a continuing process of perfection. The process continues through creative human labor which occurs when all people recognize that there is a need to reform everything in life and that everyone has to begin this labor by themself. In his *Consultatio* (Comenius 1966) he concentrated on the reform of philosophy, politics, and religion as the areas where, in the course of historical development, men could manifest their humanity; that is why these areas could represent human affairs (*res humanae*).

6. Conclusion

In his endeavor to integrate aims, content, and methods of education for everybody, Comenius developed principles of easy, rapid, and pleasant—but thorough—learning and teaching. Through this method, in which universality, simplicity, and spontaneity were leading principles, all people ought to be educated in everything that is significant for human life, and necessary for the development of individual personality and the reformation of the whole of society.

In his "mosaic physics" Comenius did not step across the boundaries of the emerging natural sciences. But in his endeavor to discover the laws governing human development and education, in the broadest ramifications of life and peaceful development, he was far ahead of his time.

See also: Historiography of Education

References

Comenius J A 1966 *De rerum humanarum emendatione consultatio catholica*. Academy of Science, Bohemoslovaca, Prague
Comenius J A *Opera didactus omnia* from 1969. Vols. 1, 2, 3, 4, 9I, 11, 12, 13, 14, 15I, 15II, 17, 18, 23. Academia Praha, Prague
Comenius J A 1986 *Pampaedia or Universal Education*. Buckland Press, London
Comenius J A 1987 *Panaugia or Universal Light. Being Part 2 of his Consultation on the Reform of Human Affairs*. Peter I Drinkwater, Shipston-on-Stour
Comenius J A 1989 *Panglottia or Universal Language*. Peter I Drinkwater, Shipston-on-Stour
Comenius J A 1990 *Comenius's Panegersia or Universal Awakening*. Peter I Drinkwater, Shipston-on-Stour
Comenius J A 1991 *La Labyrinthe du Monde et le Paradis du Coeur*. Desclée, Paris

Further Reading

Acta Comeniana from 1969. Academia Praha, Prague
Blekastad M 1969 *Comenius: Versuch eines Umisses von Leben, Werk und Schisksal des Jan Amos Komenský*. Academia Praha and Universitets-forlaget Oslo, Prague and Oslo
Čapek J B 1972 *Zur Frage des Wesens und der Funktion des Comenismus*. Independent supplement to *Studia Comeniana et historica* 2–1972č 4. Muzeum J.A. Komenského, Uherský Brod
Čapková D 1987 *Myslitelsko-vychovatelský odkaz Jana Amose Komenského*. Academia Praha, Prague
Červenka J 1970 *Die Naturphilosophie des Johann Amos Comenius*, Vol. 1. Academia Praha-Hanau, Prague
Comenius J A 1992 *Obecná porada o nápravě věci lidských*. Svoboda Praha, Prague
Internationales Comenius Kolloquium 1992 Evangelisches Bildungszentrum Bayreuth, Hussitisch-Theologische Fakultät, Prague
Pánek J 1991 *Comenius, Teacher of Nations*. Východoslovenské vydavatel'stvo Košice, Orbis Praha, Prague
Patočka J 1981 *Jan Amos Komenský. Gesammelte Schriften*

zur Comeniusforschung. Comeniusforschungsstelle Institut für Pädagogik, Ruhr-Universität, Bochum
Peskova J, Cach J, Svatos M (eds.) 1991 *Homage to J A Comenius*. Karolinum Praha, Prague
Turnbull G H 1947 *Hartlib, Dury and Comenius: Gleanings from Hartlib's Papers*. Liverpool Press, London
Schaller K 1958 *Die Pampaedia des Johann Amos Comenius*. Quelle & Meyer, Heidelberg
Schaller K (Hrsg) 1985 *Comenius. Erkennen-Glauben-Handeln*. Hans Richarz, Sankt Augustin
Studia Comeniana et historica from 1971. Comenius Museum, Uherský Brod
Symposium Comenianum 1982 1984. Comenius Institute of Education Praha Comenius Museum, Uherský Brod
Webster C 1975 *The Great Instauration. Science, Medicine and Reform 1626–1660*. Duckworth, London

D. Capkovà

Communication, Media, and Instrumentation

Media play a number of roles in education that have to do with communication and instrumentation. These roles fall into three categories: (a) the delivery of instruction, in which media are used to convey specific content, (b) the construction of mediated environments, in which media help students explore and construct understanding of a body of knowledge, and (c) the development of cognitive skills, where media are used to model, engender, or extend mental skills. Three types of theory support these roles of media. Semiotic theories are concerned with how media represent what they refer to. Cognitive theories account for how students decode and learn from the messages media convey. Contextual theories are concerned with learning contexts that media create.

This entry describes the three educational roles that media play, reviews the three types of theory, and discusses issues that arise from the roles and theories. It concludes by identifying current trends that are likely to shape the future of the way media are used in education.

1. The Educational Roles of Media

1.1 The Delivery of Instruction

Historically, the role of media in instructional delivery has received the most attention. Advocates of media have felt compelled to demonstrate, first, that media are at least as effective in teaching as teachers and, second, that certain media are particularly effective at delivering certain types of content to particular kinds of student. Although the value and validity of media comparison studies, which purport to demonstrate both of these effects, have been questioned on the grounds that instructional methods and not delivery systems are what really make a difference in learning (Clark 1983), the notion persists that media do enable students to learn in unique ways. However, a review by Kozma (1991) suggests that the contribution of media to learning may not lie in the way they deliver instruction, but rather in their construction of learning environments and the development of cognitive skills.

Building on the premise that media can deliver instruction, the instructional role of media has become well-established in both public education and in corporate and military training. In public education, media usually play a subordinate role to the teacher, acting as simple audiovisual aids, like slides or videotapes, or serving as self-instructional systems intended to deliver portions of the curriculum to students who do not need the constant attention of a teacher. Heinich (1970) has proposed different roles for media in schools, where they would share instructional responsibility with teachers, or even supersede them. This has not happened to any significant extent. On the one hand, teachers are resistant to such a radical change in their instructional responsibility. On the other, media-based instructional systems are not yet capable of doing all that teachers do.

In the area of corporate and military training, media have often assumed a more central instructional role because few professional instructors work in these areas. Here, instruction may simply be guided by comprehensive course notes. Alternatively, a rich multi media environment might be embodied in a training simulator in which trainees can master all the skills they require with virtually no intervention from a human instructor.

Since the mid-1970s educators have become increasingly sensitive to the need to select media on the basis of their instructional function (Heidt 1976). Consequently, the role media play in instruction is determined from a careful analysis of the goals and content that students are expected to master, and from an analysis of the students themselves. The selection or design of the mediated portions of instruction is therefore guided by knowledge of which media are the most effective for delivering which kinds of content to which kinds of students.

An increasingly important role for media in the delivery of instruction is in distance education. Telecommunications and related technologies have been used in large and modest projects in many countries to deliver instruction. The United Kingdom's Open University is a good example of a large-scale project and exemplifies many of the characteristics of mediated distance education. University courses are delivered by correspondence, radio, and television to students' homes. The Satellite Instructional Television Experiment (SITE) in India is typical of mediated distance education in developing countries. Programs in basic education, agriculture, and health care are broadcast to communities around the country in a variety of languages. Members of local communities are involved in many aspects of the project.

1.2 Mediated Educational Environments

Since the early 1980s, media have been used increasingly to construct rich learning environments whose purpose is not didactic, but rather to encourage students to explore the knowledge that the environment contains and to construct their own knowledge of it. The chief distinguishing characteristic between this use of media and media that deliver instruction is that, here, media environments are largely content-free.

The oldest, and probably the best known example of this kind of learning environment is the LOGO microworld (Papert 1980). LOGO is a computer language. Its graphic commands (at least) are simple enough for young children to master and use in constructing interesting images. The ease with which youngsters can control the computer and the attractiveness of the output make LOGO a motivating environment. However, Papert's intention was not to develop a system that simply allowed students to draw pictures, but rather to create an environment in which children could develop what he called "powerful ideas" about how to approach and solve problems. What children draw is not specified. Instead, students wrestle with problems of their own choosing and develop problem-solving skills in doing so (see *Logo, Educational Applications of*).

Many other examples of mediated environments in which students can construct knowledge involve "hypermedia" computer software. The first commonly available program in this genre was Apple Computer's Hypercard, which simulates a card file in a number of interesting ways. Users put whatever information they want on a card; they may place the cards in any order and link the cards together in any sequence they wish. In addition to text and graphics, cards may contain sounds, voice, music, still and motion pictures. Multimedia environments can be constructed as "stacks" of cards that contain any of these formats (see *Hypertext, Educational Applications of*).

Hypermedia environments have two characteristics that make them ideal for knowledge construction. The first is the potentially limitless flexibility in the order in which users can access information. The second is the ease with which users can create databases. If users are students, they can construct their own materials and learning environments. Several projects in this genre are described by Nix and Spiro (1990). They include the work of Spiro and Jehng (1990), where random access videodisk under the control of a hypermedia program allows students to explore the film Citizen Kane and gain an understanding of such literary concepts as theme and character. The Cognition and Technology Group at Vanderbilt University (1991) have likewise used videodisks to promote problem-solving skills in mathematics, social studies and science. McMahon and O'Neil (1991) use Hypercard to allow students to construct imaginary dialogs among characters in which both overt speech and unspoken thoughts are written. Their "Bubble Dialog" program is used in a range of activities, from writing to social issues.

1.3 Development of Cognitive Skills

The third role for media is the development of students' cognitive skills. As researchers began to question the intrinsic capability of media to improve learning, interest developed in the ways in which the symbol systems of media interact with cognitive processes. This role for media is based on the premise that thinking involves the manipulation of symbols that are created when external representational forms (media), such as those employed in speech, television, or computer programs, are internalized and made directly available to cognition.

The corollary of the idea that cognition relies on internal media-like symbols is that internal representations and the cognitive processes that operate on them can be augmented if students are induced to internalize new symbol systems. Salomon (1979) has shown that this is in fact the case. Exposure of young Israeli children to "Sesame Street" led to their developing the mental skills necessary for viewing the program. Similar evidence for the internalization of reading-related metacognitions has been reported for subjects using a computer program (Salomon et al. 1989).

Finally, now that it is acknowledged that cognitive skills can be developed by exposure to the symbol systems of different media, scholars have adapted the approach that media can be used to "distribute" cognition. Media are not just tools for the thoughts that occurs internally, but can become tools for storing and sharing those thoughts. It is by no means new to think of media as storehouses of ideas. However, the sharing of thoughts that the archival and distributive functions of media allow raises a whole host of questions that media scholars are only now beginning to answer. These include the educational and social contexts within which mediated experiences take place, and the redefinition of literacy to include skills with a variety of media.

2. Media Theories

Students learn from media, construct knowledge from mediated environments, and develop cognitive skills to the extent that they interact with, comprehend, and react to the messages media convey. The three types of media theory focus on this interaction, but with emphasis on different aspects. Semiotic theories emphasize the message side of the interaction. They are concerned with how messages are constructed to represent objects and events. Cognitive theories emphasize the student side of the interaction, stressing the processing, interpretation, and comprehension of messages. Contextual theories emphasize the context in which the interaction takes place and focus on students' perceptions of media and the ability of media to motivate students. While these types of theory are closely related, it is useful to examine each type separately (see *Media and Learning*).

2.1 Semiotic Theories

The earliest attempts to establish a theory of educational media were based on the idea that the instructional effectiveness of media depends on the way in which objects and events are represented. Models and pictures capture realistically a number of the features of objects, whereas text and mathematical formulae do not. For some, the greater the resemblance of the message to its referent, the greater its instructional usefulness. Realistic pictures, for example, make it easier to identify objects and to remember them, and "realism theories" became prominent in research on educational media and in the development of instructional materials.

The early advocacy of realism in educational media was tempered somewhat by the suggestion that the resemblance of a message to its referent sometimes hinders communication and instruction. Pictures have such specific referents that they are not good at teaching about broad categories of things. A series of studies by Dwyer (1978) demonstrated that reducing the realism of pictures to create more abstract forms, such as line drawings, is effective for teaching about the working and structure of objects, rather than about their appearance. In the early 1990s, it is accepted that the way in which media represent their referents, whether, for example, as pictures, text, diagrams, or charts, should be determined by the function the illustration is to perform.

2.2 Cognitive Theories

Cognitive theories of media are concerned with the relationships between the symbolic elements of media and internal representation and processes. Salomon (1979) argued that a message's meaning is more likely to be influenced by its degree of correspondence to a person's internal representations than by its resemblance to some external object or event. This is because interpretation and learning are the product of the interaction between established knowledge and new information. The form of a mediated message is still important in cognitive theories in the early 1990s. However, the media's impact is ascribed to their direct effect on cognitive processes.

It is useful to distinguish between two aspects of cognitive theories of media. The first is concerned with how different forms of representation affect the way in which information is encoded, stored, and retrieved. The second is concerned with how different forms of representation, once encoded, affect the way in which knowledge is processed and transformed by the cognitive system.

The human ability to recall details of visual images is quite phenomenal, with experimental subjects accurately recognizing more than 80 percent of the pictures they see after viewing thousands of slides over periods of several days. Achievements such as this, compared to relatively poor memory for verbal information, are best explained if pictorial and verbal are encoded separately. Paivio (Clark and Paivio 1991) has proposed "dual coding theory" built on precisely this premise. Verbal memory encodes information in arbitrary word-like symbols. Imaginal memory encodes information as representations that are similar to the percept experienced when an object or event was apprehended. In other words, information may be encoded and stored either in language-like symbols or as images. Pictures of recognizable objects are encoded directly as images and also, verbally, as their labels. This redundancy is why pictures can be easier to recall than words.

While encoding and retrieval are necessary conditions for learning, they are not sufficient. For learning to occur, new information must be assimilated to existing knowledge, which in turn has to be modified to accommodate it. This means that internal representations have to be acted upon and transformed by cognitive processes. Internal representations that have this necessary dynamic property are known as "mental models."

The dynamic nature of mental models arises from their ability to be "run" in memory in the same way that programs are run in a computer. Thus, the events that occur in an electrical circuit when a switch is closed can be examined in the mind's eye as the mental model of the circuit passes through a series of transformations brought about by the operations of the components in the circuit.

The running and examination of a mental model involve "envisionment." Understanding of the modelled phenomenon evolves as discrepancies between what is envisioned and what is observed are reduced. What is observed is often a mediated presentation of something rather than the thing itself. There is therefore an important link between media and the development and running of mental models (Seel and Strittmatter 1989). For example, still or animated line drawings and diagrams make it easy for a student to envision such things as the opening and closing of valves and the movement of pistons, and lead to a more rapid and better understanding of physical systems.

2.3 Contextual Theories

The social effects of media have been described and debated in many books and articles. In order to keep attention focused on educational media, the discussion will be confined to an examination of two closely related factors that affect the context in which students learn from media. The first is motivation. The second is the attribution of characteristics to media by students.

Generally speaking, students like mediated instruction. Many media researchers have developed the habit of assessing students' motivation to learn from media at the same time as assessing instructional effectiveness. The positive effects that these assessments provide can be attributed to the novelty of mediated instruction and to its ability to cater to students who are less verbally oriented. However, the novelty of instruction by media wears off over time, as it loses its allure.

Motivation that arises when media cater to processing modes in which students have skill is less ephemeral. If, by seeing pictures or diagrams or videotape, students come to understand something they could not understand before, they will be motivated to learn more from that medium. The problem that arises here is that the media are used to adapt instruction to students' ways of thinking rather than challenging them to develop new cognitive skills. While this makes it easier for students to learn from material designed especially to match their abilities, it may make it harder for them to learn from material that is not designed in this way.

Related to motivation are students' beliefs about the ability of the media to teach them. Instead of intrinsic characteristics of media influencing learning, a more likely influence is students' attributions of their success or failure in learning from a medium. Salomon (1984) found that students tend to think it is easy to learn from television and hard to learn from text. Not only do their attributions of success or failure vary as a result of these beliefs, but the amount of effort they invest in learning is affected as well. If they think it is easy to learn from a medium, they will not try as hard and consequently will not learn as much.

3. *Issues and Trends*

A number of issues arise from this review. The first is whether or not media have intrinsic properties that influence learning. The consensus among researchers seems to be that they do not. However, they certainly enable a variety of instructional activities that would be extremely difficult to realize without them. In particular, these involve the development of informationally rich multimedia environments that allow students to construct knowledge for themselves rather than simply absorb information presented to them by someone else. As a result, there is a move away from simply using media to teach predetermined content toward using media to create learning environments and microworlds. Research on the effectiveness of these uses of media is ongoing and results are promising.

A second cluster of issues concerns the influence of media on internal representation and cognitive processing. Much evidence exists to show that the symbol systems that different media employ are internalized and can be used as tools for thought. The extent to which this internalization occurs naturally, or can be deliberately induced is not entirely clear, however. To judge from past experience, it will be necessary at some point to re-examine what it means to be literate. Simple observation shows that young people who have lived all of their lives in a highly mediated environment interact with information and with each other in very different ways from their parents.

Encouraging students to develop ways of thinking that are derived from the ways media represent and handle information raises a third set of issues. These are ethical issues, and they deserve far more attention than they are typically given in research. Students' beliefs in the value of media, as well as their beliefs in media's ability to educate, need to be studied extensively. Moreover, technologies are not neutral. The "goodness" or "easiness" attributed to a particular medium is quickly associated with the messages the medium conveys.

Finally, the applications of media and the media theories described above have implications for the day-to-day conduct of schooling. Early predictions that media would change schools beyond all recognition have not turned out to be true. This is partly because, until recently, media have been given primarily a didactic role that is in direct competition with the teacher. In the early 1990s, media can achieve many things that a teacher cannot, especially through the integration of many formats and sources of information, and the creation of environments that students can manipulate directly. The new varieties of pedagogy that these uses of media allow are different from the traditions of practice of teachers, providing teachers with alternatives rather than competition. As a result, it is possible that media will act as a catalyst in attempts to restructure schooling.

See also: Logo, Educational Applications of; Hypertext, Educational Applications of; Cognition and Learning; Media Selection; Instructional Design Theories

References

Clark J M, Paivio A 1991 Dual coding theory and education. *Educ. Psychol. Rev.* 3(3): 149–210

Clark R E 1983 Reconsidering research on learning from media. *Rev. Edu. Res.* 53: 445–59

Cognition and Technology Group at Vanderbilt University 1991 Technology and the design of constructivist learning environments. *Educ. Technol.* 31 (5): 34–40

Dwyer F M 1978 *Strategies for Improving Visual Learning: A Handbook for the Effective Selection, Design, and Use*

of Visualized Materils. Learning Services, State College, Pennsylvania
Heidt E U 1976 *Medien und Lernprozesse*. Beltz Verlag, Weinheim [1978 *Instructional Media and the Individual Learner: A Classification and Systems Appraisal*. Kogan Page, London]
Heinich R 1970 *Technology and the Management of Instruction*. Association for Educational Communication and Technology, Washington, DC
Kozma R B 1991 Learning with media. *Rev. Educ. Res.* 61(2): 179–211
McMahon H, O'Neill B 1991 Zones of engagement in learning. Paper presented at the NATO Advanced Research Workshop on The Design of Constructivist Learning Environments, Leuven, Belgium
Nix D, Spiro R J (eds.) 1990 *Cognition, Education and Multimedia: Exploring Ideas in High Technology*. Erlbaum, Hillsdale, New Jersey
Papert S 1980 *Mindstorms: Children, Computers and Powerful Ideas*. Basic Books, New York
Salomon G 1979 *Interaction of Media Cognition and Learning*. Jossey-Bass, San Francisco, California
Salomon G 1984 Television is "easy" and print is "tough": The differences in investment of mental effort in learning as a function of perceptions and attributions. *J. Educ. Psychol.* 76(4): 647–58
Salomon G, Globerson T, Guterman E 1989 The computer as a zone of proximal development: Internalizing reading-related metacognitions from a Reading Partner. *J. Educ. Psychol.* 81(4): 620–27
Seel N M, Strittmatter P 1989 Presentation of information by media and its effect on mental models. In: Mandl H, Levin J R (eds.) 1989 *Knowledge Acquisition from Text and Pictures*. Elsevier, Amsterdam
Spiro R J, Jehng J C 1990 Cognitive flexibility and hypertext: Theory and technology for the nonlinear and multidimensional traversal of complex subject matter. In: Nix D, Spiro R J (eds.) 1990

Further Reading

Anglin G J 1991 *Instructional Technology Past, Present, and Future*. Libraries Unlimited, Englewood, Colorado
Clark R E, Salomon G 1986 Media in teaching. In: Wittrock M (ed.) 1986 *Handbook of Research on Teaching*, 3rd edn. Macmillan, New York
Fleming M L, Levie W H (eds.) 1993 *Instructional Message Design*, 2nd edn. Educational Technology Publications, Englewood Cliffs, New Jersey
Greenfield P M 1984 *Mind and Media: The Effects of Television, Video Games and Computers*. Fontana, London
Houghton H A, Willows D M 1987 *The Psychology of Illustration. Vol. 2: Instructional Issues*. Springer Verlag, New York
Jonassen D, Mandl H (eds.) 1990 *Designing Hypermedia for Learning*. Springer Verlag, Berlin
Seel N M 1991 *Weltwissen und mentale Modelle*. Hogrefe, Göttingen
Spencer K 1991 *The Psychology of Educational Technology and Instructional Media*, 2nd edn. United writers Press, Liverpool

W. D. Winn

Community and Parents' Participation in Curriculum Decisions

An examination of the issues surrounding community and parent participation in curriculum decision-making is embedded in the much larger discussion of parent and community involvement in education in general. Community and parent involvement in schools has become a goal for many educators in light of theoretical and empirical work suggesting that increased school–parent interaction can result in significant educational benefits (Seeley 1984, Bronfenbrenner 1974). Furthermore, reform efforts in numerous countries have increased the legitimacy of parent involvement in school affairs, including curriculum (Goldring 1991). For the purposes of this discussion, community involvement will refer to the participation of citizens from the general school neighborhood, while parent participation refers to those specific community members who have children in the school.

Community and parental involvement may be reflected in numerous aspects of the educational process from a variety of perspectives. This involvement may be implemented through different parental roles such as volunteer, paid employee of the school, teacher at home, audience, decision maker, or adult learner (Gordon 1979). The involvement may reflect specific action arenas such as teaching, providing resources, learning, or decision-making (Flammer 1981). Additionally, parental participation may result in different levels of involvement. For example, Schickendanz (1977) proposes three different levels of parental involvement: level one involves activities where parents receive information and provide limited help in the school (bazaars, etc.); level two includes activities where parents provide assistance in the school under the direction of the professional (either the teachers in general or the school principal); and level three includes activities in which parents participate in making decisions regarding educational policy. Emerging from these various typologies of parental involvement is the fact that participation in curriculum transcends many areas of involvement. For instance, parents can help mobilize resources to help the school acquire new instructional materials, or community members can volunteer to tutor at-risk children in school. The rationale behind community and parent participation in curriculum decisions follows the reasoning that learning is most effective when there is congruence among school, home, and community. Following the Coleman and Hoeffer (1987) study that compared public and private schools in the United States, the extent to which parents and schools have a shared value orientation, a common definition of the school's ideology and mission, or are part of a "functional community," is considered to be an important aspect of school effectiveness. In this light, curriculum is not conceived of as a printed course of study, but as learning environments (Tyler 1980). The aim of participation mechanisms is to provide productive environments of learning which complement one another.

This is a complex task as parents and community members do not necessarily agree on the values which should be embraced in a curriculum. For example, court cases in the United States have had to decide the extent to which a group of parents has the right to demand that certain books be withdrawn from the school curriculum, as the books did not coincide with the group's religious values (Will 1986). Furthermore, there are numerous controversies over the rights of parents in curriculum decisions compared with the responsibility of professional educators to make these decisions. Some suggest that when curriculum decisions are likely to be controversial, it is extremely important to involve a wide range of parents to avoid such conflicts (Helm 1982). In contrast, some parents do not want to participate in curriculum decisions, even when educators try to recruit them. Parents are often concerned about their children's welfare in school and do not want to become involved beyond solving problems of their individual child.

This entry summarizes these complex issues by addressing four general topics: (a) avenues for community and parent participation in curriculum decisions; (b) modes of participation; (c) community schools and curriculum participation; and (d) issues for consideration.

1. Avenues for Community and Parent Participation

Participation in curriculum decision-making is both individual and collective in its form. Citizens, that is, parents and members of the community, can be involved in schools as individuals or as members of committees, councils, and groups (Davies 1978). Individual participation is increasing as reports indicate that parental involvement contributes to student achievement. A survey of parents in Israel indicates that the primary motive for parent participation is to help their individual child (Shapira and Goldring 1991). Individual participation includes volunteering, tutoring, working in the school as teacher aides, parent training programs, and parental choice of schools. Parents often volunteer in classrooms by helping teachers and students, giving guest lectures, and reading.

As individuals, parents may find it difficult to gain influence, but once formally organized, they have a greater potential for influence. Parent and community groups can be classified according to their origins, scope, auspices, and focus (Davies 1978). The origins of parent groups are either mandated or citizen initiated. Mandated parent groups include advisory committees, while voluntary groups include parent–teacher associations, grassroots organizations, and business organizations concerned with education. The scope of parent groups ranges from the local school, such as a school curriculum committee, to the city or the national level. Auspices are related to the scope of parent groups. Some groups are affiliated with larger organizations, including religious groups or political parties, and other collective parent groups are unaffiliated and independent. Lastly, some parent groups limit their focus to one specific issue, while other groups focus on multiple issues.

The type of parent group has important implications for the impact of the participation. For example, parents interested in a particular issue create a coalition to achieve a specific goal. This voluntary issue group often links with larger, more powerful national organizations to help them influence the educational establishment (Goldring 1991). When the goal has been achieved, the group may disband. The effectiveness of parent groups is often influenced by the extent to which members of the group are representative of the community, and the extent to which relevant, not merely ritualistic, issues link the group with the school.

2. Modes of Participation

There are several mechanisms by which parents and communities can influence curriculum decisions that will create congruent learning environments between home and school. Three types of participation, including both individual and collective forms, are discussed here: participation at home (home schooling, tutoring at home), participation in school forums (committees, school boards), and participation through exercising choice. Although these three mechanisms are by no means exhaustive of all the types of participation in curriculum decisions, they encompass the most commonplace modes of parental involvement.

2.1 Participation at Home

Parent participation at home is usually of three types: (a) home education, (b) parental involvement in home curriculum, and (c) parents as tutors.

In many countries, education is compulsory, but schooling is not required and parents may educate their children at home. This is referred to as home instruction, home education, or home schooling, and seems to be on the rise. In the United States over 120,000 children are taught at home, while some estimate that the number may be 260,000—less than 1% of the total school-age population (Lines 1987). In Europe, Germany does not have a home education provision, while in other countries, such as Denmark, Luxembourg, Ireland, and the United Kingdom, there are no restrictions on home instruction. In the

United Kingdom, as well as in the United States, there are organizations that assist families in educating their children at home (Macbeth 1988).

Parents seem to choose home schooling for two main reasons, both related to curriculum: ideology and pedagogy (Van Galen 1988). Parents who choose home schooling for ideological reasons object to what they believe is being taught at school. They hold specific beliefs and values (e.g., fundamentalist religious doctrines), and they want to provide their children with a curriculum that supports these values. Parents who choose home schooling for pedagogical reasons believe that they can provide their children with a "better" education at home, both in terms of academic achievement and emotional well-being. Parents vary in the extent to which they rely on curricular materials at home. Some parents subscribe to specific curricula through correspondence courses, while other parents rely on a totally unstructured approach to learning. Therefore, the way home schooling impacts on curriculum is that in this case, parents are completely in control of the curriculum in terms of deciding both what should be taught and how it should be presented to the child.

Specific programs targeted to increase parent involvement at home rather than at school are a second mode of parent participation at home. In this mode, the children do attend school and parents work with their children on school-related curricula. This type of parent participation at home is based on the assumption that parents can support and supplement school programs by working with their children at home. These types of programs are widespread and are usually geared to preschool or elementary age children. These programs in the United States, Israel, and the United Kingdom usually have three components. Most include a home visitor component where paraprofessionals train parents to be effective teachers; a curriculum materials component where instructional materials, including television, are presented for parent–child interaction; and a classroom component where groups of parents and children meet together to reinforce the activities presented in the home curriculum (Wallace and Walberg 1991).

Parent-as-tutor programs are a third type of participation at home. These programs are aimed at helping parents support their child's school program by tutoring them at home. The tutoring programs are usually quite structured and provide parents with specific learning objectives in reading, language, mathematics, and study skills. Curriculum workshops help parents understand specific curricula and provide ways in which parents can help their children at home. Hence, parent tutoring is a way for individual parents to work with their children at home to reinforce the curriculum presented at school.

2.2 Participation in School Forums

In the United States many forums exist for community participation in curriculum decisions. In fact, citizen participation is guaranteed because local schools are governed by lay school boards which are the trustees for local school systems nationwide. This basic right of lay control of schools has translated into numerous forms of community participation in school governance: community councils, parent advisory councils, and parent associations. All of these types of participation vary as to the level of actual influence parents have. Fantini (1980) summarizes the level of participation in these types of forums from relatively low levels of influence where parents are clients responding to school requests, to much higher levels of influence where parents are equal partners in the educational process and educators rely on community groups to set policies.

Numerous examples exist across different countries for meaningful participation in curriculum decisions. Curriculum advisory councils often meet, where parents and teachers discuss curriculum concerns such as homework, class projects, and instructional materials. Councils serve as a source of input when making curriculum decisions. For instance, council members may visit other schools to see how instructional programs are being implemented and then provide their own school with information to help form policies (Hinton 1986).

A unique type of curriculum advisory council are parent associations which administer extracurricular programs. These associations have been responsible for developing and financing independent school programs by collecting a monthly fee from parents. The stated aim of these programs is to supplement and enrich school activities eliminated by budget cuts. The curriculum of the programs is decided upon by a committee of parents together with the principal. In many cases, the parents hire teachers and negotiate their salaries. The programs are usually held at the end of the school day or during one-day workshops (Bar-Simon-Tov and Langerman 1988).

Parents can also be involved in specific aspects of the curriculum decision-making process. After a new curriculum has been adopted, an evaluation often takes place. Parents can take important roles in the evaluation process. For example, Donmoyer (1990) describes a deliberative approach to curriculum evaluation. In the deliberative approach, parents are actively involved in the evaluation of a program in all of its stages, from defining the issues, selecting and collecting data, and judging the findings.

It is important to note that in some countries there is little tradition of parental participation in curriculum decisions in school forums. For instance, Krum (1991) indicates that in Austria, although there is legislation that provides for parental participation in school forums, there is very little meaningful cooperation around pedagogical issues. Similarly, in the United Kingdom, Johnson (1991) found that working class families keep in touch with secondary schools by discussing educational issues with their children. These parents feel their role is to prepare their children to assume responsibility. In Japan parents are relatively passive in their influence on decisions in the elementary and junior high schools. Parents typically come to school for school events, such as awards, sports, or the Parent–Teachers' Association (PTA), but they have no voice in determining policies and curriculum (Benjamin 1991). In Japan the focus of parental participation is in the home. "The success of home–school cooperation is often evaluated by teachers on the basis of parents coming to the school. . . . Many home-based forms of parental support and interest are invisible to teachers" (Johnson 1991 p. 180).

2.3 Participation Through Choice

One of the major educational issues facing families pertains to questions of choice in education. More and more parents are being called upon to make choices regarding their children's school. Simply stated, public choice models of education advocate that parents should have the right to choose their child's school both within the public school system and between the public and private sectors. The aims of parental choice plans include increased accountability, social integration, and parental involvement in public education (Maddaus 1990). Although the debate surrounding school choice is not typically placed in the context of curriculum decision-making, curriculum is often one of the criteria cited for choosing a particular school. Parents can choose to send their children to a school where the curriculum and pedagogy are congruent with their own culture and value systems. Hence, a very important form of individual participation in curriculum decision-making is through choosing a school other than an assigned neighborhood school.

In most countries parents are responsible for their children's education through a mandatory education law, and it is the parents' responsibility to see that this law is upheld. Choice advocates suggest that parents should be given some authority commensurate with the responsibility. This authority would allow parents to choose their child's school according to their religious, philosophic, or pedagogic preferences and simultaneously give them influence over the curriculum.

Parents often cite curriculum and values as the reason they chose an alternative to their neighborhood school. Parents surveyed in Minnesota about their reasons for choosing schools indicated that 67 percent choose because of better curriculum options (Martin and Burke 1990). In Australia and many European countries parents choose alternative schools according to religious preference.

The important point is that through choice parents can influence curriculum decisions. The chosen schools are highly dependent upon parent satisfaction with curriculum—if parents are dissatisfied, they can leave the school and enroll their children elsewhere. For instance, a recent study of schools of choice in the United Kingdom documents ways in which the schools are responding to parental concerns. A choice school is systematically involved in soliciting parent feedback, and the parents are active in changing aspects of the school policies and practice in regard to homework and examinations (Woods 1992).

3. Community Schools and Curriculum Participation

Community schools form a special case of educational programs that emphasize community participation in education and are part of many educational systems, including developing countries. Community schools view the community as the center of learning and the focus of education. The goal of community schooling is to link the culture of the pupil's home community with the culture of the school. The community school concept implies a much broader view of the functions of the school building, the curriculum, and the students. School facilities are available to all residents of the community, school activities are integrated into the community, and the curriculum coincides with broad community values and needs (Totten and Manley 1969).

In Papua New Guinea, for example, community schools are central to the national curriculum development. Community schools are defined according to the way in which schools function in relation to their communities and the way in which schools provide opportunities for lifelong learning of community residents. These community schools, like many of the community schools in developing nations with large rural populations, include aspects of community life in their curricula such as festivals, customs, musical instruments, and local business activities. Furthermore, community leaders such as healthcare officers, village leaders, and agricultural officers teach in the schools, and many community groups such as welfare groups, church groups, and elders utilize the school's buildings, (Aarons 1982).

The major distinguishing factor of community schools is that the school is viewed as an integral part of the community. These schools are major institutions in their communities responsible for implementing changes and providing services for all residents. These schools aspire to be central to the life of the community by encouraging active community involvement to achieve mutual goals (Friedman 1988). Many developing Third World nations are relying on community schools as mechanisms of social reform to integrate education into the local community for all citizens. In countries such as India, China, and Tanzania, innovative community school programs are adopting existing curricula to the unique circumstances of local villages (Roy 1980, Maliyamkono 1980).

By definition, community schools offer a much broader role for parent and community participation in curriculum decisions. All decisions require community involvement. Research has documented that community schools promote more participation than neighborhood schools without a distinct community orientation. Research of community and non-community schools in Alberta, Canada indicates there is more parental and community involvement in community schools; however, there is a need to delineate the boundaries of decisions made at the community–school level from those decisions made at the district and provincial levels (Lazaruk 1982). This finding highlights some of the problems of community schools. One of the main problems is related to the allocation of power in decision-making. Although community schools may increase participation in curriculum decision-making, the balance of power between the community and other educational authorities may lead to a decrease in the scope of decision-making to restricted arenas.

4. Issues for Consideration

Pressures for community and parental participation in all aspects of the educational process are increasing. As community and parent participation in curriculum decisions becomes more extensive, a number of issues must be considered which were inconsequential before. The first issue pertains to the impact of participation on the curriculum. With increased participation there are more parties who have potential influence on curriculum decisions. Not all parties have the same values and ideas regarding what a curriculum should be. Not all parents of a particular school agree on what should be taught and how it should be taught. Numerous questions must be considered, for example: How can multicultural curricula be realized? How are different parties (e.g, parents, local school professionals, state and federal planners) able to participate in curriculum decisions in order to arrive at a curriculum that meets the needs of varied groups? What happens when a local community's curriculum needs are in conflict with a national curriculum, such as in the case of minority cultural groups (e.g., the Native Americans in the United States or the Aboriginals in Australia)?

A second issue which must be deliberated is the impact of increased involvement on the role relationships between the various parties involved in the participation processes. In other words, how can participation best be facilitated? Community and parent participation places numerous constraints on the typical, centralized school administration. In order for participation to be meaningful, mechanisms must be adopted which allow for significant collaboration. Thus, shared decision-making among school professionals, parents, and communities requires a reorganization of power and authority relationships. However, questions remain. Should there be boundaries on the scope and domain of this participation? Without some level of restructuring, participation will be reduced to ritualistic, unimportant arenas.

A third issue which must be considered pertains to questions regarding who participates. Efforts must continue to facilitate the participation of low-income, disenfranchised parents of at-risk children so they may become active partners in the school–home participation process. Family structures (e.g., single parents, or working mothers) do not always support the mechanisms of participation which are advocated by the school. These families often lack the time and organizational sophistication to become active partners. Schools must provide the necessary assistance, awareness, and value systems that encourage all parents to participate (Education Studies Group 1991, Pink and Borman 1986).

Lastly, research and development needs to provide practical guidelines for implementing and evaluating different types of participation programs. Some programs have documented success, but dissemination must be encouraged.

See also: Family and Schooling; Family, School, and Social Capital; School Choice, Foundations of

References

Aarons A 1982 What is a community school? Decentralizing curriculum planning in Papua New Guinea. In: 1982 *Proc. Annual Conf. Australian Comparative and International Educational Society*. Australian Comparative and International Educational Society, Sydney

Bar-Simon-Tov R, Langerman S 1988 *Extracurricular Classes Administered by Parents in Elementary Schools*. The Henrietta Szold Institute, Jerusalem

Benjamin G R 1991 Choices of education in Japan. *Int. J. Educ. Res.* 15: 251–64

Bronfenbrenner U 1974 *Is Early Intervention Effective?* DHEW Publication No. (OHD) 74–25, US Department of Health, Education, and Welfare, Washington, DC

Coleman J, Hoeffer T 1987 *Public and Private High Schools*. Basic Books, New York

Davies D 1978 *Patterns of Citizen Participation in Educational Decisionmaking*. Institute for Responsive Education, Boston, Massachusetts

Donmoyer R 1990 Curriculum evaluation and the negotiation of meaning. *Lang. Arts* 67: 279–86

Education Studies Group 1991 *Resources and Actions: Parents, Their Children and Schools*. National Opinion Research Center, Chicago, Illinois

Fantini M D 1980 Community participation: Alternative patterns and their consequences on educational achievement. In: Sinclair R (ed.) 1980 *A Two-way Street: Home–school Cooperation in Curriculum Decisionmaking*. The Institute for Responsive Education, Boston, Massachusetts

Flammer M G 1981 *Parent Involvement Programs in New*

Jersey. ERIC Document Reproduction Service No. ED 213533, Washington, DC
Friedman I 1988 *Education and Community*. The Henrietta Szold Institute, Jerusalem
Goldring E 1991 Parents: Participants in an organizational framework. *Int. J. Educ. Res.* 15: 215–28
Gordon I J 1979 The effects of parent involvement in schooling. In: Brandt R S (ed.) 1979 *Partners: Parents and Schools*. Association for Supervision and Curriculum Development, Alexandria, Virginia
Helm V 1982 Curriculum changes require support. *Am. Sch. Brd. J.* 169: 38
Hinton J 1986 Seven ways to fire up parents about your elementary school. *Executive Educator* 8: 39–40
Johnson D 1991 Parents, students and teachers: A three-way relationship. *Int. J. Educ. Res.* 15: 171–82
Krumm V 1991 Whose school is it anyway? *Int. J. Educ. Res.* 15: 265–76
Lazaruk W A 1982 *A Comparative Analysis of Selected Designated Community Schools and Non-designated Schools in Alberta*. Alberta Department of Education, Planning and Research Branch, Edmonton, Alberta
Lines P 1987 An overview of home instruction. *Phi Del. Kap.* 68: 510–17
Macbeth A 1988 *Parental Choice in School in Europe*. European Parents' Association
Maddaus J 1990 Parental choice of schools: What parents think and do. *Rev. Res. Educ.* 16: 267–95
Maliyamkono T L 1980 The schools as a force for community change in Tanzania. *Int. Rev. Educ.* 26: 335–47
Martin M, Burke D 1990 What's best for children in the schools-of-choice movement? *Educ. Policy* 4: 73–91
Pink W T, Borman K M 1986 Building community-school programs in two cities. *Urban Review* 18: 105–16
Roy A 1980 Schools and communities: An experience in rural India. *Int. Rev. Educ.* 26: 369–78
Schickendanz J A 1977 Parents, teachers and early education. In: Persky B, Colubcheck L (eds.) 1977 *Early Childhood*. Avery Publishing Group, Wayne, New Jersey
Seeley D 1984 Home-school partnership. *Phi Del. Kap.* 65: 383–93
Shapira R, Goldring E 1991 *Parental Involvement and Schools of Choice*. Discussion Paper 15–90 The Pinhas Sapir Center for Development, Tel Aviv University, Tel Aviv
Totten W F, Manley F 1969 *The Community School*. Allied Education Council, Galien, Michigan
Tyler R 1980 Parental involvement in curriculum decision making: A review and critique. In: Sinclair R L (ed.) 1980 *A Two-way Street: Home–school Cooperation in Curriculum Decisionmaking*. The Institute for Responsive Education, Boston, Massachusetts
Van Galen J 1988 Ideology, curriculum and pedagogy in home education. *Educ. Urb. Soc.* 21: 52–68
Wallace T, Walberg H 1991 Parental partnerships for learning. *Int. J. Educ. Res.* 15: 131–46
Will G 1986 Free exercise of Ignorance is no "right." *Los Angeles Times*, November 11
Woods P 1992 Responding to the consumer. Parental choice and school effectiveness. Paper presented at the International Congress for School Effectiveness and Improvement, Victoria, California

E. B. Goldring

Community Colleges

Educational systems in all nations are called on to accommodate people who are past the age of compulsory schooling but who desire further education that is not provided by the traditional universities. That group includes students seeking preparation for jobs or low-cost access to prebaccalaureate studies, and adults who want culturally and socially relevant recurrent education. The systems are also expected to supply properly trained workers for the nation's business and industry, and to retrain the workforce to meet the demands of emerging technologies. These challenges have led many countries to develop various forms of schooling in which one or a combination of these functions are carried out.

1. Scope and Definition

The postcompulsory, nonuniversity sector includes structures organized in association with the nation's formal school system as well as numerous unique enterprises standing apart. Although this area of education is a loosely defined sector, its outlines can be traced in the formally recognized institutions that perform its functions in the nations of Asia, Europe, and North America where the concept is most generally recognized.

The names applied to the institutions in this sector suggest its multiple purposes. In the United States, the term "community college" is used generically for all publicly supported institutions accredited to award the associate degree as their highest degree. Elsewhere these institutions may be known as "junior colleges" (still used in the United States for some privately supported colleges), regional or district colleges, technical or technological institutions, or by a number of other names, as shown in Table 1. "Short cycle institution" is sometimes used in Europe to encompass the entire group of of postsecondary schools that do not award baccalaureate degrees. But in this entry "community college" is used as the collective term.

Distinctions within the category may be made by reference to curricular classifications or modes of institutional organization. The colleges may offer general or foundation studies, pre-university courses, technical and vocational programs, and cultural and social education. None of these terms is definitive and the same institution may provide several types of curricula, with overlaps among them. The colleges may be organized as branches of a university, locally governed schools, or as independent state or national systems. In some nations, specialized curricula are provided in two or three types of community colleges, each governed and funded differently.

Overall, community college education is less a definable institutional sector than an area of education that serves several purposes in the interstice

Table 1
Institutions providing community college functions

Institution	Country
College of Advanced Education	Australia
College of Applied Arts and Technology	Canada
Collége d'Enseignment Général et Professionnel (CEGEP)	Canada
College of Further Education	Australia United Kingdom
Community College	Canada New Zealand United States
Fachhochschule	Germany
Folk High School	Denmark
Higher School	Yugoslavia
Higher Technicians' Section	France
Institut Teknologi	Malaysia
Junior College	Japan Republic of China United States
Regional (or District) College	Norway Israel
Regional Technical College	Ireland
Special Training School	Japan
Technical College (or Institute)	United States Malaysia New Zealand
Technological Education Institution	Greece
Two-year Vocational University	People's Republic of China
University Institute of Technology (IUT)	France
Upper Secondary School	Sweden
Volkhochschule	Germany
Workers' College	People's Republic of China

between compulsory and higher education or, in some cases, after higher education. It tends to follow patterns of workforce differentiation and is more generalized in countries where student tracking is delayed (as in the United States), and more specialized where streaming students according to their likely place in the workforce is made earlier (as in some northern European countries).

Nevertheless, the community colleges worldwide share certain characteristics. Their fees are usually lower than those charged by universities, and students may enroll without satisfying the rigorous requirements that many university systems impose. The institutions employ large numbers of part-time faculty members. They may provide undergraduate studies that can be used as credits toward baccalaureate degrees if the student eventually gains admission to the university, a function that is especially prominent in the United States and Canada. Where educational expectations are expanding they relieve the pressure placed on university systems by people seeking admission for postsecondary studies. And they act as flexible institutions that can organize programs to resolve short-term problems of language preparation for immigrant groups, workforce retraining in the face of technological change, and community expectations for ad hoc postsecondary education of general interest to the local populace.

2. Development of Community Colleges

The development of community colleges in the various nations has followed different patterns. In the United States, where 1,250 community colleges serve more than 5.5 million students, the institutions date from the early years of the twentieth century. As long ago as 1930, community colleges were operating in nearly every state. The general expansion of postsecondary education that began in the 1940s led to rapid growth as institutions were organized to provide first-year and second-year courses for students for whom the universities had no space. Many additional students appeared who either were not qualified for university entrance because of their poor prior academic preparation, or who could not afford the higher tuition charges. The colleges also grew because they organized programs to prepare people for middle-level or semitechnical occupations that the universities had ignored. These two central functions, prebaccalaureate and technical training, were subsequently joined by two others: cultural and educational programs for lifelong learning, in which people might participate for their personal interest, and remedial courses for the students who failed to learn basic literacy skills during their previous schooling. By the 1980s nearly half the undergraduates enrolled in publicly supported higher education in the United States were in community colleges, found now in all 50 states. And if the proprietary trades schools are added to the category, the number of students in community colleges exceeds the total enrolled in universities.

Although the community colleges in other nations are not as comprehensive or ubiquitous, they share many of the same developmental characteristics. Canada's were founded in each province to meet rising demands for access to postsecondary studies, workforce preparation, and adult education. The Republic of China's (Taiwan) junior colleges, organized in the late 1970s, provide programs that vary in length from 2 to 5 years, with the latter accepting students from middle schools (Ministry of Education 1990). The Swedish system was reformed in 1970 when pre-university preparatory schools were combined with vocational programs to form single upper-secondary schools. The University Institutes of Technology (IUTs) were founded in France in the 1960s in an attempt to channel more students into programs connected with the workplace. Their selective admissions policies and technological emphases differentiate them from that nation's higher technicians' sections which are more nearly terminal vocational schools.

3. *Goals and Functions*

The emphasis placed on the functions assigned to community colleges varies considerably. Occupationally related studies are prominent in many systems. Some of the community colleges in the United States provide vocational and technical programs exclusively, and a few states have organized dual systems, with university branches providing the general education and technical institutes, the occupational studies. Sweden's upper-secondary schools integrate general subjects with vocational training that includes a workplace-based component. Vocational courses are also featured in the regional technical college system in Ireland, the Japanese special training schools, and the junior colleges in the Republic of China (Taiwan).

Pre-baccalaureate programs are prominent in community colleges in nations where the universities have been unable to matriculate a rising number of degree seekers. Colleges in the United States enroll sizable numbers of students who seek the first 2 years of a bachelor's degree program. Such students form a high proportion of the enrollment in numerous institutions, especially in states such as Kentucky and Wisconsin where the colleges were organized as branches of the state university, and in states where the public universities' first-year class is kept deliberately small so that the community colleges serve as feeders to the upper division; Arizona, California, and Florida are notable examples. The credits earned in the Canadian community colleges and in the Japanese junior colleges can also typically be applied to the baccalaureate degree, but this feature is rare in other nations.

The cultural and social education of adults, often called "lifelong learning," is emphasized in the regional colleges in Norway, the *Volkshochschulen* in Germany, the folk high schools in Denmark, and the colleges of further education in the United Kingdom and Australia. The lifelong learning programs in these institutions have a widespread scope. Cultural and leisure-time activities are a part, along with programs that are attentive to social objectives in the local communities. The British and Australian systems rely heavily on open or distance learning provided through electronic media. Table 2 displays the major emphases and orientations of community colleges in different countries.

4. *Organization*

Governance and organizational patterns vary. United States community colleges were formed originally by public school districts, churches, independent agencies, universities, or under special state authorization, with the state-coordinated system gradually becoming the prevalent pattern. In Austria, Denmark, Indonesia, Sweden, and, more recently, France, short-cycle postsecondary programs were attached to the secondary school system. In South America, the colleges were more likely to be founded as branches of the university or the polytechnic colleges. Separate systems were developed to govern community colleges in Canada, and New Zealand has formed a technical institute system to link its community colleges with its polytechnics and technical institutes (Kintzer 1990). Japan's junior colleges and special training schools are privately supported in the main, but there is also a small system of public technological colleges. Norway's short-cycle programs are conducted through district colleges, Israel's through regional colleges, Germany's through *Fachhochschulen*, nationally coordinated but with a strong component of local governance.

The age limits for compulsory schooling affect the

Table 2
Major emphases of institutions providing community college functions

	General	Pre-university	Technical	Vocational	Cultural/Social
Australia					×
United Kingdom					×
Canada	×	×	×	×	
Denmark					×
France			×	×	
Germany					×
Greece			×		
Ireland				×	
Israel	×		×		
Japan	×	×	×	×	
Malaysia				×	
New Zealand			×	×	
Norway		×		×	
People's Republic of China			×	×	
Republic of China			×	×	
Sweden	×			×	
United States	×	×	×	×	
Yugoslavia			×		

way community colleges are organized. In nations where the compulsory years end early, the community college may take the form of an institution offering programs that extend for 4 or 5 years. The programs in these institutions serve upper-secondary as well as early collegiate functions. But where the students are obliged to attend school for 10 years, the community colleges operate as postsecondary institutions offering prebaccalaureate, occupational, and/or leisure-oriented studies. Such programs may be of only 1 or 2 years' duration, or even shorter in the case of specific occupational-certificate programs.

The formation of community colleges usually follows the recommendations of some state or national body commissioned to study ways of accommodating the rising demand for postsecondary studies and for relevant occupational and technical training. These types of commissions were organized in numerous countries in response to the population bulge of the 1960s. During that decade, 50 community colleges a year opened in the United States. The Israeli colleges, along with those in such African countries where they have been developed, also date from that time. The colleges in Scandinavia grew out of the older, locally governed adult schools but those systems, too, have been broadened since the 1960s.

The community colleges may be integrated into a single postsecondary system that includes the universities; they may be extensions of the secondary school system; or increasingly, they may take form as separately organized postsecondary structures. Most of the community colleges in the United States are governed by state or local boards of trustees and local boards are influential in the German and Scandinavian systems. In general, the community colleges operate under state or national laws with local boards more prominent than they are in the university sector.

5. *Clientele*

Enrollments in each nation's community colleges vary greatly depending on the level of institutional development, especially the number of sites, and the accessibility of the universities. Since the 1970s enrollment growth worldwide has been greater in the community colleges than in the universities. In Australia and the United Kingdom, further education enrolls twice as many students as the universities. In some of the states in the United States where a campus is within reasonable commuting distance for nearly the entire population, as many as 85 percent of the students who begin higher education do so in a community college. But the proportion of postsecondary enrollment in community colleges in France, Israel, and Italy is considerably lower, principally because the universities are open to a broader range of matriculants.

The people attending community colleges tend to reflect the characteristics of the adult population in the districts where the colleges are located. Their ages range from upper teenage all the way to the most elderly, with the former concentrated in the prebaccalaureate programs and the latter in leisure-oriented education. Half the students in the United States community colleges are aged 25 or younger, and one-third of them are under age 22 (Cohen and Brawer 1989). In systems where lifelong learning is emphasized, the median student age is higher.

Most community college students attend on a part-time basis, commuting from their nearby residences. The students' aspirations and age affect their attendance patterns. The younger students, typically enrolled in vocational entry or prebaccalaureate programs, are more likely to attend full-time. Most of the older students who enroll in education for their personal interest or in occupational recertification or career upgrading courses are employed in local business, industry, or service occupations and attend part-time.

Data on the positions held by the students after they leave the community colleges are difficult to aggregate because the institutions serve as continuing learning centers with sizable numbers of students entering and leaving as their educational aspirations and life circumstances shift. Nearly one-third of the students receiving a university diploma of technology from a French IUT, and two-thirds of those obtaining associate in arts or sciences degrees from United States community colleges matriculate at universities. But these figures are misleading because most of the community college attendees do not complete the degree programs, and many of the programs in all systems lead to certificates that do not qualify the holder for university study. Similarly, the figures on job entry are unclear. Many students already hold jobs and use the colleges for further education qualifying them for advancement. The data that are available suggest that as many as 90 percent of the graduates of programs leading to positions in selective-entry fields, such as the health and engineering technologies, obtain employment, whereas as few as 20 or 30 percent of the students who are prepared as office workers or sales personnel gain immediate employment. The job market in a college's locality constitutes a major variable.

6. Finance and Facilities

The financing of community colleges is varied, ranging from full support by national governments to a majority of support coming from local communities. Many systems are funded by monies coming from a combination of sources. The pattern in the Nordic countries is for the national government to fully support the institutions, whereas in Japan tuition paid by the students accounts for a sizable proportion of the funding. Community colleges in the United States rcccivc practically no money from the federal government except for that which is paid on behalf of students who receive federal grants and loans. Overall public community colleges in the United States receive 10 percent of their income from the federal government whereas tuition and fees account for 16 percent, local aid 17 percent, and state aid 47 percent (Cohen and Brawer 1989). The junior colleges in Japan receive 9 percent of their income from the government, 62 percent from student fees, 10 percent from endowments, and 11 percent from loans (National Institute for Educational Research 1990). In both nations, auxiliary services and private gifts and grants account for the remainder.

The cost per student per credit hour is from one-third to one-half as much as in universities, with the difference a result of many factors. The faculty in community colleges teach longer hours and are paid less, the libraries and laboratories are considerably more modest, and class size is larger on average. The tendency in most nations is for the community colleges to have limited facilities, often to have no exclusive campuses of their own. They offer courses in school buildings, in public administration facilities, and in businesses and factories, especially for the people working there. However, although the community colleges of the United States and Canada often started in such donated and rented facilities, in the early 1990s most of them now have developed full-service campuses.

7. Faculty and Staff

The community college faculty have more in common with secondary school teachers than with university professors. They rarely engage in research or scholarly publication. Their credentials may be trades experience or baccalaureate degrees for those teaching the vocational courses, and masters degrees for those teaching in prebaccalaureate programs. Some, such as the Danish folk high schools operate with noncertificated faculty. The part-time instructors in United States community colleges outnumber the full-timers by 58 to 42; just under one-fourth of the instructors hold a doctoral degree. The doctorate is even less common among community college instructors in other countries where continuing and vocational studies are more prevalent.

The faculty often have close ties with local industries or governments, working in the plants or agencies and teaching during off hours. The full-timers teach for more hours (12–20 per week) and are paid less than the university professors. The part-timers are on hourly pay scales and usually have little security of employment. Instructional innovation is encouraged and community college systems around the world rely heavily on cooperative learning, multimedia presentations, peer tutorials, and open-broadcast output, as well as on traditional classroom activities.

8. Curriculum

Each of the curricular areas—general, pre-university, technical, vocational, and cultural–social—covers a broad scope. General studies include reading, writing, and arithmetic for students who passed through the compulsory school years without being adequately prepared for life in the community, or who dropped out of secondary school before completing the requirements for a diploma. The programs may also emphasize rudimentary work habits, study skills, and personal hygiene and social practices.

The pre-university curricula feature introductory courses in the sciences, social sciences, mathematics, humanities, and fine arts, often arrayed in two-year programs leading to a university specialization. They are heavily influenced by the university faculty who often have authority over which courses are acceptable for credit toward the baccalaureate; therefore the courses rarely deviate greatly from the content and text of their university counterparts.

Technical studies apply science to the workplace. Most of the health fields fall in this category, along with engineering, some mechanical operations, business management, information processing, and professional support areas such as laboratory technician training. In nations where teacher education does not require a bachelor's degree, those studies are provided through the community colleges.

Vocational studies prepare people for jobs in factories, offices, and farms. They center on specific workplace functions and may be provided through programs that take only a few months to complete. The type of vocational study that is offered varies with labor force demands in the college's vicinity and the programs often have direct links with local employers or labor organizations.

Cultural and social studies are provided for adults who may or may not have participated in prior postsecondary education. The courses are often presented as short, discrete offerings for a few days or months, with a focus on specific topics; for instance, child care, art appreciation, cooking, foreign languages, labor union or small business management, civic issues, and consumer education. Certificates of completion may also be awarded.

9. National Profiles

As the following profiles illustrate, the organization and operation of community colleges in the various nations takes different forms. The curricular emphases, control, and student populations are the major differences. However, the absence of a community college system or of a particular curricular function within one does not necessarily mean that the function is not offered; it may be provided by that nation's university or adult school system.

9.1 People's Republic of China

The two-year vocational or polytechnic institutions in the People's Republic of China were developed in the 1970s and 1980s, initially under World Bank financing. By 1982, 53 such institutions were in operation, offering courses in secretarial work and accountancy. Adult education through various inservice courses and two-year and three-year vocational courses presented through the universities are also provided, but the tendency is to promote more two-year vocational schools. In general, the workers' colleges provide the technologies, especially engineering, while the two-year vocational universities are directed toward local community requirements for vocational studies (Shiqi 1984) (see *China, People's Republic of: Adult Education*).

9.2 Germany

The *Volkshochschulen* began in the nineteenth century as open-access, low-cost institutions. They now total 900 institutions offering a varied curriculum including language training for foreigners, personal interest courses in the arts and humanities, and a potpourri of courses and activities relating to local community social objectives. They tend to operate without permanent campuses, and with courses taught by part-time instructors in various types of facilities. Local governance is strong in their operation, but they are funded by a combination of state and national monies (Bogart 1985).

9.3 Japan

Japan's 561 junior colleges, 3,152 special training schools, and 62 technical colleges together enroll more than 25 percent of the students who graduate from high school. This compares with less than 19 percent who go to the universities. Women form 91 percent of the junior college students, but men form the majority of the students in the special training schools. Beginning in 1976, the latter schools have taught technologies, paramedical fields, business, accounting, and foreign languages. The junior colleges are heavily weighted toward the liberal arts, with more than 70 percent of the students majoring in humanities, home economics, or education (National Institute for Educational Research 1990). There is little transfer to the universities from either set of institutions. As compared with the universities, the colleges enroll students from the lower socioeconomic groups and their programs lead to less prestigious employment. Adult education is not featured, but is provided instead through locally organized social education centers. General vocational studies are undertaken in more than 3,000 miscellaneous postsecondary schools privately organized to offer business and health-related studies and to prepare students for the university examinations (Abe 1989) (see *Japan: Adult Education and Training*).

9.4 New Zealand

The 20 technical institutes and community colleges in New Zealand enroll 80 percent of all students in higher education in that nation. They offer short courses in business for local interest to a population comprising mainly part-time students. Certificate programs in nursing and applied sciences are also offered by a faculty made up of approximately equal numbers of full-timers and part-timers (Kennedy 1981).

9.5 Norway

The Norwegian regional colleges enroll just over 6 percent of all students in higher education in that nation. They tend to be more vocationally oriented than the universities but they do offer certain courses which can be credited toward traditional university degrees. Some 70 percent of the students are in vocational programs, and 20 percent in university preparation. Funding was originally based on local sources for buildings and national sources for operations, but the colleges have since become totally funded by the government (Kyvik 1981).

10. Trends and Issues

The worldwide expansion of postcompulsory, non-university education will continue as national development, technological change in the workplace, and rising demand for further education focus attention on this sector. The major inhibitors to this expansion are competition from the universities and the lower school systems, and limitations on public finance of education. In most nations the tendency is for technological studies and vocational education to be provided at public expense while cultural and social education is often seen as a consumption item to be paid for by the participants. Free or heavily subsidized postcompulsory education for everyone on a recurrent basis is not feasible; therefore, cooperative arrangements, with financing and facilities provided in cooperation with local industries, continue to be sought so that the burden of paying for the instruction can be shared.

Issues of national planning versus local option come continually into play. In many nations the central agencies attempt to anticipate workforce needs and to encourage development of programs that prepare people in those specialty areas. At the same time, the locally based community colleges value their ability to respond to local demands on the part of industries that need especially trained workers and individuals who want access to programs of their choice. The organization of the community colleges within national education systems often conflicts with these local and individual expectations.

Within the community colleges the necessity of serving masses of people economically and sustaining curricular relevance make for continual modifications. Instructional systems that differ from the traditional labor-intensive teaching are sought and the proper training for instructors is always a concern. The amount of credit that should be awarded for work experience is an issue, along with the capacity of the institutions to maintain control over their own curricula while not jeopardizing their students' ability to transfer credits to other post-secondary institutions.

The various types of institutions that make up the community college sector in any nation present a problem of coordination. Duplicating and competing systems magnify problems of finance and articulation. The United States has publicly funded community colleges, private junior colleges, and proprietary trade schools. Japan has private junior colleges, national technological institutes, and special training schools with a strong component of local governance. The lines between France's university institutes of technology and higher technicians' sections are not clearly drawn. And within every nation institutional drift occurs continually as the local colleges become regional, the specialized institutes become comprehensive, and the competition for students and funding leads all of them to organize new programs continually.

The community college sector attempts to retain its flexibility so that it can respond to changing student populations and labor force demands. But this flexibility and the absence of familiar academic degrees results in the public's holding a murky view of what the institutions are. Institutional evaluation is often misguided because traditional paradigms of educational research focus on degree attainment and students' cognitive learning developed through sequentially organized programs, neither of which is a feature of community college education.

In the nations where the community colleges have not developed, studies repeatedly point to the need for some type of institution to perform the functions that could be provided by this sector. In Italy, for example, where the universities have been open to all petitioners, the need for two-year vocational programs and other types of intermediate diploma-related activities is apparent. In the United Kingdom, where the proportion of 18-year olds entering higher education continually expands each year, the case for an increase in the number of two-year diploma courses and for a breakdown in the barriers between the universities and the community colleges can be recognized. In general, expansion of the community college sector is assured because of rising demand worldwide for further education at reasonable cost.

See also: Lifelong and Continuing Education; Recurrent and Alternation Education; University Adult Education; Adult Secondary Education; Polytechnical Education; Folk High Schools; Sociology of Adult Education; Adult Education, Planning Public Policy for

References

Abe Y (ed.) 1989 *Non-university Sector Higher Education in Japan*. Hiroshima University Research Institute for Higher Education, Hiroshima

Bogart Q J 1985 The community college and the Volkshochschule: An international comparison of leadership objectives in the adult teaching/learning process. Paper presented at the Annual National Convention of the American Association of Community and Junior Colleges, San Diego, California

Cohen A M, Brawer F B 1989 *The American Community College*, 2nd edn. Higher Education Series. Jossey-Bass, San Francisco, California

Kennedy P J 1981 *New Zealand: A Study of the Educational System of New Zealand and a Guide to the Academic Placement of Students in Educational Institutions of the United States*. World Education Series. American Association of Collegiate Registrars and Admissions Officers, Washington, DC

Kintzer F C 1990 Education for employment: An international perspective. *Higher Educ. Eur.* 15 (4): 97–104

Kyvik S 1981 *The Norwegian Regional Colleges: A Study of the Establishment and Implementation of Reform in Higher Education*. Studies in Research and Higher Education. Norwegian Research Council for Science and the Humanities, Oslo

Ministry of Education, Taiwan 1990 *Educational Statistics of the Republic of China, 1990*. Ministry of Education, Taipei

National Institute for Educational Research 1990 *Basic Facts and Figures About the Educational System in Japan*. National Institute for Educational Research, Tokyo

Shiqi H 1984 On some vital issues in the development and reform of higher education in the People's Republic of China. Paper presented at the World Congress on Comparative Education, Paris

Further Reading

Assefa A M 1988 *France: A Study of the Educational System of France and a Guide to the Academic Placement of Students in Educational Institutions of the United States*. World Education Series. American Association of Collegiate Registrars and Admissions Officers, Washington, DC

Dennison J D, Gallagher P 1986 *Canada's Community Colleges: A Critical Analysis*. University of British Columbia Press, Vancouver

Furth D 1973 *Short-cycle Higher Education: A Search for Identity*. OECD, Paris

Gilliland R J 1986 Folkhighschool: The people's college of Scandinavia. *Community Tech. Jr. Coll. J.* 56(5): 22–25

Kintzer F C 1984 Short-cycle higher education: Purposes and issues. *Higher Educ.* 13: 305–28

Organisation for Economic Co-operation and Development 1985 Educational reforms in Italy. In: OECD (eds.) 1985 *Reviews of National Policies for Education*. OECD, Paris

Squires G 1987 *Education and Training after Basic Education: Organisation and Content of Studies at the Post Compulsory Level. General Report*. OECD, Paris

A. M. Cohen

Community Education and Community Development

This entry is about community education and community development and its many faces. Included are programs known as "community schools," "community education," and "community development." Also described are forms of grassroots endeavors seeking social transformation by means of popular education, participatory research, and education provided by social movements. Finally, the role of popular theater and popular culture in the education of adults is discussed.

Education is not a neutral activity. Hence the discussion of the various manifestations of community education must be placed in a social and political context. Accordingly, the "functionalist–development" and "conflict–change" sociological concepts are utilized to interpret the varying ideologies that drive educational practice.

1. The Conceptual Framework

In adult education there has been continued debate regarding the extent to which the main purpose of schooling is to reproduce the power relationships existing in a society, or whether the school and adult education serve as the sorting mechanisms by which complex modern societies assign, through an egalitarian process, particular roles to their citizens based on meritocratic achievement (Rubenson 1989). The first interpretation, in which power is the key concept, leads to a conflict model in which variables such as race, class, and gender are powerful means for explaining education for domestication. The concept of domestication is central in analyses of class struggle and resistance (Giroux 1983). Key concepts in the second, functionalist interpretation are modernization and evolutionary change through development in which consensus and integration are emphasized. Schools prepare citizens, both cognitively and through socialization, to take their social and economic roles based on their achievement in a competitive system (see *Meritocracy*).

Table 1 describes aspects of community education and community development from both analytical perspectives. To illustrate the categories in Table 1, one can contrast community education and community-based education in the United States.

1.1 Community Education

Community education developed from the Mott-funded community school movement in Flint, Michigan. Defined as "an educational and community development process for the development of human potential and participation in the local decision making process" (Kerensky 1989 p. 63), it is in practice associated with the functionalist paradigm. The process assumes equality regardless of race, class, or gender. It also assumes equality in the democratic decision-making process. The ubiquitous nature of the public primary school and a desire for its efficient use is the rationale for making the school a community resource, intended to increase participation of the community by providing for financial, edu-

Table 1
Functionalist/development and conflict/change theories of community education and community development

Theory	Functionalist/development	Conflict/change
Characteristics	consensus–integration reformation	conflict–transformation
Definition of community	geographical communities	geographical; racial/ethnic, gender, social class communities; social issue (environment, peace) groups
Forms	centered in formal; use of nonformal	centered in nonformal; use of formal
Educational program	community education community development community college	community-based education popular education social movement learning
Knowledge production	logical positivistic research	participatory research; transformative research
Culture	"High Culture"—e.g., museums and libraries	"Popular Culture"—e.g., popular theater and popular art
Historical roots	Henry Morris—England Frank Manley—USA	Father Coady—Canada Paulo Freire—Brazil Rajesh Tandon—India Myles Horton—USA Julius Nyerere—Tanzania

cational, recreational, and avocational needs. The idea is that, with citizen participation in education, other community problems may be identified and addressed. Formal societal structures are not seen as the problem; the problem is the involvement of citizens in a community. Accordingly, some theorists in the United States promote the use of community education organized around the local school as one way of solving problems such as schools failing to prepare competitive workers, the perceived failure of the family, and the apparent disintegration of moral values in the society. The emphasis is on making the community function as it should (Kerensky 1989).

1.2 Community-based Education

In contrast, Community-based Education (CBE) assumes a more radical stance. The Association for Community Based Education defines the concept as responding to underserved populations by carrying out a range of activities that include economic development, housing rehabilitation, health services, job training, adult literacy, and continuing education programs. The premise is that education cannot be separated from the culture and community in which it occurs—it is linked to community development and the empowerment of communities. In this definition the commitment is to bring about development and empowerment in poor communities. In practice CBE's may be organized around special populations such as women, or an environmental concern as well as a geographic community. Rarely would a community-based organization be located in a public school. The definition of the problem is poverty and power relationships, not citizen participation.

To make the language even more complex the term "community education" in the United Kingdom may encompass both types described above. There are community education programs based on what is termed a "liberal" philosophy, while others operate with a "liberating" philosophy (Fletcher 1980 p. 10). These types parallel the functionalist and conflict models indicated in Table 1.

2. Definitions of Community

The complexity of the term, "community" is captured by the editors of the two volumes of *Harvard Educational Review* issued in 1989 and 1990 dedicated to community-based education:

> Community is the configuration of people we live next to, as well as of people with whom we share deep common bonds: work, love, an ideology, artistic talent, a religion, a culture, a sexual preference, a struggle, a movement, a history, and so on. Community can be difficult to define uniformly in terms of where people live; for within the same geographical area there can exist different communities, and it is not uncommon for their interests to clash. Such is the case with Palestinian communities within Israeli communities, Black South Africans under apartheid; communities of women within patriarchal culture; Asian, African American, Latinos and Native Americans in racist cities and rural areas in the United States; poor and working class people struggling against homelessness while right next door affluent communities prosper; and gay and lesbian communities within a larger homophobic society. (Munoz and Garcia-Blanco 1989 p. 5)

Not only is the definition of the word "community" complex but "one of its central features is that it is used to avoid the discomfort of being understood exactly" (Jackson 1980 p. 39). Jackson notes there is a significant "difference between being part of a pleasant, cozy, residential neighborhood where one can be certain that everyone will be socially acceptable and being in a community organized by professional social workers. Again the idea of community obscures the most important social and economic relationships involved. Local social relationships are important to people but the nature and strength of those relationships are determined by factors beyond the locality" (p. 42). Accordingly, Jackson (1980) challenges the definition of community as a local neighborhood. Such a definition plays an important ideological function since it promotes the ideal that "local factors determine the nature of social and personal problems while diverting attention from criticism of fundamental, political and economic institutions or dominant social belief" (p 43).

In community education or community development, one's definition of community and assumptions about the forces that define the community will in turn define one's educational ideology and the goals that one subsequently formulates. The following anecdote is illustrative: A folk school teacher in the United States was approached for help by a community group called "Not in My Back Yard," which was fighting toxic waste being deposited in their community. The teacher asked, in whose back yard should it be deposited? By asking that question the problem was redefined and communities joined together to educate and organize around the newly framed problem, "Not in Any of Our Back Yards." The problem was not toxic waste dumping in a community, but a society which allows industrial plants to pollute any local community which cannot protect itself.

3. Community Education

In the affluent countries of the northern hemisphere, "community education" is usually defined as a participative educational process based within a local public school or occasionally a community college or other adult education institution. The school, formerly limited to children, is opened up to the entire community for both academic and social education, recreation, and avocational pursuits.

One of the major issues in community education is whether it is a process or a program. This fundamental distinction has encouraged elaborations on process as the one proposed by Warden (1979):

(a) process as procedure where process is used to involve people in achieving a specified goal by a specified time;

(b) process as community problem-solving where problems are identified and solutions attempted;

(c) process as community power where the community organizer assists the mobilization of power against a particular adversary;

(d) process as psychological and social development in which persons through their activity grow and become self-actualized.

Only (c) utilizes a conflict orientation. Thus, the program–process argument is not always ideological, but rather one of procedure.

Martin (1987 p. 24), reflecting the United Kingdom experience, divides community education into universal, reformist, and radical models. In the universal model, professional leadership operates out of a formal setting; the reformist model targets low-income communities and through partnership aims for positive discrimination; the radical model involves issue-oriented, "class"-based approaches to change community structure.

Thorpe (1985), with a similar analysis and speaking from the Australian context, assumes community education is about change. She defines three models of social change: consensus (based on cooperation and participation); pluralist (recognizes inequality and negotiates social planning); and structuralist (feminist, socialist, Marxist, or anarchist analysis supporting consciousness raising and direct action).

All of the above authors attempt to specify the differences one finds in philosophy, goals, and method in analyzing practice; what is clear is the diversity of community education.

Community education programs which are consensual in nature are characterized by educational offerings for all ages, recreational programs which make full use of the resources available, and avocational training. Intergrated approaches to education such as family education and age-mixed events are planned to overcome the separateness of modern age groupings. Administration of the community school tends to be lean, and the director may report directly to an advisory council; teachers and facilitators are usually hired part-time or volunteers are utilized. Financing can be mixed with public funds, private or philanthropic funding, and, in some cases, tuition fees from participants.

Community education which is more process-oriented goes beyond programming activities to solving problems. The process-oriented community education administrator would help mobilize persons or resources to work on a solution. Community education which is conflict-oriented would operate more as popular education does and is discussed below.

A National Center for Community Education has been developed in Flint, Michigan in the United States. It is dedicated to leadership development and community education training. There are over 100 community education centers located in universities or state departments of education providing training (Brown 1990). In the United Kingdom, a Community

Education Development Center (CEDC) was built in Coventry for promoting the concept and providing consultative services to local communities (Watts 1990). There are national community education associations in each country, as well as advanced degree programs in community education. Organized in 1978 and based at Coventry in the CEDC, an International Community Education Association has as its purpose the extension of the community education model worldwide.

4. *Popular Education and Community-based Education*

Popular education (known as community-based educaiotn in North America) is based on the conceptual work of Paulo Freire (1970). It is defined as a social behavior situated within a framework broader than that dealing with education. It aims at making persons self-aware political subjects. Popular education is characterized by horizontal relationships between facililators and participants, popular participation in the planning of training and action, and the assumption that problems and solutions must emanate from the community.

Popular education is about understanding and interrogating one's own oppression. It utilizes the means of problem posing, develops a collective response, acts on the response, and then critically reflects on the quality of the response as parts of the process. However, there is no one methodology. This is because popular education is always contextualized and action must be organically related to the context. The final result is the development of the capacity to transform reality and the ability to challenge oppressive power relationships. Put simply, the end result of popular education is the ability to read one's world. Cadena (1984) states that the results should be an increasing ability of people to: (a) consciously appropriate their own reality; (b) influence and control the processes in their own lives, including equalization of the distribution of goods and services; (c) defend their own interests and the kind of society that would serve them best; and (d) make the society less hegemonic and more responsive to them.

Conceptually, popular education proceeds from the understanding that knowledge is socially produced, that there are intellectuals in all social classes, and that collectively, seemingly powerless groups can mount strong counterhegemonic forces through producing their own knowledge and challenging the official knowledge of the dominant group. Popular education is also driven by the dialectical concepts of the base (economic production) and the superstructure (cultural reproduction). Accordingly, popular education recognizes the importance of culture as well as economic power (see *Conscientization and Mobilization*).

4.1 Popular Culture

Those popular educators who make their analysis through a conflict model recognize that culture is a place to make war on hegemony. Hegemony (defined as the making common to all social classes the cultural and social formations of the dominant, high culture in order to impose control through consent) can only be opposed by countering cultural imposition. High culture is found in museums, libraries, galleries, and concert halls; pop or mass culture is the culture of fashion, celebrity, and popularity spread, for example, through television. Traditional popular culture comes from the grass roots: folk art, folk songs, folk dance, folk tales, and folk medicine.

Popular theater is an important part of popular culture because participants can creatively enact the dilemmas, induced by hegemony, which they face in society. This is a cultural expression for those who produce it; it is equally an educative event for the spectators. Popular theater can, according to Lambert (1982), be divided into agitprop (produced by professionals around local themes), participatory (produced by and for people with spectators), or conscientization (produced by and for people without spectators). Boal (1979 p. 122), a primary interpreter of popular theater, states: "I believe that all the truly revolutionary theatrical groups should transfer to the people the means of production in the theater, so that people themselves may use them. The theater is a weapon, and it is the people who should wield it."

4.2 Participatory Research

One object of participatory research is the creation of popular knowledge. Participatory research is an important part of popular education because those who learn to read their world are able to participate in the production of knowledge.

Participatory action research has a rich history with origins in Latin America, Asia, and Africa (Fals-Borda and Rahman 1991). It is based on the existential concept of experience proposed by José Ortega y Gasset: "through actual experiencing we intuitively apprehend its essence—thereby place our own being in a wider more fulfilling context" (quoted in Fals-Borda and Rahman 1991 p. 4). This concept of *experience* along with the idea of *authentic commitment* allows those external or internal to the exploited class to recognize that knowledge is the basis for social transformation, thus allowing them to work together in a subject–subject relationship.

4.3 Popular Education Programs

Popular education, like community education, is also manifested in many different ways. Popular education as used in Latin America is best described in the words of the local people who practice it. Archer and Costello (1990), for example, collected 10 case studies of popular education projects in Latin American countries. They conclude that Freirean approaches to literacy education cannot "be simply grafted on; they must be relevant to the concrete reality of the situation. Thus television, radio, and video may be more relevant when communication is less dependent on the written word" (pp. 200–01). A second conclusion is that appropriate organizational structures to give learner's demands a collective voice are needed.

In contrast, Melo and Benavente (1978) present their own analysis of the popular education movement in Portugal following the fall of the dictatorship. They carefully contextualized the rise of hundreds of local popular groups which helped to define adult education in modern Portugal and whose work helped to bring significant changes in the new Constitution. Worthy of note is the study by Chené and Chervin (1991), who provide an excellent description of popular education in Québec.

4.4 Folk High Schools

Folk high schools, which originated in Denmark in the nineteenth century, continue to respond to community needs and popular social movements (see *Folk High Schools*).

In Tanzania, with the help of the Swedish Government, folk development colleges were established in 52 districts with mixed success. Local funds to support the colleges and student enrollment were not always forthcoming from the villages. Few of the colleges were able to raise funds through self-reliance efforts (Mosha 1983).

In Chile, a network of folk schools has been developed for the purpose of training local leaders in appropriate technology techniques, literacy, ecology, and women's programming. *El Canelo*, a major resource center, receives "monitors" from a feeder system of community centers to do short-term (2–4 weeks) residential training. This Center is successful in engaging the poor. Grass root leaders studying at the Center may never have previously been away from their district.

4.5 Study Circles

Study circles have spread from the Nordic countries to many parts of the world. They have become an integral part of the idea of "circles of culture" advocated by Freire (see *Study Circles*).

With the assistance of the Kettering Foundation and the National Issues Forum, the publishing of a book on study circles by Oliver (1987), and the establishment of a Study Circles Resource Center, the study circle has taken root in North America. The goal of study circles is to advance deliberative democracy and improve the quality of public life and to promote small-group democratic, participatory discussions on social and political issues. Sometimes study circles may be utilized by community education, as in the state of Minnesota where 420 of the 432 school districts have publically supported community education.

Through a similar program, *La Mesa*, study circles are being used by popular educators in Chile and Brazil. Study circles played an important part in the mobilization of literally hundreds of thousands of mothers in Sao Paulo, who took action because of the difficulties they faced in feeding their families in a high inflation economy. Eventually, the popular mothers' groups in Brazil delivered over 1 million signatures to the president to demonstrate the depths of their dilemma.

4.6 Social Movements

Communities of special interest such as peace, environment, and women's rights, provide natural contexts for the development of popular education within a social movement. Community here is defined as a group assembled around a common interest. For example, learning for environmental action is one of four major concerns of the International Council for Adult Education. With an international office in Sao Paulo and networks organized in each of its six regions throughout the world, there is an effort to link local environmental groups into an international coalition to bring pressure to bear on environmental concerns.

5. Community Development

"Community development" also has many definitions; it can be a process, a method, a program, or a movement. By definition, the value positions on what constitutes development are normative. Much of so-called "community development" has been used by dominant groups to exploit weaker sectors of the society. Such development is top down, benefits either internal or external elites, and may do cultural violence to existing community members. The imposition of Western institutions on indigenous persons in the name of development has been well-documented. Accordingly, the defining characteristics of liberating community development must be participatory, broadly educative, and in harmony with community values. International examples to illustrate this view of community development are examined below.

5.1 Khit-Pen

The term *"Khit-Pen,"* coined by Kowit Varapipatana in 1974, signified a new approach to community development by Thai adult educators and a rejection of Western economic and technocratic definitions of development. Based on a mixture of Buddhism and Western humanistic thought, *Khit-Pen* works along three axes: information on methods of Buddhist introspection, information on society and environment as defined by sociopsychological and ecological fields, and technical information or book knowledge.

By emphasizing problem posing, the ultimate goal is to transform the Thai adult into a critical thinking person. This objective connects *Khit-Pen* to Freire's conscientization movement (Nopakun 1985). *Khit-Pen* has been translated into a national strategy for adult education aimed at the transformation of Thai rural villagers into more independent persons.

5.2 Saemaul Education

Faced with the need to develop rural villages in Korea, a national economic strategy called "*Saemaul Undong*" was initiated to promote community development. The idea was to use seasonally unemployed workers in productive work. Almost immediately the need for education of leaders emerged. *Saemaul* education was established to train village leaders in good thinking, leading to good action, leading to national development. Values taught were diligence, self-reliance, and cooperation. *Saemaul* training is done nonformally, through both residential and distance education, with an emphasis on experiential learning from successful case studies. This integrated plan of nation-building based on village-building has reportedly been successful. Benefits include the will toward development and cooperation, an active role for women, adoption of a work ethic, and a sense of village community (Cheong 1987 p. 11).

5.3 A European Cooperative Plan

The Council of Europe, through its Council for Cultural Cooperation, initiated in 1975 a cooperative program to investigate how education through community development could contribute to economic, social, and cultural innovation. Three priority groups were considered: women, the elderly, and the illiterate. Three areas were identified for study: (a) participation of women and men in decisions affecting their daily lives, (b) responses to unemployment and economic restructuring, and (c) evolution of the social and cultural roles of men and women. A number of projects were identified as exemplary and were monitored for 2 years. The monitors reported the results, and in 1987 recommendations were made to all member countries through a "Declaration" on practical strategies to solve problems arising in community development (Council of Europe 1987).

5.4 Tribal Colleges

Worthy of note are the 27 tribal colleges which have emerged since 1969 in the United States when the first—the Navajo Community College—was founded. Organized and administered by Native Americans, they now enroll over 5,000 full-time students. Though their work includes a formal college curriculum, the tribal college has a strong outreach into the entire community process. Almost all are located on reservations. Boyer (1989 p. 53) states: "Tribal Colleges are in the vanguard of cultural renaissance in all of their communities. On the Senta Gleska College Campus, the Lakota studies department offers classes in Sioux history, oral literature, Lakota thought and a [series of Lakota language courses]."

In Canada, the Gabriel Dumont Institute of Native Studies and Applied Research in Saskatchewan organizes both formal and nonformal educational programs and native teacher education programs, and promotes both cultural and historical research on the activities of native peoples. Community development is defined as "taking back" the village and reservation schools, encouraging indigenous language and cultural expression, and diffusing information throughout the sparsely populated region using indigenous language broadcast by radio stations controlled by the community.

The Saskatchewan Indian Federated College (SIFC) is the only North American Indian-controlled university offering graduate as well as undergraduate studies. Elders from the five Indian tribal groups in the province are employed as staff to counsel and advise faculty and students. While the College seeks to strengthen local community leadership, it also has a program to link the indigenous people of Canada to indigenous peoples worldwide.

These tribal community colleges in North America parallel the community colleges in Australia and the South Pacific that likewise are controlled by indigenous people. The agenda is for colleges and their communities to recapture lost history, songs, dances, language, tales, medicines, and the healing arts. These are then utilized to contextualize and understand modern day experience, which is markedly alienating to indigenous communities.

5.5 Development and Social Justice

In India, an experiment in micro action by grass roots groups was initiated in 1980 because of the ineffectiveness of established, large organizations in improving the lot of the poor (Bhatt 1989). The large and comprehensive community development programs of the 1950s and 1960s had not made a difference in alleviating poverty.

Instead, in many communities poverty had become even more acute. In the 1970s a new, concentrated effort was made through separate, exclusively targeted programs such as the Tribal Development Plans, Integrated Rural Development, and the Child Health and Nutritious Schemes. Again there was documented failure, as economic exploitation continued.

It is in this context that different grass root organizations developed and began to redefine politics to include health, rights over forests and community reserves, education, and ecological and cultural issues. Working with advocates of poor people in the voluntary sector these spontaneous groups provided critiques and alternatives to strategies of development masterminded by governmental and nongovernmental organizations (NGOs). Bhatt (1989) studied 38 of these spontaneous groups in two districts in India. He found that with modest small grants from Oxfam, an international NGO, these grass root groups (with leaders as young as 21) accomplished an extraordinary amount of work which directly affected the quality of community life. His recommendation is that more funds should be allocated directly to grass root groups, with minimal or no external intervention, to bring about change organized and directed by the poor themselves.

5.6 North American Community Development

Community-based development organized around economics received its impetus in the late 1960s when readiness was high to bring about social change. It was in this context that the Community Development Corporation (CDC) was set up in North America by young community activists. The Corporation is defined as "a coalition organization of neighborhood residents to carry out their own comprehensive program of local renewal activities, especially including business development" (Perry 1987 p. 8). The success of local organizations of poor people bringing economic vitality to their community has kept alive federal funding through community development grants given directly to poor communities. These funds have allowed the development of community-based education programs as well as economic development schemes. Gaventa et al (1990) documented efforts by rural community-based researchers to facilitate poor communities in learning about the reasons for their economic plight. Working with Appalachian and southern communities they reported on studies examining attempts to strengthen the informal sectors of the economy by means of community-based education. These case studies demonstrate how participatory research can be linked to social, cultural, and economic development.

See also: Formal, Nonformal, and Informal Education; Conscientization and Mobilization; Adult Education for Development; Ideologies in Adult Education; Critical Approaches to Adult Education; Participatory Research; Community and Parents' Participation in Curriculum Decisions; Community Education and Community Schools; Community Financing of Education

References

Archer D, Costello P 1990 *Literacy and Power: The Latin American Battleground*. Earthscan, London

Bhatt A 1989 *Development and Social Justice: Micro Action by Weaker Sections*. Sage, New Delhi

Boal A 1979 *Theater of the Oppressed*. Urizen Books, New York

Boyer E L 1989 *Tribal Colleges: Shaping the Future of Native America*. Princeton University Press, Princeton, New Jersey

Brown D 1990 USA: The National Center for Community Education. In: Poster C, Krüger A (eds) 1990 *Community Education in the Western World*. Routledge, London

Cadena F 1984 Popular education and peasants movements for change. *Convergence* 17(3): 31–36

Chené A, Chervin M 1991 *Un(e) Air(e) Populaire: L'education populaire authonome au Quebec* (Popular Education in Quebec: Strengthening Social Movements) (In both French and English). American Association for Adult and Continuing Education, Washington, DC

Cheong J W (ed.) 1987 *Promising Education for Community Development*. National University Press, Seoul

Council of Europe 1987 *Adult Education and Community Development*. Council for Cultural Cooperation, Council of Europe, Strasbourg

Fals-Borda O, Rahman M A (eds.) 1991 *Action and Knowledge. Breaking the Monopoly with Participatory Action-Research*. Apex Press, New York

Fletcher C 1980 Developments in community education: A current account. In: Fletcher C, Thompson N (eds.) 1980 *Issues in Community Education*. Falmer Press, Lewes

Freire P 1970 *The Pedagogy of the Oppressed*. Herder and Herder, New York

Gaventa J, Smith B E, Wellingham A (eds.) 1990 *Communities in Economic Crises: Appalachia and the South*. Temple University Press, Philadelphia, Pennsylvania

Giroux H 1983 *Theory and Resistance in Education*. Bergin and Garvey, South Hadley, Massachusetts

Jackson K 1980 Some fallacies in community education and their consequences in working class areas. In: Fletcher C, Thompson N (eds.) 1980 *Issues in Community Education*. Falmer Press, Lewes

Kerensky V M 1989 *The Sovereign New Perspectives on People, Power and Public Education*. Kendall/Hunt, Dubuque, Iowa

Lambert P 1982 Popular theatre: One road to self determined development action. *Comm. Dev. J.* 17(3): 242–49

Martin I 1987 Community education: Towards a theoretical analysis. In: Allen G, Bastani J, Martin I, Richard K (eds.) 1987 *Community Education: An Agenda for Educational Reform*. Open University Press, Milton Keynes

Melo A, Benavente A 1978 *Experiments in Popular Education in Portugal*, No. 29. UNESCO, Paris

Mosha H F 1983 United Republic of Tanzania: Folk development colleges. *Prospects* 13(1): 95–103

Munoz B, Garcia-Blanco A M 1989 *Harvard Educational Review* 59(4) (Special issue on Community Based Education, Part I)

Nopakun O 1985 *Thai Concept of Khit-pen for Adult and Non-Formal Education*. Chulaongkorn University, Bangkok

Oliver L 1987 *Study Circles*. Seven Locks Press, Washington, DC

Perry S 1987 *Communities on the Way*. State University of New York Press, Albany, New York

Rubenson K 1989 The sociology of adult education. In: Merriam S, Cunningham P (eds.) 1989 *Handbook of Adult and Continuing Education*. Jossey-Bass, San Francisco, California

Thorpe R 1985 Community work and ideology: An Australian perspective. In: Thorpe R, Petruchenia J (eds.)

1985 *Community Work or Social Change*. Routledge and Kegan Paul, London
Watts J 1990 UK: Community Education Development Centre. In: Poster C, Krüger A (eds.) 1990 *Community Education in the Western World*. Routledge, London
Warden J 1979 *Process Perspectives: Community Education as Process*. Mid-Atlantic Community Education Consortium, Charlottesville, Virginia

Further Reading

Bookman A, Morgen S 1988 *Women and the Politics of Empowerment*. Temple University Press, Philadelphia, Pennsylvania
Christie P 1985 *The Right to Learn: The Struggle for Education in South Africa*. Ravan Press, Johannesburg
Epskamp K 1989 *Theater is Search for Social Change*. CESO, The Hague
Hinzer H 1991 *Adult Education and Development* 37: September (Special issue on Environment)
Lovett T 1988 *Radical Approaches to Adult Education: A Reader*. Routledge, London
Mangione J 1985 *A Passion For Sicilians: (The) World Around Danilo Dolci*. Transaction Books, Oxford
Maguire P 1987 *Doing Participatory Research: A Feminist Approach*. Center for International Education, University of Massachusetts, Amherst, Massachusetts
Matwana M, Walters S, Groever Z 1989 *The Struggle for Democracy: A Study of Community Organizations in Greater Capetown from the 1960's to 1988*. Centre for Adult and Continuing Education, University of the Western Cape, Capetown
Munoz B, Garcia-Blanco A M 1990 *Harvard Educational Review* 60(1) (Special issue on Community Based Education, Part II)
Osteria T, Okamura J (eds.) 1986 *Participatory Approaches to Development Experiences in the Philippines*. De La Salle University, Manila
Reed D 1984 *Evaluating Community Organizing in the Philippines*. La Ignacia Centre Printing Press, Manila
Welton M 1987 *Knowledge for the People: Adult Life, Learning and Social Change in Canada*. OISE Press, Toronto

P. M. Cunningham

Community Education and Community Schools

In the past, community education was "normally understood as the process of transforming schools and colleges into educational and recreational centers for all ages" (Fletcher 1985 p. 845). In the 1990s, although the school remains a valued center and resource for community education, there is now a wide diversity of location and practice appropriate to local needs and conditions. New concepts that link education and industry, or use the streets as places of learning for homeless children, are developing rapidly. In the Third World, adult literacy and overpopulation remain great and related issues that community education is addressing. Thus, community education cannot be divorced from community development and community action. This entry provides an overview of the history of community education and of recent developments and directions taken in this field.

1. The Origins of Community Education

Community education dates from the early 1930s. This was the time of the pioneering work in the United States of Frank Manley and his philanthropic friend and sponsor Charles Stewart Mott (see Young and Quinn 1963), and in the United Kingdom of Henry Morris, Secretary for Education in the county of Cambridgeshire (see Rée 1985). The period is certainly significant: the collapse of the economy in these two powerful Western countries had led to widespread unemployment, rural depopulation, increased crime, and feelings of despair and frustration, particularly among the young.

Manley worked initially in Flint, Michigan, on relatively small-scale projects designed to extend the work of the schools into this new dimension of "community." Over the next 40 years, largely through the beneficence of the Mott Foundation, community education developed apace, with ever-widening remits for the schools, now not merely for youth but additionally in the fields of the environment, home–school relationships, senior citizens, leadership development, and other nationwide initiatives. These culminated in federal legislation (the Community School Development Act of 1974), which empowered states to set up bureaus or departments of community education.

Progress in the United Kingdom was far slower and of a different kind. By the start of the Second World War in 1939, Morris had managed to found only four "village colleges," as he named these institutions designed specifically to serve both the secondary school population (then 11–14) and the adult education needs of the inhabitants of the neighboring rural areas. His view of adult education was all-embracing: adult literacy, continuative education, recreation, the arts. The colleges bore little physical resemblance to the formal school buildings of the time: Impington College, designed by Walter Gropius and Maxwell Fry, remains to this day an exemplar of excellence in educational architecture.

It was not until the 1950s that the movement began to burgeon. Community schools, whether so designated or merely including elements of educational provision beyond those required for the statutory age range, now exist in well over half the education authorities in the United Kingdom, mainly in secondary schools (11–16 or 11–18) but increasingly also in primary schools (5–11).

Curiously, until attempts were made to trace the international development of community education (e.g., Poster 1982), community educators in the United States and United Kingdom were largely ignorant of the routes taken and the achievements made in each other's country. New Zealand had been influenced by the United Kingdom model; Australia and Canada by that of the United States. In all these countries the much earlier innovation of residential adult learning communities pioneered in the 1860s by Nikolai Grundtvig (1783–1872), the Danish Folk High Schools (Rørdam 1980), was, regrettably, largely unknown prior to the 1970s and 1980s. Only since the foundation in 1974 of the International Community Education Association and its rapid expansion during the 1980s has there been an opportunity for an understanding and evaluation of community education worldwide.

The work by Poster and Krüger (1990) illustrates the wide diversity of community education practice in a sample of European, North American, and Australasian countries. New concepts that link industry and education are being piloted and disseminated (Organisation for Economic Co-operation and Development 1989, Shuttleworth 1993). The freeing of East European countries from their former isolation has opened up possibilities for a dozen more countries to develop their own concepts of community education.

The country that has undoubtedly been in the forefront of community education development since 1983 is the Federal Republic of Germany. This is not merely because of the outstanding initiatives taken in Berlin and some of the *Länder* (States) (Krüger 1990, Petry 1990), but is also a consequence of Germany's considerable investment of human resources and funds in Third World countries.

2. Community Education in the Third World

Community education in the developing countries is richly varied and significantly dependent on local circumstances and needs. In these countries the term "community education" is rarely used: in Latin America, for example, *educación popular* is current; in Africa, the African Association for Literacy and Adult Education (AALAE) is at the heart of the movement. In all these countries community education has come about as a natural response to local social conditions.

In Trinidad and Tobago, for example, the riots of 1970 were the catalyst. The appalling conditions in the ghetto areas were seen by Father Gerard Pantin as the root cause. The breakdown of the nuclear and the extended family, drug abuse, large-scale unemployment, dropout from the educational system, an absence of lifelong learning programs, and neglect of the handicapped were the symptoms of social malaise.

Pantin founded a nursery school which attracted parents, children, the "boys on the block," indeed, a whole cross section of the deprived in the community. The school became an open forum for people to speak out about themselves, their area, leaders, hopes, disappointments, and plans for the future (Montrichard 1980). Out of this early experiment was born SERVOL (Service Volunteered for All), which built or converted many education centers for preschool learning, vocational training, recreation, leisure, adult learning, and community participation.

In Thailand the rural areas have undergone a rapid transition, threatening the survival of village communities. In a Third World country that has, exceptionally, an abundance of land easily capable of sustaining its population of 30 million, modern agro-industry is destroying the peasant economy. The success of agro-industry depends on large-scale monoculture, which makes peasant farmers wholly dependent on world markets. As the market fluctuates, the small farmer, formerly self-sufficient, becomes indebted and at best a tenant farmer, at worst landless.

The solution offered in Thailand to this ever-worsening situation is based on a fundamental concept of community development: self-reliance, which is deeply rooted

> in what might be called a Buddhist concept of economics. The self-reliance farmer must refrain from greed and the desire to be rich. He must be satisfied with basic needs, seeking in spiritual values a richness more meaningful for life than material richness. (Puntasen 1992 p. 103)

The Thai concept is holistic, and regards the forest as the source of all basic human needs: food, medicine, clothing, and shelter. Through skillful planting policies and by preserving centuries-old community skills and knowledge, the Thai farmer can sustain his family and, through historical barter systems, the community in which he lives. In view of the worldwide need to provide for an ever-expanding population in the face of the threat of ecological disaster, Thai silviculture may represent a model that other emerging countries might be able to adopt or adapt.

The Philippines and Brazil are two of the many countries that are seeking, through community education, to provide an answer to the complex problems of orphaned and homeless children. In the Philippines the problem has its origins mainly in the civil war of the 1970s and 1980s, which by no means ended with the overthrow of the totalitarian regime of Ferdinand Marcos in 1986. Many children were separated from their families by the murder, imprisonment, or forced relocation of their parents, or were simply turned out of poverty-stricken shanty homes to fend for themselves. Child prostitution is rife, and in the larger cities children subsist by scavenging. In and around "Smokey Mountain," as the world's largest garbage tip in Manila is called, children pick over refuse for anything salable, wearable, or eatable, risking serious injury or death from the bulldozers constantly at work there.

On islands nearer the centers of armed conflict, hundreds of children have been traumatized by the effects of war. Some have seen whole villages destroyed, usually without warning and at night, on suspicion that they were harboring or sustaining rebels. Children have themselves been wounded and killed, in the crossfire of opposing forces or by mines in boobytrapped fields. Some have been "salvaged," the euphemism used in official reports for murder by death squads.

In 1985 a university psychologist, Elizabeth Protacio Marcelino, herself once briefly imprisoned under the Marcos regime and a prominent member of the international organization Children Under Torture, set up the Children's Rehabilitation Center (CRC) in Quezon City (the official capital of the Philippines). With her students, paid workers, and volunteers, Marcelino devised programs to provide schooling wherever possible, but above all to give psychological and therapeutic support for the children of that area. There are now four regional centers, in Davao, Bicol, Iloilo, and Negros, in addition to the original national center. The center held its first national conference in August 1991. The mission statement of the CRC is worthy of inclusion in this outline of the work being done:

> The CRC takes it upon itself to facilitate psychological structures primarily for children in war and secondarily for children-survivors of social and natural disasters at the grassroots/community level which will lay the groundwork for people's initiative, creativity, responsibility and communal concern for children. (Marcelino 1991)

In Brazil, as in a number of Latin American countries, the city streets are filled with destitute children and young people. According to Graciani, a leading community worker and theoretician in that country, the reasons for this are obvious:

> They are obliged to contribute to the maintenance of their families through street trading, car cleaning, window cleaning, shoeshining. This need for early earning forces them out of school onto the street. What is more, the configurations of street work are founded on existing social relations that contradict accepted norms. This in turn justifies models of repression maintained by mechanisms of social control: the police and the adults among whom they work. The majority of these children are gradually drawn into work contexts which are exploitative, cruel and violent. (Graciani 1992 p. 45)

Graciani set out a well-conceived praxis for education for work, which accepts that traditional schooling is an irrelevance and seeks to promote strategies for group income-generating activities. Work is seen as a collective project and as an educational process that takes place in the classroom of the street pavements. The curriculum is based on costing products, establishing sources of raw materials, planning the production process, accounting for plant depreciation, maintenance and repair, exploring markets, and seeking new openings. Each young person is involved at some time or other in every aspect of the enterprise. Some become seed members of other street groups. This system of education for work represents a community education alternative to the horrific exploitation of children and young people by criminal and immoral elements in the adult population.

3. Community Education and Adult Illiteracy

Community education is about movements that empower the people, not about leaders. Yet this entry would be incomplete without mention of the profound influence on community education worldwide of Paulo Freire. Of his many seminal works, *Pedagogy of the Oppressed* (1972) is probably the best known. The main thrust of his activities, both in exile in Europe and later as minister for education in São Paulo, Brazil, has been in the field of adult literacy. He has argued that literacy and liberation go hand in hand, and his motto of "Each one teach one" has been realized widely throughout the Third World.

In India, a national policy firmly rooted in local communities has been rapidly emerging in response to the two most urgent problems facing the subcontinent: population control and the eradication of adult illiteracy. The interrelation between these two issues can best be appreciated from government statistics: in the 30-year period from 1955–85, the adult literacy rate more than doubled to 36 percent of the population; yet in the same period the actual number of adult illiterates rose by 140 million.

India's national program for adult education recognizes that, since three-fourths of the population live in rural areas, it is essential to devolve responsibility for mass education down to district, subdistrict (*tehsil*), and local (*thana*) levels. This implies the establishment of over 100,000 village community education centers. India's civic and religious cultures require that those who have benefited from higher education repay their good fortune by spending some time working for the deprived and underprivileged. Under the auspices of the Association of Indian Universities, students and lecturers work to transform conventional colleges in rural areas into community colleges, providing vocational and cultural education.

In the South Pacific there has been a growing awareness of the injustice done by colonialism to indigenous populations—among others, to the Australian, Polynesian, and Melanesian aboriginal inhabitants. Community educators seek to empower them to recreate their cultures, replacing or supplementing imposed Western values. It is now realized that their beliefs, and their methods of decision-making, and lawgiving are worthy of respect and consideration. Thus, in New Zealand, community schools accept the value of the traditional *maraes* or community meeting grounds of the indigenous population and adopt and adapt them to meet the needs of the aboriginal and White populations alike.

4. The Management of Community Education

To become genuine centers of community education, schools will have to undergo radical managerial change. Effective two-way communication is an essential step toward opening up the decision-making process: "Community education is not the dispensing of education to the community, but the involvement of the community in the content and style of its own education" (Poster 1982). Schools will need to become open institutions: with open access, and open to ideas from professionals, parents, and the community.

Education is too often equated with schooling, yet the traditional school has contact with the average schoolchild for less than 20 percent of the year. Of prime importance, then, is the recognition by the school of the host of other influences—above all the family and the peer group—upon the child or young person. Nor can community education be isolated from community development and community action. There are times when involvement in community education cannot be a neatly encapsulated, easily controllable, and safe activity. Management structures and strategies must be based on flexibility and responsiveness. The loose-coupling concept of management (Weick 1976), in which organizational subsystems have a high degree of autonomy, is particularly relevant to community education, provided that there is also clarity about and adherence to the organizational mission statement, aims, and objectives.

Schools throughout the world have the potential to be central to the expansion of community education. Yet there are dangers in viewing them as the only, or even necessarily the best, route to achieving greater popular involvement in the vast and diverse enterprise called "education." Many are still hidebound by tradition, or too beset with problems of their own to consider becoming involved in what they regard as the concern of others. Education in the developed world has not grown organically, but has been imposed by the state. Most teachers have been socialized out of the culture of the majority of their pupils and their parents (Musgrave 1973). Evidently, there must be a reconstruction of the role and training (both initial and in-service) of teachers if they are to serve community education.

There are times when the ideal role for teachers in all countries is that of facilitator for initiatives that have come from the community itself. There are even times when they have no role to play at all, but must learn to be listeners rather than activists. Much in community education requires spontaneity and a sensitive response—apparently instinctive, but in fact the result of a deep understanding of principles. It is to the development of these skills that community educators in all countries are increasingly turning.

See also: Community Education and Community Development; Folk High Schools

References

Fletcher C 1985 Community education and community development. In: Husén T, Postlethwaite T N (eds.) 1985 *International Encyclopedia of Education*, 1st edn. Pergamon Press, Oxford

Freire P 1972 *Pedagogy of the Oppressed*. Penguin, Harmondsworth

Graciani M S S 1992 Brazil: Children of the streets. In: Poster C D, Zimmer J (eds.) 1992 *Community Education in the Third World*. Routledge, London.

Krüger A 1990 West Berlin: The youth and culture centre, Schlesische 27. In: Poster C D, Krüger A 1990

Marcelino E 1991 *C R C First National Conference on Treatment and Rehabilitation*. Children's Rehabilitation Center, Quezon City

Montrichard R 1980 SERVOL Faces the Eighties. SERVOL Printing Services, Port of Spain

Musgrave P 1973 A comparative study of the statutory links between school and community. In: FitzGerald R (ed.) 1973 *Community Participation and School Policy*. Australian National University, Canberra

Organisation for Economic Co-operation and Development 1989 *Towards an "Enterprising" Culture: A challenge for Education and Training*. CERI Paris

Petry C 1990 RAA: An innovation agency in the Ruhr. In: Poster C D, Krüger A 1990

Poster C D 1982 *Community Education: Its Development and Management*. Heinemann, London

Poster C D, Krüger A 1990 *Community Education in the Western World*. Routledge, London

Puntasen A 1992 Thailand: Agro-industries and self-reliance. In: Poster C D, Zimmer J (eds.) 1992 *Community Education in the Third World*. Routledge, London

Ree H 1985 *Educator Extraordinary: the Life and Achievement of Henry Morris*. Peter Owen, London

Rørdam T 1980 *The Danish Folk High Schools*, 2nd edn. Det Danske Selskab, Copenhagen

Shuttleworth D E 1993 *Enterprise Learning in Action*. Routledge, London

Weick K E 1976 Educational organisations as loosely coupled systems. *Adm. Sci. Q*. 21(1): 1–9

Young C, Quinn W 1963 *Foundation for Living: The Story of Charles Stewart Mott and Flint*. McGraw-Hill, New York

C. D. Poster

Community Financing of Education

Issues relating to community financing of schools have come increasingly to the fore in many countries. The chief reason is negative: governments find themselves financially hard-pressed, and admit that they cannot shoulder the total cost of education by themselves. Communities generate their own resources to bridge the gap, for they realize that the alternative to self-help is no help at all.

More positively, expanded community financing may encourage participants to value education more highly, and greater parental involvement can promote the effectiveness of school systems. However, in official policy statements these positive rationales generally receive less weight than the negative economic one, except as justifications when governments find themselves gaining unfavourable publicity.

In this entry the term "community" is defined broadly and includes geographic, religious, ethnic and racial groups. It also includes alumni and parents. The entry commences with comments on the scope and potential for community financing. It then turns to mechanisms for raising funds, issues of quality, social and geographic inequalities, and questions of guidance and control.

1. The Scope and Potential for Community Financing

Community support is heavily influenced by cultural and economic factors, and similar amounts of finance cannot be generated in all contexts. Nevertheless, a few examples can illustrate the scope and potential.

One of the best examples is the *harambee* movement in Kenya (Anderson 1973, 1975). *Harambee* is a Swahili word meaning "let's pull together," and the concept has been strongly promoted by the nation's politicians. In the mid-1980s, 50 percent of Kenya's secondary schools were unaided *harambee* institutions, and another 20 percent were aided *harambee* or private schools. Most primary schools also had a strong element of community funding, especially in the physical infrastructure. As well as providing cash, communities contributed land, labor and materials.

Zimbabwe is also well-known for its community support. Chung (1990 p. 192) states that between 1979 and 1989 the number of primary schools increased from 2,401 to 4,504, and the number of secondary schools from 177 to 1,502. Construction was heavily dependent on community financing. Communities also contributed significantly to running costs.

Other statistics from Trinidad and Tobago, the Dominican Republic, Panama, Honduras, and Cuba indicate that between 15 and 30 percent of both recurrent and capital costs may be financed by community inputs. In Nepal, 60 percent of the labor for school construction is said to be provided free of charge by communities; and in parts of China over 60 percent of primary school teachers are community-employed (Bray and Lillis 1988 p. 7)

The industrialized countries of Europe, North America, and Australasia also have important elements of community financing, particularly through Parent–Teacher Associations (PTAs) and comparable bodies. In most of these countries, communities only supplement government provision but nevertheless provide some important "extras." Parallel systems of profit-making private schools may also exist, though these cannot be classified as community efforts.

2. Mechanisms for Raising Resources

2.1 School Fees

In most self-help institutions, fees are the greatest source of income. Fees can of course be put to any use, but are particularly important for financing recurrent expenditure because it is often difficult to find other ways to do so. Fund-raising schemes for capital works have the advantage that they aim at visible outcomes. Moreover, donors like to think that their gifts will have a lasting impact rather than being dissipated on salaries or materials. Most schools therefore set the fees aside for recurrent needs, and utilize other mechanisms for generating capital resources.

2.2 Levies

It might be argued that the difference between a fee and a levy is merely semantic, particularly when levies are imposed every year and are destined for expenditure that would otherwise be covered from a general fee. Certainly there are cases in which communities have been prohibited from charging fees, and have therefore changed the name to levies but have used the money for the same purposes. Fees are sometimes conceptualized as payments for services, however, whereas levies are more commonly methods of raising funds for specific projects. In many systems, levies are particularly important for capital works.

2.3 Launching Ceremonies

When properly managed, launching ceremonies can generate considerable funds for capital works. Mbithi and Rasmusson (1977) describe practices in Eastern Kenya:

> In a typical self-help project, participants walk to the project site from the sublocation and surrounding areas. Those representing special groups such as clans are provided with transport by their groups . . . The dignitaries such as the chief, headman, clan leaders, project committee members, visiting politicians and wealthy businessmen and citymen sit near the table of the Master of Ceremonies. The local clans normally prepare food and supply water, and young men act as marshals, dance partners and general handymen.
>
> As all expected participants arrive the tempo of work and dance increases as each group attempts to outperform its neighbour . . . All contributions are announced publicly and all sing songs of praise to the contributor. If contributions are meagre, the songs will exalt the wealth of the conspicuously rich and appeal to their love for their local area . . . Donations which continue to pour in may be money, eggs, poultry, food, cement, a lorry full of sand or even the land on which the project stands. (Mbithi and Rasmusson 1977 pp. 27–28)

This account is culturally specific. However, some of the general principles, for example, of encouraging competition to donate, and of making the event highly visible, are applicable in many other cultures.

2.4 Community Taxation

Communities sometimes raise additional resources by imposing taxes on members. Igwe (1988 pp. 112–3) indicates that community members in Eastern Nigeria are taxed by Councils of Elders. The men generally pay higher rates than the women, and age groups are a valuable instrument for collection of the dues. Sons and daughters who are no longer resident in the village may also be taxed, with the sanction of ostracism in the event of nonpayment.

Religious communities may also impose taxes on themselves. In Indonesia, for example, part of the funds for the *pesantrens*, which teach both Islamic religious knowledge and secular subjects, comes from tithes (Bray and Lillis 1988 p. 41). Donation of the compulsory tax known as *zakat* is one of the pillars of Islam, and other religions also emphasize the importance of charity.

2.5 PTA Collections

Collections by Parent–Teacher Associations can be another major source of income in both industrialized and less developed countries. While not focusing specifically on financing, Beattie (1985) presents extensive information on parental participation in the education systems of France, Italy, Germany, and England and Wales. Examples from less developed countries are provided by Berthe (1985) who focuses on Mali, and Kaluba (1988) on Zambia.

2.6 Other Mechanisms

Other types and sources of community funds include contributions from alumni, grants from cooperatives, assistance from overseas churches, and donations from local business people.

3. Implications for Quality

When communities supplement the resources of government schools, one may assume that their efforts improve the quality of education. Many churches also have a reputation for strong discipline and high-quality teaching. However, major problems have arisen in some countries from the poor quality of independent self-help schools. Wellings (1983 p. 24) concluded that the quality of education in Kenya's *harambee* schools was "low, and quite often abysmally low" in both relative and absolute terms. These schools have suffered from poor resource bases, untrained teachers, and academically weak students. Wellings considers *harambee* schools more a blight than a blessing.

Mkandawire (1985) was not so forceful about the situation in Malawi, but reached a similar conclusion:

> Community financing of schools has indeed helped to expand the school system, but the variation in its financing has made it difficult to achieve acceptable standards . . . It would appear that unless there is an expansion in central government financing of schools, we shall live with a situation where high academic standards are hard to achieve. (Mkandawire 1985 p. 3)

One should of course distinguish between the quality of the school intake and the quality of the teaching process, and recognize that many self-help schools are handicapped at the outset by their inability to attract the best students. However, Kenyan research shows that *harambee* schools have compounded the problems of poor intakes by giving their students poor teaching. Robinson's (1988) comments on the People's Republic of China imply that similar factors have operated there.

4. Social and Geographic Inequalities

In some countries, community financing of education has exacerbated social inequalities. To cite just one example, Galabawa (1985) indicates that Tanzanian nongovernment secondary school fees exceed 2,000 Tanzanian shillings (TShs) per pupil per annum.

> The ordinary peasant in Tanzania cannot afford this amount. But many of the schools are built with the help of money or labor of the very poor peasant . . . A striking example is that of Omumwani Secondary School in Kagera which was opened by TAPA [Tanzanian Parents' Association] in 1968. The school fees are exorbitant and yet the Kagera Region Cooperative Union was paying TShs 600 per annum for every pupil. Here one may question the justification for the common cooperative funds being used to educate children of the few members of the cooperative. (Galabawa 1985 p. 18)

Self-help operations can also exacerbate regional inequalities, for the rich areas are in a better position to fund operations than poor ones. It has been shown in Kenya, for example, that the *harambee* movement has widened the gap between the economically developed central highlands and poorer regions in the rest of the country. Similar findings appear in the literature from Tanzania and elsewhere.

5. Central Guidance and Control

The problems of quality and equity emphasize the need for central guidance and control. However, strong control raises the danger that local initiatives will be stifled, and governments have to seek an appropriate balance. The nature of this balance varies in different societies. In Eastern Nigeria, for example, the tradition of self-help is so great that it seems to flourish under almost all circumstances. Elsewhere, seeds might require more careful nurture.

Government control on community initiative may be direct, through regulations on registration of schools, class size and fees. Alternatively, influence may be indirect, through provision of grants, training programs for teachers, general advice through district education officers, and so on.

In most systems, regulations lay down a series of steps which communities must follow before a school can gain full approval. Community leaders must first secure approval in principle before proceeding with construction, and they must secure final approval before they are allowed to operate the school. The initial stage allows the government to check whether the location and nature of the school matches its own priorities, and the second stage allows it to see whether the facilities meet required standards.

Governments may also set regulations on accounting procedures. Misuse of money, or allegation of misuse, is one of the most common causes of strife in community-funded projects. Improved recordkeeping could discourage the temptation to embezzle funds and could protect the innocent. Even when individuals have not stolen school money, they often find it difficult to demonstrate that fact when they have poor accounts, and allegations of theft can severely damage community spirit.

Indirect influences may be exerted through grants of various kinds. The grants encourage the communities to provide the facilities for which the money is intended, and allow the government to set requirements on the types and nature of facilities. Special grants may be made for disadvantaged communities in order to reduce social and regional inequalities, and help may be in the form of government-paid staff.

Governments may also hold workshops for boards of governors and PTA officials. Experience in Papua New Guinea has suggested that at least in some contexts these need not be costly (Bray 1988). Communities are often willing to provide accommodation and travel expenses for their own nominees, and the workshops can be valuable forums for headteachers, community leaders, and government officers to exchange views.

Offers of government takeover of community schools may also be an effective indirect influence. Most Kenyan communities are very keen for the government to take over their institutions and to relieve them of heavy financial burdens. The government sets clear criteria on which it decides whether or not to take over a school, among which are the nature of the facilities and the standard of academic achievement. This acts as a guideline and incentive for the communities.

However, many of these controls are limited. Bureaucracies are frequently overworked and inadequately staffed, and it is hard to devote optimum attention to these matters. Governments often find it difficult to encourage communities which are fragmented and do not have strong traditions of self-help. Occasionally, they also find it difficult to restrain eager communities, the activities of which may have a detrimental effect on social and regional inequalities.

Some governments operate through overcentralized administrations. Hanson (1986) indicates that, prior to a 1968 reform, the Venezuelan Ministry of Education was responsible for all major and minor decisions about schools, personnel, and instructional programs. The ministry, Hanson contends, became a huge bureaucratic job bank which often took 9–12 months even to reply to simple requests on such matters as building repairs or payment of teachers in newly opened institutions. It would be hard in such a structure either to encourage desirable community initiatives or to discourage undesirable ones.

6. Conclusion

Mechanisms for community financing are diverse and dependent on local conditions. Nevertheless, in many parts of the world community financing plays a crucial role in supporting education systems and sometimes in providing an alternative track to the mainstream. Too often, government figures are quoted as if they represent the only expenditure on education. In many settings a full picture of financing would have to include community and private expenditures.

Although governments and international agencies have become more interested in community financing, it is not a panacea. Authorities would be unwise to allow schools to be starved of government funds on the assumption that communities would necessarily bridge gaps. Furthermore independent self-help schools are sometimes of inferior quality, and can exacerbate social and regional imbalances. Only a heavily qualified recommendation could be made to other governments to try to emulate Kenya's strategy of *harambee*, even assuming that it can be emulated and that its roots are not exclusive to that country. Authorities also need to pay careful attention to guidance and controls, yet to be sufficiently flexible to avoid stifling initiatives.

See also: Private and Public Costs of Schooling in Developing Nations

References

Anderson J 1973 *Organization and Financing of Self-Help Education in Kenya*. International Institute for Educational Planning (IIEP), Paris

Anderson J 1975 The organisation of support and the management of self-help schools: A case study from Kenya. In: Brown G N, Hiskett M (eds.) 1975 *Conflict and Harmony in Education in Tropical Africa*. George Allen and Unwin, London

Beattie N 1985 *Professional Parents: Parent Participation in Four Western European Countries*. Falmer, London

Berthe A 1985 *Participation des Communautés Locales*

au Financement de l'Education au Mali. Division of Educational Policies and Planning, UNESCO, Paris.
Bray M 1988 Community management and financing of schools in Papua New Guinea. In: Bray M, Lillis K (eds.) 1988
Bray M, Lillis K (eds.) 1988 *Community Financing of Education: Issues and Policy Implications in Less Developed Countries*. Pergamon, Oxford
Chung F 1990 Government and community partnership in the financing of education in Zimbabwe. *Int. J. Educ. Dev.* 10(2/3): 191–94
Galabawa J C J 1985 Community financing of schools in Tanzania. Paper presented at the Commonwealth Secretariat workshop on community financing of schools, Gaborone
Hanson M 1986 *Educational Reform and Administrative Development: The Cases of Colombia and Venezuela*. Hoover Institution Press, Stanford, California
Igwe S O 1988 Community financing of schools in Eastern Nigeria. In: Bray M, Lillis K (eds.) 1988
Kaluba L H 1988 Education and community self-help in Zambia. In: Bray M, Lillis K (eds.) 1988
Mbithi P M, Rasmusson R 1977 *Self-Reliance in Kenya: The Case of Harambee*. Scandinavian Institute for African Studies, Uppsala
Mkandawire D 1985 Academic standards in Malawi schools. Paper presented at the Commonwealth Secretariat workshop on community financing of schools, Gaborone, Botswana
Robinson J C 1988 State control and local financing of schools in China. In: Bray M, Lillis K (eds.) 1988
Wellings P A 1983 Unaided education in Kenya: Blessing or blight? *Res. Educ.* 29(1): 11–28

Further Reading

Bray M 1986 *New Resources for Education: Community Management and Financing of Schools in Less Developed Countries*. Commonwealth Secretariat, London
Kemmerer F 1992 Community support of schools. In: Chapman D W, Walberg H J (eds.) 1992 *International Perspectives on Educational Productivity*. JAI Press, Greenwich, Connecticut
Okoye M 1986 Community secondary schools: A case-study of a Nigerian innovation in self-help. *Int. J. Educ. Dev.* 6(4): 263–74
Ota C C 1986 Community financing of schools in Zimbabwe. *Prospects* 16(3): 355–68
Shaeffer S 1991 *School and Community Collaboration for Educational Change: Report of an IIEP Seminar*. International Institute for Educational Planning, Paris
Williams P 1986 Non-government resources for education with special reference to community financing. *Prospects* 16(2): 231–41

M. Bray

Community–School Relations, Anthropological Study of

Anthropological research in education covers a wide range of units of analysis such as the classroom, the school, and the community, each of them relevant to the examination of different theoretical and practical topics. Studies centered on community–school relations, which are the most faithful to the holistic tradition of anthropology, lend themselves more easily to an analysis of the effects of both structural and situational factors on schooling, and to a search for connections between the school and other social institutions. Existing work conducted in France, England, and the United States provides answers to important questions, such as the role of the school in maintaining or reducing cultural diversity, and in favoring or impeding the educational success and vertical mobility of different social and ethnic groups.

1. Schools in Rural Communities: Local Cultures versus National Culture

Anthropologists have traditionally centered their analyses on small, relatively homogeneous, and self-sufficient communities around the world. A strong relationship between community and education was postulated by the culture-and-personality school of thought which defined communities as central units for the transmission of culture. However, a direct transposition of the cultural-transmission model to the study of schools in modern societies was impossible for two reasons: communities which belong to a nation-state are part of a global society that influences them in many different ways; and schools, and particularly the school systems that came into existence in the United States and several European countries at the turn of the nineteen century, were clearly instruments of acculturation, designed not only to raise the level of instruction of the population but to modernize the economy, diffuse urban values, and develop a sense of national identity. The persistence of great cultural diversity, even in countries as centralized as France, nevertheless shows that schools still transmit traditional, local orientations or, at least, that they do not prevent them from developing alongside the dominant culture. One of the main contributions of anthropological studies of community–school relations in rural areas has been to explore how this was made possible.

1.1 Community Resistance and Community Accommodation

Anthropologists have carefully studied the effects of community resistance and community strategic adaptation to outside pressure via schools. Working on communitarian societies in the United States, Hostetler and Huntington (1971) showed that those communities that successfully managed to preserve their own culture engaged in "defensive structuring." This type of adaptation involved either the establishment of communities' own private institutions or the formal and informal control of the functioning of public institutions, as well as the reinforcement of other community agencies to counteract the influence of schools, particularly at critical periods for the pupils, such as adolescence. Work such as that of Reed-Danahay (1987) in a rural French community analyzed how resistance to the imposition of the dominant culture manifests itself at school through children's various strategies to reinforce group cohesion and subvert the teacher's emphasis on individual learning and achievement. These strategies allow the children to cope daily with the conflicting demands of home and school. Through their influence on school failure and consequent vocational orientation, these strategies also favor the pupils' integration into the local community and into farming as a professional activity.

This work calls into question Wylie's (1964) earlier study of a Provençal village, which concluded that there existed an important correspondence between the values transmitted by the community and the school: the main difference being that, at school, core principles such as respect for elders, politeness, and social control of emotions had a more normative character. While this contradiction clearly arises from two different theoretical positions, one that emphasizes the impact of the strategic behavior of individuals and one that stresses the role of the social structure, it is important to note that it also partly reflects different historical contexts. In the 1950s, Wylie was studying a French society where rural values were still dominant and where rural communities were still fairly homogeneous and relatively impervious to outside influence. He centered his attention on the primary school, which had progressively been accepted by peasants who attributed to it an instrumental function (to teach the basics and encourage the social promotion of a handful of "bright children") and did not expect it in any large measure to transmit local values. This was the role of families, peer groups, and professional groups. Therefore, as long as parents and teachers were careful not to encroach upon each other's domain, school could assimilate children into a wider national culture without sacrificing their local identity.

1.2 Local Cultures at School

It is, however, simplistic to assume that even the most centralized of educational systems can operate without adapting in one way or another to the local environment. In his study of schooling in a German village, Spindler showed that even though schools were operating in a context of rapid urbanization and change, they seemed to favor the formation of a conservative rural identity. In the first account of this research, Spindler (1974) emphasized the role of the formal curriculum. However, the same study undertaken a decade later (Spindler and Spindler 1982) led the authors to underline the more lasting influence of the "hidden curriculum" of teachers. Although sweeping curricular reforms had been conducted with the overt objective of reducing localism, which was perceived as politically suspect and economically dysfunctional, teachers continued to teach revised versions of the local culture under new curriculum headings. The authors concluded that in periods of great social transformation, schools could contribute to cultural stability by transforming changes into "substitute changes": innovations brought in from the outside would not be rejected but be made to serve local, rather than national, aims.

In countries where communities enjoy considerable power over educational decisions, schools can more easily adapt national directives to fit local orientations. In his study of an American Midwest community and its high school, Peshkin (1978) noted the central role played by the group of farmers who control the local school board. Although these "educational guardians" of the community did not explicity orient the curriculum to local needs and interests, they influenced—by countless microdecisions—curriculum choices, teacher recruitment, and school activities so that they fit a "country" world view. Teachers were also encouraged by their own upbringing in rural towns and their professional training in the smaller branches of the state university system to reinforce local values and locally appropriate levels of intellectual attainment. This "symbiosis" between community and school, which strongly contributes to a sense of personal identity and low alienation among the inhabitants, may have a strong appeal to anthropologists and educators committed to the value of cultural diversity. It also has a dark side that Peshkin does not omit to present: lower academic opportunities, lower standards of academic performance, and the reproduction of religious beliefs and anti-Black feelings that conflict with the achievement-oriented, rationalist, egalitarian, and pluralist society that the nation seeks to promote.

2. Schooling in the City: Social and Ethnic Cultures versus Mainstream Culture

After the 1960s, anthropological community–school studies became strongly urban oriented. Lower-class and ethnic neighborhoods largely replaced the village as a unit of analysis. In fact, early community studies in the United States and the United Kingdom had already analyzed, to some extent, the relationship between schooling and social and racial stratification in urban communities. Those studies which focused specifically on youth socialization and schooling in working-class neighborhoods have analyzed "the conflict of loyalties" experienced by the first boys who attended secondary schools. Schools did not only expect them to comply with the formal requirements of instruction, but also to embrace school values through their language, their manners, their way of dressing, and their participation in extracurricular school activities. These expectations greatly disrupted the organization of and social relations within the families of the elected few; they also set them definitely apart from the "street corner society" of the peer group. Nevertheless, at that time, neither the schools' orientation toward the perpetuation of mainstream middle-class values nor the communities' orientation toward the reproduction of their own culture were greatly affected by a phenomenon which was perceived as marginal both in scope and character (Whyte 1955, Jackson and Marsden 1962).

2.1 School Adaptations: Compensation and Cultural Awareness

By the 1960s, community–school relations in the city had become a central political issue. Schools were seen as key elements in efforts to reduce poverty and social and racial segregation in urban areas. Anthropologists were called upon to supply theories and methodological tools, and to evaluate the impact of various educational programs. The first anthropologist to enter the educational debate was Lewis (1966) who had developed the notion of a "subculture of poverty" to explain the attitudes and behaviors of ghetto dwellers. Although Lewis did not directly analyze community–school relations, his statements concerning the definitive impact of negative cultural dispositions on childrens' preschool learning and achievement had a great influence on the development of preschool compensatory programs. Both as a reaction to Lewis's theories and to their applications, several anthropologists produced theoretical argumentations (Leacock 1971) and empirical research results (Rosenfeld 1971) to show that children from the ghettos suffered not from a substantive "cultural deprivation" but from their inadequate responses to cultural expectations that were radically different from those of their own culture, and from differential teacher treatment.

The effect of cultural differences in aspirations, values, learning styles, and communications patterns between ethnic communities and schools subsequently became an important field of study in the United States. One of the most interesting studies of this kind was conducted by Philips (1983) in an Indian reservation. She showed how the participant structures that Native Americans learn in their community, which encourage an egalitarian relationship and discourage individual public performance, contrast sharply with the participant structures that teachers use in the classroom, which are teacher-centered and emphasize the public evaluation of individuals. Indian children performed best in the classes where teachers used participation structures, such as group work, that were most congruent with their cultural tradition. This line of research has also been pursued by Heath (1983) who analyzed the linguistic socialization of children from a White working-class community and a Black working-class community and its effects on the learning difficulties they experienced at mainstream town schools. Heath's study goes further toward developing a cultural theory that simultaneously takes into account the effect of ethnic and social factors and that examines how language reflects and reinforces other historical cultural patterns such as the relationship to work, recreational habits, and the use of space.

2.2 Students' and Parents' Opposition and Strategic Action

Despite their undeniable contribution to the understanding of the problems faced by lower-class and minority children at school, and to the development of curriculum and teacher-training programs more sensitive to cultural diversity and its impact on schooling, these studies provide an incomplete picture of community–school relations because, as noted by Ogbu (1981), they focus mainly on a transactional level of interaction between school and community. Ogbu's own work has more clearly taken into account structural factors. In his study of "Burgherside," a neighborhood in Stockton, California, he showed how the interpretation of Black school failure must take into account sociohistorical, political, and economic factors such as residential segregation and its effects on school segregation, the existence of a job ceiling and an objective inadequate educational payoff. As a consequence of this, Ogbu argues that Blacks develop a "folk theory of getting ahead" which has not led to the formation of a strong tradition of academic work or academic work optimism, but to a perception of school learning as a threat to their own identity. This makes it very difficult for Black youths to accept and follow school rules conducive to school success. It leads them rather to pursue alternative ways of "making it": on an individual basis (through engaging in activities such as prostitution), or on a collective basis (through protest or legal action) (Ogbu 1974, 1989).

Ogbu's recent theoretical developments partly integrate the results of other community–school studies that emphasize class or ethnic opposition to schooling. This line of interpretation was first developed in the United Kingdom where several school ethnographies have shown how secondary educational institutions give rise to "antischool" cultures among working-class youth (Lacey 1970). The link between this oppositional culture (which manifests itself at school through the students' way of dressing and talking and through a myriad of "deviant" behaviors) and the working-class culture of the community was analyzed by Willis (1977). He showed how this culture constitutes a creative response of students to the imposition of middle-class values at school while helping them integrate their parents' culture and the culture of the workplace.

There is also considerable debate concerning the interplay between class and racial factors. Foley's

(1990) research, for instance, showed how middle-class Mexican–Americans in south Texas are able to integrate elements from their parents' culture and elements from the mainstream culture in such a way as to develop "communicative styles" that are not only perceived positively at school but actually help them to win favor with the school authorities during sport, peer group, and classroom interactions.

Many of these studies focus on youth attitudes and behaviors. Community–school studies in urban areas, however, have also explored parents' opposition and strategic adaptation to school. Henriot-van Zanten's (1990) study of education in a lower-class neighborhood in France analyzed how the relative heterogeneity of the population in terms of social class, ethnic identity, and geographical origins leads the inhabitants to develop "avoidance strategies" which have an impact both on the neighborhood and on the school. In the neighborhood, desire to avoid social and racial mixing leads to retreat into the family and the home, to a selective use of public places and local institutions, and to a low participation in associations. At school, parents avoid meetings and social events that involve contact with other parents, and a growing number of those who are French and financially better-off, and whose children have good results at school, choose to leave the neighborhood school altogether (Léger and Tripier 1986). These strategies are not directly conducive to school failure or to school success. They can have diametrical effects depending on whether they are coupled with fear of teachers and lack of interest in the school, or whether they become part of a global strategy of individual mobility that emphasizes the importance of distinguishing oneself from other "bad parents," the follow-up of school activities at home, and personal interaction with teachers.

3. Conclusion

Although anthropological studies of community–school relations conducted since the 1950s in rural and urban areas share common characteristics concerning themes and methods of investigation, there have been important changes in their scope and in their theoretical and practical focus. Until the end of the 1960s, comprehensive studies, conducted mainly in rural areas, tried to analyze the global role of the school in modern, complex societies from an academic perspective strongly influenced by a cultural-transmission model. From the 1960s to 1980, studies in urban settings narrowed the scope of research to the analysis of face-to-face interaction between members of the community, and became both more theoretically sophisticated with the introduction of sociolinguistic theories, and more service-oriented as researchers participated in the elaboration of curriculum and teacher-training programs. Studies since 1980 show a will to combine a sociological orientation that incorporates Marxist and radical perspectives with a sophisticated anthropological analysis of cultural confrontation and adaptation. Immediate responses to problems faced by educators are not provided, but a greater effort is made to show the political, social, and pedagogical implications of the attitudes and behaviors of administrators, teachers, parents, and students in and out of the school.

See also: Anthropology of Education: History and Overview; Multicultural Education

References

Foley D 1990 *Learning Capitalist Culture: Deep in the Heart of Tejas*. University of Pennsylvania Press, Philadelphia, Pennsylvania

Heath S B 1983 *Ways with Words: Language, Life and Work in Communities and Classrooms*. Cambridge University Press, Cambridge

Henriot-van Zanten A 1990 *L'Ecole et L'Espace Local. Les Enjeux des Zones d'Education Prioritaires*. Presses Universitaires de Lyon, Lyon

Hostetler J A, Huntington G E 1971 *Children in Amish Society: Socialization and Community Education*. CSEC/ Holt, Rinehart and Winston, New York

Jackson B, Marsden D 1962 *Education and the Working Class: Some General Themes Raised by a Study of 88 Working-class Children in a Northern Industrial City*. Routledge and Kegan Paul, London

Lacey C 1970 *Hightown Grammar: The School as a Social System*. Manchester University Press, Manchester

Leacock E B (ed.) 1971 *The Culture of Poverty: A Critique*. Simon and Schuster, New York

Léger A, Tripier M 1986 *Fuir ou Construire l'Ecole Populaire?* Méridiens-Klincksieck, Paris

Lewis O 1966 *La Vida: A Puerto Rican Family in The Culture of Poverty, San Juan and New York*. Random House, New York

Ogbu J U 1974 *The Next Generation: An Ethnography of Education in an Urban Neigborhood*. Academic Press, New York

Ogbu J U 1981 School Ethnography: A multi-level approach. *Anthropol. Educ. Q.* 12(1): 3–29

Ogbu J U 1989 Cultural boundaries and minority youth orientation toward work preparation. In: Stern D, Eichhorn D (eds.) 1989 *Adolescence and Work: Influence of Social Structure, Labor Markets and Culture*. Erlbaum, Hillsdale, New Jersey

Peshkin A 1978 *Growing Up American: Schooling and the Survival of Community*. The University of Chicago Press, Chicago, Illinois

Philips S 1983 *The Invisible Culture: Communication in Classroom and Community on the Warm Springs Reservation*. Longman, New York

Reed-Danahay D 1987 Farm children at school: Educational strategies in rural France. *Anthropol. Q.* 6092: 83–89

Rosenfeld G 1971 *"Shut Those Thick Lips!" A Study of Slum School Failure*. Holt, Rinehart and Winston, New York

Spindler G 1974 Schooling in Schönhausen: A study of cultural transmission and instrumental adaptation in an urbanizing German village. In: Spindler G (ed.) 1974

Education and Cultural Process: Toward an Anthropology of Education. Holt, Rinehart and Winston, New York

Spindler G, Spindler L 1982 Roger Harker and Schönhausen: From the familiar to the strange and back again. In: Spindler G (ed.) 1982 *Doing the Ethnography of Schooling: Educational Anthropology in Action*. Holt, Rinehart and Winston, New York

Whyte W F 1955 *Street Corner Society: The Social Structure of An Italian Slum*. University of Chicago Press, Chicago, Illinois

Willis P 1977 *Learning to Labour: How Working-Class Kids Get Working-Class Jobs*. Saxon House, Farnborough

Wylie L 1964 *Village in the Vaucluse*. Harvard University Press, Cambridge, Massachusetts [1968 *Un Village du Vaucluse*. Gallimard, Paris]

Further Reading

Anderson-Levitt K 1989 Degrees of distance between teachers and parents in urban France. *Anthropol. Educ. Q.* 20 (2): 97–117

Arensberg C M, Kimball S T 1965 *Culture and Community*. Peter Smith, Gloucester

Hargreaves D H 1967 *Social Relations in a Secondary School*. Routledge and Kegan Paul, London

Henriot-van Zanten A 1990 L'Ecole et la communauté: problématique surannée ou renouveau d'un champ de recherches? In: *Sociologie de l'éducation. Dix ans de recherches*. L'Harmattan/INRP, Paris

King M 1967 *The School at Mopass: A Problem of Identity*. CSEC/Holt, Rinehart and Winston, New York

Siegel B 1974 Conceptual approaches to models for the analysis of the educative process in American communities In: Spindler G (ed.) 1974 *Education and Cultural Process: Toward an Anthropology of Education*. Holt, Rinehart and Winston, New York

Warren R L 1967 *Education in Rebhausen: A German Village*. CSEC/Holt, Rinehart and Winston, New York

Weis L 1985 *Between Two Worlds: Black Students in an Urban Community College*. Routledge and Kegan Paul, Boston, Massachusetts

A. Henriot-van Zanten

Comparative and International Education: Overview and Historical Development

"Comparative education" and "international education" are often confused. The former term refers to a field of study that applies historical, philosophical, and social science theories and methods to international problems in education. Its equivalents in other fields of academic study are those dedicated to the transsocietal study of other social institutions, such as comparative government, comparative economics, and comparative religion. Comparative education is primarily an academic and interdisciplinary pursuit.

International education (see *International Education*) fosters an international orientation in knowledge and attitudes and, among other initiatives, brings together students, teachers, and scholars from different nations to learn about and from each other. International education also includes the analysis and description of such activities. Many practitioners of international education are experts on international exchange and interaction. Their activities are partly based on a knowledge of comparative education. However, there is some disagreement on the specific range of activities encompassed by international education. Halls (1989) categorized it as a subfield of comparative education, consisting of "international pedagogy." This would include such items as education for international understanding, internationalization of teaching norms, and the study of international education institutions. Others characterize it as an applied field attached to comparative education.

Comparativists, as distinct from international educators, are primarily scholars interested in explaining why educational systems and processes vary and how education relates to wider social factors and forces. International education tends to focus more directly on descriptive information about nations and societies and their educational systems and structures. International educators use findings derived from comparative education to understand better the educational processes they examine, and thus to enhance their ability to make policy relating to programs such as those associated with international exchange and understanding.

International education and comparative education complement each other. Although they are now concurrent pursuits, comparative education grew out of, and was inspired by, international education. Comparativists and international educators often work closely together and both participate in several international organizations, such as the Comparative and International Education Society of the United States (see *International Education*).

1. Historical Development

International education and comparative education emerged out of a desire to know more about other peoples and their education than could be learned from travelers' perfunctory reports. These fields took root in modern form with the development of organized national systems of education in the nineteenth century, when models for schooling large numbers of people were sought, and when technological advances made travel and communication easier, principally in Europe and the United States. France, in particular, was the cradle of these pursuits.

1.1 Origins of International Education

In 1808, César Auguste Basset called for the appointment of a scholar "free from national and methodological prejudices" to travel in an official capacity to other countries to observe education outside of France (Basset 1814). In 1831 the french Minister of Education Victor Cousin published his internationally influential report on public education in Germany (Cousin 1836). Throughout the nineteenth century, several notable scholars traveled abroad and produced reports that contrasted education in different countries. In the twentieth century, this means of gathering information was continued by many celebrated educators including John Dewey. However, as travel became easier, observations conducted by teams of individuals became the norm. Schools organized group study programs abroad, and after the Second World War several countries developed cooperative international aid efforts and founded international education organizations. The largest is probably the United States-based organization, the National Association for Foreign Student Affairs (NAFSA): Association of International Educators, which was founded in 1948. It is dedicated to assisting universities and community organizations to deal with the legal, social, administrative, and academic complexities of international exchange. It issues a newsletter, magazine (the International Educator), books, and papers. NAFSA has also encouraged and supported international research. In 1990 it had almost 7,000 individual members, working in almost 2,000 colleges and universities in 60 countries.

1.2 Origins of Comparative Education

Comparative education, as a distinct field, originated with the publication in 1816–17 by the French scholar Marc-Antoine Jullien of a series of five articles in the *Journal d'education* and reprinted in a pamphlet entitled *L'Esquisse et vues préliminaires d'un ouvrage sur l'éducation comparée* in 1817 (Jullien 1817). In this work Jullien set out a method for comparison: standard questionnaires were to be used to collect information and the findings were to be arranged into comprehensive tables so that differences in education among countries could be grasped at a glance. These tables would show the elements that could be productively conveyed from one country to another, taking into account local peculiarities and, especially, differences in "mentality." Jullien's aim was to "deduce true principles and determined rules so that education would be transformed into an almost positive science."

Although he laid the foundation for systematic transnational studies of education early in the nineteenth century, Jullien's impact on the development of comparative education was only felt much later. For many decades after Jullien there was little interest in comparative education. Some progress was made by the English poet and school inspector Matthew Arnold, who, in a series of reports on France, Holland, Switzerland, and Germany, published between 1861 and 1888, addressed requirements for the comparative treatment of educational data. It was not until the turn of the century, however, that comparison came to be viewed in a different light. In a momentous public lecture delivered in 1900, the English educator Michael Sadle contended: "We cannot wander at pleasure among the educational systems of the world, like a child strolling through a garden, and pick off a flower from one bush and some leaves from another, and then expect that if we stick what we have gathered into the soil at home, we shall have a living plant" (Sadler 1900). Sadler urged that the use of simple descriptions of education cross-nationally be avoided as data for use in reforming educational systems. Yet neither did he advance the kind of method proposed by Jullien or social scientists such as Emile Durkheim. Instead, Sadler said that comparison should be used "to find out what is the intangible, impalpable spiritual force which, in the case of any successful system of education, is in reality upholding the school system and accounting for its present efficiency." That "spiritual force" was something extraneous to education, so that successful inquiry required an examination not only of schooling but also of the social context in which schools functioned.

Jullien and Sadler shared certain ideas that distinguish the field of comparative education. They opposed the application of simplistic characterizations of school systems for the purposes of educational reform. They also believed that the comparativist had to take into account factors beyond the school in order to understand education. Yet despite these common grounds, they had fundamentally different epistemologies and methods.

Jullien's approach was basically nomothetic: isolate a few social factors to identify underlying trends and patterns and apply these to schooling to arrive at a general explanation of a class of educational actions or events. The use of the scientific method to test hypotheses cross-culturally, developed by Durkheim in the late nineteenth century, was particularly instrumental in opening the way for nomothetic studies. Thus, to give a contemporary example, comparison could be used to test whether social class differences explain variations in school achievement on a regional or even global scale.

By contrast, Sadler's method was ideographic: analyze the special social and cultural circumstances that differentiate schooling in one society from that in another. For Sadler, genuine comparative education yielded *Verstehen*, or understanding. The comparativist would be uniquely equipped to reform education not because of precision gained by the scientific cross-national testing of hypotheses involving social and educational variables, but because of the special insight he or she had derived from intensive study of school–society relationships in a few countries. Ideographic and nomothetic approaches have delineated the contours of comparative education right up to the present (see *Comparative and International Education: Paradigms and Theories*).

1.3 Comparative Education 1900–45

The early promise of comparative education went

unfulfilled during the first decades of the twentieth century. This period encompassed the two World Wars. Preoccupation with conflict retarded the field's development. Comparison was often placed in the service of ideological competition. The best scholarship emerged in the form of a few key books and yearbook series. The most important book published during this period was Kandel's (1933) classic, *Comparative Education*. Kandel, in the United States (based at the International Institute of Teachers College, Columbia University) argued that the comparative approach should use certain common concepts or problems to contrast the forces that make for differences between national systems of education. His impact was also felt in other ways. For two decades, from 1924 to 1944, he edited *The Educational Yearbook*. He used the *Yearbook* to publicize his approach. Problems on which Kandel focused included church and state (1932), rural education (1938), adult education (1940), and higher education (1943). Other important yearbooks were also started, especially the *Yearbook of Education* (founded in 1932) and the *International Yearbook of Education* (initiated in 1933 by the International Bureau of Education in Geneva).

During this period the field's first scholarly journal appeared, the *International Education Review*. Unfortunately, it fell victim to the depredations of international conflict. It was founded in Cologne, Germany, in 1931 under the editorship of Friedrich Schneider, who was joined immediately by Paul Monroe (from the United States). The journal was hailed as a "new enterprise in international understanding." After overcoming early critical financial difficulties, the journal developed promisingly until 1934, when Schneider was dismissed from his positions at the Academy of Pedagogics in Bonn and the University of Cologne, and was replaced as coeditor by a Nazi, Alfred Baeumler, professor of philosophy and political education at the University of Berlin. Monroe left by 1938, but was replaced by another American, Isaac Doughton, dean of instruction at State Teachers College in Mansfield, Pennsylvania, with Baeumler continuing as coeditor. With the 1940 edition, Baeumler was made sole editor, an open acknowledgment of Nazi control. (After the war the *Review* moved to Salzburg, Austria. Schneider returned as editor.)

Few centers of comparative education were created during this period to train future generations of scholars. The most important new institutions were the International Institute at Columbia University Teachers College in the United States and the Institute of Education at the University of London. Scholars in the field generally emerged from "mother" disciplines, mainly history and philosophy. Nevertheless, the first courses and programs were developed during this time. The content of comparative education courses at United States institutions (e.g., Columbia, Syracuse, and Michigan Universities) was descriptive and focused largely on the school systems of England, France, Germany, and the United States. Course content evolved mainly by expanding the range of countries viewed for "comparison" rather than by a progressive inclusion of issues for analysis. National systems of education continued to be juxtaposed in terms of such items as organizational structure, teacher training, and methods of instruction. There was little effort to look beyond the manifest functions of schools. Nevertheless, the number of institutions that introduced courses in the field grew rapidly after 1920, again largely in the United States and England.

1.4 Comparative Education after 1945

Unlike the fitful growth of comparative education during the first half of the twentieth century, the field blossomed after the Second World War. The War itself turned out to be a catalyst. Soldiers returning to their home countries brought fresh insights into the way others lived, worked, and learned, and an appreciation for the complexities of social order. The purpose of comparative education expanded to include not only using national school systems as models for reform and development, but also understanding the role of education in shaping social structures and influencing economic development. Sociologists, economists, political scientists, anthropologists, and psychologists joined historians and philosophers in fashioning the field. Nomothetic and ideographic analytical approaches displaced sterile descriptions of national education systems. The social sciences came to play a paramount role.

In the 1960s voluntary assistance agencies, such as the Peace Corps in the United States, brought large numbers of young people into close contact with people abroad and promoted ever greater interest in comparative education. Returning assistance workers were more interested in studying the school's role in economic development than in using schools elsewhere as models for reform in their own country; they helped to refocus comparative education as a social science activity.

At the end of the Second World War, except for a few independent university and documentation centers, there were no organized structures to bring these varying interests together. If the field was to advance, forums had to be created for discussion among scholars from different institutions, different countries, and from the traditional background disciplines of history and philosophy and the newly important social sciences.

The first professional association of comparativists of education was founded in the United States in 1956. It was organized as the Comparative Education Society and sponsored an annual conference, a journal (*Comparative Education Review*), and regional conferences. In 1969 it changed its name to the

Comparative and International Education Society, to reflect the close connection between the two fields. In 1961 European comparativists founded the Comparative Education Society in Europe (CESE). It developed several national and regional "sections," which functioned as mini organizations. Most of these sections, such as the francophone group, eventually evolved into independent associations, with their own meetings and administrative structures. National organizations also developed in other parts of the world, beginning in 1964 with the formation of the Comparative Education Society in Japan.

With the formation of national organizations, some comparativists saw the need for a network connecting scholars around the world. In 1968 Joseph Katz of the University of British Columbia in Canada convened an International Committee of Comparative Education Societies. In 1970 the Committee changed its name to the World Council of Comparative Education Societies, to reflect the organization's anticipated role in the development of the field. Its most important function has been to plan the World Congress of Comparative Education Societies (see *Comparative Education Societies*).

After the War comparative education continued to expand within major universities and elsewhere. In the United States the creation of the University of Chicago's Comparative Education Center in 1958 was a notable development. Within a decade under the directorship of C Arnold Anderson and later Philip Foster, it became plausibly the most influential institution in the field. Its emphasis was on social scientific applications, particularly the role of education in economic and social development. Stanford University and the University of Michigan established strong programs during this period, as did the University of Wisconsin. In the 1970s programs were developed at several public institutions in the American Midwest, including the Universities of Iowa, Illinois, Indiana, and Kent State University and notable centers emerged at the State University of New York at Buffalo, the University of California at Los Angeles, and Harvard University. During the 1970s, Canada established important centers at the Ontario Institute for the Study of Education and the University of Calgary. In the 1980s outstanding work was produced at the University of Pittsburgh and Florida State University.

In Europe the University of London continued to operate notable programs. The University's continuing impact is attributable in large part to the work of exceptional scholars, such as Nicholas Hans, Edmund J King, and Brian Holmes. In Germany, important programs were established at universities in Frankfurt, Hamburg, Bochum, and Berlin (Humboldt). In Spain, the *Universidad Nacional de Educación a Distancia* in Madrid, under the leadership of José-Luis García-Garrido, has had an important influence. In Sweden, an Institute of International Education, the only one in the Nordic countries, was established at Stockholm University in 1970.

Certain national and multinational organizations have also been influential in comparative education. Among multinational agencies, the United Nations and the World Bank have been preeminent. The research produced by these organizations matches that of universities in its quality. UNESCO's *Statistical Yearbook* and other UN and World Bank publications are major resources in the field.

In 1959–61, the UNESCO Institute for Education conducted a pilot study comparing achievement of 13-year olds. This led to the first major international study, in which mathematics achievement of 13-year olds and terminal-grade students was compared across a dozen countries. There then followed cross-national studies of achievement in science, reading, literature, French and English as foreign languages, and civic education. Both the areas of learning tested and the number of countries were later expanded (see *United Nations Organizations: Research and Service in Comparative and International Education*).

Regional organizations have sponsored comparative research that has had a strong impact on human resource development and collaboration in policy-making. For example, the Council of Europe, in association with Oxford University, studied the content of academic secondary leaving examinations in Western Europe to assess the degree to which harmonization among them was possible. Some national governmental and quasi-governmental organizations have also played an important role in the development of comparative education. In this regard, the United States Agency for International Development, the Max Planck Institute for Educational Research in Berlin, the *Centre Internationale d'Etudes Pedagogiques* in Sèvres, the Academy of Pedagogical Sciences in Moscow, the National Institute for Educational Research in Tokyo, and the *Centro de Estudios Educativos* in Mexico City are notable examples. Specialized organizations, such as the International Association for Educational Assessment (IAEA), have had great impact on certain domains of scholarship in the field (see *Organisation for Economic Co-operation and Development (OECD): Educational Activities*).

During this period academic journals replaced yearbooks as the scholarly lifeblood of the field. Journals have the advantage of disseminating a greater volume of scholarship more quickly than books and yearbooks, and are therefore better suited to the field's rapid expansion of knowledge. In 1955 the *International Education Review* was renamed the *International Review of Education* reflecting a new editorial perspective and sponsorship by the UNESCO Institute of Education. In 1957 the *Comparative Education Review* was founded as the principal organ of the Comparative Education Society of the United States. Other new journals included *Comparative*

Education, *Compare*, and the *International Journal of Educational Development*.

2. Comparative and International Education: A Nexus

International education, by setting the framework for observations of education in other countries, is the starting point for comparative education. Comparison gives meaning to the observations made possible by international education, by expanding the possibilities of analysis. To understand why and how something functions requires inquiry into the relationship among its parts. To grasp why some students achieve at a higher level than others, factors that may differentiate high achievers from low achievers need to be identified, to see if some of these do account for the differences. Such a study can be undertaken for one particular country, but to do so limits the range of factors that can be used to explain achievement. Country X, for example, may display low gross domestic product and a low level of technology; hence the scope of academic achievement there would be limited to students not only of a particular culture but also in an economically lesser developed country. But if the inquiry is extended to students in a variety of countries, both developing and developed, then the range of factors to be considered can be broadened, which will increase the likelihood of discovering valid reasons for variations in achievement levels, for both Country X and other countries. Countless statistics can be amassed on education in a particular country, but unless they are incorporated within a comparative framework, the analysis will be limited.

Comparative education tends to draw its inspiration from the social sciences. In doing so it makes certain assumptions about schooling. For one thing, the field views schools as integral parts of culture, as never inert but susceptible to social change and in turn as contributing to the tempo and direction of change. Social change makes common demands on education; comparativists can study how these demands produce differential results among societies. They can also observe how the content of culture conveyed through schools varies because of the advance of science and technology and realignments in social and political structures.

Comparative research on education may take different forms. An inquiry can view a society as a unique whole, using other societies to throw the particular one into relief. Alternatively, it can hold constant those qualities that a given society has in common with others, in order to discern the differential impact of its distinctive features, these latter constituting independent variables. In the first instance, the society is "compared" in the sense that its school system and other institutions are found in a cross-cultural context to be parts of a unique configuration. In the second approach, commonalities of culture with other societies or nations are first discerned and then distinctive features of education are studied comparatively to see if they produce invariant results (see *Comparative Methodology in Education*).

Comparisons can be either explicit or implicit. Explicit comparisons may involve a variety of contemporary societies that display reasonably similar characteristics or societies separated in time. They can also focus on different historical periods in a particular society. Implicit comparisons do not give equal attention to two or more societies or time periods. Inquiry into issues in a particular society or historical period may qualify as being comparative as long as the analytic scheme can be extended to problems in other societies and periods.

As knowledge in comparative education expands, it becomes an increasingly important source for informing international education activities. For example, the November 1992 (36:4) issue of *Comparative Education Review* presented two articles that empirically examined conditions of international students in the United States. One article identified factors considered important in predicting Indonesian students' academic success. The other article examined the impact of time spent in the host country on Chinese students' attitudes toward their home country's ideology. The findings of such research have important practical implications for structuring international students' learning environments.

Indeed, such studies yield results that are of considerable value for both the development of theory and for schools catering to, and third-party sponsors of, international students. They have theoretical import by extending the discourse in comparative education to the factors that influence student behavior in varying settings, and have practical value in international education by furnishing knowledge on how learning structures for international students can be shaped most effectively to produce intended outcomes.

See also: Comparative and International Education: Paradigms and Theories; Comparative Education and International Education: Organizations and Institutions; International Education; Comparative Methodology in Education; Education as a Field of Study, Origins of; Educational Research, History of

References

Basset C A 1814 *Essais sur l'organisation de quelques parties d'instruction publique*, 2nd edn. Brundt-Labbe, Paris

Cousin V 1836 *Report on the State of Public Education in Prussia*, 2nd edn. Wilson, London

Halls W D 1989 *Comparative Education: Contemporary Issues and Trends*. Jessica Kingsley, London

Jullien de Paris M-A 1817 *L'Esquisse et vues preliminaires d'un ouvrage sur l'education comparée*. Colas, Paris

Kandel I L 1933 *Comparative Education*. Houghton Mifflin, Boston, Massachusetts
Sadler M 1900 How far can we learn anything of practical value from the study of foreign systems of education? The Surrey Advertiser, Guildford

E. H. Epstein

Comparative and International Education: Paradigms and Theories

Comparative and international education studies comprise a synthetic field using ideas, methods, and data from a wide variety of disciplines, research traditions, and educational practices. Accordingly, efforts to type, juxtapose, and interrelate knowledge perspectives being used in the field at any particular time through use of conceptual constructs—such as paradigms and theories—will be a complex and, at best, heuristic activity. This entry examines changing representations of knowledge in the field since the 1950s by means of textual interpretation; identifies dominant paradigms and theories; and suggests how these increasingly diverse constructs may be mapped both as an intellectual field, and in practice (see *Comparative and International Education: Overview and Historical Development*).

1. Changing Representations of Knowledge

While comparative educators have explicitly discussed their theoretical framing choices only since the Second World War, implicit knowledge perspectives can be identified in work of the field's founding fathers. The eighteenth- and nineteenth-Century foundational texts, for example Jullien, all advocate encyclopedic description and macro comparisons of public instruction in order to generalize on its efficiency. With the ensuing construction of national systems of education in the industrial or modern world, and their transfer, in part, to the colonized world, comparative education knowledge concerns shifted to the study of social forces and contexts in the shaping and differentiation of these systems. Here, the work of Sadler, Kandel, and Hans, among others, helped by 1950 to consolidate the functionalist paradigm as the dominant, albeit implicit, way of seeing both national and cross-national educational phenomena.

Table 1 below summarizes textual knowledge orientations in comparative education during three major periods: that is, in the 1950s and 1960s when functionalist and positivist orthodoxy dominated; in the contentious 1970s and 1980s when the radical functionalist, humanist, and radical humanist paradigms challenged orthodoxy and unresolved heterodox struggles prevailed; and in the emergence of a more heterogeneous period (with the acceptance of the complementarity of different paradigms) in the 1990s. To facilitate comparison, Table 1 distinguishes between the text's representation of knowledge control and organization; of knowledge and ontology, framing, and style; of knowledge and gender or emotions; and of inquiry products. Textual representations in comparative education, it should be noted, have closely tracked the ascendancy of the functionalist paradigm in sociology, in social anthropology, in political science, and in modernization and human capital theories, though usually with a time lag of half a decade or so.

1.1 Early Orthodoxy

Following the Second World War, with the crises of decolonization and the Cold War, comparative education studies—especially those in North America—continued to be framed in evolutionary and functionalist perspectives while moving closer to the social sciences and to their concerns to explain and inform social and economic development using the vocabulary of nomothetic science. This florescence of comparative and international education studies during these decades of functionalist and positivist orthodoxy also saw the creation of scholarly journals in the field, governmental and foundation support, and the founding of several comparative education centers in leading United States and European universities. At the Comparative Education Center at the University of Chicago, for example, the first director argued in a foundational text that the ultimate aim of comparative education is systematic knowledge of causation; i.e., the shaping of the results of analyses into law-like generalizations (Anderson 1961). Where earlier educational research and educational psychology programs had gained methodological respectability in European and North American higher education using statistics and experimental methods, Anderson proposed that comparative education should seek acceptance via a threefold strategy of: (a) integration with the functionalist social sciences; (b) the use of the natural sciences model of hypothesis testing and analysis of covariation; and (c) a commitment to theoretical explanation and generalization (see *Comparative Methodology in Education*).

To this end, he proposed a strengthening of the two broad, yet complementary, approaches to comparative education espoused since its origins and their integration into social science research. The first, i.e., intraeducational analysis generating strictly educational data, viewed education as if it were an autonomous social system. This strand would generate the statistical correlations seen as indispensable for comparing educational systems and practice. The second approach, namely, interdisciplinary research on educational–societal relations, would examine the social, political, and economic functions and tasks laid upon the schools by a society. Anderson's threefold agenda for the creation of a more systematic and

Table 1
Changing representations of knowledge in comparative and international education texts, 1950s–1990s

Characteristics of textual representations	Linear 1950s–1960s	Branching 1970s–1980s	Interwined 1990s
Knowledge control and organization:	Orthodoxy; hierarchial and centralized	Heterodoxy: emergence of "neo" variants and new inquiry perspectives	Heterogeneity: Disputatious yet complimentary knowledge communities
Knowledge relations:	Hegemonic and totalizing	Paradigm clash, i.e., "either/or" competition of incommensurable world views	Emergent post-paradigmatic, i.e., rhizomatic and interactive
Knowledge ontology:	Realist views predominate	Realist and relativist views contest reality	More perspectivist views encompass multiple realities and perspectives
Knowledge framing:	Functionalism and positivism dominant	Functionalist, critical and interpretative views compete and decenter	More eclectic, reflextive, and pragmatic
Knowledge style:	Parsimonious and value-free	Agonistic and partisan	Increasingly intertextual, ecologistic, and contingent
Knowledge gender:	Maleness: logic dominant	Feminist ideas emerge, compete, decenter	Gender issues more open and indeterminate
Knowledge emotions:	Optimism and confidence	Disdain, incredulity, or exhilaration	Ambivalence, i.e., nostalgia for certainty; delight in diversity
Knowledge products:	Law-like crossnational statements the ideal	Competing ideologies	Explanation, interpretation, simulation, translation and mapping
Illustrative texts:	Adams and Farrell (1969), Anderson (1961), Bereday (1964); Husén (1967); Noah and Eckstein (1969)	Anderson (1977), Bourdieu and Passeron (1977), Bowles and Gintis (1976), Carnoy (1984), Clignet (1981), Epstein (1983), Heyman (1979), Husén (1988), Karabel and Halsey (1977), Kelly and Nihlen (1982), Paulston (1977)	Altbach (1991), Cowen (1990), Lather (1991), Masemann (1990), Paulston (1990, 1993), Paulston and Tidwell (1992), Rust (1991), von Recum (1990)

social scientific comparative education found strong support in related efforts to establish the field both in the United States and in Western Europe. Anderson saw only hypothesis-testing using evolutionary and functional approaches as suitable knowledge-framing ideas if comparative education aspired to capture relevant aspects of "the concrete reality."

Bereday (1964) also proposed a comparative methodology that built upon positivist and evolutionist assumptions, yet chose instead to stress the need for an inductive, nonsocial science comparative methodology capable of simultaneous analysis of educational practice across national frontiers and, ideally, hypothesis-testing to advance the identification of laws in comparative education. Bereday's methodology-driven approach sought to develop an increasingly analytical but dispassionate field akin to comparative politics and comparative religion; in other words, a field "unhampered by ethical or pragmatic considerations."

In a closely related text, Noah and Eckstein (1969) sought to develop a more scientific comparative education, not based on the comparative method, as advocated by their teacher, Bereday, but in a research model taken from Sir Karl Popper and the natural sciences. They saw the attainment of rigorous scientific explanation in comparative education as a difficult goal, but one most likely to result from a methodological empiricism grounded in functionalist assumptions. Instead, research-framing choices focused on testing propositions about the relationship of education to society. Questions about the form and function of schooling would be restricted to questions of pedagogical efficiency and correlational analysis of educational relations with more complex systems. Here the comparative method is seen as a defining, if imperfect, substitute for experimentation. Explanation in comparative education is presented as an evolutionary process proceeding from curiosity, description, and primitive quantification to sophisticated quantification offering a means of rigorous scientific testing to support policy and planning. Ultimately, it will yield "scientific prediction." The empirical science model would, Noah and Eckstein contended, bring comparative education into the traditions of mainstream social science at a time, ironically, when the very foundations of modernity would come under serious attack in the social sciences and the humanities as well (Rust 1991).

The International Evaluation of Educational Achievement Project (IEA), reported by Husén (1967), brought to fruition these calls for a more scientific comparison of educational practice in schools around the world. Driven in part by fears in the United States caused by the Soviet Union's launch of the Sputnik satellite (1957) and Western European concerns related to the emergence of mass secondary education, the IEA project drew most heavily on positivistic and nomothetic traditions in educational measurement. For the first time, comparative educators would measure international differences in school achievement using objective tests to account for variations in test results. New levels of insight into the educational inputs and processes generating particular educational outputs would suggest ways of producing more efficient and predictable instructional practices. The project also provided a working model of a new comparative education, seeking causal explanation via correlational studies rather than the narrative description and moral exhortation commonly found in earlier studies. With the involvement of comparative educators from Teachers College at Columbia University, the Universities of Chicago and Stockholm, and numerous ministries of education around the world, the project promised to validate the scientific aspirations of the field in the 1950s and 1960s. Viewing the world as an educational laboratory and using comparative and correlational methods, the IEA project initially expressed the aim of discovering cognitive universals. Experience demonstrated instead the importance of unintended outcomes of schooling, the dangers of too much data and too little conceptual modeling, and the problems inherent in comparison itself, given that each school and educational system is embedded in complex and unique webs of cultural, economic, and political relations (see *Educational Achievement: Comparative Studies*).

By the late 1960s several funding agencies and comparative educators turned their attention to international education, a new branch of comparative education. This addressed problems of educational planning, development, and theory construction in macrostudies of educational and social change in largely poor, newly independent countries. In a canonical text representing a variation of the prevailing orthodoxy, Adams and Farrell (1969) proposed that the primary purpose of comparative and development studies is the generalization and specification of testable propositions or statements of relations between variables. However, because scholars in comparative education are seen to have been most reluctant to undertake this task "our knowledge remains scattered and unsystematic." The authors' corrective would be to order knowledge about relations within and across educational systems according to Parsonian notions of unilineal structural differentiation, a process that "will follow an approximately similar sequence in all societies" undergoing modernization.

1.2 Heterodoxy

By the early 1970s functionalist theory and positivist methods had achieved the status of orthodoxy in comparative and education studies at the same time they came under attack in the social sciences and in development studies from a combination of emergent critical and interpretive knowledge communities. The reasons for the vulnerability had many sources including: the shift from a segregated to a plural society in the United States—that is with cultural pluralism came epistemological and ontological pluralism; the limitations of functionalist theory in adequately directing or explaining development efforts; the defeat of the United States in Vietnam (1972); and, among other things, the creation of numerous new academic centers (Cowen 1990) and the arrival of new scholars, many from the Third World, using antithetical neo-Marxist critical theory and feminist and dependency perspectives.

A major decentering of the structural functionalist world view began following the publication of Berger and Luckmann's seminal text (1967) *The Social Construction of Reality*. Here the humanist paradigm and its support of the intersubjective or social origin of all ideas branched into ethnomethodological and phenomenological perspectives (see Figure 1) while strengthening the arrival of a new ethnographic approach in comparative education.

The radical functionalist worldview, first elaborated by Althusser (1990) and later by Bowles and Gintis (1976) among others to explain how education functions to reproduce capitalist structures, also rather quickly and effectively mounted a telling critique of structural-functionalist explanations of educational reform and modernization failures. Carnoy (1984) documented the subsequent appearance of a variety of neo-Marxist texts rooted in the historical materialist worldview in the early 1970s as early examples of paradigm clash in comparative education discourse.

Texts drawing on radical functionalist counterorthodoxy greatly increased in number and influence to produce a powerful critique of entrenched Parsonian structural functionalism and its variants in modernization and human capital theories. But, because traditional Marxist–Leninist texts portray education as a repressive state apparatus, they paid little attention to how education might contribute to a revolutionary socialist strategy. By the 1970s neo-Marxist researchers had given this question their highest priority.

In France Althusser's 1960s interpretations of Marx (1990) regarded the superstructure, including education, as determined by the relations of production. Here the hegemony of the dominant class lies in the very relations of the means of production and directly defines the purposes and functioning of the educational system. Thus the educational system is seen hyperfunctionally; that is, it necessarily reproduces the relations of production and any counterhegemonic response from educators or students is largely precluded.

In the United States Bowles and Gintis (1976) applied Althusser's theory of structural correspondence and sought to demonstrate the reality of American education as the values and relationships of capitalist production. Attempts to reform schools without corresponding changes in the structure of production, they argued, would always fail.

In the United Kingdom B. Bernstein and the New Sociology of Education school elaborated a neo-Marxist project to study educational institutions as agents of cultural transmissions and reproduction. While Bernstein's seminal work on the influence of social class in the classification and framing of educational knowledge was clearly tied to the radical wing of the "old" sociology of education, he also drew widely upon both the humanist, or interpretive, and functionalist world views (see Figure 1). In a perceptive assessment, Karabel and Halsey (1977) concluded that the macrosociological conflict approach of the American neo-Marxists and the essentially microsociological interpretative studies of the British are highly complementary and that both have "waged war" against the common enemies of functionalist theory and methodological empiricism without ever coordinating their critiques.

During the 1970s numerous structuralist Marxist texts also provided penetrating structuralist explanations of why many of the Third World modernization efforts foundered on structured inequality and class interests. But because these texts left out contingency, the human actor, and individual subjectivity, they could, as with the more conservative structural functionalist texts, only offer critique and deterministic, top-down solutions predicated on a single view of social process (Schrag 1986).

By the early 1980s a more humanistic Marxism, or radical humanism, began to gain prominence in critical studies. Texts framed in this knowledge orientation drew on the critical theory of the Frankfurt School—in Germany led by Jürgen Habermas, in North America by Henry Giroux, and in the Third World by Paulo Freire. As a branch of this intellectual movement, feminist texts also began to draw upon critical theory's agenda for the liberation of consciousness, using a negative dialectical argument to expose how education serves the patriarchal domination of women, much as capitalists were seen to dominate workers in Marxist texts. Kelly and Nihlen (1982), for example, critized all existing comparative education texts for their silence on education's role in the reproduction of gender inequality. They also presented a valuable reflexive critique of their own reproduction framework and found that it "fails both to deal with 'deviations' and chart how and when they occur or become significant." The answers will not come, they contended, from deterministic functionalist or radical functionalist analysis of structure or history, but from interpretative research rooted in the humanist and radical humanist paradigms that tell us how women experience and interpret education in their everyday lives, and how they come to see and resist domination.

With the spread of epistemological pluralism and the decentering of positivist dominance in the social sciences in the 1970s and 1980s, interpretative research-framing choices also began to appear in comparative education texts. An illustrative text by Heyman (1979), for example, laid out an alternative ethnomethodological knowledge orientation, a rationale discarding functionalist approaches, and an agenda for ethnographic inquiry in the field. Heyman's text contended that comparative education has not provided useful knowledge to educational planners, policymakers and reformers because of its decontextualized commitment to social "facts" (i.e., in the IEA study), its narrow interest in functional and structural relationships (i.e., modernization and Marxist research), and its focus on social science indicators rather than on interaction among participants in actual social and educational environments. Research based on the measurement of indicators as proxies for theoretically related concepts result, according to Heyman, is a gross distortion of the very social reality that comparatists seek to reveal and understand.

His heterodox argument built upon Garfinkel's work in the 1960s and called for the replacement of positivism with interpretative approaches better able to observe, describe, and interpret "this reality" of everyday existence. Ethnomethodology, i.e., the study of how individuals engage in reality-making processes, is proposed because it promises to capture more of the continuous production of social reality in human interaction than do correlational studies that assume that objects cannot be two things at once; or that they have stable, discreet, and permanent properties—assumptions more appropriate for inquiry in the physical sciences. For Heyman, the level of analysis in comparative studies must shift from macro to micro, from an objectivist–realist to a subjectivist–relativist ontology, and to the study of everyday life. Research in comparative education must stop "pretending to be scientific" and seeking grand generalizations and instead become microscopic, steer a heuristic course, and build its comparative interpretations and theories through replication.

In a related paradigmatic text, Clignet (1981) also rejected both functionalist and radical functionalist worldviews. Despite their apparent differences, Clignet demonstrated that both share a number of weaknesses. Both give a privileged position to functionalist explanation, i.e., they use effects to explain events; both stress vertical hierarchical relations at the expense of horizontal interactive relations. In their focus on structure, both ignore how assimilation and replication processes performed by schools are contingent on critical sets of interaction among individuals and social groups located within the same layers of social reality. Both perspectives prevent researchers from analyzing the variability of the mechanisms used by schools in assimilation and replication functions and both prevent researchers from differentiating between the process of educational interactions and their outcomes in students' life chances.

Instead, Clignet looked to behavioral science and proposed a biological or psychological framework that distinguishes the perspective of each individual organism and differentiates its modes of adaption to the environment—in this case the school environment of teachers and students. This ecologistic approach rejects the notion of universal viability found in functionalist and critical arguments. Instead, it starts at the micro level, with biographies of individual actors, and examines the relationship between educational structures and actions. It sees local adaptation and differentiation as an integral part of social reality, and the necessity of historically and culturally contingent strategies if change efforts are to be effective. Accordingly, Clignet argued, the failure of most educational development policies and planning efforts follow from their rigid and uniform top-down pedagogical treatments that "reflect ideological rather than scientific principles." By the mid-1980s all foundational knowledge in the field had become vulnerable to this attack (Paulston 1977, Epstein 1983).

The first summary of texts on comparative education, seeking to reveal and map paradigmatic and theoretical perspectives in the field, appeared in the mid-1970s. Paulston's (1977) phenomenographic typing of how the international educational reform literature represented and explained national reform efforts and outcomes produced a heterodox, or bipolar, juxtaposition of texts framed in either equilibrium or conflict worldviews. Theories, or reform explanations, found linked with these two paradigmatic orientations included the evolutionary, functionalist theory, and systems with the equilibrium pole; while the various Marxist, cultural revitalization, and anarchistic utopian theories attached to the conflict pole. As interpretativist or feminist explanations of national educational reform process and outcomes had yet to appear, they are absent from the summary figure. This was not be the case in the 1990s, as may be seen in Table 2 and Figure 1, where the consequences of subsequent branching and entwinement of functionalist, critical, and interpretativist knowledge perspectives and the emergence of radical hermeneutic critique and explanation are clearly apparent and burgeoning (Masemann 1990, Lather 1991).

By the mid-1970s, Anderson (1977) had come to qualify somewhat his earlier strong advocacy of an exclusive structural-functionalist approach to comparative education. In response to attacks from advocates of competing holistic–interpretative and critical perspectives, he warned that confusion and vulgar functionalism arise when investigators "too readily infer ostensible functions of schools from putative societal needs" rather than from strict adherence to "confirmation of many a priori hypotheses" concerning complex matrices of variables explaining functional equivalents among the educational practices of different systems. Despite some pessimism about the state of the art in comparative education, Anderson predicted continued progress in the identification of "functional equivalents for the basic structures and functions of educational systems." He also argued against the utility of a "holistic" view of society: "Perhaps, we should cease to speak of society as a 'seamless web' and see it rather as a matrix of .5 correlation coefficients. Accordingly, holistic conceptions of society should be espoused with heavy qualifications, even when we would do not put conflict at the center of our conceptual scheme" (Anderson 1977 p. 413).

In his presidential address to the Comparative and International Education Society Epstein (1983), a student of Anderson at Chicago, also found comparative education texts in chaotic disarray over "appropriate methodology" and a battleground of seemingly irreconcilable and competing ideologies. In his dichotomizing of supposedly incommensurable and irreconcilable realist and relativist knowledge orientations, and defense of Anderson's interpretation of positivism, Epstein's text captures well the heterodox knowledge relations of the 1970s.

1.3 Emergent Heterogeneity

In the late 1980s representations of knowledge in comparative education texts began a major shift away from heterodoxy (Altbach 1991). While a few researchers still claimed orthodox purity and remained within their exclusive paradigmatic utopias, and many continued unsuccessful partisan efforts to replace one worldview with another, the collapse of paradigms and grand theory in the social sciences meant that no particular knowledge community could now claim a monopoly on truth. Rather, a growing number of researchers saw all foundational knowledge as incomplete and problematic.

Husén (1988), for example, pointed the way past heterodoxy with his recognition that no single paradigm can answer all questions, that all serve to compliment supposedly conflicting and incommensurate

Table 2
A heuristic taxonomy of knowledge perspectives in comparative and international education texts

Root paradigms/ world views	Branching "theories"	Illustrative texts
Functionalist "Must be"	Modernization/human capital	Boli & Meyer (1985), Coombs (1985), Schultz (1989)
	Neofunctionalist	Adams (1988), Plank (1990), Rondinelli et al. (1990)
	Rational choice/micro-macro	Coleman (1987), Turner (1987)
	Conflict theory	Archer (1984), Bourdieu & Passeron (1977), Paulston (1980), Weiler (1989)
	Dependency	Altbach (1989), Arnove (1980)
Radical Functionalist "Will be"	Historical materialist	Althusser (1990), Bowles & Gintis (1976), Schrag (1986)
	Neomarxist/postmarxist	Carnoy (1984), Carnoy and Samoff (1990)
	Cultural rationalization	Habermas (1987), Weiler (1983), Welsh (1991)
Radical Humanist "Can be"	Critical theory/critical ethnography	Avalos (1986), Foley (1991), Weis (1990)
	Feminist	Kelly & Nihlen (1982), Lather (1991), Stromquist (1989, 1990)
	Poststructuralist/postmodernist	Cherryholmes (1988), Rust (1991), von Recum (1990)
	Pragmatic interactionist	Holmes (1988), Husén (1988), Paulston and Rippberger (1991)
Humanist "Be-ing"	Ethnographic/ethnological	Gibson and Ogbu (1991), Spindler and Spindler (1987)
	Phenomenographic/ ethnomethodological	Clignet (1981), Heyman (1979), Paulston (1993)

worldviews. Paulston (1990, 1993) saw the field moving from paradigm wars to something of a disputatious community as the use of knowledge became more eclectic and reoriented by new ideas and knowledge products, such as interpretations, simulations, translations, probes, and conceptual mapping. Here data do not claim to represent some objective reality embodied in universals or foundations. Rather, they are presented "as if" reality in an increasingly fragmented, interwoven, and contingent field might be thus partially seen, read, and interpreted.

With the appearance of poststructural (Cherryholmes 1988) and postmodern (von Recum 1990, Lather 1991, Rust 1991) texts, comparative education discourse then also began another fundamental shift in knowledge framing, from traditional social, behavioral and Marxist science models to those of language, culture, and the interpretative humanities.

2. *Intellectual Communities in the 1990s*

Table 2 presents a taxonomy or synchronic mapping of knowledge perspectives in the 1990s. Four major root paradigms, or worldviews, are identified: i.e., the functionalist, the radical functionalist, the radical humanist, and the humanist. Some 21 branching theories, drawing upon one or more paradigms, are identified and linked using a number of illustrative texts. Together the interaction of paradigms and theories within texts comprises dynamic intellectual communities. While this figure captures something of the range and diversity of knowledge perspectives in the field, it can only suggest the intense eclectic borrowing taking place across intellectual communities, not only in comparative eduation but in almost all areas of intellectual work. Figures 1 and 2 present an indication of this knowledge interaction and growth via the mapping of knowledge relations at macro- or metatheoretical and at micro- or practice levels.

2.1 *Functionalist Neofunctionalist Theory*

Functionalist theory has seen the growth of numerous vital new branches while the traditional structural–functional root paradigm has continued to be attacked from all quarters. Humanist texts, for example, have critiqued its "anti-individualism" and "downward conflation," where a supposedly integrated cultural system is seen to create a consensus that engulfs the social and personality systems. Radical functionalist texts have attacked its "conservatism," "idealism," and willingness to accept structured inequality and human misery as the price of social efficiency, progress, and homeostasis, or moving equilibrium. Neofunctionalist texts have sought to address and move beyond these problems by synthesizing core paradigmatic assumptions with opposing paradims and other theoretical traditions.

Modernization theory, for example, has several branches. The evolutionary functionalist branch (Boli et al. 1985) has drawn heavily on the writings of Emile Durkheim and Talcott Parsons to explain how the functional requirements of increasingly complex differentiated societies create a functional need for mass schooling. Interventionist attempts to modernize educational systems via planning and innovation based on idealized Western models and applied science have led to crises (Coombs 1985), despite efforts by the World Bank and other international agencies to improve efficiency and productivity using human capital and related economic perspectives (even though there have been discredited for decades as a result of frequent failure in practice) (Schultz 1989).

Neofunctionalists have retained the general social system perspective of Parsons while opening their texts to hermeneutic approaches and interpretative perspectives (Adams 1988), to an acceptance of conflicting social and cultural factors in educational reform projects (Rondinelli et al. 1990), and to a recognition of the centrality of structured inequality and interest group conflict in explanations of failed educational reform (Plank 1990).

Rational choice theory, as well, has sought to move action theory away from the macro system level and back toward the actor and possibilities for human agency and more contingent understanding. One branch of rational choice theory has drawn upon empirical game theory to explain how actors interpret and act in situations of social change (Turner 1987). Rational choice theory has undergone rapid growth as both neofunctionalists and neo-Marxists have tried to put into place an empirical base of rational choice microtheory to support a diverse variety of macrotheoretical constructs. Coleman (1987) especially has contributed to the development of a broader action theory which synthesizes interests in actors and systems to clarify the meaning of voluntaristic action. Analytical Marxists, as well, have come to borrow freely from rational choice and game theory—even from general equilibrium theory and neoclassical economics—to elaborate the empirical microgrounding of what their radical texts see as macrosocial, historical materialist processes.

Conflict theory has drawn on both functionalist and macrohistorical sociological theory to explain education in contexts of privilege, domination, and reproduction. Building on paradigmatic texts by Weber, Simmel, Dahrendorf, and Coser, conflict theory has focused on consequences of conflict within social and educational systems. Archer (1984) for example, presented a "morphogenetic" explanation in which mutual causal processes are seen to counteract systemic stress and to facilitate structural differentiation and increased information flow. Texts emphasizing conflict theory have willingly incorporated Marxist ideas such as cultural reproduction (Bourdieu and Passeron 1977), yet have rejected historicism and see only continued conflict into the future (Paulston 1980, Weiler 1989). With its predilection for intellectual eclecticism, orientation to empirical research methods, and micro-macro interaction, conflict theory has become increasingly attractive as a perspective to study how changing stratification and organization structures are grounded in the interactions and intersubjectivity of everyday life.

2.2 *Radical Functionalist Neo-Marxist Theories*

While the sort of traditional Marxist structural determinism associated with the texts of Althusser and Bowles and Gintis of the 1970s has now largely disappeared, neo-Marxist and post-Marxist theory has continued, albeit in something of a state of shock following the collapse of socialist theory and practice in Eastern Europe, in the former Soviet Union, and in much of the Third World. Anticipating this debacle to some extent, Bowles and Gintis (1987) moved far beyond their earlier rigid social class reproduction model and called for a new post-Marxist theoretical discourse combining features of liberalism and Marxism. Carnoy and Samoff (1990) have also been concerned to rid their earlier Marxist analysis of its more teleological, metaphysical, and hyperfunctionalist features. They have attempted to break with orthodox Marxist social class theory and have presented a less deterministic neo-Marxist "transition-state theory," now giving a privileged place to the role of the state over productive forces and class conflict in explaining attempted Third World transitions to socialism. Yet the theory's inability to recognize, let alone to explain, reverse transitions from socialism to market economies in, for example, Nicaragua, Eastern Europe, and elsewhere, indicate a continuing and debilitating adherence to the historicism and emancipatory idealism in this perspective.

2.3 *Radical Humanist Critical Theory*

Cultural rationalization theory (Weiler 1989, Welsh 1991) has also drawn upon a number of what were earlier viewed as ideologically incommensurable perspectives. The Sociologist Jürgen Habermas, a leading theorist in this community, has constructed a sweeping reconstruction of Marx's grand emancipatory narrative. Rejecting utopian and structuralist notions of base and superstructure, Habermas has sought a new normative foundation for reconstructing Marxism in critical theory, in the intersubjective theory of communicative democracy of G H Mead, in Weber's theories of bureaucracy and progressive cultural rationalization, and in the action theory of Talcott Parsons.

Critical theory, the main branch growing out of radical humanism, has played an important role in paradigmatic contention since the 1950s. It is closely related to cultural rationalization theory but has more directly attacked the repressive character of Western reason, culture, and society. Herbert Marcuse and Paulo Freire have, perhaps, most directly influenced comparative educators' use of this perspective in their advocacy of emancipatory modernity (Arnove 1980), and studies of distorted knowledge relations (Altbach 1989), and oppressive gender relations (Kelly and Nihlin 1982, Stromquist 1989,

Lather 1991). A vital and growing variation of this theoretical framing perspective, drawing upon Horkheimer's negative dialectics, is also found in several critical ethnographic studies (Foley 1991, Weiss 1990), which offer thick descriptions of cultural and economic domination and reproduction and prospects for resistance supposedly from the actor's viewpoint.

Examples of poststructuralist theory (Cherryholmes 1988) and postmodernist theory (von Recum 1990, Lather 1991, Rust 1991) in comparative education texts are the most difficult to categorize and to map. While they are for the most part rooted in both the humanist and radical humanist paradigms (see Figure 1) in their privileging of language and rejection of domination, they have also rejected the truth claims of positivist science, of history, and of classical rationalism (i.e., the notion that knowledge claims can be ranked according to intuitive standards of truth). Instead, the social world is usually portrayed as a collage of multiple narratives or traces tied to specific forms of empowerment. The time of total relativity is seen to be present everywhere. Postmodern texts have attacked everything that claims to be free of contradiction, closed, uniform, or unequivocal. Rather, paradox, diversity, ambiguity, and chance have become the new social determinants.

From this perspective's extreme relativism, both society and values disintegrate and the subject is decentered and diminished. Science shifts from attempts to discover truth to the creation of new ideas with preference for paralogical analysis. In redefining educational goals, the postmodern perspective avoids the imposition of normative decisions and looks instead to a better understanding of the discursive field in which education occurs, to local knowledge, and to "decentralized small units" (von Recum 1990, Rust 1991).

It seems likely that postmodern theory, because of its provocative new ideas, has the potential to occupy a good deal of the space vacated by the collapse of Marxist structuralism with its tired global philosophy of the subject and its teleological vision of social evolution. Instead, postmodern theory, because it rejects modernity as an historical movement toward control based on foundational knowledge, replaces rationality and logic with paralogy or counterlogic. Its radical perspective links power with knowledge and views emancipatory moral rhetorics as merely another of the forms assumed by power.

Comparative education texts have made valuable contributions to understanding educational relations in earlier transformations to capitalism, urbanism and democracy. Poststructural and postmodern theories offer difficult yet challenging new ideas in attempts to theorize the present transformation into, as yet, unknown educational and cultural patterns.

2.4 *Humanist Interpretativist Theory*

The pragmatic interactionist perspective in comparative education texts also rejects totalizing theory and accepts most methods in attempts to understand how social actors come to consciousness within social structures. It is concerned with understanding the larger questions of human experience; it seeks to determine, through the testing of knowledge in practice and community, which perspectives have pragmatic, i.e., operational and heuristic, value (Holmes 1988, Husén 1988). Drawing upon Dewey and Mead, and later on neopragmatic texts by Habermas and Rorty, pragmatic interactionism has offered a central space at the paradigmatic margins (see Figure 1), where all worldviews and perspectives might interact in the context of educational change practice (Paulston 1990).

Equally central to the humanist paradigm, the ethnographic perspective favors local knowledge and interpretation over exclusive paradigmatic constructs and modernization agendas for progressive change. In comparative education this perspective has been used to describe participant perception of classroom experiences among poor Latin American students (Avalos 1986) and patterns of academic persistence and achievement among immigrant and "involuntary minority" children (Gibson and Ogbu 1991). While the ethnographic perspective provides rich description of how ethnic communities and others view and interpret educational practice, ethnographic data have little, if any, comparative value without the imposition of an antithetical ethnological or ideological overlay (Spindler and Spindler 1987).

Accordingly, neither Heyman's proposal (1979) to replace positivism with ethnomethodological method and perspective, nor Clignet's (1981) call for an exclusive phenomenological approach to comparative education have garnered much support. But with the field entering a stage of eclectic critical postpositivism, the humanist paradigm with its concerns for consciousness, creativity, and emotion has been combining with other perspectives in the void left by the reduction in credibility of the scientific functionalist and emancipatory grand metanarratives.

Because of the increasingly diverse knowledge communities interacting within the dynamic intellectual field of comparative and international education texts, efforts at conceptual mapping, such as phenomonography, have also shown promise (Paulston and Tidwell 1992, Paulston 1993).

Phenomenography is about the qualitatively different ways in which people experience or think about various phenomena and about the relations between human beings and their world. In comparative education, phenomenographic studies have sought, as in this Entry, to characterize how researchers see, apprehend, and think about knowl-

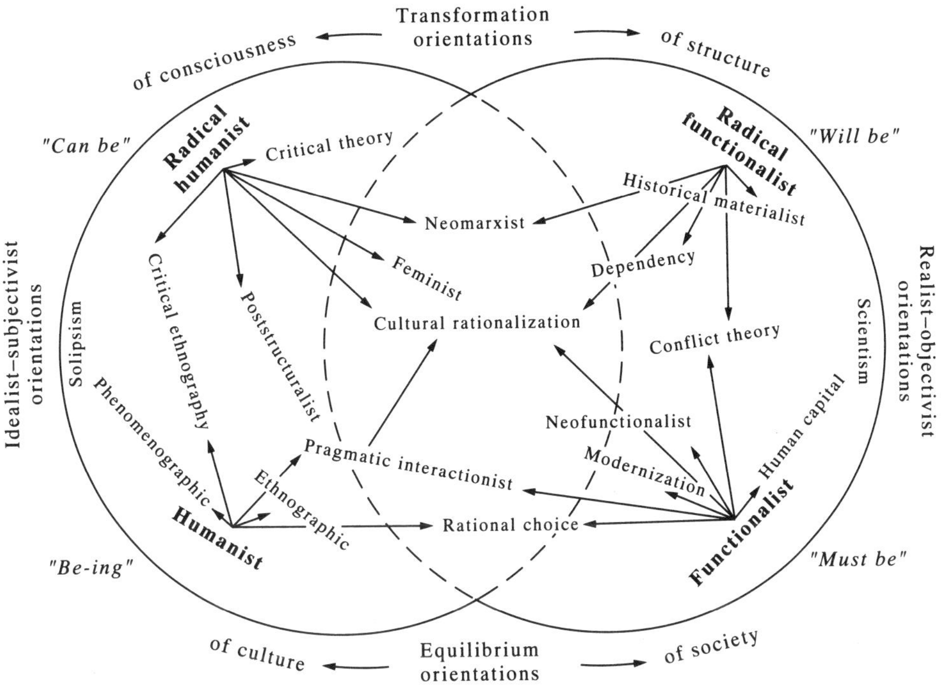

Figure 1
A macromapping of paradigms and theories in comparative and international education seen as an intellectual field

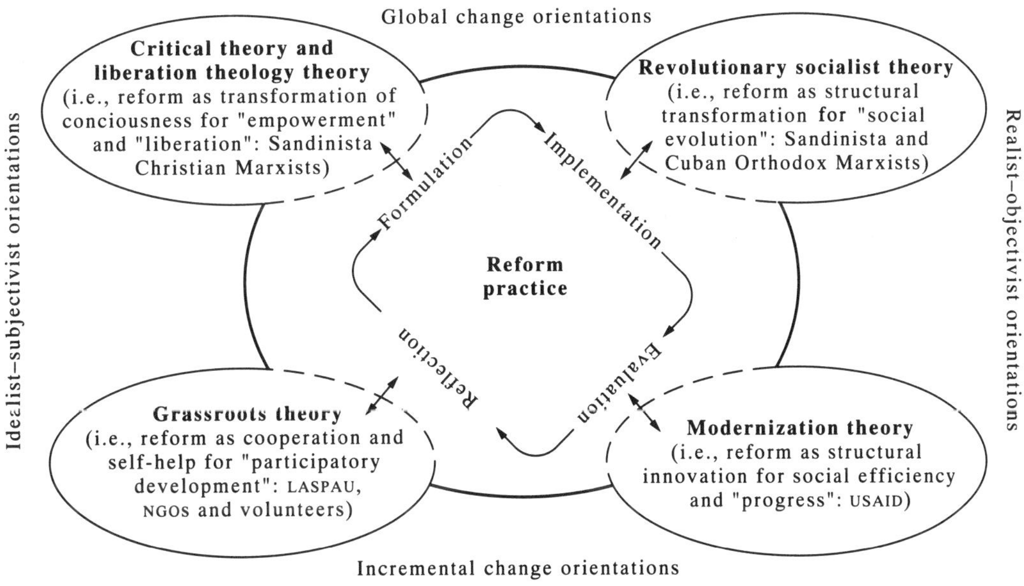

Figure 2
A micromapping of educational and social change theories in Nicaraguan higher education reform practice

edge constructs such as "paradigms and theories" at different times and in different knowledge cultures and subcultures. Through textual analysis, phenomenographic studies have sought not to describe things "as they are," but how they have been presented as ways of thinking about the world. The categories of description (see Figs. 1 and 2, Tables 1 and 2) are seen as a form of discovery and as the main outcomes of such research activity. Comparison of alternative perspectives has tried to identify distinctive characteristics or essential structures of each conceptualization so that they may be described and mapped.

3. Mapping Knowledge Perspectives

Earlier examples of mapping knowledge in comparative and international education texts can be seen in Anderson (1961), where implicitly structural functionalism occupied all space; in Paulston (1977), where polarized equilibrium and conflict paradigms contested space; in Epstein (1983) where three distinct and supposedly irreconcilable paradigms labeled "neopositivist," "neo-Marxist," and "neo-relativist" contested space; in Adam's (1988) presentation of Burrell and Morgan's multidimensional typology; and in the interactive typologies and "maps," presented here.

3.1 Macromapping

Maps are a distinct mode of visual representation that use space to represent space. As with textual and discourse analysis, they offer a system of possibility for knowledge. In Fig. 1, paradigms and theories in the field of comparative education are presented in heuristic fashion as a macrointellectual field derived from intratextual and crosstextual analysis. Textual dispositions regarding social and educational change (the vertical dimension) and characterization of reality (the horizontal dimension) are the coordinates used to type and locate texts within the field. Several advantages of Fig. 1 may be noted. It facilitates, for example, the understanding of particular intellectual perspectives within broader movements. It suggests a dynamic and rhizomatic field, that is, comparative education may be seen as an exploration and comparison of the eclectic interweaving of knowledge communities rather than the more structural and linear image presented to the world in earlier foundational texts. The strength of modern social theory in the field is firmly grounded in this very multiplicity of its perspectives and tools. Simultaneously, in cataloging and reinscribing discourse communities and relations, Figs. 1 and 2, and Tables 1 and 2 order and discipline this world, discover hierarchies, and represent an act of control. Despite interpretative and heuristic intent, they are only one researcher's perspective. Other readings may lead to different interpretations.

3.2 Micromapping

A representation of the micromapping of paradigmatic world views and theoretical perspectives intertwined in a specific educational reform practice is presented in Fig. 2.

This visual representation, in contrast to Fig. 1, seeks to map educational practice at a particular time and place. Practice is viewed as a hermeneutic circle into which major stakeholders in an educational reform practice bring their guiding world views and ideas, creating a goal-oriented interactive process (Paulston and Rippenberger 1991). It suggests an examination, in Parsonian terms, of energy, behavior, and accomplishments in the context of social action rather than, as done in Fig. 1, a global juxtaposition of the sources of intellectual energy identified in illustrative texts.

4. Conclusion

This entry has used textual analysis to examine the emergence of paradigmatic and theoretical conceptions of knowledge in comparative and international education over time as history; as a synchronic, taxonomic structure; and as conceptual maps, both at macro and micro levels. Three major representations of knowledge in the field are identified as the orthodox, the heterodox, and the enfolding heterogeneous. Convergent trends across knowledge communities are also identified and discussed, noting that comparative educators and their texts are becoming more reflexive and eclectic, thus allowing new theory to emerge from often paradoxical combinations of existing theories.

See also: Comparative and International Education: Overview and Historical Development; Comparative Methodology in Education

References

Adams D 1988 Extending the educational planning discourse: Conceptual and paradigmatic explorations. *Comp. Educ. Rev.* 32(4): 400–15.

Adams D, Farrell J P 1969 Societal differentiation and educational differentiation. *Comp. Educ.* 5(3): 249–62

Altbach P 1989 Twisted roots: The western impact on Asian higher education. *Higher Educ.* 18(1): 9–29

Altbach P 1991 Trends in comparative education. *Comp. Educ. Rev.* 35(3): 491–507

Althusser L 1990 Theory, theoretical practice and theoretical formation. In Althusser L (ed.) 1990 *Philosophy and the Spontaneous Philosophy of the Scientists and other Essays.* Verso, London

Anderson C A 1961 The methodology of comparative education. *Int. Rev. Educ.* 7: 1–23

Anderson C A 1977 Comparative education over a quarter of a century: Maturity and challenges. *Comp. Educ. Rev.* 21(2/3): 405–16

Archer M 1984 *Social Origins of Educational Systems.* Sage, London

Arnove R 1980 Comparative education and world system analysis. *Comp. Educ. Rev.* 24(1): 48–62.

Avalos B 1986 *Ensenando a los Hijos de los Pobres: Un Estudio Ethnografico en America Latina*. International Educational Research Center, Ottawa
Bereday G Z F 1964 *Comparative Method in Education*. Holt, Rinehart and Winston, New York
Berger P, Luckmann T 1967 *The Social Construction of Reality*. Penguin, Harmondsworth
Boli J R, Ramirez F O, Meyer J 1985 Explaining the origins and expansion of mass education. *Comp. Educ. Rev.* 29(2): 145–70
Bourdieu P, Passeron J C 1977 *Reproduction, Education, Society, and Culture*. Sage; Beverly Hills, California
Bowles S, Gintis H 1976 *Schooling in Capitalist Society (Educational Reform and the Contradictions of Economic Life*. Routledge and Kegan Paul, London
Carnoy M 1984 Marxism and education. In: Ollman B, Vernoff E (eds.) 1984 *The Left Academy: Marxist Scholarship on American Campuses*, 1984, Vol. 2. Praeger, New York
Carnoy M, Samoff J 1990 *Education and Social Transition in the Third World*. Princeton University Press, Princeton, New Jersey
Cherryholmes C 1988 *Power and Criticism: Post-structural Investigations in Education*. Teachers College Press, New York
Clignet R 1981 The double natural history of educational interactions: Implications for educational reforms. *Comp. Educ. Rev.* 25(3): 330–52
Coleman J 1987 Micro-foundations and macrosocial behavior. In: Alexander J, Giesen B, Munch R, Smelser N J (eds.) 1987 *The Micro-Macro Link*. University of California Press, Berkeley, California
Coombs P H 1985 *The World Crisis in Education: The view from the 80s*. Oxford University Press, New York
Cowen R 1990 The national and international impact of comparative education infrastructures. In: Halls W D (ed.) 1990 *Comparative Education: Contemporary Issues and Trends*. UNESCO, Paris
Epstein E H 1983 Currents left and right: Ideology in comparative education. *Comp. Educ. Rev.* 27(1): 3–29
Foley D E 1991 Rethinking school ethnographies of colonial settings: A performance perspective of reproduction and resistance. *Comp. Educ. Rev.* 35(3): 532–51
Gibson M A, Ogbu J U 1991 *Minority Status and Schooling: A Comparative Study of Emigrant and Involuntary Minorities*. Garland, London
Heyman R 1979 Comparative education from an ethnomethodological perspective. *Comp. Educ.* 15(3): 241–49
Holmes B 1988 Causality, determinism and comparative education as a science. In: Schriewer J, Holmes B (eds.) 1988 *Theories and Methods in Comparative Education*. Peter Lang, Bern
Husén T (ed.) 1967 *International Study of Achievement in Mathematics: A Comparison of Twelve Countries*. Almqvist and Wiksell, Stockholm
Husén T 1988 Research paradigms in education. *Interchange* 19: 2–13
Karabel J, Halsey A H (eds.) 1977 *Power and Ideology in Education*. Oxford University Press, New York
Kelly G P, Nihlen A S 1982 Schooling and the reproduction of patriarchy. In: Apple M (ed.) 1982 *Cultural and Economic Reproduction in Education*. Routledge and Kegan Paul, London
Lather P 1991 *Getting Smart: Feminist Research and Pedagogy within the Post-Modern*. Routledge, New York
Masemann V 1990 Ways of knowing: Implications for comparative education. *Comp. Educ. Rev.* 34(4): 465–73
Noah H J, Eckstein M A 1969 *Toward a Science of Comparative Education*. Macmillan, New York
Paulston R 1977 Social and educational change: Conceptual frameworks. *Comp. Educ. Rev.* 21(2/3): 370–95
Paulston R 1980 Education as anti-structure: Nonformal education in social and ethnic movements. *Comp. Educ.* 16(1): 55–66
Paulston R 1990 From paradigm wars to disputatious community. *Comp. Educ. Rev.* 34(3): 395–400
Paulston R 1993 Ways of seeing education and social change in Latin America: A phenomenographic perspective. *Latin Amer. Res. Rev.* 28(1): 177–202
Paulston R, Rippberger S 1991 Ideological Pluralism in Nicaraguan University reform. In: Ginsburg M (ed.) 1991 *Understanding Educational Reform in Global Context*. Garland, London
Paulston R, Tidwell M 1992 Latin American education—Comparative. In: Alkin M (ed.) 1992 *Encyclopedia of Educational Research*. Macmillan, New York
Plank D 1990 The politics of basic education reform in Brazil. *Comp. Educ. Rev.* 34(4): 538–60
Rondinelli D A, Middleton J, Verspoor A M 1990 *Planning Education Reforms in Developing Countries: The Contingency Approach*. Duke University Press, Durham, North Carolina
Rust V 1991 Postmodernism and its comparative education implications. *Comp. Educ. Rev.* 35: 610–26
Schrag F 1986 Education and historical materialism. *Interchange* 17(3): 42–52
Schultz T W 1989 Investing in people: Schooling in low income countries. *Econ. Educ. Rev.* 8(3): 219–40
Spindler G, Spindler L 1987 *Interpretive Ethnography of Education: At Home and Abroad*. Erlbaum, Hillsdale, New Jersey
Stromquist N P 1989 Determinants of educational achievement of women in the Third World: A review of the evidence and a theoretical critique. *Rev. Educ. Res.* 59(2): 143–83
Turner D A 1987 Problem solving in comparative education. *Compare* 17(1): 39–45
Von Recum H 1990 Erziehung in der Post-moderne. *Die Politische Meinung* 237: 76–93
Weiler H 1989 Why reforms fail: The politics of education in France and the Federal Republic of Germany. *J. Curric. Stud.* 21(4): 291–305
Weis L 1990 *Working Class without Work: High School Students in a De-industrializing Economy*. Routledge, New York
Welsh A R 1991 knowledge and legitimation. *Comp. Educ. Rev.* 35(3): 508–31

R. G. Paulston

Comparative Education and International Education: Organizations and Institutions

Research in international studies and comparative education will intensify during the 1990s and beyond as the "global village" becomes reality, and researchers and policymakers work together to apply theory, research, training, and policy to monitor schooling worldwide. Fulfilling tasks such as these have dominated the past work of Comparative International Education Organizations (CIEOs). In the light of shifting task environments, many international organizations are rethinking their long-term strategies better to promote education in the 1990s, since attaining the proper mix of theory, research, and policy is essential for educational development. In this entry a brief sketch of the workplace facing key CIEOs provides a context for understanding the history, scope, funding, and clients of, and the demands placed on, comparative education organizations. In addition, the organizational role played by universities, research institutes, and planning agencies is profiled, which when linked to tasks shows how institutions fulfill their overall purpose. Finally, an annotated description of 30 major educational organizations is presented in the above context to give the reader a sense of the variation found among international organizations working in education.

1. Universities as Paradigm Builders

Comparative education has always been fraught with great uncertainty and problems of coordination because education is full of competing paradigms practiced by millions of teachers around the world. Key universities and foundations have always been highly dependent on prominent faculty to safeguard their theories and guarantee prestige under extremely uncertain conditions and this has affected the way such organizations plan their work (see *Comparative and International Education: Paradigms and Theories*). Historically, universities have fulfilled the role of generating intellectual paradigms which explain educational behavior, by acting as a final point for academics to train a worldwide cadre of researchers, professors, and educational planners. While some universities emphasize theory over research, others stress policy and training. For example, comparative education departments at Chicago, Stockholm, and London have advocated theory with research, while universities such as Sussex in the United Kingdom, Liège in Belgium, and Ibadan in Nigeria have stressed theory with training. In all cases, the scientific strategy predominates as institutions give validation and recognition to the international education enterprise. To prosper in the 1990s, comparative education departments must influence educational policy, management, and data-collecting techniques by blending theory with practice.

2. Research and Information Institutes

Research and information pose less risk than theory building, especially when the methodologies and technologies that support analytical strategies are already known. However, close coordination is still required to manage information. Logically, those research institutes specializing in survey research endeavor to refine evaluation techniques while a few private institutes may simply conduct contract research for profit. Traditionally, methodologists, statisticians, and educators who enjoy the challenge of a good puzzle have been the driving force behind this educational research enterprise. Research and informatics institutes serve a practical role, by providing information to ministries (e.g., the *Deutsches Institut für Internationale Pädagogische Forschung* in Frankfurt, and the *Instituto Ajijc sobre Educación Internacional* [IASEI] in Mexico). They contract evaluation research for national agencies (e.g., the National Institute for Educational Research [NIER] in Japan, the Australian Council for Educational Research [ACER], the Centre International des Etudes Pedagogiques [CIEP] in France, the Centro Europeo dell' Educazione [CEDE] in Italy, etc.). While their main thrust is survey research, the orientation may be toward data collection, information generation designed for policy clients, or perfecting better technological procedures and information flow. In the 1990s these institutions must improve survey technology and data handling, while forging forward links to policymakers and support linkages to universities.

3. Education Policy-oriented Organizations

In the latter part of the twentieth century, international agencies such as the World Bank, UNESCO, OECD, major foundations, and bilateral donors (the Japanese Overseas Economic Cooperation Fund, IDRC in Canada, USAID in the United States, and NORAD in Scandinavia) including some ministries of education worldwide have promoted human resource development both at home and abroad. Since education is a key element in accomplishing this end, policy has always been aimed at promoting education and training among the world educational research and training community. A shift in policy emphasis toward administration/management has become apparent. This pursuit of quantity with quality is now the main aim of the major international policy organizations whose concern is with monitoring education (see *Educational Policy and Decision-making: Comparative Data*). Ministries of education sometimes fall within this category but major organizations such as the Spencer and Bertelsmann Foundations, or action groups like the International Testing Association and the International Reading Association also qualify. A range of non-governmental associations also provides information to the public (e.g., the International Association for the Evaluation of Educational Achievement, the World Association for Education Research, and The European Institute of Education and Social Policy).

Political roles often dominate in this sphere, as these organizations adopt central resource allocation, planning, and lobbying functions to influence education. When educational decision-making runs smoothly, there is little uncertainty and bureaucratic structures predominate. When policy decisions become uncertain, however, these organizations adopt a more cross-disciplinary strategy, to ensure that policy research does affect change. Essentially, without adequate research information and theory, policy and planning clients are condemned to subjective decision-making. Owing to rapid political change, many foundations and policymakers fund "action programs" rather than invest long-term in coordinated research which combines training, theory, policy, and informatics. In the future, these organizations will place greater reliance on sustained research planning while simultaneously drawing on new paradigms useful in solving educational problems.

4. *Integrating Functions and Roles*

Regardless of organizational affiliation, the 1990s must see international education organizations working more closely in consort to link policy, information, educational theory, and training, otherwise CIEOs will not contribute successfully to the next generation of comparative and international education ideas. Organizations concerned with the comparative international studies must determine goals before combining strategies. Although no organization can maintain control over its task environment indefinitely owing to leadership gaps, coordination problems, and rapidly changing technologies, collaboration among institutes may offer the best chance of maintaining an impact on comparative education in the long term. Most bilateral aid agencies and international foundations with strong policy or training missions already rely on universities to provide a theoretical base and train education staff. Government ministries, too, can contract out survey research to universities and research institutes when seeking answers to specific policy questions.

The following survey outlines the relationship between key elements of the international education industry by mapping the task boundaries in the early 1990s for major organizations that have made significant contributions in defining comparative and international education. Each organization treated below engages in various tasks, usually stressing one particular function above others. A profile of these tasks weighted by effort spent on research, theory, policy, or training, reveals the preferred strategy deployed by each institute in attempting to alter education.

5. *A Survey of Comparative Education Organizations*

Figure 1 presents the spatial arrangement found in the field of international comparative education summarized above. Organizations close to the periphery are in this position because certain task functions (e.g., policy, research etc.) predominate in their strategy. The figure highlights the world task environment faced by major international studies and comparative research organizations in the 1990s and beyond. Placement on this map is schematic rather than precise.

University of London Institute of Education. It is perhaps not surprising that the origins of comparative education may be traced to the University of London's Institute of Education, given its interest, beginning in the 1930s, in comparative European studies, followed in the 1960s by comparative research among Commonwealth nations. These included many Third World countries in Africa and on the Indian subcontinent. The Institute of Education was well-positioned both geographically and historically first to develop and then to export research paradigms linking comparative education to society at large (usually by thematic content such as social class, teacher education, politics of education, etc). Early graduates and lecturers went abroad schooled in comparative education, spreading the influence of the London Institute throughout North America, Asia, and Africa.

From its earliest years, the Institute attracted degree candidates from all over the world, who returned home to work in planning ministries and universities. In the areas of international development, the Institute cooperated with and influenced OECD, UNESCO, and the Council of Europe on a number of educational paradigms, published an influential *World Yearbook of Education* (until 1974), and helped form the Comparative Education Society of Europe in 1961, which in 1970 developed into the World Council of Educationalist Societies. Over time, the London Institute has developed and published research and theoretical paradigms which defined the field of comparative education, trained and educated comparative educationists, and influenced the educational thinking of OECD, UNESCO, and the Council of Europe. It continues this tradition in the 1990s (see *Comparative Education Societies*).

The Chicago Comparative Education Center. During the 1950s and 1960s, transatlantic international education was taught in universities at New York (Columbia Teachers' College), Pittsburgh (University of Pittsburgh International Studies Center), and Chicago. It was perhaps the University of Chicago which took the lead in 1957 with the formation of a comparative education center which blended a cross-national interdisciplinary approach (sociology, economics, and psychology) with the study of education and the social order. Although focusing initially on Europe and Africa, the center

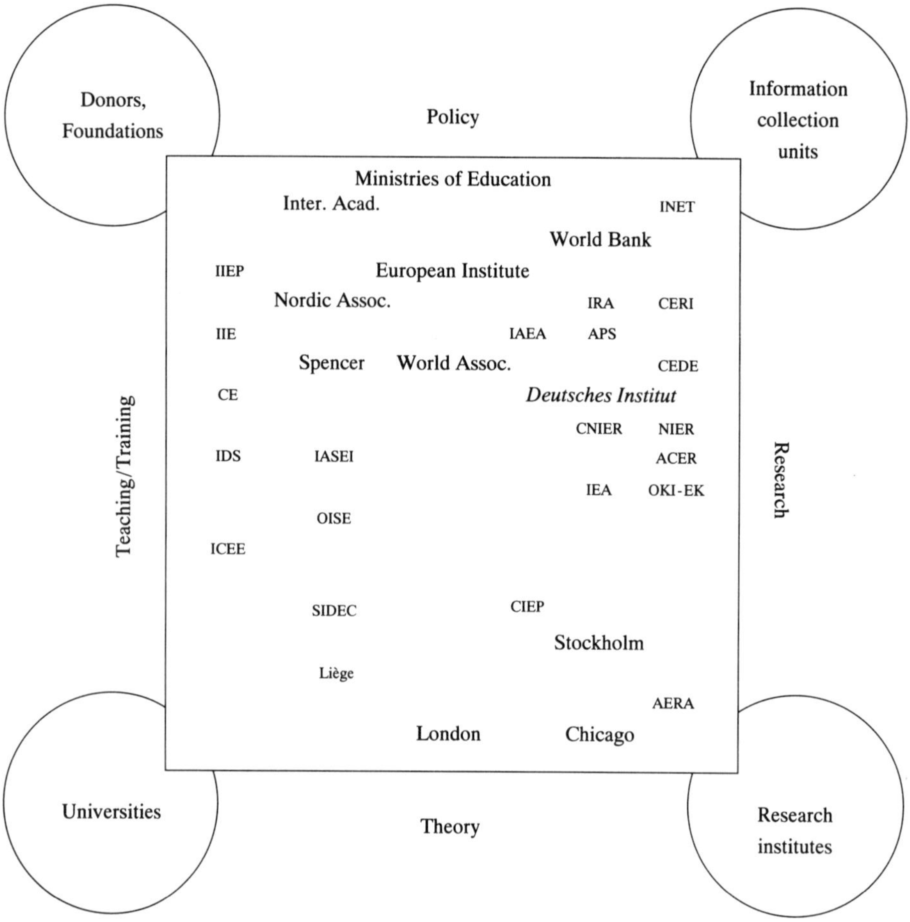

ACER: Australian Center for Educational Research
AERA: American Educational Research Association
APS: Academy of Pedagogical Sciences, Moscow
CEDE: *Centro Europeo Dell 'Educazione*, Rome
CERI: Center for Educational Research and Innovation, Paris
Chicago: University of Chicago, Comparative Education Center
CIEP: *Centre International d 'Etudes Pédagogique, Serves*, France
CNIER: Chinese National Institute for Educational Research, Beijing
CE: Council of Europe, Strasbourg
Deutsches Institut: *Deutsches Institut für Internationale Padagogische Forschung*, Frankfurt
European Institute: The European Institute of Education and Social Policy
IAEA: The International Association for Educational Assessment
IASEI: *Instituto Ajijc sobre Educación Internaciónal*, Mexico
ICEE: International Center for Educational Evaluation, Ibadan, Nigeria
IDS: Institute of Developmental Studies, University of Sussex
IEA: International Association for the Evaluation of Educational Achievement, The Netherlands
IIE: Institute of International Education, New York
IIEP: International Institute of Educational Planning, Paris
INET: International Networks in Education and Development, Michigan
Inter. Acad.: International Academy of Education
IRA: International Reading Association
Liège: *Laboratoire de Pédagogie Expérimentale*, University of Liège, Belgium
London: University of London Institute of Education
NIER: National Institute for Educational Research, Japan
Nordic Assoc.: Nordic Association for the Study of Education in Developing Countries, Oslo
OISE: Ontario Institute for Studies in Education, Toronto
OKI-EK: The Hungarian Center for Evaluation, Budapest
SIDEC: Stanford International Development Education Committee
Spencer: The Spencer Foundation, Chicago
Stockholm: The Institute of International Education, Stockholm
World Assoc.: World Association for Educational Research, Paris
World Bank: World Bank Education and Employment Division, Washington, DC

Figure 1
International education organizations in their task environment

later expanded to include the entire Third World. By diversifying away from African studies early on, the center was able to concentrate on universal themes of educational planning, development, and modernization. These themes influenced thinking about cognitive and noncognitive schooling outcomes and led to new perspectives on the way education altered society.

Chicago's major contribution combined economic decision theory in time allocation, equity/efficiency in school finance, and economic, sociological, and psychological perspectives of achievement performance among the world's student population using survey research methods including multivariate analysis. For example, the first large-scale mathematics achievement survey was carried out in 12 countries during the mid-1960s using computers, card sorters, and elementary programming at Chicago. The center developed quantitative research methodologies and, from the very outset, greatly influenced the field of United States comparative education during the period of expansion in the 1960s and 1970s. Given the cross-disciplinary approach in which graduates receive degrees in the social sciences rather than education per se, students of comparative education at Chicago draw on the university's overall subject discipline base, while the comparative education center focuses on linking theory to practice.

Institutionen för Internationell Pedagogik, Stockholm. The University of Stockholm's Institute of International Education (a graduate student institute), founded in 1971, played an important role in Europe in applying quantitative survey research of instruction, especially in the area of international curriculum. Stockholm undertook large-scale international survey data collection in school achievement during the early 1970s, and trained survey researchers in data processing and analysis. These researchers, with their new skills in hand, went on to staff the major institutions in Europe and the rest of the world. In the 1990s, the institute continues student surveys of academic achievement, and is involved in training and advancing structural-equations-modeling in comparative education and curriculum development.

The Stanford International Development Education Committee (SIDEC). This institution is part of the Stanford School of Education in California. Formally organized in 1965, this program stresses a social science approach to educational planning and policy-making, with a broad emphasis on both quantitative and qualitative (anthropology, political science) reporting. Its situation on the west coast of North America put the center in a favorable position to influence Asian and South American educational regions during their periods of high growth in the 1970s and 1980s. Since its inception, SIDEC has graduated a large number of competent comparative educationists who have had a major influence in shaping Third World thinking on the educational process.

Successful project fund-raising has enabled a steady investment in high-quality education and training in the field of education development at Stanford. Staff there have influenced and continue to influence the advancement of theory and practice in comparative education—especially policy research.

Laboratoire de Pédagogie Expérimentale, Liège. The University of Liège in Belgium has a long and influential history in the field of comparative education in Europe. In the 1960s and 1970s, the *Laboratoire de Pédagogie Expérimentale*, using empirical methods uncommon to Europe at that time, examined many issues of European comparative education including language learning and civics education. In the 1990s, the *Laboratoire de Pédagogie Expérimentale* is divided into a center for empirical educational research which has links to the post-Piagetian tradition of cognitive language learning, preprimary schooling, and teacher evaluation; a center for technology of education which examines school computer usage; and a center for the development and evaluation of educational programs. This latter center plays a key role in carrying out international studies and training in survey methods, and providing technical assistance to the World Bank in North and West Africa. Liège stresses research and training practice in addition to theory building.

The Institute of Developmental Studies (IDS). The Institute of Development Studies at the University of Sussex in England was organized in 1966 and has had an immense impact in training Third World educators and researchers, especially in the area of education and underdevelopment—poverty alleviation, rural development programs, and so on. Funded heavily by the British Government (Overseas Development Administration), along with tuition fees and contract research grants, the IDS blends intellectual pluralism with its training mission, in the hope of yielding innovative responses to poverty alleviation in Third World settings.

Typical research topics include: qualifications and selection in education systems; student orientations to learning; the transition from school to work; educational resource distribution; and adult learning. Educational programs consist mostly of short courses, although doctoral degrees can be granted through the University of Sussex. Stressing research for decision-making, IDS publishes *The Digest of Development Research* and is closely associated with the *International Journal of Educational Research*.

The Ontario Institute for Studies in Education (OISE). The Ontario Institute for Studies in Education was established in 1965 as an independent agency with university status, providing graduate-level education and training in conjunction with Canada's largest university, the University of Toronto. Closely linked to Canadian development assistance programs, OISE provides academic, computer, and quantitative data-handling expertise to governmental development assistance programs. With an annual research budget approaching US$10 million, interests in second language, computer-assisted instruction, and evaluation methodologies predominate.

The International Centre for Educational Evaluation (ICEE). Founded in 1957, this institute of the University of Ibadan, Nigeria, represents one of Africa's finest international education centers for teaching and conducting international research. With links to the United Kingdom, the ICEE administers examinations in affiliated institutions, conducts inservice educational training among Anglophone countries in the region, and provides graduate- and undergraduate-level training in research evaluation and methodology. The center also serves as an educational R&D consortium for West Africa and publishes the *West African Journal of Education*.

The education centers listed above represent key universities which influence trends in comparative and international education. These organizations are housed within universities, drawing on cross-disciplinary academic resources, which allow the integration of theory with research methodology, training, and policy. These universities engage in theory building and validation primarily through dissertation and faculty research. They serve a worldwide network of educational researchers working in ministries of education, international donor agencies, and information dissemination agencies. Some of these are examined below.

6. Autonomous Institutes of Educational Research Outside Universities

Key institutes of educational research have been established outside universities, either privately or by governments, to conduct experimental and large-scale empirical surveys. These institutes may have either a strong empirical research base, or a strong theoretical base. In the former case, they often collect data for ministries of education. In the latter case, data interpretation is also carried out, which requires university know-how using the latest educational theories and methods.

The Academy of Pedagogical Sciences (APS). Located in Moscow, the APS was created in 1967 and is fully funded by the national government to conduct research in pedagogy and educational psychology, and to collect information on schooling nationally. It reports all research findings to the Ministry of Education and teachers' societies. The Academy employs over 1,600 professional staff (with a budget of US$14 million in 1990), working in 15 research centers located mainly in Moscow. Moves toward decentralization in the former Soviet Union will undoubtedly affect the influence this organization has on education since the larger republics have their own state education academies. In 1990 the APS underwent major division into 15 departments covering theory and history of pedagogy, theory of methods, educational psychology, developmental physiology, special education, administration, preschool education, general secondary education, vocational education, informatics, teaching aids, aesthetic education, specialized education, adult education, and bilingualism. These divisions are responsible for disseminating all findings relating to education among government agencies, teachers, and parents.

International cooperation has focused mainly on Eastern European countries and UNESCO. In the early 1990s, APS has participated in collaborative research with Japan, the United States, the United Kingdom, Germany, Finland, the People's Republic of China, Canada, Norway, and Italy. The APS has participated in mathematics surveys with the international survey community and traditionally has managed experimental laboratory schools readily accessible to academy researchers. Drawing only on these laboratory schools, the APS has little experience in conducting large-scale survey sampling. Major journals published by the Academy, as well as textbooks and educational brochures for teachers and parents, include *Sovietskaja Pedagogika*, *Kvant*, and *Voprosy Psikhologii*.

Centre International d'Etudes Pédagogiques Sèvres (CIEP). Located in Paris, CIEP was founded in 1945 to train internationally qualified teachers in the French language, and conceptualize, conduct, and disseminate survey research on educational innovations. The center is a state institution attached to the National Ministry of Education. Its four major functions are: (a) research in French as a foreign language, (b) comparative research on evaluation of educational systems, (c) training French foreign language teachers, and (d) hosting meetings on comparative education.

These CIEP functions interrelate well because in the process of bringing together teachers, educators, researchers, and educational administrators from various organizations around the world, creative educational dialogue about French language training methods, teaching, and other academic disciplines is enhanced, resulting in a close relationship between theory and educational need.

The Center publishes *Dossiers de Sèvres*, *Echos*, and the review *Amis de Sèvres*. It provides documentation services for a number of national systems of education designed to facilitate comparative approaches. It is involved in cooperation with the province of Quebec, Canada, the United States, Belgium, Germany, and several North and West African countries. Within France, the CIEP conducts survey research in reading literacy, mathematics, and computers in education. It provides an interesting blend of large-scale empirical research with curriculum and policy analysis.

The Hungarian Center for Evaluation (OKI-EK). The Hungarian Center for Evaluation, in Budapest, is a semi-independent unit of the Hungarian National Institute of Public Education, financed mainly by the Ministry of Education. The Center develops new national core curricula and examinations, carries out national achievement surveys, conducts research in pedagogical instruction, curriculum research, and evaluation, and publishes series in curriculum history and theory.

The Center for Evaluation has participated in Western-style positivist–empirical research since the early 1970s, despite political and ideological constraints. Institutes in Poland and Romania also attempted such research at various times but were not successful. The Center for Evaluation has prided itself on adapting methodological innovations devised worldwide to all kinds of educational assessment in Hungary. The Center has used these international paradigms to conduct national surveys which have set benchmarks for mathematics, science, and language learning. Survey findings indicate that the Hungarian system attains high levels of achievement, by international standards, in mathematics and science but not in reading and language learning. The Center for Evaluation is one of the few institutions in the world which has tested empirically a wide range of education programs over two decades using international benchmarks. It continues to carry out surveys and is moving to assist its neighboring countries in developing similar educational research skills.

Deutsches Institut für Internationale Pädagogische Forschung. The German Institute for International Educational Research was founded by the State of Hesse in 1951 in Frankfurt am Main, Germany, to engage in empirical research in school organization, curriculum development, and educational planning, with the intention of submitting all research findings to the German Federal Ministry of Education. In 1964 the institute was restructured into a full-time research institution and given the legal status of an independent foundation, while retaining government funding.

Over time, the institute's international perspective has shifted from Western Europe and North America to Eastern Europe and the Third World. Since comparative education is not its primary focus, the institute also engages in contact with organizations around the world studying the history of education, vocational education, special education, economic development, test construction, educational statistics, and data processing. Consequently, educational research projects may fall in any of these categories, whether or not the comparative aspect is accentuated.

The institute advises the European Community, the Council of Europe, UNESCO, and OECD on educational matters by providing information exchange. The institute's journal, *Zeitschrift für Erziehungs- und Sozialwissenschaftliche Forschung*, is published biannually along with a number of scholarly books and journal articles. The *Deutsches Institut* stresses practical empirical research over theory-based studies.

Japanese National Institute for Educational Research (NIER). The NIER, located in Tokyo, was established in 1948 as a branch of the Ministry of Education, Science and Culture. It expanded in the 1960s on two fronts: research capacity was expanded dramatically to conduct scientific and practical research in education, and international involvement with UNESCO was broadened to exchange information and personnel. In 1967, NIER inaugurated its regional program with UNESCO for the enhancement of educational research activities (seminars, workshops, etc.) in Asia. This led to the Academic Program of Educational Innovation for Development (APEID) in the 1970s, to which Japan made a major contribution.

Research at NIER, whose budget exceeded US$7 million in 1990, is undertaken in the areas of educational philosophy/history, and higher education; educational planning; measurement; guidance/counseling; infant education; school curriculum; comparative studies; teaching methods; and content of science and mathematics. The NIER publishes regularly in Japanese with occasional English language reports. It has participated in international survey research since the early 1960s, and in the 1990s routinely tests in mathematics, science, and computer studies.

The Australian Council for Educational Research (ACER). The Australian Council for Educational Research (ACER), an independent nongovernmental organization located in Hawthorn, Victoria, is financed by grants and research contracts from the Commonwealth and State Departments of Education, private sector grants, and the sale of educational and psychological tests, books, and other educational materials. The Council was started in 1930, and by 1990 professional research staff exceeded 50, with an annual budget of US$2.7 million. Essentially, the function of ACER is to develop its own research and development program in Australian education including training research methodologists and disseminating results. Well-known ACER publications include the *Australian Journal of Education* as well as reports on literacy and numeracy and school-achievement monitoring studies in mathematics and science, and the transition from school to work. The Council is engaged in international mathematics and science surveys.

Instituto Ajijc sobre Educatión Internacional (IASEI). The ISAEI is a private, nonprofit international organization, instituted in 1978, and affiliated to the Autonomous University of Guadalajara, Mexico. The institute explores higher education issues in a comparative framework. It focuses on Latin American issues; the organization conducts and then publishes its research results internationally in journals such as *Docencia-Postsecundaria*, published in Guadalajara. Topics addressed include higher education and scientific research, education and employment, and international cooperation. The advisory council to IASEI includes many well-known educators from around the world.

The Chinese National Institute for Educational Research (CNIER). The CNIER, situated in Beijing, was reconstituted in 1978 after the Cultural Revolution as a comprehensive educational research institution affiliated with the Chinese Ministry of Education. The institute undertakes research and studies on major theoretical and practical educational issues in China to render policy decision-making for educational reform consistent with a strong modernization drive. With a staff of over 250 researchers, the CNIER is conducting studies in preprimary education, computers in education, and science curriculum development. It serves a ministry of education which is responsible for over 400 million school children.

Centro Europeo Dell'Educazione (CEDE). The European Centre for Education (CEDE) is located at Villa Falconieri, outside Rome. The institute was organized in 1960 as one of several didactic centers in Italy and is associated with the University of Rome ("*La Sapienza*"), and four other Italian universities. These offer research doctorates in the field of experimental pedagogy including survey methodology, to which CEDE researchers lend guidance and support. About 50 professors and teachers are chosen nationally to work at CEDE (though they keep their tenure in the state school system). The institutional aims of CEDE, as set out in 1974, include collecting, elaborating, and disseminating Italian and foreign (mostly European) educational documentation through comparative studies and research. Organized around departments which carry out research on programming costs, education and employment, learning processes, educational innovation and inservice training, and use of educational technology, CEDE departments act in consort when carrying out international large-scale research projects.

With a budget of over US$1.5 million in 1991, CEDE advises UNESCO, OECD, the Council of Europe, and the European Economic Community on educational matters. In addition, the Italian Comparative Education Society is located at CEDE. Included among national research projects underway in schools in the early 1990s are studies in the teaching of Italian and foreign literature, computers in schools, and contemporary art. International survey participation by CEDE is also extensive: preprimary childcare, written composition, and mathematics and science through IEA; CERI international activities in the school environment initiatives project; and the Youth in Europe project organized jointly with the Italian Comparative Education Society. Many conference papers and reports are published in the *Quaderni di villa Falconieri*, as well as the institution's quarterly review, *Ricerca Educativa*, published by La Nuova Italia in Florence, Italy, where articles appear in Italian, French, or English with abstracts in all languages.

7. Associations and Nongovernmental Organizations (NGOs)

In addition to univerisities and research institutes, there are a host of associations and NGOs that collect, process, and disseminate data to both policymakers and universities, and that provide training in educational research and policy-making.

International Reading Association (IRA). The International Reading Association is a service organization of over 80,000 teachers and institutions dedicated to the improvement of reading instruction worldwide. In promoting reading, the association publishes a newspaper, articles, and books including *The Reading Research Quarterly*, *The Reading Teacher*, *Journal of Reading*, and *Lectura y Vida*, which is a Spanish-language journal of reading. The organization is typical of large-scale interest groups which lobby on behalf of teachers favoring the support of reading. The association sponsors an annual convention and a world congress every 2 years, and is developing a network of national reading associations in Europe.

The International Association for Educational Assessment (IAEA). Founded in 1974 at Princeton, New Jersey, as an association of measurement agencies, the IAEA is responsible for disseminating information on educational assessment. The objectives specified in the organization's bylaws include providing readily available expertise in assessment techniques, while engaging in activities leading to the improvement and use of assessment techniques. Membership of IAEA is institutional and includes over 80 measurement agencies around the world. Annual conferences are held in rotation among geographical regions. In 1991, Nairobi in Kenya was the venue for the meeting. The organization has produced *A Teacher's Guide to Assessment*, carried out a higher education survey for UNESCO and training workshops for the World Bank, and developed prototypes of International Tests of Developed Abilities in several languages useful for college students contemplating study abroad.

World Association for Educational Research. In 1977, the former International Association for the Advancement of Educational Research was renamed The World Association for Educational Research (*Association Mondiale des Sciences de l'Education*). The organization's secretariat is located at the University of Ghent in Belgium, within the *Seminarie en Laboratorium voor Experimentele Psychologische en Sociale Pedagogiek*. The aim of this nonprofit association is to foster the development of high-quality international educational research through exchange of information and dissemination of research studies. Membership of the association is open to university professors and others who engage in educational research. The organization holds congresses every 4 years and publishes *Communications* twice a year as part of the *International Journal of Experimental Research in Education* (see *International Education; UNESCO and Adult Education*).

The Nordic Association for Study of Education in Developing Countries. The Nordic Association was created at the University of Oslo in the early 1980s. This association encourages exchange experiences among students and institutions through the promotion of North–South dialogue and serves as an intellectual stimulus to student researchers as well as a contact point with Nordic donor agencies. Topics on educational planning, universities, and national development are held periodically and symposium papers are published annually in an attempt to improve teaching and research in Third World and Nordic universities (see *Education and Development*).

International Networks in Education and Development (INET). The International Networks in Education and Development (INET) is a resource center located at Michigan State University which facilitates collaboration among educators interested in international development. It fulfills its mission by maintaining a library of research reports for exchange worldwide. It also collaborates with other universities to write proposals and administer international research projects. Linkages exist between Michigan and universities in countries including China, Pakistan, Thailand, and Zimbabwe.

The International Academy of Education. The International Academy was founded in 1986 as a nonprofit scientific association in Brussels with a coordinating office in Hamburg, Germany. The academy promotes cooperation and exchange in assessing and reviewing educational research in Europe and the Third World. It does so by commisioning state-of-the-art reports, forming task forces to review and synthesize research for decision-making, and holding seminars. Membership of the academy is restricted to individuals who conduct scholarly work in international research.

The Institute of International Education (IIE). The IIE in New York City had its origins in the internationalism of the 1920s under the presidency of Woodrow Wilson, and since 1950 has served to administer programs and training grants to foreign students studying in the United States. In addition, the institute produces statistical data on the flow of foreign students into the United States and addresses policy-related issues concerning this flow. The center has designed training programs for individuals from developing countries along with administering grant programs on behalf of foundations and government aid programs, totaling over US$100 million each year.

The European Institute of Education and Social Policy. The European Institute was renamed in 1982 having originally been founded in 1975 in cooperation with the European Commission, Brussels, the International Council for Educational Development in New York, and the European Cultural Foundation of Amsterdam. The policy institute, headquartered at the *Université de Paris* with offices in Brussels, is underwritten by means of grant assistance and contract research with the aforementioned founders. With full-time staff and consultants, the policy institute examines issues associated with post-secondary schooling and employment in Europe. Typical topics include student mobility in Europe and European educational cooperation through the EC. The institute currently operates grant assistance for joint study programs throughout the EC. Its official academic quarterly is *The European Journal of Education*.

Council of Europe. Instituted in 1949, the Council of Europe, located in Strasbourg, France consists of over 25 member states within and around Europe which cooperate on a number of social and economic issues. Since 1976, the Council of Cultural Cooperation (CDCC) within the Council of Europe has established aims for its international programs in education and culture. These include: (a) educational projects such as improved language teaching, or adult education across Europe; (b) educational conferences and publications on practical studies; (c) public services such as scholarship and exchange programs, exhibits, and so on; and (d) education and programs in support of human rights, migrant workers, youth employment, and so on.

From year to year, council members debate a wide range of educational topics affecting Europe, then projects are decided upon and funded nationally with international overheads for meetings, publications, and so on. Research is applied rather than theoretical, and process-oriented instead of focused on organization and outcomes. The Council of Europe publishes and administers the database EUDISED (European Documentation Information System in Education).

The Centre for Educational Research and Innovation (CERI). Formally organized in 1971 within the Organisation for Economic Co-operation and Development (OECD) in Paris, CERI's work is designed to support educational research among OECD member states, promote pilot programs to test innovations in education, and in general build consensus among the 24 industrialized countries' education systems. Research is carried out by members of the OECD Secretariat according to the dictates of a governing board. Within this framework, CERI undertakes projects of several years' duration. A major CERI project is concerned with developing science and technology indicators in education for member states.

One product of that project is *A Handbook on International Educational Indicators*. The organization is effective in mobilizing consensus building among government educational research institutes within OECD countries (see *Organisation for Economic Co-operation and Development (OECD): Educational Activities*).

The World Bank Education and Employment Division. Situated in Washington DC, the World Bank Education and Employment Division is an internal unit within the World Bank which helps to write education sector policy and disseminate educational information to staff within the regions, and conduct research—both original and secondary analysis—on topics central to bank lending. This division is expanding its role in international education by developing capacity building through empirical research training aimed at educational research centers around the world.

The International Association for the Evaluation of Educational Achievement (IEA). The IEA was founded in 1959 in Stockholm. The organization has its Secretariat in The Hague. Membership of IEA is restricted to ministries of education and universities and educational research institutes which carry out survey research and represent educational systems around the world. Activities are paid for with funds from membership, grants, and contract research. In 1992 the IEA international budget reached US$3.3 million.

Since the 1960s IEA has carried out large-scale curriculum-based survey research at the primary and secondary school level in over 60 countries around the world. Topics include mathematics, science, reading literacy, and foreign languages. Each involves worldwide samples exceeding 250,000 students, 10,000 teachers, and thousands of schools (see *Educational Achievement: Comparative Studies*). Research employs highly empirical sampling, test and questionnaire construction, and data collection, processing, and analysis at the national level which leads to reports interpretable in the context of worldwide achievement norms. The testing is diagnostic. The organization holds its general assembly annually and publishes scholarly volumes through Pergamon Press in the United Kingdom. It combines descriptive with explanatory analysis and theory and methodology with policy, all suggesting how systems work best under differing conditions.

See also: International Education; Organisation for Economic Co-operation and Development *(OECD):* Educational Activities

Bibliography

Ayres R 1983 *Banking on the Poor: The World Bank and World Poverty.* MIT Press, Cambridge, Massachusetts
Cowen R 1987 *International Directory of Research Institutions on Higher Education*, 2nd edn. UNESCO, Paris
Debeauvais M 1990 *National Educational Research Policies: A World Survey.* UNESCO, Paris
Hodson H V (ed.) 1986 *The International Foundation Directory*, 4th rev. edn. Europa, London
Huczynski A 1987 *Encyclopedia of Organizational Change Methods.* Gower, Adershot
Lehming R (ed.) 1982 *Directory of Research Organizations in Education.* Far West Laboratory for Educational Research, San Francisco, California
Ronnen S 1986 *Comparative and Multinational Management.* Wiley, New York
UNDP/UNICEF/UNESCO/World Bank 1990 *World Declaration on Education for All* and *Framework for Action to Meet Basic Learning Needs.* UNDP/UNICEF/UNESCO/ World Bank, Paris
UNESCO 1987 *Directory of Educational Research Institutions.* International Bureau of Education, UNESCO, Paris
Union of International Associations 1991 *Yearbook of International Organizations 1991/92: Organization Descriptions and Index*, 28th edn. K G Saur, Munich

W. Loxley

Comparative Education Societies

Academic and professional societies in comparative education have played a major role in allowing scholars access to each other's work and in promoting educational exchanges of students and teachers among various countries. The founding of these societies, their goals, the composition of their membership, their financial support base, conferences, and thematic concerns are discussed here. The major emphasis is on the Comparative and International

Education Society (CIES), founded in the United States, the Comparative Education Society in Europe, and the World Council of Comparative Education Societies. Information where available is also given on various national societies (see *Comparative and International Education: Overview and Historical Development*).

1. Comparative and International Education Society

The oldest professional scholarly organization in comparative education in the modern era was founded as the Comparative Education Society in New York in 1956, the outcome of a series of annual conferences organized by William Brickman and Gerald Read at the School of Education of New York University. The objectives of the Society were "to encourage scholarly research in comparative and international studies in education . . . to promote intervisitation of educators and on-the-spot studies of education throughout the world . . . to facilitate the publication of studies and up-to-date information on comparative education" (Brickman 1985 p. 852).

Since its inception, the purpose of the Society has been neatly circumscribed in the words of its constitution, namely to "promote teaching and research in comparative education and international studies in institutions of higher learning; promote the study of education as a phase of the work of other comparative and international disciplines, area studies, and centers of international studies; and facilitate publication and distribution of comparative, cross-cultural, interdisciplinary, and international studies contributing to interpretation of developments in the field of education in their broad and interrelated political, economic, and social context; and encourage exchanges and other visits by educators" (Comparative and International Education Society 1990).

The CIES is composed of individual members who pay an annual membership fee which entitles them to receive the *CIES Newsletter* and the Society's journal, *The Comparative Education Review*, and to participate in the business and scholarly work of the Society, both at the annual conferences and the regional meetings. Although it is based in the United States, the Society is open to members worldwide. In 1991, there were 974 individual subscribers to the *Comparative Education Review* (707 from the US and 267 from other countries). In the institutional category, there were 1,327 subscribers (735 US and 592 from other countries), mainly libraries (Epstein 1992). Income from memberships, special issues of the journal, and conference registration, as well as financial and other forms of support from academic and other institutions enable the Society to maintain a relatively healthy financial state. The eminence of the *Comparative Education Review* is without doubt an attraction for scholars to join the Society. While its earlier focus tended toward the study of formal school systems, with contributions from those who regarded themselves as educationists, more recent issues have reflected the more eclectic, multidisciplinary membership of the Society and have grappled with some of the theoretical debates and current issues in the field which are of interest to a wider audience than simply educators.

It is customary for CIES vice-presidents to be elected for a four-year term, progressing through the offices of president-elect (in which year it is their responsibility to organize the annual conference), president, and immediate past president. The other terms of elected office are for three years. The editor of the *Comparative Education Review* and the secretary are appointed by the board after proposals have been reviewed from various institutions in an open bidding process. Support from the host institution is considered to be an important element in the success of proposals. The Society is a registered charitable organization under United States law, but there is no legal obligation for the secretariat to be based in any particular location in the United States.

The Society has held annual conferences since its inception on a variety of themes which have usually provided a general focus for the conference, but which do not limit the acceptance of other proposals. The themes generally reflect the interests of the Organizing Committee and the President-Elect. The conferences are organized as a series of separate workshops or panels on any number of topics, some of which may be linked together conceptually by their organizers. There is, therefore, a very eclectic mix of many topics at any single conference. Conferences are held annually, most commonly in the United States, but several have also been held in Canada, one in Mexico City, and one in Kingston, Jamaica. One of the most notable conferences took place in Toronto in 1986 on the occasion of the thirtieth anniversary of the founding of the Society. This conference attracted an unusually large attendance and expanded the scope of future CIES conferences.

Typically midway between annual meetings, the Society also holds regional meetings which are arranged by CIES members in the various regions of the United States. Although there are no separate regional associations of CIES, these meetings have provided an opportunity for students and colleagues from a particular area to participate in a smaller forum. In the Western region, colleagues have met to collaborate in the production of books on topics of common interest, for example, human rights (see Tarrow 1987), and education's role in national development plans (see Thomas 1992). The working language of all CIES meetings is English.

In the years since its inception, the CIES has attracted scholars from a wide range of disciplines, but there have been some discernible shifts in the characteristics and interests of the members (see *Comparative and International Education: Overview and Historical Development; Comparative and International Education: Paradigms and Theories*). In the early years, members were heavily representative of the social foundations of education and international educational interests. Later, they tended to have more specialized training in various academic disciplines, such as sociology, anthropology, political science, or economics, and were primarily based in university departments. A trend in the 1980s was for increasing numbers of members, although still a minority, to be based in the private sector, in small and large educational consulting firms, or in major aid and financial agencies. The impact of this shift on the character of debate and the nature of the Society's activities remains to be seen.

The CIES has formal contacts with other professional organizations in the United States which are involved in aspects of educational research, teacher education, and global education. Furthermore, its members have been consulted in an advisory role by governments and international agencies, both in the United States and elsewhere. It is also a founding member of the World Council of Comparative Education Societies.

2. The Comparative Education Society in Europe

The founding of the Comparative Education Society in Europe (CESE) took place in 1961 in London, during a meeting organized by Professor Joseph Lauwerys (1902–81) at the University of London Institute of Education. Nearly 60 people were present, from 12 European countries and 3 non-European countries (see *European Community: Educational Goals and Plans*).

The first constitution of the CESE was adapted from the CIES constitution and accepted by the general assembly of the first CESE conference in Amsterdam in 1963. When the CESE secretariat moved from London to Belgium in 1978, the statutes were altered to accord with Belgian law. The legal status of the CESE was granted and its statutes approved by royal decree of King Baudouin of Belgium in 1980.

The purpose of the CESE is to "encourage and promote comparative and international studies in education by: promoting and improving the teaching of comparative education in institutions of higher learning; stimulating research; facilitating the publication and distribution of comparative studies in education; interesting professors and teachers of other disciplines in the comparative and international dimensions of their work; encouraging visits by educators to study educational institutions and systems throughout the world; cooperating with those who in other disciplines attempt to interpret educational developments in a broad cultural context; and organizing conferences and meetings" (CESE *Statutes* 1980). It also works with other comparative education societies to further international action in this field. It is a founding member of the World Council of Comparative Education Societies.

The general assembly of the CESE meets at least once every two years and elects the members of the executive committee. The term of office is two years, renewable once. The executive committee is composed of the president, the immediate past president, two vice-presidents, and two members. The secretary general is appointed annually by the executive committee.

Membership of the CESE is open to individuals who are nominated by two existing members, and whose application is ratified by the executive committee. Members of the CESE are academics who teach comparative education in institutions of higher learning, and persons concerned with comparative and international education or related areas in educational agencies and organizations. Membership is not limited to Europeans, and the members are drawn from several continents. Revenue is derived primarily from memberships, conferences, and support from educational institutions and agencies. The CESE publishes the *CESE Newsletter* and proceedings of CESE conferences.

In various countries of Europe, sections of the CESE have been established, some of which later became independent societies during the 1970s; for example, the British Comparative and International Education Society, the *Association francophone d'éducation comparée* (AFEC), the *Nederlandstalig gezelschap voor de vergelijkende studie van onderwijs en opvoeding* (NGVO), and the *Sociedad Española de Pedagogía Comparada*. The German comparativists have a commission for comparative education which is part of the German Society for Educational Sciences and remains a section of the CESE. In the 1980s an Italian section was formed. These sections of the CESE have their own annual meetings, but for the smaller societies, the biannual CESE conference is the main opportunity to meet. Some societies, such as AFEC, hold working meetings on themes to prepare their members for the CESE meetings.

The CESE has tried to establish and maintain contacts with colleagues in Eastern Europe. For example, the fourth CESE conference held in Prague in 1969 was organized by Professor S Singule of Charles University, who, just before his death in 1991, was engaged in organizing the eighth World Congress of Comparative Education in Prague. The world congress is held usually every three years, sponsored by the World Council of Comparative Education Societies and hosted by an individual member society. Various other groups of comparative educators and social scientists in countries formerly considered to be in Central and Eastern

Europe are now in the process of organizing their societies. New organizations are at an embryonic stage in several other countries in Europe (Portugal, Greece, Poland, the Scandinavian countries, Hungary, and Bulgaria).

Conferences have been held every two years since the founding of the CESE in major cities throughout Europe. The working languages of the CESE are English, French, and German. When conferences are held elsewhere, the language of the host country is added (Italian, Hungarian, and Spanish).

The organization of CESE conferences has always been more structured than the American model. When conference themes are announced, several commissions are formed, each of which treats an aspect or a subtheme. Commission chairs solicit papers for their commissions, or proposals may be submitted for approval. These commissions form the basic structure of the conference; and the proceedings are recorded during the sessions and presented in summary form at the concluding plenary session. Themes of past conferences have included such topics as policy development, teacher education, educational reforms, school and community, and the field of comparative education itself.

A particular role is played by the CESE in the development of the European dimension in education. It has individual members in all parts of Europe, and its executive committee has members from various national and linguistic backgrounds. Its conferences are held throughout Europe, and several of its members have served the Council of Europe or the European Community as consultants or experts.

3. The World Council of Comparative Education Societies

The seeds of the idea for the World Council of Comparative Education Societies lay in the vision of Joseph Katz of Canada who conceived the idea of International Education Year in 1960. The idea was supported by the officers of CIES, members of the Phi Delta Kappa Commission on International Relations in Education, the staff of the Canadian National Commission for UNESCO, and the comparative education experts at the UNESCO Institute in Hamburg. In 1967, UNESCO declared 1970 to be International Education Year (Read 1985).

Katz was also the driving force behind the founding of the Comparative and International Society of Canada in 1967. It hosted the first World Congress of Comparative Education at the University of Ottawa in 1970. To continue the impetus of the International Education Year, the International Planning Committee for the congress was renamed the World Council of Comparative Education Societies (WCCES). It was made up of representatives from the Comparative and International Education Society of Canada, the Comparative Education Society in Europe, the Japan Comparative Education Society, the Korean Comparative Education Society, and the Comparative and International Education Society of the United States.

In 1971, the WCCES met at the UNESCO Institute of Education in Hamburg. Since no funding for a secretariat could be secured from the founding societies, it was agreed to house the secretariat at the Palais Wilson in Geneva, at the International Bureau of Education. A newsletter was produced during this period, but the financial base was not supported by subscriptions from member societies.

In 1973, the WCCES was given ad hoc consultative status within UNESCO as a nongovernmental organization, category C. In 1991, this status was upgraded to category B. The relationship with UNESCO has meant that the WCCES has been invited to various consultations with members of other international educational organizations and has been involved in a number of research projects supported by UNESCO, most notably the project on national educational research policies conducted during the period 1983–87 (Debeauvais 1990). The World Council was also represented on the steering committee of the World Conference on Education for All held in Jomtien, Thailand in March 1990.

The draft statutes of the World Council were drawn up and adopted in 1972 and entered into force in 1974. A revised version was adopted and came into force in 1984. The legal status of the World Council is that of "an international non-governmental organization representing at international level the duly constituted societies and groups of comparative educationists which are accepted as members in accordance with the by-laws" (WCCES *Statutes* 1984). In this respect, its structure is unlike that of any of the other member organizations. It is a society comprised of societies, although ongoing attempts are being made to establish an associated group of individual members from countries where formally organized societies do not exist.

Since membership is open to formally constituted societies which apply for membership, the process of adding to the total is slow, but the number has grown substantially. In 1992, about 25 societies from every continent were members of the World Council. The participation of countries of the southern hemisphere is less than that of countries in the northern hemisphere, a feature that has been noted with great regret by several members. The reason for this is the lack of financial assistance which the World Council can provide for travel expenses, the absence of a comparative education focus at many institutions of higher education, and the scattered geographical dispersal of comparative educationists. A membership levy and annual dues of US $200 were requested from societies, but problems of currency exchange and transfer prevented many countries from making any subscription. The World Council has also received funds from educational institutions, from governments of countries which hosted world congresses, and from UNESCO. World congresses have, in some cases, generated cash reserves which have assisted the work of the Council until the next congress. However, the general picture for the World Council is one of financial stringency, and a great deal of invisible support which does not translate into fiscal reserves or financial liquidity.

The goals of the World Council are expressed as follows: "to advance education for international understanding in the interests of peace, intercultural co-operation, mutual respect among peoples and observance of human rights; and to improve education systems so that the right to education may be more fully realised" (WCCES *Statutes* 1984). The specific professional aims of the World Council are: "to promote the study of comparative and international education throughout the world and enhance the academic status of this field; and to bring comparative education to bear on the major educational problems of the day by fostering co-operative action by specialists from different parts of the world" (WCCES *Statutes* 1984). The specific activities by which the World Council is to achieve these aims are very similar in scope to those outlined for the CIES and the CESE with the exception that it works specifically at encouraging the formation of new societies of comparative educationists.

The structure of the World Council is based on an executive committee consisting of the president, a vice-president or vice-presidents, the secretary general, representatives of constituent societies, other members, (such as chairs of commissions), and coopted nonvoting members. It normally meets once a year and is empowered to delegate its work to a bureau consisting of the president, the secretary general, and at least two other members appointed by the executive committee.

The history of the various world congresses, which the Council has sponsored, and their themes reflect most clearly the interests and concerns of its members. From an earlier focus on fairly specific and Eurocentric topics such as the secondary school (1974), the themes have broadened to more global concerns such as the effect of the world economic crisis in 1987.

After the founding congress in Ottawa in 1970, the second congress was held in Geneva in 1974, with the theme "Efficiencies and Inefficiencies in Secondary Schools." Organization of world congresses at that time followed the European model, with papers being closely linked to the theme, and commissions being established as part of the structure of the congress.

By 1975, the membership of the Council had grown to nine, with the addition of representatives from Australia and New Zealand, France, the Netherlands, and Spain. The third world congress met in London in 1977, with the theme "Unity and Diversity in Education." Approximately 350 people from 40 countries participated.

At that congress, the decision was taken to hold the fourth world congress in Japan in 1980, and the secretariat was moved to Tokyo. Because of the willingness of the Korean Comparative Education Society to share responsibilities as host, there was a pre-congress held in Seoul which was attended by some 220 scholars and teachers from 35 countries. The congress in Tokyo was attended by about 465 people from the same number of countries (Epstein 1981 p. 262).

Clearly, interest in comparative and international education had grown throughout the 1970s. However, the World Council was still a federation of societies and was not financially supported by individual members. After the fourth world congress, its fiscal state was enhanced by revenue from the congress.

By the 1980s, the organization of congresses by the World Council had become a far more complex affair, not least of all due to the large increase in attendance numbers since the founding years. The scale of world congresses was altogether larger, and the necessity for liaison among societies and communication with individual scholars was increasing. Various other member societies were admitted during the 1980s: Argentina, the United Kingdom, Colombia, the People's Republic of China, the Federal Republic of Germany, India, Egypt, the London Association of Comparative Education (LACE), Nigeria, Italy, and Brazil. In the early 1990s, colleagues from the former Soviet Union were admitted, as well as those from the Czech and Slovak Federal Republic (their society had existed in one form or another for over 30 years), the Chinese Comparative Education Society–Taipei, Hong Kong, and Bulgaria. Several other countries were in the process of preparing their membership applications.

The fifth world congress was originally scheduled to be held in Monterey, Mexico, in 1983. However, several organizational problems led to the cancellation of plans to hold it at this venue, and it was held instead in 1984 in Paris, hosted by the *Association francophone d'éducation comparée.*

The sixth world congress was held in Rio de Janeiro, with the theme "Education, Crisis, and Change." This was the first time a world congress had been held in the southern hemisphere, and it was an outstanding success. At the Rio congress, it was decided that the seventh world congress would be held in 1989 in Montreal (the two hundredth anniversary of the Declaration of "Les droits de l'homme"). The theme was "Development, Communication, and language."

The organizational model of the seventh world congress in Montreal was a synthesis of the European tradition of commissions and the North American "free market" of workshops. It was held in July 1989, and attracted even greater numbers than previous congresses.

The major question at issue was whether it would be possible to hold the 1991 congress in Beijing in the light of the violent suppression of the student demonstration in Tiananmen Square, which had taken place only a few weeks prior to the 1989 congress. It was decided to defer a decision to the following year in Madrid, where it was resolved to hold the eighth world congress in Prague in 1992, and the ninth world congress in Beijing in 1995. The eighth world congress in Prague had as its theme "Education, Democracy, and Development."

Thus the history of the World Council demonstrates both the increasing complexity of its own organization and the impact of external events on its development. With the fragmentation of power blocs, there will be a proliferation of national societies. However, there are also centripetal forces in all of the large societies which draw members from small countries toward some of the larger groups. There is still a North–South divide which has not been adequately bridged, and the East–West relationship continues to create complexities. The relationship of the World Council to UNESCO will remain affected by developments in the world and in the role of the large aid agencies and financial institutions.

4. Conclusion

It is a testament to the commitment of many of those in the three organizations described in this entry that they have managed to build up a voluntary network of scholars and teachers who have been able to record great achievements in the field of comparative education between the 1950s and the 1990s.

The success of these societies has probably been most marked in the enhancement of possibilities for scholars to meet and share their work. There is now a regular "circuit" of meetings held every one, two, or three years, attended by a growing network of scholars, consultants, and educationists. Another success is in the nature of the development of comparative education as a field. It has brought together scholars from many diverse disciplines, who may all be interested in one geographical area or a particular theoretical approach. The societies have also assembled those with often divergent opinions, and have provided international forums for discussion on some of the major contemporary theoretical and practice-related issues.

In terms of publications, these societies have had mixed success. The CIES has succeeded in supporting a journal for its subscribers, financed by fees and by the support of the institutions at which the editors are employed. The international societies are not able to provide this service because of their membership structure, in which individual members do not provide a financial base, and because of the difficulty of finding institutional support. They have published proceedings from their conferences, and their members publish in various independent journals of comparative education.

In the relationship between the world of theory and the world of practice, these societies have produced some strong links. There has been an ongoing interest in teacher and student exchange programs and in the role of overseas students and overseas training programs among a significant minority of the members. Moreover, current issues of educational reform and policy development are discussed increasingly at the meetings of comparative and international educationists.

Within higher education institutions, comparative educationists have lobbied for the inclusion of the subject in the foundations of education component of their teacher training programs and also for its inclusion in graduate programs. They have met with mixed success in these endeavors, since comparative education is sometimes seen as a "frill" which can be eliminated in times of financial stringency. In other cases, national reforms of teacher training may have an impact on the content of teacher education which no academic society can predict.

The avowedly apolitical nature of the academic societies results in little inclination to lobby politically on any issues which may be within the purview of comparative educators. The emphasis on the technical or logistical problems of implementing reforms at the international level means that comparative educationists participate in activities that ultimately have political agendas, but the academic societies discussed here do not have any articulated position on the political issues that may exist.

One live issue that is of public interest in many countries in the 1990s is how the national education system compares or ranks with others. Comparative education societies have not played a major role in illuminating this debate for the general public, but they have explored many of its aspects in their meetings.

See also: Comparative Education and International Education: Organizations and Institutions; Comparative and International Education: Overview and Historical Development

References

Brickman W W 1985 Comparative and International Education Society. In: Husén T, Postlethwaite T N 1985 *The International Encyclopedia of Education*, 1st edn. Pergamon Press, Oxford

Comparative and International Education Society in Europe (CESE) 1980 *Statutes*. CESE, Brussels

Comparative and International Education Society (CIES) 1990 Constitution. *CIES Newsletter* 95:14–18

Debeauvais M 1990 *National Educational Research Policies: A World Survey*. UNESCO, Paris

Epstein E H 1981 Toward the internationalization of comparative education: A report on the World Council of Comparative Education Societies. *Comp. Educ. Rev.* 25(2): 261–71
Epstein E H 1992 *Comparative Education Review*. Annual Report for 1992
Read G H 1985 The World Congress of Comparative Education Societies. *CIES Newsletter* 77: 1–3
Tarrow N B 1987 *Human Rights and Education*. Pergamon Press, Oxford
Thomas R M (ed.) 1992 *Education's Role in National Development Plans: Ten Country Cases*. Praeger, New York
World Council of Comparative Education Societies 1984 *Statutes*. WCCES, Manchester

Further Reading

Bereday G Z F, Brickman W W, Read G H 1960 *The Changing Soviet School*. Houghton Mifflin, Boston, Massachusetts
Canadian and International Education. Journal of the Comparative and International Education Society of Canada
Comparative Education Society in Europe (CESE) *Newsletter* (3–4 times annually). CESE, Brussels
Compare. Journal of the British Comparative and International Education Society
Plancke R L 1973 The Comparative Education Society in Europe: Ten years of meetings. *Paedag. Hist.* 13(2): 552–56
Ryba R 1989a The contribution of the *Association francophone d'éducation comparée* (AFEC) to comparative studies of education. Paper delivered at the CIES Annual Conference, Harvard Graduate School of Education, March 30–April 2
Ryba R 1989b The Contribution of Comparative Education Societies: A Case Study of the British Society in Comparative Perspective. Paper delivered at the 7th World Congress of Comparative Education, Montreal, June 26–30
Song Y, Wilson D N 1989 A Brief History of the Comparative and International Education Society of Canada. OISE, Toronto
The Comparative Education Review. Journal of the Comparative and International Education Society
Van Daele H 1991 CESE is 30 years old. *CESE Newsletter* 31: 2–3
World Council of Comparative Education Societies (WCCES) 1988 *Annals of the VIth World Congress of Comparative Education: Education, Crisis, and Change*. Brazilian Society of Comparative Education, Rio de Janeiro

V. L. Masemann

Comparative Methodology in Education

This entry examines the methodologies employed in the making of comparisons in educational research. Scholarly inquiry in the field of education employs two essentially different investigatory strategies. These strategies are referred to as the "holistic" or "systemic" approach and the "comparative" or "contrastive" approach. Within the systemic approach the characteristics of the parts are seen to be largely determined by the whole to which they belong. Thus the emphasis in inquiry is on the study of the interrelationships between the elementary parts which are assumed to be interdependent within the whole. Inquiry here involves the study of patterns and processes. The test that is applied is whether the characteristics of an elementary part, a relationship, or a pattern, that is under examination may be considered to exist. Within the comparative approach, characteristics of an elementary part are compared across two or more research situations. Where a difference is observed, a reason for the difference may be sought. Alternatively, where a difference is not observed, the reason for the similarity may be of interest. It is of course possible to apply initially a systemic approach and having established the existence of a pattern or a set of interrelationships between the parts within a whole, to undertake comparisons of the patterns or interrelations observed across two or more research situations. The test that is applied is whether the characteristics of two or more elementary parts, or two or more relationships, or two or more patterns can be said either to differ or to be the same.

Logically, establishing the existence of the characteristics of a part, a relationship, or a pattern, must precede the making of comparisons between two or more such entities. However, one of the tests of existence is whether a difference can be observed in particular research situations. Thus the distinction between the two strategies lies, at least in part, in whether the emphasis is on providing an account of wholes and the need to emphasize holistic qualities, or whether the emphasis is on the decomposition into parts and a comparison and further examination of the characteristics of the parts in two or more situations.

Comparative studies may be undertaken using either a scientific approach or a humanistic approach. The former commonly involves measurement and statistical analysis, the latter tends to be ethnographic and largely descriptive. Both approaches are considered in this entry.

1. Field of Comparative Education

During the twentieth century travel to other countries has greatly increased, communication with people from other lands has been made much easier, and barriers to cross-national trade have been steadily removed. This has led to increased interest among educators as to how education is provided in different cultures and societies. As a result comparisons have commonly been made between countries with respect to many different aspects of educational provision. A field of scholarly work in education has emerged that is primarily concerned with cross-national comparisons in the provision of education. While initially the work undertaken in this field was solely descriptive and information-seeking, without the explicit making of comparisons between countries, interest in the making of such comparisons increased to such an extent that the field acquired the name of comparative education. The field has identified a founding father in Marc-Antoine Jullien, whose seminal work *L'Esquisse et vue préliminaire d'un ouvrage sur l'éducation comparée* in 1817 emphasized objective observation, the collection of documents, thoroughness, and systematic analysis. The field is also able to trace its roots back into Antiquity (see Brickman 1960, 1966). There are, however, several fallacious ideas concerned with the methods and nature of comparative education that must be dispelled.

1.1 Fallacy of a Single Scientific Method of Comparative Education

In his work *Problems in Education: A Comparative Approach*, Holmes (1965) provided a statement on the scientific method that he advocated for comparative education. He drew on the writings of Dewey (1933) on problem-solving and proposed a sequence of eight major steps in comparative education which for him was both an instrument of reform or planned development in education as well as a method of investigation that led to the production of new knowledge. These steps may be listed as follows: (a) selection of a problem; (b) identification of possible solutions; (c) reflection on the problem, leading to a clearer formulation; (d) analysis of the context of the problem; (e) advancement of hypotheses on policy choices: (f) testing of hypotheses; (g) drawing of conclusions; and (h) reexamination of the processes. The key steps were step (a) which not only involved selection but also analysis; step (b), which involved the formulation of policy proposals; step (d), which involved the identification of relevant factors; and step (f), which involved prediction and the testing of possible solutions against the context analyzed.

In spite of the coherence of Holmes's ideas, educational research workers who are interested in questions that require the investigation of educational provision in one or more countries and who bring to the investigation perspectives drawn from one or more disciplinary areas, such as psychology, sociology, anthropology, geography, economics, history, demography, philosophy, and law, cannot consistently be constrained by a particular sequence of steps in inquiry. Moreover, the conceptual or methodological problems in comparative research are not unique to a single discipline or investigatory approach. Comparative educators are free to draw on those methods of inquiry that seem most appropriate to them to answer the research questions that have been posed. Frequently, multiple methods are useful in achieving greater understanding. The methods that are chosen may involve perspectives and knowledge drawn from one or more disciplines, as well as the methods of investigation traditionally employed in those disciplines. There is no single scientific method of investigation in comparative education.

1.2 Fallacy of a Choice between Qualities or Quantities

A fallacy widely held among comparative educators is that a choice exists in investigation between, on the one hand, the examination of qualities rather than quantities and, on the other hand, the examination of quantities rather than qualities. Both are misconceived when they are taken to be clear-cut alternatives since quantities are measures of qualities (Kaplan 1964). Moreover, complex procedures of statistical analysis are now available for the rigorous examination of qualitative data, where information is recorded in two or more categories, without any attempt being made to measure, just as there are similar rigorous statistical procedures available for the examination of quantitative data that involve accurate measurement. The issues are simply those concerned with the meaningfulness and consistency of the measurement procedures employed that indicate whether quantitative or qualitative information or both are best used in a particular research situation. Admittedly improving the accuracy of measurement involves refining the abstract concept being measured, and this commonly involves eliminating from consideration certain aspects of the quality under examination. However, increased precision of measurement increases the likelihood of establishing a relationship that may be hypothesized.

1.3 Fallacy of Distinction Between Policy-oriented and Discipline-oriented Studies

While for Holmes (1965) comparative education was an instrument of planned development in education, he also recognized that such inquiry led to a greater understanding of educational systems. The interest shown by politicians and the media in the "horse race" aspects of international studies of educational achievement without concern for developing a coherent explanation of why such differences arise is one consequence of the artificial dichotomy between policy-oriented and discipline-oriented studies or between applied and pure research. Most research workers would wish the results of their research to be useful, but any demand for policy-oriented research at the expense of discipline-oriented research can involve a gross misunderstanding of the nature of social action and the power of ideas. Moreover, it assumes that research in the social and behavioral sciences finds application in the same manner as research in the physical sciences does through technology and applied science. There is, nevertheless, an important role for such institutions as the World Bank, the Centre for Educational Research and Innovation at the Organisation for Economic Co-operation and Development (OECD) and the International Institute of Educational Planning to provide an international platform for discussion, where the results of comparative research studies are translated into terms that policymakers understand. Thus the powerful ideas that emerge from comparative research are made accessible for translation into policy and practice across countries.

1.4 Fallacy Concerning Exclusive Attention to Processes and not Products

In part, in reaction to the interest of policymakers in the outcomes of education and in policy-oriented research, there is a fallacy that comparative research should be concerned with the elaboration and understanding of the processes involved in the provision of educational services. While some naive input–output models of educational provision that are advanced must be cast aside as incomplete and inadequate, so too must the limited study of the processes involved in educational provision. In seeking an indepth understanding of educational provision, it would seem unsatisfactory merely to investigate the processes that operate in a particular educational situation without detailed consideration of the outcomes or products of that system. Thus, to achieve greater understanding of education and educational changes, it is necessary to develop and examine models of educational provision and operation that incorporate both the *products* of a system and the *processes* at work as well as the *context* in which the system is set. The methods to be employed in such investigations depend on the nature of the research questions being asked, and on the extent of understanding that has been achieved of the problem situation being investigated.

2. Types of Research in Comparative Education

Research workers in comparative education undertake research studies that involve one or more countries or regions, which can be classified into three types, namely: (a) descriptive studies; (b) developmental studies; (c) analytical, relationship, and process studies. Studies that fall into the second and third categories require theoretical perspectives that are discussed in a later section. In this section the methods employed are considered and examples of such research studies are given.

2.1 Descriptive Studies

An initial and necessary task in the field of comparative education is the development of understanding through studies that provide a descriptive account of the state of education at a specific point in time in generally one, but sometimes more than one country. Examples of these studies are provided in this encyclopedia for more than 130 countries in the articles on National Systems of Education or in the important series of Studies in Compulsory Education in particular countries which were issued around 1950 as joint publications of the International Bureau of Education and UNESCO. A further example involves the examination of the teaching of a school subject, science, in 20 countries, which is provided in a report of the Second IEA Science Study by Rosier and Keeves (1991) based on case studies conducted in each of the participating countries. Such studies may or may not contain a historical component. Any historical information that might be included is generally more descriptive than explanatory of the provision of education in a particular country. These descriptive studies serve an important purpose since they provide relatively concise accounts of educational policies and practices in a particular country and assist in the building up of an understanding both within that country and outside of the systems of education that operate.

The United Nations Educational, Scientific and Cultural Organization (UNESCO) in Paris, which was established after the Second World War (in 1946) and the International Bureau of Education in Geneva, which was established in 1925, have both played an important role over the past half-century in this field. Not only have they published resource material, they have also maintained international surveys on "the condition of education" in each country. In these surveys a questionnaire has been completed by the ministry of education within each country and the responses have been classified and published. Such work is beset with many problems. The major ones are: (a) the absence of a list of the most important educational indicators agreed upon by scholars in the field; (b) the cost and practical difficulties of obtaining data from so many sources; (c) the lack of comparability in the data collected, in spite of efforts made to obtain uniformity; (d) the lack of sufficient analysis of context without which data have limited meaning; and (e) uncertainties about the consistency or meaningfulness of the data returned, because of the tendency for ministry officials to wish to present the conditions of education within their country in the best possible light.

In the later decades of the twentieth century, greatly increased opportunities have become available for travel and study in schools, colleges, and universities outside a person's country of origin, for example, the ERASMUS scheme, which aims to promote student mobility within the European Community and which is also being taken up by countries outside the EC. There are, however, the very practical problems of: (a) obtaining proficiency in a second language to study effectively; (b) supplying sufficient information on the portability of qualifications; and (c) undertaking meaningful comparisons of the nature and standard of courses. However, problems

(b) and (c) listed above are being met by the work of EUROSTAT with benefits both between and within countries. The long-term effects of such student exchange schemes and the increased emphasis on foreign language learning beyond the commercial sphere are difficult to foresee, but are likely to be substantial and highly beneficial. There is, nevertheless, little doubt that descriptive studies in the field of comparative education must play an increasingly important role in the development of a greater understanding of educational provision in other countries. This goes well beyond the aims and purposes of the traditional courses in comparative education that are provided. However, comparative educators led by Kandel (1933), Hans (1949), Bereday (1964), King (1968), and Noah and Eckstein (1969) have all come to recognize that in their field of inquiry both descriptive and historical studies are not enough.

2.2 Developmental Studies

The influence of the social and behavioral sciences on life in different parts of the world is achieved not so much through the implications for policy and practice of a particular research study, but through the power of the ideas and concepts that are generated. In no field of life is this greater than in that of education, where ideas are traded, debated, and successively advanced and promulgated. The remarkable changes in the way of life of both men and women across the world during the past 2,000 years may be ascribed primarily to those ideas that flowed from Greece and Rome, but also from the countries of the Middle East, China, India, and from other centers of learning. In the field of education and through education the changes that have occurred since the mid-nineteenth century have been quite spectacular, particularly in the areas of compulsory education, universal secondary education, the establishment of universities, and more recently in programs of lifelong and recurrent education. The stories of many developments, such as that of the curriculum and methods of science education, remain to be told.

Frequently, accounts of the developments that have occurred in an area of education in a particular country have been merely descriptive and have attributed change to the influence of a certain individual and to the borrowing of particular policies and practices. However, the changes that have taken place have been too rapid and too widespread to be attributed to chance. Kandel (1933) sought to ascribe the developments in education that took place within a particular country to national character. Furthermore, Mallinson (1957) contended that "common identity of interest, that common purpose, leads over the centuries to a kind of fixed mental constitution" which influenced educational development within a country. While a national mental constitution or culture may be employed to explain certain unique features of German and Japanese education, it cannot be used to explain the widespread commonalities in educational growth that have developed since the mid-nineteenth century.

Hans (1949) moved to a higher level of generality through identifying certain factors that influenced educational development, namely: (a) natural factors (racial, linguistic, geographic, and economic); (b) religious factors (Catholic, Anglican, and puritan); and (c) secular factors (humanism, socialism, nationalism, and democratic ideals). While these factors shift explanation of educational development beyond national boundaries to more widespread regions, they are more concerned with unique factors than with the common or universal factors that would appear to have operated across the world.

Meyer and Hannan (1979) have argued that the thrust for universal primary education, initially in Western Europe from the middle of the nineteenth century onwards, had little to do with national educational policies and must be viewed in a cross-national context. It might be argued that the powerful ideas of this period arose from the Darwinian concept of evolution, the drive to establish a national identity and to strengthen the power of the state, and from the need in an industrialized state for a workforce that could read, write, and count. Likewise, the impact of Marx's ideas influenced educational policies and practices in a substantial region of the world, including the former Soviet Union and China, from early in the twentieth century onward.

More detailed studies into the nature of particular aspects of educational development across countries have also been carried out. For example, the character of an educational system, whether tightly centralized or largely decentralized, Archer (1979) argued, is related to its origins. Those systems with restrictive origins emphasize unification and systematization and those with substitutive origins feature differentiation from other social institutions and a high degree of internal specialization. These characteristics in turn affect the nature and speed of change in an educational system.

Developments that have occurred cross-nationally which particularly warrant examination include: (a) the interaction of educational, social, and economic ideas; (b) the equality of educational opportunity programs built around ideas of social justice; (c) programs for equality between the sexes which have been built from psychological and sociological research into sex and gender differences; and (d) developments in science and mathematics programs that have flowed from a demand for scientific and technological growth to raise standards of living within countries. Studies of the history of education in the twentieth century tend to be encyclopedic and do not seek to reveal how the ideas that have been generated since the mid-nineteenth century have spread across the world to influence the growth and development of education.

2.3 Studies of Relationships and Processes

These studies seek to increase understanding of how variables relate to one another, to explain better the dynamics of learning, teaching, and educational change, and to examine how such relationships and processes vary across systems and countries. The objective frequently is to specify functional or cause-and-effect relationships and outcomes. Such studies often focus on a set of actors (e.g., teachers, students, parents) or roles (e.g., teaching, learning, supporting) to explain the behavior of schools and educational systems. Studies falling within this broad range include input–output studies, production function studies, effective school studies, and process–product studies.

The need and potential for comparative research on educational relationships and processes are reflected in the work of the International Association for the Evaluation of Educational Achievement (IEA). In the late 1950s a group of educational research workers meeting at the UNESCO Institute of Education in Hamburg came to recognize that within a particular country there was commonly insufficient variation in the conditions of education to make it possible to detect by existing methods of statistical analysis the effects of particular factors on learning outcomes. They contended that if research studies could be conducted cross-nationally, then the greater variation that existed across countries could assist in identifying common factors of importance. The feasibility of undertaking research studies across countries into factors influencing educational outcomes was tested through a pilot study (Foshay et al. 1962). The success of this work led to the formal establishment of the IEA. Since that time, the IEA has carried out a series of research studies, primarily survey and cross-sectional investigations, into factors that have an effect on educational achievement, participation rates, and attitudes toward school and school learning. The data collected have been examined across countries, between schools within countries, and between students within countries, and where possible relationships have been sought after controlling for other factors that might affect the educational outcomes under consideration. The specific relationships that have been detected fall into one of several types, namely: (a) relationships between predictor and criterion variables across countries; (b) similar relationships between predictor and criterion variables between students and schools within countries; (c) a relationship between predictor variables and criterion variables and between students and schools within countries that is unique to a particular country or a small group of countries; and (d) the absence of a relationship where current opinion within educational circles believes such a relationship should exist (see *Evaluation of National Comparisons*). The extensive body of international research assembled by the IEA has established many generalizations that explain the processes by which education is more or less effective.

The existence of these general relationships involving factors that influence, for instance, science achievement and attitudes, has raised the need to examine in a systematic manner whether similar or different processes operate within schooling in different countries, at different age or grade levels, and across different subject areas. Before the systematic examination of processes can take place, advances must be made along three major fronts. First, it is necessary for theory to be developed and models postulated of specific processes of school learning. One such very influential model in this field has been Carroll's (1963) model of school learning. Second, it is necessary to develop procedures for the collection of data that are sufficiently comparable across countries that the testing of models in a comparative manner is worthwhile. Third, procedures for the testing of models need to be further developed in order to provide better estimates of effects and appropriate estimates of error. Problems arise on all three fronts.

The lack of relevant theory has resulted in the collection of massive amounts of data, in cross-national empirical studies, some of which are never effectively examined, because there is little guidance provided by theory as to what hypotheses or models could be tested or what questions could be asked. However, sometimes models have been advanced long after the data collection and it has been fortuitous that data were available for the testing of a model in secondary analyses. Sometimes, only weak relationships are observed because of bias in samples, or because of marked error of measurement in the data. Such shortcomings generally serve to reduce greatly the possibility of observing an expected relationship within a model, rather than enhancing the possibility of detecting relationships.

Inadequate theory limits all types of studies in the field of comparative education. Naturalistic, ethnographic, and other descriptive techniques have generated rich, detailed analyses of teaching and learning processes and the organizational contexts of education. Yet, generalizations beyond culturally specific meanings are constrained by lack of theory and adequate tests of comparability across countries. However, advances are being made in the requisite conditions for improvements in studies of relationships and processes. Experience in crosscultural ethnographic research and increased sophistication in techniques of interviewing, document analysis, and observation are contributing to more accurate descriptions of schooling and educational activities in their natural or normal setting. Equally significant are the technical advances in analytical methods which have also been made in recent decades, particularly in the areas of multivariate and multilevel analysis. The procedures employed in such statistical analyses are essentially those of making comparisons and testing models when large bodies of data are available.

3. Nature of the Data Collected in Cross-national Statistical Studies

The focus of comparative research in education may be at the individual, institutional (school or classroom) or system level. Yet it is necessary to recognize that the effects of education are experiences in the lives of individual students at a particular point in time. It is, therefore, instructive to consider in greater detail the nature of the data to be collected in crossnational studies, assuming that the basic unit of inquiry is of necessity that of the individual student at a specified time point.

Studies of learning necessarily involve change in student behavior between two or more occasions. Where only one time point is considered, as in a crosssectional study, it must be assumed that the learning being measured has taken place during the life of a student up to that time point rather than change in learning between occasions. (see *Cross-sectional Research Methods*).

It is necessary to recognize that in studies of the effects of schooling, the treatment conditions that operate are provided for some treatments at the level of the school or school district, and for other treatments at the level of the teacher or the classroom. There is thus a series of levels commonly present in the policy-making and practice of education that has to be taken into consideration in both the sampling design and the examination of the effects of treatment conditions. These levels are: (a) within a student between occasions; (b) within a classroom between students; (c) within a school between classrooms; (d) within a school system between schools; (e) within a country between regional or local school systems; and (f) within a sample of countries between countries.

These different levels not only influence the nature of the data to be collected and the drawing of samples of students, but they necessarily also influence how the analyses of data must be carried out to separate the effects associated with differences between occasions, between students, between teachers and classrooms, between schools, between school systems, and between countries. For simplicity a particular level may be ignored; for example, only cross-sectional data may be used and the first level is ignored; or students may be sampled from across classrooms within schools, and the third level is ignored; or the effects of a school system within a country may not be of interest and the fourth and fifth levels are combined.

The statistical significance of the comparisons made between students, or between teachers, or between schools, are only valid and generalizations can only be made to other students, teachers, and schools if random samples have been chosen with a known probability of selection. Where random sampling is not possible (as with occasions, systems, and countries), the nature and magnitude of a relationship can be established as well as its statistical significance but with limited generalization. The other great benefit derived from the use of fully random samples from a defined target population is that the unknown effects of bias arising from the selection procedure employed is reduced (see *Selection Bias in Educational Research*).

In IEA studies of the 1980s and 1990s (e.g., the Second IEA Science Study—Keeves 1992, Postlethwaite and Wiley 1992), the practice has emerged, largely for administrative convenience in testing in order to avoid the splitting of class groups, of drawing a stratified random sample of schools with a probability proportional to size and with the school as the primary sampling unit. At the second stage of sampling an intact class is drawn from within each school at the specified grade level and all students in that class are tested. Unless two classes per school are sampled it is impossible to separate out in statistical analysis the effects of schools in contrast to the effects of classrooms or teachers. A similar difficulty arises if a specified number of students is sampled from across classrooms within the chosen schools, for although some separation of the effects of schools and classrooms is possible, unless large numbers of students are tested the estimates of effect are unlikely to be accurate enough for meaningful findings to be obtained at the classroom level. In part, the limited success of such empirical survey studies, whether cross-sectional or longitudinal in design, to detect strong effects associated with the characteristics of teachers and classrooms, or the characteristics of schools arises from the practical problems of sample design which result in school and classroom effects being confounded with student effects. Moreover, the difficulty of detecting school and teacher effects is due in part to the fact that in most educational systems bad schools and bad teachers are not permitted to operate, and there is limited variation to be explained. However, there are also problems arising in the methods of analysis used with such data.

The major problem that arises from the existence of the different levels at which data are collected and at which treatment effects operate is that the analysis must be carried out in such a way that the variance is appropriately partitioned between levels. If this is not done then the estimates of effect must be expected to be biased and distorted by the effects of aggregation or disaggregation of data. Furthermore, the significance tests employed must inevitably use incorrect estimates of error unless appropriate partitioning of error into its specific components has been carried out. Consequently care must be taken to partition the effects of error if the significance tests are to be meaningful. Testing for statistical significance is a great deal more complicated than is generally acknowledged and a tendency is emerging merely to consider the magnitude of an effect obtained with a large sample rather than to apply what are considered to be erroneous tests of statistical significance. Such tests are all too commonly based on simple random sampling theory, which clearly does not apply where complex sample designs have been employed and where treatments operate at levels above that of the individual student (see *Sampling Errors in Survey Research*).

4. Quantification of Cross-national Comparisons

In comparative education the typical activity is the drawing of comparisons between national systems. There is, however, the ever-present danger that conclusions are drawn on differences between countries on the basis of observations that are primarily superficial and are largely unrelated to factors that influence learning. For example, age of entry to school differs markedly across countries, largely for historical reasons. However, the effects of age of entry on achievement in reading has proved to be a complex problem to unravel in an appropriate manner unless effective controls are provided for other factors that influence reading achievement (see Thorndike 1973, Elley 1992). As a consequence considerable effort is required in planning the collection and analysis of data to ensure that sound and relevant information is obtained. The second major difficulty encountered in the making of comparisons in cross-national studies of education is that there are many variables involved that interact with each other to influence educational outcomes. The analysis of the data collected must thus proceed through a series of stages to ensure that valid findings are obtained, and this involves multilevel and multivariate analyses.

4.1 Simultaneous Analyses of Data

Powerful statistical techniques have become available that should help to tease out complex relationships between variables at several levels of analysis. One such technique is linear structural relations analysis (Muthén 1991). Although linear structural relations analysis does not currently permit the examination of random effects at both micro and macro levels in cases where complex sample designs have been employed, it does provide a strategy for the comparison of structural equation models simultaneously for up to 10 different data sets. This option transforms the nature of research and analysis into the study of processes across different countries. It provides a strategy by means of which the processes operating within schools and school systems or between sexes can be investigated using structural equation models, and the parameters of the models estimated can be effectively compared across country groups. Reports of crossnational studies have been presented by Yli-Luoma (1990) and Tuijnman and ten Brummelhuis (1991) where up to six countries have been compared in the simultaneous testing of models of educational processes. In these studies the same path model is employed across countries, but with significant differences in the magnitudes of the estimated effects, which would appear to have meaningful explanations in terms of general knowledge and understanding of educational provision within those countries. The methods of analysis employed in these two studies represent a considerable methodological advance in comparative research. Unless it can be shown that similar processes are operating in all countries under survey, it may prove seriously misleading to pool data across countries and merely estimate using least squares procedures the magnitude of national effects using dummy variables. As a consequence, the growing emphasis on the conjoint study of both processes and product, rather than the investigation of product or processes alone is of considerable importance.

5. Theoretical Perspectives

The increased elegance of the quantitative and qualitative methods that can be employed in comparative research studies in education serves to highlight the deficiencies that exist in the theory that might guide cross-national comparative research in the future. Efforts need to be made in the field of new theoretical perspectives if future studies are to achieve their potential. Three areas where developments have occurred recently in this field are provided for purposes of illustration.

5.1 Curriculum Implementation Theory

From the Granna Workshop conducted by IEA in Sweden in 1971, which examined in detail the seminal work *The Handbook of Formative and Summative Evaluation* (Bloom et al. 1971), came the theoretical view of curriculum implementation that has been tested, in part, in reporting the results of the First and Second IEA Science Studies and the Second IEA Mathematics Study (Keeves 1974, Garden and Robitaille 1988, Rosier and Keeves 1991, Postlethwaite and Wiley 1992, Keeves 1992).

The curriculum can be considered to exist at three levels: (a) the intended curriculum, (b) the implemented curriculum, and (c) the achieved curriculum, which are influenced by the antecedent and the contextual factors operating at the systemic, classroom, and student levels respectively. The *intended curriculum* is usually specified by political bodies and/or authorities in charge of an educational

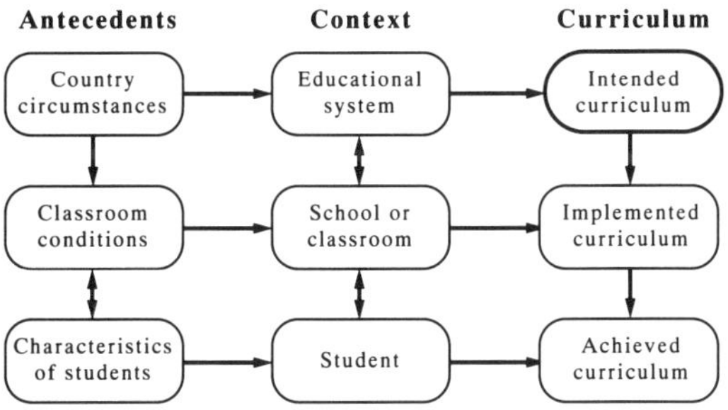

Figure 1
The context and components of the science curriculum

system. However, in some systems the responsibility to specify what is taught resides with the board of an individual school, or with each individual teacher within a school. The *implemented curriculum* is the second level in the curriculum sequence. It is the task of each individual teacher to interpret the intended curriculum by translating it into a set of learning experiences which are considered appropriate for the particular group of students in a class. The *achieved curriculum* is the third stage. It refers to the extent to which individual students have learnt from the experiences that were planned and organized for them. Figure 1 shows that the intended curriculum is set in the context of the educational system; the implemented curriculum is located in the context of the school or classroom; and the achieved curriculum occurs in the context of the individual student. Moreover, it is clear that the implemented curriculum is dependent on the intended curriculum, and the achieved curriculum upon the curriculum that is implemented in the classroom. A further refinement of this model might include separation of the implemented curriculum into: (a) textbook and materials, and (b) opportunity to learn the items included in a test that is administered. Some work has been done to show the importance of access by students to a textbook (Heyneman and Loxley 1983).

A more detailed discussion of this theory and model is given by Rosier and Keeves (1991). To date the links between the intended and the achieved curricula, and between the implemented and achieved curricula have been examined, but other relationships in the model shown in Fig. 1 remain to be tested (see *Testing and the Curriculum*).

5.2 A Causal Model of School Learning

The model of school learning advanced by Carroll (1963) has been the source of many theoretical discussions of the factors influencing educational achievement. The IEA studies provide opportunities for such theory and the derived models to be tested empirically (Carroll 1975). In the planning of the Second IEA Science Study a causal model derived from Carroll's model of school learning was advanced in 1981 which was subsequently tested in the analyses

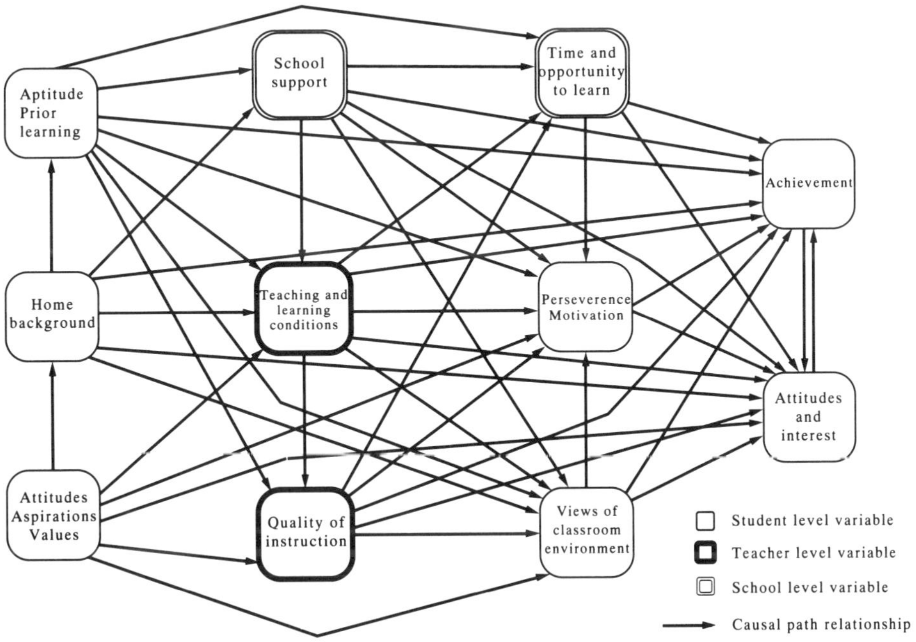

Figure 2
A simplified model of student performance

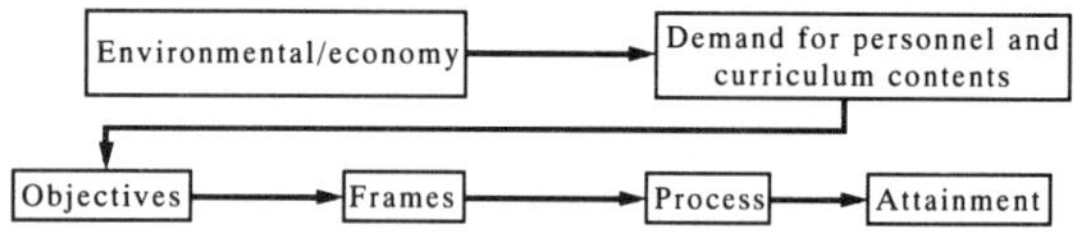

Figure 3
Model of educational process in cross-national settings

of the data collected in that study at the 10-year-old, 14-year-old, and terminal secondary school levels (Keeves 1992). This causal model has also been examined in detail in several doctoral theses.

The model of performance in science is shown in Fig. 2 and its dependence on Carroll's ideas is immediately evident. However, consideration must be given as to the best measurable variables that are manifestations of the latent variables shown in the model. A more detailed discussion of the development of this model is given in Keeves (1992).

5.3 A Cross-national Model of Educational Achievement in a National Economy

In 1967 during the planning phase for the IEA Six-subject Study, a conference was held at Lake Mohonk in the United States which sought to develop "a cross-national model of educational achievement in a national economy" A paper by Dahllöf (1967) developed a scheme for the *educational process* that applied in cross-national settings—see Fig. 3.

Of particular interest for policy-making in education are the frame variables. However, their dependence on: (a) the environment and economy, (b) demand for personnel (c) curriculum content, and (d) objectives cannot be denied.

IEA studies have shown the marked difference in levels of achievement between the developed and the developing countries, with much lesser variation between the countries within each group (Inkeles 1977). Moreover, Lietz (1991) has shown that a causal model that explained well the influence of individual student factors on reading achievement at the 14-year-old level in developed countries was inadequate in two developing countries, India and Iran. Several possible reasons were hypothesized for these results. First, the reading tests employed were possibly inappropriate in the context of developing countries, leading to low scores and reduced variance in the outcome measures. Second, effects of selection probably operated and only students from higher status homes could afford to remain at school to the secondary level. This led to less variance on explanatory constructs. Selection bias in turn led to less explained variance in the outcome measure. Third, there were the probable effects of limited resources in the homes. The reduced availability of reading resources in the homes of most students in developing countries restricted the explanatory power of this variable. Finally, in many, but not all, developing countries a high proportion of the students were learning and were tested in a language that was substantially different from their mother tongue, and this may also have accounted for the lower average level of performance.

Cross-national studies of educational achievement are, as pointed out above, in need of more highly developed theory and more specific models that can be subjected to testing in order to account for the general uniformity in achievement between developed countries, as well as the marked differences in achievement between developed and developing countries. The Lake Mohonk Conference advanced an input—output—utilization model of education (Super 1967) that included many significant components, namely: (a) inputs (human, financial); (b) production conditions, (c) structure and operations (educational structure, equipment, agents, curriculum, and instructional methods); (d) outputs (knowledge, skills, attitudes, participation, attainment level); and (e) utilization (employment, community involvement, and family activity). While causal influences, student movement, and financial flow were taken into consideration, insufficient thought was given at that stage to the testing of such a complex model. The task still remains for more specific hypotheses and multilevel causal models to be advanced that are amenable to testing, and rejection or refinement.

6. *Future Developments*

Comparative methodology in educational inquiry reflects both the variety in the disciplinary training of researchers and the limited range of available theories and models that may be examined. Contemporary comparative research in education, following trends in the social sciences, is clearly in a period of methodological diversity. However, a pluralism has emerged emphasizing the complementarity of different research approaches.

In addition to the fundamental need for theoretical developments in the field of comparative education, other advances should be sought. First, there is a need for studies using a multiplicity of methodological approaches. In particular, it should be recognized that the meaning of the context of education and richness of details of educational provision can be provided by painstaking, lengthy, on-site observation and analysis. Second, there is the need for research workers in certain more highly developed countries to adopt more rigorous procedures of sampling, so that genuinely random samples that are representative of a specified target population and that yield unbiased data are studied. Third, there is a need for all countries to recognize the value of complete and high-quality data that are consistent across countries, so that sampling error and systematic bias in data collection are reduced. This requirement also involves a reduction in the amount of erroneously coded data, which can be largely eliminated through the use of appropriate data entry routines. Fourth, there is a need for the development of computer programs for the analysis of multilevel data that involve latent variables which are fixed or random in nature, and operate at the student, school, and national or sytemic levels. Finally, there is a major need for organizations such as UNESCO and the OECD to continue efforts to develop indicators that can be used in comparative educational studies to assist in the teasing out of cross-national explanatory relationships. The publication of the volume *Education at a Glance: OECD* Indicators (Bottani et al. 1992) is a valuable start in this field. Areas where the information available has been found to be seriously deficient include simple participation rates at the twelfth year of schooling, and in higher education, particularly gender-related participation rates in general and in specific fields. Indexes of the role of women in society and indicators of home learning environments are also needed. Current indicators, while useful for certain planning purposes, fail to provide much insight into the processes of teaching and learning or why educational organizations and systems develop the way they do. Only when relatively straight-forward but conceptually more meaningful indexes of social and educational change are available will it be possible to examine the effects of change over time both between and within countries.

See also: Comparative and International Education: Paradigms and Theories; Comparative Statistics in Education; Educational Achievement: Comparative Studies; Research Paradigms in Education; Research in Education: Epistemological Issues

References

Archer M 1979 *Social Origins of Educational Systems*. Sage, London

Bereday G Z F 1964 *Comparative Method in Education*. Holt, Rinehart, and Winston, New York

Bloom B S, Hastings J T, Madaus G F *Handbook of Formative and Summative Evaluation of Student Learning*. McGraw-Hill, New York

Bottani N, Duchene C, Tuijnman A 1992 *Education at a Glance: OECD Indicators*. OECD, Paris

Brickman W W 1960 A historical introduction to comparative education. *Comp. Educ. Rev.* 3(3): 6–13

Brickman W W 1966 Prehistory of comparative education to the end of the eighteenth century. *Comp. Educ. Rev.* 10(1): 30–47

Carroll J B 1963 A model of school learning. *Teach. Coll. Rec.* 64(8): 723–33

Carroll J B 1975 *The Teaching of French as a Foreign Language in Eight Countries*. Wiley, New York

Dahllöf U 1967 Relevance and fitness analysis on comparative education. In: Super D E (ed.) 1967

Dewey J 1933 *How We Think*. Heath, New York

Elley W B 1992 *How in the World do Students Read*? IEA, Hamburg

Foshay A W et al. (ed.) 1962 *Educational Achievements of 13-year-olds in Twelve Countries*. UNESCO Institute of Education, Hamburg

Garden R A, Robitaille D F 1989 *The IEA Study of Mathematics 2: Context and Outcomes of School Mathematics*. Pergamon Press, Oxford

Hans N 1959 *Comparative Education: A Study of Educational Factors and Traditions*. Routledge and Kegan Paul, London

Heyneman S, Loxley W 1983 The effect of primary-school quality on academic achievement across twenty-nine high and low income countries. *Am. J. Sociology* 88(6): 1162–94

Holmes B 1965 *Problems in Education: A Comparative Approach*. Routledge and Kegan Paul, London

Inkeles T (ed.) 1977 The international evaluation of educational achievement: A review of *International Studies in Education* (9 vols.) by the International Association for the Evaluation of Educational Achievement. *Proceedings of the National Academy of Education* 4: 139–200

Kandel I L 1933 *Comparative Education*. Houghton Mifflin, Boston, Massachusetts

Kaplan A 1964 *The Conduct of Inquiry: Methodology for Behavioral Science*. Chandler, San Francisco, California

Keeves J P 1974 The IEA Science Project: Science achievement in three countries—Australia, the Federal Republic of Germany, and the United States. In: *Implementation of Curricula in Science Education*. German Commission for UNESCO, Cologne

Keeves J P (ed.) 1992 *The IEA Study of Science III: Changes in Science Education and Achievement: 1970 to 1984*. Pergamon Press, Oxford

King E J 1968 *World Perspectives in Education*. Methuen, London

Lietz P 1991 Factors influencing reading achievement at the 14-year-old level in 15 educational systems (MEd dissertation, The Flinders University of South Australia

Mallinson V 1957 *An Introduction to the Study of Comparative Education*. Heinemann, Melbourne

Meyer J W, Hannan M T 1979 *National Development and the World System: Educational, Economic, and Political Change*. University of Chicago Press, Chicago, Illinois

Muthén B O 1991 Analysis of longitudinal data using latent variable models with varying parameters. In: Collins L M, Horn J L *Best Methods for the Analysis of Change*. American Psychological Association, Washington, DC

Noah H J, Eckstein M A 1969 *Toward a Science of Comparative Education*. Macmillan, London

Postlethwaite T N, Wiley D E (eds.) 1992 *The IEA Study of Science II: Science Achievement in Twenty-Three Countries*. Pergamon Press, Oxford

Rosier M J, Keeves J P 1991 *The IEA Study of Science I: Science Education and Curricula in Twenty-Three Countries*. Pergamon Press, Oxford

Super D E (ed.) 1967 *Toward a Cross-national Model of Educational Achievement in a National Economy*. Teachers College Press, New York

Thorndike R L 1973 *Reading Comprehension Education in Fifteen Countries: An Empirical Study*. International Studies in Evaluation 3. Wiley, New York

Tuijnman A C, ten Brummelhuis A C A 1993 Predicting computer use in six systems: Structural models of implementing indicators. In: Pelgrum W J, Plomp T

(eds.) 1993 *Computers in Education: Implementation of an Innovation in 20 Countries*. Pergamon Press, Oxford
Yli-Luoma P V J 1990 *Predictors of Moral Reasoning*. Almqvist and Wiksell, Stockholm

Further Reading

Husén T, Tuijnman A, Halls W D 1992 *Schooling in Modern European Society*. Pergamon Press, Oxford
Purves A C (ed.) 1989 *International Comparisons and Educational Reform. Association for Supervision and Curriculum Development* (ASCD), Alexandra, Virginia
Thomas R M (ed.) 1990 *International Comparative Education: Practices, Issues, and Prospects*. Pergamon Press, Oxford
Øyen E (ed.) 1990 *Comparative Methodology: Theory and Practice in International Social Research*. Sage, London

J. P. Keeves; D. Adams

Comparative Statistics in Education

One result of the rapid growth of the education sector since the 1960s and of the emphasis given to educational planning in relation to the targets of economic and social development was the greater attention devoted to educational statistics at both the national and the international level. In the early 1990s, the importance of comparable statistics is being recognized, since education in any given country is increasingly studied with reference to other countries or within a regional context. Comparability can only be achieved through the adoption and implementation by all countries of the same general concepts and definitions. However, ensuring international comparability of data is a long and difficult process in view of the wide variations existing in national systems of education. Significant progress has been made in this area, but much remains to be accomplished. This entry discusses education statistics mainly from the viewpoint of international comparability. The focus is on sources of data, international standardization, and uses of comparative data.

1. National and International Sources for Statistics

1.1 National Level

The primary sources for statistics on education are the educational institutions of all types, public or private, from preschool to university level. In most countries the responsibility for collecting and presenting the data lies with the statistical service of the ministry of education or the central bureau of statistics. The function of data collection is usually shared with several other governmental and nongovernmental agencies. The collection of data is basically carried out by means of regular questionnaires filled out by the schools. However, certain types of data—for example, statistics on educational expenditure—are obtained from central administrative records and more detailed statistics, including individualized data, depend on special enquiries and sample surveys. Statistics on educational characteristics of the population (e.g., literacy and educational attainment) are obtained from population censuses or surveys.

Most countries issue at least one annual publication containing detailed education statistics. The data are based on their own definitions, classifications, and tabulations. As international standards develop, national statistics systems are transformed to reflect them.

1.2 International and Regional Sources

At the international level, UNESCO is responsible for statistics in the field of education, in the same way as the United Nations is responsible for demographic statistics and the International Labour Organisation for labor statistics.

One of the main activities of the Division of Statistics of UNESCO is the collection and dissemination of statistical data on education from all countries and territories. Data are collected on institutions, pupils, teachers, expenditure, and other subjects by means of annual questionnaires, complemented by national publications. In addition, ad hoc surveys are conducted to meet specific needs.

The Statistical Data Bank of UNESCO contains a large amount of data from 1960 onward. Topics covered include: enrollment by level, gender, age, and field of study for higher education; teaching staff by level and gender; illiteracy; educational attainment; foreign students and graduates.

UNESCO publishes the *Statistical Yearbook*, a principal source of internationally comparable statistics on education, and the *Statistical Digest*. Reports of a more analytical nature are issued in two main series: the Statistical Reports and Studies, and the Current Surveys and Research series. These reports cover subjects such as the quantitative development of education, illiteracy projections, enrollment projections, trends and patterns of wastage (repetition and dropout), foreign students, and educational expenditure. In addition, statistical reviews of education trends are prepared for the regional conferences of ministers of education. A list of the documents is given in the UNESCO *Statistical Yearbook*.

Apart from UNESCO, several other international and regional organizations publish data on education, for example: the United Nations in the *Statistical Yearbook*, the Regional and Social Commissions of the United Nations in their main statistical publication, the Organisation for Economic Co-operation and Development (1967, 1990), and the World Bank in the *World Report*. In 1981 the Statistical Office of the European Communities (EUROSTAT) produced *Education Statistics 1970–1975*. The Nordic

Table 1
Distribution of education systems in 199 countries by entrance age to first-level education

Age (in years)	Number of countries
4	2
5	32
6	115
7	47
8	3

Source: UNESCO *Statistical Yearbook* 1990

Council and the Nordic Statistical Secretariat produces the *Yearbook of Nordic Statistics*.

In other cases organizations request data directly from their member countries. In general there has been coordination between the various organizations with a view to ensuring comparability of education statistics and also to avoiding repeated demands for the same information to national statistical services. However, as might be expected, the data shown for the same country by the various organizations are not always consistent or comparable due to differences in one or another respect, for example, definition, coverage, methodology, or even sources and reference date.

2. *International Standardization of Educational Statistics*

To achieve comparability, statistics should be based on uniform concepts, definitions, classifications, and tabulations. International comparisons of education statistics are more difficult to obtain than in many other fields due to the wide differences in the structure of national education systems and in institutional arrangements. Information on these structural differences is thus essential when attempting international comparisons of education data. As an illustration, Tables 1 and 2 show the variations existing over 199 countries in entrance age to first-level education and in duration of compulsory and first- and second-level education. Obviously, national education systems differ in many other respects, such as the distinction made in secondary education by types (general, teacher training, vocational/technical); admission examinations; regulations on repetition of grades. Figure 1 shows some of these complexities as regards the flow of pupils after entering Grade g of primary education. When the statistics on enrollment do not define and quantify these different flows, overestimation of the real coverage of the education system may occur and comparisons between countries are rendered more difficult. Figure 1 further illustrates that work on international comparisons of education statistics also implies the development of appropriate statistical methodology and analytical techniques.

Table 2
Distribution of education systems in 199 countries by duration of studies

	Number of countries		
Duration (in years)	Compulsory education	First-level education	General education at the second level
0	26	—	—
1	—	—	—
2	—	—	2
3	—	1	2
4	1	8	25
5	9	35	33
6	40	101	66
7	9	25	64
8	31	26	5
9	28	3	2
10	38	—	—
11	9	—	—
12	7	—	—
Not specified	1	—	—

Source: UNESCO *Statistical Yearbook* 1990

The work on standardization of education statistics was first taken up in 1926 (UNESCO 1961). Although the work is far from complete, very significant progress has been achieved since then. The two major international instruments developed and adopted in this field are the *International Standard Classification of Education* (ISCED), approved by the 1975 International Conference of Education, and the *Recommendation Concerning the International Standardization of Educational Statistics* adopted by the General Conference of UNESCO in 1958 and subsequently revised in 1978 to make it compatible with ISCED.

2.1 *The International Standard Classification of Education* (ISCED)

ISCED has been designed as an instrument suitable for assembling, compiling, and presenting statistics of education both within individual countries and internationally. It is expected to facilitate international compilation and comparison of education statistics as such, and also their use in conjunction with personnel and other economic statistics.

The classification, which is essentially a dictionary of educational programs, is designed for assembling data on current educational phenomena, such as enrollment, teaching staff, and finance, as well as for statistics of the "stock" of educated people as obtained, for example, by a census of population. In this sense, it is a multipurpose system within which comparable data can be assembled on various features of education systems and processes.

As a classification of education, ISCED classifies programs within broad fields of education according

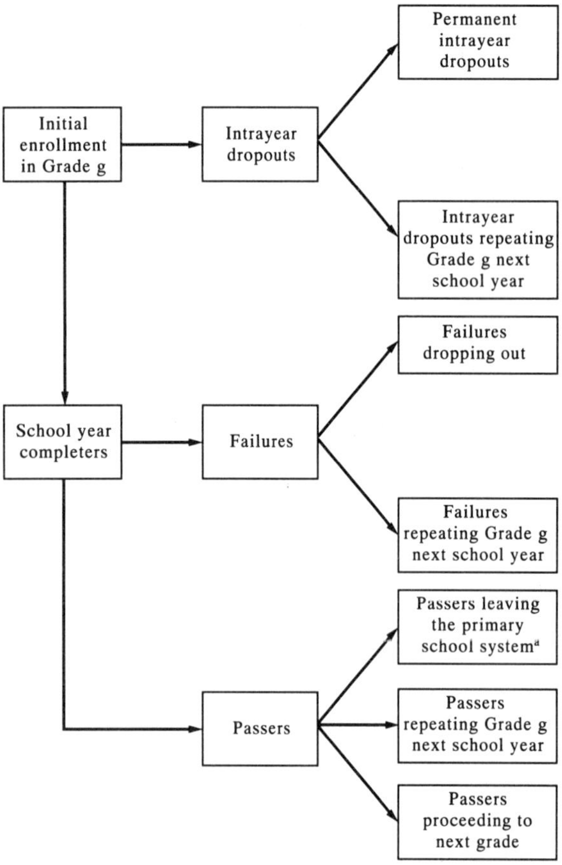

Figure 1
Flow of pupils entering Grade g of primary education
Source: UNESCO 1981

a If Grade g is the last grade of a cycle, these pupils are graduates leaving primary education, who may or may not enter secondary education in the following school year. Otherwise, they are dropouts

to their educational content. In addition, each program and field is designated to its level category. ISCED is presented in full in a UNESCO document (UNESCO 1976). This document contains codes and definitions for 518 programs of education, 21 fields of study, and 8 levels of education for classifying statistics on regular, special, and adult education.

Several countries have prepared handbooks to relate their national education classification to ISCED. The Classification has also been incorporated in international and regional recommendations for population censuses.

2.2 Revised Recommendation Concerning the International Standardization of Educational Statistics

This recommendation proposes concepts, definitions, classifications, and tabulations under four sections: (a) statistics of illiteracy; (b) statistics of the educational attainment of the population; (c) statistics of enrollment, teachers, and educational institutions; and (d) statistics of educational finance.

For the full text of the Revised Recommendation see UNESCO 1978, and for further details on various aspects of the Recommendation, the UNESCO *Manual of Education Statistics* (1961).

The adoption of international instruments such as ISCED and the Recommendation constitutes a first stage in the work to promote improvement of international comparability. The work should be continued with their actual application by all countries. It is not expected, however, that countries replace their national statistical systems or classifications, but rather that they be made compatible with ISCED and the Recommendation so that countries can provide internationally comparable data in addition to statistics reflecting national needs.

Work on standardization is a long and laborious process. In spite of the significant progress achieved in this area so far, there are still many basic statistical series that cannot yet be covered in international surveys due to lack of comparability, as for example on teachers' qualifications.

Apart from the need for common terminology and classifications, comparability of data depends on the use of standard methods and techniques in analyzing education statistics. Significant work has been carried out by UNESCO to develop methods for enrollment and literacy projections, for the analysis of wastage at school resulting from repetition of grades and dropout, and to develop methods for the analysis of educational expenditure.

3. Uses of Comparative Data

Education statistics are collected for use in research, policy-making, administration, and planning. These functions are primarily of national concern. However, specific problems of education in a given country are increasingly studied with reference to the situation in other countries or within a regional framework. Extensive use of comparative data and indicators by country is made in the statistical background papers prepared by the UNESCO Division of Statistics for the international and regional conferences on education organized at regular intervals by UNESCO in conjunction with other organizations. Comparable data are essential for the quantification of regional targets such as those on universal primary education adopted for Africa, Asia, Latin America, and in the Arab states, and for evaluation of progress made. The reference document (WCEFA 1990) prepared for the World Conference on Education for All held in March 1990 in Jomtien, Thailand (see *International Conferences, Commissions, and Reforms in Education*) is a valuable example of the use of comparative indicators in education and of related indicators in other fields (see also UNESCO 1990a).

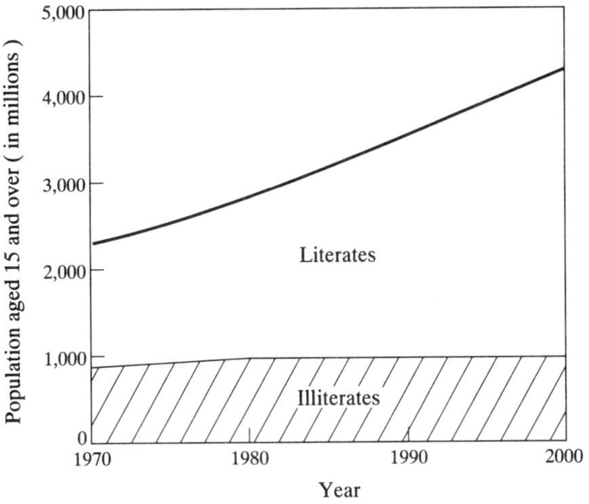

Figure 2
World proportion of literates and illiterates aged 15 and over
Source: UNESCO 1990b

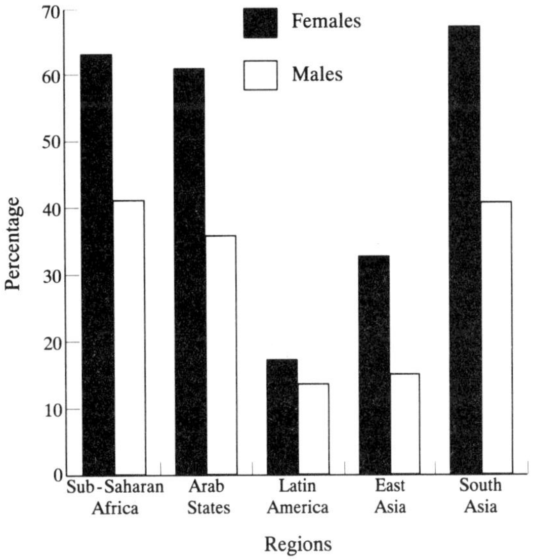

Figure 3
Female and male illiteracy rates (population aged 15 and over) by region 1990
Source: UNESCO Division of Statistics

In order to illustrate further the use of comparative data, a few examples selected from UNESCO publications will be discussed below. These examples refer mainly to comparison of regional aggregates but the data presented allow similar analyses by country.

3.1 Adult Illiteracy in the World

Figure 2 provides an illustration of the world literacy situation for the population aged 15 years and over. Estimates show that the illiteracy rate has been declining: from 38.5 percent in 1970 and 26.5 percent in 1990, it is projected to be 21.8 percent by the year 2000. However, the absolute number of adult illiterates continues to increase: 890 million in 1970 and 948 million in 1990. This apparent contradiction is explained by the very large increase in the population aged 15 years and over which took place during the same period. By the year 2000 a slight reduction in the number of illiterates is projected (935 million). Nearly all the illiterate population is to be found in the developing countries; 10 of these countries accounting for 75 percent of the world's illiterates. Figure 3 shows further detail on the distribution of the illiterate population. It highlights the disparities in illiteracy rates by gender and between regions. The eradication of illiteracy has been adopted as a major objective by the international community. The standardized estimates and projections prepared by UNESCO are very useful for evaluating progress toward this goal. The projected results serve as a warning that regular primary schooling will be insufficient for reducing substantially, let alone eradicating, illiteracy before the end of the twentieth century (see UNESCO 1990b).

3.2 Distribution of Enrollment by Level of Education and by Gender

Disparities in enrollment between boys and girls at each level of education are common to most countries. Figure 4 compares trends on this subject in the aggregates for the developed countries and the developing countries. For the developing countries, the enrollment of females was markedly lower than for males, particularly in secondary and higher education. Nevertheless, over the period 1960 to 1990, there was a distinct improvement. For the developed countries, parity between the sexes in enrollment now exists for all three levels of education. A more precise picture of enrollment disparities by sex may be obtained by looking at male and female enrollment ratios, thereby taking into account the age composition of the school population (see UNESCO 1989).

3.3 Enrollment Ratios

The enrollment ratio (ER) is a basic indicator of the coverage of the education system. It relates enrollment at a given level of education or in a given age group to the relevant population. Thus various types of enrollment ratios can be calculated according to need and to the data available: ERs, gross or net, by level, age-specific ERs, disaggregated by gender, by urban–rural, or by geographical divisions. For example, the gross enrollment ratio (GER) for primary education relates total enrollment at that level (regardless of the age of the pupils) to the population in the "official" age group for primary education. The

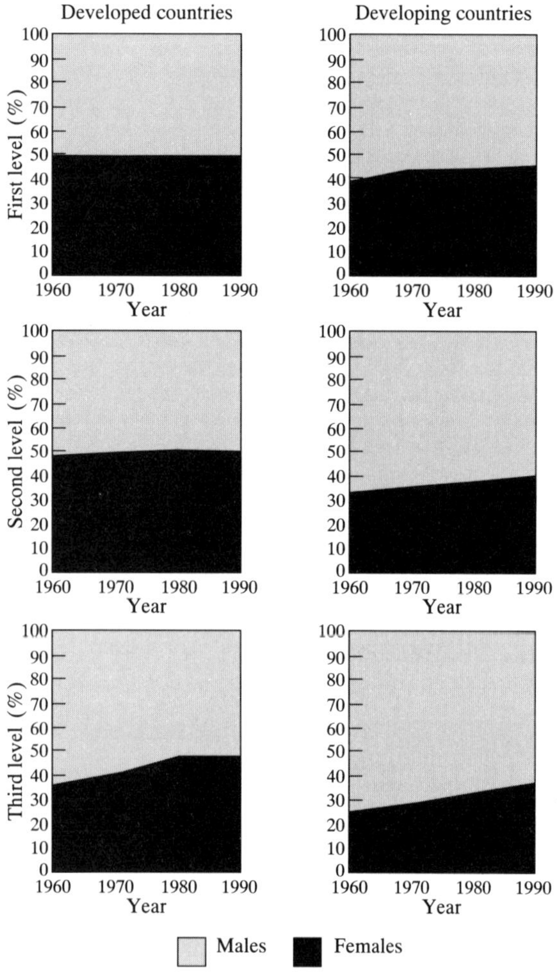

Figure 4
Male and female enrollment by level of education
Source: UNESCO Division of Statistics

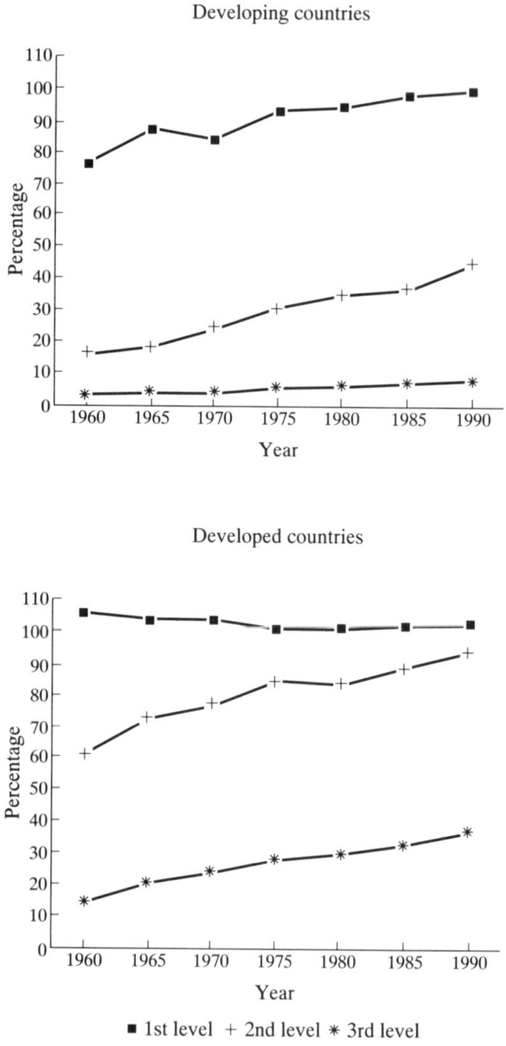

Figure 5
Adjusted gross enrollment ratios by level and by region 1960–90 (both sexes)
Source: UNESCO Division of Statistics

GER is the most commonly available for comparative studies but its interpretation is somewhat difficult, since the ratio can surpass 100 percent, due to the inclusion of under- and over-age pupils. The gross enrollment ratio can be interpreted as a measure of the capacity (i.e., number of pupil places) of the primary education system to enroll all the children in the official age group. Figure 5 shows trends in adjusted gross enrollment ratios at each level for the developing countries and the developed countries, for the period from 1960 to 1990. The term "adjusted" is applied to regional data to indicate that the school-age population used is the aggregate of the school-age population of the individual countries (rather than a fixed age group).

Figure 6 illustrates the wide variation existing in African countries in the capacity of the primary school system.

3.4 Public Expenditure on Education

Any attempt to assess expenditure on education on a comparative basis meets with great difficulties. This is due to lack of complete data. For example, coverage may be limited to public education or to the ministry of education only. Moreover, currency conversion problems and price fluctuations make comparisons over time difficult. Statistics on expenditure by level reflect different durations and the part of expenditure not distributed varies considerably between countries and from year to year for the same country. Despite such shortcomings, estimates of regional education expenditure are regularly pub-

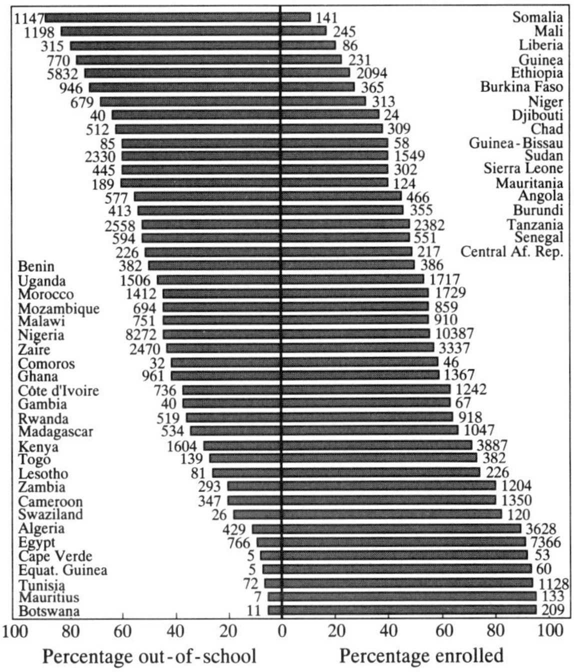

Figure 6
African Region: Primary school-age population 1988—enrolled and out-of-school children (in thousands and as a percentage)[a]

Source: UNESCO 1991

a The enrollment figures refer to the net enrollment for primary education which is lower than the total primary enrollment because students outside the official age of primary education are not included

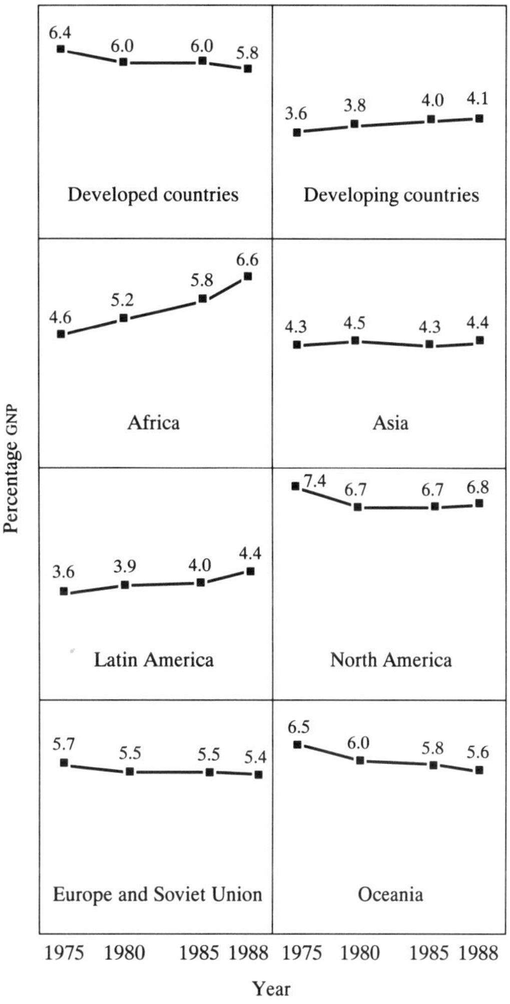

Figure 7
Public expenditure on education as a percentage of Gross National Product (GNP)

Source: UNESCO *Statistical Yearbook* 1990

lished by UNESCO. Figure 7 shows public expenditure on education related to gross national product (GNP), from 1975 to 1988, by major regions. A significantly higher proportion of GNP is spent on education by the developed countries (5.8 percent in 1988) as compared to developing countries (4.1 percent). During this period, however, the percentage increased in the developing countries, whereas it decreased in the developed countries.

4. Conclusion

This entry has described some of the work that has been carried out to promote the improvement of international comparability of education statistics. It has stressed that, because of the structural and other important differences in national education systems, international comparisons of education statistics are more difficult than in other fields. The application of international standards by national statistical services has continued but is far from complete. An examination of the statistical documents mentioned in this article shows evidence of both the very positive results that have been achieved throughout the world as regards availability and comparability of education statistics, and of the existing gaps and difficulties where further work is necessary.

See also: Educational Policy and Decision-making: Comparative Data; Area Studies: Comparative and International Education; Documentation and Information in Comparative and International Education; Education and Development

References

Organisation for Economic Co-operation and Development 1967 *Methods and Statistical Needs for Educational Planning*. OECD, Paris

Organisation for Economic Co-operation and Development 1990 *L'enseignement dans les pays de l'OCDE 1987–88: Recueil d'informations statistiques*. OECD, Paris
UNESCO 1961 *Manual of Educational Statistics*. UNESCO, Paris
UNESCO 1976 *International Standard Classification of Education*. COM/ST/ISCED, UNESCO, Paris
UNESCO 1978 *Revised Recommendation Concerning the International Standardization of Education Statistics*. UNESCO, Paris
UNESCO 1981 *Analysing and Projecting School Enrollment in Developing Countries: A Manual of Methodology Prepared by Professor Tore Thonstad*. STS 24, UNESCO, Paris
UNESCO 1989 *Trends and Projections of Enrollment by Level of Education and by Age, 1960–2025*. CSR-E-60, UNESCO, Paris
UNESCO 1990a *Basic Education and Literacy—World Statistical Indicators*. ST-90/WS-1, UNESCO, Paris
UNESCO 1990b *Compendium of Statistics on Illiteracy*. STS 31, UNESCO, Paris
UNESCO 1991 *Development of Education in Africa: A Statistical Review*. ED-91/MINEDAF/REF.1, UNESCO, Paris
WCEFA 1990 *Meeting Basic Learning Needs. A Vision for the 1990s*. Background document for the World Conference on Education for All, Jomtien, WCEFA Interagency Commission, New York

J. Porras-Zúñiga

Comprehension, Teaching and Testing for

This entry is about comprehension as a central aspect of meaningful learning in the context of teaching. First, basic characteristics of human comprehension are described. Comprehension is considered as a mental construction process. Based on these considerations, possibilities for educational guidance of these construction processes through teaching are discussed. Then, methods for testing and evaluating certain aspects of comprehension are described. Finally, perspectives for further research activities are pointed out.

1. Components of Human Comprehension

Understanding human comprehension requires an understanding of the major components of comprehension. Five primary components are addressed in this section.

1.1 Effort after Meaning

A central task of education is to help people orientate themselves in a complex real and symbolic world and understand its various phenomena. Comprehension can be considered as the most demanding human mental activity since it can encompass perception, memory, thinking, and problem solving. Humans principally assume that information about the world is understandable. Bartlett (1932) has called this basic anthropological attitude an "effort after meaning." Within interpersonal communication a distinction can be made between comprehension on the content level and comprehension on the communication level. One can understand the conveyed information about the content and one can understand the intention of message.

1.2 Mental Construction

Findings from hermeneutics, psycholinguistics, cognitive psychology, and artificial intelligence since the early 1980s gave rise to a constructive theory of comprehension (Bransford 1979, Hörmann 1978). The theory's basic assumption holds that comprehension is an active and goal-oriented construction of coherent mental representations based on newly acquired information and prior knowledge. In most cases, comprehension of verbal information has served as a paradigm for the analysis of comprehension. Other forms of comprehension as, for example, comprehension of situations or social behavior have received only little attention.

1.3 Interaction Between External and Internal Influences

Comprehension is not a single act. It results from a complex interaction between different levels of information processing influenced by external and internal conditions (Engelkamp 1984). On the one hand, comprehension activities are usually triggered by external information which provides the material for mental constructions. Teaching can influence these mental construction processes by presenting certain verbal or pictorial information in an appropriate learning environment. On the other hand, comprehension is being controlled by internal conditions, especially prior knowledge, aims, interests, and expectations. In order to comprehend then, a student must assimilate the new information into pre-existing cognitive structures and/or accomodate these structures according to the new information. Trying to make new information as meaningful as possible by forming coherence with already existing knowledge can sometimes lead to misunderstandings (as when a learner comprehends the presented information in his or her own way but misinterprets the teacher's meaning). The integration of old and new information into a coherent whole requires knowledge-based inferences and can be controlled by metacognitive processes.

1.4 Open-ended Processes

Comprehension is principally an open-ended process. Neisser (1976) has developed a comprehension cycle to explain comprehension. New information enlarges prior knowledge which influences subsequent processing, leading again to a knowledge modification, and so on. Depending on the number of processing cycles, comprehension can be deeper or more superficial. An individual can break off further comprehension efforts for practical reasons. Nevertheless, already understood material can be put into a new context and then be comprehended again in a new way or at a deeper level.

1.5 Context Dependency

Information is always embedded in a context which influences its meaning (Bransford 1979). Actions, for example, are embedded in social situations, words are embedded in sentences and these again are embedded in texts, and so on. The respective context serves to avoid ambiguity and misunderstandings. The context dependency of comprehension is a central issue in situated learning and cognitive apprenticeship.

2. Teaching for Comprehension

Teaching can only lead to comprehension by stimulating an individual to engage in certain mental construction processes. On the one hand, the learner needs sufficient guidance to interrelate new information into prior knowledge. On the other hand, mental construction processes require a certain degree of individual freedom which should not be unnecessarily limited. A balance has to be found between necessary instructional guidance and the required cognitive independence of the learner.

2.1 Activation of Prior Knowledge

In meaningful learning an individual is expected not only to pick up information about isolated facts but to assemble pieces of knowledge to coherent higher order structures. Coherence formation requires the activation of prior knowledge. According to the theory of cognitive subsumption by Ausubel (1968), a teacher should activate clear, stable, and distinct concepts which allow anchoring of the new information in the learner's knowledge structure. This activation, using advance organizers, provides a general framework which can then be further elaborated through progressive differentiation. A similar notion can be found in the elaboration theory of instruction (Reigeluth 1983). According to this theory, prior knowledge is activated through a preceding epitome which provides a conceptual framework for the integration of new information. Such an epitome contains a few simple central concepts and interconnects them using semantic relations. The subject matter is then described first in a crude, general way. Subsequently, more detailed descriptions follow step by step.

Activation of prior knowledge can also be achieved by the use of examples. On the one hand, examples can help to illustrate general statements and to make instructions more lively by personally affecting the learner. On the other hand, learners often consider an example in isolation without recognizing their relationship to the more general content (Marton and Wenestram 1978). Examples often have a stronger influence on comprehension than explicitly conveyed general information. A frequent recommendation, therefore, is to start with typical examples and then gradually to reduce typicality.

2.2 Triggering of Comprehension Activities

There frequently exists a gap between what learners can do and what they actually do. Many students think that comprehension is a passive reception of knowledge from a teacher or textbook rather than a generative constructive process. Therefore, the question arises how to stimulate learners to engage in the appropriate comprehension activities. Instead of simply presenting ready-made knowledge structures with the help of advance organizers or epitomes, teachers can use genetic or inquiry-oriented teaching. Here, the learner is being stimulated to discover essential coherence relations on his or her own. The teacher requires students to structure problem situations independently, to infer global interrelations from presented examples, and to generate hypotheses and to test them (Wagenschein 1989). Epistemic motivation is stimulated through inducing cognitive conflicts (Berlyne 1960). In these less structured learning situations, however, the correlation between general intelligence of the learner and learning outcome usually becomes higher than in highly structured learning environments.

Comprehension activities can also be triggered by adjunct aids like the explication of educational objectives or adjunct questions. A teacher can make educational objectives explicit through providing information about tasks which will have to be solved later on. On the one hand, such information gives learners an orientation basis for directing their processing. On the other hand, however, there is the danger of learners being too selective with regard to the conveyed information. They might then only concentrate on seemingly goal-relevant contents and neglect the other information with the consequence that higher order relations are not recognized.

Well-suited adjunct questions can stimulate reflection or deeper-level processing, evoke cognitive conflicts, or demand an application of what has been understood. Rothkopf (1970) has used the term "mathemagenic activities" for such deeper processing initiated by adjunct questions. In order to support coherence formation, such questions should aim especially at establishing higher order relations. Questions can either precede each instructional section and therefore enhance mainly intentional learning of question-relevant contents, or can follow each instructional section. Then they initiate, on the one hand, intentional learning through recapitulation of the conveyed content, and on the other, incidental learning through generating a specific cognitive orientation. The learner comes to expect similar questions in the following instructional sections and organizes his or her processing activities accordingly (Rickards and Denner 1978).

The application of such adjunct aids has to be well-measured and matched with the cognitive-processing capacity of the learner. Too many educational objectives and adjunct questions can be quite confusing instead of being supportive for the learner. The efficiency of such aids seems to follow a u-inverse function. In the case of very favorable conditions (for example, good individual learning prerequisites, well-structured teaching materials, and sufficient learning time), studies often show no effect since such aids are actually not needed. Under very unfavorable conditions there is again no effect since the aids cannot be utilized appropriately. However, a supportive effect with regard to comprehension and learning can be expected in case of average processing conditions (Hartley and Davies 1976).

2.3 Metacognitive Control and Self-regulation

Comprehension as a mental construction is a goal-directed process. Learners are capable of adapting their cognitive processing to context conditions and expected demands. In order to achieve flexible and adaptive cognitive processing, metacognitive strategies concerning comprehension monitoring and control of one's own processing are necessary. Flavell (1979) has emphasized the importance of metacognitive knowledge (i.e., knowledge about human cognition) for monitoring and controlling one's own processing. However, the role of this metacognitive knowledge is being disputed; even experts often have difficulties in verbalizing their metacognitive self-regulation. Furthermore, existing metacognitive knowledge is often not used.

The regulation of cognitive processing is usually automatized. Only in the case of comprehension problems which cannot be solved with automated procedures is cognitive processing consciously controlled through metacognitive knowledge (Brown et al. 1986). However, learners frequently have inadequate standards for evaluating their comprehension. They often do not realize that they do not really understand. They establish coherence only at the specific level and not at the global level or they ignore inconsistencies but are nevertheless under the asumption that they understand well. Glenberg et al. (1982) have called this the "illusion of knowing."

2.4 Strategy Training

Various methods exist aimed at preventing learners from superficial comprehension by teaching them certain processing strategies (Mandl and Friedrich 1992). Some of these strategy training programs, for example, instruct the learner to emphasize central information through self-questioning and to connect this information with other information. Learners can also be supported in independently summarizing what they have understood with the help of certain techniques, such as mapping procedures. Using mapping procedures, the learner graphically depicts the superordinate structure of the learning content. The results are two-dimensional maps which represent the basic structure of a subject area in the form of a diagram and which can be considered as graphical summaries (Anderson 1979). These procedures require the learner to go beyond specific coherence and to direct his or her attention also to the higher-order global relations. The techniques usually require many hours of intensive training until they can be mastered and used relatively efficiently. Other strategy training programs emphasize time-planning, concentration management, self-perception, motivational–affective factors, individual learning styles, and social–psychological aspects of learning in groups (e.g., McKeachie et al. 1985, Weinstein 1988).

Studies on the effectiveness of strategy training programs frequently show positive effects with inexperienced learners whereas experienced learners often either profit little or show a decline in comprehension and learning performance. Experienced learners usually follow certain habits in their processing which are relatively resistant to change. If a training program is to have positive effects on learning it must first dismantle these old learning habits before it can establish a new regulatory system. Furthermore, the learner has to concentrate during strategy training on the subject matter and, simultaneously, on the learning techniques to be acquired. Due to this division of attention the cognitive capacity available for the subject matter itself is reduced, which can result in temporarily impaired learning performance. Strategy training programs are probably most efficient when they aim at global coherence formation with less experienced learners.

Newly acquired strategies are often dropped under the pressure of a specific learning situation. The learner then returns to his or her usual processing style. This finding suggests the need to engage in indirect promotion of strategies. The learner is placed in a learning situation and given certain tasks which stimulate the desired processing activities. Such indirect training makes the acquisition of strategies a by-product of subject matter learning. Strategies should not just be practiced. Rather, learners should be convinced of their usefulness in order to increase their willingness to apply them. Furthermore, strategy application depends on motivational transfer, attributional beliefs, and on the learner's self-concept (Borkowski et al. 1988). Comprehension strategies need to be supplemented through socioemotional coping strategies in order to help less efficient learners overcome the negative emotions associated with learning (Lehtinen 1992).

2.5 Situatedness

Context dependency of comprehension implies that

the cognitive processes are embedded into situations of everyday life. Therefore, the social aspect of comprehension must be considered. This view has been emphasized by Palincsar and Brown (1984) in what they "reciprocal teaching" which supports comprehension activities by embedding them into a social context. Teachers and learners alternately conduct dialogues on instructional text-sections and summarize, make predictions, ask questions, and clarify where necessary. This interaction provides many possibilities to uncover misunderstandings on the part of the individual learner.

The context dependency of comprehension is especially emphasized in the situated learning approach. According to this view, comprehension is best supported in authentic situations with meaningful goal-oriented activities which provide the possibility for a cognitive apprenticeship. The teacher shows the learners, for example, a specific action (modeling) and conveys an orientation base for its execution (scaffolding). The learners then carry out the action themselves while the teacher observes and supports them (coaching). The more the learners become able to master the task, the less help they receive (fading out). Comprehension is viewed here as a process of enculturation whereby the learner adopts knowledge, abilities, and beliefs of social groups (Collins et al. 1989).

3. Testing for Comprehension

Comprehension cannot be measured directly. It is only possible to measure performances which require comprehension as a prerequisite. These indicators can be measured during comprehension (on-line) or after comprehension (off-line). The methods used for testing comprehension only address aspects of these complex comprehension processes (Anderson 1972, Ballstaedt and Mandl 1988).

3.1 Questions

Answering questions is probably the oldest and the most versatile method for testing comprehension (Graesser and Black 1985). Such questions require not only the retrieval of facts, but also additional processing which goes beyond the previously presented information. There is a distinction between open questions which allow answers to be constructed and closed questions which allow only a choice among various possible answers. Multiple-choice questions have proved very efficient in testing. Several variants of such questions are distinguished depending on how many possible answers are being provided and how many of them are correct. The difficulty of constructing multiple-choice questions lies in finding optional answers which require higher order cognitive processing to check their correctness.

3.2 Free Recall

The free recall of a previously learned content using one's own words is also a common method for testing comprehension. The corresponding evaluation can take into account both the quantity and the quality of the response, especially the coherence of recall. The basic assumption that comprehension allows correct reproduction assumes that the learner has created a conceptual representation of the presented information which he or she can then verbalize if required. Different learners will, of course, produce different sequences of the content, use different words, and generate different sentences. This creativity is considered as proof of the integration into prior knowledge. The connection between comprehension and remembering, however, is sometimes rather weak. There are contents which learners understand and then forget and there are contents which they do not understand but can nevertheless remember.

3.3 Summarizing

The task of summarizing the most important elements from a large amount of information is especially well-suited for written testing. Here as well, the quantity and quality of the summary can be of interest; the most important information has to be included and the summary has to be coherent. Summaries are quite valid indicators for comprehension since their mental construction requires higher order coherence formation processes. The reduction processes involved in summarizing have been analyzed in detail and a list of macro-operations such as deletion, selection, integration, and generalization has been produced (van Dijk 1980).

3.4 Thinking Aloud

This method requires the verbalization of ongoing cognitive processes while solving a task. Recording and transcribing a protocol are necessary to preserve the material for further evaluation. Thinking aloud is only possible in a single learner situation. Furthermore, it requires that systematic quantitative and qualitative evaluation criteria be developed according to the respective goals of the analysis. The method usually costs a great deal of time, but it allows on-line insight into the actual development of comprehension or misunderstanding (Graesser 1981).

The protocols provide qualitatively rich and distinctive material which reflects various comprehension processes: knowledge activation, inferences, establishment of coherence, and metacognition. Nevertheless, thinking aloud brings only the tip of the iceberg of all the processes of comprehension into view. Much more is going on in the head of a learner than he or she can verbalize. Furthermore, the central assumption that ongoing mental processes can be verbally expressed without distortions has repeatedly been doubted. The objection is that the unusual task of continually verbalizing actually interferes with the comprehension processes.

3.5 Cloze Procedures

The standard form of a cloze procedure consists in a text presented to the subject in which one word out of five is missing. The learner has to fill in the missing words. The percentage of correctly filled blanks is used as the measure of comprehension. There are numerous variants (e.g., only one out of five content words can be deleted, or the learner is presented with the fragment of a text or sentence which he or she has to complete appropriately). Cloze procedures can also be applied for visual tests of comprehension, when empty spaces have to be correctly filled within a picture or a graph. There is disagreement about what kind of comprehension processes are being measured with cloze procedures. Some researchers doubt that comprehension is being measured at all. The question remains to what extent guessing plays a role since due to pre-existing content and linguistic knowledge a number of empty spaces can be filled without any comprehension of the passage.

3.6 Structure Displays

These testing procedures can be viewed as a variant of the mind-mapping technique. Subsequent to a comprehension process the learner externalizes his or her knowledge through writing concept words on cards and connecting them with a set of given content relations. The procedure has been standardized, but it can easily be modified for various aims (Scheele 1992). Unfortunately, no theory-based set of relations has been developed. The possibilities of quantitative and qualitative criteria of formal and content-related analyses are manifold. Measures for the internal coherence and differentiatedness of the knowledge can be calculated. The concepts can also be categorized using content analysis. Structure displays exhibit coherence relations and can be used for knowledge diagnosis. If the prior knowledge about a certain topic is displayed before learning, then the new conceptual interrelations acquired during teaching can be identified.

3.7 Application

In many cases the application of what has been understood in performing a certain behavior is the most valid method for testing comprehension. Examples of this method include conducting an experiment, using an apparatus, and similar activities. The quality of such a performance can be judged by the number of mistakes, the required amount of time, or other appropriate criteria. The use of videorecording allows repeated observation, also with slow motion. Since this procedure requires individual sessions and since the evaluation is costly in terms of time, practical application as a test for comprehension is accordingly rare. In addition, successful performance can sometimes occur on the basis of procedural knowledge rather than conceptual knowledge. In this case, the person being tested acts correctly although he or she did not grasp the meaning of that action. Therefore, tasks have to be constructed so that they are only solvable with the comprehension of the entire context.

4. Future Perspectives

Further research on teaching and testing for comprehension should analyze more deeply the interaction between cognitive, motivational, emotional, and social aspects of understanding. Furthermore, research should not be restricted to language comprehension, since nonverbal comprehension processes also play an important role in education.

In order to promote comprehension processes, a deeper analysis of the interplay between cognitive and metacognitive processes in the self-regulation of comprehension seems to be promising. Related to this analysis is the question of how direct training of comprehension and learning strategies and indirect support of such strategies should be combined. Another important problem is the optimal combination of the cognitively oriented strategies and the motivationlly oriented supportive strategies for specific learner groups.

The provision of indirect support for comprehension strategies is closely related to the situated learning approach to teaching comprehension since in both cases teaching is tied to authentic social and pragmatic contexts. Formal objective tests for comprehension play a limited role in these approaches since comprehension is constantly being evaluated in the social context (communicative validation). The complexity of the field requires multidisciplinary research from the perspectives of cognitive psychology, psycholinguistics, educational psychology, and instructional design.

See also: Learning Potential and Learning Potential Tests; Cognition and Learning

References

Anderson R C 1972 How to construct achievement tests to assess comprehension. *Rev. Educ. Res.* 42(2): 145–70

Anderson T H 1979 Study skills and learning strategies. In: O'Neil H F, Spielberger D (eds.) 1979 *Cognitive and Affective Learning Strategies*. Academic Press, New York

Ausubel D P 1968 *Educational Psychology: A Cognitive View*. Holt, Rinehart and Winston, New York

Ballstaedt S-P, Mandl H 1988 The assessment of comprehensibility. In: Ammon U, Dittmar N, Mattheier K J (eds.) 1988 *Sociolinguistics. An International Handbook of the Science of Language and Society*. Walter de Gruyter, Berlin

Bartlett F C 1932 *Remembering. A Study in Experimental and Social Psychology*. Cambridge University Press, Cambridge

Berlyne D E 1960 *Conflict, Arousal, and Curiosity*. McGraw-Hill, New York
Borkowski J G, Weyhing R S, Carr M 1988 Effects of attributional retraining on strategy-based reading comprehension in learning-disabled students. *J. Educ. Psychol.* 80(1): 46–53
Bransford J O 1979 *Human Cognition: Learning, Understanding, and Remembering*. Wadsworth, Belmont, California
Brown A L, Armbruster B B, Baker L 1986 The role of metacognition in reading and studying. In: Orasanu J (ed.) 1986 *Reading Comprehension. From Research to Practice*. Erlbaum, Hillsdale, New Jersey
Collins A, Brown J S, Newman S E 1989 Cognitive apprenticeship: Teaching the crafts of reading, writing, and mathematics. In: Resnick L B (ed.) 1989 *Knowing, Learning, and Instruction*. Erlbaum, Hillsdale, New Jersey
Engelkamp J 1984 Verstehen als Informationsverarbeitung. In: Engelkamp J (ed.) 1984 *Psychologische Aspekte des Verstehens*. Springer, Berlin
Flavell J H 1979 Metacognition and cognitive monitoring: A new area of cognitive-developmental inquiry. *Am. Psychol.* 34(10): 906–11
Glenberg A M, Wilkinson A C, Epstein W 1982 The illusion of knowing: Failure in the self-assessment of comprehension. *Memory and Cognit.* 10(6): 597–602
Graesser A C 1981 *Prose Comprehension Beyond the Word*. Springer-Verlag, New York
Graesser A C, Black J B (eds.) 1985 *The Psychology of Questions*. Erlbaum, Hillsdale, New Jersey
Hartley J, Davies I K 1976 Preinstructional strategies: The role of pretests, behavioral objectives, overviews and advance organizers. *Rev. Educ. Res.* 46: 239–65
Hörmann H 1978 *Meinen und Verstehen. Grundzuge einer psychologischen Semantik*. Suhrkamp, Frankfurt
Lehtinen E 1992 Lern- und Bewältigungsstrategien im Unterricht. In: Mandl H, Friedrich H F (eds.) 1992
Mandl H, Friedrich H F (eds.) 1992 *Lern- und Denkstrategien*. Hogrefe, Göttingen
Marton F, Wenestram C G 1978 Qualitative differences in understanding and retention of the main points in some texts based on the principle-example structure. In: Gruneberg M M, Morris P E, Sykes R N (eds.) 1978 *Practical Aspects of Memory*. Academic Press, London
McKeachie W J, Pintrich P R, Lin Y G 1985 Learning to learn. In: d'Ydewalle G (ed.) 1985 *Cognition, Information Processing, and Motivation*. North-Holland, Amsterdam
Neisser U 1976 *Cognition and Reality. Principles and Implications of Cognitive Psychology*. Freeman, San Francisco, California
Palincsar A M, Brown A L 1984 Reciprocal teaching of comprehension-fostering and comprehension-monitoring activitics. *Cognition and Instruction* 1(2): 117–75
Reigeluth C M (ed.) 1983 *Instructional-design Theories and Models: An Overview of Their Current Status*. Erlbaum, Hillsdale, New Jersey
Rickards J P, Denner P R 1978 Inserted questions as aids to reading text. *Instr. Sci.* 7(3): 313–46
Rothkopf E Z 1970 The concept of mathemagenic activities. *Rev. Educ. Res.* 40(3): 325-36
Scheele B (ed.) 1992 *Struktur-Lege-Verfahren als Dialog-Konsens- Methodik*. Aschendorff, Munster
van Dijk T A 1980 *Macrostructures*. Erlbaum, Hillsdale, New Jersey
Wagenschein M 1989 *Verstehen lehren*. Beltz, Weinheim
Weinstein C E 1988 Assessment and training of student learning strategies. In: Schmeck R R (ed.) 1988 *Learning Strategies and Learning Styles*. Plenum Press, New York

W. Schnotz; S-P. Ballstaedt

Computer and Information Sciences: Educational Programs

What do primary and secondary students need to know about computers? Should they learn how to program? What are the cognitive effects of learning how to program? How can computers be used to help students learn to program? These are the curricular and pedagogical questions addressed by this entry.

One curricular approach to computer and information science emphasizes learning the nontechnical aspects of computers, their capabilities, limitations, and uses, as well as their social, vocational, and educational implications (Moursund 1976). This "applications approach" has become the dominant way in which computer knowledge is taught in the United States and countries in Europe. A second approach takes the position that studying the computer, and more specifically computer programming, is an appropriate end in its own right (Luehrmann 1972); such study provides students with the skills needed to master the power of the new technology rather than be mastered by it. A third approach argues that students should learn to program but not as an end in itself; rather, programming is learned for the higher order thinking and problem-solving skills that are claimed to result from acquiring ability in programming—its cognitive effects (Papert 1980). This entry examines these approaches in more detail, reviews the research on the cognitive effects of learning to program, and examines two ways by which computers themselves can be used to teach programming.

1. Computer Science Curriculum

"Computer science" is the discipline and study of computers and how they operate. "Information science" or "informatics," the term more often used in Europe, refers to the organization, structure, and use of information. "Computer programming" is the use of a computer programming language to provide computers with the instructions and data they need to operate. "Computer literacy" refers to the knowledge and skill needed to use computers and understand their impact on everyone's lives. These terms also reflect the range of objectives and purposes that have been proposed for studying information and computers, from the acquisition of knowledge and skills needed to understand and apply computers in everyday life, to the knowledge and skill needed to make computers carry out specialized tasks.

1.1 Learning the Applications of Computers

It is clear that computers are becoming pervasive in modern society. They are to be found in businesses, laboratories, schools, and homes. One curricular approach to the computer science curriculum is to teach students to use computers effectively in their personal and professional lives.

At the primary level, Hunter (1982) identified four main areas for curricular objectives that represent this approach: using computer programs, procedural thinking, computer applications, and social and values implications of computer and communications systems. The purpose of this curriculum at the primary level is to provide students with the skills and concepts they need to learn subsequently about any particular computer application or system. These general skills and abstract concepts would be acquired while learning to use specific applications, such as information-retrieval software, word processing, spreadsheets, and so on. Hunter recommends that these skills, experiences, and applications be infused throughout the United States primary curriculum rather than be taught as a separate course.

At the secondary level, the professional society for the computer science field in the United States, the Association for Computing Machinery (ACM), issued a report recommending several types of computer science courses that students might take (Rogers et al. 1985). One course is "Applications and implications of computers." This course is intended to provide skills in computer applications as problem-solving tools that become integrated in their lives. The course is also intended to provide students with an understanding of the individual and societal implications of computer applications. As a result of the course, students would have an appreciation of the roles computers and information can and do play in society.

There has been considerable curriculum development in other countries which parallel developments in the United States. An International Federation for Information Processing (IFIP) World Conference in 1990 demonstrated that many countries were actively developing national curriculum policies, policies that reflected the alternative curricular approaches described above. Most countries have taken the applications approach to computer and information science described in this section. Of these countries, some, such as Israel (Barta 1990), have had considerable experience with this curriculum; others, such as Japan (Nishinosono 1990), were only beginning to experiment in the early 1990s.

1.2 Learning Computer Science as a Profession

The study of computers and computer science can be considered an end in itself. Computer science is often studied as a formal discipline or profession and the curriculum emphasizes the acquisition of the knowledge and skills needed to make computers work, particularly the ability to program computer software. This approach is encountered more often at secondary level. The ACM report (Rogers et al. 1985) cited above also recommends a one-semester course entitled "Introduction to high-level computer language." This is a prerequisite for more advanced programming courses. Its goal is to provide students with an understanding of programming concepts and the basics of a programming language. There is considerable discussion in the report about the languages that might be used in the course. Both BASIC and Logo are easy for novices to use and are likely to result in early success, in part because as interpreted languages they execute commands immediately and students can see the effects of their programming. But some computer scientists argue against the use of BASIC because it is not structured like more professional languages, such as Pascal, and students may acquire poor programming habits. A more recent ACM report (Merritt et al. in press) updates the curriculum for this introductory programming course and recommends that the course should include fundamental concepts in the field of computer science, such as algorithms, programming languages, operating systems, computer architecture, and the social, ethical, and professional contexts of computing. A laboratory component would use computers and a programming language to conduct experiments that explore the power of computers and illustrate the abstract concepts in the course.

Internationally, this approach to teaching computer science and computer programming as a profession or formal discipline is used primarily to supplement a curriculum that emphasizes the applications approach. Curricula that emphasize programming are used in a relatively small number of countries. They include countries in the former Soviet Union (Kerr 1987) and in Eastern Europe.

1.3 Programming and its Cognitive Effects

Papert (1980) argued that computer programming should be taught in primary and secondary schools but not as an end in itself. Rather, Papert believed that, through programming, students would come to think more about the domain within which they were programming and think more about their own thinking. Students would acquire higher cognitive skills, such as planning and problem-solving, and metacognitive skills that would allow them to think reflectively about these processes. Presumably, these higher level skills would be transferred to other cognitive tasks. These goals have come to be referred to as the "cognitive effects of programming."

While positive cognitive effects have been claimed for programming in general, perhaps the strongest claims have been made for the effects of programming in Logo. Logo is a powerful but easy to use programming language. It is characterized by a graphic interface that, at its simplest level, allows a user to control the movement of an object (i.e., a "turtle") on the screen. It is an extensible language, which means that with relatively few primitive commands users can write procedures that Logo then treats as elements of its syntax. Logo has a modular structure, preferred by computer scientists, which allows students to write program codes in meaningful components. Logo is also an interpreted language, which allows the user to see immediately the effects of the program. Noninterpreted, or "compiled" languages require the user to finish writing the program before it can be run. In part for these reasons, and in part because of the philosophy and persuasiveness of Papert, the use of Logo has become widespread in the United States, particularly at the primary level.

2. *Research on the Cognitive Effects of Logo*

The claimed cognitive effects of learning Logo programming are also an important reason for its widespread use. Initially these claims were not based on empirical studies. The widespread adoption of Logo prompted a number of research studies to examine the cognitive effects of learning Logo.

2.1 *Cognitive Effects and Their Transfer*

Among the more prominent research studies on the cognitive effects of Logo is a study by Clements and Gullo (1984). This examined a group of first-grade students who received Logo lessons on the skills involved in deciding on a goal, separating the goal into subgoals, translating subgoals into Logo code, and so on. The intent was to see if these programming skills would transfer to other cognitive skills, such as reflective thinking and cognitive monitoring. A control group received computer-assisted instruction (CAI) on specific skills from the reading and arithmetic curriculum.

The programming group demonstrated significant gains in measures of creativity and reflectivity and outperformed the CAI group on tests of cognitive monitoring processes. Clements (1987) extended this study by testing a subset of the students in the original study 18 months after the end of the original training. He found that, compared with the control group, the Logo treatment resulted in a moderate effect on the total score of test of cognitive skills, a strong and significant effect on total language achievement, and a moderate effect on total mathematics. On the other hand, the CAI evidenced a weak positive effect on memory abilities.

Studies have not uniformly supported the cognitive effects of Logo programming. For example, Pea et al. (1987) examined two primary school classes over a two-year period. During the first year of the study, students received some simple instruction in Logo, occasional teacher-led group sessions, two sessions per week programming with the computers, and additional optional access at other times. The researchers were interested in the effect of such extensive experience on a "far transfer" task. Far transfer refers to the appropriate use of a skill on tasks different from those used with the original learning. The researchers selected a planning task judged to be isomorphic in deep structure, though different in surface structure from planning tasks required during programming. The hypothesis was that students who learned the skills needed to plan a Logo program would also plan better during the transfer task, as would be demonstrated by their think-aloud protocols and overt planning behaviors. However, compared to a control group of students who had not taken programming lessons, the plans generated by Logo students were no more efficient or structured and the Logo students did not differ from nonprogrammers in their planning decisions. Near the end of the second year of more structured experience with Logo, the researchers looked at the effect on a more similar, "near transfer" task; that is, a task designed to be isomorphic with programming tasks at both a deep and a surface level. Again, an analysis of plans and protocols found no differences between programming and nonprogramming groups in their plans or planning processes.

Pea et al. (1987) concluded that Logo may allow for but does not necessarily result in the development of cognitive skills. They suggest that programming be used within a classroom culture that builds bridges between programming activities and thinking about other domains of school and life, and one in which students, peers, and teachers talk about thinking skills and display them aloud for others to share and learn from.

2.2 *Logo and the Culture of Learning*

Harel and Papert (1990) have designed an integrated programming–learning culture of the sort recommended by Pea et al. (1987). Called the Instructional Software Design Project (ISDP), the Logo-based environment creates a pervasive programming culture in which learning to program is integrated with other school content and assignments. Students work with each other on their projects and regularly engage in structured planning or design activities. With ISDP, students begin by using Logo everyday to work on different computer projects as an integral part of their homeroom activities. After five months of this, students spend another five months designing and producing educational software to teach fractions to younger aged children. Students are involved in teacher-led focus sessions on topics related to programming and design and in daily sessions when they plan and program their software. Students record their daily plans, problems, and changes in their "designer's notebooks." Students are free to circulate in the specially designated classroom to work individually or with friends and share ideas about fractions, design, and programming. In addition, once each month the project fourth-graders would be joined by third-graders to try out and discuss the software.

At the end of the first school year, the ISDP group was compared with two control groups on a posttest of fraction knowledge. One control group had learned Logo in an integrated fashion without ISDP and the other had learned Logo separate from other school activities (Harel and Papert 1990). All three groups received only two weeks of formal instruction on fractions during the school year. The ISDP group scored significantly higher on the fractions test and higher on tests of Logo knowledge than either of the control groups. The researchers also contend that the ISDP students developed a range of cognitive and metacognitive skills, such as planning, self-management, and thinking about these processes. Harel and Papert (1990) concluded that the observed cognitive effects were due to the fact that the ISDP children were actively involved in their own learning, learned Logo through integration into their daily activities, used it in conjunction with learning-by-teaching design activities, participated in a community actively involved in the sharing of knowledge and products, and so on. They claim it is this culture of learning, along with the use of Logo, rather than the teaching of Logo per se, that fostered cognitive effects.

In summary, it appears that as Pea et al. (1987) have pointed out, learning to program Logo may, but need not, have the effect of developing cognitive and metacognitive skills, such as planning and self-monitoring. These effects seem to depend on building an entire school curriculum, not just a programming curriculum, around activities related to higher level cognitive and metacognitive skills.

3. Computer-based Approaches to Programming

Computers themselves are beginning to play a direct role in the teaching and learning of programming. Programming software environments are being developed that are based on models of how experts program. Two basic approaches have emerged: one uses the computer as an intelligent programming tutor; the other uses the computer as a specialized planning tool.

3.1 Intelligent Tutor for Programming LISP

Anderson and his group at Carnegie Mellon University (Anderson et al. 1990) have developed a sophisticated, intelligent tutor to teach LISP programming. Underlying the tutor is an ideal model of how students should solve programming problems based on studies of expert programmers and a model of how students err. The ideal model includes approximately 500 production rules that are needed to solve problems of the sort that appear in introductory LISP textbooks. The model guides students along a correct solution path, if necessary. The error model is used to recognize and remediate errors. There are four basic features of the tutoring system: (a) the tutor constantly monitors the student's problem-solving and provides direction whenever the student wanders off one of the correct solution paths; (b) the tutor tries to provide help with both the overt parts of the problem solution and the planning; (c) the interface tries to eliminate aspects such as syntax checking, which are irrelevant to the problem-solving skill being tutored; (d) the interface is highly reactive in that it makes some response to every symbol the student enters.

The LISP tutor was systematically evaluated in a college programming course. All students attended the same lectures and did the same problems as homework. One group did these problems with the LISP tutor; another group did them with the standard LISP environment. The tutored group did significantly better on a mid-course performance examination and on the final examination.

3.2 Tools to Support the Design of Pascal Programs

Soloway and his group at the University of Michigan (Guzdial et al.) have developed an "editing" environment that supports students as they design and run Pascal computer programs. Called the Goal-Plan-Code editor (GPCeditor), the environment is also derived from studies of human expert software-designers. In contrast to Anderson's intelligent tutor, the GPCeditor does not have expert knowledge built into the system. As a consequence, the system is not limited to a specific set of prespecified problems. It is also more responsive to the problems that students identify and the knowledge and experiences they have accrued.

The GPCeditor is designed to provide students with work spaces and functionality that explicitly support, enable, and constrain the user to engage in the kinds of behaviors that experts exhibit. For example, students must explicitly state the goals and subgoals that they have for a problem. The goals are the objectives to be met and each goal corresponds to a plan (subroutine or code fragment) by which it is attained. In the Plans Library, students can select a plan that corresponds to their goal from a set of plans they previously wrote. If a plan does not exist, one must be constructed. Plans cannot be entered without specifying a corresponding goal; goals that do not have plans are identified by the system.

4. Conclusion

In summary, research on the knowledge of expert and novice programming performance is important to the development of programming curricula. As this knowledge accrues so will the sophistication of the software designed to support novice programmers and computer-based approaches will make an increasingly important contribution to computer science education.

See also: Computer Literacy; Computer Programming, Learning and Instruction of; Computers and Learning; Computers in Education, Organizations and Journals on

References

Anderson J, Boyle C, Corbett A, Lewis M 1990 Cognitive modeling and intelligent tutoring. In: Clancey W, Soloway E (eds.) 1990 *Artificial Intelligence and Learning Environments*. MIT Press, Cambridge, Massachusetts

Barta B 1990 Computers in the Israel education system: Implementation aspects (1984–1989). In: Mc Dougal A, Dowing C (eds.) 1990 *Computers in Education*. North-Holland, Amsterdam

Clements D 1987 Longitudinal study of the effects of Logo programming on cognitive abilities and achievement. *Journal of Educational Computing Research* 3 (1): 73–94

Clements D H, Gullo D F 1984 Effects of computer programming on young children's cognition. *J. Educ. Psychol.* 76 (6): 1051–58

Guzdial M et al. 1992 The future of CAD: Technological support for kids building artifacts. In: Balestri D, Ehrmann S, Ferguson D (eds.) *Learning to Design, Designing to Learn: Using Technology to Transform the Curriculum*. Ablex, Norwood, New Jersey

Harel I, Papert S 1990 Software design as a learning environment. *Interactive Learning Environments* 1: 1–32

Hunter B 1982 Computer literacy curriculum for grades K–8. In: Seidel R, Anderson R, Hunter B (eds.) 1982 *Computer Literacy: Issues and Directions for 1985*. Academic Press, New York

Kerr S 1987 Soviet applications of microcomputers in education: Developments in research and practice during the Gorbachev era. *Journal of Educational Computing Research* 3 (1): 1–17

Luehrmann A 1972 Should the computer teach the student or vice-versa? In: Taylor R (ed.) 1980 *The Computer in the School: Tutor, Tool, Tutee*. Columbia University Press, New York

Merritt S et al. in press *ACM Model High School Computer Science Curriculum*. Pace University, New York

Moursund D 1976 What is computer literacy? *Creative Computing* 2 (6): 55

Nishinosono H 1990 International cooperation for educational use of computers in Asia and the Pacific through UNESCO and recent trends in Japan. In: Mc Dougal A, Dowing C (eds.) 1990 *Computers in Education*. North-Holland, Amsterdam

Papert S 1980 *Mindstorms: Children, Computers, and Powerful Ideas*. Basic Books, New York

Pea R, Kurland D, Hawkins J 1987 Logo and the development of thinking skills. In: Pea R, Sheingold K (eds.) *Mirrors of Minds: Patterns of Experience in Educational Computing*. Ablex, Norwood, New Jersey

Rogers J et al. 1985 Computer science for secondary schools: Course content. *Communications of the ACM* 28 (3): 270–74

Further Reading

Cummings T C, Brown S W (eds.) 1986 *The Information Age Classroom: Using Computers as a Tool*. Franklin, Beadle and Associates, Irvin, California

Davidson J I 1988 *Children and Computers Together in the Early Childhood Classroom*. Delmar, Albany, New York

Nix D, Spiro R (eds.) 1990 *Cognition, Education, and Multimedia: Explosing Ideas in High Technology*. Erlbaum, Hillsdale, New Jersey

R. B. Kozma

Computer Literacy

Computer literacy is not a stable, invariant concept, but one that has developed over time along with technological developments and the changing role of new information technologies in global societies. In general, the term is used to refer to basic general education in computing, as distinct from more specialized, advanced, or vocational courses (Eraut 1991). Many publications reflect the intensive discussions and the many—often very creative—efforts made to determine what concepts should be included in computer literacy education (often called introductory computer education) in secondary and sometimes in elementary education. This entry reviews the development of computer literacy as a concept since the late 1970s and of trends in computer literacy education in the early 1990s.

1. Computer Literacy: Not an Invariant Definition

In the literature many labels can be found referring to forms of computer literacy or introductory computer education, such as computer awareness, computer appreciation, computer initiation, and computer familiarization. No consensus exists as to the meaning of these terms, although they are often used to indicate distinct levels of computer proficiency (Plomp and van de Wolde 1985). Culbertson (1986) illustrated this perception by distinguishing the following four meanings of computer literacy:

(a) operational literacy: knowing the basic components of hardware and software and being able to demonstrate the operational skills needed to make computers work;

(b) instrumental literacy: using computers as an instrument in accomplishing certain tasks (for students in schools, learning tasks);

(c) algorithmic reasoning: literacy acquired through computer programming;

(d) education for altered roles: notable components include consumer literacy, worker literacy and citizen literacy.

A representative and illustrative definition of computer literacy comes from the Minnesota Educational Computing Consortium, "computer literacy is whatever understanding, skills and attitudes one needs to function effectively within a given social role that directly or indirectly involves computers" (Anderson and Klassen 1981). However, a similar but more elaborate definition is proposed by Lockheed et al. (1983) in a publication of survey items for assessment of computer literacy in schools:

> computer literacy may be defined as whatever a person needs to know and to do with computers in order to function competently in our information-based society. Computer literacy includes three kinds of competence: skills, knowledge, and understanding. It includes (1) the ability to use and instruct computers as aids in learning, solving problems, managing information; (2) knowledge of functions, applications, capabilities, limitations, and social implications of computers and related technology; and (3) understanding needed to learn and evaluate new applications and social issues as they arise (Lockheed et al. 1983 pp. 8–9).

Both definitions illustrate that computer literacy is not an invariant concept. Computer literacy courses vary greatly, depending on the social role of the learners (e.g., adults or high school students), the state of technology, and the way of thinking about this concept at a certain moment. In this entry the term computer literacy will refer to all kinds of introductory computer education.

2. *Developments over Time*

Ways of thinking about computer literacy have changed over the years. Plomp and van de Wolde (1985) summarized goals of "early" computer literacy courses (at the beginning of the 1980s):

(a) development of proficiency in using computers (programming) and computer applications;

(b) development of understanding of a variety of present and future computer applications, and their implications for life at both the social and individual level;

(c) elimination of computer-related phobias and anxieties; this goal was especially of importance at the early 1980s when microcomputers started to pervade the workplace and many adults appeared to show concerns and even resistance toward computer technology (Jay 1981);

(d) promotion of a deeper understanding of the capabilities and limitations of computers.

In addition to these computer-related goals, computer literacy is often connected with two general educational goals, which in themselves were emphasized in education long before new information technologies were introduced:

(e) development of skills in problem-solving and procedure specification: in order to become a productive user of information technology one has to acquire skills in the analysis, synthesis, and evaluation of models and algorithms;

(f) development of information-handling skills: to be literate in an information society one needs to be competent in both formal and informal aspects of information handling.

The latter general goal makes computer literacy part of a much broader skill called "information literacy," which refers to familiarity with hardware beyond computers (Hade 1982).

Differences between computer literacy curricula and later efforts do not so much reflect the nature of the above goals as the weighting of these goals. Technological developments influenced this process, although goals (c) and (d) were common for almost all early computer literacy teaching. The development of the concept can be illustrated by subdividing computer literacy curricula into categories according to their content structure (Plomp and van de Wolde 1985).

The earliest type of computer literacy curricula—emphasizing the first goal of computing skills, focused heavily on the bits and bytes of computing, as well as programming (often supported by mainframes in the late 1970s)—can be characterized as "computer (hardware) oriented." From the late 1970s hardware developed at an increasing rate and related knowledge became obsolete, with the consequence that only a few curricula placed hardware facts and procedures in a central position. It was often argued that computer education should only stress invariant aspects of information technology, and be built up in such a way that technological developments will not necessarily affect its content. One of the influential proponents of this approach was Luehrman (1981), who advocated that to become a computer literate person it was insufficient just to learn about computers; it was necessary to "do" computing; that is, to do programming. Until the mid-1980s many teachers still paid much attention to "peeks and pokes," taking for computer literacy education an elementary course in BASIC programming. This may have been partly due to the fact that the background in mathematics or science of many computer literacy teachers at that time did not necessarily make them feel comfortable in teaching "soft" subjects, such as the impact of new technologies on society.

In the early 1980s, as microcomputers were introduced, the hardware became cheaper and more powerful, while computers were introduced in many jobs and workplaces as important tools. This led many countries to increase the number of schools equipped with computers, and many teachers started to use ready-made applications and tool software of better quality than they would ever be able to produce themselves. These developments resulted in "application oriented" computer literacy courses, emphasizing application environments (goal (b) rather than programming environments; goals (c) and (d) (aimed at providing a correct mental image of computers) were included most of the time as well.

The belief that computers can play a role in realizing general educational goals such as the development of problem-solving skills (goal (e) and information-handling skills (goal (f)) led to two other types of computer literacy courses in the same period. The first was "algorithmic-oriented" courses, mainly structured around problem-solving strategies and principles of algorithm construction. The other type (less frequently found) was the "information-oriented" course, tending to deal with information or information needs rather than with computers, as Marland (1981) showed. In this approach, information technology based on microelectronics is integrated with older forms of information technology and the computer is considered as just one of the means available (albeit a very powerful one) for producing, storing, retrieving, using, and/or communicating information.

Although courseware development remained a major problem in the process of introducing computers in education, especially in the Anglo-Saxon and many Western European countries, an increasing number of good educational software packages in the "traditional" subject matter domains have been developed. Besides, a trend toward open, content-free software (educational use of word processors, databases, etc.) could be observed, allowing teachers in almost all subject-matter areas to adjust computer applications to their style and content of teaching. All these developments, in many countries in combination with the stimulation policies of national, regional, and/or local educational authorities, resulted in the mid-1980s in many schools having many computers. The use of computers in existing subject matter areas became a feasible option. Hawkridge (1990) discussed the social rationale for using computers (preparing students through computer literacy for their place in society) and the pedagogical rationale (using computers to improve teaching and learning in existing subject matters) as major developments in the schools (see *Educational Technology: Developing Nations*).

These parallel developments led to the question of whether separate courses in computer literacy were still needed or whether computer literacy goals could be better attained in other ways. Separate courses were criticized for creating yet another content area to be learned, unrelated to the rest of the curriculum, and probably resulted in the common view of teachers that the computer is "another person's problem." By the end of the 1980s separate computer literacy or introductory computer education courses still existed (Pelgrum and Plomp 1991). Many countries still subscribed to a policy that separate computer literacy or introductory computer education courses should be taught. Two other approaches could also be observed.

The first approach (strongly represented in Anglo-Saxon countries) was the integration of computer literacy goals with "traditional" educational goals by promoting the instrumental use of computers in existing courses, Hunter (1983) and Collis (1988). An assumption was that schools have no choice but to adapt to the information age and that learning about computers was only a part of that adaptation. However, Hunter and Collis took the position that there is no need for a separate computer literacy course or unit, but that computer-related objectives and activities must be integrated in the curricula of mathematics, social studies, science, and language arts. Having separate computer literacy courses has several negative aspects:

(a) given the rapid technological developments, such a course would be soon obsolete;
(b) teachers of other subjects may think that they would have no personal need to change their instructional practice;
(c) computer resources would be underutilized, even though they are in principle powerful tools in teaching fundamental objectives such as problem-solving and information-handling in already existing subjects in the curriculum.

The trend in the second half of the 1980s was that application programs became a major focus for computer literacy experiences. It was proposed that computer literacy objectives and activities should be integrated in the existing school curriculum. This approach was found broadly in the United States as well as in England and Wales, and Germany.

The second approach was related to the question of whether the characteristics of the new information technologies are not such that it is justifiable to have a separate course, in combination with the instrumental use of computers in other subject-matter areas. This plea is for a so-called "mixed" approach, with some of the computer literacy goals being realized via "traditional" subject matter courses, while the more specific information-handling goals are addressed in a separate course. This approach has been adopted in The Netherlands.

3. Examples of Different Computer Literacy Approaches

3.1 Computer Literacy Courses

In many countries (e.g., Austria, Belgium, Bulgaria,

Greece, Japan, Luxembourg, Romania, and Sweden) computer literacy or introductory computer education has been introduced as a new, often compulsory subject in general secondary schools. Courses vary in size, and usually have a major emphasis on programming while also attending to general applications (database, spreadsheet, etc.). A typical example of the aims of such an initial course is taken from Bulgaria (Nikolov et al. 1988):

(a) to obtain the basic skills and habits required for using computers and other products of new technologies;

(b) to obtain ideas of some basic computer applications;

(c) to acquire skills and habits of applying software tools in various fields;

(d) to determine what problems can be solved with the help of a computer;

(e) to acquire and use some basic notions of informatics;

(f) to use Logo in a good programming style when solving problems in various fields (mathematics, languages, physics, etc.);

(g) to become familiar with some basic information structures in order to apply them effectively when solving problems.

The data from the international survey on computers in education (Pelgrum and Plomp 1991) showed that in 1989, in many countries, students learned about computers in separate courses. In other words, the use of computers was not integrated in existing subjects. Some data for lower secondary education are as follows: Belgium 89 percent, Germany 81 percent, the Netherlands 91 percent, Switzerland 90 percent, and 51 percent in the United States, a country that has a strong movement of having computer literacy integrated in the curriculum.

3.2 Computer Literacy as Curriculum—Computer Integration

The attainment of computer literacy goals through the use of computers in existing subjects is the path followed, for example, in Germany (Eraut 1991) and England and Wales. The National Curriculum of England and Wales, introduced by the Educational Reform Act (ERA) of 1988, provides minimal requirements for information technology (IT), making it a compulsory topic for pupils and teachers. (In this context, information technology is concerned with the storage, retrieval, processing, and transmission of information, which makes objectives in this area similar to the "context" of this computer literacy entry.) The aims of IT in education are that the curriculum should ensure that each pupil (a) has the opportunity to use IT whenever its use is helpful to his or her task; (b) uses IT to enhance and enrich his or her learning in every area of the curriculum; (c) has the scope of their learning potential extended by the appropriate use of IT; (d) acquires IT capability; and (e) has a coordinated and coherent program of relevant IT experiences (Griffin and Davies 1990).

Aims (a), (b), and (c) refer to the instrumental use of computers and other information technology in all subjects across the curriculum. Aim (d) acknowledges that there is a body of skills, knowledge, and understanding relating to IT that it is important for all pupils to acquire. It is defined (Griffin and Davies 1990) as the pupil's ability to use IT for the following purposes: (a) to communicate and handle information; (b) to design, develop, explore, and evaluate models of real or imaginary situations; and (c) to measure and control physical variables and movement.

In principle, the ERA does not prohibit schools from teaching IT capability as a separate course, but there is considerable discouragement for this approach, partly based on the nature of IT capability and partly because of the overlap between IT as content and IT as method (Birnbaum 1990). All subject groups set up to define areas of the national curriculum have been asked to include relevant aspects of IT; the requirements for the subject of Technology specify a separate attainment target for IT.

3.3 The "Mixed" Approach

The Netherlands provides an example of a mixed approach. For the reformed junior secondary education (grades 7, 8, and 9), the government decided to achieve goals in the area of computer literacy (known in the Netherlands as information and computer literacy or ICL) through a separate course as well as through the integration of computer use in other school subjects, such as language arts, mathematics, and technology. In doing this, a distinction was made between the subject matter domain of information and computer literacy (ICL), and the small course on ICL which is only a part of this domain.

The operational goals and objectives for the subject matter domain of ICL reflect an information-handling and computer applications orientation. They are organized in the following four categories (Plomp and Van Weering 1990):

(a) data, data processing, information: students gain insight into processes of purposive data-collection, processing, and retrieval, and are able to deal comprehensively with data and information;

(b) data processing systems: students receive a correct functional image of data processing systems (such as the computer) and, on the basis of this, can use these systems;

(c) applications of information technology: students learn application possibilities of information technology, and can use applications;

(d) social impact of information technology: students acquire insight into the societal impact of information technology.

The starting point for this approach is teaching a basic introduction to new technologies which has three components: elements from information science, elements from computer science, and computer applications (Plomp and van Weering 1990).

In the *computer science aspects* the central focus is on hardware and software, and their operation, but only from an operational angle (i.e., students must be able to operate the computer as a machine) and an instrumental angle (i.e., students must have a correct mental image of the computer to be able to use the computer purposefully).

ICL has also *information science aspects*, because it will deal with knowledge and skills needed for data-collection, organization, and processing, which usually come up only implicitly in applications in existing subject-matter areas. Here we have to do with a class of skills for which the computer is an important versatile aid. The general idea behind emphasizing information-handling skills is that data and information are different concepts and the second component will be dealt with in a short separate course.

As data-collection and processing (with or without the computer) have to be related to "contents," ICL is also a domain that will be applied in other subject-matter areas. Whenever there is a reference in Dutch policy plans to elements of ICL and IT in other subject-matter domains, it is to *computer applications*. Here two clearly different aspects have to be distinguished. First, certain goals and objectives of information and computer literacy can best be realized in the context of other subject-matter areas. But it is also supposed that certain goals and objectives of those other subject-matter areas can be realized better by the instrumental use of the computer.

See also: Computer and Information Sciences: Educational Programs; Computer Programming, Learning and Instruction of; Computer-managed Learning

References

Anderson R E, Klassen D L 1981 A conceptual framework for developing computer literacy instruction. *AEDS Journal* 14(3): 128–41

Birnbaum I 1990 The assessment of IT capability. *Journal of Computer Assisted Learning* 6(2): 88–97

Collis B 1988 *Computers, Curriculum, and Whole-class Instruction: Issues and Ideas*. Wadsworth, Belmont, California

Culbertson J 1986 Whither computer literacy? In: Culbertson J A, Cunningham L L (eds.) 1986 *Microcomputers in Education*. National Society for the Study of Education, University of Chicago Press, Chicago, Illinois

Eraut M (ed.) 1991 *Education and the Information Society: A Challenge for European Policy*. Cassell, London

Griffin J A, Davies S 1990 Information technology in the national curriculum. *Journal of Computer Assisted Learning* 6(4): 255–64

Hade D D 1982 Literacy in an information society. *Educ. Technol.* 22(8): 7–12

Hawkridge D 1990 Machine-mediated learning in Third-World schools. *Machine-mediated Learning* 3: 319–28

Hunter B 1983 *My Students use Computers: A Guide for Literacy in the K–8 Curriculum*. Reston Publishing, Reston, Virginia

Jay T B 1981 Computerphobia: What to do about it. *Educ. Technol.* 21(1): 47–48

Lockheed M E, Hunter B, Anderson R E, Beazly R M, Esty E T 1983 *Computer Literacy: Definition and Survey Items for Assessment in Schools*. National Center for Educational Statistics, Washington, DC

Luehrmann A 1981 Computer literacy—What should it be? *Math. Teach.* 74(9): 682–86

Marland M (ed.) 1981 *Information Skills in the Secondary Curriculum: The Recommendations of a Working Group Sponsored by the British Library and the Schools Council*. Methuen Educational, London

Nikolov R, Sendova E, Dicheva D 1988 What to teach in informatics and how: A Bulgarian experiment. In: Lovis F, Tagg E D (eds.) 1988 *Computers in Education*. Elsevier, Amsterdam.

Pelgrum W J, Plomp T 1991 *The Use of Computers Worldwide*. Pergamon Press, Oxford

Plomp T, van de Wolde J 1985 New information technologies in education: Lessons learned and trends observed. *Eur. J. Educ.* 20 (2–3): 243–56

Plomp T, van Weering B 1990 Information literacy and computer literacy: The "mixed" approach in The Netherlands. In: McDougall A, Dowling C (eds.) 1990 *Computers in Education*. Elsevier, Amsterdam

T. Plomp; I. Janssen Reinen

Computer Networking for Education

The use of computer networks for educational activity at all levels—primary, secondary, tertiary, adult, and distance education—has introduced new options to enhance and transform teaching and learning opportunities and outcomes. Since the late 1960s computer networks (electronic mail, bulletin board services, and computer conferencing) have been adopted and adapted by educators to enhance the curriculum by expanding access to expertise and educational resources, to increase student interaction and peer collaboration both within and between classrooms, and for the delivery of credit and non-credit courses and programs. Computer networks enhance traditional forms of face-to-face and distance education and enable new and unprecedented educational interactions, creating the basis for a new paradigm: network learning.

The new opportunities, however, also introduce new challenges for educators and learners. This entry describes this emerging field and provides examples from around the world to illustrate the applications, outcomes, and issues involved in computer networking for education (see *Computers in Education*).

1. Background and Overview

Human communication and interaction are the major uses of computer networks. Educational uses of computer networks on time-sharing computers can be traced to the late 1960s (i.e., the PLATO system) while the application of email networks for course activities and information exchange began in the early 1970s (Hunter 1992). Computer conferencing and bulletin board systems, first developed in the early 1970s, were used for educational communication from the 1970s and by 1981 computer conferencing was used for course delivery (Feenberg 1993, Harasim et al. 1994).

1.1 Classroom Adjunct

One of the earliest educational applications of computer networking was the use of electronic mail to complement traditional face-to-face classroom activities by expanding opportunities for class discussion (Quinn et al. 1983). Computer conferencing and bulletin board systems were also adopted for information exchange and collaborative projects among learning peers, for sharing assignments, communicating with the instructor, and to access expertise and resources beyond what was available locally. As early as 1969, Stanford University began delivering mathematics education to low-income students in Mississippi, Kentucky, and California via computer networks (Hunter 1992). The use of computer networks as a classroom adjunct has been adopted at all levels of education.

1.2 Networked Classrooms

The networked classroom approach links classes in different geographical locations (local and global) for information exchange and group activities (Harasim et al. 1994). One of the earliest examples was a network of secondary schools linked by Dartmouth's time-sharing computer in 1969 (Hunter 1992). The InterCultural Learning Network (ICLN), implemented in 1983, used email to link schoolchildren in San Diego, California, with peers in Alaska and other American states and eventually Japan, Mexico, Puerto Rico, and Israel (Levin et al. 1990). The Canadian RAPPI network (1985–87) linked schoolchildren and teachers in over 70 different schools in Canada, France, Italy and the United Kingdom, to facilitate information exchange with peers in different regions and countries (Hart 1987). Other notable examples of school-level networks are the National Geographic KIDSNet, the AT&T Learning Network, Australia's Computer Pals Across the World, Canada's Southern Interior Telecommunication's Project (Teles and Duxbury 1992), and the Japan-based APICnet. University examples include the European Campus 2000 (Mason 1993) and BESTnet and AFRINet which link university students and courses in the United States, Canada, Latin America, and Africa (Bellman et al. 1993).

1.3 Online Courses and Programs

Since the mid-1980s, networks have been used to deliver credit and noncredit courses. This application is primarily employed by university and adult education institutions. Graduate schools such as the Ontario Institute for Studies in Education (OISE is a graduate school of education affiliated with the University of Toronto) and Connected Education (affiliated with the New School for Social Research, New York) began to offer graduate-level courses entirely online in late 1985. Other institutions—such as those associated with the Virtual Classroom Project—developed the use of computer conferencing for undergraduate course delivery (Hiltz 1990, 1993). Full degree or professional programs are offered entirely online. Training programs are also adopting networks for online course delivery.

1.4 Distance Education and Open Learning

Distance education institutions and programs use computer conferencing and networking in adjunct and full course delivery mode. The American Open University began using computer conferencing in 1984 to supplement learner–tutor communication and to provide a forum for group discussion. In 1989 the British Open University introduced the first mass-based distance education course that incorporated computer conferencing (Mason and Kaye 1989). European initiatives in computer networking provide valuable models and lessons for open and distance education opportunities (Mason 1993, Collis 1991).

1.5 Professional Development Networks

Networks are also used within a broader educational framework, not restricted to curriculum integration. Thousands of specialist forums and user groups on networks such as the Internet, bulletin boards, and commercial services (CompuServe, America Online) support professional collaboration among teachers and educators and provide teacher education and enhancement. Electronic newsletters are published and disseminated over the networks. Professional development activities in the form of mini courses, special lecture seminars, workshops, and formal courses are also available on-line.

1.6 Community Learning

Networks offer a variety of community education and

support services. The Big Sky Telegraph network, launched in Montana in 1988, serves rural schools, communities, and cooperatives. Public free-nets are active. The Cleveland Free-Net (the National Public Telecomputing Network) was established in 1986 as a community computer service to offer free networking services in areas such as health, education, technology, government, arts, recreation, and the law. The menu is built around a metaphor of a community which includes an administration building, a public square, a library, and a university circle. GeoNet supports a consortium of Electronic Village Halls throughout Europe (Mason 1993). Computer networks are also used to link the home and school, to enhance educational opportunities for students and in some cases to provide for parent involvement and education as well.

2. *Theoretical Framework*

2.1 Overview

The use of computer networking in education has been referred to variously as online education (Harasim 1990), the virtual classroom (Hiltz 1994), and learning networks (Harasim et al. 1994). The paradigm underlying educational networking should be distinguished from other educational applications of computing: (a) computer-based education, such as computer-assisted instruction (CAI), computer-managed instruction (CMI), computer-based training (CBT), and other like terms, which broadly represent those uses of the computer in which the student is tutored by the computer; (b) programming, in which the student designs instructions that tell a computer how to carry out a particular processing task; and (c) the use of the computer as a tool, exemplified in such applications as word processing, spreadsheets, or database management. These application involve an individualized interaction between the student and the computer and do not facilitate human communication and interaction among members of an educational community (see *Computer Assisted Learning; Computer-managed Learning*). Learning networks are characterized by human communication and require attention to instructional design to organize the message-based computer networks into an educational environment.

2.2 A New Paradigm: Network Learning

Computer networking for educational purposes represents a new learning paradigm: network learning. Network learning shares certain fundamental characteristics with the face-to-face educational environment; that is, interactive group communication. However, participants are geographically separated and thus network learning also shares attributes common to distance education. However, distance education is based on a transmittal model (Burge 1988) which in theory and practice emphasizes individual rather than group learning. The unique combination of place-independent, asynchronous interaction among groups of people linked by a network system yields the new educational model and set of learning outcomes called network learning.

The attributes of the networking environment present unique opportunities as well as constraints for learning. The first attribute is that networking technology supports group communication. Electronic mail networks enable one-to-one (interpersonal) and one-to-many (broadcast) communication, while a group mail facility or distribution list supports some group communication activities. Computer conferencing and some bulletin boards support personal and broadcast modes but provide system features specifically designed to support many-to-many (group) communication.

As a group communication system, the networking environment is in certain respects familiar territory. Topics are discussed, teachers introduce new subjects, and "spaces" may be created to facilitate various types of learning activities. Learners network with peers, experts, and mentors to ask questions, share information, and engage in discussion, debates, apprenticeship, or collaborative work. Learners may work together in groups of 2 or 20 to discuss a topic, undertake a joint research project, create a newspaper, or compose a short story.

There are also significant and fundamental differences to learning online. Among the most obvious is that the group interaction is place-independent. Users are not limited by where they live. By using networks, learners and teachers can form linkages with counterparts in other parts of the world with relative ease, to access ideas, perspectives, cultures, and information beyond the local resources (teacher, library, textbook, etc.).

Time-independence or asynchronicity is a third characteristic of most learning networks. While a few networks support synchronous mode (i.e., real-time systems such as audiographics, videoconferencing, and audioconferencing) most computer networks operate primarily as asynchronous communication environments. The asynchronous network is always "open," and class discussions and interaction can occur at any time, 24 hours a day, seven days a week.

Currently, most networks are text-based although multimedia networking is becoming increasingly available. The text-based nature of communication on the network encourages articulation and exchange of ideas. Participants must formulate a comment in order to be "present" and once the idea is entered into the group forum, it invites response and group interaction. The availability of a text-based archive, moreover, provides a form of group memory and also enables retrospective analysis of the proceedings.

The final characteristic is computer-mediation. The mediation of the computer enables the first four attributes and introduces new tools to enhance communication and intellectual work. The computer enables the storage, retrieval, processing, and manipulation of data. Various software programs, from spell checkers to hypertext and information management systems, can be applied to computer networks. Educational software programs can assist the user in structuring messages and with interconnecting new ideas with previous ones to support the creation of personal and group knowledge bases.

3. Design and Implementation of Learning Networks

Attention to design of the applications is one of the single most critical factors in successful learning networks, whether course activity is delivered totally online or in adjunct mode. Network learning, just as face-to-face education, involves intervention by a content and/or process expert (the instructor) to organize the content, sequence the instructional activities, structure task and group interaction, and evaluate the process.

3.1 Learning Approaches used in Computer Networks

Six main types of learning approaches are found in educational computer networks (Harasim et al. 1994): (a) ask-an-expert, (b) mentorship, (c) tutor support, (d) peer interaction, (e) structured group activity, (f) access to relevant information. The first three approaches require online resource persons such as mentors, experts, and instructors to support student work. The latter three are student-centered. The choice of model depends on the content area and course design. These approaches seem to be most successful when structures and roles are well-defined, or when the information accessed is relevant to a particular learning task.

3.1.1 Ask-an-expert. Learning networks facilitate access, local or global, to subject area experts (scientists, writers, professionals, etc.). Teachers first establish a list of experts willing to undertake this role and set up a set of procedures for undertaking that activity. Students send questions to the expert on a given area and obtain responses in a few days. The main benefits of this model are quick access to up-to-date relevant information and the positive feedback of receiving an answer.

3.1.2 Mentorship. Mentorship is a time-honored educational approach. An online mentor is a professional in a particular subject area who provides ongoing feedback until the apprentice masters the learning task. At that point the mentor "fades" away and the apprentice engages in the exploration of expert practice. For example, a student submits a poem or a short story to an online mentor who provides coaching in how better to craft the writing. The student–mentor interaction may continue over several weeks or even months as the student submits or resubmits the work and obtains ongoing feedback from the mentor. Online mentorship is a technique used in the humanities and sciences.

3.1.3 Tutor support. Learners at all levels can be provided with tutoring to support educational activities. Tutoring complements face-to-face and on-line classes, while in distance mode online tutors provide the primary source of instructional support and interaction.

3.1.4 Peer interaction. Peer interaction is based on principles of collaborative learning, and has been effective in online environments (Harasim 1990). There are two types of peer interaction: informal and structured. Informal peer interaction may take various forms: "electronic pen pals"; special interest group discussions (i.e., newsgroups and distribution lists); and social interaction, as in a "virtual cafe" or public square on the free-nets set up for informal socializing. Often, interactions initiated through such public spaces then move on to the exchange of personal email messages, as learners find peers with similar interests. These forms are common to most learning networks. Structured peer interaction is discussed below under structured group activity.

3.1.5 Structured group activity. This is a curriculum-based approach designed to be implemented within deadlines for submissions and responses. There are many types of curriculum group activity: long and very structured, short and less structured, based on peer interaction and guided coaching.

Group learning structures that have been effectively reformulated for network environments include: seminars, small group discussions, learning partnerships and dyads, small work groups, learning circles, simulations and role plays, and debating teams. In addition, such group spaces as a "virtual cafe" or student lounge and a mutual "assist" space where students help one another with technical and other problems are valuable.

3.1.6 Access to network resources. Global networks such as the Internet, provide access to online databases and archives (data files), libraries, as well as to thousands of special interest forums, on topics ranging from nuclear physics to environmental issues.

4. Educational Outcomes

4.1 Active Learning

The network environment has been found to support active participation as well as active contruction of meaning. In order to be "present" online, students must formulate and send a message. Articulating that idea and sharing it in a group forum has important cognitive benefits and the ongoing group interaction on the idea can enhance the knowledge building process. Research indicates that with an appropriate course design, most students actively and regularly message online (Riel 1992, Harasim 1989) and that the volume of communication is distributed fairly evenly (Harasim 1989). Several factors are cited by users. The opportunity to control the pace, place, and time of participation enables increased participation. Asynchronicity reduces competition for airtime. Moreover, such features as the opportunity to edit a message as well as the anonymity afforded by text-based communication further contribute to students taking a more active role in on-line discussions (Bellman et al. 1993).

Networking can also contribute to facilitating active construction of meaning (Harasim 1990). Group interaction on a network generates a database of ideas and responses. The exposure to positive and negative feedback on one's ideas stimulates cognitive restructuring in response to new information and perspectives. Cognitive learning strategies such as making multiple passes or directed searches through the rich corpus of ideas are rewarding. Moreover, access to real audiences is more motivational and has been found to contribute to improved writing skills (Cohen and Riel 1989).

4.2 Achievement and User Characteristics

Research on user characteristics has been conducted primarily on online course delivery for university students. Hiltz (1990, 1994) found that outcomes for the virtual classroom are at least as good as outcomes for traditional face-to-face courses. The average student reported that both access to and quality of the educational experience were improved. Research indicates high levels of student satisfaction, with a high percentage reporting that they would take another course online (Hiltz 1990, Phelps et al. 1991).

Hiltz (1990) found that improved outcomes were generally contingent upon providing adequate access to equipment, instructional effort and skill in teaching with networks, and student characteristics. Students who were motivated to explore the learning network environment were self-disciplined, and those who had average or better verbal skills were likely to experience superior outcomes, compared with achievement on traditional courses. Students who lacked this motivation and basic college-level skills, or who had to travel to use a computer for access, were more likely to drop out of an online course, to participate more irregularly, and to perform more poorly than they would in a traditional course.

4.3 Global Education

Computer networks facilitate communication across national boundaries, to enable learners to "meet" and interact with peers and experts from other cultures. Cross-cultural communication and understanding and the perception of the interconnectivity of the world's population can be enhanced by global networks. Students can network to discuss or gather geographically and socially significant data about today's problems and to explore ways to resolve them.

Global education via networks also poses challenges. Conducting group work among people who are geographically separate can be difficult. Issues related to cross-cultural communication, choice of language of communication and different curricula need to be resolved (Mason 1993). Differing cultural and economic perspectives on an event (e.g., a war) or activity (e.g., whaling) challenge as well as enrich global education (Riel 1993, Teles 1993).

4.4 Teacher Revitalization

Teachers who use computer networks report a sense of revitalization as a result of the enhanced learning opportunities that they can offer their students as well as the opportunities for teacher networking (Teles and Duxbury 1992, Riel 1992). Network access to peer support and teacher resources also facilitate teacher adoption of educational change and modification of teaching approaches (Lenk 1992).

5. Research Directions

Despite its short history, significant research has been conducted on educational computer networking, especially with regard to learner participation (i.e., frequency, volume, distribution of communication), learner satisfaction, impacts on teaching, and issues in curriculum design and implementation. The data gathered have proven the viability of this pioneering new field and have illuminated critical organizational and pedagogical issues. There is a need now for systematic study of learning processes in online environments, examining patterns of human interaction in decision-making, problem-solving, and knowledge building. Such research is valuable for the purposes of designing software that supports network learning, for instructional design of online environments, and for understanding the cognitive and affective processes in learning networks. Computer mediation enables an archive of the proceedings to be established, enabling retrospective content and interaction analysis of the transcript.

As networks become increasingly multimedia, there is a need for research into the relationship between different forms of learning and media. Studies are needed on such issues as the fit between specific educational tasks and media form and content, teaching and learning approaches in multimedia networks, and determining the relative costs and effectiveness of the different media. Finally, there is a critical need for theory building regarding educational technologies such as computer networking. Theories from education or communication or which, like the concept of network learning, build on field experience and research are needed to guide developments in computer networking for education.

6. Conclusion

Rapid progress in the technology of computer networking (email and conferencing) has enabled new educational opportunities that transcend geographic and temporal boundaries. Educators around the world, at all levels of education, have adopted computer networking. A new paradigm for education has emerged: network learning. This entry has described network learning applications and attributes and has outlined instructional design and implementation issues. Network learning, based upon group collaboration in knowledge building, collectively shared goals, active participation, and cross-cultural communication will offer important training for life in the twenty-first century.

See also: Computers and Learning; Computer Assisted Learning; Computer Literacy

References

Bellman B, Tindimubona A, Arias A Jr 1993 Technology transfer in global networking: Capacity building in Africa and Latin America. In: Harasim L M (ed.) 1993 *Global Networks: Computers and International Communication.* MIT Press, Cambridge, Massachusetts

Burge L 1988 Beyond andragogy: Some explorations for distance learning design. *Journal of Distance Education* 3(1): 5–23

Cohen M, Riel M 1989 The effect of distant audiences on students' writing. *Am. Educ. Res. J.* 26(2): 143–59

Collis B 1991 Telecommunications-based training in Europe: A state-of-the-art report. *Am. J. Distance Educ.* 5(2): 31–40

Feenberg A 1993 Building a global network. In: Harasim L M (ed.) 1993 *Global Networks: Computers and International Communication.* MIT Press, Cambridge, Massachusetts

Harasim L M 1989 On-line education: A new domain. In: Mason R, Kaye T (eds.) 1989 *Mindweave: Communication, Computers, and Distance Education.* Pergamon Press, Oxford

Harasim L M 1990 Online education: An environment for collaboration and intellectual amplification. In: Harasim L M (ed.) 1990 *Online Education: Perspectives on a New Environment.* Praeger, New York

Harasim L M, Hiltz S R, Teles L, Turoff M 1994 *Learning Networks: A Field Guide.* MIT Press, Cambridge, Massachusetts

Hart R 1987 Towards a third generation distributed conferring system. *Canadian Journal of Educational Communication* 16(2): 137–52

Hiltz S R 1990 Evaluating the virtual classroom. In: Harasim L M (ed.) 1990 *Online Education: Perspectives on a New Environment.* Praeger, New York

Hiltz S R 1994 *The Virtual Classroom.* Ablex, Norwood, New Jersey

Hunter B 1992 Linking for learning: Computer-and-communications network support for nationwide innovations in education. *Journal of Science Education and Technology* 1(1)

Lenk C 1992 The network science experience: Learning from three major projects. In: Tinker R F, Kapisovsky P M (eds.) 1992 *Prospects for Educational Telecomputing: Selected Readings.* TERC Publication, Cambridge, Massachusetts

Levin J, Kim H, Riel M 1990 Analyzing instructional interactions on electronic message networks. In: Harasim L M (ed.) 1990 *Online Education: Perspectives on a New Environment.* Praeger, New York

Mason R 1993 Computer conferencing and the new Europe. In: Harasim L M (ed.) 1993 *Global Networks: Computers and International Communication.* MIT Press, Cambridge, Massachusetts

Mason R, Kaye T (eds.) 1989 *Mindweave: Communication, Computers, and Distance Education.* Pergamon Press, Oxford

Phelps R, Wells R, Ashworth R, Hahn H 1991 Effectiveness and costs of distance education using computer-mediated communication. *Am. J. Distance Educ.* 5(3): 7–19

Quinn C N, Mehan H, Levin J A, Black S D 1983 Real education in non-real time: The use of electronic message systems for instruction. *Instructional Science* 11(4): 313–27

Riel M 1992 Learning Circles: A functional analysis of educational telecomputing. *Interactive Learning Environments* 2: 15–30

Riel M 1993 Global education through learning circles. In: Harasim L M (ed.) 1993 *Global Networks: Computers and International Communication.* MIT Press, Cambridge, Massachusetts

Teles L 1993 Cognitive Apprenticeship on Global Networks. In: Harasim L M (ed.) 1993 *Global Networks: Computers and International Communication.* MIT Press, Cambridge, Massachusetts

Teles L, Duxbury N 1992 *The Networked Classroom.* Simon Fraser University, Burnaby

Further Reading

Canadian Journal of Educational Communication 1987 16(2): Spring (issue devoted to computer-mediated communication in education)

Roberts N, Blakeslee G, Brown M, Lenk C 1990 *Integrating Telecommunications into Education.* Prentice-Hall, Englewood Cliffs, New Jersey

Tinker R F, Kapisovsky P M (eds.) 1992 *Prospects for Educational Telecomputing: Selected Readings.* TERC Publication, Cambridge, Massachusetts

Waggoner M D (ed.) 1992 *Empowering Networks: Computer Conferencing in Education.* Educational Technology Publications, Englewood Cliffs, New Jersey

L. M. Harasim

Computer Programming, Learning and Instruction of

A computer program is a list of formal instructions to a computer to make it accomplish a goal. Computer programming is a problem-solving activity that includes creating, comprehending, modifying, and debugging computer programs. In creating a program, the originator produces computer code that solves a problem stated in natural language. In comprehending a program, the user describes in natural language what a given computer program accomplishes. Modifying a program occurs when a person changes an existing program to accomplish a different goal from the one it was originally designed to accomplish. Debugging involves detecting and correcting errors in a program.

During the 1980s, computers became commonplace in elementary and secondary schools—increasing 50-fold over 10 years in some countries. To a lesser extent, computer programming became a major new subject-matter area for many students (Becker 1991, Pelgrum and Plomp 1991). Research also began in this period on how people learn and use computer programming languages and developed into one of the most active psychologies of subject matter (Mayer 1988a, Soloway and Spohrer 1989). Although there are over 1,000 programming languages, the languages most commonly taught in schools and studied by educational researchers are Logo, BASIC, and Pascal.

This entry addresses three major lines of research on the educational psychology of computer programming: (a) how to teach computer programming to novices, (b) what novices learn from instruction in computer programming, and (c) how expert programmers differ from novices.

1. Teaching Computer Programming

One of the major research issues concerns how to teach computer programming. Should students be free to discover how to use creatively a computer programming language in a "hands-on" environment or should teachers also provide more guidance concerning the learning and use of a programming language? In spite of strong claims for the power of allowing students to learn programming on their own, educational researchers have found that students often fail to discover even the fundamentals of programming on their own in nondirective, hands-on instructional programs (Linn 1985, Pea and Kurland 1984). For example, an analysis of students who learned to program by discovery revealed that "students often produced programs without really comprehending how the programs worked" (Nickerson et al. 1985 p. 277). In contrast, teaching that emphasizes structure and mediated guidance results in better learning and transfer than unstructured and nondirected teaching methods (Lehrer and Littlefield 1991, van Merrienboer 1990). Structuring insures that the learner receives the basic information in a useful order whereas mediation insures that the learner connects the presented information with relevant existing knowledge. In a review, Mayer (1988a p. 5) concluded that "the overwhelming consensus . . . is that, for most children, a hands-on discovery environment should be complemented with direct instruction and mediation by a teacher."

Students' ability to use a programming language to solve problems can be enhanced by instructional methods that help the student build a mental model of the computing system. A mental model of a computing system is a simplified representation of the major locations (such as memory space or output screen), objects (such as data or pointers), and actions (such as find or erase) within the computer. For example, when low-ability students are taught to understand BASIC instructions (such as LET A = B + 1) in terms of the underlying activity within the computer (such as "find the number in space B, add 1 to that number, put the result in space A") they build more accurate mental models of the BASIC machine and are better able to solve novel programming problems than comparable students who are given conventional training (Bayman and Mayer 1988).

2. Learning Computer Programming

A second major issue concerns the cognitive consequences of learning to program. Does learning to program affect the way a student thinks? Soloway and Sleeman (1986 p. 1) noted that "some claim that programming is the new Latin of our times" so that "learning to program develops general intellectual skills that are needed in all endeavors." The search for transfer of programming skills to other domains has often yielded disappointing results (Linn 1985, Mayer 1988a, Pea and Kurland 1984). However, transfer has been achieved in some cases, especially when students successfully learned to solve programming problems, instruction emphasized the transferability of the learned programming skills, and the transfer tests were analogous to the programming problems (Clements 1990, Clements and Gullo 1984, De Corte et al. 1992, Mayer and Fay 1987, Mayer et al. 1986, Salomon and Perkins 1987).

Building on Linn's (1985) model of the "chain of cognitive accomplishments," Mayer and Fay (1987) proposed a "chain of cognitive changes" theory to account for the conditions under which learning to program will transfer to nonprogramming domains. The theory asserts that learning the fundamentals of a programming language is a prerequisite for learning to solve programming problems, and that learning to think about programming problems is a prerequisite for solving similar kinds of problems outside the domain of programming. For example, students who learned the underlying syntax and semantics of Logo showed a pretest to posttest improvement in their ability to generate and comprehend English-language instructions for how to navigate with a map, whereas students who did not show improvements in learning the syntax and semantics of Logo did not show signs of transfer (Mayer and Fay 1987). Similarly, students who were able to transfer from learning of BASIC to other domains showed gains on near transfer, such as comprehending English-language instructions, but not on far transfer, such as general reasoning (Mayer et al. 1986).

3. Expertise in Computer Programming

A third research issue concerns the knowledge required to become an expert computer programmer. A cognitive analysis revealed four kinds of programming knowledge: syntactic, semantic, schematic, and strategic (Mayer 1985, 1992). Syntactic knowledge is knowledge of the language units (such as keywords and variable names) and rules for combining language units (such as the legal placement of a line number on a line of code). Semantic knowledge refers to a person's mental model of how the computing system works. Schematic knowledge represents categories of program types (such as various routines for sorting or looping). Finally, strategic knowledge includes methods for devising and monitoring plans (such as breaking a programming task into meaningful parts).

What does an expert know about programming that a novice does not know? Expert and novice programmers differ in their syntactic, semantic, schematic, and strategic knowledge of computer programming (Mayer 1988b). Differences in syntactic knowledge have been investigated by asking students to judge whether or not a line of programming code is grammatically correct. Novices are slow and have to expend mental effort in order to recognize grammatically incorrect code; in contrast, experts make judgments rapidly and effortlessly, suggesting that they have automatized their recognition processes (Wiedenbeck 1985). Differences in semantic knowledge can be measured by asking students to describe what happens inside the computer when it carries out an instruction. The protocols of novices suggest the lack of useful mental models, whereas experts' protocols display the effective use of mental models of the computing system (Bayman and Mayer 1988). Differences in schematic knowledge have been evaluated by asking students to recall programs that are presented in normal or scrambled order. Experts and novices do not differ greatly in recall of scrambled programs, whereas experts perform much better than novices in recall of normal programs (McKeithen et al. 1981). Paralleling earlier research on expert–novice differences in memory for chess pieces on a chess board (De Groot 1965), expert programmers may possess a repertoire of typical combinations of statements that enable them to cluster the lines of a program into several meaningful chunks. Finally, expert–novice differences in strategic knowledge have been measured by asking students to think aloud as they solve programming problems. Experts tend to break a problem into finer parts than novices, are more likely to consider alternative ways to solve a programming problem than are novices, and engage in more planning before beginning to write a program than do novices (Soloway and Erhrlich 1984, Vessey 1985).

See also: Computers and Learning; Computers in Education; Logo, Educational Applications of; Problem-solving and Thinking, Development of Learning Skills in

References

Bayman P, Mayer R E 1988 Using conceptual models to teach BASIC computer programming. *J. Educ. Psychol.* 80(3):291–98

Becker H J 1991 How computers are used in United States schools: Basic data from the 1989 IEA computers in education survey. *J. Educ. Computing Res.* 7(4):385–406

Clements D H 1990 Metacomponential development in a Logo programming environment. *J. Educ. Psychol.* 82(1):141–49

Clements D H, Gullo D F 1984 Effects of computer programming on young children's cognition. *J. Educ. Psychol.* 76(6):1051–58

De Corte E, Verschaffel L, Schrooten H 1992 Transfer of cognitive skills through powerful Logo-based teaching–learning environments. In: De Corte E, Linn M, Mandl H, Verschaffel L (eds.) 1992 *Computer-based Learning Environments and Problem Solving*. Springer-Verlag, Berlin

De Groot A D 1965 *Thought and Choice in Chess*. Mouton, The Hague

Lehrer R, Littlefield J 1991 Misconceptions and errors in Logo: The role of instruction. *J. Educ. Psychol.* 83(1):124–33

Linn M C 1985 The cognitive consequences of programming instruction in classrooms. *Educ. Researcher* 14(5):14–16, 25–29

Mayer R E 1985 Learning in complex domains: A cognitive analysis of computer programming. In: Bower G (ed.) 1985 *The Psychology of Learning and Motivation*, Vol. 19. Academic Press, San Diego, California

Mayer R E (ed.) 1988a *Teaching and Learning Computer Programming: Multiple Research Perspectives*. Erlbaum, Hillsdale, New Jersey

Mayer R E 1988b From novice to expert. In: Helander M (ed.) 1988 *Handbook of Human–computer Interaction*. North-Holland, Amsterdam

Mayer R E 1992 Psychology of learning and teaching computer programming. In: De Corte E, Linn M, Mandl H, Verschaffel L (eds.) 1992 *Computer-based Learning Environments and Problem Solving*. Springer-Verlag, Berlin

Mayer R E, Dyck J, Vilberg W 1986 Learning to program and learning to think: What's the connection? *Communications of the ACM* 29(2): 605–10

Mayer R E Fay A L 1987 A chain of cognitive changes with learning to program in Logo. *J. Educ. Psychol.* 79: 269–79

McKeithen K B, Reitman J S, Rueter H H, Hurtle S C 1981 Knowledge organization and skill differences in

computer programmers. *Cognitive Psychol.* 13(3): 307–25
Nickerson R S, Perkins D N, Smith E E 1985 *The Teaching of Thinking*. Erlbaum, Hillsdale, New Jersey
Pea R D, Kurland D M 1984 On the cognitive effects of learning computer programming. *New Ideas in Psychology* 2 137–68
Pelgrum W J, Plomp T 1991 *The use of Computers Around the World: Results from the IEA "Computers in Education" Survey in 19 Educational Systems*. Pergamon Press, Oxford
Salomon G, Perkins D N 1987 Transfer of cognitive skills from programming: When and how? *J. Educ. Computing Res.* 3(2):149–69
Soloway E, Erhrlich K 1984 Empirical studies of programming knowledge. *IEEE Transactions on Software Engineering* 10(5):595–609
Soloway E, Sleeman D 1986 Introduction to special issue on novice programming. *J. Educ. Computing Res.* 2(1):1–3
Soloway E, Spohrer J C (eds.) 1989 *Studying the Novice Programmer*. Erlbaum, Hillsdale, New Jersey
van Merrienboer J J G 1990 Strategies for programming instruction in high school: Program completion vs. program generation. *J. Educ. Computing Res.* 6(3):265–85
Vessey I 1985 Expertise in debugging computer programs: A process analysis. *Int. J. Man–Machine Studies* 23(5):459–94
Wiedenbeck S 1985 Novice/expert differences in programming skills. *Int. J. Man–Machine Studies* 23(4):383–90

Further Reading

Carroll J M (ed.) 1987 *Interfacing Thought: Cognitive Aspects of Human–computer Interaction*. MIT Press, Cambridge, Massachusetts
De Corte E, Linn M, Mandl H, Verschaffel L (eds.) 1992 *Computer-based Learning Environments and Problem Solving*. Springer-Verlag, Berlin
Helander M (ed.) 1988 *Handbook of Human–computer Interaction*. Elsevier, Amsterdam
Mayer R E (ed.) 1988 *Teaching and Learning Computer Programming: Multiple Research Perspectives*. Erlbaum, Hillsdale, New Jersey

R. E. Mayer

Computer Simulations and Modeling

Computer simulations and modeling tools are now available for many different school subjects, providing learning environments to challenge pupils' ideas about a domain. This entry describes some of the tools now available and presents examples of how these might be used in the curriculum.

1. Definitions

A computer simulation is a representation of a real world situation, which can be investigated by the learner through changing the values of specified factors or properties, or meanings of specified conditions. The simulation has an underlying model, usually in the form of one or more mathematical relationships, or a set of qualified objects, or a set of textual rules and conditions. Computer modeling is the process that involves building a model, whereas using a simulation can be regarded as exploring an existing model.

2. Simulations

Many early simulations were written in the programming language BASIC, and the underlying mathematical model was hidden from the user. Pupils could investigate the simulation by changing the values of variables, and observing the results, usually displayed in the form of graphs or tables. With the rapid development of computer technology, simulations now include those based on models that can be modified by the user, producing multiple displays running in parallel, including moving film sequences, controlled by a pointer on the screen operated by a hand-controlled device called a "mouse."

2.1 Designing Simulations

Designing the early simulations often required knowledge and competence in mathematics and in a programming language such as BASIC. However, developers have since produced simulations based on different types of models, which can be modified and extended by the teacher.

Van Schaick Zillesen and Min (1988) have developed a system for designing educational simulations called MACTHESIS (and THESIS). This system, based on their "Parallel Instruction" theory (Min 1992) can display several windows on the screen at the same time, showing: the conceptual model of the simulation in diagrammatic, mathematical, or graphical form; graphical functions of the relationships between two or more variables in the model; and instructions and guidelines for the user and the teacher. There is also a window editor for the teacher, who can change the visualization of the conceptual model.

Other types of authoring systems enable developers to produce simulations based on qualitative models, databases, and semiquantitative models (described later in this entry). There is considerable overlap between simulations whose models can be modified by the teacher or pupil and computer modeling environments which enable the user to build the underlying model completely, as well as run the simulation.

3. Modeling

Modeling on the computer might involve constructing the following: one or more mathematical relationships to represent a physical process; or a set of statements linked together in a logical framework; or a network of concepts linked through causal loops;

or some other type of representation. Models can be roughly grouped into quantitative, semiquantitative, and qualitative models. The following tools are being used to provide modeling opportunities in education: (a) programming languages; (b) authoring tools; (c) general purpose software; (d) educational modeling packages.

3.1 Programming Languages

Computer models can be built using any programming language such as BASIC, but the skills and time required often exceed those available in schools. However, the programming language Logo, which was pioneered by Papert (1980) for modeling in education, enables learners as young as 6 years to build quantitative models and use the Turtle facility for diagrammatic displays or qualitative relationships. Its use is relatively widespread in schools, especially in mathematics. Other advanced languages including Prolog and Smalltalk can also be used for different types of modeling, though the use of these in the classroom is very rare. An additional difficulty in using most programming languages is that the routines for the input and display have to be created as well as the model itself.

3.2 Authoring Tools

Authoring tools have been designed to facilitate the development of a computer "program" without the need for skills in the use of a general purpose programming language. On microcomputers, systems such as Hypercard or MACTHESIS on the Apple Macintosh, Linkway for IBM systems, and the Alternative Realities Kit provide modeling tools that can be used by teachers to design and create their own simulations or, when sufficiently simple, can be used by pupils to create their own models in the classroom.

3.3 General Purpose Software

General purpose software includes commercial software now widely available in schools such as data-analysis programs, spreadsheet packages, and word-processors. Using data-analysis software pupils can propose a model representing the relationships between two or more variables and test their model through an analysis of the data (Webb and Hassell 1990). Using spreadsheets, pupils can enter variable values and mathematical equations into cells in an array, to build quantitative models, which can be displayed in the form of graphs, pie charts, and so forth.

Modeling with general purpose software is limited to the framework of the software and the extent to which it fits the kind of modeling required. This type of software has been considered by teachers to be complicated and often difficult to use, although with the advent of a Windows-type environment, and the production of curriculum support materials, its use in the classroom is growing.

3.4 Modeling Packages

In order to overcome some of the difficulties encountered by more general purpose software, often designed for the adult market, modeling packages have been developed specifically for education. One of those first produced for science education was the Dynamic Modelling System (DMS)—see Ogborn (1985). Originally produced with examples of physics models, it was later extended to include biology, chemistry, geography, economics, and mathematics models, and is now available in Dutch and in a more extended version in German (Comet 1991). A model can be built up from a series of fairly simple mathematical relationships which the computer then calculates by looping through them in an iterative process. The relationship between the variables can be displayed in the form of graphs or tables.

Other modeling packages useful for dynamic, quantitative modeling include Stella, the Cellular Modelling System, Numerator, and the Algebraic Proposer, all described by Bliss et al. (1992), and THESIS, described earlier. One development of a quantitative modeling environment, Model Builder (Webb et al. 1991), designed for pupils aged from 10 years, has a more natural language syntax than DMS for creating models. It features boxes on the screen containing each variable and submodel, and also includes facilities for creating pictures as well as graphs and tables.

The modeling packages referred to above are principally designed for quantitative model-building through algebraic relationships. The semiquantitative system IQON, developed by the Tools for Exploratory Learning Programme (Bliss et al. 1992), enables pupils to develop models through causal loops linking together different variables, but without having to write formal algebraic relationships. Qualitative tools, such as the expert system shell Expert Builder (Webb et al. 1993) have been developed to allow the learner to construct a logical network of phrases in the form of questions, facts, rules, and advice, displayed on the screen in the form of boxes linked together through logical connectors. While the model is being constructed, it can be interrogated by pupils to test their logic and the reasoning behind the model. This kind of system is based on formal logic and inference rules.

These are just a few of the many modeling environments that are growing in use in schools as teachers become more confident and aware of their value for pupils' learning.

4. Curriculum Examples of Simulations and Modeling

Laurillard (1978) formulated a series of descriptions of the learning interactions that take place when pupils are using simulations, which equally apply to modeling. They include: checking knowledge and understanding, experimenting, visualizing, reasoning, and interpreting. Computer simulations and modeling also promote social skills amongst pupils, which include: working in groups, communicating ideas, organizing activities, and experimental skills. The examples described below illustrate a range of simulation and modeling activities that can engage pupils in such learning experiences.

4.1 Simulations

There are many examples of topic-specific computer simulations (Cox 1992) based on a theoretical model, designed for use in science teaching, where a real experiment would be too dangerous, expensive, or time-consuming to perform in the school laboratory. Examples of these include: predator–prey systems, plant competition, and human energy expenditure for use in biology; Millikan's oil-drop experiment, satellite motion, atomic orbitals in physics; and rates of reactions, organic synthesis, and chemical bonding in chemistry.

Another use of computer simulations in education is the simulation of industrial processes and their development; for example, the manufacture of sulfuric acid in chemistry, the operation of a nuclear reactor in physics, the location of an iron and steel factory in geography and economics.

Simulations have also been developed with a focus on role-playing and decision-making for many topics in the humanities and social sciences. For example, pupils can adopt the role of an engineer designing a high-pressure gas pipeline to satisfy national gas demands and to consider the cost involved, or follow the work of the service center from receipt of a customer's call through to the engineer mending the appliance in the customer's home, or plan a new major installation. Other examples of simulations in the humanities and social sciences include human population growth for use in geography and the shaping of the settlement of the American West in the nineteenth century in history.

Although there is now research evidence that using simulations enhances pupils' learning, there is increasing support for the encouragement of model-building in education, to extend the creative activities of the pupils and provide opportunities for them to express their own ideas about a given domain.

4.2 Modeling

With the tools now available, modeling can be applied to almost any curriculum area. For example, pupils studying the population growth of rats in biology might build a quantitative model that relates the population of rats to the initial population and the number of offspring for each generation. This simple model can then be extended to include, for example, a dependency of the number of births on the total rat population using a fertility factor, and other variables such as a death rate, availability of food, and so on.

Pupils using the semiquantitative modeling tool IQON built a model to study the relationships between sleep, fitness, running, and food, each of which could increase or decrease depending on the links between them and the initial change in one of the variables. Pupils using Expert Builder in the classroom built a logical network of symptoms and advice representing the kind of advice a medieval doctor might give to his patients who revealed various symptoms of ill health.

Using Model Builder in science, pupils can study radioactive decay involving the half-life of an element, probability of decay, nuclear disintegration, and randomness of nuclear decay. Pupils building a geography model that simulates the movement and storage of rainwater on a small area of ground can investigate the concepts of rainfall intensity, water stores, stream discharge, and water evaporation. Pupils studying economics can investigate relationships between the balance of payments of a country and its monetary inflation, import tariffs, and devaluation.

One distinct advantage of "content-free" modeling software over topic-specific software for education is that, with the appropriate supporting materials, the same modeling package can be used in many different curriculum areas and for pupils of different ages. See, for example, Cox et al. (1993), who have developed an energy curriculum pack based on the use of three different modeling environments, which includes materials for mathematics, science, design and technology, and information technology. Using such software enables pupils to investigate their own ideas about different processes and concepts at the same time as learning information technology skills about model-building, graphical representations, and using computers for simulating complex physical, economical, or geographical processes.

There is also no inbuilt teacher control except for the constraints imposed by the modeling framework. The subject and level of understanding are determined by the learner and not the software developer.

5. Conclusion

The use of computer simulations and modeling in education has been shown by numerous researchers to enhance the learning experience of pupils and to provide a challenging learning environment (e.g., Brna 1991). However, the ethos of individual and group work that can arise from the increased use of simulation and modeling requires considerable changes to the organization of learning. These changes to the learner's traditional method of working challenge the more traditional roles of the teacher, as a purveyor of knowledge and as a director of learning, which in turn has significant implications for teacher training.

See also: Educational Computer Software, Production of; Software Tools in Courseware Design; Models of Learning

References

Bliss J et al. (eds.) 1992 *Tools for Exploratory Learning*. Lancaster University, Lancaster
Brna P 1991 Promoting creative confrontations. *Journal of Computer Assisted Learning* 7(2): 114–22
Comet (Software Company) 1991 *Katalog—Software für Schüle und Lernen*. Comet, Duisburg
Cox M J 1992 The computer in the science curriculum. *Int. J. Educ. Res.* 17(1): 19–35
Cox M J, Webb M, Booth B, Robbins P 1993 *Energy Expert*. Advisory Unit for Microtechnology in Education, Wheathampstead
Hassell D, Webb M 1990 MODUS: The integrated modelling system. *Comput. Educ.* 15(1–3): 265–70
Laurillard L M 1978 Evaluation of student learning in CAL. *Comput. Educ.* 2(3): 259–65
Min F B M 1992 *Parallel Instruction: A Theory for Educational Computer Simulation*. Interactive Learning International
Ogborn J 1985 *Dynamic Modelling System*. Computers in the Curriculum Project, AVP, Chepstow
Papert S 1980 *Mindstorms, Children, Computers, and Powerful Ideas*. Basic Books, New York
van Schaick Zillesen P G, Min F B M 1988 A design system for educational computer simulation programs for computers used in secondary education in the Netherlands. In: Lovis F, Tagg E D (eds.) 1988 *Computers in Education*. North-Holland, Amsterdam
Webb M, Booth B, Cox M, Robbins P 1991 *Model Builder*. Advisory Unit for Microtechnology in Education, Wheathampstead
Webb M, Booth B, Cox M, Robbins P 1993 *Expert Builder*. Advisory Unit for Microtechnology in Education, Wheathampstead

Further Reading

AVP 1992 Educational Software for the BBC, RM Nimbus, IBM PC and Archimedes. Computers in the Curriculum Project, AVP, Chepstow
Centre for Educational Research and Innovation 1987 *Information Technologies and Basic Learning: Reading, Writing, Science and Mathematics*. OECD, Paris
Kent A, Lewis R (eds.) 1987 *Computer Assisted Learning in the Humanities and Social Sciences*. Blackwell, Oxford
Watson D M 1992 The computer in social science curricula. *Int. J. Educ. Res.* 17(1): 51–61

M. J. Cox

Computer-assisted Learning

Computer-assisted Learning (CAL) covers the various ways in which the computer is used for learning. Thus drill and practice exercises, tutorial packages, statistical routines, modeling, simulations, word processing, desktop publishing, art packages, exploring with Logo, manipulating satellite images—all come within the umbrella of CAL. The main attraction of CAL for education is the direct interaction between the software and the user; thus it is an active rather than a passive resource. Its main weakness is that, as with other educational tools, its value critically depends on the environment in which it is used. Its potential as a medium for making learning more active and learner-oriented has always excited educational innovators, while the technically oriented promote CAL because they believe it heralds a new age of Information Technology. Despite substantial attention and investment, the amount of CAL that actually takes place in educational institutions is modest. Moreover, the evidence of its effectiveness is relatively sparse.

1. Classification of CAL by Type of Program

1.1 Drill and Practice

This program requires learners to perform specified tasks, gives feedback on their performance, and graduates the sequence and difficulty of tasks according to their performance. For example, arithmetic tests are set asking students to perform subtractions. If the learners provide the correct answer, the program moves on to harder tasks; if the learner does poorly, and repeatedly produces the wrong answers, the program selects a simpler set of subtractions. Some programs may recognize a pattern of failure, and present a series of tasks geared to this problem.

These programs, by focusing on the learner's recall of particular segments and sequencing of knowledge, are of most value where accurate content is important, such as in language translation. As an accuracy-learning and testing environment for individual students, their value lies in the freeing of the teacher, enabling them to concentrate on other learning activities.

1.2 Tutorial

The tutorial program extends the drill and practice type by first providing information or a demonstration to learners, and then requiring them to perform some input. It also provides feedback on that input. For example, to teach the operation of a piece of equipment, the program shows an animation of the equipment being assembled, asks learners the sequence required, analyzes the learner's input, and tells them if they have got it right or what kind of mistake they are making.

1.3 Simulation

This program simulates an environment. Built around a model of a system, it allows learners to change the values of parameters in the system, and provides feedback in the form of graphical or diagrammatic display of how the system's behavior changes. For example, in a simulation based on a model of a pond with three main inhabitants, phytoplankton, herbivores, and fish, the learners may change the numbers of one or more populations and see the effect on the others.

Simulations provide a means for learning about an environment that may otherwise not be available to learners to explore, for reasons of safety, time, expense, or general practicality. A simulation focuses on exploration and discovery learning; it is not an exercise that necessarily has a fixed or correct solution, and the route to a solution may be varied.

Simulations may be based on models of known relationships as in the scientific world, on theoretical models as in economics, or on models of the past as in history. Concepts in many subjects are so lacking in concreteness that their definitions often need to be constructed around models of some kind. Teachers have long searched for methods of describing models in a way that makes them accessible and useful to learners. Complex relationships can often only be explored through simplification. A computer simulation offers the opportunity for relationships to be explored and exposed by the student's direct manipulation of the variables in the model.

1.4 Games

Some simulations are designed as a game, often including role-playing. For example, in a simulation based on a model of the world's wind zones, the learner adopts the role of a sailing ship's captain, selecting their starting and finishing ports, and responding to the wind patterns they meet by steering their ship to their destination. In other simulations, a group of learners may adopt different roles in order to take decisions about what actions to take. For example, in a simulation of a planning inquiry, different roles might include representing a local amenities society, a group of farmers, a property developer, an environmental protection agency, and the local planning officer. Sometimes a competitive element is introduced and learners compete to produce a solution.

In such simulations the program focuses not only on the underlying model but also on the way in which the learner interacts with the model. Learning may be built up by discovery and conjecture; the simulation encourages learning by inquiry and decision-making. Role-playing simulations may stimulate learners' interest in underlying problems through this indirect exposure to the model.

1.5 Modeling

These programs allow learners to build up models for themselves and explore their properties. They are a natural extension of the use of models for simulations, and enable the learner to experience and manipulate the fundamental structures and dynamism of models in order to appreciate their behavior and the role of models in organizing concepts of knowledge. The increase in the availability of modeling tools with sophisticated user-interfaces has brought modeling out of computer laboratories and into the range of normal classrooms.

1.6 General Purpose Packages

Packages such as word-processing, data-interrogation, and spreadsheets are more than single programs. They consist of two parts: (a) the program, which contains a variety of routines that enable data to be manipulated and displayed; (b) the data files, which are used to store the data, thus making it available for interrogation. These are often called utilities or open-ended packages; though used for CAL, these may be similar or even identical to packages used in the world of business and commerce.

The database is the raw material of an inquiry in the same way that a model is for a simulation. Previously teachers could only present learners with an organized synopsis of evidence; now the evidence itself is made available for students to explore, search for patterns, and analyze for themselves. The interrogation design enables them to set up inquiries by sorting the data into subsets, to use routes for seeking matches across fields, and to produce graphical representation of the results. Large data sets, such as census returns, parish records, United Nations and Government national and regional statistics, can be used to test hypotheses such as "Countries with low populations per doctor are the wealthiest."

These programs encourage the collecting and encoding of data from local field studies or experiments. Learning from direct experience through locally collected data is as important as sorting through large sets from other sources. Many subjects are evidence-based, placing equal weight on the value of the collection of data and on the subsequent interrogation. They demand the basic skills associated with information acquisition and measuring, sorting and classifying, leading to higher-order skills of enquiry and data-analysis.

1.7 Tools for Specific Purposes

There are packages designed for specific purposes, such as desktop publishing, synthesizing music, and capturing and encoding satellite images. These reflect, but are usually simpler than, the same style of package as is used in the adult world. Thus in Logo, which is essentially an authoring programming language, the educational function is drive a symbolic turtle around the screen. In learning the commands that control the turtle the learner is exposed to complexity in the notation and actuality of geometry as well as to programming principles.

2. Classification of CAL by Type of Use

Another way of considering and understanding the

nature of CAL is through a classification of use. Some such classifications are based on the the role that the computer plays. Taylor (1980) suggested three roles: tutor, tool, and tutee. The computer is a tutor when it leads the learner step by step through the program; for example, in drill and practice packages, where the learning is clearly driven by the tight framework of the software. The computer is a tool when used with content-free, general-purpose software such as word-processing or data-interrogation; the learner defines the agenda for use. The computer is a tutee when it is programmed by the learner in order to gain understanding, such as with Logo, or real-time control of experiments.

An alternative perception is that of Kemmis et al. (1977), who devised a framework that focused on student interactions when using CAL. It is based on four paradigms of learning: instructional, revelatory, conjectural, and emancipatory. The instructional draws on the ideas of programmed learning and is manifested in drill and practice exercises. The revelatory guides the learner through the process of learning by discovery: the content, key concepts, and related theory are revealed by progress through the software. Computer simulations provide a classic example of this paradigm.

The conjectural paradigm centers on the student learning through exploring explanations of any topic, assisting the articulation, and testing ideas and hypotheses. This suggests use of modeling and data-interrogation, through both general purpose and specific tools. The emancipatory hinges on the concept of the computer reducing the amount of inauthentic labor, thus releasing students from mental drudgery for the more significant work. This paradigm more often stands in conjuction *with*, rather than separate from, the others.

3. *Evidence of Use*

Evidence of how CAL is actually used (and the value that can be ascribed to its use) is mixed and uneven. Some evidence derives from systematic academic research and analysis using a variety of methods; other evidence comes from publications in which practicing teachers describe what has worked for them.

3.1 Cognitive Gains

Much academic research has been based on measurable cognitive gains (Roblyer et al. 1988). Niemiec and Walberg (1992) concluded from a comprehensive literature survey that focuses entirely on quantitative research that CAL is moderately effective in enhancing student outcomes; their survey suggested that such a conclusion has been reached many times. Collis (1988) supported this, though questioned the validity of some of the studies. Most studies in these surveys have focused on content, usually using instructional programs, often concentrating on lower-level skills.

Some studies however, focusing on particular populations and subjects, have been concerned with higher order thinking skills. Driver and Scanlon (1989) concluded that the development of an enhanced understanding of difficult concepts in science is possible through the revelation and conjecture of simulations, while Hoyles et al. (1989) argued for pupil achievements in their own cognitive goals from using Logo. Collections of readings such as Boyd-Barrett and Scanlon (1991) have reported a wide range of individual studies. Particular subjects (science and mathematics and languages) and particular packages (such as Logo and wordprocessing) have dominated this work.

3.2 Social and Cultural Dimensions

A different range of studies has emerged that focuses more on the social and cultural dimensions of using CAL. Discourse among students when working on and around a task has emerged as an important dimension associated with CAL (Chatterton 1985). This is related to the value of group work and in particular to learner cooperation and collaboration on task. Johnson et al. (1985) showed the benefits of work in groups: learners in collaborative groups achieved more. Pea and Sheingold (1987) supported this in their long-term studies at one institution. A component related to group collaboration and discourse is the level of intrinsic interest and motivation that CAL appears to generate from learners. A variety of case studies (Blomeyer and Martin 1991, Watson 1992), often using ethnographic rather than quantitative research methods, have focused on the positive learning environment generated, rather than attempting to measure specific cognitive gains.

3.3 CAL and the Teacher

A third and growing area of research is the exploration of the combination of factors that appears to influence the take-up of CAL. Some studies focused on the style of teaching and attitude of the teacher who does use CAL. Olson (1988) firmly focused on the role of the teacher for whom CAL either supports their style, and so is acceptable, or threatens it, and so is rejected. Others have considered the organizational and management problems associated with CAL. Moonen and Collis (1992) concluded that even in a technologically rich environment, incremental change with the use of CAL will be slow and complex. Van den Akker et al. (1992) concluded that the disappointing experiences of using CAL are related to poor and ill-considered introduction strategies—indeed, the failure to consider the complexity inherent in the use of such a technological innovation.

4. Agreed Attributes of CAL

Drawing from this research evidence and large scale reports (United States Congress, office of Technology Assessment 1988) a number of known or potential beneficial effects for CAL can be listed:

(a) developing skills in: (i) problem-solving; (ii) the observation, collection, classification, analysis, interpretation, and appropriate representation of data; (iii) language competence;

(b) encouraging: (i) creative work; (ii) the collection of fieldwork data; (iii) using data from a wider variety of sources; (iv) individual attainment amongst those with special needs;

(c) promoting: (i) inquiries in the humanities; (ii) conceptual understanding in the sciences and mathematics; (iii) logical thinking with Logo; (iv) predictive and deductive work with databases; (v) creative explorations with new tools; (vi) collaboration and social skills; (vii) focused discourse.

Computer-assisted Learning can also be used inappropriately. Word processors are often used as a method of producing fair copy, and data packages for graphical representations of simplistic analysis that is equally well-done manually. It can be used to reinforce less desirable aspects of learning: the use of drills and repetitive exercises may simply replicate tedious classwork of little proven value.

5. Concluding Issues

Examples of successful use of CAL are rare. Pelgrum and Plomp (1991) have clearly shown that in most countries only a small percentage of teachers are using computers, and the pedagogic aspects of using computers are mentioned by them the least.

Part of this problem can be attributed to a confusion as to why computers have been introduced into education. Hawkridge (1990) has identified four rationales for the introduction of computers into schools: social, vocational, pedagogic, and catalytic. The role of CAL is often perceived to be vocational (i.e., used in schools to prepare learners for the use of IT in the adult world) rather than pedagogic (i.e., to facilitate learning itself). The catalytic is predicated on the assumption that using computers will facilitate a complete change in the nature of learning and educational institutions; a message similar to that espoused by Papert (1980). This is in direct contradiction to the work that claims disinterest in CAL to be due to the poor integration within educational institutions and existing pedagogy.

A much greater corpus of research is needed to enable the picture to be sounder than it is at present. One of the biggest problems facing research communities is that if CAL produces a new and unique interactive environment, it is less easy to chart its benefits because it is not amenable to standard forms of research. This is compounded by the fact that benefits of CAL appear to be in the development of higher order thinking skills, with the outcomes being process-rather than product-oriented.

See also: Courseware Design; Computers in Education; Tutoring

References

Blomeyer R L, Martin D (eds.) 1991 *Case Studies of Computer Aided Learning*. Falmer Press, London

Boyd-Barrett O, Scanlon E 1991 *Computers and Learning: A Reader*. Addison Wesley, Wokingham

Chatterton J L 1985 Evaluating CAL in the classroom. In: Reid I, Rushtoon J (eds.) *Teachers, Computers and the Classroom* Manchester University Press, Manchester

Collis B 1988 *Computers, Curriculum and Whole Class Instruction: Issues and Ideas*. Wadsworth, Belmont, California

Driver R, Scanlon E 1989 Conceptual change in science. *Journal of Computer Assisted Learning* 5(1): 25–36

Hawkridge D 1990 Who needs computers in schools and why? *Comput. Educ.* 15(1–3): 1–6

Hoyles C, Noss R, Sutherland R 1989 Designing a Logo-based microworld for ratio and proportion. *Journal of Computer Assisted Learning* 5(4): 208–23

Johnson R T, Johnson D W, Stanne M B 1985 Effects of cooperative, competitive and individualistic goal structures in computer assisted instruction. *J. Educ. Psychol.* 77(6): 668–77

Kemmis S, Atkin R, Wright E 1977 *How do Students Learn? Working Papers on Computer Assisted Learning*. Centre for Applied Research in Education, University of East Anglia, Norwich

Moonen J, Collis B 1992 Changing the school: Experiences from a Dutch technology-enriched school project. *Education and Computing* 8(1–2): 97–102

Niemiec R P, Walberg H J 1992 The effects of computers on learning. *Int. J. Educ. Res.* 17(1): 99–107

Olson J 1988 *Schoolworlds—Microworlds: Computers and the Culture of the Classroom*. Pergamon Press, Oxford

Papert S 1980 *Mindstorms: Children, Computers and Powerful Ideas*. Basic Books, New York

Pea R D, Sheingold K (eds.) 1987 *Mirrors of Mind: Patterns of Excellence in Educational Computing*. Ablex, Norwood, New Jersey

Pelgrum W J, Plomp T 1991 *The Use of Computers in Education Worldwide*. Pergamon Press, Oxford

Roblyer M D, Castine W H, King F J 1988 Assessing the impact of computer based instruction: A review of recent research. *Computers in Schools* 5(3–4)

Taylor R P 1980 *The Computer in the School: Tutor, Tool, Tutee*. Teachers College Press, New York

United States Congress, Office of Technology Assessment 1988 *Power On! New Tools for Teaching and Learning*. United States Government Printing Office, Washington, DC

van den Akker J, Keursten P, Plomp T 1992 The integration of computer use in education. *Int. J. Educ. Res.* 17(1): 65–76

Watson D M 1992 Case studies of classroom processes

using geography simulations. In: Plomp T J, Pieters J M, Feteris A (eds.) 1992 *European Conference on Educational Research*. University of Twente, Enschede

Further Reading

McDougall A, Dowling C (eds.) 1990 *Computers in Education*. North Holland/Elsevier, Amsterdam
Underwood J D M, Underwood G 1990 *Computers and Learning: Helping Children to Acquire Thinking Skills*. Blackwell, Oxford

D. M. Watson

Computerized Educational Testing

Test developers have always had a keen interest in automating their operations. The reasons for this interest are twofold. First, inherent in the use of objective tests is the attempt to standardize all steps in the testing process. Examples of such steps are processing the answer sheets, scoring the test, sending out reports, and filing the test scores. Even before computers were available, developers in charge of large-scale testing programs had well-defined routines to deal with these activities. Where possible, technical devices were used to reduce the amount of labor involved in running the programs—as was illustrated by the widespread use of the so-called Hollerith machine for processing punch cards until the 1960s. As soon as computers became available, most of the routines were immediately transferred to application software. Efficiency was further enhanced by combining the use of computers with optical scanners for reading answer sheets.

Second, educational testing relies heavily on psychometric analyses for the evaluation of the quality of its measurements. These analyses are necessary to provide information on the difficulty of the test items, the factorial structure of the test, the accuracy of test-based predictions, or to estimate the transformation that equates scores on new test forms to the scale of an old form. The analyses must usually be done under time pressure—after the test is administered, but before it can be scored. In the pre-electronic era, ingenious computational schemes and mechanical calculators were employed to make efficient use of the amount of time available. Small wonder, then, that test specialists were among the first to use the computer for running their analyses.

The applications of the computer to educational testing outlined above will not be reviewed in this entry. Though convenient, they are straightforward and represent no major shift in technology. Rather, the interest will be in the *new* testing technology generated by the introduction of the computer in the field of educational testing. This technology capitalizes not just on the computer's ability to process data at high speed, but also on the interactivity it offers, the immediate access to mass storage of data, the novel use of graphics and the power to control multimedia environments. Examples of this new technology can be found in such applications as adaptive or response-contingent testing, innovative use of graphics to implement new response test formats, measurement of response time, computerized test design, authoring systems for test-item writing, use of test scores in support systems for instructional decision-making, and the simulation of real-life processes and the use of multimedia environments to increase test validity. This new technology is rapidly expanding. It has influenced the work of test developers profoundly, and has already reached the schools through software for personal computers (PCs).

It is important to note that all these applications are not the sheer result of the availability of powerful computer hardware or the introduction of efficient programming methodology. A fortunate coincidence was the simultaneous development of a completely new class of models in test theory. The theory underlying these models is known as Item Response Theory (IRT). IRT supports the use of computers in educational testing in a natural way. It can be used to provide each item stored in the computer with independent estimates of their properties, to have the computer select tests from item banks, to govern item administration procedures, or to design models for scoring tests with new computer-based response formats. The last example shows that IRT has not only made computerized testing feasible, but that the use of computers in testing has also stimulated the development of psychometric models that would never have existed without the presence of computers. The principles on which IRT models are built and their role in computerized testing will be briefly outlined below.

The remainder of the entry has been organized into five sections, each dealing with a different aspect of computerized testing: (a) computerized adaptive testing; (b) item banking systems; (c) automated test design; (d) authoring systems for item writing; (e) multimedia testing.

Due to developments in information technology, computer hardware quickly becomes obsolete. Therefore, no attempt will be made to review available hardware. For the same reason, existing computer software will be referred to only incidentally. Reviews of hardware and software, however, can be found in Baker (1989), Hsu and Yu (1989), and Roid (1989).

1. Computerized Adaptive Testing

Since the first standardized test was developed, test designers have been aware that they must solve the following paradox. Suppose a test has to be designed to measure the ability of an examinee in a certain domain. If the ability of the examinee were known, it would be possible to design a perfect test. None of the items the examinee would pass or fail for sure would be included in the test; it would be more efficient to just fill out the answer sheet for these items in advance. Instead, the test would concentrate on those items for which it would be uncertain if the examinee could pass. A test with this content would not waste any time, but be maximally informative about the ability of the examinee. However, the ability of the examinee is *unknown*; otherwise there would be no reason whatsoever to administer a test.

It is known that Stanford and Binet tried to solve this paradox for their first intelligence test, published in 1905, by continuously adapting the content of the test to the ability level of the examinee during the session. A description of the adaptive aspect of the Stanford–Binet test is given in Reckase (1989). Others have followed the same path, introducing such procedures as two-stage testing and flexi-level testing.

In two-stage testing, the format of a single test is replaced by a short routing test along with a series of second-stage tests of varying difficulty. The routing test is administered first. It is quickly scored, and then the scores are used to select an optimal second-stage test. Of course, the scores on the routing test have restricted reliability. In fact, the above dilemma now takes the form of a trade-off between the lengths of the routing test and the second-stage tests. But it can be shown that scores based on the combination of a routing test and an optimal second-stage test generally are more reliable than scores on a single test of the same total length. A more ingenious design offers the flexi-level test. With a flexi-level test the examinee codes his or her answer by scratching a certain area on the answer sheet, and then finds information on the next item to continue with.

Both the two-stage and flexi-level testing procedure are described in Lord (1980). Though these procedures are more efficient than traditional standardized tests, they suffer from such constraints as a restricted number of items in the test form and a fixed order in which the difficulties have to be present in the test.

For testing to be fully adaptive, the following conditions have to be realized:

(a) a delivery system that is able to retrieve items quickly from a large pool and display them to the examinee;

(b) a rule for scoring the ability of the examinee on the basis of the responses to the items already displayed;

(c) a rule for selecting the next item to be displayed as a function of the score on the previous item;

(d) a rule for selecting the item in the pool to start the testing procedure with;

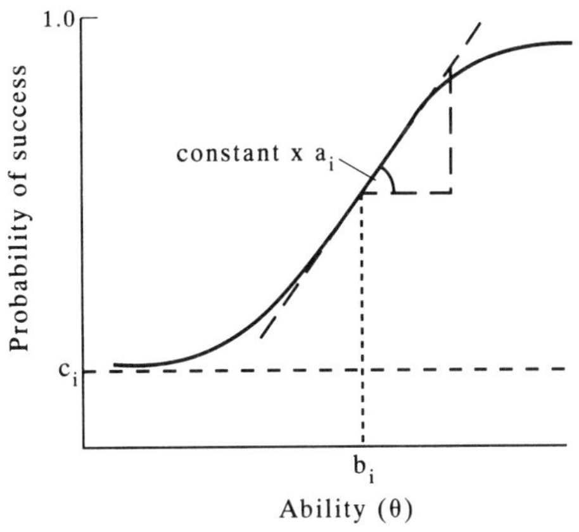

Figure 1
Response curve of a test item

(e) a rule for stopping the procedure.

A computer, with its capacity for storing huge amounts of text and graphics, its quick access to memory, its video monitor for displaying the items, its keyboard for recording the responses, and its enormous power to perform calculations according to complex rules, forms an ideal environment for adaptive testing. Hence it was not until mass production of computers started that adaptive testing became practicable.

Nowadays most test publishers sell adaptive versions of their standardized tests. Adaptive tests are delivered in the form of software for PCs along with a data file that contains the test items. A typical file has 200–500 items. It is not uncommon to find that computerized adaptive testing (CAT) realizes the same accuracy with 30–40 percent of the items needed previously in roughly 50 percent of the time. The gain in time can be used to test abilities in a larger series of domains and increase the predictive validity of the test. A favorite application in education is therefore testing for placement in educational programs; for example, at college entry level.

Introductions to CAT can be found in Bunderson et al. (1989), Lord (1970, 1980), van der Linden and Zwarts (1989), Wainer et al. (1990), and Weiss (1983).

1.1 IRT Models

As was observed above, to implement a CAT procedure, in addition to a computer environment, rules are needed to select the items, score the examinees, and stop the procedure. At the same time, these rules need statistical information about the items on which to operate. It is here that IRT plays its role.

The power of IRT resides in the fact that it par-

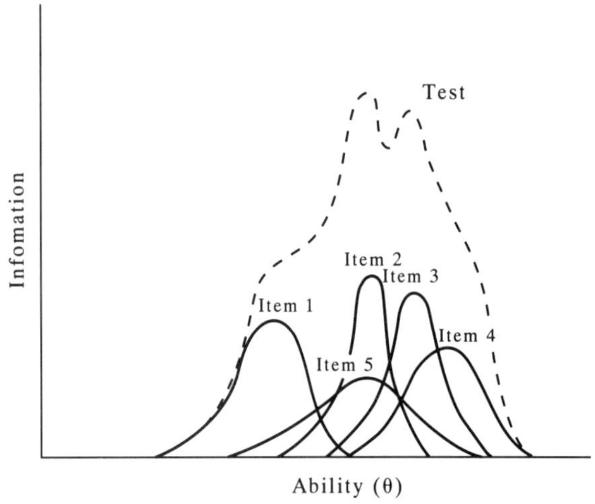

Figure 2
Item and test information functions

ameterizes the ability of the examinees and the properties of the items *separately*. Due to the presence of these separate parameters, estimates of the item parameters can be used to correct for the properties of the items when scoring the ability of an examinee. This correction is an instance of statistical adjustment. It allows scoring of different selections of items from a pool on the *same* scale—a feature on which CAT capitalizes by adapting the properties of the items to a current estimate of the examinee's ability.

A graphical representation of an IRT model is given by a response curve, as in Fig. 1. The curve displays the probability of a correct response on item i as a function of the value of ability parameter of the examinee. The item parameters determine the shape and the location of the curve. A common mathematical form of the curve is given by the so-called three-parameter logistic formula:

$$P(+|\theta) = c_i + (1 - c_i)[1 + \exp\{-a_i(\theta - b_i)\}]^{-1} \quad (1)$$

where θ is the ability of the examinee, b_i is the difficulty (location), a_i the discriminating power (slope), and c_i the guessing parameter (lower asymptote) of item i.

A practical feature of IRT models is the presence of a measure generally known as the information function. An information function gives the information in the responses to an item or a test as a function of the true ability of the examinee. For five items as well as the test composed of the items, the information functions associated with the model in Eqn. 1 are given in Fig. 2. Conceptually, it is convenient to view information functions as a related but more fundamental concept than classical reliability.

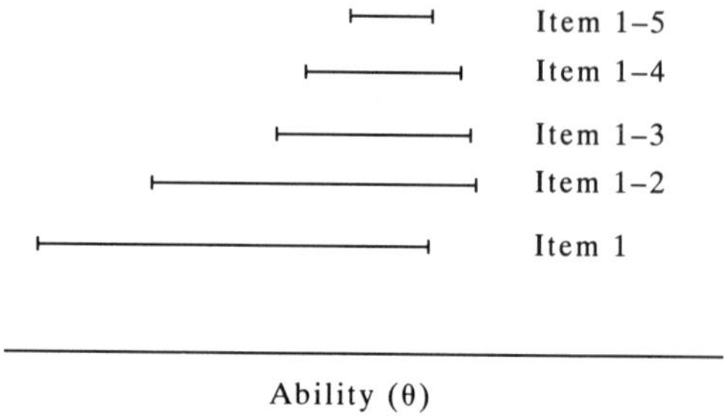

Figure 3
Increase of accuracy of ability estimation in CAT

Unlike classical reliability, information functions are no single coefficients but functions showing how "reliably" the test or the item measures examinees at each possible value of the ability scale. It should be observed that the information functions for the five items in Fig. 2 sum to the function for the test. Also, the reciprocal of the square root of the information function is a measure that gives the standard error of measurement as a function of the ability value.

Full introductions to IRT models are given in Hambleton and Swaminathan (1984), Lord (1980), and Rasch (1980) (see *Item Response Theory*).

1.2 Rules for CAT

An obvious way to select items in a CAT procedure is to base the selection of subsequent items on the information functions of the items in the pool. Each next item could then be selected such that it has maximum information at the ability value where the examinee is estimated to be. In fact, this *maximum information* rule is the most popular item assignment rule in CAT. It is not the only rule; an alternative is a Bayesian rule in which the next item is selected such that the expected variance of the posterior distribution for the examinee's ability value is minimal (see Owen 1975; *Bayesian Statistics in the Analysis of Data*).

The two item assignment rules can only be operational if an estimate of the examinee's ability from his or her responses to previous items is obtained in realistic time. A natural partner of the maximum information rule is *maximum-likelihood estimation* of ability. In this estimation method, the ability value that maximizes the likelihood of the response pattern obtained from the examinee is defined to be his or her ability estimate. The use of modern hardware and software gives quick estimates for the IRT models currently in use. For Owen's rule, Bayesian ability estimation is the appropriate choice (see *Factor Analysis*).

The choice of the first item in a CAT procedure is important, because considerable gain of information, and hence reduction of test length, can be obtained

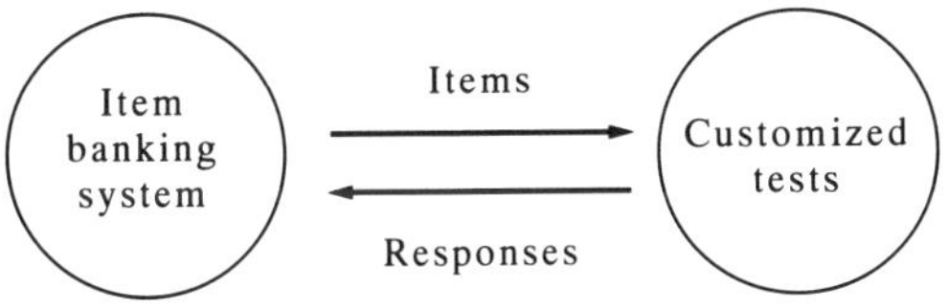

Figure 4
Diagram of test item banking system

if the first item is not too far off target. If no prior information about the ability of the examinee is present, the best choice is to start with an item that is optimal at a (subjective) estimate of the location of the ability distribution of the population of examinees the test has been designed for. If prior information is available, for example, in the form of information on background variables with a known regression on the ability variable, better choices are possible. It is also possible to have the computer collect information on the background variables and update the regression function with each new examinee.

A CAT procedure is stopped if enough information on the examinee's ability is gathered. Fig. 3 gives an account of the information gathering process for maximum-likelihood estimation of ability. For convenience, confidence intervals derived from the test information function are depicted, rather than the information functions themselves. For each item added to the test, the width of the interval decreases. At the same time the location of the interval converges to a certain ability value. As soon as the width of the interval is below a prespecified threshold value, the procedure stops.

Presenting the above examples of CAT rules, it has been assumed that all item parameters in the IRT model have been estimated earlier. This point will now be taken up.

2. *Item Banking Systems*

The traditional instrument in educational measurement is the standardized test. Standardized testing is based on the paradigm of experimental control as it has evolved in the literature on experimental design earlier in the twentieth century (van der Linden 1986b). The steps involved in developing a standardized test are as follows. First, a blueprint of the test is established that will guarantee a test with appropriate content validity. Then the items are written and field-tested. If the final version of the test is assembled, another field test is done to crossvalidate the reliability of the test and to estimate norm distributions. After this, the test is fixed and any change of content will invalidate its use.

Though of practical value, standardized tests are inflexible and their use if often less than optimal. For example, the same test can never be used twice for the same group of examinees without running into security problems. Also, if a test has to serve a population of examinees varying widely in ability, it is likely to be suboptimal for most examinees. This is the paradox of test design referred to earlier. A related point is the problem of test use in educational research with a pretest–posttest design. If the treatment in this design is effective, a standardized test is likely not to be—one test can never reliably measure large differences in ability. More fundamentally, standardized tests may have low content validity, as the number of items in the test is usually much smaller than the number of items that defines the domain to be tested.

A new conception of educational measurement is test item banking. The paradigm of test item banking is not experimental control, but the idea of statistical adjustment already alluded to earlier (van der Linden 1986a). In test item banking a computer is used to store a pool of items covering the content domain. In addition to the item, initial estimates of their parameters, like those defined by the IRT model in Eqn. 1, are stored. If the item banking system is operational, it functions as in the diagram in Fig. 4. First, items are retrieved from the system to assemble tests. If test delivery is on-line, CAT is an attractive choice. However, if on-line delivery is not possible, tests can also be assembled in the form of paper and pencil tests tailored to their specific applications. Though not as efficient as CAT, such customized tests are much better than standardized tests. The tests may be of any length not exceeding the size of the item bank. They may be selected to be very difficult or easy, or to cover a broad or a small range of ability. Whatever the selection of items, when scoring the test, the item parameters in the system automatically correct the ability estimates of the examinees for the incidental properties of the items in the test.

Second, all responses on the items in the tests are fed back into the system. They are kept, for example, for a periodic update of the estimates of the item parameters. This feature allows the system to improve the fit of future tests with the users' specifications. Another possible use of item responses is to combine them with information on background variables to update estimates of norm distributions for various populations of examinees or to find optimal start items for use in CAT procedures.

Item banking systems cannot be run without the use of a computer. They need the use of database software, a text editor, and graphics software to store, catalog, and retrieve test items and their statistical information. If printed versions of tests have to be delivered, desktop publishing software is needed to edit the tests into their final form. Statistical software for parameter estimation and update, test scoring, and test assembly requires the power of

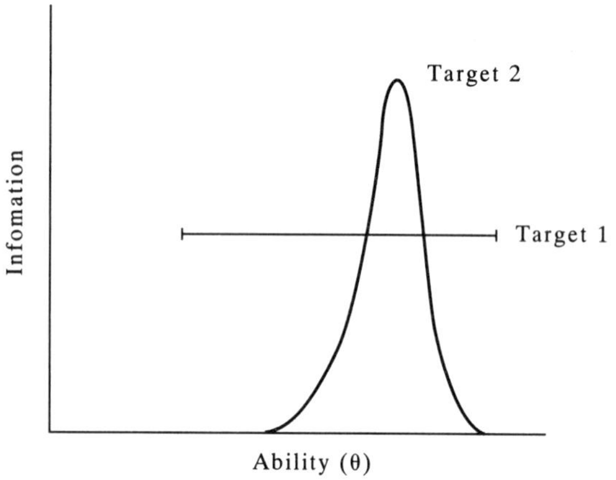

Figure 5
Two target information functions in automated test design[a]
a 1 = diagnostic test, 2 = mastery test

modern processors. In fact, the combination of all these resources into a single application makes item banking systems unique. An item banking system that shares many of the features reviewed here is MicroCAT (Stone 1989).

3. *Automated Test Design*

The process of designing customized tests assembled from an item banking system can be automated. As has already been demonstrated in Fig. 2, information functions have the property of additivity. This feature allows the following design process.

First, the test constructor decides on a *target* for the information function of the test. The first step in reaching this decision is to determine what interval of ability values the test should measure. Then the shape of the target is chosen. The shape commonly depends on the intended use of the test. Fig. 5 gives two possible targets, one for a diagnostic test, the other for a mastery test.

Second, items are selected from the pool to fill up the area below the target. This selection is subject to various constraints on the content of the items to guarantee a valid test.

To automate the design process, linear programming modeling can be used. A simple example shows the principles involved. The items in the pool are represented by index $i=1, \ldots, N$. For each item a decision variable $x_i \in \{0,1\}$ is defined to indicate whether or not the item will be selected for the test. The information in item i at ability value θ_k is denoted by $I_i(\theta_k)$. Now, let $T(\theta_k)$ be the value for the target information function of the diagnostic test in Fig. 5 at ability values θ_k for $k=1, \ldots, K$. Then, for an arbitrary test, non-negative numbers u_k and v_k can be used to denote the positive and negative slack between the actual information in the test at the values θ_k and the values of the target, $T(\theta_k)$. The following linear programming model selects the items from the pool such that the sum of the values of the slack variables is minimal:

$$\textit{minimize} \sum_{k=1}^{K} (u_k + v_k) \qquad (2)$$

subject to

$$\sum_{i=1}^{N} I_i(\theta_k)x_i - u_k + v_k = T(\theta_k), \quad k = 1,\ldots,K; \qquad (3)$$

$$\sum_{i=1}^{N} x_i = 1; \qquad (4)$$

$$u_k, v_k \geq 0, \quad k = 1,\ldots,K; \qquad (5)$$

$$x_i \in \{0,1\}, \quad i = 1,\ldots,N. \qquad (6)$$

The objective function in Eqn. 2 minimizes the sum of values of the slack variables. In Eqn. 3 the slack variables are defined as the positive and negative deviation of the test information function from the target values. The only constraint added to the model is the requirement in Eqn. 4 which states that the length of the test be equal to n items. The possible values of all variables in the model are defined in Eqns. 5–6.

Linear programming software can be used to solve the model for the values of the variables that minimize the objective function and satisfy all the constraints. These values identify an optimal test.

In its present form, the above model is too simple to be realistic. In practice, additional constraints with respect to test content, cognitive level, such attributes as item readability or gender orientation, or various statistical criteria are needed to produce acceptable results. A catalog of constraints to deal with these and other specifications is given in van der Linden and Boekkooi-Timminga (1989). The paper also lists alternative objective functions. Theunissen (1985) presented a model that minimizes the length of the test. Another possibility is the simultaneous selection of a set of parallel tests (Adema 1992, Boekkooi-Timminga 1987). These references are only to a small portion of the methodology available now. It is recommended that the models always be applied in an interactive mode in which the computer program makes a proposal and the test constructor reviews the results, deciding which items to retain and which the computer has to replace. The process is iterated until a satisfactory result is obtained.

A software program that can be used to solve a model of minimal test length is *Optimal Test Design* (Verschoor 1991). A general-purpose test assembly program with an interface that allows the user to make his or her own selection of objective function and constraints is *Contest* (ProGamma 1993).

4. Authoring Systems for Test Item Writing

Item writing is a time-consuming process, mostly with several stages of review by content experts and field testing. It is surprising to note that the quality of the first versions of the items is often far less than optimal. It is not unusual to find that more than half of the items never reach the final stage. Typical errors involve poor use of language, response options with equivocal truth values, or the inability to produce items within a desired range of difficulty. As the quality of the items imposes an upper bound on the quality of the test, technology to improve the item writing process would be a major step forward.

Though the use of computers has penetrated the art of item writing, its potential has not been fully realized yet. Some of the developments will be briefly outlined here. In so doing, it is not the intention to suggest that the human item writer should be replaced by computer software. Human involvement will always be needed to produce text, make critical decisions, or approve products. However, computer technology may provide a convenient environment for item writers to fulfill all those functions.

A first level of computerized item writing involves the use of word processors to draft and edit test items. It was only recently that the use of word-processing programs added efficiency to the item writing process. The first reason for this fact is the amount of text in items usually is not large. Even a language test seldom has more than a few pages of text. Further, most test items have nontext materials, such as graphs, diagrams, drawings, mathematical symbols or expressions, or high-resolution photographs. Fortunately, nowadays most word processors have spellcheck or thesaurus options and work with graphics programs for drawing graphs, preparing diagrams, or creating mathematical expressions. It is the integration of all these facilities that has made the word processor an attractive tool for item writing.

Though word processing may increase the efficiency of item writing, it is unlikely that the mere use of word processing will improve the effectiveness of the items produced. One possible exception is the fact that repeated use of the same word-processor may lead to better standardization of materials and hence to multiple test forms that better realize the ideal of parallel tests.

Significant improvement in the quality of item writing may be reached with a next generation of word-processing software, which will check for errors in grammar and style. Most item formats are sensitive to errors in the use of grammar and style. Examples of critical errors are: (a) inconsequent continuation of grammar in alternatives of multiple-choice items; (b) nonuniform style in checklist items, or between alternatives in matching items; and (c) failure to meet the requirement that fill-in items should allow wrong answers compatible with the grammar or style of the text presented.

Ultimate support of item writers would be provided by authoring systems specially designed for item writing. Such systems would integrate the above two levels of support with several new facilities to create an environment that fully supports each step in the item production process. The following facilities are attractive.

(a) The first is support of the selection of item format; for example, through a dialogue leading the item writer to an appropriate format for the application at hand.

(b) Second is guidance through the item writing process once a format is chosen. Options include the definition of a template for each individual item, lists of suggestions for typical text elements in items, routines for including nontext materials, procedures for ordering or randomizing alternatives or making layout decisions. Ideally, at each decision the system would provide the item writer with projections of the effects of the alternatives on the expected difficulty of the item.

(c) Third is check of quality of the items. This includes not only the checks for spelling and grammar, but also for features such as the readability of the item and typical item writing errors that now figure in extensive checklists circulating in the testing literature on various item formats. A third level of item checking would be a search of collections of items for clues in one item to right answers on other items.

(d) Finally there is project management. Item writing typically is a process with many participants. If installed on networks of computers, authoring systems could provide communication between the participants and standardization of their output. In principle, the next participant could immediately continue working on a half product delivered by his or her predecessor.

A review of item writing software is given in Roid (1989), whereas Rikers (1988) described the design of an ideal authoring system for item writing.

5. Multimedia Testing

For some content domains, test developers have had a tradition of using media other than paper and pencil to enhance the validity of their tests. Examples are the use of audio equipment in tests of listening comprehension in foreign languages and the use of slide presentations, for example, in traffic licensing exams.

With the availability of new electronic media, it is possible that these trends will expand. With built-in processors or in a computer-controlled mode, these media have the power to represent real-life situations convincingly in the test or to simulate processes in real time. Examples of these media are videodisc, CD-I, and special-purpose simulators. Their potential for use in educational testing has not been fully explored, but their impact on the validity of tests may be enormous. The first applications can been found in computer simulations of patient–management problems that are now introduced to test knowledge and skills in medical programs around the world. It is anticipated that other applications will follow soon. In particular, the use of computer-controlled multimedia environments in testing is attractive. Digital technology has reached the point where these environments are capable of simulating almost any process in "virtual reality." Applications of this technology are waiting to be used in educational testing. The only current obstacle is the cost of these media, which tend to prohibit large-scale application in education. However, if prices decrease, the number of applications in testing can be expected to increase immediately.

6. Conclusion

The use of information technology will no doubt further penetrate educational testing. Its effect on the flexibility and measurement quality of test procedures is enormous. At an increasing rate the field of educational testing will show tests delivered in novel formats and at unusual places. It is expected that this increased flexibility will provide a major impetus to further integration of educational testing and instruction.

See also: Tests: Different Types; Item Response Theory

References

Adema J J 1992 Methods and models for the construction of weakly parallel tests. *Appl. Psychol. Meas.* 16 (1): 53–63

Baker F B 1989 Computer technology in test construction and processing. In: Linn R L (ed.) 1989 *Educational Measurement*, 3rd edn. Macmillan, New York

Boekkooi-Timminga E 1987 Simultaneous test construction by zero-one programming. *Methodika* 1(2): 101–12

Bunderson C V, Inouye D K, Olsen J B 1989 The four generations of computerized educational measurement. In: Linn R L (ed.) 1989 *Educational Measurement*, 3rd edn. Macmillan, New York

Hambleton R K, Swaminathan H 1984 *Item Response Theory: Principles and Applications*. Kluwer-Nijhoff, Boston, Massachusetts

Hsu T-C, Yu L 1989 Using computers to analyze item response data. *Educational Measurement: Issues and Practice* 8(3): 21–28

Lord F M 1970 Some test theory for tailored testing. In: Holtzman W H (ed.) 1970 *Computer-assisted Instruction, Testing and Guidance*. Harper and Row, New York

Lord F M 1980 *Applications of Item Response Theory to Practical Testing Problems*. Erlbaum, Hillsdale, New Jersey

Owen R J 1975 A Bayesian sequential procedure for quantal response in the context of adaptive mental testing. *Journal of the American Statistical Association* 70(350): 351–56

ProGamma 1993 *Contest* (Software and manual). ProGamma, Groningen

Rasch G 1980 *Probabilistic Models for Some Intelligence and Attainment Tests*, rev. edn. University of Chicago Press, Chicago, Illinois

Reckase M D 1989 Adaptive testing: The evolution of a good idea. *Educational Measurement: Issues and Practice* 8(3): 11–15

Rikers J A H N 1988 *Towards an Authoring System for Item Construction*. Department of Education, University of Twente, Enschede

Roid G H 1989 Item writing and item banking by microcomputer: An update. *Educational Measurement: Issues and Practice* 8(3): 17–20

Stone C A 1989 Testing software review: MicroCAT. *Educational Measurement: Issues and Practice* 8(3): 33–38

Theunissen T J J M 1985 Binary programming and test design. *Psychometri.* 50(4): 411–20

van der Linden W J (ed.) 1986a Special issue on test item banking. *Appl. Psychol. Meas.* 10(4)

van der Linden W J 1986b The changing conception of measurement in education and psychology. *Appl. Psychol. Meas.* 10(4): 325–32

van der Linden W J, Boekkooi-Timminga E 1989 A maximin model for test design with practical constraints. *Psychometri.* 54(2): 237–47

van der Linden W J, Zwarts M A 1989 Some procedures for computerized ability testing. *Int. J. Educ. Res.* 13(2): 175–87

Verschoor A 1991 *Optimal Test Design* (Software and manual). Cito, Arnhem

Wainer H et al. (eds.) 1990 *Computerized Adaptive Testing: A Primer*. Erlbaum, Hillsdale, New Jersey

Weiss D J (ed.) 1983 *New Horizons in Testing: Latent Trait Test Theory and Computerized Adaptive Testing*. Academic Press, New York

Further Reading

Boekkooi-Timminga E, van der Linden W J 1994 *Linear Models for Optimal Test*. Sage, Newbury Park, California

Gutkin T B, Wise S L (eds.) 1990 *The Computer and the Decision-making Process*. Erlbaum, Hillsdale, New Jersey

Hambleton R K, Zaal J N, Pieters J P M 1991 Computerized adaptive testing: Theory, applications, and standards. In: Hambleton R K, Zaal J N (eds.) 1991 *Advances in Educational and Psychological Testing*. Kluwer, Boston, Massachusetts

W.J. van der Linden

Computer-managed Learning

This entry addresses the practice of managing instruction and individual student learning using networked computers. The entry provides a brief history of computer-managed learning in the United States from early computer-assisted instruction (CAI) to growing use of integrated learning systems (ILS) and describes the characteristics of such systems. It also discusses international applications of computer-managed learning, its further evolution, and the paucity of systematic research of its effect on learners, teachers, and curriculum.

1. Nature and Origins of Computer-managed Learning

Computer-managed learning is an evolving pedagogical practice in which networked computers are used to provide individual learners with access to instructional software, productivity software, and electronic information resources. The defining characteristics of such systems are: (a) integration of computer-based instruction and other learning-related software applications; (b) capability to manage a flow of information related to use of the system by individual learners; (c) system-generated progress reports on student progress and achievement.

The origins of computer-managed learning are traceable to the development and use of computer-assisted instruction at a few universities, military training centers, and corporations in the United States during the 1960s. These early efforts were designed as means for providing individualized, interactive instruction to many learners simultaneously. Such systems employed mainframe computers and a network of terminals to store, distribute, and manage instructional programming and a flow of information required to sustain individualized electronic teaching and learning.

2. Growth and Evolution

During the first two decades of school-based application of computer-managed learning, the 1960s and 1970s, it was restricted to a prescriptive, linear approach to teaching basic mathematics and language skills. Although experimental applications in some universities went beyond such limited applications, those experiments had little effect on the type of applications available to school users.

In United States schools, the growth and evolution of computer-managed learning have been shaped by a complex mix of technical, economic, social, and educational realities. Throughout the 1970s, when school applications still required the use of costly mainframe or minicomputers, plus a level of technical expertise that made most educators wary, the growth in applications of computer-managed learning systems in United States schols was slow. However, during the 1980s cost and technical barriers were lowered considerably by the appearance of lower cost, technically less daunting, networkable microcomputers. This was followed by a significant increase in the number of commercial providers of computer-managed learning systems. This increase coincided with metaresearch findings (Kulik 1985) indicating that CAI was often equal to, or superior to, conventional teaching.

The initial markets for these commercially developed systems were schools and job-training centers looking to improve: (a) remedial instruction in basic skills, and (b) instructional accountability. In time a wider market developed among schools and colleges interested in innovative approaches to teaching through the use of technology. In response to this wider market, such systems have begun to address learning that goes beyond instruction in basic skills. As a result, the number of installations of computer-managed learning in the United States schools grew from a few thousand in the early 1980s to an estimated 20,000 in the early 1990s.

2.1 Integrated Learning Systems

Most installations of computer-managed learning in the United States have been commercially marketed to schools as "integrated learning systems"—a name used by those in marketing to indicate that such systems, in addition to delivering CAI, may also include other applications such as word-processing, electronic encyclopedias, and other productivity and research tools. As of the mid-1990s, the term "integrated" in such systems refers to a system's capability to integrate and to manage the use of a variety of computer software applications in addition to each system's distinguishing proprietary instructional software. However, such integration does not usually imply an integrated approach to curriculum and learning across content areas.

Although integrated learning systems vary in complexity and sophistication, as well as in quality of instruction and management, their common functions and features may be outlined as in Table 1.

3. International Applications of Computer-managed Learning

As of 1993, in addition to the United States, countries with a significant base of networked computers installed in schools were Israel, Japan, and Sweden. However, among these only Israeli schools had a significant amount of computer-managed learning installed and in use.

Computer-managed learning in Israel began in the mid-1970s, when rights for the use of a system developed in the United States were granted to an Israeli university. That resulted in the employment of computer-managed learning in a few Israeli schools, and led to a continuing expansion of computer-managed learning in Israel. This acceptance prompted commercial development of a number of systems, two of which are marketed in both Israel and the United States. Although the percentage of Israeli

Table 1
Functions and features of integrated learning systems

Distribution of software	
Instructional software	Sequential lessons (supplied with system) – preset sequencing of lessons – resequencing of lessons and teacher lesson planning Nonsequential supplemental lessons (added by users)
Tool software	Word processing, spell checker, note pad, etc. Database or filing system Calculator Spreadsheet
Reference software	Electronic encyclopedia, dictionary, etc. Research database
System access and security	
Hierarchical access	By students, teachers, systems managers
Passwords	Required, optional, or unavailable
Backup of system-generated data	On system's hard disk or on tape
Student testing	
Diagnostic	
Achievement	
Report generation	
Individual student, by lesson	Percentage completed/percentage correct Time spent Text of student's responses Analysis of responses to lessons Aggregate performance on multiple lessons
Progress report to parents	
Reports on class, multiple classes and special groups	
Reports on whole school or multiple schools	
Integrated computer-management of all of above	

schools using computer-managed learning is estimated to be comparable to use in United States schools, official government statistics are not available for either country.

In Sweden, national education authorities established a national policy during the 1980s that called for the use of networked (rather than stand-alone) computers in schools throughout the country. Since then, responsibility for education management has been decentralized, but the policy on networked computers has resulted in the widespread use of networks to provide students with access to software for carrying out writing, computation, and other productivity tasks. There has been only modest development of curriculum-related software by a few commercial publishers. No official statistics are available on the use of software in Swedish schools.

The only country for which detailed statistics exist on the use of networked computers in schools is Japan. The figures in Table 2 from the Japanese Ministry of Education, provide a profile of the base of networked computers installed in schools throughout Japan as of 31 March 1992. It is important to note that these figures pertain only to the presence of networked computers, and not to whether those networks are being used to implement computer-managed learning. The Japan Council for Educational Software reports that appropriate software is still in the early stages of development. The objective is to create networkable software that will meet the requirements of the national curriculum that is widely followed by Japanese schools.

Other applications of computer-managed learning internationally seem to be at much earlier stages of development. In Australia, for example, the use of such learning seems to be limited to the schools secondary level utilizing mainframe computers. Schools in most other countries lack both networked computers and sources of appropriate software. However, if conditions similar to those that have fostered growth of computer-managed learning in the United States develop in other countries, international use of computer-managed learning may increase. Among these conditions are: (a) willingness of education authorities and/or teachers to use networkable computers to individualize instruction; (b) availability of computer networks in schools; (c) sources of appropriate and sufficient educational software; (d) financial resources necessary to

Table 2
Networked computers installed in schools in Japan

Type of school	Percentage with installations	Numbers of schools
Primary (age 6–12)	6.3	1,529 of 24,267
Secondary (age 13–15)	28.4	2,998 of 10,551
High (age 16–18)	37.5	1,554 of 4,144
All schools	15.6	6,081 of 38,962

Source: Japanese Ministry of Education

implement computer-managed learning; and (e) a concern about accountability for learning.

4. Questions about Future Development

There is little doubt that computer-managed learning will continue to evolve and develop. However, because so much of its evolution has been dependent on the development and marketing to schools of proprietary computer-managed learning systems that are installed, maintained, and updated by commercial vendors, is it to be assumed that future evolution will be as heavily dependent on commercial development of similar proprietary systems? If such systems continue to be based on the use of one vendor's proprietary software, how technically and pedagogically open will such systems be to the integration of other competing proprietary software?

As has been noted, current state-of-the-art computer-managed learning evolved from the CAI systems of the 1960s and 1970s. Although ILS systems now go well beyond early CAI, they retain enough of CAI's well-ordered, diagnostic–prescriptive, sequential approach to individualizing instruction to put them in sharp contrast with current constructivist views about learning. To what extent will constructivist ideas about learning and teaching affect the ongoing evolution of computer-managed learning?

All computer-managed learning is "managed" through the use of management software. Such software is at the heart of all current ILSs. It not only manages the system, but it enables a teacher to plan and adapt the use of the system by learners. To what extent will future computer-managed learning systems enable learners themselves to plan and adapt a system to their personal learning needs and interests? How will the increasing use of non-ILS-related, instructional management systems, and the increasing availability of large amounts of networkable, non-ILS-related educational software by schools affect the evolution of computer-managed learning?

5. Paucity of Research and Evaluation

All of the above questions suggest a need for systematic research on many aspects on computer-managed learning. Extant research says little about the effects of computer-managed learning on learning and teaching, and on learners and teachers. Most relevant research has addressed the effectiveness of CAI as measured by standard tests of performance of basic skills. A comparative evaluative report on the eight major ILSs used in United States schools as of 1990 found broad user acceptance of computer-managed learning, but many specific criticisms of particular systems by both teachers and learners (EPIE 1990). It also found wide variation in the quality of instructional software and management systems.

As of 1992, only one multiyear, international research study existed (Hativa 1991, Hativa and Lesgold 1991). The study is an integration of findings from the use of four commercially developed ILSs (two United States and two Israeli) in United States and Israeli schools over a period of six years. The research was limited to "arithmetic practice." The research concluded that all four systems fell short of meeting the curricular and instructional management needs of school users. Given such findings, it is evident that a broad base of ongoing systematic research is needed to shape future development of computer-managed learning in educationally productive ways. However, it remains to be seen whether continuing research or continuing market forces will play the major role in such future development.

See also: Computers and Learning; Computer Literacy; Computers in Education

References

EPIE Institute/Komoski P K 1990 *The Integrated Instructional Systems (IIS) Report: A Comparative Evaluation Report on Eight Integrated Learning Systems*. EPIE Institute, Hampton Bays, Author New York

Hativa N 1991 Cognitive, affective, and social impacts of arithmetic practice with ILS: An integration of findings from six-years qualitative and quantitative studies. ERIC Document Reproduction Service No. ED 336 060, Washington, DC

Hativa N, Lesgold A 1991 The computer as tutor: Can it adapt to the individual learner? ERIC Document Reproduction Service No. EJ 43 1610, Washington, DC

Kulik J A 1985 Consistencies in findings on computer-based education. ERIC Document Reproduction Service No. ED 269 012, Washington, DC

Further Reading

McLaughlin P 1990 Computer-based education: The best of ERIC 1989. ERIC Document Reproduction Service No. ED 341 386, Washington, DC
Plomp T, Moonen J (eds.) 1991 Implementation of computers in education. ERIC Document Reproduction Service No. EJ 436 930, Washington, DC

P. K. Komoski

Computers and Learning

The introduction of computers in schools in the early 1980s was accompanied by high expectations about the potential of this new technology for improving student learning at school. However, by the end of the decade, these high expectations, which were raised for various forms of educational computer use, had not been fulfilled. In this entry, expectations, research outcomes, and new developments will be considered in relation to three prevailing educational computer applications; i.e. computer-assisted learning, word processing, and Logo.

1. Computers and Learning: Expectations and Reality

Computer programs can fulfill a variety of functions in teaching–learning processes, such as: (a) drill and practice, (b) tutorials, (c) instructional computer games, (d) simulations, (e) spreadsheet, (f) word processing, (g) database management, and (h) computer programming (Makrakis 1988, Taylor 1980). In Taylor's (1980) well-known classification schema, the first four types involve the computer as a *tutor*; in types (e) to (g) the computer is used as a *tool*, while in type (h) the computer is considered as a *tutee*. These different computer uses can be ranked in a hierarchical order from low to high, according to several dimensions: the level of cognitive/mental thinking evoked, the degree of learner–computer interaction, and the amount of learner initiative allowed (Makrakis 1988, Scott et al. 1992). As will be demonstrated, these categories tended to merge from the late 1980s onward (Kaput 1992).

In 1989 the International Association for the Evaluation of Educational Achievement (IEA) conducted a survey about the use of computers in education in 20 countries (Pelgrum and Plomp 1991). While big differences between countries were reported, there were also some remarkable similarities. Some overall trends, based on Becker's (1991) survey of the situation in the United States—a country that has played and still plays a pioneering role in the use of computers in education—can be summarized as follows. In the early 1980s educational computer use was largely restricted to drill-and-practice programs, playing instructional games (mostly in mathematics and language), and learning to write simple programs in BASIC. Because most schools at that time had few computers, students had only a limited amount of computer experience. By the end of the decade, systematic and regular hands-on computer experience had become somewhat more common. Especially in middle and high schools, there was an increase in computer applications that score high in terms of the major dimensions of evoked cognitive level and student–computer interaction, such as simulations, word processing, and database management. Learning to program (in BASIC), however, was the only curriculum area where a decline became evident by the end of the 1980s.

From the beginning, the effects of various forms of computer use on students' learning, motivation, and social behavior have been a source of heated debate and a topic of continuing research (Lepper and Gurtner 1989). However, questions about the impact of computers on students' learning and thinking have not always been clearly asked. According to Salomon (1992), one must distinguish between two different ways in which computers can affect human learning and intellect. One way concerns the changes in performance that people display *while* being equipped with a technology; for example, the quality of the student's thinking while using a computer-based graphic tool for solving word problems, or the level of sophistication in the writing process when using a word processor. It has been argued that in these and many other cases, working with a computer affects what one does and how well one does it. A second category of effects concerns relatively lasting changes in people's capacities, as a *cognitive residue* of interaction with a computer (i.e., transfer effects). A typical example here is whether learning to solve word problems or to compose text with the computer will have beneficial effects on those activities when carried out without the technology. Salomon (1992) referred to the former as cognitive effects *with* technology and to the latter as cognitive effects *of* the technology.

It is impossible to give a complete overview here of the state of the art concerning the effects on learning of the whole range of potential applications of computers in education. The entry will therefore focus on three major applications that differ widely in terms of the major dimensions referred to above to put the different educational computer uses in a hierarchical order, namely: (a) computer-assisted learning and intelligent tutoring, (b) the computer as a learning tool, and (c) computer programming.

2. Computer-assisted Learning and Intelligent Tutoring

The oldest and still the most common educational

application of the computer is computer-assisted learning (CAL), especially the use of the computer to drill and practice particular concepts or skills in traditional school subjects such as mathematics or language. In typical drill-and-practice programs, the computer generates a set of tasks and provides immediate feedback about the correctness of the student's answer. Many programs also contain stored comments or help of one kind or another associated with different response options.

In some sense, traditional CAL changed little, and is rather an add-on to an existing and unchanged classroom setting. It was, nevertheless, expected that this shift would affect student learning very positively. As long ago as 1966, Suppes (1966 p.206) predicted that "in a few more years millions of school children will have access to what Philip of Macedon enjoyed as a royal prerogative: the personal services of a tutor as well-informed and responsive as Aristotle."

There is some research evidence supporting this claim. Based on a meta-analysis of almost 200 studies on effects of CAL, Kulik and Kulik (1987) concluded that it has positive effects: students generally learned more in classes where they received help from computers, they learned their lessons with less instructional time, they enjoyed their classes more when they received computer help, and they developed more positive attitudes toward computers. However, even with respect to this most intensively studied educational computer use, the literature is less than compelling. Indeed, many of the studies reporting moderate or strong effects of CAL can be seriously criticized on methodological grounds (Kulik and Kulik 1987, Lepper and Gurtner 1989). Moreover, researchers as well as practitioners raised severe criticisms of the CAL programs that prevailed and still prevail in educational practice. A first criticism stresses the lack of individualization of instruction in traditional CAL, because of the limited "intelligence" built into the computer system. A second major criticism involves the mismatch between the content and organization of the CAL programs, on the one hand, and the new developments within the different subject-matter areas of the school curriculum and pedagogy, on the other. Both criticisms have stimulated new developments aiming at overcoming those shortcomings.

Dissatisfaction with the lack of individualization in traditional CAL was one of the major incentives to design a new generation of programs, originally called "intelligent computer-assisted instruction" (ICAI) or "intelligent tutoring systems" (ITS). In contrast to traditional software, these programs are not static, preprogrammed systems; on the contrary, the computer's decisions about what problem or what information to present next to the learner, and when and how exactly to intervene, are *generated*, taking into account a set of built-in components, namely: (a) knowledge about the cognitive structures and solution strategies underlying expertise in that particular domain (i.e., the expert modeling component); (b) a model of the student's knowledge and skills at a given moment in comparison to the expert system, derived from his or her answers and reactions on the previous problems (i.e., the student modeling component); (c) a set of principles about how to control and influence the student's learning process (i.e., the tutorial component); and (d) knowledge about how to organize the interface with the student (i.e., the communication component).

Intelligent tutoring systems have been developed for a variety of topics, such as learning classical mechanics, geometric optics, economic rules, elementary algebra, arithmetic place value, grammar, computer programming, and so on (see Sleeman and Brown 1982, Wenger 1987). In contrast to traditional CAL, systematic data about the achievements of the ITS approach are scarce. Moreover, they are mostly "soft" in character, compared to the hard and quantitative nature of the research findings for traditional CAI (Scott et al. 1992).

While fascinating research and developmental work relating to ITS continues, there is already some opposition to this approach. First, there is the question of how far one *can* go in building the necessary simulation components of the ITS. As was argued above, intelligent tutoring is only possible if the system accurately understands what the student is actually doing when he or she either solves the problem correctly or commits an error. Building such a simulation is not always possible. Take, for example, the processes involved in understanding and solving college algebra word problems. According to Kintsch (1991), the real-world situations described in college algebra problems are so numerous and so varied that only a system that knows essentially as much about the world as students do, would be able to simulate these problem-solving processes. But if simulation is impossible, then so is intelligent tutoring.

A second issue is not whether computer-based tutoring systems can, but rather whether they *should* aim at building a perfect and detailed model of the student's knowledge and skills as a basis for diagnosis and for taking decisions about instructional interventions. Indeed, this can easily lead to a preponderance of highly structured and directive learning situations lacking sufficient opportunity for active and constructive learner involvement and participation—a learning principle that is heavily stressed in instructional theory. Anderson's *Geometry Tutor* (Anderson et al. 1985), one of the most frequently quoted examples of an ITS, is an illustration of such a directive system. As was remarked by Kaput (1992), suggested attempts to make this tutor more flexible and educationally adjustable will not change its underlying educational philosophy: "the knowledge and the underlying authority of the tutor reside in the computer" (p. 545). Paraphrasing Papert (1990), who opposed "constructivism" to "instructionism," one could say that the *Geometry Tutor* will continue to reflect an "instructivist" rather than a "constructivist" view of learning. In this respect, Kintsch (1991) has launched the idea of unintelligent tutoring: "A tutor should not provide the intelligence to guide learning, it should not do all the planning and monitoring of the student's progress, because those are the very activities the students must perform themselves in order to learn. What a tutor should do is to provide a temporary support for learners that allows them to perform at a level just beyond their current ability level" (p. 245). Kintsch (1991) and many others (see, e.g., Scardamalia et al. 1989) have argued that computers are also ideally suited for this type of cognitive scaffolding, which accords better with the constructivist view of learning and teaching.

Traditional CAL has also been severely criticized because of the dated views about learning goals, content, and learning and teaching of the disciplines embedded in these programs. In the domain of mathematics, for example, the large majority of the available software aims mainly at exercising computational skills, replacing in this respect traditional worksheets (Kaput 1992). In other words, computers are mainly used to reproduce—or sometimes even to restore—the traditional, mechanistic approach toward mathematics education. (This also holds for most ITS programs.) But this mechanistic approach toward mathematics education has already been sharply criticized, and major efforts have been made to transform mathematical learning and teaching from the individual absorption and memorization of a fixed body of decontextualized and fragmented concepts and procedural skills transmitted by the teacher, into the collaborative, teacher-mediated construction of meaningful and useful knowledge and problem-solving skills based on mathematical modeling of authentic, real-life situations and contexts (De Corte et al. in press, Kaput 1992). In the domain of language, no less than in mathematics, the bulk of available software—also the ICAI—focuses on practicing rules from spelling and grammar, instead of supporting the more essential aspects of reading and writing, namely, comprehension and communication. Therefore, several authors have pleaded for implementing technology in line with reformed objectives, contents, and learning and teaching principles.

3. The Computer as a Learning Tool

Another important category of computer use in classroom instruction comprises the manifold ways in which the computer can serve as a tool in the hands of the student to facilitate the accomplishment of certain academic or creative goals. Typical examples of types of computing are word processors, calculators, spreadsheets, database programs, drawing and music composition programs. Contrary to CAL programs, such tool programs have originated outside of education. However, once available, they were often expected to be equally useful for supporting learning processes at school, such as cognitive learning, creative expression, and communication skills. The underlying idea is that computer tools will significantly affect the quality of students' thinking and learning processes, because these tools assume part of the intellectual burden, free students from lower-level operations, and trace states and processes. In line with Salomon's (1992) distinction mentioned above, some of these qualitative changes in students' cognitive processes have been assumed to occur not only while they are equipped *with* the computerized tool, but also when they do not have it at their disposal (*cognitive residue*).

As an example, word processing will be discussed. Compared with the other tools, it has been used most often in schools, albeit that much more time is devoted to learning how to use a word-processing program rather than to improving writing itself (Becker 1991).

It is no surprise that because of its peculiar features, word processing is perceived to be a powerful vehicle for language learning in schools. Indeed, composing text is essentially subjected to a cyclical control of its quality during a series of steps, such as planning, production, revision and editing at the textual levels of word, sentence, and structure. Moreover, word processing is compatible with a process view on writing, in contrast with the earlier emphasis on the written product (see Fitzgerald 1987, Lepper and Gurtner 1989).

In line with the enthusiasm of professional writers regarding the potential power of word processing compared to the laborious writing activity with paper and pencil, it was initially expected that word processing as an open learning tool could substantially improve students' writing effectiveness (Cochran-Smith 1991). However, there is almost no evidence to show that word processing in schools has clear-cut effects on text quality, length of text, amount and quality of revision, differences between revision with and without computers, and overall writing improvement (Cochran-Smith 1991). A clear example derives from research on revision. Although word processing seems most suitable for this subprocess, it remains unclear whether it affects the amount of students' revision (Cochran-Smith 1991, Fitzgerald 1987). Some reports indicate more revision activities with word processors than with pens or typewriters, while others indicate the reverse. Moreover, the quality of revisions seems not to fit with the expectations. Indeed, more surface revisions are made with word processors and more expanded revisions may occur with pens (Fitzgerald 1987).

It became clear that effectiveness of word processing tools highly depends upon the quality of the support available in a specific context. Consequently, the question is not whether mere word processing is effective, but how word processing interrelates with instructional goals, target groups, organizational and social structures of schools, curricula, teachers and concrete learning contexts (Cochran-Smith 1991). In order to make the tools powerful for learning, explicit support by teachers, peers, and/or supplementary computer programs is needed. In most cases, word-processing programs are accompanied by computerized tools or writing aids, such as text-analysis programs (spelling checker, vocabulary control, style analysis) and prompting programs (writing coaches, text help) which all offer additional support and comfort (Piolat and Blaye 1989). For instance, it is expected that text planners may help students to organize their thoughts before and during the writing process, and revision facilities may elicit and support control strategies.

If computer-based learning environments, and more specifically word processing programs, aim at supporting the active and constructive learning processes in students, both cognitive-oriented writing tools for students must be designed (Salomon 1992, Scardamalia and Bereiter 1991) and additional support for teachers offered (Cochran-Smith 1991). Moreover, the systematic development of tools for knowledge construction needs to be considered, be it for individual use or in computer network systems (Salomon 1992, Scardamalia and Bereiter 1991). Developments along those lines should aim at linking and integrating in a flexible way several computer tools, in which databases of text and graphics will support the organization of knowledge of individuals and groups (see Scardamalia and Bereiter 1991), and in which writing processes are embedded in specific subject-matter domains.

4. *Computer Programming and Learning to Think*

A third major educational computer use is computer programming. In this case the computer is a tutee. As was mentioned above, learning to program a computer (in BASIC) was one of the foremost applications in the early days of computers in education. It was mostly considered as a crucial aspect of acquiring computer literacy. But another argument for learning and teaching programming was the so-called "cognitive effects hypothesis"; that is, the claim that this experience would result in lasting positive changes in students' thinking and problem-solving skills as a cognitive residue of interaction with this programming language (De Corte et al. 1992, Salomon 1992). In this sense, learning to program was seen as a substitute for Latin and Greek, where learning the particulars of the language leads to the acquisition of general thinking skills which can be transferred to other content domains.

In connection with the second argument, the Logo computing language was very popular in the 1980s. Logo originates from an AI approach to educational computing that is at right angles not only to traditional CAL, but also to the early stages of ITS. Indeed, according to Papert (1980), Logo should be acquired in a constructive and self-discovering way, which he called "learning without curriculum."

Despite the evident enthusiasm of many practitioners and investigators in this area, a series of studies about the effects of Logo programming on children's problem-solving skills conducted in the early 1980s did not report any positive results supporting the cognitive effects hypothesis (De Corte et al. 1992). Interestingly, these investigations have not led to a rejection of this hypothesis, a major reason being the poor quality of the Logo learning environments that were designed and implemented in those studies: systematic and direct intervention was kept to a minimum, and it was hoped that the acquisition of the programming skill would somehow "happen" to the pupils as a result of the unique characteristics of the Logo language. In the second half of the 1980s the latter viewpoint was largely abandoned, and most researchers agreed that Logo learning environments should involve systematic guidance and mediation aiming at the acquisition of problem-solving skills in programming and, eventually, at their transfer to other contexts and situations. Most investigations that attempted to overcome the shortcomings of the earlier work have reported more positive results (De Corte et al. 1992).

Taken as a whole, the available research evidence suggests that Logo is not in itself a genuine vehicle for learning to think, but that it can be a very useful device for the acquisition of thinking skills, if embedded in a powerful teaching–learning environment that aims particularly at the mastery and transfer of these skills. This instructional support can, of course, be provided by the teacher in the form of prepared written materials and assignments, explicit task requirements, individual help, and so forth. But part of this support can also be built into the Logo software itself. Therefore, several attempts have been made to enrich the original Logo software with computer-based tool kits and coaching devices that support the development of problem solving skills. These developments with respect to Logo can also be considered as indicative of the trend toward integration between the different categories of educational computer applications: tutor, tool, and tutee.

5. *Conclusion*

When microcomputers began to be introduced in schools in the early 1980s, it was predicted that this new interactive and dynamic medium would significantly change the quality and the outcomes of school learning, even before the end of the decade. However, neither traditional computer-assisted instruction nor intelligent tutoring systems have been able to fulfill these initial high expectations. A critical examination of these prevailing forms of educational computer applications, based on findings of media research and on the understanding of the constructive and social nature of the learning process, has shown that this is not at all surprising. Indeed, underlying these educational uses of computers—albeit often implicitly—are both the wrong assumption that computers will by themselves elicit effective learning, and a conception of learning as a rather passive and highly individual process of knowledge absorption and accumulation. Initial disappointing results were also obtained with respect to the other two major forms of educational computer use, namely the computer as a tool (e.g., word-processing) and the computer as a tutee (e.g., Logo). For these applications it also quickly became obvious that the mere "add-on strategy" of computer use in schools cannot produce the improvements in the quality and the outcomes of learning that were originally anticipated. By the early 1990s, it was accepted that the productive educational application of computers requires that they be embedded in powerful teaching–learning environments, that is, instructional settings that elicit from students the acquisition processes necessary to attain worthwhile and desirable educational objectives in different curriculum domains. Embedding means that the computer is not just an "add-on," but is judiciously integrated in the environment, capitalizing on its specific strengths and potential to present, represent, and transform information, and to induce effective forms of interaction and cooperation. In this new conception, the role of the computer has changed from an authoritarian and directive tutor toward a supportive system that is less structured and less directive, that encompasses student-controlled tools for the acquisition of knowledge and skills, and that attempts to integrate both tools and coaching strategies in collaborative learning environments (Kaput 1992, Scardamalia et al. 1989).

See also: Computer-assisted Learning; Computers in Education; Computer Literacy; Computer Programming, Learning and Instruction of; Constructivism and Learning; Learning Environments; Hypertext, Educational Applications of; Logo, Educational Applications of; Media and Learning; New Information Technology and the Curriculum; New Information Technology in Mathematics Education; New Information Technology in Science Education; New Information Technology in Language Education; Tutoring; Learning Strategies and Learning to Learn

References

Anderson J R, Boyle C F, Reiser B J 1985 Intelligent tutoring systems. *Science* 228: 456–662

Becker H J 1991 How computers are used in the United States schools: Basic data from the 1989 IEA Computers in Education survey. *Journal of Educational Computing Research* 7(4): 385–406

Cochran-Smith M 1991 Word processing and writing in elementary classrooms: A critical review of related literature. *Rev. Educ. Res.* 61(1): 107–55

De Corte E, Greer B, Verschaffel L in press Mathematics. In: Berliner D, Calfee R (eds.) in press *Handbook of Educational Psychology*. Macmillan Inc., New York

De Corte E, Verschaffel L, Schrooten H 1992 Cognitive effects of learning to program in Logo: A one-year study with sixth-graders. In: De Corte E, Linn M C, Mandl H, Verschaffel L (eds.) 1992 *Computer-based Learning Environments and Problem Solving*. Springer-Verlag, Berlin

Fitzgerald J 1987 Research on revision in writing. *Rev. Educ. Res.* 57(4): 481–506

Kaput J J 1992 Technology and mathematics education. In: Grouws D A (ed.) 1992 *Handbook of Research on Mathematics Teaching and Learning*. Macmillan Inc., New York

Kintsch W 1991 A theory of discourse comprehension: Implications for a tutor for word algebra problems. In: Carretero M, Pope M, Simons R J, Pozo J I (eds.) 1991 *Learning and Instruction: European Research in an International Context*, Vol. 3. Pergamon Press, Oxford

Kulik J A, Kulik C-L C 1987 Review of recent research literature on computer-based instruction. *Contemp. Educ. Psychol.* 12(3): 222–30

Lepper M R, Gurtner J L 1989 Children and computers: Approaching the twenty-first century. *Am. Psychol.* 44(2): 170–78

Makrakis V 1988 *Computers in School Education: The Cases of Sweden and Greece*. Institute of International Education, University of Stockholm, Stockholm

Papert S 1982 *Mindstorms: Children, Computers, and Powerful ideas*. Basic Books, New York

Papert S 1990 An introduction to the fifth anniversary collection. In: Harel I (ed.) 1990 *Constructionist Learning: A Fifth Anniversary Collection of Papers*. MIT Media Laboratory, Cambridge, Massachusetts

Pelgrum W J, Plomp T 1991 *The Use of Computers in Education Worldwide*. Pergamon Press, Oxford

Piolat A, Blaye A 1989 Effects of word processing and writing aids on revision processes. Paper presented at the Third Conference of the European Association for Research on Learning and Instruction, Madrid

Salomon G 1992 Effects *with* and *of* computers and the study of computer-based learning environments. In: De Corte E, Linn M C, Mandl H, Verschaffel L (eds.) 1992 *Computer-based Learning Environments and Problem Solving*. Springer-Verlag, Berlin

Scardamalia M, Bereiter C 1991 Higher levels of agency for children in knowledge building: A challenge for the design of new knowledge media. *The Journal of the Learning Sciences* 1: 37–68

Scardamalia M, Bereiter C, McLean R S, Swallow J, Woodruff E 1989 Computer-supported intentional learning environments. *Journal of Educational Computing Research* 5(1): 51–68

Scott T, Cole M, Engel M 1992 Computers and education: A cultural constructivist perspective. In: Grant G (ed.) 1992 *Review of Research in Education*, Vol. 18. American Educational Research Association, Washington, DC

Sleeman D, Brown J S (eds.) 1982 *Intelligent Tutoring Systems*. Academic Press, London
Suppes P 1966 The uses of computers in education. *Scientific American* 215(3): 206–21
Taylor R 1980 *The Computer in the School: Tutor, Tool, Tutee*. Teachers College Press, New York
Wenger E 1987 *Artificial Intelligence and Tutoring Systems: Computational and Cognitive Approaches to the Communication of Knowledge*. Morgan Kaufmann, Los Altos, California

E. De Corte; L. Verschaffel; J. Lowyck

Computers in Education

This entry presents an overview of the uses of computers in education. After a general definition of terms, two different approaches to categorizing computer functionality in education are given, and then factors related to realizing this potential are summarized. Finally, new functions that are emerging and factors that are likely to affect their realization are outlined briefly.

1. Defining the Domain of Computers in Education

Since the early 1960s there has been a steady stream of discussion and literature pertaining to computers in education (for an overview, see Hunter 1982). Thus, while the topic is not new, new developments, dimensions, and experience continue to proliferate. This overview will address the topic from a functionality perspective—how can computers be used in education, and what factors relate, either positively or negatively, to the realization of their potential uses? Only a limited sketch can be given here, but many of the key aspects are developed further in the more detailed sections of this Encyclopedia. First, the domain of discussion needs to be clarified, relative to the terms computer and education.

1.1 Defining the Term "Computer"

The term "computer" covers all environments of which a computer is an integral part. This definition thus ranges from the familiar stand-alone microcomputer to computers linked conceptually to other learning resources, and those linked electronically to other computers, electronically connected resources, other types of apparatus, or to all of these (see Moonen and Collis 1991 for an elaboration of these levels of complexity).

The essential factor is that the user is interacting with a computer in a deliberate way (rather than as a consequence of using another piece of equipment, such as a telephone). Given the technological convergence of computers with other media, information sources, and communications technology, it is not realistic to think of computers as referring only to the familiar stand-alone unit. In this entry, the word "computer" will be used instead of more accurate, but cumbersome, nomenclature such as NCIT (new communications and information technology, the term used by the Ministers of Education from the 24 OECD countries at the 1989 Council of Ministers meeting) or "virtual computer" (Sawyer 1992).

1.2 Defining the Term "Education"

In this entry, the word "education" is used in a broader sense than merely learning and instruction. Education covers the conscious structuring of experience in order to facilitate learning and instruction, and also the communication and interaction which can lead to learning and instruction. It is thus not synonymous with the K-12 school system, but also includes higher education, vocational education, professional education, training, and educational environments outside traditional, structured educational institutions.

Thus, "computers in education" refers to the use of computers as mediators in the flow of information, communication, and instructional materials that occurs in, or relates to, educational situations.

2. Computers in Education: Perspectives on Function

The function of computers in education can be considered in a variety of ways, including: relative to types of use, and relative to the philosophical background and motivations underlying computer use in education.

2.1 Function in Terms of Types of Use

One approach to categorizing of the function of computers in education is to identify type of use in terms of the software used. The following description of learner-oriented and teacher-oriented uses is not exhaustive, and some types of use can be classified in more than one way.

Learner-oriented uses include structured, predetermined learning tasks such as the following:

(a) drill and practice and testing;

(b) tutorials (including "intelligent" varieties);

(c) educational games;

(d) simulations (some varieties, particularly those for training);

(e) "problem-solving" software (some varieties); and

(f) learning about the computer and its functions as goals in themselves.

Extensive research on these types of functions appears in literature from the 1960s to the present (for example, Atkinson and Wilson 1969, as well as the seminal work of pioneers in the field such as Bork, Luehrmann, and Suppes—see Taylor 1980 for a selection of their early work). "Intelligent" tutoring and coaching, coupled applications of artificial intelligence and advances in student modeling, are areas of ongoing research and development (see, e.g., Mandl and Lesgold 1988, Wenger 1987). There has been much study of computer-based training, relative to the use of computers for skill learning in training settings (see, e.g., Dean and Whitlock 1988). Alessi and Trollip (1991) are a representative source of the considerable literature on tutorials, drills, tests, instructional games, and simulations.

The issue of if, or to what extent, computers in educational settings should be used to learn about computers themselves, rather than used as agents for learning experiences relative to other topics, has long been discussed (see, e.g., Tinsley and Tagg 1984), yet there is still no consensus on what the optimum level might be. In the early 1990s, computers are used in school settings in many countries, predominately in courses about computers (or information technology) rather than as agents for learning activities more generally (see Pelgrum and Plomp 1991 for an international survey).

Other learner-oriented uses include those in the educational environment, tailored to a particular learning task or content, but allowing flexiblity of use:

(a) simulations (some varieties, including some varieties of "microworlds");

(b) problem-solving software (some varieties);

(c) MBLs (microcomputer-based laboratory materials);

(d) electronically organized data sets in relational databases, hypertext-linked stacks, or "electronic books" (Barker 1992)—any of these data sets may be text-only or multi-media; and

(e) expert systems (some varieties).

Learner-oriented uses also include tools or content-free environments used for educational purposes:

(a) writing environments, including word processing and desktop publishing;

(b) database environments (not already organized around a particular topic or goal, as in the categories above—these may be on-line, or resident in local computer or local external storage);

(c) calculation, projection, and statistical software (including spreadsheets);

(d) programming environments (particularly LOGO);

(e) telecommunications-mediated communication environments (including those for messaging, bulletin boards, and computer conferencing);

(f) electronic environments for visual and audio production and manipulation (including environments for graphing mathematical functions as well as environments for supporting creative visualizations and compositions); and

(g) "cognitive tools" (such as cognitive mapping, idea organizers, and some other types of software, including expert systems provided their function is to extend cognitive functioning during learning in a constructivistic way).

These categories also have an extensive literature. For example, microcomputer-based laboratory tools have been widely discussed, and their characteristics relative to student learning analyzed (see Thornton and Solokoff 1991). The implications of experiences with LOGO programming have commanded long-lasting and widespread attention (see Papert 1982 for the seminal work, and Pea et al. 1985, for an example of the many sorts of subsequent analyses of LOGO experiences that have occurred). The investigation of the educational applications of telecommunications is also commanding international attention (see, e.g., Roberts et al. 1990, Mason and Kaye 1989). Finally, a rapidly emerging area of interest in computer applications in education is that of cognitive tools—computer-based tools that facilitate generative processing of information by learners in a way that "amplifies the learner's cognitive processing" (Kommers et al. 1992).

Teacher oriented uses involve the use of teacher productivity tools, and tools for resource acquisition and handling, and for communication, including

(a) all of the tools noted above for learner use;

(b) student management and record-keeping software (for various types of data including individual student performance records and data for accumulation in system-wide administrative information systems); and

(c) software for production of specialized types of learning material (ranging from print materials, such as puzzles or tests from test banks, to the production of demonstration materials, such as transparencies for overhead projectors or multimedia materials for presentations).

2.2 *Function in Terms of Rationale for Use*

A different way of categorizing the function of computers in education is to consider the rationale behind their use, rather than to group different types of software. There are many different purposes for which computers are used in education. Hawkridge (1990), for example, identifies the following categories: (a) social—to prepare students in a general way, through computer awareness, for their place in society; (b) vocational—to give students skills related to success in future jobs or study directions; (c) pedagogical—to improve teaching and learning in traditional subject areas; (d) catalytic—to use computers as catalysts of significant change in some aspect of the educational system, including the learner; (e) information technology industry—to build up the local information technology industry either through large-scale stimulation of use of its hardware and software products or by the eventual supply of a work force experienced with local products; and (f) cost-effectiveness—to reduce the overall cost of education or improvement of its results in relation to the traditional system. These categories illustrate the range of functions of computers in education.

While Hawkridge focused on schools and goal-directed motivations, Willis (1991) examines the field of computers in education in terms of the different background traditions and orientations of those who take leadership roles in various aspects of the field. Willis sees six "models" behind computer use in education, each relating to "different perspectives, different traditions, and different definitions of the essence of educational computing" (p.335): the computer science model, the educational psychology model, the programmed instruction model, the instructional design model, the information center model, and the audiovisual equipment model. (To this list could be added the communications model.) A representative of these background orientations would interpret the functions of computers in education in different ways, or at least give a different order of importance to the ways in which computers could be used.

3. *Factors Related to Realizing the Potential of Computers in Education*

Just as there is an extensive collection of literature describing ways in which computers can be used in education, there is also considerable information about factors that affect the realization of this potential. Some of these factors can increase the likelihood of successful realization while others serve to complicate or block the realization (see, e.g., van der Akker et al. 1992, Sheingold and Hadley 1990). The factors form an interrelated system in which the status of an individual component is continuously affected by the status of many others (the "ecological framework" conception of Peled et al. 1992 is a way of conceptualizing this). Another way of conceptualizing the factors is to group them in terms of macrolevel, mesolevel, and microlevel influences on the implementation of computers in an educational setting (Pelgrum and Plomp 1991). The following is a reworking of Pelgrum and Plomp's approach in terms of a school-type educational setting; this approach can also be applied to training situations or informal educational settings. As with the categorization of functions of computers in education, the following list is not exhaustive and, in many cases, categories overlap.

3.1 Macrolevel Influences on the Realization of Computers in Education

These influences include the following:

(a) attitudes of communities (social, cultural, political) to the value of a particular function of computers in education, and their ethical/philosophical positions relative to priorities for education;

(b) the range of possibilities for computers in education relative to economic constraints and economic motives and pressures relative to decisions about various aspects of computer use;

(c) the direction, degree, range, and level of support relative to funding, leadership, coordination, dissemination, and stimulation of possibilities;

(d) the system for development, dissemination, and follow-up support relative to the resources and support needed for computer use in education, such as educational software, lesson and curriculum materials, appropriate teacher education, and hardware and related equipment; and

(e) the extent to which successful completion of a curriculum area, relative to system-wide norms for that area, relates to computer use.

These layers of influence form the embedding environment in which computer use in education is contained. Factors here are very much interrelated. For example, the availability of a certain category of educational software in a system depends on how the development and distribution of that software was organized, which in turn reflects a chain of economic, political, and organizational decisions operating within a particular cultural and social framework. As another example, society's attitude toward respect of copyright versus software piracy can have a significant impact on the emergence of a viable education software market. Without financial incentives for educational software development, a local industry will not naturally develop, and software availability will then have to rely on government subsidy, which in turn depends on policy and the expedients that shape it. More generally, the efficiency with which software development and dissemination is organized critically affects the availability, and thus eventual impact, of affordable resources in a system. (For further analyses of the macrolevel influences on computers in education see: Murray-Lasso 1990 for social and cultural aspects; Fullan et al. 1987 for leadership aspects; Walker 1986 for curriculum relationship aspects; Moonen and Plomp 1987 for national policy and the organization of software production aspects; and Collis and Oliveira 1990 for policy and economic aspects.)

3.2 Mesolevel Influences on the Realization of Computers in Education

These influences may be broadly enumerated as follows:

(a) institutional framework relating to policy, availability of resources, and "social climate";

(b) support available to teachers relative to computer use, including provision for an in-house computer coordinator, and provision of adequate time and access to computers for teachers to develop personal skills and lesson preparation;

(c) organization of computer-related resources within the institution, relative to equity and ease of access;

(d) leadership characteristics of significant persons within the institution relative to support and stimulation of computer use; and

(e) general social and demographic characteristics of the institution, including its teachers and students.

Every educational institution has its own culture and history relative to computer use, and these are factors in the realization of any particular type of computer function (Fullan et al. 1987). In particular, the attitudes and support of the institution leadership have a strong impact on computer implementation within an educational setting (Cox et al. 1988). Organizational decisions, such as who gets access to school computers and for how long, and the procedures by which such decisions are made critically affect the range of computer functions available within an institution. The approach and insight of the persons responsible for computer coordination within a system also affect implementation. Moreover, the general demographic characteristics of the institution, including the level of experience of its teachers and students with computers or, more generally, with innovation in the educational setting, set a frame around whatever occurs in terms of computer use (Collis 1988, Fullan et al. 1987).

3.3 Microlevel Influences on the Realization of Computers in Education

These influences include the following:

(a) characteristics of the particular teacher and students in a computer-use situation, including background experiences, attitudes, and capabilities;

(b) organization of the learning experience in which the computer use occurs, including integration with other learning activities, and strategies for student–student and teacher–student interaction during the learning experience; and

(c) characteristics of the computer-related resources themselves, with hardware and peripherals as constraining factors, but with the instructional design of the resources a critical factor.

Much of what is written about computer use in education relates to these so-called microlevel considerations. Many books and resources suggest lesson integration and management strategies for the teacher, and the more sophisticated of these take into account the teacher's and students' background characteristics in terms of their being able to handle a different level of complexity in lesson organization (see Boyd-Barett and Scanlon 1990, Kearsley et al. 1992). The design of educational software is a field unto itself, with a voluminous literature on design considerations that is continually being expanded by the emergence of new functions for computer use in schools and new complexities of computer systems, such as those related to multimedia and interconnectivity (see Moonen and Schoenmaker 1992, Venezky and Osin 1991).

3.4 The Realization of the Potential of Computers in Education

A large amount of research and comment is available on the extent to which the potential of computers in education has been realized. In general, there is agreement that the meaningful implementation of computers in educational settings is a complex, difficult, and time-consuming process requiring much insight and support, in which the teacher plays a critical and central role. While many instances can be cited of positive effects of computers in education in specific settings, the overall impact of computer use in education has not yet demonstrated "results" relative to the goals of any of the six rationales identified by Hawkridge (1990) except, perhaps, the first category, social preparation. The massive influx of computers into educational settings has likely, through sheer exposure, raised the general level of awareness of computers and their applications among students and teachers. (See summaries of the literature in van der Akker et al. 1992, Collis 1991, Kurland and Kurland 1987.)

4. Emerging Directions for Computers in Education

Emerging directions for computers in education are

related to the evolution of technological possibilities, new conceptualizations of computer use in an educational context, and to the need for better understanding and consolidation of past experiences. Again these categories often overlap, and many different perspectives are possible.

4.1 Toward Interconnectivity and Integration

Technically, educationally, and socially there is strong movement toward interconnectivity with respect to computers in education. On a technical level, computers are increasingly being integrated with video and audio resources, and—through networks—connected with other computers and educational resources. Educationally there is a growing movement toward acknowledging the value of cooperative work, and "computer-supported cooperative work" is a multidisciplinary growth area. The conception of the world as a global village, reinforced by social and economic realities, is also helping to promote the movement toward interconnectivity in computers in education. Interconnectivity and integration also refer to the movement toward regarding computer use as an integrated part of the educational environment, integrated in terms of computer application in "traditional" subject areas, but also in terms of computers as a catalyst to stimulate more integration of subject areas.

4.2 Toward Pervasiveness as a Personal Educational Tool

Another perspective of integration relates to computer use becoming ever more integrated in study, work, and communication processes in education. Word processing, desktop publishing, computer-mediated communications, and access to electronically stored information are aspects of computer use that are increasingly becoming commonplace features of educational activity. The emergence of "cognitive tools" and "intelligent agents" (as a new metaphor for computers), accompanied by advances in natural-language communication between persons and computers, will have a pervasive effect on learning; however, their effects on education as an organized system will take considerably longer to become apparent.

4.3 Toward Clarification of Priorities

Finally, after more than a decade of extensive (and expensive) experimentation with computers in education, a tendency to appraise the benefits of various applications of computers in education relative to their costs of implementation in a system is emerging (OTA 1988). Given the limitations on funds and resources in educational systems, there may be less willingness to fund broad-scale exploration of computer use in education than to strategically fund areas with the largest predicted payoff. Thus, for example, there may be more interest in computer use in vocational and professional education than in primary and lower secondary school applications. (This is already becoming the case in Europe.) Also, a critical reexamination of the degree of government subsidy to educational software supply, or even overall educational computer use, is now taking place in a number of countries in which significant government investments in these areas occurred in the 1980s, such as the Netherlands (Netherlands Ministry of Education and Science 1992). Finally, the viability of some of the types of computer applications in education listed in Sect. 2.2 above may be doubtful if system-wide cost-effectiveness criteria are applied to their use.

See also: Computer-assisted Learning; Computer-managed Learning; Computers and Learning; Instructional Design Theories

References

van der Akker J, Keursten P, Plomp T 1992 The integration of computer use in education. *Int. J. Educ. Res.* 17(1): 65–76

Alessi S M, Trollip S R 1991 *Computer-Based Instruction: Methods and Development*, 2nd ed. Prentice-Hall, Englewood Cliffs, New Jersey

Atkinson R C, Wilson H A (eds.) 1969 *Computer-Assisted Instruction: A Book of Readings*. Academic Press, New York

Barker P 1992 Electronic books and libraries of the future. *The Electronic Library* 10(3): 139–49

Boyd-Barrett O, Scanlon E (eds.) 1990 *Computers and Learning: A Reader*. Addison-Wesley, Wokingham

Collis B A 1988 *Computers, Curriculum, and Whole-Class Instruction: Issues and Ideas*. Wadsworth Publishing, Belmont, California

Collis B A 1991 Anticipating the impact of multimedia in education: Lessons from the literature. *International Journal of Computers in Adult Education and Training* 2(2): 136–49

Collis B A, Oliveira J B 1990 Categorizing national computer-related educational policy: A model and its applications. *Information Technology for Development* 5(1): 45–68

Cox M, Rhodes V, Hall J 1988 The use of computer-assisted learning in primary schools: Some factors affecting the uptake. *Comput. Educ.* 12(1): 173–78

Dean C, Whitlock Q 1988 *A Handbook of Computer Based Training*, 2nd edn. Kogan Page, London

Fullan M G, Miles M B, Anderson S A 1987 *Strategies for Implementing Microcomputers in Schools: The Ontario Case*. Ministry of Education, Toronto

Hawkridge D 1990 Machine-mediated learning in Third-World schools? *Machine-Mediated Learning* 3(4): 319–28

Hunter B 1982 Computer literacy: 1949–1979. In: Seidel R J, Anderson R E, Hunter B (eds.) 1985 *Computer Literacy Issues and Directions for 1985*. Academic Press, New York

Kearsley G, Hunter B, Furlong M 1992 *We Teach with Technology: New Visions for Education*. Franklin, Beedle & Associates, Wilsonville, Oregon

Kommers P A M, Jonassen D H, Mayes J T (eds.) 1992) *Cognitive Tools for Learning*. Springer-Verlag, Berlin
Kurland D M, Kurland L C 1987 Computer applications in education: A historical overview. *Annual Review of Computing Science* 2: 317–58
Mandl H, Lesgold A (eds.) 1988 *Learning Issues for Intelligent Tutoring Systems*. Springer-Verlag, Berlin
Mason R, Kaye A (eds.) 1989 *Mindweave: Communication, Computers and Distance Education*. Pergamon Press, Oxford
Netherlands Ministry of Education and Science 1992 *Enter the Future: Long-Term Considerations for the Use of Information Technology in Education*. OPSTAP Series 33. Ministry of Education and Science, Zoetemeer
Moonen J C M M, Collis B A 1991 *Multimedia in het onderwiis: Een verkenning*. Ministry of Education, Zoetemeer
Moonen J C M M, Plomp T 1987 *EURIT* 86: Developments in Educational Software and Courseware. Pergamon Press, Oxford
Moonen J C M M, Schoenmaker J 1992 Evolution of courseware development methodology: Recent issues. *Int. J. Educ. Res.* 17(1): 109–21
Murray-Lasso M 1990 Cultural and social constraints on software portability. *Journal for Research in Computing in Education* 23(2): 252–71
Office of Technology Assessment (OTA) 1988 *Power On! New Tools for Teaching and Learning*. US Government Printing Office, Washington, DC
Papert S 1982 *Mindstorms: Children, Computers, and Powerful Ideas*. Basic Books, New York
Pea R D, Kurland D M, Hawkins J 1985 LOGO and the development of thinking skills. In: Chen M, Paisley W (eds.) 1985 *Children and Microcomputers: Research on the Newest Medium*. Sage, Beverly Hills, California
Peled E, Peled Z, Alexander G 1992 Computerization of an Israeli school system: Project Comptown 1985/86–1989/1990. In: Collis B A, Carleer G (eds.) 1992 *Technology-Enriched Schools: Nine Case Studies, with Reflections*. International Society for Technology in Education, Eugene, Oregon
Pelgrum W J, Plomp T 1991 *The Use of Computers in Education Worldwide*. Pergamon Press, Oxford
Roberts N, Blakeslee G, Brown M, Link C 1990 *Integrating Telecommunications into Education*. Prentice-Hall, Englewood Cliffs, New Jersey
Sawyer W D M 1992 The virtual computer: A new paradigm for educational computing. *Educ. Technol.* 32(1): 7–14
Sheingold K, Hadley M 1990 *Accomplished Teachers: Integrating Computers into Classroom Practice*. Center for Technology in Education, Bank Street College of Education, New York
Taylor R P (ed.) 1980 *The Computer in the School: Tutor, Tool, Tutee*. Teachers College Press, New York
Thornton R, Sokoloff D 1991 Learning motion concepts using real-time microcomputer-based laboratory tools. *American Journal of Physics* 59(4): 375–76
Tinsley J D, Tagg E D 1984 *Informatics in Elementary Education*. North-Holland, Amsterdam
Venezky R, Osin L 1991 *The Intelligent Design of Computer-Assisted Instruction*. Longman, New York
Walker D F 1986 Computers and the curriculum. In: Culbertson J A, Cunningham L L (eds.)
Wenger E 1987 *Artificial Intelligence and Tutoring Systems: Computational and Cognitive Approaches to the Communication of Knowledge*. Morgan Kaufmann Publishers, Los Altos, California
Willis J 1991 Graduate training in educational computing: Training the next generation of technology leaders. *Computers in the Schools* 8(1/2/3): 333–47

Further Reading

Ambron S, Hooper K (eds.) 1990 *Learning with Interactive Multimedia: Developing and Using Multimedia Tools in Education*. Microsoft Press, Redmond, Washington
Center for Educational Research and Innovation 1987 *Information Technologies and Basic Learning: Reading, writing, Science, and Mathematics*. OECD, Paris
Ministerio de Educacion y Ciencia 1992 *Information Technology in the Curricula of the Different* EC Countries. Task Force Human Resources, Education, Training and Youth, Commission of the European Community, Brussels
Ragsdale R G 1988 *Permissable Computing in Education: Values, Assumptions, and Needs*. Praeger, New York

B. A. Collis

Computers in Education, Organizations and Journals on

The 1980s was a decade of rapid technological improvement, and as a result, there was a reduction in prices and a growth of personal computers in educational settings. The number of supporting organizations and journals increased dramatically. In 1993, there were more than 1,000 organizations worldwide dealing with computers in education and related areas. To select and filter from all of the organizations, they were first divided into two main categories: (a) institutions of further and higher education, and (b) other organizations with an interest in computers in education. The first category covers university departments, computing centers and special centers for software and hardware development and implementation in the education and training area (primary, secondary, and university level). The second category covers professional profit and nonprofit organizations (international and national) with a profile of activities related to computers in education.

Similar clustering can be found in Osborne's (1991) *International Yearbook of Educational and Training Technology*. The selection was undertaken by taking into account detailed descriptions of all these organizations and the existence in all large universities of specialized departments and centers. In the second category national organizations from a limited number of countries are given. The selection criteria were: the size of the country, the sphere of influence of the country, and the geographical representation around the globe. All organizations are listed in Sect. 2 of this entry with reference addresses. More information about organizational mission and major activities and publications can be found in Osborne (1991).

On the national level some organizations (for example the United Kingdom National Council for Educational Technology) are producing catalogs of research and development in the area of information technology in education. International and regional organizations (see, e.g., ISTE and DELTA listed in Sect. 2) produce directories of the organizational affiliates with addresses and short profile descriptions (in cases of nonindividual membership).

For the selection of journals, magazines, and bulletins on computers in education listed in this entry, *Ulrich's International Periodicals Directory* (1992) was used. Most of the journals are published in English because of the acceptance of the English language as "official" for the professional community in the areas of research, development, and implementation of the new information technologies in education.

All information about publishers and distributors is available from *Ulrich's Periodicals Directory*. A similar strategy for selection of the organizations was followed for the journals and the magazines listed in Sect. 1. An additional criterion was to try as far as possible to include in the list of journals, magazines, newsletters, and bulletins, those published by the professional organizations listed in Sect. 2.

1. Journals, Magazines, Newsletters, and Bulletins on Computers in Education and Related Areas

AV Magazine (The Netherlands)
Boletín de Informática Educativa (Colombia)
British Journal of Educational Technology
Computer Education
Computers and Education
Computers in Education
Computers in Human Behavior
Computers in New Zealand Schools
COS (The Netherlands)
The CTISS File
Datorn I Utbildningen (Sweden)
DLT News—New Technologies and Learning in Europe
Education and Computing
Educational Computing Research
Educational Media International
Educational Technology
Educational Technology—Research and Development
Educational Technology Systems
Educational and Training Technology International
Electronic Learning
Eurostep Courier
Human–Computer Interaction
Hypermedia
Informática Educativa (Argentina)
Informatik og Undervising (Denmark)
Information Technology and Learning
Intelligent Tutoring Media
Interacting with Computers: The Interdisciplinary Journal of Human–Computer Interaction
Interactive Learning Environments
Interactive Learning International
Interactive Multi Media
International Journal of Instructional Media
International Journal of Technology and Design Education
Journal of Artificial Intelligence in Education
Journal of Computer Assisted Learning
Journal of Computer Based Instruction
Journal of Computers in Mathematics and Science Teaching
Journal of Computing in Childhood Education
Journal of Computing in Teacher Education
Journal of Educational Multi Media and Hypermedia
Journal of Hypermedia and Multimedia Studies (Hypernexus)
Journal of Research on Computing in Education
Journal of Structural Learning
Login (Germany)
Machine Mediated Learning
Multi Media Computing
Multimedia Review
Multimedia and Videodisc Monitor
Performance and Instruction
School and Computer (The Netherlands)
Simulation/Games for Learning
Social Science Computer Review
Teaching and Computers
Technology and Learning
Tech Trends for Leaders in Education and Training
The Computing Teacher
THE Journal (Technological Horizons in Education)

2. Organizations Concerned with Computers in Education and Training

2.1 International Organizations

Association for Educational and Training Technology (AETT), c/o Centre for Continuing Education, City University, Northampton Square, London EC1V 0HB, United Kingdom

ERIC Clearinghouse on Information Resources, Syracuse University, Syracuse, NY 13244–2340, USA

The Intergovernmental Informatics Programme (IIP), Secretariat, UNESCO, 7 Place de Fontenoy, F-75700 Paris, France

International Communications Institute (ICI), Box 1414, Main Post Office, Rockhampton, Queensland, Australia

International Council for Educational Media (ICEM), 28 rue d'Ulm, 75230 Paris, Cedex 05, France

International Federation for Information Processing

(IFIP), Secretariat, 16 Place Longemalle, CH-1204 Geneva, Switzerland

International Simulation and Gaming Association (ISAGA), c/o Professor Dr Jan H G Klabbers, Faculty of Social Sciences, RUU, PO Box 80140, 3508 TC Utrecht, The Netherlands

International Society for Technology in Education (ISTE), University of Oregon, 1787 Agate Street, Eugene, OR 97403, USA

United Nations Development Programme (UNDP), 1 United Nations Plaza, New York, NY 10017, USA

UNESCO Institute for Education, Feldbrunnenstrasse 58, D-2000 Hamburg 13, Germany

UNESCO International Bureau of Education (IBE), Case Postale 199, CH-1211 Geneva 20, Switzerland

UNESCO Section of Innovation, Technology and Research within the Division of Higher Education and Research, 7 Place de Fontenoy, F-75700 Paris, France

2.2 Regional Organizations

The Arab States Educational Technology Centre (ASETC), PO Box 24017, Safat, Kuwait 13101

Asia and the Pacific Programme of Educational Innovation for Development (APEID), UNESCO Principal Regional Office for Asia and the Pacific, 920 Sukhumvit Road, PO Box 967, Prakanong Post Office, Bangkok 10110, Thailand

Development of European Learning through Technological Advance (DELTA), Rue de la Loi 200, B-1049 Brussels, Belgium

EuroPACE, CNIT-INFOMART, B.P. 529, 2 Place de la Défense, F-92053 Paris-La Défense, France

European Association of Users of Satellites in Training and Education Programmes (EUROSTEP), Rapenburg 63, 2311 GJ Leiden, The Netherlands

European Information Centre for Further Education of Teachers (EIC–FET), Charles University, Kaprova 14, 11000 Praha, Czech Republic

European Interactive Media Ltd., 22 Brook Street, London W1Y 1AE, United Kingdom

European Open Learning Network (a partnership between industry and distance teaching and training institutions), (SATURN) Office, Keizersgracht 756, 1017 EZ Amsterdam, The Netherlands

Regional Center for Educational Innovation and Technology (INNOTECH), Commonwealth Avenue, University of The Philippines, Diliman, Quezon City, The Philippines

2.3 United Kingdom

Ace Centre (Aids to Communication in Education), Ormerod School, Waynflete Road, Headington, Oxford OX3 8DD

Advisory Unit for Microtechnology in Education, Endymion Road, Hatfield, Hertfordshire AL10 8AU

CIMTECH (National Centre for Information Media and Technology), College Lane, Hatfield, Hertfordshire AL10 9AB

Computer Education Group (CEG), c/o Staffordshire Polytechnic, Computer Centre, Blackheath Lane, Stafford ST18 0AD

Educational Media Association of Ireland (EMAI), Dr David Ruddick, Educational Technology, University of Ulster, Jordanstown, Co Antrim, BT37 0QB

Eurotech, Oakfield Road, East Wittering, West Sussex PO20 8RP

Microcomputers in Computer Education (MICE), c/o Computer Education Group, BCS, 13 Mansfield Street, London W1M 0BP

Micros and Primary Education, Administration (MAPE), The Old Vicarage, Normanton-on-Trent, Nottinghamshire NG23 6RR

Micro Users in Secondary Education (MUSE), PO Box 43, Houghton on the Hill, Leicester LE7 9GX

National Council for Educational Technology, Sir William Lyons Road, Science Park, Coventry CV4 7EZ

The Scottish Council for Educational Technology (SCET), Dowanhill, 74 Victoria Crescent Road, Glasgow G12 9JN

Society for the Advancement of Games and Simulation in Education and Training (SAGSET), c/o Centre for Extension Studies, University of Technology, Loughborough, Leicestershire LE11 3TU

Sundridge Park Management Centre, Plaistow Lane, Bromley, Kent BR1 3TP

2.4 United States

Association for the Advancement of Computing in Education (AACE), PO Box 2966, Charlottesville, VA 22902

Association for the Development of Computer-based Instructional Systems (ADCIS), 229 Ramseyer Hall, 29 W. Woodruff Ave., Columbus, OH 43210

Association for Educational Communications and Technology (AECT), 1126 Sixteenth Street NW, Washington, DC 20036

CALICO (Computer Assisted Language Learning and Instruction Consortium), 3078 JKHB, Brigham Young University, Provo, UT 84602

EDUCOM, 1112 16th Street NW, Washington, DC 20036

Minnesota Educational Computing Corporation (MECC), 3490 Lexington Ave North, St. Paul, MN 55126–8097

National Society for Performance and Instruction (NSPI), 1300 L Street NW, Suite 1250, Washington, DC 20005

Society for Applied Learning Technology (SALT), 50 Culpeper Street, Warrenton, VA 22186

2.5 Other Worldwide Organizations

Australia

Australian Society for Educational Technology (ASET), PO Box 372, Hawthorn, Victoria 3122

National Software Coordination Unit, ASCIS Information Services, Curriculum Corporation, 141 Rathdowne Street, Carlton South, Victoria 3053

Austria

Institut für Unterrichtstechnologie und Medienpädagogik (Institute of Educational Technology and Media Pedagogics), Universitätsstrasse 65–67, 9020 Klagenfurt

Belgium

Centrum Voor Informatieve Spelen vzw (formerly Informatief Spelmateriaal vzw; Centre for Informational Games), Naamsesteenweg 164, 3000 Leuven

Canada

ACCESS Network, Educational Technology Centre, Alberta Educational Communications Corporation, 295 Midpark Way SE, Calgary, Alberta T2X 28A

Association for Media and Technology in Education in Canada (AMTEC), 163 Princess Street East, Clinton, Ontario N0M IL0

Canadian Information Processing Society (CIPS), 243 College Street, 5th Floor, Toronto, Ontario M5T 2Y1

Educational Computing Organization of Ontario (ECOO), Box 2699, Station B, Richmond Hill, Ontario, L4E 1A7

Educational Technology Program, Infotech Centre, Manitoba–Education and Training, 1970 Ness Avenue, Winnipeg, Manitoba, R3J 0Y9

Open Systems Group, 4252 Commerce Circle, Victoria BC, V8Z 4M2

China, People's Republic of

East China Normal University (ECNU), Institute of Modern Educational Technology, 3663 Zhong-Shan North Road, Shanghai 200062

The Educational Administration Institute, Beijing 100875

Institute of Modern Educational Technology, Xin Jie Kou Wai Street, Beijing

France

Centre National de Documentation Pédagogique (CNDP), (National Teaching Resource Centre), 29 rue D'Ulm, 75230 Paris Cedex 05

Institut National de Recherches Pédagogique (INRP), Département des Technologies Nouvelles et de l'Education, 91 rue Gabriel Péri, 92120 Montrouge

Observatoire des Technologies pour l'Education en Europe, 38 rue de Bourgogne, 75007 Paris

Unité de recherche "Télématique" INRP—Département Technologies nouvelles et enseignement, 91 rue Gabriel Péri, 92120 Montrouge

Germany

Deutscher Didacta Verband eV, Eppsteiner Strasse 36, D-6000 Frankfurt am Main 1

FWU Institut für Film und Bild in Wissenschaft und Unterricht Gemeinnützige GmbH, Bavaria-Film-Platz 3, D-8022 Grünwald

Zentralstelle für Computer im Unterricht (The Central Organization for Computers in Education and Programmed Learning in Bavaria), Schertlinstrasse 9, D-8900 Augsburg

India

All India Association for Educational Technology (AIAET), c/o National Institute of Educational Planning and Administration, 17-B, Sri Aurobindo Marg, New Delhi 110016

Israel

Centre for Educational Technology, 16 Klausner Street, Ramat Aviv

Italy

Centro Televisivo Universitario (CTU), Via Celoria 20, 20133 Milan

Instituto Technologie Didattiche (ITD), National Research Council (CNR), Via Opera Pia 11, 16145 Genoa

Japan

Centre for Research and Development of Educational Technology (CRADLE), 2–12–2 Ohokayama Meguro-ku, Tokyo 184

Laboratory of Educational Technology, Tokyo Institute of Technology, 2–12–1 Ohokayama, Meguro-ku, Tokyo 152

Laboratory of Educational Systems Technology, Graduate School of General Science and Technology, Tokyo Institute of Technology, 2459 Nagatsuta-cho Midori-ku, Yokohamashi Kanagawa 227

The Netherlands
Centre for Education and Information Technology (COI), PO Box 217, 7500 AE Enschede

Media Design BV, Van Diemenstraat 200, 1013 NH Amsterdam

Nederlands Instituut voor Audio-Visuele Media (NIAM), Neuhuyskade 94, 2596 XM The Hague

Spain
EPISE, SA, Ensenanza Programada e Ingenieria de Sistemas Educativos, Muntaner 430, 08006 Barcelona

FUNDESCO, Alcalá 61, 28014 Madrid

See also: Comparative Education and International Education: Organizations and Institutions

References

Osborne C W (ed.) 1991 *International Yearbook of Educational and Training Technology*. Oryx Press, Phoenix, Arizona

R R Bowker Staff 1992 *Ulrich's International Periodicals Directory: A Classified Guide to a Selected List of Current Periodicals, Foreign and Domestic*, 31st edn. Bowker, New York

I. Stanchev

Concept Learning

Concepts form the basic elements of human knowledge, and the learning of concepts includes the cognitive processes of: (a) acquisition of newly encountered concepts, (b) elaboration of existing concepts, and (c) development of cognitive strategies to employ concepts in previously encountered and unencountered situations. Concepts are defined as classes of instances that represent objects, symbols, or events and can be characterized as either having well-defined dimensions (i.e., constant) or ill-defined dimensions (i.e., variable). Acquisition of concepts occurs by abstracting information from examples and forming prototypes within memory based on a given situational or contextual culture. Employment or application of concepts occurs through the cognitive strategies of generalization and discrimination.

This entry reviews the nature of concept learning and integrates such learning within the context of a cognitive system model. The cognitive system model is presented as a foundation for the design of instruction to improve concept learning. Implications of concept learning for teaching are twofold: first, learners acquire concepts within meaningful contexts associated with their existing knowledge; and, second, the development of the cognitive strategies can be improved by instruction that provides opportunities for learners to contribute to their own construction of the knowledge base.

1. The Nature of Concept Learning

1.1 Nature of Concepts

Concepts can range from one-of-a-kind elements (e.g., the Hope diamond) to a whole set or class of specific objects, symbols, or events. In this latter situation, a concept may have a finite set of members or an infinite set. Regardless of type of class (i.e., finite or infinite), the members are grouped together on the basis of shared characteristics and can usually be referenced by a particular name or symbol. In addition to class membership, concepts can exhibit either well-defined dimensions or ill-defined dimensions. Well-defined concepts have characteristics that are constant within any situation or context and can be transferred across situations without changes in their definitions (e.g., mathematical concepts, physical science concepts, etc.). On the other hand, ill-defined concepts have characteristics that are variable according to given situations and are not easily transferable from one context to another without being embedded within the different situation (e.g., humanities concepts, language concepts, etc.).

For purposes of understanding concept learning, the three types of concept classes (objects, symbols, and events) are defined as follow: object concepts exist in time and space and can easily be represented by drawings, photographs, models, or the object itself. Many object concepts can be found by merely scanning the pages of a school textbook. Symbol concepts consist of particular kinds of words, numbers, marks, and numerous other items that represent or describe objects, events, or their relationships, either real or imagined. Many of the concepts learned in school are symbol concepts (e.g., in mathematics and science). Event concepts are interactions of objects, either living or inorganic, in a particular period of time (e.g., history and literature). Event concepts are difficult to learn in the abstract because they require the interaction of previously known object concepts. As stated above, each of these three classes can contain concepts that are either constant in definition or variable according to context. The classification of a given concept is then based on the type of class and definitional structure (i.e., well-defined or ill-defined).

1.2 Nature of Instances

The word "instance" is a general term used to refer to both members and nonmembers of a concept class. There are two kinds of instances: examples and nonexamples. An example is an instance which is a member of the concept under consideration. Members of a given concept class are sometimes called by other names, such as exemplar, positive instance, and positive example. A nonexample, on the other hand, is any instance which is not a member of the concept under consideration but is a member of any other concept; it can also be referred to as a negative instance or negative example.

Examples are the primary or initial element of information learned about concepts. In early childhood, all concepts are actually examples of a given concept: each dog that a child sees is an object concept. In memory, the child is storing each example as a separate concept. As the child matures, the separate example-concepts become increasingly associated and start forming abstractions (prototypes) of given concepts. From the initial formation of a concept from a single example, the child learns that specific examples are only instances of a class of objects, symbols, or events. Thus, over time the child forms in memory prototypes that are abstractions from the examples encountered in the environment.

1.3 Classification Behavior

A concept has been learned when a person can correctly identify the class membership of a specific object, symbol, or event. This type of cognition is termed "classification behavior."

Classification behavior occurs when, given a specific object, symbol, or event, the learner can name or point to the general word that refers to a class to which the specific instance belongs; or, when given the general name of the class and shown representations of specific instances of this and other classes, the learner will be able to identify those objects, symbols, or events which are members of the class and those which are not members of the class. Classification behavior does not occur if the learning task is to state a definition or make an association.

There are two cognitive strategies involved in classification behavior: generalization and discrimination. Generalization occurs when a learner exhibits a particular response in one situation which was acquired in a similar situation. All learners have general cognitive strategies to generalize both within and between concept classes. Knowledge which is learned in one situation can usually be tried again in similar situations. It is this transfer process (combined with discrimination) which enables a learner to adapt to new circumstances.

Discrimination occurs when a learner exhibits a particular response in one situation but a different response in another, similar situation. Discrimination allows the learner to make distinctions between very similar situations. Discrimination provides the cognitive strategy for the learner to differentiate between changes in situations, to communicate precisely, and to deal with the complexity of the environment.

2. Cognitive System Model of Learning

An important aspect in understanding the learning of concepts is the way concepts are formed and employed in memory. Because concepts form the basic knowledge elements in memory, this section will describe a cognitive system model of learning that deals with both concept formation and employment. The importance of such an understanding of a cognitive learning system is that prescriptive models of instruction can be developed that take into account internal cognitive processing as well as the usual teaching methods that manipulate the instructional environment.

2.1 Concept Learning Model

The basic components of the cognitive system model include the following processes: sensory receptors, executive control, affective variables, working memory, and long-term memory. The model also indicates two primary sources for concept formation: external and internal. External concepts enter the cognitive system through the standard sensory mechanisms, while internal concepts are constructed by the exchange between the various system components. External classification behavior is exhibited through the output of the executive control component.

This cognitive system model differs from information-processing models because it is a highly dynamic, interactive system that assumes constant integration of the various components. Each of the components is now discussed in a linear fashion although this is not an accurate representation of how the system operates. For the purposes of this entry, direct reference to the psychomotor domain is not included; other sources present that domain in a more explicit manner (see, e.g., Tennyson and Breuer 1984).

2.2 Sensory Receptors

This component includes the various ways in which external information is entered into the cognitive system. Conceptual information is conveyed through the sensory component and is passively registered in sensory buffers in more or less complete analogical form. These sensory registers are sometimes referred to as "primary memory." Information in these registers decay rapidly and are easily interrupted. Attention and perception-driven processes in the executive control component determine which subset of this information is selected for further processing, as far more information is registered than can be processed and acquired.

External stimuli include those aspects of instruction referred to as "delivery systems," such as text materials, visuals, audio/verbal sources, graphics, illustrations, and drawings. Instructional theory is especially influenced by research dealing with the manipulation of the environment to improve concept learning. For example, computer-based technology has had an effect on how concepts can be represented in visual form. Also, techniques for analyzing concepts for the purposes of improving higher cognitive processing contribute to the importance of this component (Tennyson et al. 1992).

2.3 Executive Control

Control of the cognitive system is usually referenced by some form of an executive processor that regulates the various components of the system by either active or automatic means. Although cognitive theories differ on specific functions and their distribution in the complexity of the system, for the purposes of this entry it is convenient to consider three executive functions: perception, attention, and resources.

Conceptual information coming from either external or internal sources passes through the perception function which performs the processes of being aware of, and assessing the potential value of, the external and/or internal information. In this function, the perception component services the cognitive system for the purposes both of directing attention and of determining effort. The attention function maintains an active interaction with the processes associated with the working memory component. Resources assist in the coordination of the various components of the entire system. Evaluation of effort associated with a given concept learning situation is important in this function. For example, in most situations, there is an abundance of resources available, so determination is made on allocation of necessary resources.

2.4 Working Memory

There is considerable debate as to the divisions or architecture of memory, but in a broad sense, the exact details are not important as regards the instructional implications of the theories (Shuell 1990). In general, there is agreement that memory comes in two forms, a store for previously learned concepts and a store for concepts which are currently being processed. This latter form, working memory, is defined with these salient aspects:

(a) It is limited in capacity.

(b) Concepts in working memory are subject to manipulations such as rehearsal, comparison, or matching and reordering by the processes that operate in working memory.

(c) Concepts are selected for inclusion in working memory either by some consciously active process or by automatic action of well-developed processes in such activities as reading, processing of verbal discourse, and imagery-evoking processes.

The exact processes which operate in working memory vary from theory to theory, but there are a set of processes which most theories have in common. These include the following four processes:

(a) encoding processes which, in concert with the executive control component, deposit incoming concepts into working memory for purposes of employment;

(b) storage processes which interact with long-term memory to create permanent prototypes and increase the strength of existing prototypes;

(c) retrieval processes to obtain necessary existing knowledge (i.e., prototypes, skills, and strategies) from long-term memory;

(d) maintenance processes that keep concepts in working memory so that they are not lost before they are stored in long-term memory.

2.5 Long-term Memory

Long-term memory is the repository for all previously acquired concepts and other information. In contrast to the limited capacity of working memory because of its role of dealing with immediate concerns of concept processing, long-term memory focuses on the nature of knowledge representation in terms of concepts, skills, and strategies. There is agreement among researchers in the field that long-term memory has no capacity limits and that knowledge is considered permanent, although it may become difficult to retrieve.

Within long-term memory there are various types of conceptual knowledge: declarative, procedural, and contextual (Tennyson and Rasch 1988). Declarative knowledge implies an awareness of knowledge and refers to "knowing that," for example, understanding that the concept of underlining keywords in a text will help recall. Procedural knowledge implies a "knowing how" to use given concepts. Contextual knowledge implies an understanding of "knowing why, when, and where" to employ specific concepts. This knowing of why, when, and where, is governed by selection criteria embedded within the organization of the knowledge base. Selection criteria are integrated within the knowledge base because of the interaction with the affective variables component during the learning process. The term "contextual" implies direct association with cognitive skills, which are defined below as domain-dependent cognitive strategies.

The value of conceptual knowledge is its employment in the classification behaviors of generalization and discrimination. The cognitive strategies of generalization and discrimination can be distinguished as either domain-dependent or domain-independent. The concept of cognitive skill describes a specific application of a cognitive strategy within a given situation (or context) whereas cognitive strategy implies domain-free abilities. The cognitive strategies of generalization and discrimination include three primary cognitive abilities (although skills are further refined to specific situations and embedded in contextual knowledge): differentiation, integration, and construction. Differentiation is defined as the twofold ability to understand a given situation and to apply appropriate contextual criteria (i.e., the standards, situational appropriateness, and/or values) by which specific concepts can be selectively retrieved from storage. Integration is the ability to elaborate or restructure existing concepts and/or conceptual networks in the service of previously unencountered problem situations. Construction is the ability to both discover and create new concepts in novel or unique situations.

2.6 Affective Variables

Just as cognitive theories differ in details but have many common features, the same is true of the affective variables component. Given the complexity of the affective domain, and the space limitations of this entry, only some of the more identifiable affective variables that may have implications for concept learning will be addressed. Also, because of their interactive nature and variability, the various types of affect are described without reference to the hierarchy or value of each.

The list includes such variables as motivation, feelings, attitudes, emotions, anxiety, and values. The immediate interaction of this component within the cognitive system is with the executive control component which interfaces with the working memory. For example, motivation influences both attention and maintenance processes. On the other hand, values and feelings would influence the criteria associated with acquisition of contextual knowledge. Anxiety as an affect variable influences both the acquisition and employment processes (e.g., test anxiety may interfere with both generalization and discrimination). Together with emotions, anxiety can be a serious interfering variable in concept learning.

3. Conclusion

Concept learning includes both acquisition of concepts and employment through the classification behaviors of generalization and discrimination. Because of the central dominance of concepts in the content of a knowledge base, and given the complexity of the cognitive system, instructional strategies for concept learning should expand beyond the standard format of definition, example, and practice. Additional instructional variables would improve the organization of new concepts by presentation within a meaningful context. Thus, concepts could be more readily connected with existing networks and prototypes. Second, acquisition of contextual knowledge would be improved by instruction that requires the learner to solve complex problems that would employ knowledge of why, when, and where. Too often learners fail to receive instruction that goes beyond the simple per concept declarative and procedural knowledge.

Additionally, the presented cognitive system model emphasizes the role of cognitive strategies as an integral condition in concept learning. These cognitive strategies can be improved by instruction that provides an environment for learners to engage in dynamic and complex problem situations. The purpose of such instruction is twofold. First, learners will further develop the cognitive abilities of differentiation, integration, and construction. Second, learners will expand and elaborate their knowledge base (i.e., declarative, procedural, and contextual knowledge).

This entry has presented a model of concept learning that describes both the internal processes of learning and the external. The purpose is to establish the construct that learning is more than mere reaction to reinforced responses: that is, learners have the cognitive capability to participate in the constructing of their own knowledge base. Learning occurs in part through the development of internal cognitive strategies and abilities as well as through the manipulation of the environment. Another entry in this *Encyclopedia* describes the variables and conditions that are needed to design a learning environment which would improve the acquisition and employment of concepts (see *Concept Learning, Teaching and Testing for*).

See also: Architecture of Cognition; Attention in Learning; Concept Learning, Teaching and Testing for; Declarative and Procedural Knowledge; Knowledge Representation and Organization; Learning Processes and Learning Outcomes; Perception and Learning; Preconceptions and Misconceptions

References

Shuell T J 1990 Phases of meaningful learning. *Rev. Educ. Res.* 60(4): 531–47

Tennyson R D, Breuer K 1984 Cognitive-based design guidelines for using video and computer technology in course development. In: Zuber-Skerritt O (ed.) 1984 *Video in Higher Education*. Kogan Page, London

Tennyson R D, Elmore R, Snyder L 1992 Advancements in instructional design theory: Contextual module analysis and integrated instructional strategies. *Educ. Tech. Res. Dev.* 40(2): 9–22

Tennyson R D, Rasch M 1988 Linking cognitive learning theory to instructional prescriptions. *Instr. Sci.* 17(4): 369–85

Further Reading

Bransford J D, Sherwood R, Vye N, Rieser J 1986 Teaching thinking and problem solving. *Am. Psychol.* 41: 1078–89

Clark R E 1989 Current progress and future directions for research in instructional technology. *Educ. Tech. Res. Dev.* 37(1): 57–66

Fleming M L 1987 Displays and communication. In: Gagné

R (ed.) 1987 *Instructional Technology: Foundations*. Erlbaum, Hillsdale, New Jersey
Merrill M D, Tennyson R D, Posey L 1992 *Teaching Concepts: An Instructional Design Guide*, 2nd edn. Educational Technology, Englewood Cliffs, New Jersey
Tennyson R D, Cocchiarella M J 1986 An empirically based instructional design theory for teaching concepts. *Rev. Educ. Res.* 56(1): 40–71
Tennyson R D, Park O 1980 The teaching of concepts: A review of instructional design research literature. *Rev. Educ. Res.* 50(1): 55–70
Winn W D 1989 Towards a rationale and theoretical basis for educational technology. *Educ. Tech. Res. Dev.* 37(1): 35–46

R. D. Tennyson

Concept Learning, Teaching and Testing for

Concepts represent the fundamental elements of all content areas. In formal content situations, concepts are classes of objects, symbols, and events that are grouped together in some fashion by shared characteristics. An important purpose of education is to provide a learning environment in which students can both readily learn new concepts and improve the use of acquired concepts. The purpose of this entry is to present the instructional design guidelines for the preparation of instruction to improve concept learning and employment.

1. Overview of Design Guidelines

The learning of concepts involves three basic cognitive behaviors: (a) understanding the characteristics of a given concept and the association of that concept within a content area; (b) applying a given concept; and (c) knowing when, where, and why to employ a given concept. These cognitive behaviors are best learned when acquired within meaningful contexts. That is, teaching of concepts is more than a mere presentation of information. Where possible, the instruction should draw upon students' existing knowledge to put the concepts into a context that has meaning and employment potential. For example, historical (i.e., event) concepts are meaningful when viewed within the context or culture of the current environment. When designing concept lessons, the rule of thumb is to include learning objectives that integrate behaviors of content acquisition with improving and extending cognitive strategies for employment (e.g., recall, problem-solving, creativity).

Like the learning of concepts, instructional design as it applies to concepts involves three main activities: (a) the identification of the goals and objectives of the learning environment; (b) the analysis and sequence of the concepts to be learned; and (c) the development of the instruction, which includes selecting the appropriate instructional strategies and means of delivery (e.g., lecture, print materials, electronic). Given the scope of this entry, the design process of selecting the delivery system will not be addressed.

2. Preparing Goals and Objectives

Goals are broad statements that reflect the overall educational outcomes usually associated with a curricular area. Goals can be classified as either statements dealing with acquisition of concepts or the improvement in cognitive strategies for employment of concepts. From these two broad categories, objectives can be directly referenced that specify the type of behavior to be learned and improved. Because behaviors vary according to the complexity of outcomes, objectives are usually labeled to reflect the type of behavior desired. The labeling scheme selected for this entry is influenced by contemporary educational goals associated with improving higher-order cognitive skills and strategies. By directly linking the goals and objectives of the learning environment, it is also possible directly to link the objectives to instructional prescriptions.

In Table 1, an instructional design (ID) model is presented that shows the direct integration of cognitive learning theory with prescribed instructional strategies. In addition to the direct linkages between the various memory systems and instructional strategies, the model includes direct reference to formal classroom instructional time. The times presented in the model focus on goals dealing with acquiring and employing knowledge. The suggested times should be manipulated by the individual curricular situation based upon focus of the goals. The major components of the ID model are: memory systems, learning objectives, instructional time, and instructional prescriptions.

2.1 Memory Systems

The proposed ID model is directly associated with cognitive theories of learning (see *Concept Learning*). Because the goals of the ID model include both the acquisition and the employment of knowledge, the memory systems reference the long-term memory subsystems of storage and retrieval. The storage system is composed of three basic forms of knowledge:

(a) declarative knowledge, knowing *that* about the information;

(b) procedural knowledge, knowing *how* to use information; and,

(c) contextual knowledge, knowing *when*, *where*, and *why* to use given concepts and associated cognitive skills.

The retrieval system is composed of cognitive strat-

Table 1
The Instructional Design (ID) model[a]

Model components	Educational goals: Acquisition of knowledge			Employment of knowledge	
Memory systems	Declarative knowledge	Procedural knowledge	Contextual knowledge	Cognitive complexity	Cognitive constructivism
Learning objectives	Verbal information	Intellectual skills	Contextual skills	Cognitive strategies	Creative processes
Instructional times	10%	20%	25%	30%	15%
Instructional prescriptions	Expository strategies	Practice strategies	Problem-oriented strategies	Complex–dynamic strategies	Self-directed experiences

a Tennyson 1992

egies associated with the processes of recall, problem-solving, and creativity.

2.2 Learning Objectives

The purpose of learning objectives is to elaborate further the curricular goals of knowledge acquisition and employment. Objectives are important in the planning of concept teaching because they provide the means of both allocating instructional time and identifying specific instructional strategies. Five learning objectives can be identified: verbal information, intellectual skills, contextual skills, cognitive strategies, and creative processes.

Verbal information deals with the learner acquiring an awareness and understanding of the concepts within a specified domain of information (i.e., declarative knowledge).

Intellectual skills involve the learner acquiring the skill to use correctly the concepts of a specified domain of information (i.e., procedural knowledge).

Contextual skills focus on the learner's acquisition of a knowledge base's organization and accessibility (i.e., contextual knowledge). The organization of a knowledge base refers to the modular structure of the information, whereas the accessibility refers to the complex cognitive skills that provide the means necessary to employ the knowledge base in the service of recall, problem-solving, and creativity. Contextual knowledge includes the criteria, values, feelings, and appropriateness of a given content domain's modular structure. For example, simply knowing how to classify examples or knowing how to use a concept does not imply that the learner knows when, where, and why to employ specific concepts.

Cognitive strategies deal with both the improvement and development of cognitive strategies and the extension of such strategies to domain-specific cognitive skills. Thus, this learning objective deals with two important issues in education. The first is the elaboration of cognitive strategies that will arm the students with increased domain-specific contextual knowledge (i.e., cognitive skills). The second is the development of the cognitive abilities of differentiation and integration. These abilities provide the cognitive tools to employ and improve the knowledge base effectively; therefore, they are integral to any educational goals seeking to improve higher-order cognition.

Creative processes deal with the most elusive goal of education: the development and improvement of creative abilities. Creativity is a twofold ability: (a) constructing knowledge to solve a problem from the external environment, and (b) constructing the problem as well as the knowledge to solve the problem. Integral to the construction of both the problem and knowledge are the criteria by which consistent judgment can be made. There are two sets of criteria. The first consists of criteria that are known and which can be applied with a high level of consistency. In contrast are those criteria that are developed concurrently with the problem and/or knowledge, and are consistently applied across a high level of productivity. Students should be informed of the criteria in the former and, in the latter, of the necessity to develop criteria.

2.3 Instructional Time

A key factor in implementing the cognitive goals of knowledge acquisition and employment is the allocation of learning time to defined objectives. For example, Tennyson and Rasch (1988) suggest that if improvements in problem-solving and creativity are to occur, there needs to be a significant change in how instructional time is allocated. They recommend that the conventional instructional time allocation for learning be altered so that, instead of 70 percent of instruction being aimed at the declarative and procedural knowledge levels of learning, 70 percent should be devoted to learning situations that involve acquisition of contextual knowledge and development of cognitive strategies.

Using Tennyson and Rasch's recommended figures on instructional time allocation, learning time can be divided into the two main subsystems of long-term memory: storage and retrieval. Within the guidelines illustrated in Table 1, time is assigned according to the cognitive objectives defined in the section above. In the storage system, learning time is allocated among the three memory systems making up a knowledge base as follows: declarative knowledge 10 percent, procedure knowledge 20 percent, and contextual knowledge 25 percent.

Contextual knowledge learning time should be about equal to the other two knowledge forms because of the necessity to both organize a knowledge base and develop accessibility to it once organized. The value of a knowledge base is primarily in the functionality of its organization and accessibility. Without a sufficient base of contextual knowledge, the opportunity for employment, future elaborations, and extension of the knowledge base is severely limited.

For knowledge acquisition goals, the focus of learning time allocation is on contextual knowledge, and away from the usual practice of heavy emphasis on amount of information. Declarative and procedural knowledge acquisition is believed to be an interactive process that is improved when employing the knowledge base in the service of higher-order thinking situations (i.e., those involving problem-solving and creativity). Time allocated for declarative and procedural knowledge focuses on establishing an initial base of necessary conceptual knowledge that can be used within a context of a problem situation. That is, learning time should include the opportunity for the learner to gain experience in employing the learned concepts.

The learning times presented in Table 1 do not imply a linear sequence of knowledge acquisition going from declarative to contextual. Rather, they represent total amounts in an iterative learning environment where learners are continuously acquiring each form of knowledge. For example, students may engage in contextual knowledge acquisition prior to declarative knowledge acquisition if they currently have sufficient background knowledge (i.e., a discovery method of instruction as contrasted to a structured method) (see *Discovery Learning and Teaching*).

3. Concept Analysis

An important component of instructional design is the analysis of the concepts to be learned. There are two basic types of analysis: (a) a content (task) analysis that focuses on defining the critical characteristics of the concepts and the relationship of those characteristics according to superordinate and subordinate organizations; and (b) a contextual analysis that focuses on the memory or knowledge base organization of the concepts. The first analytic method identifies the external structure of the concepts (either a taxonomy or hierarchy) but does so independently of how it might actually be stored in human memory. However, research in cognitive psychology on human memory suggests that the internal organization of concepts in a knowledge base is based more on employment needs than by attribute characteristics or taxonomic/hierarchical connections (Fodor 1983). That is, the utility of the knowledge base is attributed to its situational organization, not necessarily the amount of information. The implication of knowledge base organization is the need for a contextual analysis of the concepts better to understand their possible internal organization (Garner 1990). Better organization in memory may also imply better accessibility within the knowledge base for such higher order cognitive activities as problem-solving and creativity (Harré 1984).

To understand the nature of knowledge base organization, cognitive psychologists analyze problem complexity and the way individuals try to solve given problems (Klahr et al. 1987). By analyzing problems, it is possible to identify the concepts employed; and, by analyzing the solutions, it is possible to identify the associations of those concepts within given problem situations. The implication for concept teaching is that the sequence of concepts for instruction should be based in part on internal situational associations as well as external structures (Bereiter 1990). The assumption is that because external structures are independent of employment needs, an analysis of possible internal associations would improve the initial organization of the new concepts, resulting in better employment.

A second analytical method, contextual analysis, is proposed when the goals of the curriculum include employment and improvement of cognitive skills and strategies, such as problem-solving, decision-making, and trouble-shooting. Contextual analysis includes five basic steps:

(a) Define the context for the employment of the concepts to be learned. A context is a meaningful application of the concepts. For example, a simulation, a game, a role-playing situation, or a case study provides an instructional vehicle for presenting a meaningful context.

(b) Define the complex problems (problems requiring more than one concept for solution) associated with the context. This step follows a knowledge engineering approach where problems associated with a given context are identified.

(c) For each problem, identify concepts employed for the solution or decision-making.

(d) Identify possible clusters of concepts employed

in the solution of the various problems. That is, within a context certain concepts may be employed for a certain set of problems while other concepts may be employed in other sets.

(e) Sequence the clusters according to increasing complexity. For example, the first cluster may involve only two concepts while more complex clusters may have additional concepts. Analyzing problems within a context and then identifying the concepts and their employment organization (i.e., cluster) provides a means for sequencing the instruction to improve higher order cognition. In other words, the sequence of the instruction is based on the objective of improving employment of knowledge in addition to improvement in acquisition.

4. *Instructional Prescriptions*

This section describes instructional strategies found through empirical research to improve concept learning. Selection of the various strategies is based upon the learning objectives and the prerequisite knowledge of the students. For students with minimal prerequisite knowledge, an instructional program would probably utilize all of the strategies to insure adequate declarative and procedural knowledge. However, for students with a good knowledge base within the targeted curriculum area, an instructional program would emphasize more of the discovery type of instruction.

4.1 Expository Strategies

The category of expository strategies represents those instructional variables designed to provide an environment for learning of declarative knowledge (see Table 1). The basic instructional variables provide a context for the concepts to be learned. That is, advance organizers are used to provide a meaningful context for the concepts as well as a mental framework of the given domain's abstract structure. In addition to providing a context for the information, meaning can be further enhanced by adapting the context to individual student background knowledge.

The context establishes not only the initial organization of the domain, but also introduces both the "why" of the theoretical nature of the concepts and the "when and where" of the criterion nature of the domain's standards, values, and appropriateness (Bereiter and Scardamalia 1989). Personalizing the context to student background knowledge improves understanding of the information by connecting, within working memory, knowledge that is easily retrieved. Thus, the new knowledge becomes directly connected or associated with existing knowledge.

Following the contextual introduction of the concepts, five additional expository instructional variables are used to present the concepts in forms that extend existing knowledge and that aid in establishing new knowledge. These are as follows:

(a) *Label.* Although a simple variable, it is often necessary to elaborate on a label's origin so that the student is not just trying to memorize a nonsense word.

(b) *Definition.* The purpose of a definition is to connect the new concepts with existing knowledge in long-term memory; otherwise the definition may convey no meaning. That is, the student should already know the critical attributes of the concept. To improve understanding of the new concepts further, definitions may, in addition to presentation of the critical attributes (i.e., prerequisite knowledge), include information linked to the student's background or personal knowledge.

(c) *Best example.* To help students establish initial prototypes or abstractions of a domain's concepts, expository examples that are clear representations should be provided first.

(d) *Expository examples.* Additional examples should provide increasingly divergent representations of the concepts, perhaps also in alternative contexts.

(e) *Worked examples.* This variable provides an expository environment in which the examples are presented to the student in statement forms that elaborate application. The purpose is to help the student in becoming aware of the application (i.e., intellectual skill) of the concept within the given context(s). For example, to learn a mathematical operation, the student can be presented with the steps of the process in an expository problem while concurrently being presented with explanations for each step. In this way, the student may more clearly understand the procedures of the mathematical operation without developing possible misconceptions or overgeneralizations.

4.2 Practice Strategies

The category of practice strategies contains a rich variety of variables and conditions which can be designed into numerous teaching methods to improve learning of procedural knowledge. The term "practice" is used because the objective is for the student to learn how to use procedural knowledge correctly; therefore, it requires constant interaction between student learning (e.g., problem-solving) and instructional system monitoring. Practice strategies should attempt to create an environment in which (a) the student learns to apply procedural knowledge to previously unencountered concepts, while (b) the instructional system carefully monitors the student's performance so as both to prevent and correct possible misconceptions of procedural knowledge.

The basic instructional variable in this strategy is the presentation of problems that have not been previously encountered. Other variables include means for evaluation of learner responses (e.g., pattern recognition), advice (or coaching), elaboration of basic information (e.g., text density), format of information, number of problems, use of expository information, error analysis, and lastly, refreshment and remediation of prerequisite information.

4.3 Problem-oriented Strategies

Problem-oriented strategies involve problem-oriented techniques (e.g., simulations). Simulations improve the organization and accessibility of concepts within a knowledge base by presenting problems that require students to search through their memory to locate and retrieve the appropriate knowledge to propose a solution. Within this context, a simulation is a problem rather than an expository demonstration of some situation or phenomenon (Breuer and Kummer 1990).

Basically, problem-oriented strategies focus on the students trying to use their declarative and procedural knowledge in solving domain-specific contextual problems. Problem-oriented simulations present problem situations that require the student to (a) analyze the problem, (b) work out a conceptualization of the problem, (c) define specific goals for coping with the problem, and (d) propose a solution or decision. Unlike problems in the practice strategies that focus on acquiring procedural knowledge, problem-oriented simulations present situations that require employment of the domain's declarative and procedural knowledge. Thus, the student is in a problem-solving situation that requires establishing cognitive skills (i.e., contextual knowledge) among the concepts of specific domains of information.

4.4 Complex-dynamic Problem Strategies

Complex-dynamic strategies require students to employ their knowledge in the generation of solutions to complex, dynamic problems. Such learning processes are expected to improve the cognitive abilities of students (i.e., differentiation and integration; see Table 1). Five basic features should be considered in the design of instruction for improving cognitive complexity:

(a) The context is meaningful and of interest to the student.

(b) The context permits the student to construct concepts through his or her own cognitive efforts and employ this knowledge in proposing solutions and making decisions.

(c) The context provides a responsive, changing environment in which the student can receive feedback relevant to his or her evolving cognitive skills and strategies.

(d) The context permits the student to move from knowledge employment and improvement to knowledge acquisition, back to knowledge employment, and so on. It is this movement from one process (employment) to another (acquisition), from the employment of discrepant information to the combination of concepts in cognitive strategies that helps overcome boredom and creates interest.

(e) The context measures the degree of cognitive strategy employment independently from the knowledge acquisition.

Complex-dynamic simulations within such domains as politics and economics have been developed. Each simulation starts from a complex scenario that allows individual information searches and decision-making processes. The simulations are responsive as they reflect the decision-making processes of students by changing the status of the variables and conditions that represent the situation. The simulations are open-ended, as all decisions entered bring about a different and usually new status of the depicted situation, which can be "improved" or "optimized" by the student again. The simulation features create steady involvement of students and the repeated need for movement between knowledge and cognitive strategies. Additionally, the need for cognitive activity is supported by organizing the learning and thinking processes within cooperative learning groups. These groups provide opportunities for explanation, argumentation, justification, and adaptation.

4.5 Self-directed Experiences

An important goal of education is the development of learners who can be responsible for not only employing their existing knowledge but for the creating of new knowledge. The purpose of this instructional strategy category is to provide an environment in which students have instructional opportunities to improve their abilities to construct new knowledge.

For the most part, this process of cognitive constructivism can be improved by instruction that is self-directed. That requires a learning environment that is rich in resources and time for the student to seek out answers to both predefined and self-defined problems. Although cognitive constructivism may occur under unplanned environments, planned instructional environments can help create spheres of domain focus. For example, if the area of interest is social studies, the environment may include resources that would benefit creation of knowledge in that area as opposed to domains in the physical sciences.

Several programs of research in writing have shown improvements in basic writing skills as well as creativity through the use of computer-based word-processing systems (Reed 1992). In less planned environments, such as computer-based interactive games, there are findings that individuals construct the necessary concepts to continue improving their performances. For example, computer-based programs provide rich facilities that are under control of the student and, with intelligent systems, allow students to query the system.

A mixed initiative learning environment simulates the interaction between a domain expert and a novice learner. Thus, the student can artificially alter the time necessary to create new knowledge. Interest in virtual reality techniques is especially high in this area because of the total landscape of the artificial environment. Students may have the opportunity to explore just about any avenue of the domain without constraints that may be inherent in the real environment.

5. Concept Evaluation

Evaluation of concepts should take place within four stages of student assessment, ranging from pre-instruction (for the purpose of evaluating entry behavior) to postcurriculum (for the purpose of evaluating educational goals). Thus, teachers should view evaluation as an integral component of classroom instruction.

5.1 Pre-instruction Evaluation

Before teaching concepts to students, the teacher should evaluate student entry knowledge. Where possible, the ideal evaluation plan would include assessing two types of knowledge: prior knowledge and prerequisite knowledge. A pretest that measures prior knowledge would identify what concepts to teach and whether any remediation for misconceptions is necessary. A pretest that measures prerequisite knowledge would identify the amount of remedial instruction required before formal instruction of the concepts to be learned begins. Additionally, preinstructional evaluation of aptitude and general achievement would help teachers to establish appropriate levels of difficulty.

5.2 During-instruction Evaluation

A major concern in concept teaching is the amount of instruction required for mastery (i.e., successful employment of learned concepts). Assessment of learning during instruction will help in determining the amount of instruction needed. Methods of evaluation should focus on products that make it possible to assess progress and effort. This type of evaluation can be integrated with the instructional prescriptions for problem-oriented and complex–dynamic strategies.

5.3 Post-instruction Evaluation

In most cases, students should not be required to take a posttest unless the teacher can assume mastery of concept employment. Students and the teacher should be well aware of progress and effort such that post-instruction measures truly evaluate the student at his or her highest level of achievement. Testing methods for learning objectives include final products and criterion-referenced objective tests. Norm-referenced tests may be useful for evaluation of curricular goals (e.g., school district outcome-based goals).

5.4 Postcurriculum Evaluation

Student success in schools is often measured by performance on standardized tests that evaluate students across curricular settings. In such testing individual student knowledge is compared to a large population; rarely does this information identify specific concept knowledge. Rather, postcurriculum evaluation informs the students of their relative level of general achievement in reference to their peers.

6. Conclusion

Teaching and evaluation of concepts can be enhanced when viewed within an integrated instructional program, that is, an instructional program planned to provide both acquisition and employment of concepts. Concepts are valuable when the learner can employ them in future situations. The instructional design (ID) model for concept teaching and evaluation described in this entry meets the educational goals of acquisition and employment. The guidelines presented are flexible and can be manipulated by teachers in reference to their given environment. As such, the guidelines are tools to be controlled by the teacher and, for the most part, improved with experience in their use.

See also: Concept Learning

References

Bereiter C 1990 Aspects of an educational learning theory. *Rev. Educ. Res.* 60: 603 24

Bereiter C, Scardamalia M 1989 Intentional learning as a goal of instruction. In: Resnick L B (ed.) 1989 *Knowing, Learning, and Instruction: Essays in Honor of Robert Glaser.* Erlbaum, Hillsdale, New Jersey

Breuer K, Kummer R 1990 Cognitive effects from process learning with computer-based simulations. *Comput. Hum. Behav.* 6: 69–81

Fodor J A 1983 *The Modular Theory of Mind: An Essay on Faculty Development.* Bradford Books, Lexington, Massachusetts

Garner R 1990 When children and adults do not use learn-

ing strategies: Toward a theory of settings. *Rev. Educ. Res.* 60: 517–29
Harré R 1984 *Personal Being: A Theory for Individual Psychology*. Harvard University Press, Cambridge, Massachusetts
Klahr D, Langley P, Neches R (eds.) 1987 *Production System Models of Learning Development*. MIT Press, Cambridge, Massachusetts
Reed W M 1992 The effects of computer-based writing tasks and mode of discourse on the performance and attitudes of writers of varying abilities. *Comput. Hum. Behav.* 8: 97–120
Tennyson R D 1992 An educational learning theory for instructional design. *Educ. Technol.* 32(1): 36–41
Tennyson R D, Rasch M 1988 Linking cognitive learning theory to instructional prescriptions. *Instr. Sci.* 17: 369–85

Further Reading

Alexander P A, Judy J E 1988 The interaction of domain-specific and strategic knowledge in academic performance. *Rev. Educ. Res.* 58: 375–404
Merrill M D, Tennyson R D, Posey L 1992 *Teaching Concepts: An Instructional Design Guide*, 2nd edn. Educational Technology, Englewood Cliffs, New Jersey
Tennyson R D 1990a Cognitive learning theory linked to instructional theory. *J. Struct. Learn.* 10: 249–58
Tennyson R D 1990b Computer-based enhancements for the improvements of learning. In: Dijkstra S, van Hout Wolters B H A M, van der Sijde P C (eds.) 1990 *Research on Instruction: Design and Effects*. Educational Technology, Englewood Cliffs, New Jersey
Wertsch J (ed.) 1985 *Culture, Communication, and Cognition: Vygotskian Perspectives*. Cambridge University Press, Cambridge, Massachusetts

R. D. Tennyson

Concept Mapping

The power of a visual representation of an idea or process is generally accepted in both the wider community and in education. Company logos, maps of subway systems, flow charts, and road signs are seen to be effective forms of representation of ideas of varying complexity in everyday life. Visual representation techniques also constitute one of the major instructional formats available to teachers, ranging from carefully prepared multi-colored diagrams of objects or processes to sketches hastily drawn on paper or even the ground. There is quite strong informal evidence available from both teachers and students that these devices assist learning. Given the long history of use of such devices in teaching it is surprising that there has been relatively little systematic study of their nature and effects. Mayer and Gallini (1990), who have carried out several studies of the effects of illustrations on learning, argue that their potential remains to be fully exploited. In their discussion of different types of illustrations Jones et al. (1988–89) propose that an effective graphical representation allows the development of "a holistic understanding that words alone cannot convey" (p. 21), because the graphical form allows representation of parts and whole in a way that is not available in the sequential structure of text.

An attractive form of visual representation, the "concept map," has emerged in a number of forms in educational research, though the term is most commonly associated with the work of Novak and his colleagues in the science education program at Cornell University (e.g., Novak and Gowin 1984). It is upon this version of concept mapping that this entry will concentrate.

Forms of visual representation have received much less attention in educational research than have verbal and text-based materials. In part this seems to be related to the lack of availability of a framework for considering ways to structure a complex array of material. While there are well-developed analyses of text structures (e.g., de Beaugrande and Dressler 1981) there is not an analytical scheme of comparable complexity that can be used in description of the structure and components of graphical displays. Kosslyn (1989) has suggested a means for beginning the study of different types of illustrations by setting out a broad framework within which he distinguishes four types of graphic representation of some phenomenon—(X)-graphs, maps, charts, and diagrams. In this framework *graphs* are seen as the most constrained form of visual display, involving representation of X in terms of values on at least two axes. The labels and the scales assigned to the axes denote the dimensions of representation of the phenomenon. *Maps* are less constrained in structure than graphs, the central feature of a map in Kosslyn's scheme being its representation of spatial relationships characteristic of X, typically relationships such as size, location, direction and distance. The map need not only be of a static structure such as a city but has also been used as a form of representation for a dynamic system like a brain. The features of charts and diagrams are less firmly established. For Kosslyn the *chart* represents discrete relationships among discrete entities, with relationships such as sequence being typically associated with charts, as in a flow chart. *Diagram* is the least specific of Kosslyn's categories, covering any visual representation not identified in the other categories.

Within Kosslyn's framework the concept map of Novak would not be regarded as a map, for as Thompson (1992) argues it is not a central feature of a concept map that spatial relationships be represented, the more typical focus being the representation of semantic relationships. This entry considers the development and use of the Novak procedure, and some related techniques, for the representation of relationships among ideas in educational research and for ease of reference the term "concept map" will be retained here.

1. The Concept Maps of Novak

Novak's initial interest in the concept map was stimulated by the need to make sense of a large body of data generated through interviews with students in elementary science classes (Novak 1990). The concept map was developed as a means of facilitating analysis of such information by application of a structural device for representing a student's understanding of a complex phenomenon. Novak sought to develop a procedure that would represent that understanding in terms of propositional relationships established among a group of related concepts. Some form of representation of the structure of student understanding was argued by Novak and Gowin (1984) to be necessary to make progress in identifying areas of difficulty in understanding that might give rise to misconceptions. For Novak a concept map satisfied this need by providing "a schematic device for representing a set of concept meanings embedded in a framework of propositions" (Novak and Gowin 1984 p. 15).

In establishing this representational format Novak drew extensively on the descriptions of learning that had been developed by Ausubel (1968). In Ausubel's theory, the most effective learning, "meaningful learning," involved the establishment of patterns of relationships among concepts with the larger more general patterns coming to *subsume*, or incorporate, the more specific concepts. The establishment of meaningful relationships among concepts was contrasted by Ausubel with "rote" learning in which concepts were not embedded in rich conceptual networks but were left relatively unelaborated and conceptually isolated within the broad conceptual structure. In the Ausubelian view the growth of knowledge in an individual was characterized by the gradual development of more complex and more differentiated structures organized in a hierarchical pattern. The different parts of this structure could be related, or integrated, through the establishment of propositional links. The hierarchical structure of a concept map was seen by Novak as instantiating the process of knowledge growth that Ausubel termed "subsumption." In this process the meaning of a new concept would be assimilated within the sphere of meaning of an existing concept/proposition complex to create a more powerful and coherent structure.

These ideas have been translated directly into the form of a concept map by Novak and his colleagues. In the form developed and used by Novak the concept map is a hierarchical structure, the focal point of which is the superordinate concept, the other concepts of concern being arranged in a manner which indicates their place and semantic relationships within this hierarchy. As noted above the structure is simple with three basic features—a list of concepts, a set of linking relationships among the concepts and, if desired, a set of labels for those relationships. Concepts, or entities, are established in a pattern of relationships. The connection of two concepts in a relationship expresses a proposition. Typically this simple structure is depicted using ellipses to represent concepts and lines to represent the relating links. If required, labels can be assigned to the linking lines in order to express the nature of a proposition.

In its hierarchical form the structure of the Novak concept map bears close similarity to the model of internal semantic network structure developed by memory researchers during the 1960s as a format for representation of long-term memory (e.g., Collins and Quillian 1969). The concept map may be seen as a system for externalizing this internal memory representation. It is not the only technique that has been designed to externalize internal psychological structure. Conceptually it is similar in nature to procedures for structuring conceptualizations that use the multivariate statistical techniques of cluster analysis and multidimensional scaling procedures, some of which are also termed "concept mapping procedures" (see Trochim 1989). The preparation of the typical Novak map does not involve use of these statistical techniques, though such techniques would be quite compatible with the central themes of Novak's work. Repertory grid techniques and semantic differential procedures share essentially the same objective as concept mapping in their concern to produce a representation of the structure of a semantic space. Each of these alternative techniques has been associated with the development of more refined statistical techniques than has Novak's concept mapping. Perhaps because of the close identification of concept mapping with a range of classroom applications its procedures for preparation and scoring have remained less formal than the representational techniques just noted.

The epistemological stance of Novak and other users of the general class of techniques for representation of cognitive structure has been questioned by Phillips (1983). Phillips questions the existence of the relationship between the behavioral representation manifested in the concept map and the internal structural state of the individual. However, as argued by Greeno (1983) in a response to Phillips, it seems that this criticism is overextended by Phillips so that the possibility of the existence of a less than perfect representation of cognitive structure is mistakenly interpreted as lack of such a relationship. Novak (1990) accepts Greeno's view that the outcomes of the use of techniques such as concept mapping do bear a systematic, though perhaps "noisy," relationship to cognitive structure, and so can be used as a basis for derivation of inferences about the state of that structure.

2. Functions of a Concept Map

It is of value to distinguish between the uses of concept maps from teacher and student perspectives.

2.1 Concept Map as Instructional Display

For a teacher the concept map can be used as a means of representing a pattern of relationships in an instructional display, a sort of diagrammatic text. The teacher can propose a structure of relationships in diagrammatic form rather than in verbal, or text, or equation formats. The display is then available for use by the teacher in part or as a whole structure.

For the student the concept map represents a way of introducing structure into the process of knowledge acquisition. This structuring can take two broad forms. In the first, the instructional display presented by the teacher, or by a text, can be inspected and used by the student to structure the relationships pertinent to the topic under study. The concept map presents a number of propositional relationships for analysis, and would also be expected to influence the form of organization of these propositions in memory. An alternative procedure could require the student to produce the map, from a list of relevant concepts, with one concept being nominated as the focus of the hierarchy. The links established by the students, and the labels assigned to these links, are argued to influence the nature of the understanding of the phenomenon that is developed.

The concept map can also be expected to have the potential to influence events at the time of retrieval of information related to the topic of the hierarchy. The visual character of the map could provide a means of structuring cognitive activity during retrieval, with the concept names and the labels having the potential to act as cues that could guide the search of memory. The use of the map would then be expected to improve the accessing of relevant knowledge because of its potential for influencing both organizational and retrieval events.

A number of researchers have reported positive effects of the use of concept maps as a form of instructional display, the majority of this research involving secondary school science students. In one of the earlier evaluation studies Novak et al. (1983) found that junior high school students who prepared a concept map were able to identify more relevant relationships in reporting on a topic in science than students who were presented with keywords prior to developing their responses. These authors also found that the concept map group solved more problems on a transfer task than did the control group. Okebukola has carried out a number of studies with secondary school science students in which the effectiveness of concept map use during learning for a topic has been evaluated. In a recent study (Okebukola 1990), the effect of adding a concept mapping strategy to discussion and practical sessions in units on genetics and ecology was assessed with students aged 15–22 years. In both units the effect of preparation and the use of concept maps during class sessions was associated with significant improvements in post-test performance. Pankratius (1990) observed a similar pattern of results in a study with high school physics students. The preparation of the maps, and their updating during study, resulted in better performance than did conventional classroom instruction that did not include use of the mapping procedure. Willerman and Mac-Harg (1991) used concept maps as an advance organizer for their eighth-grade science students and found that their mapping group scored significantly higher on a post-test than did the control group that had not used the map organizer.

While these sets of findings indicate that the use of a concept mapping procedure offers an interesting alternative means of instructional presentation to the teacher, it is important to note that not all investigations of the use of concept maps have returned positive results. Lehman et al. (1985) found no differences in achievement in comparisons of mapping and control treatments in biology classes. The results obtained in Prater and Terry's (1988) study of the use of concept maps as an aid to reading comprehension were also equivocal with an advantage for use of concept maps being observed for reading comprehension in only two of the three studies involving fifth-grade students. No advantage for use of the concept mapping approach was obtained on a writing task. Stensvold and Wilson (1990) found that the use of concept maps in chemistry classes resulted in lower scores for high ability students than did the conventional teaching procedure. Heinze-Fry and Novak (1990) noted a similar effect on their higher ability students in initial post-test performance, though this effect was not apparent after a period of five months. In this study no significant effect of concept map use was observed at either immediate or delayed testing.

As is the case for many other instructional techniques the pattern of results for use of concept maps as study devices is mixed. This pattern is not seen here to be sufficient reason to abandon use of concept maps for it is clear that there have as yet been relatively few systematic studies of the use of this form of instructional display. There is such a wide variation in design of concept maps, in manner of presentation of these to students, and in procedures for examining the effects of map use, that it would be premature to argue that a clear picture of concept map use is available. The variation just noted makes clear that it is difficult to assemble very many studies that have involved closely similar conditions, so that precise statements of effects are not available.

2.2 Concept Map as an Evaluation Device

A concept map produced by students is argued by Novak and Gowin (1984) to be as important as an evaluation technique. In very general terms the teacher may identify for a given hierarchy concepts that are incorrectly included in student maps, concepts that are omitted, or valid relationships that are either not justified in the light of current understanding or are missing. Novak and Gowin clearly see this use of the concept map as a valuable alternative to such evaluation devices as objective tests and essays, arguing that in many cases the concept map has greater sensitivity as a measuring device. The strength of this argument rests to a significant extent on the qualities possessed by both the manner of preparation of the map and those of the system used to score the map. At present both these remain issues that require further discussion and investigation before it would be reasonable to claim that the concept map had wide practicability as a formal evaluation device in school or university classrooms. These issues are discussed more fully in a following section.

2.3 Concept Map as Curriculum Organizer

Starr and Krajcik (1990) have used concept maps as a means of developing curriculum plans and sequences, and have found that teachers value the structure which the use of the procedure introduces into planning of lesson sequences. This has involved the structuring of hierarchies based around the major constructs/concepts in a given area and identification of related, subordinate concepts—a process similar to that involved in the use of Gagne's learning hierarchies (Gagne 1968). Both concept maps and learning hierarchies can be used to produce specifications of the content of a teaching/learning sequence, though the learning hierarchies have typically been developed in much greater detail for this purpose than have concept maps. Across a number of sessions Starr and Krajcik (1990) identified the development of a more coherent framework for the presentation of the life science component of the upper elementary curriculum. These authors also saw the process of development of the maps as having the effect of increasing the degree of involvement of these teachers in the curriculum planning process. There is clear scope for the development of more detailed investigation of this use of concept maps.

2.4 Concept Map as Index of Understanding

As indicated earlier the need for a form of representation of student understanding provided the impetus for development of the concept map and this continues to be one of the major uses of the technique (Novak and Musonda 1991; Wallace and Mintzes 1990). Novak and Musonda (1991) used concept maps to document changes in understanding of a wide range of scientific notions in a group of students as they moved from first grade to twelfth grade. In this study the concept maps were developed by the researchers from clinical interviews with students. The procedure used to move from interview to map is not clearly explicated by these authors, though they do claim reasonable validity and reliability for their procedures. Wallace and Mintzes (1990) trained undergraduates to produce concept maps prior to beginning their instructional intervention and then assessed the quality of the student produced maps at preintervention and postintervention times using an "expert-produced" map as a reference point. The training in production of maps followed the procedures set out by Novak and Gowin (1984).

Of these two procedures the latter is more straightforward and appears to be less prone to problems of unreliability. The analysis of interview transcripts requires the interposing of the interpretive framework of the researcher between the consideration of the concept complex and the structuring of the student's map. This places the student at some considerable distance from the process of structuring the map, a disadvantage that is overcome through use of the student-produced maps.

3. Issues

3.1 The Problem of Hierarchical Structure

Novak has maintained hierarchical structure as a central feature of the concept map (Novak 1990), deriving the basis of such a structure from the notion of subsumption as a process of knowledge development and organization. Wandersee (1990) also sees such a structure as being required to represent the "psychological structure" of understanding. It now seems more reasonable to justify the use of a hierarchically structured concept map on practical grounds, rather than arguing for an isomorphism between the structure of the map and psychological structure of meaning. While the early models of semantic memory networks were organized hierarchically (e.g., Collins and Quillian 1969), the psychological evidence for such a pattern of organization is not strong (e.g., Anderson 1990). The recent interest in distributed memory organization moves away from the simple hierarchical pattern of internal representation. Network models, in which the structure of conceptual elements was likened by Anderson (1990) to a massed tangle of marbles with strings attached, are more compatible with current thinking about mental structure. The limited dimensionality of the hierarchy suggests that it is an impoverished representation of memory structure.

Even a limited experience in constructing a concept map within a hierarchical format highlights the problem of variations in degree of generality of a concept that emerge when different features of the concept are highlighted. The analogy drawn by Novak and Gowin between a concept map and a rubber sheet of concepts, part of which (the superordinate concept) is elevated into prominence for purposes of discussion, suggests that they have some appreciation of the limitations of the hierarchical structure. Novak and Musonda (1991 p. 129) acknowledged the difficulty of recognizing hierarchies in a map and scored the maps in their study using level as a broad indicator of hierarchy. The limitations noted here have also been raised in discussions of other hierarchical structures popular in discussions of learning and instruction during the 1970s—Gagne's (1968) learning hierarchies (Merrill and Gibbons 1974). Phillips (1983) has also noted a number of problems that arise in drawing relationships between individual knowledge structures and the structure of a knowledge discipline. A major practical limitation is one concerned with designation of concepts to levels in a hierarchy.

As indicated in Section 2.3, there is value in use of concept maps and like devices for the structuring of a curriculum, or of a lesson. The seeking by a teacher of a clear structure for presentation in an instructional sequence is a necessary activity, and will be of most value when that structure is one that mirrors, at an appropriate level for the particular students, current understanding of the topic. So the seeking of a clear structure is not the problem. The limitation, particularly in a research context, is inherent in a hierarchical representation of knowledge in which complex concepts, or complexes of concepts, are established in a superordinate/subordinate relationship. The concept complexes situated in the subordinate positions are, however, multilevel entities whose constituent parts often relate in a complex manner to the focus concept. As alluded to above, in practice this can mean that the structure being represented in a hierarchy must be accompanied by frequent qualifications that recognize the complexity, the high-level nature, of the entities being placed lower in the hierarchy. Gagne appears to have recognized this limitation in recent discussions of the nature of memory structures such as "schema" (Gagne and Glaser 1987).

Even though the hierarchy may not be a good model of memory organization, and so may be limited as a format for representation of psychological structure, the conventional concept map format, based on establishment of relationships between superordinate and subordinate concepts, may still be useful as a pedagogic device in early stages of use of concept maps. The establishment of a superordinate concept does provide a focus for consideration of relationships of a group of related terms to that focal element which may be easier for students to consider in initial stages of discussion. It seems that this may well be the position adopted by Novak in recent writing (e.g., Novak and Musonda 1991 p. 129). However, once the level of complexity of the representational format increases, the maintenance of a hierarchical format is difficult. It is relevant to note that not all researchers developing concept maps have insisted upon use of the hierarchical structure (Champagne and Klopfer 1981).

3.2 Scoring Concept Maps

One difficulty likely to attend use of concept maps in both classroom evaluation and research is the lack of a common method of scoring of concept maps. The significance of this difficulty can be overstated and it is not suggested that this difficulty is one that should cause teachers or researchers to avoid contact with the concept map. As a measuring instrument the concept map shares with all other instruments the need to provide a set of clear, valid, and consistent procedures that are appropriate for the occasion and which can be understood and applied in the same fashion by other users. The major problems associated with the scoring of concept maps are concerned with the reporting of these procedures in a manner that allows easy application in similar situations.

The basic structure of the concept map suggests a number of these procedures. If the central elements of the concept map are the concept and the relating link then the identification of the presence of concepts and of links suggests a basis for a first-level scoring system. Beyond this the scoring of features of the concept map becomes more complex as judgments are required about such qualities as the suitability of a link or of a label, and the appropriateness of the grouping of a set of concepts. In a research study the development and application of these procedures will require a significant amount of time. In the classroom informal judgments may be made more quickly, though the use of detailed procedures will also be time-consuming.

The scoring of the level structure within the hierarchy is advocated by Novak and Gowin (1984). What is not clear from their scoring procedure is what constitutes a *level*, and it is here that the hierarchy imposes what can be argued to be an artificial restriction on expression of relationships among related conceptual elements. The members of a list of concepts required to be related to a focal concept will not necessarily be intrinsically less general than the focal concept. In establishing these concepts in a network of relationships with the focal concept it seems unnecessary and artificial to insist on a hierarchical form of representation.

Related, but less serious, scoring problems arise in the identification of "segments" of a map, and in the establishment of the soundness of procedures used to justify the scoring of the quality of links within a segment and of those between segments. The problems in this case are regarded as being less serious because they are problems of definition and clarity that attend development of all measuring devices. Stewart (1979) provided an early discussion of the central issues of scoring of concept maps and other representational techniques, while Fisher (1990) has addressed many of these scoring issues in development of the semantic networking computer-based procedure. The scoring of complex relationships remains a challenge for the user of the Novak mapping procedure.

4. Conclusion

The concept map, in both a generic form and in the form developed by Novak, is of contemporary interest in education because the problem of representation tackled by Novak is of central concern to both teachers and researchers. Both groups wish to have access to sensitive indices of the nature of the understandings held by students that is associated with different levels of achievement. The growing body of research on the uses of concept maps by both groups attests to the importance of this need. A review of some of this research suggests that there is good reason to pursue investigation of the design and use of concept maps in order to increase the level of sensivity of the instrument.

See also: Concept Learning; Concept Learning, Teaching and Testing for

References

Anderson J R 1990 *Cognitive Psychology and its Implications*, 3rd edn. W H Freeman, New York

Ausubel D P 1968 *Educational Psychology: A Cognitive View*. Holt, Rinehart and Winston, New York

Champagne A, Klopfer L 1981 *Using the ConSAT: A Memo to Teachers*. Reports to Educators No. R.T.E. 4. Learning Research and Development Center, University of Pittsburgh, Pittsburgh, Pennsylvania

Collins A, Quillian M R 1969 Retrieval from semantic memory. *J. Verbal Learn. Verbal Behav.* 8: 240–57

de Beaugrande R, Dressler W 1981 *Introduction to Text Linguistics*. Longman, New York

Fisher K 1990 Semantic networking: The new kid on the block. *J. Res. Sci. Teach.* 27(10): 1001–18.

Gagne R M 1968 Learning hierarchies. *Educ. Psychol.* 6: 1–9

Gagne R M, Glaser R 1987 Foundations in learning research. In: Gagne R M (ed.) 1987 *Instructional Technology: Foundations*. Erlbaum, Hillsdale, New Jersey

Greeno J 1983 Response to Phillips. *Educ. Psychol.* 18(2): 75–80

Heinze-Fry W, Novak J 1990 Concept mapping brings long-term movement toward meaningful learning. *Sci. Educ.* 74(4): 461–72

Jones B F, Pierce J, Hunter B 1988–89 Teaching students to construct graphic representations. *Educ. Leadership*, 46(4): 20–25

Kosslyn S 1989 Understanding charts and graphs. *Applied Cognitive Psychology* 3(3): 185–225

Lehman J, Carter C, Kahle J 1985 Concept mapping, vee mapping and achievement. *J. Res. Sci. Teach.* 22(7): 663–73

Mayer R, Gallini J 1990 When is an illustration worth ten thousand words. *J. Educ. Psychol.* 82(4): 715–26

Merrill M D, Gibbons A 1974 Heterarchies and their relationship to behavioral hierarchies for sequencing instruction. Paper presented at the Annual Convention of the American Educational Research Association, Chicago, April

Novak J 1990 Concept mapping: A useful device for science education. *J. Res. Sci. Teach.* 27(10): 937–49

Novak J, Gowin D B 1984 *Learning How to Learn*. Cambridge University Press, Cambridge

Novak J, Gowin D B, Johansen G 1983 The use of concept mapping and knowledge vee mapping with junior high school science students. *Sci. Educ.* 67(5): 625–45

Novak J, Musonda D 1991 A twelve-year longitudinal study of science concept learning. *Am. Educ. Res. J.* 28: 117–54

Okebukola P 1990 Attaining meaningful learning of concepts in genetics and ecology: An investigation of the potency of the concept mapping technique. *J. Res. Sci. Teach.* 27(5): 493–504

Pankratius W 1990 Building an organised knowledge base: Concept mapping and achievement in secondary school physics. *J. Res. Sci. Teach.* 27(4): 315–33

Phillips D C 1983 On describing a student's cognitive structure. *Educ. Psychol.* 18(2): 59–74

Prater D, Terry C 1988 Effects of mapping strategies on reading comprehension and writing performance. *Reading Psychology* 9(2): 101–20

Starr M, Krajcik J 1990 Concept maps as a heuristic for science curriculum development: Toward improvement in process and product. *J. Res. Sci. Teach.* 27(10): 987–1000

Stensvold M, Wilson J 1990 The interaction of verbal ability with concept mapping in learning from a chemistry laboratory activity. *Sci. Educ.* 74(4): 473–80

Stewart J 1979 Content and cognitive structure: Critique of assessment and representation techniques used by science education researchers. *Sci. Educ.* 63(3): 395–405

Thompson M 1992 Concept mapping and essay writing in physics. Unpublished Master of Education thesis, School of Education, Flinders University of South Australia

Trochim W 1989 An introduction to concept mapping for planning and evaluation. *Evaluation and Program Planning* 12(1): 1–16

Wallace J, Mintzes J 1990 The concept map as a research tool: Exploring conceptual change in biology. *J. Res. Sci. Teach.* 27(10): 1033–52

Wandersee J 1990 Concept mapping and the cartography of cognition. *J. Res. Sc. Educ.* 27(10): 923–36

Willerman M, Mac-Harg R 1991 The concept map as an advance organiser. *J. Res. Sci. Teach.* 28(8): 705–12

M. J. Lawson

Configural Frequency Analyses of Categorized Data

This entry is intended to introduce the main principles of "classical" configural frequency analysis (CFA) as initially proposed by Lienert (1969) and subsequently presented by Krauth and Lienert (1973). Since then there have been many publications both on theoretical issues and applications. A more recent overview is contained in Lienert (1988).

The general objective of CFA is the analysis of multivariate frequency data typically summarized in the form of multidimensional contingency tables. The key idea is the search for *types* in such a body of data, possibly supplemented by an analysis of the *interaction structure*.

The typical situation is as follows. From some population a sample of n units has been drawn, the units being persons in most instances. There are a number of observable attributes, $A_1, \ldots, A_t$, say, and each attribute A_i is made up of r_i mutually exclusive and exhaustive categories, $C_{i1}, \ldots, C_i r_i$. Hence the attributes are assumed discrete. If $r_i = 2$ then A_i is a dichotomy. Any observed unit can be classified according to the categories to which it belongs. An ordered set of such categories is called a "configuration." Obviously, the total of possible configurations is the product $r = r_1, r_2 \ldots r_t$. The above notation will be adhered to throughout. For instance, let A_1 indicate "gender" with categories C_{11} = "male," C_{12} = "female." Similarly, A_2 may denote "age groups" with categories C_{21} = "under 30 years of age," C_{22} = "between 30 and 60," and C_{23} = "over 60." Finally, A_3 may designate "employment" with C_{31} = "self-employed," and C_{32} = "not self-employed." Then the configuration (C_{11}, C_{21}, C_{32}) refers to a male under 30 years of age who is not self-employed.

The frequencies with which each configuration occurs in a sample of observed units are obtained by counting. Configural frequency analysis now purports to identify such configurations that are realized more often than should be expected by chance alone. Such a configuration is called a "type." On the other hand, one may speak of an antitype if a particular configuration occurs with too low a frequency. In most cases, however, interest focuses only on types.

It is necessary to specify exactly the *base model* according to which chance is supposed to operate. The underlying assumption is total independence among all attributes. A different base model of intuitive appeal has been proposed by Victor (1989). This remark may suffice for present purposes. In each event, CFA is a residual analysis after the base model has been taken into account.

1. Statistical Definition of Types

According to the previously introduced notation C_{ij_i} with $i = 1, \ldots, t$ and $j_i = 1, \ldots, r_i$ designates the j-th category of attribute A_i. Let the corresponding marginal probability of observing C_{ij_i} in some population be π_{ij_i}, that is, the probability of C_{ij_i} occurring regardless of the categories of the other attributes to which a unit belongs. On the other hand, let the probability of observing the configuration $(C1j_1, \ldots, C_{tj_t})$ be given by $\pi_{j_1} \ldots j_t$. For ease of notation the first subscripts 1, ..., t have been suppressed as the sequence of the second subscripts serves to identify the configuration in question. It follows from the base model of total independence that

$$\pi_{j1} \ldots j_t = \pi_{1j_1} \times \ldots \times \pi_{tj_t} \tag{1}$$

If, however, the inequality

$$\pi_{j1} \ldots j_t > \pi_{1j_1} \times \ldots \times \pi_{tj_t} \tag{2}$$

holds then $(C_{1j_1}, \ldots, C_{tj_t})$ constitutes a type. It is an antitype if the reverse inequality holds.

The existence of at least one type implies the existence of at least one antitype. For, if a configuration is found that appears more often than chance alone would allow then there must be another configuration with too small a frequency and vice versa.

2. Search for Types

After collection of a body of data as previously described, the researcher will wish to search for such configurations that presumably constitute types. This can be achieved by several methods. It is necessary, however, to distinguish two stages of any such search. During the *exploratory stage* hypotheses about specific configurations being types should be generated. This may be done by inspection of the data. In each event, such hypotheses must be considered preliminary and, strictly speaking, should not be subjected to statistical tests on the basis of the same data that served to suggest them. It appears that this point is often neglected in practice. Statistical tools concerning hypotheses about types make up the *confirmatory stage* of the search process. To this end new data should be employed. They should be independent of the ones already used. Randomly splitting the initial total sample suggests itself. If hypotheses regarding types have been set up independently of the data then the researcher can immediately enter into the second stage. At any rate, when hypothesis testing is intended the following quantities apart from sample size n, that is, the number of observed units, are required.

(a) For each configuration $(C_{1j_1}, \ldots, C_{tj_t})$ the number of units exhibiting this pattern is determined. Let this frequency be $f_{j_1} \ldots {}_{j_t}$. The order of the subscripts is essential, of course. These frequencies may be regarded as the entries of a t-dimensional contingency table, the number of cells being the product $r{=}r_1 \times \ldots \times r_t$.

(b) For each category C_{ij_i} $i = 1, \ldots$, t, the number of units falling into this category is determined. Let this marginal frequency be $f \ldots j_i \ldots$ in the familiar dot notation.

(c) Under the assumption of fixed marginals and total independence of the attributes the probabilities of observing configurations $(C_{1j_1}, \ldots, C_{tj_t})$ are calculated from the data. From the multiplication theorem of probabilities the result

$$\pi_{1j_1} \ldots \pi_{tj_t} = f_{j1} \ldots \times f_{.j2} .. \times \ldots \times f \ldots j_t / n_t \tag{3}$$

is obtained.

(d) The expected frequency associated with configuration $(C_{1j_1}, \ldots, C_{tj_t})$ under the above assumptions becomes

$$e_{j1} \ldots j_t = n\pi_{1j_1} \ldots \pi_{tj_t} = f_{j1} \ldots \times f_{\cdot j2\cdot} \times \ldots \times f \ldots j_t / n^{t-1} \tag{4}$$

These are the quantities basic to all further calculations. The actual search for types can be performed by a number of methods applicable at both the exploratory and the confirmatory stages of an empirical study involving CFA.

2.1 Lienert's Original Test

According to Lienert's (1969) original proposal the following statistical criterion for a configuration $(C_{1j_1}, \ldots, C_{tj_t})$ to be a type needs to be satisfied apart from

$$f_{j1} \ldots j_t > e_{j1} \ldots e_{jt}: \tag{5}$$

$$L^2 = (f_{j_1} \ldots {}_{j_t} - e_{j_1} \ldots j_t)^2 / e_{j1} \ldots e_{jt}$$

when regarded as a chi-square value with $df = 1$ has an upper tail probability less than some prescribed significance level α. It is a prerequisite, however, that for the expected frequency $e_{j1} \ldots j_t \geqslant 5$ should hold. This is a conservative procedure of only heuristic value.

2.2 Kristof's Test

An immediate improvement over L^2 is obtained when in addition to a particular configuration $(C_{1j_1}, \ldots, C_{tj_t})$ the remaining configurations and the associated frequencies are considered. The total of the units can be divided into two classes according to whether a unit exhibits the configuration in question or not. The corresponding frequencies are $f_{j_1} \ldots {}_{j_t}$ and $n - f_{j_1} \ldots {}_{j_t}$, respectively. The expected frequencies under the same assumptions as before are $e_{j_1} \ldots {}_{j_t}$ and $n - e_{j_1} \ldots {}_{j_t}$. It follows that

$$K^2 = (f_{j_1} \ldots {}_{j_t} - e_{j_1} \ldots {}_{j_t})^2 \left(\frac{1}{e_{j_1} \ldots {}_{j_t}} + \frac{1}{n - e_{j_1} \ldots {}_{j_t}} \right) \tag{6}$$

is approximately chi-square distributed with $df = 1$. Evidently, $K^2 > L^2$. Hence (6) provides a test less conservative than (5). Through personal communication by the author test statistic (6) first appeared in Rittich (1988). With the abbreviations $f = f_{j_1} \ldots {}_{j_t}$ and $\pi = \pi_{1j_1} \ldots \pi_{tj_t}$ this relationship is equivalent to:

$$Z = (f - n\pi) / \sqrt{n\pi(1-\pi)}, \tag{7}$$

Z being a standard normal. This formula supplemented by the familiar continuity correction was given by Krauth (Krauth and Lienert 1973 p. 44, Krauth 1985a, and elsewhere). As to be expected, $Z^2 = K^2$. Obviously, Z is to be used as a one-sided test statistic.

2.3 Krauth's Test

Test statistic (7) is an asymptotic result for n large. If this condition does not hold so that the approximation by a standard normal is doubtful then Krauth's binomial test is preferable, for example, see Krauth and Lienert (1973) and Krauth (1985a). For a configuration $(C_{1j_1}, \ldots, C_{tj_t})$ with theoretical probability $\pi = \pi_{1j_1} \ldots \pi_{tj_t}$ and observed frequency $f = f_{j_1} \ldots {}_{j_t}$ the value

$$b = \sum_{i=f}^{n} \binom{n}{i} \pi^i (1-\pi)^{n-i} \tag{8}$$

is calculated. It gives the probability of observing f or an even larger frequency and may be compared with a preassigned significance level α according to a one-sided test.

2.4 Other Approaches

All of the foregoing tests are conservative. This is most pronounced with method (5) and probably least with (8). In each event, the performance of these techniques is generally known. The same cannot be said of Lehmacher's (1981) method. In this case the test statistic resembles (7) but the denominator is calculated in a different way. According to Krauth (1985a) and others it remains unknown whether the performance of Lehmacher's test is conservative or liberal in particular cases. Evidence for liberal performance has been gathered by Lindner (1984), Küchenhoff (1986), and Wüpper (1988).

Lindner's (1984) test is based on a generalization of the exact Fisher–Yates test for fourfold tables such that more than two attributes are admitted. In general the required calculations are too cumbersome to commend themselves despite the exactness of the test.

Wüpper (1988) modified Lehmacher's (1981) approach by the introduction of various continuity corrections, using Lindner's (1984) exact test as a criterion. However, Wüpper has not demonstrated generalizability of his recommendation as regards sample size or number of attributes and categories.

2.5 Alpha Adjustment

The various previously introduced statistical tests may also be employed during the confirmatory stage of the search for types. If just a *single* configuration is of interest then no problem regarding the significance level exists. For any chosen level α the corresponding critical value of chi-square with $df = 1$ or of the standard normal can be read off at once. This does not hold, however, when two or more such tests are to be carried out simultaneously. One must distinguish between a prescribed overall level α and the corresponding nominal level α^* to be used with the single tests so that the given α value for the total test may result.

Suppose it is hypothesized that k explicitly selected

configurations qualify as types, and suppose this composite null hypothesis H_0 is tested at the overall level α. Let the required level used with each single test be α^*. Acceptance of H_0 is equivalent to accepting each of the partial null hypotheses. If all the single tests are independent, then by the multiplication theorem for probabilities $1 - \alpha = (1 - \alpha^*)^k$. Since α^* is typically small, $(1 - \alpha^*)^k$ may be replaced by $1 - k\alpha^*$. Hence $\alpha^* = \alpha/k$ results. On the other hand, suppose that the single tests are totally dependent, that is, the same. Then, of course, $\alpha^* = \alpha$. Most cases, however, will assume an intermediate position somewhere between total independence and total dependence so that $\alpha/k \leqslant \alpha^* \leqslant \alpha$. Thus it is on the safe side if

$$\alpha^* = \alpha/k \tag{9}$$

is always chosen. This is the so-called Bonferroni adjustment of α. It is recommended for general use in the present context. For completeness Holm's (1979) somewhat more complicated method of adjusting α should be mentioned. Details may be found in Krauth (1985a).

There is still another variety of alpha adjustment. As has been said before, (7) is to be used as a one-sided test since only positive values of Z are in favor of $f > n\pi$. In other words, the significance level α is an upper tail probability of the standard normal. For instance, the minimal significant Z at the level $\alpha = 0.05$ is about 1.65 and not 1.96. So, when test (6) is employed, the corresponding minimal significant chi-square is not to be read off for $\alpha = 0.05$ but for $\alpha' = 2\alpha = 0.10$. It is not $3.84 \approx 1.96^2$ but $2.71 \approx 1.65^2$. The same applies when (5) is used. As a consequence, when simultaneous chi-square tests as provided by (5) and (6) are intended then the Bonferroni adjustment (9) should be modified. The previous α^* should be replaced by

$$\alpha' = 2\alpha/k \tag{10}$$

to be used with each single test so that the chosen overall α may result as a maximum. Employing the previous α^* rather than α' is unnecessarily conservative.

3. Derived Contingency Tables

So far general techniques have been described relevant to the search for types when a multidimensional contingency table is given. The case may arise, however, that new tables derived from the original one appear more adequate for further analysis. Such tables will be called "derived." The general techniques of analysis will remain appropriate nevertheless. In introducing derived tables it is convenient to follow Krauth's (1985a) enumeration of instances and also to adopt his example.

Four ways of obtaining a derived contingency table are presented. By way of illustration, an example with $t = 4$ attributes A, B, C and D, each with two categories, is employed. This yields $r = 2^4 = 16$ different configurations. The initial table is signified by $A{\cdot}B{\cdot}C{\cdot}D$, the dots separating the attributes. Combinations of attributes are indicated by AB, ABC, and so on, the categories by A_1, A_2, B_1, B_2, and so on. It is possible to apply consecutively different ways of getting a derived table.

3.1 Reduction of Dimension

A derived table with fewer dimensions results when the categories are combined across two or more attributes. By this process the total number of cells and the frequencies remain unchanged. In the extreme, all 16 configurations are strung out along one single dimension. For example, attributes A and B may be combined to form a new attribute AB with categories (A_1B_1), (A_1B_2), (A_2B_1) and (A_2B_2). This new table has only three attributes or dimensions but again $4 \cdot 2 \cdot 2 = 16$ cells. It may be signified by $AB{\cdot}C{\cdot}D$. Other derived tables of reduced dimensionality may be obtained in the same vein.

3.2 Marginal Tables

Such derived tables result if one or more attributes are deleted. This yields a lower dimensionality and a smaller number of cells. The new configurations are strings of fewer categories. Frequencies of old configurations which differ only with respect to deleted attributes are added and yield the frequencies of the new configurations. The sum of all frequencies remains unaltered. For example, if attribute D is deleted the three-dimensional table $A{\cdot}B{\cdot}C$ with $r = 2^3 = 8$ cells obtains.

3.3 Partial Tables

Fixing a category for one or more attributes leads to partial tables. In general, this will lower sample size n because only units that belong to the fixed categories are considered. The dimensionality is reduced as well. For example, if category A_1 of attribute A is fixed then the three-dimensional table $B{\cdot}C{\cdot}D \mid A_1$ is generated. It has $r = 2^3 = 8$ cells.

3.4 Anchoring to a Single Configuration

The term "anchor" is introduced here to denote a particular configuration or cell. This configuration consists of a certain sequence of categories pertaining to the attributes. Suppose that the categories not making up the selected configuration are combined attribute-wise so that each attribute is reduced to two categories. This procedure leads to another derived table. It is not applicable to the initial example $A{\cdot}B{\cdot}C{\cdot}D$ because there were only two categories per attribute anyway.

3.5 Interaction Analysis

Krauth and Lienert (1974) proposed procedures for investigating interactions of the attributes in a mul-

Table 1
CFA of attributes A_1, A_2, A_3

Configuration	Observed frequency	Expected frequency	Chi-square according to (6)
000	70	39.29	29.9
001	17	30.25	6.8
010	25	29.64	0.9
011	10	22.82	8.1
100	8	25.12	13.3
101	19	19.34	0.0
110	10	18.95	4.7
111	41	14.59	51.6

tidimensional contingency table. It may be interesting, for instance, to determine whether one or more of the initial attributes are immaterial for the existence of types. Let A be the attribute in question and form by reduction of dimension the two-dimensional table $A{\cdot}BCD$ with $2 \cdot 8 = 16$ cells. Calculate the associated chi-square value with $df = 15$ under the independence hypothesis. A will be retained only if no significant result emerges. Tables $B{\cdot}ACD$, $C{\cdot}ABD$, and $D{\cdot}ABC$ may be treated in the same vein. Suppose that A proves superfluous. Then, in a next step, the marginal table $B{\cdot}CD$ and so on may be analyzed until all irrelevant attributes have been eliminated.

The interpretability of an initially determined type becomes doubtful if the attributes can be partitioned into seemingly independent subsets of more than one attribute each. For example, the two-dimensional table $AB{\cdot}CD$ obtained by reduction of dimension with $4^2 = 16$ cells may be considered. There are no clear-cut rules on how to handle the matter, but a caveat is certainly in order.

Certain types may exist in one subpopulation but not in another. For instance, the partial table $B{\cdot}C{\cdot}D|A_1$ may yield a particular type consisting of categories of attributes B, C, D but the partial table $B{\cdot}C{\cdot}D|A_2$ may not.

Various procedures utilizing reduction of dimension and marginal and partial tables may be subsumed under the common heading "interaction analysis." The previously presented methods of searching for types remain basic. Interaction analysis is a means toward a better understanding of types although it is not a univocal and easily handled concept.

4. Numerical Example

By way of illustration, real data reported by Rittich (1988) will be used in an exploratory CFA. The area under investigation is complexity of writing styles in essays, the units being samples of such writing. Six dichotomous attributes capturing various aspects of complexity were originally defined. Three of them will be subjected to a CFA. These are A_1 = simple clause usage with categories 0 = simple clauses preferred, 1 = clauses at higher levels preferred; A_2 = complex sentence usage with categories 0 = no interrelated clauses or more complex sentences used, 1 = one or more such clauses or sentences used; A_3 = end of sentences with categories 0 = simple clauses preferred, 1 = higher levels preferred. There were $n = 200$ units. The CFA is summarized in Table 1. Under the hypothesis of independence of the attributes the total chi-square becomes 101.4 with $df = 2^3 - 3 - 1 = 4$. This is significant at a level α much lower than 0.001. Hence the existence of types (and antitypes) may be anticipated.

This being an exploratory study it is hypothesized that all configurations are either types or antitypes. To ascertain an overall significance level $\alpha = 0.05$, adjustment (9) is in order. This is so because types and antitypes are not specified so that two-sided testing with $\alpha^* = 0.05/8 = 0.00625$ is indicated. The critical chi-square value with $df = 1$ becomes 7.46. It follows from Table 1 that configurations 000 and 111 may be hypothesized to be types whereas 011 and 100 may well be antitypes.

Suppose now that the null hypothesis of independence of the three attributes had been confronted with the above alternative in a confirmatory study using the same data. Then $k = 4$. For overall significance a minimal chi-square of 8.1 is now prescribed. This corresponds to $\alpha' = 0.005$. According to (10), the null hypothesis would be rejected at an overall level $\alpha = 0.01$ in favor of the alternative. Considering the substantive content of the attributes, these results appear perfectly satisfactory.

5. Special Applications of CFA

It appears that most special applications of the general methods are analyses of tables derived from the original table by reduction of dimension, forming marginal or partial tables, anchoring to a single configuration and combinations of these operations. Hence a variety of derived tables are utilized. The methods of ascertaining types previously introduced remain basic.

One example is *prediction* CFA. Here the aim is to predict a certain combination of categories of a set 1 of attributes by means of another combination of categories of a set 2 of other attributes. References to details may be found in Krauth (1985a), for instance.

Another example is *multisample* CFA. One wishes to find *discrimination types* that distinguish between different populations of units. For instance, consider the four-dimensional table $A{\cdot}B{\cdot}C{\cdot}D$, each attribute being a dichotomy. Let D designate gender with categories D_1 = male and D_2 = female. By reduction of dimension the two-dimensional table $ABC{\cdot}D$ with

Table 2
Observed frequencies in a fourfold table

		Categories of Attribute 2		
		1	0	
Categories of Attribute 1	1	n_{11}	n_{12}	$n_{1.}$
	0	n_{21}	n_{22}	$n_{2.}$
		$n_{.1}$	$n_{.2}$	n

$8 \cdot 2 = 16$ cells is derived. Suppose it is necessary to know if configuration $(A_1B_2C_1)$ is a discrimination type by which males and females tend to differ. As a first step the table is now anchored to the configuration or cell $([A_1B_2C_1]D_1)$. This yields a fourfold table with categories $A_1B_2C_1$, not $A_1B_2C_1$ and D_1, D_2. Configuration $(A_1B_2C_1)$ will be recognized as a discrimination type as regards gender if the independence hypothesis for the attributes of said fourfold table can be refuted. The appropriate procedure in this case is the familiar chi-square test based symmetrically on all four cells, possibly with a continuity correction. The observed frequency of configuration $([A_1B_2C_1]D_1)$ must exceed its expected frequency and the test should be one-sided. This implies that the critical chi-square value for $df = 1$ and level α' should be read off for $\alpha = 2\alpha$. As an alternative, the exact Fisher–Yates test is applicable.

A further special application is *longitudinal* CFA as proposed by Krauth and Lienert (1980). Suppose there are a number of initial attributes. All combinations of categories across these attributes are formed and regarded as the categories of a new attribute. The effective attributes in a subsequent CFA are this new attribute observed on a number of units at various points in time. The dimensionality of the resulting table equals the number of time points. The search for *longitudinal types* is effected after anchoring the table to such hypothesized types. For further hints consult Krauth (1985a).

The above enumeration of special applications of the principles of CFA is by no means exhaustive. Rich materials are contained in Lienert (1988).

There are certain peculiarities worth noting as regards a fourfold table. This case has already been encountered in connection with multisample CFA. Consider Table 2. The notation is standard. The cells contain observed frequencies. Let e_{ij} be a typical expected frequency under the hypothesis of independence of the two attributes and fixed marginals. Determining the e_{ij}'s is standard. For configuration (1,1) to be a type it is necessary that $n_{11} > e_{11}$. Easy calculations show that the following equivalences hold:

$$\begin{aligned} n_{11} &> e_{11} \Leftrightarrow n_{22} \\ &> e_{22} \Leftrightarrow n_{12} \\ &< e_{12} \Leftrightarrow n_{21} \\ &< e_{21} \Leftrightarrow n_{11}\, n_{22} \\ &> n_{12}n_{21} \end{aligned} \tag{11}$$

An analogous chain of equivalences results on reversing the directions of the signs. This means that both (1,1) and (0,0) are types and both (1,0) and (0,1) are antitypes or both (1,0) and (0,1) are types and both (1,1) and (0,0) are antitypes if types occur at all. In the first case coefficient phi associated with the fourfold table is positive and in the second case it is negative. Hence both types and antitypes exist only in pairs diagonally arranged that make up the whole fourfold table.

For the search for types in the present situation the exact Fisher–Yates test may be utilized. Alternatively, the difference $(n_{11}/n_{.1}) - (n_{12}/n_{.2})$ may be tested for significance in the familiar way, that is, a one-sided test based on the standard normal results. Or else, the usual chi-square test for independence of the dichotomous attributes may be carried out equivalently. It is necessary, however, to replace α by 2α in order to ensure the required one-sidedness at level α.

6. *Relation to Other Methods*

There has been an attempt by Blasius and Lautsch (1990) to utilize CFA and correspondence analysis (CA) in a complementary way on the same data set. Correspondence analysis is an exploratory technique for the analysis of mainly two-dimensional contingency tables and has become quite popular. By combining initial attributes any contingency table can be transformed to the required format. Hypotheses may be generated by CA and then CFA may be used to test them. At present, however, any pronouncement as to the fruitfulness of such endeavors would be premature.

The relation of CFA to the analysis of multidimensional tables by log-linear modeling is quite close. The simple CFA model may be viewed as a log-linear model allowing only for main effects but no interaction effects. Configural frequency analysis is a sort of residual analysis that purports to find outliers that contradict the simple model. On the other hand, log-linear modeling is meant to describe the interaction structure as a whole. It is this particular structure which gives rise to types in the sense of CFA.

In an example analyzed by Lienert and Lehmacher (1982) three dichotomous attributes were used and all of the eight possible configurations proved to be types or antitypes. At the same time a log-linear analysis revealed only negligible correlations between any two attributes but a substantial trivariate interaction. This alone gave rise to the types and antitypes found. In a sense, CFA and log-linear modeling are two sides of a coin.

See also: Contingency Tables; Correspondence Analysis of Qualitative Data; Log-Linear Models

References

Blasius J, Lautsch E 1990 Die komplementäre Anwendung

zweier Verfahren: Korespondenzanalyse und Konfigurationsfrequenzanalyse. *ZA-Inform* 27: 110–33

Holm S 1979 A simple sequentially rejective multiple test procedure. *Scand. J. Statist.* 6: 65–70

Krauth J 1985a Principle of configural frequency analysis. *Z. Psychol.* 193(4): 363–75

Krauth J 1985b Typological personality research by configural frequency analysis. *Pers. Individ. Diff.* 6(2): 161–68

Krauth J, Lienert G A 1973 *Die Konfigurationsfrequenzanalyse* (KFA) *und ihre Anwendungen in Psychologie und Medizin*. Alber, Freiburg

Krauth J, Lienert G A 1974 Zum Nachweis syndromgenerierender Symptominteraktionen in mehrdimensionalen Kontingenztafeln (Interaktionsstrukturanalyse). *Biom. 16(3): 203–11*

Krauth J, Lienert G A 1980 Die Konfigurationsfrequenzanalyse. XII. Symptommusterfolgen (Durchgangssyndrome). *Z. Klinische Psychol. Psychother.* 28(4): 302–15

Küchenhoff H 1986 A note on a continuity correction for testing in three-dimensional configural analysis. *Biom. J.* 28: 465–68

Lehmacher W 1981 A more powerful simultaneous test procedure in configural frequency analysis. *Biom. J.* 23: 429–36

Lienert G A 1969 Die Konfigurationsfrequenzanalyse als Klassifikationsmittel in der klinischen Psychologie. In: Irle M (ed.) 1969 *Bericht über den 26. Kongress der Deutschen Gesellschaft für Psychologie in Tübingen, 1968*. Hogrefe, Göttingen

Lienert G A (ed.) 1988 *Angewandte Konfigurationsfrequenzanalyse*. Athenäum, Frankfurt

Lienert G A, Lehmacher W 1982 Die Konfigurationsfrequenzanalyse als Komplement des loglinearen Modells. In: Lienert G A (ed.) 1988

Lindner K 1984 Eine exakte Auswertungsmethode zur Konfigurationsfrequenzanalyse. *Psychol. Beitr.* 26(3): 393–415

Rittich R 1988 Configural Frequency Analysis. In: Keeves P (ed.) 1988 *Educational Research, Methodology, and Measurement: An International Handbook* Pergamon Press, Oxford

Victor N 1989 An alternative approach to configural frequency analysis. *Methodika* 3: 61–73

Wüpper N 1988 Auffindung und Identifikation konfiguraler Typen in sozialwissenschaftlichen Daten. (Doctoral dissertation, University of Hamburg)

Further Reading

Greenacre M J 1984 *Theory and Applications of Correspondence Analysis*. Academic Press, London

Lautsch E, von Weber S 1990 *Die Konfigurationsfrequenzanalyse* (KFA) Methoden und Anwendungen. Volk und Wissen, Berlin

von Eye A 1990 *Introduction to Configural Frequency Analysis*. Cambridge University Press, Cambridge

W. Kristof

Conflict and its Management in Educational Organizations

Conflict, overt or latent, is endemic to educational organizations because of their sensitive roles as regulative social agencies. From an international perspective, the wide range of conflicts which occur, remain latent, or are suppressed, and the array of strategies available for their management by administrators, make a simple taxonomy of conflict or its management of questionable use. However, even a brief discussion would illustrate that these variations offer fruitful terrain for research into the comparative relations of state and society. There appears to be a link between the nature of particular educational conflicts and the degree to which the advancement of social cohesion, technical expertise, or social mobility has been institutionalized as the responsibility of the school.

1. Origins of Conflict

One salient feature of education in modern nation-states is that it is promoted as uniquely empowered to regulate civic consciousness, human capital formation, and intergenerational mobility. Whereas in the past other morally integrative or productive agencies—e.g., the church, the army, or the crafts guild—made schooling appear dispensable for mass society, this is no longer the case anywhere in the world. On the contrary, contemporary education leaders worldwide would claim these responsibilities as justifications for expanding the boundaries and purposes of their institution.

Conflicts typically are sparked by competition over the personal or group benefits commensurate with this expansion—and the world's educational conflicts are marked by numerous intraorganizational struggles for supremacy, or simply a greater share of the benefits. Naturally, in poorer countries where education assumes the largest share of government spending, battles over proceeds are pitched. However, and more fundamentally, because of the broad role or "charter" schooling is given by most modern societies, there is a latent tension over the expanded domain that has been subsumed under the term "education."

A comparative perspective shows school systems in which, to a greater or lesser degree, education is seen as the legitimate media of mobility, training, and social integration. Conflicts are fought or managed because this legitimacy can be lost as well as won. Especially in societies undergoing rapid change, the institutionalization of school responsibilities is frequently contested. This is likely when demographic, geopolitical, or economic changes occur outside the decision-making authority of the education system. Beyond the control of the organization are such events as change in population through immigration or fertility decline, depreciation in the relative competitiveness of local labor in a world market, even (as seen in Eastern Europe) transformations of national sovereignty and identity. These events may lead the public to rethink the place of schooling in society.

Therefore, the perceived legitimacy of education in generating cohesion, expertise, and mobility is a product of larger social forces which are not manageable from within the organization. For this reason, it is often the case that educational conflicts appear (from the manager's perspective) to spill over the organizational boundaries which are imagined to exist, and to present themselves as lateral with respect to the hierarchy of the system.

At these times, managers may attempt to narrow the goals and retract the boundaries of their organization in order to buffer themselves and deflect responsibility for unfulfilled expectations. After a period of expansion in the 1960s, for example, school leaders in many industrialized nations began to emphasize a more "professional" approach to tasks which were less broadly defined as social responsibilities. Hence there was a renewed emphasis on "basic skills" and, concomitantly, on the need for families and community organizations to reclaim areas of responsibility for child development.

2. Types of Conflict

Conflicts surface not only when the potential clients, organized in other types of systems, resist encroachment by the new educational organization (e.g., in societies where religious groups resist secular education). Conflicts also surface when the very expectations raised by schooling (e.g., for meritocracy, productive employment, or political participation) come back to assert themselves as demands on the organization. Actors situated outside the system often see their interests as coincident with its integrity rather than its destabilization.

Sociologists such as Meyer see this as inevitable because, as an institution, education processes participants and nonparticipants alike by certifying and legitimating expertise and knowledge. Because education affects nonparticipants indirectly, all groups are in some sense potentially parts of the educational organization, and potential souces of conflict. As a consequence, it can be said that the ultimate power of the organization to manage conflict is not technical or instrumental but, rather, lies in the "institutional exoskeleton" of education (Meyer 1980 p. 49).

A dilemma arises because the same regulatory authority to increment knowledge and gauge expertise also has a potential to assume a life of its own. For example, once education is declared a universal right, those who aspire to the social mobility perceived in the status of "expert" will not easily be persuaded that existing educational arrangements are anything other than the exclusive mechanisms for achieving the legitimate goals of mobility, training, or political socialization. Skillful educational managers are careful to avoid engendering "unrealistic" expectations in the public, regardless of the short-term political gains for their organization.

During periods of stress, expectations remain unmet if schools are perceived to lose the authority to govern political socialization, technical training, or social mobility. In late Imperial China, for example, the perceived corruption of the examination system—through which access was gained to the bureaucracy—led eventually to the Taiping rebellion (Ho 1962). Some Black Americans resist socialization by curricula and institutions they regard as "Eurocentric," and opt for separate schools, engendering conflicts seen as separatist and tribalistic by White educators (Kirp 1991). Meanwhile, some White Americans agree the system imposes too much, and encroaches on their "traditional" communities, precisely because it *does* try to legitimate an integrated vision of society, including positive images of African, Asian, and Mexican heritage (Post 1992). In Sweden, Same (Lapp) parents have in some cases resisted integration and assimilation, partly through a revival of traditional symbols of solidarity (the Reindeer Herder's Association), but chiefly through the educational institution itself. The alternative Lapp Folk High School (Paulston 1976) illustrates the way education becomes the focus of conflicts when social cohesion is institutionalized as a goal of public schooling.

3. Responses to Conflict

In a responsive system, legitimacy is protected by incorporating into the organization disaffected elements and producing change. When systems are less responsive, or when cooptation occurs without change, conflicts may arise which appear lateral or external to administrators. Results of the former stance might include the Chinese student movement of May 1989; the 1986 student movement in Mexico exemplifies the ultimate fruits of cooptation. Because of the defensive posture of the administrative process vis-à-vis the public, and the buffering represented by professionalization, administrators who are adept at handling organizational conflict may be unprepared for the lateral demands of central governments or disaffected groups who see themselves as excluded from the system (Zeigler et al. 1984). Yet, perhaps in part because of changing demographics or the reduced economic returns from school participation, such political as opposed to organizational conflicts appear increasingly to face administrators: a study of urban superintendents in the United States (Wirt and Christovich 1989 p. 31) concluded that under progressively more stringent conditions numerous conflicts began to originate from outside of the organization.

One possible defense is a "permanent posture of reform" (Meyer 1980 p. 51) by school leaders, who may depict *themselves* as crusading outsiders. More generally, as lines of defense against conflict, the boundaries of educational organizations are subject to continual redefinition by a variety of actors, including groups at the helm as well as groups which claim to be excluded by unresponsive educational organizations. Because of this ongoing redefinition, in practical terms there is little point in distinguishing between actors within or without the bounds of the formal organization: not only do actors move back and forth across its boundaries, but the definition of the system itself responds to opportunities and threats by encroaching or retreating. Thus, even Clark's (1983) comparative study of the higher education system, which has a far narrower charter than does the educational enterprise generally, explicitly merges organizational and political conflict by ignoring whether actors are inside or outside of the organization at any given time.

4. Cases of Conflict

Four brief examples may be cited of the ways that conflict is associated with the institutionalization of the ideals of cohesion, training, or mobility as part of the educational charter. The first two examples are cases of comparative colonialism: Taiwan under the Japanese, and Hong Kong under the British. The other two cases are from modern Latin America: the unsuccessful 1972 Peruvian educational reform, and the failed decentralization of decision-making in Mexico during the 1980s.

4.1 Taiwan

Taiwan was acquired as a spoil of war by Japan in 1895. The colonial education strategy was guided by the negative example of the British in India where educational expansion had engendered nationalism instead of loyalty. In Taiwan, Japanese administrators like Uchida Kakichi felt that, "A colonial education system must correspond to social conditions and the people's cultural level. It is absolutely inadvisable to teach advanced courses . . . The people of Taiwan should be taught practical skills so they may earn a living and enjoy happiness" (cited in Tsurumi 1977 p. 49). One member of the Japanese Diet wrote for an American audience that Japan followed a different policy to that of France or the United States "which endeavor to transplant in their colonies the laws and civilization of the mother country, and to assimilate the natives in the quickest way possible . . . [Japan] must respect the manners and customs of the natives" (Tsurumi 1977 p. 82). This *laissez-faire* attitude prevailed until the end of the First World War, when the seeds of nationalism began to germinate and President Woodrow Wilson's doctrine of Self-determination began to cause unrest in the Japanese protectorate of Korea.

With the arrival of Governor-general Motojiro Akashi in 1918 assimilation became the linchpin of Taiwanese education. Whereas previously a network of traditional Chinese schools had existed alongside of newer colonial institutions, after 1918 the government aggressively pursued political socialization in the classroom, especially by promoting the Japanese language. All routes to social mobility and training were then linked with the assimilation policy, since the only higher education institutions open to Taiwanese were those located in Japan. This policy may have avoided the degree of nationalist fervor engendered among Indian intellectuals by the comparatively expanded higher educational opportunities allowed by the British. However, other unanticipated reactions occurred which led ultimately to the same consequence: because of the small number of Taiwanese who could receive advanced education, demands for access began to focus on the legitimacy of the educational system itself, and opponents eventually directed their ire against the colonists. Institutionalized, the goals of the education system affected those outside its purview, leading to demands for access which, when frustrated, helped cause a legitimation crisis in the colonial system.

4.2 Hong Kong

In Hong Kong up until 1895 public funding had been available both to Chinese- and English-medium schools. Thereafter only English-language schools remained eligible for support. The reason for this was that the rationale for government involvement had changed when Orientalists were replaced by progressive, moralistic functionaries in the newly empowered Education Department. These men held the sincere opinion that "Europe's destiny is to govern Asia," in the words of Hong Kong's chief Inspector of Schools, E J Eitel (Ng 1984 p. 85). But an unintended consequence of emphasizing English-language instruction was that the government lost its regulatory power over Hong Kong's village schools and—more importantly—over dozens of new schools established after the turn of the century by proponents and antagonists of the decadent Ching court. A 1912 inspection discovered that many students were under the mistaken impression that Hong Kong was a part of China. This led to the 1913 "Ordinance to Provide for the Registration and Supervision of Certain Schools," under which school managers could be sanctioned for failing to register with the government.

The government returned to funding Chinese-language schools. However, it avoided placing broader social responsibilities with schools to avoid the ideological penetration of the Education Department by opposing groups. By carefully insulating the bureaucracy from social demands, the government was able to delay until relatively late the institution of free primary schooling (1971) and free lower-secondary schooling (1977). Wisely, the then Governor of Hong Kong, Murray MacLehose, decided to universalize lower-secondary schooling before conflicts could arise by parents demanding it. Moreover—and most crucially in terms of maintaining the organizational boundaries of the system—MacLehose's government never presented free education as a social reform at all: in place of a social rationale, the 1974 White Paper (promoting free secondary schooling) explained only that "this program should go far to provide for the children of Hong Kong the standards of education which they need if they are to be properly equipped to fend for themselves and serve their fellows in the competitive world of the next decade." Couched apolitically, detached from a broader social agenda, and free from the influence of interest groups or parties who might later claim credit, the entire issue of public education remained a technocratic one to be resolved by the professionals who buffered the organization from conflict.

As autocracies, it never appeared essential for the state in colonial Taiwan or Hong Kong to make public schools the channels of vertical mobility, a feature which Sorokin (1927) had predicted would eventually characterize modern societies. The educational institutions of both colonies were given a narrow charter, in this regard. In Taiwan, but not in Hong Kong after 1913, the government did attempt to use schools as a legitimate means of political socialization. In a sense, conflict arose because of political movements outside the organization whose leaders could not be incorporated or completely coopted because they could never become English or Japanese. The legitimacy of the organization's charter began to be questioned at the point when its own logic of regulative norms for mobility and training were seen as inconsistently applied in the case of Taiwan (advocating assimilation, but restricting access). Japanese manipulation of education policy was aimed at defusing latent nationalism and conflict, but actually had the opposite effect. On the other hand, conflict in Hong Kong was circumvented by an even narrower charter for education. Since 1913, relatively mild attempts had been made to socialize students as British subjects. The identity of the Hong Kong Chinese was not challenged directly, and this may have contributed to the lower expectations parents had of the colonial government as compared with Taiwanese expectations of the Japanese administration.

4.3 Mexico

In Mexico, the centralized control of education is a legacy of the revolution: the architect and first head of the Secretary for Public Education (SEP) was José Vasconcellos, a leader in the establishment of modern Mexican political culture. Moreover, public education became crucially important for the nationalist project of the revolution, and the curriculum became a laboratory for various attempts to build a political culture among its unequally empowered, multilingual, multiracial populations (Vasquez 1975). With the SEP capping the highly centralized administration of education, it also became the focal point for conflict after the price of oil plummeted in the late 1970s. With falling national revenues, and amid devaluation of the peso, teachers' salaries also suffered and militancy arose within the normally quiescent, government-aligned union (the National Union of Educational Workers, the SNTE). Because Mexico has been governed continuously by the *Partido Revolucionario Institutional* (PRI), actors outside the party apparatus or its affiliated labor syndicates have been seen as threats to the integrity of the bureaucracy. Cooptation has been the preferred means of checking these potential threats. This strategy worked while there was an expanding economy, and growing benefits for all, but with a fiscal crisis and major recession in full swing by the early 1980s, cooptation within the SNTE failed to stem labor unrest among its 600,000 members.

Under the Lopez Portillo administration (1976 to 1982) deconcentration was attempted (McGinn and Street 1986). Personnel functions were delegated to Mexico's 31 state governments in an attempt to fragment the bargaining process. However, the centrality of schooling to the ideology of the PRI's development policies, and the jealousy for control on the part of the central bureaucracy, led only to a partial effort at real decentralization: teachers' salary schedules, revenue generation, curriculum, and (most important) contract negotiations remained in the hands of the SEP. Expectations of the educational organization by the public also figured prominently in the failure to stem the unions' demands on the SEP. Parents accustomed to delivery of curriculum and services from Mexico City, who had never been granted local institutions for the control of their children's schools, were unwilling to believe that decentralization was anything other than a ploy to stem teacher militancy. A new independent labor movement led by the National Coordinator of Educational Workers (CNTE) forced the government to make concessions to the PRI-dominated SNTE. More recently, the Salinas Gortari administration tried an indirect approach to reducing the federal role in education. By emphasizing "modernization" and increased competitiveness in a world market for skills, Salinas attempted to defuse the nationalist potential of education as an appeal to parents and labor groups. The success of this redirection is likely to depend upon Mexico continuing both to sustain economic growth and to satisfy teachers and the social demand for education.

4.4 Peru

Peru's 1972 educational reform (in tandem with the country's agrarian reform) ranks among the world's most ambitious attempts to refocus an entire system outside of a violent revolutionary process. The main goals were the establishment of preprimary, nonformal education for children; decentralization through the creation of school districts; bilingual (Spanish–Indigenous) instruction; and technical alternatives to university postsecondary education. There was also, as in the case of Mexico, a strong nationalist component. The 1972 law, issued by military decree, stated that education should: "awaken in the Peruvian people a critical awareness of their condition and stimulate them to adopt actions, rooted in knowledge, which will make them participants in the historical process of removal of the old structures of dependence and domination, and convert them into free men committed to forging the future of the country."

In implementing the reform, the military government sought to bypass the militant, Maoist-oriented teachers union and deal directly with the public. As in the case of Mexico, the previous centralization of authority in the hands of the Ministry of Education—albeit mediated in Peru by a truly oppositional union—eventually made the reform unworkable.

Many observers have commented on the lack of continuity within the military government, which changed leadership after 1976, and the partisan battles over control of the new school districts. Most of Peru's left-wing parties, which might have been allies in the struggle to inject anti-imperialism and nationalism into the educational organization instead became antagonists because the reform was vertically imposed. More generally, it can be seen in retrospect how little power the government had to recreate its relationship with the public. In the words of one leading educator, Luis Jaime Cisneros: "If I say: 'Come all parents, and build with me an educational reform,' that reform will go to the devil! Parents only want their children to escape from their own socioeconomic situation. And this has nothing to do with education."

On nearly every front the reform failed to refocus goals of public education because of expectations engendered during previous, neoliberal administrations (influenced in part by international development agencies). Indigenous parents opposed bilingual education because they saw it as channeling their children into "dead-end" careers. Nonformal preschool and adult education were seen as an empty gesture. The school districts were seen—perhaps rightly—only as conduits of directives issued from Lima. The clients who had been cultivated by the system to demand university access were unwilling to accept any other alternative to it.

The problems of the stymied reform were not limited to the military government however. In 1985, elected to office with Peru's best organized, best disciplined, and oldest political party, Alan Garcia's government could do no more. Its Minister of Education, Grover Pango, was reduced to exhorting the public that "the over-valuation of the university as an instrument of social change taxes it with a burden that should be shared by society as a whole." This tendency was related, said Pango, to "the widespread illusion that in university study one finds the only and the best way to achieve one's personal goals in life." As Pango's plea went unheeded students were paralyzing many of Peru's universities throughout the country, now grown to number almost 50 in the hemisphere's poorest nation.

Conflicts from outside of the educational organization were nevertheless linked to it: in the rural areas of Peru student support of a messianic insurgency (the *Sendero Luminoso,* or "Shining Path") derived partly from frustration with an education system perceived as failing to deliver social mobility or training for productive employment (Post 1988).

5. Conclusion

Drawing a single conclusion from the world's educational conflicts, and managers' responses to them, would be highly suspect. However, among the many lessons one insight into state–society relations does emerge. Because the education system exists first and foremost in the minds of its eligible participants (i.e., all members of modern societies), redefining its domain is not automatic or mechanical. Paradoxically, the degree to which conflicts arise within or without organizational boundaries depends on how successful the system was previously in monopolizing under its charter the responsibilities for cohesion, training, and mobility. Once these responsibilities are assumed by central bureaucracies, and the boundaries have been extended, retracting them (as in both the "decentralization" and "privatization" types of reform) is not easily accomplished. Conflicts arise because of the institution's inherent power to process its own environment, as well as to respond to it. For, once institutionalized, education is not a dynamic, adaptive organization which simply molds itself to the preference orderings of its clients. Rather, institutional organizations generally have the power to adapt the environment to their own capabilities, to "find" problems corresponding to the solutions they offer society (Perrow 1972 pp. 199, 162). Uniquely, as an explicit part of the social charter granted to education, that institution assumes an authority to *create* preferences in its clients: for values (e.g., patriotic), skills (certifiable), and regulative norms (meritocratic).

If the concept of power is to include at least the potential to impose outcomes on actors which may be contrary to their interests (Lukes 1974 p. 34) then, in the most literal sense, education is powerful. Nor can educational organizations be precisely understood (cf. Collins 1975 p. 289) as "arenas for conflicting interests." Rather, the organization is granted a partial authority to *define* the interests of its clients, and an authority to instill the regulative norms and beliefs necessary for their legitimacy. The Uruguayan reformer José Pedro Varela, writing in 1874, typifies this authority: "To establish a republic, the first step is to form republicans . . . And all the great necessities of a democracy, all the requirements of a republic, have only one possible means of fulfillment: to educate, to educate, and still to educate" (cited in Rama 1983 p. 18). The promise of conflict appears inherent in the promise of education in the modern nation-state.

See also: Governance: Relations among Levels of Government; Micropolitics of Schools; Religious Issues in Education; School Reform and Restructuring; School-based Management

References

Clark B 1983 *The Higher Education System: Academic Organization in Cross-national Perspective*. The University of California Press, Berkeley, California
Collins R 1975 *Conflict Sociology: Toward an Explanatory Science*. Academic Press, New York
Ho P T 1962 *The Ladder of Success in Imperial China*. Columbia University Press, New York
Kirp D 1991 Textbooks and tribalism in California. *Public Interest* 104: 20–36
Lukes S 1974 *Power: A Radical View*. Macmillan, London
Meyer J W 1980 Levels of the Educational System and Schooling Effects. In: Bidwell C, Windham D (eds.) *The Analysis of Educational Productivity*, Vol. 2. Ballinger, Cambridge, Mass.
McGinn N, Street S 1986 Descentralization educational: politica nacional o lucha de facciones? *La Education* 99: 20–45
Ng L N 1984 *Interactions of East and West: Development of Public Education in Early Hong Kong*. Chinese University Press, Hong Kong
Paulston R G 1976 Ethnic revival and educational conflict in Swedish Lapland. *Comp. Educ. Rev.* 20(2): 179–92
Perrow C 1972 *Complex Organizations: A Critical Essay*, 2nd edn. Scott, Foresman and Co., London
Post D 1988 Political goals of Peruvian students: The foundations of legitimacy in education. *Sociol. Educ.* 61(3): 178–90
Post D 1992 Through Joshua Gap: Curricular control and the constructed community. *Teach. Coll. Rec.* 93(4): 673–96
Rama G 1983 Education in Latin America. *CEPAL Review* 21: 13–38
Sorokin P A 1927 *Social and Cultural Mobility*. Harper, New York
Tsurumi E P 1977 *Japanese Colonial Education in Taiwan, 1895–1945*. Harvard University Press, Cambridge, Massachusetts
Vasquez J Z 1975 *Nacionalismo y educacion en Mexico*. El Colegio de Mexico, Mexico City
Wirt F M, Christovich L 1989 Administrators' perceptions of policy influence: Conflict management styles and roles. *Educ. Admin. Q.* 25(1): 5–35
Zeigler H, Kehoe E, Reisman J 1984 *City Managers and School Superintendents: Response to Community Conflict*. Praeger, New York

Further Reading

Street S 1983 Burocracia y educacion: hacia un analisis politica de la desconcentracion administrativa. *Estudios Sociologicos* 1(2): 239–62

D. Post

Confucian Theory of Human Nature and Development

Over the centuries in Chinese culture four books have represented the core of the Confucian philosophical tradition. The first of these is the *Analects of Confucius*, a collection of brief proverbial sayings attributed to the teacher and social philosopher after whom the tradition was named, Confucius or Kung Fu-tzu (551–479 BC). Second is *The Book of Mencius*, composed by the sage Mencius or Meng-tzu (c. 372–289 BC), a student of Confucius' grandson. The last two books, *The Great Learning* and *The Doctrine of the Mean*, were written somewhat later but are still considered to be faithful representations of Confucius' beliefs.

In Chinese society prior to the twentieth century, these four classics served as the material to be mastered by candidates for the civil service examinations that determined who would be awarded positions in the imperial government. In the late twentieth century, the four continue to be viewed by followers of Confucian philosophy as the most authentic description of the proper conduct of life in the well-ordered political state. The four can also be used as the source of a Confucian theory of proper human development.

The version of Confucian theory offered here has been formulated by the writer's addressing a series of questions about human development to the contents of the four books, then organizing the derived answers under four topics: (a) personality structure, (b) the goal of development, (c) learning theory, and (d) implications for child rearing and education.

1. Personality Structure

From a Confucian perspective, human nature is divided into two general types, the physiological and the virtuous. The physiological represents lower level characteristics and is disposed toward certain aspects of the world of behavior—the mouth disposed to tastes, the eye to colors, the ear to sounds, the nose to odors, and the four limbs to ease or rest. The higher level of human nature is that of virtue, which makes the difference between humans and brutes. Unlike animals, humans innately possess a heart that is sensitive to the suffering of others. This sensitive heart is a composite of the four hearts containing virtues—hearts of compassion, of shame, of courtesy and modesty, and of a sense of right and wrong.

In the heart of compassion is the seed of the virtue of humanity (*jen*). The heart of shame is the basis for righteousness (*i*). The heart of courtesy and modesty is the source of the observance of the Confucian rites (*li*). And the heart of right and wrong is the source of wisdom (*chih*). These four are the origin of all other virtues people develop.

Although human nature consists both of physiological needs and of virtues, in Confucian philosophy the fulfilment of physiological needs is chiefly in the hands of fate, while achieving the virtues depends upon the individual.

According to Mencius, although a person at birth is endowed with a positive human nature (a sense of virtue), he or she does not necessarily preserve it forever. Environmental influence can exert a profound impact on the preservation and nurturing of this nature. Mencius illustrated this point by comparing life to a forest. The trees can be felled by the axe, and even though new seedlings spring up, cattle can consume them, so the hillside remains denuded. It is not because the forest was never there but that it has been cut down. In like manner, each person is born with a virtuous nature, but the circumstances of his or her life thereafter will determine whether he or she will nuture or lose that nature.

However, people are not simply the victims of life's circumstances. External influences are not so crucial in determining a person's development as is self-cultivation. Virtue will be maintained and developed only if the individual continues to cultivate it throughout the lifespan. Even under difficult conditions, people should not cease cultivating their original nature. Indeed, a person can benefit from unfavorable circumstances, gaining strength of character by struggling against adversity. Mencius wrote: "When Heaven is about to place a great burden on a person, it makes him suffer starvation and hardship, frustrates his efforts so as to shake him from his mental lassitude. It thus toughens his nature and corrects his deficiencies" (Liang Cheng-t'ing 1958 p. 324).

In summary, all people are endowed by Heaven with the same nature at birth. The differences observed among people as they develop are due to how well they nurture their original endowment. People behave badly because they have allowed themselves to lose virtue. However, even when apparently lost, the inner strength of human nature always exists in the mind and is rediscoverable if a person seeks to recover it.

2. The Goal of Development

The goal of development and of life is to maintain and enhance *jen*, which is the sense of humanity. By achieving *jen*, the individual becomes a superior person. The key characteristics of *jen* are sincerity, righteousness, filial obligation, and reciprocal respect in relationships with others. *Jen* is founded on love—first, love of one's parents, then of neighbors, and ultimately of all humans. Proper social relations are built on *li*, meaning courtesy and modesty as defined by the rules of traditional social patterns. A person who possesses *jen* is sincere in speech and behavior and without pretense. What he or she says or does is the true expression of what he or she thinks.

Jen is formed by giving attention to two agents, self and others. As for the self, individuals develop their own personalities through recognizing the meaning and value of their own natures and through accepting the responsibilities of life. Then they draw inferences about others on the basis of the way they perceive themselves. In a passive mode of interacting with others, if an individual does not want something done to him or her by others, he or she will in turn not do it to others. In an active mode, he or she not only performs acts of self-development but also helps others develop themselves as well. As Confucius wrote in the *Analects*, "You yourself desire rank and standing; then help others achieve rank and standing. You want to turn your own merits to account; then help others turn theirs to account" (Ch'ien Mu 1964 Book 6, p. 90).

In summary, the goal of development is *jen*, the perfection of self-understanding and the extension of this understanding and love to encompass others and their welfare. By achieving these characteristics, it is possible to become a superior person, evidencing all of the human virtues. Thus an individual attains the perfect life.

In pursuit of self-development, a person bears the responsibility constantly to: (a) sharpen sensations—visual and auditory—in order to examine people and events clearly, (b) be gentle and respectful in manner, (c) speak sincerely and with care, (d) ask others' advice on matters about which he or she has doubts, (e) control his or her temper when angry, and consider carefully the likely result of different sorts of reactions when angry, and (f) when seeing an opportunity for personal gain, think primarily about what would constitute righteous behavior in such a situation.

Of overriding concern in a person's social relationships is that of filial obligation—the responsibility to parents. Sons and daughters of all ages are to accept and execute their parents' commands and to support their parents with worldly goods, love, and personal service.

3. Learning Theory

A learning theory derived from analysis of Confucian writings can be viewed in terms of a learning hierarchy, how a person learns, and the relationship of ability to effort.

3.1 Steps in the Learning Hierarchy

The book *The Great Learning* postulates a learning hierarchy which consists of seven levels, each built on the successful completion of the levels below it. At the top of the hierarchy, the ultimate aim is that of producing peace and enlightenment for all humankind. Starting at the bottom of the hierarchy, it is possible to identify the way each successive level becomes a necessary foundation for the next higher one and thus contributes to the final goal of universal peace and enlightenment.

(a) *Step 1: Investigating objects and events.* The author of *The Great Learning* proposed that everything in the world operates according to principles, and the human mind is formed to understand these principles. The first step of learning is to use the intellect to investigate the principles, to understand the essence of each object and event. This is called knowing the roots.

(b) *Step 2: Extending one's knowledge.* After analyzing the principles of all events perceived over a long period of time, an individual is able to apprehend the quality of every object and event, whether internal or external, refined or coarse. Through such a process knowledge is extended to its limits.

(c) *Step 3: Making the will sincere.* Sincerity or authenticity means no self-deception. It is the process of becoming true to oneself and then of extending this understanding and sincerity to others.

(d) *Step 4: Controlling one's mind so as to cultivate one's life.* According to Confucianism, such emotions as wrath, fear, fondness, and worry or anxiety all exist in people's hearts. When these emotions are kept in balance, the person can control them. But when the emotions are unduly aroused, they control the individual. Thus, by means of sincerity, which enables a person to examine his or her emotions clearly, a person can control the emotions and prevent his or her behavior from being misguided. This ability to control the emotions is called cultivating one's life.

(e) *Step 5: Regulating the family.* When the members of a family achieve each of the first four steps, they are equipped to carry out their individual responsibilities within the group in an amicable manner, with the parents in charge of the group and the sons and daughters willingly performing the tasks they are assigned. In essence, step 5 consists of the members learning to operate efficiently as a small social system.

(f) *Step 6: Bringing order to the state.* Confucian belief holds that since the state is composed of families, if all of the families are well-regulated, then the state will be properly regulated as well. The individual family members' knowledge, sincerity, self-cultivation, and skills of living within the family social system form the elements that ensure the state operates efficiently.

(g) *Step 7: Achieving world peace and enlightenment.* When each state operates efficiently on the basis of knowledgeable, sincere, and socially skilled individuals, peace and enlightenment for all of humanity are achieved.

As the hierarchy illustrates, the ultimate aim of Confucian theory is the good society and not simply the good or efficient or happy individual. However, since the goal of the good society can be achieved only if the individuals composing it are good, the theory necessarily centers initial attention on developing each individual into a superior person.

3.2 How People Learn

The learning process consists of the interaction of "doing" and "thinking". Doing means the learner searches for varied sources of knowledge. For example, the learner first reads books or gains wider personal experiences. However, it is useless merely to memorize what has been read or experienced. Rote memorization is not learning. What is needed in addition is thinking, in the sense of organizing and comprehending how new experiences relate to other aspects of life and knowledge.

Both processes, the doing and the thinking, are necessary for learning. Doing, in the sense of reading widely or encountering life experiences, can result in useless memorization, while thinking based on limited reading or experience leads to error, for the individual lacks the breadth of resources to verify conclusions.

3.3 Ability and Effort

Confucianism holds that most people are born with similar mental capacity or ability to learn. Therefore, differences among individuals in their knowledge or virtue result chiefly from the effects of learning and, to a lesser degree, from such environmental factors as opportunities to learn or the models of behavior of the people around the individual. In Confucian theory, only a very few "naturally superior persons" have an innate ability to "know" without having to learn what they come to know. And, at the other end of the ability scale, few people are mentally incapable of learning.

Consequently, since it is assumed that most people have similar potential, what they know and how virtuous they are is the result of effort, of how diligently they have dedicated themselves to study. The assumption is that no matter how difficult the task, a person can succeed if he or she tries hard enough. Therefore, failure is not attributed to level of ability or the difficulty of the task, but rather to the amount of effort expended. *The Doctrine of the Mean* (Liang Cheng-t'ing 1958 p. 107) urges:

> When there is anything not yet studied, or studied but not yet understood, do not give up. When there is any question not yet asked, or asked but its answer not yet known, do not give up. When there is anything not yet thought over, or thought over but not yet apprehended, do not give up. . . . When there is anything not yet practiced, or practiced but not yet earnestly, do not give up.

4. *Implications for Child Rearing and Education*

Confucian theory does not distinguish between characteristics of childhood and of adulthood. The general process of developing *jen* and becoming a superior person is essentially the same at all stages of life. Therefore, no special suggestions are offered for child rearing. However, from the theory's postulates about the nature of humans and the goal of life, it is possible to infer several implications for child-raising practices.

First, since children are born with a basically virtuous nature (including the seeds of compassion, shame, courtesy, modesty, and a sense of right and wrong), adults should recognize the child's good nature and further develop it. The child should also be taught such traits as honesty, good faith, and respect for others that are founded on his or her original virtuous nature. More specifically, Confucian writings suggest that the child learn poetry and music to nourish his or her nature, since these arts not only harmonize the emotions but also stimulate the mind.

As noted above, Confucianism stresses the development of people as social beings, as elements of the family and of the broader society. As a consequence, the child needs to learn the rules of social relationships (li) so as to become a mature participant in society. This process is called ritualization. For instance, in the parent–child relationship, children are to obey parents in all things. In the sibling relationship, older children take precedence over younger ones, with the older guarding the younger and the younger respecting and obeying the older. In relations with friends, a person should always be sincere and faithful.

While environmental forces are not as crucial in development as personal effort, the environment can exert some influence in terms of the opportunities for learning that are available. Parents and teachers should arrange the child's environments so as to furnish proper models to imitate and a wide range of useful experiences. To illustrate, a well-known story of Mencius' boyhood describes the boy and his mother living near a funeral parlor, and as a consequence young Mencius was soon imitating the way funeral processions were conducted. Since his mother wished to avoid such an influence, she moved their abode to a market district, where Mencius began imitating the buying and selling activities. Again his mother disapproved of the neighborhood's influence, so she moved to a dwelling adjacent to a school where Mencius learned to study. Accordingly, Confucian doctrine would suggest that a proper environment is one in which people behave according to *jen* and *li*.

A further recommendation to parents and teachers is that they urge the growing child to concentrate diligently on learning tasks and not give up readily, since the main ingredient of success in Confucian theory is the amount of effort expended to achieve a goal.

Finally, since rote memorization is regarded as an inadequate form of learning, the growing child should not only be provided with a wider range of experiences to remember (including such vicarious experiences as are found in books) but should also be guided to analyzing the remembered experiences so as to decide what generalizations can be drawn and what implications they hold for achieving personal *jen* and a peaceful and enlightened society.

See also: Human Development: Cross-cultural Approaches; Human Development: Cultural and Religious Concepts; Philosophy of Education: Historical Overview

References

Ch'ien Mu 1964 *Lun-Yo Yao Lueh*. Shang-wu, Taipei
Liang Cheng-t'ing 1958 *Kuang Chiai Ssŭ Shu Chin Ku*. Hsa-sin, Taipei

Further Reading

Kuo Chieh-ming 1969 *San-tzŭ-ching Ching Chiai*. Hung-yeh, Taipei
Liu I-Shêng 1963 *Lun-Yu Piao Chiai*. Chinese Publishing Committee, Taipei

Lin Huey-Ya

Conscientization and Mobilization

The experience of educators, concerned clergy, and community workers in Latin America produced the realization that traditional approaches to education for adults were largely irrelevant for those who lived in poverty and misery, and, even worse, served to further entrench the structures and power relationships that were the causes of the problems. An alternative form of education was needed, one which allowed the learner to see the situation differently, understand the larger causes, and take personal responsibility to create changes. While many have been involved in the evolution of these ideas, they were crystallized by the thought and writing of Paulo

Freire, a Brazilian educator, in his seminal work *Pedagogy of the Oppressed*, which introduced the concept of "conscientization." This and later writings proved enormously influential in the following decades, spreading slowly from Latin America to North America, and then echoed by the work of others in Asia and Africa (see *Critical Approaches to Adult Education*).

Application of the insights of Freire and others to adult education took many forms, encapsulated by terms such as "conscientization," "nonformal education," "popular education," and "education for social mobilization." The use of these terms is varied and frequently overlapping, although distinctions are often argued fiercely on the basis of the ideological beliefs of proponents.

1. Conscientization

Although the concept of "conscientization" was known and used by other radical Catholics in Brazil before Paulo Freire, the term has come to be synonymous with him and his explication of it as an idea and a process. Mackie (1981) describes Freire's philosophy as an eclectic mixture which was not built up systematically, but which emerged and continues to be shaped through praxis—the continuing cycle of action and reflection. Freire drew upon a variety of European philosophers and from the many radical Catholics writing in the context of Latin America, yet his philosophy originated in his experiences with poor adults in the Third World and was addressed explicitly to the oppressed of the Third World. His pedagogy for adults is grounded in the social reality of the poor and the need to address their reality as the first priority in any approach to adult education.

1.1 Adult Literacy—Learning to Read the World and the Word

Initially, Freire's approach to adult education arose from his experiences with poor adults in Recife, Brazil in his role as municipal coordinator for adult literacy. There he developed "culture circles" as alternative learning environments for adults where active, critical dialogue could take place. Work with the culture circles evolved into a more fully developed literacy method which can be briefly summarized in a few lines. Working with community members, Freire and his colleagues chose generative themes which reflected the social and political realities of the learners' lives—themes which engaged workers in problematizing their situation. These themes were then captured in a series of generative words which had the emotional impact needed to stimulate discussion and which contained the core phonemes of Portuguese. Typically they chose words with two or three syllables, beginning with words containing simple syllables common to the language such as "*tijolo*" (brick) or "*favela*" (slum). Each of the syllables could then be used to explore the family of syllables so that the "*ti*" in *tijolo* expands into the syllables "*ta te ti to tu*." From these syllables new words can be formed. A total of about 16 or 17 words was sufficient to cover the basic sounds for syllabic languages like Portuguese or Spanish (for a sample list of words, see Freire 1973 pp. 82–84). In Latin America, this approach is known as the "psychosocial method."

The first step, though, was to use a picture or drawing of the concept contained in the word to discuss its meaning in the local context. The picture of a brick provokes discussion of building with bricks, housing as a community problem, and the obstacles to better housing. The word itself was presented only after this discussion took place. He explicitly rejected primers which use an external message rather than the words and thoughts of the learners because he believed that they lead to domesticating rather than liberating education by encouraging uncritical acceptance.

Freire's approach to literacy has stimulated the development of literally hundreds of adaptations to a wide variety of literacy and adult education situations throughout the world. Srinivasan (1977) reports another approach, the Apperception–Interaction Method (AIM), that was used in functional literacy programs in the United States, Thailand, the Philippines, and Turkey. This method uses problem themes from the daily lives of learners, starting with a provocative photograph or drawing complemented by a short drama or narrative to stimulate discussion. A word or phrase is then introduced based on the theme. The Nicaraguan Literacy Crusade of the early 1980s also provides a good example. Miller (1985) describes the evolution of the methodology which used pictures, dialogue, and a series of 23 keywords beginning with the word "*la revolución*."

In many cases, there is tension between the desire to create primers which contain content viewed as essential, particularly in immediate postrevolutionary situations like Nicaragua, and Freire's pedagogy which argues that the themes and the conclusions must come from the learner if they are to be truly liberational. Srinivasan (1977 p. 91) feels similarly that materials must be truly open to local concerns rather than constraining the learners to react to content chosen by the curriculum designers. Most programs confront this tension when they move beyond pilot activities to larger scale implementation.

1.2 Conscientization—Overcoming the Psychology of Oppression

To interpret Freire's theory of conscientization as solely, or even primarily, a method for achieving adult literacy would seriously underestimate his importance. Following in the footsteps of Fromm, Fanon, and Memmi, Freire's theory is a description of the psychology of the oppressed, an analysis of how the oppressed and the oppressor behave, and a pedagogy for freeing both from the structures of oppression.

Conscientization is the humanization of people, transforming them from objects to subjects, from dehumanized individuals trapped in oppressive structures to more fully human beings (see Freire 1970 pp. 27–56). Since both oppressed and oppressor are trapped in the same structure, both are dehumanized and both need to be liberated. Liberation comes about through a painful process of rebirth in dialogue between humans, and between humans and the world. Critical and liberating dialogue must be part of a dialectical process between action and reflection, which Freire calls "praxis." Neither reflection nor action alone is sufficient.

The central point of Freire's philosophy is mirrored in the title of his book—*Pedagogy of the Oppressed* (1970). Oppression cannot be overcome by well-intentioned actions on the part of individual oppressors. Only the oppressed can initiate the process of praxis which has the power to free both themselves and their oppressors. The oppressed must move from seeing themselves as objects to people engaged in the vocation of becoming more fully human. In the process, they will come to understand that the oppressors are also trapped in the same dehumanizing structure. Only the oppressed can free themselves through a process of reflection and action to transform the dehumanizing situation. Conscientization is the process by which the oppressed liberate themselves and their oppressors.

Freire articulates three levels of consciousness which characterize individuals in the struggle to overcome oppression: magical, naive, and critical. In each stage, individuals name (problematize), reflect, and act in characteristic ways which reflect their stage of consciousness (see discussion in Smith 1976). These levels are characterized as follows:

(a) The magical state—conforming—is characterized by problem denial or avoidance, simplistic causality which focuses on things like lack of money or poor health, and inaction justified by fatalism or passively playing "host to the oppressor."

(b) The naive state—reforming—names the problem as individual oppressors who are bad, accepts the oppressor's ideology and explanations for what is essentially a good system, and actively plays "host to the oppressor" by defending them and blaming the oppressed for acting inappropriately.

(c) The critical state—transforming—names the problem as the whole dehumanizing structure, affirms the goodness of the oppressed and their values, and understands the contradictions that trap both the oppressors and the oppressed. The critical individual is self-actualizing, seeking to transform the system through acting as a subject, having faith in one's peers, and working to change the structure.

Conscientization is the process of growth through these stages, although the process is uneven, with individuals often regressing or being in different states simultaneously in different contexts.

Freire's lifetime of writing, speaking, and doing, the veritable library of references and writings which it has inspired, and the legion of followers who have been energized by his insights have all combined to have a significant effect on adult education efforts around the world. Anywhere there is a group which feels oppressed, one is almost certain to find an educational effort informed in part by Freire's analysis of oppression and his vision of a pedagogy which can liberate. These efforts are as much present in the First World—gays and lesbians, racial or ethnic groups, women's groups, native peoples—as they are in the Latin American setting in which Freire first worked.

2. *Popular Education*

La Belle (1986) documents a conceptual split between consciousness raising, as exemplified by Freire and others, and popular education for structural change. Torres (1990 p. 18) traces popular education back to at least the socialist education process in Mexico during the 1930s. Popular education, then and now, is characterized as being oriented toward political development, is highly participative and mobilizing with an emphasis on social change, and is sensitive to the structure of power in society. Freirean approaches became so well-known in the 1970s that they tended to be co-opted into official, government adult education programs which kept the rhetoric without being liberatory in nature. Partly in response to the perceived failure of consciousness raising and the nonformal education programs which sometimes incorporated it, popular education has gained new prominence, emphasizing social class, participatory organizations, and strategies for the transformation of society.

Current popular education is heavily influenced by the Marxist perspective of Antonio Gramsci, particularly his vision of cross-class coalitions to support change movements rooted in the lower classes and his concept of organic intellectuals—peasants and workers who serve as linkages between concrete knowledge and general knowledge, local and national issues, and social formation and the mode of production (Fals-Borda 1981). Gramsci argued for the organization of workers to counteract the hegemony of the state and its support for the interests of the dominant classes. The focus of popular education is therefore on preparing the lower classes to take advantage of opportunities to exercise power in an organized manner that will alter the balance of power in capitalist societies. This emphasis is in contrast to the more individualistic psychological and intellectual awareness produced by consciousness raising efforts. Popular education recognizes that consciousness raising is an important component of social change, but that it is inadequate on its own. Current popular education activities often begin with some form of participatory investigation by the community (referred to also as "action research," "participatory action research," or "participatory education"). Using a dependency perspective, Fals-Borda, for example, says that knowledge is produced by and reflects the class interests of the dominant groups. He promotes four techniques: collective research by the group to gather information, a critical recovery of local history from the perspective of the people, valuing and using popular culture to support social mobilization of the people, and production and diffusion of new knowledge generated by these methods. The organizations and the awareness created by participatory research constitutes the foundation for ongoing education and action for social change.

A typical example of a popular education activity is provided by the Learning Workshops Program in Chile which has been in operation since 1977 and has served over 10,000 children (Vaccarro 1990). The Learning Workshops are alternative learning centers for poor children who have dropped out of school. The workshops are run by community adults who serve as monitors and coordinators. They are trained with a participatory process which leads them to problematize the reality which has created the poverty and the children who are unable to learn in school. The workshop becomes an activity which is "appropriated" by the community as one way in which they can begin to transform their reality. The process of appropriation begins immediately, when the initial proposal offered by an external agent is subject to discussion and modification by the participants and grows throughout the process until they become independent.

La Belle (1986 pp. 210–14) uses three goals to assess the outcomes of popular education: development of local participatory organizations, forging of linkages across and within social classes to generate power for the poor, and designing strategies to shift concentrations of power to the poor. He concludes that the evidence to date of success with popular education is limited: not being noticeably more successful than earlier community development approaches in building nondependent, participatory organizations, making some gains in forging within class alliances, and having little impact on power concentrations. However, the support for popular education approaches remains strong, partly because it provides a means for the oppressed to participate effectively in local development.

3. Conclusion

Conscientization and popular education are unique as development approaches because they originated in the Third World and speak from the realities of that setting, not from those of the First World. The rich ferment generated by peasants, workers, local leaders, intellectuals, and scholars, initially in Latin America but now increasingly throughout the world, has forced the development industry to recognize the social and human costs of dominant approaches to development. Yet within conscientization and popular education tensions continue to emerge between local generation of knowledge and the use of these techniques as a means for mobilizing a society in support of new national ideologies. The role of conscientization and social mobilization will continue striving to build effective linkages between micro-level and macro-level development, trying to balance national economic power with the rights and needs of people. For many knowledgeable and concerned educators, these approaches offer the only hopeful alternatives.

See also: Ideologies in Adult Education; Politics and Governance of Education; Critical Approaches to Adult Education; Adult Literacy Programs in Developing Nations; Nonformal Education Policy in Developing Nations; Adult Education: Concepts, Purposes, and Principles; Empowerment Skills, Acquisition of; Marxism and Educational Thought

References

Fals-Borda O 1981 The challenge of action research. *Development* 23(1): 55–61

Freire P 1970 *Pedagogy of the Oppressed.* Herder and Herder, New York

Freire P 1973 *Education for Critical Consciousness.* Seabury Press, New York

La Belle T J 1986 *Nonformal Education in Latin America and the Caribbean: Stability, Reform or Revolution?* Praeger, New York

Mackie R 1981 Contributions to the thought of Paulo Freire. In: Mackie R (ed.) 1981 *Literacy and Revolution: The Pedagogy of Paulo Freire.* Continuum, New York

Miller V 1985 *Between Struggle and Hope: The Nicaraguan Literacy Crusade.* Westview Press, Boulder, Colorado

Smith W A 1976 *The Meaning of Conscientizacao: The Goal of Paulo Freire's Pedagogy.* The Center for International Education, University of Massachusetts, Amherst, Massachusetts

Srinivasan L 1977 *Perspectives on Nonformal Adult Learning: Functional Education for Individual, Community, and National Development.* World Education, New York

Torres C A 1990 *The Politics of Nonformal Education in Latin America.* Praeger, New York

Vaccarro L 1990 Transference and appropriation in popular education interventions: A framework for analysis. *Harv. Educ. Rev.* 60(1): 62–78

Further Reading

Arnold A et al. 1991 *Educating for a Change. A Handbook*

for Community Educators. Between the Lines/Doris Marshall Institute for Education and Action, Toronto
Barndt D 1989 *Naming the Moment: Political Analysis for Action: A Manual for Community Groups*. The Jesuit Centre, Toronto
de Kadt E 1970 *Catholic Radicals in Brazil*. Oxford University Press, Oxford
Fals-Borda O, Rahman M A (eds.) 1991 *Action and Knowledge: Breaking the Monopoly with Participatory Action-Research*. Apex Press, New York and Intermediate Technology Publications, London
Freire P 1972 *Cultural Action for Freedom*. Penguin, Harmondsworth
Freire P 1978 *Pedagogy in Process: The Letters to Guinea-Bissau*. Seabury Press, New York and Writers and Readers Publishing Cooperative, London
La Belle T J 1987 From consciousness raising to popular education in Latin America and the Caribbean. *Comp. Educ. Rev*. 31(2): 201–17
Magendzo S 1990 Popular education in nongovernmental organizations: Education for social mobilization. *Harv. Educ. Rev*. 60(1): 49–61
Zachariah M 1986 *Revolution through Reform: A Comparison of Sarvodaya and Conscientization*. Praeger Greenwood, New York

D. R. Evans

Constructivism and Learning

The idea that learning is a constructive process is widely accepted; learners do not passively receive information but instead actively construct knowledge as they strive to make sense of their worlds. Empirical support for this position is provided by numerous studies that demonstrate that the understandings that students acquire in instructional situations are frequently very different from those that the teacher intended. Three general instructional implications that follow from constructivism are: (a) priority should be given to the development of meaning and understanding rather than the training of behavior, (b) researchers and teachers should assume that students' actions are rational given the way that they currently make sense of things, and (c) students' errors and unanticipated responses should be viewed as occasions to learn about students' understanding (von Glasersfeld 1989).

Although the basic notions and implications of constructivism are generally supported, it is possible to distinguish between realist and radical positions. The key issue that differentiates the two positions concerns the general function of cognition. From the realist perspective, cognition is the process by which learners eventually construct mental structures that correspond to or match external structures located in the environment. In contrast, radical constructivists consider that cognition serves to organize the learner's experiential world rather than to discover ontological reality.

1. Realist Constructivism

1.1 Assumptions and Tensions

The assumption that students learn by reorganizing their mental structures while interacting with the physical and symbolic environment is common to the various theoretical accounts of cognitive functioning proposed by realist constructivists. A philosophical dilemma arises because learners do not have direct access to the external environment; they can only interpret it in terms of their current knowledge structures. Consequently it is impossible, in principle, to explain how they can construct internal knowledge structures that correspond to the structure of the environment. At a deeper level, the dilemma can be traced to the Cartesian dualism that is created by separating the knower from the environment to be known. In practice, most realist constructivists ignore the philosophical dilemma by making the working assumption that it is useful to treat true or correct knowledge as a reflection of ontological reality. Cognitive research can then pursue the task of specifying increasingly sophisticated knowledge structures, culminating with those that are assumed to match the structure of the environment.

1.2 Implications

A wide variety of instructional approaches have been proposed and studied by realist constructivists. In general, approaches that characterize thinking as a sequence of cognitive behaviors that manipulate incoming information to generate responses have fallen from favor since the 1980s. The more influential approaches of the 1990s instead focus explicitly on the development of conceptual understanding and attempt to ensure that this understanding guides the performance of skills and procedures. For example, analyses conducted in this tradition lead to the recommendation that the construction of procedures for adding and subtracting multidigit numbers should be related to the development of place value understanding. One instructional strategy is to use Dienes blocks that represent 1, 10, 100, and 1,000, and to develop instructional tasks so that students' actions with the blocks will inform their paper and pencil procedures (Fuson 1990). The results of a series of studies conducted by Fuson demonstrate that the computational performance of 7- and 8-year old students taught in this way is significantly superior to that of students who received traditional United States textbook-based instruction. Fuson's work also illustrates the more general strategy of designing external instructional representations that are said to embody the structures or relationships to be learned in a transparent or readily apprehensible way. In the course of the learning process, students construct mental representations that accurately mirror the structure of the instructional materials in their environment.

Other realist approaches concentrate on the teachers' knowledge rather than instructional tasks. For example, Carpenter et al. (1989) reasoned that teachers who understand research-based models of students' conceptual development will make more informed interpretations of their students' thinking. These interpretations would then guide the teachers' selection of developmentally appropriate tasks. Carpenter and his colleagues have used this approach in the area of elementary addition and subtraction word problems with promising results. A working hypothesis of this work is that students construct internal cognitive structures that mirror the semantic structure of increasingly complex arithmetical word problems.

1.3 New Challenges

The basic assumption that viable mental structures mirror the structure of ontological reality implies that what counts as correct or true knowledge does not depend on social or cultural circumstance. Vygotsky (1934) argued that knowing is relative to the situations in which knowers find themselves and numerous more recent studies have demonstrated that cognition is both socially and culturally situated. This is true even of the seemingly most objective type of knowledge, namely mathematics (Carraher et al. 1987). These findings have led several prominent researchers to reconsider the assumption that a fixed, given physical and symbolic environment is the primary source of knowledge. Increasingly, the view of isolated students interacting with the environment is being displaced by the notion that students are members of classroom communities. Knowing then becomes a social as well as an individual activity in which students explain and justify their thinking as the teacher guides their enculturation into the intellectual practices of their society. The challenge that lies ahead for realist constructivism is to reconcile the characterization of knowing as the ability to participate in the intellectual practices of their society, with the view that it involves the construction of cognitive structures which mirror an environment that exists independently of human activity, culture, and history.

2. Radical Constructivism

2.1 Assumptions and Tensions

Radical constructivism has its roots in a variety of disciplines, but has been most profoundly influenced by the theories of the Swiss psychologist Jean Piaget as interpreted and extended by von Glasersfeld 1989). In general, radical constructivists believe that learners construct increasingly sophisticated ways of knowing solely on the basis of their personal experiences as they attempt to achieve their goals by resolving situations that they find problematic.

Radical constructivists have repeatedly challenged realist constructivists' working hypothesis that true knowledge mirrors ontological reality. However, in stressing that each person lives in the world of his or her own personal experience, radical constructivists have implicitly accepted the Cartesian dualism between ontological reality and the knower. Realist constructivists locate the knowledge to be learned at one pole of the dualism, ontological reality, and radical constructivists locate it at the other pole, subjective experience. Realists have argued that the radical position is solipsistic in that it implies each person inhabits their own private world. In addition, they contend that the notions of truth and certainty thereby have to be relinquished. Radical constructivists typically refute the first charge but usually accept the second.

In practice, radical constructivists necessarily assume that certain aspects of their experiential worlds are given, fixed, and shared with others when they conduct their investigations. For example, when conducting a study of university students' learning of, say, calculus, radical constructivists typically assume without question that students share their understanding of whole number arithmetic. Implicit working hypotheses of this type are, however, subject to revision if a student's activity calls them into question.

2.2 Implications

Given the emphasis on personal experience, radical constructivists initially tended to derive general instructional aphorisms from analyses of individual students' learning. However, since 1987 an increasing number of researchers have used radical constructivism as a general orienting framework within which to develop instructional approaches, frequently in collaboration with teachers. In addition, several approaches developed by researchers working outside the radical constructivist framework are highly compatible with this theoretical position. For example, an approach called Realistic Mathematics Education (RME) described by Treffers (1987) reflects the view that mathematics is an experientially based human activity. Treffers and his colleagues at the Freudenthal Institute in the Netherlands argue that learning occurs as students develop effective ways to solve problems, and involves the reorganization of thinking at increasingly sophisticated levels. One of the characteristics of RME is its contention that the first phase of the learning process should involve an extensive exploration of a range of specific situations drawn from everyday life or from students' physical or imagined reality. This view can be contrasted with the instructional representation approach advocated by some realist constructivists. There, the knowledge to be learned is embodied in physical materials, diagrams, or computer graphics in ways designed to make it readily apprehensible to students. From the perspective of

RME, the instructional challenge is to develop sequences of tasks that support students' reorganization of their initially informal activity at increasingly sophisticated levels. Textbooks based on this approach have been used widely in the Netherlands at a range of age levels with considerable success.

In addition to considering the design of instructional tasks, radical constructivists have broadened their focus from the individual student by analyzing the role that social interaction plays in learning. As a consequence, instructional approaches that emphasize small group collaborative work and whole class discussions in which students are expected to justify their thinking have become increasingly prominent since the 1980s. In these approaches, great emphasis is placed on the teacher and students openly negotiating their interpretations of and solutions to instructional tasks. One of the teacher's responsibilities is then to guide the classroom community's establishment of consensual meanings. These meanings in turn become part of the basis for further discussions. Human et al. (1989) have implemented such an approach to elementary school mathematics on a wide scale with promising results. In developing their approach, these researchers have questioned whether it is necessary for students to learn the standard procedures for arithmetical computation. They argue instead that students should be encouraged to construct their own personally meaningful computational algorithms. This approach can be contrasted with the program developed by Fuson. There, the objective is to help students learn the standard computational algorithms in a meaningful way. This difference between the two programs brings to the fore a more general issue, namely, to what extent students' constructions in school should conform to those currently institutionalized in wider society in this era of rapid technological change.

2.3 New Challenges

Like realist constructivists, radical constructivists have been influenced by studies that demonstrate that knowing is socially and culturally situated. On the one hand, the finding that intellectual practices in subject-matter areas differ from one cultural community to another is consistent with radical constructivists' rejection of knowledge as a mirror of ontological reality. On the other hand, the relative homogeneity of these practices within a community sits uncomfortably with radical constructivists' emphasis on the personal experiences of the individual. In particular, it would seem that social interaction is not merely a catalyst for individual cognitive development, but that knowing is, in some sense, intrinsically social. Radical constructivists are therefore faced with the challenge of elaborating their theoretical orientation so that it encompasses both collective activity and individual experience. In this regard, analyses that relate cognitive development to either didactical situations (e.g., Brousseau 1986) or to classroom social interaction patterns (e.g., Bauersfeld 1988) would appear to be of great relevance.

3. Emergent Trends and Issues

Realist and radical constructivists' developing views of the teacher and students as members of a classroom community indicates that a rapprochement could be possible. However, each group will have to transcend the Cartesian dualism it has erected between ontological reality and subjective experience if this possibility is to be realized. For their part, realist constructivists would need to question their working hypothesis that knowledge can be given fixed, ahistorical foundations. The view that what counts as true or certain knowledge evolves historically and differs from one cultural group to another is now widely accepted in a variety of disciplines ranging from literary criticism to the philosophy of mathematics. It is also becoming increasingly clear that this view does not lead to an intellectual anarchy in which any interpretation or opinion is as good as any other. In contrast, radical constructivists might come to the conclusion that their rejection of the possibility of true and certain knowledge both feeds on the realist position and contradicts personal, common sense experience. They would therefore have to develop ways to rehabilitate the notions of truth and certainty.

The theoretical problem of transcending the Cartesian dualism has its correlate in the activity of teachers. The view that true knowledge corresponds to the structure of a pregiven environment carries with it the risk that the adult's view of the world might be imposed on students at the expense of their individual needs and interests. Conversely, a view which focuses solely on students' personal experiences might downplay the teacher's obligation to enculturate students into the intellectual practices of their society. According to Lampert (1985), this tension between accommodating students' interests and pushing them to act in accordance with institutionalized intellectual practices is an endemic aspect of teaching. Perhaps constructivists who transcend the Cartesian dualism will be in a better position to help teachers cope with this deep-seated tension that pervades their attempts to help students learn with understanding.

See also: Culture and Learning; Learning Theories: Historical Overview and Trends; Preconceptions and Misconceptions

References

Bauersfeld H 1988 Interaction, construction, and knowledge: Alternative perspectives for mathematics education. In: Grouws D, Jones D (eds.) 1988 *Effective Mathematics Teaching*. National Council of Teachers of Mathematics and Lawrence Erlbaum Associates, Reston, Virginia

Brousseau G 1986 Fondements et methodes de la didactique des mathematiques. *Recherches en Didactique des Mathematiques* 7(2): 33–115

Carpenter T P, Fennema E, Peterson P L, Chiang C, Loef M 1989 Using knowledge of children's mathematics thinking in classroom teaching: An experimental study. *American Educational Research Journal* 26(4): 499–532

Carraher T N, Carraher D W, Schliemann A D 1987 Written and oral mathematics. *Journal for Research in Mathematics Education* 18(2): 83–97

Fuson K C 1990 Conceptual structures for multiunit numbers: Implications for learning and teaching multidigit addition, subtraction, and place value. *Cognition and Instruction* 7(4): 343–403

Human P G, Murray J C, Olivier A I 1989 *A Mathematics Curriculum for the Junior Primary Phase*. University of Stellenbosch, Research Unit for Mathematics Education, Stellenbosch

Lampert M L 1985 How do teachers manage to teach? Perspectives on problems in practice. *Harv. Educ. Rev.* 55(2): 178–94

Treffers A 1987 *Three Dimensions: A Model of Goal and Theory Description in Mathematics Instruction—The Wiskobas Project*. Reidel, Dordrecht

von Glasersfeld E 1989 Constructivism in education. In: Husén T, Postlethwaite T N (eds.) 1989 *The International Encyclopedia of Education*, 1st edn., Supplementary Vol. 1. Pergamon Press, Oxford

Vygotsky L S 1934 Voprocy detskoi vozrastnoi psikhologii. In: El'konin D B (ed.) 1984 *L. S. Vygotskii. Sobranie Sochineni: Detskaia Psikhologiia*. Pedagogika, Moscow

Further Reading

Davis R B, Maher C A, Noddings N (eds.) 1990 *Constructivist Views on the Teaching and Learning of Mathematics*. Journal for Research in Mathematics Education Monograph No. 4. National Council of Teachers of Mathematics, Reston, Virginia

Piaget J 1970 *Genetic Epistemology*. Columbia University Press, New York

Saxe G B 1991 *Culture and Cognitive Development: Studies in Mathematical Understanding*. Erlbaum, Hillsdale, New Jersey

Steffe L P, Wood T (eds.) 1990 *Transforming Children's Mathematics Education: International Perspectives*. Erlbaum, Hillsdale, New Jersey

von Glasersfeld E (ed.) 1991 *Radical Constructivism in Mathematics Education*. Kluwer, Dordrecht

P. Cobb

Consumption Benefits of Education

The consumption benefits of education are treated in this entry as the nonmonetary returns accruing from education to the individual throughout his or her lifespan. As such, they include not only the nonmonetary satisfactions enjoyed by the student while in school, but also the contribution made by education to the efficiency of household production and final consumer satisfaction during leisure time before and after retirement, plus the contribution made by homemakers during the nonmarket time spent in household management and child rearing.

Many of these consumption benefits have been measured. This research has largely followed the lament by Schultz in surveying the earlier literature that "all these studies omit the consumption value of education . . . It is a serious omission . . . The available estimates of earnings from education in this respect all underestimate the real value of education" (1967 p. 300). The most fruitful empirical results have been achieved by use of the theory of household production as developed primarily by Becker (1975 pp. 67–68, 1976 Chap. 7) and as extended and surveyed by Michael (1972, 1982). The results of further empirical research, which are summarized below, find that education makes positive contributions to many types of nonmarket activities involving significant cognitive or education-related affective attributes—activities such as maintaining the health of family members, earning a higher rate of return on savings, improving the children's school achievement and preschool IQ, increasing the efficiency of household purchasing, and staying out of jail. Some studies find education counterproductive for the more mundane household (and workforce) tasks, since it causes time to be diverted from those tasks where education contributes less to productivity, such as dishwashing, mending, ironing, and the more time-intensive aspects of child rearing. For example, the findings of Lemennicier (1978) and Levy-Garboua and Jarousse (1978) are analogous to similar counterproductive effects found for comparable time-intensive tasks in the workplace by Rumberger (1981) and others.

The following material focuses on those studies that control in some way for the purely market benefits of education to avoid double-counting the satisfactions secured through the use of education in the workplace. This summary excludes nonmonetary satisfactions of the job (Duncan 1976), since these derive from the use of market time. The private consumption benefits from education considered below exclude externalities and spillover benefits which accrue to the society (or to other jurisdictions) above and beyond those that accrue to the individual. This entry also focuses on those microeconomic studies that test for measurable nonmarket effects—there is some work on the macro level, however, by Eisner and Nebhut (1981), McMahon (1981), and Kendrick (1979) that expands imputed values in the national income and product accounts to include an imputed value for the services of the education of homemakers in total consumption, and hence in total product and total productivity.

1. Consumption Benefits

Consumption benefits of education can be regarded

as those that fall within the "new theory of consumer behaviour" (see, e.g., Becker 1976 pp. 87–150), even though most occur later in the life cycle and therefore can alternatively be viewed as a nonmonetary return on an investment. Higher earnings are a pure investment return, however, and hence are considered separately under investment returns (Psacharopoulos and Hinchliffe 1973, Psacharopoulos 1993) and under expected rates of return to education (McMahon and Wagner 1982). In considering consumption benefits, those studies will not be included that do not eliminate the benefits from education due to higher earnings.

1.1 Pure Current Consumption Effects

There are the current satisfactions enjoyed when schooling itself is enjoyable—particularly at high-school and college levels and in leisure-time courses—plus current services provided by local schools to the family such as hot lunches, community center services, and childcare. Although these can be observed, little has been done to measure them beyond one study by Lazear (1977) and aspects of some cost–benefit studies of daycare services by Gustafson (1978) and others.

1.2 Health

There is strong evidence that education contributes to better health. Numerous studies show that education is highly correlated with good health, and highly significant work by Grossman (1976) considerably refines this. He controls for the individual's income, IQ, health status as a teenager, and wife's schooling, to find an effect of education on health status by age 46 that is about 40 percent as strong as the effect of education on wages. He finds that the wife's schooling has an even bigger positive effect on the man's health than does his own schooling. Those with more education live longer; each additional year of schooling lowers the probability of death by 0.4 percent. Lando (1975) finds less work-disability, and in a later study, Grossman, again holding income and other factors constant, finds that the children of more educated women tend to have healthier teeth, are less likely to be anemic, and are less likely to be obese. Cochrane and her coresearchers estimate that one additional year of the mother's education is associated with a reduction of nine per thousand in infant mortality, and an additional year of the father's education with a reduction of one-half that amount (Cochrane et al. 1980). Although the positive effects of schooling on the individual's own health, and of the woman's education on the health of her children are now well-documented, no study has yet examined the effect of the education of the husband on his wife's health.

1.3 Other Effects on Family Life

Leibowitz (1974), using Ben-Porath's well-known model of the household production of human capital over time, finds that a mother's education and pre-school home investments in children significantly raise the child's IQ. Benson (1982) finds that families of high socioeconomic status tend to limit television viewing and pay more attention to whether or not the child does his or her homework, factors positively related to school achievement. The number of years of college planned by White male and by Black male college freshmen has been found by McMahon (after controlling for family income, ability, and all financial aids) to be positively influenced by the education of the parents (McMahon 1976 p. 322).

Ben-Porath neutrality implies that the young person's past education is productive in further education, as every school admissions officer knows, but also that this is only at the cost of its equal productivity in the market. This is not an issue when considering the productivity of education in the home during leisure time, however (since in this case there are no forgone earnings), or when considering how the education of the parents contributes to the further education of the child in exchanges within the family.

1.4 Returns on Savings

Solomon (1975) finds that the level of education among respondents in a survey of members of the Consumers Union, after controlling for income and occupation, has the strongest relation to choosing the best inflation hedge for their savings.

1.5 Consumption Behavior

Michael (1972, 1982) finds that those consumers with higher levels of education shift their spending patterns among consumption items, behaving as if they have more real income (over and above the higher money earnings that they also have). He estimates this real income effect of schooling on nonmarket production of consumption satisfaction to have an elasticity of 0.5, an effect about 60 percent as great as the comparable relation of schooling to money earnings.

1.6 Expected Consumption Benefits

From preliminary evidence, consumption benefits appear to average 50–60 percent of the monetary returns expected by students from their higher education. In a survey in which 5,000 students were each asked to appraise the value of the nonmonetary leisure-time returns to them relative to the expected monetary returns, McMahon (1974) finds that students in fields such as music placed the expected nonmonetary returns above the expected monetary returns, while those in medicine and business tended to place them far below. In a 1984 study, McMahon also finds that expected earnings tend to have a relatively stronger influence on most student and family educational investment decisions, an influence that is even more pronounced at the more advanced levels.

Within the sphere of nonmarket behaviour, however, education is more productive in some household activities than in others. Lemennicier (1978) challenges Michael's important simplifying assumption that education is technologically neutral among these activities—an assumption that eventually had to be challenged—which allows schooling to affect the relative price of time within the household. He finds that this causes time to be diverted from those types of activities which are time-intensive, so that in these activities education is counterproductive. He finds, for example, that a very large proportion of the time budgets of French housewives is occupied by dishwashing, and although he agrees with the positive effects of education on health, schooling, and saving behavior, which require cognitive and affective skills, the overall shifts away from dishwashing, mending, ironing, and analogous activities in the time budgets of the more educated French housewives leads him to conclude that education is counterproductive in these forms of household production. This is consistent with the now numerous research studies by Gustafson (1978), Levy-Garboua and Jarousse (1978), Ferber and McMahon (1979), and others documenting the time shifts of more educated women in Sweden, France, and the United States toward entry into the labor force.

1.7 Home Management

The simultaneous technological revolution within the home, however, may require even less time-intensive labor and increasing levels of education for effective home management which uses fewer hours. The advent of dishwashers, automatic washing machines, wash-and-wear clothing, and monthly payment of bills by check means that less time is required for such tasks than by earlier methods. However, they do require knowledge of home repairs and repair management, plus some accounting skills. Tele-shopping for groceries and sundries is now in use in 217 United States cities, tele-bill-paying and tele-banking are spreading, and home computers are now available at increasingly reasonable cost for managing household energy use, adjusting savings portfolios, teaching the children, preparing income tax returns, and even life-cycle planning—all requiring more (and changing) education for their effective use.

There are many studies, not all accompanied by adequate controls for differences in money income, which provide evidence that those with more education tend to adopt new products more quickly. Of those that do attempt to hold real income constant, Mandell (1972) finds that those with more education adopted credit cards faster; Michael (1982) reports on several studies, including his own, that indicate that more educated women are more likely to use contraception and to have fewer unplanned babies; and Hettich (1972) finds that more educated women are more efficient in market search, with potential savings as the result of more efficient purchasing behaviour that raises the estimated rate of return to a college education by 1.5 percent. No study has yet examined whether or not persons with more education realize more of the deductions to which they are entitled on their income tax.

1.8 Affective Attributes Created by Education

As distinct from the more cognitive attributes, affective attributes affect productivity in consumption in addition to their effect on earnings.

The clearest measures are of the comparative advantage schooling confers in the selection of a desirable spouse. Michael (1982) develops the point that a person's own schooling and that of their mate are positively correlated by at least 0.4, making education a good investment in securing a spouse whose earning capacity (and presumably other attributes also (are more desirable. The amount of college education planned by students is also found to be positively and significantly related to "finding a spouse with college values" in a study by McMahon (1984), who controls for expected monetary returns, as well as for financial aids and other influences on student decisions. It is interesting that the coefficient for this expected nonmonetary return is four times as large, and the t-statistic twice as large, for men as it is for women students. Benham (1974) and Welch (1974) find that a wife's schooling raises her husband's annual earnings by about 3.5 percent.

Such affective returns from education as meeting, and conversing with more interesting people, capacities for entertaining guests, and community service (although the latter is an external benefit discussed elsewhere) are recognized by students and expected to be positive, although only meeting more interesting people was found by McMahon to have significant effects on student decisions. Becker (1981 Chap. 4) suggest that schooling can contribute to greater happiness in marriage, since it facilitates a more nearly optimal sorting among mates in the marriage market. However, women with more education are also more prone to divorce, generating disutility for the husband and children, a fact that Becker (1981 p.231) and others have usually associated with the growth in women's earnings that lessen the economic advantages of marriage, rather than with education per se.

Education facilitates readjustment for divorced persons with more education who are known to remarry more quickly. Furthermore, in the broader role stressed by Schultz (1975), it allows individuals to adapt more easily to changes at work, disequilibria in the job market, and new technology in the home. It also changes tastes—from drag racing or horse racing, for example, toward concerts and reading editorials. Yet the net effects of pure shifts in tastes on consumer satisfaction cancel out to some extent. Rather than concentrate on taste shifts, the research focusing on the effects on productivity in household production has been far more fruitful.

In summary, it has been seen that many good studies exist which provide evidence of positive consumption benefits of education—benefits (after holding earnings constant) to the family's health, schooling, return on savings, purchasing efficiency, home management skills, and affective sources of happiness. Against this, the counterproductive effects relating to divorce and to the time-intensive activities in the home requiring less skill must be netted out. Beyond testing for additional effects, further work is needed such as extending the work by Michael and others using shadow prices to impute values (both positive and negative) to each of these nonmonetary benefits for individual families, and also for total consumption and total product at the macro level in the national income and product accounts. These would have to include the value of education in facilitating adjustment to disequilibria, whether they be caused by market opportunties, divorce, or new technology within the family.

See also: Benefits of Education; External Benefits of Education

References

Becker G S 1975 *Human Capital: A Theoretical and Empirical Analysis, with Special Reference to Education*, 2nd edn. National Bureau of Economic Research, New York

Becker G S 1976 *The Economic Approach to Human Behavior*. University of Chicago Press, Chicago, Illinois

Becker G S 1981 *A Treatise on the Family*. Harvard University Press, Cambridge, Massachusetts

Benham L 1974 Benefits of women's education within marriage. In: Schultz T W (ed.) 1974

Benson C S 1982 Household production of human capital: Time uses parents and children as inputs. In: McMahon W W, Geske T G (eds.) 1982

Cochrane S, O'Hara D J, Leslie J 1980 *The Effects of Education on Health*. World Bank Staff Working Paper No. 105, The World Bank, Washington, DC

Duncan G J 1976 Earnings functions and non-pecuniary benefits. *J. Hum. Resources* 11: 462–83

Eisner R, Nebhut D H 1981 An extended measure of government product: Preliminary results for the United States, 1946–76. *Rev. Income Wealth* 27: 33–64

Ferber M A, McMahon W W 1979 Women's expected earnings and their investment in higher education. *J. Hum. Resources* 14: 405–20

Grossman M 1976 The correlation between health and schooling. In: Terleckyj N (ed.) 1976 *Household Production and Consumption*. Columbia University Press, New York

Gustafson S 1978 Cost benefit analysis of early childhood care and education. Working Paper, Industrial Institute for Economic and Social Research, Stockholm

Hettich W 1972 Consumption benefits from education. In: Ostry S (ed.) 1972 *Canadian Higher Education in the Seventies*. Information Canada, Ottawa

Kendrick J W 1979 Expanding imputed values in the national income and product accounts. *Rev. Income Wealth* 25: 349–63

Lando M 1975 The interaction between health and education. *Soc. Secur. Bull.* 38(12): 16–22

Lazear E P 1977 Education: Consumption or production? *J. Pol. Econ.* 85: 569–97

Leibowitz A 1974 Home investments in children. In: Schultz T W (ed.) 1974

Lemennicier B 1978 *Education et technologie de consommation. Incidences de l'éducation sur la consommation.* Centre de Recherche pour l'Etude et l'Observation des Conditions de Vie (CREDOC), Paris

Levy-Garboua L, Jarousse J 1978 *Education, aptitudes perceptives, et valeur extraite des choses familiales. Incidences de l'éducation sur la consommation.* Centre de Recherche pour l'Etude et l'Observation des Conditions de Vie (CREDOC), Paris

McMahon W W 1974 Policy issues in the economics of higher education and related research opportunities in Britain and the United States. *High. Educ.* 3: 165–86

McMahon W W 1976 Influences on investment by Blacks in higher education. *Am. Econ. Rev.* 66(2): 320–23

McMahon W W 1981 The slowdown in productivity growth: A macroeconomic model of investment in human and physical capital with energy shocks. Faculty Working Paper No. 752, Bureau of Economic and Business Research (BEBR), University of Illinois, Urbana, Illinois

McMahon W W 1984 Why families invest in education. In: Sudman S, Spaeth M (eds.) 1984 *The Collection and Analysis of Economic and Consumer Data; Essays in Honor of Robert Ferber*. University of Illinois Press, Urbana, Illinois

McMahon W W, Wagner A P 1982 The monetary returns to education as partial social efficiency criteria. In: McMahon W W, Geske T G (eds.) 1982

Mandell L 1972 *Credit Card Use in the United States*. Institute for Social Research, University of Michigan, Ann Arbor, Michigan

Michael R T 1972 *The Effect of Education on Efficiency in Consumption*. Columbia University Press/ National Bureau of Economic Research, New York

Michael R T 1982 Measuring nonmonetary benefits of education. In: McMahon W W, Geske T G (eds.) 1982

Psacharopoulos G 1993 Returns to investment in education: A global update. Education and Employment Policy Research Working Paper No.1067, Latin American and Caribbean Region, The World Bank, Washington, DC

Psacharopoulos G, Hinchliffe K 1973 *Returns to Education: An International Comparison*. Elsevier, Amsterdam

Rumberger R W 1981 *Overeducation in the US Labor Market*. Praeger, New York

Schultz T W 1967 The rate of return in allocating investment resources to education. *J. Hum. Resources*. 2: 293–309

Schultz T W 1975 The value of the ability to deal with disequilibria. *J. Econ. Lit.* 13: 827–46

Solomon L C 1975 The relation between schooling and savings behavior. In: Juster F T (ed.) 1975 *Education, Income, and Human Behavior:* McGraw-Hill, New York

Welch F 1974 Comment. In: Schultz T W (ed.) 1974

Further Reading

Cohn E 1990 *The Economics of Education*, 3rd edn. Ballinger, Cambridge, Massachusetts

Haveman R, Wolfe B 1984 Schooling and economic well-being: The role of nonmarket effects. *J. Hum. Resources* 19(3): 377–407
Levhari D, Weiss Y 1974 The effect of risk on the investment in human capital. *Am. Econ. Rev.* 64(6): 950–63
McMahon W W, Geske T G (eds.) 1982 *Financing Education: Overcoming Inefficiency and Inequity*. University of Illinois Press, Urbana, Illinois
Mincer J 1963 *Social and Economic Factors in Spending for Public Education*. Syracuse University Press, Syracuse, New York
Mincer J 1974 *Schooling, Experience, and Earnings*. Columbia University Press for the National Bureau of Economic Research, New York
Schultz T W (ed.) 1974 *Economics of the Family: Marriage, Children and Human Capital*. University of Chicago Press, Chicago, Illinois
Weisbrod B A 1964 External benefits of education: An economic analysis. Research Report 105, Industrial Relations Section, Department of Economics, Princeton University, Princeton, New Jersey

W. W. McMahon

Contemporary History of Education

This outline of worldwide developments in education since 1945 is based on the view that Western and communist experience have been seen as the two main influences. Education is first set in its global context, and then treated from the viewpoint of levels and institutions, processes, instruments, agents, and vocational considerations. One section deals with developments specific to nonindustrialized areas, and the important theme of equity is analyzed, before a tentative conclusion is drawn.

It is necessary to be very selective: there cannot be just *one* contemporary history; there are *many*, particularly when the focus is the world.

1. Contextual Factors: An Overview

The end of the Second World War heralded worldwide political changes. Within a few years humanity became split into three camps: the Western democracies; the socialist countries, particularly the Soviet bloc in Europe, and which initially included China until it followed its own devices; and the nonaligned countries—mainly the nonindustrialized areas of the world. At the same time, the process of decolonization began: India achieved statehood in 1947 but most African countries had to wait until the late 1950s and early 1960s before attaining independence. The Arab countries emerged as a powerful grouping, through the exploitation of their mineral wealth. South American countries also developed mutually closer ties. These very diverse phenomena had repercussions upon educational systems, which were as much founded on political and economic ideologies as upon strictly cultural and pedagogical prescriptions.

A postwar recovery stage meant that from 1945 until the mid-1950s little was accomplished educationally. The birthrate explosion lasting until the mid-1960s placed industrialized societies in a situation where they could do little more than provide a bare minimum—the requisite school places. Education took second place to priorities such as housing and communications. At the same time there was much educational idealism expressed in France, for example, in the Langevin–Wallon Plan for an *école unique* and, in the United Kingdom, in the 1944 Education Act. Not until the 1960s did much concrete movement take place, when education came almost to be regarded as a panacea for all ills. Secondary education for all began to be realized, and some kind of comprehensive system for this level was envisaged, except in the Federal Republic of Germany where, after the disastrous Nazi experience, "*keine Experimente*" was the watchword. Expansion of preschool and higher education occurred, with the latter creating new, more practically oriented institutions.

In contrast to the recent upsurge of idealism, the 1970s were for some a decade of disillusionment: it was realized that education and economic growth did not go hand in hand, and that equal schooling did not produce an egalitarian society. A new decade, marked by stringent economies, shifted the focus of reform to the relationship between education and work, a theme that chimed well with cost-effectiveness and value for money. However, the 1980s finished in great confusion with the ending of the Cold War and the breakup of the Soviet bloc. Speculation was rife as to what form the educational systems of the former socialist countries would take and how they would modify their Marxist–Leninist approach.

Dichotomies also crystallized over the period, with important educational consequences: the division into industrialized and nonindustrialized (developing) nations; the so-called "North–South divide," also characterized by differences in wealth and natural resources; and religious divisions, particularly related to the resurgence of Islam. Globally, international bodies such as UNESCO and the World Bank facilitated many educational changes.

Social and economic evolution since 1945 likewise impinged greatly upon education, particularly in the developed world. The structure of the family was modified. By the late 1960s family size in Europe had dropped from 2.6 children per family in 1947 to just over 2. This could have been providential for the education system, since less children had then to be educated, but this was balanced by the perceived need for longer schooling. The "nuclear family" also signaled a declining interest in the classroom: in the early 1960s some 40 percent of families had at least one child passing through school or university; by the mid-1980s this had diminished by half. On the other hand, the divorce rate rose spectacularly; "broken homes" and one-parent families became more common. The educational repercussions of this were self-evident: the school was often obliged to act as a surrogate for the home, the teacher being *in loco parentis*. Furthermore, increased wealth meant that adolescents no longer regarded the school as a major focus for their interests. Young persons' attitudes and expectations as regards schooling were modified accordingly.

Changes in employment structures also impacted upon education. The move away from primary occupations (farming, fisheries, and mining) and, to a lesser extent, from the secondary sector (manufacturing) to the tertiary sector (service industries) was accomplished by extensive changes in schooling. From the 1960s onward formal educational qualifications became the passport to social and economic mobility. At the same time rationalization in the manufacturing sector and automation in the services sector represented diminished job opportunities—indeed some unemployment became endemic. Early school-leavers suffered most from this situation. Whereas previously they had no difficulty in finding work, by the 1980s it was estimated that in OECD countries up to 50 percent of the 16–19-year old, if not still in school, were unemployed.

One solution, in countries such as the United States—where such students were dubbed "seat-warmers"—and France, was to retain as many as possible in school. This was deemed to be justified also because occupations required increasingly high standards of skills competence. However, this gave rise to a further problem: retaining those who, for all practical purposes, were adults rather than adolescents aroused their resentment. The 1968 riots in the Western world were not confined to higher education, but spread to the schools. Political reaction to them was to demand that the school change its external "caretaking," child-minding image to a more utilitarian one. This internal ethos, which in the 1960s was widely regarded as being one of cooperation, was transformed into one of competition, a concept earlier played down by "progressive" educationists. The growth of the "diploma disease" signified what Husén et al. (1992) called the creation of an educational "underclass," for whom any qualifications were beyond reach. Since the school was widely viewed as a main vehicle for economic and social success, their status of underdogs was likely to be carried over into adult life. Indeed, the relation of school to work had a profound effect upon schooling, which is considered elsewhere.

During the period a migration of peoples occurred such as had not been seen since the Dark Ages. In 1945 refugees from war-torn Europe migrated massively to the New World; within Europe they fled either East or West, depending upon their political allegiance. The former European colonial powers, short of labor, recruited from their former overseas dependencies. Meanwhile members of the poorer European nations either emigrated to the richer northern areas of the continent, or elsewhere. Melbourne, for example, became the second largest Greek-speaking city in the world; the EC hosted 15 million migrants—a "thirteenth state" within the Community. The educational consequences of such large-scale movements were profound. In the Federal Republic of Germany, for example, the proportion of foreign children in German schools rose between 1977 and 1987 from about 7 to 9.5 percent. In France throughout the 1980s the proportion of foreign children fluctuated at around 8.5 percent. In Belgium (in the French-speaking sector) in 1982 just under 22 percent of children in school were foreign. In Luxemburg in the same year they amounted to 30 percent. The educational difficulties this influx raised were cultural and linguistic. Initially, problems were simply ignored or treated as temporary, on the assumption that migrants would eventually return home. Then various educational policies were tried: assimilation, which, however could only be a long-term eventuality; multiculturalism, which nevertheless in practice seemed to accentuate differences and placed migrant children in an educational ghetto; and finally, integration, which implied stressing what all ethnic groupings held in common, while respecting divergences. In the United States the "melting-pot" policy was continued, although concessions had to be made to the large numbers of Spanish-speaking children. Everywhere some curricula revision took place to accommodate the new situation; in particular, special measures were devised to intensify teaching migrant children the vehicular language, while maintaining the language of the home.

Table 1
Global number of students 1970–83 (in thousands)

Year	1970	1975	1980	1983
Primary	433,287	517,162	558,465	572,140
Secondary	160,719	207,197	241,984	250,143
Higher	28,179	36,619	47,185	51,513
Total	622,185	763,978	847,634	873,795

2. Development of Educational Institutions

Table 1 represents the growth in numbers in education worldwide between 1970 and 1983 according to UNESCO figures.

The table demonstrates that between 1970 and 1975, enrollments increased exponentially.

If universal primary education was the goal to be achieved for developing countries, the problem of universal secondary education bulked large for the industrialized nations, where the demand for the generalization of secondary education had begun in 1945 as part of the democratization process. On a world scale the problem of secondary schooling was immense. The global population of the 10–19 year old age group numbered 776 million in 1970, 950 million in 1980, and more than a billion by the mid-1980s. For the developed countries the numbers were fairly steady from 1970 to 1980, but then began slowly to decline; on the contrary, for the developing countries, if an index of 100 is postulated for 1970, this had risen to 145 by 1985. The steepest growth in potential secondary students was in non-Arab Africa; the steepest decline was in North America.

For the developed world the question was: what kind of secondary school(s) should be founded to accommodate initially all children? Based on research, the Swedish unitary school was designed to take youngsters up to 16 with practically no differentation. Founded on ideology, the main Soviet bloc countries followed the example of the former Soviet Union and established a "general polytechnical" school for students from 7 to 18 years of age (although most students left at 16), which sought to combine schooling with work experience. In North America the high school(s) were "comprehensive" with academic, technical, and vocational tracks. In Western Europe, with its traditional grammar school, *lycée*, or *Gymnasium*, evolution was slow. In England and Wales the move away from a three-track system from the age of 11 took off in earnest in 1965 with the introduction of 6 types of comprehensive education. In France a comprehensive lower secondary school finally evolved in the mid-1960s. In the Federal Republic of Germany a tripartite system prevailed. In some countries (e.g., the former Soviet Union, Sweden and France) a separate upper secondary school or schools evolved as a means of meeting the needs of the labor market. The rise of vocational education sparked off a debate as to the age this should begin: in lower or upper secondary education, or in work-based postcompulsory schooling, as in Germany.

In higher education from the 1960s onward, alongside the traditional universities there evolved institutions more directly related to working life: polytechnics in the United Kingdom *Instituts universitaires de technologie* in France, *Gesamthochschulen* in the Federal Republic of German, colleges of advanced education in Australia, and *Tanki-daigaka* in Japan.

The content and assessment of education underwent many changes. Traditionally the primary school was mainly devoted to the mastery of the "three Rs," and this continued, although elementary science was also introduced. The updating of the traditional secondary curriculum in industrialized countries marked the virtual disappearance of the classics, supplanted by a rigorous emphasis on science. New programs, some emanating originally from North America, transformed conventional approaches to the scientific disciplines. The trend was toward a hands-on form of teaching, using a heuristic method. In the mid-1960s the social sciences—economics, sociology, and even psychology—entered the *Kanon der Fächer*. Syllabuses that had grown by accretion were drastically pruned.

By the early 1970s the cry went up for curricula to be related more closely to the world of work. At the UNESCO International Conference on Education in 1973 the ministers and their representatives proposed a reform of secondary education "to associate in one balanced, harmonious and flexibly diversified system the general, technical, and vocational processes of education." Accordingly technology, including craft and design, was included in the general secondary curriculum as was a little later, computer studies. In socialist countries and, to a lesser extent, elsewhere work-related experience formed part of the *cursus studiorum*. Meanwhile in the humanities stress was laid on communication skills. Thus the time-honored Renaissance concept of a liberal education ("*Allgemeinbildung*," "*culture générale*") was broadened to reflect these new developments.

In developing countries, after independence an academic approach prevailed, but was quickly supplanted by vocationalism. The Indian Minister of Education, V K Rao, expressed a consensus view that education must be linked to production. In Tanzania "education for self-reliance" became the slogan. Technical and vocational subjects, deemed necessary for swift economic growth, were introduced, although, by late 1960s Philip Foster, drawing upon Ghanaian experience, and other experts were skeptical as to whether they were producing the desired effect. By 1970 the Third World began seriously to question the value of much that was taught. The charge was that the link between schooling and employment remained unclear. Parents feared that school learning left their children unfit for rural life, which remained the norm. Western aid shared some of the blame. Students learned about vehicle maintenance, when how to repair a bicycle would have been more useful. In any case, adequate resources for technical education were lacking.

The one facet of schooling on which all were agreed was its use in stamping out illiteracy. Here some progress was made: in 1970, 32.4 percent of the total adult population, mainly in developing countries, were illiterate; in a decade this had dropped to 28.9 percent. (These figures masked, however, an ominous situation. The absolute number of illiterates continued to grow: from 760 million in 1970 to 850 million in 1985, and by the year 2000 the figure looked likely to top a billion.) The language of instruction remained a burning issue. Some Arab countries devoted 25 percent of teaching time to Arabic so as to shake free from the domination of European languages in teaching; however, in other countries such as Chad and Ghana, the vehicular languages for secondary education remained respectively French and English.

Examinations remained the traditional means of assessment, although the introduction of multiple-choice and short-answer questions to supplement essay-type questions and semistructured oral examinations did represent a revolution in technique. The American high school graduation model—"achieving the grades"—was not widely adopted; nor were innovatory Swedish assessment procedures. The preservation by former colonies of the old secondary school leaving examinations was described as a renewed form of cultural imperialism: France and the United Kingdom imparted models to their former overseas possessions that survived for a long while. Even the comparative homogeneity and cooperation that characterized assessment in Latin America was a result of nations adhering largely to an evolved Spanish model. Likewise some socialist countries of Central Europe broadly followed Soviet practice.

3. Control, Finance, and Planning

To control the much enlarged educational systems more elaborate agencies were necessary. Bureaucracies flourished. The management of education had always been debatable. However, the question was decisively resolved in authoritarian regimes: total political control was essential to ensure conformity. Likewise, in many of the "new" countries that arose in the 1960s centralism was imperative where resources were minimal, in order to ensure their efficient distribution. For the Western democracies, however, the position was less clear. In the United States a rationalization of the 25,000 school boards was undertaken, with a drastic reduction in their number; at the same time, individual states strengthened their control. Federal intervention was strictly limited. At the height of the Cold War, however, this position could not be sustained, and Congress passed laws pouring large sums into the promotion of science, technology, and foreign language programs. Centralization from 1938 to 1944 induced the Federal Republic of Germany subsequently to devolve responsibility for education (except for higher education) to its constituent parts. In France the Revolutionary tradition of maintaining a firm grip at the center was continued. In the United Kingdom, which until 1944 had lacked even a ministry of education, a partnership between the central government and local authorities was established. In Sweden an elaborate system of checks and balances appertained, involving Parliament (which had the ultimate say), a central ministry, the municipalities, and an independent national board, which proposed innovations.

However, in about 1965 participation became the order of the day. In Sweden, as noted, all interested lay parties were automatically consulted before reforms were formulated. Because of the principle of subsidiarity that had been applied through school boards, parent power in the United States had always been influential. Elsewhere, the uprisings of 1968 brought the "consumers" of education much more into the picture. In France, "*participation*," and in Germany, "*Mitbestimmung*," became watchwords. From about 1970 onward Western countries ensured that the views of parents, teachers, students, future employers, and other interest groups were sought before new measures were introduced. In the United Kingdom, the 1944 Education Act stipulated, children were to be educated in accordance with the wishes of their parents: this principle now began to be applied. Since the mid-1980s a new tendency emerged, particularly in the United Kingdom: the shifting of responsibility increasingly to the individual school, even allowing it freedom to dispose of its own budget. In their turn, schools not only consulted more closely their immediate "customers," both parents and pupils, but worked in closer cooperation with the "consumers" of their "products" (local employers). By some these moves were perceived as reflecting a desire of the center to exercise control without responsibility—an "arm's length" approach; in the United Kingdom they were even seen as a bid to foster the "privatization" of the school system. However, in countries such as France power was not devolved to the local level, but merely delegated. It remains to be seen whether these procedures in Europe have halted or merely shifted to local level the increasing politicization of education that has been the hallmark of the last 50 years.

At the same time, at the level of higher education the reverse process was under way: the rein of central government was applied more strongly, as post-compulsory education, with its inevitable corollary—access to higher education—underwent massive expansion. The upshot is that universities and para-university institutions, except in the United States, now exercise much less autonomy than they did in 1945.

The financing of the public education system had become an increasing burden, particularly in the developing countries. In these, the average percentage of GNP spent on education rose from 2.55 in 1960 to 4.35 in 1980. However, expenditure in some countries fell pitifully low: in 1970 Somalia devoted 1 percent of its GNP to education, and in 1980 Uganda spent 0.6 percent. In the industrialized countries the comparable average figures rose from 3.47 percent to 5.55 percent; in North America they rose from 4.14 percent to 7.28 percent. The trend, however, was for the increase to become proportionately less. This is confirmed by a scrutiny of yearly public expenditure, which everywhere showed a downturn from about 1976 onward. Thus, in Western Europe, average public expenditure on education in relation to the total annual budget in 1965 was 16.5 percent, but by 1980 this had fallen to 13.3 percent. This reflected the lesser priority ascribed to education, as human resource and cost–benefit theories formulated by economists in the late 1960s did not seem to be borne out by the results.

A feature of the period since 1945 was the development of educational planning. The concept of planning was at first relatively novel, although the Soviet Union had followed five-year plans since 1928, and planning had been essential in many countries after the Second World War in order to prioritize reconstruction, including education. In the early 1960s the view that education and economic growth were correlated was strong. In 1961 OECD sponsored in Washington the "Policy Conference on Economic Growth and Investment in Education." From then on planning units in ministries of education began to be set up in Europe, and planning—under UNESCO or regional auspices—also became an integral aspect of education in the newly independent countries. In 1963 UNESCO established an International Institute for Educational Planning (IIEP) specifically for this purpose. Meanwhile, from 1960 to 1967 OECD largely concerned itself with the relationship between education and workforce requirements, initiating such studies as the Mediterranean Regional Project (in 1965).

Although in the early 1970s the workforce approach was called into question, in the late 1980s a revival began. Other approaches to measurement of educational yield were also tried in an effort to improve the efficiency and effectiveness of education. Attempts to measure rates of return achieved some success in relation to primary education in the Third World.

4. *Latin America, Africa, Arabia, and Asia*

Although reference has already been made to features common to developing and industrialized countries, historical trends specific to the Third World or to "advanced" countries geographically located in their midst deserve special mention.

In the developing countries changes, some of which have been touched upon already, have been as far reaching as elsewhere. Characterizing them have been problems relating not only to resources, but also to communications (which greatly hindered the centralized management of education), illiteracy rates (with their corollary, the nonachievement of universal primary education), linguistic diversity, attrition rates, the mismatch of vocational education and local needs, and religious and tribal diversity, all set against a background of neocolonialism.

Indeed, the former colonial nations at first continued to look to their erstwhile rulers for assistance. However, since the late 1950s international or regional organizations such as UNESCO and the World Bank have provided substantial aid programs. Thus, various intergovernmental conferences of developing nations were able to drawn up plans for achieving primary education for all: the Karachi Plan (1960) aimed to provide seven years of schooling in Asian countries by 1980; the Addis Ababa Plan (1961) proposed a similar goal for Africa by the same year; and the Santiago Plan (1962) sought the realization of universal primary education in Latin American countries by 1970. Only the last of these three plans came near to achieving its goal.

It was in fact Latin America that made the greatest progress in the provision of institutions and facilities. In South America in 1965, for example, 16 percent of the entire student population were in secondary schools; by 1982 this proportion had risen to 21 percent.

In Africa, from 1956 onward 35 countries achieved independence in less than a decade. In colonial Africa the British had attempted to provide an education suitable to local conditions, making a bid to establish an educational partnership after the Second World War. By contrast, the French had aimed at assimilation, so much so that Africans, following the programs for French schools, even learned about "*nos ancêtres les Gaulois*." Both policies failed.

Independence brought about an upsurge of national feeling, coupled with a desire to achieve at least some schooling for everybody since, at first, this was deemed the key to economic and social progress. Modernization was an urgent priority. Thus a few countries began by devoting as much as 30 percent of annual resources to education: enrollment in primary schools more than doubled. Under colonialism, fees had to be paid even for primary education. However, the richer African countries were able to abolish tuition fees for basic education, which Kenya did in 1974 for example; two years later Nigeria followed suit. However, by the early 1970s disillusionment, accentuated by bleak economic conditions worldwide, had set in. Even with help from the developed nation and international agencies in the provision of equipment and expatriate teachers the expected "take-off" in the economy had not occurred. Education was downgraded as a priority, to make way for more pressing needs.

Attempts to give aid in terms of vocational and technical education were likewise unsuccessful. Rather than the provision of large-scale equipment unsuitable to African conditions, what was required was intermediate technology, the use and construction of which could be taught locally. The expansion of primary education led merely to a large dropout rate and to a shortage of secondary school places. Even when secondary education was expanded it was found that its graduates lacked jobs to go to. Higher education was woefully inadequate except for training a white-collar elite to enter government service or the professions. Science and technology could not cater for sufficient numbers of graduates. Teachers at all levels, once trained, sought more lucrative salaries than the classroom could offer. The chase for paper qualifications meant that formal education was considered preferable to informal or nonformal education, which might well have been more suitable to local conditions.

South Africa, though by no means falling into the category of an underdeveloped nation, merits special mention. The introduction of the apartheid laws in 1948 effectively reinforced a segregated educational system. By 1953 the Bantu Education Act had inaugurated a second-class schooling for the Black majority: the syllabus was different from that of the Whites, instruction was given in the vernacular in the primary school and in English or Afrikaans in lower secondary education. In 1959 this segregation was also enforced in higher education. In the early 1990s, with the abolition of apartheid, this system was in a slow process of dissolution but much remained to be done before equal facilities and complete racial intermixing would be realized.

For the Arab states the picture turned out somewhat brighter. Until 1945, some 20 Arab states, stretching from the Atlantic to the Persian Gulf and characterized by the unifying force of Islam, looked to Egypt as their educational role model. With the achievement of independence (Syria in 1944; the Maghreb, 1956–1962) for the remaining major Arab nations and the formation in 1945 of the Arab League, which enjoyed notable scientific and cultural success, the foundations were laid for close educational cooperation between the 110 million Arabic speakers. For schools and universities this meant Arabizing programs as far as possible, while retaining the religious elements of the curriculum; in Tunisia an Arabic baccalaureate examination even replaced the French examination of the same name.

The centripetal forces for pan-Arab cooperation were increased by the foundation in 1964 of the Arab League Educational, Scientific and Cultural Organization (ALESCO), an offshoot of the Arab League. The League itself sponsored a yearbook (*Hawiiyat at-taquafa—The Annals of Arab Culture*) authored by the Syrian educator Sati al-Husari, which appeared from 1950 to 1963 and did much to promote a unified approach to education. This was further fostered after 1964 by conferences of Arab ministers of education. The emphasis was on educational planning, and in particular on working out a common development strategy. Various subsidiary organizations, such as the Arab Bureau of Education for the Gulf States, also sprang up. Between 1970 and 1985 ALESCO carried out almost 600 research projects, many of which concerned literacy and Arabization of secondary and higher education.

Meanwhile, traditional education also continued in the Koranic schools as well as in schools for girls, which taught Moslem customs and homecraft.

The following aims set out for education in Saudi Arabia may well apply to most of the Islamic area—although in some countries, such as Algeria, the stress is also on socialism:

(a) the correct understanding of Islam and the inculcation and dissemination of the Islamic creed;
(b) the imbuing of the student with Islamic values, doctrines and ideas;
(c) the social, economic, and cultural development of society;
(d) the preparation of the individual to be a useful participant in the building of society.

Asia represents a peculiar blend of the ancient and modern. Here, although Japan, China, and Australia were not role models as such, it was their influence, rather than European, that was felt most in the postwar era.

The dominant power in the Asian region was Japan. Its educational system had been reorganized after the Second World War on American lines, with a Fundamental Law on Education introduced in 1947 that stressed equality of opportunity. A strongly centralized system ensured the maintenance of high standards—national testing was introduced as early as 1956. Indeed one salient feature of the system was the stress on performance. What has been called the "entrance examination hell" for entry to higher education ensured that young people, having been at school all day, then attended evening "cramming" classes to improve their chances of success. The system still applies. Candidates have been known to sit at least seven times the entrance examination to prestigious universities such as Tokyo. This competitive atmosphere filtered downward and created a similar pressure on younger students to gain entrance to the "best" upper secondary schools. The Japanese have attributed their economic success to the efficiency of their education system.

China, a communist state after 1949, set out under Mao to produce through education high quality students that were "Red and expert." Failing that, workers that were socialist-inspired and imbued with communist culture should be the products of the education system. Science and technology were stressed. A kind of *Gleichschaltung* placed peasants and intellectuals on an equal footing. Administration, as befitted a communist country, was highly centralized. The concept of the collective also found favor, and all education had to be subordinated to this political dimension. Thus the theory and practice of the Soviet education system was much studied in China in the 1950s and 1960s. It was followed, however, by the "Ten Years of Turmoil" of the Cultural Revolution (1966–76), with the deliberate destruction of intellectual elites. This would lead, according to Mao, to a greater egalitarianism in education. The utopian vision faded with the death of its protagonist (1976), and education in China became more pragmatic and less dependent on Marxist theory, although the relationship between education and work continued to be stressed.

In Australia, to which countries such as Papua New Guinea looked, a decentralized school system functioned satisfactorily, but with one thorny problem: that related to immigration. After 1945 the official policy was one of "populate or perish." Today the population is more than double what it was after the Second World War. Throughout the period, the annual flood of "new Australians" never dropped below 40,000 until 1972; in the 1950s at one point it rose to over 140,000. Although even in the early 1990s Australians of Anglo-Celtic origin constitute 60 percent of the population, the immigrants have come from very diverse parts of the world: from southern Europe, for example, and eventually, from Asia. It fell to the schools to undertake the process of integration. How this has been accomplished may well provide an object-lesson for Europe, faced with the same problem.

India, the great democracy of the undeveloped nations, battled with intractable educational problems after independence. Its size and population meant that control of education was devolved to its constituent States, with a Union ministry acting in the role of coordinator. The British left it with a few good schools, though many were private and designed for only a tiny minority, and a sound network of universities. But the masses came off badly. In the mid-1960s 32 percent of the population were still illiterate, a situation compounded by the multiplicity of languages. A policy of the generalization of Hindi has achieved a modicum of success, although much advanced education is still taught in English.

Many of the other nations in Southeast Asia are experiencing the same problems as Africa. Between independence in 1946 and 1960 a fourth of all Filipinos were in school, but attrition rates were so great that in 1959 only 4 percent had completed high school. As in Africa, one of the priorities was to resolve the question of the 87 languages that were spoken. In Cambodia attrition rates were also the problem. In Papua New Guinea a plan drawn up in 1961 to achieve universal primary education by 1975 was only partially fulfilled. The former South Vietnam had some success, contriving by 1967 to enroll three times more students in primary education than in 1954. In Thailand education suffered from a chronic shortage of teachers.

5. *Equality of Opportunity*

Like a golden thread running through all postwar educational history, whether East or West, North or South, has been the concept of equality of opportunity. "*Démocratisation*" in France and "*Chancengleichheit*" in Germany dominated the educational debate until the end of the 1970s, as did the concept elsewhere. Its implications were far reaching. Preschool education would allegedly start the culturally and socially deprived off on the same footing as their more fortunate fellows. Secondary education for all had to become a reality. Although by 1980, in the developed world, this had largely been achieved, the developing nations had to be satisfied with the goal of universal primary education: this was unfortunately not so achievable. In 1987 the world population topped 5,000 million for the first time; this was of great educational portent. It meant that the majority of the earth's children would be lucky to receive a full primary education, let alone any secondary education, before well into the next millenium. Equity, in a global context, was therefore very problematic.

In the West, however, the comfortable assertion of sociologists, such as Schelsky, in the 1960s that the school was the main distributor of life chances—a powerful argument particularly for those committed to a comprehensive secondary school—was modified by the Coleman Report (See Coleman 1966) which showed that variance in school attainment arose more from causes external to the school. As a result the American Project "Head Start" was begun. In England it was followed by the Educational Priority Areas (EPA) project, which was also imitated on a smaller scale in France. However, confidence was further shaken by the publication of Jencks' *Inequality* (1972), which demonstrated that equality was nowhere near within reach: resources available differed from school to school, as did the quality and quantity of what was offered, and cognitive skills differed between children—a regrettable oversight of nature. Above all, the most important factor in achievement was not the school but the home. Jencks concluded that equal opportunity could only be attained by equalizing incomes. Subsequent sociological studies—as well as some previous psychological studies—confirmed this pessimism, as did empirical studies of the effects of schooling: in capitalist and communist societies alike, higher education—the route to high incomes and power—remained, except in a minority of cases, the preserve of privileged elites. In effect, taxation, including the taxes of those in the lower socioeconomic categories, was financing, at least as regards higher education, the education those already more fortunate.

In the former Soviet Union and its satellites, the philosophy was different. The passage from a socialist to a truly communist society, where equality would allegedly become reality, demanded the sacrifice of the individual for the realization of this Arcadian dream. "All-round development" of the individual should be achieved for social ends: "from each according to his ability, to each according to his needs"—but the latter premise was qualified: "if those needs correspond to those of society." The collapse of the system in the late 1980s signaled that this doctrine, applied to education, was inoperable.

By the mid-1970s, although politicians continued to pay lip-service to this concept, alternative philosophies for schooling were being sought. As mentioned elsewhere, they revolved round the school as an instrument of preparation for employment, and better education as a *sine qua non* for prosperity. Individual development, it was argued, must be largely for this (social) goal.

A prime factor in equality of opportunity is the concept of differences in enrolment between boys and girls. This has left its mark in education. The last half of the twentieth century has shown a struggle by women to achieve equal educational status with men. In the industrialized world, one yardstick—that of parity in numbers in higher education—is on the way to being achieved. But parity was particularly difficult to accomplish in areas of study leading to the higher social cadres—the professions, industry, business, and academia (in Australia, e.g. only 3 percent of university teachers are women. After 1945, curricular stereotyping occurred in secondary education; efforts, for example, to persuade girls to follow technical rather than general education courses proved unsuccessful. The outcome was that only in the former Soviet Union were women engineers trained in large numbers. Whereas in secondary school boys opted for mathematics, science, and technology courses, girls exhibited a marked preference for languages, social sciences, and the humanities—whether this choice was conditioned by nature or nurture remains problematic.

Nevertheless progress was made. The case of Hungary may be cited. In the late 1940s the majority of girls had only 4–6 years of schooling; by 1965 only 30 percent of girls over 15 years had successfully completed 8 years of elementary schooling, and only 6 percent had secondary or higher qualifications. By 1986 the latter figure had risen to 25 percent, and 40 percent of university graduates were female. Yet in countries including the United Kingdom, it was found necessary to pass legislation as late as 1975 formally decreeing that in all spheres, including education, girls should not be discriminated against. It was recognized that the problem was cultural as well as social and economic, and that educational measures alone could not remedy it.

The situation, however, was most acute in the Third World. A UNESCO statistical review in 1972, after a decade marked by the independence of many African countries, showed the female adult illiteracy rate still running at 84 per cent. Since school failure was high, students who dropped out when they were literate, quickly fell back into functional illiteracy. This reduces a mother's ability to maintain her child's literacy standards and the effectiveness of her educative function in terms of health, population control, and family welfare. Yet where money was scarce, it was argued, education should be given to boys, who would normally become the chief family breadwinner. One notes again the basic noneducational aspects of the problem.

In Islamic countries the situation was varied, also largely dependent upon resources. In the oil-rich nations, progress was made in women's education. In Saudi Arabia the first girls' school was opened in the 1960s. An international conference on Islamic education in 1977, while giving priority to religious education and forbidding coeducation, encouraged female education although still considered that preparation for some occupations, such as engineering, was not suitable for girls. Meanwhile, closer study of the Koran did much to dispel the opposition of some religious leaders to the education of girls.

Elsewhere in the world the situation was problematic. In South America great strides were made in achieving sexual equality in schooling. In Asia the situation paralleled that in Africa, with the exception of India, where Ghandism gave a fillip to female education.

Overall, however, women remained in the minority at all levels of education, despite efforts of agencies such as UNESCO, which designated 1975–85 as the "Decade for Women."

6. Conclusion

Educational history since 1945 has been a patchwork of ideas and events. Since education follows, rather than leads society, it was peculiarly subject, during the period, to fashionable political dogmas and trends. There was a gradual move away from individualism and from education for its own sake, culminating in the early 1990s, which ushered in a decade of "realism" and utilitarianism in schooling. The cry was for cost-effectiveness and efficiency and that the "product" of schools and universities should be of tangible, measurable benefit to society. This acted in accordance with the general politicization of the educational enterprise since the early 1940s. Nineteenth-century ideas of education as being for the individual, and for the happy development of character and personality, had to take a back seat. However, the next millenium may see the pendulum swing in the opposite direction.

See also: Sociology of Education: Overview; Historical Methods in Educational Research

References

Coleman J S 1966 *Equality of Educational Opportunity*. US Government Printing Office, Washington, DC

Husén T, Tuijnman A, Halls W D 1992 *Schooling in Modern European Society*. Pergamon Press, Oxford

Jencks C et al. 1972 *Inequality: A Reassessment of the Effect of Family and Schooling in America*. Basic Books, New York

Further Reading

Bereday G Z, Lauwerys J (eds.) 1967 The World Year

Book of Education: University of London, Institute of Education, London
Broadfoot P, Sutherland M (eds.) 1987 Sex differences in education. *Comp. Educ.* 232(1): whole issue
Cremin L 1976 *Public Education.* Basic Books, New York
Coombs P H 1968 *The World Crisis in Education: A Systems Analysis.* Oxford University Press, Oxford
Davenport T R 1978 *South Africa. A Modern History*, 2nd edn. Macmillan, London
Fauré E et al. 1972 *Learning to Be: The World of Education Today and Tomorrow.* International Commission on the Development of Education, UNESCO, Paris
Frazier N, Sadke M 1973 *Sexism in School and Society.* Harper Row, New York
Garcia Garrido J L 1986 *International Yearbook of Education. Vol. 38: Primary Education on the Threshold of the Twenty-first Century.* UNESCO, Paris
Haby R 1975 *Pour une modernisation du système éducatif.* Paris
Kelly G, Elliot C 1983 Women's education in the Third World. *Comp. Educ.*
Malkova Z A, Vulfson B L 1987 *International Yearbook of Education. Vol. 39: Secondary Education in the World Today.* UNESCO, Paris
National Commission on Excellence in Education 1983 *A Nation at risk. The Imperative for Educational Reform.* US Government Printing Office, Washington, DC
Price R F 1970 *Education in Communist China.* Routledge and Kegan Paul, London
Scanlon D 1964 *Traditions of African Education.* Columbia University Press, New York
Shapovalenko S G 1963 *Polytechnical Education in the USSR.* UNESCO, Paris

W. D. Halls

Contemporary Sociological Theories of Education

The development of social theory in any particular domain of human endeavor typically reflects more general movements in sociology. This is especially true in education, where both professionals and scholars tend to see themselves as engaged in applying social analysis to a practical field of activity—using and evaluating theory rather more than creating it. As a result, there has been an ebb and flow in the prominence and popularity of various general theories as they have been pressed into service to interpret the complex and often controversial dynamics of educational institutions and practices in modern societies.

As might be expected, the popularity of particular theoretical perspectives has varied with national settings and political ideologies. Over the long term, however, a general diffusion of major theoretical alternatives has produced a robust debate about the virtues and limitations of each in accounting for the social meaning and ends of education. Virtually all major theories have been called upon to explain some aspects of educational phenomena in all countries where sociology is an established discipline.

1. General Theoretical Perspectives and the Sociology of Education

Social theories generally tend to emphasize one or more of three distinct levels of human activity. At the micro level, sociological theory tackles the problem of individual actions. Such micro theories treat societies and institutions as contexts or constraints which elicit, interpret, direct, or constrain individual actions. Attention is focused on the acquisition of social consciousness, the creation of patterns of interaction and meaning, the differentiation and taking of social roles, or the study of leadership and other mechanisms of individual influence.

At an intermediate level, sociological theories tackle the analysis of institutions and social organizations. These meso theories focus attention on social groups and structures, analyzing such phenomena as authority development and decision-making, role formation, work and play, social careers, occupational identities, or program and policy impacts. Organizational and occupational sociologists confine their attention almost entirely to this level of analysis.

At the broadest level of social behavior, sociological theories tackle questions of social order, social stratification, and the nature of interactions among social institutions. These macro theories concentrate on the foundations of social orderliness and influence and probe the relationships between social activity and the physical, historical, cultural, political, and economic forces shaping human societies.

The emphasis in the sociology of education on applied problems has tended to blunt theoretical development at the micro and meso levels. At the macro level, however, education theorists have displayed a more systematic interest in the development and elaboration of theoretical thought. Thus, the review presented here concentrates on macro social theory as it has been developed and applied to education, although micro level approaches will also be examined.

Contemporary macro social theories can be categorized into a number of broad frameworks or theoretical orientations—sometimes loosely described as competing sociological "paradigms" (Turner 1991). Four of these frames of reference dominate modern sociological theorizing about education. One is functional theory, in which the institution of education and its various organizational components are analyzed with respect to their consequences for the needs or requisites of the larger society. A second perspective is utilitarianism, in which educational systems are analyzed with respect to cost–benefit calculations and exchanges of resources among actors. Another general perspective, which often takes functional and utilitarian theory as its critical foil, is conflict theory, in which the effects of educational structures on maintaining inequality and stratification are emphasized. The final perspective is interactionism, in which face-to-face interactions of individuals in school contexts and the nature of the construction of meanings are given prominence. Within each of these four general perspectives lies a wide range of competing theories. Moreover, considerable overlap, borrowing, and diffusion occur across the borders of each overarching perspective.

2. *Functional Theorizing on Education*

All functional theorizing is ultimately concerned with how social structures meet the needs or requisites of a more inclusive social system (Turner and Maryanski 1979). In the context of the macro level sociology of education, this mode of theorizing analyzes the consequences of educational structures on the society as a whole. The most common type of functional analysis is a listing of the functions of education in modern societies. For example, Goslin has argued that "each of the different institutions within the society, including educational systems, have important functions in relation to the system as a whole and to its other parts" (1965 p. 1); he then proceeded to list three basic functions of education for society: the maintenance and transmission of culture (knowledge, beliefs, values, etc.); the innovation, discovery, and transmission of new knowledge; and the allocation of individuals to positions in society.

Macro functional analysis has developed substantially through efforts to analyze the problem of modernization. Analysts ask why political leaders of modernizing and developing societies institutionalize systems of mass education; their answer to this inquiry is a list of the functions of schools for these societies. For instance, functionalists in the area of development are likely to stress that education teaches new skills, preserves intellectual systems, indoctrinates the young into a political culture, and generates as well as transmits new technologies necessary for development (Turner 1972). Somewhat more theoretically sophisticated modernization approaches have examined the evolutionary trend toward increased structural differentiation and the effects of education on such differentiation—concerns that go back to the early works on education by Spencer (1874–96) and Durkheim (1893, 1922). In these types of analyses, structural differentiation generates needs for separate structures that can facilitate the integration of individuals into the more complex system. Education evolves as a response to this broader system's need for specialized training and the credentialing of individuals who are then inserted into the economy, while simultaneously inculcating individuals into a common civic culture or societal community (Parsons 1971). Parsons (1959) was the most persistent advocate of this position, arguing that educational structures nurture the value of achievement so necessary for a market-oriented economic system, while legitimating inequalities associated with differential rewards attached to varying levels of achievement.

While the most familiar functionalist theories have treated education as a source of social integration, others have emphasized functional differentiation and the "selective functions" of the educational system. From this perspective, education is viewed as the mechanism by which various categories of people are selected for particular positions in society. For example, Turner (1971) compared the norms of the British and American educational systems in terms of "sponsored" as opposed to "contest" mobility. In contest systems, such as the United States, upward mobility is a race in which the rules are known by all, the sorting of individuals is delayed as long as possible, the hope for mobility is kept alive, and the responsibility for failure falls on the individual. In sponsored systems, new and future elites are assigned to positions by existing elites who use high prestige schools to sort the designated out early. In either case, the norms of the educational system have the function of selecting, while also mitigating the inequalities associated with differential mobility and privilege.

Still relying on macro level functionalism, some scholars have focused on the effects of specific aspects of education on society as a whole. One of the most prominent of these more focused explorations was the investigation of American universities conducted by Parsons and Platt (1973). In their analysis, the general theory of action as developed by Parsons (1949, 1952) and various colleagues (e.g., Parsons et al. 1953) was used to analyze the nature of the American university. In this kind of analysis the overall functions of the university system in America were established: universities have consequences for the "fiduciary" subsystem by virtue of their effects on the value of "cognitive rationality." Next, American higher education was seen as a "full university" composed of four differentiated units corresponding to Parsons' four functions scheme: undergraduate education, research and graduate training, professional schools, and relations with the broader society. Each of these was viewed as employing specialized media of exchange, such as influence and intelligence, to produce commitments to the value of cognitive rationality. In turn, such commitments facilitated the operation of other institutional structures: economy, polity, and law.

Macro-level functional theorizing about education reached its zenith in the 1960s and early 1970s. A revival of conflict sociology in the 1960s challenged the adequacy of functional analysis which thereafter receded significantly. Though functionalists then often became the "straw men" for various conflict theories, functionalism did not so much disappear as move to the meso level of organisation analysis, becoming a dominant theoretical framework for graduate training programs and surfacing in the day-to-day "folk orientations" of those who administer school systems. That is, while theoretical discourse moved to conflict theories, actual practices within the schools themselves continued to be concerned with the "functions of" this or that structure or program. A key work facilitating this transition was Waller's (1961) largely functionalist analysis of how sociological processes shape teaching and learning in schools. Despite Durkheim's (1893) and Parson's (1949) early polemics, much functional analysis was imported and blended with its arch enemy—utilitarianism—to produce a new way for the conceptualization of how education functions for the general social body.

3. Utilitarian Theorizing on Education

As a theoretical doctrine, utilitarianism emphasizes that actors reveal clear hierarchies of value (i.e., preferences for resources or "utilities"). Actors are also rational in that they calculate the resources to be used (costs) to secure those valued resources high in their preference hierarchy. Most utilitarian theories add a "maximization of utilities" corollary, arguing that actors seek to maximize their profits in exchanges of resources with other actors. This simple set of assumptions, borrowed from the Scottish economist Adam Smith (1776) and subsequent thinkers in the eighteenth and nineteenth centuries, has been elaborated into a number of general theoretical approaches in sociology, most notably exchange theory (e.g., Emerson 1986, Cook 1986, Willer 1987) and rational choice theory (Coleman 1990, Hechter 1987). None of these theories has penetrated theorizing in the sociology of education in nearly as a comprehensive way as have various functional or conflict theories. However, the basic assumptions of utilitarianism can be found in both conceptual and policy statements as enumerated by economists and economically oriented theorists.

A prominent application of utilitarian assumptions in the field of education has been the "human capital" approach (e.g., Levin and Shank 1970, Juster 1975, Becker 1975, Schultz 1961, United States National Commission on Excellence in Education 1983, Sobel 1978). Often using analytic techniques borrowed from quantitative economics, this approach operates at both the micro and macro levels. At the micro end, individuals are conceptualized as calculating the benefits of attending school (i.e., the likelihood of obtaining higher pay and a prestige job) against the costs of school (e.g., time and lost income). Such calculations are facilitated by media-sponsored information on the income differentials between college and noncollege graduates, as well as by marketing by both colleges and trade schools. Moreover, the types of schools and majors in schools (e.g., business vs humanities) can be explained in terms of such calculations. Thus the amount and type of "human capital" represented by educational credentials can be viewed as a resource that individuals use in their exchanges with employers who, for their part of the bargain, assume that these credentials increase the productivity of their workers. At the macro end, societies as a whole are seen as "investing" in education in order to improve the pool of human capital that can increase productivity. Thus expenditures on education, especially technical and higher educational facilities, can be considered by political leaders to be an investment that will be returned through higher productivity and economic growth.

In policy debates in the 1970s and 1980s utilitarian theory shifted from discussions of the rate of return on educational investment to analysis of individual and group decision-making behavior. Buchanan (1978) is credited by Sichel (1989) with the development of modern public choice theory. This utilitarian theory has been applied to such diverse topics as school desegregation (Rossell 1990), educational vouchers (Levin 1991), parental choice plans (Goldring 1991), and the behavior of school board members (Rada 1988) and of school administrators (Crowson 1989). Public choice theory draws attention to the logic of participation in decisions and the formation of public conceptions of efficiency and effectiveness in educational service provision. It has been extended through agency theory (Crowson and Morris 1990) to address the behavior of individuals whose utility functions depend on costs and benefits that actually accrue to others. While this approach has been applied to schooling in most developed nations only during the 1970s and 1980s, its roots can be traced in the United States to Callahan's (1962) vitriolic critique in *Education and the Cult of Efficiency*.

There have been many criticisms of utilitarian explanations of educational system performance—those in more general sociological theory (Blaug 1976, O'Toole 1977, Hurn 1985 pp. 54–61). These criticisms question, at the micro level, the rationality of actors' calculations in the light of imperfect information and sociocultural constraints. At more macro level, they question assumptions about the payoffs of education for societal productivity and economic development. Many of those who offer these critiques propose an alternative to both functionalism and utilitarianism: conflict theory.

4. Conflict Theorizing on Education

The conflict perspective is far and away the dominant mode of theorizing about educational processes. Conflict theories are highly diverse, although they all emphasize that the dynamics of education revolve around, and are implicated in, the unequal distribution of resources in society. Conflict theories have been utilized to explore such diverse educational phenomena as local versus state control;

labor relations; class, ethnic, and racial segregation; student grouping or tracking; teacher–student conflict; and the distribution of educational attainment. It is difficult to establish clear labels for all of the conflict theories within the sociology of education, but intellectual poles can be established toward which various theories gravitate. One set of approaches, inspired by Karl Marx, has emphasized the ways in which schools reproduce class relations (Sarup 1978, Levitas 1974). Another set of theories, more indebted to Weber, stresses the effects of education on the formation of, and competition among, status groups whose boundaries are more permeable and less enduring than those attributed to Marx's conception of social classes.

4.1 Marxian-inspired Conflict Theories

Marxian theories on educational processes tend to be mediated by European adaptations of Marx, especially the works of Gramsci (1971) and Althusser (1971). In both of these scholars' works, emphasis is given to the impact of ideology and its transmission on the maintenance of capitalist class relations. For while Marx's concept of "false consciousness" anticipated some of this emphasis, his actual work on ideology—for example, *The German Ideology* (Marx and Engels 1845–46)—does not fully capture the shift to the analysis of superstructural processes.

Althusser (1971) has remained closest to Marx in emphasizing that social structure consists of an infrastructure of economic forces and relations of production linked to a superstructure consisting of a political–legal repressive apparatus and an ideological state apparatus. Ultimately the political–legal and ideological apparatuses are grounded in conditions within the material economic infrastructure, but they also operate with a certain autonomy. The ideological state apparatus influences all institutional spheres, but its power is especially evident in the schools in which children learn the "know-how," "logics," and "dispositions" appropriate to the material relations of production.

Gramsci (1971) argued in a similar vein, but his work has given much more emphasis to the autonomy of ideology and the role of intellectuals in society (Mouffe 1979). Intellectuals, Gramsci argued, elaborate the dominant culture into complex ideologies, hiding and obfuscating the connection between symbols and power. The result is that intellectuals produce knowledge, logics, and ideas that are hegemonic, subtly justifying a system of domination. This thrust on the role of intellectuals has come to be generalized in to consideration of the role of teachers in the schools. Teachers have hegemony in the classroom: they impart and impose the ideas of the ruling class into the minds of children, thereby reproducing a system of domination. Since schools and ideology become the most significant repressive forces in society, it should not be surprising that many of the conflicts over the material base (both the forces and relations of production) manifest themselves in the cultural arena and in the schools.

These kinds of arguments, which can also be found in a number of other continental European interpreters of Marx, have perhaps had the greatest influence on Anglo-American scholarship, especially in the United States where the decline of the Cold War McCarthyism of the 1950s combined with civil rights politics during the 1960s to produce a burst of Marxian theorizing in the 1970s and 1980s.

As Hurn (1985) noted, there are two types of radical theories that, to some degree, take off from the positions of Althusser and Gramsci. One is the "hidden curriculum" position or, as it is sometimes called, the "correspondence" argument, in which the school produces the traits and attitudes necessary for the maintenance of the capitalist class system. The most prominent advocates of this theoretical position are Bowles and Gintis (1976) and such empirical researchers as Anyon (1980). A somewhat different, though overlapping, type of radical theory has stressed the effects of the more "explicit curriculum" in the "reproduction of a consciousness" that helps sustain or reproduce the capitalist system. The most prominent scholars who have maintained this position are Illich (1971), Apple (1979, 1982a, 1982b, 1988) and Giroux (1981). Others, such as Carnoy (1974, 1984, 1989) as well as Carnoy and Levin (1978) have taken a position between the Althusserian and Gramscian poles, though leaning toward Althusser. To provide a sense for these theoretical differences, the discussion will emphasize Bowles and Gintis's correspondence theory and Apple's more Gramscian argument, closing with a review of Carnoy's and Levin's more intermediate position.

Bowles and Gintis's conceptualization is more Althusserian in that it emphasizes the correspondence between the material relations of production in capitalist societies and the superstructural processes operating in schools. In essence, the structure of the workplace is mirrored in the classroom where there is an emphasis on obedience to rules, deference to authority, punctuality, and external evaluation (Gintis 1972). For example, the authoritarian structure corresponds to the hierarchy of corporate organizational structures and the system of grades corresponds to wage incentive systems. Such a structure penalizes students who are creative, aggressive, and independent and rewards those who obey and conform. In so doing, the school trains students from different class backgrounds to adapt to their ultimate occupational niche, thereby perpetuating the relations of production and class structure of capitalist societies.

Later empirical work by Anyon (1980, 1983) has added refinements to the kinds of arguments made by Bowles and Gintis. For example, a comparison of different types of schools serving the children of varying social classes (working class, middle class, affluent professional, and elite executive) revealed that there is a hidden agenda, revolving around curricular, pedagogical, and evaluation processes that emphasize different cognitive and behavioral skills and which, thereby, develop dispositions to act toward physical and symbolic capital, authority, and work processes in ways corresponding to their class background. This differentiation is particularly poignant in schools that track children into different academic programs (Oakes 1985).

At the more Gramscian end of the Marxist spectrum is Apple (1979, 1982a, 1982b, 1988) who has argued that there is no simple correspondence between the material infrastructure and superstructure. Rather, schools operate to produce the ideological hegemony of the dominant classes. The economy influences these ideological processes, but they reveal a certain independence; their effects on the reproduction of class relations is subtle and indirect. Moreover, schools are the major sites in which ideological conflicts are often fought. While these to some degree reflect material class interests, they often reveal a more autonomous ideological character concerning the ends and goals a society should pursue and deciding which means for realizing these goals are legitimate. Schools thus become a place where complex ideological struggles occur; and these struggles result from contradictions between the material and ideological superstructure as well as contradictions within both. Thus, the texts, curriculum, pedagogy, and other facets of the educational system work to reproduce class relations, but because of their autonomy as "cultural institutions," they become themselves arenas for conflicts emanating from complex relations between base and superstructure (McLaren 1989).

Giroux (1981, 1990a, 1990b) has added refinements to this Gramscian line of argument. The school is an oppressive system that, to a degree, corresponds to class relations, but it has a certain degree of independence. Hence it is best to examine school processes precisely, especially those in the classroom, in order to assess how they reproduce and contradict prevailing ideologies and social relations in the broader society (Giroux and McLaren 1989). One can see, Giroux argued, both contradiction and correspondence between the school, on the one side, and sociocultural arrangements in the larger society, on the other, with respect to such matters as curricula, teaching techniques, texts, and administrative philosophies and practices.

Between this attack on Bowles and Gintis's Althusserian correspondence approach and the more Gramscian autonomy of ideology and superstructure position are several mediating positions. Carnoy and Levin's writings (1978, 1985), as well as independent work by Carnoy (1984), best illustrate this moderation.

For Carnoy and Levin, conflict in schools is ultimately between the dominant and the dominated sectors of society. Much of this conflict is ideological because the dominant business class seeks to impose its values, norms, purposes, and goals on schools and to socialize the young into its ideology, thereby perpetuating the social relations of production and the class system. Schools thus operate to "colonize" students and their parents into accepting the legitimacy of the meritocracy implemented by the schools (as in the use of "objective tests," "tracking," and "grades") which reproduces the class system (Carnoy 1975). Yet the schools reflect the contradiction between capitalism and the modern democratic state which, on the one hand, uses schools to socialize children in ways reproducing relations of production and, on the other hand, must respond to protests and movements demanding greater equality in the distribution of resources. Thus, there are both "reproductive" and "democratizing" forces operating in capitalist societies (Carnoy 1989) and these can work at cross purposes with each other in the schools because dominant educational ideologies must make concessions to the demands of the dominated for greater access to those credentials and other resources provided by the schools. This is ultimately a conflict over relations of production and access to material resources, but it often occurs at an ideological level as dominant and dominated struggle over school organization, curricula, grades, tests, tracks, and other tools perpetuating the ideology of the business class (i.e., the belief in "meritocracy"). While the schools often coopt the dominated by making it seem as though greater fairness and access to resources have occurred, some real gains in equality of opportunity are recorded. As a consequence, the school structure and its culture do not completely mirror the interests of the business class but rather some negotiated compromise with various dominated populations who have mobilized to pursue their interests and who, because of the "forces of democracy," can realize at least some of those interests against those of the dominant business class. Thus the school is an arena for intense ideological conflicts over credentials, curriculum, pedagogy, and other aspects of school culture and structure; these conflicts reflect the contradictions of a democratic state apparatus that seeks to reproduce relations of production and, at the same time, to respond to the pressures of dominated subpopulations. Therefore, while much struggle is ideological, it is nonetheless connected to the material relations of production and distributions of resources.

4.2 Weberian-inspired Conflict Theories

Like all Marxist theories, those inspired by Weber's (1922) analysis of domination also address the question of how schools "reproduce" the class system and how cultural ideas or ideology are implicated in this reproduction. Yet there is a clear shift in emphasis toward concerns with competition among "status groups," or how subpopulations compete over honor, prestige, and cultural capital. For to the degree that the economic class system is reproduced by the educational system, the intervening mechanisms revolve around the formation of status groups.

Collins (1979) has developed the most explicitly Weberian conflict approach. For Collins, schools are not so much a tool or "apparatus" of the capitalist class as they are instruments for maintaining cultural differences among individuals. Status groups compete with each other for honor and prestige, and the distribution of educational credentials is one major arena in which this conflict occurs. In contrast to functional approaches, where the expansion of the school system is seen as related to societal needs, Collins has argued that the expansion of the school system, especially the higher educational system, reflects status group competition that has little to do with actual societal needs or job requirements. The educational establishment has encouraged the use of credentials as "markers" of honor and prestige; as it has been sucessful in this pursuit of its own interests, educational credentials and the cultural capital they imply have become necessary for access to jobs with higher pay and power which, in turn, further denote status group membership. As a result, the pursuit of credentials becomes more intense as people seek markers of status and access to jobs with higher paying-power; as more and more people demand and earn ever more credentials, inflation occurs, lowering the value of credentials for both status group membership and job access. Ironically, as the value of one level of credential declines (e.g., a university degree), then more credentials are sought, thereby ratcheting up the inflationary cycle and the competition for markers of cultural capital. Thus, the conflicts in schools and the demands for ever greater access to more credentials are not just a class-driven process; status group membership as defined by educational credentials is also involved and, in advanced capitalist systems, becomes a mechanism for gaining access to class positions.

Bourdieu (1984), and Bourdieu and Passeron (1977) approached this kind of argument in a somewhat different way. The dynamics of education, Bourdieu argued, must be understood in terms of more general stratifying processes in which various types of "capital"—economic (money, objects), social (positions, networks, group affiliations), cultural (skills, credentials, tastes, speech), and symbolic (legitimating codes)—are unequally distributed. Social class position is determined by the total amount as well as the configurations of these four types of capital. Moreover, divisions within classes are also reflected in the amount and configuration of capital. Hence, the dominant class is high in all forms of capital, although its three factions reveal different amounts of various types of capital; similarly, the middle class has moderate amounts of capital, with factions evidencing somewhat different levels and configurations of capital; and the same is true of the lower classes who have, on the whole, low levels of all forms of capital. For each class and faction, there is a distinct culture or "habitus" which is the largely unconscious perceptions, choices, preferences, and behaviors of members with a given level and configuration of economic, social, cultural, and symbolic capital. Children learn within the habitus, and they acquire capital from their parents and peers that they can then use to acquire academic credentials (a type of cultural capital) which, in turn, can be exchanged for other forms of capital. Thus, educational credentials become one of the key media of exchange for converting one kind of capital into another. By virtue of acquiring from parents and from class peers levels and types of economic, social, symbolic, and cultural capital, children are able to perform with varying degrees of success in schools, thereby acquiring differentially valued credentials. The credentials are then used to "purchase" other types and amounts of capital—jobs, networks, money, prestige, tastes, life-styles, speech, legitimacy, status group membership—which maintain class position. Thus, not only is class itself a composite of varying types of capital, the processes of class reproduction are subtle and indirect, operating through habitus and school structures. Upper-class children start with high levels of all forms of capital and can use these to secure prestigeful educational credentials that can sustain their class position. Lower-class children can be upwardly mobile, but their lack of economic capital (money), social capital (networks, group memberships), and most importantly, cultural capital (speech, styles, manner, knowledge, tastes, demeanor) ultimately keeps them from penetrating the dominant classes in any numbers. Middle-class children encounter similar obstacles, especially with respect to their lower levels of cultural capital. These processes operate in an educational system that, itself, is stratified and that has its own interests in producing and reproducing itself as the arbitrator of cultural capital. Because of this fact, there is a lack of tight correspondence and synchronization between relations of economic production and educational processes.

Meyer (1977) has extended this theme, arguing that education is not the passive servant of elites but, in fact, is an active agent in creating "new classes of knowledge and personnel." Moreover, as modern capitalist economies have increasingly become "knowledge economies," this power to create and certify positions that bring income, prestige, and power has grown. Indeed, educational levels become status positions, entitling individuals to certain resources and responses from others, while shaping how adult roles are played. Since educational credentials bestow membership in a status group, people in modern societies demand increasing access to the educational system. This pressure for education to provide access to elite positions cannot be fully successful because of the tendency for higher access to deflate credential values (Collins's argument) without overcoming the persistence of unequal distribution of other types of capital (Bourdieu's position). The critical conclusion from Meyer's theory, however, is that education cannot be merely a tool of elites for class reproduction; it remains institutionally too autonomous as a creator of status and too vulnerable to demand for the extension of credentials to ever more people.

In sum, then, the major difference between Marxian and Weberian conflict theories is over the degree to which school structures and processes correspond to, reflect, or reproduce relations of the means of production. For both Gramscian and Althusserian Marxists, there is a relatively tight connection between sub-and superstructure, even if this connection is mediated by somewhat autonomous cultural and ideological forces. Within the Weberian tradition, however, class itself is a multidimensional phenomenon, involving more than relations of production, with the result that schooling creates and sustains class relations (through credentialing) as much as it is controlled by class interests. While the vocabularies and thrusts of the theories vary, their concerns are the same: to document how the distribution of status and resources in the larger society are sustained and reproduced, or challenged and redistributed, as schools mediate life chances in modern, capitalist societies. So long as theorists like Meyer convincingly argue that schools themselves have the power to create new high income-prestige positions, despite mass pressures for increasing access to the system, education will continue to be seen as more than merely an "apparatus" of the state used to promote the interests of a dominant elite.

5. *Interactionist Theorizing on Education*

While functional and conflict theories emphasize attention to the macro-level relationship between school and society, symbolic interaction sociologies tend toward meso- and micro- level analysis of individual behavior within educational settings. Interactionist theorizing has three distinct traditions, each of which makes a significant contribution to understanding contemporary work in education. One is the tradition initiated by Mead and Morris (1962) and personified in the 1990s in symbolic interactionism and role theory. Another is the line of work inspired by the late Durkheim (1912, Durkheim and Mauss 1903) which has evolved into either linguistics and structuralism or interaction ritual theory. The third has resulted from Schutz's (1932) sociological adaptation of Husserl's phenomenological project, creating modern-day phenomenology and ethnomethodology.

With the applied emphasis of most educational research, distinctions among these interactionist approaches tend to become blurred, but a conceptual emphasis on one of the three approaches is typically dominant. In general, symbolic interactionists' emphasis on self and definition of the situation is, by far, the most common conceptual imagery. The dramaturgy of Goffman that Durkheim inspired is given less emphasis than the linguistic structuralism stimulated by Durkheim via Saussure (1949). The phenomenology emphasis on categorization and knowledgeability, coupled with ethnomethodological concerns about the construction of a sense of reality, is often stressed but is frequently blended into symbolic interactionist concerns about definitions of situations. What emerges, therefore, is a somewhat eclectic mix of interactionist traditions. Moreover, these more micro approaches are often infused with concerns of functional theory (e.g., Woods 1983) and Marxist conflict theorizing (e.g., Bernstein 1977) making them even more eclectic.

5.1 *Symbolic Interactionism and Role Theory*

Hargreaves's early work (1967, 1975) laid out the basic tenets of interactionist role theory: the self-conception of teachers and pupils, the perceptions of relevant roles by teachers and pupils, the categorizing or stereotyping of others, the playing of roles, and the creation and maintenance of definitions of situations. All of these processes interact and intersect in complex ways, but like all interactionist theory, particular emphasis is given to self-conceptions as a mediating influence on definitions of situations, categorizations of other, and performances in roles. As teachers and pupils interact, these can be renegotiated, but given the power and authority of teachers, it is their self, definitions, stereotypes, and role performances that have a disproportionate influence on pupils.

Works by various interactionist sociologists have examined all of the forces enumerated by Hargreaves, but the most prevalent have focused on categorizations by teachers, definitions of situations, and role-playing style (e.g., Hammersley 1977, Hammersley and Turner 1984, Delamont 1976, Nash 1976, Sharp and Green 1975). There is also a large literature on pupils' self-conceptions, definitions of the classroom/school situation, and role-playing styles (e.g., Pollard 1984, Woods 1983, Furlong 1976). Of particular note is a large body of theory and research, inspired by Lemert's seminal work (1951), on the effects of labeling processes by teachers, testing systems, and school culture on students' self-conceptions and consequent role-playing and performance in schools (e.g., Rosenthal and Jacobsen 1982, Eder 1981, Rist 1977, McDermott 1977, Entwhisle and Hayduk 1981, Mercer 1992).

As micro level analysis of school structures, especially classroom interactions, proliferated, some began to emphasize that macro level processes set parameters for roles, definitions of situations, and categorizations and stereotypes. For example, Archer (1984) has argued that the historical processes creating educational systems "structurally conditions" the interaction processes; and while such interactions can "structurally elaborate" macro level structural conditioning, it is still essential to visualize micro level encounters among teachers, students, and administrators as highly circumscribed by the larger system of education as it evolved as a result of political and economic forces.

5.2 Dramaturgical Interactionism

One line of analysis runs from Durkheim's interpretation of rituals and their effects on social structure to Goffman's dramaturgical perspective which, in turn, has influenced educational research and theory. This perspective has emphasized that ordered interactions or encounters among individuals are embedded in a more macro context. Analysis of these encounters has focused on the presentations of "self" and "face," the constructions of lines of conduct (Goffman 1959), the strategic nature of interaction (Goffman 1972), the importance of talk and ritual in interpersonal relations (Goffman 1972), and the framing of situations in terms of what is to be excluded and included (Goffman 1975). No single conceptualization exists of how all of these dynamics operate in school, but researchers have included a number of these processes in their analyses. For example, Woods (1983) made the connection to Durkheim explicit in adopting and then adapting to the school context Merton's (1938) famous classification of responses to cultural success goals and institutional means to reach them. Perhaps in response to criticisms that such a classification of students' responses did not capture the complexity of pupil–teacher interaction, Woods (1990) moved more explicitly into the Goffmanian tradition, invoking the concepts of encounters and strategic interactions. Yet in Woods's and other work, the full Goffmanian legacy has yet to be employed systematically to the study of the school and classroom encounters (for exceptions to this conclusion see Pollard 1985, Hatch 1987).

5.3 Interactionist Structuralism

A second Durkheimian legacy is structuralism, as this evolved through Saussure (1949), Levi-Strauss (1953), and a host of modern French thinkers (Lemert 1990). Bernstein (1977) has been perhaps the most prominent thinker in education, using quasi-structuralist ideas with a Marxian twist (another well-established French tradition, including Althusser's work and that of later Europeans). Moreover, he also added what appear to be some Goffmanian elements to his analysis, reflecting the dramaturgical lineage from Durkheim.

Bernstein's most famous idea is the distinction between "restricted" and "elaborated" linguistic codes. Restricted codes operate to leave implicit much of the meaning and context of utterances, whereas elaborated codes work to make explicit and universalistic the context, meaning, and intent of utterances. Since schools are biased toward the elaborated code, and since the use of such codes is more typical among children from the middle classes, lower-class children, who are more likely to use restricted codes, are placed at a disadvantage. Differential socialization practices—"positional" with "strong classification" versus "personal" and "weak classification"—produce these differences. Positional socialization has generated a restricted code and classification schema that partitions the world, whereas personal socialization fosters an elaborated code and weak classification system that enables relationships among elements of the world to be seen and spoken. In schools, which have moved from a mechanical basis of solidarity (common values, one class, ascribed teacher status and authority, tight external control) to a more organic basis of solidarity (plurality of values, ability groupings instead of classrooms, achieved teacher authority, and weakened external control), those who use elaborated codes, weak classification systems, and weak frames (over what is to be included and excluded from the classroom) will enjoy an advantage over those who use restricted codes, strong classification, and strong frames. Bernstein's analysis is vague, like so much structuralism, but his debts to Durkheim and, to a lesser extent, Goffman and Marxian class analysis are clear.

5.4 Interactionist Phenomenology

Alfred Schutz's (1932) reconstruction of Husserl's (1913) phenomenological project has produced a concern for the "taken-for-granted" nature of much reality and the interpersonal processes that produce and sustain people's sense of reality. At a more general theoretical level, this line of argument is found in constructionist theory (Berger and Luckman 1967), ethnomethodology (Garfinkel 1967) and its offspring, conversational analysis (e.g., Schegloff 1968), and more modern versions of phenomenology. When applied to educational processes, this more phenomenological version of interactionist theory emphasizes how knowledge, truth, ability, intelligence, and other supposedly "objective" realities are, in fact, socially constructed (Blackledge and Hunt 1985, Young 1971, Keddie 1971, Esland 1971, Mehan 1987).

As Young has emphasized, schools are structured around a biased view of knowledge: that academic, abstract knowledge is superior to commonsense or everyday knowledge (Young 1971). This view of knowledge is imposed upon students, with those able to enter the teachers' realm of abstracted knowledge being defined as bright, intelligent, and motivated. In contrast, those who remain at the everyday level are defined as less bright and less able to achieve in school. Tracking in schools on ability thus involves an implicit assumption about superior knowledge which defines and labels students, pushing them into ability tracks in terms of whether or not they can enter the realm of abstract knowledge.

Keddie (1971), for example, examined "classroom knowledge" in these terms, noting that subtle and implicit class labels put on students affect judgments about which students can and will enter the realm of academic and abstracted knowledge and which cannot. The reality of school tracking, then, is not so much based on actual abilities but on a constructed framework which differentially values and rewards certain types of knowledge, usually to the disadvantage of non-middle-class students. The seeming "rationality" of the evaluation systems in schools is nothing more than an imposition of one form of knowledgeability on students.

6. Conclusion

Sociological theorizing about education has tended to reflect the ebb and flow of broader theoretical perspectives. The application of these perspectives has generally involved the extraction of certain analytical elements and application of these elements to either macro or micro level processes in schools. Though more educational researchers have relied on functional or interaction theories in interpreting problems of practice, conflict theory has been the focus of more theoretically oriented scholars. The ascendance of conflict theory may have peaked, however. At the very least it is being supplemented in many countries by a shift from concern about class inequalities to those revolving around sex/gender and race/ethnicity (e.g., Weis 1988).

Virtually all educational sociology is only loosely theoretical. Theoretical work focuses primarily on macro processes, with little theoretical attention given to meso-and micro-level analyses. Most theorizing on education is highly derivative, rarely offering to general theory comprehensive analysis or new insights. The reason for this situation is that research in education is overwhelmingly applied to problems of policy and practice, frequently by the ideological questions of research sponsors or professional reformers. In such an environment, theory will be used for ad hoc policy and ideological purposes. The result will be loose, imprecise, and vague use of theory to interpret educational processes.

See also: Classical Sociological Theories of Education; Sociology of Education: Overview; Political Socialization and Education; Philosophy of Education: Historical Overview; Marxism and Educational Thought; Philosophy of Education: Western European Perspectives; Political Philosophy and Education

References

Althusser L 1971 Ideology and ideological state apparatuses. In: Althusser L (ed.) 1971 *Lenin and Philosophy and Other Essays*. New Left Books, London

Anyon J 1980 Social class and the hidden curriculum of work. *J. Educ.* 162(1): 67–92

Anyon J 1983 *Social Class and Gender in U.S. Education*. Routledge and Kegan Paul, London

Apple M W 1979 *Ideology and Curriculum*. Routledge and Kegan Paul, Boston, Massachusetts

Apple M W 1982a *Education and Power*. Routledge and Kegan Paul, Boston, Massachusetts

Apple M W (ed.) 1982b *Cultural and Economic Reproduction in Education: Essays on Class, Ideology and the State*. Routledge and Kegan Paul, London

Apple M W 1988 *Teacher and Texts: A Political Economy of Class and Gender Relations in Education*. Routledge and Kegan Paul, London

Archer M 1984 *Social Origins of Educational Systems*. Sage, London

Becker G 1975 *Human Capital*, 2nd edn. Columbia University Press, New York

Berger P, Luckman T 1967 *The Social Construction of Reality*. Allen Lane, London

Bernstein B 1977 *Class, Codes and Control. Vol. 3: Towards a Theory of Educational Transmission*, 2nd edn. Routledge and Kegan Paul, London

Blackledge D A, Hunt B D 1985 *Sociological Interpretations of Education*. Routledge, London

Blaug M 1976 The empirical status of human capital theory: A slightly jaundiced view. *J. Econ. Literature* 14(3): 827–55

Bourdieu P 1984 *Distinction: A Social Critique of the Judgement of Taste*. Routledge, London

Bourdieu P, Passeron J 1977 *Reproduction in Education, Society and Culture*. Sage, London

Bowles S, Gintis H 1976 *Schooling in Capitalist America: Educational Reform and the Contradictions of Economic Life*. Routledge and Kegan Paul, London

Buchanan J M 1969 *Cost and Choice: An Inquiry into Economic Theory*. University of Chicago Press, Chicago, Illinois

Callahan R E 1962 *Education and the Cult of Efficiency*. University of Chicago Press, Chicago, Illinois

Carnoy M 1974 *Education as Cultural Imperialism*. McKay, New York

Carnoy M (ed.) 1975 *Schooling in a Corporate Society: The Political Economy of Education in America*. McKay, New York

Carnoy M 1984 Marxism and education. In: Ollman B, Vernoff E (eds.) 1984 *The Left Academy: Marxist Scholarship on American Campuses*, Vol. 2. Praeger, New York

Carnoy M 1989 Education, state, and culture in American society. In: Giroux H, McLaren P (eds.) 1989 *Critical Pedagogy. The State and Cultural Struggle*. SUNY Press, Albany, New York

Carnoy M, Levin H (eds.) 1978 *The Limits of Educational Reform*. Longman, New York

Carnoy M, Levin H (eds.) 1985 *Schooling and Work in the Democratic State*. Stanford University Press, Stanford, California

Coleman J S 1990 *Foundations of Social Theory*. Belknap, Cambridge, Massachusetts

Collins R 1979 *The Credential Society*. Academic Press, New York

Cook K S (ed.) 1986 *Social Exchange Theory*. Sage, Newbury Park, California

Crowson R L 1989 Managerial ethics in educational administration: The rational choice approach. *Urban Educ.* 23(4): 412–35

Crowson R L, Morris V C 1990 *The Superintendency and School Leadership. The National Center for School Leadership Project Report*. Office of Educational Research and Improvement, Washington, DC

Delamont S 1976 *Interaction in the Classroom*. Routledge, London

Durkheim E 1933 (1st edn. 1893) *The Division of Labor in Society*. Free Press, Glencoe, Illinois

Durkheim E 1961 (1st edn. 1922) *Moral Education*. Free Press, New York

Durkheim E 1976 (1st edn. 1912) *Elementary Forms of the Religious Life*, 2nd edn. Allen and Unwin, London

Durkheim E, Mauss M 1969 (1st edn. 1903) *Primitive Classification*. Cohen and West, London

Eder D 1981 Ability grouping as a self-fulfilling prophecy: A micro-analysis of teacher–student interaction. *Sociology of Educ.* 54(3): 151–62

Emerson R 1986 Toward a theory of value in social exchange. In: Cook K S (ed.) 1980 *Social Exchange Theory*. Sage, Beverly Hills, California

Entwhisle D, Hayduk L 1981 Academic expectations and the school attainment of young children. *Sociology of Educ.* 54(1): 34–50

Esland G 1971 Teaching and learning as the organization of knowledge. In: Young M F D (ed.) 1971 *Knowledge and Control*. Collier-Macmillan, London

Furlong V 1976 Interaction sets in the classroom. In: *Hammersley M*, Woods P (ed.) 1976 *The Process of Schooling*. Routledge and Kegan Paul, London

Garfinkel H 1967 *Studies in Ethnomethodology*. Prentice-Hall, Englewood Cliffs, New Jersey

Gintis H 1972 Toward a political economy of education. *Harvard Educ. Rev.* 42: 1–24

Giroux H A 1981 *Ideology, Culture, and the Process of Schooling*. Falmer Press, London

Giroux H A 1990a *Schooling and the Struggle for Public Life*. University of Minnesota Press, Minneapolis, Minnesota

Giroux H A 1990b *Teachers as Intellectuals: A Critical Pedagogy for Practical Learning*. Bergin and Garvey, South Hadley, Massachusetts

Giroux H A, McLaren P (eds.) 1989 *Critical Pedagogy, the State and Cultural Struggle*. SUNY Press, Albany, New York

Goffman E 1959 *The Presentation of Self in Everyday Life*. Doubleday, New York

Goffman E 1972 *Interaction Ritual*. Allen Lane, London

Goffman E 1975 *Frame Analysis*. Penguin, Harmondsworth

Goldring E B (ed.) 1991 Parental involvement and public choice in education. *Int. J. Educ. Res.* 15(3–4): 229–352

Goslin D A 1965 *The School in Contemporary Society*. Scott, Foresman, Boston, Massachusetts

Gramsci A 1971 *Selections from The Prison Notebooks of Antonio Gramsci*. Lawrence and Wishart, London

Hammersley M 1977 Teacher perspectives. *Schooling and Society (Unit 9 of E202)*. Open University Press, Milton Keynes

Hammersley M, Turner G 1984 Conformist pupils. In: Hammersley M, Woods P (eds.) 1984 *Life in Schools: The Sociology of Pupil Culture*. Open University Press, Milton Keynes

Hargreaves D H 1967 *Social Relations in a Secondary School*. Routledge and Kegan Paul, London

Hargreaves D H 1975 *Interpersonal Relations and Education*. Routledge and Kegan Paul, London

Hatch J A 1987 Impression management in kindergarten classrooms. *Rev. Educ. Res.* 57: 437–66

Hechter M 1987 *Principles of Group Solidarity*. University of California Press, Berkeley, California

Hurn C J 1985 *The Limits and Possibilities of Schooling*, 2nd edn. Allyn and Bacon, Boston, Massachusetts

Husserl E 1969 (1st edn. 1913) *Ideas: General Introduction to Pure Phenomenology*. Allen and Unwin, London

Illich I 1971 *Deschooling Society*. Calder and Boyars, London

Juster T (ed.) 1975 *Education, Income and Human Behavior*. McGraw-Hill, New York

Keddie N 1971 Classroom knowledge. In: Young M F D (ed.) 1971 *Knowledge and Control: New Directions for the Sociology of Education*. Collier-Macmillan, London

Lemert C C 1990 The uses of French structuralisms in sociology. In: Ritzer G (ed.) 1990 *Frontiers of Social Theory: The New Syntheses*. Columbia University Press, New York

Lemert E 1951 *Social Pathology*. McGraw-Hill, New York

Levin H M 1991 Views on the economics of educational choice. A reply to West. *Econ. Educ. Rev.* 10 (2): 171–75

Levin M R, Shank A 1970 *Educational Investment in An Urban Society: Costs, Benefits and Public Policy*. Teachers College Press, New York

Levi-Strauss C 1953 Social structure. In: Kroeber A (ed.) 1953 *Anthropology Today*. University of Chicago Press, Chicago, Illinois

Levitas M (ed.) 1974 *Marxist Perspectives in the Sociology of Education*. Routledge and Kegan Paul, London

Marx K, Engels F, Arthur C J 1947 (1st edn. 1845–46) *The German Ideology*. Lawrence and Wishart, London

McDermott R P 1977 Social relations as context for learning. *Harv. Educ. Rev.* 47(2): 198–213

McLaren P 1989 *Life in Schools: An Introduction to Critical Pedagogy in the Foundations of Education*. Longman, New York

Mead G H, Morris C W 1962 *Mind, Self, and Society: From the Standpoint of a Social Behaviorist*. University of Chicago Press, Chicago, Illinois

Mehan H 1987 Language and schooling. In: Spindler G, Spindler L (eds.) 1987 *Interpretive Ethnography of Education*. Erlbaum, Hillsdale, New Jessey

Mercer J R 1992 The impact of changing paradigms of disability on mental retardation in the year 2000. In: Rowitz L (ed.) 1992 *Mental Retardation in the Year 2000*. Springer-Verlag, New York

Merton R H 1938 Social structure and anomie. *Am. Sociol. Rev.* 3(6): 672–82

Meyer J W 1977 The effects of education as an institution. *Am. J. Sociol.* 83(1): 55–77

Mouffe C (ed.) 1979 *Gramsci and Marxist Theory*. Routledge and Kegan Paul, London

Nash R 1976 *Teacher Expectations and Pupil Learning*. Routledge and Kegan Paul, London
Oakes J 1985 *Keeping Track: How Schools Structure Inequality*. Yale University Press, New Haven, Connecticut
O'Toole J 1977 *Work, Learning and the American Future*. Jossey-Bass, San Francisco
Parsons T 1949 *The Structure of Social Action*. Free Press, Glencoe, Illinois
Parsons T 1952 *The Social System*. Free Press, New York
Parsons T 1959 The school as a social system: Some of its functions in American society. *Harv. Educ. Rev.* 29(4): 297–318
Parsons T 1971 *The System of Modern Societies*. Prentice-Hall, Englewood Cliffs, New Jersey
Parsons T, Bales R F, Shils E A 1953 *Working Papers in the Theory of Action*. Free Press, Glencoe, Illinois
Parsons T, Platt G 1973 *The American University*. Harvard University Press, Cambridge, Massachusetts
Pollard A 1984 Goodies, jokers, and gangs. In: Hammersley M, Woods P (eds.) 1984 *Life in Schools: The Sociology of Pupil Cultures*. Open University Press, Milton Keynes
Pollard A 1985 *The Social World of the Primary School*. Cassell, London
Rada R D 1988 A public choice theory of school board member behavior. *Educ. Eval. Policy Anal.* 10(3): 225–36
Rist R C 1977 On understanding the process of schooling: The contributions of labelling theory. In: Karabel J, Halsey A H (eds.) 1977 *Power and Ideology in Education*. Oxford University Press, New York
Rosenthal R, Jacobsen L 1982 *Pygmalion in the Classroom*. Irvington, New York
Rossell C H 1990 The carrot or the stick for school desegregation policy? *Urban Affairs Quarterly* 25(3): 474–99
Sarup M 1978 *Marxism and Education*. Routledge and Kegan Paul, London
Saussure F de 1949 *Course in General Linguistics*. Payot, Paris
Schegloff E A 1968 Sequencing in conversational openings. *American Anthropologist* 70(4): 1075–95
Schultz T 1961 Investment in human capital. *Am. Econ. Rev.* 51(March): 1–17
Schutz A 1932 (republished 1967) *The Phenomenology of the Social World*. Northwestern University Press, Evanston, Illinois
Sharp R, Green A 1975 *Education and Social Control*. Routledge and Kegan Paul, London
Sichel W (ed.) 1989 *The State of Economic Science: Views of Six Nobel Laureates*. W E Upjohn Institute for Employment Research, Kalamazoo, Missouri
Smith A 1937 (1st edn. 1776) *An Inquiry into the Nature and Causes of the Wealth of Nations*. Random House, New York
Sobel I 1978 The human capital revolution in economic development: Its current history and status. *Comp. Educ. Rev.* 22(2): 278–308
Spencer H 1969 (1st edn. 1874–96) *The Principles of Sociology*. Macmillan, London
Turner J H 1972 *Patterns of Social Organization*. McGraw-Hill, New York
Turner J H 1991 *The Structure of Sociological Theory*, 5th edn. Wadsworth, Belmont, California
Turner J H, Maryanski A 1979 *Functionalism*. Benjamin-Cummings, Menlo Park, California
Turner R H 1971 Sponsored and contest mobility in the school system. In: Hopper E (ed.) 1971 *Readings in the Theory of Educational Systems*. Hutchinson, London
United States National Commission on Excellence in Education 1983 *A Nation at Risk*. United States Government Printing Office, Washington, DC
Waller W 1961 *The Sociology of Teaching*. Wiley and Sons, New York
Weber M 1968 (1st edn. 1922) *Economy and Society*. University of California, Berkeley, California
Weis L (ed.) 1988 *Class, Race and Gender in American Education*. SUNY Press, Albany, New York
Willer D 1987 *Theory and the Experimental Investigation of Social Structures*. Gordon and Breach, New York
Woods P 1983 *Sociology and the School: An Interactionist Viewpoint*. Routledge and Kegan Paul, London
Woods P 1990 *The Happiest Days? How Pupils Cope with Schools*. Falmer Press, London
Young M F D (ed.) 1971 *Knowledge and Control*. Collier-Macmillan, London

Further Reading

Apple M W (ed.) 1982 *Cultural and Economic Reproduction in Education*. Routledge and Kegan Paul, London
Becker G 1975 *Human Capital*, 2nd edn. Columbia University Press, New York
Bennett K, LeCompte M D 1990 *The Way Schools Work: A Sociological Analysis of Education*. Longman, New York
Blackledge D, Hunt B 1985 *Sociological Interpretations of Education*. Routledge, London
Carnoy M, Levin H 1985 *Schooling and Work in the Democratic State*. Stanford University Press, Stanford, California
Hurn C 1985 *The Limits and Possibilities of Schooling*, 2nd edn. Allyn and Bacon, Boston, Massachusetts
Karabel J, Halsey A H (eds.) 1977 *Power and Ideology in Education*. Oxford University Press, New York
McLaren P 1989 *Life in Schools*. Longman, New York

J. H. Turner; D. Mitchell

Content and Text Analysis

Content analysis,sometimes referred to as document analysis, includes the methods and techniques researchers use to examine, analyze and make inferences about human communications. Typically, communications consist of printed or written text but may also comprise photographs, cartoons, illustrations, broadcasts, and verbal interactions. Text analysis, by contrast, has a narrower focus and is restricted to analysis of text features, and usually as these relate to comprehensibility or writing style. The widespread use of computers has seen a resurgence of research studies using methods of content and text analysis.

The techniques of content and text analysis are used by researchers across a range of disciplines: anthropology, psychology, sociology, psychiatry, history, literature, political science, education, linguistics, artificial intelligence. This entry adopts an educational, psycholinguistic perspective and, although there is often overlap, content and text analysis are discussed separately. The focus in this entry is on written communication, on purposes and techniques commonly employed by educational researchers, and on methodological issues.

1. Definitions of Content Analysis

Berelson's chapter in *Handbook of Social Psychology* Vol. 1 (1952) is still regarded as a basic reference for content analysis. (This chapter is a condensed version of Berelson's book *Content Analysis in Communication Research* published two years previously and republished in 1971). Here Berelson defines content analysis as a "a research technique for the objective, systematic, and quantitative description of the manifest content of communication" (p.489). In a further major review of content analysis in the second edition of *The Handbook of Social Psychology*, Holsti (1968) adopts essentially the same definition.

A slightly different interpretation was made by Osgood who defined content analysis as "a procedure whereby one makes inferences about sources and receivers from evidence in the messages they exchange" (Osgood 1959 p. 35). This changed emphasis was taken up by Weber who defined content analysis as "a research methodology that utilizes a set of procedures to make valid inferences from text" (Weber 1985 p. 9). Weber continues: "These inferences are about the sender(s) of message, the message itself, or the audience of the message."

In successive editions of *Foundations of Behavioral Research*, Kerlinger adopts this wider view of content analysis as going beyond description to making inferences about variables. Thus content analysis is defined by Kerlinger (1986 p. 477) as "a method of studying and analyzing communications in a systematic, objective, and quantitative manner to measure variables." While many earlier studies using content analysis focused on descriptions of various communications—for instance, analyzing the content of newspapers, radio and television programs, studies of propaganda, public opinion, bias and prejudice, and studies of literary style, reading difficulty, and error analysis—for Kerlinger, content analysis is also a method of observation and measurement. "Instead of observing people's behavior directly, or asking them to respond to scales, or interviewing them, the investigator takes the communications that people have produced and asks questions of the communications" (p. 477).

2. A Framework for Studies of Content Analysis

A model widely applied to biological, psychological, social, and other systems was that proposed by Shannon and Weaver (1949). Developed to deal with signal transmission, this model incorporates a source, transmitter, channel of communication, noise, receiver, and destination. The model has been adapted to language communication (Anderson 1976), as shown in Fig.1, and provides a framework for studies of content analysis, both in its narrower and wider connotations.

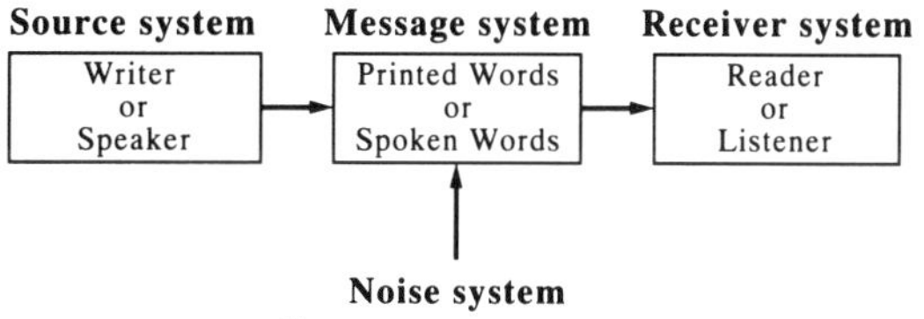

Figure 1
A model for the correspondence of source, message, noise, and receiver systems

Not only does the language communication model in Fig.1 provide a useful framework for reviewing the field of content analysis, it can also serve as a fruitful source for generating hypotheses. First, studies that focus primarily on the source system typically deal with the psychological states, motivations, or characteristics of encoders and the effects of these upon messages produced. Many of these studies fall into the category of "language style." Second, studies focusing mainly on the receiver system and which investigate attitudes, values, motives, and other psychological characteristics of decoders in relation to messages received, come into the realm of "audience analysis." Third, other studies where the primary focus is on the *message* itself or on *noise* and the effect of distortion in the message upon receivers belong to the field of content analysis in its narrower sense. Insofar as these three categories of studies involve the message system however, they are all embraced by content analysis in its wider connotation as a method of observation and measurement.

Typical of numerous studies in the first category noted, where the focus of attention is on the message in order to make inferences about encoders of messages, is that of Mahl (1959) who examined the speech of psychotherapy patients in order to assess their anxiety. Exemplifying the second category, where the focus of attention is again on the message but this time to make inferences about decoders, is a study of supporters' and critics' reactions to a television news program aimed at high school students (Wulfemeyer and Mueller 1991). Focusing more directly on the message itself is Anderson and Yip's (1987) study which examined the content of two editions of an Australian reading scheme to see what changes took place in the presentation of sex roles over a decade and a half when the roles of women in western societies changed quite markedly.

The numerous investigations into methodological questions relating to "cloze procedure" (a measure of reading comprehension discussed below where subjects attempt to replace deleted parts of text), such as the effect on comprehension of frequency of deletions, type of deletions, and scoring procedures, are illustrative of studies into noise or message distortion.

3. Purposes and Techniques of Content Analysis

The research investigations cited demonstrate the wide range of uses of content analysis. Content analyzed by researchers covers the gamut of human communication: letters, stories, poetry, essays, diaries, obituaries, minutes, biographies, newspapers, radio, television, conversations, cartoons, drawing, photographs, film. As others have remarked, communication content is the *what* in the classic description of communication: *who* says *what* to whom, how, and with *what effect*. The widespread use of computers, together with the increasing ease of inputting text via scanners and text recognition software, are multiplying the number of studies utilizing text analysis.

Although there are several ways to do content analysis, there are, nevertheless, recognized procedures that do not differ markedly from many other procedures in educational research. These procedures are illustrated by reference to specific studies. First and foremost is the need to identify the corpus or universe to be studied. In the investigation cited of sex roles in young children's books (Anderson and Yip 1987), the corpus of reading content for analysis comprised the first nine books from the *Young Australia Language Scheme* (first published in 1966) and the first nine basic readers from *Young Australia Readers* (published in 1980). These 18 books constituted the content for analysis.

The second essential step is to define the categories into which the universe is to be partitioned. According to Kerlinger (1986), this is the most important part of content analysis because it reflects the purposes of the research and the theory underlying it. Categories must be objectively defined and mutually exclusive. Further, if comparisons are to be made with other studies, generally agreed upon or standard categories need to be adopted. Considerations like these led Stone and his associates to develop *The General Inquirer*, a computerized approach to content analysis (Stone et al. 1966). The bases of this approach are specially developed dictionaries which allow computer tagging of words of text entered into the computer program. The tagged words then serve as indicators of, for example, need-achievement, or discipline, or for whatever the dictionary has been designed.

After defining categories, the next step is to determine units for analysis. In the preceding example, the computer tags words indicating need-achievement. Other units may be themes (often phrases or even sentences), characters, items, or space-and-time measures (like the number of pages in a book or the length of a discussion in minutes). Anderson and Yip (1987) adopted as one form of category the total number of characters (human, animal, fantasy figure, inanimate object) presented in the text and/or accompanying illustrations. Characters were counted for each story in each of the readers, noting the gender of all characters. Where the gender of characters was ambiguous, it was recorded as "other". As another form of category, all activities of male and female characters were categorized under a number of themes established in another study: themes like leadership, triumphing over foe or adversity, rescuing, exploring, showing bravery, showing fear, and so on. The units of analysis determine the level of measurement in statistical analyses.

The techniques of content analysis such as defining categories and determining units for analysis prove useful, too, in a number of investigations where the focus is not primarily on analyzing content. One example is in coding open-ended questionnaire responses. In an evaluation of curriculum materials, for example, rather than ask teachers to tick or otherwise indicate their views by choosing from a series of predetermined responses or multiple-choice questions, Anderson (1981) preferred to ask users to write down their views. The copious detail provided a rich data source, but to capture the depth of detail and allow responses to be analyzed by computer, some data reduction was necessary. Users' comments to individual questionnaire items became the universe. Each universe was examined and a set of categories or a coding scheme developed, as illustrated below in a request for suggestions to produce further language materials.

Code	
10–19	Produce materials other than those already available
11	Special materials for "enquiry–approach" projects
12	Materials for infants/younger children
13	Accompanying comprehension exercises or workbooks
14	More evaluation materials
15	Extending the scheme to accommodate advanced students
16	Review workbooks
17	Very basic materials for non-English-speaking children
18	Miscellaneous exercises (e.g., music with sentence drills)

Further codes were for suggestions to expand existing materials (20–29), for suggestions about general presentation (30–39), and for missing data where the question was not answered (99).

Following a decision about units of analysis, a further step is to determine which units may be reliably quantified. In early studies of readability, for instance, researchers looked for factors thought to contribute to reading difficulty, such as sentence complexity, vocabulary load, interest level, and so on. Reliably quantifying the different factors often resulted in a much reduced list. Questions of reliability inevitably raise questions of validity since some argue that there is little use in achieving high reliability if what is left to be measured has little utility or content validity.

Quantification may take the form of a simple "frequency count," as in counting the number of male and female characters per story. Ranking texts in terms of perceived reading difficulty is "ordinal measurement." Space measures like inches of newspaper type, or time measures such as minutes of teacher talk, are "interval measurement."

4. *Text Analysis and Comprehensibility*

Teachers and librarians have an obvious interest in content analysis since best results in learning are usually achieved by judicious matching of student with appropriate learning materials. This interest has long been manifest, particularly in analyses of characteristics of text as these relate to "comprehensibility." One characteristic of appropriate learning materials in this context is text reading difficulty or "readability." This entry focuses on this aspect, though the interest level of reading materials and students' motivation clearly impact on comprehensibility.

The readability movement was born in the 1920s with the publication of Thorndike's epic work on word frequency, *A Teacher Wordbook of 10,000 Words*. Shortly after this book was published, the first formula for ranking books in relative order of difficulty appeared, a formula based on Thorndike's word list. Since then many readability formulas have been developed for estimating the reading difficulty of texts in English, Japanese, Spanish, French, and other languages. The method used to construct a readability formula essentially comprises four steps, the first two of which are similar to the procedures of content analysis described above. The first is to search for factors thought to contribute to reading difficulty like, for instance, use of affixes, sentence complexity, or unfamiliar vocabulary. This step is what content analysts term "defining the categories." The second step is to determine which of these factors or categories can be reliably quantified. The third, and possibly the most difficult step, is to establish a criterion or exterior measure of reading difficulty against which the quantified factors may be validated. The final step is to incorporate into a regression

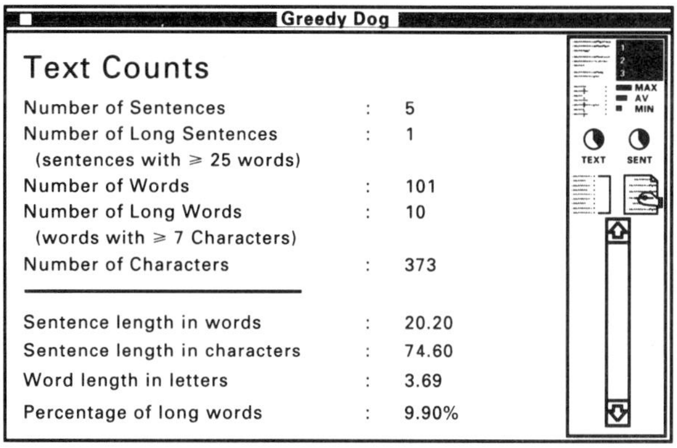

Figure 2
Text counts in Aesop's *The Greedy Dog*

equation those quantified factors which predict the criterion best. The regression equation becomes the readability formula. Two readability formulas described in Klare (1975) are those by Flesch and Spache:

$$\text{ReadingEase} = 206.835 - 0.846\text{wl} - 1.015\text{sl} \qquad \text{[Flesh]}$$

$$\text{GradeLevel} = 0.141X_1 + 0.086X_2 + 0.839 \qquad \text{[Spache]}$$

where wl, sl, X_1, and X_2 are all text factors (different measures of word difficulty and sentence complexity). The widely used Fry readability graph (see Klare 1975) is also a regression equation in graphical form.

The use of computers has had a marked effect on readability measurement, as on measurement generally. Thus, while word length in Flesch's formula (developed in 1948) involved a count of syllables which is relatively easy for human analysts, more recent formulas compute word length by counting characters. Such character counts would rarely have been conceived when analyses were done manually since they were too time-consuming and unreliable. For computers though, character counts are quicker and certainly more accurate than counting syllables.

A research instrument developed at Flinders University for use on microcomputers to analyze text features (Anderson 1992) displays the following text counts when the Text Count icon (the one selected in Fig. 2) is clicked.

Similarly, clicking on the Sentence Profile icon (seen in Fig. 3) displays a sentence profile for a given text.

The same text analysis tool computes an estimate of text reading difficulty, base on the "Rix" index, a measure that traces its origins to an index termed "Lix" which was developed in Sweden by Björnsson (1968). Clicking on the Text Difficulty icon (see Fig. 4) displays information about text difficulty.

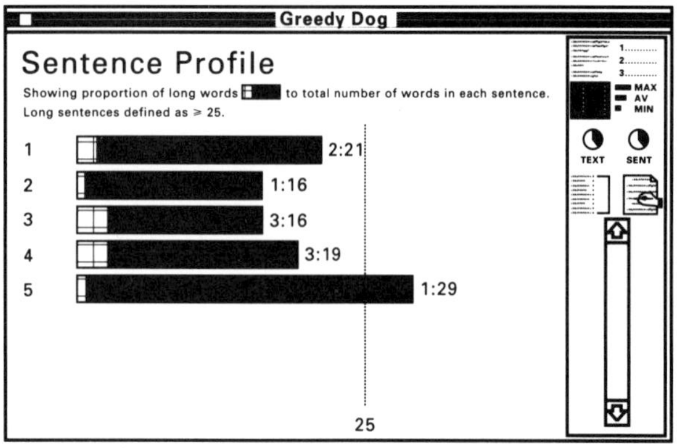

Figure 3
Sentence profile for Aesop's *The Greedy Dog*

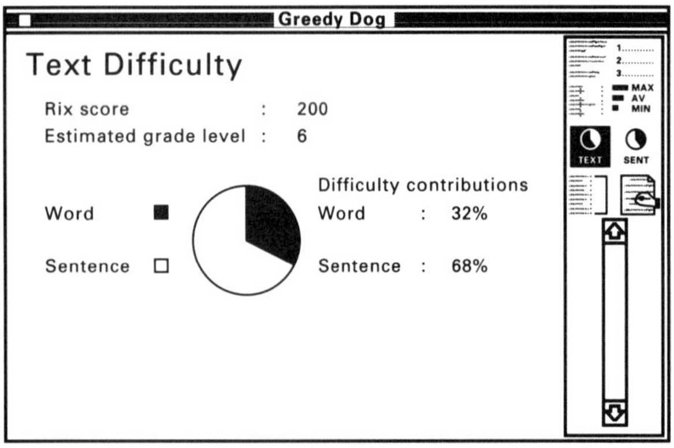

Figure 4
Text difficulty for Aesop's *The Greedy Dog*

Further options compute the reading difficulty of individual sentences and list the number of different words in a text (ordered alphabetically, by frequency or by word length).

5. Cloze Procedure and Cohesion

Readability measurement as a form of text analysis has obvious advantages and equally obvious shortcomings. Among the advantages are that it is objective and, with computers, quick and easy to apply. Indices such as Flesch, Lix, or Rix provide estimates of readability, that is, predictions of the ease or difficulty that readers are likely to experience in comprehending texts. Herein, however, lies the inherent weakness of such measures because no account is taken of the reader, at least in any direct way.

5.1 Cloze Procedure

Cloze procedure was developed to overcome this precise problem and to involve readers directly. It is basically a straightforward technique, consisting of a set of rules for constructing cloze tests over samples of written (or spoken) materials, administering these tests to subjects and scoring them, and determining from the cloze scores the degree of comprehension of the written (or spoken materials). To construct a cloze test, the words of a passage are systematically deleted in some mechanical way, for example, every seventh word, and replaced by blanks, usually of a standard length (though this condition is not a necessary one). The task for subjects is then to replace the missing words, and their scores, that is, the number of words correctly replaced, is an index of the comprehension of the passage. Thus the technique measures two aspects: the readability or reading difficulty of text and subjects' comprehension of text.

There are many reviews of cloze procedure since it is now included in the repertoire of techniques employed by classroom teachers, as well as being a useful measure in language research. The application of cloze procedure in foreign language testing, and especially with English learned as a foreign language in Southeast Asia as well as with Malay and Mandarin Chinese, is comprehensively reviewed in Anderson (1976).

5.2 Cohesion

"Cohesion" is yet another aspect of text which is receiving increased attention from educational researchers. Cohesion is based on the linguistic concept of cohesive ties, the mechanisms in text that make a text a text, thus differentiating connected discourse from a set of unrelated sentences. The most complete linguistic description of cohesive ties in English is to be found in Halliday and Hasan (1976). Researchers at The Open University in the United Kingdom, in a large-scale longitudinal study and in a series of fine-grained analyses, have tested the educational and psychological validity of cohesion by demonstrating that students' perception of cohesive ties in text is related to other measures of linguistic and verbal ability (see especially Chapman 1983). The *Australian Journal of Reading* (1983) devoted a special issue to the topic of cohesion and the reading teacher.

6. Content and Text Analysis: Retrospect and Prospect

Content and text analysis deal with essential forms of human interaction, the messages that the human species has developed for communication. As Holsti (1969 p. 1) remarked:

> It therefore follows that the study of the processes and products of communication is basic to the student of history, behavior, thought, art, and institutions. Often

the only surviving artifacts that may be used to study human activity are to be found in documents.

Yet, as Berelson (1952 p. 518) even earlier remarked: "Content analysis, as a method, has no magical qualities." The methods of the content or text analyst are open to the same strictures faced by all educational researchers: the need to select the universe of materials for analysis carefully if unwarranted generalizations are not to be made, to select categories that are meaningful, and to pay heed to questions of reliability and validity.

The computer, as a research tool, has had an enormous impact on content and text analysis and this impact is likely to increase even further. Not only does the computer facilitate all statistical analyses, it is a tool that is ideally suited for making routine counts of whatever categories researchers adopt, provided these can be fully defined and therefore quantified. The bottleneck that used to exist when entering text into computers is fast losing force as an obstacle, as scanners linked to computers become more widespread. Improvements in software are making text recognition more rapid and efficient, across a range of languages and alphabets. When voice recognition becomes a reality, the amount of human communication content available for ready analysis will increase even more dramatically.

See also: Linguistics and Language Learning; Reading Comprehension in Second and Foreign Language; Reading Comprehension, Learning of

References

Anderson J 1976 *Psycholinguistic Experiments in Foreign Language Testing*. University of Queensland Press, St Lucia

Anderson J 1981 *A National Survey of User Opinion of Commonwealth-produced Curriculum Materials for Teaching English as a Second Language*. Flinders University, Adelaide

Anderson J 1992 *MacTexan a Tool to Analyze Texts*. Flinders University, Adelaide

Anderson J, Yip L 1987 Are sex roles represented fairly in children's books? A content analysis of old and new readers. *Unicorn 13(3): 155–61*

Australian Journal of Reading 1983 Vol. 6, No. (issue devoted to Cohesian and the Reading Teacher)

Berelson B 1952 Content analysis. In: Lindzey G (ed.) 1952 *Handbook of Social Psychology. Vol. 1; Theory and Method*. Addison-Wesley, Reading, Massachusetts

Björnsson C H 1968 *Läsbarhet*. Bokförlaget Liber, Stockholm

Chapman L J 1983 *Reading Development and Cohesion*. Heinemann, London

Halliday M A K, Hasan R 1976 *Cohesion in English*. Longman, London

Holsti O R 1968 Content analysis. In: Lindzey G, Aronson E (eds.) 1968 *The Handbook of Social Psychology. Vol. 2: Research Methods*, 2nd edn. Addison-Wesley, Reading, Massachusetts

Holsti O R 1969 *Content Analysis for the Social Sciences and Humanities*. Addison-Wesley, Reading, Massachusetts

Kerlinger F R 1986 *Foundations of Behavioral Research*, 3rd edn. Holt, Rinehart, and Winston, New York

Klare G R 1975 Assessing readability. *Read. Res. Q.* 10(1): 62–102

Mahl G F 1959 Exploring emotional states by content analysis. In: Pool I D S (ed.) 1959 *Trends in Content Analysis*. University of Illinois Press, Urbana, Illinois

Osgood C E 1959 The representational model and relevant research methods. In: Pool I D S (ed.) 1959 *Trends in Content Analysis*. University of Illinois Press, Urbana, Illinois

Shannon C E, Weaver W 1949 *The Mathematical Theory of Communication*. University of Illinois Press, Urbana, Illinois

Stone P J, Dunphy D C, Smith M S, Ogilvie D M 1966 *The General Inquirer: A Computer Approach to Content Analysis*. MIT Press, Cambridge, Massachusetts

Weber R P 1985 *Basic Content Analysis*. Sage, Beverly Hills, California

Wulfemeyer K T, Mueller B 1991 Television commercials in the classroom: A content analysis of Channel One ads. *Communication Journalism Education Today* 24(4): 10–13

J. Anderson

Contingency Tables

In an investigation of solvent abuse and examination attainments, Chadwick et al. (1990) considered the influence of a number of background domestic factors. The results for two of these, living with both natural parents and employment status of main breadwinner, are shown in Table 1. Such an arrangement of data, where a number of individuals have been classified with respect to two qualitative variables, is known as a "*contingency table*" and such tables rise very frequently in the social sciences, generally as a result of surveys of one type or another. The entries in the cells of Table are counts or frequencies. These may be transformed into proportions or percentages, but it is important to note that in whatever form they are finally presented the data were originally frequencies or counts rather than continuous measurements.

Table 1 is a 2 × 2 contingency table since the variables involved each have two categories. Table 2 shows a 3 × 2 table, also from the solvent abuse study of Chadwick et al., and Table 3 a 4 × 4 table resulting from the cross classification of 4,353 individuals with respect to occupational group and educational level. Tables 1 to 3 are specifically two dimensional; they involve the classification of the individuals with respect to two variables. Higher dimensional tables arise when a sample of individuals is cross-classified with respect to more than two variables. Table 4, for example, shows a three-dimensional contingency table displaying data concerned with the examination results of children. The first

Table 1
Living with both natural parents and employment status of main breadwinner

	Controls	Solvent abusers	Total
Living with both natural parents			
No	35	41	76
Yes	68	60	128
Total	103	101	204
Employment status of main breadwinner			
Unemployed	3 (7.77)	12 (7.22)	15
Employed	96 (91.22)	80 (84.77)	176
Total	99	92	191

Table 2
Relationships with teachers

	Controls	Abusers
Gets on with most teachers	92(77.18)	60(74.82)
Some problems with most teachers	4(14.72)	25(14.28)
Marked antipathy toward most teachers	2(6.09)	10(5.91)

Table 3
Occupational group versus educational level

	Educational level				
	E1(low)	E2	E3	E4(high)	Total
Self-Employed business	239	309	233	53	834
Self-employed professional	6	11	70	199	286
Teacher	1	7	12	215	235
Salaried	794	781	922	501	2998
Total	1040	1108	1237	968	4353

Table 4
Examination results

Band	1			2			3		
Occupation of parent	1	2	3	1	2	3	1	2	3
Exam result									
No O-level passes	6	5	2	17	29	35	4	16	21
At least 1 O-level pass	5	6	3	21	22	10	2	2	2

variable is the verbal reasoning band that the child occupied at age 10 years, the second is the occupation of the parent when the child was 14 years of age and the third relates to examination results based on O-level passes. The table gives the number of children falling in each of the 18 categories defined by the combination of these three variables.

This entry considers the ways in which contingency tables can be analyzed in educational research studies.

1. *Independent Classifications: Association*

The question of most interest about contingency table data is usually whether the qualitative variables forming the table are independent or not. To address this question it is clearly necessary to examine just what independence between the classifying variables would imply. In the case of a 2 × 2 table this is readily seen. Take for example, Table 1. In this table it is clear that if employment status of the main breadwinner is independent of group, then the proportion of controls with unemployed main breadwinners will be the same as the corresponding proportion for solvent abusers. If these proportions differ, unemployment of the main breadwinner tends to be *associated* more with one of the groups than with the other. Of course, the two proportions might be expected to differ in some measure due solely to chance factors of sampling and for other reasons which might be attributed to random causes. What needs to be ascertained is whether or not the difference between the observed proportions is too large to be attributed to such causes, and for this purpose the statistical significance test outlined in the next section is used.

2. *Chi-Square Test of Independence*

To test for an association in a contingency table, the observed cell frequencies must be compared with those frequencies to be expected when the variables forming the table are assumed to be independent. The comparison involves the well-known "*chi-square statistic*". For example, in Table 1, if unemployment status is independent of group then the best estimate of the probability of the main breadwinner being unemployed is obtained from the relevant marginal total as 15/191. So the number of control children with an unemployed main breadwinner would be estimated to be 99 × 15/191 = 7.77. Similarly for solvent abusers the corresponding figure would be 7.22. All four estimated expected values are shown in brackets in Table 1. The chi-square statistic is calculated from summing the (observed frequency − expected frequency)^2/expected frequency, for each cell. For Table 1 this gives:

$$X^2 = \frac{(3-7.77)^2}{7.77} + \frac{(12-7.22)^2}{7.22} + \frac{(96-91.22)^2}{91.22} + \frac{(80-84.77)^2}{84.77} = 6.61$$

Since, given the marginal totals, only one of the cells of a 2 × 2 contingency table is not fixed, this statistic is known as a "chi-square with a single degree of freedom." From the appropriate chi-square distribution it is possible to determine that the probability of observing a value as large or larger than 6.61 assuming that the variables forming the table are independent is 0.013. Consequently, there is some evidence that unemployment status and group are not independent. It appears that the proportion of solvent abusing children whose main breadwinner is unemployed is higher than the corresponding proportion for the control children.

The extension of the chi-square test of independence to contingency tables with more than two row and/or column categories is straightforward. Expected values under independence are calculated as row total × column total/total number of individuals, and the chi-square statistic is again calculated as described previously. For a table with r rows and c columns the statistic has $(r-1)(c-1)$ degrees of freedom. For example, the expected values for Table 2 are shown in brackets next to the observed values and the chi-square statistic takes the value 27.2 with 2 degrees of freedom. The associated p value is less than 0.001. It appears that solvent abusing children have more difficult relationships with their teachers.

Similar calculations for Table 3 give a chi-square value of 1,254.1, which with 9 degrees of freedom is highly significant. Clearly occupation and educational level are related.

3. *Small Expected Frequencies*

The derivation of the chi-square distribution as an approximation for the distribution of the statistic X^2 is made under the rather vague assumption that the expected values are not "too small." This has, for many years, been interpreted by most users of the chi-square test as meaning that all expected values in the table should be greater than 5 for the chi-square test to be valid. But as long ago as 1954, Cochran pointed out that such a "rule" is too stringent and suggested that if relatively few expectations are less than 5 (say 1 cell out of 5), a minimum expectation of unity is allowable. Even this suggestion may be too restrictive since work by Lewontin and Felsenstein (1965) and Larntz (1978) shows that many of the expected values may be as small as 1 without affecting the test greatly.

Nevertheless for small, sparse, or skewed data the asymptotic theory may not be valid, although it is often difficult to predict *a priori* whether a given data set may cause problems. In the case of 2 × 2 tables, approaches which have been used for many years to overcome this problem have been "Fisher's exact test," and "Yates's correction", both of which are described in Everitt (1992). More recently Mehta and Patel (1983, 1986a, 1986b) have derived methods which allow exact significance levels to be computed for the general $r \times c$ table. To illustrate the differences that can occur between the exact approach and the usual procedure involving the chi-square distribution consider the following 3 × 9 contingency table:

0	7	0	0	0	0	0	1	1
1	1	1	1	1	1	1	0	0
0	8	0	0	0	0	0	0	0

For this table $X^2 = 22.9$. The corresponding p value from the chi-square distribution is 0.1342. The true p value is, however, 0.0013. The exact analysis indicates that the row and column classifications are not independent. The asymptotic analysis fails to show this relationship. (For interest, the exact p value for Table 1 is 0.014, very similar in this case to the approximate value given earlier.)

A procedure which has been used almost routinely for many years to overcome the problem of small expected frequencies is the pooling of categories. Such a procedure may be criticized on several grounds. First, a considerable amount of information may be lost by the combination of categories and this may detract greatly from the interest and usefulness of the study. Second, the randomness of the sample may be affected. The whole rationale of the chi-square test rests on the randomness of the sample and on the categories into which the observations may fall being chosen in advance. Pooling categories after the data are seen may affect the random nature of the sample with unknown consequences. Lastly, the manner in which the categories are pooled can have an important effect on the inferences drawn. As an example consider the following data set given by Baglivo et al. (1988):

	Column				
	1	2	3	4	5
Row 1	2	3	4	8	9
Row 2	0	0	11	10	11

When this table is tested for independence using the usual approximate methods, the calculated significance level is 0.086 which agrees with the exact

Table 5
Truancy in matched samples of smoking and nonsmoking schoolchildren

		Smokers No	Smokers Yes	Total
	No	30	10	40
Nonsmokers	Yes	3	7	10
Total		33	17	50

probability to two significant figures although a standard statistical package will issue a warning like "some of the expected values are less than 2, the test may not be appropriate." If the first two columns are ignored, however, the p value becomes 0.48; and if the first two columns are collapsed into the third, it becomes 1.00.

The practice of combining classification categories should be avoided and is no longer needed because of the availability of the exact tests referred to previously.

4. Matched Samples

One-to-one matching is frequently used by research workers to increase the precision of a comparison. The matching is usually done on variables such as age, sex, weight, and so forth, and other such variables which might possibly affect the response variable. Two samples matched in this way must be thought of as correlated rather than independent, so the usual chi-square test is no longer strictly applicable.

The appropriate test for comparing frequencies in matched samples is one due to McNemar (1955). The test statistic is given by:

$$X^2 = \frac{(b-c)^2}{b+c}$$

where b is the number of matched pairs where members of sample I have the attribute of interest, and those of sample II do not; and c is the number of pairs where members of sample I do *not* have the attribute while those of sample II do. Under the hypothesis of no difference between the matched samples with respect to the attribute, X^2 has a chi-square distribution with a single degree of freedom.

As an example, consider an investigation of schoolchildren who admit to being smokers. A total of 50 such children were matched one-to-one on sex, school year, and school with children who claimed to be nonsmokers. The children were then asked about various behavioral and emotional problems such as sleeping difficulties, headaches, truancy, and loneliness. The results for truancy, for example, are given in Table 5. The result of McNemar's test is

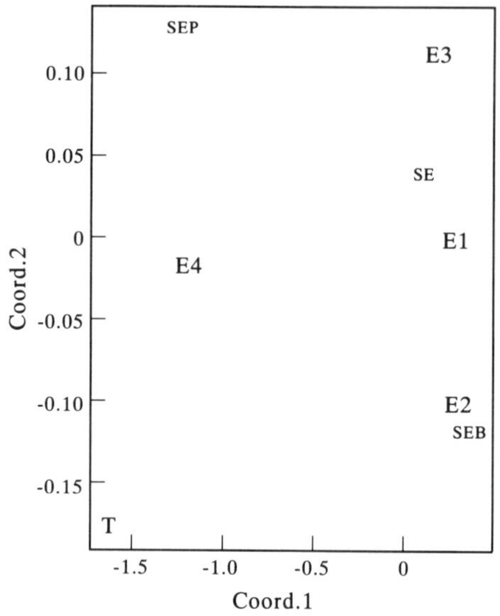

Figure 1
Correspondence analysis of occupation and educational level data: Two-dimensional solution

$X^2 = \frac{(10-3)^2}{13} = 3.77$. The associated p value is 0.052. The data give some fairly weak evidence perhaps that smokers and nonsmokers differ with respect to truancy.

5. Displaying Contingency Tables Graphically—Corespondence Analysis

Recent years have seen a growing interest in a technique which attempts to display the relationship between the variables forming a contingency table graphically. The method, "correspondence analysis," has in fact been known for a long time but its use until recently was, for some reason, largely confined to French data analysts.

Correspondence analysis works by finding a set of coordinate values to represent the row and column categories of the table. These coordinates are analogous to those derived from a principal component's analysis of multivariate, continuous data (see Everitt and Dunn 1992), except that they are derived by partitioning the chi-square statistic for the table rather than variance. A full account of correspondence analysis is given in Greenacre (1984)—here the method will be illustrated by its application to Table 3. The two-dimensional correspondence diagram is shown in Fig. 1. This diagram can be interpreted by noting the positions of the points representing the row and column categories relative to each other *and* relative to the origin. Row and column category points close to each other and relatively far from the origin imply that the frequency in the correspondence cell of the table is larger than would be expected if the two variables were independent. Row and column points distant from one another and from the origin suggest a negative association so that the corresponding cell in the table will have a smaller frequency than expected under independence. Here the diagram indicates that the individuals in the self-employed business category (SEB) tend to have educational level E2 more than would be expected if occupation and educational level were independent. Similarly teaching (T) and self-employed professional (SEP) are positively associated with educational level E4.

6. *Higher Dimensional Contingency Tables*

Three and higher dimensional contingency tables arise when a sample of individuals is cross-classified with respect to three (or more) qualitative variables. An example has already been given (see Table 4). The analysis of such tables presents problems not encountered with two-dimensional tables, where a single question is of interest, namely, that of the independence or otherwise of the two variables involved. In the case of higher dimensional tables, the investigator may wish to test that some variables are independent of some others, that a particular variable is independent of the remainder, or some more complex hypothesis. Again the chi-squared statistic is used to compare observed frequencies with those to be expected under a particular hypothesis.

The simplest question of interest in a three-dimensional table is that of the mutual independence of the three variables; this is directly analogous to the hypothesis of independence in a two-way table and is tested in an essentially equivalent fashion. Other hypotheses which might be of interest are those of the partial independence of a pair of variables, and the conditional independence of two variables for a given level of the third.

A more involved hypothesis concerns whether an association between two of the variables differs in degree or in direction in different categories of the third. All such hypotheses are assessed by comparing the frequencies to be expected under the model with the corresponding observed frequencies by means of chi-square statistic. For some hypotheses, expected values cannot be obtained simply from particular marginal totals but must be calculated interatively (for details, see Everitt 1992 Chap. 5). Such hypotheses are best assessed by the use of the models which are described briefly in the next section.

7. *Log–Linear Models for Contingency Tables*

A major development in the analysis of contingency tables occurred in the 1960s with the introduction by Birch (1963) of the "log–linear model." Such models propose some conceptual framework for the observations, and the parameters of the model represent the effects that particular variables or combinations of variables have in determining the observed frequencies. Such an approach is commonly used in other branches of statistics, for example, regression analysis and analysis of variance.

Table 6
Log–linear models for Table 4

Model (terms omitted from saturated model)	G^2	*df*	Change in G^2 from model 1	*df*
1. u_{123}	3.84	4	—	—
2. u_{12}, u_{23}, u_{13}, u_{123}	40.14	12	36.30	8
3. u_{12}, u_{123}	12.66	6	8.82	2
4. u_{13}, u_{123}	15.73	6	11.89	2
5. u_{23}, u_{123}	10.37	8	6.53	4

To introduce the log–linear model consider a two-dimensional table which, in the population, has frequencies m_{ij} in the ij-th cell. (The expected values met previously may be thought of as estimates of the m_{ij}.) If the two variables forming the table are independent then it is relatively simple to demonstrate that m_{ij} may be expressed in the form

$$\ln m_{ij} = u + u_{1(i)} + u_{2(j)} \quad (1)$$

where u, $u_{1(i)}$, and $u_{2(j)}$ are parameters of the model representing respectively a "grand mean" effect, and "row" and "column" effects (for details, see Everitt 1992 Chap. 5).

If this model fails to provide an adequate fit to the data, an "interaction" term can be added giving

$$\ln m_{ij} = u + u_{1(i)} + u_{2(j)} + u_{12(ij)} \quad (2)$$

The extra term represents discrepancies between the actual cell frequencies and those to be expected under independence. Such a model would provide a perfect fit since the number of parameters is the same as the number of cells in the table. For this reason it is known as the "saturated" model for a two-dimensional table.

For a three-dimensional table the corresponding saturated model is

$$\ln m_{ijk} = u + u_{1(i)} + u_{2(j)} + u_{3(k)} + u_{12(ij)} + u_{13(jk)} + u_{23(jk)} + u_{123(ijk)} \quad (3)$$

In this model the parameters $u_{123(ijk)}$ represent the possibility that associations between a pair of variables may differ in degree or direction in each category of the third variable. By dropping parameters from Eqn.(3), models corresponding to the mutual, partial, or conditional independence of the variables may be obtained. For example, the model corresponding to the mutual independence of the three variables has the form

$$\ln m_{ijk} = u + u_{1(i)} + u_{2(j)} + u_{3(k)} \quad (4)$$

When assessing the fit of particular log–linear models, expected and observed frequencies are again compared by the usual chi-square statistic or, more commonly, by a "likelihood ratio" statistic, G^2 given by

$$G^2 = 2 \sum \text{observed} \ln \frac{\text{observed}}{\text{expected}} \quad (5)$$

where summation is over all cells of the table.

The degrees of freedom of G^2 are the degrees of freedom for the model—that is, the number of independent parameters subtracted from the number of cells in the table. For large sample sizes G^2, like X^2, is distributed as a chi-square variate.

To illustrate the application of log–linear models, several will be applied to the data in Table 4. The results are summarized in Table 6. Clearly a number of models provide an adequate fit and a question that might be asked is how does one choose between models? Differences in fit can be measured by differences in the G^2 statistic. The aim is for the model with the least number of parameters which provides an adequate fit. For example, moving from Model 1—no second order relationship between the three variables, to Model 2—mutual independence of the three variables, leads to an increase in G^2 of 36.30 and an increase in degrees of freedom of 8. This indicates a significant *decrease* in the ability of the model to account for the data and so Model 2 would not be retained. Judgments between the other models considered in Table 6 can be made in a similar fashion. Model 5 appears to hold most promise—this model implies that, given the verbal reasoning band, parental occupation and examination result are independent.

Log–linear models allow a systematic approach to be taken to discover the relationships that may be present in complex multidimensional tables and provide a powerful addition to methods available for the analysis of contingency table data.

See also: Correspondence Analysis of Qualitative Data; Log–Linear Models

References

Baglivo J, Oliver D, Pagano M 1988 Methods for the analysis of contingency tables with large and small cell counts. *J. Amer. Statist. Assoc.* 83: 1006–13

Birch M W 1963 Maximum likelihood in three-way contingency tables. *J. Roy. Statist. Soc. B.* 25: 220–33

Chadwick O, Yule W, Anderson R 1990 The examination attainments of secondary school pupils who abuse solvents. *Brit. J. Educ. Psychol.* 60: 180–91

Cochran W G 1954 Some methods for strengthening the common X^2 tests. *Biometrics* 10: 417–77

Everitt B S 1992 *The Analysis of Contingency Tables*, 2nd edn. Chapman and Hall, London

Everitt B S, Dunn G 1992 *Applied Multivariate Data Analysis*. Edward Arnold, London

Greenacre M J 1984 *Theory and Applications of Correspondence Analysis*. Academic Press, London

Larntz K 1978 Small-sample comparison of exact levels for chisquared goodness-of-fit statistics. *J. Amer. Statist. Assoc.* 73: 253–63

Lewontin R C, Felsenstein J 1965 The robustness of homogeneity tests in 2 × *N* tables. *Biometrics* 21: 88–117

McNemar Q 1955 *Psychological Statistics*. 2nd edn. Wiley, New York

Mehta G R, Patel N R 1983 A network algorithm for performing Fisher's exact test in *r* × *c* contingency tables. *J. Amer. Statist. Assoc.* 78: 427–34

Mehta G R, Patel N R 1986a A hybrid algorithm for performing Fisher's exact test in unordered *r* × *c* contingency tables. *Commun. in Statist.* 15: 387–403

Mehta G R, Patel N R 1986b FEXACT: A Fortran subroutine for Fisher's exact test on unordered *r* × *c* contingency tables. *ACM Trans. Mathemat. Software* 12: 154–61

B. S. Everitt

Continuing Education, Effects of

The purpose of this entry is to present a summary of evaluative research on the relationships between adult and continuing education and training, on the one hand, and several economic and sociological outcome variables on the other. The focus is on the external, productivity-relevant effects of organized and structured learning activities engaged in by adults. These activities may be conducted at the workplace or on other premises, irrespective of whether any direct outlays are covered by the individual or by the employer. However, the possible effects on productivity of self-planned study, apprenticeships, work experience programs, and informal learning at the workplace are not taken into account. The effects of distance education and public training programs for employment are also excluded (see *Distance Education: Economic Evaluation; Evaluation of Public Training: Industrial Countries*).

1. Levels of Impact Assessment

Kirkpatrick (1967) noticed four levels of assessing the effectiveness of a human resource development program:

(a) Measuring the reactions of the participants to the course. Did they like it? Did they perceive the course to have been useful?

(b) Measuring learning and transfer. Did the participants acquire the desired level of proficiency as defined by the program objectives?

(c) Measuring the utility of learning. Are the participants making use of the knowledge and skills they acquired, either on the job or for other purposes?

(d) Measuring the outcomes of learning. What are the external effects of the knowledge, skills, and behaviors acquired through continuing education on variables such as individual income and life career, the productivity of firms, and the economic growth of the nation?

This entry is mainly concerned with the effects of continuing education as approached in level 4 studies. Although the emphasis is on the relationships between continuing education, the economy, and the labor market, some social–psychological effects will also be considered (see *Evaluation of Adult Education*).

2. An Emerging Area in Educational Research

Many arguments support the necessity for increasing investment in continuing education. An overview of these often prescriptive arguments is given in OECD (1991). These statements reflect the belief that the value of continuing education has been greatly enhanced as a result of recent demographic change, new technology, and increased trade competition. The growth of investment in continuing education during the 1980s, which can be noted in many industrialized countries, can be understood against a new appreciation of its economic significance. Increased investment in continuing education can, of course, also be triggered by a decrease in the direct costs of education, low or reduced quality and efficiency in initial education, an extension of working life, and increases in wealth.

Support for the conviction that continuing education constitutes a major productive factor and an instrument for success in the competition among individuals, firms, and nations has, until very recently, come mainly from indirect evidence based on general work in the economics of education, which shows that initial formal education influences personal income. However, the belief that continuing education increases productivity "is premised mainly on very indirect empirical evidence found in the concavity of age-earnings profiles" (Hanushek and Quigley 1985 p. 381). Systematic studies of the hypothesis that continuing education improves productivity by enhancing the skills of the labor force and the value of technology and has benefits in the form of increased competitiveness and income, have only become available during the 1980s (see *Market Failure in Firm-based Education and Training*).

Data on the precise quality of these relationships were generally not available until the 1980s. This dearth of empirical information limited the possibility of examining some of the hypotheses concerning the value of postinitial education. Funds for assembling large-scale data sets on adult learning and training have only become accessible since continuing education became a priority on the agenda of policymakers from the mid-1980s. The number of studies investigating the effects of continuing education has grown concomitantly with this increase in research funding and data. The aim of this entry is to discuss some of the results obtained in this emerging field of study.

3. Microscopic and Macroscopic Assessment

The people involved in continuing education form a very heterogeneous group (see *Populations and Special Clienteles: Adult Education*). Continuing education is, moreover, characterized by a wide range of offerings (see *Providers of Adult Education*). A diversified approach is needed, therefore, in measuring the outcomes. The assessment of the nonmonetary benefits of continuing education, for example its effects on perceived quality of life, is as important a topic for research as the economic returns.

It follows from the above that the possible effects of continuing education can be measured in different ways and at different levels. Microscopic evaluations tend to be focused on variables that carry meaning for individuals, for example, whether a qualification was obtained, or whether improvements in life satisfaction, employment opportunity, and income were recorded. By contrast, macroscopic evaluations are concerned with the effects of continuing education on the supply of skilled labor, the functioning of labor markets, and aggregate economic growth.

Both approaches are indicated in Table 1, which also presents some major assumptions concerning the benefits of continuing education. These beliefs reflect not only the rhetoric of the stakeholders in postinitial education but also a certain body of empirical knowledge (see *Benefits of Education; External Benefits of Education*).

Implicit in Table 1 are two crucial assumptions. The first is that there may be interaction among the economic, social–psychological, and labor market related benefits of continuing education. The second assumption is that the microscopic and macroscopic benefits of a human investment program are interrelated. If the balance of costs and benefits is positive for employers and individuals, then there may well be an aggregate gain also for the nation. This postulate is at the heart of the interest of policymakers in the outcomes of continuing education. Policymakers who want to optimalize the gains for society—if necessary by intervening in the training market—require information regarding such matters as the determinants of successful training programs, the distribution of economic benefits, and the causes of possible under-investment in continuing education (see *Market Failure in Firm-based Education and Training*).

4. Consumption and Investment Education

The concept of continuing education is open to varying interpretations. This has implications for the out-

Table 1
Some hypothesized benefits of continuing education

Outcomes	Individual	Institution	Society
1. Gain in net income (co-varying with an increase in the effectiveness and productivity of workers and work organizations; future increase in taxes paid)	X	X	X
2. Increased employment stability (co-varying with reduced unemployment and increased mobility; future decrease in transfer payments and unemployment insurance)	X	X	X
3. Increased job satisfaction and life satisfaction (future decrease in transfer payments due to, for example, lower absenteeism, high morale, and lesser need of welfare intervention)	X	X	X

come variables used in effectiveness research. A distinction is often made between consumption and investment education. Consumption education is directed mainly to personal goals, often in connection with the development of leisure. By contrast, investment education is concerned mainly with the development of skills relevant to work tasks.

Variables indicating how the costs of the investment are shared among individuals, employers, and society are often used in determining the orientation of an educational program. Another way is to consider whether a program affords a degree, diploma, or credential upon successful completion. The usefulness of a dichotomy between continuing education for consumption and investment is limited, however. Problems arise since many learning activities which can reasonably be considered as investment also have a leisure component and vice versa. Hence it can be difficult to locate a given educational program on the consumption–investment dimension.

Yet despite this difficulty the dichotomy offers an attractive means of conceptualizing the outcome variables used in previous research. The range of possible assessment criteria can be limited by considering an educational program in relation to its capacity to achieve certain objectives. For example, the effectiveness of education aimed at personal development or the enrichment of leisure is appropriately assessed against other criteria than those used in evaluating industrial training programs. Accordingly, continuing education for consumption can be evaluated with dependent variables measuring aspects of, for example, social interaction and the satisfaction adults derive from participation. Investment education tends to be evaluated in cost–benefit terms.

5. *Theories and Derived Hypotheses*

It is useful to review briefly some theories on the relationships between continuing education, the economy, and the labor market before examining the research evidence. Studies on the benefits of continuing education can be summarized in different ways. One alternative is to order the research in terms of the dependent variables that are employed. Another is to group the studies in accordance with the disciplinary orientations they represent, or the major theories from which the hypotheses are derived. Both approaches are used in this entry. Three relevant economic theories and two perspectives from sociology are discussed in the paragraphs below.

Table 2
Three economic theories and derived hypotheses

Theories	Emphasis on:	Criteria	Main hypothesis
Human capital	Factors influencing individual return	Productivity Personal income	Continuing education increases productivity because observed increases in personal income reflect the value-added of productive skills, knowledge, and abilities acquired by means of continuing education and training
Screening	Factors influencing the social distribution of income	Selection Sufficient information	Continuing education raises productivity not only because it improves the capacity of workers to perform certain tasks, but also because it provides employers with a means to identify individuals with high expected marginal productivity
Job matching	Factors influencing the allocation of investment and the individual and social returns	Allocation Insufficient information	Continuing education increases productivity because it increases the capacity of both workers and employers to gather information concerning the most efficient match between offered and demanded abilities and skills

5.1 Economic Theories on Continuing Education

Three theories seem particularly salient for a discussion of the economic benefits of continuing education: the human capital perspective, the screening theory, and the job matching theory (see *Human Capital Concepts; Screening Models and Education; Internal Labor Markets and Education*). The hypotheses to which these perspectives give rise are summarized in Table 2.

Continuing education and human capital theory. The individual benefits of education are emphasized in the human capital approach, using personal income as the criterion. The relationship between continuing education and productivity is considered straightforward: continuing education results in a higher wage because education confers knowledge and skills which increase the capacity of workers to perform efficiently on the job. Two relationships are hypothesized: first, an effect of continuing education on labor productivity and, second, an effect of productivity on individual income. The focus of studies conducted in the human capital tradition is on the relationship between education and income. The relevance of education for productivity is often taken for granted.

Continuing education and screening theory. Compared with the approach outlined above, screening or signaling theory hypothesizes a different connection between adult education and individual earnings (Cohn and Geske 1990). The theory holds that a person invests in continuing education because the qualifications and credentials which are acquired by means of adult education can be used to inform employers that the person possesses certain scarce skills and other desirable personality traits which are likely to make him more productive in a given job than competitors who lack these specific characteristics. Continuing education thus presents a means to identify and select workers with a high expected marginal productivity. It is not productivity but self-selection which forms the basis for the relationship between continuing education and earnings. In this view continuing education is not necessarily a strategic investment that will raise productivity; it may also be given as a reward.

Continuing education and job matching theory. Information is a central variable in both screening and job matching theory. The two approaches are therefore closely related. In screening theory the emphasis is on the comparative advantage of the individual, who holds vital information, vis-à-vis the employer, who lacks such information. In job matching theory it is considered that *both* the worker and the employer can derive useful information from the fact that a given person participates in a given adult education program. This information can be used by both parties to improve the efficiency of the "match" between the skills possessed by the worker and the skills demanded on a certain job. The central hypothesis is that continuing education raises productivity not only because it provides workers with updated knowledge and skills but especially because it helps in "getting the right person on the right job." However, the theory also predicts that skill formation does not necessarily lead to productivity gains and increased wages. These returns are only forthcoming if the skills acquired by means of continuing education are actually utilized on the job—that is, if continuing education improves the job match of an employee. But if continuing education increases the discrepancy between the qualifications of the workforce and labor demand then the effect on productivity may be nil or even negative.

Continuing education and overschooling. Screening and job matching theories call the idea that continuing education necessarily represents a productive investment into doubt, since it may also lead to overschooling. Although the individual tends to derive a positive return on overschooling (research suggests that the rate of return may be as high as 3–5% for each year of schooling over and above the level required for the job), the costs may outweigh this return. The problem of overschooling is often eschewed by research workers in adult education. Yet it must be addressed, especially in the light of the renewed emphasis on the development of lifelong education.

5.2 Sociological Theories on Continuing Education

A central theme in the sociology of education concerns the role of both initial and continuing education in influencing social stratification. Whereas much research has focused on the role of school education, much less effort has gone into the study of the influences of continuing education. There are essentially two approaches to investigating the social and labor market outcomes of continuing education. The effects on indicators of individual life career are studied in the status attainment approach. Reproduction theory, which comes under a variety of labels, gives rise to the examination of the function of continuing education in the perpetuation of social inequality (see *Social Mobility, Social Stratification, and Education*). Several hypotheses may be derived from these two perspectives. These are indicated in Table 3.

Continuing education and status attainment. In the status attainment tradition, stratification is commonly interpreted as an individuated pattern of positions in social space that closely reflect a finely graded hierarchy of prestige, wealth, and influence. These scales are measured in terms of the exchange value of people on a supposedly open and competitive labor market. A central question for research is to discern the degree to which occupational and social standing depend on competence acquired by means of both initial and continuing education, compared

Table 3
Two sociological theories concerning the effects of continuing education

Theories	Emphasis on:	Criteria	Main hypothesis
Status attainment	Individual life career	Occupational status measured on the basis of a finely graded hierarchy of social prestige	Continuing education has a *net* effect on the life career and occupational status of the individual, independent of the effects of other structural determinants in an economic and social system
Social reproduction	Group, labor markets, society	Social class, measured in terms of power, capital, and education	Continuing education is a factor in the intergenerational transmission of ascribed rather than attained positions in the social, cultural, economic, and political dimensions

with the influences of other determinants of life career within a given social and economic system. As in the human capital approach, status attainment research emphasizes the role monetary rewards play in the forming of assumptions about the kind of jobs individuals aspire and search for (see *Aspirations and Expectations of Students*).

Continuing education and reproduction theory. Studies examining the effects of continuing education on the perpetuation of social inequality often place much emphasis on the historical and relational context within which a person is located. It is assumed that the social position to which groups of persons are assigned on the basis of their background and previous education not only influences the pricing on the market of their skills, but also limits the degree of openness and fair competition in labor markets. Opposed to the image of society implicit in the status attainment approach, the basic tenet of the reproduction perspective is that meritocratic competition is illusionary, and that opportunity and barriers to mobility within and across labor markets derive from the relations of people to the factors of production (for a discussion, see Knotterus 1987). In analyzing the relationship between continuing education and labor market outcomes, proponents of this perspective tend to emphasize the correspondence between the goals, means, and ends of work and those of further education and training. Thus, the focus is on the complementary roles of initial and continuing education in transmitting and reproducing cultures, ideologies, and ascribed structural positions in a society. Rather than considering participants in continuing education as a self-selected group, they tend to be defined by their position in the social structure. Compared with the advocates of the status attainment perspective, reproduction theorists are also more likely to conceptualize participation as an outcome rather than an antecedent of the production process determining life career. Instead of concentrating on the benefits of continuing education, this approach leads to the study of economic and structural barriers to participation, and attempts to analyze their significance in relation to nonparticipation and economic exclusion.

6. An Overview of the Research Evidence

The central findings of the research into the economic and labor market effects of continuing education are reviewed below. The implications for economic and sociological theories are also indicated. The focus is on the following dependent variables: (a) productivity, (b) technology, (c) earnings variation, (d) labor market variables such as occupational attainment and employment stability, and (e) social–psychological variables such as job satisfaction and the quality of life.

6.1 Continuing Education and Productivity

Productivity can be assessed in terms of the aggregate output of an economy, a branch of industry or a specific workplace, and an individual worker. These criteria are considered below.

Continuing education and macroeconomic growth. Neoclassical theory is at the heart of most studies of the relationship between education and macroeconomic growth. These studies have often used simple production functions, which hold that the output of an economy depends, first, on the amount of financial capital and labor employed and, second, on the flow of new technology. Increases in capital and labor typically account for nearly half of the growth in output. The residual variance is attributed to technology. Education is usually not entered explicitly but it is assumed to influence both labor quality and technological progress. Hence studies estimating simple production functions with aggregate data support the view that initial and continuing education and macroeconomic growth are related (Cohn and Geske 1990) (see *Education Production Functions*).

A new theory of growth has been gaining in importance since the mid-1980s. Extended production functions take not only capital and labor, but also knowledge into account. Knowledge, which is usually measured in terms of the level of education in a population, is therefore considered as a primary rather than a secondary production factor. Recent studies comparing growth rates in many different countries found that lack of human capital and education, not lack of labor or investment in physical capital, is what prevents economic growth in poor countries. Since there is ample evidence that continuing education "adds to" the "stock" of human capital in a population, it may be concluded that not only formal initial education but also adult education and training contribute to the growth of output in an economy.

Continuing education and labor productivity. The effects of continuing education on the productivity of firms are investigated in several studies. In this case possible indicators are: (a) the turnover of the firm multiplied by the average percentage share of value-added in the turnover of the relevant branch, (b) the annual growth of turnover by worker, (c) the growth of production volume minus the growth of labor volume, (d) profitability, and (e) changes in market shares over time (see *Education and Productivity*).

Studies of the relationship between continuing education and productivity growth in industry have usually concentrated on firm-specific job training. Blakemore and Hoffman (1989) and Bishop (1990), among others, report a positive correlation between training investment and output. Yet the direction of this relationship is often unclear. Profitable companies and firms with high turnover tend to invest more in training than small firms. But studies unequivocally showing that this investment also raises output are scarce. Exceptions are Bishop (1987), Barron et al. (1989), and Mendes de Oliviera et al. (1989). These authors show in well-designed studies that continuing education has a significant effect on labor productivity. Barron et al. (1989) find that a 10 percent increase in training investment leads to a growth of 3 percent in labor productivity. If training raises the productivity of workers, then it is also likely to have an effect on the aggregate output of firms.

It is often assumed that the positive relationship between continuing education and personal income (see Sect. 6.3 below) is indicative of differences in productivity between workers according to the acquired level of education. However, it is found in microscopic studies that income, although predicted by the level of education, does not equal the real value of the marginal product (Brown 1989, Bishop 1991). The theory of implicit wage contracts explains this in terms of the distribution of risk-taking between employees and employers. Another explanation is that employers who carry most of the costs of specific training will offer incomes lower than the value of the marginal product. The extent to which continuing education is an investment in general human capital is seen as an important determinant of the distribution of the costs and benefits of continuing education between employers and workers. Since the value-added of specific training falls in large measure to the employer, the return on continuing education

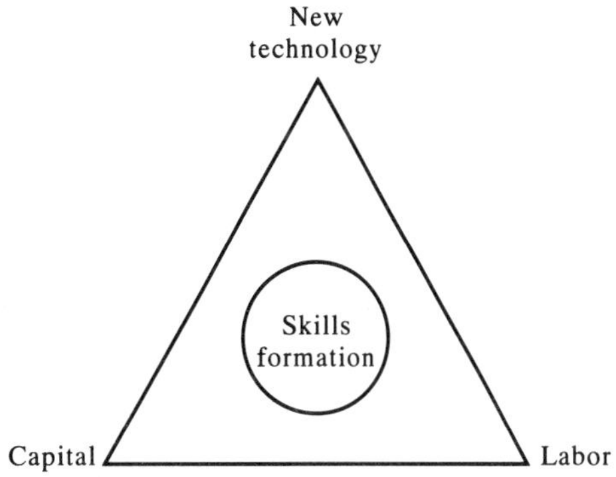

Figure 1
A theory of productivity and skills formation

in terms of increased productivity is therefore likely to be greater than the return suggested by wage growth.

6.2 Continuing Education and Technology

As noted above, studies in which measures of initial and continuing education are specified in extended production functions show that education has a direct effect on productivity. But there is also evidence that continuing education may have important indirect effects as well, since it influences the efficiency of employing other relevant factors of production such as capital and new technology (Levin 1987, Eliasson 1987, and Romer 1990). This insight is behind the rapidly rising interest in the economics of skills formation since the mid-1980s.

Technology is conventionally seen as a primary factor in production. The huge investment in new technology since the 1970s should have raised output, at least in theory. But the results in the industrialized countries were generally disappointing. This apparent contradiction gave rise to the formulation of the new theory of growth mentioned previously. According to the current position, the effect of technology on productivity is not linear and direct but dependent on interaction with other variables, of which skills formation and the organization of work are particularly important. Continuing education is thus seen as a *sine qua non* for realizing the economic benefits that are, potentially at least, associated with an investment in new technology.

The new approach to growth theory is shown in Fig. 1, which depicts skills formation at the heart of the economic production function. With the human factor assuming pre-eminence as a factor of production, concern with the consequences of under-investment in continuing education (and with inefficient and unequal participation) has come to the foreground of the debate at present (see *Further Education and Training: Demand, Supply, and Finance*).

6.3 Continuing Education and Earnings Variation

Age–earnings profiles and continuing education. Studies of average age–earnings profiles in industrialized countries show, according to Blaug (1976) and Psacharopoulos (1987), that the relationship between formal education and earned income increases in strength up to a point between 40 and 45 years of age, and then levels off. The age at which this peak is manifested tends to be higher the higher the level of initial education. This can be interpreted as a reflection of decreasing marginal productivity, where depreciation sets in earlier for the poorly educated than the well-educated workers. The later in life the effects of formal education on earnings are estimated, the more likely it is that these are mediated by other variables, notably by the labor market positions previously held. There is evidence that continuing education is also implicated: the turning point in earnings power arrives at a later age for workers with additional training compared to workers who lack training (Mincer 1991).

Individual returns to continuing education. Estimates of the individual rate of return on formal education show a great deal of cross-national consistency (Psacharopoulos 1985). Most industrial countries show returns on higher education similar to those found in the United States, where the individual return varied from 6 percent in the 1970s to between 7 and 11 percent in the mid-1980s (Cohn and Geske 1990). It is of interest to note that studies conducted in both developed and developing countries find that the return on continuing education for young workers seems to be at least as high as that on higher education (Lillard and Tan 1986, Brown 1989, Bishop 1991, Psacharopoulos and Velez 1992). Some authors report that the effects of continuing education on wage growth diminish with increasing age (Duncan and Stafford 1980). However, the cumulative effects of continuing education on wage growth seem to increase with age (Brown 1989, Tuijnman 1989).

Mincer (1991) reanalyzed data collected in the United States in the 1970s and 1980s. Using an eight-year timespan for depreciation, he finds a return on one year with training of 23.5 percent for all male workers, 26.5 percent for the newly hired, and 37.5 percent for older cohorts. If the training investment is written off over 25 years, then the corresponding estimates are 12.8 percent for all workers, 16 percent for the newly hired, and 26 percent for older cohorts. These estimates compare well with those reported by Tuijnman (1989) who used longitudinal data collected for the "Malmö Study"—a fifty-year study of a cohort of Swedish men—to estimate the cumulative effects of continuing education on the earnings of these men. The results show a return of 6 percent at age 35, 11 percent at age 40, 19 percent at age 43, and 26 percent at both ages 52 and 56. Thus, there is reason to assume that the individual rate of return on continuing education exceeds the return on both schooling and higher education. A similar conclusion is reached by Psacharopoulos and Layard (1979). Mincer (1991) concludes:

> The range of estimates of *worker* returns to training based on several data sets seems to exceed the magnitude of rates of return usually observed for schooling investments. Given the data on worker's firm tenure, it appears also that training remains profitable to *firms*, even in the face of average worker mobility. The rates of return here calculated may be large enough to suggest underinvestment in training relative to that in schooling.

Social returns to continuing education. Screening theory predicts that the individual returns will exceed the social returns, and that this imbalance will be most pronounced in continuing education. The findings of research studies seem to confirm this hypothesis (Psacharopoulos 1981). There is evidence showing that the imbalance between individual and social rates of return is greater in continuing education compared with both secondary and higher education. It seems that the larger the distance to compulsory education, the more the social rate of return diminishes relative to the private return.

Because employees seem to sacrifice little or no pay to get continuing education (Bishop 1987), and since both the employers and the society subsidize a major part of the direct costs of this education (see *Training Costs: Measurement*), the individual returns are likely to be high compared with the social return. Given that the individual returns on certain education and training programs tend to be higher for women than men (Psacharopoulos 1985, Barnow 1987), and that the returns on general education seem to exceed those of specific vocational training (Kang and Bishop 1989), it appears moreover that self-selection is implicated in the imbalance between the social and individual returns to continuing education.

Path models of earnings effects. The effect of continuing education on individual earnings can also be studied by means of path models (see *Path Analysis and Linear Structural Relations Analysis*). Studies employing longitudinal data and path models show that this relationship may not be as straightforward as the rate-of-return analyses reviewed above seem to suggest. The regression of earnings on continuing education yields insignificant estimates in both Swedish and Dutch longitudinal studies if variables such as cognitive ability in childhood, initial education, and job level are held constant (Tuijnman 1989, Van Leeuwen and Dronkers 1992). Yet the correlations between continuing education and earnings measured at successive ages are moderate. Although a significant direct effect of continuing education on earnings is not found, continuing education nevertheless has a significant indirect effect mediated by occupational status. This indirect effect becomes increasingly important with increasing age.

Job matching theory may provide an explanation for the finding that the effect of continuing education on earnings is not significant once job level is held constant in the equation. The theory holds that continuing education only increases productivity, and hence income, if the skills acquired by means of continuing education efficiently correspond to those demanded and actually used on the job. Hence the pay-off to the individual depends on factors such as whether the education confers instrumental qualifications, whether a person receiving further education is in a position to make effective use of the acquired skills, and whether the productivity gain warrants promotion to another job carrying higher responsibility and pay. Support for this interpretation of the relationship between education and income is provided by sociological studies pointing to the crucial role of the firm and other labor market variables in determining the economic return on continuing education (Kalleberg and Lincoln 1988).

6.4 Labor Market Outcomes of Continuing Education

Empirical work on the labor market outcomes of continuing education has focused on many variables. Only a few are considered below, namely: (a) occupational attainment, (b) employment security and mobility across internal labor markets, (c) unemployment incidence, (d) social inequality, and (e) sex differences in the labor market outcomes of continuing education.

Continuing education and occupational attainment. There is much support for the hypothesis that the acquisition of skills, knowledge, and attitudes by means of continuing education is a factor of significance in explaining differences in occupational attainment between workers with similar levels of initial education and work experience, even if other contributing variables such as cognitive ability, achievement motivation, and personal work histories are held constant. Bishop (1991) finds that job-relevant continuing education of a formal type results in greater occupational mobility than on-the-job training and informal learning at the workplace. The explanation seems to be that knowledge and skills acquired by means of formal programs are easier to certify than skills acquired informally on the job.

Findings from the "Malmö Study" indicate that the direct effects of initial education on occupational status reach a maximum at around age 30 and then gradually decrease in strength. By contrast, the effect of continuing education cumulatively increases from early to late career (Tuijnman 1989). As workers get older, the effect of initial education on earnings is increasingly mediated by continuing education and positions previously held on the labor market. Hence the total impact of initial education on earnings is far greater than the regression effect seems to indicate at first sight. For workers beyond 50 years of age the direct effect of continuing education on occupational status exceeds that of initial education. Even though the direct regression of earnings on continuing education is not significant, the cumulative effect on earnings mediated by job status is positive and moderate.

Continuing education, employment security, and mobility. The question of the relationship between continuing education, employment security, and mobility across labor markets is important. Continuing education is often seen as a policy instrument for enhancing employment security and facilitating mobility. There is some indication that these two goals are at odds, however. Theory predicts that firm-specific continuing education improves employment security. This is so because workers who have acquired skills that are central to the operations of the firm run less risk of being laid off at times of economic hardship than workers with a general training. However, customized education also limits the free flow and turnover of labor. By contrast, continuing education of a general type may reduce employment stability, but facilitate mobility across internal labor markets.

The pay-off from continuing education to the firm depends on how long workers remain employed at that company after receiving training. Firms are therefore likely to invest more in those workers who are likely to stay. The research evidence bears this out. Trainees who receive firm-based education are on the average less mobile prior to receiving the education than other workers, and their mobility is further reduced by that education (Mincer 1989). Employment security apparently promotes training investment, and training investment in turn promotes employment stability, since both employers and employees will try to maximize their returns. The implication is that a macroeconomic policy aimed at both creating conditions for and sustaining full employment can be effective in encouraging individuals and firms to invest in continuing education.

Continuing education and unemployment incidence. The incidence of unemployment is generally lower the higher the level of education. There is evidence that this applies also to continuing education. Compared with untrained workers, those who receive continuing education show a lower incidence of unemployment. Because continuing education influences the job level independent of initial education, it seems likely that it helps to consolidate or strengthen the labor market attachment of workers. Van Leeuwen and Dronkers (1992) confirm this. Using longitudinal data collected in the Netherlands, they show that the likelihood of becoming unemployed in mid-career is significantly and negatively related to both initial and continuing education, although the relationships are not strong and the influence of initial education is twice that of continuing education.

Much continuing education is job relevant. In many cases it can be considered vocational education. Some studies show that the employment chances of labor market entrants with a vocational education are higher than those of generalists, although the private returns on vocational education tend to be lower. Continuing education has similar positive effects: it increases employability and decreases both the chance of becoming unemployed and remaining unemployed once laid off (Mincer 1989). The disadvantage of vocational education in schools is that the jobs students get often do not correspond to those for which they are trained. Insufficient information often leads to a poor job match. The problem of insufficient or misleading information, which lowers the efficiency and productivity of vocational schooling, is less pronounced in continuing education. This is an important finding since it implies that continuing education can be effective in preventing and reducing unemployment in information-poor labor markets. It may also indicate that vocational education in schools is a less cost-effective way of training for certain skills than employer-provided education, since in the latter case the skills are almost certain to be used and retained.

Continuing education and social reproduction. Studies in industrial societies consistently show that the delivery system for continuing education caters most efficiently for the initially well-educated population. Workers in low technology-intensive sectors, workers who have not received an adequate training from the beginning, and people lacking experience of work tend to be underrepresented in continuing education. Hence continuing education is not only a factor in occupational mobility, but also in the maintenance of the status quo and the reproduction of the relations of workers to the working world.

The research findings also show that continuing education is a cumulative phenomenon. Both initial and postinitial education are good predictors of recurrent participation in continuing education. This applies not just to adult education of a formal type. For example, Mincer (1989) notes that the amount of training received on the present job correlates with training taken in both previous and future jobs. This result indicates that initial education and continuing education may be considered complementary. Psacharopoulos and Velez (1992) and others note that there is an interaction effect between initial schooling and continuing education: the former increases the productivity, and thus the value-added, of continuing education. This may be one explanation why employers tend to invest more in the training of professionals and other well-educated workers compared to workers with an initially low level of education.

Continuing education and sex differences. Moderate effects of continuing education on employment opportunities and job promotions for women are reported by Felmlee (1988). The effect of educational attainment on occupational achievement seems to be larger for women than for men, but the income effects of education tend to be lower. Felmlee (1988) finds that for young women continuing education yields only a modest increase in wages but a substantial increase in the prestige associated with subsequently held jobs. Using a Dutch longitudinal data set, Van Leeuwen and Tuijnman (1993) have found that not only do men more frequently take part in adult and continuing education than women, but also that they tend to realize a greater raise in their educational level compared to women. Both structural and cognitive factors are behind this imbalance between the sexes.

Surveys show that men more often than women mention career advancement as the main reason for taking part in continuing education. Women seem more often to take part for emancipatory and recreational reasons (see *Participation in Adult Education: Antecedent Factors*). However, structural factors also play a role in the differential allocation and use of continuing education by sex. Men have a greater labor market participation rate than women, and they tend to be overrepresented in supervisory and professional occupations that not only confer more social prestige and pay, but also offer better chances of obtaining job-related continuing education. If initial and continuing education are complementary not only for men but also for women then it seems likely that continuing education does not function to offset but to reinforce the sex-based differences in the labor market outcomes of education.

6.5 Social–Psychological Effects of Continuing Education

It is important to acknowledge that continuing education also serves goals other than economic ones. Hence the effects of continuing education cannot and should not be solely assessed and interpreted in terms of criteria such as productivity, life career, and earnings. The fact that the activities subsumed under the generic label "continuing education" are heterogeneous must be taken into account in searching for evidence of program impact. Two social–psychological variables are considered below: quality of life and job satisfaction. There are of course many other attitudinal and dispositional variables that may be of interest, but these cannot be dealt with here.

Continuing education and the quality of life. The influence of educational experience on preferences, expectations, feelings, and emotional states can be seen as a multiple force which contributes not only to the shaping of personality characteristics such as trainability and attitudes to work and leisure, but also to traits such as self-esteem and perceived personal well-being. Research studies have shown that employment, income, age, and health, but also previous experience of education, are factors which facilitate or limit opportunities for participation in continuing education. Since education influences life chances, the shaping of perceptions of self and society, and ultimately role acquisition, it can be assumed that experiences of education gained through adult education also influence the way people assess their own life situation. Studies provide some support for this assumption. For example, the desire to improve one's social network is a frequently noted factor which motivates people to become active in social and cultural activities, including voluntary adult education (Tuijnman 1990). Some people clearly consider continuing education not as a means for advancing their career and increasing earnings, but as a means for coping with role discontinuity and transitions in the lifespan.

Continuing education and job satisfaction. Judging by the number of articles in scholarly journals, the study of the sources and consequences of job satisfaction has been a popular activity since the 1970s. A general finding is that characteristics such as sex, age, social background, tested cognitive ability, and initial education account for very little of the variance in measures of job satisfaction. Another consistent finding is that job satisfaction is only weakly related to income. Locke (1976) and Michalos (1986) conclude on the basis of previous studies that job satisfaction increases if one or more of the following factors is optimalized: (a) general enrichment of the work environment, (b) enrichment of job content, (c) industrial democracy and worker participation in decision-making, (d) workers' perceptions of personal development through work, (e) task autonomy and task involvement, (f) perceived significance of the job task, (g) employment security, and (h) coworker assistance and social interaction at work.

Continuing education and human resources development are often considered key elements in a strategy to create a "post-Taylorist" workplace characterized by multiskilling, job rotation, quality circles, and informal learning at the workplace (Barra 1989). In this view, continuing education presents a means not only for the development of productive skills, but also for increasing the job satisfaction of workers by optimalizing some of the factors mentioned above. There is an abundance of research evidence pointing to a positive association between firm-based human resource development and job satisfaction (see Cascio 1989).

7. Conclusion

Within the area of adult education there has, until very recently, been little interest in empirical research on the social, economic, and labor market outcomes of continuing education. Large-scale evaluation studies of program effectiveness have typically not been carried out by adult educators, who have tended to be skeptical of quantitative research, but by researchers with a different disciplinary footing: in educational sociology and the economics of education. Adult educators have traditionally adhered to a different conceptualization of research questions. For them, the emphasis was, and still is, on practical problems arising in the teaching of adults (Rubenson 1989). So the little empirical work on the effects of adult education that is currently available has come mainly from research workers with a loose connection to the adult education field. This has advantages, since the interaction enriches the field in many ways, but there are also disadvantages. A problem arises because the kind of questions economists and sociologists ask inevitably put an emphasis on investment education. Compared with the vast body of research on training effects, little systematic evidence has cumulated concerning the short- and long-term benefits of general adult education. There is a need for specialists in adult education to become concerned with effectiveness research. Decisions with respect to the worthwhileness of a program of continuing education cannot, and should not, be based only on an assessment of external economic returns. Yet it is clear that this is happening. Adult educators may help in broadening the perspective so that nonmonetary benefits and even unexpected outcomes are taken up.

See also: Further Education and Training: Demand, Supply, and Finance; Adult Education and Training Markets; Nonformal Education, Economics of; Evaluation of Adult Education; Lifelong and Continuing Education; Adult Education, Reform Strategies in; Human Resource Development

References

Barnow B S 1987 The impact of CETA programs on earnings: A review of the literature. *J. Hum. Resources.* 22(2): 157–93

Barra R 1989 *Putting Quality Circles to Work: A Practical Strategy for Boosting Productivity and Profits.* McGraw-Hill, New York

Barron J M, Black D A, Loewenstein M A 1989 Job matching and on the job training. *J. Labor Econ.* 7(1): 1–19

Bishop J 1987 The recognition and reward of employee performance. *J. Labor Econ.* 5: S36–S56

Bishop J 1990 Job performance, turnover, and wage growth. *J. Labor Econ.* 8(3): 363–86

Bishop J 1991 On-the-job training of new hires. In: Stern D, Ritzen J M M (eds.) 1991 *Market Failure in Training? New Economic Analysis and Evidence on the Training of Adult Employees.* Springer-Verlag, Berlin

Blakemore A, Hoffman D 1989 Seniority rules and productivity: An empirical test. *Economica* 56: 359–71

Blaug M 1976 *Introduction to the Economics of Education.* Penguin, Harmondsworth

Brown J 1989 Why do wages increase with tenure? On the job training and life cycle wage growth observed within firms. *Am. Econ. Rev.* 79(5): 971–91

Cascio W F 1989 *Managing Human Resources: Produc-*

tivity, Quality of Working Life, Profits, 2nd edn. McGraw-Hill, New York
Cohn E, Geske T G 1990 *The Economics of Education*, 3rd edn. Pergamon Press, Oxford
Duncan G, Stafford F 1980 The use of time and technology by households in the United States. *Res. Lab. Econ.* 3: 335–74
Eliasson G, Ryan P 1987 *The Human Factor in Economic and Technological Change*. OECD, Paris
Felmlee D H 1988 Returning to school and women's occupational attainment. *Sociol. Educ.* 61(1): 29–41
Hanushek E A, Quigley J M 1985 Life-cycle earning capacity and the OJT investment model. *Int. Econ. Rev.* 26(2): 365–85
Kalleberg A L, Lincoln J R 1988 The structure of earning inequality in the United States and Japan. *Am. J. Sociol.* 94: S121–53
Kang S, Bishop J 1989 Vocational and academic education in high school: Complements or substitutes? *Econ. Educ. Rev.* 8(2): 133–48
Kirkpatrick D 1967 Evaluation of training. In: Craig R L, Bittel L (eds.) 1967 *Training and Development Handbook*. McGraw-Hill, New York
Knotterus J D 1987 Status attainment research and its image of society. *Am. Sociol. Rev.* 52(1): 113–21
Leeuwen S van, Dronkers J 1992 Effects of continuing education: A study on adult education, social inequality and labour market position in the Netherlands. *Int. J. Educ. Res.* 17(6): 609–24
Levin H M 1987 Improving productivity through education and technology. In: Burke G, Rumberger R M (eds.) 1987 *The Future Impact of Technology on Work and Education*. Falmer Press, London.
Lillard L A, Tan H W 1986 *Private Sector Training: Who Gets it and What are its Effects*? RAND Corporation, Santa Monica, California
Locke E A 1976 The nature and causes of job satisfacion. In: Dunette M (ed.) 1976 *Handbook of Industrial and Organizational Psychology*. Rand McNally, Chicago, Illinois
Mendes de Oliviera M E, Cohn E, Kiker B 1989 Tenure, earnings, and productivity. *Oxford B. Econ. Statis.* 51(1): 1–14
Michalos, A C 1986 Job satisfaction, marital selection and the quality of life: A review and a preview. In: Andrews F M (ed.) 1986 *Research on the Quality of Life*. Institute for Social Research, University of Michigan, Ann Arbor, Michigan
Mincer J 1989 Human capital and the labour market. A review of current research. *Educ. Researcher* 18(4): 27–34
Mincer J 1991 Job training: Costs, returns, and wage profiles. In: Stern D, Ritzen J M M (eds.) 1991 *Market Failure in Training? New Economic Analysis and Evidence on Training of Adult Employees*. Springer-Verlag, Berlin
OECD 1991 *Further Education and Training of the Labour Force in OECD Countries: Evidence and Issues*. OECD
Psacharopoulos G 1981 Returns to education: An updated international comparison. *Comp. Educ.* 17(3): 321–41
Psacharopoulos G 1985 Returns to education: A further international update and implications. *J. Hum. Resources* 20(4): 583–604
Psacharopoulos G 1987 Earnings functions. In: Psacharopoulos G (ed.) 1987 *Economics of Education: Research and Studies*. Pergamon Press, Oxford
Psacharopoulos G, Layard R 1979 Human capital and earnings: British evidence and a critique. *Rev. Econ. Stud.* 46(3): 485–503
Psacharopoulos G, Velez E 1992 Does training pay independent of education? Some evidence from Columbia. *Int. J. Educ. Res.* 17(6): 581–91
Romer P 1990 Endogenous technical change. *J. Pol. Econ.* 98: S71–S102
Rubenson K 1989 Adult education research: General. In: Titmus C J (ed.) 1989 *Lifelong Education for Adults: An International Handbook*. Pergamon Press, Oxford
Tuijnman A C 1989 *Recurrent Education, Earnings, and Well-being: A 50-year Longitudinal Study of a Cohort of Swedish Men*. Acta Universitatis Stockholmiensis. Almqvist and Wiksell, Stockholm
Tuijnman A C 1990 Adult education and the quality of life. *Int. Rev. Educ.* 36(3): 283–98

Further Reading

Baldwin S, Godfrey C, Propper C 1990 *Quality of Life: Perspectives and Policies*. Routledge, London
Dougherty C 1992 Evaluation of the economic and labour market effects of continuing education: Practice and policy issues. *Int. J. Educ. Res.* 17(6): 549–69
Gordon J 1991 Measuring the "goodness" of training. *Training* 28(8): 19–25
Layard R, Psacharopoulos G 1974 The screening hypothesis and the returns to education. *J. Pol. Econ.* 82(5): 985–98
Mosier N R 1990 Financial analysis: The methods and their application to employee training. *Hum. Resource Dev. Q.* 1: 45–63
Psacharopoulos G 1989 Time trends of the returns to education: Cross-national evidence. *Econ. Educ. Rev.* 8(3): 225–31
Romer P 1983 *Dynamic Competitive Equilibria with Externalities, Increasing Returns and Unbounded Growth*. Doctoral dissertation. University of Chicago Press, Chicago, Illinois
Rumberger R W 1987 The impact of surplus schooling on productivity and earnings. *J. Hum. Resources* 22(1): 24–50
Scott M 1989 *A New View of Economic Growth*. Clarendon Press, Oxford
Spencer L M 1984 How to calculate the costs and benefits of a HRD program. *Training* 21(7): 40–51

A. C. Tuijnman

Cooperative Learning

Organizing students to work together in small groups is an ancient practice in education throughout the world. While practice varies widely within the various countries, there is a sharp distinction between the approaches to cooperative learning prevalent in the United States and those prevalent in Europe, Israel, and the British Commonwealth. In the United States cooperative learning most frequently takes the form of relatively structured programs focused on mastery of skills, concepts, and information. These programs are likely to involve four-member, heterogeneous learning groups which remain together over a period of several weeks or more. In most cases, the groups receive recognition or occasionally grades based on their learning or performance as a group. In contrast, cooperative learning outside of the Unites States is more likely to focus either on relatively unstructured discussions or on group projects. Group membership is more likely to change from discussion to discussion and project to project. Furthermore, the purpose of the activity is at least as much socialization and general higher-order thinking or problem-solving skills as it is the learning of specific subject matter content.

Research on these different approaches to cooperative learning also differs sharply. Research on approaches developed in the United States (including that conducted in other countries) emphasizes experiments comparing cooperative and traditional methods, with a primary focus on academic achievement as the outcome of interest. Group Investigation, a structured technique based on Dewey's project method that was developed in Israel, has also been studied in experiments of this kind (e.g., Sharan and Shachar 1988). In contrast, there is far less research done on more informal cooperative learning approaches, and that which does exist tends to provide rich descriptions of the cooperative activities rather than any assessment of the outcome of those activities (e.g., Barnes and Britton 1969).

This entry presents a review of research on cooperative learning involving comparisons of cooperative and traditional approaches. With the exception of Group Investigation, all of these programs were developed in the United States. However, research on these and other closely related programs has also been conducted in Canada, Israel, Germany, the Netherlands, and Nigeria.

1. Cooperative Learning Methods

While social psychological research on cooperative learning dates back to the 1920s (see Slavin 1989), research on specific applications of cooperative learning to the classroom did not begin until the early 1970s. At that time, three independent groups of researchers in the United States and one in Israel began to develop and research the use of cooperative learning methods in classroom settings. In the early 1990s, there are researchers all over the world studying practical applications of cooperative learning principles, and there are many cooperative learning methods in use. The most widely researched are described in the following sections.

1.1 Student Team Learning

Student team learning methods are cooperative learning techniques developed and studied at Johns Hopkins University. More than half of all experimental studies of practical cooperative learning methods involve student team learning methods.

All cooperative learning methods share the idea that students work together to learn and are responsible for one another's learning as well as their own. In addition to the idea of cooperative work, student team learning methods emphasize the use of team goals and team success which can only be achieved if all members of the team learn the objectives being taught. In student team learning, therefore, the students' tasks are not to do something as a team but to learn something as a team.

Three concepts are central to all student team learning methods: "team rewards," "individual accountability," and "equal opportunity for success." In these techniques, teams may earn certificates or other team rewards if they achieve at or above a designated standard. The teams are not in competition to earn elusive rewards; all (or none) of the teams may achieve the standard in a given week. Individual accountability means that the team's success depends on the individual learning of all team members. Thus, the activity of the team members is focused on tutoring one another and making sure that everyone on the team is ready for a quiz or other assessment which students will be expected to complete without teammate help. Equal opportunity for success means that students contribute to their teams by improving over their own past performance. This ensures that high, average, and low achievers are equally challenged to do their best, and the contributions of all team members will be valued.

Research on cooperative learning methods has indicated that team rewards and individual accountability are essential elements for producing basic skills achievement (Slavin 1983a, 1983b, 1989). It is not enough simply to tell students to work together. They must have a reason to take one another's achievement seriously. Further, research indicates that if students are rewarded for doing better than they have in the past, they will be more motivated to achieve than if they are rewarded based on their performance in comparison to others, because rewards for improvement make success neither too difficult nor too easy for students to achieve (Slavin 1980).

There are four principal student team learning methods that have been extensively developed and researched. Of these, two are general cooperative learning methods adaptable to most subjects and grade levels: Student Teams–Achievement Divisions (STAD) and Teams–Games–Tournament (TGT). The remaining two are comprehensive curricula designed for use in particular subjects at particular grade levels: Team Assisted Individualization (TAI) for mathematics in grades 3–6, and Cooperative Integrated Reading and Composition (CIRC) for reading and writing instruction in grades 3–5.

1.1.1 Student Teams–Achievement Divisions (STAD). In STAD (Slavin 1986), students are assigned to four-member learning teams that are mixed in performance level, sex, and ethnicity. The teacher presents a lesson, and then students work within their teams to make sure that all team members have mastered the lesson. Finally, all students take individual quizzes on the material, at which time they may not help one another.

Students' quiz scores are compared to their own past averages, and points are awarded based on the degree to which students can meet or exceed their own earlier performance. These points are then summed to form team scores, and teams which achieve certain standards may earn certificates or other rewards. The whole cycle of activities, from teacher presentation to team practice to quiz, usually takes from three to five class periods.

This method has been used in a wide variety of subjects, from mathematics to language arts to social studies, from Grade 2 through college. It is most appropriate for teaching well-defined objectives with single right answers, such as mathematical computations and applications, language usage and mechanics, geography and map skills, and science facts and concepts.

*1.1.2 Teams–Games–Tournament (*TGT*).* Teams–Games–Tournament (DeVries and Slavin 1978, Slavin 1986) was the first of the Johns Hopkins cooperative learning methods. It uses the same teacher presentations and teamwork as in STAD, but replaces the quizzes with weekly tournaments in which students compete with members of other teams to contribute points to their team scores. Students compete at three-person "tournament tables" against others with similar past records in mathematics. A "bumping" procedure keeps the competition fair. The winner at each tournament table brings the same number of points to his or her team, regardless of which table it is. Thus, low achievers (competing with other low achievers) and high achievers (competing with other high achievers) have equal opportunities for success. As in STAD, high-performing teams earn certificates or other forms of team rewards.

*1.1.3 Team Assisted Individualization (*TAI*).* Team Assisted Individualization (TAI) (Slavin et al. 1986) shares with STAD and TGT the use of four-member mixed ability learning teams and certificates for high-performing teams, but where STAD and TGT use a single pace of instruction for the class, TAI combines cooperative learning with individualized instruction. Also, where STAD and TGT apply to most subjects and grade levels, TAI is specifically designed to teach mathematics to students in Grades 3–6 (or older students not ready for a full algebra course).

In TAI, students enter an individualized sequence according to a placement test and then proceed at their own rates. In general, team members work on different units. Teammates check each others' work against answer sheets and help one another with any problems. Final unit tests are taken without teammate help and are scored by student monitors. Each week, teachers total the number of units completed by all team members and give certificates or other team rewards to teams which exceed a criterion score based on the number of final tests passed, with extra points given for perfect papers and completed homework.

Because students take responsibility for checking each others' work and managing the flow of materials, the teacher can spend most of the class time presenting lessons to small groups of students drawn from the various teams who are working at the same point in the mathematics sequence. For example, the teacher might call up a decimals group, present a lesson on decimals, and then send the students back to their teams to work on decimal problems. The teacher might next call the fractions group, and so on.

*1.1.4 Cooperative Integrated Reading and Composition (*CIRC*).* The newest of the student team learning methods is a comprehensive program for teaching reading and writing in the upper elementary grades called Cooperative Integrated Reading and Composition, or CIRC (Stevens et al. 1987). In CIRC, teachers use basal readers and reading groups, much as in traditional reading programs in the United States. However, students are assigned to teams composed of pairs of students from two different reading groups. While the teacher is working with one reading group, students in the other groups are working in their pairs on a series of cognitively engaging activities including reading to one another; making predictions about how narrative stories will come out; summarizing stories to one another; writing responses to stories; and practicing spelling, decoding, and vocabulary. If the reading class is not divided into homogeneous reading groups, all students in the teams work with one another. Students work as a total team to master main idea and other comprehension skills. During language arts periods, students engage in writing drafts, revising and editing one another's work, and preparing for publication of team books.

In most CIRC activities, students follow a sequence of teacher instruction, team practice, team pre-assessments, and quiz. That is, students do not take the quiz until their teammates have determined that they are ready. Certificates are given to teams based on the average performance of all team members on all reading and writing activities.

1.2 Jigsaw

Jigsaw was designed by Elliot Aronson and his colleagues (Aronson et al. 1978). In the original Jigsaw method, students are assigned to six-member teams to work on academic material which has been broken down into sections. For example, a biography might be divided into early life, first accomplishments, major accomplishments, major setbacks, later life, and impact on history. Each team member reads his or her section. Next, members of different teams who have studied the same sections meet in "expert groups" to discuss their sections. Then the students return to their teams and take turns teaching their teammates about their sections. Since the only way students can learn sections other than their own is to listen carefully to their teammates, they are motivated to support and show interest in one another's work.

Slavin (1986) developed a modification of Jigsaw at Johns Hopkins University and then incorporated it in the Student Team Learning program. In this method, called Jigsaw II, students work in four- or five-member teams as in TGT and STAD. Instead of each student being assigned a unique section, all students read a common narrative, such as a book chapter, a short story, or a biography. However, each student receives a topic on which to become an expert. Students with the same topics meet in expert groups to discuss them, after which they return to their teams to teach what they have learned to their teammates. Then students take individual quizzes, which result in team scores based on the improvement score system of STAD. Teams which meet preset standards may earn certificates.

1.3 Learning Together

Researchers at the University of Minnesota developed the Learning Together model of cooperative learning (Johnson and Johnson 1987). The methods they have developed and studied involve students working in four- or five-member heterogeneous groups on assignments. The groups complete a single assignment and receive praise and rewards based on the group product. Their methods emphasize team building activities before students begin working together and regular discussions within groups about how well they are working together.

1.4 Group Investigation

Group Investigation, developed by Shlomo Sharan at the University of Tel-Aviv (Sharan and Sharan 1992), is a general classroom organization plan in which students work in small groups using cooperative inquiry, group discussion, and cooperative planning and projects. In this method, students form their own two- to six-member groups. After choosing subtopics from a unit being studied by the entire class, the groups further break their subtopics into individual tasks and carry out the activities necessary to prepare group reports. Each group then makes a presentation or display to communicate its findings to the entire class.

2. Research on Cooperative Learning

More than 70 high-quality studies have evaluated various cooperative learning approaches over periods of at least four weeks in regular elementary and secondary schools; 63 of these have measured effects on student achievement. These studies all compared effects of cooperative learning to those of traditionally taught control groups on measures of the same objectives pursued in all classes. Teachers and classes were either randomly assigned to cooperative or control conditions, or they were matched on pretest achievement and other factors.

2.1 Academic Achievement

Of the 63 studies of the achievement effects of cooperative learning, 36 (57%) have found significantly greater achievement in cooperative than in control classes; 26 (41%) found no differences; and in only one study did a control group outperform the experimental group. However, the effects of cooperative learning vary considerably according to the particular methods used.

As noted earlier, two elements must be present if cooperative learning is to be effective: group goals and individual accountability (Slavin 1983a, 1983b, 1989). That is, groups must be working to achieve some common goal and the success of the group must depend on the individual learning of every group member. In studies of approaches which include these elements, effects on achievement have been consistently positive; 34 out of 41 such studies (83%) found significantly positive achievement effects. In contrast, only 4 out of 22 studies (18%) lacking group goals and individual accountability found positive effects on student achievement.

Cooperative learning generally works equally well for all types of students. While occasional studies find particular advantages for high or low achievers, boys or girls, and so on, the great majority find equal benefits for all types of students. Sometimes a concern is expressed that cooperative learning will hold back high achievers. The research provides absolutely no support for this claim; high achievers gain from cooperative learning (relative to high achievers in traditional classes) just as much as do low and average achievers (Slavin 1989).

2.2 Intergroup Relations

Social scientists have long advocated interethnic cooperation as a means of ensuring positive intergroup relations in desegregated settings. Contact theory (Allport 1954), the dominant theory of intergroup relations in the United States, predicts that positive intergroup relations will arise from school desegregation if and only if students are involved in cooperative, equal-status interaction sanctioned by the school. Research on cooperative learning methods has borne out these predictions. Specifically, students were asked to list their best friends at the beginning of the study and again at the end. The number of friendship choices students made outside their own ethnic groups was the measure of intergroup relations. Positive effects on intergroup relations have been found for STAD, TGT, TAI, Jigsaw, Learning Together, and Group Investigation models (Slavin 1985).

Two of these studies, one on STAD (Slavin 1979) and one on Jigsaw II (Ziegler 1981), included followups of intergroup friendships several months after the end of the studies. Both found that students who had been in cooperative learning classes still named significantly more friends outside their own ethnic groups than did students who had been in control classes. Two studies of Group Investigation (Sharan et al. 1984, Sharan and Shachar 1988) found that students' improved attitudes and behaviors toward classmates of different ethnic backgrounds extended to classmates who had never been in the same groups. Similarly a study of TAI (Oishi 1983) found positive effects of this method on cross-ethnic interactions outside as well as in class.

The United States studies of cooperative learning and intergroup relations involved Black, White, and (in a few cases) Mexican–American students. A study of Jigsaw II by Ziegler (1981) took place in Toronto, where the major ethnic groups were Anglo-Canadians and children of recent European immigrants. The Sharan (Sharan et al. 1984, Sharan and Shachar 1988) studies of Group Investigation took place in Israel and involved friendships between Jews of European and Middle Eastern backgrounds.

2.3 Mainstreaming and Integration

Although ethnicity is a major barrier to friendship, it is not so large as the one between physically or mentally handicapped children and their normal-progress peers. The movement called "mainstreaming" in North America and "integration" in Europe seeks to place as many children as possible in regular classrooms. This movement has created an unprecedented opportunity for handicapped children to take their place in the mainstream of society. It has also created enormous practical problems for classroom teachers, however, and thus often leads to social rejection of handicapped children. Cooperative learning has been used to increase the social acceptance of the mainstreamed student.

The research on cooperative learning and mainstreaming has focused on the academically handicapped child. In one study, STAD was used to attempt to integrate students performing two years or more below the level of their peers into the social structure of the classroom. The use of STAD significantly reduced the degree to which the normal-progress students rejected their mainstreamed classmates, and increased the academic achievement and self-esteem of all students, mainstreamed as well as normal-progress (Madden and Slavin 1983). Other research using cooperative teams has also shown significant improvements in relationships between mainstreamed academically handicapped students and their normal-progress peers (Cooper et al. 1980, Slavin et al. 1984).

2.4 Self-esteem

Students in cooperative learning classes have been found to have more positive feelings about themselves than do students in traditional classes. These improvements in self-esteem have been found for TGT and STAD (Slavin 1983a), for Jigsaw (Blaney et al. 1977), and for the three programs combined (Slavin and Karweit 1981). Improvements in student self-concepts have also been found for TAI (Slavin et al. 1984).

2.5 Other Outcomes

In addition to effects on achievement, positive intergroup relations, greater acceptance of mainstreamed students, and self-esteem, effects of cooperative learning have been found on a variety of other important educational outcomes. These include liking of school, development of peer norms in favor of doing well academically, feelings of individual control over the student's own fate in school, cooperativeness, and altruism (see Slavin 1989). In addition, TGT (DeVries and Slavin 1978) and STAD (Janke 1978) have been found to have positive effects on students' time on-task. Finally, a remarkable study in the Kansas City (Missouri) schools found that lower socioeconomic-status students at risk of becoming delinquent who worked in cooperative groups in sixth grade had better attendance, fewer contacts with the police, and higher behavioral ratings by teachers in seventh through eleventh grades than did control students (Hartley 1976).

3. Conclusion

Research on cooperative learning supports its usefulness for improving such diverse outcomes as student achievement at a variety of grade levels and in many subjects, intergroup relations, relationships between mainstreamed and normal-progress students, and student self-esteem. The widespread and growing use of cooperative learning demonstrates that, in addition to its effectiveness, cooperative learning is practical and attractive to teachers.

See also: Group Processes in the Classroom; Mainstreaming; Group Dynamics

References

Allport G 1954 *The Nature of Prejudice*. Addison-Wesley, Cambridge, Massachusetts

Aronson E, Blaney N T, Stephan C, Sikes J, Snapp M (eds.) 1978 *The Jigsaw Classroom*. Sage, Beverly Hills, California

Barnes D, Britton J 1969 *Language, the Learner, and the School*. Penguin, Harmondsworth

Blaney N T, Stephan S, Rosenfeld D, Aronson E, Sikes J 1977 Interdependence in the classroom: A field study. *J. Educ. Psychol.* 69(2): 121–28
Cooper L, Johnson D W, Johnson R, Wilderson F 1980 Effects of cooperative, competitive and individualistic experiences on interpersonal attraction among heterogeneous peers. *J. Soc. Psychol.* 111: 243–52
DeVries D L, Slavin R E 1978 Teams–Games–Tournament (TGT): Review of ten classroom experiments. *J. Res. Dev. Educ.* 12: 28–38
Hartley W 1976 Preventive outcomes of small group education with school children: An epidemiologic follow up of the Kansas City School Behavior Project. Education Report. National Institute of Mental Health, Rockville, Maryland
Janke R 1978 The Teams–Games–Tournament (TGT) method and the behavioral adjustment and academic achievement of emotionally impaired adolescents. Paper presented at the annual convention of the American Educational Research Association, Toronto, April
Johnson D W, Johnson R T 1987 *Learning Together and Alone*, 2nd edn. Prentice-Hall, Englewood Cliffs, New Jersey
Madden N A, Slavin R E 1983 Cooperative learning and social acceptance of mainstream academically handicapped students. *J. Spec. Educ.* 17: 171–82
Oishi S 1983 Effects of team assisted individualization in mathematics on cross-race interactions of elementary school children. Doctoral dissertation, University of Maryland, College Park, Maryland
Sharan S et al. 1984 *Cooperative Learning in the Classroom: Research in Desegregated Schools.* Erlbaum, Hillsdale, New Jersey
Sharan S, Shachar C 1988 *Language and Learning in the Cooperative Classroom.* Springer-Verlag, New York
Sharan Y, Sharan S 1992 *Expanding Cooperative Learning Through Group Investigation.* Teacher's College Press, New York
Slavin R E 1979 Effects of biracial learning teams on cross-racial friendships. *J. Educ. Psychol.* 71(3): 381–87
Slavin R E 1980 Effects of individual learning expectations on student achievement. *J. of Educational Psychology* 72: 520–24
Slavin R E 1983a *Cooperative Learning.* Longman, New York
Slavin R E 1983b When does cooperative learning increase student achievement? *Psych. Bull.* 94(3): 429–45
Slavin R E 1985 Cooperative learning: Applying contact theory in desegregated schools. *J. Soc. Issues* 41(3): 45–62
Slavin R E 1986 *Using Student Team Learning*, 3rd edn. Center for Research on Elementary and Middle Schools, Johns Hopkins University, Baltimore, Maryland
Slavin R E 1989 *Cooperative Learning: Theory, Research, and Practice.* Prentice-Hall, Englewood Cliffs, New Jersey
Slavin R E, Karweit N 1981 Cognitive and affective outcomes of an intensive student team learning-experience. *J. Exp. Educ.* 50:29–35
Slavin R E, Leavey M B, Madden N A 1984 Combining cooperative learning and individualized isntruction: Effects on student mathematics achievement attitudes and behaviors. *Elem. Sch. J.* 84:408–22
Slavin R E, Leavey M B, Madden N A 1986 *Team Accelerated Instruction—Mathematics.* Mastery Education Corporation, Watertown, Massachusetts
Stevens R J, Madden N A, Slavin R E, Farnish A M 1987 Cooperative integrated reading and composition: Two field experiments. *Read. Res. Q.* 22(4): 433–54
Ziegler S 1981 The effectiveness of cooperative learning teams for increasing cross-ethnic friendship: Additional evidence. *Human Organization* 40:264–68

R. E. Slavin

Copyright

Daily, it seems, the laws regulating society multiply, and educational institutions in particular are required to cope with a multitude of regulations. The question of copyright poses some of the most difficult problems in this regard, since the law itself usually fails to address specifically educational situations. This entry highlights the evolution of copyright, the components of a copyright law, the major international copyright agreements, and the copyright issues facing educators today.

1. Historical Overview

Although Renaissance Italy saw the enactment of the first copyright-type legislation, copyright as a moral interest in a work dates back at least as far as Ancient Greece and Rome. These civilizations condemned plagiarism as dishonorable. St Columba's clandestine copying (circa AD 567) of Abbot Finnian's *Psalter* became a medieval *cause célèbre*, leading to the civil war that deposed King Diarmid. Hence the manuscript's name, *Cathac* ("the fighter") (see UNESCO 1981, Sinofsky 1984).

The medieval Italian city-states began granting authors and inventors exclusive rights in the form of patents. One example of such a patent was that granted in 1421 to Filippo Brunelleschi, architect of the dome of Florence Cathedral, for a shallow-draft boat design (unfortunately, the completed boat sank!). These early patents later developed into printing monopolies granted to encourage the new technology of printing. The question of authorship was only a secondary consideration.

In sixteenth- and seventeenth-century England such grants became tools of censorship, which were used to suppress religious and political dissent. For example, the Stationers' Company, chartered on 4 May 1557 by Queen Mary Tudor, was granted a printing monopoly as long as it ensured that nothing offensive to the Crown reached print. When the Company's charter finally expired in 1695 commercial plagiarism reigned until Parliament passed the Statute of Anne in 1710, the first modern statutory copyright law. Under this statute, copyright was vested in the author, not the publisher, thus breaking the printers' monopolies. In 1735 the "Engravers'

Act," or "Hogarth's Act," was passed—the first visual copyright law.

On 31 May 1790 the United States passed its first federal copyright law, the second nation to provide such legislation. In 1777 Louis XVI of France had issued six decrees recognizing an author's right to publish and sell works, and in 1793 France became the third country to adopt a national statutory copyright law. In Germany, the first federal law was enacted in 1837, although recognition of an author's rights can be found as early as 1686. Russia's first copyright law relating to literary works appeared in 1830.

2. *General Provisions of a Copyright Act*

A full discussion of copyright law and all its ramifications for a single country (let alone for three or more countries), far exceeeds the scope of this brief entry. Rather, this section explores the basic ideas and provisions generally found in a copyright law.

The underlying principles of copyright are that the creators of intellectual property have a right to their own intellectual property, to protection against unauthorized use, and to any monetary rewards from public use of their work. Copyright stimulates creativity through these monetary rewards, and protects the author's expression of an idea, not the idea itself. This allows others to use the idea. However, the line between idea and expression is blurred, especially where visual media are concerned, and this often results in accusations of copyright infringements.

Copyright laws set forth who is the author, who owns the copyright, who owns works-made-for-hire or commissioned, and who is a joint author. They also outline how copyrights may be transferred, for how long, which rights may be transferred, and which rights may be transferred after death. The laws indicate the duration of copyright protection and any formalities needed to implement copyright protection, such as registration, deposit, and copyright notice requirements. They also include remedies for copyright infringement, such as statutory damages and prison terms.

The moral rights (*droit moral*) of authors differ from copyrights because they focus on "the right to protect the integrity and the paternity of the work" (Patterson and Lindberg 1991 p. 165). The moral right distinguishes between the work and copyright ownership; that is, the moral rights of the author are distinct from the economic rights of the bookseller. "Moral rights are personal in nature, whereas economic rights are essentially proprietary" (Patterson and Lindberg 1991 p. 166). Thus moral rights often merit special mention within copyright law.

Copyright laws define the subject matter to be accorded protection (e.g., literary works) but not judicial decisions. They include derivative works (i.e., works derived from preexisting works) within their ambit. Thus translations, adaptations, arrangements, collections, anthologies, and other transformations and compilations can be copyrighted.

Copyright provides limited protection for works. Once the copyright has expired, a work falls into the public domain. Anyone may use a work in the public domain without seeking authorization. Official acts, some government documents, facts, and the day's news are usually not extended the protection of copyright. But as with ideas, the actual expression of the news or facts may be copyrighted.

"Fair use" or "fair dealing" also limits copyright protection by allowing others to use a work without the copyright owner's consent. The justification for this apparent infringement of the copyright owner's rights lies in the intended purpose of the copying. Originally, fair use allowed authors to use another author's work in creating their own work, but it is no longer restricted to such a narrow definition. In determining whether a given use is fair, the courts usually consider four criteria: (a) the purpose and character of the use; (b) the nature of the copyrighted work (e.g., informational versus entertaining); (c) the amount of the copyrighted work used (both quantitatively and qualitatively); and (d) the economic effect of the use on the copyrighted work's market value.

Other limits may include special exemptions for copying by archives and libraries for preservation, research, or interlibrary loan. Compulsory licenses (i.e., the copyright owner is legally obligated to grant third parties the right to use a work for a set fee) also limit a copyright owner's rights.

3. *International Copyright Agreements*

Before the nineteenth century, intellectual property protection remained the concern of individual countries. As international trade and contact increased, so the need for an international copyright code arose. Nations realized

> that intellectual property [was] not merely a matter of exchanges of goods and services, but [had] an outstanding part to play in the dialogue of nations through the contribution which the creations of the mind [could] make to the advancement of all peoples. (World Intellectual Property Organisation 1978 p. 3)

Bilateral agreements originally satisfied this need, but lacked the convenience of an international agreement. This led to the creation of the Berne Convention for the Protection of Literary and Artistic Works, also referred to as the "Berne Union," in 1886. Yet some countries, such as the United States, were not able to become signatories to the Berne Convention because their national copyright laws included formalities (e.g., notice, registration, and deposit requirements, and protectionist printing laws) and other provisions incompatible with those of Berne. This, in turn, led to the creation in 1952 of the Universal Copyright Convention (UCC). The World Intellectual Property Organization (WIPO) administers the Berne Convention, whereas the United Nations Educational Scientific and Cultural Organization (UNESCO) oversees the UCC. The United States finally joined the Berne Convention in 1989. Russia and the People's Republic of China (as of 1993) do not belong to Berne, although the former Soviet Union did belong to the UCC.

3.1 The Universal Copyright Convention

As was mentioned above, the UCC was created as an international alternative to the Berne Convention. Its requirements are less stringent than those of the Berne Convention. It is the UCC that requires a copyright notice composed of the copyright symbol ©, the year of publication, and the copyright owner's name to be appended to all published copies of a work in order to establish the copyright. This notice, modeled after the United States copyright notice, "in effect, allowed the United States to continue to require the very formality that multilateral copyright treaties are designed to avert" (Nimmer and Nimmer 1992, ¶ 17.01[B][2]).

> The U.C.C. [*sic*] is not a "rival treaty to Berne, the founding members of the Berne Union assisted in its creation to assure participation of the American Republics in the world copyright community. Moreover, the U.C.C. itself explicitly grants priority to the Berne Convention insofar as a relation between two members of the Berne Union (which are also U.C.C. members) is involved. Thus, Berne is acknowledged to be the premier multilateral copyright treaty, with the highest standards of protection. The U.C.C. ranks second on that scale. (Nimmer and Nimmer 1992, ¶ 17.01[B][2])

3.2 The Berne Convention

The Berne Convention is the oldest and, on account of its higher standard of copyright protection, the premier international copyright agreement. It automatically assures foreign works the same rights as those accorded to indigenous works in the countries that are signatories to the Convention. Even better, an author need not worry about formalities. However,

> [b]ecause there have been so many revisions to Berne over the years, countries that have joined the Berne at different times in history belong to different versions or "Acts" of the Convention. For example, a country that joined in 1950 belongs to the Brussels Act of Berne and is not technically required to adhere to the Berne Convention changes that have been made by the Paris Act of 1971. The Paris Act is now the only version open to accession. (Motyka 1992 p. 111)

The Berne Convention provisions fall into two broad categories: (a) rules governing substance, and (b) rules handling administrative and structural Issues. WIPO's *Guide to the Berne Convention* (1978) interprets each of the Convention's provisions. What follows is a summary.

The Preamble states three key points. First, that Berne members desire to provide literary and artistic works with a high level of protection. Second, they wish to do so in a uniform manner. Third, they choose copyright as the best method for offering this uniform protection. Article 1 deals with the formation of a union by those countries signing the Convention.

Article 2 defines "literary and artistic works" and clarifies that copyright extends to the expression of an idea, not the idea itself. Furthermore, originality, *not* novelty, is the basis for copyright protection. Thus more than one author may write a science textbook. Each author's expression of the basic scientific principles will be original although the scientific principles expressed are not novel. This article also covers derivative works, official texts, news and facts, and speeches.

Articles 3 and 4 deal with conditions for protection, while Article 5 enunciates the Convention's fundamental principles; that is, that foreigners are treated like nationals and no formalities exist. Article 6 allows reprisals against non-Berne countries that fail to provide adequate protection. Article 6 *bis* addresses the moral right of authors. Article 7 declares a copyright duration of the life of the author plus 50 years.

Articles 8 and 9 give authors the exclusive rights to translation and reproduction, while Article 10 slightly limits these rights. Article 10 outlines the rules for quotations and the use of works in teaching situations, in broadcasting, and in similar instances. Articles 11, 12, 13, and 14 return to the topic of exclusive rights, this time for public performances, broadcasting, public recitation, adaptation, recording musical works, and cinematographic rights.

Article 15 considers authorship in terms of who is entitled to bring actions for copyright infringement; Article 16, the seizure of infringing copies. Articles 17 through 21 clarify such topics as Berne not superseding a country's law, the retroactive effect of Berne, bilateral agreements, and provisions for developing countries. Articles 22 through 38 handle administrative provisions.

4. Issues Facing Education

New technologies and copyright law itself form the basis for education's continual problems in applying the law to itself. The problems reflect three intertwining strands: "changes in education wrought by the new technologies, gaps in the copyright law itself, and strains the new technologies place upon the copyright law" (Sinofsky 1984 p. 7). Technology makes duplication increasingly easy. Photocopiers, video recorders, and computers allow educators to improve instruction by providing a variety of materials to supplement textbooks. However, this necessarily means that students' needs come into conflict with the interests of copyright owners.

National copyright laws themselves are often silent on the issue of educational use. In many instances, the judicial doctrine of fair use is used to reconcile educational needs with those of the copyright owners. But reconciliation often comes only after years of negotiations or litigation, during which educators and copyright owners find themselves as adversaries rather than collaborators.

The rapid proliferation of new technologies far outstrips the ability of copyright law to address the new issues they raise. For example, if two computer spreadsheets look similar, does this constitute an infringement? Such questions never arose with regard to books, but computer programs raise different concerns. Wincor presented a daunting scenario which highlights the quagmire that is copyright law:

> [W]hen a device landed on Jupiter transmits pictures with text of its own composition, [w]ho owns Japanese language rights? Was the work done for hire, and under whose law? Can the rights claimant give proper warranties? Do the contracts collide with treaties? (Wincor 1990 pp. xii–xiii)

Back on earth, the new technologies have raised a broad array of questions. For instance, does the purchase of a satellite reception antenna allow an educational institution to show and/or record the televised program thus received without a license? To cite another example: a question is posted on an electronic bulletin board. Someone answers by scanning in a copyrighted work. Is this a fair use? Take it a step further: who is legally responsible if someone downloads this copyrighted work and retransmits it? The electronic bulletin board? The first person who scanned in the copyrighted work? The person who downloaded it? Under which country's laws does the copyright owner sue over alleged infringement if the electronic bulletin board is in one country, the copyright owner another, the person who scanned in the response in still another, and the person who retransmitted in yet another? Computerized databases pose similar problems.

Two final hypothetical examples serve to illustrate the legal complexities arising from new technologies. A teacher purchases a videocassette while in a foreign country to show in class. However, the foreign videocassette's format is incompatible with the equipment in the teacher's country. May the teacher transfer the program from its original format to one compatible with the equipment? In an academic setting, educators develop marketable software programs. Who owns the copyright? The educator, or the educational institution?

These are but a few of the copyright questions facing educators. Answers to them vary from country to country as copyright law revisions, court decisions, and negotiations continue. For this reason, educators are well-advised always to check the current copyright laws when dealing with intellectual property rights.

References

Motyka C 1992 US participation in the Berne Convention and high technology. In: ASCAP *Copyright Law Symposium (39)*. Columbia University Press, New York

Nimmer M B, Nimmer D 1992 *Nimmer on Copyright: A Treatise on the Law of Literary, Musical and Artistic Property, and the Protection of Ideas*. Matthew Bender, New York

Patterson L R, Lindberg W 1991 *The Nature of Copyright: A Law of Users' Rights*. University of Georgia Press, Athens, Georgia

Sinofsky E R 1984 *Off-air Videotaping in Education: Copyright Issues, Decisions, Implications*. Bowker, New York

UNESCO 1981 *The ABC of Copyright*. UNESCO, Paris

Wincor R 1990 *Copyrights in the World Marketplace: Successful Approaches to International Media Rights*. Prentice-Hall Law and Business, Englewood Cliffs, New Jersey

World Intellectual Property Organization (WIPO) 1978 *Guide to the Berne Convention for the Protection of Literary and Artistic Works (Paris Act. 1971)*. WIPO, Geneva

Further Reading

UNESCO 1956 *Copyright Laws and Treaties of the World*. UNESCO, Paris

Nimmer M B, Geller P E 1992 *International Copyright Law and Practice*. Matthew Bender, New York

1992 North American free trade agreement has provisions on intellectual property. *BNA's Patent. Trademark & Copyright Journal*. 44: 398–99

Sinofsky E R in press *A Copyright Primer for Educational and Industrial Media Producers*, 2nd edn. Copyright Information Services, Washington DC

E. R. Sinofsky

Core Curriculum

The term "core curriculum" has been used in two different senses in the twentieth century's educational literature. In the 1930s it denoted a curriculum focusing on content of immediate significance for the learner. This involved topics such as adolescent needs or social problems. The planning of such programs required cooperation between teachers and pupils, and it handled contents from two or more school subjects in an integrative way (Foshay 1985).

Since the 1960s the term has been used mainly in the context of determining what elements of the school program should be strongly emphasized and taught to all students.

Typically, school curricula specify what subjects are to be taught in schools and/or what students are expected to learn. Most of these curricula also list the topics within each subject that are included in the plan.

Traditionally, this plan included what the developers considered essential for education, but as new subjects arose which had produced organized bodies of knowledge their proponents sought to have them included in the school and college curriculum. More subjects were being proposed for inclusion than could be accommodated in practice within the time and with the resources available. As these constraints were recognized the basic question was shifted to: what is the common core of knowledge that all students should be expected to learn? The curriculum has come to be viewed as composed of two parts: common core subjects and peripheral subjects which provide instruction for differences in student populations, environmental contexts, and purposes. Throughout the twentieth century the debate over the composition of the core curriculum has continued and reached its peak in the 1980s when several educational systems around the world introduced a national core curriculum.

According to Skilbeck (1986), "the core curriculum defines those structured and organized studies and other learning activities which, by virtue of their fundamental importance for individuals and society, are, in some form or another, required of all students during the compulsory years of schooling." Tripp and Watt (1984) questioned the need to have a core curriculum, and Holmes (1988) went even further, claiming that there was no consensual basis to shore up a significant common core beyond the ABCs. In his opinion, the idea of a common core contradicts the centrifugal and individualistic tendencies of modern times.

Despite such critical comments, formally defined and prescribed core curricula were established by the educational authorities in countries including England and Wales, the Netherlands, France, Spain, Norway, Bavaria, and several states of the United States during the 1980s.

1. *Factors Influencing the Debate*

It might appear to some educators that this debate should have been settled once and for all, but it still continues. By examining the ongoing discussions several factors that account for this can be recognized. One is the continuing development of new subjects or new divisions within subjects. Eventually some of these subjects are recognized as potentially appropriate for teaching and student learning. For example, science based on empirical studies began to develop organized knowledge nearly 500 years ago. By the early nineteenth century it was recognized as a subject for the college curriculum and 50 years later it was given a place in the secondary school curriculum.

As another example, sociology, based on empirical studies, began to develop a body of knowledge around 1900, but it has not become part of the core curriculum of the secondary school. Examples of other new subjects or new subdivisions of subjects that are not part of the core curriculum include linguistics, molecular biology, genetics, and political science.

A second factor in maintaining a continuing debate over the core curriculum is the recognition by educators that a subject title does not define the things being taught. For example, modern European history is often taught as a series of wars and battles and a succession of kings and political parties which students are to memorize; alternatively, it may be taught as lessons in the development of nations from feudal fiefdoms. Again, it may be taught as examples of economic production growing from rural farms to industrial factories and the resulting changes in occupations and ways of life of ordinary people. There are various other ways in which the content of modern European history is defined. As educators discovered these different courses all listed as the same subject, they sought more appropriate ways to define the content of the core curriculum. The one most commonly used is to define a curriculum in terms of the subject, the topics to be included, and the aims or objectives to be attained. As teachers are finding new possibilities for student learning in different subjects, these discoveries stimulate debates over the potential value of teaching the subject, with these new purposes to guide the teacher and learner. Such debates have been continuing for many years.

A third factor influencing the continuing debate has been the changing interests of students. When students believe that the curriculum enables them to learn what they consider important, they will try to learn what the teachers are teaching. When they see no connection between their own concerns and interests and the content of the curriculum, they may try to do the school assignments and pass the school tests but will quickly forget what they have been taught because they see no way to use what they are taught except to pass school tests. John Dewey wrote in 1913 of his experience with the Chicago Experimental School, reporting that when students were interested in the school work they made much more effort to learn. In the early 1990s, a large number of students come from homes where parents have had little or no education. Many of these families think of schooling only as a means to get better jobs for their children. When they see no connection between the school tasks and good jobs, the students lose interest in doing their school assignments. The solution to this problem is seen by some educators to be a core curriculum of vocational education for these students and a core curriculum of academic subjects for those who are interested in academic activities. Other educators see the solution to the problem to be the development of a core curriculum that emphasizes academic work carried on in the activities of interest to the students, including occupational interests. There are other variants, such as cooperative education in which students alternate between periods in the work force and periods in school, aided by a coordinator to help them see how the school assignments assist them in carrying out the work effectively.

A fourth factor influencing the continuing debate is the implicit belief of the public that most social problems can be solved by education in the schools. Some aspects of contemporary social problems can be successfully treated by education of school children and youth. Racial attitudes of students, for example, have been and can be strongly influenced by what students learn in school, both in courses and in the way in which the school community is operated. Sometimes the attitudes developed by children in the school influence their parents and other adults in the community, but the beliefs and practices of adults are usually affected very little by school programs that present positions in contrast to their own. In most cases, adults themselves must be involved in study and action programs to accept ideas in conflict with the beliefs they have held for many years.

2. *Pressures for Inclusion in Core Curriculum*

In spite of the 200 years of experience that many nations have had in dealing with serious social problems, schools have had few successes and many failures in this area. When asked to solve these problems leaders of the public still place responsibility upon the schools for dealing with unexpected crises. Pressure groups, for example, are trying to get their agenda into the core curriculum. Among proposals are courses in AIDS prevention, in the prevention of smoking, in the battle against teenage pregnancy, in the prevention of war, and so on. This pressure for the inclusion of ad hoc subjects creates serious debate among educators regarding the proper criteria for the identification of bodies of knowledge to include in the core curriculum.

Pressures for inclusion in the core curriculum come not only from individuals and groups seeking effective attacks on serious social problems but also from selfish interests seeking to promote their products or services. For example, organizations of milk producers distribute a syllabus for a course in nutrition which emphasizes the importance of milk in the diet of children and adults. The producers of mason jars used in canning fruits and vegetables distribute a syllabus for a course in food preservation for use in home economics programs that are being recommended for the core curriculum. Some computer companies seek to influence the sale of computers to schools and families by offering to furnish some leading schools with computers together with course work for a basic computer course to be part of the core curriculum. This kind of marketing seeks to circumvent the selection of curriculum content on the basis of experience and experiment, the results of which are verified and judged by educators making the decisions.

3. *Essential Components of Core Curriculum*

As educators have participated in the debates, their leaders have identified certain subjects to be included in the core curriculum and have also recognized the need for each generation to redefine the content of these subjects for different age levels of students and to include consideration of new knowledge and new demands for knowledge arising from societal changes.

The study of language has continued over the years to be one component of the core curriculum. Language includes developing understanding and skill in the use of language in speech, in listening, in reading, in writing, and for the many purposes in which each age group can effectively utilize language.

Closely associated with language in the core curriculum is the study of literature. Literature has many functions in the lives of modern people. It serves much more than providing amusement to fill one's leisure time. It can furnish exploration into many aspects of the human condition, providing vicarious experience of matters not readily obtained through direct experience. This enables the reader not only to perceive and understand these situations but also to sense their emotional appeals and pains.

Mathematics is a third subject that continues to be an essential component of the core curriculum. To guide one's life as well as to understand the society in which one lives requires answers to questions such as: When did this happen? How long was it? When will I do these things? Where do I go? How far is it? How heavy is it?

As one gains understanding of the environment and of one's self, conceptual maps are developed which serve as guides to action and to clearer understanding. These maps involve mathematical relations expressed by answers to such questions as those listed above. One uses some form of mathematical thinking in developing answers to such questions. The process may be crude or more refined as one studies mathematics, including actual and possible quantitative relations.

History is the fourth subject that continues to be a component of the core curriculum. To understand most complex issues and appreciate the current situation of peoples and of nations, requires knowledge of the developments over long periods of time. It is necessary to understand both the successful steps that have been taken and the tragic ones. Without an understanding of historical experiences, nations and individuals are likely to make the same mistakes as in the past.

Science is the subject most recently accepted by educators as a major component of the core curriculum. By the mid-nineteenth century, bodies of knowledge had been developed and organized by scientists using the methods of empirical inquiry and experimentation. It was then clear that science provided a means of exploring and understanding the world of nature that could be of great importance in the education of children, youth, and adults.

In the early 1990s the usual core curriculum included five major subjects: language, literature, mathematics, history, and science. The inclusion of other subjects in the core curriculum is still being debated.

4. *Defining the "Core": The Subject Structure and the Cultural Literacy Approaches*

In the late 1980s arguments were advanced in various countries in favor of centrally defining a new core curriculum for schools. Well-articulated essays on topics such as "the impact of living in a multicultural society on defining educational objectives and selecting curriculum contents" have generated consensus about the desirability of such steps. Nevertheless, difficulties have been encountered whenever attempts were made to translate these ideas into curriculum documents such as laws, decrees, orders, curriculum frameworks, or syllabuses.

4.1 The Subject Structure

Some theorists attempted to suggest new ways to facilitate the translation of innovative ideas into curriculum documents. They suggested strengthening the relevance of the curriculum for life in a democratic society and for cultural participation. Walker (1990) described some cross-curricular issues related to these attempts, which may be summarized as follows:

(a) Try to identify a set of broadly defined life skills (e.g., being able to use a variety of communication means and/or channels in various situations), or identify a set of broadly defined cultural domains (e.g., being able to cope with different moral systems valid in one's national culture).

(b) Break down these broad skills or domains into statements of educational goals (e.g., being able to recognize and interpret body language and being able to recognize various moral beliefs reflected in one's behavior).

(c) Design educational situations in which these goals can be mastered and bring these designed situations together in meaningful "units" (projects or courses). If some of these units can be integrated into traditional subject syllabuses (e.g., communication in one's mother tongue) that is fine. Alternatively, new patterns of curriculum structure may arise.

In practice, however, most innovative topics were integrated into the prevailing subject structure and only a few cross-curricular topics emerged in the form of cross-disciplinary or interdisciplinary areas of study. The most notable among them are: consumer education, environmental education, human rights education, peace education, and family life education.

Even these topics, however, have been frequently integrated into subjects such as history, biology, and economics. This has been done in England and Wales, Baden Württemberg, the Netherlands, Spain, Bavaria, and other countries. In most countries there is also a separate list of cross-curricular issues, prescribed by law and obligating schools to cover these issues in their elaboration of the attainment targets. The subject structure as it has developed since the mid-nineteenth century in university sciences, teachers' associations, teacher graduation, and so on, is too strong and too valuable, although the content of traditional subjects does change gradually.

4.2 Cultural Literacy

A new approach to defining core curriculum emerged at the end of the 1980s in the United States which affected thinking about the subject in numerous countries of the Western world. It became known as the cultural literacy approach. Hirsch's (1987) publication on the topic is the benchmark in the spread of this idea. The underlying idea of this approach is that one of the main tasks of the school is to motivate and enable students to participate in, and communicate about, issues pertaining to their national culture. This, claims Hirsch, requires more than mastering reading, writing, thinking, and vocational skills. It is necessary to get acquainted with specific contents that constitute a part of the national culture. Hirsch drew up a list of concepts and terms from various disciplines (including science and mathematics), names of persons and geographic locations (including fictional characters), works of art and literature, and famous proverbs, expressions, quotations, and so on. He also published a dictionary of these items. Hirsch claimed that without being familiar with the meanings of these items one is not culturally literate. An example of items included is Martin Luther King's saying "I have a dream." A culturally literate person in the United States is supposed to know the historical context and significance of this saying. An illustrative set of these items, appearing in alphabetical order, is presented in Table 1.

Hirsch's ideas generated an educational movement. Several school districts in the United States have adopted his ideas as a basis for curriculum

Table 1
What literate Americans know—a selection

amphibian	antonym
amplifier	Antony's speech at Caesar's funeral
Amsterdam	Archimedes
anaerobic	archipelago
analogy	Arctic Circle
anal personality	Arctic Ocean
anarchy	aria
Anchorage, Alaska	aristocracy
antimatter	as the crow flies
antipodes	astrology
anti-Semitism	astronomy
antitrust legislation	asymmetry
Antony and Cleopatra (title)	As you make your bed so must you lie in it

Source: Hirsch 1987

construction. Moreover, in several other countries, such as the Netherlands, Sweden, and Israel, similar lists were compiled and disseminated. The validity of these lists was established through the involvement of specialists in judging the importance of each item on them. While one may strive to obtain stronger evidence about the validity of the list, it should be noted that expert judgment is a commonly accepted data type in studies of curriculum validation (Bloom 1977).

Hirsch's approach to defining the core curriculum became a topic of debate among researchers. Westbury (1988) criticized his way of compiling a list of cultural literacy and suggested that such a list should not be produced by a single team of experts, but rather by separate subject teams (for example, experts dealing with issues of "man's physical environment and biological inheritance"; "man's social inheritance and social responsibilities"; "health and physical development," etc.).

In general, however, Westbury favored Hirsch's approach and conceived it as a rejection of the traditional attitude which viewed cultural literacy as being associated with status and aptitude. Hirsch's conception of cultural literacy represents an aspiration that may sound utopian; earlier in the twentieth century, however, universal literacy would have seemed utopian, and it has since been achieved in most industrialized nations.

A more severe criticism was voiced by Kliebard (1989) who expressed the concern that "Hirsch's list may lead to acquiring a superficial knowledge of the vocabulary of educated people, which is hardly a substitute for becoming truly educated. The terms listed [in Hirsch's dictionary] do not represent a coherent body of knowledge. Students will trivialize cultural information, without really possessing it."

5. Significance for Schools

Theoretically, a core curriculum imposed by the state could be a starting point for curriculum development initiatives at the school level. It may also serve as a signal from society through parliamentary democracy to impart basic knowledge to all learners. Unfortunately, many teachers do not seem to be too susceptible to such a challenge and perceive the core curriculum as an invention of "educational bureaucrats" at the ministry.

A core curriculum may promote innovation and change. Traditional contents in certain subjects have to be changed and new ones need to be infused. The core curriculum could also function as an arbiter for change in decision-making processes at the school level. For example, the Dutch core curriculum prescribed that schools had to coordinate attainment targets in economics, biology, and in an innovative subject called "personal care and home economics." This demand may promote increased coordination between different departments of the school. The coordination may also, for instance, be increased by joining environmental education with the curricula of biology, geography, and chemistry.

There is, however, no guarantee that this will happen in practice. Rassekh and Vaideanu (1987) pointed out the difficulties in changing the content of teaching. They observed a growing resistance to change generated at the system level. This is due to the expansion of the bureaucratic and administrative branch of educational systems, the expansion of rational management at the system level, the increased standardization of assessment procedures, and the decrease of opportunities for teachers' genuine participation.

The success of implementing a core curriculum across educational systems may be highly enhanced by sharing decision-making about the details of such programs between the central authorities and the teachers.

See also: Curriculum Theory; Curriculum: Sociological Perspectives; Curriculum: Philosophical Perspectives

References

Bloom B S 1977 Tryout and revision of materials and

methods. In: Lewy A (ed.) 1977 *Handbook of Curriculum Evaluation*. Longman, New York
Foshay A 1985 Core curriculum. In: Husén T, Postlethwaite T N (eds.) 1985. *The International Encyclopedia of Education*, 1st edn. Pergamon Press, Oxford
Hirsch E D Jr 1987 *Cultural Literacy: What every American needs to Know*. Houghton Mifflin, Boston, Massachusetts
Holmes M 1988 The fortress monastery: The future of the common core. In: Westbury I, Purves A (eds.) 1988. *Cultural Literacy and the Idea of General Education*. University of Chicago Press, Chicago, Illinois
Kliebard H 1989 Cultural literacy and the curate's egg. *J. Curric. Stud.* 21(1): 61–70
Rassekh S, Vaideanu G 1987 *The Contents of Education: A Worldwide View of their Development from Present to the Year 2000*. UNESCO, Paris
Skilbeck M 1986 *Guides for Experts in Preparing Reports for the Country Studies on the Core Curriculum*. OECD, Paris
Tripp D H, Watt A J 1984 Core curriculum: What it is and why we don't need one, *J. Curric. Stud.* 16(2): 131–41
Walker D 1990 *Fundamentals of Curriculum*. Harcourt, Brace, Jovanovich, San Diego, California
Westbury I 1988 Who can be taught what: General education in the secondary school. In: Westbury I, Purves A (eds.) 1988 *Cultural Literacy and the Idea of General Education*. University of Chicago Press, Chicago, Illinois

Further Reading

Faunce R C, Bossing N L 1958. *Developing the Core curriculum*, 2nd edn. Prentice-Hall, Englewood Cliffs, New Jersey
Foshay A W (ed.) 1963 *The Rand McNally Handbook of Education*. Rand McNally, Chicago, Illinois
Goodlad J I 1987 A new look at an old idea: Core Curriculum. *Educ. Leadership* 44(4): 8–16
Jozefzoon E O J, Gorter R J 1985 *Core Curriculum: A Comparative Analysis*. National Institute for Curriculum Development, Enschede
Parkinson K J, Broderick J S 1988 An Evaluation of the Implementation of National Core Curricula in Australia. ERIC Document Reproduction Service No. ED 292 954, Washington, DC
Tyler R W 1953 The core curriculum. *Nat. Educ. Ass. J.* 42(9): 563–65
United Kingdom Department of Education and Science 1989 *National Curriculum: From Policy to Practice*. DES, London

R. Tyler; J. Van Bruggen

Correlational Procedures in Data Analysis

In its most general sense, the term "correlation" refers to a measure of the degree of association between two variables. Two variables are said to be correlated when certain values of one variable tend to co-occur with particular values of the other. This tendency can range from nonexistent (all values of variable 2(Y) are equally likely to occur with each value of variable 1(X)), to absolute, (only a single value of Y occurs for a given value of X). A correlation coefficient is a numerical index of the strength of this tendency. This entry is concerned with the properties and uses of correlation coefficients.

There are many special types of correlation coefficients. All share the characteristic of being measures of association between two variables. The difference lies in how the variables are defined. What is commonly called the "correlation coefficient" (or, more properly, the "Pearson product–moment correlation coefficient" or PMC) is an index of association between two variables where both variables are considered as single observed variables. The association between scores on a reading readiness test and a later measure of reading achievement is an example of such a correlation. Although each measure is the sum of scores on several items or subtests and represents a complex human characteristic, it is treated as a single undifferentiable variable for the purposes of analysis.

At the other end of the spectrum is a procedure called set correlation (Cohen 1982). Like the ordinary PMC, it is a measure of the association between two variables; however, in this case the association is between two unobservable variables that are weighted additive combinations of multiple measured variables. The unobserved variables are often called latent variables or composite variables. If, for example, the reading readiness and achievement measures each yielded several subscales, the correlation between a weighted combination of one set of subscales and a weighted combination of the other would be a canonical correlation. Set correlation is a generalization of canonical correlation in which additional sets of variables can be statistically removed from one or both of the sets being correlated (see partial correlation below).

1. Mathematical Definition of Correlation

The mathematical definition of an index of correlation is quite straightforward in most cases, although its actual computation may be very involved and time consuming. Adopting the notation conventions that

X_i is the score of individual i on variable X
Y_i is the score of individual i on variable Y
$\bar{X}$ is the mean of X scores $= \Sigma X/N$
$\bar{Y}$ is the mean of Y scores

where X and Y may be measured variables or composites, the variances of X and Y are both of the general form

$$S_X^2 = \sum_{i=1}^{N} (X_i - \bar{X})^2/N \tag{1}$$

For any given set of measurements, the mean of the set is a least-squares description of the entire set. That is,

$$1/N \sum_{i=1}^{N} (Y_i - \bar{Y})^2 = \text{minimum} \tag{2}$$

For a single variable, this is clearly S^2_Y. However, if a second variable (X) is available it may be possible to use that second variable to form subgroups such that some value other than $\bar{Y}$ is a least-squares description within each subgroup. Since for any group or subgroup its mean on the variable in question is the least-squares descriptor, the subgroups must have different mean values if group information is to improve on the overall mean. Letting $\bar{Y}_j$ stand for the mean of group j, an individual's deviation from the overall mean $\bar{Y}$, can be seen as composed of two parts:

$$(Y_{ij} - \bar{Y}) = (\bar{Y}_j - \bar{Y}) + (Y_{ij} - \bar{Y}_j) \tag{3}$$

The deviation of the ith individual in group j from the overall mean is the sum of the deviations of the group's mean from the overall mean and the individual's score from the group mean.

By going through the process of computing a variance, that is, squaring, summing over N cases, and dividing by N, the above equation becomes:

$$\left[\sum\sum (Y_{ij} - \bar{Y})^2\right]/N = \left[\sum\sum (\bar{Y}_j - \bar{Y})^2\right]/N + \left[\sum\sum (Y_{ij} - \bar{Y}_j)^2\right]/N \tag{4}$$

The term on the left is clearly an ordinary variance of the form found in Eqn. (1). The terms on the right are also variances, but the first is the variance of group means around the overall mean and the second is the pooled variance within groups. The numerators of these two terms are the sums of squares between and within groups from the analysis of variance.

Recall that groups were formed on the basis of the other variable, X. The differences among the subgroup means are due to the X variable in the sense that it was the X variable that led to the identification of groups. Therefore, the second term in Eqn. (4) is the variance in Y that is due to X or is related to X. The third term, then, is the variance in Y that is unrelated to X or independent of X. This is sometimes called the "residual variance."

Equation (4) may be rewritten in terms of variances as:

$$S^2_Y = S^2_{\hat{Y}} + S^2_{Y \cdot X} \tag{5}$$

where $S^2_{\hat{Y}}$ is the Y variance due to X. $S_{Y \cdot X}$ is the residual variance and is the quantity to be minimized in Eqn. (2). With these variance terms defined, the general form for an index of correlation is

$$\text{corr} = (S^2_{\hat{Y}}/S^2_Y)^{1/2} = [1 - (S^2_{Y \cdot X}/S^2_Y)]^{1/2} \tag{6}$$

That is, an index of correlation is the square root of the proportion of Y variance that is related to X. This mathematical definition of correlation is based on the assumption that Y is measured on an interval scale and has a normal distribution, but X can be a nominal variable. The basic definition in Eqn. (6) is called the correlation ratio and is usually given the symbol η (eta).

2. *Product–Moment Correlation*

The definition given above is a general definition of correlation in which no assumptions are made about the nature of the X variable (Y is assumed to have a normal distribution). It is frequently the case in educational research that both X and Y variables can be assumed to be measured on interval scales with normal or approximately normal distributions. When both variables are continuous, measured on an interval scale, and normally distributed their joint frequency distribution is bivariate normal.

When X is a discrete or group-membership variable, it is clear that the Y scores of people at any given value of X form a frequency distribution and the mean, $\bar{Y}_j$, is the least-squares description for the group. Likewise, when X is continuous there is a distribution of Y scores for people with a particular X score (X_i), and the mean of these Ys (call it $\hat{Y}_i$), is a least-squares description for these individuals taken as a group. The assumption that X and Y have a bivariate normal distribution means that there is a consistent relationship between changes in X and changes in $\hat{Y}$. The graph of X and $\hat{Y}$ is a straight line of the form

$$\hat{Y}_i = B_{Y \cdot X} X_i + A_{Y \cdot X} \tag{7}$$

At any particular value X_i, the variance in Y scores around $\hat{Y}_i$ is the unexplained variance, $S^2_{Y \cdot X} = \Sigma(Y_i - \hat{Y}_i)^2/N$. The values of $B_{Y \cdot X}$ and $A_{Y \cdot X}$ are determined such that, across the entire set of data, $S^2_{Y \cdot X}$ is minimum. By the logic used in developing Eqns. (4) and (5), the total variance of Y may be expressed as

$$S^2_Y = S^2_{\hat{Y}} + S^2_{Y \cdot X} \tag{8}$$

It can be shown that the value of $B_{Y \cdot X}$ is given by

$$B_{Y \cdot X} = \sum x_i y_i \Big/ \sum x_i^2 = \sum x_i y_i / N S^2_X$$
$$A_{Y \cdot X} = \bar{Y} - B_{Y \cdot X} \bar{X} \tag{9}$$

where $x_i = X_i - \bar{X}$ and $y_i = Y_i - \bar{Y}$. When X and Y are expressed in the standard score form

$$B_{Y \cdot X} = \sum Z_{y_i} Z_{x_i} / N \tag{10}$$

The symbol $r_{y \cdot x}$ is used to represent the slope coefficient in Eqn. (7) when X and Y are expressed in standard scores.

$$r_{y \cdot x} = \sum Z_y Z_x / N. \tag{11}$$

This is one of several definitional formulas for the product–moment correlation. Since the intercept (A) must be zero ($\bar{Z}_Y = \bar{Z}_X = 0$), Eqn. (7) may be written as

$$\hat{Z}_{Y_i} = r_{YX} Z_{X_i} \tag{12}$$

Rewriting the least-squares function in Eqn. (2) for Z scores produces

$$1/N \sum (Z_{Y_i} - \hat{Z}_{Y_i})^2$$
$$= 1/N \sum (Z_{Y_i} - r_{YX} Z_{X_i})^2 = \text{minimum} \qquad (13)$$

By squaring, summing, dividing by N, simplifying the result, and recalling from Eqn. (3) the expression for the residual variance, the following is obtained:

$$S^2_{Z_Y \cdot Z_X} = 1 - r^2_{YX}. \qquad (14)$$

In terms of the original raw scores, this equation becomes

$$S^2_{Y \cdot X} = S^2_Y (1 - r^2_{YX}). \qquad (15)$$

Solving for r^2_{YX} yields

$$r^2_{YX} = [1 - (S^2_{Y \cdot X}/S^2_Y)] = S^2_{\hat{Y}}/S^2_Y \qquad (16)$$

which is identical to Eqn. (6). A useful computing formula for r is

$$r = \sum y_i x_i / N S_X S_Y \qquad (17)$$

or its raw-score equivalent

$$r = \frac{N\sum Y_i X_i - \sum Y_i \sum X_i}{\left[N\sum Y_i^2 - \left(\sum Y_i\right)^2\right]^{1/2}\left[N\sum X_i^2 - \left(\sum X_i\right)^2\right]^{1/2}} \qquad (18)$$

To this point, three meanings of the product–moment correlation coefficient have been developed. They are

(a) The slope of the least-squares regression line for standard score variables is r (Eqn. [11]).

(b) The strength of association between two variables $S^2_{\hat{Y}}/S^2_Y$ is r^2 (Eqn. [16]).

(c) The residual variance in Y, which may be viewed as the inaccuracy of prediction, is $S^2_Y\,(1 - r^2_{YX})$ (Eqn. [15]).

There are several additional interpretations of the PMC that are discussed by Harman (1976), McNemar (1969), or Thorndike (1978). Interested readers should consult these sources for a complete presentation.

3. Other Bivariate Correlations

The product–moment correlation is the most widely used and understood correlational index. It has several advantages, such as its numerous interpretations, that accrue when the conditions for its use are met. However, there are numerous research situations in which not all variables are continuous, represent an interval scale, and have normal distributions. A number of alternative correlation coefficients are available for situations that do not meet all the assumptions of the product–moment correlation.

Perhaps the most common case occurs when one or both of the variables is represented in the data as a set of categories. The correct procedure then depends on the basis for the categorization and the number of categories. If the variable is truly categorical and dichotomous, no special treatment is required. If the measured variable represents a categorization of a variable that could in theory be measured on a continuum, special procedures are needed to estimate what the correlation would be for a continuous variable. Truly categorical polychotomous variables can be analyzed in some situations, but because they seldom possess ordinal properties, measures of association that involve such variables are few and interpretations are severely restricted.

3.1 Special Product–Moment Coefficients

Truly dichotomous variables have two values (male or female) while polychotomous variables have several categories (geographic region). When one or both of the variables in a correlation is truly dichotomous, the analysis results in a special PMC with restricted interpretation and perhaps restricted range. If one variable is polychotomous, eta may be used. Chi-square is the statistic of association for two polychotomous variables. As measures of association, eta and chi-square cannot be used in further analyses.

A correlation between one dichotomous variable and one continuous variable is called a point-biserial correlation (r_{pb}). The correlation between two dichotomous variables is called the "fourfold point correlation" or "phi" (ϕ). Both of these coefficients are PMCs and may be computed by the usual formulas as well as by special formulas given in some statistics books. They require no special attention on the part of the investigator in that dichotomous variables included in a computer run for correlation analysis will be properly processed by the usual equations and the results will be either r_{pb}s or ϕs. However, the investigator should be aware that neither of these coefficients should be used in Eqns. (11) or (14). They may be interpreted as indicating strength of association and they are the appropriate coefficients to use when truly dichotomous variables such as gender occur in a multivariate analysis. Because they are dichotomous, their variances will be smaller than is the case for continuous variables, and the resulting correlations will also tend to be smaller.

A second situation that is encountered occasionally in educational research is that the data occur as rankings or other ordinal forms of measurement. While several methods exist for analyzing ordinal data, one popular bivariate procedure is the Spearman rank-order correlation (*rho*). This index is a PMC that may be computed from two sets of ranks by the usual formulas for r (Eqns. (17) or (18)) or by the classic formula developed by Spearman and given in most statistics texts. *Rho* is properly interpreted as an index of degree of association only, but it is the appropriate index to use (with caution) when rank variables are included with interval variables in multivariate analyses. When more than one observation occupies the same rank, special procedures are required.

3.2 Estimates of Product–Moment Correlations for Ordered Categories

It is often the case that a categorical variable represents an attribute that may reasonably be considered continuous and normally distributed. A classic example is the multiple-choice test item which dichotomizes the ability continuum into passes and fails. For bivariate situations where it is reasonable to assume an underlying normal distribution in one dichotomous variable and with the other variable measured as a continuum (e.g., 0/1 item scores and total test scores) the appropriate index is the biserial correlation (r_b). This coefficient is an estimate of what the PMC would have been, had the dichotomous variable been measured as a continuous variable. The biserial correlation, using the subscripts 1 and 2 to indicate the higher and lower portions of the dichotomy, is as follows:

$$r_b = (\bar{Y}_1 - \bar{Y}_2)(pq)/hS_Y \tag{19}$$

where p is the proportion in the upper group, q is the proportion in the lower group, $\bar{Y}_1$ is the mean of the continuous variable in the upper group, $\bar{Y}_2$ is the mean in the lower group, S_y is the standard deviation of Y, and h is the height of the normal curve at p.

The biserial correlation is an appropriate statistic for certain bivariate applications, but it is not a product–moment correlation. It can, on occasion, exceed unity and is not a directly computable function of the scores themselves. Experience has shown that inclusion of biserial correlations multivariate analysis can result in singular correlation matrices. r_b should be used with caution in multivariate analyses.

A situation that arises with some frequency in educational research is the case of one truly dichotomous variable and one artificial dichotomy: for example, inclusion in a treatment program (1) or not (0) (a true dichotomy) and passing (1) or failing (0) a test (continuous underlying trait). Under these conditions the appropriate index is the biserial-phi coefficient (Becker and Thorndike 1988, Thorndike 1949). For the four-fold table where $a = (1,0)$, $b = (1,1)$, $c = (0,0)$, and $d = (0,1)$ the biserial-phi is given by

$$\phi_{bis} = (bc - ad)/h(pq)^{1/2} \tag{20}$$

where a, b, c, and d are the frequencies in the four cells; p and q are the proportions of cases in each category of the truly dichotomous variable; and h is the ordinate of the normal curve at p.

Another coefficient, the tetrachoric correlation (r_{tet}), is analogous to ϕ, in that it is based on the assumption that each of two dichotomous variables represents an underlying normally distributed continuous variable. The coefficient estimates what the relationship between two continuous variables would be in order to produce the four-fold pattern found in the data. In some multivariate analyses where tetrachoric correlations have been used they have caused singularity, so they must be used with caution.

Olsson has presented generalizations of the biserial and tetrachoric correlations that are appropriate for the case where one or both variables represent a series of three or more ordered categories (Olsson 1979, Olsson et al. 1982). These coefficients have been called "polyserial" and "polychoric correlations" respectively. Their computation is impractical without a computer, but maximum likelihood estimates of both coefficients are available through the LISREL program (Jöreskog and Sörbom 1989). Experience indicates that when the necessary assumptions are met and the coefficients have been estimated by the algorithm in LISREL the results can be used with confidence in further analyses. However, they may cause singularity of the correlation matrix, which will result in problems with some multivariate analyses.

The primary reason for using polyserial or polychoric correlations (or their special cases, the biserial and tetrachoric) rather than ϕ or r_{pb} (or their multicategory generalizations) is that categorization of a variable reduces its variance. This has the effect of restricting the range of PMCs that involve categorical variables so they underestimate the actual degree of association between the variables when the assumptions necessary for the polyserial and polychoric coefficients are met. Such underestimates can affect the results of factor analyses and other multivariate procedures.

4. Significance Tests

The topic of statistical significance is most fruitfully viewed from the perspective of sampling distributions. Assume that there is a population that reasonably approximates infinite size and that every member of this population has or could have a value on every variable of interest. If random samples are drawn from this population, measured on the variables of interest, and summary statistics computed, it is possible to make frequency distributions of these summary statistics. Such frequency distributions are called "sampling distributions," and they exist for all descriptive statistics.

Of course, the population is never really completely available, and it is unusual to draw more than one sample, but mathematical statisticians have derived theoretical sampling distributions for many statistics. These theoretical distributions form the basis for statistical inference and significance testing.

Tests of statistical significance are usually applied to means, but they may be used with any statistic, such as a correlation coefficient. Suppose, for example, that an investigator wishes to test the hypothesis that the correlation between two variables such as number of books in the home and reading ability at age 10 is greater than zero. This implies a one-tailed null hypothesis of the standard form that ρ (*rho*, the correlation in the population) is zero or negative ($\rho \leqslant 0$), and this hypothesis creates a hypothetical sampling distribution of the correlation coefficient, r for samples of size N. The investigator obtains a sample, computes r and the appropriate test statistic (described below), determines the probability of obtaining this large a value of the test statistic, and reaches a conclusion. If the value of the test statistics is unlikely, given the hypothesized sampling distribution, the investigator concludes that $\rho > 0$ in the population from which the sample was drawn.

4.1 Tests for a single r

Tests of statistical significance are more complicated for correlation coefficients than for means. With sufficient sample size the sampling distribution of the mean is symmetric around the population parameter regardless of the value of that parameter. For the correlation coefficient the shape of the sampling distribution depends on both ρ and N. When ρ is zero or close to zero, the sampling distribution is symmetric; however, when ρ exceeds about ± 0.25 the sampling distribution becomes skewed with the direction of skew toward zero. The degree of skewness increases as ρ increases.

Asymmetry of the sampling distribution is not a problem for most simple tests of hypotheses because for most cases the null hypothesis is $\rho = 0$. However, for nontypical nulls, such as $\rho = 0.60$, and for confidence intervals on larger correlations, the problem is more serious.

When testing the hypothesis that $\rho = 0$, the appropriate statistic depends upon N. For $N > 50$, the standard error of r is $\sigma_r = 1/(N^{\frac{1}{2}})$ and the statistic $z = r/\sigma_r$ is normally distributed. Smaller samples require that $t = r/[(1-r^2)/(N-2)]^{\frac{1}{2}}$ with $df = N-2$ be used instead.

The solution to the asymmetry problem for the PMC was derived by R A Fisher. The transformation

$$z_F = ln(1 + r) - ln(1 - r) \tag{21}$$

which is known as Fisher's z, results in a statistic that has a sampling distribution that is very nearly normal in shape for any value of ρ. The standard error of z_F is $1/(N - 3)^{\frac{1}{2}}$, and the statistic $z = (z_F - K)/\sigma_{z_F}$ is a normal deviate. In this case K is the z_F transformed value of ρ specified in the null hypothesis. Tables for transforming r to z_F and back are provided in some statistics texts, such as McNemar (1969), Thorndike (1982), and Hays (1988).

4.2 Significance of r_{pb}, ϕ, r_{b}, *and rho*

For small samples ($N < 100$) the best way to test the hypothesis ($\rho = 0$) for r_b and r_{pb} is to test the significance of the difference between group means. If the value of t exceeds the critical value with $N - 2$ degrees of freedom, the correlation is statistically significant. When $N > 100$, r_{pb} may be treated as any other PMC, while the standard error of r_b is approximated by $\{[(pq)^{1/2}/h] - r_b^2\}/N^{1/2}$.

The ϕ coefficient may be tested for significance by the relationship $\chi^2 = N\phi$, where χ^2 has $df = 1$. If the value of χ^2 exceeds the critical value, it is appropriate to conclude that $\phi > 0$. When the sample size is fairly large, the approximate standard error of ϕ is $1/N^{\frac{1}{2}}$.

A word of caution is necessary with regard to tests of significance for these coefficients. If the frequencies in the two categories of a dichotomous variable are very unequal, tests of significance may be inappropriate. McNemar (1969) suggests that when the proportion of cases in either category of a dichotomous variable exceeds 0.90 the significance tests should be viewed with caution. Tests of significance have not been developed for the biserial-phi, polyserial, and polychoric correlation coefficients.

Rank order coefficients such as *rho* are seldom used with large samples because of the difficulty of obtaining a clear ranking of large numbers of observations. Therefore, the statistic for testing significance will usually be a t test of the form $t = \rho/[(1 - \rho^2)/(N - 2)]^{\frac{1}{2}}$, which is identical to the small sample test for r. Tables of critical values for as few as five pairs of ranks are included in several introductory statistics books.

4.3 Testing Differences between r's

The situation occasionally arises when it is desirable to test a hypothesis about the equality of two correlation coefficients. Such tests may take either of two forms. The correlations being tested may be correlations between same variables in different samples, or they may be correlations between one variable and two different variables in the same sample. In the first case, both *rs* are transformed to z_Fs. The standard error of the difference between two z_Fs is $\sigma(z_{F_1} - z_{F_2}) = [1/(N_1 - 3) + 1/(N_2 - 3)]^{\frac{1}{2}}$ and the test statistic $z = (z_{F_1} - z_{F_2})/\sigma(z_{F_1} - z_{F_2})$ is a normal deviate.

The second situation is a little more complicated. Three variables have been measured on a sample of N individuals, so there are three correlations, r_{12}, r_{13}, and r_{23}. If an investigator wishes to test the null hypothesis that $\rho_{12} = \rho_{13}$, the necessary test is

$$t = \frac{(r_{12} - r_{13})[(N-3)(1+r_{23})]^{1/2}}{[2(1 - r_{12}^2 - r_{13}^2 - r_{23}^2 + 2r_{12}r_{13}r_{23})]^{1/2}} \quad (22)$$

with $df = N - 3$.

4.4 Other Uses of z_F

There are two other useful applications of Fisher's z transformation in correlational research. The first of these is averaging correlations. Since the correlation coefficient itself does not represent an interval scale, it is not proper to average correlations directly. However, z_F is an interval scale measure of association, so it is appropriate to compute an average z_F weighted by N. After converting each r to z_F, a mean z_F is found:

$$\bar{z}_F = \frac{(N_1-3)z_{F_1} + (N_2-3)z_{F_2} + \ldots + (N_j-3)z_{F_j}}{(N_1-3) + (N_2-3) + \ldots + (N_j-3)} \quad (23)$$

The standard error of $\bar{z}_F$, $1/[(N_1 - 3)\ (N_2 - 3) + \ldots + (N_j - 3)]^{\frac{1}{2}}$, may be used to test hypotheses about $\bar{z}_F$. Once $\bar{z}_F$ has been calculated, the mean correlation, $\bar{r}$, may be found by reversing the original transformation. Finding $\bar{z}_F$ to be statistically significant is equivalent to finding r significant.

An alternative approach that is common in the literature is to use the unweighted median of a set of correlations to represent the central tendency of the set. This procedure is acceptable, but it does not use all the information in the original data. Correlations based on larger samples should ordinarily have greater influence on the average. Also, there is no standard error to use for hypothesis tests.

The second application for z_F is the determination of a confidence interval for ρ. Since the sampling distribution of r is not symmetric except when ρ is zero, the confidence interval for any nonzero ρ cannot be symmetric. However, the sampling distribution of z_F is symmetric. A proper confidence interval for any ρ can be obtained by transforming r to z_F, finding the standard error of z_F, multiplying σ_{z_F} by the appropriate critical values from the normal distribution, adding these products to z_F and finally transforming the resulting limits for z_F back into correlations. For example, if $r = 0.65$ and $N = 19$, then $z_F = 0.775$ and $\sigma_{z_F} = 0.25$. To find the 95 percent confidence interval the critical values are $+1.96$ and -1.96. Multiplying these by 0.25 yields $+0.49$ and -0.49, and adding these values to z_F gives 1.265 and 0.285 as the upper and lower limits for z_F. These are transformed back to correlations, yielding 0.85 and 0.28 as the limits of the 95 percent confidence interval for ρ. Note that this confidence interval is symmetric around r in terms of probability, but not in the scale of r. The procedure for confidence intervals can also be applied to mean correlations.

5. Partial and Semipartial Correlation

There are many occasions in educational research where it is desirable to control or remove statistically the effect of one or more variables. One way by which this can be accomplished is through sampling. A characteristic that is constant for all subjects in a study cannot be a source of variance in the results. The effect of gender can be removed by using only male or only female subjects. Likewise, maturational factors can be controlled, at least in part, by studying children who are all the same age.

However, control at the sampling stage of a study has some definite drawbacks, the most important of which is that the generalizability of the finding may be severely restricted. Also, there are many research situations in which it is impossible to control variables by selection or it may be undesirable to do so because one or more of the questions of interest in the study involves the control variables as independent or dependent variables in the study. For example, in a study of the relationship between pupil attitudes and achievement the investigator might wish to remove or hold constant the effect of differences in age and measured intelligence. Selecting pupils of only a particular age and intelligence level would be wasteful of subjects and might distort the sample on other relevant variables such as socioeconomic status. In addition, the investigator might wish to include one or both of the control variables in a later phase of the analysis.

The solution to this problem is to collect data on an unrestricted sample, a sample that is representative of the population to which generalizations are to be extended, and then remove the control variables statistically. Note that the term "control variable" is being used in a restricted way in this discussion. Some potential variables such as conditions under which measurements are obtained should be held as constant as circumstances allow. It is to other variables, particularly status characteristics of the subjects, such as age, intelligence, and gender, that this discussion is directed. These variables may be measured during the data collection phase, and their effects removed during analysis. It is therefore important to include measures of all relevant variables in the design and data collection stages of a study.

If X is a student motivation variable, Y is a performance measure, Z is ability, and S is sex, then it might be of interest to examine the relationship between motivation and performance both with and without controlling for ability and gender. The effect of one variable on another may be removed by analyzing the residual variance. For example, the residual variance in Y after controlling S is the variance in Y within levels of S, pooled across levels of S. The Y variance is found for males and for females independently, and the weighted average of these two variances is the variance in Y that is independent of S.

The analysis of residual variance is equivalent to using deviation scores of the form $y_{ij} = Y_{ij} - \bar{Y}_j$, or, for continuous variables, $y_i = Y_i - \hat{Y}_i$. Each individual's residual score is his or her deviation from the least-squares prediction made from the variables being removed or controlled. The residual scores are then analyzed like scores on any other variables. For example, the correlation between motivation and performance with the effect of sex differences removed from the motivation variable would involve correlating residual scores on motivation ($x_{ij} = X_{ij} - \bar{X}_j$) with raw scores on performance. It is given the symbol $r_{Y(X \cdot S)}$, where the subscript indicates that S is controlled in X but not in Y. The subscript $YX{\cdot}S$ would indicate that S is controlled in both Y and X.

Correlations that involve residual variances are called "partial correlations." When residual scores appear on both sides of the equation the term partial correlation is used if the same variable is controlled in both X and Y. Bipartial correlation is used when one variable is controlled in X and a different variable is controlled in Y. Semipartial or part correlations are those that involve residual scores on only one side of the relationship.

While the logic of partial correlations involves residual scores, the computations can generally be performed with the ordinary bivariate correlations themselves. Starting with the definitions of the residual scores as deviations from least-squares predictions, that the partial correlation of X and Y with Z removed is

$$r_{XY \cdot Z} = (r_{XY} - r_{XZ}r_{YZ})/[(1 - r^2_{XZ})^{1/2}(1 - r_{YZ})^{1/2}] \tag{24}$$

There is only one partial correlation between X and Y controlling Z, but there are two possible semipartial correlations, one where Z is controlled in X and one where it is controlled in Y. The formulas for these correlations differ from Eqn. (24) only in the denominator:

$$r_{Y(X \cdot Z)} = (r_{XY} - r_{XZ}r_{YZ})/(1 - r^2_{XZ})^{1/2} \tag{25}$$

$$r_{X(Y \cdot Z)} = (r_{XY} - r_{XZ}r_{YZ})/(1 - r^2_{YZ})^{1/2} \tag{26}$$

5.1 Higher Order Partial Correlations

There may be occasions when it is desirable to control more than one variable statistically. The logic is a direct generalization of the case of a single variable. That is, the analysis involves residual scores in one or both of the variables being correlated. The difference is that now the residuals are more complex. For example, the partial correlation between motivation and performance with sex and ability controlled (a second-order partial correlation) would first involve the residual scores on X, Y, and Z from sex. The X and Y residuals would then be entered into analyses with the Z residuals and the residuals of the residuals obtained. Finally, the correlation between second-order X and Y residuals yields the desired second-order partial correlation. Higher order semipartial correlations can be conceptualized in the same way; however, they are very closely related to the standardized regression weights of multiple regression analysis and are usually obtained in that way (see *Regression Analyses of Quantified Data*).

Partial correlations of any order are correlations between residual scores of that order. As was the case with the first-order partial, the analysis may be performed starting with ordinary bivariate correlations. The procedure is a sequential one involving repeated use of Eqn. (24). First, all first-order partials removing one variable (say Z) are computed. Then Eqn. (24) is repeated for a second control variable, but with each term replaced by the appropriate first-order partial.

For problems involving more than two control variables the procedure described is quite cumbersome. Although it would be conceptually and computationally sound to continue in such a sequential fashion, the analysis would almost certainly be performed by one of the computer programs that uses a matrix algebra solution.

5.2 Test of Significance

The statistical significance of a partial correlation may be tested by procedures analogous to those used for simple rs. The z_F transformation is appropriate and with large N the standard error of z_F is $1/(N - p - 3)$ where p is the number of variables being partialled out of the relationship. z_F may be used either to test a hypothesis about the partial correlation or to set up a confidence interval for ρ.

An alternative way to test the hypothesis that $\rho = 0$ for small N is available. The statistic $t = r_p/[(1 - r_p^2)/(\text{N} - p - 2)]^{1/2}$, in which r_p is the partial correlation and p is as above, is distributed as t with $df = (\text{N} - p - 2)$.

Tests of significance for semipartial correlations are closely related to multiple correlation. In general, the significance of a semipartial correlation is tested by exploring the significance of the difference between the multiple correlation with the relevant variable both included and excluded. If the difference between multiple correlations is statistically significant, the semipartial correlation of the excluded variable with the dependent variable of the multiple correlation analysis is significant.

6. Multiple Correlation

Correlation was defined as an index of the degree of association between two variables. Common bivariate correlations describe the relationship between a pair of observed variables. Partial correlations are PMCs between sets of residual scores after the effect of one or more variables has been removed. In all of these cases the correlation coefficient is an index of maximum relationship in terms of a least-squares criterion.

Multiple correlation extends the concept of least-squares association to the relationship of one dependent or outcome variable with more than one independent or predictor variable. The multiple correlation coefficient is the bivariate product–moment correlation between the outcome variable (Y) and some combination of the set of predictor variables (X_1, X_2, . . . X_p). The combination of X variables (call it P) is determined in such a way that the correlation r_{YP} is the largest possible correlation that could be obtained from the given set of data.

The majority of work with multiple correlation in education and the behavioral sciences defines P as a weighted linear combination of the Xs. That is, if the array (B_1, B_2, . . . B_p) is a set of weights to be applied to the Xs, then P is of the general form

$$P = B_1X_1 + B_2X_2 + \ldots + B_pX_p + A \quad (27)$$

To say that P is a weighted linear combination of the Xs means that no term in Eqn. (27) involves a product of X terms or any X term other than the first power. The restriction of linearity is not a necessary one, and there are some situations where a particular theory may postulate nonlinear relationships, but for most applications the linear model is best for two reasons: its simplicity and its generalizability.

The definition of the best- or least-squares composite of the set X is relatively simple, but is most easily accomplished if all variables are expressed as standard scores. In standard score form Eqn. (27) becomes

$$z_P = \beta_1 z_{X_1} + \beta_2 z_{X_2} + \ldots + \beta_p z_{X_p} \quad (28)$$

It can be shown that for the special case of $p = 2$ the values of β_1 and β_2 are given by

$$\beta_1 = (r_{1Y} - r_{2Y}r_{12})/(1 - r_{12}^2) \quad (29)$$

$$\beta_2 = (r_{2Y} - r_{1Y}r_{12})/(1 - r_{12}^2) \quad (30)$$

These equations are very similar to semipartial correlations; β_1 represents the contribution of X_1 to P that is independent of X_2, and β_2 is the independent contribution of X_2 to p. They differ from semipartial correlations only by the scaling factor $(1 - r_{12})^{\frac{1}{2}}$ in the denominator. The squared multiple correlation, $r^2{}_{YP}$, can be shown to be equal to the sum of products of the βs and the bivariate predictor–criterion correlations, $r_{YP}^2 = (\beta_1 r_{YX_1} + \beta_2 r_{YX_2})$, and the multiple correlation itself is the positive square root of r_{YP}^2.

Generalization to the multivariable case is most easily handled by using matrix algebra. The solution, which is simply a substitute for solving p linear equations in p unknowns, is given by $\boldsymbol{\beta}_p = \boldsymbol{R}_{PP}^{-1}\boldsymbol{R}_{PY}$, where $\boldsymbol{\beta}_p$ is a $p \times 1$ vector of β-weights for use in Eqn. (28), $\boldsymbol{R}_{PP}^{-1}$ is the inverse of the $p \times p$ matrix of correlations among the p predictors, and $\boldsymbol{r}_{PY}$ is the $p \times 1$ vector of correlations between the predictor variables and Y. The squared multiple correlation is then given by $r_{YP}^2 = \boldsymbol{\beta}_{YP}\boldsymbol{r}_{PY}$.

The β-weights may be expressed in the metric of the original variables appropriate for use with Eqn. (27) by the transformation $B_{X_j} = \beta_{X_j}(S_Y/S_{X_j})$. The value of the intercept, A, is given by

$$A = \bar{Y} - \sum_{j=1}^{P} B_j\bar{X}_j \quad (31)$$

Of course, the correlation between Y and P is unchanged by this transformation.

6.1 Asymmetry of Multiple Correlation

There is an important restriction on the interpretation of r_{YP}^2. Whereas r_{XY}^2 was a symmetric index of the degree of association between two variables, r_{YP}^2 is not. The simple squared bivariate correlation reflects the proportion of variance in Y that is related to X and the proportion of variance in X that is related to Y. It is bidirectional. The multiple correlation is unidirectional in the sense that r_{YP}^2 is the proportion of variance in Y that is related to the set of X variables but not the proportion of variance in the set of X that is related to Y. The relationship is symmetric in the observed variable Y and the latent variable P.

The reason for this asymmetry is the fact that P does not contain all of the variance of the set X. The correlation of each variable X_j with P is given by $r_{PX_j} = r_{YX_j}(1/r_{YP})$. These correlations of observed variables with a latent variable are factor loadings. The mean of squared loadings

$$\bar{r}_{PX}^2 = \sum r_{PX_j}^2/p$$

is the proportion of X set variance that is related to P, and the product $(\bar{r}_{PX}^2) \cdot (r_{YP}^2)$ is the proportion of variance in the set X that is related to Y.

6.2 Tests of Significance

There are several types of hypotheses that can be tested in a multiple correlation analysis. The most obvious is $\rho_{YP} = 0$. The appropriate test of this hypothesis is an F test of the ratio of the mean square due to the multiple regression equation (MS_P) to the mean square residual (MS_R). Note that the total sum of squares of Y is

$$SS_Y = \sum (Y_i - \bar{Y})^2 \quad (32)$$

and that this is a combination of SS due to regression (SS_P) and residual (SS_R). That is, $SS_Y = SS_P + SS_R$.

It can be shown that these SS terms are given by $SS_P = r_{YP}^2 SS_Y$ and $SS_R = (1 - r_{YP}^2)SS_Y$. Each, divided by its degrees of freedom, is a mean square [$MS_P = SS_P/p$; $MS_R = SS_R/(N - p - 1)$]. The ratio of these

MS s canceling where possible, is an F with $df_1 = p$ and $df_2 = N - p - 1$:

$$F = (r_{YP}^2/p)/[(1 - r_{YP}^2)/(N - p - 1)] \tag{33}$$

A second hypothesis of interest relates to the contribution of some subset of the set X. The significance of the contribution of a subset of variables may be determined by the equation

$$F = \frac{[(r_{YP_1}^2 - r_{YP_2}^2)/(p_1 - p_2)]}{[(1 - r_{YP_1}^2)/(N - p_1 - 1)]} \tag{34}$$

where $r_{YP_1}^2$ is the squared correlation between Y and a set of p_1 X variables and $r_{YP_2}^2$ is for some subset of the variables in the first correlation. If F with $df_1 = p_1 - p_2$ and $df_2 = N - p_1 - 1$ is statistically significant, the contribution of the variables that were omitted from p_1 in p_2 is statistically significant. By applying Eqn. (34) repeatedly with each single variable omitted in turn, the significance of each β-weight in Eqn. (28) can be determined. Eqn. (34) is also used with the general linear model to perform tests on hypotheses related to the analysis of variance.

6.3 Stepwise Analysis

When many predictor variables are available, a small subset of these variables will usually account for most of the predictable variance in the outcome variable. It is generally desirable to determine the smallest set of predictors that will do a satisfactory job of prediction for reasons of economy and simplicity. The method by which such a minimum subset is identified is stepwise analysis.

A stepwise analysis may be either a step-up or a step-down procedure. In the former, the analysis starts with the best single predictor and variables are added in order of the magnitude of their contribution. A step-down analysis begins with the complete set of predictors and deletes those variables that make the smallest contribution at each stage. The decision about which variables to add or delete is usually made by selecting the variable that results in the largest (step-up) or smallest (step-down) F as computed by Eqn. (34) (see *Regression Analyses of Quantified Data*).

7. Canonical Correlation

A canonical correlation is the bivariate correlation between two latent variables or composites where each composite has been determined in such a way as to maximize its relationship to the composite of the other set. Given a set of X variables (measures of student achievement, for example) and a set of Y variables (interest or motivation measures) a canonical analysis finds a weighted linear combination, P, of the X set and a weighted linear combination, Q, of the Y set such that the correlation between them, r_{PQ}, is maximized. This is similar to the multiple correlation problem except that it involves the simultaneous solution for two sets of regression weights.

There is an additional complication in canonical analysis. Where there was only one multiple correlation coefficient, there are as many canonical correlations as there are variables in the smaller set. The first canonical correlation (R_{c_1}) is the highest possible correlation between composites of the two sets of original variables. The second correlation, (R_{c_2}), is the highest possible correlation between composites of the two sets of residual variables with the first pair of composites partialled out. In general, R_{c_i} is the correlation between composites of residual variables with all preceding composites partialled out. Thus, each succeeding pair of composites is statistically independent of all other pairs and each R_c describes an independent dimension of association between the sets.

A canonical analysis begins with three correlation matrices: $\boldsymbol{R}_{PP}$, the within set matrix of correlations among the X variables, $\boldsymbol{R}_{QQ}$, the within set matrix for the Y variables, and $\boldsymbol{R}_{PQ}$, the between set correlations of the X variables with the Y variables. The solution of a series of complex matrix equations (Tabachnick and Fidell 1989, Thorndike 1978) results in two matrices of standardized regression weights (βs) that define the latent variables for the X and Y sets and the R_cs between the pairs of composites.

However, interpretation of a canonical analysis is complex and requires additional information. While the regression weights indicate the relative contributions of the variables to the composites of their own set, the correlations between the observed variables and the composites, which are akin to factor loadings, may be of greater interest. There are four matrices of such loadings, two matrices of intraset canonical loadings of the X variables on the P composites and the Y variables on the Q composites, and two matrices of interset canonical loadings of the X variables on the Q composites and the Y variables on the P composites. These loadings, both intra- and inter-set, enable the investigator to treat the composites as factors and interpret them in a similar fashion (see *Factor Analysis; Canonical Analysis*).

7.1 Tests of Significance

The statistical significance of canonical correlations is is tested sequentially. If there are J canonical correlations (the number of variables in the smaller set), then the first hypothesis tested is that all of them are zero. A significant value of the test statistic (χ^2 implies that at least R_{c1} is nonzero. R_{c1} is removed and the hypothesis that the remaining R_{ci} are zero is tested. The sequence is repeated, removing the largest remaining correlation, until the hypothesis cannot be rejected. The pairs of composites associated with statistically significant correlations may then be interpreted. The test of statistical significance is an aid to the investigator in determining the dimensionality of the space in which the relationships among the variables will be interpreted. Rotation of the composites is sometimes used to aid interpretation.

7.2 *Redundancy*

The problem of asymmetry in interpreting the relationship described by a canonical correlation is more acute than for multiple correlations because R_c is an index of association between two latent variables, not the observed variables or the sets of variables. Proper interpretation of a canonical analysis requires computation of an index which was given the unfortunate name "redundancy" (see Thorndike 1978).

Although there are alternate ways to conceptualize the redundancy index, perhaps the simplest is in terms of the interset canonical loadings. An interset loading is the correlation between an observed variable of one set and a composite of the other. The square of this loading is the proportion of variance of the observed variable that is related to the composite. The mean of squared loadings across observed variables in the set is the proportion of variance of that set that is accounted for by the composite of the other set. There are therefore two sets of redundancies: those of the X set of variables with the Q composites and those of the Y set of variables with the P composites. The sum of the redundancies for a set is the total redundancy of that set with the other set. In general the redundancy of set X with set Y will not equal the redundancy of Y with X (see *Canonical Analysis*).

8. *Set Correlation*

Canonical analysis is a general and flexible data-analytic model that has only briefly been described here. It has been shown (Knapp 1978) that most commonly used hypothesis-testing procedures such as analysis of variance are special cases of the canonical model (see *Variance and Covariance, Analysis of*).

Cohen (1982) has provided a more complete generalization of correlational procedures, and therefore a very general model of data analysis which he has called "set correlation." This approach views the covariance matrices of sets of variables in a manner similar to individual variables. It is possible to partial one covariance matrix out of another one, producing a residual covariance matrix which contains partial covariances. For example, given a set of aptitude measures, W, a set of demographic characteristics, X, a set of motivational variables, Y, and a set of achievement measures, Z, one might ask what is the relationship between aptitude and achievement with demographic characteristics partialled out of the aptitude variables and motivational variables partialled out of the achievement measures? The set correlation $r_{(W\ X)(Z\ Y)}$ would be the (bipartial) canonical correlation between the residual part of the aptitude set (demographics controlled) and the residual part of the achievement set (motivation controlled). Semipartial and partial variations are also possible. As Cohen has pointed out, multivariate analysis of covariance is a special case of semipartial set correlation, just as ANOVA is a special case of multiple correlation analysis and MANOVA and discriminant function analysis are special cases of canonical correlation analysis.

However, proper interpretation of analyses such as these is complex and requires a deeper grasp of their technical aspects than can be developed here. Potential users of canonical analysis should consult a source such as Harris (1985), Tabachnick and Fidell (1989), or Thorndike (1978) for a more detailed explanation and examples. Cohen's (1982) paper is the best source for set correlation.

9. *Cross-validation*

Whenever an index of relationship is developed on a sample using the least-squares criterion, the result is optimum for that sample. However, a least-squares equation in one sample will not be a least-squares solution for another sample from the same population. In the bivariate case the degree of correlation and the equation of the regression line will fluctuate from sample to sample. In multiple correlation the problem is compounded because the least-squares equation depends not only on the correlations of the predictors with the criterion but also on the correlations among the predictors. To the extent that the pattern of correlations in a sample deviates from the pattern in the population or in other samples—a condition called sample-specific covariation—the equation developed in that sample will give poorer results with new sets of data. Of course, the problem is worse with canonical analysis because two sets of regression weights are being fitted simultaneously.

The tendency of multiple and canonical correlation analyses to capitalize on sample-specific covariation raises two related issues: (a) the degree to which the description (magnitude and pattern) of relationships generalizes to future samples, and (b) the accuracy of predictions made from the regression equation itself. A useful response to both of these issues is the procedure called "cross-validation."

Cross-validation involves applying the least-squares regression equation from one set of data to a new set of data. The correlations between predicted and observed scores provide a good indication of how well "real" predictions would work if the criterion measures were yet to be obtained. Since the regression equation is not a least-squares equation in the new sample, it will be unaffected by sample-specific covariation in the data.

Likewise, the degree and pattern of relationships in the new set of data as described by the multiple or canonical loadings indicates the generalizability of the original equations as a model for new samples. The multiple or canonical correlations in cross-validation provide an index of the degree of fit of the model. A more complete discussion of issues relating to cross-validation may be found in Thorndike (1978).

See also: Multivariate Analysis; Factor Analysis

References

Becker G, Thorndike R L 1988 The biserial-phi correlation coefficient. *J. Psycholo.* 122(5): 523–26

Cohen J 1982 Set correlation as a general multivariate data-analytic method. *Multivariate Behav. Res.* 17(3): 301–41

Harman H H 1976 *Modern Factor Analysis*, 3rd edn. University of Chicago Press, Chicago, Illinois

Harris R J 1985 *A Primer of Multivariate Statistics*, 2nd edn. Harcourt Brace Jovanovich, San Diego, California

Hays W L 1988 *Statistics*, 4th edn. Harcourt Brace Jovanovich, San Diego, California

Jöreskog K G, Sörbom D 1989 *LISREL VII User's Reference Guide*. SPSS, Chicago, Illinois

Knapp T R 1978 Canonical correlation analysis: A general parametric significance-testing system. *Psych. Bull.* 85(2): 410–16

McNemar Q 1969 *Psychological Statistics*, 4th edn. Wiley, New York

Olsson U 1979 Maximum likelihood estimation of the polychoric correlation coefficient. *Psychometrika* 44(4): 443–60

Olsson U, Drasgow F, Dorans N J 1982 The polyserial correlation coefficient. *Psychometrika* 47(3): 337–47

Tabachnick B G, Fidell L S 1989 *Using Multivariate Statistics*, 2nd edn. Harper Collins, New York

Thorndike R L 1949 *Personnel Selection*. Wiley, New York

Thorndike R M 1978 *Correlation Procedures for Research*. Gardner, New York

Thorndike R M 1982 *Data Collection and Analysis: Basic Principles*. Gardner, New York

R. M. Thorndike

Correspondence Analysis of Qualitative Data

The factorial analysis of correspondence is one of the procedures recently developed for the analysis of information in the form of contingency tables, where nominal data are presented for examination. This procedure is one of the most efficient for describing and establishing relationships in qualitative data and was initially proposed by Benzecri (1963). It stands alongside contingency table analysis, configural frequency analysis, Galois Lattices, log–linear models and the scaling of nominal data, as one of a battery of new techniques that can be employed for the investigation of qualitative data. This procedure has as its principal characteristic an exchange of the roles of variables and observations and seeks to represent them in the same space. This type of representation was initially suggested by Kendall, but for a long time remained unused.

Table 1
Contingency table of numbers of records and buyers

	Buyers				
Type of Music	Young people	Female adults	Male adults	Old people	Total
Songs	69	172	133	27	401
Jazz	41	84	118	11	254
Classical music	18	127	157	43	345
Total	128	383	408	81	1,000

1. An Illustrative Example

The following hypothetical example was employed by De Lagarde (1983) to illustrate the procedure.

Let us suppose that a store has sold 1,000 records and has filed information on the characteristics of the records (jazz, songs, or classical music) and on the characteristics of the buyers (young people, male or female adults, and old people). It is then possible to construct a contingency table (see Table 1) in order to analyze relationships between age, sex, and type of music.

Let the proportional frequencies of the cells in the contingency table be denoted by f_{ij} for cell (i,j) where $i = 1,\ldots, I$, $J = 1,\ldots, J$. The marginal frequencies are denoted by

$$R_i = \sum_j f_{ij} = r_i \quad \text{for rows, and}$$

$$C_j = \sum_i f_{ij} = c_j \quad \text{for columns}$$

The values of the proportional frequencies are recorded in Table 2. The variable "type of music" is

Table 2
Contingency table of cell proportions of records and buyers

	Buyers (j)				
Type of music (i)	Young people	Female adults	Male adults	Old people	Total
Songs	0.069 (f_{11})	0.172 (f_{12})	0.133 (f_{13})	0.027 (f_{14})	0.401 (r_1)
Jazz	0.041 (f_{21})	0.084 (f_{22})	0.118 (f_{23})	0.011 (f_{24})	0.254 (r_2)
Classical music	0.018 (f_{31})	0.127 (f_{32})	0.157 (f_{33})	0.043 (f_{34})	0.345 (r_3)
Total (N = 1,000)	0.128 (c_1)	0.383 (c_2)	0.408 (c_3)	0.081 (c_4)	1

Table 3
Contingency table of relative cell proportions (by columns) of records and buyers

Type of music	Buyers: Young people	Female adults	Male adults	Old people
Songs	0.539	0.449	0.326	0.333
Jazz	0.320	0.219	0.289	0.136
Classical music	0.141	0.332	0.385	0.531
Total (N = 1,000)	1.000	1.000	1.000	1.000

obviously recorded on a nominal scale. Likewise the variable "buyers" is also on a nominal scale. The aim of correspondence analysis is to represent graphically the data contained in this two-dimensional contingency table.

In this example, it would clearly be possible to use three rectangular axes (songs, jazz, and classical music) to represent the four categories of buyers in this three-dimensional space. However, such a direct representation is limited to small contingency tables and is not very useful. Correspondence analysis permits more complex bodies of data to be represented in simplified form.

Correspondence analysis is based not on the proportional frequencies recorded in Table 2, but on the relative proportions which are obtained by dividing f_{ij} by c_j for columns or f_{ij} by r_i for rows. The relative frequencies for columns are presented in Table 3.

If we denote f_{ij} divided by c_j as x_i, then $\Sigma x_i, = 1$ for each value of j. Thus it is possible to state this as the equation of a plane

$$x_1 + x_2 + x_3 = 1$$

If we have l dimensions with $(l > 3)$ the equation of the corresponding hyperplane will be

$$x_1 + x_2 + x_3, \ldots, x_l = 1.$$

In this example the four points representing young people, female adults, male adults and old people belong to a plane since their three coordinates will satisfy Eqn.(1). Moreover, this plane will intersect the three axes at points A, B, and C which are at a distance of one unit from the origin of the three-dimensional space. These three points will therefore form an equilateral triangle. As shown in Fig. 1, it is possible to represent the data for each group of buyers by a circle of area proportional to the value of c_j.

The reciprocal analysis is also possible in which the three points (songs, jazz, and classical music) are located on a hyperplane in four-dimensional space.

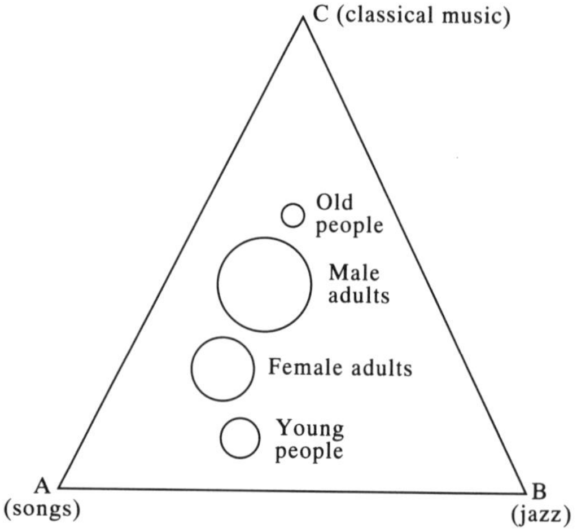

Figure 1
Type-of-music plane with buyer groups shown

In the reciprocal analysis, Benzecri (1973) weights the values of x_i by $(r_i)^{\frac{1}{2}}$ for the first analysis, and the values of x_j by $(c_j)^{\frac{1}{2}}$ for the reciprocal analysis.
In the first analysis:

$$x_i = \frac{f_{ij}}{r_i(c_j)^{1/2}}$$

and in the reciprocal analysis:

$$x_j = \frac{f_{ij}}{c_j(r_i)^{1/2}}$$

By proceeding in this way, the three poles of the triangle in the first analysis are no longer equidistant from the origin. The perpendicular line from the origin to the four dimensional hyperplane intersects the plane at a point G. Thus, OG becomes the initial axis of the four-dimensional scatter plot. By considering the reciprocal analysis, it is a simple task to identify the second axis. Mathematical procedures have been developed for computing these different axes. In the example concerned with buyers and type of music there are only two axes and the total proportion of variance extracted by these two factors is 100 percent. The four types of buyers and the three types of records can consequently be accurately represented in two-dimensional space as in Fig. 2. It should be noted that G is the centroid at which the proportions would be the same for each buyer or type of music category. When a point is far from G it contributes significantly to the location of the axes. Distances between points are also meaningful. For instance, in the example, note the relative proximity of the positions of female adults and songs, and between old people and classical music. In addition, it is clearly possible to identify the meaning of the

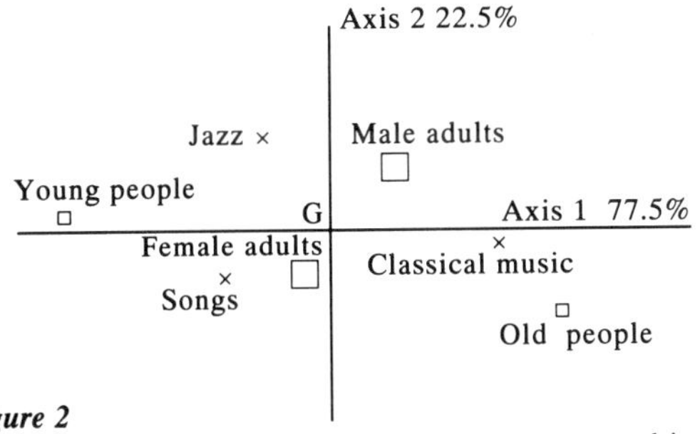

Figure 2
Positions of types of music and buyers represented in two-dimensional space.

Table 4
Proportion of data accounted for by each axis

Axis	Proportion of data explained
1	33.07
2	30.41
3	8.05
4	7.47
5	7.01
Total	86.01

two axes. The horizontal axis (axis 1) in Fig. 2 represents the relationship between young people and old people, while the vertical axis (axis 2) distinguishes between jazz and non-jazz music.

One advantage of this procedure is that more complex mathematical operations can be carried out, but they will not be developed in this entry. For example, it is possible to calculate the relative contribution of each dimension to each of the factorial axes in order to identify more clearly the nature of the axes. It is also of value to calculate the expression

$$R = \sum_{ij} \left(\frac{f_{ij}^2}{r_i c_j} \right)$$

Since R is distributed with a chi-squared distribution, it is possible to proceed beyond a description of the sample and to employ inferential statistics.

Moreover, it is possible to generalize correspondence analysis to a $m \cdot n$ table. If j is the lowest dimension of the table then j–1 axes of reference can be identified, and as with traditional factor analysis, the first two or three axes generally account for a high proportion of the total variance. These features of the procedure will be illustrated in the following example drawn from educational research.

2. *A Study of Teaching Behavior*

In a study reported by Crahay (1987) of teaching behavior, 21 lessons were observed of one teacher teaching the same sixth grade class. The verbal interactions between the teacher and the students were recorded on audiotape. The tape recordings of the first 20 minutes of each lesson were transcribed for more detailed analysis. Since the extracts of each of the lessons sampled and examined are of the same duration, the absolute frequencies of teaching behavior are comparable between lessons.

From an examination of the transcripts, the verbal behavior of the teacher was coded using a nine-category system developed by De Landsheere (De Landsheere and Bayer 1969, De Landsheere et al. 1973). The directions of the teacher–student interactions were also coded, namely, whether the teacher spoke to the whole class or to a specific student. In addition, the verbal participation of the students was coded into one of three categories. In this system of classification of teacher behavior there was thus a total of 14 categories of teacher or student behavior.

Five axes were identified as significant by correspondence analysis. The proportion of the data accounted for by each of the five axes has been recorded in Table 4.

The first two axes account for 63.48 percent of the data, which is sufficient to restrict further analysis to consideration of these two axes only. Distances in this two-dimensional space and the relative contributions of each variable can be calculated, but limitations of space prevent such information being presented here. However, a diagrammatic presentation of the lessons and teaching behavior variables in the two-dimensional space has been recorded in Fig. 3.

In Fig. 3, each of the 21 lessons is indicated by a number and each of the teaching behaviors by a combination of letters. In the following discussion only those teaching behaviors and lessons which have a relative contribution equal to or greater than 0.20 are considered. Two groups of lessons can be identified and contrasted on the horizontal axis (axis 1). The first group are shown clustered on the left hand side of Fig. 3, namely lessons: 19, 3, 21, 17, 9, 14, and 15. The second group of lessons lie on the right hand side of Fig. 3, namely lessons: 4, 10, 1, 6, 7, and 11. The first group of lessons is associated with five teaching behavior variables: TC (teacher speaks to the whole class); RSC (a student responds to a request that the teacher has addressed to the whole class, without specifying who has to respond); IMP (imposed instruction); FB + (positive feedback) and CONC (concretization by the teacher).

The second group of lessons may be characterized by five teaching behaviors: TP (teacher speaks to a specific student); RSP (a student responds to a request that the teacher has addressed specifically to the student); PS (a student spontaneously asks a question or reacts to the teacher's comment without specifically being asked); DEV (content development in the lesson); and A + (positive affectivity).

The first group of lessons reflect a traditional teach-

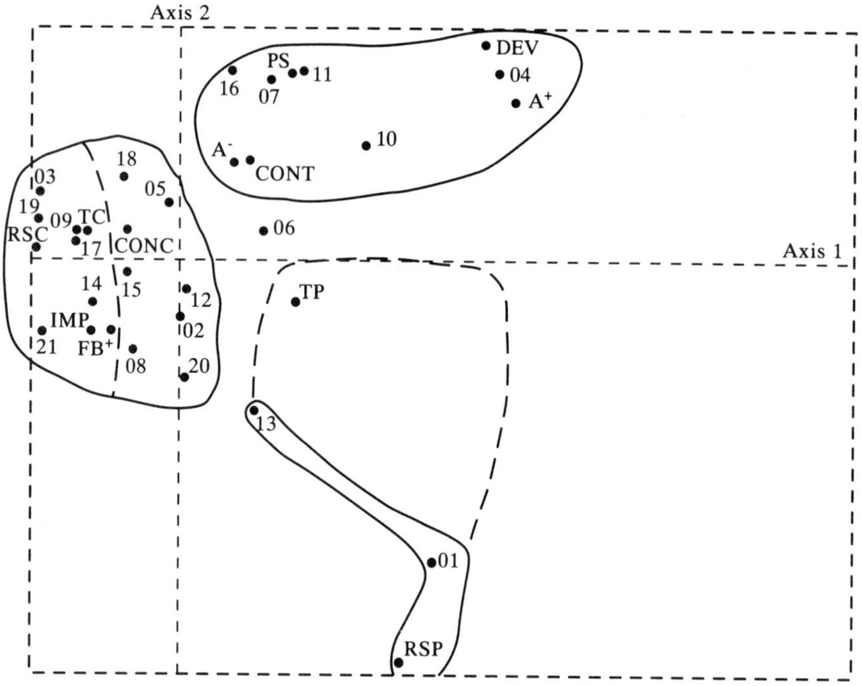

Figure 3
Spatial representation of categories and lessons

ing style. During these lessons, the verbal behavior of the teacher is mostly directed toward the whole class (TC). The teacher lectures and frequently asks questions of the whole group without specifying who has to respond. We may assume that those students who participate verbally are those who know the correct answer. This would account for the high level of positive feedback (FB^{+}).

The second group of lessons reflects another pattern of interaction: (a) where a specific student questions the teacher (PS); (b) the student responds (RSP); (c) the teacher's verbal behavior is oriented toward a particular student (TP); (d) the teacher develops (i.e., accepts, classifies, and amplifies what the student says) (DEV); and (e) the teacher gives more positive affect than usual (A^{+}). In the first group of lessons verbal participation by the students is quite different in comparison to the second group of lessons where the students participate spontaneously or respond to questions directed to them personally.

Before discussing the second group of lessons in greater detail, it is necessary to examine the vertical axis in Fig. 3 (axis 2). Few teaching behavior variables show high relative contributions. The axis is clearly polarized on two forms of verbal participation by the students. On the one hand there is a student responding to a request that the teacher has specifically addressed to the student (RSP). On the other hand there is a student spontaneously asking a question or reacting to the teacher's comment without being specifically asked (PS). Four other teaching behavior variables were found to have substantial loadings along this second axis: imposed instruction (IMP) and positive feedback (FB^{+}) on the negative side; and content development (DEV) and controlling function (CONT) on the positive side. However, the roles that these four teaching behavior variables play in the definition of the second axis is slight, since their relative contributions do not exceed 0.28.

Five lessons are located on the negative side of this second axis (namely, 1, 8, 13, 20, 21). On the positive side, four lessons (namely, 4, 7, 11, 16) show a high relative contribution on this axis (greater than 0.44) and three others (namely, 3, 10, 18) show a lower positive loading on this axis (between 0.22 and 0.25). The six lessons which belong to the positive side of the first axis are split into three groups by the second axis. Four lessons (4,7,10,11) are characterized by a high frequency of spontaneous participation by the students, and by a low frequency of personally solicited participation, whereas lesson 1 is characterized by a low frequency of student spontaneous participation, and by a high frequency of personally solicited participation.

3. Conclusion

Correspondence analysis has therefore allowed the

construction of a typology of lessons and their characterization according to two main dimensions. These two main dimensions take into account the different types of variables which have been observed. In one sense this technique of correspondence analysis may be compared with factor analysis and the scores assigned along the two axes to the calculation of factor scores, but the mathematical model is very different, and the technique is suitable for use with nominal data, whereas factor analysis is suitable for use with scores associated with an underlying normal distribution. Correspondence analysis seeks to account for the distribution of data in the specified categories, and factor analysis seeks to account for the variance in the scores obtained with respect to specified variables.

See also: Log–Linear Models; Galois Lattices; Factor Analysis

References

Benzecri J P 1963 *Cours de linguistique mathématique*. University of Rennes, Rennes
Benzecri J P 1973 *L'analyse des données. Vol. 2: L'analyse des correspondances*. Dunod, Paris
Crahay M 1987 Stability and variability of teachers' behaviors: A case study. *Teaching and Teach. Educ.* 4(4)
De Lagarde J 1983 *Initiation a l'analyse des données*. Bordas and Dunod, Paris
De Landsheere G, Bayer E 1969 *Comment les maîtres enseignent*. Ministère de l'Education Nationale, Brussels
De Landsheere G, Nuthall G, Cameron M, Wragg E, Trowbridge N 1973 *Towards a Science of Teaching*. National Foundation for Educational Research (NFER), London

Further Reading

BMDP *Statistical Software Manual 1990. Vol. 2: Procedure* CA *Parts 1 and 2*. University of California Press, Los Angeles, California
Lefebvre J 1976 *Introduction aux statistiques multidimensionelles*. Masson, Paris
SAS/STAT User's Guide 1990. *Vol. 1: Anova-freq, Version 6*, 4th edn. SAS Institute Inc., Cary, North Carolina
SPSS/PC+ Procedure ANACOR. SPSS, Chicago, Illinois

G. Henry

Cost Analysis in Education

Many important decisions in education are concerned with the costs of education. Cost analysis can reveal the cost implications of an educational policy, assess the financial feasibility of an educational reform, provide diagnosis of past and current resource utilization in education, project future educational cost requirements, and evaluate the relative efficiency of alternative educational policies or interventions. Cost studies can contribute significantly to decision-making, planning, and monitoring in education. The purpose of this entry is to introduce the different types of educational cost analysis and explain how they can contribute to improved policy-making in education. The discussion is grounded in a review of educational cost studies in both developed and developing countries in order to provide a brief summary of the current state of knowledge and gaps in educational cost analysis.

1. An Economic Classification of Cost Studies in Education

An economic framework is useful for analysis of costs and efficiency in education (Hanushek 1979). According to this framework, educational production is likened to economic production, whereby inputs to education (such as students, teachers, instructional materials, school facilities, equipment, etc.) are transformed through an educational process (encompassing, e.g., the curriculum, pedagogical methods, school organization, management and monitoring procedure) into educational outputs (schooling effects such as cognitive and noncognitive skills, and schooling benefits such as higher productivity and earnings). The costs of education refer to the economic value of the inputs used in education. The cost or economic value of an educational input is defined as its opportunity costs and is measured by the value of the input in its best alternative use. This definition of cost implies that the costs of education consist not only of public educational expenditures on personnel, school facilities, supplies, and equipment, but also parental and students' expenditures on education (direct private costs, such as tuition and other education-related fees, textbooks, uniform, transportation, etc.), students' forgone opportunities (indirect private costs, such as forgone earnings or other productive activities), as well as private contributions to education (contributions in cash or in kind, by individuals, parents, or private organizations).

Efficiency in education production is concerned with a comparison of the costs of education to the output of education. Educational production is said to be efficient when the maximum amount of educational output is produced for given educational costs; or alternatively, the least amount of educational cost is required to achieve a given level of educational output.

There is a large body of literature on educational cost studies in both developing countries and developed countries that demonstrates the applications of cost analysis to improved policy-making in education (Tsang 1988, Levin 1983, Cohn and Geske 1990). It is a diverse literature which includes studies that vary in the type of cost analysis, the purposes and applications in education, and in the scope of analysis. Nevertheless these studies can be conveniently classified into three categories based on the economic framework described above: costing and feasibility-testing studies, behavioral studies of educational costs, and input–output studies.

2. *Educational Costing and Feasibility Testing Studies*

Studies in the first category are concerned with educational inputs only. Their major tasks are to identify, classify, and measure the costs of various inputs to education. They are conducted for purposes of costing, and testing the financial feasibility of an educational activity.

Educational costing is one of the earliest and most common applications of cost analysis in education. There are numerous studies which illustrate the broad scope of cost estimation in traditional education (Coombs and Hallack 1972). They range from the costing of an educational intervention in the classroom, an education project, or an education program, to the costing of the reform in a subsector of education, or the five-year plan for the entire education system. They demonstrate that for a given educational activity, cost estimation can inform the policy-maker about: (a) the total cost and thus financial requirement of the activity, (b) the economic feasibility and thus the likelihood of successful implementation of the activity, (c) the short-term and long-term cost implications (such as start-up costs and recurrent costs of the activity when fully operated), and (d) the distribution of the cost burden among various parties involved and thus equity/inequity in cost sharing. All such information is relevant to the decision about whether or not to undertake the educational activity.

The estimation of the costs of new educational technology is another important area of educational costing. A significant number of cost studies have been conducted on new educational media projects (Eicher et al. 1982). They indicate that such projects have high start-up costs, but the cost per student generally decreases with student enrollment. Depending on how the operation is conducted, the cost per broadcast hour can vary significantly among countries. A positive result of these cost studies is the standardization of the measurement and classification of the various costs of new educational media. Estimating the costs of new educational media is a necessary part of the comparison of its cost-effectiveness with that of traditional education.

A number of conceptual and methodological advances have been made in the understanding of educational costs. First, the cost of an education input is defined in terms of its opportunity costs and is thus not necessarily equal to public expenditure on the input. Consideration of public educational expenditures alone can significantly underestimate the real cost of an educational activity, usually due to omission of direct and indirect private costs of education, as well as private contributions. Second, care has to be exercised in estimating capital costs. In particular, the facilities and equipment purchased through a capital investment can last for many years; thus the annualized costs of such capital inputs have to depend on the expected life of service of the items, the rate of discount, and the opportunity cost of the undepreciated part of the items. Also, if future expenditures that are required as a result of capital investment (such as maintenance, repair, and staff) are ignored, the total cost of an educational activity will be underestimated. Third, it is useful to distinguish between educational costs in current dollars and educational costs in constant dollars; the latter reflect real resources to education and are obtained by adjusting the former with price indexes showing changes in the price level. If the rates of inflation are high, the cost figures in current dollars will differ substantially from those for in constant dollars. Teachers are often victimized by inflation as their salary increases fall behind the rates of inflation. To assess the amount of real resources to education, educational costs in constant dollars should be estimated. Finally, since the prices of education inputs can vary significantly among regions, cost-of-education indexes reflecting such price disparities are needed in determining the costs of education for different regions (Chambers 1978). Failure to take account of these conceptual/methodological issues can lead to error in costing and in the choice of policies based on such costing information.

Despite these advances and the obvious relevance of cost analysis for informed decision-making in education, "technical" and "sociopolitical" barriers do exist that could limit the usefulness of cost analysis in education. On the technical side, a major barrier is the lack of relevant cost data. There are tremendous gaps between what data are required and what data are available for cost analysis, especially for studies in developing countries. For example, data are often available for public educational expenditures, but not for the other costs of education. Even public educational expenditures are sometimes available in terms of planned public expenditures, not actual public expenditures. Public educational expenditures by the central government are available, but not necessarily those by lower levels of education. Similarly, educational expenditures by the ministry of education are available, but not necessarily those by noneducation ministries or departments. Finally, expenditures on a number of items are sometimes lumped together; such aggregated data are not useful when information on individual items is needed.

Besides data-related difficulties, a failure in the evaluation of educational activities may result from a lack of awareness of the relevance of cost analysis on the part of decision-makers or a shortage of competent cost analysts.

On the sociopolitical side, policy-makers may not have genuine interest in determining the financial requirements and feasibility of an educational plan. Educational plans may be drawn up by policy-makers for symbolic purposes, for legitimizing the power and actions of a regime, or for complying with the requirements for obtaining external financial assistance. Analysis of educational costs may yield findings inconsistent with the hidden agenda of such policy-makers. It may also expose glaring inequalities or inequities in the distribution of educational resources by social class, gender, ethnicity, and region, which a regime would like to cover up. Obviously, technical barriers are easier to overcome than the sociopolitical ones.

3. *Behavioral Studies of Educational Cost*

Studies in the second category are concerned with the relationships among inputs and the utilization of inputs in the educational production process. They are conducted for purposes such as ascertaining behavioral patterns in educational costs, revealing the extent of underutilization of inputs in educational production process, and uncovering problematic cost patterns in education. They provide "diagnostic" signals to policy-makers about existing or potential problems in education. Their scope of analysis also ranges widely, from "macro" investigations of national education systems to "micro" investigations of individual schools. These studies can be further subdivided into two groups: studies of educational expenditures and unit costs of education, and studies of resource utilization in education.

3.1 *Studies of Educational Expenditures and Unit Costs*

These studies are based largely on national data over time. The major tasks are focused on understanding the trend in educational expenditures, and uncovering the determinants of educational expenditure and unit costs.

Most cross-national studies on educational expenditures are concerned with public educational expenditures. There are three major findings on the trend of public educational expenditures in developing and developed countries over time (Eicher 1984 pp. 45–47). First, despite variation among countries and regions, the overall effort in favor of education in the 1960s and 1970s has been phenomenal. Total public educational expenditure increased by 250 percent in real terms. Public educational expenditure as a proportion of gross national product ("national-effort" cost indicator) increased by 75 percent in developing countries and by 50 percent in developed countries. Public educational expenditure as a proportion of total public expenditure ("fiscal-effort" cost indicator) increased by over 30 percent in both developing and developed countries. Second, there are discernible trends in the national-effort and fiscal-effort cost indicators. The average national-effort cost indicator increased from 2.9 percent to 4.2 percent during the 1960s; it continued to increase at a slower rate between 1970 and 1974. However, after 1974 the pattern between countries differed: the national-effort cost indicators began to stabilize for developed countries and Asian countries, but continued the upward trend for sub-Saharan African countries. As for the fiscal-effort cost indicators, the trend was rising for all countries between 1960 and 1974 (from about 11% to 15%). Developed countries began to reduce their fiscal effort in the 1970s. In contrast, developing countries stabilized their fiscal effort after the mid-1970s. Third, the effort in favor of educational expenditure is now leveling off for all countries except the sub-Saharan African region. The slowdown in national and fiscal efforts is widespread.

The changes in public educational expenditures are due to both supply factors (such as the growth rate of the national economy, the ranges of competing demands of other public services, etc.) and demand factors (such as demographic changes, the importance of education for national development, etc.) which are often outside the locus of control of educational policy-makers and school administrators. The slowdown in public educational expenditures can be attributed to three factors: slower rates of economic growth, a relative decrease in the demand for education, and a change in government attitude toward education (Eicher 1984 p. 55).

Lack of data makes cross-national comparison of private costs of education difficult. Available evidence indicates that the direct and indirect costs of schooling are significant compared to public costs (Wolff 1985, Tilak 1985, Tsang and Kidchanapanish 1992). The costs of private schools relative to those of government schools may be significantly underestimated if private costs are omitted (Tsang and Taoklam 1992).

Unit costs of education have been estimated for a wide range of situations, usually in terms of expenditure per student. Two major findings are obtained from unit cost studies: there are significant disparities in unit costs for different situations, and there are identifiable patterns in unit costs. For example, significant differences often exist in unit costs between rural areas and urban areas, between states or provinces in a country, and among countries. There are also significant differences in unit costs between different levels of education, between different types of curriculum or subjects, and between different types of schools (e.g., boarding schools vs. day schools; government schools vs. private schools).

On the other hand, per-student expenditure exhibits common patterns across education systems: (a) it rises with the level of education, (b) it is dominated by personnel costs with higher proportion for personnel costs at lower levels of education, (c) it is higher for boarding schools than for day schools at the secondary level, (d) it is generally higher for vocational/technical education than for academic/general education at the secondary level, (e) it is higher for engineering and science subjects than for arts and humanities at the tertiary level, and (f) it has a built-in tendency to rise over time (Psacharopoulos 1982, Tsang 1988, Coombs and Hallak 1988). These common patterns can be understood by examining the determinants of unit costs.

An important factor affecting unit cost is the technology of educational production. Education in countries across the world takes place predominately in the traditional school and university, with similar organization, curriculum, pedagogy, management, and monitoring procedure. The adoption of a common technology is the major reason for the similar patterns of unit costs. The labor-intensive technology of traditional education accounts for the dominance of teacher costs. Different provisions in terms of class size, staffing pattern, and facilities explain the cost differences among levels of education, types of curriculum, and types of schools. Furthermore, pay scales based on qualifications, years of service, and automatic promotion practice make personnel costs rise over time.

3.2 Studies of Resource Utilization in Education

The other group of studies assesses the rates of utilization of inputs in educational institutions, and the findings have direct implications for unit costs and educational efficiency. If there is considerable underutilization of resources, the number of students served can be increased without incurring additional cost; alternatively, cost can be reduced without affecting the number of students served. In either situation, unit cost is lowered and educational efficiency is raised.

Survey studies have been conducted to study the utilization rates of resources in educational institutions in a number of developing countries, based on measures such as the number of contact hours per week for a teacher, the student–teacher (or student–faculty) ratio, the building area per student, and the percentage use of laboratory time and equipment. Low rates of utilization are reported for both secondary schools and for universities, indicating real potential for cost savings and efficiency improvement.

Econometric studies have also been conducted to assess resource utilization by estimating education cost functions (ECFs) and determining the presence or absence of economies of scale in educational production. An ECF relates the minimum cost of education to the level of educational output, given input prices and the technology of production; it shows how the cost of education varies with educational output. Education cost functions can be estimated statistically, though there are a number of theoretical and methodological difficulties (Tsang 1988 p.208). The presence or absence of economies of scale can be determined from an estimated ECF. Educational production is said to exhibit economies (or diseconomies) of scale if each additional unit of output becomes cheaper (or more expensive) to produce.

Studies of ECFs in developed countries (Canada, the US, and the UK) show that there are economies of scale in primary and secondary education, and in higher education (Kumar 1983, Fox 1981, Verry and Davies 1976, Brinkman and Leslie 1987). There are very few studies of ECFs in developing countries. Available evidence indicates that higher education production demonstrates economies of scale (Psacharopoulos 1982), but no definite conclusion can be drawn for primary and secondary education in developing countries.

Studies of cost functions of new educational-media projects in developing countries indicate the presence of economies of scale (Jamison et al. 1978, Perraton 1982). They found that these projects have large start-up costs, so that large enrollments and a long period of operation are needed to lower their unit costs to levels comparable to that of the traditional school. In addition, "small" media (such as radio) are much less costly than "big" media (such as television).

3.3 Behavioral Cost Studies and Educational Policy-making

Studies in the second category illustrate how cost analysis can contribute to improved policy-making in a number of ways. First, examination of cost patterns and resource utilization can uncover opportunities for improving the efficiency of educational investment, for example, in terms of reallocation of resources between levels or types of education, improved utilization of existing personnel or facilities, or the adoption of alternative technologies of education.

Second, the studies find considerable disparities in educational expenditures and unit costs across diverse settings. This finding has several policy implications. Policymakers should be warned against designing an "average" policy to be applied to diverse settings. Schools in different settings may have different needs and thus require different treatment. The diversity of educational setting also implies the need to base policies on disaggregated data. Moreover, disparities in educational costs often reflect inequities in access to educational resources; reducing such inequities can be a desirable policy objective. Finally, differences among countries and regions warn against uncritical adoption of practices found useful elsewhere.

Third, indicators of education costs can be used in an anatomical examination of resource utilization in education. They include, for example, measures of national effort and fiscal effort, unit costs by level of education, type of education, curriculum, region, and time, as well as indicators related to the distribution of costs by sources and input categories. From a policy perspective, indicators are useful for a number of diagnostic purposes: they indicate the state of affairs in education, uncover areas of abnormalities, and provide the bases for gauging progress in educational interventions. They should be regularly constructed and examined.

4. *Input–Output Studies in Education*

In contrast to the previous two categories of cost studies which examine input costs and characteristics of educational costs only, studies in the third category consider both the costs and outputs of education. They are conducted for the purposes of choosing among alternative educational investment so that educational resources are allocated efficiently. These studies can be divided into two distinct groups: cost-benefit studies which compare the benefits of education (such as increased productivity and earnings) to the costs of education, and cost-effectiveness studies which compare the effects of education (such as student learning) to the costs of education. A brief summary of the findings of these studies and their policy implications is presented here. More detailed discussion of the theory and methodology of these analyses is available elsewhere (Cohn and Geske 1990, Levin 1983).

4.1 Cost–Benefit Studies in Education

These studies use the rates-of-return approach to evaluation. The measurement of educational benefits is based on human capital theory. According to this theory, education enhances the skills (human capital) of individuals and thus raises their productivity; and in a competitive labor market, a more productive individual is paid a higher wage. Thus differences in education among individuals result in differences in earnings, other things being equal. Since human capital is durable, the productive benefits of education can be measured in terms of lifetime earning differentials. One can distinguish between private rates of return and social rates of return. Private rates of return compare the benefits of education to an individual to the costs of education to the individual; they inform investment decisions for an individual. Social rates of return compare the benefits of education to society to the costs of education to society; they inform public investment decisions to achieve "external" efficiency in education.

A large literature on cost–benefit studies in education exists for both developing countries and developed countries. The major findings are: (a) educational investment is very profitable, with rates generally above the benchmark rate for physical capital (10%); (b) primary education has the highest rates of return among all education levels; (c) private rates of return are higher than social rates of return, especially at the level of higher education; (d) at a given level, the rate of return to education in developing countries is higher than that in developed countries; (e) the rates of return to women's education are higher than those for men in developing countries; and (f) at the secondary level, academic education has a higher rate of return than that of vocational/technical education (Psacharopoulos 1985).

The implications for educational policies are obvious, if one accepts human capital theory and the rates-of-return approach. The findings suggest a top priority of investment in primary education, increasing private costs of university education, expanding access to schooling for females, and offering academic education at the secondary level.

The social rates-of-return approach to public investment is adopted by some cost analysts because it is grounded in economic theory, is analytically straightforward, and has clear policy implications. Yet it is not without its limitations, especially with regard to the measurement of educational benefits. Besides, there are alternative explanations of the relationship between education, productivity, and earnings (Tsang 1988 pp. 213–15). Policymakers should be informed about both the advantages and limitations of cost–benefit analysis.

4.2 Cost-effectiveness Studies in Education

Cost-effectiveness analysis in education is used to choose among alternative educational interventions so as to maximize educational effects given cost, thus improving "internal" efficiency in education.

A prominent application of cost-effectiveness analysis is in new educational media. Despite some methodological difficulties, several tentative conclusions can be drawn on the cost-effectiveness of new educational media (Eicher et al. 1982, Jamison and Orivel 1982): (a) students do learn from new educational media, but their use within the traditional school setting is not cost-effective; (b) small media have been found to be more cost-effective than big media; (c) distance teaching may be the only way to educate children in thinly populated areas; (d) distance teaching projects for school equivalency appear to be effective and cost-effective; (e) the effective use of new educational media requires technical staff for operation and maintenance; and (f) in any given situation, it is difficult to determine which particular medium is most suitable; in practice several media are used together in a project.

Compared to cost-benefit analysis, the applications of cost-effectiveness to traditional education are relatively few, especially in developing countries. Most studies on school improvement have focused on educational effectiveness (primarily measures of cognitive outcomes), without also considering educational costs. Among the few applications, a conspicuous example is studies on textbooks which

Table 1
Applications of cost analysis in education

Type of cost studies	Domains of Educational policy analysis	Applications Educational planning	Educational monitoring
Costing/feasibility studies			
Cost estimation	Costing	Costing	-
Economic feasibility	Evaluating feasibility	Evaluating feasibility	-
Behavioral studies of costs			
Expenditure/unit costs	-	Costing and cost projection	Diagnosis
Other cost indicators and indices	-	Cost projection	Diagnosis
Resource utilization surveys	Improving efficiency	-	Assessing resource utilization
Estimation of cost functions and economies of scale	Improving efficiency	-	-
Input–output studies			
Cost-benefit studies	Improving efficiency	-	-
Cost-effectiveness studies	Improving efficiency	-	-

find that the provision of textbooks is a cost-effective strategy to improve student achievement (Heyneman et al. 1984). Another example includes the study of alternative approaches to computer-assisted instruction (Levin et al. 1987). The cost-effectiveness information on other traditional education inputs or processes is lacking, incomplete, or not yet generalizable.

In short, not much has been learned about alternative school interventions for improving the internal efficiency of traditional education. This state of affairs is indeed unsatisfactory given the pressing need to improve educational efficiency under conditions of tight fiscal constraints and unmet social demand for education. This situation may be improved by efforts to strengthen the research basis of cost-effectiveness analysis and the utilization of research findings in educational policy-making. In particular, educational evaluation should be based on the cost-effectiveness approach, efforts should be made to collect reliable cost data, and measures of school effectiveness should include not only cognitive effects, but noncognitive effects as well.

5. Summary and Recommendations

Table 1 summarizes the applications of cost analysis in education. It shows that there are eight common types of cost studies (within the three categories discussed) which can be used in at least three domains of educational analysis, for different purposes or type of applications in each domain. The scope of cost analysis can be very broad; it may range from the analysis of school activities and educational institutions to the analysis of a subsector of education and the system of education.

While cost analysis can contribute significantly to informed decisions in education, its use in the different domains of educational analysis remains inadequate to date. This state of affairs is especially unsatisfactory in light of the need to improve educational quality and provide basic education to all, the severe fiscal constraints facing many countries, and the importance of raising the efficiency of educational investment in the years to come. At least three tasks are necessary to alter this situation. One task is to strengthen the informational basis of cost analysis. As indicated previously, there often exist wide gaps between what cost data are available and what cost data are needed. The need to develop a database for cost analysis is both self-evident and urgent (Tsang 1988 pp. 223–24). Another task is to encourage research on educational costs. Studies of cost-effectiveness in traditional education are especially limited and should be encouraged. Studies of unit costs and other cost indicators and indexes should be conducted periodically to monitor and diagnose resource allocation and utilization in education. The third task is to heighten the awareness of educational decision-makers about the usefulness of cost analysis and to encourage them to incorporate the findings of cost studies in educational policy-making (Levin 1988).

See also: Education Production Functions; Cost–Benefit Analysis; Cost-effectiveness Analysis

References

Brinkman P, Leslie L 1987 Economics of scale in higher education: Sixty years of research. *Rev. Higher Educ.* 10(1): 1–28

Chambers J 1978 Educational cost differentials and allocation of state aid for elementary secondary education. *J. Hum. Resources* 13(4): 459–81

Cohn E, Geske T 1990 *The Economics of Education*, 3rd edn. Pergamon, Oxford

Coombs P, Hallak J 1972 *Educational Cost-Analysis in Action: Case Studies for Planners*, Vols. 1–3. UNESCO/IIEP, Paris

Coombs P, Hallak J 1988 *Cost Analysis in Education: A Tool for Policy and Planning*. Johns Hopkins University Press, Baltimore, Maryland
Eicher J C 1984 *Educational Costing and Financing in Developing Countries: Focus on Sub-Saharan Africa*. World Bank Staff Working Paper No. 655, World Bank, Washington, DC
Eicher J C, Hawkridge D, McAnany E, Mariet F, Orivel F (eds.) 1982 *The Economics of New Educational Media, Vol. 3: Cost and Effectiveness. Overview and Synthesis*. UNESCO, Paris
Fox W 1981 Reviewing economies of size in education. *J. Educ. Finance* 6: 273–96
Hanushek E 1979 Conceptual and empirical issues in the estimation of educational production functions. *J. Hum. Resources* 14(3): 351–88
Heyneman S, Jamison D, Montenegro X 1984 Textbooks in the Philippines: Evaluation of the pedagogical impact of a nationwide investment. *Educ. Eval. Policy Anal.* 6(2): 139–150
Jamison D, Klees S, Wells S 1978 The costs of eductional media: Guidelines for planning and evaluation. Sage, Beverly Hills, California
Jamison D, Orivel F 1982 Cost-effectiveness of distance teaching for school equivalency. In: Perraton H (ed.) 1982
Kumar R 1983 Economies of scale in school operation: Evidence from Canada. *Appl. Econ.* 15: 323–40
Levin H 1983 *Cost-effectiveness: A Primer*. Sage, Beverly Hills, California
Levin H 1988 Cost effectiveness and educational policy. *Educ. Eval. Policy Anal.* 10(1): 51–69
Levin H, Glass G, Meister G 1987 Cost-effectiveness of computer-assisted instruction. *Eval. Rev.* 11(1): 50–72
Perraton H (ed.) 1982 *Alternative Routes to Formal Education*. Johns Hopkins University Press, Baltimore, Maryland
Psacharopoulous G 1982 The economics of higher education in developing countries. *Comp. Educ. Rev.* 26(2): 139–59
Psacharopoulos G 1985 Returns to education: A further international update and implications. *J. Hum. Resources* 20(4): 583–604
Tilak J 1985 Analysis of costs of education in India. Occasional Paper No. 10, National Institute of Educational Planning and Administration (India), New Delhi (ERIC Document Reproduction Service No. ED 261 946)
Tsang M 1988 Cost analysis for educational policymaking: A review of cost studies in education in developing countries. *Rev. Educ. Res.* 58(2): 181–230
Tsang M, Kidchanapanish S 1992 Private resources and the quality of primary education in Thailand. *Int. J. Educ. Res.* 17(2): 179–98
Tsang M, Taoklam W 1992 Comparing the costs of government and private primary education in Thailand. *Int. J. Educ. Dev.* 12(3): 177–90
Verry D, Davies B 1976 *University Costs and Output*. Studies on Education 6, Elsevier, Amsterdam
Wolff L 1985 Controlling the Costs of Education in Eastern Africa: A Review of Data, Issues, and Policies. World Bank Staff Working Paper No. 702, World Bank, Washington, DC

Mun C. Tsang

Cost–Benefit Analysis

Cost–benefit analysis represents an important tool for analyzing the desirability of social investments. It has been applied widely to educational investments at the national and sub-national levels, particularly in evaluating the ability of such investments to raise productivity and earnings. Cost–benefit analysis compares the costs and outcomes of alternatives when the outcomes can be assessed in monetary terms (Mishan 1976).

Cost–benefit analysis enables a direct comparison of the costs and benefits of an alternative or a comparison of their magnitudes with those of other types of social investments in education or in other sectors. Not only is it possible to ascertain which educational investment has the largest benefits relative to costs; it is also possible to compare these results with investments in health, transportation, physical capital such as plant and equipment, and other sectors. In this way governmental units can use cost–benefit analysis to compare the desirability of alternative educational investments, as well as in determining the balance between investing in education and other sectors. In contrast, cost-effectiveness can only evaluate alternatives with the same goals and measures of effectiveness, such as improvements in student achievement (see *Cost-effectiveness Analysis*).

Cost–benefit analysis was developed in the 1930s by the United States Corps of Army Engineers. The US Congress was overwhelmed with requests for massive regional investments in water-resource projects (e.g., hydroelectric dams, deep-water harbors, major canals) which the various regional interests viewed as powerful stimuli for reducing unemployment at a time of national economic depression. A bewildered Congress asked the Corps of Army Engineers to recommend only projects whose benefits were at least equal to costs (Eckstein 1958). By the 1960s, cost–benefit analysis was used widely by economists to assist in the search for efficiency in government spending. At the same time it began to be used to scrutinize educational investments.

1. Measuring Costs and Benefits

In contrast to cost-effectiveness analysis, cost–benefit analysis requires that both costs and benefits be expressed in monetary terms. In this respect, the costs are measured in the same way for both types of analyses using the ingredients or resource-recovery approach (Levin 1983). However, benefits must be measurable in terms of their monetary value rather than in terms of educational effectiveness as reflected in cost-effectiveness analysis.

1.1 Assessing Benefits

Since cost–benefit analysis requires that benefits be measured in monetary units, it is only possible to apply it to subjects where that is feasible. This means that cost–benefit analysis lends itself especially well to those alternatives or interventions in which the outcomes are market-oriented. For example, educational and training programs that are designed to improve employment and earnings or reduce poverty can be evaluated with a cost–benefit approach when the benefits are the additional earnings associated with the interventions (Ribich 1969).

Many educational projects and investments are dedicated to raising labor force productivity and income. These include commitments to vocational education, workforce training, dropout prevention and even much of the effort at general education which is dedicated to improving the labor force (Becker 1964, Psacharopoulos and Woodhall 1985). Thus, educational programs that have labor market outcomes are the most appropriate ones for using cost–benefit analysis. The most typical method of measuring the benefits of such interventions is to compare the earnings of similar persons with different amounts of education. Under assumptions of the competitive marketplace, long-run differences in earnings associated with education are equivalent to the higher productivity of such persons.

It is difficult to estimate such benefits through experimental studies in a democratic society. An experiment would require that persons be assigned randomly to different levels of education—and perhaps their lives would have to be controlled in other ways—to assure comparability in examining the role of education. More typically the studies observe cross-sections of workers or follow them longitudinally in attempting to measure the connection between specific levels and types of educational investments and earnings. However, it is reasonable to expect that persons with more education also have other resources that can account for higher earnings. For example, persons with more education are generally of a higher social origin, leading to better connections in labor markets. They may also have higher ability and discipline, two factors which are associated with greater educational attainments and which should also reap dividends in labor markets. Accordingly, the measurement of benefits in cost–benefit analysis must attempt to control statistically for noneducational differences that may affect earnings and that are associated with education.

Thus, the benefits of a specific vocational education program relative to an alternative can be measured according to the earnings associated with participation in that program rather than the alternative. The benefits of expanding schooling can be assessed according to the additional earnings of those who benefit from that expansion. Of course, these represent the gross benefits to the investment. Net benefits can only be determined after subtracting the cost.

There are a number of other concerns in the measurement of benefits. The first is that the additional earnings that represent the benefits of more education or training are not received immediately. They are distributed over the working lives of the educated labor force following education and training. Yet economists and psychologists have long recognized that benefits that are received over time have a lesser value than those received at present. In order to make the value of benefits indifferent to the time pattern over which they were conferred, it is important to obtain a standard measure of their value. Accordingly, the stream of benefits from an investment that is generated over time is converted to a single measure of "present value" by penalizing or discounting future benefits by an interest rate to make them comparable with benefits received at present. This is a fairly straightforward conversion which provides a present value of benefits that can be compared directly with a present value of costs (Mishan 1976 pp. 199–224).

A second concern is that the benefits of educational investments extend beyond increases in productivity and earnings to improvements in health, consumption, labor market information, and reductions in criminal justice and public assistance burdens. Haveman and Wolfe (1984) have estimated that the total value of benefits from educational investments is probably double that of the additional earnings alone. Therefore it is likely that the education-induced increase in earnings will understate the true value of benefits from educational investments.

A final concern is that the aggregate benefits and costs that comprise a cost–benefit estimate reveal nothing about the distribution of who pays the costs and receives the benefits. The question of who receives the benefits and who pays the costs may be an important issue. For example, if social investments tend to redistribute income, most democracies prefer investments that are redistributive from wealthier to poorer populations. There is some evidence that educational subsidies in higher education represent a net transfer of resources from lower-income groups to upper-income ones (Fields 1980, Leslie and Brinkman 1988. pp. 107–21). Lower-income groups participate less in higher education than upper-income groups, but they must still pay taxes to support such a system. In this case, the investment may have high benefits relative to costs, but may redistribute income from the poor to the rich. Accordingly, the distributive consequences of investments must be analyzed as well as the ratio of costs to benefits (Psacharopoulos and Woodhall 1985 pp. 244–86).

1.2 Measuring Costs

The costs of an intervention are defined as the value of the resources that are given up by society to effect the intervention. These resources are referred to as the ingredients of the intervention, and it is the social value of those ingredients that constitute its overall cost. At a later stage one can assess the distribution of these costs between the decision-making agency and other entities. Accordingly, the method sets out systematically to identify and ascertain the value of the ingredients that are required for each alternative that is under consideration. From an economic perspective the costs of an action are determined by the value of the resources that are entailed in their best alternative use. This is known as "opportunity cost," in the sense that it is the value of the forgone opportunities that must be considered when one refers to the cost of an endeavor. The ingredients method represents a straightforward way of estimating cost within this framework.

The ingredients approach to cost estimation entails three distinct phases: (a) identification of ingredients; (b) determination of the value or cost of the ingredients and the overall costs of an intervention; and (c) an analysis of the costs in an appropriate decision-oriented framework. These three phases are discussed more fully elsewhere (see *Cost-effectiveness Analysis*), but they hold some particular implications for cost–benefit analysis.

1.3 Identification of Ingredients

The identification of ingredients refers to the delineation of all of the resources that are required for the particular intervention that forms the basis for the cost–benefit analysis. For example, in the case of a study of expansion of technical education, the personnel, facilities, materials, and other ingredients required for the activity need to be identified.

Educational interventions use not only these resources, but also the time of students who might otherwise be able to use their time productively in the workplace or through self-employment. Even the time of primary school youngsters in developing societies is likely to have some value in terms of household or farm tasks. If a student is required to spend four additional academic years in the educational system, those years could have been used for other productive activities that, when forgone, have a cost to both the individual and society. Accordingly, an important element of specifying ingredients for cost–benefit analysis is that of student time.

1.4 Determination of Costs

Once the ingredients have been identified and stipulated, it is necessary to ascertain their costs (Levin 1983 Chap. 4). In doing this, all ingredients are assumed to have a cost, including donated or volunteer resources. That is, they have a cost to someone, even if the sponsoring agency did not pay for them in a particular situation. At a later stage the costs will be distributed among the constituencies who paid them, but at this stage the aim is to ascertain the total costs of the intervention.

Ingredients can be divided into those that are purchased in reasonably competitive markets, and those that are obtained through other types of transactions. In general, the value of an ingredient for costing purposes is its market value. In the case of personnel, market value may be ascertained by determining what the costs would be for hiring a particular type of person. Such costs must include not only salary, but also fringe benefits and other employment costs that are paid by the employer. Many of the other inputs can also be costed by using their market prices. There are a number of techniques for determining the values of resources that cannot be readily priced in the marketplace (see *Cost-effectiveness Analysis*).

Of particular concern is the value of student time. The usual measure of the value of student time is the earnings forgone by the student by enrolling in school or a training program rather than being employed in the workplace. This should approximate to the value of productive activity that was lost because the student was in school. Typically the cost of student time is estimated from the earnings of persons of similar gender, race, and socioeconomic status who are in the workforce rather than in schools or training programs. Of course, such estimates must be adjusted for the probability of unemployment.

1.5 Combining Benefits and Costs

Costs and benefits can be combined in several ways in order to do a cost–benefit analysis. The most common forms of cost–benefit comparison are rate of return, cost–benefit (or benefit–cost) ratios, and net present values. One form of cost–benefit analysis is that of estimating internal rates of return on investment, that rate of interest that equates the present values of benefits and costs (Psacharopoulos and Woodhall 1985 pp. 31–41) In general, no investment should be undertaken that does not have a rate of return that is at least equal to that of other alternatives (see *Rates of Return to Education*).

A more typical cost–benefit analysis takes the form of a comparison of cost–benefit ratios among alternative endeavors. The necessary condition for considering an educational investment is that its benefits exceed costs where both benefits and costs represent present values, that is, benefit and cost streams that are properly discounted. The sufficient condition is that the benefit–cost ratio is greater than that of all alternative investments, both educational and noneducational.

The third form of cost–benefit analysis is the calculation of net present values of investments. Net present value is simply the difference between the present benefits and present costs, using the same discount rate to ascertain present values of each. The necessary condition for considering an investment is that its net present value be positive. The sufficient condition is that the net present value of an alternative exceed the net present value of all other alternative investments whose costs are of the same magnitude.

2. Examples of Cost–Benefit Studies

Cost–benefit studies have been carried out in many areas of education. These include the prevention of dropouts, preschool education for disadvantaged children, vocational education, and college loan programs among others.

2.1 Dropout Prevention

A study of dropout prevention found large net present benefits (Stern et al. 1989). This evaluation was based upon the success in reducing dropouts among 11 academies created in public high schools in California. These academies were special programs or schools within the larger high school setting that provided vocational training for careers in which students stood a good chance of placement, as well as academic training. Students were given special attention from their teachers and representatives of local employers. When students were matched with a similar group of students in the regular school programs, it was estimated that the academies had saved 29 persons who would have been expected to drop out.

The marginal costs of the academy program beyond the costs of the regular school program for all 327 students were compared to net present benefits in terms of the additional earnings of the 29 persons who were "saved" from dropping out. The overall net present benefits of the program were found to exceed overall costs by considerable amounts, the specifics depending upon which assumptions were used regarding benefits.

In contrast to studies of a single dropout program, Levin undertook a national study on the economic consequences of high school dropout (Levin 1972). This study calculated the additional lifetime earnings and tax revenues that would have been generated if the entire cohort of 25- to 34-years old males in 1970 had graduated from high school. It was assumed that, even if existing dropouts had graduated, they would not have done as well as those who had actually graduated from high school. Thus, additional earnings of dropouts who would be induced to graduate were assumed to be only 75 percent of those of conventional high school graduates. However, it was also assumed that a portion of the induced graduates would continue into higher education with additional earnings from that source as well.

The total loss of lifetime earnings for this group as a result of failure to complete at least high school was estimated at about US $237 billion. The additional cost for achieving this result was comprised of two parts: first, there was the cost of the additional years of schooling undertaken by members of the group; second, there was the cost of the additional expenditures to prevent dropping out. It was assumed that it would have been necessary to increase annual schooling expenditures on those at risk of dropping out by 50 percent a year for all of their elementary and secondary schooling to keep them in school until completion of high school. On this basis it was estimated that the total costs of achieving at least high school graduation for all members of the cohort was about US $40 billion, producing a benefit of six dollars for each dollar of cost. The additional lifetime earnings would have generated about US $71 billion in government revenue or about US $1.75 in tax revenues for each US $1.00 in cost. The study also estimated that inadequate education was contributing about US $6 billion a year to the costs of welfare and crime in 1970.

2.2 Preschool Educational Investment

Barnett (1985) undertook a cost–benefit analysis of the Perry Preschool Project in Ypsilanti, Michigan. The Perry Preschool approach is one that has been studied since its inception in the 1960s, and it has been used as a model for hundreds of preschools for disadvantaged students across the United States, including the national Head Start Program. Students who had been enrolled in the preschool project were followed until age 19. It was found that relative to a matched control group, enrollees in the project experienced better school achievement, educational placement, educational attainment, and employment. Monetary values for the benefits were calculated on the basis of the apparent effect of these advantages on the value of childcare during the programs; reduced school expenditures for remediation, special services, and grade repetition; reduced costs of crime, delinquency, and welfare; and higher earnings and employment.

It was found that the benefits exceeded the costs by a large margin under a wide range of assumptions. The one-year program showed benefits of seven dollars for every dollar of costs, a benefit–cost ratio of about 7:1, and the two-year program showed a benefit-cost ratio of about 3.6:1 (Barrueta-Clement et al. 1984 p. 60). About 80 percent of the net benefits were received by taxpayers in the form of higher tax contributions and lower expenditures on education, crime, and welfare and by potential crime victims in the form of lower costs for property losses and injuries.

2.3 Higher Educational Loans

A study of benefits and costs for financial aid to stimulate participation in higher education for low-income students has also indicated high benefits relative to costs for government investment (St. John and Masten 1990). This study compared tax revenues generated by the additional income produced by the higher levels of college participation among low-income students with the costs of financial aid that induced these higher enrollments. The net present value of additional tax revenues was four times as great as the cost of the aid program for students in the high school class of 1980. In other words, from the perspective of the federal treasury, such programs had a benefit–cost ratio of 4:1.

2.4 Developing Countries

Cost–benefit analysis has been carried out in education for developing countries by several international agencies including The World Bank (Psacharopoulos and Woodhall 1985). But, usually the analysis is done in the form of a rate-of-return analysis rather than a cost–benefit ratio or net present value. That is, the benefits of the investment are expressed in terms of the equivalent of an annual return on investment rather than in the form of a cost–benefit ratio or a net present value. However, the basic data that are used to estimate internal rates-of-return can be used to calculate net present values or cost–benefit ratios.

See also: Consumption Benefits of Education; Education and Economic Growth; Benefits of Education; Cost Analysis in Education; Returns to Vocational Education in Developing Nations

References

Barnett W S 1985 Benefit-cost analysis of the Perry Preschool Program and its Policy implications. *Educational Evaluation and Policy Analysis* 7(4): 333–42

Becker G S 1964 *Human Capital*. Columbia University Press, New York

Berrueta-Clement J R, Schweinhart L J, Barnett W S, Epstein A S, Weikart D P 1984 *Changed Lives: The Effects of the Perry Preschool Program on Youths Through Age 19*. High/Scope Press, Ypsilanti, Michigan

Eckstein O 1958 *Water-Resource Development: The Economics of Project Evaluation*. Harvard University Press, Cambridge, Massachusetts

Fields G S 1980 Education and income distribution in developing countries: A review of the literature. In: King T (ed.) 1980 *Education and Income*. Staff Working Paper No. 402, The World Bank, Washington DC

Haveman R, Wolfe R 1984 Schooling and economic well-being: The role of nonmarket effects. *J. Hum. Resources* 19(3): 377–407

Leslie L L, Brinkman P T 1988 *The Economic Value of Higher Education*. Macmillan, New York

Levin H M 1972 *The Costs to the Nation of Inadequate Education*. Report of the Select Senate Committee on Equal Educational Opportunity, 92nd US Congress. Government Printing Office, Washington DC

Levin H M 1983 *Cost-Effectiveness: A Primer*. Sage, Beverly Hills, California

Mishan E J 1976 *Cost-Benefit Analysis: An Informal Introduction*. Praeger, New York

Psacharopoulos G, Woodhall M 1985 *Education for Development: An Analysis of Investment Choices*. Oxford University Press, New York

Ribich T I 1969 *Education and Poverty*. Brookings Institution, Washington, DC

St John E P, Masten C L 1990 Return on the federal investment in student financial aid: An assessment for the high school class of 1972. *J. Stud. Financial Aid* 20(3): 4–23

Stern D, Dayton C, Paik I W, Weisberg A 1989 Benefits and costs of dropout prevention in a high school program combining academic and vocational education: Third-year results from replications of the California Peninsula Academies. *Educ. Evaluation and Policy Analysis* 11(4): 405–16

H. M. Levin

Cost-effectiveness Analysis

Cost-effectiveness analysis refers to the consideration of decision alternatives in which both their costs and consequences are taken into account in a systematic way. It is a decision-oriented tool, in that it is designed to ascertain which means of attaining particular educational goals are most efficient. For example, there are many alternative approaches for pursuing such goals as raising reading or mathematics achievement. These include the adoption of new materials or curriculum, teacher training, educational television, computer-assisted instruction, smaller class sizes, and so on. The cost-effective solution to this challenge is to ascertain the costs and effects on reading or mathematics achievement of each alternative and to choose that alternative which has the greatest impact on raising achievement scores for any given resource outlay.

Cost-effectiveness analysis is closely related to cost–benefit analysis in that both represent economic evaluations of alternative resource use and measure costs in the same way (see *Cost-Benefit Analysis*). However, cost–benefit analysis is used to address only those types of alternatives where the outcomes can be measured in terms of their monetary values. For example, educational alternatives that are designed to raise productivity and income, such as vocational education, have outcomes that can be assessed in monetary terms and can be evaluated according to cost–benefit analysis. However, most educational alternatives are dedicated to improving achievement or some other educational outcome that cannot be easily converted into monetary terms. In these cases, one must limit the comparison of alternatives to those that have similar goals by comparing them through cost-effectiveness analysis.

The purpose of cost-effectiveness analysis in education is to ascertain which program or combination of programs can achieve particular objectives at the lowest cost. The underlying assumption is that different alternatives are associated with different costs and different educational results. By choosing those with the least cost for a given outcome, society can use its resources more effectively. Those resources that are saved through using more cost-effective

Table 1
Examples of effectiveness measures

Program objective	Measure of effectiveness
Program completions	Number of students completing program
Reducing dropouts	Number of potential dropouts who graduate
Employment of graduates	Number of graduates placed in appropriate jobs
Student learning	Test scores in appropriate domains utilizing appropriate test instruments
Student satisfaction	Student assessment of program on appropriate instrument to measure satisfaction
Physical performance	Evaluation of student physical condition and physical skills
College placement	Number of students placed in colleges of particular types
Advance college placement	Number of courses and units received by students in advance placement, by subject

approaches can be devoted to expanding programs or to other important educational and social endeavors.

Cost-effectiveness analysis was developed in the 1950s by the United States Department of Defense as a device for adjudicating among the demands of the various branches of the armed services for increasingly costly weapons systems with different levels of performance and overlapping missions (Hitch and McKean 1960). By the 1960s it had become widely used as a tool for analyzing the efficiency of alternative government programs outside of the military, although its applications to educational decisions have been much slower to develop. Indeed, in the early 1990s the use of the tool in considering educational resource allocation is restricted largely to the United States and has not emerged as a decision approach to resource allocation in other countries.

1. Measuring Cost-effectiveness

The basic technique has been to derive results for educational effectiveness of each alternative by using standard evaluation procedures or studies (Rossi and Freeman 1985) and to combine such information with cost data that are derived from the ingredients approach. The ingredients approach was developed to provide a systematic way for evaluators to estimate the costs of social interventions (Levin 1983). It has been applied not only to cost-effectiveness problems, but also to determining the costs of different educational programs for state and local planning (Hartman 1981).

1.1 Assessing Effectiveness

Before starting the cost analysis, it is necessary to know what the decision problem is, how to measure effectiveness, which alternatives are being considered and what their effects are. If a problem has risen on the policy agenda that requires a response, a careful understanding of the problem is crucial to addressing its solution (Levin 1983 pp. 34–35). Once the problem has been formulated, it will be necessary to consider how to assess the effectiveness of alternatives. For this purpose, clear dimensions and measures of effectiveness will be needed. Table 1 shows examples of effectiveness measures that respond to particular program objectives.

Given the problem and criteria for assessing the effectiveness of proposed solutions, it is necessary to formulate alternative programs or interventions. The search for such interventions should be as wide-ranging and creative as possible. This procedure sets the stage for the evaluation of effectiveness of the alternatives, a process which is akin to the standard use of evaluation methods (e.g., Rossi and Freeman 1985). Estimates of effectiveness can be derived from previous evaluations or from tailored evaluations for the present purpose.

It is important to emphasize that the evaluation of effectiveness is separable from the evaluation of costs. Most standard evaluation designs for assessing the effectiveness of an intervention are also suitable for incorporation into cost-effectiveness studies. These can be found in the standard evaluation literature (see e.g., Cook and Campbell 1979, Rossi and Freeman 1985). The cost analysis is not typically found in the general evaluation literature and has been developed independently as a subspecialization (Levin 1983).

1.2 Cost Estimation

The costs of an intervention are defined as the value of the resources that are given up by society to effect the intervention. These are referred to as the ingredients of the intervention, and it is the social value of those ingredients that constitute its overall cost. At a later stage the distribution of these costs among the decision-making agency and other entities can be assessed. Accordingly, the method sets out systematically to identify and ascertain the value of the ingredients that are required for each alternative that is under consideration.

The ingredients approach to cost estimation entails three distinct phases: (a) identification of ingredients; (b) determination of the value or cost of the ingredients and the overall costs of an intervention; and (c) an analysis of the costs in an appropriate decision-oriented framework.

The first step is to ascertain which ingredients are required for an intervention (Levin 1983 Chap. 3). Most educational interventions are labor-intensive, so an initial concern is to account for the number and characteristics of personnel. It is important to stipulate whether personnel are part-time or full-time and the types of skills or qualifications that they need. Beyond this it is necessary to identify the facilities, equipment, materials, and other ingredients or resources which are required for the intervention.

Identification of ingredients requires a level of detail that is adequate to ensure that all resources are included and are described adequately to place cost values on them. For this reason, the search for ingredients must be systematic rather than casual.

The primary sources for such data are written reports, observations, and interviews. Written reports usually contain at least a brief history and description of the intervention. Other sources of information must be used to corroborate and supplement data on ingredients from evaluations and descriptive reports. If the intervention is present at a nearby site, it may be possible to visit and gather additional data on ingredients through observation. A third valuable source is that of interviews, where present or former personnel are asked to identify resources from among a number of different classifications. The three principal types of information—reports, observations, and interviews—can be used to assure the accuracy of the data by comparing the findings from each source and reconciling differences, the process of triangulation.

Once the ingredients have been identified and stipulated, it is necessary to ascertain their costs (Levin 1983 Chap. 4). In doing this, all ingredients are assumed to have a cost, including donated or volunteer resources. That is, they have a cost to someone, even if the sponsoring agency did not pay for them in a particular situation. At a later stage the costs will be distributed among the constituencies who paid them, but at this stage the need is to ascertain the total costs of the intervention.

Ingredients can be divided into those that are purchased in reasonably competitive markets, and those that are obtained through other types of transactions. In general, the value of an ingredient for costing purposes is its market value. In the case of personnel, market value may be ascertained by determining what the costs would be for hiring a particular type of person. Such costs must include not only salary, but also fringe benefits and other employment costs that are paid by the employer. Many of the other inputs can also be costed by using their market prices. These include the costs of equipment, materials, utilities, and so on. Clearly the cost of leased facilities can also be ascertained in this way.

Although the market prices of some ingredients such as personnel can often be obtained from accounting data for educational enterprises, such data are not reliable sources for ascertaining overall program costs. The accounting systems that are used by schools were designed for ensuring consistent reporting to state agencies rather than for providing accurate and consistent cost data on educational interventions. For example, they omit completely or understate the cost of volunteers and other donated resources. Capital improvements are charged to such budgets and accounts during the year of their purchase, even when the improvements have a life of 20–30 years. Normal cost accounting practices would ascertain the annual costs of such improvements by spreading them over their useful lives through an appropriate method (Levin 1983 pp. 67–71). Thus, data from accounting and budgetary reports must be used selectively and appropriately and cannot be relied upon for all ingredients.

There exist a variety of techniques for ascertaining the value of ingredients that are not purchased in competitive markets. For example, the method for ascertaining the value of volunteers and other contributed ingredients is to determine the market value of such resources if they had to be purchased. The value of facilities can be determined by estimating their lease value. The annual value of facilities and equipment can be estimated through a relatively simple approach that takes account of depreciation and interest foregone by the remaining capital investment. Details for these techniques are found in Levin (1983 Chap. 4).

1.3 Combining into Cost-effectiveness

Once each of the ingredients is costed, these can be added to obtain a total cost for the intervention. The next stage entails the use of these costs in an analytic framework (Levin 1983 Chap. 5). The two most important concerns for cost summary and analysis are (a) the appropriate unit for expressing costs and (b) who pays the costs.

Clearly, the question of the appropriate unit for expressing costs depends upon how effectiveness is measured and the nature of the decision. Usually, educational effectiveness is measured in terms of achievement gains per student or some other per-student measure. In that case, it is necessary to convert total costs to a per-student cost figure for comparing cost-effectiveness of alternative interventions. Cost-effectiveness ratios are usually based upon the average effects and costs per student. However, it is possible to do an analysis on total project or program costs and effects. In other cases it may be the additional or marginal costs versus additional or marginal effectiveness that is the subject of scrutiny. For example, one may want to ascertain the number of additional students who will graduate from high school relative to the additional costs of alternative approaches for reducing dropouts.

A very different issue is who pays the costs. The overall cost-effectiveness ratio may be irrelevant to a decision-maker who pays only part of the costs for one intervention, but all of the costs for an alternative. For this reason, it is important to ascertain total costs of an intervention and to separate out those that are borne by the decision-maker in considering different alternatives. However, it should be remembered that since different decision-making units have different opportunities to obtain volunteers and contributed resources, it is inappropriate to assume any particular cost subsidy to the decision-maker. The basic estimate of costs that is used for all subsequent cost analyses is the overall cost of the intervention. Subsequent analyses can distribute the costs among those who will bear them to ascertain the implications of that distribution for decisions.

The most common measure of cost-effectiveness is the cost-effectiveness ratio, namely, the effectiveness of an alternative divided by its cost. When this is done for each alternative, it is possible to see which of the alternatives yields the best outcomes per unit of cost. For example, one might wish to examine different alternatives for raising student achievement by comparing the cost per additional achievement gains. In principle, the alternative with the lowest cost per achievement gain would be the most desirable. However, it is important to know if differences in cost-effectiveness ratios are large or small. If the differences are small, it is probably wise to weigh more fully other criteria in making the decision such as the ease of implementation or previous experience of staff. If the differences in cost-effectiveness are large, it is important to place greater weight on the cost-effectiveness criteria while still considering other factors that were not considered in the analysis.

Finally, it is important to mention the issue of scale. In general, those alternatives with high fixed costs such as those with large investments in facilities and equipment will require a high enrollment or utilization to reach their best cost—effectiveness ratios. The reason for this is that fixed costs represented by a building or an educational television network of transmitters and receiving stations cannot be readily adjusted to demand and must be fully utilized to obtain the lowest level of cost per unit of output. In contrast, alternatives that are constituted largely of variable costs such as personnel will have costs that are less sensitive to the scale of output. Variable costs are derived from inputs or ingredients that can be readily increased or decreased. Thus, a comparison of cost-effectiveness of alternatives that differ in terms of their intensities of fixed versus variable costs may produce very different results depending upon the scale of enrollment or output. Accordingly, estimates should be made among the alternatives for the specific levels of output that are pertinent rather than assuming a general pattern from cost estimation at only one level of scale.

2. Educational Applications

Cost-effectiveness studies have been carried out on teacher training (Tatto et al. 1991), teacher selection (Levin 1970), educational television and radio (Jamison et al. 1978), choice of a mathematics curriculum (Quinn et al. 1984), computer-assisted instruction (Levin et al. 1987) and also increasing the school day, reducing class size, and cross-age tutoring (Levin et al. 1987). Lockheed and Hanushek (1988) have provided a good summary of cost-effectiveness studies of educational radio and of textbook provision for several countries. Their comparisons among studies and interventions should be viewed cautiously given that the studies were done independently for different years (with no standardization for changes in price levels or exchange rates) and are not necessarily based upon the same cost methodology.

2.1 Educational Television

The 1970s witnessed a great interest in educational television as a way of improving educational quality in developing countries, as well as expanding their educational systems (Mayo et al. 1975, Jamison et al. 1978). In many developing societies adequate numbers of trained teachers are unavailable—particularly in rural areas—or populations are so sparsely distributed that there are not adequate numbers of students in school attendance boundaries to justify minimum personnel requirements. Educational television has been viewed as an alternative for delivering instruction that might be less costly and that also might raise the quality of education. Studies were undertaken of educational television as a partial replacement for teachers in rural areas where examination test scores were used as a basis for effectiveness. Such studies found that the television was relatively cost-effective in comparison with traditional schools in that it produced comparable student achievement at lower cost (Mayo et al. 1975). However, these results depended heavily on certain assumptions which were highly controversial, illustrating the fact that cost-effectiveness comparisons must be reviewed carefully before using them for decision-making (Carnoy and Levin 1975).

2.2 Curriculum

Curriculum is an area that is very appropriate for cost-effectiveness analysis. In the quest for educational improvement, schools face numerous ways in which they can organize the pace, content, and method of instruction. Some are likely to be more effective than others, and there may also be substantial differences in resource requirements with respect to such ingredients as teacher time, materials, equipment, and so on. As with many other areas of education, the potential for using cost-effectiveness analysis has barely been tapped in the curriculum field.

An excellent cost-effectiveness study of fifth grade mathematics curriculum was carried out by Quinn et al. (1984). Their evaluation compared two approaches to teaching mathematics, a traditional curriculum and an alternative one. Using the ingredients method, the researchers found that the alternative mathematics program cost about 50 percent more than the traditional mathematics program, but the effectiveness of the alternative program was also higher. Depending upon how student achievement was measured, the alternative mathematics program was found to be from 60 percent to 300 percent more cost-effective—cost per point of achievement score—than the traditional program.

2.3 Teacher Training

A study of teacher training in Sri Lanka compared the cost-effectiveness of training in colleges of education and in teachers' colleges as well as through distance education (Tatto et al. 1991). Teacher performance and pupil achievement were used as measures of effectiveness. Teachers who had received distance education were almost as effective as those trained in colleges of education and teachers' college, but the costs of their training were a small fraction of the costs of institutional training. In a country that has a shortage of teachers, it appears that expansion of qualified teachers could be done more efficiently using distance education.

2.4 General Comparisons of Reform Alternatives

An attempt was made to compare a variety of educational reforms that had been suggested for improving schools in the United States. In the early 1980s, such reports suggested a general reform agenda that included a large variety of alternatives. Levin et al. (1987) investigated four of these for which there were adequate effectiveness data as well as a basis for estimating costs. These four alternatives included computer-assisted instruction (CAI), a longer school day, smaller class sizes, and peer tutoring. Each was associated with acceptable effectiveness studies that had assessed the effects of the reform on student achievement scores at the elementary level in both mathematics and reading.

More specifically, the CAI consisted of daily sessions of 10 minutes of drill and practice on a computer using an approach that has received wide adoption both in the United States and in other countries. The increase in the length of the school day comprised a total of one hour, divided equally between instruction in mathematics and reading. Changes in class size were evaluated for reductions from 35 to 30 students; 30 to 25 students; 25 to 20 students; and 35 to 20 students. Peer tutoring was evaluated for a program in which fifth and sixth grade students tutored second grade students for 15 minutes a day.

Costs were estimated by using the ingredients approach. They were summarized according to the cost per student for each subject. The least costly interventions were reductions in class size of five students and increasing the length of the school day. The most costly was peer tutoring because it requires adult coordinators. The costs of peer tutoring were about four times as great as reducing class size by five students or increasing instructional time by one half hour a day per subject and twice as great as the daily sessions of CAI.

In terms of effectiveness, peer tutoring showed the largest effects, nearly a year of achievement gain in mathematics and about one-half year in reading. The longer school day and reduction of class size by five students showed the smallest effects. CAI was associated with gains in the middle of the range of results.

Cost-effectiveness was determined by combining costs and effectiveness in terms of the estimated annual costs to obtain an additional month of student achievement per year of instruction. According to this study, an additional month of mathematics achievement would cost about US$200 a year with a longer school day, but only about US$22 a year with peer tutoring. In fact, a longer school day was less than half as cost-effective in raising mathematics achievement as was CAI or reducing class size, despite the prominence of calls for longer school days in the national reports on educational reform. The most cost-effective approach, peer tutoring, required only one-ninth of the resources to obtain the same effect on mathematics achievement as increasing the school day.

To obtain an additional month of reading achievement would cost about twice as much for increasing the school day as using peer tutoring, with CAI almost as efficient as the latter. Reducing class size appears to be particularly inefficient with respect to raising reading achievement. Although its effectiveness is very high, its cost is also high. These results provide useful information in comparing instructional strategies to raise achievement.

See also: Education Production Functions; Cost Analysis in Education; Cost-Benefit Analysis

References

Carnoy M, Levin H M 1975 Evaluation of educational media: Some issues *Instr. Sci.* 4(3/4): 385–406

Cook T D, Campbell D T 1979 *Quasi-Experimentation*. Houghton Mifflin, Boston, Massachusetts

Hartman W T 1981 Estimating the costs of educating handicapped children: A resource–cost model approach summary report. *Educ. Eval. Policy Anal.* 3(4): 33–48

Hitch C J, McKean R N 1960 *The Economics of Defense in the Nuclear Age*. Harvard University Press, Cambridge, Massachusetts

Jamison D, Klees S, Wells S 1978 *The Costs of Educational Media: Guiddiness for Planning and Evaluation*. Sage, Beverly Hills, California

Levin H M 1970 Cost-effectiveness analysis of teacher selection. *J. Hum. Resources* 5(1): 24–33

Levin H M 1983 *Cost-Effectiveness: A Primer*. Sage Beverly Hills, California

Levin H M, Glass G V, Meister G 1987 A Cost-effectiveness analysis of computer-assisted instruction. *Eval. Rev.* 11(1): 50–72

Lockheed M E, Hanushek E 1988 Improving educational efficiency in developing countries: What do we know? *Compare* 18(1): 21–38

Mayo J, McAnany E, Klees S 1975 The Mexican telesecundaria: A cost-effectiveness analysis. *Instr. Sci.* 4(3/4): 193–236

Quinn B, VanMondfrans A, Worthen B R 1984 Cost-effectiveness of two math programs as moderated by pupil SES. *Educ. Eval. Policy Anal.* 6(1): 39–52

Rossi P H, Freeman H E 1985 *Evaluation: A Systematic Approach*, 3rd edn. Sage, Beverly Hills, California

Tatto M T, Nielsen D, Cummings W, Kularatna N G, Dharmadasa K H 1991 *Comparing the Effects and Costs of Different Approaches for Educating Primary School Teachers: The Case of Sri Lanka.* Bridges Project, Harvard Institute for International Development, Cambridge, Massachusetts

H. M. Levin

Cost-effectiveness of Training Courses

The question of cost-effectiveness is important for instructional systems, such as training courses in business and industry. This entry discusses the concept of cost-effectiveness in relation to efficiency and productivity, cost factors, and models for analyzing the cost-effectiveness of training courses.

1. *Effectiveness, Efficiency, and Productivity*

Jobs in many organizations are changing rapidly; new duties and tasks are being replaced by old ones, and new jobs are being created. This change causes a multitude of training needs, and organizations respond with a variety of interventions, often labeled human resource development (HRD). Nadler (1984) describes training, education, and development as HRD interventions. Training is an activity aimed at a current job, education is aimed at a future job, and development is aimed at enhancing flexibility of the organization.

This entry will concentrate on training. Employers conceive of training as one human resource development tool that can be integrated into a broad approach of human performance improvement in organizations. McLagan and Bedrick (1983) distinguish the following areas of human resources that employers can use to improve human performance:

(a) organization development: assuring healthy interunit and intraunit relationships and helping groups initiate and manage change;

(b) organization/job design: defining how tasks, authority, and systems will be organized and integrated across organization units and in individual jobs;

(c) human resource planning: determining the organization's major human resource needs, strategies, and philosophies;

(d) selection and staffing: matching people and their career needs and capabilities with jobs and career paths;

(e) personnel research and information systems: assuring a personnel information base;

(f) compensation/benefit: assuring compensation and benefits fairness and consistency;

(g) employee assistance: providing personal problem-solving, counseling to individual employees;

(h) union/labor relations: assuring healthy union–organization relationships;

(i) training and development: identifying, assessing and—through planned learning—helping develop the key competencies (knowledge, skill, attitudes) which enable individuals to perform current or future jobs.

The relatively high costs of training justify closer scrutiny of its cost-effectiveness. Mulder et al. (1991) reported that in a complex training project for several hundreds of counter personnel within the Post Office division of the Dutch Postal Service PTT, a careful analysis and revision of the training program resulted in a cost reduction of over 2 million dollars on a budget of about 20 million dollars.

The concept of cost-effectiveness includes three related terms: effectiveness, efficiency, and productivity. Effectiveness is reached when better results are achieved at the same cost. It is the amount which training enhances in the solution of a performance problem in the organization or in the need for competency development felt by the employees. Efficiency is achieved when a given objective is realized with minimum cost. Productivity is realized when better results are achieved at lower cost.

2. *Cost-effectiveness and Cost–Benefit*

Cost-effectiveness and cost–benefit are concepts that are frequently confused. The difference in their meaning is substantial, and refers to fundamentally different criteria of evaluating training. In both concepts the common element is that of costs. Costs are the financial means that are needed for realizing training in the organization. Cost-effectiveness is the amount to which a given training alternative with an expected level of effectiveness can be realized with a minimum of financial means. Cost–benefit is the relationship between the financial results of training and the costs required to produce these results.

The difference between cost-effectiveness and cost–benefit lies in the outcome component. The effectiveness of a solution is answered in relation to the initial problem, whereas benefits are expressed as a monetary unit. Cost–benefit analysis approaches will not be elaborated in this entry (see *Cost-Benefit Analysis*). Those approaches are less promising than cost-effectiveness because outcomes of training are partly intangible and cost–benefit ratios do not aid the decision as to whether a training course is necessary. Such investment decisions are based on competency needs in the organization, for instance in air transportation, where pilots need extensive training and retraining at high costs. For an airline organization it is less interesting to know what they "gain" from these training programs; the mere knowledge of what they can lose with insufficiently trained professionals is reason enough to justify the considerable training expenditure. The fundamental question is what instructional system guarantees the required performance standards at the lowest cost. This is the cost-effectiveness approach to training:

> Cost-effectiveness . . . is specifically useful for decisions involving the comparison of alternative approaches to a given goal. For such decisions, the dollar costs of the alternatives are generally identified while their effectiveness is considered on a scale chosen to reflect the nature of the particular goal (e.g., achievement test scores). This ability to consider two kinds of measures makes cost-effectiveness analysis a very useful technique but limits its application to the comparison of alternative approaches to the same goal. If choices have to be made between competing goals achieved through completely different activities, then outcomes must be measured in the same units as costs to structure an interpretable comparison. Under such circumstances, the more specialized economic technique of cost-benefit analysis (comparing costs and benefits on identical scales of estimated monetary value) is more appropriate. (Lent 1980 p. 4ff.)

If the instructional design model in an organization comprises human performance analysis, and instruction is (part of) the solution, and training needs analysis results in a specific definition of the outcomes of the instructional system, the costs of the alternatives may be compared to see whether the total expenditure on training can be minimized.

3. *Cost and Effectiveness Factors*

To determine the cost-effectiveness of training courses, costs as well as effectiveness factors have to be distinguished. These factors will be described below.

3.1 Cost Factors

If the costs of training courses are to be analyzed, the first question is what cost factors have to be included. Head and Buchanan (1981) have reduced the cost factors for training courses to a manageable set of five factors: (a) trainee costs, (b) instructor costs, (c) costs of facilities, (d) overhead costs, and (e) instructional development costs. Summation of these cost factors determines the total costs for the training course at the organizational level. The authors have presented a set of formulas for calculating the cost factors and the formula for calculating trainee costs is as follows:

$$\mathrm{T}' = (\mathrm{NT} \times \mathrm{L})(\mathrm{TS} + \mathrm{TPD} + \mathrm{LO}) + \mathrm{NT}(\mathrm{TTC}) \qquad (1)$$

where T' is the total trainee costs; NT is the number of trainees; L is the course length in days (travel time included); TS is the trainee salary per day; TPD is the housing costs per day (housing, meals, tips); LO is the lost opportunity cost per trainee; and TTC is the trainee travel cost (return fare and local travel cost).

Most of the cost factors in this model are clear, but one component needs further clarification: lost opportunity costs. This factor means the productivity loss of trainees and instructors, while they are learning and teaching. When they are not in training, trainees and instructors would have opportunities to increase the productivity of their organization. The quantity of lost opportunities can vary considerably, depending on the job of the trainee and instructor. This ambiguity creates considerable difficulties in calculating the lost opportunity costs. Head and Buchanan (1981) give different examples of practical situations in which lost opportunities are calculated in specific ways. Examples are:

(a) multiplying the salary costs of trainees with an estimated weighting factor;

(b) adding costs of replacements to the salary costs;

(c) dividing the return of the workforce for the organization by the number of employees and adding this amount to the salary costs.

Productivity loss is quite often forgotten in calculating the costs of training, but on a corporate level it can amount to substantial sums of money.

In the list of cost factors that are distinguished in the model, two categories of costs can be differentiated: fixed costs and variable costs. Fixed costs are independent of the number of trainees, and the number of training days. An example of fixed costs is the rent of facilities, and an example of variable costs is the total trainee costs.

3.2 Effectiveness Factors

Smith (1987) distinguished many effectiveness factors that are based upon 28 evaluation studies in various business and industry contexts. This overview presents the scope of the criteria that can be employed to evaluate the impact of training courses. These factors are aimed at studying the relationship between the training course and job performance. The different evaluation studies are compared on five categories: the function of the evaluation, the category of intervention, the productivity standard, the standard for quality of the performance, and the standard for the description of the group workers. *Productivity* refers to the quantity of production per time unit. This can be calculated on different levels: the individual employee, a group of employees, and the whole organization. *Quality* refers to the discrepancy between the actual and the ideal products and services. These discrepancies can be determined by the organization itself, for instance by a quality check within the organization, or by private organizations, customers, or administrative bodies. Quality standards are measured by such matters as the quantity of trash, customers' complaints, machine stoppages, accuracy, and client service. Finally, with a *group of employees*, the stability and the competency profiles of the employees are used for assessment. Standards in this respect are mobility (to other employers), absenteeism, complaints, and promotions or lateral transfers.

The study performed by Smith (1987) comprises a broad scope of jobs, varying from production to service personnel in the automotive trade, inspectors of machine parts, extruder operators, assembly-line workers, welders, welding inspectors, and car-tire salespeople, to production supervisors, programmers, bank employees, and branch managers. The types of training vary considerably too, from on-the-job training and "job aids" to all kinds of off-the-job training courses on different topics. On the basis of this study, effectiveness standards are distinguished for productivity, performance quality, and the group of employees.

Effectiveness of training courses can be evaluated at different system levels. Mulder (1992) distinguishes the supra-, macro-, meso-, and microlevel. The supralevel denotes the business environment, the macrolevel the business as such with respect to the training department, the mesolevel the training department itself, and the microlevel denotes the learning and instruction process. Training course effectiveness can be determined at the micro-, meso-, and macrolevel. It is not practicable to think of evaluating the training course effectiveness at the supralevel, for this would require searching for training impact at the business environment level. Although there may be a certain amount of impact, it seems impossible to isolate the training factors from various other factors that influence the business environment, such as the world economy and politics. It is also extremely complicated to isolate the training course effectiveness at corporate level, as other interventions in the organization, such as corporate strategy, organizational structure, and human relations, make it almost impossible to separate the training factor from intervening variables. Measuring training course effectiveness at the micro-, meso-, and macrolevel in organizations implies testing learning results, job performance results, and organizational results.

4. Models for Determining the Cost-effectiveness of Training Courses

There are several models for determining the cost-effectiveness of training courses. On the one hand a cost-effectiveness analysis can be conceived of as a problem-solving strategy, on the other hand it can be seen as the cost-effectiveness calculation technique. One example of each category will be described below.

4.1 Cost-effectiveness Analysis as a Problem-solving Strategy

Performing a cost-effectiveness analysis of training courses is a complex task. In many cases, business and industry do not keep records of training data. Recommendations to plan and implement cost-effectiveness studies as a problem-solving strategy are given by Doughty and Lent (1987). Their perspective on cost-effectiveness analysis consists of a problem-solving perspective. They suggest the following six steps in planning and implementing cost-effectiveness studies: (a) describing the context, (b) determining discrepancies between the actual and the ideal situation, (c) identification of criteria, (d) clarification of alternatives, (e) defining the solution, and (f) justification of the solution. In many cases the initial stages of cost-effectiveness studies are neglected. Doughty (1986) developed a procedural guideline structured by five questions: (a) what are the goals of the study? (b) what is the nature of the target group of the study? (c) who will be designing and implementing the study? (d) what are the essential design elements? (e) what methods will be used?

4.2 Cost-effectiveness Calculation

Cost-effectiveness calculation can be performed for *a priori* investment justification or for *a posteriori* investment evaluation. *A priori* calculation, or precalculation of the potential cost-effectiveness, is done in the context of determining objectives for the training course, establishing achievement or performance standards, selecting or designing training course alternatives, determining expected effects, and comparing the costs of the alternatives. The cheapest alternative that yields the minimum acceptable quality will be chosen for implementation or development. *A posteriori* calculation, or postcalculation, is performed by analyzing achievement or performance objectives, assessing effects of the training course (on the level of trainee satisfaction, learning gains, performance results, or organizational effects). Costs and effects are calculated separately, because the units in which these variables are expressed are different.

The costs of training courses can be calculated with costing forms such as the one described by Spencer (1984). Swanson and Sleezer (1987) developed a practical system for training effectiveness evaluation

(TEE) which can be employed as an example of how to determine training course effects. This system consists of three components: an evaluation plan, a toolkit for measuring the effectiveness of the training course, and an evaluation report.

5. Conclusion

Cost-effectiveness analysis is fundamentally different from cost–benefit analysis. The former is the more promising analysis approach to assess the value of training courses to organizations. Cost–benefit analysis assumes that the benefits of training can be measured in monetary units, which is usually of less interest because of the qualitative nature of the training results for the individual and the organization.

See also: Cost-effectiveness Analysis; Cost Analysis in Education

References

Doughty P L 1986 *Planning Cost-effectiveness Studies of Training Development and Implementation: A Procedure Guide.* Area of Instructional Design, Development and Evaluation, Syracuse University, Syracuse, New York

Doughty P L, Lent R M 1987 *Case Studies of the Cost Justification of Interactive Applications in Key Industries in Interactive Video in Education.* Area of Instructional Design, Development and Evaluation, Syracuse, Syracuse University, Syracuse, New York

Head G E, Buchanan C C 1981 Cost/benefit analysis of training: A foundation for change. *NSPI Journal* (November): 25–27

Lent R M 1980 An examination of the methods of cost-effectiveness analysis as applied to instructional technology. Unpublished doctoral dissertation. Area of Instructional Design, Development and Evaluation, Syracuse University, Syracuse, New York

McLagan P A, Bedrick D 1983 Models for excellence: The results of the ASTD training and development competency study. *Train. Dev. J.* 37(6): 10–20

Mulder M 1992 Toward a comprehensive framework on training and development in business and industry. *Int. J. Lifelong Educ.*

Mulder M, Spitholt W E, Barents A M C 1991 Cost-effectiveness of curriculum revision. *Journal of European Industrial Training* 15(7): 8–16

Nadler L (ed.) 1984 *The Handbook of Human Resource Development.* Wiley, New York.

Smith M E 1987 Measuring results. In: Craig R L (ed.) 1987 *Training and Development Handbook. A Guide to Human Resource Development*, 3rd ed. McGraw-Hill, New York

Spencer L M Jr 1984 How to calculate the costs and benefits of an HRD program. *Training* 21(7): 40–51

Swanson R A, Sleezer C M 1987 Training effectiveness evaluation. *Journal of European Industrial Training.* 11(4): 7–16

Further Reading

Cascio W F 1982 *Costing Human Resources: The Financial Impact of Behavior in Organizations.* Van Nostrand Reinhold, New York

Cohen S I 1985 S Cost-benefit analysis of industrial training. *Econ. Educ. Rev.* 4(4): 327–39

Jackson T 1989 *Evaluation: Relating Training to Business Performance.* Kogan Page, London

Kearsly G 1982 *Costs, Benefits, and Productivity in Training Systems.* Addison-Wesley, Reading, Massachusetts

Niemic R, Baker E T 1987 *Cost-effectiveness in Business and Industrial Training.* Temple University, Center for Research in Human Development and Education, Philadelphia, Pennsylvania

Schmidt F L, Hunter J E, Pearlman K Assessing the economic impact of personnel programs on workforce productivity. *Personnel Psychology* 35: 333–47

Spencer L M Jr 1986 *Calculating Human Resource Costs and Benefits. Cutting Costs and Improving Productivity.* Wiley, New York.

Swanson R A, Gradous D B 1988 *Forecasting Financial Benefits of Human Resource Development.* Jossey-Bass, San Francisco, California

M. Mulder

Costa Rica: System of Education

1. General Background

Costa Rica is a country of 50,900 square kilometers located in Central America, bordering on Nicaragua in the north, Panama in the southeast, the Caribbean Sea in the east, and the Pacific Ocean in the west. Costa Rica gained independence from Spain in 1821 and emerged as a state after the break-up of the Federal Republic of Central America in 1829. Education has been a cornerstone of the political and economic system of Costa Rica and an important foundation for one of the oldest democracies in the region.

For many years, Costa Rica has had higher literacy and school enrollment rates than its neighbours in Central America and other Latin American countries. In 1990, only 7 percent of the population was illiterate and the average number of years of schooling of the population aged 25 years or over was 5.7. In 1990, Costa Rica had a population of 3,015,000, of which 47 percent lived in urban areas. Population growth between 1980 and 1988 was 2.8 percent. Some 36 percent of the population was aged 14 years or less. Most of the population is of European descent from the colonial period, with the exception of some regions in the Atlantic coast populated by Blacks who came from the Carribbean at the end of last century. Spanish is the prevalent language.

The Gross National Product (GNP) per capita in 1989 was US$1,780. In terms of the Gross Domestic Product (GDP), 17 percent came from agriculture, 27 percent from industry, and 56 percent from services. In 1983, 10 percent of the population in urban areas lived on only 1.1 percent of the income, while 10 percent received 40 percent of the income. The poorest 50 percent of the population lived on 19 percent of the income. The distribution of income is not significantly different in rural areas. The predominantly agricultural economy of Costa Rica is structured in a variety of patterns of land ownership, with many small and medium-sized farms. In 1973, about 55 percent of the owners had plots of 200 hectares or more, 4 percent had plots smaller than 9 hectares, 4 percent had plots from 10–19 hectares, 25 percent had plots between 20–99 hectares, and 13 percent from 100–199 hectares.

During the 1980s, Costa Rica experienced a severe economic crisis which saw a deterioration in living conditions which also affected the education sector. This crisis originated in the major slump in coffee prices in 1978 (coffee is the main commodity export of the country), the deterioration of demand of the Central American Common Market, oil crises, recession in the United States, and the debt crisis. The public debt increased from US$134 million in 1970 to US$3,480 million in 1989. In 1989, the total external debt was equal to 236 percent of the exports of goods and services and 91 percent of GNP, and debt servicing was 19 percent of exports of goods and services. Since 1980, the country has had seven stabilization/adjustment loans with the IMF and three with the World Bank. The exchange rate went from 8.6 colones per US$1 in the 1970s to 120.6 colones per US$1 in 1991; inflation reached 51 percent in the early 1980s. GNP growth which had averaged 2.5 percent in the 1970s became negative in the 1980s.

2. Politics and the Goals of the Education System

In the mid-nineteenth century, Costa Rica embarked on a liberal democratization project, of which education was a mainstay. The Constitution devised in 1869 established that primary education should be free and compulsory, under the direction of the municipalities. Between 1870 and 1882, the country was ruled by a dictatorship. From 1882 to 1888, education received a new stimulus from the Minister of Education Mauro Fernandez, a lawyer who had written extensively on the role of education in society. He proposed an education reform that would proceed in stages, addressing first primary education, then sceondary education, and lastly university. In 1885, a general Law of Education was passed, influenced by the ideas of Fernandez. The Law aimed to centralize educational administration which until then was in the hands of the municipalities.

Between 1908 and 1948, several reforms, influenced by the ideas of the "active school" were carried out to make schools instruments for national development. The curriculum was simplified to make it more relevant to everyday life, and education began to be perceived as an instrument for national development.

José Figueres, who won the Civil War of 1948, laid the foundations of modern Costa Rica. The Constitution approved in 1949 gave education a preeminent role. In the same year, the national armed services were abolished—in a symbolic act, the keys to the main military barracks were given to the Minister of Education. A new Law of Education was passed in 1957 to promote the reform and development of the education system.

Since 1953, Costa Rica has had democratic governments with a strong social democratic agenda. The Costa Rican social democracy, represented by the *Partido de Liberación Nacional* (PLN) (established by José Figueres) has virtually controlled the legislature and alternated in the presidency with a coalition of smaller parties espousing neoliberal views. The platform of the PLN assigns the state the role of main agent in the promotion of development and general welfare. The Party espouses heavy state intervention in the economy and an aggressive social welfare policy.

The Costa Rican Constitution establishes that basic education is mandatory and free. Preschool and secondary education are also free. University students pay nominal tuition fees. The Constitution also establishes that the state will help students without means to pursue higher education and will provide food and clothing to poor students at the basic levels.

Though there has been much continuity in the goals assigned to the education system under democracy, personalism and the lack of institutional development account for substantial policy discontinuities with every change of minister. In 1970–71, a plan for education development was prepared as a result of a broad-based national consultation. This plan was the result of analytic work of 18 committees which involved ministry staff, the planning ministry, the teacher union, retired teachers, and the university. A total of 16 working sessions were organized in the 14 regions of the country to promote participation of community representatives in the diagnosis and programming of the plan. The plan had three main objectives: (a) to raise average levels of education of the population, (b) to modernize the education system to meet the needs of economic development, and (c) to maintain the present share of education in the budget. A new system of basic education was created which included the old primary education of 6 years and the first cycle of secondary of 3 years. These 9 years were proposed as the minimum level of education for all the population and the National Constitution was amended in 1973 to include this extension of mandatory education from 6 to 9 years.

The teachers' unions, however, opposed the plan for the proposed education reform and embarked on a strike which lasted until the election of 1973. Although the *Partido de Liberación Nacional* won the election, the new Minister of Education was from a different faction of the Party and hence shelved the numerous reforms proposed in the document, which never reached schools and classrooms. The new Education Law proposed in this plan was never passed by Congress:

> Thus, three years after exceptional national efforts supported by considerable international assistance had been deployed in a movement which the Minister hoped would make history, changes in the classrooms were few and far between. Mention of the Plan now evoked no more than cynical smiles or regretful sighs. (Lourie 1989 p.108)

3. *The Formal System of Education*

The education system is structured in the formal system and in the parallel system. The formal system includes four levels: preschool education of two years' duration, nine years basic education divided into three cycles of three years each, diversified secondary education which may last two years (academic branch) or three years (technical branch), and higher education. Special education is also offered in the three cycles of general basic education. In practice, the first two cycles of basic education are typically offered in the same institutions while the last cycle is offered in the same secondary schools offering secondary diversified education; this reflects the institutional arrangements of the pre-reform model of 5–6 years.

The parallel system includes adult education administered by the Ministry of Education and vocational education administered by the National Institute for Learning (*Instituto Nacional de Aprendizaje*).

3.1 Primary, Secondary, and Tertiary Education

There have been sustained improvements in the expansion of education since the early 1960s. The number of primary school teachers and schools doubled between 1960 and 1990, while the number of secondary schools increased fourfold and the number of secondary schools doubled. The percentage of the population with incomplete primary education decreased from 75 percent in 1960 to 25 percent in 1990. The percentage of illiterate population aged 15 and over declined from 11.6 in 1973 to 7.4 in 1984. Figure 1 and Table 1 summarize basic statistics of the formal education system.

In 1990, 90 percent of the relevant age group was enrolled in basic education. Most of the enrollments in the first six years (94%) and in the last cycle of basic education (84%) are in public schools. While all children enter school in Grade 1, only 80 percent complete six years; 99 percent of 8-year olds are enrolled in school. There are wide regional disparities in educational opportunity. While half of those children who enter Grade 1 complete the nine years of basic education in San José, only one student in four will complete the cycle in regions which are predominantly rural (e.g., Coto and Perez Zeledón). This is related to the fact that there are proportionately more untrained teachers and multigrade schools in rural areas. While only 5 percent of the schools have only one teacher in San José, in areas like Coto this figure is 49 percent. While 31 percent of the schools in the country have only one teacher, in rural areas this figure is 45 percent.

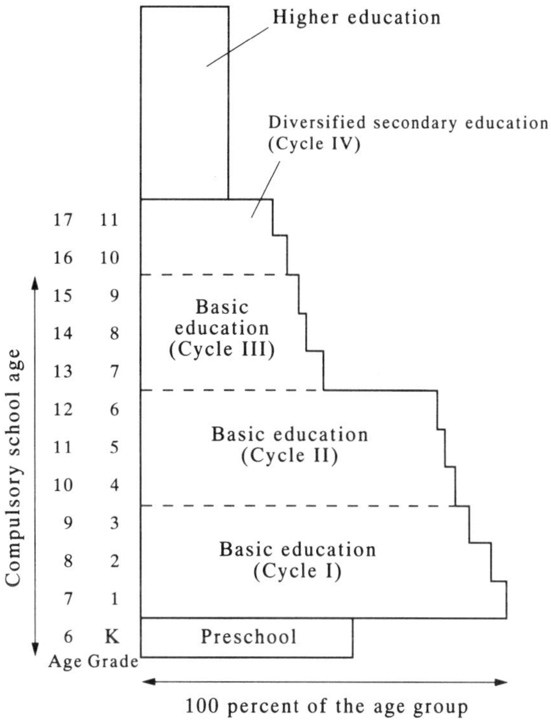

Figure 1
Costa Rica: Structure of the formal education system 1991

Grade repetition is a serious constraint on internal efficiency. Over 20 percent of the students in Grade 1 repeat. In basic education, the estimated cost of grade repetition is US$11 million. However, 90 percent of the students stay in school for at least five years. Among the students who complete the basic cycle, 10 percent do it after repeating three or more times. On average, students need 1.2 years to pass one year in school (Schiefelbein and Heikkinen 1992).

Students are learning too little, as indicated by the results of achievement tests administered in 1987 to students in Grades 4 and 12; less than 30 percent of the students passed those tests of basic subjects. The scores of rural students were 37 percent below those of urban students.

In theory the school year lasts 171 days, though in practice there is wide variation between regions. The school day lasts 4.5 hours in double-shift schools, which represent the majority (98.4%). The curriculum assumes 925 lesson hours a year of 40 minutes

Table 1
Enrollments in Costa Rica 1990

Level	Students	Teachers	Schools
Preprimary	50,377	2,373	755
Primary (cycles I-II)	422,021	15,671	3,236
Secondary	—	8,160	247
cycle III	104,807	—	—
cycle IV	42,214	—	—
Higher			
university	65,531	3,954	13
other	9,483	—	4
Expenditure per student (colones)[a]			
Preschool		20,545.21	
Primary		23,143.91	
Lower secondary		38,861.64	
Higher secondary		41,721.92	
University		123,985.83	

Source: World Bank 1991 *Staff Appraisal Report: Costa Rica*
a Unit costs were computed dividing total public education expenditures per level in 1990 over public enrollment in that level (in 1990, 91.58 colones = US$1).

each. Urban schools provide 29 lesson hours per week of 48 minutes each, for a total of 600 lesson hours per year. In schools taught by a single teacher, teaching time is divided among the different grades, hence students receive 22 lesson hours of 40 minutes each, while per year they receive an average of 450 lesson hours.

While enrollment in private institutions amounts to a very small share of total enrollments (5%), the number of students in private schools increased 73 percent between 1980 and 1987 as a response to the widespread perception of declining quality in public schools.

The economic crisis of the 1980s affected secondary education the most dramatically. Salaries of secondary school teachers declined 42 percent between 1980 and 1987. Only 61 percent of the students who complete basic education go on to secondary, and 41 percent of the relevant age group is enrolled in this level. In 1990, there were 42,214 students in secondary schools, of whom 8 percent are in private institutions.

Enrollments at this level declined by 20 percent between 1980 and 1988. The subsector was influenced by disproportionate cuts in public expenditures, by the number of students who dropped out in order to contribute to the household economy, and by the increase in the price of school supplies.

There are four public and nine private universities, and four public institutes of higher education. In 1990, there were 2,478 university students for every 100,000 persons in the country, or 25 percent of the relevant age group. Enrollments in Universities are disproportionately from higher-income groups; 43 percent of those enrolled belong to families in the top quintile of the income distribution, while only 10 percent come from the bottom quintile of the income distribution.

In the early 1970s, a university reform attempted to increase the equality of educational opportunity in higher education to all income groups. A study of that reform, however, found that even though more students from lower-income groups were admitted, the system became more stratified, with a higher proportion of well-to-do students gaining access to better universities. The reform did not change the distribution of students from different social groups (Mendiola 1989).

Enrollment trebled in the 1970s. The University of Costa Rica was converted into a multi-campus university. Most of the expansion in enrollments took place in satellite campuses, and the University of Costa Rica became more socially homogeneous. While 22 percent of entering students in 1972 came from private schools, in 1979, 33 percent of the new entrants came from private schools.

3.2 Preschool Education

Preschool education lasts one or two years and takes place in special centers or in classrooms attached to a primary school. There are 50,377 students enrolled in this level, of which 11 percent attend private institutions. Some 58 percent of the 5-year olds are enrolled in preschool institutions. The government has given priority to expansion at this level, and between 1980 and 1987 enrollments grew at an annual rate of 10 percent per year. The decline in birth rates has allowed services to expand at this level and for the relocation of primary school teachers.

3.3 Special Education

There is public special education at each of the three

cycles of the basic education level. All special education takes place in special classrooms in regular schools; there is no mainstreaming in Costa Rica. In 1987, there were 10,478 special education students of which 86 percent lived in urban areas, and 531 teachers worked in these special education classrooms.

3.4 Technical, Adult, and Nonformal Education

Technical education is provided by the Ministry of Education and by the National Institute of Learning (INA). A technical stream exists for lower secondary (the last cycle of basic education) and higher secondary, in which students learn technical job-related skills in addition to the academic curriculum. Technical education receives 7 percent of all expenditures of the Ministry of Education. In addition, INA is financed by a 2 percent payroll tax

Enrollments in the Ministry's adult education classes decreased sharply during the 1980s, from 43,329 in 1980 to 28,343 in 1987. The number of teachers declined from 1,270 to 1,178 in the same period, and the number of schools from 92 to 59.

INA provides two types of training: apprenticeship and on-the-job training. Apprenticeship is a three-year program including education for students 15–20 years of age (e.g., carpentry). After completing the program, students are placed as apprentices in industry. This program includes instruction of basic and secondary education and provides funding to the students. On-the-job training is provided in the form of short courses lasting less than 6 months. There have been a number of changes in INA in the last few years to make it more responsive to an increasingly open economy. For example, public workshops in poor communities teach skills such as masonry, metal mechanics, welding, carpentry, and so forth, in which by using equipment from the INA, community members build products which are then sold in the local market. INA is also promoting micro-enterprise development, helping small entrepreneurs establish their own firms.

4. Administrative and Supervisory Structure and Operation

The state manages education through the Ministry of Education, the universities, and the *Instituto Nacional de Aprendizaje* (INA). The National Education Council is the highest education authority in the country. It includes the Ministers of Education and Planning and Economy, representatives from the universities, the national council of rectors, and the INA. The Ministry of Education is responsible for the implementation of policies designed by the National Education Council and it administers public education at the preschool, basic, and secondary levels. The Ministry is also responsible for the supervision of education in private institutions.

Universities are administered autonomously. There is a National Council of University Presidents which, together with the National Planning Office, coordinate education policy at that level. The National Institute of Learning (INA) is an autonomous institution, financed from a 2 percent tax on the payroll.

The Ministry of Education is organized into 5 divisions, 23 directorates, and 39 departments. It has a staff of 31,572, of which 87 percent are teachers. There are 17 regional directorates. Each regional directorate is nominally in charge of all basic and secondary schools in the area. Each region is divided into 5 to 12 districts each containing some 20 schools. Each district is administered by a school supervisor and each school has an association, made up of parents and the principal, that is responsible for oversight of school expenditures and the mobilization of resources.

In practice, administration is highly centralized as suggested by the fact that 90 percent of the administrative staff work out of the capital city, San José. All personnel management, school supervision, and resource allocation decisions are all made in the Ministry offices in San José.

Operating procedures in the Ministry are outmoded and inefficient. Many systems of information and control rely on old manual-based procedures, and computer equipment is rarely used. Budgeting is a process lacking all rationality, since the input of regional directorates is minimal. Budget requests are prepared by the Ministry in San José based on a 10 percent increment formula every year.

5. Educational Finance

Between 1980 and 1985, education expenditures in real terms declined 33 percent, and decreased from 26 percent of the government budget in 1980 to 22 percent in 1989. As a percentage of the GNP, they fell from 5.6 percent in 1980 to 4 percent in 1989.

The decline in education expenditures have affected the primary level disproportionately. Expenditures for this level declined from 66 percent in 1980 to 60 percent in 1989. Transfers to the universities increased from 22 percent of the education budget in 1980 to 36 percent in 1989, partly as a result of a constitutional provision that establishes a special fund for higher education which cannot be abolished nor reduced. Increases in primary school enrollment, together with decreases in resources for this level, reduced per pupil spending at this level by 32 percent between 1980 and 1988. Capital expenditures were slashed, declining from 23 percent of total education expenditures in 1980 to 1 percent in 1989. About 3 percent of education expenditures goes to administration, 35 percent to higher education, 58 percent to basic education, and the rest to other programs. The economic crisis which affected the sector severely constrained all nonsalary expenditures, with consequent declines in quality. For instance, no new textbooks have been printed since 1984. Parents are asked to contribute 1,000 colones per year in primary school toward school supplies. In addition, the cost of notebooks, supplies, and uniforms add up to 7000 colones per year, which, added to the per pupil expenditure reported in Table 1, suggests that families bear over 20 percent of direct primary education costs in public schools. This share is higher in secondary education.

6. *Supplying Personnel for the Education System*

In 1990, there were 21,535 teachers working in 3,551 schools. Of these teachers, 13,651 taught in primary education and the rest in secondary schools.

In response to fiscal austerity affecting the sector, teacher salaries for primary level declined 33 percent between 1980 and 1987. As a result, the quality of education has continued to decline. For instance, enrollment growth between 1981 and 1989 was served with an increased number of untrained teachers. Of the 6,200 teachers hired during this period 44 percent were untrained ("*aspirantes*"). An achievement test administered to some of these *aspirantes* showed that only 10 percent of them attained pass marks in the four basic subjects at a Grade 6 level.

In 1989, 23 percent of the primary school teachers were untrained, with most of them teaching in rural and urban-marginal areas.

Since 1986, the Ministry of Education has developed a program where untrained teachers sign a contract committing themselves to enroll in a one-year certification program while they teach. Classes take place at weekends and during the summer. There is a shortfall in the output of the training programs which currently train 588 new teachers every year, while 1,377 new teachers will be required annually between 1991 and 1996.

7. *Curriculum Development and Teaching Methodology*

Curriculum development is the responsibility of the Ministry of Education. This curriculum is followed in all schools in the country. The Ministry inspects and approves all textbooks, to assess that they conform to the national curriculum.

In 1990, the Ministry carried out a curriculum reform in basic education which emphasizes core subjects while adding a strong social curriculum focusing on ecology, health, and values education.

The document which outlines the new curriculum policy emphasizes the role of learning from real life activities, as well as having a regional emphasis and a student-centered learning approach. The new curriculum highlights the importance of teaching using democratic approaches, active and participatory learning, and assessment focused in products as well as processes (Ministerio de Educación 1991b). To implement the curriculum reform, the Ministry printed new programs for each subject and various teacher guides, such as the book entitled *The Teaching and Learning Processes in a Democratic Society* which was distributed to all teachers. An additional mechanism to implement the new curriculum are the new textbooks which will be produced under the new education reform.

8. *The System of Examination, Promotions, and Certifications*

Promotion from one grade to the next, at all levels of education, depends on the grades given by the teacher based on performance throughout the year and in a final examination in each subject.

Costa Rica was one of the first Latin American countries to experiment with automatic promotion in basic education in the 1960s. Within each of the cycles, students were automatically promoted from one grade to the next. In addition, the entrance examination to secondary education was eliminated. Many educators in Costa Rica attribute to this the decline of the quality of education—more students were promoted but with less effective knowledge.

Concern with the decline in the quality of education stimulated the research carried by the University of Costa Rica at the request of the Ministry of Education, which developed criterion tests in all basic subjects (Spanish, mathematics, science, and social studies) to be administered to all students at the end of each cycle of basic education and at the end of secondary education. These tests were used for certification and university entrance. All students were tested in 1986 and 1987, and a random sample was tested in 1989. One of the consequences of the widespread concern generated by the poor performance of students in the basic achievement tests administered in 1987 was a revision of the system of promotion. At the end of each of the cycles of basic education, students will be tested in all basic subjects and a minimum passing score will be required for promotion to the next grade. Similarly, at the end of secondary education, students will be required to pass the test. While the original idea was to implement a national test to determine promotion, there has been a shift toward tests developed by each district on the basis of national criteria. These tests establish a minimum level required to graduate from primary and secondary school. The final grade received by each student is a combination of 50 percent of the test score and 50 percent continuous evaluation from the teacher.

9. *Educational Assessment, Evaluation, and Research*

Although there is a research unit ascribed to the

planning division in the Ministry of Education, there is very limited research and policy analysis capacity within the Ministry. Research was one of the activities which was devalued during the economic crisis of the 1980s.

The Ministry collects standard educational data (enrollments, teachers) and computes a number of indicators (e.g., completion and repetition rates) of internal efficiency. In addition, there has been experience administering national achievement tests, and the education reform in operation in the early 1990s proposes establishing a regular system to monitor student performance.

The University has an Institute of Educational Research (*Instituto de Investigaciones para el Mejoramiento de la Educación en Costa Rica*) which has produced a number of influential reports, focusing especially on the low levels of achievement of students and teachers.

By and large, decision-making is informed by political and other considerations and technical analysis plays a relatively unimportant role in this process.

10. Major Reforms in the 1980s and 1990s

In spite of the financial strain on the education sector, there has been innovation and experimentation in Costa Rica to try to address the fundamental problems of inefficiency and inequity facing the education system.

In 1986, the Ministry of Education started an experiment in community participation in the formulation of the curriculum in the rural region of Los Santos. This coffee-producing area, 70 kilometers south of San José, was characterized by low completion rates in basic education, and the Ministry assumed that this was due to the fact that the curriculum was irrelevant to this community. This action-research project was launched to identify appropriate planning methodologies to design a curriculum responsible to local needs. The core of the experiment were a series of consultations and community mobilization activities which helped to design a profile of basic learning needs.

During the 1980s, the government financed the creation of a foundation (the Omar Dengo Foundation) chartered to develop a five-year experiment to introduce computers in some schools. This project was continued with subsequent funding from the World Bank and the Inter-American Development Bank in the 1990s. It was initially implemented in about 1,000 primary schools which were provided with Logo software, microcomputers, and teacher training. Pupils receive 80 minutes of Logo instruction per week. In addition, the Ministry established the Costa Rican Scientific Colleges, which are schools for gifted children.

As mentioned earlier, the Ministry supported several exercises to assess student performance which were carried by the University of Costa Rica. The ultimate aim is to establish a national testing system.

In 1990, Costa Rica requested and received loans from the Inter-American Development Bank (US$28 million) and the World Bank (US$23 million) to finance a program to improve the quality of basic education and to strengthen management in the Ministry of Education. An additional US$10.5 million of local financing went toward the project. This project will involve school repair and maintenance, curriculum development, textbook and teaching materials development including school libraries, teacher training, assessment systems, computers in schools, and management development in the Ministry of Education.

In 1991, the Ministry of Education initiated a reform which would devolve some of the administrative functions to the regions. The current system of administration based on 17 regions would be replaced by one of 6 regions, 12 subregions, and 150 zones. In 1992, the Ministry developed a new curriculum for basic education as a result of studies and a consultation to students, teachers, parents, university faculty, and private firms. There are four new areas that have been added to the curriculum: ecology, cultural revitalization, personal and collective security, and health and nutrition. Values education is included in the last three areas.

11. Major Problems for the Year 2000

Costa Rica faces the challenge of repositioning education at the core of its strategy of economic and political development. While the education sector has enjoyed this position since the consolidation of the modern Costa Rican state, the economic crisis of the 1980s took a severe toll in the education sector. The morale of teachers fell, partly as a result of lower teacher salaries, but especially as a result of continued confrontations between the Ministry of Education and the Teachers' Union. As part of the increasing confrontation, the Ministry blamed the teachers for the low achievement scores in the tests administered at the end of the 1980s.

The education sector's response to the adjustment programs made the distribution of benefits of public spending in education among income groups more inequitable. While 30 percent of the poorest households captured 31 percent of the education resources in 1977, by 1986 their share had declined to 27 percent. In contrast, 40 percent of the richest households increased their share from 38.6 percent in 1977 to 45.4 percent in 1986 (World Bank 1990).

A major challenge for the year 2000 will be the financing of necessary improvements in efficiency and equity in basic education. This will involve issues of overall allocations to education within the public budget, but especially the need to redistribute the education budget to make it more equitable. This requires exploring options to generate additional resources for higher education.

The decline in the working conditions of teachers, and the sustained confrontations between the Ministry of Education and the teachers' unions are likely to have a negative effect on the quality of education. This has resulted in the most highly trained teachers looking for alternative jobs. Furthermore, the signaling value of salaries is likely to further lower the quality of the supply of teachers in the future. The implicit policy in operation in the early 1990s of replacing teachers with candidates with lower levels of formal education, and providing them with short periods of inservice training, has yet to show its merits.

The education reforms initiated in 1991, and the attempts to enhance a social curriculum that place a premium on educating for democracy, are positive signs in the direction of helping the sector recuperate from the devastating damage of the 1980s.

As the political and economic situation improves in the Central American region, it might be easier for Costa Rica to return to human development as a central pillar of its democratic project. Solving the challenges of low efficiency and equity of the education sector will be a true test of the commitment to that project.

References

Lourie S 1989 *Education and Development: Strategy and Decisions in Central America.* UNESCO, Paris

Mendiola H 1989 Reform of higher education in Costa Rica: Effects on social stratification and labor markets. *Comp. Educ. Rev.* 33(3): 334–56

Ministerio de Educación Pública 1991b *Sintesis de la Política Curricular.* Ministerio de Educación, San José

Schiefelbein E, Heikkinen S 1992 Costa Rica: Acceso, permanencia y eficiencia en la educación básica. UNESCO-OREALC, Santiago (Unpublished manuscript)

World Bank 1990 *Costa Rica. Public Sector Social Spending.* World Bank, Washington, DC

World Bank 1991a *Staff Appraisal Report. Costa Rica: Basic Education Rehabilitation Project.* World Bank, Washington, DC

Further Reading

Carnoy M, Torres C 1991 Educational change and structural adjustment: A case study of Costa Rica. (Unpublished manuscript)

Horn R, Wolff L, Velez E 1991 *Developing Educational Assessment Systems in Latin America.* LATHR Regional Studies Program No. 9. World Bank, Washington, DC

Ministerio de Educación Pública 1990a *Serie de Documentos del Proyecto de Planificación Educativa.* Ministerio de Educación, San José

Ministerio de Educación Pública 1990b *Plan General de Educación. 1990–1994.* Ministerio de Educación, San José

Ministerio de Educación Pública 1991a *Memoria Anual de Labores 1990.* Ministerio de Educación, San José

Ministerio de Educación Pública 1991c *Programas de Estudios.* Ministerio de Educación, San José

Pérez Cordoba R et al. 1991 *Los Procesos de Enseñanza y Aprendizaje en una Sociedad Democrática.* Ministerio de Educación, San José

Reimers F 1991 The impact of economic stabilization and adjustment on education in Latin America. *Comp. Educ. Rev.* 35(2): 319–53

Rojas Y 1984 The politics of an educational reform process in Costa Rica: A case study. Unpublished doctoral dissertation, University of Wisconsin, Madison, Wisconsin

Sanguinetty J 1988 *La educación general en Costa Rica: La Crisis y sus posibles soluciones.* Development Technologies, San José

UNESCO-OREALC (annual) *Situación Educativa de América Latina y el Caribe. 1980–1987.* UNESCO-OREALC, Santiago

World Bank 1991b *World Development Report 1991.* Oxford University Press, New York

F. Reimers

Costs of Continuing Education: Industrialized Countries

The costs of continuing education are related to important issues such as the scope, amount, and profitability of investment in continuing education, the cost-effectiveness and financial feasibility of alternative programs, and the planning and management of continuing education programs. Despite substantial resources devoted to continuing education in industrialized countries, cost analysis still remains a neglected area in continuing education in these countries. By drawing upon studies in industrialized countries, this entry discusses several aspects of the costs of continuing education including: definition and classification of costs, amount of spending, determinants of costs, applications of cost analysis, and emerging cost issues.

1. Definition and Classification

The costs of continuing education refer to the economic value of the various inputs used in the production of continuing education. The economic value or cost of an input is measured in terms of opportunity cost, that is, the value of the input in its best alternative use. The total cost of a continuing education program is the sum of the costs of the inputs to the program. This implies that the costs of continuing education include not only the actual expenditures on inputs, but also the opportunity costs associated with inputs such as participants' time, donated equipment or materials, or "free" facilities.

There are some common distinctions among cost categories, such as the distinction between social costs and private costs, between direct private costs and indirect private costs, between direct institutional costs and indirect institutional costs, between recurrent costs and capital costs, between personnel costs and nonpersonnel costs, and so on. However, there is no one standard system of classification of the costs of continuing education across countries. This is not surprising because of the great variety of programs in terms of objectives, method of financing, sponsorship, mode of training, and method of delivery (OECD 1977). Presumably costs may be classified according to one or more of these aspects of continuing education. Costs may also be further broken down according to the type/category of inputs, or the function of the inputs in the education and training process. Thus a variety of schemes for cost classification is possible and different techniques are available for measuring these costs (Eicher et al. 1982, Jones 1986, Tsang 1988).

For most applications, three cost classification schemes can be considered. The first one is a classification by input categories only. This scheme provides basic information for the costing and planning of continuing education. The second scheme is a cost matrix which classifies costs by both input categories and sources of finance. It provides additional information which is useful for the financial management of continuing education. The third scheme is a cost matrix which classifies costs by both input categories and function of inputs. It provides additional information which is useful for program evaluation (see *Training Costs: Measurement; Education Production Functions*).

2. *Problems in Estimating Training Costs*

Studies of continuing education in industrialized countries have pointed out the lack of information on the costs of continuing education (OECD 1977, 1979, Anderson and Kasl 1982, Carnevale and Gainer 1988). Lack of relevant information is certainly a barrier to a precise estimation of costs. The nature of continuing education also makes the estimation of national resources devoted to it more difficult than that for regular or youth education (i.e., elementary, secondary, and postsecondary education). First, the tremendous diversities of public and private continuing education programs make the task of properly identifying relevant programs and collecting cost information almost impossible. Second, many continuing education programs are run by government agencies or institutions for which continuing education is a secondary service or of peripheral concern. There is no provision to separate the cost of continuing education programs from the overall budget of these agencies or institutions. In other nongovernmental organizations (such as labor unions, community organizations, or professional organizations), continuing education programs are administered by staff members with other responsibilities. It is very rare for these organizations to record the portion of the salaries and benefits of these staff members which is related to continuing education. Similarly, many enterprises (especially the smaller ones) do not have a separate budget for training. Third, the costs of some employer-based occupational training (such as formal or informal on-the-job training) are rather difficult to measure. Fourth, there is a danger of double counting expenditures on continuing education as the government may often provide substantial education and training grants to nongovernmental organizations, and there may be intergovernmental grants from higher levels of government to lower levels of government.

3. *Magnitude of Training Costs and Expenditures*

The following discussion presents the findings of studies on the costs of continuing education in a number of industrialized countries. Given the limitations in cost information described above, most of the figures indicated here are meant to provide order-of-magnitude estimates of the costs of continuing education. Also, because of differences in methodology, coverage of continuing education programs, and quality of data employed by these studies, cross-national comparison has to be undertaken with extreme caution.

Most of the studies on the magnitude of national resources devoted to continuing education are based on expenditures by the government, the private sector, and individuals; though some studies did include estimates of the opportunity cost of participants' time.

Table 1 shows the magnitude of national expenditure on continuing education in a number of industrialized countries as well as how such expenditure compares with that on youth education in these countries. Though these figures are rough estimates and out of date, they nevertheless indicate that significant amounts of national resources have been devoted to continuing education in industrialized countries. In the United States, in particular, national expenditure on continuing education was about 90 percent of national expenditure on youth education.

For the United States, Christoffel (1978) estimated that, in 1976, the various federal departments and agencies provided a total funding of US$14 billion for continuing education programs serving various lifelong learning needs and population groups. Carnevale (1986) estimated that total government (all levels of government) spending on adult training amounted to US$5 billion in 1984. The large difference between the two figures may be due partly to a difference in the coverage of government continuing education programs and to the reduced federal spending on education and training in the early 1980s. For general (nonvocational) adult education in Sweden, the government spent 475 million kronas in 1970 (OECD 1977 p. 62).

Table 1
National expenditure on continuing education

Country (year)	Amount (national currency)	As a % of national expenditure on youth education
Canada (1970–71)	683 million	14
France (1970–71)	6,280 million	24
Japan (1970)	325 billion	14
Sweden (1970–71)	1,116 million	10
United Kingdom (1970–71)	1,300 million	46
United States (1984)	218 billion	90
West Germany (1970–71)	8,371 million	46

Sources: For Canada, France, Sweden, United Kingdom, and West Germany, see OECD 1977. For Japan, see Noda and Watanabe 1977. For United States, see Carnevale 1986

Employers are large contributors to continuing education, especially in terms of formal and informal occupational training. There are three measures of employer expenditure which can be examined: total expenditure, expenditure per employee, and total expenditure as a percentage of total payroll cost.

For the United States, in 1984, employers spent an estimated US$12–30 billion (Brown 1989) in direct costs on formal training that they either provided themselves or purchased from outside suppliers of training. Firms in the United States with 100 or more employees budgeted US$44 billion and US$46 billion dollars respectively in 1989 and 1990 for formal training (Geber 1990 p. 39). The total cost of informal training is even greater; a rough estimation puts it at US$180 billion in 1984 (Carnevale 1986). These figures indicate that, in the United States, employers are much bigger contributors to continuing education than the government.

From a survey of personnel executives of 159 firms in the United States, the Bureau of National Affairs (1985) found that the median expenditure on in-house training was US$122 per trainee in 1983 and US$250 per trainee in 1984. However, such figures were based on a response rate of less than 16 percent. According to Japan's Ministry of Labor, employers spent an average of about 30,000 yen (about $150) per employee in 1983 (Weber 1984). In Canada, the average expenditure per employee was CDN $160 in 1986–87 (OECD 1991 p. 156).

Table 2 shows training expenditure as a percentage of payroll cost (or labor cost) in industrialized countries. It shows that although there is some variation among countries, training expenditure was between 1 and 2 percent of payroll cost in the majority of these countries.

Finally, individuals also contribute a significant amount of resources to continuing education. In the United States, surveys of participation in adult education conducted by the Bureau of Census show that for the year ending May 1981, 21 million participants in adult education took over 37 million courses. Some 48 percent of these participants or their families paid for the courses themselves, with a total private expenditure of US$2.2 billion. The average cost was US$120 per course. During the year ending May 1984, 23 million participants in adult education took over 43 million courses, with 47 percent of these participants or their families paying for the courses themselves, with a total private expenditure of US$3 billion. The average cost was US$152 per course (National Center for Educational Statistics 1982, 1986).

4. *Variation in Training Costs in Industry*

There are large variations among industries and firms in their expenditure on occupational training. According to the American Society for Training and Development, total expenditure on training by industry in the United States in 1984 ranged from a low of US$90 million for the agricultural production and services industry, to a high of US$8.7 billion for services (see Table 3). Total expenditure per industry obviously depends on the number of employees per industry, the percentage of employees receiving training, and the cost of training per employee.

The percentage of employees receiving training in an industry is related to the occupational structure of the firms in an industry. For example, employer-based formal training is disproportionately concentrated in industries with large numbers of professionals, managers, and technicians (Carnevale and Gainer 1988).

Table 2
Employer expenditure on training as a percentage of payroll cost

Country	Year	Training expenditure as % of payroll
Australia	1989–90	1.7
Denmark	1984	2.1
France	1984	1.6
France	1987–89	2.5
Germany	1984	1.8
Italy	1984	0.3
Japan	1988–89	0.4–0.7
Netherlands	1986	1.5
United Kingdom	1984	1.3
United States	1984–85	1.0

Sources: For United States, see Carnevale and Gainer 1988. For other countries, see OECD 1991 p. 156

The cost of training per employee (CPE) also varies significantly among industries. For industries in the United States in 1984, it ranged from a low of US$54 per employee for agricultural production and services, to a high of US$645 per employee for public administration (see Table 3). Variations in CPE across industries were also reported in the former West Germany and the United Kingdom. The Edding Commission on apprenticeship training in the former West Germany found that, in the early 1970s, the gross expenditure per trainee per year ranged from DM86 in the health industry to DM8,912 for large firms belonging to the Chambers of Industry and Commerce (OECD 1979 p. 56). For the United Kingdom, Jones (1986) found that, in 1984, the net cost (gross cost minus trainee output) of apprentice training was £8,900 per trainee for engineering firms, and £11,800 per trainee for nonengineering firms.

5. Determinants of Training Costs

CPE is influenced by a variety of factors. One way to understand the determinants of CPE is by relating it to the amount of training per employee (in terms of hours per employee) and the unit cost of training (in terms of dollars per training hour).

5.1 Amount of Training per Employee

The amount of training per employee depends on the nature of jobs, the characteristics of a firm, and the background characteristics of employees.

Nature of job. Different jobs require different amounts of training. A survey of firms in the United States with 100 or more workers in 1990 found that the number of hours of training ranged from 19 hours per administrative/office worker and 31 hours per production worker, to 36 hours per professional worker and 41 hours per salesperson (Gordon 1990 p. 52). The distribution of the total training time (estimated to be 1.3 billion hours for all such firms) by occupation was: 2.1 percent for executives, 17.1 percent for professionals, 2.8 percent for senior managers, 8.0 percent for middle managers, 11.9 percent for first-line supervisors, 23.7 percent for production workers, 12.7 percent for salespersons, 16.2 percent for customer-service workers, and 5.5 percent for administrative/office employees (computed from Gordon 1990 p. 52).

Characteristics of firms. In general, larger firms provide more training to employees than smaller firms (OECD 1991 Chap. 5). But Bishop (1982) found that the smallest firms (less than 10 employees) did not provide the least amount of training per employee. In other words, the relationship between amount of training and firm size is a U-shape curve. Also, he found that firms with higher rates of employment

Table 3
Training expenditure by industry, United States 1984

Industry	Total expenditure (million dollars)	Expenditure per employee ($/employee)
Agriculture production and services	90	54
Construction	720	127
Durable goods	4,710	314
Finance, insurance, and real estate	3,480	529
Manufacturing	6,450	258
Mining	720	566
Nondurable goods	1,740	260
Public administration	3,960	645
Services	8,700	283
Trade	2,910	136
Transportation and public utilities	2,610	351

Source: Carnavale 1986 p. 20

growth provided more training than firms with lower rates.

Characteristics of workers. In the United States, White workers receive disproportionately more training than minority workers. In general, workers with more formal education receive more training than workers with less formal education, though it is not clear whether a worker with a doctoral degree or professional degree receives more training than workers with a master's degree. Part-time workers receive less training than full-time workers. Though there are some inconsistencies among the findings of different studies, work experience generally enhances the training opportunities for a worker. However, there is no consensus among studies on whether male workers receive more training than female workers, and whether union workers receive more training than nonunion workers (Brown 1989).

A recent study of OECD countries has made several discoveries regarding access to training (OECD 1991 p. 161). First, there are two broad patterns regarding training access by age. In some countries (especially those with strong apprenticeship systems, like Germany), incidence of training decreases with increasing age. In other countries, incidence of training increases with age, reaches a maximum for the 30–44 age group, and then declines afterwards. Second, there is little difference between men and women. Third, more educated workers have more access to training then less educated workers. And fourth, in general, higher level nonmanual and skilled manual workers have more access to training than lower level and less skilled workers.

5.2 Unit Costs of Training

The cost per training hour depends on the technology of training and the prices of inputs to training (Tsang 1988).

Technology of training. The technology of training refers to how training is provided; it concerns such matters as the curriculum, pedagogy, class size, organization, and the mode of delivery.

Anderson and Kasl (1982) found large differences in unit costs of continuing education among different sponsors; the cost per training hour was US$2 for public school systems, US$5 for colleges and universities, US$8 for community organizations, and US$15 for professional organizations. One reason for the low unit cost of the public school system is its above average class size.

In addition, when a training organization can increase its output without increasing inputs proportionately (known as "economies of scale"), unit costs will be smaller. Continuing education programs through the new educational media (such as television, radio, and satellite) draw attention to the importance of achieving economies of scale. Since continuing education programs through new educational media demand heavy capital investment in their initial development, such programs require a large enrollment and a relatively long period of operation (Eicher et al. 1982).

Prices of inputs. For most continuing education programs, the payment to personnel is the key determinant of unit cost. Part-time instructors are often paid less then full-time instructors, on an hourly basis. The use of volunteers can reduce the direct cost of training.

Different providers of continuing education appear to differ significantly in how costs are distributed among different inputs to training (Anderson and Kasl 1982). For example, as a proportion of total expenditure (excluding private costs of participants), instructor costs amount to 60 percent for public school systems, 44 percent for colleges and universities, 35 percent for community organizations, and only 17 percent for professional organizations. Such variation may be due to a combination of differences in the technology of training and in the type (and thus price) of inputs employed.

6. Applications of Cost Analysis

Analyses of the costs of continuing education are important for decision making, planning, and management in continuing education.

6.1 Cost–Benefit Analysis and Investment in Continuing Education

A key application of cost analysis in continuing education is economic evaluation of the profitability of investment in continuing education. The technique of cost–benefit analysis (or rate-of-return analysis) as applied to continuing education is most relevant here (see *Cost-Benefit Analysis*). It can be applied to the evaluation of continuing education programs for which the benefits can be quantified in monetary terms, such as higher earnings or productivity.

Obviously, there are many cost–benefit analyses that can be undertaken, for example, with respect to the sponsor, the mode of training, the type of industry and trades within an industry, the objective or kind of continuing education program (occupational, basic literacy, civic/political competence, etc.), and others. The literature on cost–benefit analysis in continuing education is much smaller than that on youth education. The available cost–benefit studies on continuing education are mostly out of date, and other economic studies on continuing education tend to focus on the earnings or productivity effects of continuing education. Previous studies on occupational training indicate that the rates of return were either near to or much above the benchmark of 10 percent (Mangum 1989). More current estimates are needed to inform public and private investment decisions.

6.2 Cost-effectiveness Analysis

Decision-makers in continuing education are often

faced with the task of choosing between alternative programs or methods with a common objective (better verbal skill) which cannot be measured in monetary terms. An analysis of the effectiveness and costs of the alternatives can be conducted to assist decision-makers in selecting the most cost-effective alternative (see *Cost-effectiveness Analysis; Vocational Education and Training: Improving Cost-effectiveness in Developing Nations*). For example, when two programs yield similar training effects, the less costly program should be selected, other things being equal. By incorporating cost-effectiveness analysis in the decision-making process, continuing education organizations will make more efficient use of their scarce resources.

6.3 Cost Functions in Training

Cost functions relate the total cost of production to the output of production (see *Education Production Functions*). Cost functions can be estimated for different modes of (or approaches to) training. They are useful in two ways. First, given a mode of training, an estimated training cost function shows how the unit cost of training varies with the amount of training provided under that mode. Second, cost functions for different modes of training provide cost information necessary for investment decisions regarding the choice of training modes for human resource development. Cost functions have been estimated for new educational media as a training mode for continuing education (Eicher et al. 1982). Little attention has been paid to study of the cost functions of other training modes.

6.4 Cost Information in Planning and Management

Information on costs is necessary to monitor and improve the utilization of existing resources in a continuing education organization. By more fully utilizing existing resources, an organization can raise its output without increasing costs, thus increasing the "internal" efficiency of the organization. The key to increased internal efficiency is to identify "slack" in the organization, such as underutilized personnel, facilities, or equipment.

Cost analysis is an integral part of the planning and management of continuing education programs. A careful estimation of the total cost of a continuing education program is necessary for several reasons. First, it simply shows how much a program costs, for accounting or budgetary purposes. Second, if some important indirect or hidden costs are not included in the proposal or contract for a program, there are likely to be financial difficulties when the program is implemented. Third, the total cost estimate is needed in assessing the financial feasibility of a program.

Cost data are needed for planning future developments in continuing education. Historical data on unit costs (such as cost per trainee or cost per training hour) provide a basis for projecting the costs of programs in the future.

Information on cost is also indispensable for controling or reducing the costs of continuing education programs. In general, there are three strategies for cost reduction. First, given a program or method of delivery, cost can be reduced by employing lower cost inputs. Thus, instead of using a qualified full-time instructor, a part-time instructor or an instructor with a lower qualification may be employed. In some situations, volunteers may fill certain personnel needs of the program; the direct cost of the program to the sponsor thereby will be reduced. It should be noted that there is often a trade-off between the cost of an input and its quality. Second, given a program or a set of programs run by a continuing education organization, unit costs can be reduced by more fully utilizing the existing resources for the program or the organization. When there is organization slack, cost can be reduced without affecting the level of output. Third, given a training objective, alternative technology of production of training or training programs can be evaluated to determine their costs and effectiveness. Thus, other things being equal, an alternative with a lower cost should be preferred to another alternative with a higher cost.

Finally, there is a long-standing observation by analysts and practitioners alike about the lack of information on the costs of continuing education programs. To improve the planning and management of such programs, cost information should be regularly collected and analyzed. For large organizations which provide continuing education programs on a regular basis, a model for analyzing and estimating cost can be developed.

7. Emerging Cost-related Issues

In industrialized countries, there is an emerging need for both governments and employers to reassess investment activities in continuing education because of rapid production changes and intensifying economic competition among countries. Investment in human capital is often seen as a key strategy to deal with these changes. This raises at least four questions regarding investment in continuing education: is the current level of investment in continuing education adequate? What kind of adult education and training should be provided? How should access to continuing education for disadvantaged members of society be expanded? And how should the costs of continuing education programs be financed? Further research and public discussion are needed to address these questions.

Because of the current economic difficulties in industrialized countries, decision-makers or managers of continuing education programs in both the public and private sectors have to face increasing scrutiny of their demands for resources. There is a more urgent need for running efficient programs, cutting unnecessary costs, and improving the planning and management of continuing education programs.

See also: Recurrent and Alternation Education; Employment Policy: Adult Education and Training; Adult Education and Training Markets; Paid Educational Leave and Collective Bargaining; Nonformal Education, Economics of; Training Costs: Measurement; Measurement of Industry Training

References

Anderson R, Kasl E 1982 *The Costs and Financing of Adult Education and Training*. D C Heath–Lexington Books, Lexington, Massachusetts

Bishop J 1982 *The Social Payoff for Occupationally Specific Training: The Employers' Point of View*. National Center for Research on Vocational Education, Columbus, Ohio

Brown C 1989 Empirical evidence on private training. In: Commission on Workforce Quality and Labor Market Efficiency 1989 *Investing in People*. US Department of Labor, Washington, DC

Bureau of National Affairs 1985 *Training and Development Programs*. Bureau of National Affairs, Washington, DC

Carnevale A 1986 The learning enterprise. *Train. Dev. J.* 40 (January): 18–26

Carnevale A, Gainer L 1988 *The Learning Enterprise*. American Society for Training and Development, Alexandra, Virginia

Christoffel P 1978 Current federal programs for lifelong learning: A $14 billion effort. *Sch. Rev.* (May): 348–59

Eicher J, Hawkridge D, McAnany E, Orivel F (eds.) 1982 *The Economics of New Educational Media. Vol. 3: Cost and Effectiveness: Overview and Synthesis*. UNESCO, Paris

Geber B 1990 Budget barely budge. *Training* 27(10): 39–47

Gordon D 1990 Where the training goes. *Training* 27(10): 51–69

Jones I 1986 Apprentice training costs in British manufacturing establishments: Some new evidence. *British Journal of Industrial Relations* 24(3): 333–62

Mangum S 1989 Evidence on private sector training. In: Commission on Workforce Quality and Labor Market Efficiency 1989 *Investing in People*. Department of Labor, Washington, DC

National Center for Educational Statistics 1982 *Participation in Adult Education, 1981*. Department of Education, Washington, DC

National Center for Educational Statistics 1986 *OERI Bulletin*. US Department of Education, Washington, DC

Noda T, Watanabe T 1977 Educational expenditure in Japan. In: Levy-Garboua L et al. (eds.) 1977 *Educational Expenditure in France, Japan, and the United Kingdom*. OECD, Paris

OECD 1977 *Learning Opportunities for Adults*, Vol. 1. OECD, Paris

OECD 1979 *Policies for Apprenticeship*. OECD, Paris

OECD 1991 *Employment Outlook*. OECD Paris

Tsang M 1988 The cost of vocational training. In: Middleton J, Ziderman A (eds.) 1988 *Vocational and Technical Education and Training*. Population and Human Resources Department, The World Bank, Washington, DC

Weber D 1984 An eye to the East: Training in Japan. *Train. and Dev. J.* (October): 32–33

Further Reading

Levin H 1983 *Cost Effectiveness: A Primer*. Sage, Beverly Hills, California

Lillard L, Tan H 1986 *Private Sector Training: Who Gets It and What are Its Effects?* Rand Corporation, Santa Monica, California

Lusterman S 1985 *Trends in Corporate Education and Training*. The Conference Board, New York

Phillips J 1983 *Handbook of Training Evaluation and Measurement Methods*. Gulf Publishing Company, Houston, Texas

Ryan P 1980 The costs of job training for a transferable skill. *British Journal of Industrial Relations* 18(3): 334–52

Ziderman A 1975 Costs and benefits of manpower training programmes in Great Britain. *British Journal of Industrial Relations* 13(2): 223–44

Zymelman M 1976 *Economic Evaluation of Vocational Training Programs*. Johns Hopkins University Press, Baltimore, Maryland

M. Tsang

Côte d'Ivoire: System of Education

1. General Background

Côte d'Ivoire is a West African country, roughly square in shape, which is bordered by the Atlantic Ocean to the south, the Republics of Liberia and Guinea to the west, the Republics of Mali and Burkina Faso to the north, and the Republic of Ghana to the east. Its land mass covers 322,462 square kilometers, which represents only 1 percent of the African continent's surface. The country is divided into two quite distinct bioclimatic zones: a two-season regime (dry and rainy seasons) in the north and a four-season one in the south (short and long rainy seasons and two dry periods).

Large-scale immigration to Côte d'Ivoire by other West African groups began in the sixteenth century. Hence, when the country was declared a full-fledged colony by France on March 10, 1893, cultural zones had already been established by six major sociolinguistic communities: (a) Krou or Mangwé; (b) Southern Mandé or Peripheral Mandé; (c) Mandingo or Nuclear Mandé; (d) the Voltaic family of the Senoufo, Koulango, and Lobi subfamily; (e) the Angi-Baoulé subgroup of the Akan group; and (f) the "lagoon people" (i.e., the few small Akan groups who live by the lagoons that stretch along the coastal areas).

These cultural and linguistic zones still exist. In 1989, 46 percent of the population aged 15 years and above in Côte d'Ivoire were regarded as illiterate (World Bank 1989 p. 326). Different local languages are used for intercommunication purposes. Ivoirian leadership, however, has chosen French as the only acceptable and official language. Since the 1960s, it has been used for all official transactions—from church to educational activities, from politics to cultural contests, from small business to economic deals, and from administration to judicial practices. In 1986, the Ivoirian government announced that the official name of the country would thenceforth be "Côte d'Ivoire" rather than the "Ivory Coast."

In 1990, Côte d'Ivoire had a total population of 11,730,000, growing at an average annual rate of 4.3 percent (World Bank 1992 p. 11). The country's urban dwellers represented 46.6 percent of the total population with an average annual growth rate of 5.6 percent. In 1980, Abidjan was the only city with over 500,000 people, and it comprised 34 percent of the urban population of Côte d'Ivoire at that time. Indeed, Abidjan's population grew from 1.3 million inhabitants in 1978 to 2 million in 1988, including 500,000 African immigrants vying for jobs with Ivoirians (Lamb 1988 p. 120).

In the 1980s, Côte d'Ivoire's labor force totaled 3,547,000 (World Bank 1992 p. 282), with an average annual growth rate of 2.7 percent. Some 65 percent of this labor force was in agriculture, 8 percent in industry, and 27 percent in services. Their earnings at minimum wage decreased from US$1,581 per annum in 1980 to US$1,061 per annum in 1986 (World Bank 1992 p. 287). The education level attained by Ivoirian workers, in the 1980s, was estimated at an average of only 2.1 years.

In 1985, 11.2 percent of Côte d'Ivoire's school-age population was enrolled in the private primary institutions and 29.3 percent in private secondary institutions (World Bank 1992 p. 330). Thus far, the private sector has not invested in tertiary education. Its main investment has been in preschool education, whether of the "traditional" or modern type. In 1985, the gross enrollment ratio in primary schools was 70 percent, but for females it was some 18 percent less (World Bank 1992 p. 327). The dropout rate of the primary school population was 32 percent, while the number of repeaters per 100 pupils enrolled was estimated at 28. In that same year, the secondary school gross enrollment ratio was 19 percent, with the female rate trailing 8 points behind (World Bank 1992 p. 333). The number of repeaters per 100 students enrolled was 19, but for females it was 22 (World Bank 1992 p. 334).

These statistics are a sad reflection on the efforts and reforms in education introduced by the Ivoirian government since the 1960s. This high rate of dropout and school leaving may be due to the following reasons: (a) the insistence of the government on following the French system, hence abrogating the deep cultural forms of education already extant in Ivoirian society; and (b) the lack of political will to make the necessary changes.

2. Politics and the Goals of the Education System

Three decades after regaining its independence from France on August 7, 1960, Côte d'Ivoire's educational system is still modeled on the French school system. Like the French system, education in Côte d'Ivoire is regarded as the sole concern of the state and, therefore, is mainly secular. Historically, however, education in Côte d'Ivoire was initially a matter of family units, village communities thereafter, and eventually ethnic groups. This responsibility was taken away from those groups by the French colonial power and given over to denominational groups, mostly Christian and a few Muslims. In the early twentieth century, education became the charge of the French colonial power itself, and finally the sole responsibility of the Ivoirian government after Independence.

The educational system in the early 1990s appears to be well-structured, but a closer look reveals conflicting elements which are the result of a lack of cohesion between traditional and modern education systems. These conflicting elements did not surface during the years of prosperity in the 1960s and 1970s. The hardships of the 1980s have revived some of the unresolved problems. The Ivoirian government faces new (and old) challenges of educational reform.

3. The Formal System of Education

Côte d'Ivoire had an educational system in existence before the nineteenth century and the arrival of the French colonists. This "traditional education system" began during early childhood, as early as the "mother's back" stage (a reference to children always being carried on the mother's back) and extended to "age-group" settings. This traditional education system has continued up to the early 1990s. Based entirely upon the two basic concepts of "orality" and "apprenticeship," it still flourishes at the individual family level in urban areas. It is practiced more extensively by rural dwellers where the majority of Ivoirians continue to entrust the charge of dispensing education to a respected family unit elder, generally an aunt or uncle, or another knowledgeable adult. The lack of such an education is believed to detract from the active participation needed for the preservation of family values and economic survival.

In contrast, the modern educational system is so totally different that it relies exclusively on "writing" and "analysis procedure." Ong (1990 p. 9) portrayed the ways in which mental and social structures operate in "primary oral cultures." Ong argued that people from these oral cultures, who have been untouched by any writing system, learn by "apprenticeship." In other words, they acquire knowledge through the practice of listening and repetition and by assimilating a repertoire of common folk wisdom. Battestini points out, however, that it would be mis-

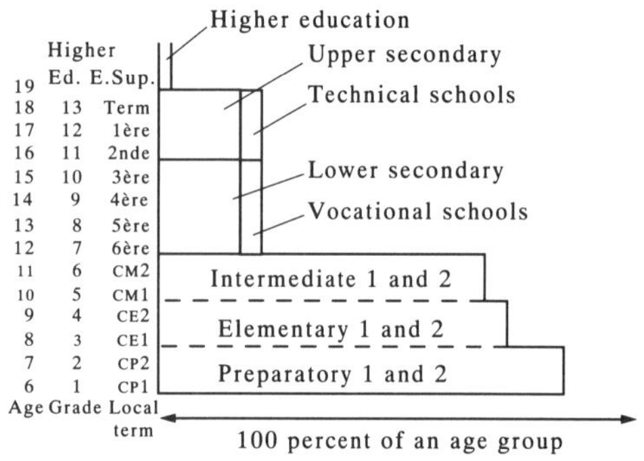

Figure 1
Côte d'Ivoire: Structure of the formal education system

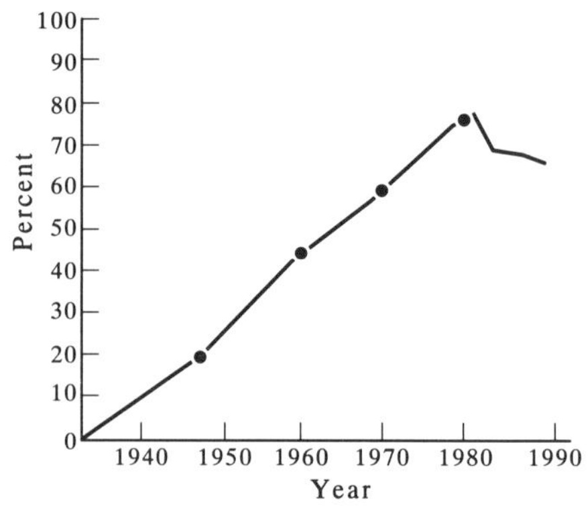

Figure 2
Primary school enrollment 1940–90

leading to rule out any book-oriented knowledge in the traditional education system, given the existence of writings in African languages (Vaï, Bété, Mandé, Fulani). Traditional education has produced literates whose duties in their social group included diffusing knowledge for legal matters, medical purposes, geomantic predictions, ethical questions, and so on. Books were still scarce, and owned only by a few literates. The knowledge contained in these books was available to everyone through the "master of speech," or "alkitabi" (the man of the book). By contrast, the book-oriented knowledge which illustrates the trend of the modern educational structure focuses mainly on analytical and analogical skills (Bendor-Samuel 1984).

3.1 Primary, Secondary, and Tertiary Education

The Ivoirian school system is organized into a three-tiered system, each of which has a general goal (see Figure 1). The primary tier ensures an elementary education, the secondary tier secures a general and technical education, and the tertiary tier is intended to provide higher education for people to develop elite skills and be trained as professionals.

Primary education aims to reach all children aged 6 through 11 and is subdivided into three steps with a double entry per step: Preparatory classes I and II, Elementary classes I and II, and Intermediate classes I and II—identified here by their French acronyms CP1 (*Cours Préparatoire 1ère année*), CP2 (*2ème année*), CE1 (*Cours Elémentaire 1ère année*), CE2, CM1 (*Cours Moyen 1ère année*), CM2.

Figure 2 presents primary school enrollment statistics. In 1948, school attendance of all school-age children was estimated to be 20 percent. There was a steady increase up to 1983 (77%). Enrollment then started to decline and, by 1992, it was estimated to be 66.5 percent.

General secondary education is available to pupils who have passed their secondary school entrance examination and whose full names have been registered on a nationwide list. The candidates are from 11 to 15 years of age, depending on how many times they repeated the final grade of primary school. The secondary tier is divided into first and second cycles: (a) lower general secondary, which extends over a four-year curriculum and leads to the middle course final examination called the *Brevet d'enseignement du premier cycle*, BEPC; and (b) upper general secondary, which lasts three years and prepares students to take the *Baccalauréat* examination. Upper general secondary students enter major areas of study, casually referred to as series "A, B, C, D, E, F, and G." These letters correspond respectively to the following domains of studies: (a) letters, arts, and human sciences—A; (b) economy and social sciences—B; (c) pure sciences and physics—C; (d) sciences of experimentation—D; (e) sciences and technology—E; (f) applied sciences, office techniques, trade and management—F and G. Success in the *Baccalauréat* examination in any of these disciplines ensures the candidate automatic access to higher education and to student allowances. However, the economic disarray of the 1980s forced the Ivoirian education authorities to modify this practice in higher education, in terms of both accessibility and financial support strategies.

In 1960, the general secondary school enrollment was 12,000. A decade later, it stood at 70,000, an almost sixfold increase, and by 1980, it had reached 238,000. Although the enrollment of 1983 totaled 269,000 students, the average annual growth rate of the 1960s and 1970s (16%) drastically decreased to 4.1 percent in the early 1980s (World Bank 1989 p. 126).

Higher education has a two-track curriculum: the university schools called "*facultés*" and specialized professional schools known as "*grandes écoles*." The first track is composed of schools, such as law, medicine, and pharmacy. However, there are no specific job prospects as students progress toward their degree or diploma. Few jobs are available even for university graduates. The *facultés*-track also includes higher educational institutes devoted to fundamental and applied research (see Sect. 9). The National University of Abidjan (with only one campus until the academic year 1992–93) was founded in 1959 as the Center for Higher Education, under the leadership of the University of Paris. Starting in 1964, its internal schools were granted full autonomous status as required, but only when they satisfied the French university criteria of administrative and pedagogical autonomy.

University enrollment at Abidjan campus was 300 in 1960. It climbed to 4,400 in 1970 and reached a peak of 19,600 in 1980. In 1982, however, enrollment decreased slightly to a total of 17,900, but rose again in the late 1980s. In 1992, the student body totaled 20,000 regular full-time students and 3,000 evening students, enrolled in FIP (*Formation individuelle permanente*) training. All University facilities are used to their maximum capacities. The 23,000 student population makes for overcrowding in the institution, especially since the University was built to accommodate only 7,000 students. For this reason, policymakers decided to open, for the academic year 1992–93, a second campus in the city of Bouaké, which will accommodate about 3,000 new baccalaureate graduates.

3.2 Preschool Education

In the traditional educational setting, preschooling was quite different from the system implemented in Côte d'Ivoire in the 1970s. In the former case, the child received an informal preschool education while on the "mother's back." The parents' home, the field, or the village market were the natural milieu where this informal education was dispensed. This form of education was the beginning of the training of young Ivoirians into active membership in their communities—their first "contact with the adult world" (Roberts et al. 1973 p. 114). This was a serious undertaking, as it constituted the very foundation of any subsequent education.

In Côte d'Ivoire in the early 1990s, preschool education does not appear to be as serious a matter of concern for policymakers as primary, secondary, and higher education. Indeed, there are no specialized administrative or supervisory structures to run preschools. This is understandable—in fact, the issue is not really discussed in the public arena—insofar as the vast majority of rural women are self-employed workers who are not constrained to wage-earners' time as in the urban areas. Thus, these women satisfactorily meet the educational needs of their preschool-age children.

Nonetheless, Côte d'Ivoire policymakers have had to address the problem of the high mortality rate of children under 5 years of age (163 per thousand in the 1980s), who constitute a large percentage of the 1–14 age-group. This 1–14 age-group has shown a serious decline, from 48.3 percent in 1980 to 46.7 percent in 1990. The preschool population and its education has been considered more a matter for the Ministry of Social Affairs (with 91 maternal or kindergarten schools under its tutelage in 1987) rather than the responsibility of the Ministry of National Education.

3.3 Special Education

Special education endeavors to find a viable solution to the ever more pressing scholastic problems faced by policymakers as a result of the failure of the formal educational system to adapt to Ivoirian sociocultural settings. For instance, with 80 percent of students enrolled in the first grade of primary school, both private and public, Côte d'Ivoire may justifiably be proud of its record in making considerable progress toward universal primary education. However, the disadvantage of this progress is the high dropout and grade repetition rate (see Sect. 1). Special education is therefore an ad hoc response to limit the negative effects of the dropout and repetition phenomena affecting the overall school population.

The alternative education system does not usually fall under the supervision of the ministries in charge of formal education. Curricula and classes are organized by concerned ministries. For instance, the *Lycée agricole* of Bingerville is under the tutelage of the Ministry of Agriculture. The *Ecole de police* is supervised by the Ministry of the Interior. The *Ecole des infirmiers/infirmières ou des sages femmes* is under the tutelage of the Ministry of Health. The *Ecole des assistantes sociales* as well as the *Institut des aveugles et des mal-voyants* and the *Village des enfants d'Abobote* are all under the supervision of the Ministry of Social Affairs, Youth, and Sports. Other specific ministries which take on educational responsibilities are: the former Ministry of Scientific Research and Culture; the National Defense Ministry; the Civil Service (*la Fonction publique et emploi*); the Ministry of Industry and Planning; the Ministry of Public Labors, Transportation, Construction, and Urbanization; and the former Ministry of Agriculture, Water, and Forest (Gideppe 1990 p. 197).

3.4 Vocational, Technical, and Business Education

In keeping with its ideology towards the colonized, French educational policy concentrated on vocational training. In fact, as early as 1892, the first school of agriculture was opened on Verdier's farm, in the Aboisso area of southeastern Côte d'Ivoire. Nevertheless, the history of vocational, technical, and business education in Côte d'Ivoire demonstrates that it was first considered only as an adjunct to general education, before gaining recognition through the creation of a full-fledged ministry, called the "Ministry of Technical Education and Vocational Training" (the autonomy of which was interrupted by a short-lived superministry of national education between 1983 and 1986). Roberts et al. (1973 p. 123) give the following appraisal of Côte d'Ivoire's vocational school policy: "The 20-odd institutions which existed in 1962 offered a variety of programs leading to certificates, diplomas and degrees covering a range of proficiency from craftsman to engineer." Hence, from its earliest beginnings, education was regarded by decision-makers as an investment in an academic education leading to white-collar jobs, rather than being considered a practical vocational or technical training. The Ministry of Technical Education and Vocational Training manages all the technical- and vocational-related institutions at the secondary and tertiary levels, except for those coming under specific ministries (see Sect. 3.3).

3.5 Adult and Nonformal Education

The longstanding debate about the link between education and the labor market can be traced to colonial administration policies in all African countries. In an effort to contribute to a better understanding of the role of education, some educationists (Speak 1982 p. 98) have proposed a three-way classification of education: (a) "formal" education, (b) "informal" education, and (c) "nonformal" education. Speak argues that "formal" education is concerned with "the highly structured, chronologically graded system running from primary school through university." This mode of education has already been addressed above. "Informal" education is viewed as a "truly lifelong process whereby every individual acquires attitudes, values, skills and knowledge from daily experience and the environment" (this approach will be examined in Sect. 7). "Nonformal" education, in Speak's terms, "refers to organized activities outside the formal system intended to serve identifiable clienteles and learning objectives." Any range of activities from "literacy classes to driving instruction" comes under this category, which is discussed below.

The illiteracy figures quoted in Sect. 1 indicated that 60 percent of females and 33 percent of males aged 15 years or more were illiterate. In other words, the illiterate female population outnumbered male illiterates by 2 to 1. In an attempt to reach this population, the Côte d'Ivoire government has participated in "nonformal" education mainly through two of its ministries—the Ministry for Social Affairs, Youth and Sports, and the Ministry of Technical Education and Vocational Training. The former has a "center for literacy" through which French reading and writing skills are taught. The latter has within it the National Bureau of Vocational Training, which is in charge of inservice training of workers. In both cases, the teaching objectives seem to be limited to the training of holders of blue-collar jobs. The teaching objectives claim to reach the self-employed, in rural areas as well as urban environments. In Speak's terms, "nonformal" education as monitored by the two ministries has been limited to include the improvement of reading and writing skills for urban wage-earners.

Indeed, the concept of "nonformal" education extends beyond literacy viewed as the acquisition of reading, writing, and arithmetic. At variance with "formal" education, it aims at the acquisition of job skills. A study has shown convincingly that "formal" and "nonformal" education are not substitutes for each other but "prepare people for different careers" (Grootaert 1990 pp. 309–19).

4. Administrative and Supervisory Structure and Operation

Education is the sole responsibility of the state, and hence is always referred to as "national education." For a short period, between 1983 and 1986, a superministry was created which was committed to managing the whole educational system directly with the intent of realizing the ideal of a unified system of national education.

These years were the worst in the history of the school system management in Côte d'Ivoire. The depth of the school crisis in the early 1990s can be directly attributed to those three years of demagoguery and mistaken enactment of so-called "Moral Rearmament" (Gideppe 1990 p. 192). Indeed, under this leadership, state responsibility towards the Ivoirian school system was actually on the decline, notwithstanding the uplifting rhetoric about the "new Ivoirian school."

In reality, in 1983–84, only three new public schools were built under the new centralized system, in contrast to 20 new private institutions (FPI 1987 p. 141). At the same time, and without allowing any transition period, the state left to new and inexperienced mayoral authorities the planning and development of primary schools (Gideppe 1990 p. 192). The ensuing chaos resulted in a return to the multi-approach management policy which was still in effect in the early 1990s.

The Ministry of National Education is in charge of secondary and tertiary education. This ministry directly oversees the institutions of general education (the *collèges et lycées du secondaire*). Moreover, it sets the standards for all the private secondary education institutions. It is divided into as many regional directorates as necessary to cover the country's territorial divisions. It is the only institution which decides the validity of all diplomas earned and recognized from any other training institution, inside and outside the country (Gideppe 1990 p. 197). In 1991, the national university (*Université nationale de Côte d'Ivoire*), the teacher college (*Ecole normale supérieure*), and student union affairs (*Centre national des oeuvres universitaires*) came under the auspices of a new ministry called "*Enseignement supérieur et recherche scientifique*."

Primary education falls under the supervision of the Ministry of Primary Education. This ministry was created when Côte d'Ivoire decided to launch a large-scale television teaching program—*le programme d'éducation télévisuelle* (PETV)—from October 1971 to June 1983. The Ministry oversees all the public grade schools at the primary level and sets the standards for all private schools at that level. It functions through regional directorates composed of as many primary education inspection personnel (*les inspections d'enseignement primaire* (IEP) as necessary. The head of each inspection unit monitors the competence of the teachers as well as the quality of the content of the teaching.

After a lengthy period of neglect (see Sect. 3.4), technical education and vocational training was put under the supervision of an autonomous administrative and academic ministerial authority which directly manages all the institutions of technical education and vocational training at the secondary and tertiary levels. At the secondary level, education and training are offered through the *Institut national de formation technique et professionnelle* (INFTP). At the tertiary level, the schools are known as the *Grandes écoles*, *Institut supérieur de l'enseignement technique* (INSET), *Institut pédagogique de l'enseignement technique et professionnel* (IPNETP). There are two other vocation-related institutions which come under the control of this ministry: the *Office national de la formation professionnelle* (ONFP) and *Fonds national de régulation* (FNR).

5. Educational Finance

The Ivoirian authorities have repeatedly maintained that education must be the overriding priority ("*la priorité des priorités*") because "education and culture are seen by them as one of the best investments if we [the Ivoirian people] want our country to reach in a short period of time to its full development" (Gideppe 1990 p. 188). Therefore, they were willing to devote up to 43 percent of the country's budget to creating several structures and hiring a full complement of teachers, with a highly attractive salary scale to encourage more candidates to apply and to retain those already in service. Thus, a special teacher salary scale was established within the Ivoirian civil servants' (*les fonctionnaires ivoiriens*) salary scale. This was known as "*le décrochage*," referring to the uncoupling of the teachers' category from all other civil servants' categories (Gideppe 1990 p. 192; also Komenan and Grootaert 1990).

During the first half of the 1980s, Côte d'Ivoire's expenditure and lending (minus repayments) on education was estimated at an average of 18.2 percent of the state budget (World Bank 1992 p. 191). Nonetheless, one may wonder whether mere lip service is being paid to the sacred principle of "*la priorité des priorités*" in matters of education in Côte d'Ivoire. One yardstick of comparison is the educational statistics of Cameroon, a quite similar country in terms of population size; these might provide an indication of whether the huge Ivoirian educational budget has been managed efficiently.

In mid-1990, the population of Cameroon, a middle-income African country like Côte d'Ivoire, was 11.6 million, compared with 11.7 million in Côte d'Ivoire. In 1985, primary school enrollment in Cameroon was 94 percent, as against 60 percent in Côte d'Ivoire. In 1989, secondary enrollment in Cameroon reached 27 percent, compared with 19 percent in Côte d'Ivoire. For the first half of the 1980s, Cameroonian government expenditure on education was only 11.0 percent of total expenditure and lending (minus repayments), as against 18.2 percent in Côte d'Ivoire. During the same period, Cameroon registered only 23.1 percent in real per capita education spending, compared with 67.6 percent in Côte d'Ivoire, almost three times higher. In 1980, the number of Cameroonian primary school staff was 26,760 including 20 percent females compared with 26,460 with 15 percent females in Côte d'Ivoire.

The Côte d'Ivoire–Cameroon comparison reveals that greater per capita public expenditure is not a necessary prerequisite of better achievement. Cameroon budgeted less per capita public expenditure than Côte d'Ivoire, yet the former had a better return to investment in education than the latter (Ogbu and Gallagher 1991).

6. Supplying Personnel for the Education System

Historically, education training has taken a variety of forms in Ivoirian society. Within the context of one such traditional education system, the sacred forest during "Poro" initiation among the Senoufo people was the required institution for supplying the personnel needed for their education purposes. In the pre-Independence era, personnel for educational tasks were supplied through a three-year normal course aimed at training teachers at the *Ecole primaire supérieure*, founded in 1925 in Bingerville, on the Ebrié lagoon, 17 kilometers from Abidjan.

In the 1930s, the *Cours normaux* teacher-training institutions were established in Dabou at the other end of the Ebrié lagoon. This new training policy was implemented throughout the country as Côte d'Ivoire gained more autonomy from the educational policy of *l'Afrique occidentale française*, based in Dakar, capital city of the West African Federation of French colonies. Guiglo and Bouaké were established as all-male training institutions in 1946 as well as Korhogo in 1953 and Bouaké as the all-female teacher-training institution, in 1957. With Independence, these institutions were transformed into *collèges d'enseignement général* (CEG), and lost their teacher-training institutions' characteristics.

In the early 1990s, there were two types of institutions supplying teachers for the Ivoirian primary and secondary education system: the *Ecole normale supérieure*, founded in 1964 in Abidjan; and the *Centres d'animation et de formation pédagogiques* (CAFOP). The latter were founded as supporting institutions to the nationwide *Programme d'éducation télévisuelle* (PETV) in the 1970s.

Teachers at the tertiary level (this applies to the university rather than the *grandes écoles* level) are hired upon obtaining a doctoral degree (*troisième cycle*) with a high pass mark. In the early 1980s, the francophone African countries created the *Conseil africain et malgache pour l'enseignement supérieur* (CAMES) which functions as a tenure committee overseeing the promotion of university teachers from assistant, associate, and to full emeritus professorship.

7. Curriculum Development and Teaching Methodology

A study (Roberts et al. 1973 p. 114) has described the different steps of a curriculum development and teaching methodology in *informal* education of the traditional type. They affirm that the 0 through 5 age-group is a period of "constant contact with the adult world," conveyed to the child via every gesture of the mother. There then follows the 5 or 6 through 8 age-group, which corresponds to a period of individualization and personal relationship with the environment. The curriculum for the period from age 8 until puberty is organized according to two criteria: age-group activities and gender job specialization.

However, the traditional curriculum was not based solely on an informal environment. In some ethnic communities, such as the Senoufo people in northern Côte d'Ivoire, there was quite an impressive formal curriculum. The "Poro" as an institution of initiation can be regarded as the survivor of the kind of formal education system indigenous to Côte d'Ivoire before the European-oriented system was imported. Indeed, the "Poro" is said to be a comprehensive school curriculum as well as a lifelong education system. The first three stages last seven years each and are compulsory for males of ages 7, 14, and 21.

The Senoufo female goes through a different and simplified "Poro" test from her early childhood to puberty, at which point the initiation process is suspended. After reaching her menopause, she is considered asexual and, therefore, is again eligible to pursue this lifelong education system. As a rule, the "Poro" initiation spans the Senoufo's life from cradle to grave, gradually teaching him or her self-control techniques and also the bulk of knowledge necessary to assume his or her social and professional status.

The 1990s public school curriculum is designed and monitored by central authorities operating at the level of the different ministries in charge of the educational system. The main task of these authorities consists in producing syllabuses for nationwide use. They assume more a pedagogical role than an administrative one. At the level of the primary school system, there is the *Direction générale des études et des programmes* (DGEP). Its counterpart at the secondary school level is the *Sous-Direction de la coordination pédagogique*. Finally, there is the *Commission nationale de pédagogie* which is more administrative than didactic. It is composed of the *Conseillers pédagogiques* and *Inspecteurs de l'enseignement* (one inspector per subject matter). The Commission periodically gathers its commissioners to discuss curriculum matters and to establish the national list of the different textbooks used in the country's primary and secondary schools. There is very little in this curriculum that reflects the cultural environment of indigenous Côte d'Ivoire.

8. The System of Examinations, Promotions, and Certifications

At the end of the first cycle of study (i.e., CP1 through CM1), pupils sit for two tests, the results of which will have different impacts on the course of their futures. The first is a school leaving certificate which provides neither social nor economic returns to the holder. The second test is a nationwide examination which allows the successful candidates to apply for entrance to the first grade of secondary education (CEG). It used to be the case that any Ivoirian who passed the second examination successfully was automatically eligible for a scholarship covering textbooks and school supplies. This is no longer the case, as resources are scarce, and parents are encouraged to share the financial burden of their children's education.

During the 1980s, there was a steady decline in primary education enrollment. In 1992, an average of 34.5 percent of all school-age children in Côte d'Ivoire were still denied access to formal primary education, despite the goal set for universal primary education in accordance with the 1961 Addis Ababa Educational Proclamation.

In addition, the system contains a severe factor of selectivity that produces a 30 percent dropout rate following the first grade and a 20 percent rate of primary school repetition. These three negative factors (34.5% non-school-attendance rate; 30% dropout rate, and 20% repetition rate) confirm the impression that the Ivoirian educational system is of low effectiveness at best and provides low equitable access to the school system.

As the secondary school level is reached, further unduly selective factors are encountered which further curtail Ivoirians, access to education: the Secondary School Entrance Examination (*Examen d'entrée en sixième*), the Secondary School First

Cycle Examination (*Brevet d'études du premier cycle* [BEPC]), and the University Entrance Examination (*Baccalauréat*). These three consecutive parameters of selection result in a pyramid-shaped Ivoirian educational system characterized by a large base (82% of school-age children in the first grade of the primary level) narrowing sharply toward tertiary education (17% at middle-course, in the first year of the secondary level and 1% at the top, in the first year of higher education).

In the school year 1991–92, there were 241,489 candidates who sat for the CEPE (the second sixth grade) examination. The total number who succeeded was 147,045 (61%). At the BEPC level, the total of the candidates was 81,272, and 19,414 students passed (24.5%). Finally, 45,075 students registered for the *Baccalauréat* examination. The total number of successful candidates was 10,685 (23.7%). Again, at 61 percent, the pyramidal structure has a large base. Four years later, the steepness of the pyramid slope produces a loss of 36.5 points and the percentage drops to 24.5 percent. There is only 0.8 point in loss between those sitting the BEPC and the *Baccalauréat*.

9. Educational Assessment, Evaluation, and Research

Since Independence in 1960, Côte d'Ivoire has made various adjustments to the inherited colonial educational system. Early endeavors were aimed at achieving universal primary schooling by the mid-1970s. The launch of a nationwide television educational program formed an essential part of this first educational assessment (Egly 1986). A subsequent decision based on a tenuous evaluation that correlated education to the labor market (Bertrand et al. 1981) produced a measure by which the leadership attempted to subordinate educational needs to development and economic potentials. The 1977 Reform Law (which was never enacted) aimed at improving the integration of Ivoirian youth into the economic system.

In 1975, the Ivoirian leadership added an evaluation tool known as *Service d'évaluation* to the primary education system. The rationale behind the creation of this tool of educational performance measurement was to enable the Ivoirian policymakers to monitor simultaneously the multiple components of national distance education through television. This evaluation tool drew a great deal of support from internationally renowned scientific institutions, such as the *Laboratoire de pédagogie expérimentale* at the University of Liège, Belgium, and the Stanford University Institute for Communication Research. However, twelve years after its creation, the television program and its supporting evaluation structure collapsed, not due to economic, technical, and pedagogical difficulties, but because of sociocultural factors that policymakers did not address beforehand (Egly 1986 p. 343).

Since 1990, Higher Education and Scientific Research, which were under two separate ministries, have been combined into one department. At first glance, it appears as if Higher Education, which is concerned with teaching, and Scientific Research, traditionally an individual activity, are now being considered as two sides of the same coin. This policy has positive ramifications, since the two areas can now inform each other rather than operate autonomously.

Fundamental and applied research are performed in order to establish or consolidate the credentials of the university or the higher education institution. Between 1966–74, several university research institutes were created: the *Institut d'ethnosociologie* (IES), the *Institut de géographie tropicale* (IGT), the *Institut d'écologie tropicale* (IET), the *Institut de linguistique appliquée* (ILA), the *Institut d'histoire, d'art et d'archéologie africains* (IHAAA), the *Centre d'études et de recherches en communication* (CERMOM), the *Criminologie*, the *Institut de littérature et d'esthétique négro-africaine* (ILENA), the *Institut de recherches mathématiques* (IRMA), the *Centre ivoirien d'études et de recherches en psychologie appliquées* (CIERPA), the *Centre ivoirien de recherche économique et sociale* (CIRES), the *Centre universitaire d'études françaises* (CUEF), the *Centre de recherches en architecture urbaine* (CRAU), the *Groupe de recherches en tradition orale* (GRTO).

10. Major Reforms in the 1980s and 1990s

Experts on education in sub-Saharan Africa have called for a "revitalization" of the 1960s and 1970s "existing educational infrastructure" that could lead to "a properly conceived educational strategy" in the 1980s and 1990s (World Bank 1989 p. 3). In Côte d'Ivoire, the period from 1983–90 was described as a taking-in-hand of the educational system in order to rejuvenate it at both the moral and managerial levels (Gideppe 1990 p. 192). However, the serious school crisis of the early 1990s has shown this period to have been more political rhetoric and wishful thinking rather than actual reform. The main reason appears to be the superficial analysis of the real educational needs of the country's primary and secondary school population. In other words, the condition of the educational picture in Côte d'Ivoire in the early 1990s is troubling because there never has been a properly conceived educational strategy, only a series of innovations with no real plan for following them through.

The 1977 *Etats généraux* on education under the authority of Usher Assouan (the name of the Commission's President) and their output were never properly enacted. The 1983–90 educational reform in Côte d'Ivoire was assessed as a three-phase action conducted by the supervising ministry at that period. The first phase, called the "Third Education Project of the World Bank," in fact ran from 1980 to 1985 and was dubbed the "Moral Rearmament" endeavor. Its supposed aim was to win the trust of all the educational system's partners. The second phase, from 1986 to 1988, was launched by the *Etats généraux* on education, and set as its goals the reconstruction of the existing educational system by targetting definite objectives, such as the introduction of civic and moral education, pledging allegiance to the national flag, and singing the national anthem every morning. The third phase, starting in 1989, emphasized the administrative as well as the pedagogical management of the human and financial resources available, by decentralizing the primary and secondary schools' planning and development. In other words, education is now in the hands of the local jurisdictions.

11. Major Problems for the Year 2000

The phenomenon of rapid urbanization, with its series of socioeconomic and politico-cultural challenges in modern Côte d'Ivoire, will have tremendous impact on all educational issues for the rest of this century. During the 1980s, the urban portion of the total Ivoirian population saw an additional 1 percent increase per year. If this trend continues at the same pace the urban population will reach 57 percent of the total population by the year 2000. One implication is that by the beginning of the twenty-first century, more than half the Ivoirian population will be city dwellers and will rely less on the traditional channels of education, such as the "Poro" initiation ceremony.

Based on the history of education reforms and the emerging demographies, some tentative conclusions can be drawn in identifying the major education problems of the next century. These may be enumerated as follows:

(a) The reforms of the 1980s and 1990s, such as pledging allegiance to the country's flag and singing of the national anthem, will no longer be a viable ingredient of educational reform.

(b) The advent of multiparty rule on April 30, 1990 has brought to the forefront the necessity of a real debate on the kind of education the country wishes to implement. The student body has changed since 1990: student demands are no longer limited to increases in their allowances or the social concerns of previous decades. The claims are of a political and academic nature, regarding, for example, the change of leadership at the head of the ministry in charge of the education system, or the university presidency, or the student union directorate. Irrespective of whether these claims are justified or not, they must in any event be taken into account as Côte d'Ivoire prepares for a national dialogue on the educational system.

(c) The debate on the "new Ivoirian school" includes a variety of aspects which can be summarized as follows: economic returns to investment in education, equitable access to educational opportunities, and the education–labor ratio.

These are among the important issues to be tackled. Both government and opposition leaders will need to cooperate in laying down principles for the foundation of a new Ivoirian school system.

References

Bendor-Samuel D 1984 On the study of literacy. In: Kaplan R B (ed.) 1984 *Annual Review of Applied Linguistics 1983*, Vol. 4. Newbury House, Rowley, Massachusetts

Bertrand O, Timar J, Achio F 1981 The planning of training in the Third World. *International Labor Review* 120(5): 531–44

Egly M 1986 L'utilisation de la télévision scolaire au Niger, en Côte d'Ivoire et au Sénégal. *Int. Rev. Educ.* 32: 338–45

Front Populaire Ivoirien (FPI) 1987 *L'Education: Propositions pour gouverner la Côte d'Ivoire.* L'Harmattan, Paris

Gideppe (ed.) 1990 Education: La priorité. *Jeune Afrique Economi.* JAE, Paris

Grootaert C 1990 Returns to formal and informal vocational education in Côte d'Ivoire. *Econ. Educ. Rev.* 9(4): 309–19

Komenan A G, Grootaert C 1990 Pay differences between teachers and other occupations: some empirical evidence from Côte d'Ivoire. *Econ. Educ. Rev.* 9(3): 209–17

Lamb D 1988 A different path. *Wilson Q.* 12(4): 114–31

Ogbu S M, Gallagher M 1991 On public expenditures and delivery of education in sub-Saharan Africa. *Comp. Educ. Rev.* 35(2): 295–318

Ong W J 1990 *Orality and Literacy: The Technologizing of the World.* T J Press (Padstow) Ltd, Padstow

Roberts T D et al. (eds.) 1973 *Area Handbook for Ivory Coast.* US Government Printing Office, Washington, DC

Speak G (ed.) 1982 Education and literacy. In: *Cultural Atlas of Africa.* Mayfield House, Oxford

World Bank 1989 *Education in Sub-Saharan Africa: Policies for Adjustment, Revitalization, and Expansion.* The International Bank for Reconstruction and Development/The World Bank, Washington, DC

World Bank 1992 *African Development Indicators.* The International Bank for Reconstruction and Development/The World Bank, Washington, DC

Further Reading

Appleton S, Collier P, Horsnell P 1990 *Gender, Education, and Employment in Côte d'Ivoire: Social Dimensions of Adjustment in Sub-Saharan Africa.* Working paper No. 8, Policy Analysis. World Bank, Washington, DC

Chaudenson R, De Robillard D (eds.) 1989 *Langues et Développement: Langues, Economie et Développement, Vol. 1.* Didier Erudition, Paris

Glaze A J 1981 *Art and Death in a Senufo Village*. Indiana University Press, Bloomington, Indiana
Grootaert C, Kanbur R 1990 *Policy-oriented Analysis of Poverty and the Social Dimensions of Structural Adjustment*. World Bank, Washington, DC
Kanbur R 1990 *Poverty and the Social Dimensions of Structural Adjustment in Côte d'Ivoire*. World Bank, Washington, DC
World Bank 1989 *Sub-Saharan Africa: From Crisis to Sustainable Growth*. World Bank, Washington, DC
World Bank 1990 *Primary Education*. World Bank, Washington, DC

P. Kokora

Counseling Adult Students

The counseling of learners—or potential learners—is a vital activity within adult education and one which is integral to its philosophy and goals. Although considerable ground has been gained in promoting an understanding of counseling for adult students and in establishing these services, many challenges remain. This entry provides a discussion of the nature and importance of counseling for adult learners, and reviews selected emerging issues.

1. Concepts and Definitions

Woolfe et al. (1987) describe counseling as being "about helping people to help themselves to live their lives more effectively" (p. 35), and as involving four stages—exploring, understanding, decision-making, and acting. But what does this mean for adults in an educational context? The answer is not a simple one nor is it a singular one.

Adult learners or potential learners bring many strengths to an educational setting as a result of life experience. That same complexity and richness, however, also implies that they present a variety of needs which may include the need for information about learning opportunities; for help in overcoming the residual pain of previous encounters with the educational system; for assistance in determining career and learning directions; for financial assistance; for help in learning how to learn; for help with personal or family concerns; for assistance in dealing with the educational system; or for emotional or psychological support. Counseling in an adult education context, then, may involve any of these activities and more, and may take place at any stage in the learning process—pre-entry, entry, during, or at exit (Schlossberg 1984a, Lynch and Chickering 1984).

Considerable variation exists in terminology used to articulate this helping function. "Guidance" and "counseling" are the two most common terms and are, on occasion, used interchangeably as, for example, by the Council for Cultural Cooperation (1982); frequently, however, distinctions are drawn. Woolfe et al. (1987) are among the clearest in distinguishing between two approaches. Guidance, according to them, emphasizes advice-giving and is advisor-directed; the major concern is with the decision or product which is specific to the situation at hand. Counseling, on the other hand, is more concerned with the process of decision-making and assumes that learning from one situation can be transferred to another. This activity is more nondirective and client-driven, with the counselor acting as an enabler or facilitator. Paulet (1988) draws a similar distinction between advising and counseling. Others (e.g., Brown 1991) use "guidance" as the more generic term and list "counseling" as a specific activity within a framework which also includes informing, advising, assessing, enabling, advocating, and feeding back.

2. Functions of Counseling

Educational counseling may serve a number of important functions for the individual, the institution, and for adult education in general. In broadest terms, counseling helps to remove or reduce barriers for the individual, barriers which may be informational, dispositional, situational, or institutional in nature. As a result, counseling provides improved access to educational opportunities for adults and increases the likelihood of successful completion. As recognized by the Council for Cultural Cooperation, adult education is still largely a privilege of the already educated; educational guidance and counseling, therefore, have an outreach function to help extend equality of opportunity to underserved groups. The Council report (1982) refers to guidance and counseling as the "hinge-pin" between supply and demand in adult education.

Counseling can also be vital in helping adults deal with change. Schlossberg (1984b) builds upon earlier research by Aslanian and Brickell which indicated that a high proportion of adults seeking to continue their education are facing a transition in their lives. She offers a model for helping adults which assists them in exploring their transition, in understanding their resources, and in coping with the process of change. In a later work (Schlossberg et al. 1989), she applies the notions of adults in transition to the institutional setting and develops comprehensive recommendations for improving educational environments for adults. Woolfe et al. (1987) examine the risks, uncertainties, and grieving associated with change and suggest that counseling in adult and continuing education is frequently directed toward helping adults cope with change.

With the increased complexity of choice faced by adults, guidance and counseling can also provide assistance with decision-making as well as with helping students or prospective students to make necessary linkages. Active mediation is also an important function in helping adult learners, both within institutions and the larger community.

Guidance and counseling services for adult learners can also provide major benefits for educational institutions by attracting and retaining highly motivated nontraditional students. Adult education, as a whole, benefits from the important information about adults' needs and preferences gained through the counseling process—information that can be used in planning adult education programs and services.

The growth in and concern for counseling of adult learners is evidenced by national and international movements as well as by an expanding literature base. A 1981 study sponsored by the Council for Cultural Cooperation, for example, investigated the provision of information, guidance, and counseling in adult education throughout Germany, Denmark, France, Italy, the Netherlands, Portugal, Spain, Sweden, the United Kingdom, and Northern Ireland. In the United States, the National Association of Educational Guidance Services initiated a Task Force on Advising Adult Learners in 1986 which resulted in a report and list of recommendations (Polson 1986). Many writers indicate a lack of satisfaction with the recognition of the need for guidance and counseling services for adult learners. The expanding number of issues related to educational guidance and counseling for adults represented in the literature, however, indicate the growth and development of this aspect of adult education. The remainder of this entry reviews a number of these issues.

3. Settings and Structures

Educational counseling for adults may be offered in a variety of settings and through a range of agencies. Woolfe et al. (1987) list adult education centers, institutions of further and higher education, government training centers, community development centers, workplaces, and voluntary organizations as possible providers.

Institutionally based counseling for adults appears to be more the norm in North America than elsewhere. Polson (1986) reports that 79 percent of institutions responding to a national survey indicated the provision of special advisory services for the adult population. These services are generally available during regular working hours; slightly more than one-half of the respondents, however, provide office hours at nontraditional times. Although these services are primarily offered on campus only, about 40 percent indicated that similar services are available in off-campus locations. The counseling services provided by tutors in the United Kingdom's Open University are another example of a means of delivering institutionally based programs. Based on its investigation, however, the Council for Cultural Cooperation (1982) recommends that educational counseling services should remain independent of educational institutions because of the likelihood that the providers will offer biased advice.

Levine and Piggins (1981) explore the issue of counseling available in the workplace and conclude that there is a need for greater flexibility in the variety of courses and programs that will be supported by employers and unions and that more attention must be paid to enabling services such as childcare. Similar criticisms are raised concerning government counseling services; for example, in reviewing educational counseling provided by the Canada Employment Centre, Edwards (1991) questions whether it is the requirements and interests of the client that are being served or rather the government's agenda.

Ironside (1981) reports on four models for community counseling for adults and describes the strengths and weaknesses of each. These include the institution-based model (Women's Resource Centre, Vancouver, Canada); the community council/consortium model (Education Information Centre, Brantford, Canada); local government model (Education Advice Centre, Cologne, Germany); and the brokerage model (Belfast Educational Guidance Service).

There is, therefore, little consistency in recommendations regarding a "best" model. Whatever the structure for delivery, writers largely agree that the need for counseling and guidance services for adult learners is not sufficiently recognized and that these services are not adequately funded.

4. Roles of Educational Counselors and Advisors

Counselors and advisors of adult learners are called upon to play many roles. The role of provider of up-to-date information is, of course, central. The counselor may also be called upon to help clients assess their current skill levels. The description of "counselor-as-advocate" appears frequently; Woolfe et al. (1987), for example, suggest that the counselor must be concerned with not only the student/client but also with the system. Schlossberg (1984b) recommends an ecological approach in which the counselor is more than a good listener, but is also a broker, an advocate, and a linker. In another work (Schlossberg 1984a), it is suggested that counselors of adults in transition move from thinking of themselves as therapists and take on the role of environmentalist to build a supportive climate and collaborative community. This theme is carried forward by Lynch and Chickering (1984) who point out that the influx of adult learners to traditional higher education settings demands new roles for student development specialists; their list of potential roles includes ecology manager/consultant, resource person, mentor/educator, facilitator, and advocate. The theme of "counselor-as-educator" also runs through the work of several authors. Students need to learn how to learn (Gelatt 1984) as well as how to transfer the learning from one life situation to others.

5. *Professionalization*

What are the elements which make for an effective educational counselor or advisor of adults? Considerable concern is in evidence regarding issues of qualifications and training for counselors of adult students. Several authors, Imeson (1991) for example, view educational guidance for adults as a relatively uncharted movement and raise questions about the necessary knowledge and skills. Schlossberg (1984b) maintains that knowledge of adult development is as essential as are process skills in helping adults. Her model for helping adults in transition depends on the integration of content and process.

An ambitious project carried out in the United Kingdom by the Unit for the Development of Adult Continuing Education (UDACE), and funded by the Further Education Unit (FEU) of the National Institute of Adult Continuing Education (NIACE), took as its objective the development of a list of competencies for counselors of adult students (Oakeshott 1991). As a basis for this work, which measures competencies as outcomes rather than as methods or processes, four major objectives for educational guidance are identified: it should help potential adult learners to identify their learning requirements and interests, to make decisions appropriate to their requirements, to pursue strategies to meet these requirements in relation to opportunities available or negotiable, and to evaluate their own learning and decision-making processes. The report identifies three major work roles for the educational advisor: to provide a service offering educational guidance to adults, to deliver educational guidance to adults, and to provide feedback on clients' requirements to agencies concerned with adults' learning. The report also defines concomitant subtasks which can be used to develop education/training standards and to assess performance. By the project officer's observation, however, there is a need to find better ways to assess competence in interpersonal fields.

Woolfe et al. (1987), working from a philosophy of counseling as an educational process and from an acceptance of the counselor's role as one of helping the student or client to understand the learning process and to transfer it from one situation to another, suggest a number of agenda items for a potential training program for helpers of adults. They recommend that counselors need to be trained in the following: to understand adult life as a process of change and development; to understand the motivation behind and the nature of adult learning; to understand cultural, social, and economic influences on adult learning; to develop bridges between educational, work, and personal lives of adults; to work within systems to promote organizational change; to understand the importance and complexity of interpersonal relationships in learning; to use basic counseling skills; to recognize the open-ended nature of the helping process; and to recognize the need for accepting personal responsibility for one's own development.

Lynch and Chickering (1984) cite many of the same recommendations for the professional development of institutional student development specialists working with adult learners. Because of the increasing use of technologies for the counseling of adults, especially those studying through distance education, they add the need for training and skill development in these new technologies.

Training opportunities for counselors of adults remain limited. To promote the professional development of counselors of adult learners, the Council for Cultural Cooperation Report (1982) points to the need for increased exchange of experience through international, national, and regional meetings, through writing, and through study visits. A cautionary note regarding the professionalization of counseling for adult learners is struck by the Council as well as by Woolfe et al. (1987); they warn that this function ought not to be limited to professionals only, but that teachers of adults must continue to view themselves as having a vital counseling role.

6. *Models and a Theory Base for Counseling Adult Learners*

The deficit of comprehensive theory to support the growing practice of counseling adult learners remains a concern. Adult development writing is rich, but there are still many unanswered questions and much potential for investigation remains to challenge adult education theorists. However, adult development theory is acknowledged widely as fundamental to counseling practice.

Schlossberg (1984b) provides one of the most fully developed frameworks for counseling adults in transition. Her model proposes three primary goals for this type of counseling—to explore, to understand, and to cope—and outlines for each goal a knowledge component and a skills component. Exploring, for example, requires a knowledge of the transition, its type, content, and impact, and calls for listening, responding, attending, and focusing skills. Likewise, to accomplish the second goal of helping the client to understand, the counselor uses knowledge concerning the interactions among the individual, the transition events, and her or his environment to determine coping resources, and also uses helping skills of interpreting, identifying themes, confronting, and presenting information in order to provide a new perspective. Coping, the third helping goal, requires knowledge of the stages in the transition process as well as the skills to help the client decide on a course of action (or inaction).

Several authors contribute to the formulation of a theory base for educational guidance and counseling for adults. Woolfe et al. (1987) build a framework using concepts of adult development and principles of counseling. They offer strategies for particular applications, for example, in working with the unemployed, the retired, or with students at a distance. Marsick (1985) describes a specific application, reevaluation counseling, which is used to examine and work through internalized patterns and preconceptions to improve learning. Developmental academic advising (Thomas and Chickering 1984), which is based on solid adult education principles, encourages advisors of students of all ages to view students as whole persons and to understand their needs using various development theories, including intellectual, moral reasoning, and life-cycle theories. Other specialized bodies of literature, in learning and career counseling to name but two examples, add to the richness of resources for the counseling of adult learners.

7. *Use of Technology*

Computer technology has been used extensively and for some time to assist with career counseling, with programs such as Choices, DISCOVER, and SIGI PLUS; these tools can help clients to assess interests and examine values as well as to identify and explore options. More recently, with the proliferation of personal computers in homes, libraries, workplaces, educational institutions, and so on, this medium is being used to disseminate up-to-date information about educational opportunities through computer networks; a project initiated by the Open Learning Agency in British Columbia is an example of this kind of service. A range of technologies, including telephone, television, cable, satellites, computers, electronic mail, videotapes, cassettes, and videodiscs provide assistance in various aspects of counseling, for example, record keeping, information provision, making assessments, and academic skill development (Lynch and Chickering 1984).

Technology is also playing an important role with a specific group of learners that are gaining greater recognition, that is, those studying through distance education formats. Woolfe et al. (1987) devote a chapter to means of counseling adult learners at a distance. Paulet (1988) points out that the significance of counseling and related support services for campus-based postsecondary education is well recognized; questions are now appearing about the need for such opportunities for distance education students as well. Paulet reminds practitioners about the social aspect of learning and about the concept of a community of scholars which still pertains to those learning away from a main campus setting. Distance education students, with their diverse backgrounds, lack of familiarity with new learning formats, and multitude of competing life concerns, need a support system as well as current and accurate information. Some services—for example, the provision of information—are being provided through nontraditional methods such as written communication, telephone, audiocassette, radio, and television, but the range of counseling content is limited. Distance education students also require help with goal-planning and decision-making skills as well as in making personal, social, and intellectual adjustments. In some cases, tutors or community representatives are employed to assist adult learners in their local communities.

Cooper (1991) raises a similar concern about the isolation which may be felt by individuals taking advantage of flexible learning alternatives such as modularization, accreditation of prior learning, and open learning as well as distance learning. He warns of the potential for a growing sense of confusion rather than empowerment and the risk of deterioration of needed support systems. Educational guidance and counseling, either through institutionally based or community-based services, are important for providing coherence of information, helping with decision-making and the acquiring of necessary skills, and providing a sense of connectedness.

8. *Ethical Issues*

Little writing appears on issues specifically related to the educational counseling and advising of adults. Day (1988) reminds educational advisors of the responsibility which is part of providing choice options for adult learners. He uses the examples of Eliza Doolittle in *Pygmalion* and Rita in the film *Educating Rita* to reinforce his assertion that the increase in choices brought about through learning may have significant implications for other aspects of the learner's life, such as for one's personal relationships. He suggests that educational counselors, in their role as educators, have a responsibility in helping learners to understand that learning cannot be viewed in isolation from the wholeness of their lives, but that it has consequences.

Oakeshott (1991) acknowledges the need to recognize the importance of adhering to professionally recognized ethical principles in competence statements for educational advisors, but admits uncertainty in determining ways to do so.

9. *Evaluation and Research*

The need for further research in the field of educational counseling and guidance for adults is noted by several authors. Knox (1981), for example, suggests that the evaluation of these services for adults requires investigation. Likewise, Oakeshott (1991), as a result of his competence project, identifies the need for research into the relationship between guidance activities and outcomes for clients. He also recommends the continuation of the work begun in this project (i.e., the identification of the competencies required by effective advisors). He also suggests that, because the effectiveness of educational guidance cannot be fully gauged simply by measuring outcomes for clients, new techniques must be developed to assess interpersonal elements of the counseling interaction.

Despite impressive developments in the counseling aspect of adult education, many writers warn that counseling is still viewed as a marginal enterprise with inadequate policies and precarious funding. Particularly in recessionary times, the message is clear that these services have a vital contribution to make to individual, social, and economic renewal.

See also: Student Support Systems: Adult Education; Student Support Systems: Administration

References

Brown J 1991 What is educational guidance? *Adults Learning* 2(10): 277–78

Cooper R 1991 Educational guidance and flexible learning. *Adults Learning* 2(10): 284–85

Council for Cultural Cooperation 1982 *Information, Guidance and Counselling in Adult Education*. Report of the seminar held in Soest, Germany, September 22–24, 1981. Council for Cultural Cooperation, Strasbourg

Day M 1988 Educational advising and brokering: The ethics of choice. In: Brockett R (ed.) 1989 *Ethical Issues in Adult Education*. Teachers College, Columbia University, New York

Edwards R 1991 Guidance and unemployment in Canada. *Adults Learning* 2(10): 279–82

Gelatt H B 1984 Excellence, equality and education: A future for counselling. *New Perspectives on Counseling Adult Learners*. In: Council for the Advancement of Experiential Learning 1984. National Institute of Education, Washington, DC

Imeson R 1991 The great training debate. *Adults Learning* 2(10): 283

Ironside D 1981 Community counseling for adults. In: DiSilvestro F (ed.) 1981

Knox A 1981 Emerging issues in counseling adult learners. In: DiSilvestro F (ed.) 1981

Levine H, Piggins D 1981 Workplace counseling: The missing link. In: DiSilvestro F (ed.) 1981

Lynch A, Chickering A 1984 Comprehensive counseling and support programs for adult learners: Challenge to higher education. In: Council for the Advancement of Experiential Learning 1984 *New Perspectives on Counseling Adult Learners*. National Institute of Education, Washington, DC

Marsick V 1985 Working with adult learners in higher education: Going against internalized norms. Paper presented at the Conference of the American Association for Adult and Continuing Education, Milwaukee, Wisconsin November 6–10, 1985

Oakeshott M 1991 *Educational Guidance for Adults: Identifying Competences*. National Institute of Adult Continuing Education, Leicester

Paulet R 1988 Factors influencing successful counseling in selected distance education programs. *J. Res. Dev. Educ.* 21(3): 60–64

Polson C 1986 Advising adult learners. National Academic Advising Association Task Force Report presented at the National Conference on Academic Advising, Seattle, October 12–15, 1986

Schlossberg N 1984a *Caught in a Dilemma: Adults as Learners*. New Perspectives on Counselling Adult Learners. National Institute of Education, Washington, DC

Schlossberg N 1984b *Counseling Adults in Transition: Linking Practice with Theory*. Springer, New York

Schlossberg N, Lynch A, Chickering A 1989 *Improving Higher Education Environments for Adults*. Jossey-Bass, San Francisco, California

Thomas R, Chickering A 1984 Foundations for academic advising. In: Winston R et al. 1984 *Developmental Academic Advising: Addressing Students' Educational, Career and Personal Needs*. Jossey-Bass, San Francisco, California

Woolfe R, Murgatroyd S, Rhys S 1987 *Guidance and Counselling in Adult and Continuing Education: A Developmental Perspective*. Open University Press, Milton Keynes

Further Reading

Allman P 1983 The nature and process of adult development. In: Tight M (ed.) 1983 *Education for Adults: Adult Learning and Education*. Croom Helm, London

Bitterman J 1985 Academic advising and adult education: An emerging synthesis. *NACADA J.* 5(2): 29–33

Dean G et al. 1987 Adults in mid-career change: Case studies for advisors. *NACADA J.* 7(1): 16–26

DiSilvestro F (ed.) 1981 *Advising and Counseling Adult Learners*. Jossey-Bass, San Francisco, California

Egan G 1982 *The Skilled Helper*. Brooks–Cole, Monteray, California

Friesen J 1986 Systems approach to adult counselling. *Guidance and Counselling* 1(3): 10–15

Marton F, Hounsell D, Entwistle N (eds.) 1984 *The Experience of Learning*. Scottish Academic Press, Edinburgh

Moore G, Waldron M 1991 *Helping Adults Learn: Course Planning for Adult Learners*. Thompson Educational Publishers, Toronto

Murgatroyd S 1985 *Counselling and Helping*. British Psychological Society, Leicester

Payne J 1985 Educational guidance services and the provision of adult education. *Int. J. Lifelong Education* 4(1): 35–54

Thomas N, Majnarich B, Lobes D 1982 Educational information centres: One answer for adults. *New Directions for Experiential Learning* 16:75–85

J. Potter

Courseware Design

Courseware, also known as computer-based instruction (CBI) or computer-assisted learning (CAL), has great appeal in education because it has the potential strengths of the three traditional media: teachers, films or videos, and books. Theoretically, courseware should have the ability to interact with students and to adapt to their individual needs, to provide easy access to structured information, and to be able to present static and dynamic graphics. This entry describes the various approaches taken to the design and implementation of courseware, and some of the issues contributing to its success or lack thereof.

There have been two distinct formal approaches to courseware design. One focuses on the content, the other on the process. The former is typified by the ideas of Reigeluth (1983), who differentiated between design, development, implementation, and evaluation. In Reigeluth's view, the design phase places the emphasis on structuring the content properly for learning to take place. This is in contrast to, and separate from, the development phase, which deals with taking the content and developing it into an instructional episode. Process-oriented models, on the other hand, deal with all aspects of producing a finished piece of courseware and take the attributes of the medium into account.

1. Content Models

Typical of the content approach are the models of Gagné and Briggs (1979) and Merrill (1983), as well as the traditional Instructional Systems Design models (see *Instructional Design Models*). Of these models, the one most commonly applied to courseware design is the well-known model of Gagné and Briggs with its nine events of instruction: gaining attention; informing learner of lesson objectives; stimulating recall of prior learning; presenting stimuli with distinctive features; providing learning guidance; eliciting performance; providing feedback; assessing performance; enhancing retention and learning transfer. Each event has a different purpose. Some may be omitted if the knowledge or background of the learner allows it. However, each needs to be considered as the lesson is designed in terms of both learners, content, and desired outcomes. The Gagné–Briggs model is general and can be applied to the design of all instruction. It has no specific attributes that apply to courseware design, although its application to courseware has been discussed frequently (e.g., Wager and Gagné 1988).

A similar situation applies to Merrill's Component Display Theory (Merrill 1983). It is also a general model for instructional design and deals primarily with the content and sequencing of a lesson. It does not deal specifically with courseware design. However, Merrill (1988) showed how it can be used for the production of courseware and provided numerous examples of its application.

1.1 Content Structure

In addition to the general models mentioned above, there are several other areas of research whose purpose is to influence the structure of courseware content, such as research into individual differences, including learning preferences and learning styles (e.g., Carrier and Jonassen 1988), adaptive instruction (see Tennyson and Cocciarella 1986), and the application of artificial intelligence (for overviews, see Alessi and Trollip 1991, Camstra 1986) (see *Artificial Intelligence as a Contributing Field to Instructional Design*). Each of these research themes seeks to find ways by which courseware can differentiate more finely between students, thus providing more individualized instruction. Results of this research have not been conclusive.

2. Process Models

In contrast to the content-oriented models, the process-oriented models deal with all aspects of courseware production rather than just the structuring of its content. These models specifically take into account the nature of the medium being used to deliver the instruction. Three such models will be discussed, namely those of Alessi and Trollip, Roblyer and Hall, and Steinberg.

Alessi and Trollip (1991) proposed a 10-step model comprising the following steps: determine needs and goals; collect resources; learn the content; generate ideas; design instruction; flowchart the lesson; storyboard displays; program the lesson; produce supporting material; evaluate and revise.

In the model, the first five steps make up the primary content and content structure phase of courseware design. Unlike the traditional models, where analysis occurs at the beginning of the design process, task and concept analyses in the Alessi and Trollip model are undertaken only after a creative brainstorming phase ("generate ideas") has been completed. "We believe that poor CBI is often developed as a result of cookbook-style instructional design wherein the developer never engages in activities resulting in creative ideas. Creativity is necessary in this new field, and without it, it is unlikely that the computer's capabilities will be fully exploited" (Alessi and Trollip 1991 p. 245). Following this advice, the possibilities of the medium are explored before the more traditional analyses take place.

With respect to content and content structure, Alessi and Trollip paid more attention to the process of ensuring that the strengths of the medium are taken into account in the design than they did to the details of content analysis and instructional sequencing. For that part of the design process, they recommended using the traditional content models (e.g., Gagné and Briggs 1979, Merrill 1988). One other feature of the Alessi and Trollip model that affects content and structure is the iterative nature of the model. Formative evaluation is undertaken at each major point in the model. After the lesson has been designed in outline form, it is appraised by

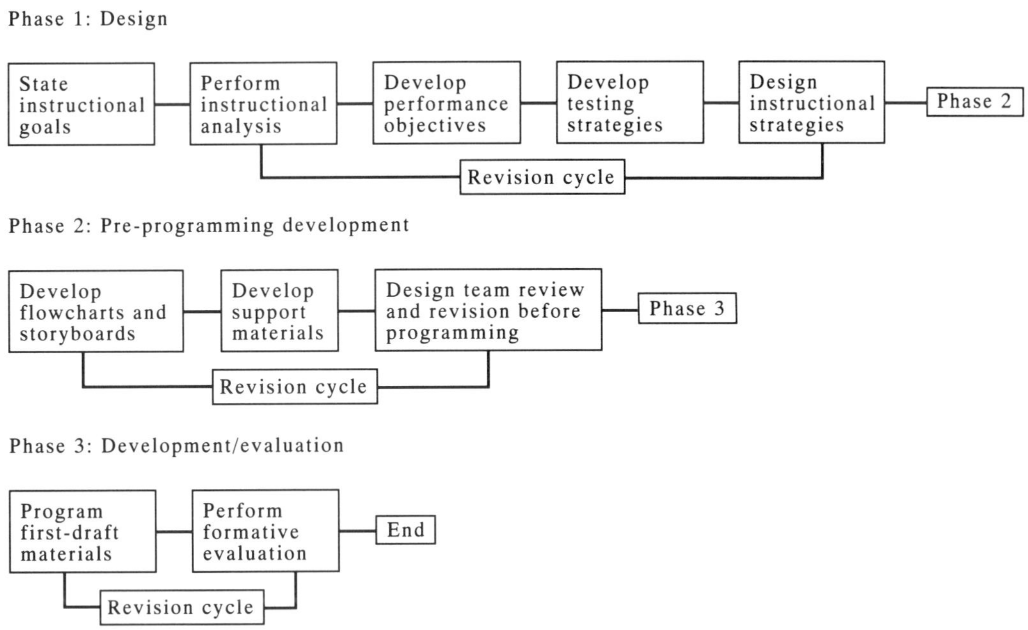

Figure 1
Courseware design model (adapted from Roblyer and Hall 1985)

content experts and potential students. This happens again after a prototype of the lesson has been prepared (either on paper or on screen), but before the programmer starts work. A final evaluation occurs after implementation. Each round of criticism has the potential to influence the structure of the lesson and, to a lesser extent, the content. This iterative approach minimizes the possibility that the end product will be ineffective.

Roblyer and her colleagues (Roblyer 1988) developed a courseware design model with three phases (see Fig. 1): design; preprogramming development; development evaluation.

The design phase of Roblyer's model is identical to the first five steps of the Alessi and Trollip model, except that it does not formally include a brainstorming session. The second and third phases are also very similar to the Alessi and Trollip model. The model as a whole emphasizes an iterative design, test, and revise paradigm. Roblyer and Hall (1985) did not elaborate a formal content structure approach, but suggested using Gagné and Briggs as a basis for designing instructional strategies.

Steinberg (1984) dealt with the development of content and content structure of courseware in her three-phase plan (Fig. 2). In phase one the initial planning takes places with the analysis of the task and the specification of prerequisite skills. In phase two, units of instruction are programmed, evaluated with students, and then revised, expanding the available information whenever necessary. Each iteration has a ripple effect on the instruction, resulting in only necessary information and interactions being developed. One potential drawback of the model is that each iteration requires units to be developed on the computer before evaluation. If major changes are required, it can be very time-consuming to undo and redo program codes. As with the two models

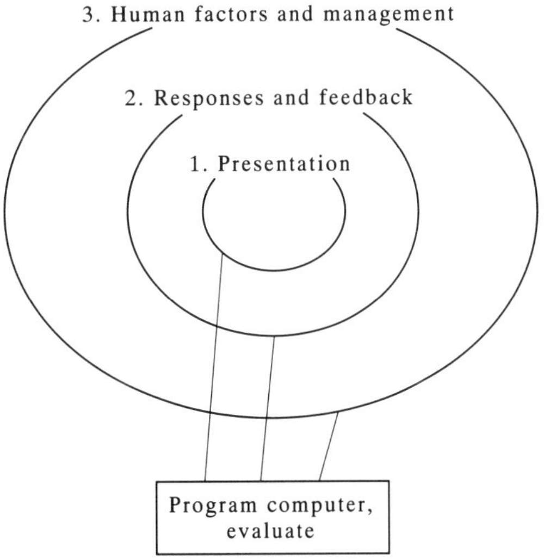

Figure 2
The Ripple Plan (adapted from Steinberg 1984)

above, Steinberg drew upon traditional instructional design approaches to supplement her model.

3. Commentary

It would be very useful to know whether the content-oriented models are more effective for designing courseware than the process models. Unfortunately, conclusions cannot be reached because there are virtually no data evaluating the effectiveness of the different design approaches. On the other hand, there is a wealth of practical experience on how to develop courseware that works—often in the form of what not to do rather than what to do. As with classroom teaching, there is no magic formula to ensure high-quality instruction. There are only guidelines that increase the probability of success, which may best be described as the necessary conditions for success. There are, as yet, no sufficient conditions.

3.1 Necessary Conditions

If courseware design is considered as a multidisciplinary activity demanding expertise in content, content structure, presentation, interaction, implementation, and evaluation, then these necessary conditions may be stated as follows:

(a) The content must be accurate.

(b) The content must be structured to facilitate learning.

(c) Information must be presented succinctly in both textual and graphic formats, taking into account the constraints of the size and resolution of the computer screen.

(d) Interactions between the learner and the courseware must be meaningful.

(e) The courseware must be robust and implemented so efficiently that it never malfunctions.

(f) Courseware must be the product of a rigorous, iterative formative evaluation process.

The content-oriented design models discussed earlier can only provide the first two of these necessary conditions. Merrill (1988) argued that as long as the nature of the medium is taken into account any good instructional design theory can be used for courseware design. The weakness of the argument is the assumption that designers will take the nature of the medium into account. Practical experience and anecdotal evidence suggest that because these models were not developed specifically for an interactive medium, designers usually overlooked the constraints of the medium and produced courseware with limited interactivity, violating one of the necessary conditions stated above. In other words the nature of the content-oriented models appears to constrain the creativity of the designer, particularly in the area of interactivity.

The process-oriented design models, for the most part, provide sufficient direction for a designer to satisfy all the necessary conditions and, consequently, have a greater chance of success. It is important to realize that even satisfying all the necessary conditions will not ensure effective courseware, but only improve the chances of doing so.

Experience shows that three of the conditions are particularly difficult to satisfy. First, screen design is often poor. Second, most designers find it very difficult to conceive and implement meaningful interactions. Third, the rigorous, iterative formative evaluation process is often ignored.

One aspect of the whole courseware design process that can have a major impact on effectiveness is the way the content is presented visually. Many good lesson designs have been marred by lack of attention to principles of screen layout. Issues such as presenting information from left to right, top to bottom, not overdoing any form of highlighting (such as color or underlining), providing adequate "white" space, ensuring that graphics and animations are pertinent and clear, and making clear what the student has to do, are well-known and thoroughly documented (e.g., Alessi and Trollip 1991, Sampath and Quaine 1990). The other point to be remembered is that some people prefer to learn from text and others from graphics. Incorporating both into courseware usually facilitates learning (Alesandrini 1987, Rieber and Kini 1991).

If designers have had little experience with courseware design, their years of experience of working with either stand-up instruction or paper-based media will usually result in their courseware having inadequate interactions. This usually means that the interactions comprise no more than answering multiple-choice questions or pressing a key to advance. More sophisticated interactions, such as occur in complex simulations or when allowing and then judging extended answers, are very difficult to design, let alone implement. They require both familiarity with the medium and access to a high level of technical ability for implementation.

Inadequate interactions can also mean that the power of the computer is not used effectively. A good example of this is in the area of drills. Most computerized drills are based on either a static or randomized presentation of information that mimics a flashcard presentation. However, a more effective approach is to build on what is known about learning, and to design a drill that incorporates feedback, discrimination, and reinforcement. The Variable Interval Performance (VIP) drill (Alessi and Trollip 1991) does this by presenting items in an order that depends on how the learner is performing. Furthermore, feedback for incorrect responses varies according to whether the incorrect answer is the answer to another item in the drill or not.

The one area in which some progress has been made, although the benefits are still in doubt, is that of adaptive instruction. Not unlike the VIP drills mentioned above, adaptive courseware assesses how the learner is performing, hypothesizes what the learner's misconceptions are, or optimizes the order of instruction (see Jonassen 1988 Pt. II for an overview). From a purely practical perspective, the algorithms that underlie adaptive instruction usually take a great deal of study, experimentation, and revision before they can be incorporated effectively into courseware. For most designers or developers the amount of effort required is too great, and consequently work in this area is left to researchers.

The final condition that is rarely met is that of rigorous, iterative formative evaluation. This may, in fact, be the most crucial of all the conditions. As stated earlier, merely satisfying the six necessary conditions will not guarantee effective instruction, but simply increases the chances of it happening. Rigorous, iterative formative evaluation and revision throughout the design process will have the greatest impact on effectiveness. Content analysis and design, screen layouts, and programming are all bound by well-known conventions or models. However, the subtleties of effective courseware are not. It appears that the best way to incorporate them is by watching students perform and react to the instruction, and then revising the instruction accordingly. This is a slow process, but this trial-and-error cycle of testing, revising, and testing again hones the instructional effectiveness of the courseware.

3.2 Motivation

Another issue that affects the quality of courseware is the motivation of students. There are two basic types of motivation: (a) extrinsic, where students are motivated by the need for good grades or the threat of punishment; (b) intrinsic, where the student is interested in learning irrespective of the external conditions. If students are not motivated to learn (which is the assumption a designer should make), even the best designed courseware may be ineffective unless it is in itself motivating.

Malone (1981) found that courseware that motivated students had three fundamental characteristics: challenge, fantasy, and curiosity. Video games clearly have these, which explains why they are so popular. Malone's work was seminal in the area, but it was Keller and his associates (Keller and Kopp 1987) who developed a model (the ARCS model) for designing motivating courseware (see *Motivation in Instructional Design*). The ARCS model uses four factors, each with three subcategories: Attention (perceptual arousal, inquiry arousal, variability); Relevance (familiarity, goal orientation, motive matching); Confidence (learning requirements, success opportunities, personal control); Satisfaction (natural consequences, positive consequences, equity).

Keller and Suzuki (1988) took the ARCS model and illustrated how it can be applied to courseware design. For each category, they provided a strategy for implementation. For example, for perceptual arousal, the strategy is: 'Gain and maintain student attention by the use of novel, surprising, incongruous, or uncertain events in instruction.'

From the perspective of a courseware designer, it is important to realize that students are not necessarily motivated to learn. The implication is that motivation needs to be designed into the courseware.

3.3 The Design Team

One other important aspect of courseware design is the question of who should design it. The diverse requirements of successful courseware design indicate that a team effort is required (Alessi and Trollip 1991, Roblyer 1988). It is the rare exception when effective courseware is produced by a single person. The design team should have several capabilities: instructional design expertise with experience in interactive media; content expertise; writing skills, with experience in succinctness; graphics design experience, with expertise in laying out information on a screen; programming or implementation skills, with a background in issues of the human–machine interface; and evaluation skills, with an emphasis on transfer of learning issues. Finally, all those involved in the team have to be managed. This is best done by the instructional designer, although there are many cases when it has been handled by other team members or even a professional manager.

4. Conclusion

There are numerous studies reporting the effectiveness of individual pieces of courseware, and meta-analyses that report on the medium as a whole (e.g., Kulik and Kulik 1986). However, the effectiveness of courseware has generally been very disappointing. Typical courseware is not as insightful or flexible as a teacher and does not have the depth of information of a book, nor the richness of the graphics or animations available in video or film. The problem is that a great deal of courseware has been developed without taking into account basic instructional design concepts. Courseware that is well-designed is often unsuccessful because it fails to satisfy one or more of the other necessary conditions discussed above. Often, courseware contains more "glitz" than good instruction, probably due more to marketing considerations than to educational ones.

As to which model to use for designing effective courseware, there are no data for guidance. Incorporating a content-oriented model into a process-oriented model is most probably the best approach. However, it is wise to remember that there is no approach that guarantees good instruction. The best chance of producing effective courseware is to ensure that each of the necessary conditions is in place, and to conduct thorough and exhaustive formative evaluations throughout the design process.

Courseware design in the early 1990s is still in its infancy. It is likely that in the late 1990s and beyond principles and procedures will be established that will make courseware design more of a science than an art. Until then, following one of the systematic approaches described above offers the best likelihood of producing effective computer-based instruction.

See also: Computer Assisted Learning; Computer-managed Learning; Computers and Learning; Computers in Education; Computers in Education, Organizations and Journals on; Instructional Design Theories

References

Alesandrini K 1987 Computer graphics in learning and instruction. In: Houghton H, Willows D (eds.) 1987 *The Psychology of Illustration. Vol 2: Instructional Issues*. Springer-Verlag, New York

Alessi S M, Trollip S R 1991 *Computer-based Instruction: Methods and Development*, 2nd edn. Prentice-Hall, Englewood Cliffs, News Jersey

Camstra B 1986 AI in computer-based training. *Interactive Learning International* 3(4): 27–30

Carrier C, Jonassen D H 1988 Adaptive designs for courseware. In: Jonassen D H (ed.) 1988

Gagné R M, Briggs L J 1979 *Principles of Instructional Design*. Holt, Rinehart, and Winston, New York

Jonassen D H (ed.) 1988 *Instructional Designs for Microcomputer Courseware*. Erlbaum, Hillsdale, New Jersey

Keller J M, Kopp T 1987 Application of the ARCS model of motivational design. In: Reigeluth C M (ed.) 1987 *Instructional Theories in Action: Lessons Illustrating Selected Theories and Model*. Erlbaum, Hillsdale, New Jersey

Keller J M, Suzuki K 1988 Use of the ARCS motivation model in courseware design. In: Jonassen D H (ed.) 1988

Kulik C-L C, Kulik J A 1986 Effectiveness of computer-based education in colleges. AEDS Journal 19: 81–108

Malone T W 1989 Towards a theory of intrinsically motivating instruction. *Cognit. Sci.* 5: 333–69

Merrill M D 1983 Component display theory. In: Reigeluth C M (ed.) 1983 *Instructional design Theories and Models: An Overview of Their Current Status*. Erlbaum, Hillsdale, New Jersey

Merrill M D 1988 Applying component display theory to the design of courseware. In: Jonassen D H (ed.) 1988

Reigeluth C M 1983 Instructional design: What is it and why is it? In: Reigeluth C M (ed.) 1983 *Instructional-design Theories and Models*. Erlbaum, Hillsdale, New Jersey

Rieber L P, Kini A S 1991 Theoretical foundations of instructional applications of computer-generated animated visuals. *Journal of Computer-based Instruction* 18(3): 83–88

Roblyer M D 1988 Fundamental problems and principles of designing effective courseware. In: Jonassen D H (ed.) 1988

Roblyer M D, Hall K A 1985 *Systematic Instructional Design of Computer Courseware: A Workshop Handbook*. Florida A & M University, Tallahassee, Florida

Sampath S, Quaine A 1990 Effective interface tools for CAI authors. *Journal of Computer-based Instruction*, 17(1): 31–34

Steinberg E R 1984 *Teaching Computers to Teach*. Erlbaum, Hillsdale, New Jersey

Tennyson R D, Cocciarella M 1986 An empirically based instructional design theory for teaching concepts. *Rev. Educ.* 56(1): 40–71

Wager W, Gagné R M 1988 Designing computer-aided Instruction. In: Jonassen D H (ed.) 1988

Further Reading

Clark R E, Voogel A 1985 Transfer of training principles for instructional design. *Educational Communication and Technology Journal* 33(2): 113–25

Dudley-Marling C, Owston R D 1987 The state of educational software: A criterion-based evaluation. *Educ. Technol.* 27(3): 25–29

Hannafin M J, Peck K L 1987 *The Design, Development, and Evaluation of Instructional Software*. Macmillan, Inc., New York.

Merrill M D 1987 Prescriptions for an authoring system. *Journal of Computer-based Instruction* 14(1): 1–9

O'Shea T, Self J 1983 *Learning and Teaching with Computers*. Prentice-Hall, Englewood Cliffs, New Jersey

Reigeluth C M (ed.) 1987 *Instructional Theories in Action: Lessons Illustrating Selected Theories and Models*. Erlbaum, Hillsdale, New Jersey

Shneiderman B 1986 *Designing the User Interface: Strategies for Effective Human-Computer Interaction*. Addison-Wesley, Reading, Massachusetts

Steinberg E R 1989 Cognition and learner control: A literature review, 1977–1988. *Journal of Computer-based Instruction* 16(4): 117–21

Wager W, Wager S 1985 Presenting questions, processing responses, and providing feedback in CAI. *J. Instr. Dev.* 8(4): 2–8

S. R. Trollip

Courseware Evaluation

The reshaping of schools and school curricula has brought about a rapid increase in the use of information technologies in education. As a result, the need has arisen for valid methods of evaluating such technologies. Courseware evaluation is a relatively new field, and one in a state of constant change. This entry discusses factors involved in the evaluation of courseware, such as the variety of courseware types and the role of each type in meeting curricular needs, as well as the methods of evaluation in use. Throughout this entry, the terms "courseware" and "instructional software" are used to refer to computerized instructional programs.

1. Goals

As society becomes more technologically and scientifically oriented, its needs become increasingly diverse and complex. These changes are clearly reflected in the restructuring of schools and curricular goals. The effort to realize the new goals is manifested in the introduction of computer technology to schools. Between 1980 and 1990, the number of microcomputers in United States schools increased nearly fifty-fold, from fewer than 50,000 to roughly 2,400,000 (Becker 1991).

Computer technology is not an end in itself but one of the means by which the new educational goals can be achieved. Computer-based instructional programs, or courseware, are expected to help reshape the circumstances of learning and teaching, to provide opportunities in education, and to restructure the way in which educational resources are distributed and delivered. Such high expectations emphasize the critical role of courseware evaluation that is adaptive to changing educational needs and computer applications.

Because courseware evaluation is a relatively new field, it lacks an established framework as well as a sound tradition based on accumulated experience. Approaches to courseware evaluation rely heavily on conventional practices; however, because of inherent differences among the various media, one cannot evaluate computer-based instructional programs in the same way as one evaluates other learning materials, particularly textbooks. Courseware is not readily accessible to inspection by scanning and the random selection of parts for detailed examination. Computerized materials must be run in real time and explored in detail from the perspectives of both an expert user and a novice learner. Hence, new and diverse methods of evaluation are called for; they must be flexible enough to accommodate varied types of computer applications and to adapt to changing needs.

Information about computerized instructional programs is in demand by diverse audiences including policymakers, school officials, producers of educational materials, potential financial backers, and, of course, teachers, students, parents, and researchers. Each sector has its own concerns, such as improving the productivity of the educational system; facilitating the learning of a particular skill across different subject areas; maintaining or increasing educational equity; redefining curricular goals in a specific subject area; and preparing both students and teachers for the technological needs of society. The increasingly diverse consumer market combined with broader curricular priorities governs the directions for the evolving field of courseware evaluation.

Evaluation covers four major areas, which are also applicable to the evaluation of courseware: (a) courseware design; (b) the effects on courseware selection; (c) courseware implementation; and (d) the formation of a theoretical basis for courseware use, including its effects on cognitive, social, and instructional processes.

2. *Factors affecting Evaluation*

Courseware evaluation as a field of study requires parameters that define valuable educational courseware. Although a vast amount of literature exists on this subject, a basis of agreed criteria is still lacking. The parameters of evaluation are influenced mainly by the multiplicity of courseware types and the role of each type, curricular needs, and actual classroom implementation.

2.1 *Courseware Types*

The field of computerized instructional programs has grown rapidly and is constantly subject to innovation. Within a relatively short period, a variety of instructional software types has emerged. In the early 1980s, the dominant types were the tutorial lesson, and drill and practice. The earliest programs, often referred to as "closed," "goal-driven," or "tutorial-model" courseware, were considered effective in developing factual knowledge. However, new types have been developed in the form of simulations, guided and open-ended explorations, microworlds, microcomputer-based laboratories, data bases, model-building activities, and learning tools such as spreadsheets and word processors. These newer types of courseware, referred to as "open," "goal-free," or "tool-model," are believed to foster strategies and skills (Yazdani 1986, Meeks 1987, Naiman 1987, Futcher 1989, Holloway 1990).

As courseware types have been evolving, the packaging of courseware programs has also undergone change. The early isolated sets of computerized activities were replaced by well-organized packages. Later, integrated learning systems (ILS) that offer both courseware and instructional management functions were introduced; some ILS packages also generate activities that are performed without the computer. These developments affect the ways in which computerized programs are used in the classroom. The settings range from a dedicated computer laboratory to a classroom with several computers; from a stand-alone program (implemented at a single computer) to the configuration of a networked system (connecting a group of computers).

The various courseware types and usages differ in their structure, function, and aims. The differences are not merely quantitative nor are they due simply to the use of more advanced technology. They stem from differing schools of thought regarding how computers should and could affect learning and instruction. One view is that courseware is a means of improving upon the teaching of current curricula; another view endows courseware with the potential to foment a fundamental curricular reorganization that would allow for novel approaches and goals unattainable with previous technologies. Earlier conceptions looked for an increase in "smartness" that would render courseware a self-contained instructional delivery aimed at supplanting the role of teachers; approaches adopted since the late 1980s, however, regard courseware as a friendly tool to be controlled by teachers and students—in other words, a teacher's and student's partner.

Such a multiplicity of courseware types and diversity of aims cannot be accommodated within a set of standardized dimensions or criteria for evaluation. For example, a typical computerized tutorial presents concepts or rules, and, through branched programming, provides practice linked to error diagnosis. An exploration environment, on the other hand, lets students search for rules and generalizations and, in this way, fosters the development of searching and learning strategies. In the traditional tutorial courseware, tasks usually build on a predefined sequence—be it from the concrete to the abstract, from the specific to the general, or from the intuitive to the formal; on the other hand, a typical exploration environment expects the learners to control the actual path of learning according to their own style, preferences, and knowledge. Hence, a single set of attributes cannot be expected to assess accurately and validly the intrinsic qualities of all courseware types or the effects of the particular courseware on students' performance and teachers' instructional effectiveness. Moreover, evaluation criteria relating to individual pieces of courseware necessarily differ from those that apply to packages or systems. A variety of learning modalities that adapt to different students may be an important attribute in a courseware package, for example, but it is less likely to be a necessary dimension in the evaluation of a single courseware activity.

2.2 Courseware Roles and Curricular Needs

Curricular change is constant in education and does not represent merely a transition between old and new. Evolving educational needs, as reflected in curricular frameworks, thus constitute the most basic and meaningful source for determining means and modes of evaluation.

All computerized activities have at least one characteristic in common: they are intended to enable students to accomplish curricular goals. The activities are conceived as providing opportunities for both students and teachers to mindfully process, integrate, and apply curricular principles. Since curricular goals and frameworks define the circumstances of instruction and learning, they determine the functions and roles of courseware in the classroom. The roles assumed by courseware shape the dimensions of evaluation in two complementary ways: first, by focusing evaluators' attention on current approaches toward instructional processes and the expected outcomes of those processes; and second, by helping define dimensions for evaluating the implementation of courseware in the classroom.

Evaluation is made more difficult in light of the changeable nature of curricular goals. Since the 1950s, the emphasis of curricular goals has moved from knowing to searching; from learning content to applying processes; and from developing isolated skills to understanding global concepts and relationships. Curricular frameworks have broken away from the restrictions of subject matter boundaries to include conceptual connections within and between disciplines; and at the same time, the goals focus on depth rather than just breadth. Finally, curricular goals manifest a new attitude toward basic literacy skills (Shane and Tabler 1981, Ravitch 1983, Sendov and Stanchev 1987, Olson 1988, Holloway 1990).

Such curricular change typically requires evaluators to base their rationale and evaluation criteria on new sets of principles, primarily psychological and pedagogical. Many existing dimensions of evaluation are built on more traditional approaches to learning and instruction. These dimensions may be invalid or totally irrelevant to new educational goals and novel types of courseware. One of the requirements of courseware evaluation, therefore, is knowledge of, and openness to, divergent views regarding effective educational practices—even though such practices may be in a state of evolution and lacking a formal and conceptual framework. For example, a relatively stable set of principles is generally accepted as governing the effective design of an interactive tutorial lesson. One of these principles is to make clear to the students the goals of the activity. The manner in which this is done is secondary—it could be via a statement of the activities' objectives or by some other means of advanced organizer. In contrast, most of the "open" exploratory activities are designed with some level of ambiguity concerning the task at hand; trial-and-error experiences and more mindful search strategies may be a desired design principle. Does this principle lead to effective learning? Is it a necessary component of exploration-type courseware? In order to relate to such issues, evaluators must be sensitive to a large spectrum of approaches and theories regarding effective learning and instruction.

Actual classroom practices and the changing roles of students and teachers introduce further complexity to program evaluation. Students are no longer viewed as passive participants and receptors of information; they are considered active, independent learners responsible for their own learning. Teachers, rather than being regarded as the only source of information and knowledge, are cast as facilitators of instruction, tutors and coaches, and curriculum planners. These newly defined roles have significant effects on the dimensions of evaluation, as they redefine educational as well as organizational conditions that are part of an evaluation rationale. Furthermore, many curricula greatly enhance cooperative learning approaches and collaborative environments. These approaches are already evident in newer courseware (Eraut and Hoyles 1989) and evaluation must be adaptive to such changes.

A curriculum serves not only as a source for establishing evaluation criteria but also as a framework for methodologies that are essential in courseware evaluation. Since a curriculum determines the roles played by courseware in the educational environment, and a particular courseware program may have divergent roles and usages in the instructional process, evaluation is likely to be meaningful only if carried out in the context of the whole classroom milieu. For example, educators generally agree that two of the most promising roles of simulation in instruction are establishing a cognitive framework or structure in students to accommodate further learning in a related subject area, and providing an opportunity for reinforcing, integrating, and extending previously learned material. The simulation's function depends on its position relative to an instructional sequence. When used prior to instruction, the simulation is likely to fulfill the first role, whereas after instruction, it will probably fulfill the second (Levin and Waugh 1988, Brandt et al. 1991). Hence, out-of-context evaluation might be limited but would most likely be invalid.

Evaluation that takes into account the specific purposes of a computerized program and its use in a particular social and physical setting can be extremely helpful in the decision-making process as well as informative of the principles underlying the program's effects.

3. *Dimensions and Indicators*

Evaluation practices, particularly those dealing with the potential value of courseware, employ lists, schemes, and models that are assumed to reflect the most valuable dimensions or targets to be evaluated in a program. The lists often confine themselves to a particular realm: a subject area (Zohar and Tamir 1986); an age group (Swick 1989, Dejoy and Mills 1989); a type of courseware (Levin and Waugh 1988, MacKenzie 1990); or integrated learning systems (Hathaway 1989). The lists contain specific items in the form of questions or statements. Examples of these items follow:

(a) "Behavioral objectives are clearly described."

(b) "The user can adjust the level of difficulty."

(c) "Selection of choices is clear and easy to follow."

(d) "To what extent can learners control and guide the activity while they are engaged with the system?"

The lists vary in size, and some include over 300 items (Micceri et al. 1989). In most cases, the items are categorized according to global themes that link the components being judged. Some researchers have proposed a taxonomic structure for these components. Carrier and Sales (1987), for example, name three components: context, which includes a range of variables dealing with assumptions about instruction and learning (such as classroom environment and groupings); strategies, which relate to instructional techniques used to encourage specific processing activities (such as analogies, metaphors, examples, and types of feedback); and features, which deal with the technical capabilities available in computer-based instruction (such as color, sound, animation, and control by the learner).

Another scheme, the Computer Courseware Evaluation Model (CCCEM) developed by the Center for Interactive Technologies Application and Research (CITAR) (Micceri et al. 1989), uses four basic fields of reference: physical, which deals with characteristics of hardware and software (e.g., screen resolution and interface tools); presentation, which relates to the physical and instructional interface between the student and the software package (e.g., design features, text, graphics, and sound); instruction, which focuses on characteristics of the learning environment (e.g., instructional techniques, lesson sequencing, and questioning); and management, which concerns features of the instructional management system (e.g., record keeping, the generation of reports, and the control of lesson content). Many other schemes exist. Although the schemes vary in structure, most of them distinguish between components that influence the ongoing learning process and those that support the delivery of the instructional materials.

In most of the existing evaluation schemes, the dimensions to be analyzed and the indicators of value are interwoven. Some schemes, however, suggest the use of more explicit determinants of quality (Levin 1986, Voogt 1990). These determinants check, for example, whether the courseware is relevant to the curriculum, congruent with curricular goals, and based on appropriate objectives; valid (relating to the educational content, the legitimacy of computer use, and fairness toward all groups of users); adaptable or alterable; usable (in the technical and mechanical sense), integrative (able to integrate various sources of learning or different disciplines); and effective (relating to both immediate and long-term learning outcomes).

4. *Evaluation Methods*

Courseware evaluation studies usually use one or more of the following methodologies: a checklist, an analytical (open-ended) review, a panel evaluation, observation, and experimentation. Each methodology serves a particular purpose, is used at a certain stage of courseware development, and yields a different type of evaluation measure.

4.1 Checklist

The checklist method provides descriptive information on courseware and is often used as an aid in courseware selection. A checklist systematizes the evaluation process. A number of people, including teachers, curriculum coordinators, computer specialists, and students, rate the courseware according to the same set of evaluative criteria. An evaluator reviews the ratings and analyzes the data to discover trends. The advantage of the method is that it focuses on predefined criteria in a relatively short amount of time. However, the data lack reliability and validity, they are highly subjective, and their degree of detail comes at the expense of an overall picture.

4.2 Analytical (Open-ended) Review

This method involves the detailed, unstructured documentation of referees' judgments regarding the features of a program. By offering users and specialists the freedom to describe and judge various aspects of a program, the evaluator attempts to detect strengths and weaknesses that the most detailed checklist may not reveal. Although the information gathered in an analytical review is subjective, it is useful, particularly in combination with other methodologies. The method is often used in the stage of formative evaluation in order to provide relevant information for program developers.

4.3 Panel Evaluation

A panel of evaluators consists of two or three members drawn from a pool of classroom teachers, subject-area consultants, and university professors. Using a checklist, the panel works in one of two possible modes. In one mode, each member makes an independent judgment of a given program, then the panel decides together on the final ratings. In the other mode, the panel works as a team in examining the software and arrives at a consensus in the process. When the ratings are complete, the panel writes a short report that explains any extreme ratings, describes unusual features of the software, and offers suggestions regarding its usage. The need for a consensus appears to lessen the degree of subjectivity that is inherent in the checklist method and analytical review, and it also produces a reasonably high level of reliability. In addition, obtaining a view of a program as a whole seems to be easier with this methodology (Owston and Dudley-Marling 1988).

4.4 Observation

Observation of courseware in use can provide the basis for valid and effective evaluation. Ideally, the studies should be conducted at three levels: (a) the observation of a number of learners, either on an individual or a group basis, under controlled laboratory conditions; (b) the observation of learners under real classroom conditions; and (c) formal field-trial research that examines the effectiveness of the instructional and learning process or, when relevant, the effectiveness of the courseware under various possible instructional conditions. If and when the type of courseware involves the classroom teacher in a meaningful way, as in integrated learning systems or computerized management systems, similar research designs will be needed but will focus on teachers and learners alike. Observational studies that help clarify how program effects are produced typically pay a great deal of attention to the program itself. Such studies attempt to conceptualize the critical features that were to be designed into the program and to document them as actually delivered.

4.5 Experimentation

The use of experimental design in evaluation is controversial, particularly in regard to media-related instructional programs. When used properly, however, it can produce valuable results. Several experimental designs for evaluating computer-based instruction have been proposed (King and Roblyer 1984); they are oriented mostly toward assessing the effectiveness of courseware in terms of its effects on learning outcomes. Experimentation is the only methodology that checks the origin of effects rather than the effects themselves; it helps the researcher understand why a program works and why it produces different results under different educational conditions, rather than whether it works and how.

4.6 Criticism of Evaluation Practices

Criticism of courseware evaluation practices revolves around several issues. The practices are claimed to be normative, in that software is judged relative to other software; subjective, since judgments reflect the evaluator's personal philosophy and biases; descriptive rather than analytical (Johnston 1987); lacking in consistency or reliability (Micceri et al. 1989); and often providing information that is so specific and detailed that it is difficult to interpret and cannot lead to meaningful decisions (Owston and Dudley-Marling 1988). Along different lines, evaluation is criticized for using superficial functional qualities as evaluation criteria (Cox 1989); for showing a bias toward individualized instructional learning; and for neglecting to consider the quality of the software tools used to produce the courseware (Eskenasi and Radev 1989). Traditional experimental evaluation methodology is viewed by some researchers as being insensitive to the specific environmental circumstances within which the courseware is being assessed (Salomon 1990), as well as lacking a long-term approach to the systematic evaluation of a program on the basis of its possible usages and effects.

5. *Curricula, Classrooms, and Courseware*

The evaluation of computerized instructional programs involves more than just the establishment of definitive sets of criteria. A broader and more complex task, it necessarily reflects an ongoing dialogue between curricular needs, classroom practices, and courseware development. In the absence of mutual awareness, the dialogue can become an exercise in futility. Effective evaluation produces judgments that are context-related; regardless of the methodology used, it takes into account the pedagogical nature of the courseware, the classroom milieu, the desired goals, and the type of usage. Such evaluation is driven by educational needs, as reflected in the curricula, and by learning theories, rather than by technology.

Evaluation in general plays a significant role in establishing educational practices, expectations, and standards. Courseware evaluation needs to adapt a broad view of the field of educational computing to continue in this tradition. In this way, it can succeed in fulfilling its varied roles by moving from a descriptive approach to an analytic one, and it can foster the development of flexible frameworks within which systematic research will be encouraged and applied.

See also: Evaluation, Nature of; Computers in Education

References

Becker H J 1991 How computers are used in the United States schools: Basic data from the 1989 IEA computers in education survey. *Journal of Educational Computing Research* 7(4): 385–406

Brant G, Hooper E, Surgue B 1991 Which comes first, the simulation or the lecture? *Journal of Educational Computing Research* 7(4): 469–81

Carrier C, Sales G C 1987 A taxonomy for the design of computer-based instruction. *Educ. Technol.* 27(10): 15–17

Cox M J 1989 The impact of evaluation through classroom trials on the design and development of educational software. *Education and Computing* 5(1–2): 35–41

Dejoy J K, Mills H 1989 Criteria for evaluating interactive instructional materials for adult self-directed learners. *Educ. Technol.* 29(2): 39–41

Eraut M, Hoyles, C 1989 Groupwork with computers. *Journal of Computer Assisted Learning* 5(1): 12–24

Eskenasi A, Radev R 1989 Evaluation of the quality of authoring systems. *Education and Computing* 5(1–2): 43–47

Futcher D 1989 Playing with numbers. *Educational Computing* 10(1): 47–51

Hathaway W E 1989 A network-based curriculum: The basis for the design of a new learning system. *Educ. Technol.* 29(4): 23–28

Holloway M 1990 The media center online catalog: A modern day instructional tool. *Wilson Library Bulletin* 65(1): 26–30

Johnston V M 1987 The evaluation of microcomputer programs: An area of debate. *Journal of Computer Assisted Learning* 3(1): 40–50

King F J, Roblyer M D 1984 Alternative designs for evaluating computer-based instruction. *J. Instr. Dev.* 7(3): 23–29

Levin J A, Waugh M 1988 Educational simulations, tools, games and microworlds: computer-based environments for learning. *Int. J. Educ. Res.* 12(1): 71–79

Levin T 1986 Formative evaluation in the context of computerized insruction. *Stud. Educ. Eval.* 12(2): 121–29

MacKenzie, S 1990 Courseware evaluation: Where's the intelligence? *Journal of Computer Assisted Learning* 6(4): 273–85

Meeks B N 1987 The quiet revolution: On-line education becomes a real alternative. *BYTE* 12(2):183–90

Micceri T, Pritchard W H, Bareet A 1989 Must computer courseware evaluation be totally subjective? *Br. J. Educ. Technol.* 20(2): 120–28

Naiman A 1987 A hard look at educational software. *BYTE*, 12(2): 193–200

Olson J 1988 *Schoolworlds/Microworlds: Computers and the Culture of the Classroom.* Pergamon Press, Oxford

Owston R D, Dudley-Marling C 1988 A criterion-based approach to software evaluation. *Journal of Research on Computing in Education* 20(3): 234–44

Ravitch D 1983 On thinking about the future. *Phi Del. Kap.* 64(5): 317–20

Shane H, Tabler M 1981 *Educating for a new millennium* Phi Delta Kappan Educational Foundation, Bloomington, Indiana

Salomon G 1990 Studying the flute *and* the orchestra: Controlled vs. classroom research on computers. *Int. J. Educ. Res.* 14(6): 521–31

Sendov B, Stanchev I (eds.) 1988 *Children in the information age: Opportunities for creativity, innovation and new activities.* Pergamon Press, Oxford

Swick K J 1989 Appropriate uses of computers with young children. *Educ. Technol.* 29(1): 7–13

Voogt J 1990 Courseware evaluation by teachers: An implementation perspective. *Comput. Educ.* 14(4): 299–307

Yazdani N 1986 Intelligent tutoring systems: An overview. *Expert Systems* 3(3): 154–62

Zohar A, Tamir P 1986 A new instrument to assess the inquiry characteristics of science computer software. *Journal of Computers in Math and Science Teaching* 6(1): 44–46

T. Levin

Creativity

Creativity is an important but elusive concept. This entry is concerned with the three focuses of the scientific study of creativity: the person, the product, and the creative process.

Most of the scientific disciplines concerned with humans, from neuropsychology to economics, have been called upon to contribute to an understanding of creativity. From whatever perspective creativity is regarded, there are heated contests among alternative theories, and between the disciplines (e.g., between psychology and sociology) the coordination often leaves much to be desired. In addition, the subject matter itself seems to inspire an individualistic approach that hampers communication and the steady accumulation of warranted fact and understanding. To bring order into such a poorly unified field, a useful first step is to select a kind of prototypical creativity. Scientific creativity fits this role best. The greater part of the literature concerns scientific creativity. When scientific creativity was compared to other kinds (e.g., in architecture or writing) typically more commonalities than differences were found (Taylor and Barron 1963). A second unifying principle is that the study of creativity has three focuses also known as the "three Ps": the creative person, the creative product, and the creative process. These three aspects of creativity will be discussed in order.

1. *The Creative Person*

The basic question about the creative person (e.g., scientist) is what characteristics distinguish more creative people from their less creative peers. Research interest may then fan out to encompass matters such as social background effects, home environment, education, developmental patterns, career, personality (temperament), and interests. It is important to realize that the personal characteristic of being creative is merely one component of what is called "eminence," or "importance." The other components of this multidimensional "summing-up concept" are productivity, scholarship, and organizational contribution. The fact that being creative is a separable aspect of eminence is often obscured due to a tendency to select only the most eminent for consideration. The most eminent are statistically likely to score highly on all four contributing traits, even though these are only moderately correlated among each other. However, when a random sample of the complete population of working scientists in a certain field (e.g., psychologists) is taken, a multidimensional picture clearly emerges. There is the phenomenon of, for example, the highly productive scientist who is seldom cited, or the scholar, much appreciated for fine reviews, but who does no original research, and so on. All four components of eminence have their own set of predictive personal characteristics associated with them. In the psychometric tradition much correlational work has been done relating tests of intelligence and data from questionnaires with creativity ratings of scientists obtained from peers and supervisors. The results are clear-cut. The scientists judged more creative are very intelligent but not much more so than their less creative peers. They are characterized by a deeply felt interest in their subject matter, often going back to their childhood. Another striking feature is their independence of mind, their strong liking for the challenge of uncharted areas of investigation, and their persistence. Most distinctive, however, is their seemingly unshakable professional self-confidence. Though the correlations are clear, this approach leaves important aspects of the creativity of a person untouched. It is easy to see how creative potential translates into long hours (50 or more a week) of concentrated intelligent work on the frontiers of science and also to see how those hours result in success; but this will only happen if the environment, as a support system, provides the opportunity for the potential to become actual. Every person, whether they are creative or not, may be viewed as the ward of an informal support system that codetermines the level of performance reached by the individual. Thus, when judging a person to be highly creative on the basis of their scientific work, the researcher into creativity is bound to realize that this judgment pertains not to a self-contained individual but to a person interacting with an environment.

For the assessment of the creative potential of students and young scientists, multipurpose tests of intelligence and aptitude (e.g., the SAT) and temperament have proved to be of limited value. More appropriate are biographical inventories that aim to measure specific correlates of the complex of contributing traits described above. An example is the question of what the respondent prefers: a research position, a teaching position, or a combination of the two (see Taylor 1988).

2. *The Creative Product*

When can a product be called "creative"? In science, more than in the arts where matters of taste dominate, it is in the interest of all that creative work is universally recognized as such. The creative scientific product solves an important problem, answers an important question, or poses an important new problem or question. Consequently, the creative scientific product is, by definition, important and novel. However, it is in the nature of science that the creative product will eventually be fully accepted and followed. In science creativity is leadership. Defined in this way, the creativity of scientific products hinges on the judgment by peers, namely the recognized experts in the field, whose status is itself a matter of peer judgment. In intellectual domains that lack the institutionalized peer-review structure of science, such as architecture and literature, a similar structure can and has been temporarily established for research purposes: using nominations by peers to select a forum of acknowledged experts and then using this forum to obtain ratings of creativity of products or persons (Barron 1969). Research of this kind brings to the fore striking commonalities between scientific creativity and creativity in other domains.

According to the definition given, creativity is measured on an absolute scale. However, for educational and pedagogical purposes a relative point of view might sometimes be more useful. The comparison is then not between the given product and the absolute best there is, but between the product and the best to be found in a chosen reference group (e.g., the group of children of the same age). For the purpose of clarity in the discussion, it is important never to confound the two perspectives. In particular, creative children should not be thought of as junior, scaled-down versions of adult creative scientists, writers, architects, and so on. There is an important qualitative difference between the promising child and the creative adult, because creative production in the absolute sense is only to be expected from experts who have built up an extensive store of knowledge of their domain. Such expertise invariably takes years and much personal investment to realize (Ericsson and Smith 1991). It is certain that the creative scientist has "what it takes"; the creative child or student still has to prove it.

3. The Creative Process

Two schools of thought exist on the creative process. One regards creating as a process of goal-directed production; the other, Darwinian view, stresses the three processes of random production, goal-directed selection, and retention. Underlying this dispute is the philosophical question of how something novel can ever purposefully be created. Only accidental production of novelty would seem possible; the unknown cannot direct its own production. Psychological theories that start from this point of view stress fast random production of new combinations of already available elements, followed by rigorous evaluation to test whether the combinations generated fit the demands. A vast store of available elements (knowledge), and the opportunity and learning ability to fill this store, are considered prerequisites for creative production. The more elements available, the more new combinations are possible and the higher the level of complexity that can be achieved. Although, according to this view, the generation of new ideas is haphazard, the process itself is a deterministic one. The generation of ideas follows laws of association, and so the inventor/creator has some degree of control (e.g., via the selective filling of the knowledge store [preparation] and through influencing the contents of working memory). From these ideas, one arrives at the now prevailing theoretical position on creative thought. This claims that, although the creative product striven for is novel and thus unknown, it need not be, and indeed rarely is, totally unknown; otherwise the proposals generated could not be evaluated. The starting point of this theory is that the goal does indeed direct the process of its creation because it is partially and/or schematically known. This view essentially reduces creative production to problem-solving. Both are seen as a process of search that is directed and restricted by approximation (or anticipation) of the end results and of the way to achieve them. To know, for example, that one wants to compose a fugue constrains the search enormously, and each partial result (lines written) constrains this space even further. The schematic approximations or anticipations of the road to the goal are called "heuristic methods." Many different heuristic methods have been described, among them random "generate and test." However, the latter is seen as one method among others, and not as the basic nature of creative production. Indeed, humans have been shown to be incapable of random generation (try to write a random string of digits; a statistical test for randomness will always show your biases.

Both accounts of the creative process must be amended. As is typical for the psychological approach to human affairs, both stress the short term, the here and now of creation. The history of science, however, shows that actual creation is most commonly a process lasting many years, and taking place in a scientific environment that itself evolves. Nevertheless, mental search may be thought of as a core element of creative production.

4. Education and Creativity

The strong relationship between creativity and expertise has implications for how to go about educating *for* creativity. Many programs have been put on the market that aim at raising problem-solving ability and creativity in general. Both, however, are always particular: productive thinking is domain-specific. Such programs therefore miss the point. When the aim is to foster creativity there are two recommendations. The first is to orient the entire standard curriculum as far as possible toward problem-solving. The second is to help students of greater promise find or construct avenues of accelerated intellectual development in the domain of their choice.

See also: Problem-solving and Thinking, Development of Learning Skills in; Creativity, Teaching and Testing for

References

Barron F 1969 *Creative Person and Creative Process*. Holt, Rinehart and Winston, New York

Ericsson K A, Smith J (eds.) 1991 *Toward a General Theory of Expertise: Prospects and Limits*. Cambridge University Press, Cambridge, Massachusetts

Taylor C W 1988 Various approaches to and definition of creativity. In: Sternberg R J (ed.) 1988 *The Nature of Creativity: Contemporary Psychological Perspectives*. Cambridge University Press, Cambridge

Taylor C W, Barron F (eds.) 1963 *Scientific Creativity: Its Recognition and Development*. Wiley, New York

Further Reading

Ochse R 1990 *Before the Gates of Excellence: The Determinants of Creative Genius*. Cambridge University Press, Cambridge

Sternberg R J (ed.) 1988 *The Nature of Creativity: Contemporary Psychological Perspectives*. Cambridge University Press, Cambridge

J. Elshout

Creativity, Teaching and Testing for

People of all ages are constantly confronted by problems and situations that require decisions and provide them with opportunities to improve the human condition and enable them to understand phenomena in their lives. Every day they must act or behave in new or different ways because they are unable to solve the problems or resolve the situations using their current repertoire of knowledge and skills. Thus, these problems and situations require creativity, that is, innovative or adaptive thinking and behavior.

Creative thinking can be taught, enhanced, or nurtured. It is a complex cognitive activity that includes the development and effective use of a large knowledge base, critical thinking skills, decision-making skills, and metacognitive control processes. This entry will focus on (a) definitions, models, and theories of creativity; (b) methods of assessing creativity; and (c) ways of teaching or developing creative ability.

While often contrasted with intelligence, creativity rarely is restricted to cognitive or intellectual functioning or behavior as is intelligence. Rather, researchers and theorists are apt to include as part of their definition of creativity, personality and a host of motivational factors, cognitive processes (perhaps the heart of the matter), press, climate, environmental or zeitgeist conditions, chance factors, and even products or the result of creative functioning.

It is possible that creative, inventive, or innovative thinking and behavior can only be understood in the context of specific disciplines. Creative functioning in science may be unique and totally different psychologically from creativity in political science, jurisprudence, or art. Much of the research on creativity has been conducted in specific domains with little effort expended on seeking generalities across domains. There is also a broad tendency in the field of creativity research to seek insights about the process of creativity by studying people at the upper end of creative functioning (for example, leaders or eminent individuals in various fields).

1 Definitions, Conceptions, Models, and Theories

Vernon (1989) suggested that there is a consensus that creativity means a "person's capacity to produce new or original ideas, insights, restructurings, inventions, or artistic objects, which are accepted by experts as being of scientific, aesthetic, social, or technological value" (p.94). Getzels (1975), on the other hand, claimed that "there is no universally agreed upon definition of creativity" (p.327). Rather, according to Getzels, conceptions of creativity tend to be product-oriented, process-oriented, or based on subjective experiences.

Torrance (1979) offered a definition which he proposed would be useful in understanding, predicting, and developing creative behavior. Torrance believed that creativity consists of a set of abilities, skills, and motivations; furthermore, it is inextricably linked to dealing with problems. In this latter regard, "no creative thinking . . . is likely to occur until there is a recognition or awareness of a problem . . ., there is some definition of the problem, and commitment to deal with it" (p. 13).

One of the major leaders in creativity research and theory development, Amabile (1987), offered one of the simplest and most straightforward definitions: "A product or response is creative if it is a novel and appropriate solution to an open-ended task" (p. 227). This definition, she argues, meets criteria of novelty, correctness or value, and nonalgorithmic or heuristic quality. Elsewhere she says that "a product or response is creative to the extent that appropriate observers independently agree it is creative" (p. 231).

Treffinger et al. (1990) proposed a comprehensive theoretical model of productive thinking (see Fig. 1). This model seeks mainly to account for creativity as a set of cognitive processes contributing to a broader process of productive thinking or problem-solving. As a foundation for productive thinking, it posits a knowledge base which in turn consists of information and skills, motivations and dispositions, and management or metacognitive systems. The intermediate "tool" skills in productive thinking are specific creative (or divergent) thinking abilities and critical thinking skills. Finally, there are the complex methods of problem-solving and decision-making.

As can be seen from the definitions and accompanying model, creativity is an extremely complex phenomenon. It manifests itself chiefly as a set of processes within individuals. Within the individual, creative or adaptive behavior is a complex of cognitive skills and abilities, personality factors, and motivations as well as styles, strategies, and metacognitive skills. However, it also can be studied by focusing on the environmental context or press surrounding creative individuals as well as the impact their products, ideas, and performances have on the world around them. Creativity can perhaps be best understood when one realizes that its manifestation in different domains such as the sciences, arts, humanities, and business depends on quite different interactions among the elements or factors delineated as the creative process.

2. Assessing Creativity

Given the complexity of the models and conceptions of creativity which involve environmental press, pro-

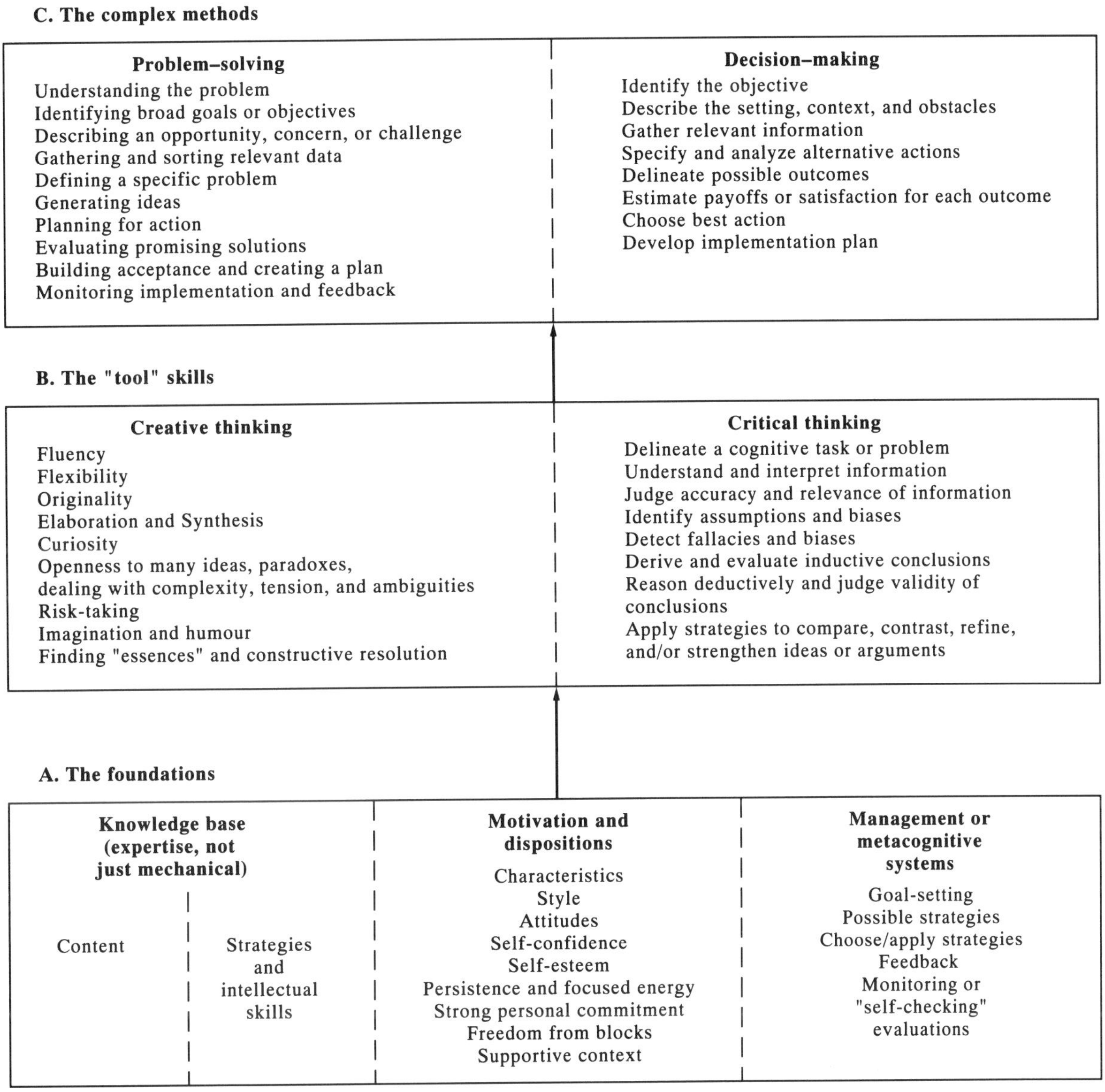

Figure 1
Organization and structure of productive thinking

cesses, and products, the assessment of creativity is equally complex. Thus, a single test instrument or battery is likely to be inappropriate. As a consequence, most efforts to assess creativity have used a variety of instruments which, in combination, have focused on individuals and on their cognitive abilities, personality characteristics, motivations, or background experiences.

Hocevar and Bachelor (1989), for example, offered a "Taxonomy and a Critique of Measurements Used in the Study of Creativity." They proposed eight categories of creativity assessment: (a) tests of divergent thinking, (b) attitude and interest inventories, (c) personality inventories, (d) biographical inventories, (e) ratings by teachers, peers, and supervisors, (f) judgments of products, (g) eminence, and (h) self-reported creative activities and achievements. They also presented examples of major instruments for each category.

Hocevar and Bachelor carried out an elaborate analysis of creativity measurements using several subtests from the Torrance Tests of Creative Thinking and from the Wallach and Kogan (1965) creativity battery in a path model using confirmatory factor analysis. Writing was the outcome variable. They concluded that verbal fluency subtests of both the Torrance Tests of Creative Thinking and the Wallach–Kogan battery were sufficiently valid and reliable.

2.1 Evaluation of Products

Amabile (1990), has been singularly successful in having subjects create products and using "expert" judges to rate their creativity. Amabile reported quite high and satisfactory levels of agreement among judges.

O'Quin and Besemer (1989) have developed the Creative Product Semantic Scale (CPSS), which was based on the Creative Product Analysis Matrix (CPAM) originally proposed by Besemer and Treffinger (1981). The CPSS consists of 71 bipolar adjectives divided into 11 subscales, each measuring one aspect of the CPAM. While some positive evidence of reliability and validity was reported, the authors suggest that more research is needed to understand more completely the nature of creativity as evidenced in subjects' products.

2.2 Self-report Measures

Kirton (1987) has addressed the problem of creativity assessment very successfully by differentiating two bipolar styles of psychological functioning: innovators and adaptors. According to Kirton, "adaption is the characteristic behavior of individuals who, when confronted with a problem, turn to the conventional rules, practices, and perceptions of the group to which they belong" (p. 294). In contrast, "innovation is the characteristic behavior of individuals who, when confronted with a problem, attempt to reorganize or restructure the problem, and to approach it in a new light" (p. 294). Kirton has developed a sound theoretical underpinning for the adaptor–innovator conception as well as an excellent instrument for assessing the construct.

Another widely used scale for creativity assessment is the Group Inventory for Finding Creative Talent (GIFT). The scale is offered at three sets of grade levels, K–2, 3–4, and 5–6, and consists of 32, 34, and 33 items respectively. Students respond "yes" or "no" to self-description and biographical items such as "I like to paint pictures" and "I ask a lot of questions." Additional instruments have also been developed for higher grade levels, GIFFI-I, Group Inventory for Finding Interests, Grades 6–9, and GIFFI-II, for Grades 9–12 and college students. Davis and Rimm (1989) reported that reliabilities and validity coefficients from a number of studies in seven countries were very high and support the use of the instruments as measures of creative ability.

2.3 Assessment of the Environment

Amabile and Gryskiewicz (1989) reported on their development of the Creative Environment Scales, Work Environment Inventory (WEI). The WEI focuses on factors or conditions in the work environment that are most likely to affect creative ideation. They conclude that work so far shows the WEI to be a reliable and valid instrument.

2.4 Assessment Batteries

Milgram (1990) has developed series of tests for use in her own research program. The first is a standardized ideational fluency measure with "lenient solution standards" meaning that all responses are considered solutions. The second test includes clearly defined verbal and nonverbal problems, and calls for solutions that are both unusual and of high quality as well as being true solutions to the problems. The third test is a self-report biographical questionnaire assessing both creative performances and leisure activities. Milgram reported that the tests have demonstrated sufficient validity and reliability in research settings.

The Structure of Intellect (SOI) tests (Meeker et al. 1985) grew out of the research and theoretical formulations of Guilford (1967), and became popular as measures of creative or divergent thinking. Serious questions were raised, however, by several researchers about the tests and the factor analyses underlying the theoretical framework for the SOI. Clarizio and Mehrens (1985) reviewed research on the SOI tests as well as the evidence available in publications related to the tests and concluded that there are major psychometric weaknesses in SOI tests which seriously limit their usefulness.

2.5 Measures of Creativity and Creative Achievement

Do tests used to assess creativity predict or link real-life creative achievements? A major criticism of creativity tests is that they do not. Torrance (1975), however, argued that a number of studies using the Torrance Tests of Creative Thinking clearly demonstrated predictive validity for creative achievement over long periods of time. Among the criteria were creativity of occupation, creativity of writing, and reported creative achievements.

2.6 Lists and Reviews of Instruments

Several lists and reviews of creativity tests have been prepared to guide practitioners and researchers in selecting instruments to measure creativity, its correlates, and its components. Hocevar and Bachelor (1989) offer a fairly comprehensive listing and evaluation of the most promising instruments. Other reviews and listings include those of Petrosko (1978), Kaltsounis and Honeywell (1980), and the Educational Testing Service (1987).

3. Teaching Creativity

Can people be taught to be more creative, to do

better creative thinking, to invent or design more creative products, to write more creatively, or to perform more creatively? If the answer is yes, how can they best be taught? What is the substance or curriculum of our teaching efforts, and how or with what teaching methods can creative thinking be taught most effectively?

3.1 Models for Teaching Creativity

Perhaps the best cues to guide the developers of creativity training programs derive from theories or models of creativity or creative thinking processes. For example, Speedie et al. (1973) reviewed the theoretical and research literature on creativity and problem-solving. Based on this review and a factor analysis of a large database of children's creativity and problem-solving test scores, they concluded that 11 skills or strategies are the key components of problem-solving and creative thinking:

(a) sensing that a problem exists;
(b) formulating questions to clarify the problem;
(c) determining causes of the problem;
(d) identifying relevant aspects of the problem;
(e) judging if more information is needed to solve the problem;
(f) determining the specific problem;
(g) clarifying the goal or desired solution;
(h) redefining or creating a new use for a familiar object or concept;
(i) seeing implications of a possible action;
(j) selecting the best or most unusual solution among several possible solutions; and
(k) sensing what follows problem solutions.

Houtz and Feldhusen (1976) developed a training program to teach these skills to fourth-grade children and found that significant gains in their creativity were made after six weeks of training.

Urban (1990) reviewed literature from research on creativity and theory development and proposed a model of creativity that could serve as a comprehensive guide to creativity training. The model embraces cognitive and noncognitive components and delineates six major areas of ability or process: (a) a general knowledge base; (b) a domain-specific knowledge base; (c) divergent thinking abilities; (d) task commitment; (e) motives; and (f) tolerance for ambiguity. From this model, guides to cognitive and noncognitive components of creative thinking can be derived.

3.2 Programs for Enhancing Creativity

Creative problem-solving is one of the most widely promulgated models for teaching creativity. Isaksen and Treffinger (1985) published a comprehensive set of training materials. Their work builds upon the model and materials for creative problem-solving developed by Parnes. Parnes (1975) reviewed the history of and research on creativity and concluded that it is eminently teachable, and the skills generalized to usefulness in real-life situations. More recently Parnes (1987) reviewed the research on the teaching of creativity, especially via the creative problem-solving model, and again concluded that the results are virtually all positive.

Perhaps the most widely known creativity training system is deBono's CoRT program (1976). This program consists of a set of training materials for use by teachers and students in the classroom. Lateral thinking or seeking alternatives is a major goal of the program. The lessons can be used across a wide age range (8–17), but are probably most effective in the 10–12 age range. The lessons can be used in any subject matter for periods of about 35 minutes at a time with children in groups of four to six. The program has been widely disseminated and used throughout the world, has been researched very little, but has come to be accepted – even acclaimed – as a major success in teaching thinking.

The Purdue Creative Thinking Program (Feldhusen 1983) is a set of 36 units of instruction on the skills and personal factors of creativity. Each program is built around historical figures: statespeople, scientists, inventors, pioneers, or famous sport figures. Their lives and their creativity are used as models and vehicles for discussions on creative thinking. Much research supports the effectiveness of the program in developing creative thinking skills and motivation.

3.3 Reviews of the Effectiveness of Teaching Creativity

Torrance (1987), a lifelong researcher and developer of creativity training programs, conducted an extensive review of materials, programs, and research on the teaching of creativity. In all, 142 studies were examined. In addition to concluding that there is ample evidence that creativity can be taught, Torrance reported that the successful programs stress both cognitive skills and personality factors, provide good motivating conditions, and involve students actively in the creative thinking process.

Feldhusen and Clinkenbeard (1986) reviewed instructional materials designed to teach creativity, focusing both on the quality of the materials and on evidence of their instructional effectiveness. They found a great deal of published material that had been neither subjected to any evaluation or research nor built upon a theoretical model of creativity, creative thinking, or creative process. Nevertheless, they did find a basic core of good programs of material such as the Productive Thinking Program (Covington et al. 1972), the Purdue Creative Thinking Program (Feldhusen 1983), and Imagination Express (Davis and DiPelo 1973) which have been built on a theoretical model of creativity and found to be instructionally effective.

Finally, Rose and Lin (1984) used meta-analysis to evaluate creativity research. They concluded that most creativity training programs have a positive effect on verbal fluency and originality but little impact on figural creativity.

4. Conclusion and Future Directions

Creative thinking and creative problem-solving are teachable aspects of human cognition and behavior. The goals of such teaching are both cognitive and noncognitive. A number of aspects of personality, motivation, styles, metacognition, and attitudes are involved in creativity.

There should be great emphasis on learning creativity in domain or subject matter contexts and on helping students see the potential use of creativity in real-life situations. Developing creativity should be viewed as a long-range process leading to adult creative achievement and self-fulfillment.

See also: Creativity

References

Amabile T M 1987 The motivation to be creative. In: Isaksen S C (ed.) 1987 *Frontiers of Creativity Research*. Bearly Buffalo, New York

Amabile T M 1990 Within you, without you: The social psychology of creativity, and beyond. In: Runco M A, Albert R S (eds.) 1990 *Theories of Creativity*. Sage, Newbury Park, California.

Amabile T M, Gryskiewicz N D 1989 The creativity environment scales: Work environment inventory. *Creat. Res. J.* 2(4): 231–53

Besemer S P, Treffinger D J 1981 Analysis of creative products: Review and synthesis. *J. Creat. Behav.* 15(3): 158–78

Clarizio H F, Mehrens W A 1985 Psychometric limitations of Guilford's Structure-of-Intellect model for identification and programming of the gifted. *Gift. Child Q.* 29(3): 113–20.

Covington M V, Crutchfield R S, Olton R M, Davies L 1972 *Productive Thinking Program*. Brazelton, Berkeley, California

Davis G A, DiPelo G 1973 *Imagination Express: Saturday Subway Ride*. DOK, Buffalo, New York

Davis G A, Rimm S B 1989 *Education of the Gifted and Talented*, 2nd edn. Prentice-Hall, Englewood Cliffs, New Jersey

deBono E 1976 *CoRT VI, Teacher's Handbook, Thinking Action*. Pergamon Press, New York

Educational Testing Service 1987 *Annotated Bibliography of Tests: Creativity and Divergent Thinking*. Educational Testing Service, Princeton, New Jersey

Feldhusen J F 1983 The Purdue Creative Thinking Program. In: Sato I S (ed.) 1983 *Creativity Research and Educational Planning*. Leadership Training Institute for the Gifted and Talented, Los Angeles, California

Feldhusen J F, Clinkenbeard P M 1986 Creativity instructional material: A review of research. *J. Creat. Behav.* 20(3): 153–82

Getzels J W 1975 Creativity: Prospects and issues. In: Taylor I A, Getzels J W (eds.) 1975 *Perspectives in Creativity*. Aldine, Chicago, Illinois

Guilford J P 1967 *The Nature of Human Intelligence*. McGraw-Hill, New York

Hocevar D, Bachelor P 1989 A taxonomy and critique of measurements used in the study of creativity. In: Glover J A, Ronning R R, Reynolds C R (eds.) 1989 *Handbook of Creativity. Assessment, Research, and Theories*. Plenum Press, New York

Houtz J C, Feldhusen J F 1976 The modification of fourth graders' problem solving abilities. *J. Psychol.* 93(2): 229–37

Isaksen S, Treffinger D J 1985 *Creative Problem Solving: The Basic Course*. Bearly, Buffalo, New York

Kaltsounis B, Honeywell L 1980 Additional instruments useful in studying creative behavior and creative talent. Part 4: Non-commercially available instruments. *J. Creat. Behav.* 14(1): 56–67

Kirton M J 1987 Adaptors and innovators: Cognitive styles and personality. In: Isaksen S G (ed.) 1987 *Frontiers of Creativity Research*. Bearly, Buffalo, New York

Meeker M, Meeker R, Roid G 1985 *Structure-of-Intellect Learning Abilities Test (SOI-LA)*. Western Psychological Services, Los Angeles, California

Milgram R M 1990 Creativity: An idea whose time has come and gone? In: Runco M A, Albert R S (eds.) 1990 *Theories of Creativity*. Sage, Newbury Park, California

O'Quin K, Besemer S P 1989 The development, reliability, and validity of the revised creative product semantic scale. *Creat. Res. J.* 2(4): 267–78

Parnes S J 1975 AHA! In: Taylor I A, Getzels J W (eds.) 1975 *Perspectives in Creativity*. Aldine, Chicago, Illinois

Parnes S J 1987 The creative studies project. In: Isaksen S G (ed.) 1987 *Frontiers of Creativity Research*. Bearly, Buffalo, New York

Petrosko J 1978 Measuring creativity in elementary school: The current state of the art. *J. Creat. Behav.* 12(2): 109–19

Rose L H, Lin H T 1984 A meta-analysis of long-term creativity training programs. *J. Creat. Behav.* 18(1): 11–22

Speedie S M, Houtz J C, Ringenbach S, Feldhusen J F 1973 Abilities measured by the Purdue Elementary Problem Solving Inventory. *Psychol. Rep.* 33(3): 959–63

Torrance E P 1975 Creativity research in education: Still alive. In: Taylor I A, Getzels J W (eds.) 1975 *Perspectives in Creativity*. Aldine, Chicago, Illinois

Torrance E P 1979 *The Search for Satori and Creativity*. Creative Education Foundation, Buffalo, New York

Torrance E P 1987 Teaching for creativity. In: Isaksen S G (ed.) 1987 *Frontiers of Creativity Research*. Bearly, Buffalo, New York

Treffinger D J, Feldhusen J F, Isaksen S G 1990 Organization and structure of productive thinking. *Creat. Learn. Today* 4(2): 6–8

Urban K K 1990 Recent trends in creativity research and theory in Western Europe. *Eur. J. High Abil.* 1: 93–113

Vernon P E 1989 The nature–nurture problem in creativity. In: Glover J A, Ronning R R, Reynolds C R (eds.) 1989 *Handbook of Creativity*. Plenum Press, New York

Wallach M, Kogan N 1965 *Modes of Thinking In Young Children*. Rinehart and Winston, New York

J. F. Feldhusen

Criterion-referenced Measurement

Criterion-referenced tests are constructed to permit the interpretation of examinee test performance in relation to well-defined objectives (Popham 1978). There are three common uses for criterion-referenced test scores: (a) to describe the level of examinee performance, (b) to assign examinees to mastery states (e.g., "masters" and "nonmasters"), and (c) to describe the performance of groups of examinees in program evaluation studies. Criterion-referenced tests are receiving extensive use in schools, industry, and the military because they provide information which is valued by instructors and policy-makers and is different from the information provided by norm-referenced tests. This entry will describe (a) basic criterion-referenced testing concepts; (b) norm-referenced versus criterion-referenced tests; (c) content specifications; (d) criterion-referenced test development; (e) measurement models, reliability, and standard setting; (f) applications of criterion-referenced tests; and (g) emerging trends and research.

1. Basic Concepts

The first article on the topic of criterion-referenced testing appeared in the *American Psychologist* (Glaser 1963). Over 1,000 papers on the topic have been published since then, and the scope and direction of educational testing has been changed dramatically. Glaser was interested in assessment methods that would provide information for making a number of individual and programmatic decisions arising in connection with specific objectives or competencies. Norm-referenced tests were seen as limited in terms of providing the desired kinds of information.

At least 57 definitions of criterion-referenced measurement have been offered in the literature. Popham's (1978) definition (see above) is the most widely used. Five points about the definition are important. First, terms such as "objectives," "competencies," and "skills" are used interchangeably in the field. Second, the objectives measured by a criterion-referenced test must be well-defined. Well-defined objectives make the process of item writing easier and more valid, and improve the quality of test score interpretations. The quality of score interpretations is improved because of the clarity of the content or behavior domains to which test scores are referenced. There is no limit to the breadth or complexity of a domain of content or behaviors defining an objective. The intended purpose of the test will influence the appropriate breadth and complexity of domains. Diagnostic tests are typically organized around narrowly defined objectives. End-of-year assessments would normally be carried out with more broadly defined objectives. Third, when more than one objective is measured in the test, examinee performance can be reported on each objective or group of objectives of interest. Fourth, Popham's criterion-referenced test definition does not include a reference to a cutoff score or standard. It is common to set a minimum standard of performance for each objective measured in a criterion-referenced test and to interpret examinee performance in relation to it. The use of criterion-referenced test scores for describing examinee performance is common (e.g., the best estimate of student A's performance in relation to the domain of content defined by the objective is 70 percent) and standards are not needed for this type of score use.

The fact that a standard (or standards) may not be needed with a criterion-referenced test may surprise some persons who have assumed (mistakenly) that the word "criterion" in "criterion-referenced test" refers to a "standard" or "cutoff score." In fact, the word "criterion" was used by Glaser (1963) and, later, by Popham and Husek (1969) to refer to a domain of content or behavior to which test scores are referenced. Finally, criterion-referenced testing is not synonymous with assessing low-level basic skills with multiple-choice items. All important educational outcomes can be assessed within a criterion-referenced framework, and the mode of assessment should be based on valid testing methods. Objective item formats, performance assessments, portfolios, as well as other formats which lead to valid information about examinee proficiency may be used in test development.

It is common to see terms like "criterion-referenced tests," "domain-referenced tests," and "objectives-referenced tests" in the psychometric literature. Popham's definition of a criterion-referenced test is similar to one that Millman and others proposed for a domain-referenced test. There are no essential differences between the two if Popham's definition for a criterion-referenced test is adopted. The term "domain-referenced test" is a descriptive one and therefore it is less likely to be misunderstood than the term "criterion-referenced test." One reason for continuing to use the term "criterion-referenced test," even though it is less descriptive and its definition has become muddled in the psychometric literature, is that there is considerable public support for "criterion-referenced tests."

Objectives-referenced tests consist of items that are matched to objectives. The principal difference between criterion-referenced tests and objectives-referenced tests is that, in a criterion-referenced test, items are organized into clusters with each cluster serving (usually) as a representative set of items from a clearly defined content domain measuring an objective, while, with an objectives-referenced test, no clear domain of content is specified for an objective, and items are not considered to be representative of any content domain. Therefore, interpretations of examinee performance on objectives-referenced tests should be limited to the particular items on the test.

2. *Norm-referenced versus Criterion-referenced Tests*

Proponents of norm-referenced and criterion-referenced tests waged a battle in the 1970s for supremacy of the achievement testing world. A third group argued that there was only one kind of achievement test from which both criterion-referenced and norm-referenced score interpretations could be made when needed. It is clear that there was no winner, although the uses of criterion-referenced tests have increased substantially around the world. Also, a reduction in the amount of norm-referenced testing has taken place.

There was no winner in the debate because it is clear that it is meaningful to distinguish between two kinds of achievement tests, and both kinds of tests should have important roles to play in providing information for test users. Norm-referenced achievement tests are needed to provide reliable and valid normative scores for comparing examinees. Criterion-referenced achievement tests are needed to facilitate the interpretation of examinee performance in relation to well-defined objectives, and the uses of these tests extend well beyond schools to include the whole area of credentialing.

Although the differences between norm-referenced tests and criterion-referenced tests are substantial, the two kinds of tests share many features. In fact, it would be a rare individual who could distinguish between them from looking at the test booklets alone. They often use the same item formats; test directions are similar, and both kinds of tests can be standardized.

There are, however, a number of important differences between them. The first difference is test purpose. A norm-referenced test is constructed specifically to facilitate comparisons among examinees in the content area measured by the test. It is common to use age-, percentile-, and standard-score norms to accomplish the test's purpose. Since test items are (or can be) referenced to objectives, criterion-referenced score interpretations (or, more correctly, objectives-referenced score interpretations) are possible but they are typically limited in value because of the (usually) small number of test items measuring any one objective in the test. Criterion-referenced tests, on the other hand, are constructed to assess examinee performance in relation to a set of objectives. Scores may be used (a) to describe examinee performance, (b) to make mastery–nonmastery decisions, and (c) to evaluate program effectiveness. Scores can be used to compare examinees but comparisons may have relatively low reliability if score distributions are homogeneous.

The second difference is in the area of content specificity. It is common for designers of both test types to prepare test blueprints or tables of specifications. It is even possible that norm-referenced test designers will prepare behavioral objectives. But criterion-referenced test designers should prepare considerably more detailed content specifications than provided by behavioral objectives to ensure that criterion-referenced test scores can be interpreted in the intended way. This point will be considered further in the next section. Thus, with respect to content specifications, the difference between the two types is in the degree to which test content should be specified.

The third difference is in the area of test development. With norm-referenced tests, item statistics (difficulty and discrimination indices) serve an important role in item selection. In general, items of moderate difficulty (p-values in the range 0.30 to 0.70) and high discriminating power (point biserial correlations over 0.30) are most likely to be selected for a test because they contribute substantially to test score variance. Test reliability and validity will generally be higher when test score variance is increased. In contrast, criterion-referenced test items are only deleted from the pools of test items measuring objectives when it is determined that they are not consistent with the content specifications, violate standard principles of item writing, or if the available item statistics reveal serious noncorrectable flaws. Item statistics can be used to construct parallel forms of a criterion-referenced test or to produce a test to discriminate optimally between masters and nonmasters in the region of a standard of performance on the test score scale.

The fourth and final major area of difference between criterion-referenced tests and norm-referenced tests is test score generalizability. Seldom is there interest in making generalizations from norm-referenced achievement test scores. The basis for score interpretations is the performance of some reference group. In contrast, score generalizability is usually of interest with criterion-referenced tests. Seldom is there interest in the performance of examinees on specific sets of test items. When clearly specified objective statements are available, and assuming test items are representative of the content domains from which they are drawn, examinee test performance can be generalized to performance in the larger domains of content defining the objectives. It is this type of interpretation which is (usually) of interest to criterion-referenced test users.

3. *Content Specifications*

Behavioral objectives had a highly significant impact

on instruction and testing in the 1960s and 1970s. But, while behavioral objectives are relatively easy to write and have contributed substantially to the specification of curricula, they do not lead to clearly defined content descriptions defining objectives. Popham (1974) described tests built from behavioral objectives as "cloud-referenced tests." Several suggestions have been made for addressing the deficiency in behavioral objectives and thereby making it possible to construct valid criterion-referenced tests. These suggestions include the use of item transformations, item forms, algorithms, and structural facet theory.

Possibly the most versatile and practical of the suggestions was introduced by Popham (1978) and is called "domain specifications," or sometimes "item specifications," or "expanded objectives." Domain specifications serve four purposes: (a) to provide item writers with content and technical guidelines for preparing assessment material; (b) to provide content and measurement specialists with a clear description of the content and/or behaviors which are to be covered by each objective, so that they can assess whether the assessment materials are valid; (c) to aid in interpreting examinee performance; and (d) to provide users with clear specifications of the breadth and scope of objectives. Some educational measurement specialists have even gone so far as to suggest that the emphasis on content specifications has been the most important contribution of criterion-referenced testing to measurement practice (Berk 1984).

Building on the work of Popham (1978), Hambleton (1990) suggested that a domain specification could be divided into four parts:

(a) Description: a short, concise statement of the content and/or behaviors covered by the objective.

(b) Sample directions and test item/assessment task: an example of the test directions and a model test item/assessment task to measure the objective.

(c) Content limits: a detailed description of both the content and/or behaviors covered by the objective, as well as the structure and content of the item pool. (This section should be clear enough so that items/assessment tasks may be divided by reviewers into those items/assessment tasks that meet the specifications and those items/assessment tasks that do not.) Sometimes clarity is enhanced by also specifying areas which are not included in the content domain description.

(d) Response limits: if objective item formats are used, a description of the kind of incorrect answer choices which should be prepared is provided. The structure and content of the incorrect answers should be stated in as much detail as possible. If performance tasks are used as the assessment mode, this section should describe the details for scoring the examinee's work.

Objective
The student will identify the tones or emotions expressed in paragraphs.

Sample directions and test item
Directions: Read the paragraph below. Then answer the question and circle the letter beside your answer.

Jimmy had been playing and swimming at the beach all day. Now it was time to go home. Jimmy sat down in the back seat of his father's car. He could hardly keep his eyes open.

How did Jimmy feel?

A. Afraid B. Friendly C. Tired D. Kind

Content limits
1. Paragraphs will describe situations which are familiar to Grade 3 students.
2. Paragraphs should contain between three and six sentences. Readability levels should be at the third grade (using the Dale–Chall formula).
3. Tones or emotions expressed in the passages should be selected from the list below:

sad	mad	angry	kind
tired	scared	friendly	excited
happy	lucky	smart	proud

Response limits
1. Answer choices should be one word in length.
2. Four answer choices should be used with each test item.
3. Incorrect answer choices may be selected from the list above.
4. Incorrect answer choices should be tones or emotions which are familiar to students in Grade 3 and which are commonly confused with the correct answer.

Figure 1
A typical domain specification in the reading area

An example of a domain specification using multiple-choice test items as the assessment mode is shown in Fig. 1. Once properly prepared domain specifications are available, the remaining steps in the test development process can be carried out.

4. *Criterion-referenced Test Development*

It is essential to specify clearly the domain of content or behaviors defining each objective which is to be measured in the test. The mechanism through which the objectives are identified will vary from one situation to the next. For high school graduation exams, the process might involve district educational leaders meeting to review school curricula and identifying a relatively small set of important broad objectives

Table 1
Steps for constructing criterion-referenced tests

	Steps	Comments
1.	Preliminary considerations: (a) Specify test purposes. (b) Specify groups to be measured and (any) special testing requirements (due to examinee age, race, sex, socioeconomic status, handicaps, etc.). (c) Determine the time and money available to produce the test. (d) Identify qualified staff. (e) Specify an initial estimate of test length.	This step is essential to ensure that a test development project is well-organized, and that important factors which might have an impact on test quality are identified early.
2.	Review of objective statements; write domain specifications: (a) Review the descriptions of the objectives to determine their acceptability. (b) Make necessary objective statement revisions to improve their clarity. (c) Write and review the domain specifications.	Domain specifications are invaluable to assessment material writers when they are well-done. Considerable time and money can be saved later in revising assessment materials if the writers are clear on what it is that is expected of them.
3.	Item writing: (a) Draft a sufficient amount of assessment material for pilot testing. (b) Carry out editing.	Some training of assessment material writers in the importance and use of domain specifications, and in the principles of assessment material writing is often essential.
4.	Assessment of content validity: (a) Identify a sufficient pool of judges and measurement specialists. (b) Review the test material to determine their match to the objectives, their representativeness, and their freedom from bias and stereotyping. (c) Review the test materials to determine their technical adequacy.	This step is essential. Assessment materials are evaluated by reviewers to assess their match to the objectives, their technical quality, and their freedom from bias and stereotyping.
5.	Revisions to test materials: (a) Based upon data from 4(b) and 4(c), revise test materials (when possible) or delete them. (b) Write additional test material (if needed) and repeat step 4.	Any necessary revisions to test material should be made at this step and, when additional test materials are needed, they should be written, and step 4 carried out again.
6.	Field test administration: (a) Organize the test material into forms for pilot testing. (b) Administer the test forms to appropriately chosen groups of examinees. (c) Conduct item analyses, and validity and bias studies.	The test material is organized into booklets and administered to appropriate numbers of examinees. That number should reflect the importance of the test under construction. Appropriate revisions to test material can be made here. Item statistics are used to identify items which may be in need of revision: (a) items/tasks which may be substantially easier or harder than other items/tasks measuring the same objectives, and (b) items/tasks with negative or low positive discriminating power.

7.	Revisions to test material: (a) Revise test materials when necessary or delete them using the results from 6(c).	Whenever possible, malfunctioning test material should be revised and added to the pools of acceptable test material. When revisions to test material are substantial, they should be returned to step 4.
8.	Test assembly: (a) Determine the test length, and the number of forms needed and the number of items/tasks per objective. (b) Select test items/tasks from the available pool of valid test material. (c) Prepare test directions, practice questions, test booklet layout, scoring keys, answer sheets, etc.	Test booklets are compiled at this step. When parallel forms are required, and especially if the tests are short, item/task statistics should be used to ensure matched forms are produced.
9.	Selection of a standard: (a) Initiate a process to determine the standard to separate "masters" and "nonmasters."	A standard-setting procedure must be selected and implemented. Care should be taken to document the selection process.
10.	Pilot test administration: (a) Design the administration to collect score reliability and validity information. (b) Administer the test form(s) to appropriately chosen groups of examinees. (c) Evaluate the test administration procedures, test items/tasks, and score reliability and validity. (d) Make final revisions based on data from 10(c).	At this step, test directions can be evaluated, scoring keys/guides can be checked, and reliability and validity of scores and decisions can be assessed.
11.	Preparation of manuals: (a) Prepare a test administrator's manual. (b) Prepare a technical manual.	For important tests, a test administration manual and a technical manual should be prepared.
12.	Additional technical data collection: (a) Conduct reliability and validity investigations.	No matter how carefully a test is constructed or evaluated, reliability and validity studies should be carried out on an ongoing basis.

(e.g., reading comprehension, mathematics computations). When criterion-referenced tests are needed in an objectives-based instructional program, it is common to define a curriculum in broad areas (and sometimes into a two-dimensional grid). Then, within the cells of the grid, the sets of relevant objectives, often stated in behavioral form, are specified, reviewed, revised, and finalized. With certification exams, it is common to first conduct a "role delineation study" with individuals working in the area to identify the responsibilities and activities which serve to define a role. Next, the knowledge and skills which are needed to carry out the role are identified.

A set of 12 steps for preparing criterion-referenced tests adapted from Hambleton (1990) is suggested in Table 1.

5. *Measurement Models, Reliability, and Standard Setting*

Throughout the 1970s and early 1980s, numerous statistical models were advanced to provide criterion-referenced measurement with a solid technical foundation. The special issue of *Applied Psychological Measurement* published in the fall of 1980 still remains in 1993 as one of the most useful single references on criterion-referenced measurement models and reliability assessment (Hambleton 1980).

The binomial test model and (less frequently) the compound binomial test model have been used as a basis for estimating examinee proficiency, determining test length, assessing reliability, and setting standards (see Hambleton et al. 1978). Other researchers have applied decision theoretic models, latent class models, random sampling models, and item response models to various technical topics (van der Linden 1980).

The major breakthrough in criterion-referenced test reliability was the recognition that, when mastery–nonmastery decisions are the focus of attention, reliability of decisions (over parallel-forms or a retest administration) is more important than test score reliability (as reflected in the myriad of norm-referenced test score reliability indices). Various single and double test administration decision consistency indices have entered the measurement literature since 1973 (see Hambleton and Novick 1973, Traub and Rowley 1980, Berk 1984).

Standard setting (see *Standard Setting in Criterion-referenced Testing*) is the most controversial aspect of criterion-referenced measurement and is central to many applications. Numerous methods currently exist for standard setting. The most popular of the judgmental methods is the "Angoff method" which involves a group of judges determining how minimally competent examinees (i.e., borderline examinees) will (or should) perform on the items/tasks in the test. The most popular of the empirical methods is the "contrasting groups method" which involves identifying groups of "masters" and "nonmasters" and then considering their actual performance on the test. The standard is set to minimize some function of the false-positive and false-negative errors. For example, it is common in testing practice to choose a standard which minimizes the sum of false-positive and false-negative errors. False-positive errors result when "nonmasters" pass the test; false-negative errors result when "masters" fail the test. When the sum of these errors is used as the function to minimize in standard setting, both errors are being considered equally important. Other loss functions may be chosen to weigh the two types of errors differently.

6. *Applications of Criterion-referenced Tests*

Criterion-referenced tests (or domain-referenced tests, mastery tests, competency tests, basic skills tests, or certification exams, as they are alternatively called) are being used in a large number of settings. Criterion-referenced tests are finding substantial use in schools. Classroom teachers use criterion-referenced test score results to locate students correctly in school programs, to monitor student progress, and to identify student deficiencies. Special education teachers are finding criterion-referenced test scores especially helpful in diagnosing student learning deficiencies and monitoring the progress of their students. Criterion-referenced test results are also being used to evaluate school programs. While it is less common, criterion-referenced tests are finding some use in higher educational programs as well (e.g., those programs based upon the mastery learning concept). Also, criterion-referenced tests are in common use in military and industrial training programs.

It has become common for departments of education and (sometimes) school districts to define sets of skills (or objectives) which students must achieve in order to be promoted from one grade to the next, or, in some states, to receive high school diplomas. The nature of these criterion-referenced testing programs varies dramatically from one place to another. For example, in some places, students are held responsible for mastering a specified set of skills at each grade level. In other places, skills which must be acquired are specified at selected grade levels, and in still other places, only a set of skills which must be mastered for high school graduation is specified.

One of the most important applications of criterion-referenced tests is to the areas of professional certification and licensure. It is common, for example, for professional organizations to establish entry-level examinations which must be passed by candidates before they are allowed to practice in their chosen professions. In fact, many of these professional organizations have also established recertification exams. A typical examination will measure the competencies which define the professional role and candidate test performance is interpreted in relation to minimum standards which are established. Hundreds of professional organizations, including most groups in the medical and allied health fields, have instituted certification and recertification exams.

7. *Emerging Trends and Research*

Without a doubt, the most important trends in criterion-referenced measurement in the early 1990s involve (a) the assessment of higher level cognitive objectives such as critical thinking, reasoning, problem-solving, and writing; and (b) more use of performance assessments such as constructed response questions, projects, and portfolios (Hambleton 1993). Both trends are being stimulated by massive school reform movements, advances in cognitive psychology, and shortcomings with the multiple-choice test item format. But, with both trends, substantial research is needed in defining these higher level objectives and assessing them with appropriate levels of reliability and validity. Standard-setting methods, which can be applied to performance task data, is an especially important topic for additional research.

See also: Measurement in Educational Research; Evaluation Models and Approaches; Evaluation, Nature of; Measurement-driven Curriculum

References

Berk R A (ed.) 1984 *A Guide to Criterion-Referenced Test Construction*. Johns Hopkins University Press, Baltimore, Maryland

Glaser R 1963 Instructional technology and the measurement of learning outcomes. *Am. Psychol.* 18: 519–21

Hambleton R K (ed.) 1980 Contributions to criterion-referenced testing technology. *Appl. Psychol. Meas.* 4: 421–581

Hambleton R K 1990 Criterion-referenced testing methods and practices. In: Gutkin T, Reynolds C (eds.) 1990 *The Handbook of School Psychology*, 2nd edn. Wiley, New York

Hambleton R K 1993 The rise and fall of criterion-referenced measurement? Paper presented at the joint meeting of AERA and NCME, Atlanta, Georgia

Hambleton R K, Novick M R 1973 Toward an integration of theory and method for criterion-referenced tests. *J. Educ. Meas.* 10: 159–70

Hambleton R K, Swaminathan H, Algina J, Coulson D B 1978 Criterion-referenced testing and measurement: A review of technical issues and developments. *Rev. Educ. Res.* 48: 1–47

Popham W J 1974 An approaching peril: Cloud-referenced tests. *Phi Del. Kap.* 55: 614–15

Popham W J 1978 *Criterion-Referenced Measurement*. Prentice-Hall, Englewood Cliffs, New Jersey

Popham W J, Husek T R 1969 Implications of criterion-referenced measurement. *J. Educ. Meas.* 6: 1–9

Traub R E, Rowley G R 1980 Reliability of test scores and decisions. *Appl. Psychol. Meas.* 4: 517–46

van der Linden W J 1980 Decision models for use with criterion-referenced tests. *Appl. Psychol. Meas.* 4: 469–92

R. K. Hambleton

Critical Approaches to Adult Education

Adult education is a field marked by conflict in which diverse ideologies have sought to define the terrain and the agendas for action. The strands which form this contested terrain of theory and practice have long histories and are not necessarily easily separable. Generally, critical approaches to adult education have been informed by the radicalism of the times, but the meanings of radicalism have shifted, not least in the 1980s across Europe and in North America where "Right Radicalism" has challenged the forged identity of radical with "Left" politics. This notion has developed historically, as a result of the identification of critical approaches in adult education with the politics of the labor movement and socialist ideals.

The purpose of this entry is to review some part of this history and the ways in which it bears upon radical approaches in adult education. The following themes are addressed: (a) adult education in early socialist ideas; (b) state, class conflict, and adult education; (c) Marxism and adult education; (d) the "community" approach; and (e) adult education and the new social movements. This entry neither addresses mainstream adult education policy and practice nor the institutional base of adult education.

1. *Adult Education in Early Socialist Ideas*

The late eighteenth century was marked by the French Revolution with its call for equality, fraternity, and liberty. This reverberated throughout Europe and influenced early attempts to create a radical adult education. In France, Germany, and the United Kingdom the early years of the nineteenth century were marked by political activism generating both the proto-socialism of Charles Fourier in France and the Owenite communities and the 1840s Chartists in the United Kingdom with their call for the vote—initially for women and men and subsequently for men alone. Within all these movements the importance of education was underlined, but it was to be an education for the people and in the interests of the people. These early forms of adult education were not specifically tied to adults, but brought adults and children together in an educational experience. These forms of learning were to be integrated with other areas of life, including work. Knowledge and learning were seen as crucial to the exercise of power.

Thus, education was not considered to be a neutral, technical attribute, but one aspect of a developing politics that was tied to "class."

The Owenites were consistently critical of "schooling" and all forms of rote learning, competition, and disciplinary modes, offering instead an emancipatory vision of learning that emphasized cooperation and a collective educational experience designed to empower the individual. The Chartists also emphasized the enabling power of education and its links with everyday life, especially through the popular press as it developed. Both the Owenites and the Chartists were deeply suspicious of the developing role of the state and of all forms of paternalism and philanthropy. This set the scene for a view of popular education which was independent of state and philanthropy, and which endures to this day. The Chartists were also concerned with citizenship and the rights of working people to a place in the nation and the polity. Their concern with citizenship and the educational forms that promote it remains a key issue for adult education across the world. The Chartist leader Ernest Jones said: "A People's education is safe only in a people's hands." This vision of an independent "peoples" education is still a powerful one in adult education.

2. *State, Class Conflict, and Adult Education*

The state became more interventionist during the nineteenth century and it became difficult to maintain a position of popular independence in adult education. The contradictions erupted in the twentieth century in the United Kingdom in the struggles over the Central Labour College. During the 1850s, philanthropy initiated the working men's colleges and fueled the university extension movement, which took Oxford and Cambridge "dons" to "the people." Those in favor of this promoted the ideals of the nation-state and consensus building through a shared literary and scientific culture into which the working classes would be inducted. This vision of nationhood and consensus building through education was located with White "English" men, and the extension of patronage to one specific section of the working class—the respectable, skilled, and organized fraction. It was a constituent part of the development of the Danish folk high schools (see *Folk High Schools; Study Circles*).

The critique of patronage was a key *motif* in the ideas developed by working people, for example, the ideas that formed the background to the development of the Workers' Educational Association in Canada, Australia, and the United Kingdom. These movements were fueled by a liberal view of adult education that saw individual advance and self-development as key elements. This was an adult education that was constructed as a public enterprise concerned with men—yet women were already involved in large numbers and had, through organizations such as the Cooperative Women's Guild in the United Kingdom, already rekindled an earlier collective radicalism which sought to place women's concerns on the agenda, both publicly and privately. Similar collective and cooperative concerns were developed in Canada through the Antigonish Movement, which brought different popular movements driving concepts such as university extension, Christian ethics, and social and economic change, together.

By the turn of the century the bifurcated vision of adult education, especially in the United Kingdom, Canada, and Australia—one radical and the other liberal—had clearly developed, but what both shared was a conception of the working class as a single unitary group. Such a view belied the ways in which the working class was simultaneously fractured by skill, region, gender, ethnicities, and the ways in which these came together in specific cultures. The radical vision was tied to socialist ideals of collective goals and mobilization for emancipation through working-class institutions. In contrast, the liberal view was wedded to notions of gradual, individual advance through education.

These two views came into sharp conflict following the events at Ruskin College, a philanthropic venture in Oxford, which sought to bring working-class people into Oxford. Founded in 1899, it brought trades union and socialist activists into full-time study programs. This group soon came into conflict with the Oxford education authorities over the curriculum and other issues of control. A strike by the students was supported by the major trade unions, which proceeded to set up their own institution, the Central Labour College, in 1909. Its journal, *The plebs*, became a major vehicle for the debate on independent working-class education. The main enemies of the working class were identified not only among the bourgeoisie, but also within the Workers' Educational Association (WEA), which received government support and was committed to liberal education. The issue was not simply one of funding, but a struggle for hegemony in relation to working-class education. The dispute between the WEA and the Labour College Movement was played out around the key themes of the role of the state, the importance of Marxism, and the relationship between education and the working-class movement; themes such as feminism and racism were conspicuously absent from the debates at that time.

The debates between the Labour College Movement and the WEA serve well as an illustration of the contested terrain of adult education as it developed in the period preceding and immediately following the First World War. Briefly, the first of these debates concerned the importance of independent working-class education, where independence meant separation from the state. State involvement was seen as contrary to the goal of emancipation of the working class. This meant, of course, that there was no space within this account for a strategic engagement with the state. All encounters with the state were seen by radicalists as a dilution of the socialist agenda. This was, of course, in a time prior to welfarism and struggles around the state which have marked the politics of adult education during the 1970s and 1980s.

The second crucial area of debate concerned the curriculum and the relationship between knowledge and power. The Labour College Movement accused the WEA of promulgating "bourgeois social science" tied to the university discourses of learning which could not, by definition, be liberatory. Instead, the Labour College Movement proposed Marxism as a route to political action. While the WEA taught Marshall and Marx, the Labour College Movement taught Marx on economics, Engels on anthropology, and Dietzgen on philosophy. The issues with which both parties struggled in the early years of the twentieth century were based on a "Manifesto Marxism" which was economistic and did not have the value of Gramscian insights on hegemonic relations that would have assisted in the development of a counter-hegemonic working-class education.

3. *Marxism and Adult Education*

The discourses surrounding the debates on the role of Marxism in radical adult education have changed over time with the development of Marxism and the incorporation of different strands from the original "Manifesto Marxism," which inspired the Labour College Movement and the radical workers movements that developed in France, Italy, Germany, Canada, Australia, and the United States. In the latter country, the IWW (Industrial Workers of the World) created and sustained the Work People's College (1903–41). It envisaged an economistic Marxism tied to the power of waged labor in the capitalist system. In Russia, a politics of adult education developed around the notion of "*Proletcult*," through socialist realism in art and film, and an attention within education to the development of the new woman and man of socialism. Within this frame the working class was treated as homogenous. The developing communist parties across Europe sought to educate their members and workers through the major trade unions which often, as in France, were allied with the Communist party. Alongside economism there was a commitment to the creation of a "vanguard"—the "advanced" section of the working class that was to be educated in Marxism in order to further the struggle against capitalism.

However, since its development from Marx's original writings Marxism has been, like adult education, contested terrain. A powerful critique of "Manifesto Marxism" and economism was developed by Antonio Gramsci in Italy during the 1920s (Hoare and Nowell Smith 1971). Gramsci sought to highlight the importance of ideologies and cultural forms in relation to the political project of the Party. His own involvement with the radical workers councils in Turin was a powerful example of collective struggle and adult education side by side in the development of both a critique of the capitalist labor process and worker-controlled alternatives. Gramsci's work emphasized the importance of ideological struggles in the revolutionary process because he believed that domination was as much a product of "consensus" as coercion. From this came his conception of ideological hegemony. Hegemony, however, implies the possibility of counterhegemonic work. Thus, radical educators in adult education have used this insight to generate counterhegemonic practices, not least in Turin. Gramsci's work has had an increasing influence on critical theorists, for example on Paolo Freire, the celebrated Brazilian educator. Much of the work of popular education in Latin America can be traced to Gramscian premises. This is reflected in the search for an understanding of hegemony, the role of the state, and the importance of civil society.

In France, in the 1970s, Louis Althusser used Gramscian insights and structuralism to develop an alternative account of Marxism. This was an attempt to break with economism and to emphasize the role of ideologies and politics offering these spheres a "relative autonomy." In his now famous essay "Ideology and Ideological State Apparatuses" Althusser drew attention to the role of the state in reproducing ideology and consensus especially through the education system which, under capitalism, not only produced workers technically skilled for their place in the capitalist division of labor, but also ideologically schooled for their place in the system (Althusser 1971).

Althusser's work emphasized "struggle in the ideological sphere." With this he drew attention to the processes and curriculum of adult education. His analysis is useful in examining the power of the state and offers one way in which to understand adult education as part of a state strategy—for example, the "Americanization" process in the United States which sought to produce "Americans" from the diverse ethnicities that were part of the migration into the United States.

4. *The "Community" Approach*

Adult education and workers' education, across Europe, became part of the post-1944 welfare state and was organized around a liberal rather than a class-based model. Radicalism resurfaced through the community education movement of the 1970s. This reintroduced the issues of knowledge and power, state intervention, and the autonomy of the adult learner—now not in relation to the state but to that of locale and the politics of community. In the same way that class had been constructed as the unitary site around which to organize, similarly "community" came to occupy this space with too little attention to the diversity of communities and the stratification of groups by class, gender, and race.

The experiments with community intervention in the United Kingdom, the Netherlands, and the United States in the 1970s were tied to the regeneration of working-class neighborhoods through education and community development. Thus, Saul Alinsky in Chicago and Midwinter and Lovett in Liverpool worked through schools and institutions pioneering forms of informal education in pubs and clubs with working-class women and men. But, although women figured strongly in Lovett's (1975) account of his community education work, there was no specific attempt to activate the role of adult education in women's lives. An alternative, and more politicized account of community education appears in the work of Ashcroft and Jackson (1974), who used the vehicle of the mass meeting as an educative forum for raising local political agendas. This was a form of experiential learning in which participants, through direct action, learned how capitalism and the local state worked.

Throughout the 1970s, many urban areas moved into community education, based on the adult education model. In the United Kingdom, these initiatives reflected a homogenizing notion of community located with a White Englishness that ignored the ethnic, racial, class, and gender diversities of the United Kingdom's urban areas. In addition, "community" became allied with consumption and with forms of familialism which further emphasized consensus building and the pursuance of common interests rather than the power relations of community or family life. Yet some authors and community workers recognized that the issues raised around power and knowledge and the debate on a "relevant" curriculum were important. It was, in fact, Paolo Freire who gave a new impetus to community education and literacy work through his reiteration of the view that education was either for domestication or liberation (Freire 1972).

5. *Adult Education and the New Social Movements*

The work of Freire had a major impact on adult education worldwide during the 1980s. Here was a vision of literacy work as popular education which was not functional but made the politics of language and symbols central. Freire's work incorporated notions of cultural struggles found in the writings of Mao Tse-tung, Che Guevera, and Antonio Gramsci, as part of a general emancipatory politics. Freirian discourse was an eclectic and heady mix incorporating Marxism within liberation ideology. Freire's radical humanism was in conflict with a productionist Marxist account. Therefore, it connected with the growing appeal of emerging social movements, such as those for women's emancipation, racial justice, gay liberation, and peace and green issues. These are issues with which community-based strategies could also connect, because they were related to struggles over public resources, collective consumption, and areas of representation and language.

Thus, in the 1980s, critical approaches to adult education became more diffuse and more clearly allied with the new social movements. This led to a feminist critique of adult education in the United Kingdom, Germany, Canada and the United States and the promotion of a women's studies agenda, while issues of social class re-emerged in much of the work with the unemployed and the unwaged more generally. Feminism has a long history, emerging in Europe with the French Revolution and the women's clubs that sought to put women's rights on the agenda and raised again in relation to the struggles around enslavement in the United States. Mary Wollstonecraft published *A Vindication of the Rights of Woman* in 1792. Across Europe, North America, and Australia, women organized in unions, guilds, and clubs throughout the nineteenth century and gave a special role to the power of education in their lives. These struggles continued into the twentieth century, foregrounding citizenship rights and access to education, training, and the professions; and a new wave of feminism arrived in the post-1968 era in Europe, Canada, Australia, and the United States where it was greatly influenced by the civil rights and Black Power movements (see *Women and Adult Education*).

Feminism, like Marxism, has never been unitary and debates between radical feminists, Marxist feminists, and "Black" feminists are ongoing. In relation to adult education, radical feminism generated a womanist perspective challenging the knowledge base of traditional subjects in relation to the patriarchal power implied. This generated a quest for women's knowledge and the development of women's studies which is now part of adult education. Marxist-feminists brought class and gender together and intervened in relation to workers' education, generating simultaneously a critique of patriarchal and capitalist relations. Both these feminisms were criticized by "Black" feminists for the ethnocentrism of their accounts of the world, and from this developed both Black feminist studies and Black studies as part of the African diaspora.

The issue of racism, however, so crucial to the 1990s, has received much less attention than feminism, and still needs to be centrally placed within the adult education agenda (Westwood 1991). The civil rights and Black Power movements of the 1960s and 1970s in the United States raised once again issues like: the relationship between citizenship and the state; and the importance of education in relation to cultural and ideological struggles (reproduced in the United Kingdom in the politics of education and in the ways in which African-Caribbean and South

Asian diasporic communities sought to unite around a political identity as Black people, in the struggle against racism). Alongside these developments has been the growth in access work which seeks to provide opportunities for adults to move into higher education. Within this sphere, the issue of racism has been highlighted and some courses have provided a specific space for African-Caribbean and Asian people to move into higher education. But there is concern that this will be seen as the "ultimate" answer to the question of racism and equal opportunities.

Peace studies, too, have become part of the agenda of adult education and the International Council of Adult Education now includes a peace education network (see *Education for Peace*). Similarly, ecological issues are well represented in the popular education movement in Latin America, and across Europe with the "Green University" in Italy. The issues raised provide an important focus for global concerns and new discourses within which to understand imperialism and underdevelopment, the relationships between the "North" and the "South," and fundamental questions on the world's resources.

In so far as much that has been named as "radical" in adult education has been located with the labor movement and the socialist agenda, these are contradictory times for critical approaches because the socialist project itself, following the events in Eastern Europe and the Soviet Union, is undergoing a profound period of reappraisal. The banners declaring the importance of citizenship against the designation "comrade" speak volumes for the failures of an economistically based account of the future tied to the command economy which has shown itself less effective than capitalism in delivering certain consumption goods. However, the demise of the Soviet bloc is no triumph for the West and the forms of capitalism that continue to lurch from crisis to crisis with poverty, unemployment, and despair in its train. The current profound restructuring of capitalism globally with the new forms of work relations have also meant the diminished effectiveness of trades union power and collective strength of working people. There is some suggestion that the new forms of the labor process will allow those with jobs the opportunity for a more democratic life at the workplace. If this is to be the case, then adult education is well placed to connect with these new forms and to bring the past and the present together around the notions of citizenship and workers' control, which have been so important throughout the history of adult education.

There is also another task related to the unemployed and to those whose work is increasingly casualized. This peripheral workforce is both feminized and racialized, and thus the issues brought to the fore by the women's and anti-racist movements need to be set firmly at the center of the adult education agenda.

This relates to the problem of nationalism and ethnic identities in Europe and globally, where a politics of difference is unfolding in very contradictory ways generating both a new sense of histories submerged, but also new racism and nationalisms which are located with a dangerous exclusivity. This calls for profound changes in the ways in which adult education curricula view the world. It is no accident that the work of Paolo Freire has had such an impact on adult educators of the North. Part of this impact has been a re-examination of the power/knowledge complex and the ways in which adult education discourses construct adult learners and their relationship to knowledge and thereby to empowerment. It is here that the work of Michel Foucault with his emphasis upon micropolitics and the diffuse nature of power has important insights for critical adult education.

6. Conclusion

Adult education faces an increasingly fractured world in which some of the old certainties have disappeared. The states in various countries seek to harness adult learning in relation to a human capital agenda and adult educators struggle for greater resources in a critical engagement with the state. A new politics for adult education across the old divide between radical and liberal, vocational and nonvocational, can also be noted. Adult education has consistently worked at the interface of economics, politics, and cultures, and in the spaces opened up by these interfaces. It may well continue to do so in the 1990s and beyond in relation to the new social movements, emancipatory views of learning, citizenship, and democracy.

See also: Community Education and Community Development; Ideologies in Adult Education; Worker Education and Labor Education; Women and Adult Education; Critical Theory and Education; Politics and Governance of Education; Adult Education, History of; Conscientization and Mobilization; Marxism and Educational Thought

References

Ashcroft B, Jackson K 1974 Adult education and social action. In: Jones D, Mayo M (eds.) 1974 *Community Work One*. Routledge, London

Althusser L 1971 Ideology and ideological state apparatuses: Notes towards an investigation. In: Althusser L (ed.) 1971 *Lenin and Philosophy and Other Essays*. New Left Books; London

Freire P 1972 *Pedagogy of the Oppressed*. Penguin, Harmondsworth

Hoare Q, Nowell Smith G (eds.) 1971 *Selection from the Prison Notebooks of Antonio Gramsci*. Lawrence and Wishart, London

Lovett T 1975 *Adult Education, Community Development and the Working Class*. Ward Lock, London

Westwood S 1991 Constructing the "Other": Minorities,

the state and adult education in Europe. In: Westwood S, Thomas E J (eds.) 1991 *Radical Agendas? The Politics of Adult Education*. National Institute of Adult Continuing Education, Leicester

Further Reading

Alinsky S 1969 *Reveille For Radicals*. Vintage, New York
Brown G 1980 Independence and incorporation: The Labour College movement and the Workers' Educational Association before the Second World War. In: Thompson J (ed.) 1980 *Adult Education For A Change*. Hutchinson, London
Fieldhouse R 1977 *The Workers' Educational Association. Aims and Achievements 1903–1977*. Syracuse University, Syracuse, New York
Freize P 1985 *The Politics of Education: Culture, Power and Liberation*. Macmillan, London
Gordon C 1980 *Power/Knowledge: Selected Interviews and other Writings 1972–77 by Michel Foucault*. Pantheon Books, New York
Hall S, Jacques M 1989 *New Times: The Changing Face of Politics in the 1990's*. Lawrence and Wishart, London
Hooks B 1984 *Feminist Theory: From Margin to Center*. SouthEnd Press, Boston, Massachusetts
Johnson R 1988 "Really useful knowledge" 1790–1850: Memories for education in the 1980's. In: Lovett T (ed.) 1988 *Radical Approaches to Education: A Reader*. Routledge, London
Rattansi A 1982 *Marx and the Division of Labour*. Macmillan, London
Simon B 1990 The struggle for hegemony, 1920–1926. In: Simon B (ed.) 1990 *The Search For Enlightenment*. Lawrence and Wishart, London
Thomas J E 1982 *Radical Adult Education: Theory and Practice*. University of Nottingham, Nottingham
Thompson E P 1963 *The Making of the English Working Class*. Gollancz, London

S. Westwood

Critical Reading: Teaching and Assessing

In conventional literature and reading instruction, critical reading has been defined in terms of personal response to literature, and in terms of the comprehension of disciplinary, nonfiction texts. However, reading has been redefined as part of a critical social literacy which entails the analysis and evaluation of textual ideologies and cultural messages, and an understanding of the linguistic and discursive techniques with which texts represent social reality, relations, and identity. This entry discusses conventional approaches and contrasts these with contemporary "critical pedagogy" and "discourse analytic" approaches to critical reading, noting future directions and unresolved issues in teaching and assessment.

1. Conventional Approaches to Critical Reading

The use of the term "critical" as a descriptor for modern curriculum and instruction has a controversial history. John Dewey and other early twentieth-century progressive educators used the term to signal the need for teaching social analysis to enable student participation in industrial development and social transformation. Of course, the degree to which state educational systems encourage and discourage student criticism of the distribution of power and wealth varies according to historical and political conditions. In this light, it should not be surprising that socially critical approaches to curriculum remain a matter of ongoing debate: they range from the encouragement of students to engage in explicit criticism of cultural, economic, and political structures, to more neutral approaches which affiliate reading with individuals' "thinking skills" and the weighing of information.

What has come to count as critical reading in United States, United Kingdom, Australian, Canadian, and New Zealand education has followed broad trends in the fields of secondary school English language and literature study, and elementary school reading and language arts instruction. Consequently, many extant approaches to critical reading have been directed by educational applications of, respectively, literary criticism and theory, and psychological theories of reading.

Since the early 1960s, secondary English teaching has been influenced by approaches to literary study which emphasize the value and variability of reader affective response to texts. In the United States and United Kingdom this movement has drawn strongly from antiformalist literary theories forwarded by Louise Rosenblatt, Stanley Fish, David Bleich, and others, and from the progressive educational aim of the development of individual identity and expression. Targeting traditional and classicist approaches to literature study, many approaches to teacher education and curriculum development emphasize exploration of personal response through literature (see Willinsky 1989). Within such models, critical reading is conceptualized according to Romantic literary criteria of "experience" and "understanding," as against more traditional emphases on literary appreciation and the reproduction of classical genres. This approach to secondary literature study has correlatives in holistic, child-centered approaches to early reading and writing, which also conceive of literacy in terms of "meaning making" and individual growth.

Drawing from sociological and poststructuralist theories of texts and subjectivity, critiques of these models make several key points. First, the search for student creativity in response to literature does not adequately consider how student response in the form of speech and writing is constructed and assessed in power relations in the classroom and, indeed, the larger culture (Gilbert 1989). Furthermore, like their classicist predecessors, these approaches tend to begin from a veneration of literature, such that the resultant classroom practices are unlikely to encourage questioning of why a specific text or genre should be studied in the first place, or of the value of personal response as an appropriate or effective way of dealing with text and identity.

A further critique of the personal response model arises from those advocates of psychologically based reading instruction, who argue that its stress on literature neglects students' needs to use nonfiction texts for the retrieval and analysis of disciplinary knowledge. Such critiques are the basis of calls for direct instruction in "content-area" reading comprehension across secondary schools. However, on closer inspection, concepts of critical literacy in reading psychology are theoretically and practically limited. Where it is mentioned, critical reading is taken to refer to "higher order skills" with text, such as the capacity to make semantic predictions, to infer and construct alternative outcomes and authorial intents, or to spot propaganda and bias. In the *Handbook of Reading Research* "critical reading" warrants only two comments. Baker and Brown (1984) define critical reading in terms which complement a neutral, information-processing model of reading. Thus, critical reading involves "not only imposing sense on the material in the way the author intended, but also going beyond the information given and critically evaluating it" (p. 356). They further observe that in most United States reading programs instruction in critical reading is developmentally delayed, and often given little more than token attention in comparison to, for example, the teaching of decoding or recall skills.

These limitations of conventional reading instruction are not simply a matter of instructional emphasis and timing, however. Research in the psychology and pedagogy of reading has a long history of shunting normative social and cultural issues to the sidelines of instruction, as subordinate to the acquisition of cognate skills, whether described as "basic," "functional," or "higher order" text-processing strategies. Over a century-long history, "basal" reading curricula have followed "technocratic" approaches that view teaching and learning as scientific procedures and processes best divorced from issues of values and ideology (Luke 1988). These key theoretical and practical omissions are continuing characteristics of cognitive and psycholinguistic approaches to reading.

Schema theories of reading, for example, recognize the relationship between structured, culture-specific background knowledge that readers bring to texts and the knowledge demands of text. However, such models stop short of recognizing how knowledges and texts can be ideological, that is, how particular knowledge structures operate in the interests of social configurations of power (Freebody et al. 1991). In this way, psychological versions of reading tend to privatize and individuate social and cultural knowledge. Where comprehension and critique are defined as matters of the personal deployment of individualized knowledge resources, a socially critical model of reading is not possible.

The two conventional approaches to reading described here remain areas of curriculum development and reform. In fact, educational systems in many developing countries have turned toward personal growth and psychologically based reading curricula to deal with the problems of mass literacy education. Although they draw upon radically different disciplinary theories and educational philosophies, these approaches construct reading along similar lines: as affective and cognitive processes internal to the student reader. What is omitted from both reader response and psychological approaches is recognition of two key aspects of reading and texts. First, reading is not a private act but a social practice, not a matter of individual choice or proclivity but of learning the reading practices of an interpretive community. Second, texts are not timeless aesthetic objects or neutral receptacles for information. Rather they are important sites for the cross-generational reproduction of discourse and ideology, identity and power within these communities.

2. *Reading and Critical Pedagogy*

Reading and writing are transitive verbs; that is, texts are always about something in the world. Reading, accordingly, always entails an engagement with problems and values of the social world. This insight is at the heart of Brazilian educator Paulo Freire's critique of traditional literacy education. Freire (1970) argues that schooling tends to be based on a "banking" model of education, where students are cast as passive, empty vessels, to be filled with knowledge and skills deemed appropriate by teachers. In this transmission model of education, the very texts and genres for reading and writing are imposed by external educational authorities and, typically, disconnected from students' lives, experiences, and immediate problems. Freire argues that in both First and Third World education systems, these approaches lead to failure, alienation and, even where successful, disempowered forms of literacy characterized by political disenfranchisement and passivity.

For Freire, literacy has the potential for "doubling" the world, for naming and renaming its human agents, structures, and elements. Critical reading is a means for holding that world up for analytic scrutiny, analysis, and social action. What Freire proposes is a "critical pedagogy" which centers on teaching students to "read the word and the world." Reading is a means of achieving "critical consciousness," an understanding of the forces and ideologies that shape one's life; writing is a means for clarification, articulation, and liberation of the oppressed's voice, position, interests, and possibilities for action (Freire and Macedo 1987).

Since the initial applications of Freire's literacy pedagogy in countries like Brazil, Peru, and Mozambique in the 1960s and 1970s, critical pedagogies have been applied in a range of United States and British educational settings, including adult literacy programs, migrant and English as a Second Language instruction, and early literacy programs. A central feature of the model is that beginning reading instruction should occur simultaneously with beginning writing, specifically the writing of those key words which "name" the everyday experience and problems of the learners. The resultant texts, in the form of life descriptions, observations, recounts, and personal narratives, become the texts for learning to read critically, for making connections between biography and larger social structures and issues.

Freire's model is thus openly ideological and political. As against skills approaches to reading which stress functional skills and, implicitly, an acquiescence to extant institutions which require those skills, he puts forward a pedagogy which aims to "identify, understand, and act to transform, social relationships and practices in which power is structured unequally" (Lankshear and Lawler 1987 p. 74). At the heart of the Freirian model, then, is an emphasis on the politics of identity.

Several criticisms have been raised about theoretical and practical aspects of critical pedagogy. Freirian pedagogy begins from the assumption of a unified, androgynous subject based on common experience. It furthermore grounds its teaching in the truth, authenticity, and accessibility of repressed "voice." This position contrasts with the feminist proposition that woman's identity is socially constructed and multiple; not fixed or unified, but rather the object of fluid and continually changing discourses (Luke and Gore 1992). A related concern regards the centrality and neutrality of the teacher/leader in critical pedagogy and the danger that she or he will simply supplant dominant ideologies with equally manipulative and patriarchal substitutes. Finally, the instructional emphasis on "voice" risks obscuring the profound differences between specialized techniques, genres, and practices of spoken language, on the one hand, and written language, on the other.

Many of these critiques are based on developments in poststructuralist and feminist educational theories, which share an undertaking that identity, everyday social relations, and understandings of social and material reality are constructed in and by categories of discourse. It is this insight into the constitutive role of discourse, texts, and textuality which is the basis of those approaches which redefine reading in terms of critical language awareness and discourse analysis.

3. *Critical Reading and Discourse Analysis*

While there is a recognition of the constitutive role of discourse in these versions of critical pedagogy, there are significant gaps in their explanatory and practical approaches to language, discourse, and text. Critical pedagogy retains an instructional emphasis on expression and negotiation of the marginal and oppressed "self." It stops short of calling for direct instruction and explicit knowledge of specialized written genres and textual techniques. Relatedly, it presupposes that critical and powerful competence with these genres and techniques can evolve from a pedagogy which is centered on "voice."

Written texts are not neutral, transparent windows on the realities of the social and natural world. Nor are they simply vehicles or vessels of ideologies and values, dominant or otherwise. Rather they are refractive; that is, they actively construct and represent the world. To read critically, then, requires awareness of and facility with techniques by which texts and discourses construct and position human subjects and social reality. Models of critical reading as discourse critique have set out to engage students in the practices of critiquing reading, writing, and speaking practices, such that the political power and knowledge relations expressed and represented by texts and discourses are foregrounded (Baker and Luke 1991). Instruction based on text and discourse analysis aims to give students insights into how texts work, and more specifically, how texts situate and manipulate readers. In so doing, its purpose is to engage readers directly and actively in the politics of discourse in contemporary cultures, to open institutional sites and possibilities for alternative readings and writings.

The theoretical parameters for a discourse-analytic approach to reading are drawn from poststructuralist discourse theory, functional linguistics, and neo-Marxist cultural studies. Kress (1985) outlines how texts construct "subject positions" and "reading positions." That is, texts both represent and construct "subjects" in the social and natural world, and they position and construct a model reader. The lexical, syntactic, and semantic devices of texts thus portray a "possible world," and they position the reader to read or interpret that possible world in particular ways. Accordingly, a discourse analytic approach to critical reading would include, for instance, an understanding of how words and grammatical structures shape portrayals of the world, human agency, cause and effect, and so forth. It would also point out many of the linguistic techniques that texts use to define and manipulate readers (e.g., imperatives, pronominalization).

Fairclough (1989) views the "critical language awareness" yielded by this kind of text analysis as a prerequisite for student readers to see how social power operates through everyday language practices, to contest texts, and to develop powerful competences with a broad range of texts and discourses. In contrast with the aforementioned models, then, a discourse-analytic approach does not aim for effective "comprehension," the valorization of the "power" of literature, the liberation of "voice" or, for that matter, the development of esoteric skills of "deconstruction." Rather, it sets out to teach critical reading as "an understanding of how texts are public artifacts available to critique, contestation, and dispute" (Freebody et al. 1991 p. 453).

In a related development, Gee (1990) defines critical literacy in terms of discourse critique. Discourses are built up from systematic and related sets of statements and texts. They comprise fields of knowledge which may be disciplinary (e.g., physics, sociology), institutional (e.g., governmental, workplace), and community-based (e.g., street or family talk). When deployed in contexts and texts, discourses are tied up with culture- and subculture-specific ways of behaving, knowing, valuing, and acting. Gee argues that both community and academic, dominant and subordinate discourses have limited, finite capacities for self-criticism, and that it is difficult to critique a discourse from within itself. In part this is because participation in a discourse and its interpretive community requires that one operate within given first principles and definitions.

Gee (1990) defines critical literacy in terms of having access to multiple discourses: "we can only talk about a literacy being 'liberating' ('powerful') if it can be used as a 'meta-language' . . . for the critique of other literacies and the way they constitute us as persons and situate us in society" (p. 153). According to this definition, critical reading entails far more than just the development of a set of analytic techniques or the embrace of particular perspectives or ideologies. It requires access to and facility with multiple discourses in order to read, critique, second-guess, and reconstruct other discourses, particularly those of dominant cultural groups and texts which tend to be taken as "truths" beyond criticism.

Classroom frameworks and practices developed for discourse-analytic approaches to critical reading include the reading of multiple texts and conflicting discourses against each other within single lessons, the encouragement of alternative readings and writings which attempt to bring community and familiar discourses to bear on those represented in texts, and the foregrounding of the histories and cultural contexts of texts and discourses under study. This instructional agenda begins from several guiding principles. First, the emphasis on juxtaposing texts and discourses to be "read against each other" (Freebody et al. 1991) aims to generate difference, conflict, and debate—focal points for teaching critical reading. Second, these classroom debates can be informed by teaching which makes explicit and foregrounds how texts work ideologically.

4. Conclusion

The question of what will count as critical reading in literate cultures cannot be addressed solely by reference to literary descriptions of the features and virtues of literature, psychological descriptions of mental processes, or linguistic descriptions of texts. How nations, communities, and school systems decide to shape the social practices of reading are normative cultural and sociological decisions, decisions tied up with how power and knowledge are to be distributed in print cultures (Luke 1993). Western late-capitalist cultures center on semiotic exchange, where signs, symbols, and discourse have become the principle modes of economic exchange and value. Reading is clearly essential for participation in the lived realities of everyday life, childhood, work, and leisure, but to become a functional reader may, quite ironically, make one more susceptible to the discourses and texts of a consumer culture which at every turn builds and defines readers' identities, actions, and their very senses of "reality." That is, possession of rudimentary decoding, pragmatic, and semantic skills to construct and use meaning from text may appear empowering, but in fact may open one to multiple channels of misinformation and exploitation (Freebody and Luke 1990).

In this kind of literate environment, conventional reader response and comprehension teaching may fall short of meeting the necessities of social participation and citizenship. Critical reading would need to entail an explicit understanding of both how texts are ideological, and how reading is a potential avenue toward constructing and remaking the social and natural worlds. Classroom instruction can be reshaped to enable students to read and write "differently," to see, discuss, and counter the techniques that texts use to position and construct their very identities and relations.

There have been significant developments toward implementing discourse-analytic frameworks for teaching critical reading in Australia and the United Kingdom, particularly in alternative approaches to literature study and "critical language awareness." However a range of questions about contexts and procedures for teaching critical reading requires continued investigation and innovation. A central issue is the viability of nonneutral, openly ideological approaches in educational systems run by conservative governments and local school authorities. In such contexts, as is evidenced in both the United States and United Kingdom, a critical reading curriculum which stresses social analysis and ideology critique may have to be lodged within progressive, personal growth models (e.g., Edelsky 1991) and curricula that stress explicit knowledge of language systems (e.g., Carter 1990).

Such attempts lead back to questions about the centrality and sequencing of critique in the programs. Conventional reading programs, both humanist and skills-based, tend to delay developmentally the introduction of critical textual analysis, assuming that basic reading and writing skills are required before students can engage with larger value and ideology systems in texts. There is, however, empirical evidence of the capacity for children at very early ages to engage with and talk about critical reading of narratives (Davies 1987, Gee 1990). If indeed children's senses of the functions, uses, and potentials for reading as a social, community, and intellectual practice are being shaped in preschool literacy activities, then there would seem to be both theoretical and practical grounds for teaching critical approaches to rewriting and contesting texts at all stages of reading instruction, especially in initial training.

A final unresolved issue concerns assessment. Reading assessment has largely been constrained by psychological theorizations of reading, and attendant models for standardized testing. That is, what has come to count as reading in both classroom and more formal assessment environments has been driven by what has been measurable by extant testing devices. With the demand for accountability in schooling, this typically leads to situations where curriculum and instruction are driven by what is visibly testable. As shown here, what is psychologically testable excludes critical, ideological, and discourse-analytic approaches to reading. Furthermore, where assessed within conventional approaches, success or failure at achieving critical reading has been evaluated in terms of student writing in response to literature (e.g., essays, journals, and literary response pieces), and via standardized tests of reading comprehension.

Since the early 1980s, there has been an expanded effort to develop reading assessments that are qualitative, descriptive, and sensitive to student and contextual variables. These include culture-appropriate practices and tasks, face-to-face task assessments in early childhood, case study approaches for adult literacy programs, and classroom observation techniques (e.g., Lytle and Schultz 1990). However, appropriate and credible means for assessing critical reading have yet to be developed. These methods would require tasks sensitive to the emergent definitions, contexts, and purposes of critical reading. For instance, the effectiveness of Freirian or discourse-analytic approaches by definition cannot be assessed by conventional pencil and paper psychometric devices. Assessment of these curricula might require evidence, for example, that the student had developed an articulated social analysis and attendant action plan, or that students were able to deconstruct ideological textual devices. All assessment of reading is premised on theoretically driven observation of student talk and writing. Consequently, the redefinitions of critical reading examined here of necessity will require the development of alternative, innovative approaches to assessment.

See also: Critical Thinking: Philosophical Issues; Reading Comprehension, Learning of; Empowerment Skills, Acquisition of

References

Baker C D, Luke A (eds.) 1991 *Towards a Critical Sociology of Reading Pedagogy*. John Benjamins, Amsterdam

Baker L, Brown A L 1984 Metacognitive skills and reading. In: Pearson P D (ed.) 1984 *Handbook of Reading Research*. Longman, New York

Carter R (ed.) 1990 *Knowledge about Language and the Curriculum*. Hodder and Stoughton, London

Davies B 1987 *Frogs and Snails and Feminist Tales*. Allen and Unwin, Sydney

Edelsky C 1991 *With Literacy and Justice for All: Rethinking the Social in Language and Education*. Falmer Press, London

Fairclough N 1989 *Language and Power*. Longman, London

Freebody P, Luke A 1990 Literacies programs: Debate and demands in cultural contexts. *Prospect: J. Aust.* TESOL. 5(3): 7–16

Freebody P, Luke A, Gilbert P H 1991 Reading positions and practices in the classroom. *Curric. Inq.* 21: 435–58

Freire P 1970 *Pedagogy of the Oppressed*. Seabury Press, New York

Freire P, Macedo D 1987 *Literacy: Reading the Word and the World*. Bergin and Garvey, South Hadley, Massachusetts

Gee J P 1990 *Social Linguistics and Literacies: Ideology in Discourses*. Falmer Press, London

Gilbert P H 1989 *Writing, Schooling and Deconstruction: From Voice to Text in the Classroom*. Routledge and Kegan Paul, London

Kress G 1985 *Linguistic Processes in Sociocultural Practice*. Oxford University Press, Oxford

Lankshear C, Lawler M 1987 *Literacy, Schooling and Revolution*. Falmer Press, London

Luke A 1988 *Literacy, Textbooks and Ideology: Postwar Literacy Instruction and the Mythology of Dick and Jane*. Falmer Press, London

Luke A 1993 *The Social Construction of Literacy in the Primary School*. Macmillan, Melbourne

Luke C, Gore J (eds.) 1992 *Feminisms and Critical Pedagogy*. Routledge, New York

Lytle S L, Schultz K 1990 Assessing literacy learning with adults: An ideological approach. In: Beach R, Hynds S (eds.) 1990 *Developing Discourse Practices in Adolescence and Adulthood*. Ablex, Norwood, New Jersey

Willinsky J 1990 *The New Literacy: Redefining Reading and Writing in the Schools*. Routledge, New York

Further Reading

Baker C D, Freebody P 1989 *Children's First Schoolbooks: Introductions to the Culture of Literacy*. Basil Blackwell, Oxford

Johnston, P 1984 Assessment in reading. In: Pearson P D (ed.) 1984 *Handbook of Reading Research*. Longman, New York

Shannon P 1989 *Broken Promises: Reading Instruction in Twentieth-Century America*. Bergin and Garvey, Granby, Massachusetts

A. Luke; C. Walton

Critical Theory and Education

Among the various theories competing for acceptance, if not dominance, in the field of education, critical theory is a vigorous and ambitious contender. It is the purpose of this entry to ask just how serious a contender critical theory is by examining its validity as a theory and its usefulness as an approach to educational research.

As a relative newcomer to education theory, the critical theory of society—whether in its original, or later Habermasian, form—has already marshaled significant support and won over a dedicated group of educators. Its arrival in educational research was greeted enthusiastically by writers such as Bredo and Feinberg (1982), for example, who believe that critical theory is able to transcend the distance between the dominant positivist school and its challenger, the interpretivist paradigm. Both schools of educational research have come under attack. Positivist research has been challenged both from within analytic philosophy of science and from interpretivists who criticize its reductionism, while the implicit relativism of the interpretivist approach is said to make it an unsuitable successor to positivism. Critical theory, as seen by its advocates, promises to solve the problems of both schools in a higher order synthesis which allocates the empirical–analytical and the historical–hermeneutic sciences to their own, mutually exclusive, object domains, complete with their respective methodologies.

In addition to relegating the sciences to their respective spheres of influence and thus deflating any claims for the superiority of one or the other methodology, critical theory has a distinctive political orientation. It suggests that the dominance of science and the rise of technology and bureaucracy are developmental tendencies of late capitalism which increasingly encroach on the domain of social life (Habermas 1976b). As a result of such imperialism which is accompanied by the decline and erosion of traditional institutions and legitimations, the legitimatory vacuum thus created is filled by the new belief in science (Habermas 1972c). What is obliterated in this process, according to Habermas, is the possibility of raising questions about social norms and values, and questions about "the good life" in the public domain. Where they are raised, they can only be perceived through the distorting lens of instrumental action, or the technical interest, which makes them appear solvable by the application of Weber's means–end scheme. Unmasking the illegitimate intrusion of science into the realm of social norms, Habermas believes, makes critical theory "critical" in the sense Marx understood the term, since science and technology have thus been shown to be ideological. The perspective which makes such insight possible is that of critical reflection which liberates or emancipates actors from false beliefs and subsequently leads to concrete proposals for overcoming oppression.

It is not difficult to see the attraction of critical theory for a number of educators who, critical of positivism, wary of the implicit relativism and conservatism of the interpretive school, and disenchanted with the so-called "economism" of Marxist education theory (e.g., Bowles and Gintis 1976), have been searching for a more appropriate foundation for a socially just educational theory and practice. Critical theory, consequently, has found application in, for example, curriculum theory (Apple 1982, Van Manen 1977), educational administration (Foster 1986, 1980, Bates 1983, Giroux 1983), action research (Carr and Kemmis 1986), teacher education (Baldwin 1987), educational policy analysis (Prunty 1985) and planning (Weiler 1984), educational theory (Young 1989), and adult education (Mezirow 1985). It has also been used to explain the crisis in formal schooling (Shapiro 1984). (For a more comprehensive list, see Ewert 1991).

Applying critical theory to curriculum making, Van Manen (1977 p. 209) notes that "Curriculum is approached as a nexus of behavioral modes which must be monitored, objectified, rationalized, and made accountable." Questions about the practical relevancy of, for example, teacher education programs, in Van Manen's view are then directly translatable into demands for increasing teacher competency and curriculum effectiveness.

In educational administration, writers such as Bates, Foster, and Giroux argue that the administration of schools, when carried out from within the scientific theory of administration (which they equate with positivism), merely emphasizes the technical–procedural aspects of their operations which are then taken as the only relevant and legitimate focuses of analysis. They contend that schools ought to be studied in all their interactional complexities. This is to be done by the method of "cultural analysis" with its emphasis on understanding and critical reflection. The rationale for cultural analysis is that, in Giroux's words, "the notion of culture [is] . . . a political force . . . a powerful moment in the process of domination" (Giroux 1983 p. 31).

The advantage of critical theory as seen by those who adopt its central concepts are, as Foster (1980 p. 499) notes, that "it is possible to have a social science which is neither purely empirical nor purely interpretative," on the assumption that critical theory thus escapes the criticisms leveled at positivism and interpretivist theory respectively. The stakes, then, are high, and the goal ambitious, for if critical theory could achieve what is claimed on its behalf, and what it claims for itself, then it would indeed be an outstanding candidate for a new, comprehensive social theory in general, and for education in particular.

The version of critical theory considered here is

that presented in the work of Habermas, since it is his version which provides the source material for most educators interested in critical theory, Giroux's emphasis on the older school notwithstanding. The task is then not only to examine critical theory's central claims, but also to explicate briefly what it sets itself to achieve. This is important since critical theory is presented by its advocates as both theoretically superior to positivist social and educational theory and as practically and politically more desirable. While neither claim is considered justified, the first will be examined since the validity of any theory depends on the justification not only of its claims to knowledge, but also on the grounds on which these claims are made. If these are inadequate, then any claims derived from them, be they "practical" or "political," are equally unjustified. If critical theory turns out to be incoherent, so is any educational theory which seeks to derive its justification from it.

This entry examines two central doctrines of the theory: (a) the conception of interests, and (b) the notion of communicative competence which culminates in the "ideal speech situation." The first concept provides the justification of the theory as knowledge, and the second is Habermas's proposed solution to the "theory–practice" problem, that is, the proposal for overcoming domination.

1. Habermasian Interests

Central to understanding Habermas's approach to social theory is what he takes to be the fundamental problem of contemporary social science: the relationship between theory and practice (Habermas 1974). He means by this that the connection between knowledge and social action has become an instrumentalist one, a relation which assumes the neutrality of science. Science is considered to be free of values and cannot, therefore, give people any guidance on how to conduct their lives. This development is the result of the victory of "scientism," or positivism, which, Habermas argues, presents itself as the only valid form of knowledge. As a consequence, it has become impossible, he suggests, to reflect critically on current forms of domination since even they appear as problems which are solvable by technical means. Habermas's aim is to restore to theory the dimension of reflection eclipsed by positivism and present a social theory which, as "ideology–critique," reunites theory with practice.

The quest for a comprehensive theory of social evolution as a theory of rationality leads Habermas to examine recent developments in the social sciences and in the analytic philosophy of science on the one hand (Habermas 1985b), and investigations in the field of philosophy of language and theoretical linguistics on the other (Habermas 1972a, Habermas 1972b, Habermas 1976a, Habermas 1979). In addition, he also re-examines the crisis potential of late capitalism (Habermas 1976b, Habermas 1976c) and the foundations of the older school of critical theory (Habermas 1982). These issues are outside the scope of this entry. For present purposes, the concept of "interests" (*Interessen*) is most important since it is the cornerstone of critical theory, aiming as it does at the re-examination of the connection between knowledge and human interests in general.

Interests, Habermas contends, are not like any other contingent empirical fact about human beings; neither are they rooted in an ahistorical subjectivity. Rather, they are grounded in the fundamental human conditions of work (following Marx) and interaction. What Habermas also calls a "cognitive" interest is consequently:

> a peculiar category, which conforms as little to the distinction between empirical and transcendental or factual and symbolic determinations as to that between motivation and cognition. For knowledge is neither a mere instrument of an organism's adaptation to a changing environment nor the act of a pure rational being removed from the context of life in contemplation. (1972a p. 197)

Cognitive, or knowledge-constitutive, interests are hence ascribed a "quasi-transcendental" status, an ascription Habermas acknowledges as being problematic (1974 pp. 8 ff.). Critical theory claims three such interests: the technical, the practical, and the emancipatory. These three are asserted to correspond to the three types of sciences. The natural sciences, in Habermas' view, incorporate a technical interest; the historical–hermeneutic sciences the practical interest; and the critical sciences (such as sociology and Freudian psychoanalysis) the emancipatory. The technical interest guides work, the practical guides interaction, and the emancipatory guides power. Work, or purposive–rational action, is defined as:

> either instrumental action or rational choice or their conjunction. Instrumental action is governed by technical rules based on empirical knowledge. In every case they imply conditional predictions about observable events, physical or social. These predictions can prove correct or incorrect. The conduct of rational choice is governed by strategies based on analytic knowledge. They imply deductions from preference rules (value systems) and decision procedures; these propositions are either correctly or incorrectly deduced. Purposive rational action realizes defined goals under given conditions. But while instrumental action organizes means that are appropriate or inappropriate according to criteria of an effective control of reality, strategic action depends only on the correct evaluation of possible alternative choices, which results from calculation supplemented by values and maxims. (Habermas 1972c pp. 91–92)

The second cognitive interest—the practical—enables the grasping of reality through understanding in different historical contexts (Habermas 1972a Chaps. 7, 8). It involves interaction patterns which provide a reliable foundation for communication. What Habermas terms "interaction" or "communicative action" is, like the technical interest, a distinct, nonreducible kind of action which demands specific categories of description, explanation, and understanding. It is this conception which provides the justification for the method of "cultural analysis" employed by some writers in education.

Habermas argues that just as human beings produce and reproduce themselves through work, so they shape and determine themselves through language and communication in the course of their historical development. While he emphasizes with Marx the historically determined forms of interaction, he nevertheless insists that symbolic interaction, together with cultural tradition, forms a "second synthesis" and is the "only basis on which power (*Herrschaft*) and ideology can be comprehended" (1972a p. 42). Marx is accused of not understanding the importance of communicative action since it does not play a separate role in, and is subsumed under, the concept of social labor which Habermas claims fits his own notion of instrumental action. Nevertheless, undistorted communication which, in Habermas's view, is the goal of the practical interest inherent in the hermeneutic sciences, requires the existence of social institutions which are free from domination themselves. On Habermas's own admission, these do not yet exist. By adding the model of symbolic interaction, he wishes to expand epistemologically Marx's conception of labor.

Finally, the notion of the emancipatory cognitive interest leads one to the most fundamental, yet also derivative, interest. It must be understood in the context of the German idealist tradition whose underlying theme, Habermas asserts, is that reason, once properly understood, "means the will to reason. In self-reflection knowledge for the sake of knowledge attains congruence with the interest in autonomy and responsibility. The emancipatory cognitive interest aims at the pursuit of reflection as such" (1972a p. 314). It is this interest which provides the epistemological basis for Habermas's notion of critique which is alleged to be the function of the critical social sciences. Consequently, this interest is of equal importance for educational theory which aims to be "interested" in just this way.

2. *Interests and Their Epistemological Status*

Habermas's conception of interests was developed in critical response to positivism. The peculiar status of the interests resulted from his desire to avoid a naturalistic reduction of quasi-transcendental interests to empirical ones. Habermas wants to say, on the one hand, that humans have transformed nature, built social systems, and developed science in the course of their evolution, a process which is analogous to the evolution of claws and teeth in animals (1972a p. 312). On the other hand, he is not content with such naturalism and claims that these achievements of human evolution are not merely accidental or contingent but have developed the way they have because of *a priori* knowledge–constitutive interests. These cognitive interests are described as being of "metalogical necessity . . . that we can neither prescribe nor represent, but with which we must instead come to terms" (p. 312). They are "innate" and "have emerged in man's natural history" (p. 312) and are located in "deeply rooted (invariant?) structures of action and experience—i.e. in the constituent elements of social systems" (p. 371). From the observation that humans have in fact transformed nature, built social systems, and created science it does not follow that they have done so because of transcendental interests. In other words, there is no equivalence between asserting that the technical, practical, and emancipatory interests have emerged in human natural history, and asserting that they are true and provide the transcendental framework for all human knowledge. How could such a transcendental framework be justified?

Two alternatives are possible. Habermas can resort to another transcendental framework or, alternatively, concede that there is a framework which exists *a priori*. In the case of the first alternative, Habermas argues that cognitive interests are rooted in the depth structures of the human species. This is merely another transcendental, anthropological concept which is itself in need of justification. This solution leads to an infinite regress of transcendental frameworks since one can press the point of justification with each new framework. This means that in the end, no justification is provided. If this regress is to be avoided one would need to fall back on an *a priori* framework, a solution Habermas wants to avoid. It would seem that no matter which of these two alternatives is chosen, the status of interests which are neither amenable to empirical demonstration nor to be sought in the transcendental realm (being "*quasi*-transcendental" entities) remains unclear. If the epistemological status of the interests remains in such jeopardy, the consequences for critical theory are serious, since the interests were meant to provide the foundation for the claims made on behalf of the sciences. This means that Habermas's assertion of the existence of two categorially distinct forms of knowledge and inquiry lapses for want of adequate justification.

In the light of various criticisms of the epistemological status of the interests (e.g., McCarthy 1981, Evers and Lakomski 1991, in particular Chap. 7), Habermas felt compelled to note: "My view is today that the attempt to ground critical theory by way of the *theory of knowledge*, while it did not lead astray, was indeed a round-about way" (1982 p. 233). This assessment leads him to ground his theory in the theory of language instead (Habermas 1979, 1985a).

3. Communicative Competence and the Ideal Speech Situation

The concept of communicative competence culminating in the ideal speech situation is the centerpiece of critical theory, since here the various strands of Habermas's investigations are drawn together. Parallel to Marx's critique of political economy, Habermas attempts to elucidate contemporary forms of alienation expressed in distorted communication. He wants to show that the potential for emancipation inheres in ordinary language which both presupposes and anticipates an ideal speech situation in which communication free from domination is possible. The full impact of Habermas's theory of communicative competence cannot be grasped adequately without taking recourse to its three underlying tenets which need further explication: (a) the notion of discourse and its relation to interaction, (b) the consensus theory of truth, and (c) the conception of an ideal speech situation.

Habermas argues that one can proceed from the fact that functioning language games, in which speech acts are exchanged, are based on an underlying consensus which is formed in the reciprocal recognition of at least four claims to validity. These claims comprise the "comprehensibility of an utterance, the truth of its propositional component, the correctness and appropriateness of its performatory component, and the authenticity of the speaking subject" (Habermas 1974 p. 18, 1979 Chap. 1). Habermas contends that in normal communication these claims are accepted uncritically. Only when a background consensus is challenged can all claims be questioned. Their justification is subject to "theoretical discourse" which is an intersubjective enterprise within a community of inquirers. This concept is adapted from Habermas' interpretation of Peirce's model of empirical science (Habermas 1972a Chaps. 5, 6). Although theoretical discourse demands the "virtualization of constraints on action," it still remains implicitly presupposed in interaction because Habermas assumes that the subjects are in fact capable of justifying their beliefs discursively. Such a capability is characteristic of a functioning language game. Yet he is also aware of the fact that there is no complete symmetry of power among the partners of communication.

If one considers a consensus to be rational and discovers after further reflection and argumentation that it is not, how is one to decide what does constitute a rational consensus? Habermas claims that the only recourse one has is to discourse itself. He is aware that this answer might lead into a vicious circle and contends that not every achieved agreement is a consensus, that is, can be considered a criterion for truth. If, for example, an agreement is reached on the basis of what Habermas calls (covert or open) "strategic" action, then that consensus is a "pseudo-consensus" (Habermas 1982 p. 237). Strategic action is that which is undertaken primarily to safeguard an individual's personal success by means of conscious or unconscious deception. In the case of systematically distorted communication (i.e., unconscious deception), Habermas believes that "at least one of the participants is deceiving *himself* or *herself* regarding the fact that he or she is actually behaving strategically, while he or she has only apparently adopted an attitude orientated to reaching understanding" (p. 264). Even in this case, he contends, the actors themselves can know—even though only "vaguely and intuitively"—which of the two attitudes they were adopting. Both kinds are seen as "genuine types of interaction" and may be mixed up with each other in practice. As a result, Habermas asserts: ". . . it is often difficult for an observer to make a correct ascription" (p. 266). If one wants to reach a true (or "founded") consensus, he argues, one must admit as the only permissible compulsion the force of the argument, and consider as the only permissible motive the cooperative search for truth (1972a p. 363).

An argument, then, qualifies as rational when it is cogent and motivates one in one's search for truth. Implicit in this thesis is Habermas's belief that there must be increased freedom for discourse to reach higher levels, that truth claims and claims to correctness of problematic statements and norms must be able to be assessed discursively, and in the course of assessment, also be able to be changed or rejected. The conditions under which such freedom can be attained are, in Habermas's view, given in the "ideal speech situation" because "the design of an ideal speech situation is necessarily implied with the structure of potential speech; for every speech, even that of intentional deception, is oriented towards the idea of truth" (1972b p. 144). The ideal speech situation is attained when the requirements of symmetrical relations obtain which involve all speakers having equal chances of selecting and employing "speech acts" and their being able to assume interchangeable dialogue roles. Since practical discourse is generally distorted, according to Habermas, and since the ideal speech situation can only be anticipated, it is difficult to assess empirically whether or not, or to what extent, the conditions of an ideal speech situation actually obtain. This problem, Habermas contends, cannot be solved in any *a priori* way. There is no single decisive criterion by which one can judge whether a consensus reached is "founded," even under ideal conditions; one can only determine in retrospect whether the conditions for an ideal speech situation obtained. This difficulty resides in the fact that:

> the ideal speech situation is neither an empirical phenomenon nor simply a construct, but a reciprocal supposition or imputation (*Unterstellung*) unavoidable in discourse. This supposition can, but need not be,

> contra-factual; but even when contra-factual it is a fiction which is operatively effective in communication. I would therefore prefer to speak of an anticipation of an ideal speech situation. . . .. This anticipation alone is the warrant which permits us to join to an actually attained consensus the claim of a rational consensus. At the same time it is a critical standard against which every actually reached consensus can be called into question and checked. (Habermas in McCarthy 1976 p. 486)

What, exactly, does this notion amount to? Stripped of its abstractions, one is left with a procedural model of negotiation which has the following characteristics in practice: (a) not everyone can participate in a given negotiation because of the existing power differential in society; (b) even when one reaches agreement practically, one is not sure whether it really is a consensus, nor does one have the means to check this (presuming that that is a worthwhile thing to do in the first place); and (c) the language one uses to reach consensus is itself a carrier of ideology. While Habermas emphasizes that his model is only an "anticipation" possessing the status of a "practical hypothesis" which does not refer to any historical society (Habermas 1982 pp. 261–62), one is nevertheless entitled to press the point regarding its potential for realization in the here and now. Recall that the solution to this dilemma is that one can only determine with hindsight whether or not its conditions obtained. Recall further that these are the postulates of symmetrical relations in which all speakers have equal chances of "selecting and employing speech acts." This still does not solve the problem because one has to repeat the question of how one would ever know that these "equal chances" did obtain. Since all one has to go by are self-reports which may be consciously or unconsciously misleading, or even false, even a retrospective assessment would not avoid the skeptical regress.

Habermas calls his model a "constitutive illusion" and an "unavoidable supposition of discourse" which, however, is possibly always counterfactual. From this, McCarthy draws the conclusion that: "Nonetheless this does not itself render the ideal illegitimate, an ideal that can be more or less adequately approximated in reality, that can serve as guide for the institutionalization of discourse and as a critical standard against which every actually achieved consensus can be measured" (1981 p. 309).

While this is not an uncommon defence of the ideal speech situation, it is nevertheless invalid. This is so because the ideal speech situation is in principle unrealizable. It cannot be "more or less" adequately approximated in reality because the condition of retrospectivity does not get Habermas out of the problem of stopping an infinite skeptical regress, as was argued above. It follows that one cannot even achieve what self-reflection and the emancipatory interest promised: the liberation from dogmatic attitudes which is, in any case, only the formal precondition for practical, political action in Habermas's scheme of things. For his theory to work, one must assume as already given, what, on his own account, does not yet exist but is supposed to come into existence as the result of the theory: namely, a world in which power and control are equalized. On the issue of social change then, this theory, which makes so much of its historical–materialist heritage, is silent. (For further critical comment on this aspect see Evers and Lakomski 1991 Chap. 7).

4. Conclusion

It is perplexing that this model of rationality (i.e., rational persons discussing their differences in an ideal speech situation) has been hailed as at least potentially the solution to the so-called "theory/practice problem" which holds that traditional (positivist) theory is incapable of informing and guiding practice. If the preceding analysis is correct, it seems that critical theory is similarly incapable of doing so. While the reasons outlined above go a considerable way toward explaining the problems of the theory of communicative competence, and hence critical theory, it finally fails because truth-as-consensus is removed from direct confrontation with the "objects of possible experience." In other words, the consensus theory of truth rules out the possibility of making true statements about empirical reality. If one cannot, in principle, know whether or not there is, as Habermas asserts, distorted communication and oppression in contemporary society, then one is left with mere speculation. However intuitively convincing this may be, speculation comes a poor second to knowledge. These fundamental problems need to be resolved if the critical theory of society is to be relevant for this world.

See also: Classical Sociological Theories of Education; Contemporary Sociological Theories of Education; Action Research; Participatory Research; Research Paradigms in Education

References

Apple M W 1982 *Education and Power*. Routledge and Kegan Paul, London

Baldwin E E 1987 Theory vs. ideology in the practice of teacher-education. *J. Teach. Educ.* 38(1): 16–19

Bates R J 1983 *Educational Administration and the Management of Knowledge*. Deakin University Press, Geelong

Bowles S, Gintis H 1976 *Schooling in Capitalist America*. Basic Books, New York

Bredo E, Feinberg W (eds.) 1982 *Knowledge and Values in Social and Educational Research*. Temple University Press, Philadelphia, Pennysylvania

Carr W, Kemmis S 1986 *Becoming Critical: Education Knowledge and Action Research*. Falmer Press, London

Evers C W, Lakomski G 1991 *Knowing Educational Administration*. Pergamon Press, Oxford

Ewert G D 1991 Habermas and education: A comprehensive overview of the influence of Habermas in educational literature. *Rev. Educ. Res.* 61(3): 345–78

Foster W P 1980 Administration and the crisis of legitimacy: A review of Habermasian thought. *Harv. Educ. Rev.* 50(4): 496–505

Foster W P 1986 *Paradigms and Promises: New Approaches to Educational Administration.* Prometheus, Buffalo, New York

Giroux H 1983 *Critical Theory and Educational Practice.* Deakin University Press, Geelong

Habermas J 1971 *Toward a Rational Society.* Heinemann, London

Habermas J 1972a *Knowledge and Human Interests.* Heinemann, London

Habermas J 1972b Towards a theory of communicative competence. In: Dreitzel H P (ed.) 1972 *Recent Sociology, No. 2: Patterns of Communicative Behavior.* Macmillan, New York

Habermas J 1972c *Toward a Rational Society.* Heinemann, London

Habermas J 1974 *Theory and Practice.* Heinemann, London

Habermas J 1976a Systematically distorted communication. In: Connerton P (ed.) 1976 *Critical Sociology.* Penguin, Harmondsworth

Habermas J 1976b *Legitimation Crisis.* Heinemann, London

Habermas J 1976c *Zur Rekonstruktion des historischen Materialismus*, 2nd edn. Suhrkamp, Frankfurt

Habermas J 1979 *Communication and the Evolution of Society.* Beacon Press, Boston, Massachusetts

Habermas J 1982 A reply to my critics. In: Thompson J B, Held D (eds.) 1982 *Habermas: Critical Debates.* Macmillan, London

Habermas J 1985a [trans. McCarthy T A] *The Theory of Communicative Action I: Reason and the Rationalization of Society.* Beacon Press, Boston, Massachusetts

Habermas J 1985b *Zur Logik der Sozialwissenschaften.* Suhrkamp, Frankfurt

McCarthy T A 1976 A theory of communicative competence. In: Connerton P (ed.) 1976 *Critical Sociology.* Penguin, Harmondsworth

McCarthy T A 1981 *The Critical Theory of Jürgen Habermas.* MIT Press, Cambridge, Massachusetts

Mezirow J 1985 Concept and action in adult-education. *Adult Educ. Q.* 35(3): 142–51

Prunty J J 1985 Signposts for a critical educational policy analysis. *Aust J. Education.* 29 (2): 133–40

Shapiro S 1984 Crisis of legitimation: Schools, society and declining faith in education. *Interchange* 15(4): 26–39

Van Manen M 1977 Linking ways of knowing with ways of being practical. *Curric. Inq.* 6(3): 205–28

Weiler H N 1984 The political economy of education and develr ment. *Prospects* 14(4): 467–77

Yor 989 *A Critical Theory of Education: Habermas ildren's Future.* Harvester Wheatsheaf, New

G. Lakomski

Critical Thinking: Philosophical Issues

Although the fostering of good thinking has traditionally been viewed by philosophers as an educational aim, it is primarily since the start of the 1970s that the interest in critical thinking has crystallized into a movement for educational reform. This development has been accompanied by considerable theoretical analysis and debate regarding how critical thinking is to be conceptualized, and by curricular innovations including the development of critical thinking courses, the revision of existing programs and curricular materials, the proliferation of critical thinking textbooks, the development of new evaluation procedures, and the institution of critical thinking requirements in various educational institutions and systems (e.g., in California). There has also been debate regarding the justification and efficacy of the practices instituted under the rubric of critical thinking.

1. Origins

Although the intellectual antecedents to contemporary views of critical thinking are evident in the work of a number of philosophers of education (Dewey 1933, Passmore 1967, Scheffler 1973), the main impetus for the development of current theory and practice was provided by Edward Glaser and by Robert Ennis. Glaser's landmark study (1941) included a conceptualization of critical thinking, the implementation of curriculum units, and procedures for evaluation. Ennis's *A Concept of Critical Thinking* (1962), in which he explicated a conception of critical thinking and detailed its aspects, was highly influential in terms of promoting interest in, and debate about, critical thinking.

A seminal contribution to the development of critical thinking theory and practice was also made by those working in the field of informal logic. Dissatisfaction with formal deductive logic, both as a model of argumentation (Perelman and Olbrechts-Tyteca 1958, Toulmin 1958, Scriven 1976) and as a pedagogical tool to help students reason more effectively (Hamblin 1970, Johnson and Blair 1983), led some logicians to concentrate their theoretical analyses and pedagogical efforts on the interpretation, evaluation, and construction of arguments in natural language (Blair and Johnson 1987).

2. Conceptions of Critical Thinking

One of the primary philosophical issues related to critical thinking centers on how it should be conceptualized.

2.1 Robert Ennis

The conception which has been most influential is that proposed by Robert Ennis. In his 1962 paper,

Ennis defined critical thinking as "the correct assessment of statements" and detailed twelve aspects of such assessment, which he further analyzed according to three dimensions: the logical (understanding relationships between meanings of words and statements), the criterial (having knowledge of the criteria for judging statements), and the pragmatic (judging sufficiency in light of the purpose of the judgment). By 1985 he had abandoned the narrow focus on the appraisal of statements (Ennis 1985). His new definition of critical thinking is "reasonable reflective thinking that is focused on deciding what to believe and do." To the list of proficiencies he has added a list of tendencies or dispositions. Judgment is also included as a necessary component of critical thinking.

2.2 Richard Paul

Another influential conception of critical thinking is that proposed by Richard Paul (1982, 1990). Paul is critical of viewing critical thinking as a set of atomic technical skills. He argues that such skills can be used simply to criticize the views of opponents and to reinforce one's existing views. This he characterizes as critical thinking in the weak sense. Critical thinking in the strong sense, on the contrary, probes the egocentric and sociocentric commitments which lie at the heart of beliefs, including one's own, and is sensitive to the self-deceptive tendencies to which thinking is often subject. Strong-sense critical thinking involves an examination of the worldviews in which particular beliefs are embedded, and an investigation of their background logic. It involves approaching issues from multiple categories and perspectives, and demands the kind of open-mindedness entailed in an empathetic understanding of points of view with which one disagrees. The approach is essentially a dialectical and dialogical one. Critical thinking is thus viewed by Paul as much more than a body of intellectual skills. It involves, as well, a complex of dispositions, values, and traits of character.

2.3 Harvey Siegel

The link between critical thinking and character also figures prominently in the conception of critical thinking put forth by Harvey Siegel (1988). Siegel characterizes the critical thinker as one who is appropriately moved by reasons, thus forging a close conceptual connection between critical thinking and rationality. Critical thinking for Siegel has two components. The reason-assessment component means that the critical thinker must be able to assess reasons and their ability to warrant beliefs, claims, and actions properly. The critical spirit means that the critical thinker must value good reasoning and must be disposed to engage in reason assessment and to believe and act on its basis. Dispositions, inclinations, habits of mind, and character traits all contribute to the critical spirit.

2.4 Matthew Lipman

Rather than focusing on belief and action, Matthew Lipman (1991) centres his account on the notion of judgment, and attempts to explicate the characteristics of the kind of judgment which characterizes critical thinking. Thus he defines critical thinking as thinking that facilitates judgment because it relies on criteria, is self-correcting, and is sensitive to context.

2.5 John McPeck

John McPeck's (1981) conception of critical thinking departs from those described thus far by focusing on the notion of skepticism. He refers to critical thinking as the appropriate use of reflective skepticism within the problem area under consideration. McPeck views his conception of critical thinking as having a broader range of applicability than do some of the alternative conceptions, in that it applies not only to the assessment of statements and arguments, but also to the conduct of virtually any activity which requires thought. A major difference between his conception and that of Siegel is that McPeck views critical thinking not as coextensive with rationality, but rather as a subspecies of rational thought deployed only when there are difficulties in the normal course of reasoning. The most significant difference between McPeck's conception of critical thinking and those of the other theorists examined is that McPeck holds that the criteria which determine the appropriateness of thinking emanate entirely from within particular disciplines or problem areas.

2.6 Commonalities Among the Conceptions

The most central feature common to all the conceptions outlined above is that critical thinking is seen as being closely connected with rationality and the appeal to good reasons. It is this characteristic which distinguishes these philosophical accounts of critical thinking from the more psychologically oriented views which come under the rubric of thinking skills. The latter focus on the processes of thinking—for example, the steps involved in problem-solving. Philosophers have criticized these accounts on the grounds that it is impossible to specify any particular set of mental events which an individual must go through in order to think well, and moreover that good thinking is determined by the quality of the reasoning produced and not by what may or may not be going on in a person's mind. Thus the philosophical approaches to critical thinking focus on the norms of good thinking. They are explicitly normative, concerned centrally with what makes thinking effective, appropriate, and reasonable—hence the critical element.

Another feature common to most conceptions of critical thinking is the inclusion of a dispositional dimension, although there is some divergence with regard to emphasis and to how this dispositional component is seen to be related to the other elements.

3. *Relationship Between Informal Logic and Critical Thinking*

"Informal logic" has been defined as the normative study of argument, the concern of which is the development of standards, criteria, and procedures for the interpretation, evaluation, and construction of arguments and argumentation used in natural language (Blair and Johnson 1987). Most theorists agree that logic and argumentation are important for critical thinking, although many theorists view critical thinking as broader in scope than informal logic. Siegel (1988), for example, views critical thinking as an educational ideal which should suffuse all educational activities. McPeck (1981), however, downplays (and at times denies) the relevance of informal logic to critical thinking, and maintains that argument analysis constitutes a very minor aspect of the activities of critical thinking.

4. *Creative Thinking*

Critical thinking and creative thinking tend to be viewed, in popular conceptions, as distinct from and even opposed one to another, and early accounts of critical thinking tended to accept this dichotomy (e.g., Ennis 1962). It has been argued, however, that critical thinking and creative thinking are not distinct and opposite kinds of thinking, but represent emphases along a continuum of good thinking, which has both generative and evaluative dimensions (Bailin 1987), and recent theorists have begun to accept this type of account (e.g., Ennis 1987, Siegel 1988). Lipman (1991), for example, argues that all creative thinking contains rational elements and all critical thinking contains an element of intuitive spontaneity.

5. *Justification*

Although the notion of critical thinking is implicit in many well-known philosophical conceptions of education (e.g., Peters 1966, Scheffler 1973), there is relatively little writing in the area of critical thinking devoted specifically to the justification of critical thinking in education. An exception is Siegel (1988), who proposes a justification in the following terms: (a) the ideal of respect for persons demands that studen- ight to question, and to seek reasons, exr , and justification be respected; (b) criti- necessary for the development of the of judgment required for self-suf- ood; (c) critical thinking fosters in spositions, attitudes, and skills which are conducive to initiation into the rational traditions; and (d) critical thinking is central to the kind of intelligent judgement which is required by citizens in a democracy.

6. *Generalizability*

Perhaps the most contentious issue in the area of critical thinking is whether critical thinking is generalizable or subject specific. The debate centres on whether there are critical thinking skills, principles, or criteria which are not dependent on particular subjects but are common to or apply across subject areas. One of the main protagonists in the debate is Robert Ennis, who views the critical thinking skills which he enumerates as general and applicable across subject domains. McPeck (1981, 1990), however, argues against the existence of such general skills on several grounds: (a) all thinking is thinking about something. Hence the idea of a general skill which is not applied to any particular subject matter does not make sense; (b) one could not possess a general ability to think critically because knowledge of the particular subject is necessary; (c) critical thinking varies greatly from field to field. Different fields have different epistemologies, meaning that different types of arguments and different sorts of reasons are employed (see also Weinstein 1990, Barrow 1991).

Ennis (1989) and others (Siegel 1988, Govier 1983, Paul 1985) have made the following points in response to these arguments: (a) the fact that critical thinking must be about something does not preclude there being general critical thinking skills which apply to a number of subjects or areas; (b) no-one who maintains that there are general skills denies the fact that knowledge is also necessary for critical thinking; (c) most supporters of generalizability acknowledge that there are some field-dependent reasons and arguments, but claim that there are also some principles common to different fields. The real disagreement between views centers, then, on whether such common principles exist, and if they do, whether they are powerful and important (Siegel 1988) or purely formal and relatively trivial until instantiated in particular contexts (Barrow 1991).

7. *Curriculum and Pedagogy*

The theorizing regarding critical thinking has been motivated largely by concerns about how to foster critical thinking through education, and a variety of approaches have been advocated. One approach involves separate courses or instructional units designed specifically to develop critical thinking—for example, informal logic courses at the college level, or critical thinking courses or units at the elementary or secondary level (Sternberg and Kastoor 1986). The infusion approach involves the teaching of subject matter in such a manner as to make explicit and encourage critical thinking principles, abilities, and dispositions (the principles may be general and/or subject-specific) (Swartz 1987). The immersion approach is simply subject-matter instruction conducted in such a manner as to promote an in-depth and critical understanding of the subject matter (McPeck 1981). A mixed approach involves some combination of the above approaches.

The Philosophy for Children Program, operating mainly in the United States but also in other places such as Canada and Latin America, involves the active engagement by children in philosophical inquiry (Lipman et al. 1980). The pursuit of metaphysical, logical, and ethical issues within classrooms structured as communities of inquiry is viewed as an effective means of developing the self-criticism, reflection on methodology, and judgment which are constitutive of critical thinking (Lipman 1991). Curricula and teaching materials have been developed for the program (e.g., Lipman 1974).

The two most widely used instruments developed to evaluate critical thinking abilities are the Cornell Critical Thinking Tests and the Watson–Glaser Critical Thinking Appraisal.

8. Recent Developments

One development in the area of critical thinking in the early 1990s is the emergence of the field of argumentation, which has developed from a cross-fertilization of the field of informal logic, with its emphasis on the logical force of arguments (Blair and Johnson 1987, Woods and Walton 1989, Fisher 1988), and the field of discourse analysis, with its concentration on the rhetorical (Barth and Krabbe 1982, van Eemeren et al. 1987).

Critical thinking theorists have also begun to show an interest in some of the findings from cognitive science, particularly with respect to the types of errors commonly committed in reasoning (e.g., Nisbett and Ross 1980, Perkins 1989).

The field of critical thinking has had to face challenges to its theory from several schools of social criticism—for example, whether the accepted conceptions of critical thinking are gender-biased or ideological, and whether accounts of critical thinking are sufficiently sensitive to the political dimensions of critical thought.

See also: Dewey, Pragmatism, and Education

References

Bailin S 1987 Critical and creative thinking. *Informal Logic* 9: 23–30

Barrow R 1991 The generic fallacy. *Educ. Phil. Theor.* 23(1): 7–17

Barth E, Krabbe E 1982 *From Axiom to Dialogue: A Philosophical Study of Logics and Argumentation.* Walter de Gruyter, Berlin

Blair J A, Johnson R H 1987 The current state of informal logic and critical thinking. *Informal Logic* 9: 147–51

Dewey J 1933 *How We Think: A Restatement of the Relation of Reflective Thinking to the Educative Process.* D.C. Heath, Boston, Massachusetts

Eemeren F van, Grootendorst R, Kruiger T 1987 *Handbook of Argumentation Theory: A Critical Survey of Classical Backgrounds and Modern Studies.* Foris, Dordrecht

Ennis R 1962 A concept of critical thinking: A proposed basis for research in the teaching and evaluation of critical thinking ability. *Harv. Educ. Rev.* 32(1): 81–111

Ennis R 1985 Goals for a critical thinking/reasoning curriculum. *Illinois Critical Thinking Project.* University of Illinois, Champaign, Illinois

Ennis R 1987 A taxonomy of critical thinking dispositions and abilities. In: Baron J, Sternberg R (eds.) 1987 *Teaching Thinking Skills: Theory and Practice.* W H Freeman, New York

Ennis R 1989 Critical thinking and subject-specificity: Clarification and needed research. *Educ. Researcher* 18(4):4–10

Fisher A 1988 *The Logic of Real Arguments.* Cambridge University Press, Cambridge

Glaser E M 1941 *An Experiment in the Development of Critical Thinking.* Bureau of Publications, Teachers College, Columbia University, New York

Govier T 1983 Review of McPeck J E 1981 "Critical Thinking and Education." *Dialogue* 22:170–75

Hamblin C L 1970 *Fallacies.* Methuen, London

Johnson R H, Blair J A 1983 *Logical Self-Defense,* 2nd edn. McGraw-Hill Ryerson, Toronto

Lipman M 1974 *Harry Stottlemeier's Discovery.* Institute for the Advancement of Philosophy for Children, Upper Montclair, New Jersey

Lipman M 1991 *Thinking in Education.* Cambridge University Press, Cambridge

Lipman M, Sharp A M, Oscanyan F S 1980 *Philosophy in the Classroom,* 2nd edn. Temple University Press, Philadelphia, Pennsylvania

McPeck J 1981 *Critical Thinking and Education.* St. Martin's Press, New York

McPeck J 1990 Critical thinking and subject specificity: A reply to Ennis. *Educ. Researcher* 19(5):10–12

Nisbett R, Ross L 1980 *Human Inference: Strategies and Shortcomings of Social Judgment.* Prentice-Hall, Englewood Cliffs, New Jersey

Passmore J 1967 On teaching to be critical. In: Peters R S (ed.) 1967 *The Concept of Education.* Routledge and Kegan Paul, London

Paul R 1982 Teaching critical thinking in the "strong" sense: A focus on self-deception, world views, and a dialectical mode of analysis. *Informal Logic* 4:2–7

Paul R 1985 McPeck's mistakes. *Informal Logic* 7:35–43

Paul R 1990 (ed. Binker A J A) *Critical Thinking: What Every Person Needs to Cope with the Modern World.* Center for Critical Thinking and Moral Critique, Rohnert Park, California

Perelman C, Olbrechts-Tyteca L 1958 *La Nouvelle Rhetorique.* Presses Universitaires de France, Paris [1969 *The New Rhetoric.* University of Notre Dame, Notre Dame, Indiana]

Perkins D 1989 Reasoning as it is and could be: An empirical perspective. In: Topping D M, Crowell D C,

Kobayashi V N (eds.) 1989 *Thinking Across Cultures*. Erlbaum, Hillsdale, New Jersey
Peters R S 1966 *Ethics and Education*. Allen and Unwin, London
Scheffler I 1973 *Reason and Teaching*. Routledge and Kegan Paul, London
Scriven M 1977 *Reasoning*. McGraw-Hill, New York
Siegel H 1988 *Educating Reason: Rationality, Critical Thinking, and Education*. Routledge, New York
Sternberg R J, Kastoor B 1986 Synthesis of research on the effectiveness of intellectual skills programs: Snake oil remedies or miracle cures? *Educ. Leadership* 44(2):60–70
Swartz R J 1987 Teaching for thinking: A developmental model for the infusion of thinking skills into mainstream instruction. In: Baron J B, Sternberg R J (eds.) 1987 *Teaching Thinking Skills: Theory and Practice*. Freeman, New York
Toulmin S E 1958 *The Uses of Argument*. Cambridge University Press, Cambridge
Weinstein M 1990 Towards a research agenda for informal logic and critical thinking. *Informal Logic* 12:121–43
Woods J, Walton D N 1990 *Fallacies: Selected Papers 1972–1982*. Foris, Dordrecht

Further Reading

Bailin S 1991 *Achieving Extraordinary Ends: An Essay on Creativity*. Ablex Publishing Corporation, Norwood, New Jersey
Blair J A, Johnson R H (eds.) 1980 *Informal Logic: The First International Symposium*. Edgepress, Inverness, California
Bomstad L, Weddle P 1989 North American perspectives on teaching critical thinking: A general bibliography. *Argumentation* 3:237–42
Coombs J 1987 Critical thinking and problems of meaning. In: Wright I, La Bar C (eds.) 1987 *Critical Thinking and Social Studies*. The History and Social Science Teacher, Toronto
Hansen H 1990 An informal logic bibliography. *Informal Logic* 12:155–84
Meyer M 1986 *From Logic to Rhetoric*. John Benjamins, Amsterdam
Norris S 1992 *The Generalizability of Critical Thinking*. Teachers College Press, New York
Norris S, Ennis E 1989 *Evaluating Critical Thinking*. Midwest Publications, Pacific Grove, California

S. Bailin

Cross-cultural Study of Education

Cross-cultural comparisons have constituted the defining characteristic of anthropological research throughout much of the twentieth century. This approach has enabled anthropologists to explore the unique and universal traits in the learning process and formal education. Cross-cultural studies of education have given researchers and policymakers perspectives on their own educational systems as well as on those in other societies. The knowledge gained has enhanced their ability to develop innovative and informed proposals for educational reform.

This entry addresses the ongoing importance of the cross-cultural study of edcuation. After a brief methodological discussion it highlights major themes and suggests directions for the future.

1. Methodological Considerations

The vast majority of cross-cultural studies in educational anthropology have involved a solitary anthropologist undertaking ethnographic fieldwork in another society or culture. The anthropologist then combines his or her own findings with existing cross-cultural data to develop a comparative analysis and draw conclusions. In a very few cases, the same individual has undertaken ethnographic research over an extensive period of time in two or more societies and has made comparisons based on their own observations. George and Louise Spindler represent, perhaps, the most prolific cross-cultural researchers in educational anthropology. Their extensive ethnographic work documents learning and education in German society and in North America. The Spindlers have also developed and perfected innovative ethnographic techniques (the Instrumental Activities Inventory, for example, and more recently methods involving video) and have tested them on different populations.

Shimahara (1979, 1985) has straddled two societies and has produced anthropological and sociological studies on education. His work details the Japanese educational system, education policy, Japanese student achievement, and the education of the Burakumin minority. He has also analyzed the relationship between Japanese culture and education. In the United States, Shimahara has examined socialization patterns and interaction within inner-city and suburban schools. His extensive cross-cultural knowledge and expertise have enabled him to assess education policy in both countries.

The work of the Spindlers and Shimahara is unusual: due to funding constraints and other problems, most late-twentieth-century educational anthropologists have focused on particular groups and subcultures within their own societies (see Spindler 1987a, 1987b). They have relied on ethnographic research undertaken in other countries to develop a comparative framework.

This entry will consider three major themes in cross-cultural research on education that have shaped the development of educational anthropology as a discipline: cultural transmission studies, the sociocultural context of the school, and the impacts of class and minority status on schooling.

2. Cultural Transmission and Education

Studies of cultural transmission represent the earliest types of cross-cultural studies on education. In most cases, these early ethnographic descriptions and analyses of education appeared as chapters or segments of larger monographs on social structure and organization in traditional societies. These ethnographic accounts enabled later anthropologists to construct models of cultural transmission and education.

2.1 Early Ethnographies

During the first half of the twentieth century, British and American anthropologists documented child-rearing practices and the transition to adolescence in traditional, preliterate societies. Mead's (1954) seminal study of adolescent girls in Samoa demonstrated that Samoan girls did not experience the conflicts and tensions associated with the teenage years among American adolescents. Mead also carried out extensive ethnographic research on child-rearing practices among the Manus and other Polynesian peoples. She later applied her findings to discussions on American educational problems (see Mead 1943).

Firth's (1957) work about the Tikopea of the western Pacific and Fortes's (1970) studies of the Tallensi of northern Ghana documented the crucial role of parents, peers, and close kin in teaching children social rules and survival skills. Nadel's (1970) study of the Nupe kingdom of central Nigeria highlighted the specialized role of age–grade associations and Mallam schools in preparing young men for their future adult roles. Likewise, Little's (1967) work among the Mende showed how initiation schools functioned to transform adolescents into responsible adult citizens.

2.2 Models

During the 1940s, 1950s, and early 1960s, culture and personality anthropologists systematically compared ethnographic accounts on child-rearing and education in traditional societies. Based on patterns in the cross-cultural data, they developed theories and models on the nature of cultural transmission and its relation to education.

Based on his field work among the Tiwi of Australia, in addition to an extensive review of the anthropological literature, Hart (1955) discovered important similarities in early childhood and post-pubertal education in traditional societies. In many of these societies, early childhood is a period when children learn from close family and peers in a relaxed, nonstandardized manner. During adolescence, young people are exposed to formal teaching of standardized knowledge in a setting away from home.

In 1960 Henry compiled an exhaustive, cross-cultural outline of education to systematize data for the study of cultural transmission. This outline presented a vast survey of how anthropologists have looked at cultural transmission, but its methodological utility has proved to be limited. Rather than producing an analytical model explaining relationships, the outline offered only a detailed list of cultural traits, often heavily weighted toward United States society.

Spindler argued that the process of cultural transmission involves discontinuity and compression: a jolting break with past behavior and expectations, and the taking on of new cultural and/or social roles. The process of discontinuity and compression may occur at any stage of the life cycle, but it is most dramatically exemplified in adolescent rites of passage. Spindler (1987c) also suggested that schools and educational systems often represent agents of discontinuity in modernizing societies. Questions involving the school as an agent of cultural discontinuity inspired anthropologists during the 1960s and early 1970s to undertake studies on the school in changing societies (Grindal 1972, Peshkin 1972, Gay and Cole 1967; and see *Social Change and Education: Anthropological Perspectives*).

Spindler (1976) eventually discarded the discontinuity/compression hypothesis due to its vague parameters and its inability to explain people's choices regarding values, behavior, and beliefs during periods of change. To analyze these questions, he developed the Instrumental Model.

The basic premise behind the Instrumental Model is the existence of a series of systematized relationships (linkages) between people's activities and goals. Cultural belief systems support these linkages, which are transmitted to children through various agents, including the school. During periods of rapid social change, individuals are exposed to new ideas challenging the existing linkages between beliefs, activities, and behavior.

Spindler tested this model among different groups in North America and Germany. In Germany, he used this model on village schoolchildren to ascertain how urbanization might affect the cultural transmission process inside and outside school (Spindler 1974). Despite the introduction of a new school curriculum promoting urbanization and modernization, the villagers' sentiments shifted toward traditional ideas and life-styles. Spindler interpreted this shift as a defensive response to rapid social change.

Other anthropologists developed cultural transmission models based on their review of cross-cultural studies. Gearing (1976) formulated a model from an interactionist perspective, defining cultural transmission as transactions of equivalence involving cognitive maps. Cognitive maps may change during social interaction, as people converse and share new information.

Dobbert (1976) criticized Gearing for being too narrow in his focus and sidestepping the concept of culture. She developed a systems model of cultural transmission which considers how cultural information stored in people's minds is transmitted between generations.

The frameworks and models mentioned here are

notable because they were derived principally from cross-cultural ethnographic data. They do not, however, represent an exhaustive list of all analytical frameworks used by anthropologists to study cultural transmission and education (see *Education as Culture Transmission and Acquisition*).

Certain cultural transmission models, such as those of Gearing and Dobbert, raise important questions about how knowledge is transmitted; whether members of different groups share fundamental cognitive processes; and how schooling might affect or alter cognitive patterns. These questions have intrigued psychologists and anthropologists alike. The cross-cultural work of Cole and his associates has had the most widespread impact on how educational anthropologists view the relationship between cognition and culture (Cole and Scribner 1973, 1974; see *Culture, Cognition, and Education, Perspectives on*).

3. The Social and Cultural Context of Schooling

The social organization and cultural context of the classroom and school represent important themes in educational anthropology which anthropologists have explored from both micro-ethnographic and macro-ethnographic perspectives. The following discussion will center on those seminal works that demonstrate a strong comparative focus.

3.1 Micro-ethnographic approaches

Micro-ethnographic studies center on questions concerning classroom interaction, student–teacher behavior, teaching methods, and the teacher's role. Insights gained from these studies can be directly applied to curriculum development and teaching methods.

The Spindlers (1987a, 1987b) carried out a controlled comparison between a German elementary school and one in the United States, in towns with demographically similar characteristics. The Spindlers' comparative study focused on teachers' styles, cultural knowledge, and students' classroom interaction. They found that the German classrooms exhibited a strong teacher-centered orientation and standardization of expectations. The American classrooms, however, demonstrated a looser structure, with the teacher acting as facilitator.

An important component of the Spindlers' study involved responses elicited from German and American teachers who viewed videos taken of classrooms in both schools. The films sparked lively discussion among teachers, prompting observations and comments about their cultural beliefs, collective standards, and expectations.

Anderson-Levitt (1987) examined French teachers' cultural knowledge for teaching first grade. Her experience as a teacher and researcher in American schools enabled her to compare French elementary school teachers with their American counterparts. She explained that her main purpose was not to describe the French but to "make American readers reflect on the cultural nature of knowledge for teaching in the United States" (Anderson-Levitt 1987 p.171). This comparative study highlighted teachers' cultural assumptions on how reading and writing should be taught in both societies.

McCollum (1989) undertook a controlled comparison of third-grade classrooms in Chicago and Rio Piedras, Puerto Rico. Her study drew upon concepts used in social interaction studies, including "turn-allocation" and "participant structures." She employed these concepts to determine how the two teachers conducted class and organized lessons. McCollum found that the Puerto Rican teacher incorporated student conversation into her lessons. Discussion during lessons closely resembled the "give and take" of everyday conversation (McCollum 1989 p.142). The American teacher, however, structured lessons in a more formal manner and directed rather than enabled student discussion. McCollum hoped her study would give American teachers insights into how to interact with and motivate Puerto Rican students.

Tobin et al. (1989) compiled a unique cross-cultural comparison of preschool in three societies: Japan, China, and the United States. Like the Spindlers, they used video to record data and elicit responses from cross-cultural audiences.

Their book, *Preschool in Three Cultures*, offers descriptions of classroom interaction in addition to insightful analysis of the relationship between preschool, socialization practices, and culture in the three societies. This work addresses vital questions regarding the effects of early education and organized day-care programs on child development and family relations in different societies.

3.2 Macro-ethnographic approaches

There have been few comparative macro-ethnographic studies on the social organization and cultural context of schooling. Anthropologists have produced numerous case studies on school organization and school–community relations in various societies. Warren's (1967) monograph on education in Rebhausen, Germany, and Singleton's (1967) on a Japanese school exemplify these types of studies.

Shimahara's (1979) *Adaptation and Education in Japan* is notable for his analysis of the cultural, social, economic, and political forces that have shaped Japanese education. In a later article (1985) Shimahara discusses Japanese educational achievement in the light of its implications for American education. He contrasts the two societies in terms of social stratification, degrees of sociocultural heterogeneity, and education. While the Japanese educational system can offer insights into how to improve America's schools, Shimahara warns that it should not be copied in every respect.

Rohlen's *Japan's High Schools* (1983) presents a valuable cross-cultural ethnographic study of social structure, culture, and schooling. Drawing upon his ethnographic field work in five secondary schools in Kobe, Japan, Rohlen analyzes the role of the high school in maintaining Japanese culture and social structure. He makes insightful comparisons between Japan and the United States with regard to high school organization, curriculum, students' academic paths, and the adolescent experience.

Comparative macro-ethnographic studies on education offer valuable insights into how schooling can be structured, and its relationship to other social institutions. These studies will be particularly valuable to policymakers in the twenty-first century, as nations around the world reevaluate their educational systems and look for ways to structure schools effectively and to promote academic achievement.

4. *Class and Minority Status*

During the late twentieth century, certain anthropologists began to compare systematically the relationship between social class, minority status, and education in different societies. Their studies addressed the important question of whether class and minority status have a universal impact upon students' educational aspirations, choices, behavior, and performance.

4.1 Social Class

Few anthropologists have undertaken cross-cultural research specifically focusing on the relationship between social class and education. Robinson's (1987) study of education and social class in Korea is notable not only because he tackles this difficult question, but because he tries to develop a transcultural model of social typing.

In studying Korea, Robinson (1987) examined a relatively homogeneous society with a rigid class stratification system. In this society, high educational achievement is crucial for success in adult life. He applied a social-typing model developed in the United States to measure teachers' expectations and "self-fulfilling prophecies" regarding students' social class backgrounds. He found children's social class influenced teachers' responses and behavior toward them and their parents. Teachers' behavior, in turn, affected children's educational performance and aspirations.

Although Robinson was aware of the many differences between the United States and Korea, he found that a similar process of social typing occurs in the two societies. In Korea, social typing centers on social class, while in the United States the focus is on ethnic and minority status. He concluded that researchers should conduct more comparative, cross-cultural studies of social typing to learn how culturally based biases are transmitted in schools.

4.2 Minority Status and Schooling

Ogbu's seminal work *Minority Education and Caste* (1978) represented the first systematic cross-cultural comparison of the relationship between minority status and school behavior, performance, and aspirations. Ogbu examined minority education in six societies and found a direct correlation between different types of minority status and academic achievement.

Based on his cross-cultural research, Ogbu identified three types of minority status: autonomous, immigrant, and involuntary or castelike (see Ogbu 1978, 1987). African–Americans, certain Hispanic Americans, West Indians in the United Kingdom, scheduled castes in India, Burakumin in Japan, Oriental Jews in Israel, and the Maoris in New Zealand all represent involuntary minorities.

Involuntary minorities face a job ceiling which inhibits economic mobility. Economic survival often necessitates developing alternative strategies for success which often run counter to mainstream rules. Involuntary minorities may also develop and maintain systems of oppositional cultural identity. Ogbu suggests that low academic performance results from involuntary minorities' awareness of limited economic opportunities, combined with an oppositional cultural identity which might negate academic striving. (For a detailed discussion of Ogbu's cultural–ecological theory. Ogbu's theories on minority schooling laid the groundwork for subsequent cross-cultural comparative studies on minority status and schooling.

Lewis (1989) undertook an ethnographic study of the Oriental Jewish minority in Sharonia, Israel. Drawing on Ogbu's data from Stockton, California, Lewis later compared the Sharonian students' responses to schooling with those of the involuntary minorities in Stockton (Lewis 1989, Ogbu 1974). Although both groups confronted socioeconomic barriers and inferior schools, they adopted strikingly different approaches to education. The Oriental Jews embraced the assimilationist ideology of Zionism and viewed their inferior socioeconomic status as a temporary condition that could be remedied through academic achievement. Thus the Oriental Jewish students competed for classroom recognition because they believed that educational achievement would result in economic success.

In contrast, the involuntary minorities in Stockton rejected the notion that educational achievement would lead to high-paying jobs and improved social status. Their awareness of the job ceiling and powerful minority sentiment inhibited academic striving and reinforced their belief that collective mobilization was the key to improving their life conditions.

Pieke (1991) studied the Dutch–Chinese community in the light of ethnic minority educational experiences in North America and Western Europe. Pieke drew on Ogbu's work, but found that the concept of "folk theories" failed to explain adequately the complex and changing realities of individual choices and strategies. In the Dutch–Chinese community, Pieke noted that conflicts between the individual and the family's needs were often resolved by a young person dropping out of school and working in a family business.

Shimahara (1971, 1984) and Kahn (1992) addressed the question of minority status and social change. Shimahara studied the Japanese Burakumin over a 20-year period and followed their collective drive to improve their socioeconomic status and educational attainment. By the 1980s, after 20 years of self-directed political mobilization, the Burakumin had significantly increased their social mobility and educational attainment. Based on his research on the Burakumin, Shimahara suggested that minority group perceptions of job opportunities directly affect educational aspirations, thus lending credence to Ogbu's job-ceiling hypothesis.

Kahn (1992) applied Ogbu's cultural–ecological theory to the case of the Québécois, who experienced economic, social, and political subordination relative to English Canadians. The Qubébécois' limited perceptions of opportunity and oppositional cultural identity were reflected in an elevated school dropout rate. From the late 1950s through the 1980s the Québécois implemented sweeping political, social, economic, and educational reforms to change their minority status. Their educational attainment rate, in turn, dramatically improved to approach that of the English Canadians in Quebec.

The cases of the Burakumin and the Québécois have direct implications for minority groups in other parts of the world who desire to alter their minority status and improve their academic performance.

There is a pressing need for further comparative, cross-cultural studies of minority education—especially between Europe and the United States. The close of the twentieth century finds the Western European nations facing a massive and rapid influx of immigrants. As today's immigrants become tomorrow's minorities, educational researchers, policy-makers, and teachers face problems that their American counterparts have confronted for over a century. The emerging nations of Eastern Europe must also decide how to structure educational systems so as to offer equality of educational opportunity to many different ethnic minority groups. Thus, cross-cultural comparisons of United States and European ethnographic cases would benefit theorists and practitioners on both sides of the Atlantic (see Suarez-Orozco 1991).

5. Conclusion

At a time of increasing demand for cross-cultural studies, educational anthropologists continue to focus on problems within their own societies. Several factors have contributed to this trend: the difficulties of securing funding for overseas research; government limits imposed on foreign researchers; and the accessibility of ethnic or minority enclaves within one's own society. As a result, educational anthropology, particularly in the United States, is in danger of losing its broad, comparative perspective and of becoming a discipline characterized by specific case studies (Spindler 1987a, Suarez-Orozco 1991).

Twenty-first-century anthropologists must meet the challenge of pursuing high-quality cross-cultural ethnographic research in an era of mounting economic and political constraints. A solution might lie in the growing accessibility of sophisticated computer and telecommunications technology. Through electronic mail, bulletin boards, publications, and international conferences, anthropologists might apply their networking skills to develop ties with researchers in other countries. While doing fieldwork in their own societies, they could share their data with colleagues in other countries and work together to further the cross-cultural study of education.

See also: Anthropology of Education: History and Overview; Education of Indigenous Peoples, Anthropological Study of; Education as Culture Transmission and Acquisition; Race and Ethnicity in Education

References

Anderson-Levitt K 1987 Cultural knowledge for teaching first grade: An example from France. In: Spindler G (ed.) 1987e

Cole M, Scribner S 1973 Cognitive consequences of formal and informal education. *Science* 182: 553–59

Cole M, Scribner S 1974 *Culture and Thought, A Psychological Introduction*. Wiley, New York

Dobbert M 1976 Another route to a general theory of cultural transmission: A systems model. In: Roberts J I, Akinsanya S K (eds.) 1976 *Educational Patterns and Cultural Configurations: The Anthropology of Education*. McKay, New York

Firth R 1957 *We, the Tikopea: A Sociological Study of Kinship in Primitive Polynesia*. Allen and Unwin, London

Fortes M 1970 Social and psychological aspects of education in Taleland. In: Middleton J (ed.) 1970 *From Child to Adult: Studies in the Anthropology of Education*. University of Texas Press, Texas

Gay J, Cole M 1967 *The New Mathematics and an Old Culture: A Study of learning Among the Kpelle of Liberia*. Holt, Rinehart, and Winston, New York

Gearing F O 1976 Where we are and where we might go from here: Steps toward a general theory of cultural transmission. In: Roberts J I, Akinsanya S K (eds.) 1976 *Educational Patterns and Cultural Configurations: The Anthropology of Education*. McKay, New York

Grindal B 1972 *Growing Up in Two Worlds: Education and Transition among the Sisala of Northern Ghana*. Holt, Rinehart, and Winston, New York

Hart C W M 1955 Contrasts between prepubertal and postpubertal education. In: Spindler G (ed.) 1987d
Henry J 1960 A Cross-cultural outline of education. *Current Anthropology* 1: 267–305
Kahn L 1992 *Schooling, Jobs, and Cultural Identity: Minority Education in Quebec*. Garland, New York
Lewis A 1989 Minority education in Sharonia, Israel, and Stockton, California: A comparative analysis. *Anthropol. Educ. Q.* 12(1): 30–50
Little K 1967 *The Mende of Sierra Leone: A West African People in Transition*, 2nd edn. Routledge and Kegan Paul, London
McCollum P 1989 Turn-allocation in lessons with North American and Puerto Rican students: A comparative study. *Anthropol. Educ. Q.* 20: 133–56
Mead M 1943 Our educational emphases in primitive perspective. *Am. J. Sociol.* 48: 633–39
Mead M 1954 *Coming of Age in Samoa: A Psychological Study of the Primitive Youth for Western Civilization*. New American Library, New York
Nadel S F 1970 Education for citizenship among the Nupe. In: Middleton J (ed.) 1970 *From Child to Adult: Studies in the Anthropology of Education*. Natural History Press, New York
Ogbu J U 1974 *The Next Generation: An Ethnography of Education in an Urban Neighborhood*. Academic Press, New York
Ogbu J U 1978 *Minority Education and Caste: The American System in Cross-cultural Perspective*. Academic Press, New York
Ogbu J U 1987 Variability in minority school performance: A problem in search of an explanation. *Anthropol. Educ. Q.* 18(4): 312–34
Peshkin A 1972 *Kanuri Schoolchildren: Education and Social Mobilization in Nigeria*. Holt, Rinehart, and Winston, New York
Pieke F N 1991 Chinese educational achievement and "Folk Theories of Success." *Anthropol. Educ. Q.* 22(2): 162–80
Robinson J 1987 Social typing at Hanseong Elementary: A transcultural model of social bias schooling. In: Spindler G (ed.) 1987d
Rohlen T P 1983 *Japan's High Schools*. University of California Press, Berkeley, California
Shimahara N K 1971 *Burakumin: A Japanese Minority and Education*. Nijhoff, The Hague
Shimahara N K 1979 *Adaptation and Education in Japan*. Praeger Scientific, New York
Shimahara N K 1984 Toward the equality of a Japanese minority: The case of the Burakumin. *Comp. Educ.* 20(3): 339–53
Shimahara N K 1985 Japanese education and its implications for U.S. education. *Phi Del. Kap.* 66(6): 418–21
Singleton J 1967 *Nichu, A Japanese School*. Holt, Rinehart, and Winston, New York
Spindler G 1974 Schooling in Schönhausen: A study in cultural transmission and instrumental adaptation in an urbanizing German village. In: Spindler G (ed.) 1974 *Education and Cultural Process: Toward an Anthropology of Education*. Holt, Rinehart, and Winston, New York
Spindler G 1976 From omnibus to linkages: Cultural transmission models. In: Roberts J I, Akinsanya S K (eds.) 1976 *Educational Patterns and Cultural Configurations: The Anthropology of Education*. McKay, New York
Spindler G 1987a Preview to Part V: Cultural process in education viewed transculturally. In: Spindler G (ed.) 1987d
Spindler G 1987b Editorial introduction to part II: Comparative and cross-cultural. In: Spindler G (ed.) 1987e
Spindler G 1987c The transmission of culture. In: Spindler G (ed.) 1987d
Spindler G, Spindler L 1987a Schönhausen revisited and the rediscovery of culture. In: Spindler G (ed.) 1987e
Spindler G, Spindler L 1987b In prospect for a controlled cross-cultural comparison of schooling: Schönhausen and Roseville. In: Spindler G (ed.) 1987d
Suarez-Orozco M M 1991 Migration, minority status, and education: European dilemmas and responses in the 1990s. *Anthropol. Educ. Q.* 22(2): 99–120
Tobin J J, Wu D Y H, Davidson D H 1989 *Preschool in Three Cultures: Japan, China and the United States*. Yale University Press, New Haven, Connecticut
Warren R L 1967 *Education in Rebhausen, A German Village*. Holt, Rinehart, and Winston, New York

Further Reading

Kneller G F 1965 *Educational Anthropology: An Introduction*. Wiley, New York
Middleton J (ed.) 1970 *From Child to Adult: Studies in the Anthropology of Education*. Natural History Press, Garden City, New York
Roberts J I, Akinsanya S K (eds.) 1976 *Educational Patterns and Cultural Configurations: The Anthropology of Education*. McKay, New York
Roberts J I, Akinsanya S K (eds.) 1976 *Schooling in the Cultural Context: Anthropological Studies of Education*. McKay, New York
Shimahara N 1983 Polarized socialization in an urban high school. *Anthropol. Educ. Q.* 14(2): 109–30
Shimahara N 1986 The cultural basis of student achievement in Japan. *Comp. Educ.* 22(1): 19–26
Spindler G (ed.) 1987d *Education and Cultural Process: Anthropological Approaches*, 2nd edn. Waveland, Prospect Heights, Illinois
Spindler G (ed.) 1987e *Interpretive Ethnography of Education: At Home and Abroad*. Erlbaum, Hillsdale, New Jersey

L. Kahn

Cross-sectional Research Methods

There is a strong and growing demand from national authorities, educational administrators, and the wider community for detailed comparative information on the organization and operation of educational systems within their own and kindred countries (Bottani et al. 1992). A cross-sectional study is required to provide such information that is concerned with the existing conditions, processes, and outcomes of an educational system at a particular point in time. However, cross-sectional studies are not limited to nation-level investigations but can range from the collection of information in a classroom, school, or school district through to a state or province, a country, or a group of countries with common characteristics that would make comparisons meaningful. Moreover, cross-sectional studies are not necessarily comparative in nature, although comparisons are commonly informative. Sometimes information on the state of affairs within a single unit is meaningful and of value and such information, in general, is obtained from a cross-sectional investigation.

Inevitably after information has been assembled, which relates to the conditions at one point in time with respect to characteristics of interest, there is concern as to whether such characteristics exhibit stability or change over time. Thus there is a second type of study, which is commonly contrasted with cross-sectional investigations in which stability and change in particular characteristics are examined over time. Such studies are referred to as longitudinal research studies (see *Longitudinal Research Methods*). The distinction between the two types of studies is more a matter of degree than of kind, and warrants further consideration because it involves an examination of the strengths and weaknesses of the two different types of investigations.

This entry considers initially the different types of research studies that can be carried out in educational research, and their relationship to cross-sectional studies, the advantages and disadvantages of cross-sectional studies, the usefulness of cross-sectional studies, the different kinds of research studies that are essentially cross-sectional in nature, as well as the gradations in types of investigation between cross-sectional and longitudinal research studies. In addition, this entry discusses issues concerned with the design of a cross-sectional study, the role of sampling the methods of data collection, the value of pretest and pilot studies, and the major sources of error in such studies. A further important issue, which is addressed, involves the analysis of data and the problems of explanation associated with the relationships reported from cross-sectional studies in contrast to longitudinal and experimental studies. While studies of change, which are necessarily longitudinal in nature, and experimental studies remain the ideal types, the difficulties encountered in such studies in the investigation of educational problems are of sufficient magnitude that studies of a cross-sectional type are likely to continue for the foreseeable future as the major source of information to guide both policy and practice and from which to build theory.

1. Strategic Choices in Research Design

Kish (1987) has identified three kinds of strategic choices that must be made in the design of a research study, whether in education or in other fields of inquiry. These choices involve: (a) representation of the target group, (b) realism, and (c) control of treatment conditions. The importance of these strategic choices in the present context is that they permit the drawing of useful distinctions and identify the strengths and weaknesses of different approaches, and are concerned with the quality and nature of inferences that can be drawn from different types of investigations.

1.1 Representation

The first major decision that must be made in the design of an investigation is the nature and extent of the generalizations that are to be drawn from the analysis of the evidence. This decision leads to the identification of the investigation's domain and of the population to which generalization will apply. The ideal is to investigate a complete population or target group, but this is rarely possible although a national census, which is a cross-sectional study, seeks information from a complete population. It is generally necessary to draw a random sample of elements from a defined target population with a known positive probability of selection. There are two main advantages of random selection of elements with known positive probability. They ensure that strong inferences can be drawn at the conclusion of the investigation with respect to the population under investigation. First, because the elements in the sample are chosen at random from the target population, the sample is unbiased and is truly representative of that population. Second, because the sample is a random sample with a known positive probability of selection of each of the elements, estimates of sample statistics for the parameters associated with characteristics of the population can be calculated together with the estimates of the sampling errors linked to these statistics. With knowledge of the sampling error, confidence limits can be specified for the statistics that are estimated, and tests of statistical significance applied. Without the use of random probability sampling there is no guarantee of representativeness or lack of bias, and there is no information about the size of the sampling errors. It is, however, necessary to recognize that the magnitude of sampling error is not related to the probability of selection but to the effective size of the sample. For a simple random sample the effective size is the number of sampling units. For a random sample of complex design, allowance must be made for the *design effect* of the sample in calculating the effective sample size. The need to guarantee representativeness or lack of bias applies with equal strength to experiments as to surveys. However, randomization serves a further purpose in experimentation.

1.2 Realism

The second major decision concerns whether or not the investigation involves subjects in a natural setting and whether a contrived situation is desirable, admissible, or indeed possible. In the investigation of some issues in education it is not acceptable to diverge too far from an existing setting, insofar as it is the lives of individuals that are being changed by the experiment. Thus it is generally necessary to undertake an investigation in a natural setting. This may not only rule out an experimental study, but may also prevent the following of individuals over time, since repeated examination of the same individual may interfere with, or distort the life of, that individual. Under many circumstances, all that is possible is a cross-sectional investigation that studies an individual once and once only in a natural setting, rather than a longitudinal study in which not only is the behavior of the individual likely to be changed but the realism of the investigation is also in jeopardy.

1.3 Treatment Control

The purpose of research is not merely to describe but also to understand and explain. Understanding and explanation are derived from the examination of the effects of treatment factors whether acting in a natural setting, through intervention, or within a designed experiment. In a longitudinal study the effects of treatment factors operating in a natural setting, or of interventions in a quasi-experimental setting are under investigation. However, in such studies the operation of divers other factors may confound the changes observed. Only by the random selection of subjects for study and the random allocation of subjects to treatment and control groups can the effects of these divers other factors be brought under control, so that cause can validly be imputed and strong generalizations made to a population under investigation. Thus experiments have three major advantages. First, the bias from disturbance factors can be eliminated by the randomization of subjects to treatment and control groups. Second, control can be exercised over the treatment factors, so that their effects can be more strongly inferred. Third, through statistical analysis confidence can be assigned with accuracy to the probability of whether or not the results occurred by chance. Longitudinal studies lack the first advantage. However, in longitudinal studies procedures of statistical analysis seek to employ statistical controls in place of randomization to adjust for the effects of disturbance factors. There is, nevertheless, no guarantee that spurious effects are not present. Cross-sectional studies can also employ statistical controls. Nevertheless, as explained in a later section, the effects of disturbance factors are less readily eliminated in such studies.

In addition to the three strategic choices listed by Kish (1987) there is a fourth choice involving time.

1.4 Time

Time has a central role in the investigation of stability and change. Both experiments and longitudinal studies, in general, require repeated measurement, and the use of repeated measurement extends the duration of an investigation. The exception occurs in situations where the treatment and control groups may be considered to be equal prior to the operation of the treatment condition. In experiments and longitudinal studies time may also become a treatment condition whose effects can be examined. However, in cross-sectional studies the effects of time can at best be only indirectly assessed, because repeated measurements are not made.

The restriction on time and the limitation of a study's duration are generally associated with the availability of personnel over an extended period and the costs of a longitudinal study. No research worker in education can ignore these two questions of personnel and costs. While an experiment or a longitudinal study may be considered desirable in many investigations into specific problem situations, the undertaking of a longitudinal study must frequently be abandoned because of cost and personnel constraints, and a study of a cross-sectional type undertaken.

It is important to recognize that cross-sectional studies do not necessarily involve sample surveys, although such procedures are often employed. It is also possible for a cross-sectional study to be: (a) a local study, in which a representative group is investigated; or (b) a census, in which data are collected for a complete population; or (c) a register study, in which data held on file in a register at a particular time point are examined; or (d) a controlled inquiry where data are collected, with care, although without random selection or from a population, and without randomization to treatment and control groups, but at a particular point in time, in order to study a clearly identifiable problem.

2. Four Major Cross-sectional Studies

Cross-sectional studies serve many purposes, although the interest is primarily in providing information on the conditions of education at a particular point in time. Where such studies have been successfully conducted, and have given rise to findings of considerable usefulness, a follow-up or repeat study is sometimes undertaken. Four major cross-sectional studies are considered in the paragraphs that follow, to illustrate the variety of uses to which such studies have been put.

The purpose of a cross-sectional study may be largely descriptive. The purpose, for example, of the first Scottish Mental Survey, carried out in 1932, was initially to ascertain the distribution of intelligence among children aged 11 years in Scottish schools. This study tested a complete population, and reported that the spread in IQ scores was greater than had been expected, and was greater among boys than among girls. In a second survey conducted in 1947, the purpose of the study was to ascertain whether IQ scores were declining and whether the national average of intelligence was falling. Whereas in the first cross-sectional survey in 1932 the difference between boys and girls in IQ was less than one point, in the second survey a difference of four points of IQ in favor of girls was recorded. This difference, while of statistical significance, was not of marked practical significance. However, it helped to account for the small gain in average IQ of the 11-year-old population between the surveys (Scottish Council for Research in Education 1949). In addition, in the second study the opportunity was taken to examine the intercorrelations between IQ scores and a number of sociological variables that were measured.

The crossnational studies conducted by the International Association for the Evaluation of Educational Achievement (IEA) were not designed to provide "league tables" of educational achievement in different school subjects, but to relate these measures of achievement to a wide range of home, student, classroom, school, and system-level variables, describing the conditions of education in the countries involved (see *Educational Achievement: Comparative Studies*). These studies, in general, have employed large national probability samples of students at three age levels, namely, near the end of primary schooling, near the end of the period when schooling is mandatory in most countries, and at the preuniversity or terminal stage of secondary schooling.

The IEA surveys are examples of studies that have had goals of both describing and explaining educational outcomes. Sometimes specific hypotheses were tested. In other cases more general models developed from theory were examined. The usefulness of these studies, as evidenced by the publications they produced, the debate that followed the release of the publications, and the changes to policy and practice induced in different parts of the world, cannot be denied. Nevertheless, such studies can be hazardous undertakings and prone to methodological errors in execution and errors in interpretation.

Two other cross-sectional studies have been of great importance for the conduct of educational research. The first study was undertaken in the United States under Section 402 of the 1964 Civil Rights Act, the Equality of Educational Opportunity Survey, which provided the evidence for a report to the President and Congress (Coleman et al. 1966). Not only was this survey of major policy importance, giving rise to widespread debate on the effectiveness of schools and programs for the bussing of students between schools, it also established the feasibility of large-scale surveys in the United States, raised numerous issues about the analysis of data, and indirectly drew attention to the problems of causal inference from cross-sectional studies.

Likewise, the Plowden Report (Central Advisory Council 1967) provided information from a number of surveys carried out in 1964 into the condition of different aspects of education in England and Wales. One study of particular significance was a survey of parents of school children, which established the importance of parental attitudes and addressed major issues of statistical analysis. A follow-up study was carried out four years later (Peaker 1971), and in the report of this study the first use of path analysis was made in the field of education. Other surveys in the Plowden Report were concerned with the standard of reading achievement, child development, and school facilities.

Both sets of studies were conducted by, or on behalf of, governments, in order that statistical accounts of the educational systems in the two countries would be available. However, cross-sectional research studies are not necessarily large-scale surveys. The analysis of data held in the register of a school can sometimes provide valuable information for the administration of that school without need to resort to the use of advanced statistical techniques or elaborate data collection methods.

3. Cross-sectional and Longitudinal Methods

Some of the cross-sectional studies referred to in the previous section involved investigations that were repeated over time, others involved the investigation of two or more age groups at the same time, with inferences being drawn regarding the differences between age levels. There are thus three classes of cross-sectional studies, namely, (a) single cross-sectional studies, (b) simultaneous cross-sectional studies, and (c) trend studies. Classes (b) and (c) may also be considered to be longitudinal studies (see *Longitudinal Research Methods*). Each of the three classes of studies is discussed below.

3.1 Single Cross-sectional Studies

These research studies consider one target population at one point of time only. The limitation to one target population and one time point is primarily determined by considerations of personnel and cost, which require that such studies can be completed relatively quickly at modest cost. While a description of conditions is readily provided by such a study, the nature and quality of the inferences derived from statistical analysis may also be modest.

3.2 Simultaneous Cross-sectional Studies

In a research study of this type, measurements are made at only one point in time and thus personnel and cost considerations are reduced. But two or more related target populations or two or more fields of inquiry are investigated simultaneously with large random samples, so that the samples may be considered both accurate and fully representative of the populations being investigated. In such studies, different age samples may be drawn from the same larger population, but each sample is drawn independently. Likewise, some surveys conducted by the IEA were designed to investigate two or more subject areas in parallel studies in order to examine differences in the conditions under which different school subjects were taught. Since information on similar predictor and criterion variables is also collected, parallel analyses can be carried out to examine differences between age levels or differences between subject fields.

A longitudinal or time dimension in the design of studies of this type is achieved through comparisons of the data for the different age samples. Not only can growth between age levels be estimated, but factors influencing growth can also be examined. The design is simple to execute, and since only one point in time is involved, the confounding effects of environmental influences are reduced. The IEA studies of science (Comber and Keeves 1973, Keeves 1992) have shown clearly the effects of differences in retention rates across countries on growth in science achievement between age levels at different measurement times. Likewise, in a study of French as a Foreign Language, Carroll (1975) showed that the effects of years spent in learning accounted for growth between age levels. The conclusions that can be drawn from this design are only valid if it can be assumed that: (a) the age samples have been drawn from the same common population; and (b) the factors influencing change in the criterion variables and their effects have remained constant across the time span during which the different age samples were exposed to those factors.

3.3 Trend Studies

In this type of study either a single cross-sectional study or a simultaneous cross-sectional study is replicated on a second or further occasion with identically defined target populations. Notable examples of trend studies are those carried out by the Assessment of Performance Unit (APU) in England and Wales (Black et al. 1984), the Australian Studies of School Performance (Bourke et al. 1981) and the National Assessment of Educational Progress. These studies have all been concerned with changes in educational achievement and have not sought to provide explanations of why the changes recorded had occurred. Two sets of problems arise in such studies of educational achievement. First, in circumstances where school curricula change over time with new curricular emphases evolving, it is difficult to design tests that assess achievement validly on two or more occasions. A second problem concerns the strength of the statistical procedures that are employed to scale the achievement test scores on the different occasions to obtain valid and reliable measures that can be compared. The first and second IEA science studies (Keeves 1992) sought to develop item response theory scaling procedures to measure change over time and to account for observed changes in educational achievement in terms of the changes in the conditions for learning science that had occurred between occasions. It should be noted that some research workers in the United States refer to such studies as a "cohort design" (Karweit 1982). Whether studies of this type are cross-sectional or longitudinal in nature is a question for debate, but they avoid the troublesome aspect of maintaining contact over a period of several years with a sample of students and the dangers of heavy attrition that could seriously bias the findings.

4. The Design and Conduct of Cross-sectional Research Studies

In many respects cross-sectional studies are similar in kind to surveys. However, the two types of studies are not necessarily synonymous. Furthermore, both types of studies do not necessarily require the drawing of random or probability samples from specified populations. Not only can a cross-sectional survey study take the form of a census in which a complete population is surveyed, but a cross-sectional study may also involve an investigation of material held in a register, from which a sample of data may be drawn. The decision on which type of cross-sectional study to employ depends on the importance of obtaining highly accurate data. In some cases a census may be preferred to a survey, because of the elimination of sampling error. However, the attempt to conduct a census may result in a high proportion of missing or incomplete data, whereas a well-conducted survey with little missing data may yield data of higher quality, without bias, and with known sampling error. Issues of both time and cost ultimately determine the choice of type of study to be employed. The planning of a cross-sectional study is similar to the planning of a survey (see *Survey Research Methods*).

There is interest in a wide range of measures and indicators concerned with the conditions, causes, and outcomes of education that can be collected from cross-sectional studies. The publication *Education at a Glance* (Bottani et al. 1992), which presents information on indicators of interest to OECD countries in 1988, illustrates this range. Of particular importance, however, since the 1960s, when Coleman et al. (1966) conducted the Equality of Educational Opportunity Survey in the United States and the IEA carried out the first IEA mathematics study in 12 countries (Husén 1967), are measures of educational achievement outcomes. The collection of data in cross-sectional surveys of educational achievement presents particular problems, which are discussed in the two sections that follow.

4.1 Methods of Data Collection in Achievement Surveys

Probably the most common method of data collection

in cross-sectional studies of educational achievement is through requiring students to answer tests and respond to self-completion questionnaires and attitude scales. Access to the school system has long been the privilege of the researcher. Teachers in some countries have willingly agreed to supervise students while they respond to tests and questionnaires. Increasingly, however, teachers are seeking some remuneration for this work, or it is necessary to employ testers or to require district educational officers to undertake the testing of students. Interviewing is necessary in some studies where the information is too detailed or complex for students to provide written responses. The interviews may be carried out by teachers, school psychologists, or social workers. However, the use of interviewers trained to work on a particular study can prove especially useful for obtaining data on family background or for probing into the students' thought processes.

Particular problems arise in situations where the target population involves young people of school-going age who no longer attend school regularly. A study of literacy and numeracy among 17-year-old youth would require a household survey since many young people who are unable to read and write are likely, by the age of 17 years, to have dropped out from school, even in countries with relatively high retention rates. In such a study it would be necessary for trained interviewers to undertake a household survey and to test the young people sampled in their homes.

In a follow-up study to obtain further information about the activities of students who were tested at school, but who have since left, a postal or telephone survey is likely to prove worthwhile. However, it should be recognized that not all young people are likely to be accessible by telephone, and in order to get people to respond to a telephone or postal survey some rapport must already have been established.

4.2 The Pretest and Pilot Studies

It is important that where achievement tests, attitude scales, and questionnaires have been developed for a study, they should be administered to a trial group as similar as possible to the population under survey in order to check, and if necessary revise, the final form of the instruments. Such a test will also provide estimates of the reliability of the instruments that are independent of the main study. A pretest study provides an opportunity to detect and remove ambiguities, to ascertain the range of possible responses (especially important for open-ended items, from which data may be processed automatically), and to ensure that the questions asked are yielding the information sought.

The pretest of instruments should not be confused with a pilot study. In a pilot study the instruments should be in their final form. The pilot study is used to test all procedures employed in the collection of data, coding, and recording of data and the initial processing of the data. Thus the pilot study also provides an opportunity to learn what the results of the main study are likely to be. Unfortunately, even where a pilot study has been scheduled it is not uncommon for delays to have occurred so that the pilot study is reduced in scope or even eliminated, in order to save time and money. This is generally false economy, since the mounting of a pilot study helps to avoid expensive mistakes in the main study. All cross-sectional investigations should include a pilot study.

5. Sources of Error

Three main types of error can be expected to arise in cross-sectional studies, namely: (a) errors of nonobservation, (b) errors of measurement, and (c) sampling errors. Sampling errors are, however, different in kind from the other two types of error, since they are a necessary consequence of, and obtainable through, the employment of a random probability sample (see *Sampling Errors in Survey Research*).

5.1 Errors of Nonobservation

The extent to which the achieved sample falls short of the designed sample arises from several sources. First, the information on which the sample was designed may have been deficient. Second, some people who were required to respond may have declined or been unable through absence to do so—this applies whether or not a sample is drawn from the population under survey. Third, some respondents may have chosen not to reply to specific questions. Fourth, some respondents may have deliberately or unintentionally provided information that is clearly erroneous. Such errors must be reduced or removed by the wild code checks and the consistency checks that are applied at the stages of data entry or data cleaning (see *Database Management Systems in Education*). Various compensatory procedures are available, such as drawing a replacement sample, using strategies for the estimation of missing data, and compensation through the weighting of the available data. All such procedures require certain assumptions that may or may not be valid. As a consequence, all these procedures introduce some bias into the estimates made, through displacing the mean or changing the variance of the estimates. There is no substitute for a well-planned investigation and a pilot study to reduce the effects of nonobservation. Elaborate procedures for compensation may help, but generally it is not possible to tell whether or not they have been effective (see *Missing Data and Nonresponse in Survey Research*).

5.2 Errors of Measurement

Errors of measurement arise from a variety of

sources. They may stem from poorly designed instruments (see *Questionnaires*), from variability in the respondents, or from errors made by the researcher in the collection and recording of data. If items are open-ended then responses have to be coded before data are recorded, and this may be a source of error. If precoded responses are used the respondent may be careless, or may give a socially desired response, or an acquiescent response as a result of a tendency to avoid conflict. Efforts should be made to increase the reliability of the instruments employed and to obtain sound estimates of reliability with a corresponding sample. Compensation for measurement error can be made by the combination of measures, preferably in ways that will maximize the reliability of the compound measure, such as with principal components analysis and the calculation of principal component scores. Alternatively, measurement error can be modeled in certain procedures of statistical analysis, such as are employed by LISREL programs (Jöreskog and Sörbom 1989) (see *Path Analysis and Linear Structural Relations Analysis*). In addition, estimates can be corrected for attenuation if the reliabilities of the measures are known (see *Reliability in Educational and Psychological Measurement*). In general, separate measurement of response variance is not possible, and the response variance has served to inflate the estimated sample variance, with the consequent effects of reducing the magnitude of estimated correlations.

5.3 Sampling Errors

The topic of sampling error is too large to be considered here. Techniques of stratification can be employed to reduce the sampling error of a mean value. This, however, requires that the effects of stratification must be removed by statistical control in estimating the magnitude of relationships through the introduction of the stratification variable into multivariate analyses. The size of sampling errors can also be reduced by efficient design in the case of cluster samples, and by increasing the number of primary sampling units in multistage samples. Where cluster samples have been employed it is necessary to proceed with great caution in all types of statistical analyses, because nearly all computer programs that provide tests of statistical significance assume that the data are associated with a simple random sample. It should be noted that procedures of multilevel analysis are now available that not only permit the estimation of unbiased effects at the different levels of treatment, but also calculate more efficient estimates of sampling error for complex sample designs (see *Multilevel Analysis*).

6. The Analysis of Data

Four problems arise in the analysis of data from cross-sectional studies where the purposes of such statistical analyses are not merely descriptive. These problems exist in addition to the calculation of appropriate sampling errors and the testing of the parameter estimates for statistical significance in comparisons between groups. In such descriptive analyses the estimates of parameters are customarily means and standard deviations. However, most educational researchers are rarely satisfied with analyses that do not present relationships between variables considered to be of interest and importance. Here problems arise because such relationships either tacitly or explicitly involve considerations of causal influence. Two approaches can be taken in the examination of these relationships. These approaches are either exploratory or confirmatory.

6.1 Exploratory Analyses

In the exploratory analysis of data, the researcher rarely postulates a model, and simply lists variables of possible interest, largely on the basis of intuition. He or she employs contingency tables and correlation matrices to screen the data for both practically and statistically significant relationships. Where one or more antecedent factors are known to be of primary importance, it is sometimes considered desirable to examine the relationships between independent and dependent variables after the effects of these antecedent factors have been removed. This is generally achieved by regressing the dependent variable on both the independent variable and the antecedent factors, under the assumption that the antecedent factor may have influenced both the independent and dependent variables. This treatment differs from a covariance adjustment which is generally inappropriate because it assumes an effect only on the dependent variable and not on the independent variable. A further exploratory strategy is to employ stepwise regression in order to select a subset of independent variables that each have a significant unique contribution to accounting for the variance of the dependent variable. In such regression analyses, causal relationships are tacitly assumed and rarely made explicit. However, these stepwise regression analyses serve the valuable purpose of identifying variables that warrant further consideration (see *Exploratory Data Analysis; Multivariate Analysis; Regression Analyses of Quantified Data*).

6.2 Confirmatory Analyses

In confirmatory analyses hypotheses and causal models are advanced—generally ones derived from theoretical considerations—and are tested with recognized procedures of statistical analysis. In general in such analyses there are several independent variables and commonly several dependent variables. Procedures of multivariate analysis must be employed (see *Multivariate Analysis; Path Analysis with Latent Variables; Path Analysis and Linear Structural Relations Analysis*). There is much to be gained from making the multivariate models developed as explicit and as fully specified as possible. Errors of specification, which involve the omission of key factors, are of considerable importance because they lead to the generation of biased estimates of effects.

The danger in nonexperimental research is that the causal models developed may not have allowed for a factor that influences both the independent and dependent variables. The observed relationships are spurious, being confounded by unobserved and unknown factors. In experimental studies the random allocation of subjects to the treatment and control groups serves to annul the effects of such unknown confounding factors. Furthermore, the administration of a specific treatment to the experimental group and not to the control group serves to identify the factor that may cause a detected relationship.

Likewise, in longitudinal studies, through the measurement of change over time in the same subjects it is possible to eliminate the effects of a large number of factors that may have in the past influenced educational outcomes, and to focus attention on those factors that have produced change. Intervention studies in which a treatment is administered to one group and not to another permits testing for the effects of the intervention within a natural setting. However, such studies do not necessarily eliminate confounding effects, since full randomization of subjects to treatments has not occurred. Even in the most elaborate longitudinal studies it is impossible to separate and test fully for the interactions of chronological age, time of measurement, and the time of birth of the cohort that are considered to be primarily and respectively associated with genetic or biological effects, environmental effects that are common to all subjects being studied, and environmental effects that operated prior to the first time point of an investigation (see *Longitudinal Research Methods*).

Furthermore, in longitudinal studies unless the *change* in the criterion or dependent variable is measured with a high degree of reliability there is little chance of detecting the factors that have caused change. This can rarely be achieved through measurement at only two points in time in educational studies, and measurement at four or more time points is to be recommended (see *Change, Measurement of*). Moreover, the analysis of change data is not without its many problems (Collins and Horn 1991). Procedures for the analysis of data at three levels are now available. These permit the investigation of intra-individual growth, of between-individual effects, and of between-class or school group effects (see *Hierarchical Linear Models; Multilevel Analysis*). As a consequence more appropriate analyses can now be carried out on longitudinal data sets in educational research studies.

7. Conclusion

There are many limitations associated with cross-sectional studies, particularly in the analysis of data and in the drawing of inferences about causal effects that have not taken into consideration spurious influences. Furthermore, such studies can only investigate factors that influence learning from birth up to the time of data collection, and not the learning that occurs in a particular educational situation, although it may be assumed that current factors are more powerful than those that operated in previous years. In spite of these limitations and the problems of execution of large cross-sectional surveys, it seems likely that cross-sectional research studies will continue to play a major role in educational research.

See also: Sampling in Survey Research; Sampling Errors in Survey Research; Regression Analyses of Quantified Data

References

Black P, Harlen W, Orgee A 1984 Standards of performance-expectation and reality. *J. Curric. St.* 16(1): 94–96

Bottani N, Duchêne C, Tuijnman A 1992 *Education at a Glance: OECD Indicators*. OECD, Paris

Bourke S F, Mills J M, Stanyen J, Holzer F 1981 *Performance in Literacy and Numeracy 1980.* Australian Government Publishing Service for the Australian Education Council, Canberra

Carroll J B 1975 *The Teaching of French as a Foreign Language in Eight Countries*. Wiley, New York

Central Advisory Committee for Education 1967 *Children and their Primary Schools. Vol. 2: Research and Surveys*. HMSO, London

Coleman J S et al. 1966 *Equality of Educational Opportunity*. Ayer and Co., Salem, New Hampshire

Collins L M, Horn J L (eds.) 1991 *Best Methods for the Analysis of Change: Recent Advances, Unanswered Questions, Future Directions*. American Psychological Association, Washington, DC

Comber L C, Keeves J P 1973 *Science Education in Nineteen Countries: An Empirical Study*. Wiley, New York

Husén T (ed.) 1967 *International Study of Achievement in Mathematics: A Comparison of Twelve Countries*. Almqvist and Wiksell, Stockholm

Jöreskog K G, Sörbom D 1989 *LISREL 7: A Guide to the Program and Applications*, 2nd edn. SPSS Publications, Chicago, Illinois

Karweit N L 1982 Survey research methods. In: Mitzel H E (ed.) 1982 *Encyclopedia of Educational Research*, 5th edn. Free Press, New York

Keeves J P 1992 *The IEA Study of Science III. Changes in Science Education and Achievement: 1970 to 1984.* Pergamon Press, Oxford

Kish L D 1987 *Statistical Design for Research*. Wiley, New York

Peaker G F 1971 *The Plowden Children Four Years Later*. NFER, Slough

Scottish Council for Research in Education 1949 *The Trend in Scottish Intelligence: A Comparison of the 1947 and 1932 Surveys of the Intelligence of Eleven-Year-Old Pupils*. University of London Press, London

P. Lietz; J. P. Keeves